ARCO

LSAT
SUPERCOURSE™

Thomas H. Martinson, J.D.

MACMILLAN • USA

Previous editions of this book were published under the title *SuperCourse for the LSAT*.

page 1 © Conklin/Monkmeyer Press

page 41 © Rogers/Monkmeyer Press

page 411 © Robert Issacs/Photo Researchers

Macmillan General Reference
A Prentice Hall Macmillan Company
15 Columbus Circle
New York, NY 10023

An Arco Book

MACMILLAN is a registered trademark of Macmillan, Inc.
ARCO is a registered trademark of Prentice-Hall, Inc.

Library of Congress Cataloging-in-Publication Data

Martinson, Thomas H.
    LSAT supercourse / Thomas H. Martinson.—4th ed.
    p.   cm.
    Revised ed. of: Supercourse for the LSAT, 1991.
    ISBN 0-671-84849-6
    1. Law schools—United States—Entrance examinations.
2. Law School Admissions Test. I. Martinson, Thomas H.
II. Title.
KF285.Z9M375   1993   92-35392
340'.076—dc20   CIP

Manufactured in the United States of America

10 9 8 7 6 5 4 3

CONTENTS

Part One   The Anatomy of a Test

Part Two   The Coaching Program

Part Three   Practice Tests

A Letter to the Reader

Dear Reader,

The book you have just purchased is literally worth hundreds of dollars! This year, tens of thousands of students will spend $500 to $800 (and even more) for expensive test preparation courses. Yet, this book can provide you with the same benefits.

I know for a fact that *LSAT SuperCourse* is the equivalent of an expensive coaching course because I taught test preparation classes for leading coaching companies for over 15 years. During that time, I also wrote and revised the coaching programs for the LSAT and trained new teachers in the use of the programs. This book contains the fruits of those 15 years of experience.

In *LSAT SuperCourse*, you get:

- hundreds of proven strategies that take you inside the LSAT
- advice that helps you understand what the testmakers want
- hundreds of practice questions that are the equivalent of 10 LSATs
- complete answer explanations that explain why wrong answers are wrong as well as why correct answers are correct
- a diagnostic English grammar exam and complete grammar review for the Writing Sample
- successful methods of controlling test anxiety

and much more. To prove this to yourself just take a look at the powerful diagramming techniques that are presented in the chapters on Analytical Reasoning (logical games), or the analysis of the LSAT theory of Reading Comprehension, or the review of fallacies frequently tested by the Logical Reasoning section of the exam.

In short, this book contains everything you need to make sure that you get your top score on the LSAT. In my professional opinion, there is little offered by most commercial test preparation courses that you cannot get for yourself by conscientious study of this book.

Best of luck,

Thomas H. Martinson

Preface

There are three very important reasons for our publishing this book at this time. One, it proves that it is possible to improve your LSAT score. Two, it offers a reasonably priced alternative to expensive schools and tutoring services that now compete among themselves for your preparation dollars. Three, it stands as an antidote to the current mania for quick fixes rather than conscientious preparation and study.

First, this book shows that the LSAT is not invincible—that it does have patterns or clues that are inherent in the structure of the test. If you understand these patterns or clues, you can pursue them to your advantage. Consider an example taken from the Analytical Reasoning section:

> Six students—Dan, Ed, Frank, Lisa, Mark, and Stan—took a test. No two students received the same score.
> Stan received the lowest score.
> Ed received a higher score than Dan.
> Mark received a higher score than Frank.
> Lisa's score was somewhere between Dan's score and Frank's score.

Which of the following could be the order of the scores, from highest to lowest, received by the six students?

(A) Frank, Mark, Lisa, Ed, Dan, Stan

(B) Mark, Frank, Lisa, Ed, Stan, Dan

(C) Mark, Dan, Lisa, Frank, Ed, Stan

(D) Mark, Lisa, Frank, Ed, Dan, Stan

(E) Ed, Dan, Mark, Lisa, Frank, Stan

Although Analytical Reasoning is agreed by students to be the most difficult section of the LSAT, questions such as this can be answered with virtually no thinking—provided you know the correct approach. The way this question is written, four of the five choices must be inconsistent with the initial information. To find the one choice that is consistent with the information, simply "read" each condition against the answer choices, eliminating those that violate an initial condition.

Start with the first condition: Stan received the lowest score. Using this condition, you eliminate choice (B) (because in that order, Stan did not receive the lowest score). Using the second condition, you eliminate (C). With the third condition, you eliminate (A). And using the fourth condition, you eliminate (D). By the process of elimination, the correct choice is (E); and (E) is, in fact, the only order that respects all of the initial conditions.

Notice that this process is purely "mechanical." With it, anyone who can read can answer this "logical puzzle."

Nor is success here a matter of luck. Since the LSAT is a multiple-choice test, any problem like this one (which asks for a possible ordering) can be attacked in a purely mechanical fashion. The correct answer is there for the testing.

Given that there are dozens of strategies like this, common sense dictates that test-takers who know the pattern of the LSAT enjoy an important competitive edge over those who do not.

Second, this book is a viable alternative to expensive coaching schools. The 400-plus pages of instructional material are the equivalent to the forty or fifty hours of lecture included in those programs.

Third, this book should help debunk a popular myth. There is currently in vogue an attitude that only a *little* preparation is needed. Exponents of this approach tout methods with names such as "cracking the test," "breaking the code," and "beating the system."

There is nothing really new in these approaches. They offer many of the strategies and methods that have been used effectively on multiple-choice tests for years. What *is* new, however, is the "hype" or indoctrination that accompanies the strategies. Students are encouraged to believe that by learning a few easy rules, they can attain a top score without really having to think.

As you can see, preparation is effective, but it requires hard work. In point of fact, the only sure way to conquer the LSAT is through conscientious study and hard work. In sum, the approach of this book can perhaps be best expressed by paraphrasing the claim often heard in a once widely aired television commercial: "Our students get higher LSAT scores the old-fashioned way—they earn them!"

PART ONE

The Anatomy of a Test

Getting Started

What is the LSAT?

SYMBOLS

strategy

eliminating
suspects

fact

estimating

common
error

inquiry/
guessing

measuring

pattern

calculating

unlocking
the mystery

Dr. Watson

Sherlock
Holmes

smoking
gun

ladder of
difficulty

What Is the LSAT?

Let's begin by sorting out some abbreviations such as LSAT, LSAS, LSAC, and ABA. Perhaps the best way to work our way through this tangle is to start at the highest level and work our way down.

The letters A-B-A stand for American Bar Association. The ABA is a national organization of attorneys that sponsors a number of programs related to professional responsibility and ethics, judicial selection, legal reform, and legal education. Through its Section of Legal Education and Admissions to the Bar, the ABA sets standards for law school education and grants accreditation to those schools that meet its standards. As of this writing, there are 175 ABA-accredited schools in the United States and Puerto Rico.

Although the ABA sets national standards for the accreditation of law schools, each state establishes its own requirements for admission to the practice of law. Most states, however, require that a candidate for admission to the bar have graduated from an ABA-accredited law school. There are some exceptions to this general rule, but they are rare. To obtain more specific information about the requirements for admission to the practice in a particular state, contact the board of bar examiners for that state.

The letters L-S-A-C stand for Law School Admission Council. The Law School Admission Council is an association of all 175 ABA-accredited law schools in the United States plus the 14 Canadian law schools that are recognized by the Federation of Law Societies of Canada. The letters L-S-A-S stand for Law School Admission Services, a nonprofit corporation that is the operating arm of the LSAC. Through the LSAS, the LSAC provides programs and services to its member schools and to persons interested in obtaining a legal education.

Perhaps the best known service provided by the LSAC/LSAS is the LSAT. The letters L-S-A-T stand for Law School Admission Test. The LSAT is a standardized, multiple-choice exam given (at this writing) four times a year. LSAT scores are required by most member schools of the LSAC as a part of the admission process. The LSAC/LSAS has contracted with Educational Testing Service, ETS, the company that produces the Scholastic Aptitude Test, the SAT) for the development of the LSAT.

Other important LSAS/LSAC services and programs are LSDAS and *The Official Guide to U.S. Law Schools: the Prelaw Handbook* (and its counterpart, the *Canadian Law Schools Admission Handbook*).

The letters L-S-D-A-S stand for Law School Data Assembly Service, and, as the phrase suggests, the LSDAS assembles and summarizes information, such as LSAT scores and transcripts for use by law schools, for each applicant. The LSDAS is required by most LSAC schools, so it is almost as essential to the law school application process as the LSAT. You obtain registration materials for LSAT/LSDAS by writing:

LSAC/LSAS
Box 2000
Newtown, PA 18940−0998

or by calling:

(215) 968−1001

The information and registration materials are provided free of charge.

The LSAC/LSAS also publishes *The Official Guide to U.S. Law Schools: the Prelaw Handbook*. The guide contains two-page summaries of important information about the 175 ABA-accredited schools, including information about library and physical facilities, degree requirements, special programs, activities, the student body, expenses, and financial aid, as well as admission standards. This guide is an extremely valuable reference tool and well worth the price. You can order your own copy of the official guide directly from the LSAC/LSAS at the address given above.

Let's Look at the LSAT

1. **Reading Comprehension**
2. **Logical Reasoning**
3. **Analytical Reasoning**
4. **Writing Sample**
5. **Format**
6. **Scoring the LSAT**

The LSAT consists of five 35-minute sections of multiple-choice questions plus a 30-minute essay question. Each section is separately timed. You will have one writing sample section, one section each of Reading Comprehension and Analytical Reasoning, two Logical Reasoning sections and one wild card section. A wild card section can contain any one of the three multiple-choice topics (Reading Comprehension, Logical Reasoning, or Analytical Reasoning), but this section will not count toward your score. The wild card section contains questions being tried out for future LSATs. You will not, however, be told which is the wild card section.

1. Reading Comprehension

Reading comprehension questions are based upon a reading selection. They ask about the author's main point, the logic of the selection, some detail mentioned in the selection, or the tone of the selection. Here is an example. (**Note:** This selection is considerably shorter and simpler than those that appear on the actual LSAT. It is included solely for illustrative purposes.)

> *Directions:* Each passage in this group is followed by questions based on its content. After reading a passage, choose the best answer to each question and blacken the corresponding space on the answer sheet. Answer all questions following a passage on the basis of what is <u>stated</u> or <u>implied</u> in that passage.

Those who discover the people of Appalachia through quiet patience and open friendliness will rediscover something characteristically American. Part of it is awareness and appreciation of the individual, which have characterized every aspect of Appalachian history and culture. Since the romance of James Fenimore Cooper's Leatherstocking Tales on the "glimmerglass" of New York's Otsego Lake, Davy Crockett's tall tales of the Tennessee frontier, and the realistic character portrayals of North Carolina's mountain son Thomas Wolfe there have been numerous efforts to "interpret" Appalachian life.

Even George Washington didn't fathom the ferocity of the Appalachians' claim to personal liberty—until the Whiskey Rebellion caused backwoodsmen to take up arms and march east in protest against excessive taxes on their mountain brew. Before and during the Civil War, mountain independence asserted itself once more: many of the Appalachian counties in Virginia, Tennessee, or North Carolina either seceded from their states or refused to support the Confederacy.

1. The author is primarily concerned with
   (A) condemning the backwoodsmen for the Whiskey Rebellion
   (B) describing the character of the people of Appalachia
   (C) listing the main geographical divisions of Appalachia
   (D) praising the people of Appalachia for ignoring the Civil War
   (E) criticizing literary attempts to interpret Appalachian life

2. According to the author, which of the following are characteristics of the Appalachian people?
   I. Ferocity
   II. Independence
   III. Dishonesty
   (A) I only   **(B)** I and II only   **(C)** I and III only
   (D) II and III only   **(E)** I, II, and III

1. (B) This question asks about the main point of the selection. (A), (D), and (E) are incorrect for much the same reasons. Though the author does mention those things, no condemnation, praise, or criticism is implied. As for (C), the author never gives such a list. (B) is the best description of the author's main point. The passage describes the important traits of the Appalachian people.

2. (B) This question asks about specific points mentioned in the selection. The first sentence of the second paragraph mentions ferocity, and the last sentence of the passage mentions independence. No mention, however, is made of dishonesty.

A typical Reading Comprehension section includes four reading selections. Each selection is approximately 550 to 600 words long and supports six to eight questions. The total number of questions for the section is 26 to 28.

2. Logical Reasoning

Logical reasoning items ask you to evaluate an argument. The argument may be a single sentence or a short paragraph.

EXAMPLES:

1. I never bother with a seat belt when I'm just going to the store because I won't be driving more than 30 miles per hour.

   The speaker above apparently assumes that automobile accidents

   (A) never occur when the car is traveling at exactly 30 miles per hour
   (B) always occur when a car is traveling in excess of 30 miles per hour
   (C) only occur when a car is traveling at 30 miles per hour or less
   (D) only occur when a car is traveling at more than 30 miles per hour
   (E) only occur when a driver is not in his own neighborhood

2. It is clear that television scenes depicting acts of violence can result in actual crimes. After a major network aired a movie in which a person is shown leaping to his death from a bridge, there were three such suicides.

   The author is primarily concerned with

   (A) refuting a theory
   (B) proving a causal connection
   (C) appealing to an authority
   (D) pointing out a contradiction
   (E) making a statistical comparison

1. (D) The question stem asks us to figure out what must have been on the speaker's mind when the statement was made. For the statement to make sense, it must be the case that the speaker feels that accidents just don't occur if you're driving at 30 miles per hour or less. If that's true, then the claim makes sense.

2. (B) The author is attempting to demonstrate that violent scenes on television can create real violence. (B) is the best description of this. Of course, the argument may not be very convincing (in the sketchy form presented here), but (B) is a good description of the author's intention.

A typical Logical Reasoning section contains 24 to 26 such items.

3. Analytical Reasoning

Analytical reasoning items are logical puzzles or games. You are given a description of a situation, for example, the need to create a seating arrangement at a party. Then you are asked to deduce logical conclusions from the description, e.g., who can sit where.

EXAMPLE:

George is hosting a dinner party with five guests, Sally, Bob, Iris, Carl, and Mark. George and his guests will sit at a round table. Around the table there are six, evenly spaced chairs.
Carl will not sit next to Mark.
Bob must have Sally on his immediate right.

1. All of the following are possible arrangements (starting with George and reading around the table from his left to his right) EXCEPT
   (A) George, Carl, Sally, Bob, Iris, Mark
   (B) George, Mark, Sally, Bob, Iris, Carl
   (C) George, Mark, Sally, Bob, Carl, Iris
   (D) George, Sally, Bob, Mark, Iris, Carl
   (E) George, Iris, Mark, Sally, Carl, Bob

2. If Iris is seated directly to Bob's left, which of the following must be true?
   I. Bob sits next to George.
   II. Carl sits next to George.
   III. Mark sits next to Iris.
   (A) I only   **(B)** II only   **(C)** I and II only
   (D) II and III only   **(E)** I, II, and III

1. (E) All of the arrangements are possible but (E). (E) violates the condition that Sally must be seated immediately to Bob's right.

2. (B) Given that Sally is seated to Bob's right, if Iris is seated to his left, then those three must be seated Iris–Bob–Sally (as they face the table). Since Mark and Carl must be separated, there are only two possible ways of seating the group:
   George, Mark, Sally, Bob, Iris, Carl
   or
   George, Carl, Sally, Bob, Iris, Mark
So statement I cannot be true, and statement III might be true (but it is not necessarily true). Statement II, however, is necessarily true.

A typical Analytical Reasoning section contains 22–24 items presented in four or five groups.

4. Writing Sample

The writing sample is a 30-minute section during which you are required to write an essay on a specific topic. The essay is not scored by the LSAC/LSAS, but copies of your essay are sent to each law school that receives a copy of your LSAT score. Then the use that is made of the essay in the admission process is determined by each individual institution. Here is a sample essay topic:

Martha is a professional dancer. Recently, based on her performances at auditions, she has received offers of employment from two dance companies. Write an essay arguing that Martha should accept one of the offers instead of the other. Two considerations should guide your decision:

—Martha enjoys performing but also wants the opportunity to choreograph and present some works of her own creation.

—Martha wants to earn a salary that will enable her to improve her standard of living. She is currently earning about $12,000 per year.

Martha is considering an offer from the Robertson Modern Dance Company. The company is a relatively small group with only eight dancers, so each member of the company is included in at least one piece on each program. Additionally, Martha would not have to wait long for the opportunity to perform solo works, and the company has a policy of introducing new works choreographed by its members. The company holds a two-week season each year at the James Theater in the city and tours at colleges and universities for the rest of the year. All in all, the company puts on 35 to 40 performances each year. The starting salary would be $12,000, but Martha could supplement that by teaching dance classes in the company's studio on a part-time basis.

Martha is also considering an offer from the New Town Jazz Company, a larger company with 35 members. Because of the larger size, Martha could not expect to be featured prominently in any pieces at first, and she could not expect the company to allow her to choreograph her own pieces. The starting salary, however, is $15,500, and the company puts on 65 to 70 performances each year.

There is no single correct essay response. Whether a response is better or worse depends upon a number of considerations, such as organization and execution —topics we take up in the lessons devoted to the writing sample.

5. Format

The sections on your test could appear in any order. Here is a summary of what your LSAT might look like.

Section 1: Reading Comprehension (28 Questions, 35 minutes)
Section 2: Logical Reasoning (25 Questions, 35 minutes)
Section 3: Wild Card Section (?? Questions, 35 minutes)
Section 4: Analytical Reasoning (24 Questions, 35 minutes)
Section 5: Logical Reasoning (24 Questions, 35 minutes)
Writing Sample (30 minutes)

6. Scoring the LSAT

The scoring procedure is very simple. You get one raw score point for each question you answer correctly. (Incorrect responses and omitted questions do not affect your score.) Raw scores are converted to scaled scores ranging from 120 (the minimum) to 180 (the maximum) using a formula that is uniquely designed for that particular LSAT. The formula for each test form "equates" that test form to previously administered tests. The process of equating irons out any score differences that might otherwise result from differences in the levels of difficulty.

You will also be provided with a table that allows you to compare your score with those of other test-takers. The following table will give you some idea of what various scores mean:

Raw Score	Scaled Score
99–100	180
90	170
80	163
70	158
60	152
50	147
40	142
30	135
20	127

(**Important Note:** This scoring table is not derived from any particular LSAT, and it is not meant for any other test. In particular, it should not be used to score the tests in this book.) Each question counts for about a half a point on the scaled score.

Summary

1. The LSAT consists of five separately timed, 35-minute multiple-choice sections plus a 30-minute writing sample.
2. The topics covered in the multiple-choice sections are:
   Reading Comprehension
   Logical Reasoning
   Analytical Reasoning
3. The LSAT score is a function of the number of questions you answer correctly.

Nuts and Bolts

1. The Guessing Gold Mine
2. As Time Goes By . . .
3. Be in Control
4. Pace Makes the Race
   - Don't Stop to Read Directions
   - The Tradeoff
   - Leapfrogging
   - Throwing in the Towel
5. The Test Booklet and the Answer Sheet
6. Go with Your Choice!
7. Special Pressures

1. The Guessing Gold Mine

As was pointed out in the last lesson, unlike some other standardized tests, the LSAT does not penalize incorrect answers. This means, of course, that you should answer every item—even when your response is nothing but a guess.

As obvious as this is, I think that students sometimes don't understand what a gold mine guessing is because they think in terms of an individual item and not in terms of the test as a whole. Suppose, for example, that by guessing you pick up two more questions in each of the sections that counts in your score. Would that be important? Yes. That could mean the difference between a 150 and a 154, a 160 and a 164, and so on. The difference would catapult you over thousands of other candidates and that could increase significantly your chances of getting admitted at many schools.

On any question that you cannot answer confidently, eliminate as many choices as you can, and then make a guess anyway. (Pick a letter, any letter!) And even if you run out of time, fill in the rest of the answer spaces. (Pick letters!) You have nothing to lose, and everything to gain.

2. As Time Goes By . . .

Your LSAT (aside from the writing sample) will consist of five *separately* timed sections. The proctors will tell you when you can begin working on a section and when your time is up. Once a section is over, you cannot go back to it. So you must answer everything you can in a section during the time given.

In order to do this, you have to keep track of the passing time. Although the proctors do this, there may be problems. A proctor may or may not announce the time at the exact moment when it changes. For example, a proctor may say "Five Minutes To Go" when there are really only four minutes left.

3. Be in Control

Bring your own watch to the exam. If you have one with a stopwatch function, then use it. A word of warning! Do not use an alarm. The constant "beep beep" will unfairly distract other test-takers, and the proctors might confiscate your watch for the duration of the exam. In some ways, a simple watch with a minute hand is the best watch to use. As each 35-minute period begins, just set the minute hand of the watch to 25 minutes past any hour (set the minute hand on the "5"). Thirty-five minutes later the minute hand will be at "12," and your time will be up. Setting the watch in this way lets you know at a glance and within a minute or so how much time remains.

4. Pace Makes the Race

Keeping track of time, however, is not your end goal. The real goal is to *use* the time—and to use it effectively. You must pace yourself, working as rapidly as possible without working so quickly that you sacrifice accuracy to speed. Here are some suggestions to help you get the most out of your time.

1. Don't Stop to Read Directions

No extra time is given for reading the instructions for a section. If you have to read the directions, you are using time that could be better spent answering questions.

There is no reason to read the instructions included in the test booklet. The directions that are used in this book are word-for-word the same directions that will be in your test booklet. The Law School Admissions Services has allowed them to be reprinted here.

2. The Tradeoff

The time limit places you in a dilemma. On the one hand, you cannot afford to work so slowly and carefully that you do not try as many questions as you otherwise could. On the other hand, you cannot afford to work so quickly that you make foolish errors. Somewhere between the two extremes is the answer.

You will develop your own sense of pacing and find the answer by doing this book's practice exercises. If you find that you are not finishing most of the questions in a practice exercise, then on the next exercise you should speed up. If you find that you are answering most questions but are making a lot of silly mistakes, then slow down.

Finding the best tradeoff is not a science. It is a practical art. Only practice will help you find the answer to the problem.

3. Leapfrogging

A third important technique of pacing is leapfrogging, that is, jumping over difficult questions. A question may seem to you to be difficult either because it really is one of the hard ones or because you just happen to have a blind spot for that particular item. Whatever the reason, you cannot afford to spend a lot of time working on a single question.

Remember that each correct answer counts exactly one point toward the raw score—not more, not less. The easiest question on the test adds one to your raw score; the most difficult question on the test adds one to your raw score. Why spend five minutes on a difficult item, when there are easy questions later in the section just waiting to be picked?

4. *Throwing in the Towel*

The final key to effective pacing is knowing when to give up. You cannot afford to keep working on a question after you have invested a reasonable amount of time with no reward. If you spend three minutes worrying about a question—just waiting for the lightning to strike, so to speak—when you could have used that time to answer four or five other questions, then you are squandering your time.

Once you reach a dead end (you know you do not know what to do or you know it will take too long), throw in the towel. Make your guess and move on to the next question.

5. The Test Booklet and the Answer Sheet

Your answers to questions must be entered on a separate answer sheet by darkening spaces on a grid. This grid is then read by a machine. The LSAT is absolutely unforgiving of mistakes in this respect. If you know the answer to a question but forget to mark your answer sheet, you get no credit. If you mark the wrong space on the answer sheet, you get no credit. If you do not mark your answer sheet clearly, the result is the same: no credit.

It is important to enter your answer choices clearly and correctly. Take a look at a portion of a sample answer sheet:

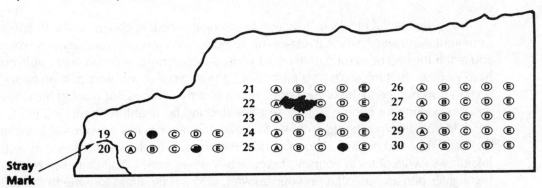

Stray Mark

The marks for questions 19 and 25 are made correctly. They are neat and dark, and they completely fill the spaces. The mark for question 20 does not completely fill the space, so the machine might miss it, giving no credit for the question. The mark for question 21 is not dark enough; again the machine might miss it, giving no credit. The mark for question 22 is messy; the machine is likely to read this as a multiple response.

Question 23 will be graded as an omitted question since there are two answers entered. (No penalty, but no credit either.)

Question 24 is blank. (A mistake, since there is no penalty for guessing.)

Questions 26 through 30 have also been left blank. If we assume that there were only 25 questions in the section, this is the correct thing to do with those spaces.

The very worst mistake that you can make with your answer sheet is to enter your responses in the wrong places. You could skip a question in your test booklet and fail to skip the corresponding answer space on your answer sheet. As a result, a whole series would be displaced by one question. The correct pattern would be there, but it would be in the wrong place. The grading machine doesn't grade your intentions; it reads the marks just as they stand.

You can avoid this error. Aside from taking care in coding answers and checking every now and then to make sure that your problem numbers and answer space numbers match up, there are two further safeguards you should use.

First, keep a separate record of your answer choices in your test booklet. Simply draw a circle around your correct answer choices. If you should make an error in coding responses, this safeguard allows you to retrieve the information without having to rework every question.

Circle the number of any question that you leapfrog over. This will enable you to locate the questions when you have finished your work and have time to go back and study them. If you do go back and arrive at an answer, then blacken in the circle around the number. This lets you know that you have already taken care of the question.

For questions that you answer but are not sure about, place a "?" beside the number. Then, if you have time, you can easily locate the questions and review your solution. For such questions, if you have definitely eliminated some choices as incorrect, place an "x" over those letters. This will let you concentrate on the remaining choices.

A second method of protecting your answer sheet is to enter the answers in groups. Why work a problem, shuffle paper, make a mark, work another problem, shuffle paper, make a mark, and so on? This is not only clumsy; it increases the danger of making a silly coding mistake. Instead, work a group of five or six questions and then mark them on the answer sheet. That will reduce the danger of such errors.

There are natural breaks in a section for doing this coding chore. In the Reading Comprehension and Analytical Reasoning sections, you can code your answers when you reach the end of a group of items. In Logical Reasoning, you can wait until you have worked all of the items on a particular page. A word of warning: as time for the section runs out, go to the one-by-one coding system. You do not want to have five answers waiting for coding in your test booklet and be unable to transfer them.

Additionally, you should feel free to make any other marks in your test booklet that you might find helpful. You can underline phrases, circle words, draw connecting arrows, write notes to yourself, or make any other marks. You can even bring a highlighter pen and use that on your booklet. Do not be afraid to write in the test booklet. You paid for it and the test booklets are not reused. They are eventually destroyed.

6. Go with Your Choice!

Many people worry about having too many of one letter and not enough of others. When an LSAT section is put together, the test writers make sure that there are approximately equal numbers of each letter—*approximately* equal. In a section like Analytical Reasoning with 24 questions, you might have five (A)s, four (B)s, three (C)s, six (D)s, and six (E)s. The distribution is not perfect.

Also, it is possible to have strings of letters, for example, two or three (D)s in a row. You will not, however, find a string of four or more letters in a row. If you find four (B)s in a row on your answer sheet, at least one of them is wrong. Unfortunately, you will not know without rechecking each question where the error is.

3

7. Special Pressures

The LSAT, as you know by now, is different in some very important respects from the teacher-prepared tests you usually get in college. These differences can put special pressures on you.

In the first place, you can expect to experience considerable time pressure. You will probably feel that you are running out of time and that if you only had more time, you could definitely answer most if not all of the questions. And this happens not just once, but five times during the test (plus in the writing sample).

Just because you feel time pressure does not mean that you are not doing well. Everyone feels the time pressure. That is part of the design of the test. The objective is to do as many questions as you can within the time allowed.

Additionally, you may get the idea that you are not doing very well because you are not answering with confidence. At the back of your mind is the gnawing thought, "I like answer (C), but it could be (B), or even (E)." Again, everyone feels this way. Use your best judgment, enter your choice, and do not second-guess yourself.

Finally, you may need to adjust your expectations about performance. What percentage of questions must you answer correctly to get an "A" or a "B" on an ordinary exam? Eighty percent to 90 percent right would usually get you a "B," and anything above that would be an "A". What would 70 percent right be? A "D," almost certainly. And no one wants to get a "D."

Things are different with the LSAT. Getting 70 percent of the questions on the LSAT correct does not result in a poor mark. For example, if you answered correctly 70 percent of 100 questions, your raw score would be 70 and your scaled score about 160. But a scaled score of 160 would put you in the top half of all test-takers—not a poor score at all.

Ninety percent correct on an ordinary test would just barely be a grade of "A." On the LSAT, a raw score of 90 would be a scaled score of 170+ or so—almost at the top!

So you must adjust your expectations slightly. Remember that to get the score you want, you will not need to answer correctly the same number of questions that you would ordinarily have to answer on other tests.

Summary

1. Learn to pace yourself. (1) Don't stop for directions; (2) learn by practice the optimal tradeoff for you between speed and accuracy; (3) know when to leapfrog over a question; and (4) learn when to throw in the towel.

2. Mark your answer sheet carefully, coding in groups. Develop your own record system to keep track of your progress in your test booklet.

3. Understand the special pressures that are created by the LSAT and learn to ignore them.

Test Anxiety

1. The LSAT and the Fear of Final Judgment

Many, even most, students experience a sense of dread or foreboding about the LSAT. For some, the feeling is no more than an uncomfortable and vague sense of uneasiness. For others, the dread can become unmanageable, leading to what is called test anxiety. In extreme cases, test anxiety can be crippling and can seriously interfere with a person's ability to take a test. This extreme anxiety, the fear of the LSAT as a final judgment, is created by a group of mistaken beliefs or impressions that work together to create the greater anxiety. You do not have to experience all of the impressions to feel the strong sense of anxiety. What are these mistaken beliefs and impressions?

2. LSAC/LSAS's Authority

Most people regard the LSAT as having a kind of natural authority over them, something like the physical laws that govern the universe. Why is there an LSAT? Well, that's like asking why is there gravity. It's just there, a fact of the world. This impression is mistaken.

To see that this impression of natural authority is an error, you need only think about the nature of your relationship to the LSAT. When you register to take the LSAT, you are entering into a legal contract with the LSAS (the nonprofit corporation that owns the LSAT). You are paying them a fee, and they agree in turn to provide you with a service. That service is to administer to you a test and to report your scores to the schools you designate. Because you pay the fee, the LSAS has a legal obligation to you.

The registration form you sign and the information booklet you receive from the LSAS set forth in detail the specific provisions of your agreement with them. Don't worry that all of this is not one single typed document (like a deed). It's still a legal contract. (In fact, most contracts are just verbal agreements, and they are still legally binding.) So you and the LSAS are parties to a business contract.

Two factors, however, tend to obscure the fact that you and the LSAS have a business relationship. First, the LSAS is a nonprofit organization. People reason that "since they are not in business to make a profit, they must administer the LSAT for altruistic reasons." This reasoning is mistaken. Though the LSAS is a nonprofit organization, the people who work there are motivated by many of the same concerns that motivate the people who run General Motors or IBM. They are concerned about income, expenses, the quality of their product, customer relations, and so on.

This doesn't mean that the people who work at the LSAS don't believe in what they do. They believe that they produce a good product and they are proud of it, but the fact that a business does not make a profit does not necessarily make it morally better than any other business.

The second factor that helps to create the impression of natural authority is the LSAS's monopoly. As I pointed out in Lesson One, to practice law in most states you must have graduated from an ABA-accredited law school, and it is the LSAC (the association of these ABA-accredited law schools) that provides for the LSAT. You don't have a choice about which test you're going to take. If you want to go to law school, you have to do business with the LSAS. But monopoly is an economic fact of life, not a natural law. You buy your electricity from a particular business because it is the one that services your area. So, too, the LSAS happens to service this particular sector of the economy.

In any event, your relationship to LSAS is that of contract—and it takes two parties to make a contract. You are an equal partner to the contract, and you have certain legal rights under the contract.

3. Superpeople?

The testing process also creates another impression. You sit down in a classroom at the testing center. You are given the test booklet and told to answer 130 or so questions in less than three hours. (Remember, you'll also have a wild card section.) You begin to think that the person who wrote these questions must really be superhuman because you are expected to answer them (and many of them are very difficult) in so short a time. This impression that a genius is behind the test is an error.

This test is not written by a single person, or by two, or even three. Rather, the test is the product of a large group of people including teachers, reviewers, and statisticians. Each question is a group effort.

In fact, you will be involved in the process of creating LSAT questions. As a final check, questions are included in non-scoring sections of the LSAT (the "wild card" section). Then computers are used to check for patterns. Do the questions work in the way they are supposed to? Student responses on the wild card sections of LSATs are essential to the development of new versions of the exam.

4. They Do Make Mistakes

A related impression conveyed by the testing process is that it is free from error. A misconception! In the first place, every so often a defective question shows up on an actual LSAT. When the LSAS catches it, the item is not scored. This happens very rarely, and a single item would not significantly affect the final scoring of the test anyway; but it is reassuring to know that the test preparers are not infallible.

The belief in the infallibility of the test preparers is a mistake for a more important reason. Built into the scoring of the LSAT is a 6-point range of error! The technical term for this is the standard error of measurement. The standard error of measurement for the LSAT is 3 points. This means that two-thirds of all scores are within 3 points above or below the so-called true score.

Thus, in a group of three students who each receive 150 on the LSAT, the "true" scores of two of those students are anywhere from 147 to 153. And the "true" score of the third student could be anything. (Imagine handling your checking account like this: "Well, my records show I have a balance of $500, which means I could have as little as $390 in the account or as much as $670. Unless, of course, this is one of those three times when I'm really wrong. Then I could have anywhere from $0 to $1,000.")

It is an error, therefore, to treat an LSAT score as though it measures anything with decimal-point precision. In fact, the LSAC and LSAS are aware of the limitations of the LSAT and take pains to advise law schools of this fact and to discourage them from placing too much emphasis on the test. (See "The Score Isn't Everything," below.)

5. Power to the Test-taker

The testing process can also create a mistaken impression that the LSAS is all-powerful and that you are powerless. The LSAS sets the testing dates, the fees, the locations, and the conditions under which you will take the exam. It is true that you have very little say in these matters. Just remember, this is the result of the LSAS's monopoly in this area.

You have to do business with the LSAS. That is an economic fact of life, like public utilities. But the LSAS is no more omnipotent than your local electric, gas, or phone company.

This impression of omnipotence can also haunt you as you take the test. You are told where to sit; what you may and may not have with you; when you can use the restroom. And when the proctor reads the rules governing the testing procedure, it may sound as though you are hearing sentence passed. It may be difficult, but try to ignore this feeling. The supervisors and proctors maintain an air of authority to make sure that they can keep control of the situation.

Finally, you may also find yourself thinking that the LSAS is a kind of priesthood that guards the mysteries of the LSAT, and to a certain extent this impression is correct. After all, the LSAS is not going to give away any secrets of the LSAT if it can avoid doing so. Time have changed, however, in one important respect. Several years ago, the State of New York enacted legislation that is popularly called the "Truth-in-Testing" law. Under this law, businesses that administer standardized tests in New York are required to release copies of the exams and other information to persons who have taken the exam.

Prior to this law, most businesses that engaged in testing released very little information about their exams—at most a handful of sample questions and a few paragraphs of descriptive material—and test-takers were not allowed to review the exams they took. You will be given the opportunity to obtain a copy of the questions that were used to create your LSAT score.

In fact, the LSAC/LSAS has been even more liberal in its disclosure policies than required by the strict letter of the law, perhaps the result of some corporate soul-searching prompted by the "Truth-in-Testing" law. Of course, the test development process must always, to a certain extent, be shrouded in mystery. After all, if the LSAT is to serve any function at all, each new test form must remain a secret until the day that form is actually administered.

6. The Score Isn't Everything

One of the most important aspects of the fear of final judgment is the impression of finality created by the testing process. To a certain extent, the result of your test (barring a mistake in scoring) is final. (You may take the LSAT more than once, but your earlier score or scores still follow you.) Once graded, that is the score you receive and it doesn't change. But many people have the mistaken impression that bad (or good) things are automatically going to happen as a result of the LSAT. In fact, the LSAT is a lot less important than you might think.

First, while it cannot be denied that LSAT scores are an important part of the admissions process, very few law schools regard LSAT scores as either passing or failing. The score is just one more factor used in making a decision, like grades, activities, motivation, and so on. So a "poor" mark will not necessarily keep you out of a school, and a "good" mark will not guarantee you will get in. (Again, I would suggest that you obtain a copy of *The Official Guide to U.S. Law Schools: the Prelaw Handbook* from the LSAS. Many law schools provide tables showing the number of applicants with particular LSAT scores and grade point averages and the number who were accepted.)

Second, a year after you take the test, no one else will care what your score was. Your professors will grade you on the basis of your course work. New acquaintances will accept you on the basis of your personality. Student associations will want you as a member for your motivation, energy, and ability.

7. Exploding the Myth of Final Judgment

I have examined several different impressions about the LSAT that I believe are mistaken. No one individual impression would be a very serious cause for concern. However, when the individual impressions are taken as a group, they can create the fear of final judgment. And it is understandable. You think you are about to be judged by some supreme authority who is both omniscient and omnipotent and that this judgment will be final.

In discussing the "myth" of final judgment, I do not mean to imply that anyone or any group set out to perpetrate a hoax. In particular, I am not suggesting that the LSAC or LSAS has consciously conspired to mislead people. In fact, if you read the information bulletin that comes with the registration materials for the LSAT, you will find that the LSAC/LSAS says many of the same things I have just said.

This mistaken impression of final judgment could be just an accident of history, but you do not have to live with it. (After all, at the time of Columbus almost everyone believed the world was flat.) If you take care to avoid falling under the spell of any one of the individual misconceptions, you should be able to keep any fears you might have about the LSAT under control.

Unlocking the Mystery

1. **Advance Warning**
2. **Multiple-Choice**
3. **Adventures of the LSAT**
   - **The Case of the Missing Reading Passage**
   - **The Case of the Hidden Clue**
   - **The Adventure of the Lengthy Solution**

Wouldn't it be great to take a test where you have all of the questions in advance and the answers are right there on the test paper? Well, the LSAT comes close. First, it is almost possible to know in advance what questions will be asked. Second, the answers are actually given to you on the test paper. These two features of the test form the basis for our system.

1. Advance Warning

Year after year the LSAT is given to tens of thousands of students; and, according to the LSAC/LSAS, scores are comparable, not just from administration to administration within a given year, but even from year to year. But how is that possible, since different test forms with completely different questions are used? The answer is found in the design specifications for the test. Each form of the exam, indeed each question, is written according to special formulas. A question is not acceptable for use on the LSAT unless it fits a particular pattern. These patterns are there for you to learn, and that is like having the questions before the test. Of course, you cannot literally have the exact questions that will appear on your particular LSAT, but certain patterns are so clearly identifiable that it almost amounts to the same thing.

2. Multiple-Choice

Additionally, you are actually given the answers to every question on your LSAT. Since every question on the exam is a multiple-choice question, the right answer is there on the page. Of course, the correct answer is camouflaged in a group of wrong answers; but even though it is partially hidden, it's there for the taking. To demonstrate how important this is, we interrupt this discussion for a:

POP QUIZ

Who was the fourth Chief Justice of the United States?

Time's up! I am not going to give you the correct answer just yet. (If you do know the answer, that's good, and I would want you as my partner in a game of trivia. But for right now, let's assume that you do not know the answer.) It is not the answer to the question that is important to us, but the form of the question.

With a question in this form, you have to come up with an answer from scratch. Either you know the name of the Fourth Chief Justice or you do not. And if not, you must either leave the question blank or make a wild guess. Either way, your chance of getting credit for the question is very small.

Things change, however, if the question is converted to a multiple-choice format:

POP QUIZ

Who was the fourth Chief Justice of the United States?
(A) xxxxx xxxxxx   **(B)** xxxxx xxxxxx   **(C)** xxxxx xxxxxx
(D) xxxxx xxxxxx   **(E)** xxxxx xxxxxx

Notice that the choices have been covered. Still, even though you cannot read the choices, you are in a much better position than you were before. Given the form of the earlier question, without the knowledge needed to answer the question you had literally no chance of getting credit for it. Now, even though you may not have knowledge that will allow you to answer with confidence, you at least have a fighting chance: pick any letter, and you have a one-out-of-five chance of getting credit for the question.

With real answer choices, you can tip the odds even more in your favor.

POP QUIZ

Who was the fourth Chief Justice of the United States?
(A) Julius Caesar   **(B)** Mickey Mouse   **(C)** Roger Taney
(D) Johnny Carson   **(E)** Madonna
Enter the letter of your choice here: _____

The correct answer is (C), and almost everyone can answer correctly even though they may have never before seen the name Roger Taney.

How is it possible to answer correctly and even confidently when you don't have the historical fact needed to answer the question? "Easy," you say. "Just eliminate the four choices that could not possibly be correct and select the one that remains."

This method of reasoning is called the Process of Elimination, and it takes advantage of an inherent weakness in the multiple-choice format. One—and only one—of the choices is correct. If you keep eliminating wrong choices, eventually only the correct choice will remain. Granted, eliminating wrong choices on the LSAT will not usually be this easy, but the principle is the same.

Patterns and answers are inherent in the LSAT. Get rid of either one, and the LSAT is no longer the LSAT. Therefore, so long as there is an LSAT there will be patterns that can be learned and there will be a multiple-choice format that can be taken advantage of.

You are surely familiar with Sherlock Holmes, the fictional detective created by the British writer Sir Arthur Conan Doyle. Using clues and logic, Holmes is able to solve case after case, even though to everyone else the situations seem to present insoluble mysteries. Most people are also familiar with the character of Dr. Watson, Holmes's good-natured friend and sometimes bachelor roommate. Watson, a medical doctor, is clearly a bright person, but his powers of investigation and logical reasoning do not quite equal those of his friend Holmes.

What would happen if these characters took the LSAT? I imagine that Watson would do fairly well. He would be able to answer many of the questions, but he would be likely to miss a lot of the more difficult ones. On the other hand, Holmes would surely do very well, getting answers to difficult questions by methods that seem almost magical.

In solving cases, Holmes relies heavily on two techniques: looking for established patterns and the process of elimination. First, in case after case, Holmes refers to his studies of patterns—footprints, cigar ashes, chemicals, and so on. Having foreknowledge of what to look for is often the key to Holmes' solution of a mystery.

Second, Holmes also uses logical reasoning, in particular, the process of elimination. In the "Adventure of the Bruce-Partington Plans," Holmes explains to Watson, "When all other contingencies fail, whatever remains, however improbable, must be the truth." That is the process of elimination.

Thus, Holmes succeeded where others failed because he was able to identify patterns and because he reasoned logically. You will notice that these two techniques are the same ones we talked about above.

If Watson and Holmes were to encounter the LSAT, here is what I think would happen.

3. Adventures of the LSAT

The Case of the Missing Reading Passage

One day Watson came to his friend Holmes with a problem. "Holmes," said Watson, "I have a reading comprehension question that I must answer, but I seem to have lost the reading selection on which the question is based. Now I'll never be able to answer the question."

"Show me the question," insisted Holmes, taking the page offered by Watson. On the page was written:

> The author's attitude toward the new technique of literary criticism is
> **(A)** apathetic   **(B)** sentimental   **(C)** scholarly
> **(D)** careless   **(E)** approving

"Why, Watson," exclaimed Holmes, "this is a multiple-choice question. My methods are perfectly suited to it. If we can eliminate four of the five choices by any means whatsoever, then the one choice that remains must be the correct one."

Holmes studied the question for a moment before he spoke further. "We can infer," he began, "from the question itself that in the missing reading selection the author discussed some new technique of literary criticism. Now let us study the answer choices.

"In the first place, Watson, (A) does not seem to be a possible answer. The question stem informs us that the author has been writing about this new development. But if the author has gone to the trouble of writing an article about something, then it hardly seems likely that the author had no interest in the topic. We conclude, therefore, that the author is not apathetic.

"Now let us examine (B). Could the author's attitude be described as 'sentimental'? Before you answer yes, Watson, let's return to the question. The question asks about the author's attitude toward some *new* development. Is it possible that you would ever describe someone's attitude toward a *new* development as sentimental?"

"No," Watson agreed. "But the author might have regarded the *old* method with affection."

"Perhaps, Watson. But literary criticism does not seem the sort of thing about which one would feel sentimental. And in any case, the question asks for the author's attitude toward the *new* literary criticism—not the old criticism. So you see, (B) cannot be correct."

"So the correct choice must be (C)," offered Watson. "Literary criticism is a scholarly endeavor, so the missing reading passage must have been a scholarly work."

"Not too fast, my dear friend," Holmes interrupted. "Although I readily grant what you say, that does not prove that (C) is the answer we seek. The question does not ask about the author's style but about the author's opinion of the new development. I think you would agree that it makes little sense to say that the author's opinion is scholarly."

"So we must eliminate (C)," said Watson. "Holmes, even if we are not successful in eliminating one of the remaining choices, at least I shall have an even chance of selecting the correct one. It must be either (D) or (E)."

"Well, Watson, it seems to me that we can eliminate (D) on very much the same ground that we eliminated (C). Although 'careless' might describe the author's method in discussing a topic, it would surely not describe the author's attitude toward the new development."

"By Jove, you're right!" Watson exclaimed. "The correct solution is probably (E)."

"Not probably," insisted Holmes. "Certainly! We have eliminated all possibilities but (E) and that *proves* (E) is the correct solution. We now know in fact that the author approves of the new development discussed in the reading selection—even though we do not have a copy of the selection."

The Case of the Hidden Clue

One wintery afternoon, Holmes and Watson were riding in the compartment of a train on their way back to London. Watson, looking up from the book he was reading, blurted out, "Blast these logical reasoning questions, Holmes! I can't figure out why the correct answer to this one is correct." And he read to Holmes the following:

"Advertising claim: Bernie's is the only department store where you can buy a 19-inch Commander color television for $195 and for that price get a six-month warranty.

"Which of the following, if true, proves that the advertising claim above is FALSE?
(A) The Commander Television Company's factory outlet sells the same model television for $195 and backs the set with the same warranty.
(B) Al's Department Store sells a 19-inch Hokusi color television for $195 and backs the set with the same warranty.
(C) Trader John's Department Store sells the same model television for $185 and backs the set with a twelve-month warranty.
(D) Honest Hal's Department Store sells a 25-inch Commander color television for $195 and backs it with a warranty containing the same terms as Bernie's warranty.
(E) Jumpin' Jack's Department Store sells the same model television for $195 and backs it with the same warranty."

Holmes furrowed his brow and read the problem carefully. After a while he said, "Yes, Watson, I can understand your perplexity. But the verbal clues are there for you to read. The correct answer is (E)."

"As you know Watson," continued Holmes, "when I visit the scene of a crime, I pay very careful attention to all details. You, too, must learn this approach in order to solve successfully problems such as this one.

"Notice how cleverly the advertising claim is worded: Bernie's is the only *department store* that offers *this particular make and model for $195* and includes a *six-month* warranty. In essence, the claim states only that Bernie's is the only establishment that meets all of these criteria.

"Choice (A) does not contradict this claim, since Bernie's is careful to distinguish itself as a department store—not a factory outlet. That a different type of commercial establishment offers a similar arrangement does not, therefore, contradict Bernie's claim. As for (B), the fact that a similar commercial entity sells a different product for the same price hardly contradicts Bernie's claim.

"As for choices (C) and (D), the fact that other emporia offer arrangements that are even more favorable than those offered by Bernie's does not contradict Bernie's claim that it does exactly what it claims to do: sell the set for $195 and back it with a six-month warranty.

"Only (E) contradicts the wording of the claim, for (E) establishes that there is another, similar commercial entity that also does what Bernie's claims to do uniquely."

At this point Watson let out a sigh of frustration and said, "Well, if logical reasoning items require this much attention to detail, I don't see that I can ever hope to succeed in solving them."

"Don't despair, Watson. Rome wasn't built in a day. As you study more and more logical reasoning items, you will gain skill in the kind of observation that is needed to do well on them."

The Adventure of the Lengthy Solution

One sultry August afternoon, Holmes returned to the rooms he and Dr. Watson shared in Baker Street to find Watson hunched over his desk scribbling madly. After several minutes, Watson stood up and declared, "At last, I have the solution!" Some seconds later he added, "But it took me nearly eight minutes, and on the actual exam I wouldn't have that much time."

Sherlock Holmes walked over to the desk and read:

> Six people, J, K, L, M, N, and O, are standing in a queue, though not necessarily in that order. J is either first or last. L is fourth. K is either directly in front of or directly in back of M, and K is not directly in front of nor directly in back of N.

> **1.** Which of the following arrangements, given in order from the front of the queue to the back, is consistent with the restrictions outlined?
>
> **(A)** J, K, M, N, L, O
>
> **(B)** K, O, N, L, M, J
>
> **(C)** M, K, N, L, O, J
>
> **(D)** M, K, J, L, O, N
>
> **(E)** N, M, K, L, O, J

Holmes spent 30 seconds looking over the problem and nodded, "Yes, the correct choice is (E)." Then Holmes looked at Watson's scribblings.

Watson explained, "I was able to work out all of the possible arrangements of the six persons. They are

1. J, K, M, L, N, O
2. J, K, M, L, O, N
3. J, M, K, L, N, O
4. J, M, K, L, O, N
5. J, N, O, L, K, M
6. J, N, O, L, M, K
7. J, O, N, L, K, M
8. J, O, N, L, M, K
9. K, M, O, L, N, J
10. M, K, O, L, N, J
11. O, K, M, L, N, J
12. O, M, K, L, N, J
13. K, M, N, L, O, J
14. N, M, K, L, O, J

And you can see that only (E) is listed there."

Holmes then said, "But, Watson, you don't need to know every single possible arrangement. You only need to find the one choice that does not violate any of the conditions that describe the arrangement. You can reach the conclusion that (E) is correct simply by examining each answer in light of the initial conditions. For example, the initial conditions state that J must be either first or last, but in (D) J is neither first nor last. So (D) cannot be correct. The initial conditions also state that L is fourth, but in (A) L is not fourth. The initial conditions state that K is either directly in front of or directly in back of M, so (B) is not a possible arrangement. Finally, the initial conditions state that K is neither directly in front of nor directly behind N, so (C) must be incorrect. By the process of elimination, then, (E) must be the correct choice."

Most people who take the LSAT are in the position of Dr. Watson. They are able to answer most of the easy questions; they answer many of the questions of medium difficulty; but they are forced to guess on many of the very difficult items. Additionally, they take longer than necessary to solve a problem. Holmes, on the other hand, with his knowledge of patterns and power of logical thinking, would fare better.

The more you are able to think like Holmes, the better you will do on the LSAT. In the lessons that follow, you will read about basic strategies of the sort that would be used by Dr. Watson. These strategies are sound, but they are not the final word on attacking the LSAT. So you will also learn Holmesian strategies, like those discussed in the stories above, that take advantage of the multiple-choice format of the LSAT. I will try not to belabor the Holmes and Watson teaching device (though I hope you enjoyed reading "The Casebook"), but I will occasionally throw in a reference to one or the other character as a reminder of what we are trying to accomplish.

5

The Coaching Program

Reading Comprehension

The typical LSAT Reading Comprehension section includes four reading passages, 500 to 600 words long, each with six to eight questions, for a total of 26 to 28 questions in the section. Here are the instructions for reading comprehension:

> **Directions:** Each passage in this section is followed by questions based on its content. After reading the passage, choose the best answer to each question, and blacken the corresponding space on the answer sheet. Answer all questions following a passage on the basis of what is *stated* or *implied* in that passage.

This seems easy enough, but the impression of simplicity is misleading.

1. Why Reading Comprehension Is Difficult

Answering reading comprehension questions on the LSAT is not nearly as easy as the directions make it sound. Some students attribute the difficulty of reading comprehension to their inability to read quickly enough. They imagine they would do better if they were able to do "speed reading."

This conclusion is completely incorrect! The LSAT is not a test of "speed reading." First, the reading selections are only one to three, or perhaps four, paragraphs long—not long enough to need "speed reading" techniques and really too short to be susceptible to them. Second, the selections are edited in such a way as to make them too dense for "speed reading." Third, the questions test depth of understanding; and, in general, "speed reading" emphasizes coverage at the expense of understanding.

Three other factors make LSAT reading comprehension difficult.

A. LSAT reading selections can treat virtually any subject. Since authors can write about any topic whatsoever, a reading comprehension selection can be about anything.

Obviously, a reading selection about some strange topic is more difficult to read than one about material you know something about, and the test-writers go out of their way to find unfamiliar material!

Let's put this into perspective. The test-writers don't select obscure reading selections simply to make the reading more difficult. Rather, they select obscure passages to make sure the questions test *reading comprehension* rather than knowledge of a subject. The theory is that if a reading selection is about, say, the obscure medieval composer Josquin des Pres, no one will be able to answer questions based on memory.

Additionally, since this is not a test of knowledge, the reading selection will contain everything needed to answer the question. For example, if a reading comprehension question asks "Why is Josquin des Pres so little known?", the basis for the correct answer will be provided in the reading selection itself.

Finally, don't let the reading selections intimidate you! Imagine the following as an opening sentence of a reading passage:

Until Josquin des Pres, Western music was liturgical, designed as an accompaniment to worship.

Your reaction to this could be "Who the dickens is this guy? I've never even heard the name before. Now, I'll never be able to answer any questions!" This reaction, while understandable, is the wrong one to have. Rather, you should be thinking "Here's one of those obscure topics that is typical of the LSAT. No one else has ever heard of this guy either; and anyway, everything I need is included in the selection."

B. A second factor that adds difficulty to the reading comprehension part of the LSAT is that you have to begin your reading without any idea of what is coming. Imagine the following opening sentence of a reading selection:

By far the most successful and visible aspect of the legal revolution in mental health has been the civil liberties and patient advocacy groups' concern for the patients' physical liberty and autonomy, as distinguished from their psychological well-being.

The sentence is really not that difficult to understand, and the topic it treats is probably one you have read about in the newspaper or in a news magazine. But the sentence seems more difficult than it really is because you don't have a point of reference from which to begin your reading.

Your reading would be much easier if a selection were accompanied by an explanatory headline:

NEW LEGAL RIGHTS FOR MENTAL PATIENTS
By far the most successful and visible aspect of the legal revolution in mental health has been the civil liberties and patient advocacy groups' concern for the patients' physical liberty and autonomy, as distinguished from their psychological well-being.

If you found this headline and article in a news magazine, you would begin your reading with an appropriate context.

Unfortunately, on the LSAT you will not be given this luxury. Instead, it's up to you to jump into the reading selection with both feet and learn as best you can what the selection is about. Just remember, however, everything you need is in the selection and everyone else is having the same problem.

C. The selections are edited so that they will "support" questions. Remember, the object of reading comprehension is not to test what you already know but how well you read. Each reading selection is taken from already published material and edited to fit the test design. The result is one or more highly compact paragraphs on which reading comprehension questions can be based.

Contrast the following two descriptions of the same events. The first is what you would expect to find in an American history textbook; the second, on the LSAT.

6

TYPICAL TEXTBOOK

Franklin D. Roosevelt became President in March of 1933. American agriculture had been nearly devastated. So, President Roosevelt promised a new farm relief program to help the farmers.

The result was the passage of the Agricultural Adjustment Act of 1933. This law created the Agricultural Adjustment Administration, or AAA for short. The legislation was based on the assumption that prosperity could be restored to the rural sector of the economy if farmers could be persuaded to control agricultural output. By controlling output, it would be possible to eliminate surplus agricultural production.

The method by which the AAA hoped to accomplish the control of surplus production was direct cash payments to farmers.

TYPICAL LSAT

When Franklin D. Roosevelt assumed the Presidency in 1933, he fulfilled his promise to bring immediate relief to the nearly devastated agricultural community by the establishment of the Agricultural Adjustment Administration (AAA). Operating on the assumption that agricultural prosperity could be restored by eliminating surpluses, the AAA offered cash inducements to farmers to control production.

Some information is lost, but not much. The second rendering uses fewer words to convey almost the same information, so it is more difficult to read.

2. The Six Types of Reading

Comprehension Questions

Every LSAT reading comprehension question is an "open-book" test; the questions ask about a selection you can look at. And every LSAT reading comprehension question falls into one of six categories.

A. Main Idea Questions. These questions ask about the central theme that unifies the passage. They are often worded as follows:

Which of the following is the main point of the passage?

The primary purpose of the passage is to . . . .

The author is primarily concerned with . . . .

Which of the following titles best describes the content of the passage?

B. Specific Detail Questions. These questions ask about details that are explicitly mentioned in the passage. This type of question differs from a main idea question in that a specific detail is a point mentioned by the author as a part of the overall development of the main theme of the selection. These questions are often phrased:

> The author mentions which of the following?
>
> According to the author, ...
>
> The author provides information that would answer which of the following questions?

C. Logical Structure Questions. This type of question asks about the logical structure of the selection. Some such questions ask about the overall development of the passage and are sometimes phrased:

> The author develops the passage primarily by . . . .
>
> The author proceeds primarily by . . . .

Others ask about the role played by a specific detail. These are sometimes phrased:

> The author mentions . . . in order to . . . .
>
> Which of the following best explains why the author introduces . . . ?

D. Implied Idea Questions. These questions ask not about what is specifically stated in the passage in so many words, but about what can be logically inferred from what is stated in the passage. For example, the passage might explain that a certain organism, X, is found only in the presence of another organism, Y. Then, an implied idea question might ask "If organism Y is not present, what can be inferred?" The answer would be "X is not present." The passage implies, and you can infer from the passage, that in the absence of Y, X cannot be present. Implied idea questions are sometimes phrased:

> The passage implies that . . . .
>
> The author uses the phrase " . . . " to mean . . . .
>
> It can be inferred from the passage that . . . .
>
> Which of the following can be inferred from the passage?

E. Further Application Questions. These question are somewhat like implied idea questions, but they ask you to go one step further and apply what you have learned in the passage to a new situation. These are sometimes phrased:

> With which of the following statements would the author most likely agree?
>
> The author would probably consider which of the following a good example of her theory?
>
> The passage is most probably taken from which of the following sources?

F. Tone Questions. These questions ask you about the tone of the selection, that is, the attitude of the author. They can ask about the overall tone of the passage, in which case they are sometimes phrased as follows:

> The tone of the passage can best be described as . . . .

Or they can ask about the author's attitude toward some specific detail, in which case they might be phrased as follows:

> The author regards . . . as . . . .
>
> Which of the following best describes the author's attitude toward . . . ?

There are many different ways of wording these six types of questions, but every LSAT reading comprehension question falls into one of the six categories.

6

The Six Types of Questions (Answers, page 69)

The passage below is followed by questions that illustrate the six different types of reading comprehension questions. Answer the questions on the basis of what is stated or implied in the passage.

To broaden their voting appeal in the Presidential election of 1796, the Federalists selected Thomas Pinckney, a leading South Carolinian, as running mate for the New Englander John Adams. But Pinckney's Southern friends chose to ignore their party's intentions and regarded Pinckney as a Presidential candidate, creating a political situation that Alexander Hamilton was determined to exploit. Hamilton had long been wary of Adams' stubbornly independent brand of politics and preferred to see his running mate, over whom he could exert more control, in the President's chair.

The election was held under the system originally established by the Constitution. At that time there was but a single tally, with the candidate receiving the largest number of electoral votes declared President and the candidate with the second largest number declared Vice-President. Hamilton anticipated that all the Federalists in the North would vote for Adams and Pinckney equally in an attempt to ensure that Jefferson would not be either first or second in the voting. Pinckney would be solidly supported in the South while Adams would not. Hamilton concluded if it were possible to divert a few electoral votes from Adams to Pinckney, Pinckney would receive more than Adams, yet both Federalists would outpoll Jefferson.

Various methods were used to persuade the electors to vote as Hamilton wished. In the press, anonymous articles were published attacking Adams for his monarchial tendencies and Jefferson for being overly democratic, while pushing Pinckney as the only suitable candidate. In private correspondence with state party leaders the Hamiltonians encouraged the idea that Adams' popularity was slipping, that he could not win the election, and that the Federalists could defeat Jefferson only by supporting Pinckney.

Had sectional pride and loyalty not run as high in New England as in the deep South, Pinckney might well have become Washington's successor. New Englanders, however, realized that equal votes for Adams and Pinckney in their states would defeat Adams; therefore, eighteen electors scratched Pinckney's name from their ballots and deliberately threw away their second votes to men who were not even running. It was fortunate for Adams that they did, for the electors from South Carolina completely abandoned him, giving eight votes to Pinckney and eight to Jefferson.

In the end, Hamilton's interference in Pinckney's candidacy lost even the Vice-Presidency for South Carolina. Without New England's support, Pickney received only 59 electoral votes, finishing third to Adams and Jefferson. He might have been President in 1797, or as Vice-President a serious contender for the Presidency in 1800; instead, stigmatized by a plot he had not devised, he served a brief term in the United States Senate and then dropped from sight as a national influence.

Main Idea Questions

1. The main purpose of the passage is to
   (A) propose reforms of the procedures for electing the President and Vice-President
   (B) condemn Alexander Hamilton for interfering in the election of 1796
   (C) describe the political events that lead to John Adams' victory in the 1796 Presidential election
   (D) contrast the political philosophy of the Federalists to that of Thomas Jefferson
   (E) praise Thomas Pinckney for his refusal to participate in Hamilton's scheme to have him elected President

2. Which of the following titles best describes the content of the passage?
   (A) The Failure of Alexander Hamilton's Plan for Thomas Pinckney to Win the 1796 Presidential Election
   (B) The Roots of Alexander Hamilton's Distrust of John Adams and New England Politics
   (C) Important Issues in the 1796 Presidential Campaign as Presented by the Federalist Candidates
   (D) The Political Careers of Alexander Hamilton, John Adams, and Thomas Pinckney
   (E) Political and Sectional Differences between New England and the South in the Late 1700s

Specific Detail Questions

3. According to the passage, which of the following was true of the Presidential election of 1796?
   (A) Thomas Jefferson received more electoral votes than did Thomas Pinckney.
   (B) John Adams received strong support from the electors of South Carolina.
   (C) Alexander Hamilton received most of the electoral votes of New England.
   (D) Thomas Pinckney was selected by Federalist party leaders to be the party's Presidential candidate.
   (E) Thomas Pinckney received all 16 of South Carolina's electoral votes.

4. According to the passage, Hamilton's plan included all BUT which of the following?
   (A) Articles published in newspapers to create opposition to John Adams
   (B) South Carolina's loyalty to Thomas Pinckney
   (C) Private contact with state officials urging them to support Thomas Pinckney
   (D) John Adams' reputation as a stubborn and independent New Englander
   (E) Support that the New England states would give to John Adams

5. The passage supplies information that answers which of the following questions?
   (A) How many votes were cast for John Adams in the 1796 Presidential election?
   (B) Under the voting system originally set up by the Constitution, how many votes did each elector cast?
   (C) Who was Jefferson's running mate in the 1796 Presidential election?
   (D) What became of Alexander Hamilton after his plan to have Thomas Pinckney elected President failed?
   (E) How many more electoral votes did Jefferson receive in the 1796 Presidential election than Pinckney?

6

Logical Structure Questions

6. Why does the author refer to the election procedure established by the original Constitution?

    (A) To prove to the reader that New England as a whole had more electoral votes than the state of South Carolina

    (B) To persuade the reader that Thomas Pinckney's defeat could have been avoided

    (C) To alert the reader that the procedure used in 1796 was unlike that presently used

    (D) To encourage the reader to study Constitutional history

    (E) To remind the reader that the President and Vice-President of the United States are chosen democratically

7. The overall development of the passage can best be described as

    (A) refuting possible explanations for certain phenomena

    (B) documenting a thesis with specific examples

    (C) offering an explanation of a series of events

    (D) making particular proposals to solve a problem

    (E) attacking the assumption of an argument

Implied Idea Questions

8. The passage implies that some electors voted for John Adams because they were

    (A) in favor of a monarchy

    (B) persuaded to do so by Hamilton

    (C) afraid South Carolina would not vote for Pinckney

    (D) concerned about New England's influence over the South

    (E) anxious to have a President from their geographical region

9. Which of the following can be inferred from the passage?

    (A) Thomas Pinckney had a personal dislike for Jefferson's politics.

    (B) The Federalists regarded themselves as more democratic than Jefferson.

    (C) The Hamiltonians contacted key Southern leaders to persuade them to vote for Adams.

    (D) Electors were likely to vote for candidates from their own geographical region.

    (E) New England states cast more electoral votes for Jefferson than did the South.

10. It can be inferred that had South Carolina not cast any electoral votes for Jefferson, the outcome of the 1796 election would have been a

    (A) larger margin of victory for John Adams

    (B) victory for Thomas Jefferson

    (C) Federalist defeat in the Senate

    (D) victory for Thomas Pinckney

    (E) defeat of the Federalist Presidential candidate

Further Application Questions

11. The electors who scratched Pinckney's name from their ballots behaved most like which of the following people?

    (A) A newspaper publisher who adds a special section to the Sunday edition to review the week's political events

    (B) A member of the clergy who encourages members of other faiths to meet to discuss solutions to the community's problems

    (C) An artist who saves preliminary sketches of an important work even after the work is finally completed

    (D) A general who orders his retreating troops to destroy supplies they must leave behind so they cannot be used by the enemy

    (E) A runner who sets too fast a pace during the early stages of a race and has no energy left for the finish

12. Hamilton's strategy can best be summarized as

    (A) divide and conquer

    (B) retreat and regroup

    (C) feint and counterattack

    (D) hit and run

    (E) camouflage and conceal

Tone Questions

13. The tone of the passage can best be described as

    (A) witty

    (B) comical

    (C) scholarly

    (D) frivolous

    (E) morose

14. The author's attitude toward Hamilton's plan can be described as

    (A) angry

    (B) approving

    (C) analytical

    (D) regretful

    (E) disinterested

6

3. Reading Techniques

"You see, Watson," said Holmes, "The tail wags the dog!"

Since Watson, like most people, believes that LSAT reading comprehension is just "reading," he would read the selections just as he might a chapter from a textbook or an article in a magazine. That is an error.

You have just learned that each reading selection is an "excuse" to ask one of the six questions. The test writers don't just find an interesting article and ask questions about it. Instead, they write a passage (by adapting and editing published material) just so they can ask several of the six questions. In other words, the tail is wagging the dog.

Knowing this, the Holmesian strategy for reading the selections is to "read for the six types of questions." Now, this does not mean that you try to anticipate the exact wording of every question that might be asked. (There are many possibilities.) Rather, this means that you adapt your reading techniques to fit the exercise.

LSAT reading comprehension questions are set up to test three levels of reading: appreciation of the general theme, understanding of specific points, and evaluation of the text. The first level, appreciation of the general theme, is the most basic. Main idea questions and questions about the overall development of the selection test whether you understand the passage at the most general level.

The second level of reading, understanding of specific points, takes you deeper into your reading of the selection. Specific detail questions and questions about the logical role of details test whether you read carefully.

The third level of reading, evaluation of the text, takes you still deeper. Implied idea questions, further application questions, and tone questions ask not just for understanding—they ask for a judgment or an evaluation of what you have read. This is why implied idea questions and further application questions are usually the most difficult.

This does not mean, however, that the three different levels are reached at completely different times. A good reader will be constantly moving back and forth, but there is a logical priority to the levels. That is, without the first level of general understanding, you can't hope to have the precise understanding of the second level. And without the precise understanding of the second level, you can't hope to evaluate or criticize the selection.

The proper method for reading an LSAT selection could be represented as a pyramid.

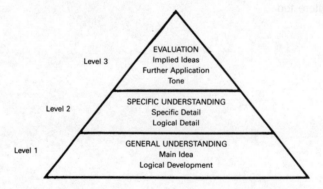

The base of the pyramid represents the basic level of reading on which the other two levels rest, and the second level is needed to support the third level. The easiest questions are usually those on the bottom level, and the most difficult questions are usually found at the top. (Note, however, that tone questions are often not very difficult.)

Although reading comprehension questions vary in difficulty, they are usually not arranged in order of difficulty. *This is an exception to the general rule of ladder of difficulty.*

Your first task when you begin reading is to answer the question "What is the topic of the selection?" If the selection consists of more than one paragraph, you may find it useful to preview the first sentence of each paragraph.

The first sentence of a paragraph is often the topic sentence, and it may give you a summary of the content of the paragraph. Here is a sample passage. Everything has been blocked out except the first sentences.

6

> In the art of the Middles Ages, the personality of the artist as an individual is never present; rather, it is diffused through the artistic genius of centuries embodied in the rules of religious art. Xxx xxx xx xxx xxxxxx xxxx xx xxxxx xxx xxxxxxxx x xxxxxx xxxxx, xxx xxxxxxx xxx xxxxxxxx xx xxxxx xxxx xxxx xxxxxxx. Xxx xxxxxxxx xxxx xxxxxx xxxxxxxxxx xxxxxx xxx xxxx xxxxxxxxx xxxxxxxxx, xxxxx xxx xxxx xxxxxxxxx xxxx x xxxxx xxxxxxxxx xxxxxxxx. X xxxxx xxxx x xxxxxx xxxxxxxxx x xxxxxxx; xxx xxxxxx xx xxxxx xx xxxxxxxx xxxx xxx xxxxxxxxxxx, xxxx xxxx xx xxxxxxx xxxxxxxxxx xx Xxxxxxxxx.
>
> Mathematics, too, was an important element of this iconography. "Xxx Xxxxxx Xxxxxx," xxxxx Xxxxx Xxxxxxxxx, "xxxxxxx xxxxxx xxxxxxxxxx xx xxxxxxx," x xxxxxxxx xxxxxxx xxxx xxx xxx-Xxxxxxxxxx xxx xxxxxxx xxx xxxxxxxxx xx Xxxxxxxxx. Xxx xxxxxxx xxxxxxx xxxxxxxx. Xx Xxxxxxxx, x xxxxxxx xxxxx xxxxxx xxxxx xxx xxxx xxxxxxxx Xxxxx, Xxxxxxx, Xxxxxx. xxx Xxxxxxxx xxxxxxxx xx xxxxx xxxxxxxxx xxx xxxx xxxxxxxxxxx Xxxxxxx, Xxxx, Xxxx, xxx Xxxx.
>
> Every painting is also an allegory, showing us one thing and inviting us to see another. Xxxxxxx xxxxxxx, xxx xxxxxx xxx xxxxx xx xxxxxxx Xxx, xxx xxx xxxxxx x xxxxxxxx xxxxxxx xxxxxx xxx xxxxxxx xxx xxx xxxxx xxxxx xx xx x xxxxx xxxxx xx xxx. Xx x xxxxxxxx xx xxx xxxxx xxxxxxx, xx xxx xxx xxxxxx xxxxxxx xx xxx xxxx xxxx xx Xxxxx xxx xxx xxxx xx xxx xxxxx, xxx xx xxxxxxxxx xxxx xxxx xxxxxxxxx xxxxx xxx xxx xxxx xxx xxxxx xxx xxx xxxxx.
>
> Within such a system even the most mediocre talent was elevated by the genius of the centuries, and the first artists of the Renaissance broke with tradition at great risk. Xxxx xxxx xxxx xxx xxxxx, xxxx xxx xx xxxx xxxx xxx xxxxx xx xxx xxx xxxxxxx xxx xxxxxxxxx xxxxxxxx xxx xxxxxx xxxxx; xxx xxxx xxxx xxx xxx xxxxxxxxxx, xxxx xxxxxxxx xxxxx xxxxxxxx xxx xxxxxxxxxxxxx xx xxxxx xxxxxxxxx xxxxx.

A preview of the first sentences should give you a pretty good idea of the subject discussed in the selection. The passage treats art in the Middle Ages. Additionally, it states that art in the Middle Ages was governed by rules and had numerical and allegorical features. Renaissance painting, however, broke with this tradition.

Given this framework, here is the selection broken down by paragraphs. As you read, consciously ask yourself what point the author is trying to make. And as you come across each new particular point, ask yourself why the author has introduced the point:

> In the art of the Middles Ages, the personality of the artist as an individual is never present; rather, it is diffused through the artistic genius of centuries embodied in the rules of religious art. For art of the Middle Ages is first and foremost a sacred script, the symbols and meanings of which were well settled. The circular halo placed vertically behind the head signifies sainthood, while the halo impressed with a cross signifies divinity. A tower with a window indicates a village; and should an angel be watching from the battlements, that city is thereby identified as Jerusalem.

In the first sentence the author introduces the topic of art in the Middle Ages. In the second sentence, we learn that this art is like a script or writing governed by rules. What function does the rest of the paragraph serve in the overall development? The author provides some illustrations of the assertion about art.

The second paragraph continues the discussion.

> Mathematics, too, was an important element of this iconography. "The Divine Wisdom," wrote Saint Augustine, "reveals itself everywhere in numbers," a doctrine derived from the neo-Platonists who revived the teachings of Pythagoras. And numbers require symmetry. At Chartres, a stained-glass window shows the four prophets Isaac, Ezekiel, Daniel, and Jeremiah carrying on their shoulders the four evangelists Matthew, Mark, Luke, and John.

Why does the author mention mathematics? Because it, too, was part of the rules for painting. And why does the author quote Saint Augustine? To show the importance of numbers in the Middles Ages.

Now, let us introduce another reading technique. This is an "open-book" test, and you can always go back to the selection. Therefore, if something is highly technical or difficult to understand, don't dwell on it. Bracket the information mentally or in writing. You can always come back to it. You should probably do this with the reference to the neo-Platonists. Who were they? It really doesn't matter. Just recognize that they had something to do with numbers, and if you need to learn more about them to answer a question, you can return to the paragraph.

What is the purpose of referring to the stained-glass window in Chartres? It illustrates the way in which numbers might influence art in the Middle Ages.

Now we move to the third paragraph.

> Every painting is also an allegory, showing us one thing and inviting us to see another. In this respect, the artist was asked to imitate God, who had hidden a profound meaning behind the literal and who wished nature to be a moral lesson to man. In a painting of the final judgment, we see the foolish virgins at the left hand of Jesus and the wise at his right, and we understand that this symbolizes those who are lost and those who are saved.

In this paragraph, the author describes another characteristic of painting in the Middle Ages: it contains an allegory. What does the next sentence mean when it compares the artist to God? That's hard to say, and again, this may be a part you should bracket. If a question asks about the analogy between art and Creation, you can always return to the selection to study. And why is the painting of the final judgment mentioned at this point? As an example of an allegorical painting.

Finally, we read the fourth paragraph.

> Within such a system even the most mediocre talent was elevated by the genius of the centuries, and the first artists of the Renaissance broke with tradition at great risk. Even when they are great, they are no more than the equals of the old masters who passively followed the sacred rules; and when they are not outstanding, they scarcely avoid banality and insignificance in their religious works.

What is the meaning of the first sentence of the final paragraph? Roughly, that even mediocre artists could produce good work as long as the rules were followed. Then the selection mentions the first artists of the Renaissance. Why? Because that was the next historical period, and also because it demonstrates how important the rules were to art in the Middle Ages.

Let's summarize the procedure for reading an LSAT reading comprehension selection.

Step 1: If the selection is more than one paragraph long, begin with a preview of the first sentence of each paragraph.

Step 2: Read the selection, consciously asking what the author is trying to do.

Step 3: When you encounter material in the selection that seems difficult to understand, bracket it. Try to understand *why* the author introduced it even if you don't understand exactly *what* it means.

A Holmesian strategy—before you begin to read the passage, preview the question stem. The question stem is everything but the answer choices. Take a question stem totally unrelated to anything we have been reading.

> Which of the following comparisons most closely parallels the relationship between specific acts and personality as described in the passage?

This stem tells you something about the passage to which it would be attached. The selection discusses some topic of psychology, specifically the relationship between personality and behavior.

Previewing the question stems may help you find your point of reference. Additionally, a stem can alert you to look for certain things as you do your reading. For example:

> The author's attitude toward corporate contributions to the arts can best be described as

You are alerted to look for the author's judgment about such contributions as you read.

This suggestion must be qualified, however, in three ways. First, some students don't find it useful. The best thing to do, therefore, is to give it a practice shot. Use it only if it helps. Second, don't try to preview the answer choices; they are too long. Additionally, four out of five choices are wrong, so they can't help you at all. In fact, they might actually lead you astray. Third, some stems are not going to be helpful, for they have no content. For example:

> Which of the following is the main point of the passage?

This question stem could go with any selection. Previewing it tells you nothing about what's to come when you read the passage. So just skip over such stems quickly. Preview only the ones that seem likely to provide some substantial information.

Previewing and Reading (Answers, page 70)

The passage below is followed by questions based on its content. Follow the suggestions indicated for previewing and reading. Then answer the questions on the basis of what is <u>stated</u> or <u>implied</u> in the passage.

The liberal view of democratic citizenship that developed in the 17th and 18th centuries was fundamentally different from that of the classical Greeks. The pursuit of private interests with as little interference as possible from government was seen as the road to human happiness and progress rather than the public obligations and involvement in the

(5) collective community that were emphasized by the Greeks. Freedom was to be realized by limiting the scope of governmental activity and political obligation and not through immersion in the collective life of the *polis*. The basic role of the citizen was to select governmental leaders and keep the powers and scope of public authority in check. On the liberal view, the rights of citizens against the state were the focus of special emphasis.

(10) Over time, the liberal democratic notion of citizenship developed in two directions. First, there was a movement to increase the proportion of members of society who were eligible to participate as citizens—especially through extending the right of suffrage—and to ensure the basic political equality of all. Second, there was a broadening of the legitimate activities of government and a use of governmental power to redress imbalances in social and

(15) economic life. Political citizenship became an instrument through which groups and classes with sufficient numbers of votes could use the state power to enhance their social and economic well-being.

Within the general liberal view of democratic citizenship, tensions have developed over the degree to which government can and should be used as an instrument for promoting

(20) happiness and well-being. Political philosopher Martin Diamond has categorized two views of democracy as follows. On the one hand, there is the "libertarian" perspective that stresses the private pursuit of happiness and emphasizes the necessity for restraint on government and protection of individual liberties. On the other hand, there is the "majoritarian" view that emphasizes the "task of the government to uplift and aid the common man against

(25) the malefactors of great wealth." The tensions between these two views are very evident today. Taxpayer revolts and calls for smaller government and less government regulation clash with demands for greater government involvement in the economic marketplace and the social sphere.

1. The author's primary purpose is to

(A) study ancient concepts of citizenship

(B) contrast different notions of citizenship

(C) criticize modern libertarian democracy

(D) describe the importance of universal suffrage

(E) introduce means of redressing an imbalance of power

2. It can be inferred from the passage that the Greek word *polis* means

(A) family life   (B) military service   (C) marriage

(D) private club   (E) political community

3. The author cites Martin Diamond (line 20) because the author

   (A) regards Martin Diamond as an authority on political philosophy

   (B) wishes to refute Martin Diamond's views on citizenship

   (C) needs a definition of the term "citizenship"

   (D) is unfamiliar with the distinction between libertarian and majoritarian concepts of democracy

   (E) wants voters to support Martin Diamond as a candidate for public office

4. According to the passage, all of the following are characteristics of the liberal idea of government that would distinguish the liberal idea of government from the Greek idea of government EXCEPT

   (A) the emphasis on the rights of private citizens

   (B) the activities government may legitimately pursue

   (C) the obligation of citizens to participate in government

   (D) the size of the geographical area controlled by a government

   (E) the definition of human happiness

5. A majoritarian would be most likely to favor legislation that would

   (A) eliminate all restrictions on individual liberty

   (B) cut spending for social welfare programs

   (C) provide greater protection for consumers

   (D) lower taxes on the wealthy and raise taxes on the average worker

   (E) raise taxes on the average worker and cut taxes on business

Step 1: Preview the first sentence of each paragraph:

   The liberal view of democratic citizenship that developed in the 17th and 18th centuries was fundamentally different from that of the classical Greeks.

   Over time, the liberal democratic notion of citizenship developed in two directions.

   Within the general liberal view of democratic citizenship, tensions have developed over the degree to which government can and should be used as an instrument for promoting happiness and well-being.

These three sentences, taken together, tell you that the topic of the passage is citizenship. The selection begins by defining the liberal view of citizenship. Then, the second paragraph states that the liberal view has evolved into two different ideas. Finally, the third paragraph apparently amplifies what was discussed in the second.

Step 2: Preview the question stems.

   Question 1 provides no useful information.

   Question 2 tells you to flag the word *polis* when you find it. It will be the basis of that question.

   Question 3 tells you that the author will quote Martin Diamond (whoever he may be) and that you will need to know why.

   Questions 4 and 5, when taken in conjunction with your preview of the first sentences, might be very helpful. They contain key words. Question 4 tells you that one of the topics for discussion will be the difference between classical Greek notions of democracy and liberal notions of democracy. Similarly, question 5 alerts you to the fact that majoritarian democracy will be discussed.

Step 3:   Read the passage.

The first paragraph defines the liberal idea of citizenship by contrasting it with the Greek idea.   Several specifics are mentioned.

The second paragraph discusses the development of the liberal view in two directions and describes each.

The third paragraph discusses the significance of the division.

Now you are in a position to answer questions.

4. Question Patterns That Clue You In

Like most test-takers, Watson is completely preoccupied with finding a correct answer to particular questions; but Holmes is keenly aware that answers fall into patterns. Once you know what makes right answers right and wrong answers wrong, you will be able to eliminate incorrect choices and spot the correct answer more easily.   Right now, just read through the following selection and familiarize yourself with it.   There are no question stems yet to be previewed.

The Aleuts, residing on several islands of the Aleutian Chain, the Pribilof Islands, and the Alaskan Peninsula, have possessed a written language since 1825, when the Russian missionary Ivan Veniaminov selected appropriate characters of the Cyrillic alphabet to represent Aleut speech sounds, recorded the main body of Aleut vocabulary, and formulated grammatical rules.   The Czarist Russian conquest of the proud, independent sea hunters was so devastatingly thorough that tribal traditions, even tribal memories, were almost obliterated.   The slaughter of the majority of an adult generation was sufficient to destroy the continuity of tribal knowledge, which was dependent upon oral transmission.   As a consequence, the Aleuts developed a fanatical devotion to their language as their only cultural heritage.

The Russian occupation placed a heavy linguistic burden on the Aleuts.   Not only were they compelled to learn Russian to converse with their overseers and governors, but they had to learn Old Slavonic to take an active part in church services as well as to master the skill of reading and writing their own tongue.   In 1867, when the United States purchased Alaska, the Aleuts were unable to break sharply with their immediate past and substitute English for any one of their three languages.

To communicants of the Russian Orthodox Church a knowledge of Slavonic remained vital, as did Russian, the language in which one conversed with the clergy. The Aleuts came to regard English education as a device to wean them from their religious faith.   The introduction of compulsory English schooling caused a minor renascence of Russian culture as the Aleut parents sought to counteract the influence of the schoolroom.   The harsh life of the Russian colonial rule began to appear more happy and beautiful in retrospect.

Regulations forbidding instruction in any language other than English increased its unpopularity.   The superficial alphabetical resemblance of Russian and Aleut linked the two tongues so closely that every restriction against teaching Russian was interpreted as an attempt to eradicate the Aleut tongue.   From the wording of many regulations, it appears that American administrators often had not the slightest idea that the Aleuts were clandestinely reading and writing their own tongue or even had a written language of their own.   To too many officials, anything in Cyrillic letters was Russian and something to be stamped out.   Bitterness bred by abuses and the exploitations the Aleuts suffered from predatory American traders and adventurers kept alive the Aleut resentment against the language spoken by Americans.

Gradually, despite the failure to emancipate the Aleuts from a sterile past by relating the Aleut and English languages more closely, the passage of years has assuaged the bitter misunderstandings and caused an orientation away from Russian toward English as their second language, but Aleut continues to be the language that molds their thought and expression.

Main Idea Questions

EXAMPLES:

The author is primarily concerned with describing

(A) the Aleuts' loyalty to their language and American failure to understand it

(B) Russian and United States treatment of Alaskan inhabitants both before and after 1867

(C) how the Czarist Russian occupation of Alaska created a written language for the Aleuts

(D) United States government attempts to persuade the Aleuts to use English as a second language

(E) the atrocities committed by Russia against the Aleuts during the Czarist Russian occupation

The best answer is (A). To answer a main idea question, look for a choice that covers the main elements of the passage without making reference to material not discussed in the passage. (B) can be eliminated because it goes beyond the scope of the passage. The passage is not concerned with the treatment of Alaskan inhabitants in general, but with the treatment of one particular group. (C), (D), and (E) can be eliminated because they are too narrow. Each of these three choices does mention one aspect of the passage, but none of them summarizes the overall point of the selection.

Here is a different kind of main idea question:

The author is primarily concerned with

(A) describing the Aleuts' loyalty to their language and American failure to understand it

(B) criticizing Russia and the United States for their mistreatment of the Aleuts

(C) praising the Russians for creating a written language for the Aleuts

(D) condemning Russia for its mistreatment of the Aleuts during the Czarist Russian occupation

(E) ridiculing American efforts to persuade the Aleuts to adopt English as a second language

Again, (A) is correct. You should be able to see that this second main idea question is really the first one presented in a different form. Here, the choices are possible completions of the question stem. Notice that each wrong choice begins with a word expressing a value judgment: *criticize, praise, condemn, ridicule.* None of those terms correctly describes the overall idea of the passage. In attacking a question in sentence completion form, eliminate as many choices as possible on the basis of the first word. Then treat the remaining choices as you would any other main idea question, looking for the one that is sufficiently broad without being overly broad.

6

Finally, a main idea question might also look like this:

> Which of the following titles best fits the passage?
> **(A)** Aleut Loyalty to Their Language: An American Misunderstanding
> **(B)** Failure of Russian and American Policies in Alaska
> **(C)** Russia's Gift to the Aleuts: A Written Language
> **(D)** Mistreatment of Aleuts During Russian Occupation
> **(E)** The Folly of American Attempts to Teach Aleuts English

The correct choice is (A). This is essentially the same main idea question presented in yet another form. The trick is to find the title that best captures the content of the passage. The criterion is the same as that for other main idea questions: it must cover all the important points without going beyond the passage.

Once more, (C), (D), and (E) fail because they describe too little of the selection, and (E) fails because it is too broad. (A), though not a perfect title, is the best of the five.

> Whatever the form of a main idea question, the answer will summarize the main theme of the selection without going beyond the scope of the passage.

Specific Detail Questions

EXAMPLE:

> According to the passage, which of the following was the most important reason for the Aleuts' devotion to their language?
> **(A)** Invention of a written version of their language
> **(B)** Introduction of Old Slavonic for worship
> **(C)** Disruption of oral transmission of tribal knowledge
> **(D)** Institution of compulsory English education
> **(E)** Prohibition against writing or reading Russian

The correct choice is (C). Since this is a specific detail question, the information you need is somewhere explicitly given in the passage—though not in exactly the same words. The reference you need is the last two sentences of the first paragraph. The Russians killed the majority of Aleut adults, so there was no one left to teach the children the Aleut traditions. All that remained for the younger generation was the language they had already learned.

As for (A), though the passage states that a Russian missionary invented the written form of the Aleut language, this is not the cause of the Aleuts' devotion to their language. (B), too, is connected with the passage. We are told that the Aleuts learned Old Slavonic, the language of the Russian Orthodox Church, but that does not explain their loyalty to their own language. (D) and (E) fail for the same reason. Though these events are mentioned in the passage, they occurred *after* the events that triggered the special devotion the Aleuts feel toward their language.

An answer choice for a specific detail question can be attractive because it is mentioned somewhere in the selection, yet still be wrong because it is not responsive to the question. Take (D) as an example. The passage does specifically mention such a requirement (end of the third paragraph), and (D) would be a perfectly good answer to a question such as "Why did the Aleuts resent the Americans?" But that is not the question asked.

> The correct choice for a specific detail question must both be explicitly mentioned in the passage and answer the question asked.

Logical Structure Questions

6

Some logical structure questions ask about the overall development of the passage. These are like main idea questions, but the focus is on the form of the passage rather than the specific content.

EXAMPLE:

The passage is developed primarily by
- **(A)** testing the evidence supporting a theory
- **(B)** describing causes and effects of events
- **(C)** weighing the pros and cons of a plan
- **(D)** projecting the future consequences of a decision
- **(E)** debating both sides of a moral issue

The answer is (B). We are looking for the best description of the overall development of the selection. The author discusses several events in terms of cause and effect. For example, the Russian brutality caused the Aleut devotion to their language, and American misunderstanding caused a renascence of Russian culture.

You can eliminate each of the other choices. As for (A), though the author uses historical evidence for his position, he is not testing evidence supporting a theory. As for (C), though the author points to some of the effects of Russian and American policies, the passage doesn't really "weigh" pros and cons. As for (D), though the author does state that the attitude of the Aleuts toward English is changing slowly, the passage is not primarily speculation about where this change might lead. Finally, as for (E), though the question of the morality of the Russian and American actions is implicit in the discussion, the passage is not developed by debating the morality of those actions.

> A logical structure question that asks about the overall development of the passage should be treated like a main idea question. Find the choice that best describes the structure of the selection.

Logical structure questions can also ask about the "why" of specific details.

EXAMPLE:

Why does the author mention that the Russians killed the majority of adult Aleuts?

(A) To call attention to the immorality of foreign conquest

(B) To urge Russia to make restitution to the children of those killed

(C) To stir up outrage against the Russians for committing such atrocities

(D) To explain the extreme loyalty Aleuts feel to their language

(E) To prove that the Aleuts have a written a language

The answer is (D). This question is somewhat like a specific detail question, except here the question is not *what* the author said but *why* he or she said it.

(A), (B), and (C) are all incorrect because they do not explain why the author mentions the atrocities. The passage is not condemning Russian behavior. As for (E), though the author does state that the Aleuts have a written language, this is not why he mentions the Russian atrocities. Rather, he mentions the devastation of the Aleuts in order to show why Aleuts are so devoted to their language.

The key to answering a logical detail question is to locate the *needed* reference and ask *why*: Why did the author do this?

Implied Idea Questions

EXAMPLES:

Which of the following statements about the religious beliefs of the Aleuts can be inferred from the passage?

(A) Prior to the Russian occupation they had no religious beliefs.

(B) American traders and adventurers forced them to abandon all religious beliefs.

(C) At no time in their history have the Aleuts had an organized religion.

(D) Aleut leaders adopted the religious beliefs of the American officials following the 1867 purchase.

(E) The Russians forced Aleuts to become members of the Russian Orthodox Church.

The correct choice is (E), and you can justify (E) as a matter of logic. In paragraph two the passage states that the Aleuts "had to learn Old Slavonic to take an active part in church services." Which church was that? It must be the Russian Orthodox Church mentioned by name in the next paragraph. And how do we know the Aleuts were forced to convert? Since Old Slavonic was required of church members, and since at the time of the Russian conquest the Aleuts did not know Old Slavonic, they could not have been members of the sect at that time. Therefore, we logically infer that the Russian conquerors forced the Aleuts to become members of the Russian Orthodox Church.

The answer to an implied idea question will not be explicitly stated in the passage, but it will be strongly supported by the passage. You can create a logical argument for the answer.

The wrong choices cannot be justified by similar reasoning. As for (A), there is no basis in the passage for the conclusion that the Aleuts had no religion at all prior to the Russians. They might have had one; they might not. The point is that the passage is logically consistent with either position. The same is true for both (B) and (D). These statements could be either true or false given the information supplied in the passage. As for (C), this is clearly false. The passage does state that at one time the Aleuts were members of the Russian Orthodox Church.

> The passage implies that
> **(A)** the Cyrillic alphabet was invented for the Aleut language
> **(B)** all of the Cyrillic characters were used in writing the Aleut language
> **(C)** Russian and the Aleut language have some similar speech sounds
> **(D)** English is also written using the Cyrillic alphabet
> **(E)** the Cyrillic alphabet displaced the original Aleut alphabet

The answer is (C). This question asks about something not explicitly stated in the passage, but only implied. (C) is logically supported by the passage. The Russian missionary Ivan Veniaminov used Cyrillic letters (which already represented certain Russian speech sounds) to represent appropriate Aleut speech sounds. This is feasible only if the sounds are sufficiently similar (even if they don't mean the same thing in both languages).

None of the other choices can be logically deduced from the selection. (A) and (E) are contradicted by the passage. The Cyrillic alphabet already existed and was adapted to the Aleut language. And since this was the first written form of the language, no Aleut alphabet could have existed before then. As for (B), Veniaminov may not have needed the entire Cyrillic alphabet, only parts of it. Finally, (D) is almost contradicted by the passage. The Cyrillic alphabet seems to be definitely not like English.

> To answer an implied idea question, look for a choice that is logically supported by the passage.

Further Application Questions

In many ways, these are the most difficult of all questions. They ask you to take what you have learned from the passage and apply it to a new situation.

> **EXAMPLE:**
>
> Distributing which of the following publications would be most likely to encourage Aleuts to make more use of English?
> **(A)** Russian translations of English novels
> **(B)** English translations of Russian novels
> **(C)** An English–Russian bilingual text devoted to important aspects of Aleutian culture
> **(D)** An Aleut–English bilingual text devoted to important aspects of Aleutian culture
> **(E)** A treatise about religions other than the Russian Orthodox Church written in English

The correct choice is (D). You must apply what you have learned in the passage to this new situation. What is the problem the author sees? The Aleuts have never really embraced English as a second language because of the events described. So what would most likely encourage them to embrace English? Something that would respect the integrity of their own culture while bringing it closer to English (and thereby minimizing the holdover effect of the Russian occupation). (A) and (B) will not do the trick since Russian–English books would not necessarily be relevant to the experience of an Aleut. (C) is closer, but still off the mark. The task is to get the Aleuts to embrace English—not Russian. As for (E), there is no reason given in the passage to believe the Aleuts have an interest in other religions. The task is to find English writings that would be of interest to the Aleuts.

> To answer a further application question, find the answer choice that is best supported by the information provided in the passage.

Tone Questions

The final category is tone questions.

EXAMPLE:

The author's attitude toward the Aleuts can best be described as one of
(A) understanding and sympathy
(B) callousness and indifference
(C) condemnation and reproof
(D) ridicule and disparagement
(E) awe and admiration

The correct choice is (A). With a tone question it is sometimes useful to arrange the choices in some kind of order. In this case, the order is from positive to negative feelings:

POSITIVE FEELINGS
awe and admiration
understanding and sympathy
callousness and indifference
ridicule and disparagement
condemnation and reproof
NEGATIVE FEELINGS

Now try to locate the author's attitude toward the Aleuts along this spectrum. First, you can eliminate the extremes of "awe and admiration." Although the tone of the passage does seem mildly positive, it is not as strong as "awe and admiration." Then start from the other end. You can surely eliminate "condemnation and reproof" and "ridicule and disparagement," because there are no strong negative feelings toward the Aleuts. Finally, you should eliminate "callousness and indifference," since the author does seem to have mildly positive feelings about the Aleuts. The best choice, therefore, is "understanding and sympathy."

5. Some Final Words of Advice from Holmes

Earlier, reading comprehension was likened to a pyramid, with easier questions as the base and more difficult questions at the top. Remember, however, that reading comprehension questions are *not* necessarily arranged according to a ladder of difficulty. The first question on a selection might be the most difficult one and the last, the easiest. So don't get bogged down by the first or second question.

Additionally, certain questions (further application questions and some implied idea questions) can be extremely difficult. But on balance, there are enough of the easier kinds for you to do well on reading comprehension even if you can't answer a further application or a difficult implied idea question. Again, don't spend too much time trying to crack a difficult nut.

Remember, also, that you have your own particular strengths, and you will react differently to different topics. For example, if you are very interested in music but relatively less knowledgeable about chemistry, you will find a passage about music easier than one about chemistry. You don't have to do the passages in the order in which they are presented. If you start on one that seems so difficult that you're going nowhere, abandon it and try another.

Finally, some questions in this section have a perfect format for Holmesean thinking.

EXAMPLE:

According to the passage, which of the following factors caused the Aleuts to resist adopting English as a second language?

  I. Government regulations prohibiting teaching in any language other than English.
 II. Threats by members of the clergy of the Russian Orthodox Church to excommunicate Aleuts who learned English.
III. Abuse suffered by the Aleuts at the hands of English speakers such as traders and adventurers.

  (A) I only   **(B)** II only   **(C)** III only   **(D)** I and II only   **(E)** I and III only

The answer is (E). With a format such as this, the process of elimination becomes a very powerful logical tool. Start with I. If you look back at the passage on the Aleuts, you will find that this is mentioned as a factor that discouraged the Aleuts from adopting English. Once you know this, you can eliminate any choice that does not include I. So you eliminate (B) and (C). Next, you try II. Nowhere is such a factor mentioned, but let's assume that you have your doubts. You are worried you have overlooked something. Go on to the next statement, III. You will find that III is specifically mentioned, which means that III must be a part of the correct choice. Now you know the correct choice must include both I and III—even though you are still in doubt about II.

But that is enough to answer the question. Only one choice includes both I and III, and that is (E). With this Roman numeral format, you must always use the process of elimination to narrow down your choices and then make a guess.

Summary

1. Reading comprehension is made difficult by the variety of topics, lack of a reference point before starting, and compactness of the selections. Don't let the passages intimidate you.

2. Reading comprehension questions fall into one of six categories: main idea, specific detail, logical structure, implied idea, further application, and tone.

3. Your reading proceeds on three levels (shown on the pyramid). Begin by previewing first sentences and question stems. As you read, try to identify as quickly as possible the main theme of the selection. Then, as each new point is introduced, try to fit it into the overall development. If material is too difficult, bracket it. Make sure you understand why it is in the passage (even if you don't understand what it says) and continue your reading.

4. Hints for answering questions.

For a main idea question, find an answer that is not too broad and not too narrow. If the choices are supposed to complete the question stem, start by checking the first words. Eliminate any choice that does not correspond to the author's treatment of the topic.

For a specific detail question, locate the reference you need in the passage. Don't be distracted by choices that make true or partially true statements but are not responsive to the question.

Logical structure questions ask either about the overall development of the selection or a particular detail. Treat a question about the overall logical development of a passage as you would a main idea question. For a logical detail question, find the appropriate reference and determine *why* the author made the point.

For an implied idea question, find a choice that is *logically* supported by the passage. The chain of reasoning will not be very long—only one or two steps. But the correct choice must be inferable from what is explicitly given.

For a further application question, find the choice that is best supported by the passage. This means you will have to apply what you have learned in the passage. Remember, this is perhaps the hardest type, but you can get a good score even if you omit some difficult items.

Explanatory Answers

6

EXERCISE 1

Main Idea Questions

1. (C) The passage describes a series of political events that resulted in the election of John Adams as President.

2. (A) The central theme is Hamilton's plan to capture the Presidency for Pinckney and why that plan failed.

Specific Detail Questions

3. (A) In the last paragraph, the passage explicitly states that Pinckney finished third in the voting, behind Jefferson.

4. (D) (A), (B), (C), and (E) are all mentioned as elements of Hamilton's plan, but (D) is not. Although the selection does say that Hamilton did not like Adams' stubborn and independent politics, it nowhere says that this was to be a part of Hamilton's plan to help Pinckney win the Presidency.

5. (B) In the next to last paragraph, it is stated that electors had two votes to cast.

Logical Structure Questions

6. (C) This question asks *why* the author mentions the fact that the 1796 election took place under the rules established in the original Constitution. (C) provides the best explanation. Under current procedures, a vote is cast specifically for a Presidential candidate and another for a Vice-Presidential candidate. Under the original system, electoral votes were cast without distinction, and the candidate receiving the most was elected President and the runner-up was elected Vice-President. Without this crucial piece of information, the author's analysis makes no sense. So in the first sentence of the second paragraph he specifically reminds the reader of this fact.

7. (C) The passage explains the series of events that lead to the election of John Adams as President in 1796.

Implied Idea Questions

8. (E) At the beginning of the next to last paragraph, the author states that sectional pride was high in New England and that John Adams, the New England politician, received the New Englanders' votes. We may infer that many of them voted for Adams because of their desire to have a President from their own region.

9. (D) At various places in the passage you can find references to the idea of regional loyalty.

10. (A) South Carolina cast 16 votes, eight for Pinckney and eight for Jefferson. So each elector cast one vote for each. Had they not voted for Jefferson, for whom could they have voted? They could not have voted for Pinckney (they had already voted for him). They could have voted either for Adams or for some unknown candidate. Either way, Jefferson loses votes and Adams does not (he could actually have gained). So the net result is a larger margin of victory for Adams.

Further Application Questions

11. (D) Here you are asked to apply what you have learned from the passage to an entirely new situation. Exactly what did the electors in question do? They wasted their second vote so that neither Pinckney nor Jefferson could benefit from them.

12. (A) Hamilton's strategy was to divide the Federalist vote: weaken party support for Adams and let Pinckney pick up the pieces.

Tone Questions

13. (C) How would you describe the tone of the passage? It is very neutral and analytical, so a good description would be "scholarly."

14. (C) The author's treatment of the series of events is neutral and objective.

EXERCISE 2

1. (B) The author discusses three different concepts of government and citizenship (classical Greek, libertarian, and majoritarian), outlining the important differences among them.

2. (E) In the first paragraph the author contrasts the Greek idea of citizenship with the more modern, liberal idea. A series of parallels is set up. The liberal notion emphasizes pursuit of individual interests and limitation of government power, while the Greek notion emphasized participation in community affairs. The *polis*, we may infer, is the location of public life. So it must mean "political community."

3. (A) This is a logical detail question. The author has already mentioned that liberalism has moved in two directions. He introduces a political philosopher as an authority to support his position.

4. (D) This is a specific detail question. (A), (B), (C), and (E) are mentioned at various points in the selection, but (D) is not.

5. (C) This is an application question. From the last paragraph we learn that majoritarians are likely to favor greater government control of the marketplace (as opposed to libertarians, who favor less government involvement).

Reading Comprehension Drills

This lesson contains three reading comprehension drills. The first drill is a "walk-through" and has answers and discussion facing the questions so that you can walk through the exercise as you read the explanations. The second and third drills are "warm-ups," which should be done within the usual 35-minute time limit. Answers and explanations for the warm-up drills begin on page 95.

7

Walk-Through

Directions: Each passage in this group is followed by questions based on its content . After reading a passage, choose the best answer to each question. Answer all questions following a passage on the basis of what is stated or implied in that passage.

"Heartily tired" from the brutal, almost daily conflicts that erupted over questions of national policy between himself and Alexander Hamilton, Thomas Jefferson resigned his position as Secretary of
(5) State in 1793. Although his Federalist opponents were convinced that this was merely a strategic withdrawal to allow him an opportunity to plan and promote his candidacy for the Presidency should Washington step down in 1796, Jefferson insisted that
(10) this retirement from public life was to be final.

But even in retirement, the world of politics pursued him. As the election grew nearer and it became apparent that Washington would not seek a third term, rumors of Jefferson's Presidential ambi-
(15) tions grew in intensity. Reacting to these continuous insinuations in a letter to James Madison, Jefferson admitted that while the idea that he coveted the office of chief executive had been originated by his enemies to impugn his political motives, he had been forced to
(20) examine his true feelings on the subject for his own peace of mind. In so doing he concluded that his reasons for retirement—the desire for privacy, and the delight of family life—coupled with his now failing health were insuperable barriers to public service.
(25) The "little spice of ambition" he had in his younger days had long since evaporated and the question of his Presidency was forever closed.

Jefferson did not actively engage in the campaign on his own behalf. The Republican party, presaging
(30) modern campaign tactics, created a grass roots sentiment for their candidate by directing their efforts toward the general populace. In newspapers, Jefferson was presented as "the uniform advocate of equal rights among the citizens" while Adams was portrayed
(35) as the "champion of rank, titles, heredity, and distinctions."

Jefferson was not certain of the outcome of the election until the end of December. Under the original electoral system established by the Constitution,
(40) each Presidential elector cast his ballot for two men without designating between them as to office. The candidate who received the greater number of votes became the President; the second highest, the Vice-President. Jefferson foresaw on the basis of his own
(45) calculations that the electoral vote would be close. He wrote to Madison that in the event of a tie, he wished for the choice to be in favor of Adams. The New Englander had always been his senior in public office, he explained, and the expression of public will
(50) being equal, he should be preferred for the higher honor. Jefferson, a shrewd politician, realized that the transition of power from the nearly mythical Washington to a lesser luminary in the midst of the deep and bitter political divisions facing the nation
(55) could be perilous, and he had no desire to be caught in the storm that had been brewing for four years and was about to break. "This is certainly not a moment to covet the helm," he wrote to Edward Rutledge. When the electoral vote was tallied, Adams emerged
(60) the victor. Rejoicing at his "escape," Jefferson was completely satisfied with the decision. Despite their obvious and basic political differences, Jefferson genuinely respected John Adams as a friend and compatriot. Although he believed that Adams had deviated
(65) from the course set in 1776, Jefferson never felt a diminution of confidence in Adams' integrity and was confident he would not steer the nation too far off its Republican tack. Within two years, Jefferson's views would be drastically altered as measures such as the
(70) Alien and Sedition Acts of 1798 convinced him of the need to wrest control of the government from the Federalists.

1. The phrase "heartily tired" (line 1) is most probably a quotation from

   (A) Alexander Hamilton
   (B) Thomas Jefferson
   (C) George Washington
   (D) John Adams
   (E) The Federalist party

2. The "escape" mentioned in the passage in line 60 refers to the fact that Jefferson

   (A) was no longer Secretary of State
   (B) would not be burdened with the problems of the Presidency
   (C) fled the country following the election
   (D) was hoping that the votes would be recounted
   (E) would no longer have to campaign for the Presidency

1. (B) This is an implied idea question. In this case, it appears that the quotation marks indicate that the phrase "heartily tired" has been taken from another source. Indeed, the question stem requires that conclusion since it asks us to identify the source. The question asks which of the five individuals named was the probable source. The first paragraph explains that Jefferson resigned his position as Secretary of State because he was tired of the political infighting. In describing his reasons for retiring, Jefferson himself might easily have used the phrase.

   None of the other men mentioned in the choices seems likely to have made such a statement—certainly neither Hamilton nor Adams, who were opposed to Jefferson and likely to see other, more selfish reasons behind the retirement. Even less likely is the Federalist party (the party of Adams).

   Finally, it is *possible* that Washington could have used the phrase, but, given that the passage is about Jefferson rather than Washington, it seems more likely (on balance) that it was Jefferson.

2. (B) Another implied idea question. This one asks us to interpret the word *escape*. What did Jefferson "escape" from? He was not elected President. Why would he regard this as an escape? He didn't want to be President in the first place. So we infer that this "escape" refers to the fact that he would not have to discharge the responsibilities of the Presidency.

   (A) must be wrong since the "escape" refers to Jefferson's defeat in the election, not his resignation from the post of Secretary of State. (C) makes the mistake of reading the word *escape* literally. (D) is contradicted by the selection. We are told that Jefferson did not want to be President. And finally, (E) is wrong since the passage also states that Jefferson did not campaign actively in the first place.

3. According to the passage, the Republican party appealed primarily to

    (A) wealthy landowners
    (B) ordinary people
    (C) prosperous merchants
    (D) high society
    (E) Washington's supporters

4. The author states that all of the following were reasons Jefferson resigned as Secretary of State EXCEPT

    (A) He was in very poor health.
    (B) He wanted to spend time with his family.
    (C) He was weary of the demands of public service.
    (D) He wished for greater privacy.
    (E) He had no further political ambitions.

5. The author is primarily concerned with revealing the

    (A) feud between Alexander Hamilton and Thomas Jefferson
    (B) difference between the Federalists and the Republicans
    (C) strategies used by early American political parties
    (D) character and personality of Thomas Jefferson
    (E) legacy of George Washington

3. (B) This is a further application question. What does the passage say about the Republican party? The Republicans touted themselves as the party in favor of equality and cast the Federalists as the defenders of privilege. We can infer, therefore, that the Republicans were appealing to ordinary people, (B). Wealthy landowners, prosperous merchants, and high society would more likely have been attracted to the Federalist party. As for (E), there is nothing in the passage to indicate that voters who liked Washington were likely to go to one party or the other.

4. (A) This is a specific detail question. Just make sure you find the right points in the passage. The question asks for the reasons given for Jefferson's resignation. (B) is specifically mentioned in the first paragraph. Then in the second paragraph, we find (C), (D), and (E).

The second paragraph does mention something about failing health, but if you read that sentence closely you will see this was not a reason for Jefferson's resignation. The sentence says all of his other reasons for retirement (those given) plus his *now* failing health were reasons for not reentering public office. In other words, Jefferson did not become ill until *after* his resignation.

5. (D) This is a main idea question. The passage focuses primarily on Thomas Jefferson and examines his feelings and reasons for resigning from and then reentering public service.

(A) is incorrect since this is only a minor point mentioned only in the first paragraph. (B) is incorrect since the focus is not on political issues, but on Thomas Jefferson, the person. As for (C), though the third paragraph does mention a campaign strategy of the Republican party, the passage as a whole is not a study of such tactics. Finally, (E) is wide of the mark. Though George Washington is mentioned by name in the first paragraph, and though the events described in the passage do come after Washington declined a third term, the focus of the passage is Jefferson, not Washington.

6. The author relies on which of the following in developing the selection?

    I. Personal correspondence
   II. Newspapers
  III. Voter registration rolls

(A) I only   (B) II only   (C) I and II only
(D) I and III only   (E) I, II, and III

6. (C) This is a specific detail question. The author specifically cites (in the last paragraph) a letter by Jefferson to Rutledge, so item I must be part of the correct answer. Additionally, in paragraph three the author quotes a newspaper description of Jefferson, so II must also be part of the correct choice. There is no mention, however, of voting registration rolls.

The mental health movement in the United States began with a period of considerable enlightenment. Dorothea Dix was shocked to find the mentally ill in jails and alms houses and crusaded for the establishment of asylums in which people could receive humane care in hospital-like environments and treatment which might help restore them to sanity. By the mid-1800s, 20 states had established asylums; but during the late 1800s and early 1900s, in the face of economic depression, legislatures were unable to appropriate sufficient funds for decent care. Asylums became overcrowded and prisonlike. Additionally, patients were more resistant to treatment than the pioneers in the mental health field had anticipated, and security and restraint were needed to protect patients and others. Mental institutions became frightening and depressing places in which the rights of patients were all but forgotten.

These conditions continued until after World War II. At that time, new treatments were discovered for some major mental illnesses theretofore considered untreatable (penicillin for syphilis of the brain and insulin treatment for schizophrenia and depressions), and a succession of books, motion pictures, and newspaper exposés called attention to the plight of the mentally ill. Improvements were made, and Dr. David Vail's Humane Practices Program is a beacon for today. But changes were slow in coming until the early 1960s. At that time, the Civil Rights Movement led lawyers to investigate America's prisons, which were disproportionately populated by blacks, and they in turn followed prisoners into the only

institutions that were worse than the prisons—the hospitals for the criminally insane. The prisons were filled with angry young men who, encouraged by legal support, were quick to demand their rights. The hospitals for the criminally insane, by contrast, were populated with people who were considered "crazy" and who were often kept obediently in their place through the use of severe bodily restraints and large doses of major tranquilizers. The young cadre of public interest lawyers liked their role in the mental hospitals. The lawyers found a population that was both passive and easy to champion. These were, after all, people who, unlike criminals, had done nothing wrong. And in many states they were being kept in horrendous institutions, an injustice which, once exposed, was bound to shock the public and, particularly, the judicial conscience. Patients' rights groups successfully encouraged reform by lobbying in state legislatures.

Judicial interventions have had some definite positive effects, but there is growing awareness that courts cannot provide the standards and the review mechanisms that assure good patient care. The details of providing day-to-day care simply cannot be mandated by a court, so it is time to take from the courts the responsibility for delivery of mental health care and assurance of patient rights and return it to the state mental health administrators to whom the mandate was originally given. Though it is a difficult task, administrators must undertake to write rules and standards and to provide the training and surveillance to assure that treatment is given and patients' rights respected.

7.   The main purpose of the passage is to
   (A) discuss the influence of Dorothea Dix on the mental health movement
   (B) provide a historical perspective on problems of mental health care
   (C) increase public awareness of the plight of the mentally ill
   (D) shock the reader with vivid descriptions of asylums
   (E) describe the invention of new treatments for mental illness

7.   (B) This is a main idea question. As discussed in the lesson, the idea is to find a statement that summarizes all of the main points of the selection without going beyond the scope of the selection. The passage does summarize the history of mental health care in the United States, so (B) is a good choice.

You can eliminate (D) on the basis of the word *shock*. There are no vivid images, and there is nothing in the passage that would shock a reader. You can eliminate (C) for a similar reason. Although a side effect of the selection may be to make some readers aware of a problem, the primary purpose of the passage is to describe, not to increase, awareness. Finally, (A) and (E) violate that part of the main idea rule that states that the correct answer cannot be too narrow.

8. According to the passage, which of the following contributed to the deterioration of the asylum system?

    I. Lack of funds to maintain the asylums
    II. Influx of more patients than the system was designed to handle
    III. Lack of effective treatments for many mental illnesses

(A) I only   (B) III only   (C) I and II only
(D) I and III only   (E) I, II, and III

9. It can be inferred from the passage that, of the following factors, which contributed to postwar reform of state mental institutions?

    I. Heightened public awareness of the unacceptable conditions in the institutions
    II. Discovery of effective treatments for illnesses previously considered untreatable
    III. Enactment of state legislation to improve conditions in mental institutions

(A) I only   (B) III only   (C) I and II only
(D) II and III only   (E) I, II, and III

10. The author's attitude toward people who are patients in state institutions can best be described as

(A) inflexible and insensitive
(B) detached and neutral
(C) understanding and sympathetic
(D) enthusiastic and supportive
(E) uncaring and unemotional

---

8. (E) This is a specific detail question. Seek out the particular references you need. All three statements are specifically supported by the first paragraph. There it is mentioned that funds dried up because of the depression, asylums were filled with too many patients, and many illnesses could not be effectively treated. So the correct choice must include I, II, and III.

9. (E) This is an implied idea question. Which of the statements can be logically deduced from the selection?

We need to focus on the second paragraph, since the question asks about the causes of postwar reform. In that paragraph, the author mentions books, motion pictures, and newspaper exposés. Why would these be effective tools of reform? By creating a new public awareness of a problem. So statement I must be part of the correct choice.

Statement II is also inferable, for the author mentions in passing that new treatments had been discovered. This, too, must have been one of the factors encouraging reform.

Finally, the author states that patients' rights groups encouraged reform by lobbying. Since these efforts were successful, we can infer that the lobbying resulted in some reform legislation.

So all three factors can be inferred to be part of the post-war reform.

10. (C) This is a tone question. Arrange all five choices to create a spectrum of attitudes ranging from positive to negative:

POSITIVE ATTITUDE
enthusiastic and supportive
understanding and sympathetic
detached and neutral
uncaring and unemotional
inflexible and insensitive
NEGATIVE ATTITUDE

Start by dividing the range in the middle. Does the passage tend toward the negative or positive direction? The author's attitude inclines more to the positive side. The passage speaks of the "plight" of the patient, a term that would not be used by someone who was detached, uncaring, or insensitive.

Now the question is one of degree. How positive is the tone? Although the attitude toward patients might be described as either "sympathetic" or "supportive," "understanding" is a better description than "enthusiastic." The author seems to understand the position of the patient, but he is not a cheerleader for the patient.

11. The passage provides information that would help answer all of the following questions EXCEPT

(A) Who are some people who have had an important influence on the public health movement in the United States?

(B) What were some of the mental illnesses that were considered untreatable until the 1950s?

(C) What were some of the new treatments for mental illness that were adopted in the 1950s?

(D) What were some of the most important legal cases that contributed to the new concern for patients' rights?

(E) What effect did the Civil Rights Movement have on the rights of prisoners?

11. (D) This is a specific detail question. You will find information in the passage that would be useful in answering four of the five questions. As for (A), two names, Dorothea Dix and Dr. David Vail, are mentioned in the passage. As for (B) and (C), help for answering these questions can be found in the second sentence of the second paragraph. And as for (E), an answer to this question is contained later in the second paragraph. (D), however, cannot be answered on the basis of the passage, for no specific case names are included.

12. It can be inferred from the passage that had the Civil Rights Movement not prompted an investigation of prison conditions,

(A) states would never have established asylums for the mentally ill

(B) new treatments for major mental illnesses would likely have remained untested

(C) the Civil Rights Movement in America would have been politically ineffective

(D) conditions in mental hospitals might have escaped judicial scrutiny

(E) many mentally ill prisoners would have been transferred from hospitals back to prisons

12. (D) This is an implied idea question. The author states that civil rights lawyers who represented black prisoners were drawn naturally into representing patients in mental hospitals. In other words, x caused y. The question stem asks us to assume that x did not occur, and on that basis we can infer that y might not have occurred. This is (D).

(A) is incorrect, for the cause of the establishment of the asylum system was Dorothea Dix's crusade. (B) is incorrect, for the passage does not state that judicial activism resulted in the discovery of any new treatments (even though it may have resulted in better treatment). (C) goes far beyond the scope of the passage. We cannot conclude that a failure in the area of prison reform would have meant complete failure of the Civil Rights Movement. Finally, as for (E), nothing in the passage suggests that judicial activism resulted in the transfer of prisoners to hospitals, so a lack of judicial activism would not necessarily have this effect.

13. The tone of the final paragraph can best be described as

    (A) stridently contentious
    (B) overly emotional
    (C) cleverly deceptive
    (D) cautiously optimistic
    (E) fiercely independent

14. Which of the following would be the most appropriate topic for the author to address in the next paragraph following the final paragraph of the selection?

    (A) An analysis of landmark cases affecting the civil rights of prisoners and patients in hospitals for the criminally insane
    (B) A discussion of the advantages and disadvantages of treatments that might result in the release of mentally ill persons
    (C) An outline of standards to guide mental health administrators in caring for mentally ill patients while respecting their civil rights
    (D) A proposal to place the administration of mental hospitals directly under the control of the judiciary
    (E) A more detailed description of the conditions in which the patients in mental hospitals lived in the 1960s and early 1970s

13. (D) This is an author's attitude question that focuses on the final paragraph. There the author makes a specific proposal, which, he acknowledges, will require effort to implement. Since the author made the proposal, he must be optimistic about its chance for success. And since he acknowledges that it will not be easy, we can call the author cautious as well.

As for (A) and (B), though the author does make an argument in that paragraph, he does so in rather neutral terms. The paragraph is not contentious or strident or emotional. As for (C), there is nothing in the selection to suggest that the author is attempting to mislead the reader. You may or may not agree with the author's suggestion in that last paragraph, but there is no warrant for the conclusion that he is trying to fool you. Finally, as for (E), although the author evidently does his own thinking, the *tone* of the final paragraph cannot be described in these terms.

14. (C) This is a further application question. Here, you must find the most logical extension of the discussion.

The best choice is (C). The selection provides a historical perspective on care for the mentally ill, but the author also has a "hidden" agenda. He is leading up to something. The point of the historical perspective is contained in the final paragraph: the evolution of the movement has reached the point at which judicial protectionism of patients is no longer critical and professional administrators should reassert their prerogatives.

As for choice (A), while it is true that the passage touches upon the role of judicial activism, judicial activism is seen by the author to be a stage in the evolution of patients' rights. Given the forward-looking development of the selection, the author would probably next discuss a further stage in this development—not return to discuss in detail a prior stage. (B) and (E) fail for the same reason. While it is true that the author does touch on these topics, further discussion of them is not consistent with the overall development of the selection. Finally, as for (D), this suggestion is directly contradicted by the passage, since the author states that it is time for the judiciary to return responsibility for patient care to the doctors.

President Roosevelt's administration suffered a devastating defeat when, on January 6, 1936, the Agricultural Adjustment Act was declared unconstitutional. New Deal planners quickly pushed through Congress the Soil Conservation and Domestic Allotment Act of 1935, one purpose of which was conservation, but which also aimed at controlling surpluses by retiring land from production. The law was intended as a stopgap measure until the administration could formulate a permanent farm program that would satisfy both the nation's farmers and the Supreme Court. Roosevelt's landslide victory over Landon in 1936 obscured the ambivalent nature of his support in the farm states. Despite extensive government propaganda, many farmers still refused to participate in the Agricultural Adjustment Administration's voluntary production control programs, and the burdensome surpluses of 1933 were gone—not the result of the AAA, but a consequence of great droughts.

In February of 1937, Secretary of Agriculture Wallace convened a meeting of farm leaders to promote the concept of the ever-normal granary, a policy that would encourage farmers to store crop surpluses (rather than dump them on the market) until grain was needed in years of small harvests. The Commodity Credit Corporation would grant loans to be repaid when the grain was later sold for a reasonable profit. The conference chose a Committee of Eighteen, which drafted a bill, but the major farm organizations were divided. Since ten of the eighteen members were also members of the American Farm Bureau

Federation, the measure was quickly labeled a Farm Bureau bill, and there were protests from the small, but highly vocal, Farmer's Holiday Association. When debate on the bill began, Roosevelt himself was vague and elusive and didn't move the proposed legislation into the "desirable" category until midsummer. In addition, there were demands that the New Deal's deficit spending be curtailed, and opponents of the bill charged that the AAA was wasteful and primarily benefited corporations and large-scale farmers.

The Soil Conservation and Domestic Allotment Act had failed to limit agricultural production as the administration had hoped. Farm prices and consumer demand were high, and many farmers, convinced that the drought had ended the need for crop controls, refused to participate in the AAA's soil conservation program. Without direct crop controls, agricultural production skyrocketed in 1937, and by late summer there was panic in the farm belt that prices would again be driven down to disastrously low levels. Congressmen began to pressure Roosevelt to place a floor under farm prices by making loans through the CCC, but Roosevelt made such loans contingent upon the willingness of Congress to support the administration's plan for a new system of crop controls. When the price of cotton began to drop, Roosevelt's adroit political maneuver finally forced congressional representatives from the South to agree to support a bill providing for crop controls and the ever-normal granary. The following year Congress passed the Agricultural Adjustment Act of 1938.

15.   The primary purpose of the passage is to

(A) analyze the connection between changes in weather conditions and the movement of agricultural prices

(B) call attention to the economic hardship suffered by farmers during the 1930s

(C) discuss the reasoning that led the Supreme Court to declare the Agricultural Adjustment Act of 1933 unconstitutional

(D) describe the events that led to the passage of the Agricultural Adjustment Act of 1938

(E) pinpoint the weaknesses of the agricultural policies of Roosevelt's New Deal

15. (D) This is a main idea question. The author begins by stating that the Agricultural Adjustment Act of 1933 was declared unconstitutional and then describes the administration's reaction to that decision. Specifically, the author details the difficulties of the administration in working out a second and permanent agricultural policy, the Agricultural Adjustment Act of 1938. This development is described by (D).

(A) is incorrect for two reasons. First, the author doesn't really analyze the connection between changes in the weather and fluctuations in farm prices. Second, the connection is only a part of the overall discussion. As for (B), though a reader might learn something about farmers during the depression, this is not the *author's* purpose in writing the selection. As for (C), though the author's starting point is the declaration of unconstitutionality, he does not discuss the Supreme Court's reasoning. As for (E), though the passage might be used to

16. Which of the following is NOT a statement made by the author about the Soil Conservation and Domestic Allotment Act?

    (A) It was intended to be a temporary measure.
    (B) It aimed at reducing agricultural production.
    (C) It aimed at soil conservation.
    (D) It was largely ineffective.
    (E) It was drafted primarily by the Farm Bureau.

17. According to the passage, the Roosevelt administration wanted agricultural legislation with all of the following characteristics EXCEPT

    (A) It would not be declared unconstitutional by the Supreme Court.
    (B) It would be acceptable to the nation's farmers.
    (C) It would dismantle the Agricultural Adjustment Administration.
    (D) It would provide loans to help farmers store surplus grain.
    (E) It would provide for direct control of agricultural production.

18. According to the passage, all of the following were impediments to the passage of the Agricultural Adjustment Act of 1938 EXCEPT

    (A) initial lack of clear Presidential support
    (B) prosperity enjoyed by the nation's farmers
    (C) opposition to the idea of a Farm Bureau bill
    (D) doubts about the constitutionality of the bill
    (E) lack of clear support for the bill in farm states

argue that Roosevelt's policy had some weaknesses, finding weaknesses is not the main point of the passage.

16. (E) This is a specific detail question—with a thought-reverser. The ideas suggested by (A), (B), and (C) are mentioned in the first paragraph. One aim of the law was conservation, but it was also intended to reduce output by taking land out of use. And it was considered a stop-gap or temporary measure. The idea suggested by (D) is mentioned in the final paragraph. In the first sentence of that paragraph, the author states that the law did not work. Finally, however, the idea mentioned by (E) represents a misreading of the selection. It was the Agricultural Adjustment Act of 1938, not the Soil Conservation and Domestic Allotment Act, that was drafted largely by members of the Farm Bureau.

17. (C) This, too, is a specific detail question with a thought-reverser. The ideas suggested in (A) and (B) are mentioned in the middle of the first paragraph. The ideas suggested by (D) and (E) are mentioned in the final sentence of the selection. (And the idea of the ever-normal granary is explained in greater detail in the second paragraph.) The idea suggested by (C) is not mentioned anywhere in the passage. In fact, in the second sentence of the final paragraph, the author states that one of the criticisms leveled at the new act was the wastefulness of the existing AAA. We can almost infer from this that the new act continued the AAA.

18. (D) This is another specific detail question with a thought-reverser. The idea suggested by (A) is clearly mentioned in the second paragraph. The idea suggested by (B) is developed in the final paragraph. The idea suggested by (C) can be found in the second paragraph and that suggested by (E) in the first. The selection does not mention, however, the idea suggested by (D). Although the administration wanted a bill that would not be struck down, the passage does not indicate that constitutional concerns were an impediment to the bill's passage.

19. The author implies which of the following conclusions?

   (A) Roosevelt's ability to gain passage of the Agricultural Adjustment Act of 1938 depended on the large harvests of 1937.

   (B) Secretary of Agriculture Wallace alienated members of the American Farm Bureau Federation by proposing an ever-normal granary.

   (C) The Agricultural Adjustment Act of 1933 was declared unconstitutional because it was written by the Farm Bureau.

   (D) The Commodity Credit Corporation was created to offer farmers incentives for taking land out of production.

   (E) The compulsory production controls of the Agricultural Adjustment Act of 1933 were effective in eliminating surpluses.

19. (A) This is an implied idea question. In the final paragraph, the author describes the sequence of events that led to the passage of the 1938 legislation, and he shows how Roosevelt used the changing economic conditions to his advantage. In this discussion, the author implies that the changing economic conditions were a critical factor in the passage of the bill.

As for (B), the author does state that some farm groups were displeased with the new bill because it was written primarily by members of the Farm Bureau, but we should not infer from this that the Secretary of Agriculture was blamed for this. (C) represents a confused reading of the passage. The author never states why the 1933 Act was voided but later does say that it was the new legislation (which would finally become the 1938 Act) that was written by members of the Farm Bureau. As for (D), there are two references to the CCC, but both mention that the CCC made loans. But you cannot infer from this that the CCC encouraged taking land out of production. That confuses the Soil Conservation and Domestic Allotment Act with the CCC. Finally, (E) is incorrect because the passage says only that the *voluntary* production controls of that legislation were not the reason for the elimination of the surplus of 1933. *Economic* conditions finally eliminated the surplus.

20. It can be inferred from the passage that the Farmer's Holiday Association opposed the bill drafted by the Committee of Eighteen because

(A) the bill was not strongly supported by President Roosevelt

(B) the Farmer's Holiday Association opposed the American Farm Bureau Federation

(C) the Roosevelt administration had incurrred excessive debt to finance its New Deal

(D) its membership consisted primarily of large-scale farmers

(E) none of its members had been invited to participate in the meeting convened by Wallace

20. (B) This is an inference question. In the second paragraph, the author states that *since* ten members of the Committee of Eighteen were members of the American Farm Bureau Federation, the bill was labeled a Farm Bureau Bill and opposed by the Farmer's Holiday Association. From this we can infer, as noted by (B), that the Farmer's Holiday Association opposed the American Farm Bureau Federation.

As for (A), while the passage does state that the bill was not, at first, strongly supported by Roosevelt, the author does not give that as the reason for the opposition to the bill by the Farmer's Holiday Association. As for (C), though the passage does state that some groups opposed the bill for this reason, the author does not give this as the reason for the FHA's opposition. In fact, it seems more likely that the FHA would favor some bill for farmers even if it did entail government spending. As for (D), although the author does mention that opponents of the bill charged that it favored large-scale farmers, the passage does not imply that this was the reason for the FHA's opposition. And finally, (E) is directly contradicted by the second paragraph.

21. It can be inferred from the passage that under the policy of an ever-normal granary

(A) the Commodity Credit Corporation would lend more money to farmers in years of good harvests than in years of bad harvests

(B) the Commodity Credit Corporation would buy up crop surpluses in years of good harvests and sell the surplus in years of bad harvests

(C) the Commodity Credit Corporation would pay farmers the difference between the actual market prices received for grain and the price needed to guarantee a reasonable profit

(D) farmers would be required by the government to store crop surpluses from good harvests until that grain was needed in years of poor harvests

(E) the government would set grain prices at levels that would encourage farmers to withhold grain from the market in times of surplus and sell in times of shortage

21. (A) This is an inference question. According to the second paragraph, under the policy of an ever-normal granary the CCC would grant loans to farmers to encourage them to store surplus grain and sell it in later years when there were shortages. Thus, we can infer that the CCC was more likely to need to make loans when harvests were good and produced surpluses than when harvests were bad and surpluses from previous years were sold off.

The remaining answer choices all represent misreadings of the role of the government under the policy of an ever-normal granary. Government intervention was to be restricted to providing inducements to store surplus grain. No direct government intervention was contemplated.

In the summer of 999, Leif Ericsson voyaged to Norway and spent the following winter with King Olaf Tryggvason. Substantially the same account is given by both the Saga of Eric the Red and the Flat Island
(5) Book. Of Leif's return voyage to Greenland the latter says nothing, but according to the former it was during this return voyage that Leif discovered America. The Flat Island Book, however, tells of another and earlier landfall by Biarni, the son of a prominent
(10) man named Heriulf, and makes of this Leif's inspiration for the voyage to the new land. In short, like Leif, Biarni and his companions sight three countries in succession before reaching Greenland, and to come upon each new land takes 1 "doegr" more than the
(15) last until Biarni comes to land directly in front of his father's house in the last-mentioned country.

This narrative has been rejected by most later writers, and they may be justified. Possibly, Biarni was a companion of Leif when he voyaged from
(20) Norway to Greenland via America, or it may be that the entire tale is but a garbled account of that voyage and Biarni another name for Leif. It should be noted, however, that the stories of Leif's visit to King Olaf and Biarni's to that king's predecessor are in the same
(25) narrative in the Flat Island Book, so there is less likelihood of duplication than if they were from different sources. Also, Biarni landed on none of the lands he passed, but Leif apparently landed on one, for he brought back specimens of wheat, vines, and timber.
(30) Nor is there any good reason to believe that the first land visited by Biarni was Wineland. The first land was "level and covered with woods," and "there were small hillocks upon it." Of forests, later writers do not emphasize them particularly in connection with
(35) Wineland, though they are often noted incidentally; and of hills, the Saga says of Wineland only that "wherever there was hilly ground, there were vines."

Additionally, if the two narratives were taken from the same source we should expect a closer
(40) resemblance of Helluland. The Saga says of it: "They found there hellus" (large flat stones). According to the Biarni narrative, however, "this land was high and mountainous." The intervals of 1, 2, 3, and 4 "doegr" in both narratives are suggestive, but mythic formulas
(45) of this kind may be introduced into narratives without altogether destroying their historicity. It is also held against the Biarni narrative that its hero is made to come upon the coast of Greenland exactly in front of his father's home. But it should be recalled that
(50) Heriulfsness lay below two high mountains which served as landmarks for navigators.

I would give up Biarni more readily were it not that the story of Leif's voyage, contained in the supposedly more reliable Saga, is almost as amazing. But
(55) Leif's voyage across the entire width of the North Atlantic is said to be "probable" because it is documented in the narrative of a preferred authority, while Biarni's is "improbable" or even "impossible" because the document containing it has been condemned.

22. The author's primary concern is to demonstrate that
    (A) Leif Ericsson did not visit America
    (B) Biarni might have visited America before Leif Ericsson
    (C) Biarni did not visit Wineland
    (D) Leif Ericsson visited Wineland first
    (E) Leif Ericsson was the same person as Biarni

22. (B) This is a main idea question. The author offers several reasons for the conclusion that the Biarni narrative does not describe the same series of events described by the Saga. And if he can pull this off, then he can claim that Biarni visited America before Leif Ericsson did. This is summarized by (B).

    (A) misinterprets the author's strategy. The author doesn't need to prove that Leif Ericsson did not visit America, only that Biarni did so before him. (C) is too narrow. It is true that the author wants to show that the two voyages are to some extent dissimilar, and that is why he tries to prove that Biarni did not visit Wineland. But this is a small part of the overall development. As for (D), as was just noted, the author needs only to argue that Biarni did not visit the same three lands later visited by Leif Ericsson. Finally, (E) would be fatal to the author's argument, so this is a point he wishes to disprove.

23. The passage provides information that defines which of the following terms?
    I. Doegr
    II. Hellus
    III. Heriulfsness
    (A) I only   (B) II only   (C) III only
    (D) I and II only   (E) II and III only

23. (E) The author explicitly defines *hellus* as meaning "stone," so II is part of the correct answer. (You can now eliminate [A] and [C].) III is defined implicitly in the passage. The author refers to Heriulfsness in the sentence following the reference to Biarni's father's home. And given the fact that Heriulf is identified as Biarni's father, we can conclude that Heriulfsness must be the father's home. Statement I, however, is not defined. For all that is stated in the selection, "doegr" could be a day, two days, a week, a fortnight, or a month.

24. It can be inferred from the passage that scholars who doubt the authenticity of the Biarni narrative make all of the following objections BUT

(A) Biarni might have accompanied Leif Ericsson on the voyage to America, and that is why a separate, erroneous narrative was invented.

(B) The similarity of the voyages described in the Saga and in the Flat Island Book indicates that there was but one voyage, not two voyages.

(C) It seems very improbable that a ship, having sailed from America to Greenland, could have found its way to a precise point on the coast of Greenland.

(D) The historicity of the Saga of Eric the Red is well-documented, while the historicity of the Flat Island Book is very doubtful.

(E) Both the Saga of Eric the Red and the Flat Island Book make use of mythical formulas, so it is probable that they were written by the same person.

24. (E) This is an implied idea question. The author doesn't give us a list of the objections to the historicity of the Biarni narrative, but we can infer what some of those objections must be from the refutations of them offered in the selection. As for (A), in the second paragraph, the author acknowledges that Biarni might have been a companion of Leif Ericsson's and that the narrative of Biarni might be a garbled tale of that adventure. We can infer, therefore, that the objectors try to explain away the "other voyage" in this way. As for (B), since the author spends so much effort in attempting to prove that the two voyages did not include exactly the same countries, we can infer that the objectors use the similarity between the two voyages as proof that there was but one voyage. As for (C), in the third paragraph the author argues that it is not unreasonable to believe that Biarni could sail directly to his father's house since the house was situated by a known navigational landmark. So we infer that the objectors argue that the event was improbable and that this makes the Biarni narrative less believable. And as for (D), the author specifically attributes this objection to them in the closing sentences.

(E), however, is not an objection that would undermine the historicity of the narrative of Biarni. The similarity of the sequence of "doegr" might suggest the two accounts were based on the same events, and this could be an objection that might be raised against the historicity of the Biarni narrative. But this would not prove the two narratives were written by the same author. Further, someone who rejects the Biarni narrative would surely not want to suggest it has the same source as the saga, the supposedly authentic story.

25. The author mentions the two high mountains (line 50) in order to show that it is

(A) reasonable for Biarni to land precisely at his father's home
(B) possible to sail from Norway to Greenland without modern navigational equipment
(C) likely that Biarni landed on America at least 100 years before Leif Ericsson
(D) probable that Leif Ericsson followed the same course as Biarni
(E) questionable whether Biarni required the same length of time as Leif Ericsson to complete his voyage

26. All of the following are mentioned as similarities between Leif Ericsson's voyage and Biarni's voyage EXCEPT

(A) both visited Norway
(B) on the return voyage, both visited three different lands
(C) both returned to Greenland
(D) both sighted Wineland
(E) both sighted Helluland

27. It can be inferred that the author regards the historicity of the Biarni narrative as

(A) conclusively proved
(B) almost conclusively proved
(C) possibly true
(D) highly unlikely
(E) conclusively disproved

28. In the final paragraph, the author suggests some authorities who regard the Saga as authentic are guilty of which of the following errors in reasoning?

(A) Oversimplification
(B) Logical contradiction
(C) False analogy
(D) Hasty generalization
(E) Circular reasoning

25. (A) This is a logical detail question. As noted above, one of the objections to the Biarni narrative is that it would have been difficult for Biarni to navigate so accurately. But the author points out that the location of Heriulf's house was clearly indicated by mountains. So the author mentions the mountains to prove that Biarni could have found the location.

26. (D) This is a specific detail question with a thought-reverser. Four of the five ideas are specifically stated in the selection. (A), (B), and (C) are mentioned in the first paragraph, and (E) is mentioned in the third. But the author is at pains to prove that Biarni did not visit Wineland as the first of his three lands.

27. (C) This is an author's attitude question. The answer choices are already neatly arranged for us on a spectrum. The best choice is (C). The author gives several arguments for the historicity of the narrative. So we can eliminate (D) and (E). On the other hand, the author does not claim to have proved his case conclusively. In fact, in the first sentence of the second paragraph, he admits that the objectors "may be justified." And in the final paragraph, the phrasing "I would give up . . ." strongly suggests that the author does not regard the issue as settled.

28. (E) This is an inference question. In the final paragraph, the author states that the Saga attributes to Leif feats similar to those attributed by the Flat Island Book to Biarni. Yet, most authorities regard Leif's voyage as probable and Biarni's as improbable. Why? Because the Saga is considered authentic and the Flat Island Book inauthentic. But why would the Saga be considered authentic? Because it describes events that are more believable. Hence, the circularity in the argument.

The other choices do describe logical errors that might make an argument fallacious, but they do not describe the argument mentioned by the author in the final paragraph.

> Directions: Each passage in this group is followed by questions based on its content. After reading a passage, choose the best answer to each question. Answer all questions following a passage on the basis of what is stated or implied in that passage.

To go into solitude, a man needs to retire as much from his chamber as from society. I am not solitary while I read and write, though nobody is with me. But if a man would be alone, let him look at the stars. The rays
(5) that come from those heavenly worlds will separate between him and vulgar things. One might think the atmosphere was made transparent with this design, to give man in the heavenly bodies the perpetual presence of the sublime. Seen in the streets of cities, how great
(10) they are! If the stars should appear one night in a thousand years, how would men believe and adore; and preserve for many generations the remembrance of the city of God which had been shown! But every night come out these preachers of beauty, and light the uni-
(15) verse with admonishing smile.

The stars awaken a certain reverence, because though always present, they are inaccessible. In fact, all natural objects make a similar impression—when the mind is open to their influence. Nature never wears a mean
(20) appearance. Not even the wisest person can extort all of her secrets nor exhaust his curiosity by finding out all her perfection. Nature never became a toy to a wise spirit. The flowers, the animals, the mountains reflect the wisdom of his best hour, as much as they delight the
(25) simplicity of his childhood.

When we speak of Nature in this manner, we have a distinct but most poetical sense in mind. We mean the integrity of expression made manifold by natural objects. It is this that distinguishes the stick of timber of
(30) the wood-cutter from the tree of the poet. The charming landscape which I saw this morning is indubitably made up of some twenty or thirty farms. This field is the property of Miller, that one the property of Locke, and that one beyond the wood the property of Manning. But
(35) none of them owns the landscape. There is property in the horizon which no man has but it belongs only to him whose eyes can integrate all the parts, that is, to poets. This is the best part of these men's farms, yet to this their warranty gives no title.
(40) To speak truly, few adult persons can see nature. Most persons do not see the sun. At least they have only a very superficial seeing. The sun illuminates only the eye of the man but shines into the eye and heart of the child. The lover of nature is he whose inward and
(45) outward senses are still truly adjusted to each other; who has retained the spirit of infancy even into adulthood. His intercourse with heaven and earth becomes part of his daily food. In the presence of Nature, a wild delight runs through the man, in spite of real sorrows. Nature
(50) says,—he is my creature, and despite his grief, he shall be glad with me.

The greatest delight which the fields and woods minister is the suggestion of an occult relation between man and the vegetable. I am not alone and unacknowl-
(55) edged. They nod to me and I to them. The waving of the bough in the storm is new to me—and old. It takes me by surprise and yet is not unknown. Its effect is like that of a higher thought or a better emotion coming over me, when I deemed I was thinking justly or doing right.
(60) Yet it is certain that the power to produce this delight does not reside in Nature but in humans, or in the harmony of both. It is necessary to use these pleasures with great temperance. For Nature is not always decked out in holiday attire. The same scene which yesterday
(65) breathed perfume and glittered is overspread with melancholy today. Nature always wears the color of the spirit.

1. The phrase "Nature never became a toy to the wise spirit" means which of the following?

(A) Educated people do not treat nature as children do.
(B) Nature will always conquer even the most learned person.
(C) Nature is unpredictable and human beings cannot understand it.
(D) A truly wise person does not lose his appreciation of nature.
(E) The best things in nature are unattainable.

2. The author implies that the difference between farms and the landscape is primarily a matter of

(A) cultivation   (B) perception   (C) ownership
(D) allegiance   (E) inheritance

3. The author uses the word *property* in the phrase "property in the horizon" (lines 35–36) to express

(A) melancholy   (B) reverence   (C) disbelief
(D) irony   (E) foolishness

4. The phrase "color of the spirit" (lines 66–67) means

(A) feelings of the observer
(B) changing seasons
(C) weather
(D) time of day
(E) rainbow

5. The author's attitude toward nature can best be described as

(A) hostile and angry
(B) awed and reverent
(C) ambivalent and confused
(D) detached and objective
(E) cynical and jaded

According to the author, the stars are a source of inspiration for which of the following reasons?

   I. They are extremely distant from us.
  II. They reappear every night.
 III. They are no person's property.
 IV. They do not shine as brightly as the sun.

(A) I and II only
(B) I and III only
(C) II and III only
(D) I, II, and III only
(E) II, III, and IV only

The beginning of what was to become the United States was characterized by inconsistencies in the values and behavior of its population, inconsistencies that were reflected by its spokesmen, who took conflicting stances in many areas; but on the subject of race, the conflicts were particularly vivid. The idea that the Caucasian race and European civilization were superior was well entrenched in the culture of the colonists at the very time that the "egalitarian" republic was founded. Voluminous historical evidence indicates that, in the mind of the average colonist, the African was a heathen, he was black, and he was different in crucial philosophical ways. As time progressed, he was also increasingly captive, adding to the conception of deviance. The African, therefore, could be justifiably (and even philanthropically) treated as property according to the reasoning of slave traders and slaveholders.

Although slaves were treated as objects, bountiful evidence suggests that they did not view themselves similarly. There are many published autobiographies of slaves, and African-American scholars are beginning to know enough about West African culture to appreciate the existential climate in which the early captives were raised and which, therefore, could not be totally destroyed by the enslavement experience. This was a climate that defined individuality in collective terms. Individuals were members of a tribe, within which they had prescribed roles determined by the history of their family within the tribe. Individuals were inherently a part of the natural elements on which they depended, and they were actively related to those tribal members who once lived and to those not yet born.

The colonial plantation system that was established and into which Africans were thrust did virtually eliminate tribal affiliations. Individuals were separated from kin; interrelationships among kin kept together were often transient because of sales. A new identification with those slaves working and living together in a given place could satisfy what was undoubtedly a natural tendency to be a member of a group. New family units became the most important attachments of individual slaves. Thus, as the system of slavery was gradually institutionalized, West African affiliation tendencies adapted to it.

This exceedingly complex dual influence is still reflected in black community life, and the double consciousness of black Americans is the major characteristic of African-American mentality. DuBois articulated this divided consciousness as follows:

> The history of the American Negro is the history of this strife—this longing to attain self-conscious manhood, to merge his double self into a better and truer self. In this merging, he wishes neither of the older selves to be best.

Several black political movements have looked upon this duality as destructively conflictual and have variously urged its reconciliation. Thus, the integrationists and the black nationalists, to be crudely general, have both been concerned with resolving the conflict, but in opposite directions.

7. Which of the following would be the most appropriate title for the passage?

(A) The History of Black People in the United States
(B) West African Tribal Relations
(C) The Origin of Modern Afro-American Consciousness
(D) Slavery: A Democratic Anomaly
(E) The Legacy of Slavery: A Modern Nation Divided

8. The author states which of the following about the Africans who were brought to America?

   I. In Africa, they had acquired a sense of intertribal unity in which all were regarded as belonging to the same group.
  II. They did not regard themselves as objects of someone else's ownership.
 III. They formed new groups to replace the tribal associations that had been destroyed.

(A) I only
(B) II only
(C) III only
(D) I and II only
(E) II and III only

9. Which of the following can be inferred about the viewpoint expressed in the second paragraph of the passage?

(A) It is a reinterpretation of slave life based on new research done by Afro-American scholars.
(B) It is based entirely on recently published descriptions of slave life written by slaves themselves.
(C) It is biased and overly sympathetic to the views of white, colonial slaveholders.
(D) It is highly speculative and supported by little actual historical evidence.
(E) It is supported by descriptions of slave life written by early Americans who actually owned slaves.

10. The author puts the word *egalitarian* in line 9 in quotation marks to

   (A) emphasize his admiration for the early Americans
   (B) ridicule the idea of democracy
   (C) remind the reader of the principles of the new nation
   (D) underscore the fact that equality did not extend to everyone
   (E) express his surprise that slavery could have existed in America

11. The tone of the passage could best be described as

   (A) informed and anecdotal
   (B) critical and argumentative
   (C) impassioned and angry
   (D) analytical and objective
   (E) caustic and humorous

12. It can be inferred that which of the following pairs are the two elements of the "dual influence" mentioned in line 45?

   (A) Slavery and West African culture
   (B) Tribal affiliations in West Africa and family affiliations in West Africa
   (C) A sense of individuality and a sense of tribal identification
   (D) The history of West Africa and modern black political movements
   (E) Integrationism and black nationalism

13. The author's argument logically depends upon which of the following assumptions?

   (A) The duality that characterized the consciousness of modern black Americans is so deeply rooted that it cannot be eliminated by political action.
   (B) African captives who were brought to North America had learned a basic orientation toward the world that remained with them.
   (C) The white Americans at the time of the beginning of the United States were not aware of the contradiction between the notion of equality and the institution of slavery.
   (D) The influence of the slavery experience on the West Africans was more powerful than the remembrance of West African attitudes.
   (E) Black Americans today are knowledgeable about the world view that was dominant in West Africa at the time of the beginning of slavery in America.

14. The primary purpose of the passage is to

   (A) advocate a new method of analysis
   (B) reconcile two opposing points of view
   (C) describe and analyze a point of view
   (D) provide historical background of a phenomenon
   (E) present examples to prove a general statement

Two techniques have recently been developed to simplify research and reduce the number of nonhuman primates needed in studies of certain complex hormonal reactions. One technique involves the culturing of primate pituitary cells and the cells of certain human tumors. In the other, animal oviduct tissue is transplanted under the skin of laboratory primates. Both culturing techniques complement existing methods of studying intact animals.

With an in vitro culturing technique, researchers are deciphering how biochemical agents regulate the secretion of prolactin, the pituitary hormone that promotes milk production. The cultured cells survive for as long as a month, and they do not require serum, a commonly used culture ingredient that can influence cellular function and confound study results. One primate pituitary gland may yield enough cells for as many as 72 culture dishes, which otherwise would require as many animals.

The other technique allows scientists to monitor cellular differentiation in the reproductive tracts of female monkeys. While falling short of the long-sought goal of developing an in vitro model of the female reproductive system, the next best alternative was achieved. The method involves transplanting oviduct tissue to an easily accessible site under the skin, where the grafted cells behave exactly as if they were in their normal environment. In about 80 percent of the grafts, blood vessels in surrounding abdominal skin grow into and begin nourishing the oviduct tissue. Otherwise, the tissue is largely isolated, walled off by the surrounding skin. A cyst forms that shrinks and swells in tandem with stages of the menstrual cycle. With about 80 percent of the grafts reestablishing themselves in the new site, a single monkey may bear as many as 20 miniature oviducts that are easily accessible for study. Because samples are removed with a simple procedure requiring only local anesthesia, scientists can track changes in oviduct cells over short intervals. In contrast, repeated analysis of cellular changes within the oviduct itself would require abdominal surgery every time a sample was taken—a procedure that the animals could not tolerate.

Scientists are using the grafting technique to study chlamydia infections, a leading cause of infertility among women. By infecting oviduct tissues transplanted into the abdominal skin of rhesus monkeys, researchers hope to determine how the bacteria cause pelvic inflammatory disease and lesions that obstruct the oviduct. Such research could eventually lead to the development of antibodies to the infectious agent and a strategy for producing a chlamydia vaccine.

15. This passage deals primarily with

   (A) reproductive organs of nonhuman primates
   (B) diseases of the pituitary glands
   (C) in vitro studies of pituitary hormones
   (D) techniques for studying hormonal reactions
   (E) new anesthesia techniques

According to the passage, the primary benefit of the new research is that

(A) scientists can study the pituitary gland for the first time
(B) the procedures are simpler and require fewer laboratory animals
(C) the study of intact laboratory animals has now been rendered obsolete
(D) reseachers were able to discover prolactin
(E) an in vitro model of the reproductive system was developed

7. Which of the following conclusions about the culturing technique can be inferred from the passage?

   I. It produces more reliable results than research done with cells requiring serum.
   II. Cultured cells can be implanted in a living animal several times without harming the animal.
   III. A single pituitary gland may generate sufficient cells for a number of experiments.

(A) I only
(B) II only
(C) III only
(D) I and III only
(E) I, II, and III

8. All of the following are true of the transplantation technique EXCEPT

(A) It avoids the need for subjecting a laboratory subject to repeated major surgery.
(B) It permits scientists to monitor changes frequently.
(C) The transplanted cells grow as they would in their normal site.
(D) The transplanted cells can be easily grown in vitro.
(E) The transplant operation is usually successful.

9. According to the passage, chlamydia causes infertility in women by

(A) causing tissue changes that block the oviduct
(B) shrinking and swelling tissues in conjunction with the menstrual cycle
(C) allowing skin tissue to encyst reproductive tissue
(D) necessitating abdominal surgery to remove damaged tissue
(E) diverting the blood supply from the reproductive organs to the skin

20. It can be inferred from the passage that an in vitro model of the female reproductive system is

(A) currently available but prohibitively expensive
(B) currently available and widely used
(C) theoretically possible but of no real scientific value
(D) theoretically possible but as yet technically impossible
(E) theoretically impossible

Because some resources must be allocated at the national level, we have created policies which reflect the aggregated attributes of our society. The federal budget determines the proportion of federal resources to be
(5) invested in social welfare programs and how these resources are distributed among competing programs. This budget is arrived at through a reiterative aggregative political process which mediates the claims of groups interested in health, education, welfare, and so on, thus
(10) socializing the continuing conflict generated by their separate aspirations. The test of whether a policy is "good" under this system is whether it can marshal sufficient legitimacy and consent to provide a basis for cohesion and action. Technical criteria may play a role
(15) in the process, but the ultimate criteria are political and social.

Whether a policy that is "good" in the aggregate sense is also "good" for a particular person, however, is a different matter. If everyone had identical attributes,
(20) these criteria of goodness would produce identical outcomes. With any degree of complexity or change, however, these criteria will always produce different outcomes. Any policy negotiated to attain an aggregate correctness will be wrong for every individual to whom the policy
(25) applies. The less a person conforms to the aggregate, the more wrong it will be.

When a policy is not working, we normally assume that the policy is right in form but wrong in content. It has failed because insufficient intelligence has informed
(30) its construction or insufficient energy its implementation. We proceed to replace the old policy by a new one of the same form. This buys time, since some time must elapse before the new policy can fully display the same set of symptoms of failure as the old. We thus continue
(35) to invest our time, energy, and other resources as if every new discovery of a nonworking policy is a surprise, and a surprise that can be corrected with some reorganized model. But if policies based on complex, aggregated information are always wrong with respect to the prefer-
(40) ences of every person to whom they apply, we should concentrate on limiting such policies to minima or "floors." Rather than trying for better policies, we should try for fewer policies or more limited aggregated ones. Such limitations could be designed to produce
(45) policies as spare and minimal as possible, for the resources not consumed in their operation would then be usable in nonaggregative, person-specific ways—that is, in a disaggregated fashion. This will require more than just strengthened "local" capacity; it will require the
(50) development of new procedures, institutions, roles, and expectations.

21. Which of the following best states the central theme of the passage?

   (A) Policies designed to meet the needs of a large group of people are inherently imperfect and should be scaled down.
   (B) Policies created by the democratic process are less effective than policies designed by a single, concentrated body of authority.
   (C) The effectiveness of a social policy depends more upon the manner in which the policy is administered than upon its initial design.
   (D) Since policies created on the federal level are inherently ineffective, all federal social welfare programs should be discontinued.
   (E) Because state, county, and city officials are more knowledgeable about local conditions, responsibility for all social welfare programs should be shifted to the local level.

22. According to the passage, the test of whether a policy is successful in the aggregate sense is whether or not it

   (A) applies to a large number of people
   (B) satisfies the needs of the people to whom it applies
   (C) appeals to a sufficiently large number of people
   (D) can be revised periodically in response to changing conditions
   (E) can be administered by existing federal agencies

23. Which of the following would the author probably regard as an example of a policy based on a process of aggregation?

   I. A school dietician prepares menus based on a survey of the taste preferences of students.
   II. A state requires licensed drivers to take an eye examination only once every ten years because most people's eyes do not change radically in a shorter period of time.
   III. The trainer for a baseball team prescribes exercises for injured team members according to the nature of the injury and the physical makeup of the player.

   (A) I only   (B) II only   (C) I and II only
   (D) I and III only   (E) I, II, and III

24. The author places the word *good* in quotation marks (line 17) in order to

   (A) emphasize that the word is ambiguous when applied to public policies
   (B) stress that no two people will agree on what is "good" and what is not
   (C) minimize the need to describe public policies in value terms
   (D) point out that the word can be applied to individuals but not to groups
   (E) remind the reader that the word is a technical term

25. Which of the following words, when substituted for the word *aggregate* in line 17, would LEAST change the meaning of the sentence?

   (A) extreme   (B) group   (C) average
   (D) quantity   (E) difference

26. The author regards the use of aggregative policies as

   (A) enlightened but prohibitively expensive
   (B) undesirable but sometimes necessary
   (C) wasteful and open to corruption
   (D) essential and praiseworthy
   (E) ill-conceived and unnecessary

27. Which of the following, if true, would most weaken the author's argument?

   (A) Many aggregative social welfare policies enacted during the 1930s are still in effect even though they have been modified several times
   (B) A study by the General Services Administration of the federal government concluded that waste and mismanagement in government programs has declined in recent years.
   (C) Many government programs can be made more efficient by applying sophisticated computer models and other advanced technology to the problems they are designed to solve.
   (D) The individuals who are the targets of aggregative policies are not required by law to accept the benefits offered by those programs.
   (E) The resources that would be freed by limiting aggregative policies exist only as tax revenues, which cannot be distributed except through aggregative policies.

28. According to the passage, a policy based on aggregation will be wrong for every person to whom it applies because

   (A) many individuals are unaware of the existence of such programs
   (B) technical criteria are not given sufficient emphasis
   (C) individuals who have no need for a program may still fit its eligibility criteria
   (D) some administrators may not apply policies uniformly to all
   (E) no individual fits precisely the group profile

Explanatory Answers

1. (D) This is an implied idea question. The phrase in question appears in the second paragraph. The author begins by stating that all of nature creates the impression of awe, at least when viewed with an open mind. Then he states that nature is inexhaustible; not even the wise person learns everything there is to know about nature. Next comes the phrase in question.

The phrase means that if one is truly wise, he will maintain this attitude of reverence toward nature. A wise person will not turn nature into an object to be played with. (D) best expresses this idea.

(A) is incorrect because the author implies that a truly wise person will continue to have the same appreciation for nature as an adult that he had as a child. (B), (C), and (E) use the word *nature*, but the statements they make have no support in the text.

2. (B) This, too, is an implied idea question. The author is drawing a contrast between property that is owned (individual parcels of dirt) and the horizon or landscape. The landscape encompasses parcels of land but it is not itself a parcel of dirt. The landscape cannot be owned. We can immediately eliminate (D) and (E) as having nothing to do with this distinction.

As for (A), while it is true that the actual dirt can be cultivated but not the landscape, this is not the main difference for the author. The real question is whether the author thinks the main difference is a matter of who owns it or a matter of perception. To answer, you must read between the lines.

While it is true that no one can own the landscape, the real difference for the author is in how things are perceived. One can see just farms, or one can see a landscape. So (B) is a better description of the difference than (C).

3. (D) This also is an implied idea question. The key to this question is contained in our discussion of question 2. The author distinguishes "property" as a bit of land (which can be owned by a person) from the landscape, which cannot be owned by deed but does "belong" to anyone who wishes to see it. So the author really is making a play on the word *property*. He is saying, ironically, anyone can have the property of the landscape but he can't own it.

Even though this is a difficult question, you can eliminate (E) as a non-answer. The author is surely not likely to say something intentionally to make himself look foolish. And by eliminating even a single answer, you are not only allowed to guess—you must guess.

4. (A) Another implicit idea question! (It seems that these literary passages are designed for such questions.) This focuses our attention on the final paragraph. The author states that nature does not always give the same impression. One day it seems happy, the next sad. Why? Because the reaction we experience "does not reside in Nature but in humans, or in the harmony of both." In other words, the important element is human perception and feeling. The author summarizes this idea by saying that "Nature always wears the color of the spirit." This means it is the human side that is the source of feelings. Only (A) mentions something from the human side.

5. (B) This is a tone question. Given the discussion above, you should be able to see that the author's attitude is one of reverence. In fact, the author even uses that word in the first paragraph.

Clearly there are no negative overtones in the selection, so you can eliminate (A) and (E). (D) must be wrong, since there is a clear positive tone in the passage. Finally, as for (C), although the passage may be difficult to understand at times (and therefore confusing), the author's attitude toward nature is not at all confused—it is a positive one.

6. (A) This is a specific detail question. In the first paragraph, the author states that the stars would be less suitable as a source of inspiration were they not frequently available. Thus, statement I must be part of the correct choice. In the second paragraph the author states that the stars inspire awe because they are inaccessible. So II must also be part of the correct choice. III is generally related to the ideas mentioned in that paragraph, but the idea suggested by III is not responsive to the question. Finally, IV is not mentioned in the selection. So the correct choice consists of I and II only.

7. (C) Here we have a main idea question presented in the "name that passage" format. We'll go down the list of choices, eliminating those that are too narrow or too broad.

(A) is too broad. Most of the discussion focuses on an early period of this country's history, even though there is one paragraph that points out the modern implications of this history. This hardly constitutes an entire history of black people in the United States. (B) is too narrow. Though the discussion of West African tribal relations is an important element of the passage, it is not the main theme. The correct answer must be a title that also includes reference to the implications of these cultural elements.

(C) gives us what we are looking for. The passage contrasts white attitudes toward slaves with the attitudes the Africans themselves held about themselves and then shows what implications this cultural history has for modern black Americans. You can eliminate (D), since the main theme of the passage is not really the relationship between slavery and democracy. The anomaly of slavery in a supposedly egalitarian society is only a small part of the discussion. Finally, (E) has the merit of using the phrase "legacy of slavery," which is an important element in the discussion. But the division mentioned in the final paragraph is a division of consciousness—not the division of a nation.

8. (E) This is a specific detail question. You will find II specifically stated in the first sentence of the second paragraph, and you will find III explicitly mentioned in the third paragraph. So II and III must be included in the correct choice. This conclusion lets us eliminate (A), (B), (C), and (D)—even without discussing statement I.

In fact, statement I is contradicted by the passage. The author states that West Africans felt a *tribal* unity, not an *intertribal* unity.

9. (A) This is an implied idea question. It's difficult because you have to pick up on the key phrase "African-American scholars are beginning to know"; but the question stem doesn't tell you that this is the key to the question.

That phrase implies that something new has been learned that has prompted scholars to change their ideas about the experience of slavery. In other words, the scholars have rejected the traditional view of what Africans thought of slavery. So we infer that the position outlined in the last two paragraphs is a new interpretation, and (A) correctly describes this.

(B) is incorrect since the author mentions evidence other than the published autobiographies. And in any case, it is the information about West African culture that has been newly discovered, not the autobiographies. (C) is incorrect since the second paragraph doesn't even deal with the attitudes of the white slaveholders.

Next, given that the author cites two sources in support of his interpretation (autobiographies and new research), we can eliminate (D). Finally, (E) is incorrect since the paragraph in question does not discuss the attitudes of those who owned slaves.

10. (D) This is a logical structure question. Why does the author place the term *egalitarian* in quotation marks? The term appears in the first paragraph, where the author is discussing the contradictions in early American attitudes, which are particularly evident in the area of race. These "egalitarian" thinkers believed that they were superior to the Africans.

The author places the term in quotation marks to indicate that he thinks the early white Americans were not really egalitarian. This surely eliminates (A) and (C). (B), however, overstates the case. The author is not implying that democracy, as a concept, is indefensible—only that the early American thinkers did not do a very good job of implementing the idea. Additionally, you can eliminate (E) because the passage does not express surprise. It treats slavery as a historical fact.

11. (D) This is a tone question using answer choices with two words. On the basis of first words, we can eliminate both (C) and (E). Although the topic is obviously of interest to the author, the treatment does not qualify as impassioned. Further, though the author's use of quotation marks to surround the word *egalitarian* might qualify as irony or even sarcasm, the overall tone of the passage is not caustic.

Next, using the second words, we eliminate (A) and (B). The author does not tell stories, so the tone cannot be anecdotal. Finally, the tone is not argumentative. Though the passage develops logically and has the form of a logical argument, it cannot be described as argumentative. *Argumentative* means "contentious and aggressive."

12. (A) This is an implied idea question. In the final paragraph, the author refers to the "dual influence" but does not name those influences. Given the context, however, we may conclude that the two influences are slavery and the elements of West African culture that survived. (B) is, therefore, only partially correct. West African culture is only one of the two influences. (C) is a dichotomy mentioned in the selection, but it is not the one to which the author is referring in the final paragraph. (D) is only partially correct. The elements of West African culture constitute one of the two influences, but modern black political movements could not be one of the *origins* mentioned by the author (though it is an outcome of the dual influences). Finally, as for (E), the author does mention these two contrasting movements, but they are a reflection of the duality, not the origin of the duality.

7

13. (B) Although this question uses the word *logically,* it is an implied idea question rather than a logical structure question. The question asks you to identify one of the choices as being a hidden premise of the argument. (B) is essential to the argument. For the argument regarding the West African influences to be valid, it must be assumed that the West Africans had learned a world view that survived their being uprooted and transported to America. Without that critical assumption, the argument about the influence of West African culture fails.

(A) is not necessary to the author's argument. The author tries to prove the existence of such a duality, but he does not make any suggestion about how it might be eliminated. (C) is incorrect because the author merely states that there was such a contradiction. Whether white Americans were aware of the inconsistency in their behavior and beliefs is irrelevant. (D) is incorrect because the author merely states that there was the "dual" influence. He does not suggest that one or the other was more important in shaping the structure of modern black American consciousness. Finally, as for (E), though the author must assume that West African culture did survive in some form, he need not assume that black Americans today are still familiar with the elements of West African culture during the time of slavery. The legacy of that culture can survive even without conscious knowledge of its elements.

14. (D) This is a main idea question that asks about the general form of the selection rather than its specific content. The best choice is (D). The author describes the historical roots of the duality that characterizes the consciousness of Afro-Americans.

As for (A), though the author does mention some evidence that may be regarded as new (the research on West African culture), he does not describe a method of analysis. As for (B), the author does not introduce opposing viewpoints, so he could not possibly attempt to reconcile opposing views. As for (C), though the author does *present* his own point of view, he does not *describe* and then *analyze* another point of view. Finally, as for (E), even though the author is at times very specific in his claims, you cannot describe the overall form of the selection as giving examples to support a generalization.

15. (D) This is a main idea question. You are looking for the choice that best describes the content of the passage. (D) fits. The passage is primarily a discussion of two new research techniques.

You can eliminate (A) as too narrow. Though the author does mention the reproductive organs of nonhuman primates such as monkeys, that is only one of the two techniques discussed. You can eliminate (C) for the same reason. The in vitro technique using cultured cells is but one half of the passage. Finally, you can eliminate both (B) and (E) because the passage mentions no *diseases* of the pituitary gland nor any new *anesthesia* techniques.

16. (B) This is a specific detail question. The task is to find the right spot in the passage. Although the passage mentions the benefits of the new research techniques at several places, the first sentence neatly summarizes the point.

(A) is incorrect since the passage does not state that this is the *first* time scientists have been able to study the pituitary gland. (C) is incorrect since the passage states only that the new techniques reduce the need for animals, not that they make laboratory animals unnecessary. (D) is incorrect for the same reason as (A). The passage does not state that the new techniques led to the *discovery* of prolactin. Finally, (E) is specifically denied in the second sentence of the third paragraph.

17. (D) This is an implied idea question. It asks about the first technique, so you will need to study the second paragraph. Additionally, the Roman-numeral format gives you an advantage over the test structure.

Statement I is inferable from the passage. The author states that cultured cells do not require serum and that serum may confuse test results. We may infer, therefore, that research using cultured cells produces more reliable results than research using cells requiring serum. At this point, you can safely eliminate choices (B) and (C).

Statement II is not inferable from the passage. Nothing suggests that these cells are implanted in animals. In fact, II represents a confusion. It is the second technique, transplantation, that implants cells. Having eliminated II, you would also eliminate (E).

Our choice has been narrowed to (A) and (D). Our decision, therefore, depends on III. III is inferable. One of the advantages of the culturing technique (mentioned in the last sentence of the second paragraph) is the large yield of these cells. So III must also be part of the correct choice, and the right answer must be (D).

18. (D) This is a specific idea question. Given the thought-reverser (EXCEPT), we are looking for the one thing that is *not* mentioned in the selection. In the third paragraph, you will find (A), (B), (C), and (E) all explicitly stated. The procedure does avoid the problem of repeated major surgery; it does allow frequent monitoring; the cells do behave normally; and the transplants are usually successful. (D), however, represents a confused reading of the selection. The in vitro culturing of cells belongs to the first technique.

19. (A) This is a specific detail question. The technique for answering this kind of question is to find the particular reference you need. In this case, you'll find the discussion in the final paragraph. There the author states that the infection causes lesions that obstruct the oviduct. This is summarized by (A).

(B) and (C) are incorrect because these ideas, though mentioned in the selection, are not responsive to the question. They provide information about how the research proceeds but not about the causes of infertility in women.

(E) is closely related to (B) and (C). In the grafting technique, blood is apparently diverted to the grafts, but this is not responsive to the question.

Finally, (D) is perhaps the second-best answer. It at least has the merit of mentioning the tissue damage. But the passage never mentions the need for surgery to remove damaged tissue. Although you might infer that this could sometimes be a proper medical procedure, such a procedure is not specifically mentioned in the selection. Remember, the answer to a specific detail question will be explicitly given in the selection.

20. (D) This is an inference question. In the second sentence of the third paragraph, the author states that the grafting technique falls "short of the long-sought goal of developing an in vitro model." From this remark we can infer, first, that an in vitro model does not yet exist, thus eliminating choices (A) and (B). Second, we can infer from the phrase "long-sought" that such a model is believed to be scientifically possible and of real value. On this basis we can eliminate both (C) and (E). Thus, (D) is the correct choice. And the remark just cited implies that such a procedure is possible but has not yet been achieved.

21. (A) This is a main idea question. In the first paragraph, the author introduces the idea of an aggregative policy, that is, a policy that is designed to meet the needs of a group of people. In the second paragraph, he explains that such policies are inherently imperfect because no single individual meets the group profile. In the final paragraph, he reaches the conclusion that we should rely less on policies that are necessarily imperfect. Choice (A) summarizes this development.

(B) is incorrect and represents a confused reading of the first paragraph. It is not the fact that the policies are created by a democratic political process that makes them ineffective; rather, it is the fact that they are aimed at a group. An aggregative policy enacted by an absolute monarch would be open to the same indictment.

(C) is incorrect because the author indicts the design, not the implementation, of the programs. (D) is wrong for two reasons. First, the author is not describing just federal programs (though he uses the federal level as an example); he is attacking all aggregative policies. Second, (D) overstates the author's point. The author calls for minimizing such programs—not totally eliminating them. Finally, (E), too, goes beyond the scope of the passage. The author does call for minimizing aggregative policies, but it is not clear that this would mean just reducing their geographic scope. The author might very well favor eliminating a lot of programs altogether.

22. (C) This is a specific detail question. In the first paragraph, the author states that the measure of whether an aggregate policy is a success is essentially political and social. That is, a "good" policy is one that commands public support. Thus, (C) is the best response. (A) is incorrect, for this is part of the definition of an aggregate policy—not the measure of its worth. (B) is incorrect because this would be the measure of the value of a policy from the standpoint of the individual (see the second paragraph). As for (D), though the author does mention that aggregate policies are often changed, he says this is done in a futile attempt to make them work. To the extent that it is possible for a policy to be revised to meet individual circumstances, it is not an aggregative policy. Finally, as for (E), though federal policies are aggregative policies, this is not the measure of the value of such policies.

23. (C) This is a further application question. You must take what you have learned about aggregative policies from the passage and apply that information to these new situations. Remember that the defining characteristic of an aggregative policy is that it is based upon the characteristics of a group. The situations in both I and II fit this description, and the author would probably say of those programs that they are defective in this respect. A menu based on a survey will meet the needs of some summary of the group, but it will not satisfy exactly the desires of any one student. Similarly, requiring eye exams once every ten years won't catch people whose eyes deteriorate more quickly than the norm and is unnecessary for those whose eyes don't change at all. Statement III, however, is not an aggregative situation. The trainer creates policies that are tailored to each individual player.

24. (A) This is an implied idea question. The author discusses two different senses of "good" in this context: the aggregate level and the individual level. We can infer he places the word in quotations to emphasize this ambiguity. (B) overstates the case. As for (C), the author himself makes such a value judgment when he says that aggregative policies are imperfect. As for (D), it is not that the word cannot be applied to groups; it's just that when the word is applied to

groups it has a meaning different from the one it has when applied to individuals. Finally, (E) might be a good choice if the word in question were a technical word such as *aggregate* or *minima,* but it is not.

25. (C) This is an implied idea question. The author never explicitly defines *aggregate,* but you can learn from the passage what it means. Aggregate policies are aimed at a group of people and take into account what the "typical" person in the group would require. Thus, such policies are based on the needs of the "average" person (even though, according to the author, no such person really exists).

26. (B) This is an author's attitude question. The author presents a fairly powerful logical argument to show the weakness in all aggregative policies. So his attitude is one of disapproval. But that disapproval is not unqualified. The author calls for reducing the number and scale of aggregative policies but not for total elimination. Thus, implicit in the argument is the recognition that it may be necessary to have some such programs (the "minima" or "floors"). This attitude is best described by (B).

    (A) can be eliminated because the author regards aggregative policies as inherently weak, not enlightened. (C), however, overstates the case. Although the author believes that such programs do not make the best use of resources, this is attributable not to corruption but to the design of the programs. As for (D), though the author does consider that some such programs are essential, he does not praise the programs. Finally, (E) overstates the point. The author does consider aggregative policies (in the main) to be ill-conceived, but he does not regard them as completely unnecessary.

27. (E) This is an implied idea question. The answer to a question that asks you to weaken (or to strengthen) an argument often focuses on an unstated premise of the argument. In the final paragraph, the author calls for reducing aggregative policies and freeing up those resources for use elsewhere. The author implicitly assumes that it is possible to reallocate those resources without using an aggregative policy. (E) attacks this implicit premise. If it is true that the resources cannot be reallocated, then the author's argument is considerably weakened.

    As for (A), the author implicitly acknowledges that such policies may survive for a long period, during which time they may be subjected to tinkering, but they still don't work. As for (B), the burden of the author's argument is not that government programs are mismanaged but that they are ill-conceived. As for (C), even if the programs can be made more efficient, "efficiency" doesn't come to grips with the logical flaw in the programs. Finally, as for (E), even though it may be true that eligible individuals don't have to accept the benefits of a program, that does not prove that the program is not poorly designed in the first place.

28. (E) This is a specific detail question. In the second paragraph, the author argues that a policy aimed at the "average" person won't apply to any real person. This is summarized by (E).

    As for (A), though this may be a weakness in some programs, it is not mentioned in the selection. As for (B), though this idea is mentioned in the selection, it is not responsive to the question. Even assuming that technical considerations are given greater weight, an aggregative policy will still be wrong for every person to whom it applies. As for (C) and (D), these ideas are not mentioned by the author as a problem, and in any event, neither is a response to the question.

> Directions: Each passage in this group is followed by questions based on its content. After reading a passage, choose the best answer to each question and blacken the corresponding space on the answer sheet. Answer all questions following a passage on the basis of what is <u>stated</u> or <u>implied</u> in that passage.

Man is the only animal that laughs and weeps, for he is the only animal that is struck with the difference between what things are and what they ought to be. We weep at what thwarts or exceeds our expectations in serious matters; we laugh at what only disappoints our expectations in trifles. We shed tears from sympathy with real and necessary distress; we burst into laughter from want of sympathy with that which is unreasonable and unnecessary, the absurdity of which provokes our spleen or mirth, rather than any serious reflections on it.

To explain the nature of laughter and tears is to account for the condition of human life, for it is in a manner compounded of these two! It is a tragedy or a comedy—sad or merry. Tears may be considered as the natural and involuntary resource of the mind overcome by some sudden and violent emotions before it has had time to reconcile its feelings to the change of circumstances. Laughter may be defined to be the same sort of convulsive and involuntary movement, occasioned by mere surprise or contrast before it has time to reconcile its belief to contradictory appearance. If we hold a mask before our face and approach a child with this disguise on, the child will at first, from oddity and incongruity of the appearance, be inclined to laugh; if we go nearer to it, steadily, and without saying a word, the child will be alarmed and be half inclined to cry. If we suddenly take off the mask, the child will recover from its fears and burst out laughing; but if, instead of presenting an old, well-known countenance, we have concealed a satyr's head or some frightful caricature behind the first mask, the suddenness of the change will not in this case be a source of merriment to the child, but will convert its surprise into an agony of consternation and will make the child cry out for help—even though he or she may be convinced that the whole display is a trick at bottom.

The alternation of tears and laughter in this little episode of common life depends almost entirely on the greater or lesser degree of interest attached to the different changes of appearance. The mere suddenness of the transition seems to give liveliness and gaiety of spirits; but the instant the change is not only sudden, but also threatens to create serious consequences, laughter gives way to tears. The serious is the habitual stress which the mind lays upon the expectation of a given order of events following one another with a certain regularity and weight of interest attached to them. When this stress is increased beyond its usual pitch of intensity so as to strain the feelings by the violent opposition of good and bad, it becomes the pathetic or the tragic. The ludicrous or comic is the unexpected unloosening or relaxing of this stress below its usual pitch of intensity, by such an abrupt transposition of the order of our ideas as taking the mind

unawares, throwing it off guard, startling it into a lively sense of pleasure, and leaving no time nor inclination for painful reflections.

The essence of the laughable, then, is the incongruous. The accidental contradiction between our expectations and the event can hardly be said, however, to amount to the ludicrous. The ludicrous is where there is the same contradiction between the object and our expectation, heightened by some deformity or inconvenience. The ridiculous, which is the highest degree of laughter, is that which is contrary not only to custom but to sense and reason as well.

1. According to the passage, tears and laughter have all the following in common EXCEPT

   (A) They are both involuntary reactions.
   (B) They are both the result of violent emotions.
   (C) They both depend on prior expectations.
   (D) They are both natural parts of the human condition.
   (E) They are both reactions to experiences of the world.

2. The author implies that animals lack the ability to

   (A) perceive emotional changes in humans
   (B) feel pain or pleasure
   (C) evoke sorrow or laughter in humans
   (D) respond strongly to external stimuli
   (E) imagine things other than as they are

3. It can be inferred from the passage that the ludicrous is most nearly the opposite of the

   (A) serious   (B) laughable   (C) comic
   (D) tragic   (E) unexpected

4. The author develops the passage primarily by

   (A) disproving a theory
   (B) citing authorities
   (C) presenting counterexamples
   (D) deducing logical conclusions
   (E) defining terms

5. In the second paragraph, the author

(A) mentions an actual laboratory experiment conducted by the author

(B) proposes an experiment that would support his theory

(C) describes a sequence of events already familiar to the reader

(D) argues that no experimental evidence is needed to prove his claims

(E) tries to prove that children are more easily frightened than adults

6. Which of the following titles best describes the content of the selection?

(A) The Psychology of Some Human Emotions

(B) Childhood Fears: The Roots of Human Emotion

(C) The Different Emotions in Man and Animals

(D) The Importance of Incongruity in Creating Fear

(E) The Causes of Childhood Fears

Open government statutes in California have proved both beneficial and harmful. In the energy commission, for example, as in other government commissions, nearly all decisions must be made in public session for which at least seven days' notice must be given. (Two notable exceptions to public participation in commission meetings are meetings that are held to discuss pending litigation and meetings held to discuss staff personnel matters.) The determination of which decisions can be made by the executive director and which are strictly reserved for the commission becomes quite important in this context. If something is a matter for the commission, there must be a public hearing with attendant publicity and preparation of materials for distribution at the meeting. (A formal delegation of authority authorizes the executive director to make purchases of goods and services, including consulting services, costing less than $5,000.)

Furthermore, no more than three of the commission's five commissioners may meet informally with one another or with the executive director or any member of his staff to discuss commission activities. Such behavior would be a violation of open government statutes. Staff briefings must take place commissioner by commissioner or through a commissioner's advisers. More frequently, commissioners or their advisers contact the staff for information, but all such requests must be submitted in writing.

An example of the impact of open government on the operating procedures of a commission is the energy commission's budgetary process. The budget for the commission, unlike that prepared in other state agencies, was prepared in public session by the five commissioners. The session was not simply a "review and comment" session, since the commissioners had not previously discussed the budget. Every item proposed for the budget could be commented on by anyone who attended the hearings. The budget was then forwarded to the governor's office prior to submission to the legislature as part of the executive budget. In a recent case involving development of regulations to ban use of gas pilot lights in new equipment sold in the state, much of the actual development of the regulations was performed by an advisory committee of both environmental and industry representatives in public workshops.

Perhaps open government's effect has been greatest in the promulgation of rules and regulations. Complaints have arisen from the news media and several legislators about the slowness of the energy commission in setting regulations. In fact, the commission may be unable to meet the original legislatively mandated deadlines for several sets of regulations, including standards for newly constructed nonresidential buildings. If, however, a commission attempts to handle fewer matters without input from state agencies and interested groups in open meetings, it will be criticized for circumventing the open government intentions of the legislation. Thus, if present practices continue, the commission will continue to be criticized for moving too slowly; but if it attempts to move more quickly, the commissioners open themselves up to charges of attempting to circumvent the letter and spirit of the open government law.

7. The author is primarily concerned with discussing the

(A) disadvantages of California's open government legislation

(B) effect of an open government statute on California's energy commission

(C) methods by which California energy commissioners obtain information

(D) energy policies adopted by the California Energy Commission under the open government statute

(E) political forces that shape California's energy policies

8. The passage implies the open government statute is intended to accomplish all of the following EXCEPT

(A) To minimize the likelihood of secret political deals

(B) To allow an opportunity for the public to influence government decisions

(C) To ensure that government officials are held accountable for their policies

(D) To guarantee that a government agency can respond quickly to a problem

(E) To publicize governmental functions

9. The passage most strongly supports which of the following conclusions about a decision that is within the authority of the executive director of an agency?

(A) It would be made more quickly than a decision reserved for a commission.
(B) It would be made with the assistance of the agency's commissioners.
(C) It would be a highly publicized event attended by members of the media.
(D) It would deal with a matter of greater importance than those handled by the commission.
(E) It would be made only after the director had notified commissioners and their aides in writing.

10. In the final paragraph, the author discusses

(A) an analogy
(B) a theory
(C) a contradiction
(D) a dilemma
(E) a counterexample

11. The author makes all of the following points about the rules governing the commission EXCEPT

(A) Public sessions can be held only on seven days' notice.
(B) At a public session, anyone wishing to be heard may comment.
(C) Meetings to discuss personnel matters do not require a public hearing.
(D) Requests by a commissioner for information from the staff must be made in writing.
(E) A meeting of commissioners cannot be held without a quorum of three commissioners.

12. It can be inferred from the passage that the executive director is authorized to make certain purchases costing less than $5,000 in order to

(A) avoid the necessity of holding public hearings on routine matters
(B) take the commission's budget outside the scope of public review
(C) allow commissioners to make their own decisions on matters of staffing
(D) protect the executive director from being sued as an individual
(E) prevent public scrutiny of private work records of staff personnel

13. Which of the following statements about a "review and comment" session can be inferred from the selection?

(A) A "review and comment" session is held to provide members of the legislature with an opportunity to ask commissioners to justify their budget requests.
(B) A "review and comment" session is likely to be much lengthier and more detailed than public sessions required by the open government statute.
(C) A "review and comment" session is held to invite those in attendance to remark on decisions that already have been made.
(D) At a "review and comment" session, the public is given an opportunity to ask specific questions of government officials.
(E) "Review and comment" sessions are held once a year to review the budgetary requests of government agencies.

14. The author's primary concern is to

(A) criticize a government agency
(B) analyze the functioning of a government agency
(C) propose changes in government regulations
(D) respond to criticisms
(E) describe a legal problem

The geological story of the Rocky Mountains is a long one, the details of which are lost in the passage of hundreds of millions of years. Some of the story has been put together by scientists from bits of scattered evidence that strongly indicate a certain chain of events, few of which can be proved to everyone's satisfaction. Most of the rocks in the Colorado region are crystalline and ancient. The gneiss and schist were, in part, once sediments formed in the seas—perhaps a billion years ago. These sediments were buried beneath thousands of feet of other sediments, cemented and hardened into layers of sedimentary rock, and later squeezed, crushed, and elevated by slow, ceaselessly working earth forces, which produced mountains. During this period, the sedimentary rocks were changed to harder metamorphic rocks, probably because of deep burial under tremendous pressure and considerable heat. Masses of molten rock welled up into these earlier deposits and hardened under the earth's surface. This later intrusive material is now exposed granite in many parts of the Rocky Mountains.

These ancient mountains were gradually worn away by wind, rain, and other agents of erosion, which must have attacked the surface of the earth as vigorously then as now. With the passage of millions of years, these mountains were gradually worn away until a new sea lapped over the land where mountains had been, and once again sediments were dropped in its bottom. This new invasion of the ocean affected the Colorado region during the many millions of years in which dinosaurs dominated the earth.

In response to little-understood rhythms of the earth's crust, which have lifted mountains ever so slowly at great intervals all over the world, the seas drained away as the crust rose again, and the rising land once more became subject to the ceaseless attack of erosion. This uplift—which began 60 million years ago—originated the system of mountain ranges and basins that today give Colorado its spectacular scenery and much of its climate. This great period of mountain-making is called the Laramide Revolution, from its early recognition in the Laramie Basin region of Wyoming. This uplift continued intermittently for many millions of years, but eventually these rocks too will be stripped away by erosion, though this will require millions of years.

An unusual feature of the present landscape is the peneplain, the rolling, sometimes flattened character of many mountain summits. These peneplains appear to be all that is left of an old land surface that may once have been continuous far eastward over the area occupied today by the Great Plains. Their presence suggests that the range had been worn down by erosion to a fairly flat upland a few million years ago, then renewed uplifting occurred, and streams draining the highland gradually cut canyons two or three thousand feet into the elevated surface. These canyons were filled by glaciers at intervals during the ice age. The glaciers, moving under their own great weight, gradually broadened, deepened, and straightened the twists and turns of the original river-cut valleys, and bit by bit scooped out cirques (or bowls) at the glacier sources. At the lower altitudes the landscape is dotted with moraines.

15. The passage deals primarily with the

(A) scenic beauty of mountains
(B) geological history of mountains
(C) classification of rock types
(D) rhythms of the earth's crust
(E) effects of glaciers

16. According to the passage, all of the following are true of metamorphic rock EXCEPT

(A) It is harder than sedimentary rock.
(B) It is formed from sedimentary rock.
(C) It is extremely old.
(D) It is a preliminary form of granite.
(E) It is created by extreme temperatures and high pressure.

17. As described by the selection, the sequence of events leading to the present landscape was

(A) erosion, uplift, submersion, uplift, erosion, submersion
(B) uplift, submersion, erosion, uplift, submersion, erosion
(C) submersion, erosion, uplift, submersion, erosion, uplift
(D) submersion, uplift, erosion, submersion, erosion, uplift
(E) submersion, uplift, erosion, submersion, uplift, erosion

18. The author regards the explanation he gives as

(A) conclusively proven
(B) complete fiction
(C) highly tentative and unsupported by evidence
(D) speculative but supported by evidence
(E) certain but unprovable

19. The author provides information that defines which of the following terms?

I. Moraine
II. Cirque
III. Peneplain

(A) III only   (B) I and II only   (C) I and III only   (D) II and III only   (E) I, II, and III

20. The author would likely agree with which of the following statements?

I. The present appearance of the landscape is only temporary.
II. The present appearance of the landscape is the product of natural forces.
III. Any changes that will occur in the appearance of the landscape cannot be predicted.

(A) I only   (B) II only   (C) I and II only
(D) I and III only   (E) I, II, and III

21. The author's primary concern is to

(A) advance a new scientific theory
(B) refute a scientific hypothesis
(C) describe the findings of a scientific theory
(D) prove the validity of a scientific theory
(E) argue against an outdated scientific theory

Most thinkers have distinguished three political entities: the individual, society, and state. It is normal to begin with the individual and then to consider society as the embodiment of his nature as a social being. Thus, the individual is considered to be both logically and historically prior to society and society both logically and historically prior to the state. But in James Burnham's vision of the future state, the logical priority of the individual over the state is inverted. Burnham changed his mind on many points of detail between one book and the next, primarily because he thought that what was happening in national and world politics at any given moment was decisive. But his general sense of the form political power would take didn't move far from the version of it he gave in *The Managerial Revolution*. In that book he predicted that the weaknesses of capitalism would eventually prove fatal, but the downfall of capitalism would not be the victory of the proletariat followed by a Marxist paradise. Capitalism would be replaced by autocracy even more extreme than that in Stalin's Russia. Under this autocracy, the instruments of production would be controlled by the state, and the state, in turn, would be controlled by a ruling elite of managers.

Burnham argued that managers would control the instruments of production in their own corporate favor and the economy of state ownership would provide the basis for domination and exploitation by a ruling class of an extremity and absoluteness never before known. The masses would be curbed or constantly diverted so that they would, as we say, go along with the managerial arrangements. In Burnham's future state, history has come to an end because existence has removed itself from historical process and become pure essence, its attributes those of official meaning. Perfection is defined as the state of completeness in accordance with the terms prescribed for it by the state, as a proposition in logic or a theorem in mathematics might be faultless.

In *We*, Yevgeny Zamyatin envisaged a one-world state, but Burnham allowed for three states. Three superstates would divide the world between them and would enter into shifting alliances with one another. In 1941, Burnham thought the three would be the United States, Europe, and Japan. The superpowers would wage war over marginal territory. "Ostensibly," Burnham said, "these wars will be directed from each base for the conquest of the other bases. But it does not seem possible for any one of these to conquer the others; and even two of them in coalition could not win a decisive and lasting victory over the third."

By 1947, several of Burnham's predictions had already proved false, a result of his irrepressible tendency to assume that present conditions would persist unchanged indefinitely; but a more damning indictment of his vision is the hypocrisy concealed behind the attack on power. Burnham was infatuated with the image of totalitarianism; he was fascinated by the power he attacked and he despised the democracy he should have defended. Ultimately, Burnham voiced the secret desire of the English intelligentsia to destroy the old, egalitarian version of Socialism and usher in a new hierarchical society in which the intellectual could at last get his hands on the whip.

22. Which of the following titles best describes the content of the passage?

(A) James Burnham and Yevgeny Zamyatin: A Critical Comparison
(B) The Political and Literary Legacy of James Burnham
(C) The Political Content of the Works of James Burnham
(D) Political and Social Forces that Shaped the Books of James Burnham
(E) *The Managerial Revolution* and *We*: Blueprints for a Future Society

23. The passage supports which of the following conclusions about the writings of Yevgeny Zamyatin?

I. They are in large part derivative of the works of James Burnham.
II. They describe a future society in which the state is all-powerful.
III. The descriptions they contain are based on conditions that existed at the time they were written.

(A) I only   (B) II only   (C) I and II only
(D) II and III only   (E) I, II, and III

24. The author's treatment of James Burnham's writing can best be described as

(A) analytical and condemnatory
(B) insightful and neutral
(C) speculative and jaded
(D) cynical and detached
(E) uncertain and hostile

25. The statement that Burnham inverted the logical priority of the individual over the state means that Burnham believed that

(A) the state came into existence before a society of individuals
(B) history culminated in the existence of an all-powerful government
(C) individuals can reach perfection only as social beings
(D) the existence of individuals can be deduced from the existence of a state
(E) people are seen as aspects of the state and not as individuals

26. The author criticizes Burnham for

(A) extrapolating from existing political and social conditions
(B) failing to show how a totalitarian state could evolve from a democracy
(C) thinking that democracy is a form of government superior to oligarchy
(D) reversing the normal relationship between the individual and society
(E) predicting that the world would evolve into a three-world state rather than a one-world state

27. According to Burnham, in the completely autocratic state, history will have come to an end because

(A) the state will define the social forms that individuals must conform to
(B) the means of production will be controlled by a managerial elite
(C) no one superpower will be able to wage war successfully against any other superpower
(D) individuals will be diverted from a study of past events by the state
(E) only the managerial elite will be permitted access to historical records

28. The author's primary concern is to

(A) present his own vision of the future
(B) prove someone else's predictions were wrong
(C) critique a political theory
(D) criticize a literary style
(E) compare two competing theories

Explanatory Answers

1. **(B)** This is a specific idea question. Somewhere in the passage, the author explicitly mentions four of the five choices. The correct answer is the one never mentioned. (A) is supported by the second paragraph, where the author specifically says that both tears and laughter are involuntary reactions. (C) can be found in the first paragraph, where the author states that laughter and weeping are both reactions to the perceived difference between what things are and what they ought to be. (D) is mentioned in the first sentence of the second paragraph. And (E) is mentioned at several points. Laughter and tears are both reactions to experiences.

   (B), however, is not stated in the passage. In the second paragraph, the author states that *tears* are a reaction to a violent emotion. He continues to explain that laughter is also a reaction, but a reaction to surprise—not violent emotion.

2. **(E)** This is an implied idea question. In the very first sentence of the selection, the author states that man is the only animal who laughs and weeps. Why? He is the only one who understands the difference between what is and what ought to be. Therefore, since animals lack the ability to laugh and weep, we may infer this is so because they do not understand the difference between what is and what ought to be.

   (A) is incorrect since animals might be able to detect human emotions even if they are not able to experience such emotions or to understand them. (B) is incorrect, since feeling pleasure or pain is not the same thing as understanding the difference between what is and what ought to be. (C) is incorrect, since animals may be the cause of laughter or sorrow in humans. Finally, (D) is wrong since the author never implies that animals are not alive at all. They just lack the human ability to react with sorrow or joy.

3. **(D)** This is a very difficult implied idea question. The information we need is in the third paragraph. There the author states that anything that is serious is so because of someone's expectations about it and the importance it has. When something becomes very important, it can become tragic. On the other hand, when something that is serious becomes less so, it becomes ludicrous. So tragedy and ludicrousness are both defined by reference to that which is serious. As for (B) and (C), they are both on the side of the ludicrous, not opposite it. As for (E), the ludicrous depends on something unexpected, so it is not the opposite of that which is unexpected.

4. **(E)** This is a logical structure question that asks about the overall development of the passage. From everything that has been said thus far, you should be able to see that the author develops the theme primarily by defining terms. (A) is wrong because there is no theory the author attacks. (B) is incorrect since no authority is cited in the selection. (C) is incorrect because no counterexamples are offered. Finally, (D) is perhaps the second-best choice since the author does seem to reason logically. But deducing a conclusion is not the same process as defining terms.

7

5. (C) The key to this question is actually the first sentence of the third paragraph. There the author refers to the incident with the child as a "little episode of common life." Thus, the author does not regard this literally as an experiment. (So we eliminate [A] and [B].) Instead, the author presumes that the reader will already be familiar with the typical reactions of a child. (So we eliminate [D] and [E].)

6. (A) This is a main idea question. The main point of the passage is to describe the causes of certain human emotions, and (A) best describes this development. (B) and (E) both make the error of elevating a part of the passage (the discussion of the child's reactions) to the status of main point. (C) makes a similar error. (The distinction between man and animals is merely the author's jumping-off point.) Finally, (D) is too narrow. The author describes not only negative emotions such as fear but positive ones as well.

7. (B) The main point of the passage is introduced in the first two sentences: the open government statutes have good points and bad points, as shown by the example of the energy commission. (A) is wrong for two reasons. One, it fails to mention that the focus of the discussion is the example of the energy commission; and two, it fails to refer to the good points of the law. (C) is too narrow. The interaction between commission and staff is mentioned only by way of illustration. (D) is wrong because the focus is the process—not the final outcome. The author is concerned with *how* the decisions are made, not with their content. Finally, (E) is incorrect since the author analyzes the energy commission in terms of its structure, not political forces.

8. (D) This is an implied idea question that covers virtually the whole passage. The term "open government" provides a clue. The general idea of the law is to ensure that the workings of an agency are open to public scrutiny, so (C) and (E) must surely be purposes of the law.

Beyond that, the second paragraph mentions that the law is so strict it prohibits private meetings between members of the commission. This fact, coupled with the general intent of an "open government" law, implies that it is intended to prevent private deals, so (A) is implied by the selection. And (B) is supported by the third paragraph. A consequence of the law is that the public is given an opportunity to participate in the decision-making process.

(D), however, is not implied by the passage. In fact, according to the last paragraph, the procedures required to implement the law have actually slowed the decision-making process.

9. (A) This is a further application question. You must use what you have learned from the passage about the administrative process. In the first paragraph, the author says decisions can be classified according to whether they can be made by the executive director or must be reserved for the commission. If the matter can be decided only by the commission, it must be done publicly. Later, the author points out that the requirements of publicity and public meetings slow the administrative process. We may conclude, therefore, that the executive director, because he or she is not bound by the open government requirements, can act more swiftly.

(B) and (C) are incorrect since a decision solely within the discretion of the executive director is made without the participation of the commission and the attendant publicity. As for (D), the "big decisions," like the one about the budget, are the ones that must be made publicly. Finally, (E) is a misreading of the passage. The passage mentions that requests for information from commissioners to staff must be in writing.

10. (D) This is a logical detail question. In the final paragraph the author discusses a dilemma. On the one hand, if the commission follows the requirements of the "open government" law, it is able to move only very slowly. On the other hand, if it tries to move quickly, it is criticized for evading the spirit of the law.

11. (E) This is an explicit detail question. In the first paragraph the author says that the public sessions can be held only on seven days' notice, so (A) is incorrect. (B) is wrong because the author specifically states that in a public session on the budget, every item proposed could be commented upon by anyone who attended the hearings. (C) is incorrect because the passage says that meetings held to discuss personnel matters are exceptions to the general rule. Finally, (D) is incorrect because the author clearly states in the second paragraph that all requests for information from the staff must be submitted in writing. (E) is the correct choice because the author does not say that the meeting of commissioners cannot be held without a quorum of three commissioners. He says that an informal meeting of the commissioners can be attended by no more than three commissioners.

12. (A) This is an implied idea question. Since the author makes the statement that the executive director may make certain purchases of up to $5,000 right after he explains that if something is a matter for the commission it requires a public hearing, the point of this authorization is obviously to avoid the need for public hearings on business matters that are small or routine. (B) cannot be correct since it is clear from the passage that the commission's budget would not be taken outside the scope of public review. (C) is not responsive to the question. An individual commissioner might or might not make such decisions, but this is not the reason that the executive director has the authorization to incur costs of less than $5,000 without a public hearing. (D) is incorrect because the passage states that the money is for goods and services, which would have nothing to do with the executive director's personal liability in a lawsuit. Finally, (E) is incorrect because, again, the money is to purchase goods and services and would have nothing to do with public scrutiny of private work records.

13. (C) This is an inference question. The author states that the budget session was not a "comment and review" session because the commissioners had never discussed the budget before and anyone attending the hearings could comment on the budget. We may infer, then, that the author is describing the opposite of a review and comment session, which is logically one about an issue that the commissioners have already discussed and decided. So (C) is the correct choice. (A) is incorrect because there is no mention in the passage of a session in which members of the legislature have an opportunity to ask commissioners to justify their budget requests. As for (B), the passage implies that a "review and comment" session would be less detailed than a public session. (D) is incorrect because according to the passage, those in attendance at a public session are permitted to ask questions. Finally, (E) is incorrect because there is no mention in the passage of budget requests of other government agencies.

14. (B) This is a main idea question and it is related to the previous question. (A) is not correct since, as we said in the previous explanation, the author is more or less neutral—he is not critical. (B) is the best answer. The author analyzes the workings of the agency. He does not propose changes, so (C) is incorrect.

Although some may criticize the open government statute, the author is not responding to these critics. He is not defending the policy; he is merely describing it. Finally, (E) is wrong because although legal issues are part of the content of the passage, describing a legal problem is not the main thrust of the passage.

15. (B) This is a main idea question. You can eliminate (A) since the passage discusses geology, not scenery. (C) is too narrow. Though the author does mention different types of rocks, the distinctions are drawn in the service of a larger point, the history of the mountains. (D) and (E) can be eliminated for the same reason. Although they are ideas mentioned in the selection, they do not constitute the main point of the selection.

16. (D) This is a specific detail question. Everything you need to know about rocks is in the first paragraph. There the author states that metamorphic rock is ancient (C); that it is created from sedimentary rock (B); that it is harder than sedimentary rock (A); and that it is created by high temperatures and pressures (E). (D), however, is a misreading of that paragraph. Granite is "later intrusive material" and not a part of the evolution of metamorphic rock.

17. (E) This is a specific idea question. According to the second paragraph, the process begins under water, so you eliminate (A) and (B). The next stage is elevation or uplift, so you eliminate (C). Then, according to the third paragraph, there is the process of erosion and another submersion, and then another elevation and erosion. (E) correctly describes the process.

18. (D) This is an application question. In essence, the question is asking with which of the judgments the author would agree. In the first paragraph, the author states that the story is a long one, the details of which are not clear, but that there is scattered evidence that strongly suggests a theory. So both (A) and (B) overstate the point—in opposite directions. Scattered evidence and a good theory are not conclusive proof of anything, but neither are they total fiction. And you can eliminate (C) and (E) for the same reasons.

19. (D) This is a specific detail question. The author states that peneplains are rolling or flattened mountain summits. In the last paragraph the author tells us that cirques are bowls. In the last sentence the author says that at lower altitudes the landscape is dotted with moraines, but there is no further explanation of what a moraine is.

20. (C) The author would probably agree with the first statement because one of the main ideas of the passage is that the landscape changed several times over the last millions of years. And he would also agree with II, since the forces he describes are natural ones (he never states that the landscape has been altered by the activities of man). He would not, however, agree with III, since at the end of the fourth paragraph he makes a prediction about the change of the appearance of the landscape. He says that the rocks of Colorado will eventually be stripped away by erosion, although that process will require millions of years.

21. (C) In the first paragraph the author says that the story of the Rocky Mountains has been put together by scientists from bits of scattered evidence that strongly indicate a certain chain of events. He then goes on to explain the theory, or rather to describe this sequence of events, so the answer is (C). He is not advancing a "new" theory, so (A) cannot be correct. He is not "refuting" anything, so (B) is wrong. He is not "proving" the theory—in fact, he says that the

theory hasn't been totally proved to anyone's satisfaction. He is not arguing against anything, so (E) is incorrect.

22. (C) This is a main idea question. As for (A), the author compares Burnham and Zamyatin, but only in passing. As for (B), the passage deals with Burnham's theories and the political events that shaped them—not with the legacy of his writings. (D) is wrong because although the author mentions the fact that political and social forces shaped Burnham's writings, he does not discuss those forces in any detail. Finally, (E) is incorrect because Burnham's book is a prediction about the future of society—not a blueprint or plan for it.

23. (B) This is an implied idea question. As for statement I, given that the author mentions *We* only in passing and then only to show in what way it differed from *The Managerial Revolution*, we can infer that *We* was in many respects similar to *The Managerial Revolution*. As for (A), the passage does not state which of the two works came first, and there is nothing to suggest that Zamyatin's work was based on Burnham's. By the same reasoning, we can conclude that II is a correct statement. III is incorrect because these works predicted an outcome of world history, and although the ideas about the outcome of history were based on current political and social conditions, the books do not describe these conditions; rather, they describe the future conditions.

24. (A) This is a tone question. The passage is mostly expository. It describes the theories of Burnham. The author does, however, criticize Burnham for being hypocritical and for making predictions based on existing conditions. (B) is incorrect because although the author is insightful, he is not neutral. (C) is incorrect because the author is not speculative; he is instead analytical. Burnham speculates and Burnham is perhaps jaded, but the author of the passage is not. Nor is he cynical, so (D) is incorrect. Finally, as for (E), the author is confident, not uncertain.

25. (E) This is an implied idea question. The author states that most thinkers identify three political entities, beginning with the individual, and consider society an embodiment of the individual and the state a logical outgrowth of the individual and the society. Burnham inverts that sequence and theorizes that the state is the logical beginning and individuals just parts of the state.

26. (A) The author states that Burnham had an irrepressible tendency to project existing conditions into the indefinite future and that this is why many of Burnham's predictions proved wrong. As for (B), though the author believes that Burnham was wrong in his predictions, this is not a criticism he aims at Burnham. As for (C), the author specifically states that Burnham failed to defend democracy —not that Burnham preferred democracy. As for (D), though Burnham inverts the traditional relationship between the individual and state in his writings, the author does not criticize him on this score. The author apparently accepts the validity of making the alternative assumption for purposes of argument. Finally, as for (E), although the author mentions that Burnham made such a prediction, the author does not make this the basis of a criticism.

27. (A) This is a difficult specific detail question. The question is difficult because it asks about a fairly abstruse idea. It is not entirely clear what the author of the selection intends to say on this point. Nonetheless, it is possible to answer this question if you keep in mind a couple of points made in the Reading Comprehension lesson. Remember that wrong answers to specific detail questions are sometimes wrong because they mention ideas found in the selection but not at

the correct location. This is the case with (B) and (C). These choices mention ideas found in the selection, but not where the author talks about the end of history. Then, the ideas mentioned by (D) and (E) are not specifically stated in the selection, so they cannot be correct answers to a specific detail question. Apparently, what the author means is that history will end because there will no longer be any change. Instead, the state will prescribe certain forms to which individuals must conform.

28. (C) (A) is incorrect because the author does not present his own vision. (B) is incorrect because although he mentions the fact that Burnham's predictions were false, this observation is only a part of his criticism of Burnham's views. (D) cannot be correct because the author never mentions Burnham's literary style. Finally, (E) is wrong because although he mentions Zamyatin's theory briefly, the author certainly doesn't compare the two theories. (C) is the correct choice. The author describes Burnham's theories and then criticizes them.

Analytical Reasoning: Part I

Analytical Reasoning: Part I

1. The Anatomy of a Group of Analytical Reasoning Items
2. Three Important Principles of Analytical Reasoning
3. Record-Keeping
4. Ordering Problems
5. Reading the Verbal Clues Carefully
6. The Science of Deduction: Understanding Problems

The Analytical Reasoning section of your LSAT will contain 22 to 24 analytical reasoning items (give or take a question). Analytical reasoning items are logical puzzles. The 22 or so items are presented in four or five groups of varying numbers of questions.

1. The Anatomy of a Group of

Analytical Reasoning Items

Analytical reasoning items come in groups. Each question in a group is based upon a set of initial conditions that describe a common situation, e.g., people to be placed into groups, objects to be arranged in order, houses to be painted one of several colors, and so on. The questions then ask that you draw further conclusions from the initial set of conditions, e.g., in which group must Jones be placed, where can object *X* be put, what color can the first house be painted, and so on.

EXAMPLES:

A group of six people—David, Ellen, Fred, Luke, Mike, and Sam—ran a series of races.
Sam finished last in every race.
Ellen finished before David in every race.
Mike finished before Fred in every race.
Luke finished somewhere between David and Fred in every race.

The questions ask that you deduce further conclusions from the initial conditions, for example, who could finish first, who could not finish fifth, who must finish third, and so on.

Which of the following is a possible order, from first to last?
(A) Fred, Mike, Luke, Ellen, David, Sam
(B) Mike, David, Luke, Fred, Ellen, Sam
(C) Mike, Ellen, David, Luke, Fred, Sam
(D) Mike, Fred, Luke, David, Ellen, Sam
(E) Mike, Luke, Fred, Ellen, David, Sam

The answer is (C). Choice (C) correctly describes a *possible* order of finish. (A) is not a possible order of finish since the initial conditions state that Mike finished before Fred in every race. Neither (B) nor (D) is a possible order of finish since the initial conditions state that Ellen finished before David in every race. Finally, (E) is not a possible order of finish since the initial conditions state that Luke finished somewhere between David and Fred in every race.

Which of the following CANNOT be the order of finish of a race, from first to last?

(A) Ellen, David, Luke, Mike, Fred, Sam

(B) Ellen, Mike, Fred, Luke, David, Sam

(C) Mike, Ellen, Fred, Luke, David, Sam

(D) Mike, Ellen, Luke, Fred, David, Sam

(E) Mike, Fred, Luke, Ellen, David, Sam

The answer is (D). The initial conditions state that Luke finished between Fred and David in every race, so (D) does not describe a possible order of finish. Each of the other choices does describe a possible order of finish.

Sometimes a question stem will supplement the information provided in the initial conditions by asking you to make an additional assumption.

EXAMPLE:

If Mike finished second in a race, then which of the following must be true of that race?

(A) David finished first.

(B) Fred finished first.

(C) David finished third.

(D) Luke finished fourth.

(E) Fred finished fifth.

The answer is (D). This question supplements the initial conditions by asking you to assume that Mike finished second. Using that assumption, try to deduce some further conclusions about the order of finish. Assuming that Mike finished second, and given that Sam finished last, Fred (who finished behind Mike in every race) finished third, fourth, or fifth. Next, since Luke finished between Fred and David, Luke must have finished either third or fourth (otherwise, he could not be between Fred and David). But since Ellen finished ahead of David, David could have finished no earlier than third. Thus, Fred, Luke, and David finished third, fourth, and fifth —though not necessarily in that order—and Ellen finished first. As for Fred, David, and Luke, Luke must have finished fourth (as choice [D] correctly notes), though the positions of Fred and David are not deducible.

2. Three Important Facts about

Analytical Reasoning

A. Many test-takers say that Analytical Reasoning is the most difficult section on the LSAT. They report that they are able to answer proportionately fewer questions in this section than in the other two sections. You may also find this to be true. You might, for example, be able to answer correctly 24 of the 28 questions in Reading Comprehension but only 15 or 16 of the 24 questions in Analytical Reasoning.

This does not necessarily mean, however, that you are not doing as well as you should in Analytical Reasoning. Remember that many other test-takers have the same reaction.

B. Since the correct answer to every analytical reasoning question is based on a logical inference from the initial conditions or the initial conditions plus some additional stipulation, a question has one of two "modalities." Either a question asks about a *necessary* relationship or it asks about a *possible* relationship. Given that a question stem might include a thought-reverser, this means that there are essentially only four different types of analytical reasoning questions:

> Which of the following can be true?
> All of the following can be true EXCEPT
> Which of the following must be true?
> All of the following must be true EXCEPT

The answer to the first type of question will be a statement that is logically possible but not logically necessary, and the wrong answers will be statements that are logically impossible.

The answer to the second type of question will be a statement that is logically impossible, and the wrong answers will be statements that are logically possible (or even necessary).

The answer to the third type of question will be a statement that is logically necessary, and the wrong answers will be statements that are merely logically possible or even logically impossible.

Finally, the answer to the fourth type of question will be a statement that is only logically possible or even logically impossible, and the incorrect answers will be statements that are logically necessary.

In this lesson and the next you will learn attack strategies for each of the two modalities.

C. As noted above, some items provide additional information to supplement the information given in the initial conditions, and any additional information or stipulation is to be used *for that question only*. Although the initial conditions govern every item in a group, additional information is used only for one question.

In fact, it may be possible that question stems will supply contradictory information. You might find, for example:

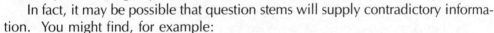

> If Ellen finishes first and Mike finishes second, then which of the following must be true?
>
> (A) ....
> (B) ....
> (C) ....
> (D) ....
> (E) ....
>
> If Mike finishes first and Ellen finishes second, then which of the following must be true?
>
> (A) ....
> (B) ....
> (C) ....
> (D) ....
> (E) ....

8

Below we will discuss various diagramming techniques for analytical reasoning groups. For now, let me just note that when you use these techniques, make sure that you don't "contaminate" a diagram for one question with information intended for another question.

3. Record-Keeping

In several of his adventures, Holmes relies on newspaper clippings and other records of events that many people might have considered trivial. But to Holmes they were an essential part of his work. Watson tells us, however, that Holmes was not the tidiest of people. Still, Holmes evidently had a record-keeping system that worked for him. So, too, you will need a record-keeping system that works for you.

You will need to make notes that summarize information for easy reference. There is no single, uniquely correct system for referencing information, but here is a system of symbols that you might find useful. In this system, I use capital letters, usually the first letter of an individual's name, to designate a concept. For example, *K* would stand for "Karen must go to the concert" and *L* for "Larry must go to the concert."

One of the most common connectives used is what logicians call conjunction, or what is ordinarily referred to simply as *and*. For *and*, you might use the plus sign, "+," or the ampersand, "&." Thus, the condition "Karen and Larry must both go to the concert" would be rendered in this system as:

$K + L$

Another common connective is called by logicians disjunction. Disjunction is simply another name for *or*. Given that *or* is a very short word, you might choose simply to write "or." Or you can use the symbol *v*, which is used by logicians. Thus, the condition "Either Karen or Larry must go to the concert" would be rendered as:

$K \lor L$

A third important connective is negation, or *not*, for which we will use the symbol ~. This symbol is called a *tilde* or sometimes just a "squiggle." To indicate negation, you simply place the tilde in front of a capital letter. Thus, the condition "Karen cannot go to the concert" would be rendered as:

$\sim K$

A fourth common logical connective is the *if, then* connection, which we will symbolize with a *horseshoe*: ⊃. The condition "If Karen goes to the concert, then Larry will go to the concert" is rendered as:

$K \supset L$

Not all conditions are as simple as these; for example: If Karen or Larry goes to the concert, then Michelle goes to the concert. We already have the symbols we need to summarize these conditions, but we have to be careful how we use them. The formulation "$K \vee L \supset M$" is ambiguous. It might be read to mean "If Karen or Larry goes to the concert, then Michelle goes to the concert," but it might be misread to mean "Either Karen goes to the concert, or if Larry goes to the concert, then Michelle goes to the concert."

How do we avoid such ambiguity? By using punctuation marks, just as we would in an English sentence. In our symbol system we use parentheses and brackets for punctuation. Thus, "$(K \vee L) \supset M$" means "If either Karen or Larry goes to the concert, then Michelle goes to the concert," but "$K \vee (L \supset M)$" means "Either Karen goes to the concert or if Larry goes to the concert, then Michelle goes to the concert."

Parentheses also make it clear to what part of a symbolic sentence the $\sim$ applies. The sentence "If neither Karen nor Larry goes to the concert, then Michelle goes to the concert" is symbolized as:

$$\sim(K + L) \supset M$$

("Neither Karen nor Larry" is equivalent to "Both not-Karen and not-Larry.")

Here is a more complex example. The sentence "If neither Karen nor Larry goes to the concert, then both Michelle and Nelson go to the concert" is symbolized as:

$$\sim(K + L) \supset (M + N)$$

There are some other symbols, taken from mathematics, for which you can find a variety of uses. The "$=$" can be used in many ways:

Karen and Larry must go to the concert together. $K = L$
Karen is the same age as Larry. $K = L$
Karen is sitting next to Larry. $K = L$
Karen is in the same grade as Larry. $K = L$

The "$=$" with a slash through it, which means "not equal," has the following uses:

Karen and Larry cannot go to the concert together. $K \neq L$
Karen is not the same age as Larry. $K \neq L$
Karen is not sitting next to Larry. $K \neq L$
Karen is not in the same grade as Larry. $K \neq L$

And you can use the symbols $>$, $<$, $\geq$, and $\leq$ in the same way:

Karen is older than Larry. $K > L$
Karen is in a higher grade than Larry. $K > L$
Karen weighs less than Larry. $K < L$
Karen takes her vacation before Larry takes his. $K < L$
Karen is not younger than Larry. $K \geq L$
(Because Karen is older than Larry or the same age.)
Karen is not in a higher grade than Larry. $K \leq L$
(Because Karen is either in the same grade as, or in a lower grade than, Larry.)

4. Ordering Problems

Certain types of analytical reasoning problems reappear frequently on the exam, so familiarity with these types is an essential part of your preparation. As we study each type, I will point out some of its special features and offer suggestions for attacking certain questions.

Over the past few years, one of the most commonly used analytical reasoning situations is what I call ordering problems. The following situations fit into this category:

A number of people stand in a single-file line.
A number of races are run with different orders of finish.
A number of houses stand side-by-side on a certain street.
A number of courses are to be scheduled for different periods during a school day.
A number of speakers are to be scheduled to give speeches, one after the other.

The conditions that determine the possible orders in such situations are statements such as:

John is not first in line.
Bill never finishes worse than third in a race.
The blue house is not next to the red house.
English must be scheduled immediately after history.
The speeches by Jones and Kelly cannot be separated by more than two speeches.

It is typical of ordering sets that the initial conditions do not establish any unique order, but they do serve to limit the number of possibilities. Let's examine some conditions to see how they work to structure the problem set. For the purpose of this analysis, assume first that there is but one initial condition:

Six people—David, Ellen, Fred, Luke, Mike, and Sam—ran a series of races. There were no ties.

There is a finite number of possible orders in which the group could have finished, and you could work out every possibility. The process would be a tedious one:

David, Ellen, Fred, Luke, Mike, Sam
David, Fred, Ellen, Luke, Mike, Sam
David, Fred, Luke, Ellen, Mike, Sam
David, Fred, Luke, Mike, Ellen, Sam
David, Fred, Luke, Mike, Sam, Ellen
Ellen, David, Fred, Luke, Mike, Sam
Ellen, Fred, David, Luke, Mike, Sam
Ellen, Fred, Luke, David . . .

And so on. By the time you finished, you would have described several hundred possibilities.

To be more precise, unless otherwise restricted, the six individuals could finish in 720 different ways, a conclusion I reached by a simple calculation. Each of the six different individuals could have finished first in a particular race. And for each possible first-place finisher there would be five possible second-place finishers. And for each of those possible second-place finishers there would be four third-place finishers, and so on. For example, if David finished first, then it is possible that Ellen, or Fred, or Luke, or Mike, or Sam finished second. And if David finished first and Sam second, then it is possible that Ellen, or Fred, or Luke, or Mike finished third, and so on. This reasoning can be represented with a diagram:

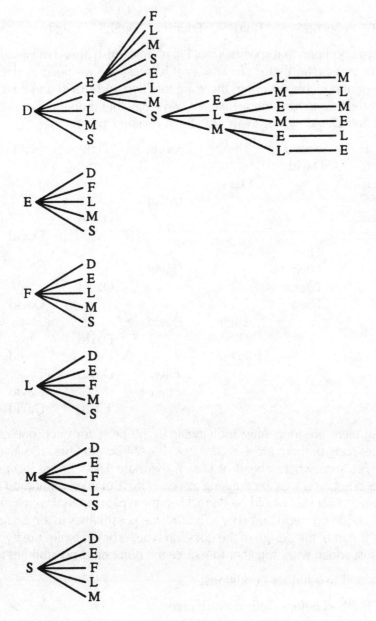

8

The diagram is not complete, but it gives you the idea of how the possibilities are ramified. To find the total number of possibilities, all we need to do is multiply:

$$6 \times 5 \times 4 \times 3 \times 2 \times 1$$

First   Second   Third   Fourth   Fifth   Sixth

You might recognize this as the formula for calculating permutations, but it's not critical that you understand fully why the arithmetic works. You can accept it as an article of faith that it does work.

Specific conditions serve to limit the number of possibilities. Take, for example, a condition that Sam finished last in each race. Given that requirement, the number of different orders of finish is only 120:

$$5 \times 4 \times 3 \times 2 \times 1 \times Sam$$

First   Second   Third   Fourth   Fifth   Sixth

Or, taking a condition that specifies that Ellen must finish ahead of David, how many possible orderings are there? To answer this question, we need to determine how many different possible orderings there are for Ellen and David and then, for each of those possibilities, in how many different ways the other individuals can be arranged. For Ellen and David alone, there are fifteen different possibilities:

First	Second	Third	Fourth	Fifth	Sixth
Ellen	David				
Ellen		David			
Ellen			David		
Ellen				David	
Ellen					David
	Ellen	David			
	Ellen		David		
	Ellen			David	
	Ellen				David
		Ellen	David		
		Ellen		David	
		Ellen			David
			Ellen	David	
			Ellen		David
				Ellen	David

Given that there are four other individuals in the race, for each one of the fifteen possibilities shown, there are $4 \times 3 \times 2 \times 1 = 24$ possibilities. So given only that Ellen finishes somewhere ahead of David, there are $15 \times 24 = 360$ possibilities.

At this point, you may be thinking to yourself, "But even a hundred possibilities is too many." And you would be correct. In the typical analytical reasoning group, the initial conditions work together to reduce the possibilities to a manageable number. This is part of the design of the question type. For example, the two conditions we have just added work together to reduce the number of possibilities to only 60.

Let us add two further conditions:

Mike finished before Fred in every race.
Luke finished somewhere between David and Fred in every race.

Now there are exactly eight distinct possibilities:

First	Second	Third	Fourth	Fifth	Sixth
Ellen	David	Mike	Luke	Fred	Sam
Ellen	David	Luke	Mike	Fred	Sam
Ellen	Mike	David	Luke	Fred	Sam
Ellen	Mike	Fred	Luke	David	Sam
Mike	Ellen	David	Luke	Fred	Sam
Mike	Ellen	Fred	Luke	David	Sam
Mike	Fred	Ellen	Luke	David	Sam
Mike	Fred	Luke	Ellen	David	Sam

I do not mean to suggest, however, that the best attack strategy is to work out all of the possibilities. In fact, "grinding" is probably the worst strategy to use. You don't know at the outset whether the initial conditions will generate eight, eighteen, or eighty possibilities; and, in any event, only a few of the possibilities will be the answers to questions. Later in this lesson, when we discuss each of the common types of problems, we will develop appropriate attack strategies. Some of these strategies will be based on a distinction uncovered by our mathematical analysis of the possibilities above: the "limiting power" of a condition. We demonstrated that the second condition reduces the number of possibilities from 720 to 360, but the first condition reduces the number of possibilities from 720 to 120. Thus, the first condition has more "limiting power" than the second. Later you will learn to recognize which conditions have the greatest limiting power and how to use that information to attack questions.

Given that the initial conditions "underdetermine" the arrangement of individuals, many students have the following concern: how can I tell whether or not I have learned all there is to learn from the initial conditions or from the initial conditions plus an additional stipulation? At least a partial answer to this question is "Use the test itself." This is a multiple-choice test, so one—and only one—of the choices is correct. If you work a problem and find only one seemingly correct choice, then you have probably done as much as you can do. There is, of course, no guarantee that you haven't made a mistake, but it does seem *likely* that you have done all that you can do.

On the other hand, if you work an item and find more than one seemingly correct answer or no possibly correct solution at all, this is a clue that you have missed something.

Here is a problem set to illustrate this strategy:

Questions 1–2

Seven people—*J, K, L, M, N, O,* and *P*—are standing in a single-file line, facing an information booth.

N is somewhere ahead of *O*.

There is exactly one person standing between *L* and *P*.

M is immediately behind *J*.

O is behind both *K* and *M*.

1. If *M* and *L* are fourth and fifth in line, respectively, which of the following must be true?

   (A) *K* is first.

   (B) *N* is first.

   (C) *O* is sixth.

   (D) *O* is seventh.

   (E) *P* is sixth.

2. If *J* is standing immediately behind *P*, then which of the following must be true?

   (A) *J* is fifth.

   (B) *L* is first.

   (C) *L* is second.

   (D) *M* is sixth.

   (E) *O* is seventh.

1. **(C)** Start by drawing further conclusions from the additional information coupled with the initial conditions. Since *M* is fourth, *J* must be third. Then, since *L* and *P* are separated by exactly one person, *P* must be seventh (because *J* is third). Now, let us suppose for the purpose of discussion that you did not see any further conclusions that could be drawn. What should you do? Go to the choices.

   Using the information we have deduced (that *P* is seventh), try to find a correct choice. The best that you can do is eliminate (D) and (E), which leaves you with more than one seemingly correct response. This indicates that you have not yet done enough work. You have overlooked something, so return to the initial conditions and the additional stipulation.

   According to the initial conditions, *O* is behind *K* and *M*, which means that *O* must be sixth. Is this enough to get a correct answer? Yes, and the correct choice is (C). What about the other two choices, (A) and (B)? The information you have doesn't dictate a specific position for either *K* or *N*; they might be first and second, respectively, or second and first. But you don't need to reach any conclusion about *K* and *N*. Once you have found a choice responding to the question, you know you have done all the work required.

2. **(E)** Here it is stipulated that *P* is immediately ahead of *J*, which means that *P*, *J*, and *M* are standing in just that order. Since only one person is standing between *L* and *P*, *L* must be ahead of *P* (the second person in front of *P*). Finally, we know that the other two individuals, *K* and *N*, must also be somewhere ahead of *O*. Although there are several possible orders, we do have enough information to answer the question: *J*, *K*, *L*, *M*, *N*, and *P* are all standing in front of *O*. So *O* must be seventh, which is choice (E). Since we are able to find a response to the question, we know we have done all that is expected.

5. Reading the Verbal Clues Carefully

The set of initial conditions supplies you with the clues you need to solve the logical puzzle, but you must interpret those clues correctly. There is, for example, a great difference between the following statements:

> John is standing somewhere behind Sally.
> John is standing immediately behind Sally.

A mistake in reading the initial conditions can affect your solution of every item in the group. In ordering problems, the following verbal clues are very important:

always, never
except, but, not
must be, cannot be
more, less, most, least, same, different
higher, lower, highest, lowest, equal, same, different
before, after, earlier, later, together
younger, older, youngest, oldest, same age
to the left of, to the right of, next to

As you read the verbal clues, make sure that you don't give the clue more limiting power than is intended. Suppose, for example, that a set involves six people seated in a row of six theater seats. You might be given one of the following clues:

> John is seated somewhere to Bill's left.
> John and Bill are sitting in adjacent seats.
> John is seated immediately to Bill's left.

The third condition has the greatest limiting power, for it reduces to five the possible arrangements of John and Bill:

1	2	3	4	5	6
J	B				
	J	B			
		J	B		
			J	B	
				J	B

The second condition has less limiting power than the third, for it allows ten different arrangements: the five just shown plus their mirror images (with Bill to John's left). The first condition is the weakest of the three, for it allows fifteen different arrangements:

1	2	3	4	5	6
J	B				
J		B			
J			B		
J				B	
J					B
	J	B			
	J		B		
	J			B	
	J				B
		J	B		
		J		B	
		J			B
			J	B	
			J		B
				J	B

You should also pay careful attention to negative assertions. For example:

John is not older than Harry.

The statement means *either* that John is younger than Harry *or* that John and Harry are the same age.

Careful Reading of Ordering Clues (Answers, page 145)

Directions: Each group in this exercise consists of an underlined statement followed by a series of numbered statements. Read the underlined statement and then indicate:

T if the numbered statement is necessarily true

F if the numbered statement is necessarily false

? if the numbered statement is possibly though not necessarily true

Questions 1–5

Norman is standing immediately ahead of Fred in the line and somewhere in front of Ed and Sally.

1. Ed is standing somewhere behind Sally.

2. Sally is standing immediately ahead of Norman.

3. Fred is standing immediately behind Norman.

4. Ed is standing somewhere behind Norman.

5. Sally is standing somewhere behind Fred.

Questions 6–10

On a certain musical scale, note _J_ is higher than note _M_, and note _K_ is immediately below note _L_.

6. _K_ is higher than _M_.

7. _M_ is lower than _J_.

8. _L_ is immediately above _K_.

9. _J_ is immediately above _M_.

10. _J_ is not immediately above _K_.

Questions 11–15

Of a group of four people, _W_ was born sometime before _X_ and sometime after _Y_, and _Z_ was born before _W_.

11. _W_ is younger than _Y_.

12. _Y_ is older than _X_.

13. _Z_ is the oldest.

14. _Y_ is the youngest.

15. _Y_ and _Z_ are the same number of years old.

Questions 16–20

Robert is taller than Fred but shorter than George, and William is not taller than George.

16. George is taller than Fred.

17. George is taller than William.

18. George is shorter than William.

19. Robert is the same height as William.

20. William is taller than Fred but shorter than Robert.

Questions 21–25

Mary will sing each of five songs, *J*, *K*, *L*, *M*, and *N*, exactly once during a performance; she must sing *K* sometime before *L* and *M* immediately after *J*, and she cannot sing *N* first.

21. Mary sings *L* first.

22. Mary sings *N* last.

23. Mary sings *N* sometime before *L*.

24. Mary sings *K* immediately before *M*.

25. Mary sings *L* immediately after *K*.

6. The Science of Deduction

(and Ordering Problems)

Holmes was famous for his chains of inferential reasoning. In one case, he astounds Watson by pronouncing that their client is a typist. He explains that the young woman has spatulate fingertips, and that spatulate fingertips derive from one of two activities, typing or playing the piano. Since the woman lacked the sensitive mien of a musician, she must, Holmes concluded, be a typist. This type of reasoning is often called the process of elimination.

The process of elimination is the key to solving any analytical reasoning problem. You must use the information you are given to limit the number of possibilities to just a few, or even one, depending on what the question stem requires. To illustrate how the process of elimination is to be used, we will need a set of initial conditions on which to base some questions:

> Six books by six different authors—*J*, *K*, *L*, *M*, *N*, and *O*—are to be placed on a bookcase with six shelves. The shelves are numbered from 1, the highest, to 6, the lowest, and exactly one book will be placed on each shelf.
> The book by *K* must be on the second shelf below the book by *J*.
> The book by *O* must be placed on either the first shelf or the sixth shelf.
> The book by *L* cannot be placed either on the shelf immediately above or the shelf immediately below the book by *M*.

We will summarize these conditions for easy reference:

> $K = J + 2$
> $O = \text{1st v 6th}$
> *L/M*

The questions associated with a linear ordering set fall into two general categories: those that supply no additional information and those that do. We will study each in turn.

A question that supplies no additional information is answerable just on the basis of the information given in the initial conditions. Sometimes you will be given five different orderings and asked to identify the one that meets all of the initial conditions.

EXAMPLE:

Which of the following is a possible order for the books from the top shelf to the bottom?

(A) J, N, K, M, L, O

(B) J, N, K, L, M, O

(C) J, M, K, L, N, O

(D) O, J, K, M, N, L

(E) N, J, M, K, O, L

The answer is (C). The best strategy for a question such as this is to use the initial conditions to eliminate choices. Using the first condition, you can eliminate (D). (The other choices respect the first condition.) Using the second condition, eliminate (E). Using the third condition, eliminate (A) and (B). The only choice that remains is (C), and by the process of elimination (C) must be correct.

A similar question could be asked using a thought-reverser.

EXAMPLE:

All of the following are possible arrangements of the books, from the top shelf to the bottom shelf, EXCEPT

(A) J, L, K, N, M, O

(B) L, J, M, N, K, O

(C) L, N, J, M, K, O

(D) M, J, N, K, L, O

(E) O, M, J, L, K, N

Here, four of the five choices are consistent with all of the initial conditions. One choice—the correct choice—violates one or more of the initial conditions. Using each condition, examine choices until you find the one that violates a condition: (B) violates the requirement that K be on the second shelf below J.

The attack strategy for the two questions just explained is purely mechanical. By that I mean that the strategy requires no logical reasoning; you just work your way down the choices until you find one that, depending on what the stem requires, is either consistent with all of the conditions or violates one of the conditions. Since this type of question is relatively easy, it often appears as the first question or the first two questions in a set.

Other questions that provide no additional information do require some logical thinking.

EXAMPLE:

Which of the following CANNOT be true?

(A) The book by J is on the second shelf.

(B) The book by J is on the third shelf.

(C) The book by M is on the third shelf.

(D) The book by L is on the fifth shelf.

(E) The book by J is on the fifth shelf.

Since the choices here do not provide complete orders, you cannot employ the purely mechanical process we used above. What would constitute a logical proof that four of the choices are possible and that one is not? You use an indirect proof.

Assume that the partial order is possible. Then, using the partial order, work out a complete order. Test that complete order against the initial conditions. If the complete order using the partial order meets all of the initial conditions, then the complete order, and the partial order contained within it, is a possible order. If the final order contradicts one or more of the initial conditions, then the final order, and with it the partial order, is not acceptable.

This strategy of creating complete orders that incorporate partial orders can be time-consuming, but sometimes it is the only way of solving the problem. So before you begin to work out complete orders for each choice (or for each choice until you find the one that generates a contradiction), you should first look for an obvious contradiction between one of the choices and the initial conditions.

Look at choice (A). The only initial condition that controls the placement of *J* is the first one, and it does seem possible for *J* to be on the second shelf:

1	2	3	4	5	6
	J		*K*		

This does not violate the condition controlling the placement of *J*. Is there a completely worked-out order with *J* on the second shelf and *K* on the fourth that is consistent with all of the initial conditions? That is a question we should not address until we have first looked at the other choices for an obvious inconsistency. So we give a similar treatment to (B):

1	2	3	4	5	6
		J		*K*	

This placement does not violate the condition controlling the placement of *J* and *K*, so we move to choice (C). The limitation on the placement of *M* is that it not be placed on a shelf just above or just below *L*, and placing *M* on shelf three doesn't seem to violate this requirement. You would quickly give the same treatment to choice (D). There is no obvious reason why *L* could not be on the fifth shelf. Finally, we come to (E). Can *J* be on the fifth shelf?

1	2	3	4	5	6
				J	

No, for this would violate the first condition.

Are the partial orders specified in the remaining choices consistent with the initial conditions? Yes, as the following complete orders demonstrate:

(A) *O, J, M, K, L, N*
(B) *O, M, J, L, K, N*
(C) *O, J, M, K, L, N*
(D) *O, J, M, K, L, N*

But as a matter of strategy, there is no need to work these out. Once we identified the inconsistency between the partial order described by (E) and the first initial condition, we had all we needed to answer the question.

In a more difficult question, the inconsistency between the partial order and the initial conditions may not be so easy to spot because it may involve the placement of some other individuals.

EXAMPLE:

Books by which of the following pairs of authors CANNOT be placed shelves three and four, respectively?

(A) J and M

(B) K and L

(C) L and K

(D) M and N

(E) N and J

The answer is (D), but the insight required to reach that conclusion is more subtle than the one we used to answer the preceding question. You should first work through the choices looking for the obvious contradiction:

(A) Placing J third and M fourth does not obviously violate either the first or the third condition.

(B) Placing K third and L fourth does not obviously violate either the first or the third condition.

(C) Placing L third and K fourth does not obviously violate either the first or the third condition.

(D) Placing M third and N fourth does not obviously violate the third condition.

(E) Placing N third and J fourth does not obviously violate the first condition.

Since no obvious contradiction between a partial order and an initial condition controlling the placement of the individuals in those partial orders is available, we are forced to work out complete orders for each choice:

(A) O, L, J, M, K, N   (Consistent with all conditions.)

(B) J, M, K, L, N, O   (Consistent with all conditions.)

(C) M, J, L, K, N, O   (Consistent with all conditions.)

(D) −, −, M, N, −, −   (Inconsistent with first condition.)

(E) O, M, N, J, L, K   (Consistent with all conditions.)

So (D), the partial order of which is inconsistent with the first initial condition, is the corrrect choice. (Of course, once you have spotted the choice that generates a contradiction, you don't have to work out orders for the following choice or choices.)

Here is another example of a question in which you must use the indirect approach.

EXAMPLE:

Books by which of the following authors can be placed on a shelf between the shelves on which are placed the books by L and M when the books by L and M are separated by exactly one shelf?

  I. N

 II. J

III. K

(A) I only   **(B)** II only   **(C)** I and II only

(D) II and III only   **(E)** I, II, and III

You must construct a complete order for each partial order. As for statement I, is it possible to have the order L, N, M or the partial order M, N, L? There are four possible positions for such a partial order:

1	2	3	4	5	6
M	N	L			
	M	N	L		
		M	N	L	
			M	N	L

The second and third are impossible because there is no place for the order *J*, —, *K*. And the first and fourth are not possible, because either *K* would be last or *J* would be first, making it impossible for *O* to be either first or sixth. So it is not possible for *N* to be placed between *L* and *M*. (**Note:** As long as *L* and *M* are separated, it doesn't matter which is above the other, so the proof just given also shows that the partial *L*, *N*, *M* is not acceptable.)

II does describe a possible partial order:

1	2	3	4	5	6
L	J	M	K	N	O

And III also describes a possible partial order:

1	2	3	4	5	6
O	N	J	M	K	L

At this point, I want to address a concern frequently voiced by students: Yes, I understand the justification for the correct answer, but I'm not sure I'll know how to attack the next problem I see. First, you have to understand that each new problem does present new difficulties, so you cannot expect to memorize a list of instructions and be able to apply them mechanically to new situations. Second, you cannot expect to see the end of a deductive chain at the very outset. In this respect, solving an analytical reasoning problem is somewhat like looking a word up in the dictionary, say the word *syllogism*.

When you first pick up the dictionary, you don't expect to know the exact location of *syllogism*; that is, you don't know on which page the word appears, or where on the page it appears, or precisely what words come immediately before and after *syllogism*. You do, however, know the *procedure* for looking up the word. Since you know that *s* comes toward the end of the alphabet, you open toward the back of the dictionary. You would be very lucky indeed if you happened to open to the page on which *syllogism* appears. Instead, you hope to find yourself somewhere in the vicinity of the word. If you happen to open to the *q* section of the dictionary, you quickly page forward until you reach the *s* section. If you page too quickly and pass through *s* into *t*, you page back. Once in the *s* section, you work backward and forward until you find the page containing *syllogism*.

Third, is there a procedure that will guide you in thinking about further deductions? Yes; in very general terms, this procedure states that you take any additional information, compare that information with the initial conditions, and draw further conclusions. But since there are several initial conditions, which should you work with first?

The answer to this question must respond to two competing considerations. On the one hand, it seems you should work first with those conditions having the most limiting power. As it turns out, however, this suggestion must be qualified for the following reason. Consider a typical linear ordering situation; for example, six people—*M*, *N*, *O*, *P*, *Q*, and *R*—are standing single file in a line. Contrast the two conditions:

> M is third in line.
> N is the second person behind O.

Which of the two would you find it easier to begin working with? Most people will probably say the first. After all, the first serves to specify the position of M exactly, but the second only narrows the placement of N and O to four possible positions:

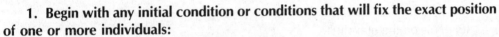

```
1       2       3       4       5       6
O               N
        O               N
                O               N
                        O               N
```

What is interesting, however, is that the second condition actually has more limiting power than the first. The first, taken in isolation, leaves 120 possible orders; but the second, taken in isolation, leaves only 96 possible orders.

Taking this into account, it seems to me that the best procedures for drawing further inferences is as follows:

1. Begin with any initial condition or conditions that will fix the exact position of one or more individuals:

John is the third person in the line.
Mary's appointment must be scheduled for Wednesday.
H is the third note in the scale.

2. Next, work with any condition that significantly narrows the possibilities for any individual:

John is either the first or the last person in the line.
Mary's appointment must be scheduled for either Wednesday or Thursday.
H is a higher note than the third note.

3. Then work with conditions that connect one individual with one or more other individuals. These conditions have more or less strength depending on how the individuals are related:

(A) Look for a condition that places an individual in an exact position relative to another individual:

John is standing immediately behind Harry.
Mary's appointment must be scheduled on the second day following Peter's appointment.
Note H is three notes higher than note M.

(B) Then look for a condition that places an individual a certain number of positions away from another individual (without regard to direction):

John is either immediately in front of or immediately behind Harry.
Mary's appointment must be scheduled either two days before Peter's appointment or two days after Peter's appointment.
Note H is separated from note M by two other notes.

(C) Finally, look for a condition that places an individual relative to another individual (without regard to number of positions removed or direction):

John is somewhere behind Harry.
Mary's appointment must be scheduled earlier in the week than Peter's.
Note H is higher than note M.

4. Use those conditions that state only that an individual may not be somewhere:
John is not the first person in line.
Mary's appointment is not on the same day as Peter's.
Note H is not immediately below nor immediately above note M.

You cannot expect to follow this outline strictly, because the limiting power of any particular condition can be affected by the limiting power of the other conditions. For example, the condition:

John is behind Harry in a line of six persons.

is not, in and of itself, a very powerful condition. But with the additional stipulation "Harry is the fifth person in line," the condition above is transformed into a first-order condition with the power to fix the position of an individual: John is sixth.

Now let's attack some questions using this general procedure:

If the book by J is on the fourth shelf, which of the following must be true?
(A) O is on the first shelf.
(B) L is on the second shelf.
(C) N is on the third shelf.
(D) M is on the fifth shelf.
(E) N is on the fifth shelf.

The answer is (A). Start by entering the additional information on a diagram:

$$1 \qquad 2 \qquad 3 \qquad 4 \qquad 5 \qquad 6$$
$$ J$$

Now return to the initial conditions and look for any condition that might specify the location of another individual with relation to J. The first condition does:

$$1 \qquad 2 \qquad 3 \qquad 4 \qquad 5 \qquad 6$$
$$ J K$$

Now look for any condition that connects either J or K to any other individual. There are none. Next, look for a condition that limits the placement of a single individual. Condition two requires that O be either first or sixth. Since K is sixth, O must be first:

$$1 \qquad 2 \qquad 3 \qquad 4 \qquad 5 \qquad 6$$
$$O J K$$

Finally, use the remaining, negative condition that requires that L and M be separated. This does not serve to fix either L or M, though it does establish that either L or M is fifth. This seems to be as far as we can go, so check the answer choices. You can see that (B), (C), and (D) are possibly, though not necessarily, true, while (E) is necessarily false. The only statement that must be true is (A).

EXAMPLE:

If the book by M is placed on the second shelf above the book by J, all of the following must be true EXCEPT

(A) The book by O is placed on a shelf somewhere above the book by M.

(B) The book by M is placed on a shelf somewhere above the book by N.

(C) The book by J is placed on a shelf somewhere above the book by L.

(D) The book by J is placed on a shelf somewhere above the book by K.

(E) The book by L is placed on a shelf somewhere above the book by K.

The answer is (A). The question stem stipulates a partial order, M, —, J, and your first impulse may be to try to put this partial order on a diagram. To follow this impulse is not an error, but there are four different positions for this partial order:

1	2	3	4	5	6
M		J			
	M		J		
		M		J	
			M		J

Before you actually enter the new information on a diagram, you should return to the initial conditions to see whether or not the placement of M or J is controlled by the placement of any other individual. The first condition connects J and K. We can expand the partial order to: M, —, J, —, K. And there are only two possible places for this partial order:

1	2	3	4	5	6
M		J		K	
	M		J		K

Now look for a condition that restricts the placement of an individual. O must be either first or sixth:

1	2	3	4	5	6
M		J		K	O
O	M		J		K

And finally, use the negative condition that separates M and L:

1	2	3	4	5	6
M	N	J	L	K	O
O	M	N	J	L	K

Thus, choice (A) makes a statement that is possibly, though not necessarily, true, while the other choices make statements that are necessarily true.

In the part entitled "Three Important Facts about Analytical Reasoning," above, I stated that analytical reasoning items are characterized by one of two modalities: what *must* be true or what *can* be true. (And, of course, each can take a thought-reverser.) There are some question forms that you might not recognize as falling into either of these categories, and we should take a look at some examples of these.

EXAMPLE:

If the book written by *L* is separated by three shelves from the book written by *M*, then which of the following is a complete and accurate list of the shelves on which the book written by *N* could be placed?

(A) Third
(B) Fourth
(C) Second, third
(D) Third, fourth
(E) Second, third, fourth

The answer to this question is (D), and the question really has the form "what can be true." *L* and *M* are governed by no initial condition except that they not be together, so enter the new information on a diagram:

1	2	3	4	5	6
L/M				*L/M*	
	L/M				*L/M*

Now look for a condition that severely limits the placement of an individual:

1	2	3	4	5	6
L/M				*L/M*	*O*
O	*L/M*				*L/M*

Only one condition remains:

1	2	3	4	5	6
L/M	*J*		*K*	*L/M*	*O*
O	*L/M*	*J*		*K*	*L/M*

And only one individual remains:

1	2	3	4	5	6
L/M	*J*	*N*	*K*	*L/M*	*O*
O	*L/M*	*J*	*N*	*K*	*L/M*

Thus, *N* could be on either the third or the fourth shelf. And this is why I call this a "could be true" question. The stem asks for the possible locations of *N*.

EXAMPLE:

If the book by *N* is placed on the first shelf, in how many different orders can the six books be placed on the shelves?

(A) 1   **(B)** 2   **(C)** 3   **(D)** 4   **(E)** 5

The answer to this item is (D). Since the additional information places *N* on shelf one, you can begin by entering this new information on a diagram:

1	2	3	4	5	6
N					

Next, look for a condition that fixes the position of an individual:

1	2	3	4	5	6
N					*O*

And the next most powerful condition is the second:

1	2	3	4	5	6
N	J		K		O
N		J		K	O

All that remains is to find the right places for M and L, but the condition that controls the placement of those individuals requires only that they be separated:

1	2	3	4	5	6
N	J	M/L	K	M/L	O
N	M/L	J	M/L	K	O

Thus, there are exactly four possible orders, and that is why this kind of question, too, should be considered a "could be" question.

The final question based on this set of initial conditions is a variation that has the "must be" modality.

EXAMPLE:

If the book by M is placed on the fifth shelf, which of the following additional pieces of information is sufficient to determine the placement of the remaining books?

I. The book by N is placed on the first shelf.
II. The book by J is placed on the first shelf.
III. The book by O is placed on the first shelf.

(A) I only   (B) II only   (C) I and II only
(D) I and III only   (E) I, II, and III

The answer to this question is (C), and the question really falls into the category of "must be true" questions. Test each statement:

I: Assume that N is on the first shelf. Since there are no conditions that connect the placement of N with the placement of any other individual, look for a condition that restricts the placement of another individual. The second condition is useful:

1	2	3	4	5	6
N				M	O

Now use the next most powerful condition:

1	2	3	4	5	6
N	J		K	M	O

And L must be on the third shelf, which completely determines the order.

II: Enter the new information on a diagram:

1	2	3	4	5	6
J				M	

The second condition now dictates the placement of O:

1	2	3	4	5	6
J				M	O

And, of course, *J* is related by that first condition to *K*:

1	2	3	4	5	6
J		K		M	O

Now the weakest initial condition (*L* and *M* are not next to each other) settles the complete order:

1	2	3	4	5	6
J	L	K	N	M	O

III: Place *O* on the first shelf:

1	2	3	4	5	6
O					

Next, *O* is not connected in the initial conditions with another individual, so try placing *J* and *K*:

1	2	3	4	5	6
O	J		K	M	
O			J	M	K

Since the only remaining condition is the separation of *L* and *M*, III does not dictate a single, unique arrangement of the individuals.

> **EXAMPLES:**
>
> An office building consists of six floors, and each floor is occupied by exactly one business. The six businesses are an insurance agency, a doctors' group, a law firm, a printing company, a dance studio, and a shirt factory.
>
> The insurance agency is located somewhere below the fourth floor.
>
> The doctors' group is separated from the insurance agency by the same number of floors that the insurance agency is separated from the law firm, though that number may be zero.
>
> The printing company is located somewhere between the dance studio and the insurance agency.
>
> The law firm is either immediately above or immediately below the printing company.

Before we look at any questions, we will summarize the information for ready reference.

$$IA < 4$$
$$(DG - IA) = (IA - LF)$$
$$DS < PC < IA \text{ or } IA < PC < DS$$
$$PC - LF \text{ or } LF - PC$$

(**Note:** This is not, of course, the only way of summarizing the information.) Notice that the arrangement of the individuals (the businesses) is not determined by the initial conditions. In fact, it isn't possible to place any business on any given floor. So we go to the questions.

Which of the following is a possible arrangement of the business, from the first floor to the sixth floor?

(A) Doctors' group, insurance agency, law firm, printing company, dance studio, shirt factory

(B) Doctors' group, insurance agency, law firm, shirt factory, printing company, dance studio

(C) Insurance agency, law firm, printing company, doctors' group, dance studio, shirt factory

(D) Shirt factory, law firm, printing company, insurance agency, doctors' group, dance studio

(E) Dance studio, printing company, insurance agency, law firm, doctors' group, shirt factory

This question stem does not supply any additional information, so it must be answerable just on the basis of the initial conditions. Use the initial conditions to eliminate choices.

Let's start with the first condition, that the insurance agency be on a floor lower than the fourth floor. (A), (B), (C), and (E) all respect this condition; (D) does not. So you eliminate (D).

Next, take the condition that the number of floors separating the doctors' group from the insurance agency be the same as the number of floors separating the insurance agency from the law firm. (A) and (B) both respect this condition; (C) and (E) do not. So we eliminate (C) and (E).

Next, take the requirement that the printing company be located between the dance studio and the insurance agency. (A) and (B) both respect this condition.

Finally, take the condition that requires that the law firm be either immediately above or below the printing company. (A) respects this condition; (B) does not. So we eliminate (B).

By the process of elimination, we have learned that the answer must be (A).

If the dance studio is on the fifth floor, on which floor is the shirt factory located?

(A) first   **(B)** second   **(C)** third   **(D)** fourth   **(E)** sixth

Since this question does supply additional information, you'll probably want to make a rough sketch to keep track of your further deductions:

1	2	3	4	5	6
				DS	

But where should you start? Look back at the summary of the initial conditions to find any condition that governs the placement of the dance studio. The third condition requires that the printing company be between the dance studio and the insurance agency, which means that the printing company must be located somewhere below the dance studio. But that doesn't allow us to fix the exact position of any individual. So we look for the most powerful initial condition. The most powerful condition is the second one, which governs the placement of three individuals. To respect that condition (and the further requirement that the insurance agency be below four), the doctors' group, the insurance agency, and the law firm must occupy three consecutive floors out of the first four:

1	2	3	4	5	6
DG/LF	IA	DG/LF		DS	
	DG/LF	IA	DG/LF	DS	

And the printing company must occupy the other floor below the dance studio. At this point, you can see that the sixth floor must be occupied by the shirt factory, which shows that (E) is the correct answer to this question.

As a matter of test-taking strategy, this is sufficient to dispose of the question; but for the purpose of discussion, we can pursue the matter to demonstrate that the additional stipulation in the question stem provides enough information to fix a single order. Since the printing company must be between the insurance agency and the dance studio and next to the law firm, the order is:

1	2	3	4	5	6
DG	IA	LF	PC	DS	SF

EXAMPLE:

If the printing company is located on the fifth floor, on what floor is the shirt factory located?

(A) first   **(B)** second   **(C)** third   **(D)** fourth   **(E)** sixth

(A) Again, start by entering this new information in a rough diagram:

1	2	3	4	5	6
				PC	

Now what is the correct move? The fourth condition stipulates that the law firm is next to the printing company:

1	2	3	4	5	6
			LF?	PC	LF?

Next, refer to that very powerful second condition. If the law firm were on floor six (and since the insurance agency cannot be higher than three), there would be at least two floors between the insurance agency and the law firm—but then it would be impossible to respect the second condition. So the law firm must be on four, which means that the doctors' group and the insurance agency are on two and three, respectively:

1	2	3	4	5	6
	DG	IA	LF	PC	

Then, the printing company must be between the dance studio and the insurance agency, so the dance studio must be on the sixth floor, which means the shirt factory is on the first.

1	2	3	4	5	6
SF	DG	IA	LF	PC	DS

EXAMPLE:

If the shirt factory is located on the fifth floor, which of the following must be true?

(A) The insurance agency is on the first floor.

(B) The doctors' group is on the second floor.

(C) The law firm is on the third floor.

(D) The dance studio is on the fourth floor.

(E) The printing company is on the sixth floor.

The answer is (C). This question stem also provides additional information, so begin by entering it on a diagram:

1	2	3	4	5	6
				SF	

Now where do you go? There is no initial condition that connects the shirt factory with any other business, so you should start with the most powerful condition available to you—the second one. The doctors' group and insurance agency (and the insurance agency and law firm) might have either no floor separating them or one floor separating them. (They cannot be separated by two businesses, for there are not enough floors in the six-story building to accommodate that arrangement.) Then, given that the insurance agency is on one of the first three floors, the three businesses, the doctors' group, the insurance agency, and the law firm, must occupy consecutive floors:

	1	2	3	4	5	6
	DG/LF	IA	LF/DG		SF	
OR						
		DG/LF	IA	LF/DG	SF	

But the law firm and the printing company are on adjacent floors, which leaves only two possibilities:

1	2	3	4	5	6
DG	IA	LF	PC	SF	DS
PC	LF	IA	DG	SF	DS

But remember that the printing company is between the dance studio and the insurance agency, so only the first of these two possibilities is valid:

1	2	3	4	5	6
DG	IA	LF	PC	SF	DS

And finally, here is yet another variation on the linear ordering theme.

EXAMPLE:

A political action group has invited six candidates—G, H, I, J, K, and L—to address a forum. Each candidate will speak exactly once.
  K must speak third.
  G must speak either first or last.
  I must speak either immediately before or immediately after L.
  H cannot speak either immediately before or immediately after I.

We begin by summarizing the information:

K = 3rd
G = 1st or 6th
I = L
H ≠ I

And you'll need a diagram to keep track of your further deductions:

1	2	3	4	5	6
G?		K			G?

8

If *H* is scheduled to speak fifth, which of the following must be true?
(A) *G* speaks first.
(B) *I* speaks second.
(C) *J* speaks second.
(D) *J* speaks fourth.
(E) *L* speaks first.

The answer is (D). Begin by setting up a figure that will keep track of your deductions:

1	2	3	4	5	6
G?		K		H	G?

Now look to see whether or not there is a condition that governs the placement of any of the individuals already entered on the diagram. The fourth condition specifies that *I* cannot speak either before or after *H*, which means that *I* must speak either first or second (depending on when *G* is scheduled to speak):

1	2	3	4	5	6
I(?)	I(?)	K		H	G
or G	I	K		H	

Now there is only one other condition to take account of: *I* must follow *L* or vice versa. The second possible arrangement above does not allow us to respect this condition. So only the first arrangement is really possible:

1	2	3	4	5	6
I/L	I/L	K	J	H	G

If *G* and *J* are first and second on the program, respectively, then which of the following must be true?
(A) *I* is fifth.
(B) *L* is fifth.
(C) *H* is sixth.
(D) *I* is sixth.
(E) *L* is sixth.

The answer is (B). Begin by entering the new information:

1	2	3	4	5	6
G	J	K			

There are only three positions left on the schedule, and the final condition requires that *H* and *I* be separated by at least one speaker. So the order must be:

1	2	3	4	5	6
G	J	K	H/I	L	H/I

It isn't possible to go any further, but you don't need to. Check the choices. (B) appears as the only correct choice, so you know you have done enough work to answer the question.

If L is the second person scheduled to speak after J, then which of the following is a complete and accurate listing of the positions in which H could speak?

(A) first, second

(B) fourth, fifth

(C) fifth, sixth

(D) second, fourth, fifth, sixth

(E) first, second, fourth, fifth, sixth

The answer is (A). The key to this question is the requirement that J and L be separated by exactly one speaker. Given that K is the third speaker, there are only two possible schedules:

1	2	3	4	5	6
	J	K	L		
		K	J		L

Then, I must be either immediately before or immediately after L:

1	2	3	4	5	6
	J	K	L	I	
		K	J	I	L

As for the first of these possibilities, H cannot speak either immediately before or after I:

1	2	3	4	5	6
H	J	K	L	I	
		K	J	I	L

And G must be either first or last:

1	2	3	4	5	6
H	J	K	L	I	G
G	H	K	J	I	L

So H can be either first or second.

Summary

1. A set of analytical reasoning questions consists of initial conditions plus questions.

2. Many test-takers agree that analytical reasoning is the most difficult section on the test. If you too find it to be a difficult section, do not jump to the conclusion that you are "weak" in this section—most other people also find this section difficult.

3. Develop a system for keeping track of information provided by the initial conditions.

4. One of the most common types of analytical reasoning sets is the ordering set:

   —The initial conditions will not determine any unique order. Remember to use the test structure to help you cope with the indeterminacy.

   —Read the verbal clues carefully.

   —Keep in mind the Holmesian strategies for ordering problems such as the "purely mechanical" process for eliminating choices to questions that provide no additional information.

Answers

1.	?	11.	T	21.	F
2.	F	12.	T	22.	?
3.	T	13.	?	23.	?
4.	T	14.	F	24.	F
5.	T	15.	?	25.	?
6.	?	16.	T		
7.	T	17.	?		
8.	T	18.	F		
9.	?	19.	?		
10.	T	20.	?		

8

(Answers, page 153)

In this section you will find ordering sets, so you can practice solving this common type of problem. There is no time limit for this exercise. I recommend that you work one group of problems and check your work on that group before going to the next group of problems.

Questions 1–7

A jazz group plans to play six pieces—*J*, *K*, *L*, *M*, *N*, and *O*—during a set. Each piece will be played exactly once. The order in which the pieces are to be played is subject to the following conditions:

N must be played before *J* and before *O*.
M must be played later than *J*.
K must be the third piece.

1. Which of the following could be the order in which the pieces are played?

   (A) *K, L, N, O, M, J*
   (B) *K, O, N, J, M, L*
   (C) *M, J, K, O, L, N*
   (D) *N, L, K, J, O, M*
   (E) *N, O, J, M, K, L*

2. Which of the following must be true of the order in which the pieces are played?

   (A) *L* is played after *K*.
   (B) *M* is played after *N*.
   (C) *N* is played after *K*.
   (D) *O* is played after *M*.
   (E) *O* is played after *J*.

3. Which of the following could be true of the order in which the pieces are played?

   (A) *J* is played sixth.
   (B) *K* is played first.
   (C) *M* is played second.
   (D) *N* is played third.
   (E) *O* is played sixth.

4. If the group plays *L* first, which piece must be played second?

   (A) *J*   (B) *K*   (C) *M*   (D) *N*   (E) *O*

5. If the group plays *M* immediately after *L* and immediately before *O*, then *J* must be played

   (A) first   (B) second   (C) fourth
   (D) fifth   (E) sixth

6. If the group plays *L* sixth, which of the following could be the first and second pieces of the set, respectively?

   I. *N* and *J*
   II. *N* and *O*
   III. *J* and *O*

   (A) I only   (B) II only   (C) I and II only
   (D) I and III only   (E) I, II, and III

7. All of the following could be played immediately after *K* EXCEPT

   (A) *J*   (B) *L*   (C) *M*   (D) *N*   (E) *O*

Questions 8–13

A film society presenting its annual film festival plans to exhibit films by four directors—two films by *J*, four films by *K*, one film by *L*, and two films by *M*. Exactly one film will be exhibited on each of nine consecutive days. Each film will be shown exactly once.

The two films by *M* will not be shown on consecutive days.

The two films by *J* will be shown on consecutive days.

On the first day, either a film by *L* or a film by *K* will be shown.

On the last day either a film by *L* or a film by *K* will be shown.

8. Which of the following is a possible arrangement of films by director?

   (A) *J, J, M, K, K, K, M, L, K*
   (B) *K, K, M, M, J, J, K, K, L*
   (C) *K, J, M, J, K, M, K, K, L*
   (D) *L, M, K, K, K, M, K, J, J*
   (E) *L, K, M, K, M, J, J, K, K*

9. Which of the following is NOT a possible schedule of films?

   (A) *L, K, M, K, M, K, K, J, J*
   (B) *K, L, M, J, J, K, M, K, K*
   (C) *K, M, K, J, J, M, K, K, L*
   (D) *L, M, K, M, J, J, K, K, K*
   (E) *K, K, K, K, M, J, J, M, L*

10. If films by *K* are shown on days 3, 4, and 5, then a film by *M* must be shown on day

    (A) 1   (B) 2   (C) 6   (D) 7   (E) 8

11. If K's films are shown on days 3, 4, 6, and 9, which of the following is (are) true?

    I. A film by M is shown on day 2.
   II. A film by M is shown on day 5.
  III. A film by J is shown on day 7.

(A) I only (B) II only (C) III only
(D) I and II only (E) I, II, and III

12. If all the films by K are shown before either of the films by M, then a film by J must be shown on which of the following days?

(A) 2 (B) 3 (C) 4 (D) 6 (E) 8

13. If all of the films by K are shown on consecutive days, then in terms of directors in how many different orders is it possible to show the films?

(A) 1 (B) 2 (C) 4 (D) 6 (E) 9

Questions 14–20

Six people—Peter, Randy, Seth, Terry, Van, and Will—were all born on the same day of the year, but each was born in a different year during a single, six-year period.

Peter is older than Seth.
Randy is older than both Terry and Van.
Will is two years older than Terry.
Peter was born either in 1962 or in 1963.
The oldest member of the group was born in 1960.

14. Which of the following could be a correct listing of the group from youngest to oldest?

(A) Seth, Peter, Randy, Terry, Van, Will
(B) Seth, Van, Peter, Terry, Will, Randy
(C) Seth, Van, Peter, Will, Terry, Randy
(D) Seth, Van, Terry, Peter, Will, Randy
(E) Van, Randy, Peter, Terry, Seth, Will

15. If Peter was born in 1962, then which of the following must also be true?

(A) Randy was born in 1960.
(B) Will was born in 1961.
(C) Seth was born in 1963.
(D) Van was born in 1963.
(E) Van was born in 1965.

16. If Will is the oldest of the group, then which of the following must be true?

(A) Randy was born in 1961.
(B) Terry was born in 1961.
(C) Peter was born in 1962.
(D) Seth was born in 1964.
(E) Van was born in 1965.

17. If Will was born in 1962, then which of the following must be true?

(A) Van was born in 1960.
(B) Randy was born in 1961.
(C) Terry was born in 1964.
(D) Seth was born in 1964.
(E) Terry was born in 1965.

18. If Peter is younger than Terry, all of the following must be true EXCEPT

(A) Will was born in 1960.
(B) Randy was born in 1961.
(C) Terry was born in 1962.
(D) Peter was born in 1963.
(E) Van was born in 1964.

19. If Van is older than Terry, which of the following must be true?

    I. Randy was born in 1960.
   II. Van was born in 1961.
  III. Peter was born in 1963.

(A) I only (B) II only (C) I and II only
(D) I and III only (E) I, II, and III

20. If Peter is older than Will, then in how many different orders could the six people have been born?

(A) 1 (B) 2 (C) 3 (D) 4 (E) 5

Questions 21–25

A teacher is planning a program for a school assembly. The program must include speeches by at least four of the six members of the student council, who are Mary, Nora, Oscar, Pam, Randy, and Tim. The program must be arranged according to the following conditions:

A student can speak only once on the program
The first student to speak must be either Mary or Nora.
The last student to speak must be either Mary or Pam.
Nora and Randy cannot both be on the program.
If both Pam and Tim are on the program, then Tim must speak sometime after Pam.

21. Which of the following students must be on the program?

(A) Mary (B) Nora (C) Pam (D) Randy
(E) Tim

22. Which of the following programs, which list students in the order in which they would speak, is acceptable?

(A) Mary, Oscar, Nora, Pam
(B) Randy, Pam, Oscar, Tim
(C) Nora, Tim, Pam, Mary
(D) Pam, Tim, Nora, Oscar, Mary
(E) Nora, Pam, Randy, Oscar, Tim, Mary

23. If both Randy and Oscar are on the program and Randy speaks before Oscar, which statements must be true?

    I. Mary speaks first.
   II. Randy speaks second.
  III. Pam speaks last.

(A) I only
(B) III only
(C) I and II only
(D) II and III only
(E) I, II, and III

24. If Nora speaks first, which of the following is a complete and accurate listing of the students who could speak second?

    (A) Pam
    (B) Mary, Oscar
    (C) Mary, Pam, Oscar
    (D) Mary, Oscar, Tim
    (E) Mary, Oscar, Pam, Tim

25. The program CANNOT comprise which of the following?

    (A) Speeches by all students except Nora
    (B) Speeches by all students except Randy
    (C) A speech by Mary sometime after a speech by Pam
    (D) A speech by Mary sometime after a speech by Nora
    (E) A speech by Nora sometime before a speech by Tim

Questions 26–31
Twelve solid-colored banners—two red, two orange, four yellow, two blue, and two green—are to be hung on a wall side by side. The positions on the wall are numbered consecutively from 1 to 12. The arrangement of the banners must conform to the following restrictions:
    The blue banners must hang side by side.
    The red banners must hang side by side.
    The green banners cannot hang side by side.
    A red banner must hang at one end of the line of banners and a yellow banner must hang at the other end.

26. Which of the following is an acceptable arrangement of the banners, from 1 to 12?

    (A) Red, red, blue, blue, green, green, yellow, yellow, yellow, orange, orange, yellow
    (B) Red, red, orange, green, blue, blue, green, yellow, yellow, yellow, yellow, orange
    (C) Red, orange, green, blue, blue, green, red, orange, yellow, yellow, yellow, yellow
    (D) Yellow, orange, yellow, yellow, blue, blue, green, yellow, orange, green, red, red
    (E) Yellow, yellow, yellow, yellow, orange, blue, green, green, blue, orange, red, red

27. All of the following are possible arrangements of the banners, from first to twelfth position, EXCEPT

    (A) yellow, green, blue, blue, orange, yellow, orange, yellow, yellow, green, red, red
    (B) yellow, green, yellow, green, yellow, blue, blue, yellow, orange, orange, red, red
    (C) yellow, orange, orange, blue, blue, green, yellow, yellow, yellow, green, red, red
    (D) red, red, orange, orange, blue, green, green, blue, yellow, yellow, yellow, yellow
    (E) red, red, green, orange, blue, blue, yellow, yellow, orange, green, yellow, yellow

28. If yellow banners are hanging in positions 9, 10, and 11, and orange banners are hanging in positions 6 and 7, then a green banner must be hanging in position

    (A) 2 (B) 3 (C) 4 (D) 5 (E) 8

29. If a blue banner is hanging in position 2, which of the following must be true?

    (A) A yellow banner hangs in position 3.
    (B) An orange banner hangs in position 4.
    (C) An orange banner hangs in position 5.
    (D) A blue banner hangs in position 8.
    (E) A red banner hangs in position 11.

30. If the orange banners hang in positions 6 and 7 and yellow banners hang in positions 5, 9, and 11, then a blue banner must hang in position

    (A) 2 (B) 3 (C) 9 (D) 10 (E) 11

31. Which of the following banners could be hanging in the six even-numbered positions?

    (A) The two green banners and the four yellow banners
    (B) The two green banners, three yellow banners, and one red banner
    (C) The two red banners, the two green banners, and the two blue banners
    (D) The four yellow banners, one red banner, and one blue banner
    (E) Three yellow banners, two green banners, and one red banner

Questions 32–34
At a certain film festival, eight films will be shown— *J, K, L, M, N, P, Q,* and *R.* The order of the showings must meet the following conditions:
    N is shown before *L.*
    J is shown third.
    Q is shown fifth.

32. If *N* is shown immediately after *P,* then *P* could be shown

    (A) third (B) fourth (C) fifth
    (D) sixth (E) seventh

33. If *N* is the fourth film shown after *M,* then *N* must be shown

    (A) third (B) fourth (C) fifth
    (D) sixth (E) seventh

34. If *K* is shown after both *L* and *R* have been shown, then which of the following must be true?

    (A) *K* is shown after *Q.*
    (B) *L* is shown before *J.*
    (C) *L* is shown before *M.*
    (D) *N* is shown after *K.*
    (E) *M* is shown before *L.*

Questions 35–38
During a certain week a sales representative must call on five customers—*J, K, L, M,* and *N.* She will call on each customer only once, and she will call on exactly one customer each day, Monday through Friday, according to the following restrictions:
    She cannot call on *L* on Monday.
    She must call on *J* before she calls on *M.*
    She must call on *K* before she calls on *N.*

35. Which of the following is an acceptable schedule for the sales representative's calls?

(A) J, M, L, K, N
(B) K, M, J, N, L
(C) L, K, N, J, M
(D) L, M, J, K, N
(E) N, L, K, J, M

36. Which of the following two calls CANNOT be scheduled after L?

(A) J and K
(B) J and N
(C) K and M
(D) K and N
(E) M and N

37. If the sales representative calls on L earlier than J, which of the following must be true of her schedule?

(A) K is first.
(B) L is second.
(C) J is third.
(D) N is second.
(E) M is fifth.

38. If L, K, and N are scheduled on consecutive days, in that order, then M could be scheduled for which day?

(A) Either Monday or Tuesday
(B) Either Monday or Wednesday
(C) Either Tuesday or Friday
(D) Either Wednesday or Thursday
(E) Either Thursday or Friday

Questions 39–44
Six members of the Jones family—J, K, L, M, N, and O—are posing for a snapshot. They are standing on the stairs to the front door of their home. There are exactly six stairs, and exactly one person is standing on each stair.

J is standing on the fourth stair.
L and N are standing on stairs below the stair on which K is standing.
M is standing on a stair below the stair on which L is standing.

39. Which of the following could be the order, from the lowest stair to the highest, in which the Joneses are standing?

(A) K, O, N, J, L, M
(B) L, M, N, K, O, J
(C) M, N, L, J, O, K
(D) O, J, M, K, N, L
(E) O, L, M, J, N, K

40. Which of the following must be true of the order in which the Joneses are standing?

(A) K is on a lower stair than J.
(B) N is on a lower stair than L.
(C) N is on a lower stair than M.
(D) M is on a lower stair than K.
(E) O is on a lower stair than K.

41. Which of the following could be true of the order in which the Joneses are standing?

(A) K is on the first stair.
(B) L is on the first stair.
(C) N is on the first stair.
(D) K is on the fourth stair.
(E) J is on the fifth stair.

42. If O is standing on the top stair, then who is standing on the fifth stair?

(A) J (B) K (C) L (D) M (E) N

43. If N is standing on a stair just below O and just above M, then on which stair is K standing?

(A) First
(B) Second
(C) Third
(D) Fourth
(E) Sixth

44. All of the following could be standing on a stair just above J EXCEPT

(A) K (B) L (C) M (D) N (E) O

Questions 45–50
A beer distributor is arranging a tasting for five imported beers, one each from Canada, England, France, Germany, and Holland. Each beer will be tasted exactly once, and the order of the tastings is governed by the following conditions:

Either the beer from Holland must be tasted first and the beer from Germany must be tasted last or the beer from Germany must be tasted first and the beer from Holland tasted last.

The beer from Canada must be tasted before the beer from France.

45. Which of the following CANNOT be true?

(A) The beer from France is tasted second.
(B) The beer from Canada is tasted second.
(C) The beer from England is tasted third.
(D) The beer from England is tasted fourth.
(E) The beer from Germany is tasted before the beer from Canada.

46. If the beer from England is tasted third, which of the following must be true?

(A) The beer from Germany is tasted first.
(B) The beer from France is tasted second.
(C) The beer from Canada is tasted second.
(D) The beer from England is tasted fifth.
(E) The beer from Germany is tasted fifth.

47. If the tastings of the beers from Canada and Germany are separated by exactly one other tasting, which of the following must be true?

(A) The beer from England is tasted second.
(B) The beer from France is tasted second.
(C) The beer from Canada is tasted fourth.
(D) The beer from Germany is tasted fifth.
(E) The beer from England is tasted fifth.

48. If the beer from France and the beer from England are tasted one after the other, though not necessarily in that order, then which of the following must be true?

   I. The beer from Germany is tasted first.
   II. The beer from Canada is tasted second.
   III. The beer from France is tasted third.

   (A) I only   (B) II only   (C) III only
   (D) I and II only   (E) I, II, and III

49. Which of the following *additional* conditions guarantees that the beer from England is tasted fourth?

   (A) The beer from Holland is tasted after the beer from France.
   (B) The beer from Canada is tasted after the beer from Holland.
   (C) The beer from France is tasted before the beer from England.
   (D) The beer from Germany is tasted before the beer from Canada.
   (E) The beer from England is tasted before the beer from Holland.

50. If the beer from Germany is tasted fifth, in how many different orders is it possible to arrange the tastings of the other beers?

   (A) 1   (B) 2   (C) 3   (D) 4   (E) 5

Questions 51–57

   Seven people—four men, Q, R, S, and T, two children, J and K, and one woman, W—are standing in a single-file line facing the ticket window of a movie house.
   Each child is standing directly behind and directly in front of a man.
   S is not standing either directly in front of nor directly behind K.
   Q is the either the fourth or the fifth person in line.

51. Which of the following could be the order in which the people are standing, from first in line to last?

   (A) J, S, R, K, Q, T, W
   (B) S, K, T, J, Q, W, R
   (C) W, T, K, Q, J, R, S
   (D) R, J, S, T, K, Q, W
   (E) W, K, R, J, Q, S, T

52. If R is the second person in line and S is the fourth person in line, which of the following must be true?

   (A) W is first.
   (B) K is third.
   (C) T is third.
   (D) T is sixth.
   (E) W is sixth.

53. If W is the fourth person in line and J is the sixth, then how many different orders for the seven people are possible?

   (A) 1   (B) 2   (C) 3   (D) 4   (E) 5

54. If J is standing directly behind R, who is standing directly behind Q, who is, in turn, standing directly behind K, then which of the following provides a complete and accurate listing of the positions in which W could be standing?

   (A) First
   (B) First or second
   (C) First or seventh
   (D) Second or seventh
   (E) First, second, or seventh

55. If J is the fifth person in line, then which of the following provides a complete and accurate listing of the positions in which K could be standing?

   (A) Second
   (B) Second or third
   (C) Second or sixth
   (D) Second, third, or sixth
   (E) Second, third, sixth, or seventh

56. If Q is the fourth person in line, then which of the following provides a complete and accurate listing of the positions in which W could be standing?

   (A) First or seventh
   (B) First, second, or third
   (C) First, second, sixth, or seventh
   (D) First, second, third, sixth, or seventh
   (E) First, second, third, fifth, sixth, or seventh

57. If R, J, and T are the first, second, and third persons in line, respectively, then which of the following must be true?

   I. K is fourth.
   II. S is sixth.
   III. W is seventh.

   (A) I only   (B) I and II only   (C) I and III only
   (D) II and III only   (E) I, II, and III

Questions 58–61

   Five people—P, Q, R, S, and T—were all born on January 1 but each person in a different year, 1961 through 1965.
   R is older than both S and T.
   P is younger than S and T.

58. If P was born in 1964, then which of the following is a complete and accurate list of the years in which could have been born?

   (A) 1961, 1962
   (B) 1962, 1963
   (C) 1963, 1964
   (D) 1961, 1962, 1963
   (E) 1962, 1963, 1964

59. If Q is the oldest member of the group, then which of the following must be true?

   I. R was born in 1962.
   II. S was born in 1964.
   III. P was born in 1965.

   (A) I only   (B) II only   (C) III only
   (D) I and III only   (E) II and III only

60. If *T* was born in 1964, then which of the following is a complete and accurate list of the years in which *Q* could have been born?

   (A) 1961
   (B) 1961, 1962
   (C) 1962, 1963
   (D) 1961, 1962, 1963
   (E) 1961, 1962, 1963, 1965

61. If *S* is two years older than *T*, then which of the following is a complete and accurate list of the years in which *S* could have been born?

   (A) 1962
   (B) 1962, 1963
   (C) 1962, 1964
   (D) 1963, 1964
   (E) 1962, 1963, 1964

Questions 62–68

Five jockeys—*G, H, I, J,* and *K*—compete in a series of races. In each race, each jockey rides one of five horses—*P, Q, R, S,* or *T*.
   G always finishes first or last.
   J always finishes ahead of *K*.
   H always finishes ahead of *I*.
   P always finishes first, and *Q* always finishes second. There are no ties.

62. Which of the following is a possible order of finish for the jockeys?

   (A) *G, H, I, K, J*
   (B) *G, J, I, K, H*
   (C) *G, H, J, I, K*
   (D) *H, J, I, G, K*
   (E) *J, K, I, H, G*

63. Which of the following is a complete and accurate list of the jockeys who could ride *Q*?

   (A) *H*
   (B) *H, J*
   (C) *H, J, I*
   (D) *H, J, K*
   (E) *H, J, K, I*

64. If *K* finished second and *S* finished fourth, all of the following must be true BUT

   (A) *J* rode *P*.
   (B) *H* rode *T*.
   (C) *I* rode *S*.
   (D) *H* finished third.
   (E) *G* finished last.

65. If *H* finished fourth aboard *S*, and *R* finished ahead of *T*, then all of the following must be true BUT

   (A) *G* rode *P*.
   (B) *J* rode *Q*.
   (C) *K* rode *T*.
   (D) *K* finished third.
   (E) *I* finished fifth.

66. If *J* rode *R*, which of the following jockeys could not have ridden *S*?

   I. *G*
   II. *I*
   III. *H*

   (A) I only   (B) II only   (C) III only
   (D) I and II only   (E) I, II, and III

67. If *H* rode *S* and finished ahead of *G*, who rode *T*, all of the following must be true BUT

   (A) *I* rode *R*.
   (B) *J* rode *P*.
   (C) *K* rode *Q*.
   (D) *S* finished fourth.
   (E) *T* finished fifth.

68. Which of the following statements is sufficient to determine the exact order of finish of both jockeys and horses?

   (A) *H* rode *R* and finished one place ahead of *I*, who rode *S*.
   (B) *H* rode *R* and finished two places ahead of *K*, who rode *T*.
   (C) *I* rode *R* and finished one place ahead of *K*, who rode *S*.
   (D) *J* rode *P* and finished two places ahead of *K*, who rode *S*.
   (E) *J* rode *Q* and finished one place ahead of *I*, who rode *T*.

Questions 69–75

An express bus carrying six passengers—*G, H, I, J, K,* and *L*—makes exactly five stops. At least one passenger gets off at each stop.
   H gets off before *I*.
   J gets off before *G*.
   K gets off before *L*.

69. Which of the following is a possible description of the stops at which the passengers got off?

	1	2	3	4	5
(A)	*H*	*G,I*	*K*	*J*	*L*
(B)	*H*	*J*	*G,L*	*K*	*I*
(C)	*J,*	*G*	*K*	*H,L*	*I*
(D)	*J,K*	*I*	*H*	*L*	*G*
(E)	*K*	*L*	*J*	*G*	*H,I*

70. Which is the earliest stop at which both *I* and *G* could get off together?

   (A) First   (B) Second   (C) Third
   (D) Fourth   (E) Fifth

71. Which is the latest stop at which both *J* and *K* could get off together?

   (A) 1   (B) 2   (C) 3   (D) 4   (E) 5

72. If *J* and *L* get off together at the stop just after *I* gets off, which of the following must be true?

(A) *H* gets off at the first stop.
(B) *K* gets off at the first stop.
(C) *I* gets off at the second stop.
(D) *J* gets off at the fifth stop.
(E) *G* gets off at the fifth stop.

73. If *I* gets off just after *G* and *L* get off together, all of the following could be true EXCEPT

(A) *H* gets off at the first stop.
(B) *J* gets off at the second stop.
(C) *K* gets off at the second stop.
(D) *K* gets off at the third stop.
(E) *I* gets off at the fourth stop.

74. If *H* and *K* get off together at the third stop, in how many different orders is it possible for the passengers to get off the bus?

(A) 1   (B) 2   (C) 3   (D) 4   (E) 5

75. If *H*, *J*, *G*, and *I* get off at the odd-numbered stops, in how many different orders is it possible for the passengers to get off the bus?

(A) 1   (B) 2   (C) 3   (D) 4   (E) 6

Explanatory Answers

Questions 1–7

Begin by summarizing the information:

$N < (J + O)$
$J < M$
$K = 3$

There is one further conclusion that can be drawn. Since N is to be played before J and J before M, N must be played before M.

1. (D) Using the first condition, that N be played before both J and O, we eliminate (B) and (C). Using the second condition, that J come before M, we eliminate (A). Finally, using the third condition, that K be played third, we eliminate (E). So the one choice that fits all of the conditions is (D).

2. (B) At the outset, we deduced one further conclusion: that N must come before M. That the other choices are not logically necessary can be demonstrated by the following possible order:

1	2	3	4	5	6
N	L	K	O	J	M

3. (E) As for (A), J cannot be played last because J is played before M. As for (B), K must be played third, not first. As for (C), M cannot be played second, because (as we learned above) both J and N must be played before M. As for (D), it is K that must be played third—not N. (E), however, is a possibility, as shown by the diagram:

1	2	3	4	5	6
N	J	K	L	M	O

4. (D) Enter the additional information in a diagram:

1	2	3	4	5	6
L		K			

   N must be played before J, and O, and also M. And this means that N must be played second:

1	2	3	4	5	6
L	N	K			

   Then the order of the other three pieces is not fixed, but these further conclusions are sufficient to answer the question asked.

5. (B) With K as the third piece, there is only one place to accommodate a series of three pieces:

1	2	3	4	5	6
		K	L	M	O

8

Then, since N comes before J, the order must be:

1	2	3	4	5	6
N	J	K	L	M	O

So J must be played second.

6. (C) Enter the additional information on a diagram:

1	2	3	4	5	6
		K			L

Since N must be played before J, O, and M, N must be first:

1	2	3	4	5	6
N		K			L

Now given that J must precede M, there are only three possibilities:

1	2	3	4	5	6
N	J	K	M	O	L
N	J	K	O	M	L
N	O	K	J	M	L

So the first and second pieces could be N and J, or N and O.

7. (D) N must be played before three other pieces (J, O, and M), so (given that K is played third) N cannot be played later than second. So N cannot be played after K. It is possible, however, to play the others immediately after K:

	1	2	3	4	5	6
	N	L	K	J	M	O
OR	N	J	K	L	M	O
OR	N	J	K	M	L	O
OR	N	J	K	O	M	L

Questions 8–13

Begin by summarizing the information:

2 by J
4 by K
1 by L
2 by M
$M \neq M$
$J = J$
1st $= L$ or K
Last $= L$ or K

8. (E) Just screen choices using the initial conditions. Using the first one ($M \neq M$), we eliminate (B). Using the second condition ($J = J$), we eliminate (C). Using the final condition, we eliminate (A) and (D). By the process of elimination, (E) must be the correct choice.

9. (A) Again, use the initial conditions as a screen. Every choice but (A) is consistent with the initial conditions. (A) fails because J cannot be the last film shown.

10. (B) Here you will probably need a diagram:

1	2	3	4	5	6	7	8	9
		K	K	K				

This means that the fourth film by K must be shown either first or ninth, with L in the other position:

1	2	3	4	5	6	7	8	9
K		K	K	K				L
L		K	K	K				K

The two films by J must be shown consecutively as either sixth and seventh or seventh and eighth, which means that one of the films by M will be shown either sixth or eighth and the other second. So it is certain that one film by M must be shown on the second day.

11. (E) Again, you will want to use a diagram:

1	2	3	4	5	6	7	8	9
	K	K		K				K

This means that the film by L is shown first:

1	2	3	4	5	6	7	8	9
L		K	K		K			K

Since the two films by J must be shown on consecutive days:

1	2	3	4	5	6	7	8	9
L		K	K		K	J	J	K

the films by M must be shown on the remaining two days:

1	2	3	4	5	6	7	8	9
L	M	K	K	M	K	J	J	K

So statements I, II, and III are true.

12. (D) If all of the films by K are shown before either film by M, then the first film must be a K film and the last must be the L film:

1	2	3	4	5	6	7	8	9
K								L

Then, we are told that the other K films and the M films have this pattern: K K K M – M. What is there to separate the M films? Only the two, consecutively shown, films by J:

1	2	3	4	5	6	7	8	9
K	K	K	K	M	J	J	M	L

So the films by J are shown on days six and seven.

13. (B) Let's start by assuming that a K film is shown on the first day and the film by L on the last day. Since K's films must be shown on consecutive days:

1	2	3	4	5	6	7	8	9
K	K	K	K					L

then, the two films by M must be separated by the films by J:

1	2	3	4	5	6	7	8	9
K	K	K	K	M	J	J	M	L

So this is one possible order. The other possible order is to assume that a *K* film is shown on the last day, in which case you will get the mirror image of the diagram above:

1	2	3	4	5	6	7	8	9
L	*M*	*J*	*J*	*M*	*K*	*K*	*K*	*K*

So given the stipulation of this question, there are exactly two possible orders.

Questions 14–20
Summarize the information:

$P > S$
$R > (T + V)$
$W = T + 2$
$P = $ '62 or '63

14. (D) Using the first condition (*P* is older than *S*), we eliminate (E). Using the second condition (*R* is older than both *T* and *V*), we eliminate (A). Using the third condition (Will is two years older than Terry), we eliminate (B) and (C). Since we are left with (D), (D) must be the one correct listing.

15. (A) Here you will probably want to use a diagram:

60	61	62	63	64	65
		P			

Since *P* was born in 1962, there are only two possible places on the diagram for *W* and *T*:

60	61	62	63	64	65
	W	*P*	*T*		
		P	*W*		*T*

As for the first possibility, *R* (who is older than *T*) would have been born in 1960, with *V* and *S* born in 1964 and 1965, though not necessarily respectively:

60	61	62	63	64	65
R	*W*	*P*	*T*	*S/V*	*S/V*

As for the second possibility, *S* (who is younger than *P*) was born in 1964, and *R* and *V* were born in 1960 and 1961, respectively:

60	61	62	63	64	65
R	*V*	*P*	*W*	*S*	*T*

Under either scenario, Randy was born in 1960.

16. (A) Use a diagram to keep track of the logic:

60	61	62	63	64	65
W					

Then *T* was born in 1962 and Peter in 1963:

60	61	62	63	64	65
W		*T*	*P*		

This means that R, who is older than T and V, was born in 1961:

```
60    61    62    63    64    65
W     R     T     P
```

S and V were born in 1964 and 1965, though not necessarily respectively. So only (A) is necessarily true.

17. (C) Again, you will need a diagram:

```
60    61    62    63    64    65
            W
```

This means that P was born in 1963 and T in 1964:

```
60    61    62    63    64    65
      W     P     T
```

Since P is older than S:

```
60    61    62    63    64    65
      W     P     T     S
```

Also, since R is older than V:

```
60    61    62    63    64    65
R     V     W     P     T     S
```

Only (C) is true.

18. (E) If P is younger than T, then (since R and W are both older than T) R, W, and T are all older than P. So P must have been born in 1963. W, T, and R are related as follows:

```
60    61    62    63    64    65
W     R     T     P
```

It is not possible to determine, however, in which order V and S were born. This is sufficient, however, to answer the questions. (A) through (D) are necessarily true, while (E) is only possibly true.

19. (C) If V is older than T, then R, V, and W are all older than T, which means that T could not have been born before 1963. T could only have been born in 1964 or 1965:

```
60    61    62    63    64    65
            W           T
            W                 T
```

We add P and S to the diagram:

```
60    61    62    63    64    65
            W     P     T     S
            P     W     S     T
```

Then, since R is older than V:

```
60    61    62    63    64    65
R     V     W     P     T     S
R     V     P     W     S     T
```

Thus, statements I and II are necessarily true, while III is only possibly true.

20. (A) If P is older than W, then P is also older than T:

60	61	62	63	64	65
	P	W			T

Since P is older than S, and since R is older than V:

60	61	62	63	64	65
R	V	P	W	S	T

So, if P is older than W, there is only one possible order in which the group could have been born.

Questions 21–25

Begin by summarizing the information:

> At least 4.
> 1st = M or N
> Last = M or P
> $N \neq R$
> $(T + P)$ ´ $(P ß T)$

21. (A) For each student, try constructing a program that omits that student. The correct choice will be the one for which omitting the student generates a contradiction.

As for (A), if Mary is not on the program, then the first and last speakers must be N and P, respectively. Then, since N is on the program, R cannot be, which means that both O and T must be on the program (to ensure the minimum of four speakers). Since P and T are both on the program, P must speak before T. Now, however, we have a contradiction. P cannot speak both before T and last. Thus, Mary is essential to the program.

That the other students are not essential is demonstrated by the following possible programs:
(B) $M \quad R \quad O \quad P$
(C) $N \quad O \quad T \quad M$
(D) $N \quad O \quad T \quad M$
(E) $M \quad O \quad R \quad P$

22. (A) Test each choice by the initial conditions. The first condition requires that M or N be first, so we eliminate (B) and (D). The second requires that M or P be last, and the remaining choices are consistent with this condition. The third condition states that N and R may not appear on the program together, so we eliminate (E). Finally, the fourth condition states that when T and P appear together, P must speak first, so we eliminate (C). By the process of elimination, we learn that (A) is the only choice that meets all of the conditions.

23. (E) Draw further conclusions from the new information. If R is on the program, then N cannot be on the program, and that means that M must speak first and P last. Since P speaks last, T cannot be on the program (because of the final condition). Thus, the program will consist of four students: $M \ R \ O \ P$.

24. (E) Draw further conclusions from the new information. If N speaks first, then R cannot be on the program. It seems, however, that no other student is specifically precluded from being on the program. This means for M, O, P, and T, we will have to try to create an order in which each is second:

    N M O P   (So M can be second.)
    N O M P   (So O can be second.)
    N P O M   (So P can be second.)
    N T O M   (So T can be second.)

Thus, (E) correctly notes that with N first, every student but R could be second.

25. (A) Notice that this question stem contains a thought-reverser: *cannot*. Four of the five choices describe possible programs; one does not. The one that does not is the correct choice. Test each one by trying to create a possible order using the individual named:

If N is not on the program, as in choice (A), then M is first and P is last. If N is the only student not on the progam, then T is on the program. If a program includes both P and T, P must speak before T and therefore cannot be last. So this is not a possible program. That the others are possible is shown by the following order:
    N P O T M

Questions 26–31

Begin by summarizing the initial conditions:

    2 R, 2 O, 4 Y, 2 B, 2 G
    B = B
    R = R
    G ≠ G
    R . . . Y or Y . . . R

26. (D) Simply screen choices using the initial conditions. All of the choices have the correct number of each color. Next, (E) fails to respect the condition that the blue banners hang together. In (C), the red banners are not together. In (A), the green banners are together, and in (B) one end banner is orange. So only (D) fulfills all of the requirements.

27. (D) Again, screen the choices. The correct choice is (D). There, the green banners hang together and the blue banners do not.

28. (E) For this question you will probably want to use a diagram:

1	2	3	4	5	6	7	8	9	10	11	12
					O	O		Y	Y	Y	

The ends must be R and Y or vice versa. Since R = R, R must be in position 1 with Y in 12:

1	2	3	4	5	6	7	8	9	10	11	12
R	R				O	O		Y	Y	Y	Y

Since B = B, there are two possible arrangements of the remaining banners:

1	2	3	4	5	6	7	8	9	10	11	12
R	R	G	B	B	O	O	G	Y	Y	Y	Y
R	R	B	B	G	O	O	G	Y	Y	Y	Y

Thus, a green banner must hang in position 8.

29. (E) If a blue banner is in position 2, the other blue banner is in position 3 and a yellow banner must be in 1. (Since the red banners hang together, they could not hang at that end.) This means that a red banner must hang on the other end and beside it the other red banner:

1	2	3	4	5	6	7	8	9	10	11	12
Y	B	B								R	R

There don't seem to be any further conclusions we can draw, but this is sufficient to answer the question. Only (E) is necessarily true.

30. (B) For this problem you will need a diagram:

1	2	3	4	5	6	7	8	9	10	11	12
				Y	O	O		Y		Y	

Since $R = R$, position 12 must be Y and 1 and 2 are filled by R:

1	2	3	4	5	6	7	8	9	10	11	12
R	R			Y	O	O		Y		Y	Y

Then $B = B$ and $G \neq G$:

1	2	3	4	5	6	7	8	9	10	11	12
R	R	B	B	Y	O	O	G	Y	G	Y	Y

So a blue banner must hang in position 3.

31. (D) Test each choice:

(A) If green and yellow banners hang in the even positions, then a yellow banner hangs in position 12. This means a red banner hangs in position 1 and next to it must hang another red banner in position 2; but this is a contradiction, so it is not a possible order.

(B) This choice avoids the problem of (A), but it is fatally flawed in another respect. Since the blue banners must hang side by side, one of the blue banners will have an even number (and the other, an odd number).

(C) Since the red banners hang side by side, one must have an odd number, and the same is true for the blue banners.

(D) This is possible:

1	2	3	4	5	6	7	8	9	10	11	12
R	R	B	B	O	Y	O	Y	G	Y	G	Y

(E) Since the blue banners hang together, one of the even-numbered positions must be occupied by a blue banner.

Questions 32–34
Begin by summarizing the initial conditions:

$N < L$
$J = 3$
$Q = 5$

There don't appear to be any further obvious conclusions to be drawn, so go to the questions.

32. (D) A diagram will probably be useful here:

1	2	3	4	5	6	7
		J		Q		

If, as the additional information requires, N is shown immediately after P, then there seem to be three possible positions on the diagram for that pair:

1	2	3	4	5	6	7	8
P	N	J		Q			
		J		Q	P	N	
		J		Q		P	N

Because N must be shown before L, the third order is not possible. So if P is shown immediately before N, P could be shown either first or sixth.

33. (D) Again, you will probably want to use a diagram:

1	2	3	4	5	6	7	8
		J		Q			

If N is the fourth film after M, then there seem to be two possible locations for the pair $M---N$:

1	2	3	4	5	6	7	8
	M	J		Q	N		
		J	M	Q		N	

The second, however, is not possible because N must be shown before L. So given the additional information of this question, N must be shown sixth.

34. (A) If K is shown after L, then K is shown after N as well. Thus, given the additional stipulation here, K is shown after L, N, and R, which (given that J and Q are shown third and fifth) means that K could be shown no earlier than sixth. Thus, K must be shown after Q. Choice (D) is not possible, since N must be shown before K. The other choices are possibly though not necessarily true.

Questions 35–38

Summarize the information:

$L \neq$ Mon.
$J < M$
$K < N$

35. (A) Just screen choices using the initial conditions. L cannot be scheduled on Monday, so we eliminate (C) and (D). J must be scheduled before M, so we eliminate (B). Finally, K must be scheduled before N, so we eliminate (E). Only (A) is a possible order.

36. (A) L can be scheduled no earlier than Tuesday, which means either J or K must be scheduled for Monday (to ensure that M is later than J and that N is later than K).

37. (A) If L is scheduled earlier than J, then L also comes before M. Then, regardless of when N is scheduled, K must come before N and L and therefore before J and M as well.

38. (C) If LKN are scheduled in that order, then they can be scheduled for Tuesday, Wednesday, and Thursday or for Wednesday, Thursday, and Friday. Then, J, which comes before M, must be Monday. This means that M could be scheduled for either Friday or Tuesday.

8

Questions 39–44

This is a linear ordering set of the most common garden variety. Start by summarizing the initial conditions:

$$J = 4$$
$$(L + N) < K$$
$$M < L$$

There is only one further, obvious conclusion to be drawn, and that is that M, who is standing below L, must also be standing below K. Now we go to the questions.

39. (C) This question provides no additional information, so you use the initial conditions to screen out the sequences that do not represent possible orders. Using the first condition, we eliminate (B) and (D). Using the second condition, we eliminate (A). Using the third condition, we eliminate (E). So the correct choice must be (C).

40. (D) This was the further conclusion we drew above.

41. (C) Test each of the choices. (A) cannot be true because K is standing above at least two persons. (B) cannot be true because L is standing above M. Neither (D) nor (E) can be true because J is standing on the fourth stair. (C) does describe a possible order:

```
6  K
5  O
4  J
3  L
2  M
1  N
```

42. (B) We know that K is standing somewhere above L and N and also M. So K must be standing above three people. Then, since J is standing on stair four, K must be higher than stair four. Given that O is standing on the top stair, K must be standing on the fifth stair.

43. (E) Here we are told to assume that M, N, and O are standing in a row:

```
O
N
M
```

But there is only one block of three consecutive stairs available:

```
6
5
4  J
3  O
2  N
1  M
```

Then, since *K* is standing above *L*:

6   *K*
5   *L*
4   *J*
3   *O*
2   *N*
1   *M*

44. (C) The stair just above *J* is number five, but we know that at least two people are standing above *M*, so it is not possible for *M* to stand on five.

Questions 45–50

Begin by summarizing the initial conditions:

1	2	3	4	5
H/G				H/G
C < F				

There are so few individuals in this situation that it would be possible to work out all of the possible orders for the tasting very quickly. For example, for the second, third, and fourth tastings, given the requirement that $C < F$, there are only three different possible orders:

$E < C < F$
$C < E < F$
$C < F < E$

Since there only two possible orders for *H* and *G*, this means there are only six possible orders for the tastings:

G E C F H
G C E F H
G C F E H
H E C F G
H C E F G
H C F E G

If you recognize this fact at the outset, then this set is very easy. If you did not realize there were so few possibilities, the set can still be handled using our standard attack strategies.

45. (A) Since either *H* or *G* is tasted first, and since *F* cannot be tasted until *C* has been tasted, it is not possible for *F* to be tasted second. That the other choices describe legitimate possibilities is demonstrated by the six sequences in the diagram above.

46. (C) If *E* is tasted third, then *C* and *F* must be tasted second and fourth, respectively; but the order of *H* and *G* is not fixed:

1	2	3	4	5
H/G	C	E	F	H/G

47. (A) If *C* is separated from *G* by one position, then *C* must be third, which means that *F* is fourth and *E* is second:

1	2	3	4	5
H/G	E	C	F	H/G

8

48. (B) Since *F* cannot come sooner than third (because *C* < *F*), *F* is either third or fourth. Given the additional stipulation that *E* and *F* are tasted consecutively, the possible orders are:

1	2	3	4	5
H/G	C	E	F	H/G
H/G	C	F	E	H/G

49. (C) If *F* comes before *E*, then the second, third, and fourth tastings must be *C*, *F*, *E*. So (C) guarantees that *E* will be fourth. As for the remaining choices, *G* and *H* can "flip-flop" between first and fifth without determining the order of the middle three tastings.

50. (C) As the diagram contained in the overview of this set shows, with *G* in fifth position, there are exactly three possible orders.

Questions 51–57

Begin by summarizing the information:

$$\male = Q, R, S, T$$
$$\circ = J, K \ (\circ = \text{child})$$
$$\female = W$$
$$\male < \circ < \male$$
$$S \neq K$$
$$Q = 4 \text{ or } 5$$

51. (C) Since this question stem provides no additional information, just use the initial conditions to eliminate choices. Using the first condition, you can eliminate (A) and (E). Using the second condition, you can eliminate (B), and using the last condition you can eliminate (D). By the process of elimination, we have determined that the correct choice is (C).

52. (A) Enter the new information on a diagram:

1	2	3	4	5	6	7
	R		S			

Now look back at the initial conditions to see if this information fixes the position of any other individual. Since *Q* must be either fourth or fifth, we deduce that *Q* must be fifth:

1	2	3	4	5	6	7
	R		S	Q		

Now place the children, *J* and *K*. Since they must stand between two men, they cannot be either first or last, so they must be third and sixth. More specifically, since *K* cannot stand next to *S*, *J* must be third and *K* sixth:

1	2	3	4	5	6	7
	R	J	S	Q	K	

Since *K* must have a man behind him:

1	2	3	4	5	6	7
W	R	J	S	Q	K	T

The diagram shows that (A) is necessarily true, while the other choices are necessarily false.

53. (B) Enter the new information on a diagram:

```
1    2    3    4    5    6    7
               W         J
```

Since W is fourth, Q must be fifth:

```
1    2    3    4    5    6    7
               W    Q    J
```

Since K must stand between two men, K must be second:

```
1    2    3    4    5    6    7
     K         W    Q    J
```

Since S cannot stand next to K, S must be seventh:

```
1    2    3    4    5    6    7
     K         W    Q    J    S
```

This means that R and T must be first and third, though not necessarily in that order. So there are two possible orders.

54. (A) The additional information stipulates that K, Q, R, and J are standing in a row, in that order. Since Q must be either fourth or fifth, J must be either sixth or seventh. But since J is a child (and must have a man standing behind him), J cannot be seventh. Therefore, J is sixth:

```
1    2    3    4    5    6    7
          K    Q    R    J
```

55. (B) Again, enter the new information on a diagram:

```
1    2    3    4    5    6    7
               J
```

And this means that Q is fourth:

```
1    2    3    4    5    6    7
               Q    J
```

Now where can K be placed? You cannot place K either first or seventh, for then K would not be positioned between two men; nor can you place K sixth, for the same reason. It appears that K can be either second or third. Let's construct complete orders to confirm this conclusion:

```
1    2    3    4    5    6    7
T    K    R    Q    J    S    W
1    2    3    4    5    6    7
W    T    K    Q    J    S    R
```

56. (A) The best way to attack this item is to place W into each of the positions mentioned. Ordinarily, you would start with the first position. As a matter of strategy, however, there is no need to test the first position, because it is mentioned by every choice. Start with the second position:

```
1    2    3    4    5    6    7
     W         Q
```

Now where should you place J and K? They cannot be placed first or second, for W is a woman. Nor can both of them be placed in positions 5, 6, and 7. This shows that W cannot be second in line when Q is fourth. Now you can eliminate all choices that mentioned "second." This is indeed fortunate, for it allows you to eliminate all but (A).

57. (A) Begin by entering the new information on a diagram:

```
1   2   3   4   5   6   7
R   J   T
```

Now Q must be either fourth or fifth. Can Q be fourth?

```
1   2   3   4   5   6   7
R   J   T   Q
```

But then K must be between Q and the only other man, S, a violation of the second initial condition. This means that Q must be fifth:

```
1   2   3   4   5   6   7
R   J   T       Q
```

Further, K is between T and Q:

```
1   2   3   4   5   6   7
R   J   T   K   Q
```

This means that S and W are sixth and seventh, though not necessarily respectively. As the diagram shows, only statement I is necessarily true, while II and III are possibly true.

Questions 58–61
Summarize the initial conditions:

$R < S$ and $R < T$ (R was born before S and T.)
$(S \ \& \ T) < P$

There is one further specific conclusion to be drawn: P is also younger than R. Additionally, you might see that R is either the oldest or the second oldest (depending on when Q was born) and that P is either the youngest or second youngest (again, depending on when Q was born).

58. (B) Enter the additional information on a diagram:

```
'61     '62     '63     '64     '65
                         P
```

Since R, S, and T are older than P (born in an earlier year), Q must be the youngest, and since R is older than S and T, R must be the oldest:

```
'61     '62     '63     '64     '65
R                        P       Q
```

So T could have been born in 1962 or 1963.

59. (D) Enter the new information on a diagram:

```
'61     '62     '63     '64     '65
Q
```

Since *R* was born before *S*, *T*, and *P*, *R* was born in 1962; and since *P* was born after both *S* and *T*, *P* was born in 1965:

'61   '62   '63   '64   '65
Q   R   P

We do not have enough information, however, to determine the years in which *S* and *T* were born, so only statements I and III are necessarily true.

60. (D) Enter the new information on a diagram:

'61   '62   '63   '64   '65
                              T

Which means that *P* was born in 1965:

'61   '62   '63   '64   '65
                              T   P

The only condition remaining is that *R* was born before *S*, but this condition does not fix the exact positions of *R* and *S*. They could be 1961 and 1962, respectively, 1961 and 1963, respectively, or 1962 and 1963, respectively. Therefore, *Q* could have been born in 1961, 1962, or 1963.

61. (A) The initial conditions establish that *S* cannot be the oldest (for *R* is older than *S*) and that *T* cannot be the youngest (for *P* is younger than *T*). So if *S* is two years older than *T*, then *S* and *T* must have been born in 1962 and 1964, respectively.

Questions 62–68
Begin by summarizing the information:

Jocks = G, H, I, J, K
Horses = P, Q, R, S, T
(1)   G = 1st or 5th
(2)   J < K
(3)   H < I
(4)   P = 1st
(5)   Q = 2nd

There do not appear to be any obvious conclusions to be drawn from this information, so go directly to the questions.

62. (C) Since this question stem does not provide any additional information, just eliminate choices using the initial conditions. Using the first condition (that *G* finish first or last), eliminate (D). Using the second condition (*J* < *K*), eliminate (A). Using the third condition (*H* < *I*), eliminate (B) and (E). So (C) is the only order that is consistent with all of the initial conditions.

63. (E) One way to handle items such as this is to attempt to construct a sample order using each of the jockeys mentioned in the choices. If you are successful, this, of course, proves that such an arrangement is possible; but if your attempt runs afoul of one or more of the initial conditions, this proves that the arrangement is not possible. That *H*, *J*, *K*, and *I* could all ride *Q* is proved by the following scenarios:

```
1    2    3    4    5
G    H    I    J    K
G    J    K    H    I
J    K    H    I    G
H    I    J    K    G
```

64. (B) Enter the additional information provided by this question on a diagram:

```
1    2    3    4    5
     K
P    Q         S
```

Since *J* finished ahead of *K*:

```
1    2    3    4    5
J    K
P    Q         S
```

And *G* must have finished fifth:

```
1    2    3    4    5
J    K              G
P    Q         S
```

Since *H* finished ahead of *I*:

```
1    2    3    4    5
J    K    H    I    G
P    Q         S
```

This seems to be as far as we can go. Our diagram proves that (A), (C), (D), and (E) are all true. As for (B), it is possibly though not necessarily true that *H* rode *T*.

65. (C) Enter the new information on a diagram:

```
1    2    3    4    5
               H
P    Q         S
```

The question stem also stipulates that *R* finished ahead of *T*:

```
1    2    3    4    5
               H
P    Q    R    S    T
```

Next, since *I* finished behind *H*:

```
1    2    3    4    5
               H    I
P    Q    R    S    T
```

This means that *G* finished first and *J* and *K* finished second and third, respectively:

```
1    2    3    4    5
G    J    K    H    I
P    Q    R    S    T
```

Our diagram proves that every choice but (C) must be true and, further, that (C) is necessarily false.

66. (C) Try to construct arrangements with the three jockeys aboard S. It is possible for G to have ridden S:

1	2	3	4	5
H	I	J	K	G
P	Q	R	T	S

And it is also possible for I to have ridden S:

1	2	3	4	5
G	H	J	K	I
P	Q	R	T	S

It is not possible, however, for H to have ridden S. Since J finished ahead of K, and since R finished third, fourth, or fifth, J and K occupy two of the three positions, third, fourth, and fifth. Then, since H finished ahead of I, it is impossible to put H in the position not occupied by J and K.

67. (D) Enter the additional information on a diagram. Given that H beat G, G must have finished last:

1	2	3	4	5
				G
P	Q			T

Since S (ridden by H) can finish no better than third, and since H finishes ahead of I, H must have been third and I fourth:

1	2	3	4	5
		H	I	G
P	Q	S		T

And that means that R ran fourth and that J and K rode P and Q, respectively:

1	2	3	4	5
J	K	H	I	G
P	Q	S	R	T

68. (B) To find out which statement is sufficient to fix the complete order of finish, construct diagrams using the additional information provided by each.

As for (A), H and I (aboard R and S, respectively) could have finished either third and fourth:

1	2	3	4	5
G	J	H	I	K
P	Q	R	S	T

or fourth and fifth:

1	2	3	4	5
G	J	K	H	I
P	Q	T	R	S

So the information provided in (A) is not sufficient to fix the complete order of finish.

8

As for (B), since *R* can finish no better than third, *H* and *R* must have finished third and *K* and *T* fifth:

1	2	3	4	5
		H		K
P	Q	R		T

This means that *S* finished fourth and *I* fourth. Finally, *G* must have finished first, which means that *J* finished second:

1	2	3	4	5
G	J	H	I	K
P	Q	R	S	T

So (B) is sufficient to fix the complete order of finish.

(C) is not sufficient, for *I* and *K* could have finished third and fourth or fourth and fifth; nor is (D) sufficient. Although (D) fixes the order in which the jockeys finished (*J*, *H*, *K*, *I*, *G*), it does not determine whether *R* and *T* ran fourth and fifth, respectively, or vice versa. (E), too, fixes the order in which the jockeys finished (*H*, *J*, *I*, *K*, *G*) but does not settle whether it was *S* or *R* that finished fourth or fifth.

Questions 69–75

Summarize the initial conditions:

$H < I$
$J < G$
$K < L$

There is one further conclusion to be drawn about the overall distribution. Since there are six passengers and five stops, given that at least one passenger gets off at each stop, two passengers will get off at exactly one of the stops.

69. (C) This item provides no additional information, so simply use the initial conditions to eliminate choices. Using the first condition, you can eliminate (D) and (E). Using the second condition, eliminate (A). Using the third condition, eliminate (B).

70. (C) Since *I* must get off sometime after *H*, and *G* sometime after *J*, and since only one pair of passengers can get off at any stop in the series, *I* and *G* must wait until both *H* and *J* have gotten off.

71. (C) This is the mirror image of the previous problem. Since *J* must get off before *G* and *K* before *L*, and since only one pair of passengers can get off at any stop in the series, *J* and *K* must get off in time to let both *G* and *L* off—which means if *J* and *K* want to get off together, they must get off no later than the third stop.

72. (E) Here the question stem isolates part of an order: *I*,(*J*&*L*). But at which stops does this sequence occur? Since *G* must get off after *J*, the order must be *I*, (*J*&*L*),*G*. Since *H* must get off before *I*, the order is *H*, *I*, (*J*&*L*),*G*. Finally, *K* must also get off before *L* and therefore before *G*, though the information does not establish which gets off first. Therefore, everyone else gets off before *G*.

73. (E) This question stem establishes the partial order (*G*&*L*), *I*. It is similar to the preceding question in that the task is to determine where this partial order fits. Notice that *G*, *L*, and *I* are the three individuals who must each get off after some other individual has gotten off. This means that *H*, *J*, and *K* must get off before *G* and *L*, and so *G* and *L* must get off at the fourth stop and *I* at the fifth.

74. (B) Start by entering the new information on a diagram:

```
1     2     3     4     5
            H,K
```

Since H gets off before I and K before L, I and L must get off at the fourth and fifth stops, though not necessarily in that order. As for the first two stops, J must get off before G:

```
1     2     3     4     5
J     G     H,K   I/L   I/L
```

So there are exactly two possible orders in which the passengers can get off.

75. (E) Given that H must get off before I and J must get off before G, there are six possibilities:

```
1     2     3       4     5
H           I & J         G
H           J             G & I
J           H & G         I
J           H             G & I
HJ          I             G
HJ          G             I
```

And in each of these, K must get off second and L fourth. So there are exactly six possibilities.

Analytical Reasoning: Part II

1. Distributed Ordering Problems
2. Scheduling Problems
3. Word Games
4. Selection Problems
5. Networks
6. Table of Characteristics
7. Maps
8. Family Trees
9. Hybrid Problems

9

In the first lesson on analytical reasoning we discussed some basic features of analytical reasoning sets. Additionally, we studied the most common type of analytical reasoning set, the ordering problem. In this lesson, we study other types of analytical reasoning problems.

1. Distributed Ordering Problems

In the linear ordering sets we just studied, only one individual could occupy a particular position in the order. In some problem sets, more than one individual can occupy a given position. Since individuals are distributed in order according to the conditions given, I call these distributed order sets. Here are brief descriptions of distributed order sets:

Seven businesses have offices in a four-story office building.
Eight people must be scheduled for interviews during a five-day workweek.
Nine books are placed on four shelves.
Eight cars are parked on six levels of a parking garage.
Seven people are sitting in the first four rows of seats in a theater.

The Holmesian strategies developed above for linear ordering problems apply to distributed ordering problems as well. But you must remember that in a distributed order situation, more than one individual can occupy a certain position. For example, two businesses might have offices on the same floor, or three people might be scheduled for an interview on the same day, or three books might be on the same shelf, or four cars might be parked on the same level of the garage, or three people might be sitting in the same row of seats. Thus, in a distributed order, you must pay careful attention to the initial conditions that govern the distribution of individuals, for example, those which specify a maximum or a minimum number of individuals in a certain location.

EXAMPLE:

A parking attendant must park seven vehicles—a compact, a sedan, a pickup, a van, a station wagon, a sports car, and a camper. There are exactly eight parking places open in the garage: two on the first level, two on the second level, one on the third level, two on the fourth level, and one on the fifth level.
At least one of the vehicles must be parked on each of the five levels.
The camper cannot be parked on the first level.
The pickup must be parked on the second level.
The compact must be parked on the fifth level.
The sedan and the station wagon must be parked on the same level.

Before looking at any questions we will summarize the information using a diagram:

Floors	(available spaces)
5 compact	(1)
4	(2)
3	(1)
2 pickup	(2)
1	(2)

$\geq$ 1 each level
camper $\neq$ 1st
sedan = wagon

As with the linear ordering sets we have seen, the initial conditions here do not dictate any single placement of the individuals. So we attack the questions.

> Which of the following is NOT an acceptable parking arrangement for the vehicles mentioned?
> **(A)** The sedan and the station wagon on level one
> **(B)** The camper and the pickup on level two
> **(C)** The van and the pickup on level two
> **(D)** The sports car and the pickup on level two
> **(E)** The van and the camper on level three

The answer is (E). This question stem, which is characterized by a thought-reverser, provides no additional information. The correct Holmesian strategy is to compare each of the initial conditions to the answer choices until you find the one choice that violates one of the initial conditions. One of the distributional conditions specifies that the third level has only one parking space available, so it is not possible to park two vehicles on that level.

> Which of the following must be true?
> **(A)** The van is parked on the second level.
> **(B)** The camper is parked on the fourth level.
> **(C)** The sports car is parked on the fourth level.
> **(D)** The station wagon and the sedan are parked on the first level.
> **(E)** Exactly two vehicles will be parked on two of the levels.

The answer is (E). This set (a distributed order) differs from the linear ordering sets we studied above in that it specifies a certain distribution. It would not be surprising, therefore, to find a question that aims at the distributional requirements. And this is one such question.

Given the flexibility of the situation, it seems unlikely that (A), (B), or (C) would be the correct answer. You can prove to yourself that none of them is correct by constructing possible arrangements in which each is false. (A), (B), and (C) all mention possible arrangements of the vehicles, but a *possible* arrangement is not a correct response to a question that asks what arrangement *must* be true. (D) suffers from this defect as well. Although it is possible that the station wagon and the sedan could be parked on the first level, they don't necessarily have to be parked there.

(E), however, is necessarily true. The attendant must park seven vehicles. Since the sedan and the station wagon will be parked on the same level, one of the levels will have exactly two cars parked on it. Of the other five vehicles, at least one must be parked on each of the other levels. This makes a total of $2 + 1 + 1 + 1 + 1 = 6$ vehicles, which means there is one more vehicle to be parked. Since the maximum number of vehicles that can be accommodated on any level is two, another level must have two vehicles. So the distribution will be 2, 2, 1, 1, and 1 (though not necessarily in that order).

> If the sports car and the camper are both parked on the same level, then which of the following must be true?
>
> **(A)** The van is parked on level two.
> **(B)** The van is parked on level three.
> **(C)** The station wagon is parked on level four.
> **(D)** The station wagon is parked on a higher level than the van.
> **(E)** The camper is parked on a lower level than the van.

The answer is (B). This question provides additional information. Since (by additional stipulation) the sports car and the camper are parked on the same level, and since the camper cannot be parked on level one, the sports car and the camper are parked on level four:

Floors	(available spaces)
5 compact	(1)
4 sports car, camper	(2)
3	(1)
2 pickup	(2)
1	(2)

$\geq$ 1 each level
camper $\neq$ 1st
sedan = wagon

Next, since the sedan and the wagon must be parked on the same level, they must be parked on level one:

Floors	(available spaces)
5 compact	(1)
4 sports car, camper	(2)
3	(1)
2 pickup	(2)
1 sedan, wagon	(2)

≧ 1 each level

camper ≠ 1st

sedan = wagon

Finally, since every level must have at least one vehicle, the remaining vehicle, the van, is parked on level three:

Floors	(available spaces)
5 compact	(1)
4 sports car, camper	(2)
3 van	(1)
2 pickup	(2)
1 sedan, wagon	(2)

≧ 1 each level

camper ≠ 1st

sedan = wagon

Our diagram shows that (B) is necessarily true, while every other choice is necessarily false.

> If the sedan is parked on level four, in how many different ways can the attendant distribute the cars among the five levels?
>
> **(A)** 1   **(B)** 2   **(C)** 3   **(D)** 4   **(E)** 5

The answer is (E). Begin your attack by processing the additional information provided by the stem:

Floors	(available spaces)
5 compact	(1)
4 sedan	(2)
3	(1)
2 pickup	(2)
1	(2)

≧ 1 each level

camper ≠ 1st

sedan = wagon

The station wagon must be parked on the same level as the sedan:

Floors	(available spaces)
5 compact	(1)
4 sedan, wagon	(2)
3	(1)
2 pickup	(2)
1	(2)

$\geq$ 1 each level

camper $\neq$ 1st

sedan = wagon

This takes care of the top two levels. Now we experiment to find how many possible arrangements there are of the remaining three vehicles (the van, the sports car, and the camper) over the lowest three levels. Given the distributional requirements, exactly one of the remaining vehicles will go to each of the lowest three levels, but the camper cannot go to the bottom level. This means that the camper is either on the second level or on the third level. If the camper is on the second level, then in order to respect the condition that each level must accommodate at least one vehicle, the van and the sports car are on levels one and three or vice versa. (That's two possibilities.) The camper might also be on the third level, in which case either the sports car or the van or both might be assigned to the first level. (That's three more possibilities.) So there are five possibilities.

2. Scheduling Problems

Some problem sets ask you to set up schedules; for example, a store manager must schedule employees to work the day and evening shifts for the upcoming week, Monday through Saturday. Conditions would then specify such restrictions as Paul cannot work on the same day as Peter or Mary cannot work on a day following a day on which Paul has worked.

The procedures for attacking a scheduling set are the same that we outlined for linear ordering sets, but here your diagram will be different.

EXAMPLE:

A music teacher is scheduling a recital for five people. The recital will consist of five pieces, and each piece will be performed by a singer with a piano accompanist.

Mary, Paula, and Samantha can sing.

Nancy, Roberta, and Samantha can accompany.

Samantha must sing the third piece on the program.

Roberta must accompany for the fourth piece on the program.

No person can perform in consecutive pieces.

You should begin by setting up a scheduling diagram:

	1	2	3	4	5
Singer					
Accomp.					

Then enter the information given:

	1	2	3	4	5
Singer			Sam.		
Accomp.				Rob.	

Are there any further conclusions to be drawn? Yes. Since Samantha is the singer for the third piece, she cannot be the accompanist for that piece. And since Roberta is the accompanist for the fourth piece, she cannot be the accompanist for the third piece. This means that Nancy is the accompanist for the third piece:

	1	2	3	4	5
Singer			Sam.		
Accomp.			Nan.	Rob.	

And since Samantha and Nancy both perform the third piece, neither is available to be the accompanist for the second piece, which means that Roberta is the accompanist for the second piece:

	1	2	3	4	5
Singer			Sam.		
Accomp.		Rob.	Nan.	Rob.	

At this point, there do not appear to be any further useful conclusions to be drawn, so we attack the questions.

> Which of the following must be true?
> **(A)** Roberta is the accompanist for the first piece.
> **(B)** Roberta is the accompanist for the second piece.
> **(C)** Samantha is the singer for the fourth piece.
> **(D)** Paula is the singer for the fourth piece.
> **(E)** Samantha is the singer for the fifth piece.

The answer is (B). The diagram confirms that Roberta is the accompanist for the second piece. As for the remaining choices, (A) must be false, for Roberta is the accompanist for the second piece (and so cannot perform the first piece). (C) is incorrect for a similar reason. Since Samantha sings the third piece, she cannot perform the fourth piece in any capacity. Finally, as for (D) and (E), these are only possibly true statements and therefore not correct responses to a question that asks, "Which must be true?".

If Samantha sings the first piece on the program, which of the following must be true?

(A) Mary sings the second piece.

(B) Paula sings the second piece.

(C) Samantha sings the fifth piece.

(D) Nancy is the accompanist for the first piece.

(E) Nancy is the accompanist for the fifth piece.

The answer is (D). Enter the additional information on the diagram:

	1	2	3	4	5
Singer	Sam.		Sam.		
Accomp.		Rob.	Nan.	Rob.	

Since Samantha is singing the first piece, she cannot be the accompanist for that piece. Since Roberta is the accompanist for the second piece, she cannot perform in the first piece, which leaves Nancy as the accompanist for the first piece:

	1	2	3	4	5
Singer	Sam.		Sam.		
Accomp.	Nan.	Rob.	Sam.	Rob.	

Are there other conclusions to be drawn? There don't seem to be any, so check your work against the choices. Choice (D) is confirmed by the diagram: Nancy is the accompanist for the first piece. The other choices describe only possibilities. Thus, since we have one and only one correct choice, we know that we did all the work required to answer this question.

If Mary is taken ill and cannot perform at all, then all of the following must be true EXCEPT

(A) Samantha sings the first piece.

(B) Nancy is the accompanist for the first piece.

(C) Paula sings the second piece.

(D) Paula sings the fourth piece.

(E) Samantha is the accompanist for the fifth piece.

The answer is (E). If Mary is unable to sing, then Samantha and Paula must share the singing duties. Since Samantha is already scheduled to sing the third piece, she cannot sing either the second or the fourth piece, so Paula must sing those:

	1	2	3	4	5
Singer		Pau.	Sam.	Pau.	
Accomp.		Rob.	Nan.	Rob.	

Then, since Paula is the singer for the second and fourth pieces, it is Samantha who sings the first and fifth pieces:

	1	2	3	4	5
Singer	Sam.	Pau.	Sam.	Pau.	Sam.
Accomp.		Rob.	Nan.	Rob.	

This means that neither Samantha nor Roberta is available to play the piano for either the first or the fifth piece, so that job goes to Nancy:

	1	2	3	4	5
Singer	Sam.	Pau.	Sam.	Pau.	Sam.
Accomp.	Nan.	Rob.	Nan.	Rob.	Nan.

We now have a complete schedule. Checking the answer choices against this schedule, we can see that (A), (B), (C), and (D) are all necessarily true. (E), however, is inconsistent with the diagram, so the correct choice must be (E).

3. Word Games

A variation on the idea of a single-file ordering is the use of letter or word sequences. In this type of problem set, certain letter or word sequences constitute "words" or "sentences" while others do not. Here is an example of a word game set:

EXAMPLE:

A certain code uses only the letters V, W, X, Y, and Z. Words in the code are written and read from left to right. The only words used in the code are those that meet the following requirements:

> A code word must be three, four, or five letters long, though words need not be made up of different letters.
>
> W cannot be the last letter in a code word.
>
> If X appears at all in a word, it must appear more than once.
>
> Z cannot be either the first or second letter of a word.
>
> V can appear in a word only if for each occurrence of V, a Y also appears in that word.
>
> Y cannot be the first letter of a word unless Z also appears in that word.

With a set like this, you won't be able to draw any further conclusions from the initial conditions, but you may want to summarize the conditions for easier reference:

$W \neq$ last
$X \supset X$
$Z \neq$ (1st or 2nd)
$V \supset Y$
$(Y = 1st) \supset Z$

(**Note:** not p unless q = if p, then q.)

EXAMPLES:

Which of the following is a code word?

(A) *VXXYV*

(B) *WYZYX*

(C) *XXZYW*

(D) *YYXXZ*

(E) *YZVXX*

The answer is (D). This set is very much like a linear ordering set. In a linear ordering set, the initial conditions establish the order of the individuals, and here the conditions establish the sequence (or order) of letters. To solve this problem, all you need to do is test each choice by the conditions (or vice versa) and eliminate choices that violate any condition.

We will start with the first condition: *W* is not the last letter of a word. (C) fails to meet this requirement, and so we eliminate (C). Next, we use the condition that *X*, if it appears at all, must appear more than once. (B) fails to respect this condition. Next, we check to see whether *Z* appears as either the first or second letter of a word, and we eliminate (E) on this ground. Next, we try the requirement that for each occurrence of *V* there must be an occurrence of *Y*. (A) fails on this score, for in that sequence there are two occurrences of *V* but only one occurence of *Y*. By the process of elimination, therefore, (D) must be the correct choice.

Be careful that you don't make the mistake of eliminating (D) as incorrect. The fourth condition requires that every *V* be accompanied by a *Y*: if *V*, then *Y*. But this is not equivalent to *if Y, then V*.

Which of the following letters could be used to create a three-letter code word having the structure "*YV—*"?

(A) V   (B) W   (C) X   (D) Y   (E) Z

The answer is (E). Test each choice by substituting the letter into the indicated blank and measuring the result by the initial conditions. As for (A), the sequence *YVV* is not an acceptable sequence because there are two occurrences of *V* and only one occurrence of *Y* (in violation of the fourth condition). As for (B), the sequence *YVW* violates the first condition. As for (C), the sequence *YVX* violates the second condition. As for (D), the sequence *YVY* violates the last condition. Finally, the sequence *YVZ* is an acceptable one because it fulfills all of the requirements.

What is the total number of different three-letter code words that can be constructed using only letters of the type *V*, *X*, and *Y*?

(A) 1   (B) 3   (C) 4   (D) 5   (E) 9

The answer is (C). We will systematically test the various possibilities. First, consider the possibility of making words using only occurrences of a single letter. No such words can be made using *V*, because *V* also requires the use of *Y*. So *VVV* is not an acceptable word. And no such words can be made using just *Y*, because *Y* cannot be the first letter of a word unless *Z* is also in the word. Thus, *YYY* is not an acceptable word. It is, however, possible to create a word using only Xs: *XXX* is a word.

Now let's ask whether it's possible to create a word using all three letters. *V*, *X*, and *Y* cannot all be combined to make a three-letter word because a single *X* violates the second condition.

Next, we see what combinations of letters could be used: *V*s and *X*s, *V*s and *Y*s, and *X*s and *Y*s. If *V* is included in a code word, then *Y* must also be included, which means that no word can be made using just *V*s and *X*s.

What about *V*s and *Y*s? If a *V* is used, a *Y* must also be used, which gives us two of our three letters. The third letter cannot be another *V* (that would violate the third condition), so the third letter would need to be *Y*. So it is possible to use the combination *V*, *Y*, and *Y*, but in what order? *Y* cannot be placed first (for that would violate the fifth condition), so the only acceptable order for this combination of letters is *VYY*.

Finally, what about words using just *X*s and *Y*s? Given the second condition, we must have at least two *X*s. So the only combination of *X*s and *Y*s that can make an acceptable word would be *X*, *X*, and *Y*. In how many different orders can these letters be arranged? *Y* cannot be placed first, so it can only be placed second or third. So there are exactly two possibilities using *X*s and *Y*s: *XXY* and *XYX*.

This accounts for all the possibilities: *XXX*, *VYY*, *XXY*, and *XYX*.

4. Selection Problems

If order problems are the most common variety used on the exam, the selection problems are the second most common. This type of problem set asks you to distribute the individuals into groups:

> A college dean is appointing five students to a committee. He must choose from among seniors—John, Karl, and Larry; juniors—Mike, Peter, and Richard; and sophomores—Sam, Ted, and William.
>
> A travel agent is selecting six cities for a package tour. The cities she is considering are London, Paris, Nice, Madrid, Barcelona, Lisbon, Rome, Florence, Zurich, Bern, and Munich.

The attack strategies for selection problems are similar to those developed for ordering problems, but there are some special twists.

The verbal clues used to structure selection sets create some special problems. Pay careful attention to connections that are not symmetrical.

> **EXAMPLES:**
>
> Symmetrical: Only couples will be admitted to the dance.
> Asymmetrical: No person under sixteen will be admitted to the movie unless accompanied by an adult.

I call the first condition symmetrical because it burdens the individuals in two groups in the same way. For example, Sally cannot go without a partner, and Bill cannot go without a partner. The second condition, however, burdens persons under sixteen in a way it does not burden adults. According to the second condition, Junior cannot see the movie unless Mother (or some other adult) goes with him, but Mother is free to see the movie without Junior.

> Symmetrical: John and Bob must go to the game together.
> Asymmetrical: If John goes to the game, then Bob must go to the game.

The first condition is symmetrical because it imposes the same burden on both individuals: John and Bob must both go. The second condition is asymmetrical because it imposes a burden on one of the two individuals but does not impose the same burden on the other. The second statement says that John's going to the game is sufficient to require Bob's going to the game—but the converse is not true. The statement does not require that John go to the game just because Bob does.

> Symmetrical: Paula and Barbara must visit City X.
> Asymmetrical: Paula cannot visit City X unless Barbara also does.

The first statement imposes the same burden on both individuals, but the second statement does not. It makes Paula's visiting City X contingent on Barbara's visiting City X: Paula cannot go without Barbara. But the statement does not require the converse. Barbara is free to visit City X with or without Paula.

The procedures for attacking a selection set are basically the same as those developed for handling ordering sets, as you will see.

> **EXAMPLES:**
>
> Eight people, M, N, O, P, Q, R, S, and T, are forming teams for a bridge tournament. Each team will have four players. One team will be designated the Blue Team and the other the Red Team.
> R cannot play on the same team as either S or M.
> O cannot play play on the same team as N.
> Q must play on the Red Team.

We have already seen problem sets similar to this. Begin by summarizing the information:

$(R \neq S) + (R \neq M)$
$O \neq N$
$Q = Red$

Here you can deduce that S and M must play on the same team. Then go to the questions.

> Which of the following is an acceptable assignment?
>
> | | Red | Blue |
> | --- | --------------- | -------------- |
> | (A) | M, R, O, Q | N, P, S, T |
> | (B) | M, Q, P, N | R, T, S, O |
> | (C) | N, R, O, Q | M, S, T, P |
> | (D) | N, M, S, T | R, O, Q, P |
> | (E) | R, Q, O, P | S, M, N, T |

The answer is (E), and the correct attack strategy is to use the initial conditions to eliminate choices. Using the condition that R cannot be on the same team as either S or M, we eliminate (A) and (B). Using the condition that N cannot be on the same team as O, we eliminate (C). And using the condition that Q must be on the Red Team, we eliminate (D).

> Which of the following groups of people could play on the Red Team?
> (A) M, N, Q, O
> (B) M, O, Q, P
> (C) N, R, Q, M
> (D) Q, P, T, R
> (E) S, M, Q, O

The answer is (E). Again, you use the initial conditions to eliminate choices. You can eliminate (C) because that group includes both R and M, and you can eliminate (A) because that group includes both N and O. But you cannot eliminate any other choice in this way. This means that you must finish constructing the entire arrangement:

(B) Blue = N, R, S, T (Unacceptable)
(D) Blue = M, N, O, S (Unacceptable)
(E) Blue = N, P, R, T (Acceptable)

> If O plays on the Blue Team, which of the following must be true?
> (A) N plays with the Red Team.
> (B) P plays with the Red Team.
> (C) R plays with the Blue Team.
> (D) S plays with the Red Team.
> (E) T plays with the Blue Team.

The answer to this fairly easy question is (A). The initial conditions stipulate that O and N cannot play on the same team. Therefore, if O plays with the Blue Team, N must play with the other team.

> If R is not on the same team as O, which of the following must be true?
> **(A)** M is on the same team as P.
> **(B)** M is on the same team as T.
> **(C)** O is on the same team as T.
> **(D)** S is on the same team as O.
> **(E)** T is on the same team as N.

The answer is (D). Use the additional information. If R is not on the same team as O, then R and N are on the same team, and O, S, and M are on the same team. Is this as far as you can carry the deductions? It seems so. It doesn't seem possible to determine who is on the Red Team and who is on the Blue Team, nor where P and T play. Don't beat a dead horse. Go to the choices, and use them to help you learn whether you have done all the work necessary to answer this question. An examination of the choices shows that there is only one choice that appears to be correct, (D). The other choices describe logically possible but not logically necessary arrangements. This indicates that we have done all the necessary work and that (D) is the correct choice.

> If T and P play on the Blue Team, then which of the following statements must be true?
> I. R plays on the Blue Team.
> II. O plays on the Red Team.
> III. M plays on the Red Team.
> **(A)** I only **(B)** II only **(C)** I and III only **(D)** II and III only **(E)** I, II, and III

The answer is (C). If T and P play on the Blue Team, we have:

Red: Q
Blue: T, P

Since O and N are not on the same team, and since S and M are on the same team, S and M must be on the same team as either O or N. But that is a total of three people together, so they cannot be on the Blue Team. Therefore, S and M plus either N or O are on the Red Team:

Red: Q, S, M, $(N \lor O)$
Blue: T, P, $(N \lor O)$

And this means that R must be on the Blue Team:

Red: Q, S, M, $(N \lor O)$
Blue: T, P, R, $(N \lor O)$

EXAMPLE:

The chair of a neighborhood association is appointing people to an ad hoc committee on traffic safety. Six people—Mary, Nancy, Opal, Peter, Ralph, and Stan—are available.

If Peter is appointed to the committee, then Mary also must be appointed to the committee.

If Ralph is appointed to the committee, then Stan also must be appointed to the committee; and if Stan is appointed to the committee, then Ralph also must be appointed to the committee.

If Mary is appointed to the committee, then Stan cannot be appointed to the committee.

If Nancy is appointed to the committee, then Opal must be appointed to the committee.

Nancy must be appointed to chair the committee.

1. Which of the following must be true?
   (A) Ralph is appointed to the committee.
   (B) Stan is appointed to the committee.
   (C) Stan is not appointed to the committee.
   (D) If Peter is appointed to the committee, then Stan is not appointed to the committee.
   (E) If Peter is appointed to the committee, then Stan is appointed to the committee.

2. If Peter is appointed to the committee, which of the following is a complete and accurate listing of the other people who also must be appointed?
   (A) Mary
   (B) Mary and Nancy
   (C) Mary, Nancy, and Opal
   (D) Mary, Nancy, Opal, and Stan
   (E) Mary, Nancy, Opal, and Ralph

3. If Mary is not appointed to the committee, then the committee could consist of exactly how many people?
   I. 2
   II. 3
   III. 4
   (A) I only   **(B)** III only   **(C)** I and III only   **(D)** II and III only   **(E)** I, II, and III

We begin by summarizing the information using the symbols introduced above. For convenience of reference, I will number each of the statements:

(1) $P \supset M$
(2) $(R \supset S) + (S \supset R)$ $[R = S]$
(3) $M \supset \sim S$
(4) $N \supset O$
(5) N

From this initial set of conditions, we can draw one further conclusion. Using statements (4) and (5):

(4) $N \supset O$
(5) N
Therefore, O.

So we know that Opal must be appointed to the committee. Aside from this definite conclusion, we can reach other hypothetical conclusions such as:

(1) $P \supset M$
(3) $M \supset {\sim}S$
Therefore, $P \supset {\sim}S$.

There are several such conclusions available to us, but too many to be immediately useful. (Remember, you cannot move from a hypothetical statement such as $P \supset {\sim}S$ to a definite conclusion such as ${\sim}S$ without a further premise.) So we proceed to the questions, knowing that the questions themselves will inform us what, if any, further conclusions are needed.

1. (D) As just noted, the initial conditions require only that Nancy and Opal be appointed to the committee, so choices (A), (B), and (C) are incorrect. Further, as was just noted, using statements (1) and (3), we can infer the conclusion given in (D), so (D) must be the correct response. (Which also shows why [E] is incorrect.)

2. (C) This question provides additional information:

(1) $P \supset M$
    P (By additional stipulation)
    Therefore, M.

So Mary must be appointed. Now that we have M as an additional conclusion, we reason as follows:

(3) $M \supset {\sim}S$
    M (Further conclusion above)
    Therefore, ${\sim}S$.

So Stan is not appointed to the committee. And finally, we use this conclusion for a further conclusion:

(2) $R \supset S$ (The first half of [2])
    ${\sim}S$ (Further conclusion above)
    Therefore, ${\sim}R$.

9

Coupling these conclusions with our conclusion above that both Nancy and Opal must be appointed to the committee, we now conclude that the committee must consist of Peter, Mary, Nancy, and Opal (neither Ralph nor Stan can be appointed to the committee).

3. (C) Using the additional premise ~M (Mary is not appointed), we reason:

(1) P ⊃ M
~M (By additional stipulation)
Therefore, ~P

And this is as far as we can go. Thus, the only person who is definitely precluded from serving on the committee (aside from Mary) is Peter. So the committee could consist of four people (Nancy, Opal, Ralph, and Stan), or it could consist of just two people (Nancy and Opal). It cannot, however, consist of exactly three people (because if either Ralph or Stan is appointed, they must both be appointed).

5. Networks

In this type of problem set, the connections joining individuals are not really spatial; they are functional. Here are some sketches of such sets:

In an office, inquiries are referred to X, who in turn refers them to Y or Z, who in turn refer them either back to X or to W, and so on.

The procedure for applying for a loan begins with completing either a green form or a red form. The green form entitles you to get a yellow form, and a red form entitles you to get a pink form, and so on.

In a certain city's subway system, from station X you can go to either station Y or station Z. From station Y you can go to either station Z or to station X, and so on.

EXAMPLE:

At a certain bank, to apply for a loan a person must submit a completed green form.

A person can obtain either a blue form or a red form at the customer service desk.

With a completed blue form, a person can obtain either a yellow form or an orange form. With a completed red form, a person can obtain either a yellow form or a manila form.

With a completed yellow form, a person can obtain a manila form, a tan form, or a white form. With a completed orange form a person can obtain a white form. With a completed manila form, a person can obtain a tan form.

With a completed tan form, a person can obtain either a white form or a pink form. With a completed white form, a person can obtain a green form.

With a completed pink form, a person can obtain a green form.

We will use arrows to indicate the connections that join the individuals. First:
A person can obtain either a blue form or a red form at the customer service desk.

B

R

Next:
With a completed blue form, a person can obtain either a yellow form or an orange form. With a completed red form, a person can obtain either a yellow form or a manila form.

```
        ↗ O
    B
        ↘ Y
    R ↗
        ↘ M
```

Next:
With a completed yellow form, a person can obtain a manila form, a tan form, or a white form. With a completed orange form a person can obtain a white form. With a completed manila form, a person can obtain a tan form.

```
        ↗ O ↘
    B          W
        ↘ Y ↗→ T
    R ↗   ↓ ↗
        ↘ M
```

And then:
With a completed tan form, a person can obtain either a white form or a pink form. With a completed white form, a person can obtain a green form.

```
        ↗ O ↘
    B          W → G
        ↘ Y ↗→ ↑
    R ↗   ↓ T → P
        ↘ M ↗
```

Finally,
With a completed pink form, a person can obtain a green form.

```
        ↗ O ↘
    B          W → G
        ↘ Y ↗→ ↑   ↑
    R ↗   ↓ T → P
        ↘ M ↗
```

   The diagram is the whole story here. There are no further conclusions to be drawn, so we go to the questions.

9

1. Any of the following could be true EXCEPT
    (A) A person with a completed yellow form can get a manila form.
    (B) A person with a completed yellow form can get a tan form.
    (C) A person with a completed yellow form can get a white form.
    (D) A person with a completed orange form can get a white form.
    (E) A person with a completed white form can get a pink form.

(E) Our diagram shows that (A), (B), (C), and (D) are all correct descriptions of the network, and it shows that (E) is not a correct description of the network. A person with a completed white form can obtain only a green form.

2. What is the maximum number of forms a person can have completed before he is given a green form?
    (A) 3   (B) 4   (C) 5   (D) 6   (E) 7

(C) This question asks you to trace possible routes through the web. Although there are many different routes, the maximum number of steps that the process could take (not counting the green form) is five. For example, a person could complete the following forms: blue, yellow, manila, tan, and white.

3. If a person completes a red form, how many different combinations of forms are available to that person to obtain a green form?
    (A) 4   (B) 5   (C) 6   (D) 7   (E) 8

(D) The trick here is to trace the possibilities. They are:
    1. red, manila, tan, pink, green
    2. red, manila, tan, white, green
    3. red, yellow, manila, tan, pink, green
    4. red, yellow, manila, tan, white, green
    5. red, yellow, white, green
    6. red, yellow, tan, pink, green
    7. red, yellow, tan, white, green

6. Table of Characteristics

In this type of problem set, individuals are said to have or to lack certain characteristics. The task is then to keep track of which individuals share which characteristics.

EXAMPLE:

Six computer users—*J, K, L, M, N,* and *O*—like to share data. Each user has one or more of the following data processing programs: Data Base, Number Cruncher, Slide Rule, Math Magic, Data Jockey. To make use of data stored on a disc, a user must have a copy of that program; but a user who has more than one program is able to convert data in one program form to any other program he has.

J has copies of Data Base and Slide Rule only.
K has copies of Number Cruncher and Math Magic only.
L has copies of Data Base, Number Cruncher, and Math Magic only.
M has a copy of Math Magic only.
N has copies of Data Base and Data Jockey only.
O has copies of Math Magic and Data Jockey only.

A user who lacks a certain program can ask another user to convert data into a form for which he does have a program.

The main problem here is to keep track of the information. A table is a good way of organizing the material:

	J	K	L	M	N	O
DB						
NC						
SR						
MM						
DJ						

Enter into each box a "yes" or a "no" to indicate whether that user does or does not have a program:

	J	K	L	M	N	O
DB	YES	NO	YES	NO	YES	NO
NC	NO	YES	YES	NO	NO	NO
SR	YES	NO	NO	NO	NO	NO
MM	NO	YES	YES	YES	NO	YES
DJ	NO	NO	NO	NO	YES	YES

With a set such as this, there are no further conclusions to be drawn, so we go to the questions.

1. The program owned by the largest number of the users is
   (A) Data Base
   (B) Number Cruncher
   (C) Slide Rule
   (D) Math Magic
   (E) Data Jockey

(D) Refer to the table and total the number of "yes"s in each row:
   Data Base = 3
   Number Cruncher = 2
   Slide Rule = 1
   Math Magic = 4
   Data Jockey = 2

2. Which of the following pairs of users can share data without the need to have a third user convert information for them?
   (A) J and K
   (B) J and O
   (C) K and N
   (D) L and O
   (E) M and N

(D) To answer this question, study the table to find which of the pairs listed as choices have the same program. For example, J has Data Base and Slide Rule but K has Number Cruncher and Math Magic. So those two users cannot share data directly, and (A) cannot be the correct choice. The correct answer is (D). Both L and O have copies of Math Magic.

3. If J wishes to share data with K, which of the following individuals could convert J's information into a form that could be used by K?
   I. L
   II. M
   III. N
   (A) I only   (B) II only   (C) I and II only   (D) I and III only   (E) I, II, and III

(A) Check the table to find whether the numbered individuals share a program with J and K. As for I, L has Data Base in common with J and Number Cruncher and Math Magic in common with K, so L could take data from J and convert it into a form usable by K. As for II, M has Math Magic in common with K but no program in common with J. So M cannot take data from J at all. Finally, as for III, N has Data Base in common with J and so can take information from J. But N has no program in common with K, so N cannot forward that information to K.

7. Maps

Some sets describe spatial relationships between individuals in terms of directions.

> **EXAMPLE:**
>
> At a certain ski resort there are seven mountains—*M*, *N*, *O*, *P*, *Q*, *R*, and *S*.
> *M* is somewhere northwest of the lodge, while *N* is somewhere southwest of the lodge.
> *R* is somewhere north of the lodge, while *Q* is somewhere east of the lodge.
> *S* is somewhere south of the lodge, and *P* is farther south of the lodge than *S*.
> *O* is due north of *Q* and due west of *R*.

The obvious and best approach to a set such as this is to use a map to show the relationships:

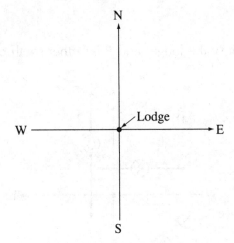

Enter information provided by the initial conditions on the map. *M* is somewhere northwest of the lodge, while *N* is somewhere southwest of the lodge:

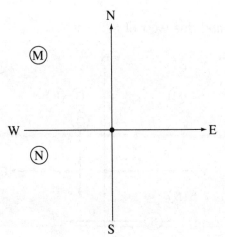

9

R is somewhere north of the lodge, while Q is somewhere east of the lodge.

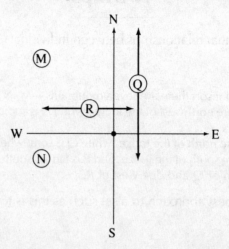

S is somewhere south of the lodge, and P is farther south of the lodge than S.

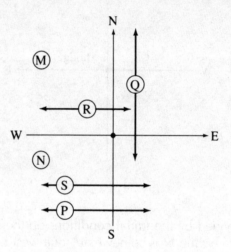

O is due north of Q and due west of R.

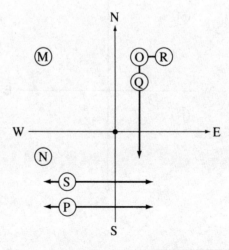

Since *Q* is east of the lodge and *O* is due north of *Q*, *O* is obviously east of the lodge. And since *O* is due west of *R*, *O* must be north of the lodge and *R* must be east of the lodge.

Questions then ask about the spatial relationships between the individuals. As you read the map, just make sure you understand that the locations shown are generally correct but are not exact. For example, *N* is in the southwest sector and is shown as being due south of *M*. The map should be read as showing that *M* is somewhere north of *N* but should not be read to show that *M* is definitely due north of *N*. It is possibly true but not necessarily true that *M* is due north of *N*.

> Which of the following must be true?
> **(A)** *M* is farther west of the lodge than *S*.
> **(B)** *N* is farther west of the lodge than *S*.
> **(C)** *N* is farther south of the lodge than *P*.
> **(D)** *Q* is northeast of *P*.
> **(E)** *R* is northeast of *Q*.

(E) As we learned above, *R* must be northeast of *Q*. As for the remaining choices, they make statements that are possibly true but not necessarily true.

> Which of the following could be true?
> **(A)** *S* is due east of the lodge.
> **(B)** *O* is due north of the lodge.
> **(C)** *Q* is due east of the lodge.
> **(D)** *M* is due west of the lodge.
> **(E)** *N* is due south of the lodge.

(C) The initial conditions establish that *Q* is somewhere east of the lodge, and that means that it is possible for *Q* to be due east of the lodge. (A) is not possible because *S* is somewhere south of the lodge, so *S* cannot be due east of the lodge. As for (B), *O* is somewhere to the east of the lodge so *O* cannot be due north of the lodge. As for (D) and (E), *M* and *N* are each in a specific sector so neither can be on the directional line.

9

If a plane flies in a straight line, its course could take it over which of the following?

   I. *N*, the lodge, and *Q*, in that order
  II. *R*, *O*, and the lodge, in that order
 III. *Q*, *P*, and *S*, in that order
 IV. *N*, *M*, and *O*, in that order
  (A) I only   **(B)** IV only   **(C)** I and II only
  (D) I and IV only   **(E)** I, III, and IV only

(E) I describes a possible course:

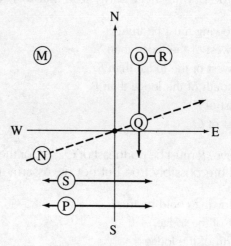

(Remember, *Q* may be north of the lodge.) II does not describe a possible course because *R* is due east of *O* and a course that included both *R* and *O* would be a due west course that would take the plane north of the lodge. III describes a possible course because *Q* could be south of both *P* and *S*. IV does describe a possible course:

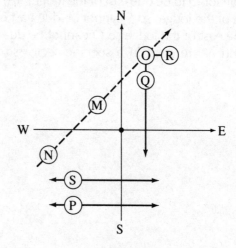

8. Family Trees

Another type of problem makes use of common family relationships, e.g., brother and sister, father and daughter, husband and wife.

> **EXAMPLE:**
>
> Dan is Bob's only brother and Alan's brother-in-law.
> Karen is Bob's daughter and Mary's niece.
> Peter, Karen and Tina's grandfather, had three children, one brother, Mark, and one sister, Odette.
> Linda, Dan's wife, is the only child of Fred and Joan.
> Mary's only daughter is Tina.

To keep track of the information, use a diagram like a family tree. There are two points to keep in mind in constructing the diagram. First, you want to keep the diagram simple, so there is no space for long notes like "the only daughter." You'll have to adopt some symbols that remind you of such restrictions. Second, the conditions are probably not presented in the most logical sequence. The third condition may introduce an individual that cannot be immediately related to anyone already on the diagram. This means you may have to go down the list of initial conditions two or even three times before you have gotten all the useful information out.

Here is one way of diagramming the information.

Dan is Bob's only brother and Alan's brother-in-law.

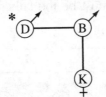

The ♂ indicates that these individuals are males; the single, horizontal connecting line indicates that they are brothers, and the star indicates that one is the only brother. Next: Karen is Bob's daughter and Mary's niece.

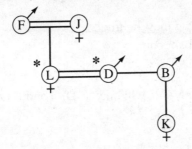

Although Karen is Mary's niece, we don't know who Mary is. She could be Dan's wife or she could be Dan and Bob's sister. So leave that information to the side and continue reading the other conditions: Peter, Karen and Tina's grandfather, had three children, one brother, Mark, and one sister, Odette. Again, it's not possible to enter the information on the diagram. Peter might be Karen's paternal grandfather and therefore Bob's father, but he might also be Karen's mother's father. The fourth condition states: Linda, Dan's wife, is the only child of Fred and Joan:

We can't enter the final condition, so we go back to the top of the list to pick up any conditions we haven't already put on the diagram. First, since Linda is an only child, Alan cannot be Dan's brother-in-law by being her brother. Therefore, Alan must be the husband of a sister to Dan, but we don't yet know her name. Next, since Karen is Mary's niece, and since Dan is married to Linda, Mary must be a sister to Dan and Bob:

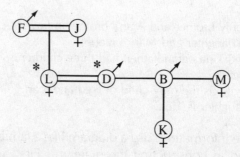

We still can't enter the third condition, so we try the fifth again. Now we can enter Tina as Mary's only daughter:

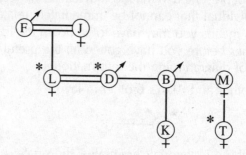

And once again back to the top. We still don't know whether Alan is Mary's husband, so skip that point again. As for the third condition, since Peter is the grandfather of both Karen and Tina, he must be the father of Bob, Mary, and Dan:

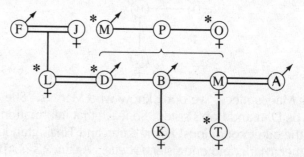

And since Peter had only those three children, Alan must be Mary's husband.

Whatever further conclusions are available from the initial conditions are already contained in the diagram, so let's go to the questions.

Which of the following must be true?
  I. Odette is older than Joan.
  II. Peter is older than Mary.
  III. Dan is older than Tina.
(A) I only   (B) II only   (C) III only   (D) I and II Only   (E) II and III only

(B) The diagram shows that II must be true since Peter is Mary's father. The other two statements, however, might or might not be true. As for I, we know nothing that would allow us to conclude that one of Dan's parents is older than one of Linda's parents. As for III, Dan is Tina's uncle; and while it is true that uncles are often older then their nieces, it is possible that the niece is older than the uncle. So III is not necessarily true, and the correct response consists of II only.

> Which of the following must be true?
>   I. Bob has only one brother.
>   II. Mark is Karen's great-uncle.
>   III. Tina is Bob's only niece.
> **(A)** II only   **(B)** III only   **(C)** I and II only
> **(D)** I and III only   **(E)** II and III only

(C) I must be true. Since Dan is Bob's only brother, Bob's only brother is Dan. (If Bob had a brother other than Dan, then Dan too would share that brother.) II must also be true. The diagram shows that Mark is Karen's grandfather's brother. III, however, is not necessarily true. Dan might also have a daughter and she would be Bob's niece as well.

> A person named Alice could be
> **(A)** Linda's sister
> **(B)** Dan's sister
> **(C)** Dan's sister-in-law
> **(D)** Tina's sister
> **(E)** Odette's sister

(C) Alice could be Bob's wife, in which case she would be Dan's sister-in-law. She could not, however, be Linda's sister, for Linda is an only child. Nor could she be another member of the second generation, for Peter had only three children. Alice could not be Tina's sister, because Tina is Mary's only daughter. Finally, Alice could not be Odette's sister, for Peter had only one sister, and that was Odette.

9. Hybrid Problems

Not every Analytical Reasoning problem set fits readily into a single category. Some problem sets incorporate features of more than one common type, so they are in essence hybrid problems. To do well with hybrids, you must be flexible and be prepared to adapt your strategies to new situations.

EXAMPLE:

A caterer is planning a meal that will include an appetizer, a soup, a main course, and a dessert—the dishes to be served in that order. From a list of possibilities, the caterer must choose one appetizer, one soup, one main course, and one dessert, according to the following conditions:

> Each dish is served either warmed or chilled; each dish is made from either vegetables or meat but not both; and each dish is either spicy or bland.
> All bland dishes, if any are included on the menu, must be served prior to the serving of any spicy dishes, if any are included on the menu.
> The meal will not include any chilled spicy dishes.

> The meal will not include any chilled vegetable dishes.
> The appetizer will be a meat dish.
> The dessert will be a vegetable dish.

This problem set combines some of the features of an ordering set with some of the features of a selection set. Since each dish must be either warm (W) or chilled (C), either vegetable (V) or meat (M), and either spicy (S) or bland (B), we can summarize the various possibilities as follows:

   CVS   CVB   CMS   CMB   WVS   WVB   WMS   WMB

Since there are no chilled spicy dishes and no chilled vegetable dishes, the list of possibilities to select from is narrowed to five:

         CMB   WVS   WVB   WMS   WMB

And the ordering feature can be summarized as follows:

Appetizer → Soup → Main Course → Dessert
      CMB   WVS
      WMS   WVB
      WMB

> Which of the following statements must be true?
> (A) The appetizer is a bland dish.
> (B) The appetizer is a cold dish.
> (C) The appetizer is a meat dish.
> (D) The dessert is a spicy dish.
> (E) The dessert is a bland dish.

The correct answer to this item is (C). As the diagram shows, the appetizer must be a meat dish (though it could be either chilled or warm and either spicy or bland). The dessert must be a warm vegetable dish, but it can be either spicy or bland.

> Which of the following statements could be true?
> (A) The meal includes a spicy, chilled meat dish.
> (B) The meal includes a bland, chilled vegetable dish.
> (C) The meal includes a spicy, chilled vegetable dish.
> (D) All of the dishes served are chilled.
> (E) Exactly one of the four dishes served is chilled.

The correct answer to this item is (E). Any of the first three dishes could be chilled. As for (A), (B), and (C), our diagram shows that these dishes are not available. As for (D), the diagram shows that the dessert must be warm.

> If exactly three of the dishes served are bland dishes, then which of the following statements must be true?
> (A) The appetizer is a warm dish.
> (B) The appetizer is a chilled dish.
> (C) The soup is a vegetable dish.
> (D) The main course is a meat dish.
> (E) The dessert is a spicy dish.

The correct answer to this item is (E). Here the ordering feature of the problem set comes into play. If exactly three of the dishes served are bland, then they must be the appetizer, the soup, and the main course, because all b'and dishes must be served before any spicy dish is served. This means that the dessert, the fourth and final course, must be spicy.

> If all of the warm dishes are vegetable dishes, then which of the following statements must be true?
>
> (A) The appetizer is a chilled, spicy meat dish.
> (B) The appetizer is a chilled, bland meat dish.
> (C) The dessert is a spicy dish.
> (D) Exactly three of the dishes are spicy dishes.
> (E) Exactly three of the dishes are bland dishes.

The correct answer to this item is (B). If we eliminate from our diagram all warm meat dishes, the appetizer must be a chilled, bland meat dish.

> If the meal includes both bland and spicy dishes but more bland dishes than spicy dishes, then which of the following statements can be false?
>
> (A) The appetizer is a bland dish.
> (B) The soup is a bland dish.
> (C) The main course is a bland dish.
> (D) The dessert is a spicy dish.
> (E) The meal includes exactly one warm dish.

The correct answer to this item is (E). From the additional information stipulated in the question stem, we can deduce that the first three courses must be bland and the last one spicy. Thus, (A) through (D) are necessarily true and cannot, therefore, be false. (E), however, can be false, for any of the first three courses could be a warm dish.

> If the appetizer is a spicy dish, then what is the minimum number of warm dishes that must be included in the meal?
>
> (A) 0
> (B) 1
> (C) 2
> (D) 3
> (E) 4

The correct answer to this item is (E). If the appetizer is a spicy dish, then it is a *warm* spicy meat dish. Since every dish that follows must also be spicy, every other dish is either a *warm* spicy meat dish or a *warm* spicy vegetable dish. Therefore, all four courses use warm dishes.

Summary

In addition to ordering problems, the other common types of analytical reasoning sets are:

Distributed Ordering Problems	Table of Characteristics Problems
Scheduling Problems	Map Problems
Word Games Problems	Family Relationship Problems
Selection Problems	Hybrid Problems
Network Problems	

(Answers, page 213)

In this section, you will find examples of the types of problems discussed above in this lesson. There is no time limit for this exercise. I recommend that you work one group of problems and check your work on that group before going to the next group of problems.

Questions 1–6

Nine professors—*G, H, I, J, K, L, M, N*, and *O*—are to appear on a series of three panels. Each panel will consist of three professors, and each professor will appear exactly once. The panels must be arranged according to the following conditions:

I and *N* must be on the same panel.

K and *L* must be on the same panel.

O and *J* cannot be on the same panel.

M must appear on the second panel.

Either *J* or *M* or both must appear on the panel with *H*.

1. Which of the following professors could appear on a panel together?

    (A) *G, L, O*
    (B) *G, J, M*
    (C) *K, I, M*
    (D) *N, I, J*
    (E) *O, I, J*

2. Which of the following CANNOT be true?

    (A) *I* appears on the second panel.
    (B) *H* appears on the third panel.
    (C) *O* appears on the third panel.
    (D) *J* appears on the first panel, and *H* appears on the third.
    (E) *G* appears on the first panel, and *K* appears on the third.

3. The third panel could consist of all of the following EXCEPT

    (A) *K, L, O*
    (B) *K, L, J*
    (C) *G, H, J*
    (D) *G, I, N*
    (E) *G, J, I*

4. All of the following could appear on the same panel as *K* EXCEPT

    (A) *G* (B) *I* (C) *J* (D) *M* (E) *O*

5. If *J* and *K* appear on the third panel, then which of the following professors must appear on the second?

    (A) *G* (B) *H* (C) *I* (D) *L* (E) *O*

6. If *N* and *M* appear on the same panel, and if *H* appears on the first panel, which professors must appear on the third panel?

    (A) *I, J*
    (B) *I, O*
    (C) *J, L*
    (D) *L, G, K*
    (E) *L, K, O*

Questions 7–13

An information processing system consists of seven stations—*M, N, P, Q, R, S*, and *T*. Every request is classified as either normal or priority. Requests for information are processed in the following ways:

All normal requests are received by either *M* or *N*, and all priority requests are received by *M* or *Q*.

All requests processed by *M* are then sent to *T*.

All requests processed by *N* are then sent to *S*.

Normal requests processed by *T* are then sent to *P*; priority requests processed by *T* are then sent to *Q*.

All requests processed by *S* are then sent either to *T* or *P*.

Normal requests processed by *P* are then sent to *Q*, and priority requests processed by *P* are then sent to *R*.

All requests processed by *Q* are then sent to either *P* or *R*.

R is the station which issues a final response.

7. Any of the following can be true EXCEPT

    (A) *M* sends a request to *T*.
    (B) *S* sends a request to *T*.
    (C) *S* sends a request to *P*.
    (D) *S* sends a request to *Q*.
    (E) *Q* sends a request to *P*.

8. A priority request could reach *R* via which of the following sequences?

    (A) *M* to *Q* to *R*.
    (B) *N* to *Q* to *R*
    (C) *N* to *S* to *R*
    (D) *Q* to *P* to *R*
    (E) *P* to *Q* to *R*

9. Any request that is first received by *M* and is finally received by *R* must also have previously been processed by

    I. *T*
    II. *Q*
    III. *P*

    (A) I only (B) III (C) I and II only
    (D) I and III only (E) I, II, and III

10. What is the minimum number of stations that must have processed a normal request *before* the request is sent to *R*?

    (A) 1 (B) 2 (C) 3 (D) 4 (E) 5

11. If a request is processed more than once by the same station, then that station could be

    I. *P*
    II. *Q*
    III. *T*

    (A) I only (B) II only (C) III only
    (D) I and II only (E) I, II, and III

12. If a request is finally processed by *R*, it is possible that which of the following stations did NOT process the request?

    I. *P*
    II. *Q*
    III. *M*

    (A) I only (B) III only (C) I and II only
    (D) I and III only (E) II and III only

13. If a normal request reaches *R*, what is the maximum number of stations through which that request could have passed before reaching *R*?

    (A) 2 (B) 3 (C) 4 (D) 5 (E) 6

Questions 14–19

The president of a college is appointing nine students—*J, K, L, M, N, O, P, Q,* and *R*—to serve on three committees to study three different aspects of student life at the college. There will be a Housing Committee, a Food Service Committee, and a Traffic Committee. Her appointments must respect the following:

Each committee must have exactly three members.
No person can serve on more than one committee.
Q must serve on the Traffic Committee.
L and *M* must serve on the same committee.
J and *K* cannot serve on the same committee.
N cannot serve on the same committee as *R*.
O must serve on the same committee as *K* or *Q* or both *K* and *Q*.

14. Which of the following groups could constitute the Housing Committee?

    (A) *J, K, N*
    (B) *J, M, P*
    (C) *L, Q, N*
    (D) *J, O, P*
    (E) *O, R, K*

15. If *P* is on the Traffic Committee and *K* is on the Food Service Committee, then which of the following must be true?

    (A) *J* is on the Traffic Committee.
    (B) *O* is on the Food Service Committee.
    (C) *R* is on the Food Service Committee.
    (D) *O* is on the Housing Committee.
    (E) *R* is on the Housing Committee.

16. Any of the following could serve on the same committee as *L* EXCEPT

    (A) *J* (B) *K* (C) *O* (D) *P* (E) *Q*

17. If *K* and *P* serve on the Housing Committee, which of the following must serve on the Food Service Committee?

    (A) *J* (B) *M* (C) *N* (D) *O* (E) *R*

18. If *O* serves on the Food Service Committee and *L* serves on the same committee as *Q*, then which of the following must serve on the Housing Committee?

    I. *J*
    II. *P*
    III. *R*

    (A) I only (B) III only (C) I and II only
    (D) II and III only (E) I, II, and III

19. If *J* is assigned to the Food Service Committee and *L* is appointed to the Traffic Committee, then which of the following must be true?

    I. *P* is appointed to the Food Service Committee.
    II. *N* is appointed to the Housing Committee.
    III. *R* is appointed to the Traffic Committee.

    (A) I only (B) III only (C) I and III only
    (D) II and III only (E) I, II, and III

Questions 20–25

The artistic director of a modern dance company is preparing two programs for the company. The two programs will include performances of three new pieces—"Lights," "Adam's Rib," and "Insanity." If a new piece is included on the first program, it cannot be included on the second program; and if a new piece is not included on the first program, it must be included in the following program. There are three exceptions to this general rule:

If all three new pieces are on the first program, then "Insanity" and "Lights" but not "Adam's Rib" must be on the second program.

If "Insanity" and "Lights" are the only new pieces are on the first program, then all three new pieces must be included on the second program.

If "Insanity" is the only new piece on the first program, then both "Insanity" and "Lights" must be on the second program.

20. If "Lights" is the only new piece on the first program, the second program will include

   (A) "Insanity" and "Adam's Rib" but not "Lights"
   (B) "Insanity" and "Lights" but not "Adam's Rib"
   (C) "Adam's Rib" but neither "Insanity" nor "Lights"
   (D) all three new pieces
   (E) none of the three new pieces

21. If the first program includes "Insanity" and "Lights" but not "Adam's Rib," then the second program will include

   (A) "Insanity" but neither "Lights" nor "Adam's Rib"
   (B) "Lights" but neither "Insanity" nor "Adam's Rib"
   (C) "Adam's Rib" but neither "Lights" nor "Insanity"
   (D) "Insanity" and "Adam's Rib" but not "Lights"
   (E) "Insanity," "Lights," and "Adam's Rib"

22. If all three new pieces are included on the second program, which of the following could have been included on the first program?

   I. "Insanity," "Lights," and "Adam's Rib"
   II. "Lights" but neither "Insanity" nor "Adam's Rib"
   III. "Insanity" and "Lights" but not "Adam's Rib"

   (A) I only   (B) III only   (C) I and II only
   (D) I and III only   (E) I, II, and III

23. Which of the following first programs results in a second program for which exactly two of the new pieces are included?

   (A) "Lights" but neither "Insanity" nor "Adam's Rib"
   (B) "Lights" and "Adam's Rib" but not "Insanity"
   (C) "Insanity" and "Adam's Rib" but not "Lights"
   (D) "Insanity" and "Lights" but not "Adam's Rib"
   (E) Neither "Insanity" nor "Lights" nor "Adam's Rib"

24. If "Lights" is the only new piece on the second program, which of the following new pieces must be included on the first program?

   (A) "Insanity," "Lights," and "Adam's Rib"
   (B) "Insanity" and "Adam's Rib" but not "Lights"
   (C) "Lights" but neither "Insanity" nor "Adam's Rib"
   (D) "Adam's Rib" but neither "Insanity" nor "Lights"
   (E) Neither "Insanity" nor "Lights" nor "Adam's Rib"

25. If "Insanity" is not on the second program, then which of the following must be on the first program?

   (A) "Insanity," "Lights," and "Adam's Rib"
   (B) "Insanity" and "Adam's Rib" but not "Lights"
   (C) "Lights" but neither "Insanity" nor "Adam's Rib"
   (D) "Insanity" and "Lights" but not "Adam's Rib"
   (E) "Insanity" but neither "Lights" nor "Adam's Rib"

Questions 26–29

Two safety inspectors, Frank and Gail, must visit seven job sites—J, K, L, M, N, O, and P. Gail will visit four sites, while Frank will visit three. Each site will be visited by one of the two inspectors according to the following restrictions:

K and M must be visited by the same inspector.
L and P cannot be visited by the same inspector.
If Frank visits site N, he cannot visit site L.
If Gail visits site O, she must also visit site J.

26. Which of the following is not a schedule of job sites that Gail could visit?

   (A) J and K
   (B) J and L
   (C) K and O
   (D) K and P
   (E) M and N

27. If Gail visits site O, which of the following must be true?

   (A) Frank visits site J.
   (B) Frank visits site L.
   (C) Frank visits site P.
   (D) Gail visits site N.
   (E) Gail visits site P.

28. If Gail visits site K, which of the following CANNOT be true?

   (A) Frank visits site J.
   (B) Frank visits site P.
   (C) Gail visits site L.
   (D) Gail visits site N.
   (E) Gail visits site O.

29. If Gail visits sites *L* and *O*, then she must visit which of the following sites as well?

   I. *J*
   II. *N*
   III. *M*

   (A) I only (B) III only (C) I and II only
   (D) II and III only (E) I, II, and III

Questions 30–35

A law firm consists of seven partners—Goldman, Hanson, Imperato, Jackson, Katz, Lippman, and Martin. The partners hold frequent but unscheduled meetings. A partners' meeting can be held on Monday, Wednesday, or Friday, and only in either the morning or the afternoon.

   Jackson cannot attend any meetings on Monday.
   Lippman cannot attend any meetings on Wednesday.
   If Imperato attends a meeting, then Katz must also attend that meeting.
   If Goldman attends a meeting, then both Hanson and Martin must also attend that meeting.
   Hanson cannot attend any morning meetings.

30. If all of the partners are to attend a meeting, then it can be held during the afternoon on which of the following days?

   I. Monday
   II. Wednesday
   III. Friday

   (A) I only (B) II only (C) III only
   (D) I and III only (E) II and III only

31. If Goldman attends a meeting on a day other than Friday, which of the following must be true?

   (A) The meeting is held on Monday.
   (B) The meeting is held on Wednesday.
   (C) The meeting is held in the afternoon.
   (D) Katz does not attend the meeting.
   (E) Jackson does not attend the meeting.

32. If a meeting is held that includes Hanson and Lippman but does not include Katz, which of the following could be true?

   (A) The meeting is held on Wednesday.
   (B) The meeting is held on Friday.
   (C) The meeting is held in the morning.
   (D) The meeting is attended by Imperato.
   (E) The meeting is attended by six partners.

33. If a meeting is held Monday morning, which of the following pairs of partners could be in attendance?

   (A) Goldman and Jackson
   (B) Goldman and Lippman
   (C) Hanson and Imperato
   (D) Hanson and Lippman
   (E) Imperato and Martin

34. If a meeting is held during the morning, which of the following partners CANNOT attend?

   (A) Goldman
   (B) Imperato
   (C) Jackson
   (D) Katz
   (E) Martin

35. If Katz is unable to attend a Wednesday morning meeting, what is the largest possible number of partners who can attend?

   (A) 1 (B) 2 (C) 3 (D) 4 (E) 5

Questions 36–38

The executive officer of a college English department is scheduling six sections of Freshman Composition—*M*, *N*, *O*, *P*, *R*, and *S*. She has available first, second, third, and fourth periods on Monday and Thursday. Each section meets once a week. Only one section can be scheduled for any period, and the schedule must be arranged according to the following restrictions.

   Section *O* must be taught on Monday.
   Sections *P* and *S* cannot be scheduled on the same day.
   Section *P* cannot be scheduled either immediately before or immediately after section *N* on the same day.
   Section *R* cannot be scheduled either immediately before or immediately after section *S* on the same day.

36. If section *M* is taught first period on Thursday, section *P* is taught fourth period on Thursday, and section *R* is taught first period on Monday, then none of the six sections can be scheduled for which of the following periods?

   (A) Second period on Monday
   (B) Third period on Monday
   (C) Fourth period on Monday
   (D) Second period on Thursday
   (E) Third period on Thursday

37. If section *P* is taught first period on Thursday and section *R* is taught third period on Monday, then which of the following must be true?

   I. *M* is taught third period on Thursday.
   II. *N* is taught fourth period on Thursday.
   III. *S* is taught first period on Monday.

   (A) I only (B) III only (C) I and II only
   (D) I and III only (E) I, II, and III

38. If *N* is taught first period on Thursday and *R* is taught third period on Thursday, then which of the following must be true?

   (A) *O* is taught second period on Monday.
   (B) *O* is taught fourth period on Monday.
   (C) *S* is taught fourth period on Monday.
   (D) *P* is taught second period on Thursday.
   (E) *P* is taught fourth period on Thursday.

Questions 39–45

The manager of a furniture store is scheduling part-time employees for a special holiday sale. The employees are Ann, Bob, Charles, Diane, Edward, Fred, and Gloria. The workday is divided into a morning and an afternoon shift. Exactly three employees will work each shift. No part-time employee can work both the morning and the afternoon shifts.

If Diane works the morning shift, then Bob must work the afternoon shift.

If Ann works the morning shift, then Edward must work the afternoon shift.

Edward will not work on the same shift as Charles.

Fred will not work on the same shift as Bob.

39. Which of the following is an acceptable work schedule?

	(A)	(B)	(C)	(D)	(E)
Morning	Ann	Ann	Bob	Charles	Charles
	Bob	Diane	Edward	Diane	Diane
	Gloria	Edward	Fred	Edward	Gloria
After-	Diane	Bob	Ann	Ann	Ann
noon	Edward	Charles	Diane	Bob	Bob
	Fred	Fred	Charles	Gloria	Fred

40. Which of the following is NOT a permissible work schedule for the morning shift?

(A) Bob, Diane, and Gloria
(B) Bob, Ann, and Gloria
(C) Bob, Edward, and Gloria
(D) Charles, Diane, and Gloria
(E) Diane, Fred, and Edward

41. If Ann and Diane work the morning shift, the afternoon shift must consist of which of the following?

(A) Bob, Charles, and Fred
(B) Bob, Edward, and Fred
(C) Bob, Edward, and Gloria
(D) Charles, Edward, and Fred
(E) Fred, Edward, and Gloria

42. If Ann works the morning shift, any of the following could work the afternoon shift EXCEPT

(A) Bob   (B) Charles   (C) Diane
(D) Edward   (E) Gloria

43. If Diane works the morning shift, which of the following must be true?

(A) Charles works the morning shift.
(B) Fred works the morning shift.
(C) Gloria works the afternoon shift.
(D) Ann does not work the morning shift.
(E) Fred does not work the afternoon shift.

44. If Charles works the afternoon shift, which of the following must be true?

(A) Ann does not work the morning shift.
(B) Bob does not work the morning shift.
(C) Diane does not work the morning shift.
(D) Edward does not work the morning shift.
(E) Fred does not work the afternoon shift.

45. If Charles does not work on a day when both Ann and Diane work the morning shift, then which of the following must be true?

I. Fred works the morning shift.
II. Gloria works the afternoon shift.
III. Bob works the morning shift.

(A) I only   (B) II only   (C) I and II only
(D) I and III only   (E) I, II, and III

Questions 46–51

A group of mountain villages is connected by a network of roads. It is possible to go

From S to T only
From T to U or V only
From U to Z or S only
From V to X only
From X to Y only
From Z to T or Y only

These are the only roads that connect the towns.

46. From which of the towns is it impossible to get to another of the towns?

(A) S   (B) T   (C) X   (D) Y   (E) Z

47. For how many of the towns is it possible to leave the town and still come back to that town?

(A) 0   (B) 1   (C) 2   (D) 3   (E) 4

48. A traveler who wishes to travel from U to V must pass through

(A) S   (B) T   (C) V   (D) X   (E) Z

49. If a traveler wishes to go from Z to X, how many other towns must he pass through en route?

(A) 1   (B) 2   (C) 3   (D) 4   (E) 5

50. From U, it is possible to get to how many other towns?

(A) 2   (B) 3   (C) 4   (D) 5   (E) 6

51. If the road from S to T is closed, then it is still possible to get to X from which of the following towns?

I. Z
II. U
III. T

(A) I only   (B) II only   (C) III only
(D) I and III only   (E) I, II, and III only

Questions 52–57

Three children—Bob, Charles, and Diane—and three adults—Ron, Stan, and Tim—are at an amusement park. The park is closing and there is time for only one more ride. The children can choose from among four rides—the roller coaster, the ferris wheel, the bumper cars, and the boat ride.

Each child will go on one ride.

Each child must be accompanied by an adult, and an adult can be responsible for only one child.

Ron will not go on the roller coaster or the ferris wheel.

Bob must go on either the roller coaster or the ferris wheel.

52. Which of the following must be true?

   (A) Bob goes on the bumper cars.
   (B) Bob goes on the boat ride.
   (C) Ron goes on the roller coaster.
   (D) Every adult goes on a ride.
   (E) The children do not all go on different rides.

53. Which of the following groups of four persons could go on the ferris wheel together?

   I. Bob, Charles, Diane, and Tim
   II. Bob, Diane, Stan, and Tim
   III. Charles, Diane, Stan, and Tim

   (A) I only   (B) II only   (C) III only
   (D) I and III only   (E) I, II, and III

54. If Tim goes on the boat ride, then Stan must go on a ride with

   (A) Bob   (B) Charles   (C) Diane
   (D) Tim   (E) Ron

55. The largest possible number of people from the group who could go on the roller coaster is

   (A) 2   (B) 3   (C) 4   (D) 5   (E) 6

56. If Stan goes on the boat ride, then all of the following could be true EXCEPT

   (A) Diane goes on the roller coaster.
   (B) Tim goes on the ferris wheel.
   (C) Bob goes on the ferris wheel.
   (D) Ron goes on the boat ride.
   (E) Charles goes on the boat ride.

57. If Stan accompanies Bob on a ride, then all of the following could be true EXCEPT

   (A) Stan goes on the boat ride.
   (B) Tim goes on the ferris wheel.
   (C) Tim goes on the roller coaster.
   (D) Charles goes on the same ride as Bob.
   (E) Diana goes on the same ride as Tim.

Questions 58–63

The board of a certain game consists of eight positions. Each position is indicated by a circle of a different color—red, orange, yellow, green, blue, black, white, and purple. Each player in turn throws a fair, evenly balanced die with faces numbered 1 through 6. A player must move his token from one colored circle to another until he has made the precise number of moves indicated on the die. A player may, if he chooses, return to a colored circle more than once during his turn. The only moves possible on the board are the following.

A player can move:

From blue to red or green, and from red and green to blue;

From red to green, and from green to red;

From red to yellow or orange, and from yellow and orange to red;

From yellow to orange, and from orange to yellow, and from yellow to white;

From green to black or purple, and from black and purple to green;

From orange to green, and from green to orange.

58. All of the following are possible series of moves for a player whose token is on the yellow circle at the beginning of his turn and rolls a two EXCEPT

   (A) White, yellow
   (B) Orange, yellow
   (C) Red, orange
   (D) Red, green
   (E) Orange, green

59. Which of the following is a possible series of moves for a player whose token is on the blue circle at the beginning of his turn and rolls a four?

   (A) Red, green, yellow, white
   (B) Red, green, orange, blue
   (C) Red, yellow, orange, purple
   (D) Green, purple, red, orange
   (E) Green, orange, yellow, red

60. If a player's token is on the purple circle at the beginning of his turn, what is the minimum number he must roll on the die if he wants to move to the yellow circle on that turn?

   (A) 1   (B) 2   (C) 3   (D) 4   (E) 5

61. If a player whose token is on the green circle at the beginning of his turn rolls a one on the die, which of the following is a complete and accurate listing of the circles on which the token could rest at the end of the turn?

   (A) Blue
   (B) Blue, red
   (C) Blue, red, black
   (D) Blue, red, black, purple
   (E) Blue, red, black, purple, orange

62. If a player whose token is on the yellow circle at the beginning of his turn rolls a two on the die, which of the following is a complete and accurate listing of the circles on which the token could rest at the end of the turn?

(A) Red, orange
(B) Red, yellow, blue
(C) Red, orange, blue, orange
(D) Red, orange, blue, green
(E) Red, orange, blue, green, yellow

63. If a player whose token is on the black circle at the beginning of his turn rolls a three and the player does not move to any circle more than once during the turn, which of the following is a complete and accurate listing of the circles on which his token could rest at the end of the turn?

(A) Blue, red
(B) Blue, red, orange
(C) Blue, red, yellow, orange
(D) Blue, red, orange, green
(E) Blue, red, orange, green, purple

Questions 64–67

During the academic year, a professor will teach one course in American literature in the fall semester and one in the spring semester. In each course, he teaches the works of exactly three of five authors—Hawthorne, Crane, Melville, Twain, and Wolfe. The professor selects the authors according to the following considerations:

If he teaches Melville in a course, he also teaches Wolfe.

If he teaches Hawthorne one semester, he does not teach Hawthorne the following semester.

In the spring semester, he teaches no more than one of the authors taught in the fall semester.

64. If the professor teaches Melville, Wolfe, and Hawthorne in the fall semester, which of the group of authors must he teach in the spring semester?

(A) Twain, Crane, and Hawthorne
(B) Twain, Crane, and Wolfe
(C) Twain, Crane, and Melville
(D) Melville, Twain, and Wolfe
(E) Melville, Hawthorne, and Twain

65. Which of the following is a possible sequence of course offerings?

	Fall	Spring
(A)	Crane, Melville, Wolfe	Wolfe, Twain, Hawthorne
(B)	Hawthorne, Melville, Wolfe	Melville, Wolfe, Twain
(C)	Melville, Hawthorne, Crane	Twain, Wolfe, Crane
(D)	Twain, Crane, Hawthorne	Hawthorne, Melville, Wolfe
(E)	Twain, Hawthorne, Wolfe	Wolfe, Melville, Twain

66. If the professor plans to teach Melville, Wolfe, and Twain in the fall semester and Twain in the spring semester, what other two authors must he teach in the spring semester?

(A) Hawthorne and Crane
(B) Melville and Wolfe
(C) Melville and Crane
(D) Wolfe and Crane
(E) Wolfe and Hawthorne

67. If the professor plans to teach Hawthorne and Melville in the spring semester, which authors must he teach in the fall semester?

(A) Wolfe, Hawthorne, and Crane
(B) Wolfe, Crane, and Twain
(C) Melville, Wolfe, and Twain
(D) Melville, Wolfe, and Crane
(E) Crane, Hawthorne, and Twain

Questions 68–73

The president of a college must appoint five persons to serve on an advisory committee. The candidates she is considering include three students—J, K, and L—and five teachers—M, N, O, P, and Q.

The committee must include two students and three teachers.

K and Q cannot both be appointed to the committee.
P and O cannot both be appointed to the committee.
N and Q cannot both be appointed to the committee.

68. Which of the following is an acceptable committee?

(A) J, K, O, M, N
(B) K, L, P, N, O
(C) K, L, O, M, J
(D) L, M, N, Q, J
(E) L, N, Q, K, P

69. Which of the candidates must be appointed to the committee?

(A) J   (B) L   (C) M   (D) O   (E) Q

70. If K is appointed to the committee, which of the following must also be appointed to the committee?

(A) J   (B) L   (C) N   (D) O   (E) P

71. If L is NOT appointed to the committee, then any of the following could be appointed EXCEPT

(A) M   (B) N   (C) O   (D) P   (E) Q

72. If Q is appointed to the committee, then which of the following pairs of candidates must also be appointed to the committee?

(A) J and K   (B) J and L   (C) L and K
(D) M and O   (E) M and P

73. For every possible acceptable committee, which of the following replacements will always result in another acceptable committee?

    (A) K for J
    (B) K for L
    (C) O for N
    (D) O for P
    (E) Q for O

Questions 74–79

A car manufacturer offers six different car models, each equipped with different options.

Model P comes equipped with automatic transmission, sun roof, and stereo system.

Model Q comes equipped with air conditioning, automatic transmission, sun roof, and stereo system.

Model R comes equipped with air conditioning, automatic transmission, bucket seats, sun roof, and stereo system.

Model S comes equipped with automatic transmission, bucket seats, and sun roof.

Model T comes equipped with air conditioning, bucket seats, and stereo system.

Model U comes equipped with automatic transmission and stereo system.

74. How many of the six models come equipped with bucket seats?

    (A) 2   (B) 3   (C) 4   (D) 5   (E) 6

75. How many of the six models come equipped with both air conditioning and a sun roof?

    (A) 0   (B) 1   (C) 2   (D) 3   (E) 4

76. How many of the six models come equipped with bucket seats but not with a sun roof?

    (A) 0   (B) 1   (C) 2   (D) 3   (E) 4

77. If a car comes equipped with air conditioning but not bucket seats, it is model

    (A) P (B) Q (C) R (D) S (E) T

78. If a car is equipped with neither sun roof nor automatic transmission, then it is model

    (A) P (B) R (C) S (D) T (E) U

79. If a car is equipped with stereo system but no air conditioning, then knowing whether the car is equipped with which of the following options is sufficient to determine the model of the car?

    I. Sun roof
    II. Automatic transmission
    III. Bucket seats

    (A) I only   (B) I and II only   (C) I and III only
    (D) II and III only   (E) I, II, and III

Questions 80–85

The dispatcher of a commuter bus service must assign five of seven commuters—J, K, L, M, N, O, and P—to seats in a van. The van has three rows of two seats. The company's driver, X, sits in the first row, and the remaining seats must be assigned according to the following conditions:

Only J, K, L, and N can sit in the first row.
Only J, K, L, M, and P can sit in the second row.
Only K, L, P, and O can sit in the third row.
J will not ride in the van with K.
M will not ride in the van with O.

80. Which of the following is an acceptable assignment of seats?

	First Row	Second Row	Third Row
(A)	X,J	K,M	P,O
(B)	X,N	J,L	O,P
(C)	X,K	M,J	L,P
(D)	X,L	J,K	P,O
(E)	X,N	J,M	O,P

81. Which of the following must be assigned to the van?

    I. J
    II. L
    III. N

    (A) I only   (B) III only   (C) I and II only
    (D) I and III only   (E) II and III only

82. If K is assigned to the third row, which commuter must sit in the same row as the driver?

    (A) J (B) L (C) M (D) N (E) P

83. If K and O are assigned to the third row, then who must sit in the same row as the driver?

    (A) J (B) L (C) M (D) N (E) P

84. If L and P are assigned to the third row, how many different groups of commuters can the dispatcher assign to the van?

    (A) 1   (B) 2   (C) 3   (D) 4   (E) 5

85. If P and O are assigned to the third row, which of the following provides a complete and accurate list of commuters who could be assigned to the first row?

    (A) N
    (B) L,N
    (C) J,K,L
    (D) J,K,N
    (E) J,K,L,N

Questions 86–90

The director of an opera company is considering five works—*J*, *K*, *L*, *M*, and *N*—for the opening night performance of the company's upcoming season. Each opera requires a tenor lead and a soprano lead. Only three sopranos—Betty, Carol, and Doris—and five tenors—John, Kelly, Mike, Orin, and Paul—are available for the leads on opening night. Each soprano can sing any lead, but the tenors can only sing according to the following conditions.

John can sing *J*, *K*, and *L* but only if Betty is not the soprano.

Kelly can sing *J* but only if Betty is the soprano and *L* and *N* but only if Carol is the soprano.

Mike can sing all five operas, but he can only sing *J* and *K* if Carol is the soprano, *L* and *M* only if Betty is the soprano, and *N* only if Doris is the soprano.

Orin can sing *J* and *L* but only if Betty is not the soprano.

Paul can sing *K* but only if Carol is not the soprano.

86. Which of the following is a complete and accurate listing of the tenors who can sing *J* if Doris is the soprano?

   (A) John
   (B) John, Kelly
   (C) John, Orin
   (D) Mike, Orin
   (E) Mike, Paul

87. Which of the following is a complete and accurate listing of the tenors who can sing *L* if Carol is the soprano?

   (A) John
   (B) John, Kelly
   (C) John, Kelly, Mike
   (D) John, Kelly, Orin
   (E) John, Kelly, Orin, Paul

88. If the director wishes to perform *N*, then the tenor and soprano must be

   (A) John and Carol
   (B) John and Doris
   (C) Mike and Betty
   (D) Mike and Carol
   (E) Mike and Doris

89. If Doris is chosen to sing the soprano role in *K*, then the tenor could be

   I. John
   II. Mike
   III. Paul

   (A) I only   (B) II only   (C) I and III Only
   (D) II and III only   (E) I, II, and III

90. If the director wishes to perform *N*, then which of the following could sing the soprano part?

   I. Betty
   II. Carol
   III. Doris

   (A) I only   (B) II only   (C) I and II only
   (D) II and III only   (E) I, II, and III

Explanatory Answers

Questions 1–6

Summarize the information:

$I = N$
$K = L$
$O \ne J$
$M = 2$
$(J \lor M) \lor \text{Both} = H$

Now attack the questions.

1. **(D)** Screen choices using the initial conditions. I must appear with N, so we eliminate (C) and (E). Then, K must appear with L, so we eliminate (A). Finally, J or M must be with H, so we eliminate (B). (D), therefore, must be the correct response.

2. **(D)** The last condition requires that either J or M or both appear with H. M is on panel 2. If J is assigned to panel one, and H to panel 3, then neither J nor M appears with H.

3. **(E)** I cannot be assigned to a panel without N, so (E) violates one of the initial conditions.

4. **(B)** The second condition requires that K and L appear together, so any panel on which K appears must consist of K and L and a third person. I cannot be this third person because the first condition requires that I appear with N. (Each panel has only three participants.)

5. **(B)** Here you may want to use a diagram to keep track of the deductions:

1	2	3
	M	J,K

   Since K appears on panel 3, L too must appear on that panel:

1	2	3
	M	JKL

   H must appear with M on panel 2:

1	2	3
	MH	JKL

   But I and N must be on the same panel:

1	2	3
IN	MH	JKL

   As for the other two professors, they could appear on either one or two. So we know only that H must appear on the second panel.

6. (E) Again, you will probably need a diagram to keep track of the logic:

         1   2   3
         H   MN

I and *N* must appear together:

         1   2   3
         H   MNI

And *K* and *L* must be on the same panel, but that panel cannot be panel one (otherwise *H* would appear without *J* or *M*):

         1   2   3
         H   MNI   KL

Then, *H* must appear with *J*:

         1   2   3
         HJ   MNI   KL

Since *O* cannot appear with *J*, we can determine the participants of each panel:

         1   2   3
         HJG   MNI   KLO

Our diagram shows that the third panel consists of *K*, *L*, and *O*.

Questions 7–13

This is a "network" set. Begin by drawing the diagram:

All normal requests are received by either *M* or *N*, and all priority requests are received by *M* or *Q*:

    NORMAL   M
                  N

    PRIORITY   M
                  Q

All requests processed by *M* are then sent to *T*:

    NORMAL   M → T
                  N

    PRIORITY   M → T
                  Q

All requests processed by *N* are sent to *S*:

    NORMAL   M → T
                  N → S

    PRIORITY   M → T
                  Q

Normal requests processed by T are then sent to P; priority requests processed by T are then sent to Q:

NORMAL $M \rightarrow T \rightarrow P$

            $N \rightarrow S$

PRIORITY $M \rightarrow T$

            $Q \swarrow$

All requests processed by S are then sent either to T or P:

NORMAL $M \rightarrow T \rightarrow P$

            $N \rightarrow S$

PRIORITY $M \rightarrow T$

            $Q \swarrow$

Normal requests processed by P are then sent to Q, and priority requests processed by P are then sent to R:

NORMAL $M \rightarrow T \rightarrow P \rightarrow Q$

            $N \rightarrow S$

PRIORITY $M \rightarrow T \qquad R$

            $Q \swarrow \qquad P$

All requests processed by Q are then sent to either P or R:

NORMAL $M \rightarrow T \rightarrow P \leftrightarrows Q \rightarrow R$

            $N \rightarrow S$

PRIORITY $M \rightarrow T \rightarrow R$

            $Q \rightarrow P$

7. (D) The diagram shows that S cannot send a request to Q, though he can send one to P, who in turn can send one to Q.

8. (D) The diagram shows that Q can forward a request to P, who in turn can forward it to R.

9. (C) A normal request received by M must be processed by T, P, and Q before it goes to R. A priority request received by M must go to both T and Q but need not go to P before it is passed to R. Q can forward a priority request directly to R.

10. (D) The two shortest routes to R for normal requests are: $M\ T\ P\ Q\ R$ and $N\ S\ P\ Q\ R$. In each case, a minimum of four stations must handle the request before it gets to R.

11. (D) A normal request can be shuffled back and forth between P and Q any number of times. T, however, is not within such a loop.

12. (D) Everything *R* receives must at some point have passed through station *Q*, so II is not part of the correct answer. There are certain requests, however, that *P* does not handle, namely, those priority requests forwarded by *Q* directly to *R*. Also, there are certain requests that *M* does not handle—namely, those normal requests that begin with *N* and those priority requests that begin with *Q*.

13. (D) A normal request that enters at *N* and passes to *S*, at which point it could pass to *T*, then to *P*, and then to *Q* (or five stations) before reaching *R*.

Questions 14–19

Here is another selection set. Begin by summarizing the information:

Q = Traffic
L = M
J ≠ K
N ≠ R
O = K or Q or both

14. (E) Using the first condition, that *Q* serves on the Traffic Committee, we eliminate (C). Using the second condition, that *L* and *M* must serve together, we eliminate (B). Using the third condition, that *J* and *K* cannot serve together n a committee, we eliminate (A). Finally, using that last condition, that *O* must serve with either *K* or *Q* (or both), we eliminate (D). By the process of elimination, therefore, the only acceptable committee listed is (E).

15. (B) You may want to diagram this:

```
FS          T          H
K           QP
```

Next, try placing *L* and *M* together. If you put *L* and *M* on the Food Services Committee, then *O* must be on the Traffic Committee (to respect the last condition), which places both *N* and *R* on the Housing Committee—in violation of the third condition. Since *L* and *M* cannot go to the Food Service Committee, they must go to the Housing Committee:

```
FS          T          H
K           QP         LM
```

Next, if *O* is assigned to the Traffic Committee, then *J* must be assigned to the Housing Committee. But that would result in both *N* and *R* on the Food Service Committee:

```
FS          T          H
K(NR)       QPO        LMJ (impossible)
```

Therefore *O* must be assigned to the Food Service Committee. The remaining individuals can be assigned in several ways.

16. (C) If *L* is on a committee, then *M* is also on that committee. This means that two members of the committee have already been assigned. *O* cannot be assigned to this committee because *O* must be assigned to one with either *K* or *Q* or both.

17. (B) This one you may want to diagram:

```
    T          FS         H
    Q                     KP
```

L and *M* must be appointed either to the Traffic Committee or to the Food Services Committee. Take the first alternative:

```
    T          FS         H
    QLM                   KP
```

So *O* must be assigned to the Housing Committee:

```
    T          FS         H
    QLM                   KPO
```

But now we cannot separate *N* and *R*. So we try the second alternative:

```
    T          FS         H
    Q          LM         KPO
```

N and *R* cannot serve on the same committee:

```
    T          FS         H
  Q N/R     LM N/R      KPO
```

So *J* must be assigned to the Traffic Committee:

```
    T          FS         H
 Q J N/R    LM N/R       KPO
```

18. (C) Again, we will use a diagram:

```
    T          FS         H
    QL         O
```

Of course *M* must serve with *L*, which means that *K* must serve with *O*:

```
    T          FS         H
    QLM        OK
```

This means *J* must serve on the Housing Committee; *N* and *R* must be appointed one to the Food Services Committee and one to the Housing Committee; and *P* is appointed to the Housing Committee:

```
    T          FS         H
    QLM        OK         JP
               N/R        N/R
```

So statements I and II are necessarily true, while III is only possibly true.

19. (A) Enter the information on a diagram:

```
    T          FS         H
    QL         J
```

So *M* must also be appointed to Traffic (filling up that committee), and *K* must be appointed to Housing (*J* and *K* cannot be together):

```
    T          FS         H
    QLM        J          K
```

So O must be appointed to Housing (to be with K), and N and R must be appointed one to Housing and the other to Food Services, with P being appointed to Food Services:

```
  T        FS        H
 QLM       JP       KO
           N/R      N/R
```

So only statement I is necessarily true.

Questions 20–25

This is a selection set. Begin by summarizing the information:

Off/On or On/Off
$(I + L + A) \rightarrow (I + L)$
$(I + L) \rightarrow (I + L + A)$
$I \rightarrow (I + L)$

The general rule here is "off/on," that is, if a piece is included on a program, it is not included on the following program and vice versa. Then there are the three exceptions to the general rule.

20. (A) An L-only program is not one of the exceptions to the general rule, so the general rule must govern here: if L is on a program and I and A are not, then the next program must include I and A but not L.

21. (E) A program that includes only I and L is the second of the three exceptions to the general rule. The next program must include all three pieces.

22. (B) There are two circumstances in which all three pieces could be included on the second program: (1) under the general rule, when none of the pieces was included on the first (so all three must be included on the second), and (2) under the second exception to the general rule, when only I and L were included on the first. The second possibility is described by statement III.

23. (A) There are three circumstances in which the second program will include two new pieces: (1) under the general rule, when only one new piece was included on the first program, (2) under the first exception, when I, L, and A are included on the first program, and (3) under the third exception, when only I is included on the first program. (A), and only (A), describes one of these circumstances.

24. (B) A second program including L is not one of the three exceptions to the general rule. So if L is the only new piece on the second program, it can only be by virtue of the general rule. So I and A were on the first program but L was not, as correctly stated by (B).

25. (B) If I is not on the second program, then none of the three exceptions govern the situation. (Under all three exceptions, I is on the later program.) This must mean that I was on the first program. But what about the other pieces? If I alone were included on the first program, then the third exception would govern, so I would have been included with one or both of the other pieces. The possibilities are: $(I + A)$, $(I + L)$, and $(I + A + L)$. The second and third, however, are the second and first exceptions to the general rule and would have resulted in a different second program. So the first program must have consisted of I and A.

Questions 26-29

26. (C) You might try screening choices by using each initial condition, but you won't be able to eliminate any pair on that basis. So you must see how the initial conditions work together with each choice:

As for (A), if Gail visits *K*, she must visit *M*. Since *L* and *P* cannot be visited by the same inspector, she must visit one of those sites. If Gail visits *J*, *K*, *M*, and either *L* or *P*, then Frank visits *N* and *O*. Since Frank visits *O*, he cannot visit *L*:

Gail	Frank
JKML	NOP

So it is possible for Gail to visit *J* and *K*. (**Note**: That last condition states that if Gail visits *O*, she must visit *J*. It does not mean if Gail visits *J*, she must visit *O*.)

As for (B), if Gail visits *J* and *L*, then she could also visit *K* and *M*, in which case Frank would visit *N*, *O*, and *P*, a schedule which we have just shown to be possible.

As for (C), if Gail visits *K*, then she must also visit *M*; and if she visits *O*, she must also visit *J*. Gail must also visit either *L* or *P*, for a total of five sites (in violation of the initial conditions). So Gail cannot visit both *K* and *O*.

As for (D), Gail can visit *K*, *M*, *P*, and *N*, while Frank visits *J*, *O*, and *L*.

As for (E), Gail can visit *M*, *K*, *N*, and *L*, while Frank visits *J*, *O*, and *P*.

27. (D) If Gail visits *O*, then she must also visit *J* and we know that she must visit either *L* or *P*, which means she cannot visit *K* and *M*. (That would bring to five the total number of her visits). Thus, we have:

Gail	Frank
OJ	KM
L/P	L/P

N must be on Gail's schedule:

Gail	Frank
OJN	KM
L/P	L/P

Although we cannot definitely fix *L* and *P*, we have sufficient information to answer the question: Gail visits *N*.

28. (E) If Gail visits *K*, then she must also visit *M* and either *L* or *P*. This means she cannot visit *O*, for that would commit her to visiting *J* as well—a total of five sites. Thus, Frank must visit *O*:

Gail	Frank
KM	O
L/P	L/P

The other sites, *J* and *N*, must be divided between Gail and Frank:

Gail	Frank
KM	O
L/P	L/P
J/N	J/N

Thus, our diagram shows that (A), (B), (C), and (D) are possible, but (E) is not.

29. (C) If Gail visits L and O, then she must also visit J, and this means that Frank will visit the pair K and M (otherwise, Gail would have too many sites on her schedule) and P (P and L cannot be visited by the same inspector):

Gail	Frank
LOJ	*KMP*

This means that Gail will visit N:

Gail	Frank
LOJN	*KMP*

(Gail visits four sites, but Frank visits only three.)

Questions 30–35

Although this set uses days of the week, it actually is a selection set: individuals are not arranged in relationships of earlier and later or before and after. Summarize the information:

$$J \neq \text{Mon.}$$
$$L \neq \text{Wed.}$$
$$I \supset K$$
$$G \supset (H + M)$$
$$H \neq \text{a.m.}$$

30. (C) J cannot attend on Monday. L cannot attend on Wednesday. The only day all partners could attend would be Friday (and that would be in the afternoon).

31. (C) The only restriction on Goldman is that if he attends a meeting, so do Hanson and Martin. The only restriction of either of those partners is that Hanson cannot attend a morning meeting. Thus, the only restriction on a meeting attended by Goldman on a day other than Friday is that it be on a Monday or Wednesday afternoon.

32. (B) If the meeting is attended by Lippman then it could be held either on Monday or Friday—but not on Wednesday. So (B) is correct and (A) is wrong. If Hanson is in attendance, then the meeting cannot be held in the morning, so (C) is wrong. Finally, if Katz is not at the meeting, then Imperato cannot be at the meeting, and the maximum number of partners who could attend would be five. So (D) and (E) are incorrect.

33. (E) Since the meeting is held on Monday, Jackson cannot attend, and (A) is wrong. Since the meeting is held in the morning, Hanson cannot attend and (C) and (D) are wrong. Further, since Goldman can attend only if Hanson also attends, Goldman cannot attend, and (B) is wrong.

34. (A) Since Hanson cannot attend a morning meeting, and since Goldman's presence is contingent upon Hanson's, Goldman cannot attend a morning meeting.

35. (B) Since the meeting is on Wednesday, Lippman cannot attend. Since it is in the morning, neither Hanson nor Goldman can attend. Since Katz cannot attend, Imperato does not attend. This leaves only two partners to attend: Jackson and Martin.

Questions 36–38

This is a scheduling set. Start by summarizing the information:

O = Mon.
P not same day as S
P ≠ N
R ≠ S

36. (E) There is a lot of additional information here, so use a diagram to keep track of it:

```
              1    2    3    4
Mon.          R
Thurs.        M              P
```

Since P is taught Thursday, S must be taught with O on Monday, though in what period is not clear. It is possible, however, to fill any of the open periods on Monday:

```
              1    2    3    4
Mon.          R    O    S
OR            R    O         S
```

(among others). The one remaining subject is N. N can be taught either Monday or Thursday. But if N is taught Thursday, it cannot come immediately before P. So third period on Thursday will be open.

37. (B) If P is taught on Thursday, then S is taught on Monday along with O. If R is scheduled for third period on Monday, then S must be scheduled for first period Monday. No further conclusions can be drawn. So only III is necessarily true.

38. (E) Enter the information on a diagram:

```
              1    2    3    4
Mon.                       O
Thurs.        N       R
```

Since R is scheduled for third period on Thursday, S must be scheduled for some time on Monday, which means that P must be scheduled for Thursday. P cannot, however, be scheduled immediately after N, so P must be scheduled for fourth period on Thursday. There are no further conclusions to be drawn, but this is sufficient to determine that (E) must be true.

Questions 39–45

This is a selection set. Begin by summarizing the initial conditions:

D (a.m.)   B (p.m.)
A (a.m.)   E (p.m.)
E ≠ C
F ≠ B

There don't appear to be any further obvious conclusions to be drawn, so go to the questions.

39. (A) Since this item does not provide any additional information, just use the initial conditions to screen choices. The second condition eliminates (B). The third condition eliminates (D). And the fourth condition eliminates (C) and (E). Only (A) is consistent with all four conditions.

40. (A) Again, you test each choice by the initial conditions. As for (A), if *D* works the morning shift, then *B* must work the afternoon shift, and that means that *B* cannot work the morning shift. (No one can work two shifts.) The remaining choices respect the initial conditions. For example:

	a.m.	p.m.
(B)	B,A,G	E,F,D
(C)	B,E,G	A,D,C
(D)	C,D,G	B,A,E
(E)	D,F,E	B,G,A

You can check these against all of the initial conditions.

41. (C) This question provides some additional information. If *A* and *D* both work in the morning, then *E* and *B* must both work that afternoon. Given that *E* will not work with *C* and that *B* will not work with *F*, the third person (who is the only other worker) must be *G*.

42. (B) If *A* works the morning shift, then *E* must work the afternoon shift. This means, however, that *C* cannot work the afternoon shift because of the third condition.

43. (E) If *D* works the morning shift, then *B* must work the afternoon shift. And if *B* works the afternoon shift, then *F* cannot work the afternoon shift.

44. (A) If *C* works the afternoon shift, then *E* cannot work that shift. And if *E* does not work the afternoon shift, then *A* cannot work the morning shift.

45. (C) If *A* and *D* work the morning shift, then both *B* and *E* must work the afternoon shift. Since *B* does not work with *F*, and since it is stipulated that *C* does not work at all on this day, the third person of the afternoon shift must be *G*. Since *C* does not work at all that day, *F*—the only remaining worker—must work the morning shift. Thus, I and II are necessarily true.

Questions 46–51
This is a network set. Create a diagram to display the connections between the individuals:
From *S* to *T* only

$$S \rightarrow T$$

From *T* to *U* or *V* only

$$S \rightarrow T \nearrow^{U}_{\searrow V}$$

From *U* to *Z* or *S* only

$$S \overset{\longleftarrow}{\longrightarrow} T \nearrow U \rightarrow Z \searrow_{V}$$

From *V* to *X* only

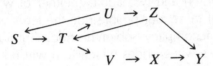

From *X* to *Y* only

$$S \xleftarrow{\quad} \rightarrow T \nearrow U \rightarrow Z$$
$$\searrow V \rightarrow X \rightarrow Y$$

From *Z* to *T* or *Y* only

With a set like this, there are no further conclusions to be drawn. Anything that you need to know is already included in the diagram.

46. (D) The arrows in the diagram show that two roads lead into *Y* but none leaves *Y*. Every other town has at least one road that leads away from it.

47. (E) If you leave *S* and go to *T*, you can then go to *U* and back to *S* or to *Z* and from there back to *T*. Thus, it is possible to create a loop for any of these four towns. Once, however, you leave *V*, you are bound for *X*, and if you leave *X*, you must go to *Y*. And it is impossible to leave from *Y*.

48. (B) There are two ways to get from *U* to *V*. You can go from *U* to *S*, from *S* to *T*, and from *T* to *V*. Or you can go from *U* to *Z*, from *Z* to *T*, and from *T* to *V*. *T*, and only *T*, is common to both of these routes.

49. (B) To get from *Z* to *X*, you must first go through *T*, then through *V*, and from there to *X*. Thus, you will pass through two towns en route from *Z* to *X*.

50. (E) As the diagram shows, from *U* you can get to every other town.

51. (E) Even without a road from *S* to *T*, you can get to *X* from *Z* by going through *T* and *V*. So item I is part of the correct answer, and you should eliminate choices (B) and (C). You can still get to *X* from *U* by going first to *Z* and taking the same route. So II is also part of the correct choice. Eliminate (A) and (D). Finally, you can, of course, go from *T* to *X* via *V*.

Questions 52–57

This is a selection set. Begin by summarizing the initial conditions:

  R ≠ *RC* or *FW* (Ron does not go on the roller coaster or the ferris wheel.)
  B = *RC* or *FW* (Bob goes on either the roller coaster or the ferris wheel.)

There is one further conclusion you can draw. Given that all three children will go on one more ride and that each child must be accompanied by an adult, one of the children must be accompanied by Ron—on either the bumper cars or the boat ride. Now attack the questions.

52. (D) This question does not provide any additional information, so you have to be able to answer it using just the initial conditions. The initial conditions do not specify a ride for any child, so (A), (B) and (C) must be wrong. (D), however, is a general conclusion inferable from the initial conditions. Since each child goes on a ride, and since each child is accompanied by an adult, each adult must go on a ride. Finally, as for (E), it is possible for all of the children to go on different rides:

Ferris Wheel: Bob and Stan
Roller Coaster: Charles and Tim
Boat Ride: Diana and Ron

53. (B) Check each statement against the initial conditions. I is not a possible combination of people for the ferris wheel, because the group contains three children and only one adult. II is a possible combination for the ferris wheel. It includes two children and two adults (neither of whom is Ron). III is not a possible group. If these four people ride the ferris wheel, then Ron, the only other adult, must accompany Bob on his ride. But Bob goes on either the roller coaster or the ferris wheel, rides which Ron will not go on.

54. (A) Given that Ron cannot accompany Bob, if Tim goes on the boat ride, then Stan (the third adult) must accompany Bob.

55. (C) Since Ron will not ride the roller coaster, Ron and one of the three children will ride either the boat ride or the bumper cars. Bob and the remaining child, accompanied by Stan and Tim, can ride the roller coaster. So the maximum number of people from the group who could ride the roller coaster is 4.

56. (A) Use the additional information provided by this question stem to draw further conclusions. If Stan goes on the boat ride, then neither Stan nor Ron can accompany Bob. This means that Tim must accompany Bob. Further, one child must go with Stan on the boat ride, and the other with Ron on either the boat ride or the bumper cars. Thus (B) and (C) are possible—if Bob decides to go on the ferris wheel. (D) and (E) are also possible, for both Diane and Charles could choose the boat ride, in which case, Ron and Stan would both go on the boat ride as well. Diane cannot, however, go on the roller coaster, for there is no adult to accompany her on that ride.

57. (A) Since Bob will go on either the ferris wheel or the roller coaster, if Stan accompanies Bob, Stan does not go on the boat ride. The other choices are possible, and you confirm this by creating examples.

Questions 58–63

This is a network problem. Use arrows to show the possible moves. First, from blue to green or red and vice versa:

From red to green, and vice versa:

From red to yellow or orange, and vice versa:

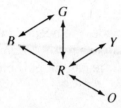

From yellow to orange, and vice versa, and from yellow to white:

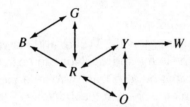

From green to black or purple, and vice versa:

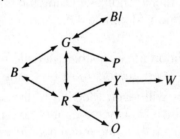

From orange to green and vice versa:

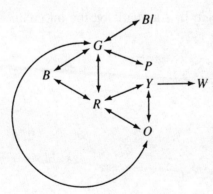

58. (A) The diagram shows that it is possible to go from yellow to white but it is not possible to return to yellow. The other choices describe possible sequences of two moves.

59. (E) The diagram shows that (E) describes a possible series of four moves and that the series described by the other choices are not possible.

60. (C) There are two equally short routes from the purple circle to the yellow circle: green to red to yellow and green to orange to yellow. Each requires three moves.

61. (E) As the diagram shows, five circles are one move away from green: blue, red, orange, black, and purple.

62. (E) As the diagram shows, if the player begins on yellow, then two moves could take him to red (or orange) and back to yellow, to orange and then to red, to red and then to orange, to red (or orange) and then to green, or to red and then to blue.

63. (C) Again the diagram provides the needed information. Given that the player does not move back to a circle already covered, a player beginning on a black circle in three moves could reach the red, blue, yellow, and orange circles.

Questions 64–67

This is a selection set, so begin by summarizing the initial conditions:
M ⊃ W
H → ~H
No more than one carry-over.

64. (B) If the professor teaches Melville, Wolfe, and Hawthorne in the fall, then he cannot teach Hawthorne in the spring. Nor can he teach Melville in the spring, for that would require that he also teach Wolfe (a violation of the third condition). Therefore, the professor must teach Wolfe, Crane, and Twain.

65. (A) This question stem doesn't provide any additional information, so use the initial conditions to eliminate choices. Using the first condition, eliminate (C). Using the second condition, eliminate (D). And using the third condition, eliminate (B) and (E).

66. (A) Given initial condition three, neither Melville nor Wolfe can be taught in the spring, so the other two authors must be Crane and Hawthorne.

67. (B) Since the professor will teach Melville in the spring, he must also teach Wolfe in the spring. Since Hawthorne cannot be repeated, Hawthorne cannot be taught in the fall. Given that third initial condition, Melville cannot be taught in the fall. Therefore, the fall offering must include Wolfe, Crane, and Twain.

Questions 68–73

This is a selection set. Begin by summarizing the information:

students = J, K, L
teachers = M, N, O, P, Q
2 students + 3 teachers = 5
K ≠ Q
P ≠ O
N ≠ Q

There is a diagramming technique that is useful for sets such as these in which there are two or more groups of individuals, e.g., students and teachers, or men, women, and children, or dogs, cats, and birds. With this technique, you use arrows to connect individuals who are logically related:

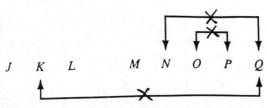

68. (A) This question stem provides no additional information, so use the initial conditions to eliminate choices. Using the distributional condition, eliminate (C) (three students). Using the condition that $K \neq Q$, eliminate (E). Using the condition, that $P \neq O$, eliminate (B). Finally, using the condition that $N \neq Q$, eliminate (D).

69. (C) In our overview of this set, we decided that there were no further conclusions to be drawn using just the initial information. As it turns out, we were wrong. The structure of this question informs us that one of the candidates must be appointed to the committee. So now we will go back and reexamine the initial conditions. Three teachers must be appointed to the committee, but there are two pairs of teachers such that one-half of the pair will not serve with the other half. This means that one of the pair N and Q must serve on the committee and that one-half of the pair O and P must also serve. The third teacher must, therefore, be M.

70. (C) Use the additional information provided by this stem to draw further conclusions. If K is appointed to the committee, then Q cannot be appointed. But we learned in our analysis of question 18, above, that either Q or N must be appointed. So N must be appointed.

71. (E) If L is not appointed to the committee, then both J and K must be appointed, and if K is appointed, then Q cannot be appointed.

72. (B) If Q is appointed to the committee, then K cannot be appointed, which means that both J and L must be appointed. As for (D) and (E), either O or P must be appointed, though the initial conditions coupled with the additional stipulation provided by this stem are not sufficient to determine whether it is O or P who is appointed.

73. (D) Of O and P, we know that one must be appointed to the committee and the other not. The alternative diagram above shows, however, that neither is related to any other individual in the problem by an arrow. Thus, it makes no difference whether we use O or P. It does make a difference whether or not we use K, for K is connected to Q. Thus, K cannot be universally substituted for J or L. Similarly, O is under a restriction that does not apply to N, so O cannot be substituted for N without some consequences. Finally, the same is true of Q and O.

Questions 74–79

Use a table to keep track of the options included on the various models:

	AT	SR	SS	AC	BS
P	✔	✔	✔		
Q	✔	✔	✔	✔	
R	✔	✔	✔	✔	✔
S	✔	✔			✔
T			✔	✔	✔
U	✔		✔		

Whatever further conclusions you need to draw are already contained within the diagram. There is nothing further to be done except go to the questions.

74. (B) As the diagram shows, three models (R, S, and T) come equipped with bucket seats.

75. (C) Three models come equipped with air conditioning (Q, R, and T), but only two of those (Q and R) come equipped with a sun roof as well.

76. (B) As the diagram shows, three models come equipped with bucket seats (R, S, and T), and only one of those (T) does not also come equipped with a sun roof.

77. (B) As the diagram shows, three cars come equipped with air conditioning (Q, R, and T), and only one of those (Q) is not also equipped with bucket seats.

78. (D) Two cars (T and U) are not equipped with sun roof, and one of those (T) is not equipped with automatic transmission. (In fact, T is the only model not equipped with automatic transmission.)

79. (A) Two cars are equipped with stereo system but not air conditioning, and they are P and U. P is equipped with a sun roof, and U is not. Therefore, knowing whether the car is equipped with a sun roof will allow you to determine the model.

Questions 80–85

Although this set involves a seating arrangement, it is actually a selection set rather than an ordering set, because the connections between the individuals are not spatial. Instead, the three rows are more like three committees or three teams. Begin by summarizing the initial conditions:

    1st = J, K, L, N
    2nd = J, K, L, M, P
    3rd = K, L, P, O
    J ≠ K
    M ≠ O

There don't appear to be any further, obvious conclusions to be drawn, so go to the questions.

80. (B) Since this question stem does not provide any additional information, use the initial conditions to eliminate choices. Choices (A), (C), and (D) can be eliminated using the condition that J ≠ K. (E) can be eliminated because M cannot sit in the van with O. So (B) must be the correct response.

81. (E) In our overview of this set, we did not find any more conclusions to be drawn. Since this question asks for "what must be true" based on just the initial conditions, we must have overlooked something. To find the individuals that must be included, try to construct possible seating assignments without them.

As for item I, it is possible to construct an assignment without *J*:

1	2	3
X,N	L,K	O,P

As for II, it is not possible to construct an assignment without *L*. Without *L*, you are left with only six commuters, and in that group *J* and *K* will not ride together and *M* and *O* will not ride together. So it is impossible to select a group of five commuters. Therefore, *L* must be included.

As for III, it is not possible to construct an assignment without *N*. Without *N*, you are left with *J*, *K*, *L*, *M*, *O*, and *P* for the other two rows. You need four people, but *J* and *L* will not ride together, and *M* and *O* will not ride together. So it is impossible to select a group of five people from that group of six.

82. (D) This question stem provides additional information. If *K* is assigned to the third row, (after eliminating *J*) the following commuters are left:

1st	L	N	
2nd	L	M	P
3rd	L	O	P

Of *L*, *M*, *O*, and *P*, three must sit in rows two and three. Since *M* and *O* cannot ride in the van together, *L* and *P* plus either *M* or *O* must ride in rows two and three. Therefore, *L* cannot ride in the first row, so *N* must ride with the driver.

83. (D) If *K* and *O* are assigned to the third row, this leaves only the following:

1st	L and N
2nd	L and P

Since it is necessary to take all three of those people in the van, *N* must be included and *N* must sit with the driver.

84. (B) If *L* and *P* are assigned to the third row, then *M* and either *J* or *K* is assigned to the second row. This means that *N* is assigned to the first row. Thus, there are only two possible assignments: *N*, *J* and *M* and *L* and *P*, or *N*, *K* and *M* and *L* and *P*.

85. (A) If *P* and *O* are assigned to the third row, then *L* and either *J* or *K* must be assigned to the second row. This means neither *L* (since he is assigned to the second row) nor *J* nor *K* (since they cannot both be assigned to the van) can be assigned to the first row. Thus, only *N* can be assigned to the first row.

9

Questions 86–90

This set may at first seem daunting; but once you have organized the information, you will find the questions are quite manageable. Here I would use a table:

	J	K	L	M	N
John	✔~B	✔~B	✔~B		
Kelly	✔ B		✔ C		✔ C
Mike	✔ C	✔ C	✔ B	✔ B	✔ D
Orin	✔~B		✔~B		
Paul		✔~C			

86. (C) As the table shows, the tenors who can sing *J* are John, Kelly, Mike, and Orin. But Kelly can sing that role only if Betty is the soprano and Mike only if Carol is the soprano. Therefore, only John and Orin can sing the role if Doris is the soprano.

87. (D) According to the table, every tenor but Paul can sing *L*; but Mike can sing only if Betty sings. Therefore, the only tenors who can sing *L* with Carol are John, Kelly and Orin.

88. (E) As the table shows, only one pair of performers can sing *N*.

89. (C) In the first place, only three tenors can sing *K*—John, Mike, and Paul. Of those three, Mike will only sing with Carol. So the other two, John and Paul, could sing with Doris.

90. (D) The table shows that Carol can sing *N* with Kelly and that Doris can sing *N* with Mike.

Analytical Reasoning Drills

1. Walk-Through Drill
2. Warm-Up Drills

10

This lesson contains three analytical reasoning drills. The first drill is a "walk-through" and has answers and discussion facing the questions so that you can walk through the exercise as you read the explanations. The second and third drills are "warm-up" drills, which should be done within the usual 35-minute time limit. Answers and explanations for the warm-up drills begin on page 255.

Walk-Through

Questions 1–6

Jack, Larry, Max, Nell, Orsen, and Peter are members of a spy network. For security reasons, only certain spies are able to contact other spies. The only contacts allowed are:

Jack can contact both Larry and Nell.
Orsen can be contacted by Larry, Max, and Peter.
Nell can contact Max.
Orsen can contact both Larry and Nell.
Peter can be contacted by Max.

A spy can receive a message from any spy who can contact him and, in turn, relay the message to any spy he is able to contact.

Questions 1–6

This group of problems is a "network" set. You can show the relationships described by the initial conditions by using arrows to connect capital letters. Begin with the first condition.

Jack can contact both Larry and Nell:

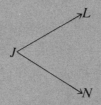

Next, Orsen can be contacted by Larry, Max, and Peter:

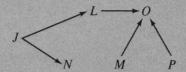

Next, Nell can contact Max:

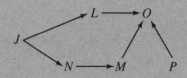

Then, Orsen can contact both Larry and Nell:

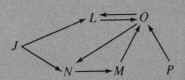

Finally, Peter can be contacted by Max:

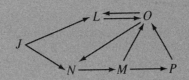

With a "network" set, any further conclusions that you might need to draw are already implicit in the diagram. For example, John can have Nell relay a message to Max, who in turn can relay the message to Orsen:

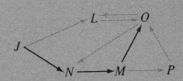

So there is no need to look for further conclusions. Go to the questions.

1. Which of the following spies CANNOT be contacted by any other spy in the network?

(A) Jack   (B) Max   (C) Nell
(D) Orsen   (E) Peter

2. Nell can get a message to which of the following spies by using exactly one intermediate contact?
I. Orsen
II. Larry
III. Peter

(A) I only   (B) III only   (C) I and III only
(D) II and III only   (E) I, II, and III

1. (A) The diagram shows no arrow leading to J, which means that Jack cannot be contacted by anyone (though he can contact others). Every other spy can be contacted by at least one other spy.

2. (C) The diagram shows that Nell can contact Max, who in turn can contact Peter and Orsen:

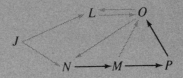

3. How can Orsen send a message to Max?

    (A) Orsen can contact Max directly.

    (B) Orsen can send a message to Max via Jack.

    (C) Orsen can send a message to Max via Larry.

    (D) Orsen can send a message to Max via Nell.

    (E) Orsen can send a message to Max via Peter.

4. If, for security reasons, Orsen cannot be contacted, which of the following messages can be sent, either directly or with an intermediary?

    (A) Jack to Peter

    (B) Larry to Max

    (C) Larry to Nell

    (D) Max to Larry

    (E) Max to Nell

5. If the following messages were sent using the smallest possible number of intermediaries, which message would require the greatest number of intermediaries?

    (A) Jack to Peter

    (B) Larry to Orsen

    (C) Max to Nell

    (D) Nell to Orsen

    (E) Orsen to Max

So, using just one intermediate contact, Nell can contact those two spies.

3. (D) Orsen can contact only Larry and Nell, and Nell is the only one who can contact Max:

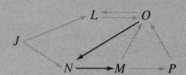

4. (A) The modified diagram looks like this:

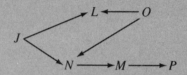

On the actual test, you would block out Orsen in your mind's eye. Our modified diagram shows that Jack is still able to get a message to Peter:

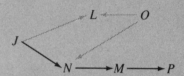

The diagram shows that none of the other communications is possible.

5. (A) Trace with your finger the various possibilities:

    (A) Jack (to Nell to Max) to Peter   (Two intermediaries)

    (B) Larry to Orsen   (No intermediaries)

    (C) Max (to Orsen) to Nell   (One intermediary)

    (D) Nell (to Max) to Orsen   (One intermediary)

    (E) Orsen (to Nell) to Max   (One intermediary)

6. If, for security reasons, Nell cannot be contacted, which of the following messages CANNOT be sent, either directly or through an intermediary?

(A) Jack to Orsen
(B) Jack to Peter
(C) Max to Larry
(D) Max to Orsen
(E) Peter to Larry

Questions 7–13
During a trial, an attorney is planning to call to the stand to testify six different witnesses—T, V, W, X, Y, and Z. She will call each witness exactly one time, and the order in which she calls them is subject to the following conditions:
The fourth witness must be T.
W and Y must both be called before V.
X must be called before W.

7. Which of the following could be the order in which the attorney calls the six witnesses?

(A) W, X, Y, T, Z, V
(B) X, W, V, T, Y, Z
(C) X, Y, W, T, Z, V
(D) Z, T, X, W, Y, V
(E) Z, X, W, T, V, Y

Note: A communication from Max to Nell could theoretically take two intermediaries, Peter and Orsen, but the question stipulates that the message takes the shortest route. Thus, (C) is incorrect.

6. (B) The modified diagram looks like this:

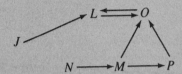

The diagram shows that the linkage between Jack and Peter has been broken, and it shows that other communication remains possible.

Questions 7–13
This is a linear ordering set, one of the most common types used on the LSAT. Begin by summarizing the information:

$$T = 4$$
$$(W + Y) < V$$
$$X < W$$

Note: The "<" is used to indicate *before* because the number of the witness called earlier will be lower than that of a witness called later; e.g., if X is called first and W is called third, $X < W$ because $1 < 3$. The initial conditions do not determine any particular order, except that T must be fourth.

There is one further conclusion: since $W < V$ and $X < W$, $X < V$. This further conclusion is the basis for the correct answer to Question 8. If you miss this further conclusion, when you get to Question 8, the fact that you don't find a correct answer will prompt you to return to the initial conditions to look for it.

7. (C) This question does not provide any additional information. Attack it by applying each of the initial conditions to the choices, eliminating impermissible orders until you are left with just one answer choice. That will be the correct choice.

The first condition specifies that T must be fourth, and you can eliminate (D) on this score.

The second condition specifies that W and Y must both be called before V is called, and you can eliminate (B) and (E) on this basis.

The third condition specifies that X must be called before W, and you can eliminate (A).

You are left with choice (C), which must be correct. (C) does describe a possible order because it does not contradict any of the initial conditions.

8. Which of the following must be true of the order in which the attorney calls the witnesses?

(A) She calls V before T.
(B) She calls X before V.
(C) She calls Y before W.
(D) She calls Y before X.
(E) She calls Z before T.

8. (B) This question does not supply any additional information, so it is answerable using just the information given in the initial conditions. As noted above, however, you must combine the second and third conditions to produce a further conclusion. If you missed this insight in your first look at the initial conditions, the fact that you would not be able to answer this question would prompt you to take another, closer look at them. Since X must be called before W, and W before V, X must be called before V.

As for the other choices, the following possible order demonstrates that they are not necessarily true:

1	2	3	4	5	6
X	W	Y	T	V	Z

9. Which of the following could be true of the order in which the witnesses are called?

(A) T is called sixth.
(B) V is called fourth.
(C) W is called first.
(D) X is called fifth.
(E) Y is called first.

9. (E) Test each of the choices to determine whether or not it describes a legitimate possibility:

(A) No. T must be called fourth, not sixth.

(B) No. T, not V, must be called fourth.

(C) No. X must come before W, so W cannot be first.

(D) No. X must be called before W and so before V, so X cannot be called fifth. (X can be called no later than third.)

(E) Yes. The only restriction on Y is that Y precede V, so Y can apparently be first.

At this point, we should raise a question about test strategy. Our analysis of (E) suggests that (E) is correct simply because it does not constitute an obvious violation of the initial conditions. We did not, however, construct a scenario in which Y is actually first. We could have done so; for example:

1	2	3	4	5	6
Y	X	W	T	V	Z

If you do this, you will confirm that it is possible to call Y first; but, of course, working out a possible order takes time. Once you have eliminated (A) through (D), you may, therefore, want to trust that your reasoning is correct and not bother to work out a complete order to prove that (E) is possible.

10. If the attorney calls Z last, which witness must be called fifth?

(A) T (B) V (C) W (D) X (E) Y

10. (B) Set up a rough diagram to keep track of the additional information and your further deductions:

1   2   3   4   5   6
            T   Z

Above we learned that X as well as W and Y must be called before V. This means that X, W, and Y must be first, second, and third (though not necessarily in that order) and that V must be fifth:

1   2   3   4   5   6
            T   V   Z

11. If the attorney calls X immediately after Y and immediately before Z, she must call V

(A) first (B) second (C) third
(D) fifth (E) sixth

11. (E) The question stem stipulates an order for X, Y, and Z: Y–X–Z. There is only one place for three consecutive letters:

1   2   3   4   5   6
Y   X   Z   T

Next, we reason that W and V must be called fifth and sixth and that W must come before V:

1   2   3   4   5   6
Y   X   Z   T   W   V

12. The attorney could call any of the following witnesses immediately before T EXCEPT

(A) V (B) W (C) X (D) Y (E) Z

12. (A) V must be called later than W and Y and X. So (since T is called fourth), V can be called no earlier than fifth. That the other four witnesses could be called third (immediately before T) is demonstrated by the following diagrams:

1   2   3   4   5   6
X   Y   W   T   V   Z
Y   Z   X   T   W   V
X   W   Y   T   V   Z
X   W   Z   T   Y   V

Remember, however, to save time you want to avoid working out these possibilities. Once you have explained to yourself why V cannot be called third, mark (A) and go to the next item.

13. If the attorney calls *Z* first, which of the following could be her fifth and sixth witnesses, respectively?

   (A) *T* and *X*
   (B) *V* and *W*
   (C) *X* and *V*
   (D) *Y* and *V*
   (E) *Y* and *X*

Questions 14–20

   Five seniors—Bob, Connie, Dan, Eileen, and Fran—and four juniors—John, Karl, Linda, and Molly —are to be divided into three debating teams of three persons each. The teams are designated as the Blue Team, the Red Team, and the Green Team.

   Dan, Eileen, and Fran must be captains of their respective teams.

   Bob and Connie cannot be on the same team.

   John and Fran cannot be on the same team.

   Linda must be on a team with either Bob or Eileen or both.

   Linda must be on the Blue Team.

14. Which of the pairs of students could be on the same team as John?

   (A) Bob and Eileen
   (B) Eileen and Fran
   (C) Eileen and Molly
   (D) Karl and Linda
   (E) Karl and Molly

13. (D) Enter the additional information on a diagram:

1	2	3	4	5	6
Z			T		

Now look for further conclusions. We know that *W*, *X*, and *Y* must be called before *V*, so *V* must be sixth:

1	2	3	4	5	6
Z			T		V

Since *X* must be called before *W*, there are three possible orders:

1	2	3	4	5	6
Z	X	W	T	Y	V
Z	X	Y	T	W	V
Z	Y	X	T	W	V

So the fifth and sixth witnesses can only be *Y* and *V* or *W* and *V*, in that order.

Questions 14–20

   This group is a selection set. Begin by summarizing the information:

Capts = *D*, *E*, *F*
B ≠ *C*
J ≠ *F*
L = *B* or *E* or (*B* + *E*)
L = Blue

There don't appear to be any further useful conclusions to be drawn, so go to the questions.

14. (C) This question provides no additional information, so just measure each answer choice by the initial conditions. The first condition requires that Dan, Eileen, and Fred be captains. Using this condition, you can eliminate (D) and (E), for a team of John, Karl, and Linda or a team of John, Karl, and Molly would lack a captain. Then, the second condition requires that Bob and Connie be separated. The remaining choices, however, all respect this condition, so it isn't possible to eliminate any more choices on this ground. Next, the third condition requires that Fran and John be separated, and we eliminate (B) for this reason. Finally, the fourth condition requires that Linda be on a team with either Bob or Eileen (or both). This eliminates (A). A team of John, Bob, and

15. Any of the following pairs of students could be on the Blue Team EXCEPT

   (A) Bob and Fran
   (B) Dan and Eileen
   (C) Eileen and John
   (D) Eileen and Molly
   (E) Eileen and Bob

16. If Bob and John are on the Red Team, then which of the following must be true?

   (A) Connie is on the Blue Team.
   (B) Dan is on the Green Team.
   (C) Dan is on the Red Team.
   (D) Karl is on the Blue Team.
   (E) Molly is on the Green Team.

Eileen is not possible because Linda would be placed on a team without either Bob or Eileen.

15. (B) This question is similar to Question 14, but here we have a thought-reverser (EXCEPT). This means that four of the five choices will describe possible teams. The correct choice is the one that violates one or more of the initial conditions. The correct choice is (B). We are told in the initial conditions that Linda must be on the Blue Team. A team consisting of Linda, Dan, and Eileen would violate the condition that Dan and Eileen be captains of their respective teams.

16. (C) Use a diagram to keep track of the new information and any further conclusions you reach:

Blue Team	Green Team	Red Team
Linda		Bob, John

Linda must be on a team with either Bob or Eileen. Since Bob is already assigned to the Red Team, we can deduce that Eileen is assigned to the Blue Team:

Blue Team	Green Team	Red Team
Linda, Eileen		Bob, John

Next, Fran cannot be on the Red Team (because John is on that team), and she cannot be on the Blue Team (because Eileen is already captain of that team). So Fran is on the Green Team:

Blue Team	Green Team	Red Team
Linda, Eileen	Fran	Bob, John

This means that the captain of the Red Team must be Dan:

Blue Team	Green Team	Red Team
Linda, Eileen	Fran	Bob, John, Dan

Have we overlooked something? Perhaps, but at this point we will look at the answer choices that are available. If we find one and only one seemingly correct response, we know we have solved the problem:

(A) This is possibly, though not necessarily, true.

(B) This is necessarily false.

(C) This is necessarily true.

(D) This is possibly, though not necessarily, true.

(E) This is possibly, though not necessarily, true.

We have only one choice that is necessarily true, so this indicates that we have solved the problem correctly.

17. If Fran is the only senior on her team, which of the following pairs could be the other members of her team?

(A) Karl and John
(B) Linda and Molly
(C) Linda and Karl
(D) Molly and John
(E) Molly and Karl

17. (E) Test each choice against the initial conditions:

(A) Fran, Karl, and John. (No. Fran and John cannot be on the same team.)

(B) Fran, Linda, and Molly. (No. Linda must be on a team with either Bob or Eileen, or both.)

(C) Fran, Linda, and Karl. (No. Linda must be on a team with either Bob or Eileen, or both.)

(D) Fran, Molly, and John. (No. Fran and John cannot be on the same team.)

(E) Fran, Molly, and Karl. (Yes. This combination does not violate any of the initial conditions.)

18. If Bob and Fran are on the Red Team, then which of the following is NOT an acceptable assignment of students for the other two teams?

Blue Team	Green Team
(A) Connie, Eileen, Linda	Dan, John, Molly
(B) Eileen, John, Linda	Connie, Dan, Molly
(C) Linda, Eileen, Karl	Connie, Dan, John
(D) Linda, Molly, Eileen	John, Connie, Dan
(E) Karl, Linda, Eileen	Molly, Dan, Connie

18. (E) You may have noticed that the questions are growing more difficult. Remember that difficulty increases not only from group to group but also within a group. This question contains a thought-reverser. You can attack it by testing each of the combinations given for the Blue Team and the Green Team. You will reach the following conclusions:

In each choice, the Blue Team and Green Team have exactly one captain.

In no choice are Bob and Connie together on either the Blue or the Green Team.

In no choice are John and Fran together on either the Blue or the Green Team.

In each choice, Linda is on the Blue Team with Eileen.

This suggests that all are possible assignments, but we know that one of them must violate some restriction. What have we failed to consider? The effect of the assignments to the Blue and Green Teams *on the third member of the Red Team*! The person not assigned to either the Blue Team or the Green Team must be assigned to the Red Team:

(A) Karl   (OK)

(B) Karl   (OK)

(C) Molly (OK)

(D) Karl   (OK)

(E) John   (No! John cannot be assigned to the Red Team because Fran is assigned to that team.)

19. Which of the following must be true?

(A) Bob is on the Blue Team?

(B) Eileen is on the Blue Team.

(C) Neither Bob nor Eileen is on the Green Team.

(D) Either Bob or Connis is on the same team as John.

(E) One team will consist of a senior and two juniors.

19. (E) This question calls your attention to a constraint on the overall distribution of individuals. First, as a matter of test-taking strategy, given the extreme flexibility of the situation here, neither (A) nor (B) is likely to be the correct choice. I would not study them too seriously. As for (C), this too seems unlikely. Make sure you don't make the mistake of assuming that just because either Bob or Eileen must be on the Blue Team (with Linda) that neither can be on a team other than the Blue Team.

(D) and (E) seem more promising, and here is where you should concentrate your attack. You can test (D) by trying to find a possible distribution in which John is not on a team with either Bob or Connie:

Red Team	Blue Team	Green Team
John	Linda, Bob	Connie

Distribute the rest of the individuals:

Red Team	Blue Team	Green Team
John, Eileen, Karl	Linda, Bob, Fran	Connie, Dan, Molly

This counter-example proves that (D) is not necessarily true.

Finally, we turn to (E). There are three teams with a total of nine positions to be filled. We know that each team has at least one senior —its captain. This leaves only two other seniors, Bob and Connie, who cannot both be assigned to the same team. So Bob will be assigned to one team and Connie to another. Their teams will be completed by two of the juniors, which means that the other two juniors will be assigned to the remaining team. So one

20. If Dan, Molly, and Karl are on the Red Team, then which of the following must be the constitution of the Green Team?

   (A) Bob, Eileen, John
   (B) Bob, Fran, John
   (C) Connie, Fran, John
   (D) Eileen, Connie, Fran
   (E) John, Connie, Eileen

team will consist of a senior (its captain) and two juniors.

20. (E) This question seems to be fairly difficult (as we might expect). The Blue Team and the Green Team will both need a captain, so Eileen and Fran must be assigned one to one of those teams and the other to the other team:

Blue	Green
Fran/Eileen	Fran/Eileen
Linda	

Since John cannot be assigned to the same team as Fran, he must be assigned to Eileen's team:

Blue	Green
Fran/(Eileen + John)	Fran/(Eileen + John)
Linda	

Bob and Connie must be on different teams:

Blue	Green
Fran/(Eileen + John)	Fran/(Eileen + John)
Linda	
Bob/Connie	Bob/Connie

We can now see that Eileen and John cannot be on the Blue Team, for that team would then consist of Eileen, John, Linda, and either Bob or Connie—four people. So Eileen and John must be assigned to the Green Team.

Blue	Green
Fran	Eileen
Linda	John

And Bob must be assigned to Linda's team:

Blue	Green
Fran	Eileen
Linda	John
Bob	Connie

Questions 21–24

The commander of a military unit participating in maneuvers has seven scouts out in the field—Johnson, Little, Markwood, Peterson, Stilton, Tucker, and Wharton.

Little, Markwood, and Tucker are somewhere east of the commander's base. Peterson, Stilton, and Wharton are somewhere west of the base.

Little is due east of Stilton, and Peterson is due west of Markwood.

Exactly two scouts are farther north than Johnson.

This is a map problem. Begin by entering the information provided on a map. First, Little, Markwood, and Tucker are east of the base, while Peterson, Stilton, and Wharton are west of the base:

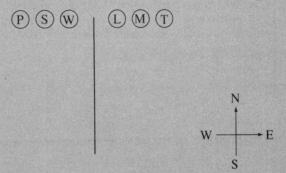

Next, Little is due east of Stilton, and Peterson is due west of Markwood:

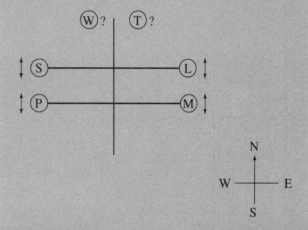

Be careful, however; the arrows indicate that the north-south placement of these individuals has not been fixed. Finally, make a note that exactly two spies are north of Johnson.

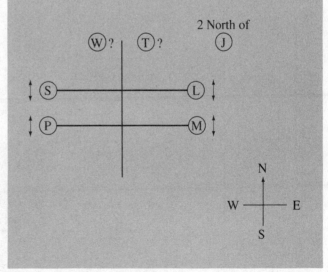

21. All of the following could be true EXCEPT:
    (A) Little is due west of Markwood.
    (B) Markwood is due east of Stilton.
    (C) Johnson is due east of Stilton and due south of Markwood.
    (D) Wharton is due south of Johnson and due north of Peterson.
    (E) Stilton and Wharton are both due north of Johnson.

21. (E) Since this question includes a thought-reverser, four of the five choices describe possible arrangements. The correct choice describes an arrangement that is not possible. Test each choice.

(A) and (B) are possible:

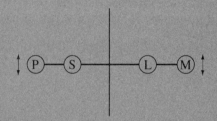

And (C) is possible:

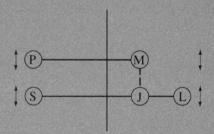

And (D) is possible:

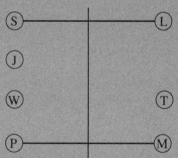

(E), however, is not a possible arrangement. If Stilton is due north of Johnson, then Little must also be north of Johnson. And that violates the condition that exactly two scouts are north of Johnson:

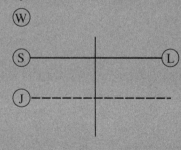

22. If Little and Markwood are both southeast of Wharton, which of the following must be true?

    I. Johnson is farther north than Stilton.
    II. Johnson is farther south than Tucker.
    III. Tucker is north of the base.

    (A) I only   (B) II only   (C) I and II only
    (D) I and III only   (E) I, II, and III

23. If Stilton is due east of Wharton, which of the following must be true?

    (A) Peterson is north of Little.
    (B) Tucker is north of Little.
    (C) Little is south of Johnson.
    (D) Tucker is north of the base.
    (E) Exactly three scouts are north of the base.

22. (B) Test each statement. I is not necessarily true. I implies that Wharton and Tucker are the two scouts who are north of Johnson, and that Stilton and Little are not north of Johnson. But the statement "Stilton and Little are not north of Johnson" does not imply "Stilton and Little are south of Johnson." They could be on the same latitude. II, however, is necessarily true. Since Little and Markwood are south of Wharton, Stilton and Peterson are south of Wharton as well. If Johnson were south of any one of those four scouts, he would be south of at least three scouts (in violation of the final condition). But there must be another scout farther north than Johnson, and that scout must be Tucker. Finally, III is not necessarily true. Although you can infer that Tucker is north of Johnson, you don't know where those scouts are in relation to the commander's base.

23. (A) If Stilton is due east of Wharton, then Stilton, Little, and Wharton are on the same latitude. So Johnson is either on the same latitude as well or farther north.

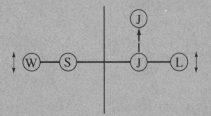

This means that Peterson and Markwood are the two scouts north of Johnson.

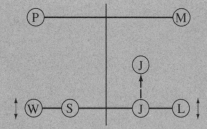

Thus, (A) is necessarily true. Peterson is north of Johnson who is not south of Little, so Peterson is north of Little. (B), however, is not necessarily true since Tucker could be anywhere south of Johnson. (C) is not necessarily true since Johnson and Little might be on the same latitude. Finally, (D) and (E) are not necessarily true since all of the scouts could be south of the base.

24. If Stilton is northwest of the base and Tucker is
     southeast of the base, what is the maximum
     number of scouts who could be north of the
     base?

     (A) 2   (B) 3   (C) 4   (D) 5   (E) 6

24. (E) The only scout who would necessarily have
     to be south of the base is Tucker:

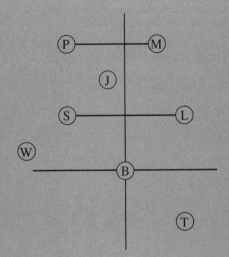

Directions: Each group of questions is based on a set of conditions. In answering some of the questions it may be useful to draw a rough diagram. Choose the best answer for each question.

Questions 1–7

A candidate for public office plans to visit each of six cities—J, K, L, M, N, and O—exactly once during her campaign. Her aides are setting up the candidate's schedule according to the following restrictions.

The candidate can visit M only after she has visited both L and N.

The candidate cannot visit N before J.

The second city visited by the candidate must be K.

1. Which of the following could be the order in which the candidate visits the six cities?

   (A) J, K, N, L, O, M
   (B) K, J, L, N, M, O
   (C) O, K, M, L, J, N
   (D) L, K, O, N, M, J
   (E) M, K, N, J, L, O

2. Which of the following must be true of the candidate's campaign schedule?

   (A) She visits J before L.
   (B) She visits K before M.
   (C) She visits K before O.
   (D) She visits M before J.
   (E) She visits N before L.

3. If the candidate visits O first, which city could she visit third?

   I. J
   II. L
   III. M

   (A) I only   (B) III only   (C) I and II only
   (D) II and III only   (E) I, II, and III

4. If the candidate visits J immediately after O and immediately before N, then she must visit L

   (A) first   (B) third   (C) fourth
   (D) fifth   (E) sixth

5. Which of the following could be true of the candidate's schedule?

   (A) She visits J first.
   (B) She visits K first.
   (C) She visits L sixth.
   (D) She visits M fourth.
   (E) She visits N sixth.

6. The candidate could visit any of the following immediately after K EXCEPT

   (A) J (B) L (C) M (D) N (E) O

7. If the candidate visits O last, which of the following could be the first and third cities on her schedule, respectively?

   (A) J and L
   (B) J and O
   (C) L and N
   (D) L and O
   (E) N and J

Questions 8–13

At a certain restaurant, above the kitchen door there are four small lights, arranged side by side, and numbered consecutively, left to right, from one to four. The lights are used to signal waiters when orders are ready. On a certain shift there are exactly five waiters—David, Ed, Flint, Guy, and Hank.

To signal David, all four lights are illuminated.

To signal Ed, only lights one and two are illuminated.

To signal Flint, only light one is illuminated.

To signal Guy, only lights two, three, and four are illuminated.

To signal Hank, only lights three and four are illuminated.

8. If lights two and three are both off, then the waiter signaled is

   (A) David   (B) Ed   (C) Flint
   (D) Guy   (E) Hank

9. If lights three and four are illuminated, then the signal of which of the following waiters might be displayed?

   I. David
   II. Guy
   III. Hank

   (A) I only   (B) III only   (C) I and II only
   (D) II and III only   (E) I, II, and III

10. If light one is not illuminated, then the signal of which of the following waiters might be displayed?

    I. Ed
    II. Guy
    III. Hank

    (A) I only   (B) I and II only   (C) I and III only
    (D) II and III only   (E) I, II, and III

11. If light three is on and light two is off, then the waiter signaled is

    (A) David   (B) Ed   (C) Flint
    (D) Guy   (E) Hank

12. If one of the five waiters is being signaled, the lights in which of the following pairs could not both be off?

   (A) one and two
   (B) one and three
   (C) two and three
   (D) two and four
   (E) three and four

13. If light four is on, then which of the following must be true?

   (A) Light one is on.
   (B) Light two is not on.
   (C) If light one is on, David is signaled.
   (D) If light two is not on, Flint is signaled.
   (E) If light three is not on, Ed is signaled.

Questions 14–20

A lawyer must schedule appointments with eight clients—*F, G, H, I, J, K, L,* and *M*—during one week, Monday through Friday. She must schedule two appointments for Monday, Tuesday, and Wednesday and one each for Thursday and Friday.

She must see *H* on Thursday.

She must see *G* on a day before the day on which she sees *I*.

She must see *J* on a day before the day on which she sees *L*.

She must see *F* on a day before the day on which she sees *L*.

She must see *K* and *F* on the same day.

14. Which of the following is an acceptable schedule for the week's appointments?

	Mon.	Tues.	Wed.	Thurs.	Fri.
(A)	G,M	I,L	K,F	H	J
(B)	G,M	I,J	K,F	H	L
(C)	G,I	M,L	J	H	K,F
(D)	L,G	I,J	K,M	H	F
(E)	G,L	M,K	F	H,J	I

15. Which of the following CANNOT be true?

   (A) She sees *M* on Monday.
   (B) She sees *K* on Tuesday.
   (C) She sees *L* on Tuesday.
   (D) She sees *I* on Wednesday.
   (E) She sees *M* on Friday.

16. Which of the following is a complete and accurate listing of the clients the lawyer could see on Friday?

   (A) *I, J*
   (B) *I, M*
   (C) *L, M*
   (D) *I, L, M*
   (E) *M, L, G*

17. If the lawyer sees *I* on Tuesday, then which of the following must be true?

   (A) She sees *J* on Monday.
   (B) She sees *M* on Tuesday.
   (C) She sees *K* on Tuesday.
   (D) She sees *M* on Friday.
   (E) She sees *L* on Friday.

18. If the lawyer sees *K* on Wednesday, which of the following must be true?

   I. She sees *I* on Tuesday.
   II. She sees *M* on Monday.
   III. She sees *L* on Friday.

   (A) I only   (B) III only   (C) I and III only
   (D) II and III only   (E) I, II, and III

19. If the lawyer sees *I* and *L* on the same day, which of the following is a complete and accurate listing of the days on which she could see them?

   (A) Monday
   (B) Tuesday
   (C) Wednesday
   (D) Monday and Wednesday
   (E) Tuesday and Wednesday

20. Which of the following, if true, provides sufficient additional information to determine on which day each client will have his appointment?

   (A) *M*'s appointment is scheduled for Monday.
   (B) *G*'s appointment is scheduled for Monday.
   (C) *G*'s appointment is scheduled for Tuesday.
   (D) *K*'s appointment is two days before G's.
   (E) *G*'s appointment is two days before I's.

Questions 21–24

Six students—Joan, Kevin, and Mark from Chamblee High School and Eugene, Flynn, and Greg from Clarkston High School—participated in a forensic tournament. Points were awarded only for the first three places—five points for first, three points for second, and one point for third—in each of three events.

Eugene, Greg, Joan, and Kevin competed in extemporaneous speaking. Eugene placed ahead of Kevin, and Joan placed immediately ahead of Greg.

Eugene, Flynn, Joan, and Kevin competed in oratory. Kevin placed ahead of Flynn, and Eugene placed immediately ahead of Joan.

Flynn, Greg, Kevin, and Mark competed in debate. Mark placed ahead of Flynn, and Greg placed immediately ahead of Kevin.

The winning school was the school with the greatest total number of points for all events.

21. Which of the following conclusions must be true?

   I. If Flynn finished fourth in oratory, then Kevin finished first in oratory.
   II. If Greg finished first in debate, then Flynn finished last in debate.
   III. Clarkston did not win the tournament unless Eugene won both of the events in which he competed.

   (A) I only   (B) II only   (C) III only
   (D) II and III only   (E) I, II, and III

22. What is the greatest number of points that could have been scored by Chamblee High School?

   (A) 15   (B) 17   (C) 18   (D) 19   (E) 20

23. Which of the following students could have scored three points in oratory?

    I. Eugene
   II. Kevin
  III. Joan
  IV. Flynn

   (A) I and II only
   (B) II and III only
   (C) III and IV only
   (D) I, II, and IV only
   (E) I, III, and IV only

24. Which of the following students could have accumulated the greatest total number of points?

    I. Eugene
   II. Flynn
  III. Greg
  IV. Kevin

   (A) I and III only
   (B) I and IV only
   (C) I, II, and IV only
   (D) II, III, and IV only
   (E) I, II, III, and IV

Directions: Each group of questions is based on a set of conditions. In answering some of the questions it may be useful to draw a rough diagram. Choose the best answer for each question.

Questions 1–7

A student planning his curriculum for the upcoming semester must enroll in three courses. The available courses fall into one of five general areas: math, English, social studies, science, and fine arts.

The student must take courses from at least two different areas.

If he takes an English course, he cannot take a fine arts course; and if he takes a fine arts course, he cannot take an English course.

If he takes a science course, he must take a math course; and if he takes a math course, he must take a science course.

He can take a social studies course only if he takes a fine arts course.

1. Which of the following is an acceptable schedule of courses?

   (A) one science course, one English course, and one fine arts course
   (B) one math course, one science course, and one social studies course
   (C) one math course, one social studies, and one fine arts course
   (D) one English course, one social studies course, and one fine arts course
   (E) one math course, one science course, and one fine arts course

2. Which of the following is NOT an acceptable schedule?

   (A) two math and one science course
   (B) two science courses and one math course
   (C) two fine arts courses and one math course
   (D) two social studies courses and one fine arts course
   (E) one social studies course and two fine arts courses

3. Which of the following courses when taken with one course in social studies is an acceptable schedule?

   (A) one course in math and one course in science
   (B) one course in fine arts and one course in English
   (C) two courses in fine arts
   (D) two courses in math
   (E) two courses in English

4. If the student wishes to take a course in math and a course in English, then he must select his third course in the area of

   (A) English
   (B) fine arts
   (C) math
   (D) science
   (E) social studies

5. Which of the following pairs of courses CANNOT be combined in an acceptable schedule?

   (A) a course in math and a course in fine arts
   (B) a course in science and a course in fine arts
   (C) a course in math and a course in English
   (D) a course in social studies and a course in science
   (E) a course in science and a course in English

6. If the student wishes to take a course in science, then which of the following pairs of courses would complete an acceptable schedule?

   (A) two math courses
   (B) two science courses
   (C) two English courses
   (D) one science course and one English course
   (E) one math course and one social studies course

7. An acceptable schedule CANNOT include two courses in

   (A) English
   (B) fine arts
   (C) math
   (D) science
   (E) social studies

Questions 8–13

A certain musical scale consists of exactly six notes: $F, G, H, I, J,$ and K. The notes are arranged from lowest (the first note of the scale) to highest (the sixth note of the scale). Each note appears once and only once in the scale, and the intervals between the notes are all equal.

J is lower than K.
G is higher than F.
I is somewhere between F and G.
H is the highest note of the scale.

8. Which of the following CANNOT be true of the scale?

   (A) *G* is the second note.
   (B) *G* is the third note.
   (C) *I* is the second note.
   (D) *I* is the third note.
   (E) *I* is the fourth note.

9. If *J* is the fourth note of the scale, which of the following must be true?

   (A) *F* is the third note.
   (B) *F* is the fifth note.
   (C) *I* is the fourth note.
   (D) *I* is the second note.
   (E) *G* is the first note.

10. If exactly two notes separate *F* and *I*, then which of the following must be true?

   (A) *F* is the lowest note.
   (B) *K* is the fifth note.
   (C) *K* is higher than *I*.
   (D) *J* is somewhere between *G* and *I*.
   (E) *K* and *J* are separated by exactly one note.

11. If *J* is the second note, then *G* and *I* could be which of the following, respectively?

   I. 4 and 3
   II. 5 and 3
   III. 5 and 4

   (A) I only   (B) III only   (C) I and II only
   (D) II and III only   (E) I, II, and III

12. If *F* and *I* are separated by exactly one note, which of the following must be true?

   (A) *G* is note 4.
   (B) *K* is note 5.
   (C) *J* is lower than *I*.
   (D) *I* is lower than *K*.
   (E) *J* is between *F* and *I*.

13. If *J* is lower than *F*, then the total number of different possible orderings of the six notes, from lowest to highest is

   (A) 1   (B) 2   (C) 3   (D) 4   (E) 5

Questions 14–20

A researcher studying organic compounds has found that five different molecules—*T, W, X, Y,* and *Z*—form chains according to the following rules.

A chain consists of three or more molecules, though the molecules in the chain are not necessarily different.

T is never found on either end of a chain.

If *W* appears in a chain, it appears more than once.

X is never found next to *Y* in a chain.

W is never found on the end of chain unless *Z* is found somewhere in the chain.

If *Y* appears in a chain, *Z* appears also.

14. Which of the following is a possible chain of molecules?

   (A) *T   X   Y   Z*
   (B) *Y   T   X   X*
   (C) *W   Z   T   Y*
   (D) *W   W   X   Z*
   (E) *Z   Y   X   W*

15. Which of the following is NOT a possible chain of molecules?

   (A) *X   X   T   Z*
   (B) *Z   X   W   W   Z*
   (C) *W   X   Z   Y   W*
   (D) *W   W   W   Z   X   W*
   (E) *Y   W   T   Z   X   X*

16. In the chain – *W W Z*, which of the following would be substituted for the dash to make a chain?

   I. *Z*
   II. *W*
   III. *T*

   (A) I only   (B) II only   (C) I and II only
   (D) I and III only   (E) I, II, and III

17. The chain *W W T Y Z X* can be changed into another chain by carrying out any one of the following EXCEPT

   (A) replacing the *T* molecule with a *W* molecule
   (B) replacing the *Y* molecule with an *X* molecule
   (C) replacing the *X* molecule with a *T* molecule
   (D) interchanging the *T* and *Z* molecules
   (E) interchanging the *Y* and the *X* molecules

18. Which of the following is not a chain but could be turned into a chain by changing the order of the molecules?

   (A) *X   Y   T   X*
   (B) *W   X   T   Y*
   (C) *T   X   X   Y*
   (D) *W   T   T   W*
   (E) *W   X   X   W*

19. Which of the following could be turned into a chain by replacing the dash with a molecule?

   (A) *W   W   –   Y   T   X*
   (B) *W   X   T   Y   –   Y*
   (C) *X   –   X   Y   T   Y*
   (D) *–   X   X   T   W   Y*
   (E) *–   X   X   T   W   T*

20. Which of the following sequences can be converted into a chain by adding *Z* and rearranging the molecules?

   I. *X Y X T*
   II. *W T T Z*
   III. *X X Y W*

   (A) I only   (B) II only   (C) III only
   (D) I and III only   (E) I, II, and III

Questions 21–24

As a sociology class project, a student is researching the history of her family. In an old family Bible, she has found the following information:

Bob was Paul's only son, and Paul's wife was an only child.

Sandra, Paul's only sister, was Eileen's aunt.

Peter was Paul's brother-in-law and Mary's uncle.

Mary's only brother, Ed, married Victoria.

Linda was Eileen's mother.

Any member of the family who married, married but once.

21. Linda could be

   I. Paul's wife
  II. Sandra's sister
 III. Paul's sister-in-law

(A) I only   (B) III only   (C) I and III only
(D) II and III only   (E) I, II, and III

22. Mary must be Bob's

(A) cousin   (B) sister   (C) niece
(D) aunt   (E) sister-in-law

23. Which of the following must be true?

   I. Sandra has more than one brother.
  II. Ed is Paul's nephew.
 III. Eileen is Mary's sister.

(A) I only   (B) II only   (C) I and II only
(D) II and III only   (E) I, II, and III

24. If the records also mention a man named Dan, then Bob could be

    I. Ed's brother
   II. Peter's brother
  III. Mary's brother
  IV. Eileen's father

(A) II only   (B) III only   (C) IV only
(D) I and III only   (E) III and IV only

Explanatory Answers

Drill 1

1. A	**11.** E	**21.** B
2. B	**12.** B	**22.** B
3. C	**13.** C	**23.** E
4. A	**14.** B	**24.** C
5. A	**15.** C	
6. C	**16.** D	
7. A	**17.** E	
8. C	**18.** C	
9. E	**19.** C	
10. D	**20.** D	

10

Questions 1–7

Here we have a common ordering set. Begin by summarizing the information:

$$(L + N) < M$$
$$J < N$$
$$K = 2$$

Note: Since the candidate cannot visit two cities simultaneously, the condition "The candidate cannot visit N before J" is equivalent to "She must visit J before N."

1. (A) This question supplies no additional information, so just take each condition and apply it to the answer choices, eliminating those that fail to comply with any condition. The first condition requires that L and N come before M. Using this condition, we eliminate (C) and (E). The second condition states that J must come before N, and we eliminate (D). The third condition requires that K be the second city, so we eliminate (B). This leaves us with (A); and (A), which respects all three conditions, is a possible order.

2. (B) M must be visited after both L and N, so given that K is visited second, M could not possibly be visited earlier than fourth, which means that K comes before M. So (B) is correct. In fact, given that J comes before N, and N comes before M, M must also come later than J. So M cannot be visited until L, N, J, and K have been visited, which means M is either fifth or sixth. As just noted, J must come before M, so (D) is necessarily false. The other three responses describe possible schedules only:

```
1   2   3   4   5   6
J   K   N   L   M   O
```

which shows that (A), (C), and (E) are possible. But:

```
1   2   3   4   5   6
O   K   L   J   N   M
```

shows that (A), (C), and (E) are not necessarily true.

3. (C) Begin by entering the additional information on a diagram:

```
1   2   3   4   5   6
O   K
```

Next, we reason that *J*, *N*, and *L* must all come before *M*, which means that *M* comes last:

```
1   2   3   4   5   6
O   K               M
```

The only condition left to take care of is the one that requires *J* before *N*, but this still leaves three possibilities:

```
1   2   3   4   5   6
O   K   J   N   L   M
O   K   J   L   N   M
O   K   L   J   N   M
```

So either *J* or *L* could be third.

4. (A) This question stipulates an order for three of the cities: *O*, *J*, *N*. Given that *J* and *N* must come before *M*, this means that the order must be:

```
1   2   3   4   5   6
    K   O   J   N   M
```

Which means that *L* must be visited first:

```
1   2   3   4   5   6
L   K   O   J   N   M
```

5. (A) This question is a good occasion to talk about test-taking strategy. A question of this form has this peculiarity: a choice like (A) may not contradict any single initial condition and may still be wrong because of the way the initial conditions work together. The only way to exclude this possibility is to devise a complete order, part of which is the segment you want to test—a time-consuming process. What should you do?

The solution to the dilemma is this: Make a first run through the choices, testing them by each single initial statement. If you can eliminate all but one, then you have your correct answer. If more than one choice remains, then the key to the question is some interaction among the initial conditions, e.g., a further inference that you have overlooked. Then, and only then, try working up an entire order to test the remaining choices.

Here we are fortunate because we can find the correct choice quickly:

(A) Doesn't contradict any single condition, so go to the next choice.
(B) No.   (*K* must be second.)
(C) No.   (*L* must come before *M*.)
(D) No.   (*M* must come after *J*, *L*, and *N* and therefore *K* as well. So *M* cannot be visited earlier than fifth.)
(E) No.   (*N* must come before *M*, so *N* cannot be last.)
  Thus, (A) must be the correct choice, so we don't have to try to construct the entire order using (A).

Just for reasons of completeness of explanation, however, here is a schedule in which *J* is the first city:

```
1   2   3   4   5   6
J   K   L   N   M   O
```

6. (C) As just noted, *M* cannot be earlier than fifth, so *M* could not immediately follow *K*. That the others could follow *K*, as shown by the following schedules:

	1	2	3	4	5	6
(A)	O	K	J	L	N	M
(B)	J	K	L	N	M	O
(D)	J	K	N	L	M	O
(E)	J	K	O	N	L	M

7. (A) Start by entering the additional information on a diagram:

1	2	3	4	5	6
	K				O

Next, we have already determined that *M* cannot be earlier than fifth:

1	2	3	4	5	6
	K			M	O

Next, since *J* must precede *N*, there are three possibilities:

1	2	3	4	5	6
J	K	N	L	M	O
J	K	L	N	M	O
L	K	J	N	M	O

(A) describes the second of these possibilities. The other choices do not describe one of the three possible schedules.

Questions 8–13

This is a "characteristics" set; each waiter has a characteristic signal. Summarize the information using a table:

	Lights			
	1	2	3	4
David	ON	ON	ON	ON
Ed	ON	ON		
Flint	ON			
Guy		ON	ON	ON
Hank			ON	ON

Whatever further conclusions you might need are already implicitly contained in the table, so go directly to the questions.

8. (C) Flint is the only waiter whose signal lights two and three are both off. For every other waiter, either two or three or both are on.

9. (E) As the table shows, if lights three and four are both on, the signal might be for David (all four on), or Guy (two, three, and four on), or Hank (three and four on).

10. (D) As the table shows, if light one is off, then the signal might be for either Guy or Hank. It could not be for David, Ed, or Flint, since their signals include an illuminated light one.

10

11. (E) As the table shows, there are three waiters whose signals include light three: David, Guy, and Hank. For David and Guy, however, light two must be on; for Guy it must be off. Therefore, if light three is on and light two is off, then Guy is the waiter signaled.

12. (B) Consult the table:

(A) Lights one and two will be off if Hank is signaled.
(B) There is no signal for which both one and three are off.
(C) Lights two and three will be off if Flint is signaled.
(D) Lights two and four will be off if Flint is signaled.
(E) Lights three and four will be off if either Ed or Flint is signaled.

13. (C) As the table clearly shows, neither (A) nor (B) is necessarily true. (C), however, is necessarily true, as the table shows. If four is on, then the signal might be for David, Guy, or Hank; but if one is also on, then the signal can only be for David. As for (D), if four is on and two is not, then it is Hank who is signaled —not Flint. As for (E), none of the five signals includes light four on and light three off.

Questions 14–20

This is a distributed order set, as opposed to a linear ordering set. Here, more than one individual can be placed in a given position (more than one appointment can be scheduled for certain days).

Start by summarizing the information:

H = Th.
$G < I$
$(J + F) < L$
$K = F$

You might notice that there is one further conclusion to be drawn. Since K and F must be scheduled for the same day, and since F must come before L, we can infer that K also comes before L. Aside from that, there do not appear to be any further important inferences to be drawn, so we go to the questions.

14. (B) Since the question supplies no additional information, we just apply each condition to the answer choices, eliminating those that fail to respect one or more conditions. The first condition states that there are two appointments for Monday, Tuesday, and Wednesday, and one appointment on the other two days. On this basis, we eliminate (C) and (E) because it is not possible to schedule two appointments on Thursday or Friday. The second condition states that H must be seen on Thursday, and our remaining choices reflect that. Then, the next condition states that G must come on a day before that on which I has his appointment, and our remaining choices respect this condition. Next, the fourth condition states that J and F must both come before L, so we eliminate (A) and (D). This leaves us with (B) as the correct choice, and you might want quickly to confirm that (B) does respect that final condition: K and F are both scheduled for the same day.

15. (C) This question allows us to talk about strategy. One way of proving that a particular partial order is possible is to construct an example of a permissible order using that part. Thus, the following example proves that (A) is a possible order (and therefore not the correct answer to this question):

M	TU	W	TH	F
M	K	L	H	I
J	F	G		

The difficulty with this approach is that constructing an example for each choice is time-consuming. Instead of trying to construct an entire order for each choice, a better strategy is to look for an answer choice that is not possible for a specific reason, e.g., because X cannot follow Y or because Z must come before W. Here is how this strategy would apply to this question.

(A) is not likely to be correct because M is not under any specific restriction, thus M could go almost anywhere. As for (B), though K is under a certain restriction, the import of that restriction is that K come earlier in the week—as (B) suggests. So (B) is probably not the correct choice. Now look at (C). L is under the restriction that he be scheduled later than both J and F and (as we learned above) later than K as well. This "pushes" L toward the latter part of the week. This choice, however, has L early in the week. So this choice merits some study.

The way to determine whether it is possible for L to have an appointment on Tuesday is to assume that he can and see whether that assumption is consistent with the initial conditions. If L is scheduled for Tuesday, then both J and F must be scheduled for Monday. But that can't be, as K would also have to be scheduled for Monday. This demonstrates that (C) cannot be true.

As for (D) and (E), you can construct schedules that show that they are possible.

16. (D) One way of attacking this question would be to try to construct all of the possibilities for Friday. For example, you would reason that K cannot be seen on Friday because K must be seen on the same day as F (and only one appointment is available on Friday). The difficulty with this "direct" approach is that you must do a lot of "grinding." Here I would use an "indirect" approach. I would go to the choices.

Since one of the choices is correct, I know that the test writer has already done the "grinding" to find all of the possibilities for Friday. I just need to find the one choice that contains all the ones that are workable schedules.

I eliminate (A) because I know J cannot be seen on Friday. As for (B), it seems to me that I and M could be seen on Friday, because they are very "flexible." (M is under no restriction, and I is under a restriction that forces him to a day later in the week.) As for (C), L is under a restriction, but that restriction pushes L to a later day, so L too seems a possibility for Friday. As for (D), this contains I, L, and M, so it begins to look like a correct choice. As for (E), I know that G cannot be scheduled for Friday, because G comes before I.

At this point, I must make a decision. My intuition is that (D) is the correct choice. I can either mark (D) as correct and move on to another item, or I can work out examples that prove that I, L, and M can be scheduled for Friday. Which I choose to do will depend on how much time I have left.

10

17. (E) Start by entering the additional information on a diagram:

M	TU	W	TH	F
	I		*H*	

G must come before *I*:

M	TU	W	TH	F
G	*I*		*H*	

K and F must be scheduled for the same day, which must now be Wednesday:

M	TU	W	TH	F
G	*I*	KF	*H*	

L must be later in the week than F, however:

M	TU	W	TH	F
G	*I*	KF	*H*	L

So *J* and *M* must have appointments on Monday and Tuesday, though not necessarily in that order. Our diagram shows that (E) is necessarily true; that (A) and (B) are possibly, though not necessarily true; and that (C) and (D) are false.

18. (C) Enter the additional information on a diagram:

M	TU	W	TH	F
	K		*H*	

This means that F is also scheduled for Wednesday:

M	TU	W	TH	F
	KF		*H*	

L must be seen sometime after F:

M	TU	W	TH	F
	KF		*H*	L

Then, G must be seen before *I*:

M	TU	W	TH	F
G	*I*	KF	*H*	L

M and J will be seen on Monday and Tuesday, though not necessarily in that order:

	M	TU	W	TH	F
	GJ	IM	KF	*H*	L
OR	GM	IJ	KF	*H*	L

Our diagram confirms that statements I and III are true. Statement II, however, is only possibly true and therefore not part of the correct choice.

19. (C) There are two ways of approaching this question. You can use a direct approach, in which you work with the initial conditions to track down all of the possibilities. The problem with the direct approach is that you will always worry that you haven't gotten all the possibilities. The alternative approach is to work backwards from the answer choices. Here's how this second approach works.

Does (A) contain all and only the possible days? No. *I* must follow *G*; therefore, *I* cannot be seen on Monday, and we eliminate (A). What about (B)? As for Tuesday, *L* must follow later in the week than *J*, *F*, and *K*, so *L* cannot be seen on Tuesday—and we eliminate (B). At this point, we should eliminate both (D) and (E), for (D) contains "Monday" and (E) contains "Tuesday." The only day on which both *I* and *L* could have appointments is Wednesday. For example:

M	TU	W	TH	F
JG	KF	IL	H	M

20. **(D)** Here, one way or another, you are going to have to test each choice. That makes this a difficult question, but that is to be expected since it is the last one. To make the question manageable, you have to think abstractly about the individuals who are most likely to determine a certain order. As for (A), as we have noted, *M* is not under any particular restriction, so he is not likely to precipitate a fixed order. As for (B) and (C), *G* and *I* are under a certain restriction, but this works primarily only between the two of them. (E) is a bit better than either (B) or (C), because it establishes that *G* and *I* are scheduled for either Monday and Wednesday, or Wednesday and Friday.

(D), however, offers even more promise. It affects not only *G* and *I*, but *K* and therefore *F* and *L* as well. Start with (D). If *K* has his appointment two days before *G*, then (given that *H* is already scheduled for Thursday) they must be scheduled either for Monday and Wednesday, or Wednesday and Friday. Here, since *G* must come before *I*, *K* and *G* must be scheduled for Monday and Wednesday:

M	TU	W	TH	F
K		G	H	

This means that *F* is scheduled for Monday and *I* for Friday:

M	TU	W	TH	F
KF		G	H	I

However, *L* cannot be scheduled before Wednesday:

M	TU	W	TH	F
KF		GL	H	I

That means that *J* and *M* must be scheduled for Tuesday:

M	TU	W	TH	F
KF	JM	GL	H	I

Questions 21–24
Begin by summarizing the initial conditions:
In extemp, Eugene placed ahead of Kevin:

K	E

Extemp: ——————————————▶

It's not possible to place the other two individuals on the diagram, so just make a note: $G < J$ (Here "<" means immediately ahead of.)

In oratory, Kevin placed ahead of Flynn:

Oratory:
$$F \qquad K$$
→

And Eugene placed immediately ahead of Joan: $J < E$

In debate, Mark placed ahead of Flynn:

Debate:
$$F \qquad M$$
→

And Greg placed immediately ahead of Kevin: $K < G$

Extemp:
$$K \qquad E$$
→ $G < J$

Oratory:
$$F \qquad K$$
→ $J < E$

Debate:
$$F \qquad M$$
→ $K < G$

21. (B) Examine each statement. Statement I is not necessarily true:

Extemp:
$$F \quad K \quad J \quad E$$
→

Statement II is necessarily true. Since Greg placed immediately ahead of Kevin in debate, if Greg finished first, then Mark finished third and Flynn fourth.

Statement III is not true. The best way to test this statement is to try to find a counterexample. Assume, for example, that Eugene did not win extemporaneous speaking but did win oratory. Is it possible that Clarkston won? A total of nine points were awarded in each event for a total of 27 for the tournament. A minimum of 14 was needed to win.

					Clarkston	Chamblee
Extemp:	K	E	G	J	4	5
Oratory:	F	K	J	E	5	4
Debate:	F	M	K	G	5	4
					14	13

So Clarkston could have won the tournament even if Eugene did not win extemporaneous speaking—provided that Eugene did win oratory and Greg did win debate.

22. (B) Take each event in turn. If Joan won extemporaneous speaking, then the order of places, from first to last, was: J, G, E, K, and Chamblee scored five points. If Kevin won oratory and Joan finished third, then the order of finish, from first to last, was K, E, J, F, and Chamblee scored six points. If Mark won debate and Kevin finished third, then the order of finish, from first to last, was M, G, K, F, and Chamblee won six points. So Chamblee could have scored a maximum of $5 + 6 + 6 = 17$ points.

23. (E) To have won three points in an event a student must have finished second. In oratory, it is possible for Eugene (*K, E, J, F*), Joan (*E, J, K, F*), and Flynn (*K, F, E, J*) to have finished second. It is not possible for Kevin to have finished second.

24. (C) Test each statement. It is possible for Eugene to have scored the most points. If Eugene finished first in his two events (oratory and debate) then he received a total of ten points, and his nearest competitor, Joan, only received six points in those two events. Since Joan did not compete in debate, Eugene would have the greatest total. Therefore, I must be part of the correct choice.

It is also possible that Flynn scored the greatest total. Flynn could have scored two seconds (in oratory and debate) for a total of six points. And if Flynn scored six points in those events, Kevin and Mark each scored five points and Eugene and Greg each scored one point. Now look at the possible results for extemporaneous speaking. If Joan won, she got five points, Greg got three points, and Eugene got one point. So the other individuals would have earned the following: Flynn = 6, Joan = 5, Kevin = 5, Mark = 5, Greg = 4, and Eugene = 2.

It is not possible for Greg to have scored the greatest number of points. If Greg placed second in extemporaneous speaking, he earned three points while Joan and Eugene earned five points and one point respectively. If Greg won oratory, he earned another five points, but Kevin and Mark earned three points and one point respectively. So far we have: Greg = 8, Joan = 5, Kevin = 3, Eugene = 1, and Mark = 1. Greg scored no points in oratory. If Eugene won, then the final scores were Greg = 8 and Joan = 8—a tie. If Kevin won oratory, then the final scores were Greg = 8 and Kevin = 8—again a tie.

It is possible that Kevin scored the greatest number of points. Kevin could have scored two seconds and a first, for a total of 11 points. No other contestant could match that total.

10

DRILL 2

1. E	**11.** E	**21.** C
2. C	**12.** C	**22.** A
3. C	**13.** D	**23.** C
4. D	**14.** D	**24.** C
5. D	**15.** E	
6. A	**16.** C	
7. A	**17.** C	
8. A	**18.** E	
9. D	**19.** A	
10. A	**20.** A	

Questions 1-7

This is a selection set. Begin by summarizing the information:

Two different areas
$(E \supset \sim FA) + (FA \supset \sim E)$
$(S \supset M) + (M \supset S)$
$SS \supset FA$

There are no further obvious conclusions to draw, so go to the questions.

1. (E) Just test each choice by the initial conditions. First, the student must select from at least two different areas, and all of the choices pass muster on this score. Next, he cannot take courses in both English and fine arts, and we eliminate (A) and (D). Next, if he takes a science course, he must take a math course, and vice versa, so we eliminate (C). Finally, if he takes a social studies course, he must take a course in fine arts, and we eliminate (B). By the process of elimination, (E) is the correct choice.

    Note: Don't misread that last condition. It states only that a course in social studies must be accompanied by a course in fine arts. It is possible to take a fine arts course without taking a social studies course.

2. (C) This question is the mirror image of the first. Just test each choice by the initial conditions. All are acceptable on the basis of the first condition (that he take courses in at least two different areas) and the second condition (English and fine arts cannot be taken together). (C), however, runs afoul of the third condition, for there we have a math course without an accompanying science course. (You can check the other choices and see that they do respect the final condition.)

3. (C) If the student takes social studies, then he must take a course in fine arts. With a course in fine arts, he cannot take a course in English; and with two courses already scheduled (social studies and fine arts), he cannot take either math or science (for those must go together). His only choice, therefore, is to take another fine arts course (as (C) suggests) or another social studies course.

4. (D) If the student takes a course in math, he must also take a course in science, so his third course must be science.

5. (D) If you simply screen choices here by the initial conditions, it seems that all of the *pairs* taken in isolation are acceptable. This means that the trick to the question must be what happens to the third course. As for (A) and (B), math requires science and vice versa, and a schedule of math, science, and fine arts is acceptable. As for (C) and (E), math requires science, and a schedule of math, science, and English is acceptable. (D), however, is not acceptable. Social studies requires fine arts, and science requires math, but there is not room on the schedule for both fine arts and science.

6. (A) Test each of the choices:

    (A) science, two math   (OK.)
    (B) three science   (No. Must schedule two different areas.)
    (C) science, two English   (No. Math must accompany science.)
    (D) two science, one English   (No. Math must accompany science.)
    (E) science, math, social studies   (No. Fine arts must accompany social studies.)

7. (A) Test each choice. As for (A), it is not possible to take two English courses. With two English courses, the student cannot take either math or science (each requires the other), nor fine arts, nor social studies (because social studies requires fine arts). It is possible to take two courses in the other areas:
    (B) two fine arts plus one social studies
    (C) two math plus one science
    (D) two science plus one math
    (E) two social studies plus one fine arts

Questions 8–13

This is a linear ordering problem. Begin by summarizing the information:

> $J < K$
> $F < G$ (G is higher than $F = F$ is lower than G.)
> $F – I – G$ or $G – I – F$
> $H = 6$

There is one further conclusion you should probably note. Since G is higher than F, and since I is between F and G, the order for those three notes is: $F < I < G$.

8. (A) Test each choice to learn which are possible and which are not. As for (A), G cannot be the second note on the scale because G must be higher than both F and I. You can grasp that the other choices are possible if you think in the following way. Imagine that FIG are consecutive notes (they may be, though they don't have to be). If they are, then they could be 1, 2, and 3; or 2, 3, and 4; or even 3, 4, and 5. This will not affect the placement of J and K since in each of those arrangements there will be two spaces left on the scale and K and can be higher than J.

9. (D) Enter the additional information on a diagram:

6	H
5	
4	J
3	
2	
1	

Since J is lower than K:

6	H
5	K
4	J
3	
2	
1	

Further, G, I, F must be notes 3, 2, and 1:

6	H
5	K
4	J
3	G
2	I
1	F

10. (A) If exactly two notes separate F and I, then they must be placed as follows:

6	H
5	G
4	I
3	
2	
1	F

J and *K* are entered as follows:

```
6    H
5    G
4    I
3    K
2    J
1    F
```

The diagram shows that (A) is necessarily true, while the other choices are necessarily false.

11. (E) Enter the new information:

```
6    H
5
4
3
2    J
1
```

If *J* is second, then *K* must be either third, fourth, or fifth:

```
6    H    H    H
5    K
4         K
3              K
2    J    J    J
1
```

For *G* to be higher than *I*, and *I* higher than *F*, they must be entered as follows:

```
6    H    H    H
5    K    G    G
4    G    K    I
3    I    I    K
2    J    J    J
1    F    F    F
```

There are three possibilities. *G* and *I* are 4 and 3, or 5 and 3, or 5 and 4. Thus, I, II, and III are all possible.

12. (C) Start by assuming that *F* is the lowest note on the scale and that *I* is therefore the third. On that assumption there are two positions for *G*:

```
6    H    H
5    G
4         G
3    I    I
2
1    F    F
```

J and K must be placed in the other two positions, with K higher than J:

```
6   H   H
5   G   K
4   K   G
3   I   I
2   J   J
1   F   F
```

Now assume that F is the second note on the scale and that I is therefore the fourth:

```
6   H
5
4   I
3
2   F
1
```

G must be higher than I:

```
6   H
5   G
4   I
3
2   F
1
```

K and J must be entered as follows:

```
6   H
5   G
4   I
3   K
2   F
1   J
```

Now try assuming that F is the third note on the scale, which would mean that I is the fifth. That is not possible, however, for G would then have to be higher than fifth. Thus, we have accounted for all the possibilities:

```
6   H   H   H
5   G   G   K
4   I   K   G
3   K   I   I
2   F   J   J
1   J   F   F
```

10

Only (C) is necessarily true. The other choices are only possibly true.

13. (D) Again, we need to approach the question systematically. First, let us assume that *J* is the lowest note and that *F* is second lowest. The possibilities are:

6	H	H	H
5	G	G	K
4	I	K	G
3	K	I	I
2	F	F	F
1	J	J	J

That makes three possibilities. Now let's try *J* as the lowest note and *F* as the third lowest note. On this assumption, there is only one possibility:

6	H
5	G
4	I
3	F
2	K
1	J

This exhausts the possibilities. It is not possible (given the additional stipulation that *J* is lower than *F*) for *J* or *F* to be any higher on the scale. So there are exactly four possibilities.

Questions 14–20

This is a letter sequence set. Start by summarizing the information:

Length = 3+
T ≠ End
W ⊃ W
X ≠ Y
(W = End) ⊃ Z
Y ⊃ Z

Now go to the questions.

14. (D) Screen each choice using the initial conditions. First, all of the sequences meet the minimum-length requirement. Next, we eliminate (A) because *T* cannot be on the end. Next, we eliminate (C) and (E) because if *W* appears in a chain it must appear more than once. Next, we look at (B) and (D) to determine whether or not *X* is next to *Y*, and we learn that (B) and (D) both pass this test. Next, we see whether *W* is on the end of a sequence and, if so, whether *Z* also appears in the chain. *W* does not appear in (B), so (B) passes this test. Although *W* is on the end of the chain in (D), *Z* also appears, so (D) passes this test. Finally, however, we eliminate (B) because *Y* appears in (B) without *Z* (and (D) passes this test because no *Y* appears in (D) at all).

15. (E) This is the mirror image of the problem above. Four of the five sequences are acceptable chains—one is not. Just screen each choice with the initial conditions. The one sequence that is not acceptable is (E), because *W* appears only once.

16. (C) Substitute each letter for the dash and test each result.

I. *Z W W Z*   This is consistent with all of the initial conditions, so this is a possible chain.

II. *W W W Z*   This is consistent with all of the initial conditions, so this is a possible chain.

III. *T W W Z*   This violates the condition that T may not be on the end of a chain, so this is not a possible chain.

17. (C) Again, test each of the resulting chains.

(A)	*W W W Y Z X*					This sequence is a possible chain.
(B)	*W W T X Z X*					This sequence is a possible chain.
(C)	*W W T Y Z T*					This is not a chain, because *T* is on one end.
(D)	*W W Z Y T X*					This sequence is a possible chain.
(E)	*W W T X Z Y*					This sequence is a possible chain.

18. (E) You first have to determine what is wrong with the sequence and then whether or not you can correct it by reordering the letters.

(A) There are two difficulties here. One, *X* is next to *Y*; two, *Y* appears with *Z*. Reordering alone will not provide a *Z*, so this cannot be changed into a chain just by reordering.

(B) Here there are three difficulties: 1) *W* appears without another *W*; 2) *W* is on the end without a *Z* in the sequence; 3) *Y* appears without *Z*. In short, you cannot supply the missing letters just by reordering.

(C) There are three problems with this sequence: 1) you have *T* on the end; 2) *X* and *Y* are together; and 3) *Y* appears without *Z*. The third cannot be corrected just by reordering.

(D) The problem here is that you have *W* on the end without a *Z* in the sequence. If you try to correct this by reordering the letters, e.g, putting the *W*s inside the sequence, you wind up with *T*s on the ends.

(E) This sequence is not a chain because *W* appears on the end without a *Z* in the sequence. You can't add a *Z* to the sequence, but you can change the order: *X W W X*. This sequence is a chain.

19. (A) Again, analyze the defect in each sequence.

(A) Here, we have a *W* on the end of the sequence without a *Z*; and we have a *Y* without a *Z*. Placing a *Z* in the space where there is a dash solves both problems, and the resulting sequence—*W W Z Y T X*—is a chain.

(B) Here a *W* appears without another *W*; *W* appears on the end without *Z*; and *Y* appears without *Z*. So we need both *W* and *Z* to turn this sequence into a chain, but we have only one missing link.

(C) Regardless of what is substituted for the dash in this sequence, the resulting sequence will have an *X* next to a *Y*, so it cannot be chain.

(D) Here we need both a *W* (for the one *W*) and a *Z* (for the *Y*) to turn this into a chain, but we have only one dash, so this sequence cannot be salvaged.

(E) Regardless of what is substituted for the dash, *T* will still be on the end of the sequence, so this sequence cannot be a chain.

20. (A) Test the three statements.

I. Adding a *Z* to this sequence will correct the problem of having a *Y* without a *Z*. Then, reordering can move *T* from the end into the interior of the sequence and separate the *X* and *Y*:

X Z Y T X

This is a chain.

II. This sequence has a *W* without a second *W*, and the addition of a *Z* will not cure that defect.

III. This sequence also has a *W* without a second *W*, and the addition of a *Z* will not cure the defect.

Questions 21–24

This is a family-tree problem. Begin by summarizing the information. First, Bob was Paul's only son, and Paul's wife was an only child:

$$[♀] = Paul$$
$$\downarrow$$
$$Bob\ [♂]$$

Next, Sandra, Paul's only sister, was Eileen's aunt.

$$[♀] = Paul —————— Sandra\ [♀]$$

Bob [♂]   Eileen   Eileen

(We don't know whether Eileen was Paul's child or the child of another sibling. Of course, if there is another sibling, it will be a brother.)

Next, Peter was Paul's brother-in-law and Mary's uncle.

$$[♀] = Paul —————— Sandra\ [♀] = Peter$$

Bob [♂]   Eileen,   Eileen,
          Mary   Mary

(Since Paul has only one sister, and since his wife was an only child, Paul's only brother-in-law has to be Sandra's husband. We have the same problem in placing Mary that we had above with Eileen.)

Next, Mary's only brother, Ed, married Victoria.

$$[♀] = Paul ————— Sandra\ [♀] = Peter\quad Brother$$

Bob [♂]   Eileen   Eileen   Mary ———— Ed [♂] = Virginia

(Since Mary has a brother, Ed, Mary cannot be Paul's daughter.) Finally, we don't know who Linda is. She could be Paul's wife, or she could be the wife of another brother.

21. (C) As just noted, Linda could be Paul's wife, because Eileen could be Paul's daughter. (The initial conditions say only that Paul has but one son.) So I must be part of the correct choice. Additionally, we noted that Eileen might be the daughter of a third, unnamed sibling (a brother), so it is possible that Linda is a wife of an unnamed brother. Therefore, III is part of the correct answer. II, however, is not part of the correct answer, for the initial conditions specifically state that Paul has only one sister—Sandra.

22. (A) Mary is a niece to Peter and therefore to Sandra and to Paul. Therefore, Mary and Bob are cousins. Since Mary and Bob belong to the same generation, she cannot be Bob's niece or aunt. And since Mary has a brother, Ed, she cannot be Bob's brother. (Bob is the only male child in his family.)

23. (C) As for I, in our summary of the initial conditions we determined that this must be true. As for II, since Sandra is Mary's aunt, and since Ed is Mary's brother, Ed is Sandra's nephew. And since Sandra's brother is Paul, Ed is also Paul's nephew. As for III, our summary of the initial conditions shows that this may or may not be true.

24. (C) As for I and III, Ed is Mary's only brother, therefore there cannot be another brother in that generation of that family. As for II, we know from the initial conditions that Bob is the only male child in his family. Finally, however, IV is possible. We do not know the identity of Eileen's father. It could be Bob, but it could also be another brother—whose name could be Dan.

10

Logical Reasoning–Part I

11

The logical reasoning section on your LSAT will contain 24–26 items.

1. The Anatomy of a Logical

Reasoning Question

All logical reasoning items consist of three parts: an initial statement or statements, a question stem, and answer choices. The initial statement or statements contain an argument, that is, a line of analysis or reasoning. The question stem then asks you to evaluate that argument, e.g., to describe it, to identify any missing parts, to defend it, or to attack it. Finally, one of the five answer choices will best respond to the question stem; the other choices will be distractors.

EXAMPLE:

In her address to the City-Wide Association of Dairy Products Distributors, the Mayor cited the success of Redwood Farms, which has increased its sales in the city by 23 percent. She encouraged all distributors to make similar efforts, concluding that the overall increase in business would benefit the city.

Which of the following, if true, points out a serious weakness in the Mayor's reasoning?

(A) Milk and other dairy products contain important nutrients that are vital to the health and well-being of citizens, particularly children.

(B) Redwood Farms achieved the increase in sales by offering discounts to businesses that purchased a complete line of Redwood Farms products.

(C) The Mayor made a speech on a previous occasion to the city's chamber of commerce in which she proposed city tax abatements to attract new industry.

(D) During the year cited, Redwood Farms showed only a 15-percent increase in before-tax profits over the previous year.

(E) The size of the market in the city is relatively fixed, so any increase in sales by one firm must come at the expense of sales by other firms.

The initial statements present an argument (or logical analysis). The question stem asks you to find a logical weakness in the argument. The answer to this critical thinking item is (E). The mayor applauds the success of one company in increasing its business and encourages other companies to do the same. If, however, the gains of Redwood Farms came at the expense of other firms in the same business, then it is logically impossible for every other firm to achieve the same success.

2. Two Important Facts about

Logical Reasoning

A. Like reading comprehension passages, the initial statement of a logical reasoning item can treat any topic—art, science, history, philosophy, government, sports, and so on. The advice you were given in the chapter on reading comprehension is applicable here as well: don't let the subject matter of the logical reasoning item intimidate you. Even if the topic is something you have never heard of, everything you need to answer the question will be given to you.

B. The Rule of 2 out of 5. A fundamental principle of the construction of logical reasoning items is that one out of the five choices must be identifiably better than the others. However, it should not be so obviously better than the others that the question becomes too easy.

This principle presents a dilemma to the writer of logical reasoning items. If a question stem asks you to attack an argument, one of the choices must represent a legitimate objection to the logic of the initial statement. This will be the "credited response." The other choices—the distractors—must be deficient in some respects, but they cannot be so deficient as to make the item ridiculously easy.

Preparing workable distractors is actually more difficult than writing the credited response. As a consequence, usually only two of the five answer choices have any real merit (one being the correct choice). The other three choices, while related to the general topic of the initial statement, ignore the logical structure of the argument.

> **EXAMPLE:**
>
> Over the past fifteen years, the largely urbanized Northeastern United States has shown more and more the influence of the Southwestern portion of the country. Once, very few people in New York City could be found sporting cowboy boots and Stetson hats, and no major radio station boasted twenty-four-hour-a-day programming of country and western music. The latest development is the rapid proliferation of restaurants serving chili, nachos, burritos, and other Tex–Mex dishes.

The passage above makes which of the following assumptions?
- **(A)** The lifestyle of people in the Northeast has been enriched by the influence of the Southwestern states.
- **(B)** Most residents of the Southwestern states regularly eat at Tex–Mex restaurants.
- **(C)** Over the last fifteen years, residents of the Southwestern United States have increasingly adopted lifestyles similar to those of the Northeast.
- **(D)** Tex–Mex dishes are an element of the regional cuisine of the Southwestern states.
- **(E)** People in the Northeastern United States eat out more frequently than they did fifteen years ago.

The best answer to this item is (D). The author claims that the Northeast has absorbed elements of the culture of the Southwest and provides three examples. A tacit assumption (one which is not proved) of the argument is that a certain mode of dress, kind of music, and type of cuisine are found in the Southwest. (D) articulates this assumption.

Three of the remaining choices are really just "flak." They lack any real plausibilty after a reasonably careful reading. These are (A), (C), and (E).

(A) goes beyond the scope of the initial statement. The author simply states that certain cultural elements of the Southwest have been transplanted to the Northeast, but no value judgment is contained in the paragraph about that process.

(C) reverses the causal linkage described by the initial statement. According to the author, the Southwest has influenced the Northeast—not vice versa.

(E) goes beyond the scope of the initial statement. Nothing in the argument suggests that people in the Northeast are eating out more frequently than they did fifteen years ago—only that there are more Tex–Mex restaurants in the region than there were fifteen years ago.

To most people, (B) will probably seem to be the second-best answer. It at least has the merit of being fairly closely connected to the argument in the initial statement. It *might* be true that people in the Southwest regularly patronize the Tex–Mex restaurants. That, however, is not necessarily an assumption of the argument. All that is required for the argument is that there exist in the Southwest such restaurants —not that residents of that area patronize those restaurants with any frequency.

3. Holmes and the Magnifying Glass

In several of the Sherlock Holmes stories, Watson describes how Holmes takes out a magnifying glass from his pocket and proceeds to study the scene of a crime in excruciating detail, a means by which Holmes finds clues that Watson, using only his ordinary vision, overlooked. On the exam, you must use a "mental magnifying glass" to study logical reasoning problems, for this part of the exam tests careful reading as well as critical thinking.

Most of the time we are reading or listening, we are just passively absorbing information. For example, when you are reading a newspaper or watching the television, you probably simply accept whatever is said as correct without studying the information too carefully. This applies to your reading of college textbooks as well. You read to learn the content of the textbook—but you take it for granted that what is written in the book is correct.

You can prove this to yourself by thinking about the advertising you encounter in the media. You are barraged by advertising; and even if you don't pay very much attention to it, you can probably recite a dozen or so key phrases from advertisements and sing parts of several jingles. Most people are surprised when they examine the actual content of the advertisements.

The claims of many advertisements are very carefully and sometimes very cleverly worded. Here are some of my old favorites, but you can probably find illustrations of your own. No brand names will be mentioned, but some of the advertisements may be familiar.

One television commercial for chewing gum runs roughly as follows:

> Chew Brand X Sugarless Gum. Four out of five dentists surveyed recommend
> sugarless gum for their patients who chew gum.

This is a claim you may have heard. On a first and casual hearing, the advertisement may give the impression that 80 percent of all dentists recommend that people chew Brand X Sugarless Gum. A closer examination reveals, however, that the claim is much less ambitious.

First, the advertisement does not claim that the dentists surveyed recommend Brand X Sugarless Gum over any other brand of sugarless gum. The advertisement states only that the dentists stated they would recommend a sugarless gum for patients who chew gum.

Second, the advertisement does not state that the dentists recommend that patients chew gum at all. The claim is that the dentists recommend that patients who intend to chew gum should chew a sugarless gum. Actually, the dentists surveyed might be universally opposed to all gum-chewing but regard the chewing of a sugarless gum as the lesser of two evils.

Finally, the advertisement does not really make a claim about dentists in general. Notice that the claim contains the qualifier "of dentists *surveyed.*" The ad does not state how many dentists were in the survey. (Given the wording, the survey might have included only five dentists. Indeed, it seems strange that a survey should yield a number so precise—instead of something like 82.1 percent or 77.3 percent.) Moreover, the ad does not state whether more than one survey was conducted. It is possible, given the wording of the claim, that several such surveys were taken, yielding unsatisfactory results, until one survey yielding the desired result was finally obtained. At that point, the company could proudly make their claim.

Once you understand the clever way in which the claim is qualified, you can see the claim really doesn't provide any really good reason for chewing Brand X Sugarless Gum.

Another tactic used by advertising copywriters is the literally true but vacuous claim. One antiperspirant is advertised on television in the following way:

> Only Brand X gives you twenty-four full hours of protection and the special Brand X scent.

The obvious intent of the advertisement is to persuade the viewer that Brand X antiperspirant has some unique advantage over all of the other antiperspirants that are available; and on a first and casual hearing, you might think that Brand X is the only antiperspirant that provides the user with twenty-four-hour protection. That is not, however, what the advertisement claims. What it really says is that Brand X is the only product to provide *both* the twenty-four-hour protection *and* the special Brand X scent. This is hardly surprising. The Brand X scent probably is unique to Brand X products.

In fact, advertisers are so confident that readers and viewers are not really attending very carefully that they sometimes even include in the advertising a disclaimer about the claim they are making. Another gum manufacturer, we will say Brand Y, used a television advertisement that claimed, "Brand Y has twice as much flavor as Brand Z." The camera focused on the pieces of gum:

Brand Y   **Brand Z**

While this image appeared on screen an actress chanted, "I can see it! I can see it!" In other words, the comparison was based on the relative size of the sticks of gum, and that is why the character in the commercial was literally able to *see* the difference in taste. (Of course, if you wanted to have the same intensity of taste from Brand Z gum, you need only put two pieces in your mouth.)

None of this is particularly new; it's been going on for years. The following anecdote appeared recently in a New York City newspaper, though the source declined to state that he knew for certain that it is true.

> At the turn of the century, the producers of canned tuna and the producers of canned salmon were pitched in a merchandizing battle against each other, and the salmon people were winning. So the tuna producers came up with a new marketing slogan that promised, "Our product is guaranteed not to turn red in the can!"

This claim was, of course, true, but not very interesting.

You might be thinking that such lack of substance might be found only in advertising. But if you carefully study news reports, you will find quite a few reports that are seemingly unbelievable. Here is the substance of a recent television news report:

> Today, the Federal Aviation Administration released the results of a study of airport safety in which agents attempted to smuggle weapons past security checkpoints at passenger boarding areas. Of a nationwide total of slightly over 2,000 attempts, 20 percent of the attempts were successful. The worst security performance was recorded at the Las Vegas airport, where nearly 60 percent of the weapons were not detected. The best security performance was found in Alaska, where the failure rate was only 1 percent.

There are many questions you might want to ask about the report before you conclude that airport security is or is not lax, for example, what kinds of weapons were used, exactly how the attempts were made, and so on. Aside from such questions, there is something very odd about the statistics—in particular, the 1 percent. According to the report, just over 2,000 agent-initiated smuggling attempts were made nationwide. If the number of attempts was divided equally among the fifty states, the result would be roughly 40 attempts in each state. If 40 tests were run at airports in Alaska (and given that Alaska is one of the less populated areas, you would expect even fewer), then the 1-percent rate translates into 1 percent of 40, or 0.4, successes. But how could part of one attempt have succeeded?

Here is another example:

> A local prosecutor had promised to reduce the incidence of crime related to drug use and to that end had established a special court to handle certain cases. After a while, the media grew critical of the plan, suggesting that virtually nothing or at best very little had really been accomplished. Few cases had been tried and fewer convictions won. To these objections, the prosecutor responded, "In 90% of the drug cases that we have pursued we have obtained convictions."

You might wonder whether the media and the prosecutor were discussing the same problem until you examine the prosecutor's claim carefully.

In the first place, the prosecutor qualifies the claim with the phrase "we have pursued." But what proportion of the cases were "pursued," and how is that term being used? It's possible that most of the arrests made were simply dismissed for any number of reasons, but even granting that a significant number of cases were pursued, the claim is weak. For what crimes were the accused convicted? It's possible that the prosecutor acccepted a plea bargain, thereby obtaining a conviction—but for a crime considerably less serious than the one actually committed.

If you examine carefully the substance of what you read and hear, you can find similar examples almost every day. This is the type of careful and considered analysis that is rewarded by the LSAT.

11

4. The Structure of Logical Reasoning

Sherlock Holmes was a scientific detective who combined acute powers of observation with chains of reasoning to reach his conclusions. In the preceding part of this lesson, I stressed the importance of reading carefully for clues; in this part, I describe how to evaluate the logic of an argument.

An argument is a group of statements, one of which is the conclusion and one or more of which are the premises. The premises and the conclusion are tied together by inference.

When we think of logical arguments, the first thing that may come to mind is something like this:

> All men are mortal.
> Socrates is a man.
> Therefore, Socrates is mortal.

In this argument, the conclusion is supported by two premises. Of course, the inference does not appear on the page. The inference is the movement of thought from the premises to the conclusion.

An argument need not have exactly two premises. An argument might have just one premise:

> No fish are mammals.
> Therefore, no mammals are fish.

An argument might have several premises:

> If John attends the party, then Ken attends the party.
> If Ken attends the party, then Lisa attends the party.
> If Lisa attends the party, then Mary attends the party.
> If Mary attends the party, then Ned attends the party.
> John attends the party.
> Therefore, Ned attends the party.

The arguments just presented are obviously valid, which is to say, they are correct. The conclusions clearly follow from the premises. This type of argument in which the conclusion *necessarily* follows from the premises is called a *deductive* argument.

In our day-to-day lives, however, we rarely have occasion to make such nice, neat, and precise deductive arguments. The kinds of arguments we ordinarily make are more apt to sound like this:

> Upon returning to the apartment I see that the mail is
> still in the mail box.
> It is my roommate's habit to pick up the mail from the
> box upon returning home.
> Therefore, my roommate has not yet returned home.

Though this argument does have its conclusion and its premises, the inference that joins them is not quite the same as the inference of the deductive arguments given above. In a deductive argument, the conclusion follows from the premises as a matter of necessity. That is, *if* the premises are true, *then* the conclusion must also be true. Here, however, it is possible for the premises to be true and yet the conclusion false.

Under what circumstances might the premises be true and yet the conclusion false? It's not difficult to imagine several possibilities: the roommate returned home before the mail was delivered or the roommate returned home but for any number of different reasons was either unable or unwilling to pick up the mail. The premises would still be true (the mail is there and it is the roommate's habit to pick it up) yet the conclusion is false.

Arguments of this sort are *inductive* arguments (as opposed to deductive arguments). They are also called probablistic arguments, because the conclusion does not follow from the premises with certainty but only with probability.

The LSAT utilizes some deductive arguments as initial statements, but most of the arguments used fall into the second category. The question stem may ask you to do one of several different things. You may be asked to find the conclusion of an argument, or to draw a conclusion from a set of premises. You may be asked to identify a premise, particularly an unstated premise of an argument. Often you are asked to examine the linkage between the premises and the conclusion and to assess the strength or weakness of the inference of the argument.

All logical reasoning items focus on one or more of these three elements, so we will examine each in greater detail.

5. Locating and Understanding the

Conclusion of an Argument

When speaking of an argument, it is customary to say that the conclusion *follows* from the premises; and often, the conclusion is the last sentence in an argument.

11

EXAMPLE:

A diet high in fiber is believed to reduce the risk of heart disease, colon cancer, and diabetes. Yet, consumers seeking to follow a high-fiber diet are hampered by the failure of food packagers to list fiber content. Congress should mandate the inclusion of fiber content on all nutrition labels.

Here the conclusion of the argument is the final sentence, "Congress should mandate the inclusion of fiber content on all nutrition labels."

There is no requirement, however, that the conclusion appear last. The same argument could be rewritten:

Congress should mandate the inclusion of fiber content on all nutrition labels. A diet high in fiber is believed to reduce the risk of heart disease, colon cancer, and diabetes. But consumers seeking to follow a high-fiber diet are hampered by the failure of food packagers to list fiber content.

Now the conclusion appears first, but the logic of the argument remains unchanged. The conclusion could even appear in the middle of the argument:

A diet high in fiber is believed to reduce the risk of heart disease, colon cancer, and diabetes. Congress should mandate the inclusion of fiber content on all nutrition labels. But consumers seeking to follow a high-fiber diet are hampered by the failure of food packagers to list fiber content.

Now the conclusion is situated in the middle of the argument. Again, the logic of the argument remains the same, but this last revision introduces certain problems of style. The argument no longer reads smoothly.

The problem of style, however, can be easily corrected by simply adding one or two transitional words to inform the reader about the logical structure of the argument:

> A diet high in fiber is believed to reduce the risk of heart disease, colon cancer, and diabetes. Therefore, Congress should mandate the inclusion of fiber on all nutrition labels, because consumers seeking to follow a high-fiber diet are hampered by the failure of food packagers to list fiber content.

With the addition of the transitional words *therefore* and *because*, the logic of the argument is once again clear.

Because the conclusion of the argument can appear anywhere, writers usually include signals for the reader. Here is a list of words and phrases that are often used to signal a conclusion:

> therefore
> thus
> so
> hence
> consequently
> as a result
> it follows that
> it can be inferred that
> which shows that
> which suggests that
> which proves that
> which means that

At other times, the author may use transitional words to signal which are the premises:

> since
> because
> for
> as
> inasmuch as
> insofar as

Sometimes, you may need to dissect the argument to find the conclusion. To do this, you must consciously ask yourself, "What is the author trying to prove here?"

EXAMPLE:

For many poor families, the desire to move from dependency to self-sufficiency founders on the problem of health insurance. A person leaving welfare for a job may earn too much to qualify for Medicaid, the Federal health insurance for the poor; and low-paying, entry-level jobs rarely provide for employee health coverage.

The argument consists of three propositions:

1. The desire to move from dependency to self-sufficiency founders on the problem of health insurance.

2. A person leaving welfare for a job may earn too much to qualify for Medicaid.

3. Entry-level jobs do not provide health coverage.

You can find the conclusion by asking, "Is this the point the author is trying to prove?" For statements 2 and 3, the answer is "no." The author is not trying to prove that a person leaving welfare may earn too much to qualify for Medicaid. That is one of the starting points of the reasoning. Similarly, the author is not trying to prove that entry-level jobs do not provide health coverage. Again, this is a starting point of the argument.

The author is, however, trying to prove statement 1. He wants to prove that lack of health insurance is a disincentive for workers to move off welfare rolls. Statements 2 and 3 provide support for the argument. The two statements cite two different factors contributing to the health insurance problem. Were we to diagram the argument, it would have the following structure:

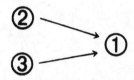

Often, a premise of an argument will support the ultimate conclusion of the argument only indirectly.

11

EXAMPLE:

It is immoral to take something that one has not earned. Gambling winnings are unearned, so gambling is immoral. Therefore, a state government that operates a lottery is acting immorally.

This argument consists of four propositions:

1. It is immoral to take something that one has not earned.

2. Gambling winnings are unearned.

3. Gambling is immoral.

4. State governments that operate lotteries are acting immorally.

The ultimate conclusion to be proved here is contained in statement 4. Statement 3 is a premise of that conclusion, but statement 3 also functions as the conclusion of a subargument, of which statements 1 and 2 are the premises. So the diagram of this argument would look like this:

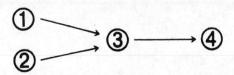

Since arguments are organized around their conclusions, finding the conclusion is the important first step in analyzing arguments. The following exercise allows you to practice identifying the conclusions of arguments. The exercise gets progressively more difficult as the arguments get more complex.

(Answers, page 295)

Directions: Underline the conclusion of each of the following arguments.

EXAMPLE:

The hammer is either in the toolbox or in the kitchen. <u>It must be in the kitchen,</u> because it is not in the toolbox.

1. Every winter for the past ten years, I have caught at least one cold. So this winter, I'll probably catch one or more colds.

2. Ann has not yet taken a foreign language course. Since only students who have passed at least one foreign language course are eligible for graduation, Ann is not a graduate.

3. All members of the Board of Trustees are graduates of the college, so Irving, who is a Trustee, is a graduate of the college.

4. Every time Allen comes to a dinner party, he brings his friend Bob, who tells that same joke about the whale and the pirate. Frank invited Allen to his dinner party tonight, so tonight I will hear the joke about the whale and the pirate.

5. The company rules require a supervisor to discipline a habitually tardy employee by either docking his pay or by firing him. Since Smith has been late every day this week, he will either be docked or fired.

6. If a nail is lost, the shoe is lost; and if the shoe is lost, the horse is lost; and if the horse is lost, the rider is lost; and if the rider is lost, the battle is lost; therefore, if a nail is lost, the battle is lost.

7. The student protest proved very effective. The day after the students first occupied the administration building, the president of the college announced he would reverse the longstanding policy of required courses.

8. Officer, I could not have been exceeding the speed limit. I was moving at the same speed as the train on the tracks that run parallel to the highway here. The speed limit for trains along that stretch of track is less than the speed limit on this highway.

9. It is possible to reduce our reliance on foreign energy sources, because the United States relies heavily on imported oil as an energy source, despite the fact that we have considerable nuclear energy capacity that remains idle.

10. This country doesn't need a five-cent cigar. What it needs is no cigar at all. There is convincing scientific evidence that smoke not only harms the smoker himself but those in proximity to him, who must breathe the smoke he creates. The federal government should enact a total ban on the sale of all tobacco products in this country.

11. The tuition and other costs of getting a college education continue to soar, and recent cutbacks in government aid for students have made it even more difficult for families of even moderate means to finance their children's education. We may soon see the day when a college education is once again the prerogative of only the very rich.

12. A band saw is more efficient than a reciprocating saw. The blade of a band saw travels at the rate of from 8,000 to 10,000 feet per minute, whereas a reciprocating saw making 200 strokes of 18 inches each minute would have a cutting speed of only 300 feet per minute.

11

13. The Federal Reserve Board must have moved last month to slow the growth of the money supply. Following a month in which prices rose more than the month before, interest rates rose noticeably, and in similar situations in the past the Board has moved to counteract inflation.

14. Contrary to the misrepresentations of my opponent, this administration has been one of the most free from corruption in the history of our city. Of the previous five administrations, a total of 23 persons were accused of criminal offenses relating to their performance of their public duties. Fifteen resigned under pressure, and four were convicted of wrongdoing. In this administration, only two people have been accused of any wrongdoing, and they quickly took leaves of absence from their positions until they were able to exonerate themselves.

15. Protectionists argue that an excess of exports over imports is essential to maintaining a favorable balance of trade. The excess can then be "cashed in" as precious metals. This means, however, that the most favorable of all trade balances will occur when a country exports its entire national product and, in turn, imports only gold and silver. Since one cannot eat gold and silver, the protectionists must surely be wrong.

16. The use of balls originated in the Middle East as part of religious ceremonies, and the earliest written references to balls of the sort we associate with games are found in the writings of Christian theologians who condemned the use of a ball as a form of Saturnalia. Apparently, the use of balls was transmitted to Europe by the Moors during the time of their invasion of Spain, for the first and condemnatory references to balls follow the time of the Moorish occupation of Europe.

17. *Nicholas Nickleby*, the second novel of Charles Dickens, has been referred to by some commentators as romantic, but the novel is actually highly realistic. Dickens collected material for his novel on a journey to Yorkshire during which he investigated for himself the deplorable conditions of the cheap boarding schools that produced broken bones and deformed minds in the name of education.

18. Given the ages and health of the justices currently on the Supreme Court, the present administration will likely get to appoint only one more nominee. Then, assuming that the Democrats win the presidency in the upcoming election, they should be able to appoint two or perhaps three new justices during the next administrations, bringing the balance between conservative and liberal forces roughly into line. Now, the Democrats should expedite the appointment of Judge Bork, so as not to antagonize the Republicans, who will surely repay in kind when considering nominees in the future.

19. A blanket ballot is one on which all the nominees of a single group or party are listed together and a voter can choose the entire "slate" simply by making one mark. With such a ballot, the support for a single popular candidate is transmitted to others on the "slate" without the voter's conscious decision to cast his vote for or against them. The Australian ballot is more democratic. All candidates are listed by office, and this requires the voter to think about each selection individually.

20. Administration officials say to scrap oil taxes, import fees, and subsidies for alternative fuels. The free market, they say, will produce the right amount of oil at the right price. That has always been a glib analysis. Now, in light of the administration's willingness to risk lives and dollars in the defense of oil from the Persian Gulf, it seems totally absurd. The real cost of oil should include the cost of military forces protecting supplies.

6. Hidden Premises

Perhaps the most striking feature of the literary genre called detective fiction is that the detective usually has certain privileged information that the reader is denied by the author. This is, after all, what makes a "whodunit" fun to read. Only at the end of the book do you learn that "the uncle's wife's lover and the parson are really the same person, and he killed the high school principal because the principal was blackmailing him." In logical terms, the detective has relied on a hidden or suppressed premise to reach his conclusion.

Above we discussed procedures for isolating the conclusions of arguments. Since every relevant proposition in an argument is either the conclusion or one of the premises, the procedures also enable you to find the explicit premises of an argument.

Most arguments, however, rely on premises that are not explicitly stated.

EXAMPLE:

Premise: Theft is an action that hurts another person.
Conclusion: Therefore, theft is immoral.

The conclusion here does not follow logically from the single, explicit premise. The argument requires yet another premise:

Premise (Explicit): Theft is an action that hurts another person.
Premise (Implicit): Actions that hurt others are immoral.
Conclusion: Therefore, theft is immoral.

Now the conclusion does follow from the two premises taken together.

Most arguments rely on such hidden premises. This is not because the speaker intends to deceive listeners by concealing information (although that may sometimes be the case). Rather, the reason most arguments rely on hidden premises is for economy of communication. If you think that you and your listener enjoy a common view, for instance, that actions that hurt others are immoral, then there is no need for you to articulate that premise. Your argument will have its persuasive appeal even though it rests upon a suppressed premise.

The role of suppressed premises is highlighted when two parties in discussion agree on all of the explicit premises of an argument but disagree about the conclusion.

EXAMPLE:

Mary: Rembrandt is the greatest painter of all times. His dramatic yet highly realistic representations give us an accurate picture of the people of his time.

Alan: No, Van Gogh is the greatest painter of all times. His impassioned use of color and authoritative brushstrokes let us feel the anguish through which he interpreted the world.

This exchange illustrates a discussion in which the two parties are probably not going to resolve their differences easily because each is committed to a host of implicit premises that the other does not share. In Mary's view, the measure of a painter is his ability to depict people or events in a highly accurate and realistic manner, while in Alan's view, the measure of a painter is his ability to communicate emotion. So, while there may not be disagreement about the explicit premises, that is, the important elements of the style of each painter, there is considerable disagreement about the import of those elements.

11

Many LSAT items ask you to uncover implicit or hidden premises. Sometimes, a careful reading of the stimulus material will allow you to anticipate one or more implicit premises, particularly if the argument is relatively simple.

> **EXAMPLE:**
>
> The legislature's decision to require doctors to prescribe generic alternatives to brand-name drugs, when an alternative is available, is an excellent one. Now, patients will be able to save a lot of money and yet get the same medical treatment.

You can probably detect a very important premise in the argument: generic alternatives have the same effect as brand-name drugs. Otherwise, patients won't pay less for the *same* treatment. This is the most obvious hidden assumption, but there are some others. For example, the speaker implicitly assumes that the difference in cost between brand-name and generic drugs is sufficient to make an important difference, and further that there are enough generic alternatives to make a difference.

Sometimes it may not be so easy to isolate the hidden premises. In that case, you will use the available answer choices as "prompts." Look at each and ask yourself, "Is the author committed to this idea?"

> **EXAMPLE:**
>
> During the miserably hot weather of the first week of June, residents of our city were unable to cool off in the municipal pools. Why? Because the pools were not scheduled to open until the first week after the end of the school year, but the school year did not end until the second week of June. To avoid this problem in the future, the Parks Department should schedule the opening of the pools for the first day of June.
>
> The argument above makes which of the following assumptions?
>
>   I. The warm weather of the first week of June is typical weather for the first week of June.
>
> II. The staff needed to operate the pools would be available during the first week of June.
>
> III. The fee charged for admission to the city's pools is not sufficient to meet the operating expenses of the pools.
>
> **(A)** I only **(B)** II only **(C)** III only **(D)** I and II only **(E)** I, II, and III

The answer to this item is (D), for I and II are hidden premises of the argument. You should test each of the statements by asking whether or not the author is (implicitly) committed to that idea. As for statement I, the basis for the demand for an earlier scheduled opening is the hot weather experienced during the first week of June. Since the author uses this as the basis for a recommendation about the future, he is implicitly committed to the idea that this year's weather is typical of June weather. As for II, the author is also implicitly committed to the general idea that opening the pools earlier is feasible and therefore to the more specific idea that staff can be found to open them. Finally, as for III, the author is not committed to this idea. If anything, he probably leans in the other direction, that is, that the increased cost of opening earlier would not be very significant.

When we talk about premises, we often say that a conclusion "rests" on its premises or that the premises "support" the conclusion. The logical function of a premise is analogous to that of the foundation of a building. For this reason, premises play an extremely important role in the attack and defense of an argument. If a key premise can be shown to be false, then the argument, like a building with a weakened foundation, will collapse.

Some LSAT questions ask you to find an idea that weakens an argument. Others ask you to find one that strengthens an argument. The correct answer to both types of question is often a hidden premise. In the case of a question that asks for an attack on the argument, the correct choice will be a statement that an implicit assumption is false, while in the case of a question that asks for a defense of an argument, the correct choice will be a statement that an implicit assumption is true.

EXAMPLES:

Now that the Federal Government has passed legislation allowing states to raise their speed limits from 55 miles per hour to 65 miles per hour, our legislature should move quickly to raise our speed limit. Most people currently drive at 65 miles per hour anyway, and this widespread disobedience tends to encourage disrespect for the law. The new speed limit would allow people to drive at a reasonable speed without encouraging people to break the law.

Which of the following, if true, would most weaken the argument above?

(A) When the speed limit is raised to 65 miles per hour, people will drive 75 miles per hour

(B) Newer, relatively more efficient cars do not use significantly more fuel driving at 65 miles per hour than at 55 miles per hour.

(C) Many people who drive in excess of the posted speed limit use electronic devices to detect police radar and avoid being caught.

(D) The legal speed at which drivers are allowed to operate their vehicles has no effect on the incidence of drunken driving.

(E) During periods in which police give extra attention to the speed limit, more speeders are apprehended and eventually required to pay fines.

The answer is (A). A hidden premise of this argument is that once the speed limit is raised, people will obey the higher limit—rather than go 10 miles per hour faster than that limit. (A) most weakens the argument because it attacks this premise.

Notice also that the question asks you to accept each of the choices as true. Of course, (A) may or may not be true in reality, but for the purpose of argument you are to accept it as true. In fact, we could transform the example above into a "strengthening" question. In that case, the correct answer would probably be something like:

(A) Most people will obey a 65-mile-per-hour limit because that is the speed at which most cars are designed to cruise. Again, I am not saying this is true—just that if we assume it is true, then it strengthens the argument above by proving one of its implicit premises.

11

Here is an example of a "strengthening" question:

> More and more couples are entering into prenuptial agreements in which they specify before the marriage ceremony a distribution of property to be implemented should the marriage end in divorce. In this way, the parties can avoid lengthy and costly divorce proceedings.
>
> Which of the following, if true, would most strengthen the analysis above?
>
> **(A)** Not every dissolution of a marriage ends in a bitter divorce.
>
> **(B)** A party to a divorce is precluded from contesting the fairness of a prenuptial agreement.
>
> **(C)** More than two-thirds of marriages end in divorce.
>
> **(D)** Couples who have lived together prior to marriage may have accumulated considerable joint property.
>
> **(E)** The emotional impact of a prenuptial agreement may actually deter some people from marriage.

The answer to the item above is (B). The argument asserts that prenuptial agreements have the beneficial effect of allowing couples to avoid lengthy and costly divorce disputes over the distribution of property. The author implicitly assumes, though it is not explicitly stated, that such agreements cannot themselves become the center of a dispute. If that implicit assumption is true, as (B) states, then the argument is much strengthened.

Thus, we see that LSAT questions often test your ability to find suppressed premises in argument, by asking you to identify them or by asking you to weaken or strengthen the argument. The exercise below will give you some practice in both types of questions. Remember, to determine whether an idea is a hidden premise of an argument, ask yourself whether the author, by the logic of the argument, is committed to that idea.

(Answers, page 297)

Directions: Each of the following items asks you to isolate the hidden premises (assumptions) of an argument. Mark the best answer.

1. Edward was just elected president of the Student Senate, so he must be a senior.
   The statement above makes which of the following assumptions?
   I. Only seniors can be members of the Student Senate.
   II. Only seniors can be president of the Student Senate.
   III. Only members of the Student Senate can be seniors.
   (A) I only **(B)** II only **(C)** III only **(D)** I and III only **(E)** I, II, and III

2. If these cabinets were built after 1975, then they were not made out of oak plywood.
   The statement above depends upon which of the following assumptions?
   (A) All cabinets made after 1975 were made out of oak plywood.
   (B) All cabinets made in 1975 or earlier were made out of oak plywood.
   (C) Only cabinets made of oak plywood were built in 1975 or earlier.
   (D) No cabinets made in 1975 or earlier were made of oak plywood.
   (E) No cabinets made after 1975 were made of oak plywood.

3. Max: Every painting done by Picasso is a masterpiece.
   Ernst: That's not true. Several masterpieces by David and Delacroix hang in the Louvre in Paris.
   Ernst apparently assumes that Max said
   (A) only masterpieces were painted by Picasso
   (B) all masterpieces were painted by either David or Delacroix
   (C) only masterpieces by Picasso hang in the Louvre
   (D) only masterpieces by David and Delacroix hang in the Louvre
   (E) some of Picasso's masterpieces do not hang in the Louvre

4. Students at Duns Scotus High must get a better education than students at Erasmus High because the grade point average of students at Duns Scotus High is higher than that of students at Erasmus High.
   The claim above depends upon which of the following assumptions?
   I. The average grade earned by students is a good measure of the quality of education that a student receives.
   II. Extracurricular activities at Duns Scotus High are given more emphasis than at Erasmus High.
   III. The grading standards at the two high schools are roughly the same.
   (A) I only **(B)** III only **(C)** I and III only **(D)** II and III only **(E)** I, II, and III

11

5. A government survey released today shows that 80 percent of the people who fly are satisfied with the service they receive from the airlines in this country. Three interviewers stood outside a major airline and asked people leaving the terminal, "Do you have any complaints about the flight you just got off?" Only 20 percent responded "yes!"

Which of the following, if true, would most undermine the conclusion of the argument above?

(A) Sixty percent of the people coming out of the airline terminal were not people who had just gotten off a flight.

(B) One percent of the people approached by the interviewers refused to respond to their inquiries.

(C) The interviewers began their inquiry just after passengers were discharged from a flight that was 40 minutes late.

(D) The interviewers were able to speak to only 70 percent of the people leaving the terminal, but those people were selected at random.

(E) For six months following the day of the interviews, no official complaints were filed by any passenger with the Federal agency that regulated the airlines.

6. Colonel Mustard did not commit the murder in the dining room with the candlestick; therefore, Mrs. Peacock committed the murder in the conservatory with the knife.

The argument above depends upon which of the following assumptions?

I. The murder was committed either with the candlestick or with the knife.
II. The murder was committed either in the dining room or in the conservatory.
III. The murder was committed either by Colonel Mustard or by Mrs. Peacock.
IV. The murder was either committed by Colonel Mustard in the dining room with the candlestick or by Mrs. Peacock in the conservatory with the knife.

(A) I only   (B) IV only   (C) I and III only   (D) I, II, and III only   (E) I, II, III, and IV

7. An efficiency expert made the following suggestion to the manager of a shirt factory: Purchase larger spools of sewing thread. With more thread to a spool, your operators will not need to stop production as often to change spools. This will reduce your labor costs.

The efficiency expert apparently assumes that

(A) thread wound on larger spools is not as strong as thread wound on smaller spools

(B) sewing machines do not break down and do not require routine maintenance

(C) workers in the factory are paid by the hour rather than on a piecework basis

(D) machine operators are not allowed to leave their machines during the work period

(E) speeding up production will improve the quality of the shirts made at the factory

8. A major insurance company reported that approximately 80 percent of all traffic accidents never result in an insurance claim. So we can conclude that about 80 percent of all losses due to theft also go unreported.

The argument above assumes that

I. Statistics about automobile insurance claims are applicable to claims for theft losses.
II. Traffic accidents represent a more serious danger to the individual than do thefts.
III. The average dollar value of a traffic accident claim is equal to the average dollar value of a theft loss claim.

(A) I only   (B) II only   (C) III only   (D) I and II only   (E) I and III only

9. The continuing and increased reliance on computers represents a serious threat to the privacy of the individual. Recently, we have seen numerous examples of teenage and other "hackers" breaking the security codes of stores and banks and obtaining sensitive financial information about customers.

The argument above depends upon which of the following assumptions?

I. People who obtain sensitive financial information about others will not share it.

II. It is not possible to develop a security system for a computer that cannot be broken.

III. Computers are not more efficient than other systems of record keeping.

(A) I only   (B) II only   (C) III only   (D) I and III only   (E) II and III only

10. The need for drug and sex counseling for teenagers has been overemphasized. Instead, we should channel the money spent on those programs into marriage counseling and other programs designed to hold the family together. Lower the rate of family dissolution, and you will reduce the incidence of teen drug use and pregnancies.

The author makes which of the following assumptions?

I. Marriage counseling and other programs are effective in maintaining the unity of the family.

II. Family dissolution contributes to problems of teen drugs and sex.

III. People presently working in teen counseling programs can be reemployed as marriage counselors.

(A) I only   (B) II only   (C) I and II only   (D) II and III only   (E) I, II, and III

11

Summary

1. In general, only two of the answer choices in a logical reasoning item have any real merit, but you will have to think carefully about those two choices.

2. Logical reasoning items are in large part a test of reading comprehension. You must read carefully—more carefully than you do in your day-to-day activities.

3. An argument consists of a conclusion, a premise or premises, and an inference. A logical reasoning item could ask about any of these elements.

4. The conclusion may or may not be the last sentence of the argument and may or may not be signalled by a transitional word such as *therefore*. Be prepared to dissect the argument by asking yourself, "Is this what the author is trying to prove?"

5. Once you have found the conclusion, every other sentence in the argument (if relevant) must be a premise of the argument. But not all premises are explicitly stated. If an item asks you to identify an assumption made by the argument, test each choice by asking, "Is this essential to the argument?"

6. Often the correct answer to a weakening or strengthening question identifies a hidden premise of the argument.

Answers

EXERCISE 1

1. Every winter for the past ten years, I have caught at least one cold. <u>So this winter, I'll probably catch one or more colds.</u>

2. Ann has not yet taken a foreign language course. Since only students who have passed at least one foreign language course are eligible for graduation, <u>Ann is not a graduate.</u>

3. All members of the Board of Trustees are graduates of the college, so <u>Irving</u>, who is a Trustee, <u>is a graduate of the college.</u>

4. Every time Allen comes to a dinner party, he brings his friend Bob, who tells that same joke about the whale and the pirate. Frank invited Allen to his dinner party tonight, so <u>tonight I will hear the joke about the whale and the pirate.</u>

5. The company rules require a supervisor to discipline a habitually tardy employee by either docking his pay or by firing him. Since Smith has been late every day this week, <u>he will either be docked or fired.</u>

6. If a nail is lost, the shoe is lost; and if the shoe is lost, the horse is lost; and if the horse is lost, the rider is lost; and if the rider is lost, the battle is lost; therefore, <u>if a nail is lost, the battle is lost.</u>

7. <u>The student protest proved very effective.</u> The day after the students first occupied the administration building, the president of the college announced he would reverse the longstanding policy of required courses.

8. Officer, <u>I could not have been exceeding the speed limit.</u> I was moving at the same speed as the train on the tracks that run parallel to the highway here. The speed limit for trains along that stretch of track is less than the speed limit on this highway.

9. <u>It is possible to reduce our reliance on foreign energy sources</u>, because the United States relies heavily on imported oil as an energy source, despite the fact that we have considerable nuclear energy capacity that remains idle.

10. This country doesn't need a five-cent cigar. What it needs is no cigar at all. There is convincing scientific evidence that smoke not only harms the smoker himself but those in proximity to him who must breathe the smoke he creates. <u>The federal government should enact a total ban on the sale of all tobacco products in this country.</u>

11. The tuition and other costs of getting a college education continue to soar, and recent cutbacks in government aid for students have made it even more difficult for families of even moderate means to finance their children's education. <u>We may soon see the day when a college education is once again the prerogative of only the very rich.</u>

12. <u>A band saw is more efficient than a reciprocating saw.</u> The blade of a band saw travels at the rate of from 8,000 to 10,000 feet per minute, whereas a reciprocating saw making 200 strokes of 18 inches each minute would have a cutting speed of only 300 feet per minute.

11

13. The Federal Reserve Board must have moved last month to slow the growth of the money supply. Following a month in which prices rose more than the month before, interest rates rose noticeably, and in similar situations in the past the Board has moved to counteract inflation.

14. Contrary to the misrepresentations of my opponent, this administration has been one of the most free from corruption in the history of our city. Of the previous five administrations, a total of 23 persons were accused of criminal offenses relating to their performance of their public duties. Fifteen resigned under pressure, and four were convicted of wrongdoing. In this administration, only two people have been accused of any wrongdoing, and they quickly took leaves of absence from their position until they were able to exonerate themselves.

15. Protectionists argue that an excess of exports over imports is essential to maintaining a favorable balance of trade. The excess can then be "cashed in" as precious metals. This means, however, that the most favorable of all trade balances will occur when a country exports its entire national product and, in turn, imports only gold and silver. Since one cannot eat or wear gold and silver, the protectionists must surely be wrong.

16. The use of balls originated in the Middle East as part of religious ceremonies, and the earliest written references to balls of the sort we associate with games are found in the writings of Christian theologians who condemned the use of a ball as a form of Saturnalia. Apparently, the use of balls was transmitted to Europe by the Moors during the time of their invasion of Spain, for the first and condemnatory references to balls follow the time of the Moorish occupation of Europe.

17. Nicholas Nickleby, the second novel of Charles Dickens, has been referred to by some commentators as romantic, but the novel is actually highly realistic. Dickens collected material for his novel on a journey to Yorkshire during which he investigated for himself the deplorable conditions of the cheap boarding schools that produced broken bones and deformed minds in the name of education.

18. Given the ages and health of the justices currently on the Supreme Court, the present administration will likely get to appoint only one more nominee. Then, assuming that the Democrats win the Presidency in the upcoming election, they should be able to appoint two or perhaps three new justices during the next administrations, bringing the balance between conservative and liberal forces roughly into line. Now, the Democrats should expedite the appointment of Judge Bork, so as not to antagonize the Republicans who will surely repay in kind when considering nominees in the future.

19. A blanket ballot is one on which all the nominees of a single group or party are listed together and a voter can choose the entire "slate" simply by making one mark. With such a ballot, the support for a single popular candidate is transmitted to others on the "slate" without the voter's conscious decision to cast his vote for or against them. The Australian ballot is more democratic. All candidates are listed by office, and this requires the voter to think about each selection individually.

20. Administration officials say to scrap oil taxes, import fees, and subsidies for alternative fuels. The free market, they say, will produce the right amount of oil at the right price. That has always been a glib analysis. Now, in light of the administration's willingness to risk lives and dollars in the defense of oil from the Persian Gulf, it seems totally absurd. The real cost of oil should include the cost of military forces protecting supplies.

EXERCISE 2

1. B
2. E
3. C
4. C
5. A
6. B
7. C
8. A
9. B
10. C

11

Logical Reasoning–Part II

1. Causal Reasoning
2. Generalization
3. Analogy
4. Appeal to Authority
5. *Ad Hominen* Arguments
6. Dilemma
7. Begging the Question
8. Ambiguity
9. Shifting the Burden of Proof
10. Contradiction

12

In the preceding lesson, you studied two of the three parts of an argument, the conclusion and the premises. In this lesson, we take up the third part, the inference. Almost every elementary text on logic makes an attempt to distribute errors of inductive reasoning under various headings such as the fallacies of *post hoc ergo propter hoc* and *ad hominem*. Fortunately, you will not be asked to classify any errors of reasoning according to such technical terms, but you probably will be asked to identify such errors or to describe a line of reasoning in nontechnical terms. I will discuss ten common forms of inductive reasoning.

1. Causal Reasoning

One of the most common forms of inductive reasoning attributes a causal connection between two events. An LSAT question might ask you to recognize that the initial statement contains a causal analysis.

> **EXAMPLE:**
>
> In May, new-home sales dropped 14.9 percent, the largest decline in over five years. At the same time, mortgage interest rates increased from 9 percent to 10.5 percent. Evidently, many first-time buyers, who normally purchase less expensive homes, were driven out of the market by higher mortgage rates.
>
> The primary concern of the argument above is to
>
> **(A)** offer an explanation of a phenomenon
> **(B)** refute a traditional theory
> **(C)** question the reliability of statistics
> **(D)** criticize government policies
> **(E)** cast doubt on the credibility of a source

The answer is (A). The initial statement seeks to provide a causal explanation for the decline of new-home sales during the month cited.

Reasoning about cause-and-effect can be good or bad, depending on whether a speaker has isolated the correct causal linkage. A question stem might ask that you find an answer choice that weakens (or strengthens) a causal explanation. Usually, the correct answer to such a question points to the existence (or nonexistence) of what is called an alternative causal linkage.

EXAMPLE:

In May, new-home sales dropped 14.9 percent, the largest decline in over five years. At the same time, mortgage interest rates increased from 9 percent to 10.5 percent. Evidently, many first-time buyers, who normally purchase less expensive homes, were driven out of the market by higher mortgage rates.

Which of the following, if true, would most weaken the conclusion of the argument above?

(A) During the first six months of the year, the economy experienced an annualized growth rate of 4.5 percent.

(B) During the first six months of the year, a nationwide strike in the building trade brought new construction to a virtual standstill.

(C) People today are able to afford their first new home at a younger age than people were ten years ago.

(D) Nationwide, per capita disposable income rose by 0.5 percent during the month of June.

(E) Many people live in urban areas where single-family homes are scarce and very expensive.

The answer to this item is (B). (B) points to a causal explanation other than the one suggested by the initial paragraph.

Sometimes the answer to a question about causal sequences will be one that mentions some unforeseen consequences of an action.

EXAMPLE:

Good health and grooming habits should be taught in school, and one such habit is the use of a cotton swab to remove wax from the ear canal. This prevents a buildup of excess wax.

Which of the following, if true, would constitute a valid criticism of the suggestions above?

  I. Some good health and grooming habits can be learned even by very young children and should be taught before a child enters school.
 II. When a cotton swab is inserted into the ear canal, it pushes wax ahead of itself, and this can result in wax buildup and infection in the inner ear.
III. Removal of ear wax exposes the delicate tissues of the ear canal to dirt and other elements which may cause infection.

(A) II only   **(B)** III only   **(C)** I and III only
(D) II and III only   **(E)** I, II, and III

The answer to this item is (D). Both II and III point to unanticipated consequences that undermine the value of the suggestion.

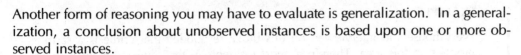

2. Generalization

Another form of reasoning you may have to evaluate is generalization. In a generalization, a conclusion about unobserved instances is based upon one or more observed instances.

> **EXAMPLE:**
>
> Every household interviewed on this block responded that crime is a serious problem in this area. Therefore, most residents in this neighborhood probably believe that crime is a serious problem here.

This is a simple illustration of a very common form of reasoning. There is nothing inherently correct or incorrect about such arguments. Rather, generalizations are stronger or weaker depending upon the evidence used to support the conclusion. The argument above could be strong or weak depending on the number of households surveyed and their "representativeness" of the area described.

Questions about generalizations are likely to focus on the issue of "representativeness."

> **EXAMPLE:**
>
> Every household interviewed on this block responded that crime is a serious problem in this area. Therefore, most residents in this neighborhood probably believe that crime is a serious problem here.
>
> The argument above depends upon which of the following assumptions?
>
> **(A)** The incidence of crime in the neighborhood surveyed is typical of the incidence of crime nationwide.
>
> **(B)** The incidence of crime in the neighborhood surveyed is growing.
>
> **(C)** The households surveyed included at least one person who had been a victim of a crime.
>
> **(D)** In the neighborhood cited, violent crime is a greater problem than nonviolent crime.
>
> **(E)** The households surveyed are representative of the households in the neighborhood.

The answer is (E), because (E) articulates the hidden assumption of the generalization—that the data upon which the generalization is based are representative.

12

Using the same initial statement, a question stem might ask you to defend the argument.

EXAMPLE:

Every household interviewed on this block responded that crime is a serious problem in this area. Therefore, most residents in this town probably believe that crime is a serious problem here.

Which of the following, if true, would most strengthen the argument above?

(A) The incidence of crime in the town surveyed is typical of the incidence of crime nationwide.

(B) The incidence of crime in the town surveyed is growing.

(C) The households surveyed included at least one person who had been a victim of a crime.

(D) In the town cited, violent crime is a greater problem than nonviolent crime.

(E) The households surveyed are representative of the households in the town.

Again the answer is (E). If the assumption of representativeness is true, then the argument is much stronger.

Conversely, a question stem might ask that you attack the argument.

EXAMPLE:

Every household interviewed on this block responded that crime is a serious problem in this area. Therefore, most residents in this town probably believe that crime is a serious problem here.

Which of the following, if true, would most weaken the argument above?

(A) The incidence of crime in the town surveyed is typical of the incidence of crime nationwide.

(B) The incidence of crime in the town surveyed is growing.

(C) The households surveyed included at least one person who had been a victim of a crime.

(D) In the town cited, violent crime is a greater problem than nonviolent crime.

(E) The households surveyed are located in the most commercial area of the town, where the crime rate is the highest.

Again the answer is (E), for (E) essentially says that the sample upon which the generalization is based is not representative of the entire town.

Another type of generalization projects conditions into the future.

EXAMPLE:

Per capita income in Country X rose from $2,000 to $2,500 from 1978 to 1988. Therefore, by the year 1998, per capita income in Country X will be $3,000.

A projection is strong or weak depending on whether or not the time period on which the projection is based is "representative" of the future, that is, whether factors which obtain will continue into the future. Question stems will likely focus on these issues.

EXAMPLE:

Archaeologist: In the past eight months, we have recovered 15 ancient weapons from this dig. At this rate, by the time we finish excavating the site next year, we will have recovered almost 40 such items.

The logic of the reasoning above is most similar to which of the following?

(A) Economist: When the money supply is tightened, the interest rates of savings and loan institutions rise more slowly than those of other state institutions because of state regulations. As a result, money flows out of savings and loans into other sectors.

(B) Attorney: The new appointment to the Supreme Court gives the conservative bloc more voting power, so we can expect to see earlier decisions on civil and individual rights read in a fairly restrictive manner.

(C) Doctor: The condition of this patient is caused by a lack of vitamin C. A vitamin supplement high in vitamin C should restore the patient to good health.

(D) Astronomer: Since no one has yet been able to prove that black holes do not exist, we can conclude that the theory that certain stars eventually become pointal masses is correct.

(E) Political Scientist: So far, six of the 15 Presidents elected in this century have been Democrats. This means the remaining three elections in this century are critical. If the Democrats are not successful again this century, we can expect to see only six Democratic Presidents in the 21st century.

The answer to this item is (E). The initial statement makes a projection based on past experience, as does (E).

You might also be asked to weaken (or strengthen) a projection, in which case the correct response would likely point out that conditions are not likely to continue (or are likely to continue) into the future.

EXAMPLE:

Political Scientist: So far, six of the 15 Presidents elected in this century have been Democrats. This means the remaining three elections in this century are critical. If the Democrats are not successful again this century, we can expect to see only six Democratic Presidents in the 21st century.

Which of the following points out a logical weakness in the argument above?

(A) The author presupposes that Democrats make better Presidents than members of any other political party.

(B) The author assumes that political conditions of one century will be repeated in the next century.

(C) The author believes that most people in the 21st century will vote in Presidential elections.

(D) The author fails to consider the possibility that a new form of government will be enacted that doesn't include elected officials.

(E) The author doesn't prove that most people prefer the policies of the Republican party to those of the Democratic party.

12

The answer to this item is (B). The initial paragraph is a straightforward projection into the future. The weakness in the argument is that it presupposes the same events will be repeated one hundred years later—without regard to possible changes in political conditions. (D) is perhaps the second-best answer. It at least has the merit of saying that political conditions may not repeat exactly. The problem with (D) is that it fails to point out the general logical flaw in the argument. Yes, it is true that the author does fail to consider this possibility, and this is one of the possibilities that might invalidate the author's prediction. But there are many others as well. And (B), because it is a more general attack on the structure of the argument, is a stronger attack.

3. Analogy

An argument from analogy is one in which the speaker draws a conclusion about one set of circumstances based upon the similarity of those circumstances to another set of circumstances.

> **EXAMPLE:**
>
> Teachers should have the authority to inflict corporal punishment on the students in their charge. During the school day, a teacher has the responsibility for ensuring the child's safety and for teaching the child right from wrong. If a parent can spank a child, then the teacher, who acts like the child's parent during school hours, should have the same option.

Some people will agree with this argument; other people will disagree. But the difference in their opinions will likely be determined by the degree to which they think the two situations are parallel.

A logical reasoning item might just ask that you identify an argument as relying on analogy.

> **EXAMPLE:**
>
> In nature, only the strong survive to reproduce themselves, thereby ensuring that nature gradually moves closer and closer to perfection. So too war is necessary to eliminate the weak and imperfect nations, for in war only the strong survive. Rather than opposing war, we should support war as the way by which the human species can perfect itself.
>
> The argument above can be criticized for
>
> **(A)** making a hasty generalization
>
> **(B)** confusing a cause with an effect
>
> **(C)** relying on a false analogy
>
> **(D)** appealing to the emotions of the reader
>
> **(E)** relying on the use of force to prove its point

The answer is (C). The author draws a parallel between the survival of the fittest in nature and the survival of political systems.

A logical reasoning item might also ask that you attack an argument based on analogy. Generally, the correct answer to a question asking you to attack an argument based on analogy will be a statement that suggests that the two situations cited in the argument are not really parallel. The correct answer might, for example, point out a significant difference between the two situations.

EXAMPLE:

A Federal lottery would not be a productive revenue-raiser. In the 27 states that have lotteries, the lotteries have yielded only 2 to 4 percent of total state-raised revenues. At the Federal level, this would mean additional revenues of only $11 billion per year—not a significant figure.

Which of the following, if true, would most weaken the argument above?

(A) A Federal lottery would offer larger prizes that would increase participation and thereby generate greater revenues.

(B) A Federal lottery would discourage participation in state lotteries, so states would lose revenues.

(C) A lottery is a form of gambling, so a Federal lottery would contribute to the problem of compulsive gambling.

(D) The proceeds from state lotteries are earmarked for special funds such as education, but proceeds from a Federal lottery would go into general revenues.

(E) Any money generated by a Federal lottery would not be used to reduce the average tax burden on individuals.

The answer is (A). The speaker draws a parallel between state lotteries and a proposed national lottery. A good attack on this argument would point to a difference between the national government and state governments. (A) does this.

4. Appeal to Authority

In making arguments, we often mention the opinion of someone else. A logical reasoning question might ask that you recognize that an argument relies upon an appeal to authority.

EXAMPLE:

To the Editor:
    While I generally agree with your call for increased efforts to combat drug dependency, I disagree with your proposal for 14-day ambulatory detoxification programs for heroin addicts. Dr. Edward McIver, head of Downtown Hospital's Detoxification Unit, notes that a two-week treatment program is not long enough to cure someone of heroin dependency. Therefore your proposal would not be effective.

The writer above relies primarily on

(A) deductive reasoning

(B) expert opinion

(C) statistical proof

(D) rhetorical questions

(E) emotional language

12

The answer is (B). The main proof for the conclusion that the two-week detoxification program would not be effective is the opinion of an expert.

Of course, reliance on authority can be more or less effective, and the persuasive force of a citation of authority depends on several factors:

(1) Is the expert cited generally qualified as an authority in the area? A medical doctor, for example, would not necessarily be a good source to cite for an opinion about the causes of unemployment in the central city, but a medical doctor would be a good authority to cite on the cause of some disease.

(2) Is the expert cited specficially qualified to speak on the particular issue? For example, a general practitioner might not be a particularly good choice to rely on for an opinion about tropical diseases.

(3) Is there any reason to believe that the opinion given by the expert is colored by self-interest? For example, an administrator of a government agency such as a subway system might very well be expert in the operations of that agency, but you should be wary of any statements made by that person about the operation of the agency: "Over the next few months, the performance of subway trains should become significantly better." Here it is possible that the speaker's opinion is colored by his interest in presenting the agency in a favorable light.

5. *Ad Hominen* Arguments

Above I said that you would not be held responsible for any technical terminology, but here I prefer to use the Latin description of this form of reasoning. I suspect that most people have heard the term before. An *ad hominem* argument is just an attack that is directed against the person making an argument—as opposed to an attack on the merits of the argument. In any event, the LSAT would not expect you to know the Latin terminology. The LSAT would likely call this type of reasoning "an attack against the person making the argument" rather than an *ad hominem* attack.

EXAMPLE:

Bob, the president of the neighborhood association, states that we should urge our state legislator to vote for a tax increase to provide more money to schools. But we all know that last year Bob was arrested for drunk driving. How can you believe what a drunk tells you?

This line of reasoning is weak because it attacks Bob's character rather than the merits of the proposal to raise taxes for educational purposes.

An *ad hominem* attack is not always an illegitimate form of reasoning. On those occasions when the character or credibility of the proponent of a position is at issue, then an *ad hominem* attack is a powerful form of reasoning.

EXAMPLE:

Sam is running for the position of president of the neighborhood association. However, we should remember that Sam was forced to resign as chairman of the softball league for using league funds for his own personal purposes.

This is a legitimate use of the *ad hominem* attack, because the character of a public official is a determinant of how well the person will discharge the duties of his office.

6. Dilemma

A dilemma is an either/or situation. For example, in a moral dilemma you are forced to choose between two equally unacceptable courses of action: you find yourself in a life-and-death situation, and you have the ability to save your brother or your sister—but not both. This is the essence of a dilemma.

As a forensic strategy, you might try to force an opponent into a dilemma, a position where an opponent must choose one of two unacceptable consequences.

> **EXAMPLES:**
>
> A young law school graduate hired an older attorney to tutor him for the bar exam. The agreement between them specified that the student would pay his tutor when he finally won his first case. After passing the bar exam, the student decided not to practice law. The tutor, tired of waiting for his fee, sued the student, and the student defended himself. The tutor argued: "If the court determines that the student has breached his contract by not going into the practice of law, then I am entitled to my fee; if the court determines that the student has not breached the contract and the student wins his case, then I am entitled to my fee by the terms of the contract."

> I have challenged my opponent to state his position on abortion. If he tells us that he favors abortion, then we know he has little respect for human life. If he tells us that he opposes abortion, then we know that he cares little for the rights of women.

As with other forms of reasoning, the use of a dilemma can be effective or ineffective, depending on whether or not the two alternatives that compose the dilemma are truly exhaustive of the possibilities. What often happens is that the person facing the dilemma is able to "escape through the horns" of the dilemma, which means that he points out that there are one or more alternatives that are not unpalatable to him.

> **EXAMPLE:**
>
> Either you will punish your puppy severely when he misbehaves, or the puppy will grow up to be a bad dog. Since your puppy just had an accident on the kitchen floor, you should punish him severely.
>
> The argument above can be best criticized by pointing out that it relies upon
>
> **(A)** a false dilemma
> **(B)** an inappropriate analogy
> **(C)** a hasty generalization
> **(D)** a nonrepresentative sampling
> **(E)** an unproved theory

The correct answer is (A). The speaker asserts that the person he addresses faces an either/or situation. In reality, however, there is considerable middle ground between the two extremes. You don't have to punish the puppy severely for an accident.

12

7. Begging the Question

"Begging the question" is a phrase that is used to describe a line of reasoning that attempts to prove a conclusion by using the conclusion itself as one of the premises of the argument.

> **EXAMPLE:**
>
> Shakespeare was a better playwright than Eugene O'Neill. After all, Shakespeare's plays are better than those of O'Neill, and the description "better" playwright must surely be applied to the person who wrote the better plays.

This argument has the structure:

Premise: The better playwright is the one who wrote the better plays.
Premise: Shakespeare wrote better plays than O'Neill.
Conclusion: Shakespeare was a better playwright than O'Neill.

But the conclusion is really just a restatement of the first premise.

This type of thinking is also referred to as "circular reasoning." If you study the argument above, you will see that the premises refer you to the conclusion and the conclusion refers you back to the premises. It is enough to make you dizzy.

Circular reasoning cannot be good (although it can be interesting). Circular reasoning is always bad reasoning, because it contains a logical fallacy.

> **EXAMPLE:**
>
> To say that humans are moral agents is to imply that they have the capacity to choose one course of action over another, but in reality humans lack this capacity. When a person seems to choose one course of action, he is really just acting on the strongest desire he has. And he must have acted on the strongest of the desires, because it is the one that finally moved him to act. Therefore, human beings cannot be considered moral agents.
>
> Which of the following is the best criticism of the argument above?
>
> **(A)** It reaches a general conclusion based on too few examples.
> **(B)** It confuses an effect with its cause.
> **(C)** It contains a logical contradiction.
> **(D)** It relies upon questionable authority.
> **(E)** It assumes what it tries to prove.

The answer is (E). To prove his point, the speaker must show that humans merely act on the strongest desire—that they never choose a less intensely felt desire over a more intensely felt desire on moral grounds. But his proof for this claim is the contention that we can determine what was the most intensely felt desire by looking at a person's actions and that the action is the effect of the strongest desire.

8. Ambiguity

Any time that a line of reasoning uses a term in more than one way, it commits the fallacy of ambiguity.   Sometimes, the results can be quite amusing.

> **EXAMPLE:**
>
> The American buffalo is disappearing.
> This shaggy beast here in this zoo exhibit is an American buffalo.
> Therefore, this beast is disappearing.

The problem with this line of reasoning is that it uses the word "buffalo" in two different senses.   In the first premise, the term is used to refer to the species, but in the second premise the term is used to refer to a particular member of the species.
   The exchange that constitutes the initial paragraph of the following problem is taken from Lewis Carroll's *Through the Looking Glass* and is a classic example of ambiguity.

> **EXAMPLE:**
>
> "Who did you pass on the road," the King went on . . . .
> "Nobody," said the Messenger.
> "Quite right," said the King, "this lady saw him too.   So of course Nobody walks slower than you."
> "I do my best," the Messenger said in a sullen tone.   "I'm sure nobody walks much faster than I do!"
> "He can't do that," said the King, "or else he'd have been here first!"
> Which of the following terms is used ambiguously in the exchange above?
> **(A)** faster
> **(B)** slower
> **(C)** nobody
> **(D)** pass
> **(E)** saw

The ambiguous term is "nobody."   In some instances, the speakers use the term in its standard sense to refer to an absence of persons, but in other instances they use the term as though it were the name of a person.

9. Shifting the Burden of Proof

The proponent of an argument has the burden of going forward with an issue. After all, it's no argument at all simply to make a statement and challenge others to disprove the statement.

> **EXAMPLE:**
>
> I am quite certain that all cats are really very cleverly built Martian robots that resemble living creatures.   They were placed here on Earth to spy on us.   Those Martians are so clever, you'd never know these robots aren't really living creatures.   Since no one has yet disproved that cats are really Martian robots, my theory must be correct.

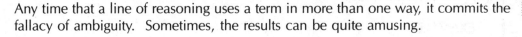
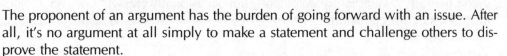

12

The fallacy in this line of reasoning is that it contains no affirmative support for the thesis. The only "proof" of the conclusion is the statement that no one has yet proved the contention false.

EXAMPLE:

For over a quarter of a century, researchers have been trying to find a cure for cancer, and they have failed. We must finally admit that cancer is simply an incurable disease.

Which of the following is most nearly like that of the paragraph above?

(A) Three students were implicated in the theft of the final exam. Two have admitted their guilt. The third must also be guilty, since she cannot prove that she is innocent.

(B) Lower-paying jobs are often filled by workers with few or no skills. Since Bob has very few skills, he will probably get a low-paying job.

(C) At 4:00 and 4:15 a city bus filled with commuters passed this corner. Therefore, at 4:30, another city bus will probably go by, and it, too, will be filled with commuters.

(D) Dr. Erskine maintains that the causes of the current outbreak of tuberculosis are poverty and poor living conditions. But Dr. Erskine is an avowed proponent of the negative income tax, so this is exactly what one would expect him to say.

(E) We must reject the President's proposal to send aid to Central America. If we become involved in politics in that region, we will soon find ourselves engaged in another Viet Nam.

The answer is (A). The initial paragraph offers no affirmative proof for the claim that cancer is incurable. Similarly, statement (A) offers no affirmative proof for the claim that the third student is guilty.

10. Contradiction

A logical contradiction is the joint assertion of two statements that cannot possibly both be true.

EXAMPLE:

No students failed the exam, but John, a student, failed the exam.

These statements cannot both be true. Of course, we rarely find anyone making such obviously contradictory statements, but occasionally you will uncover a logical inconsistency in a position.

EXAMPLE:

No one has the moral right to take the life of another person. Since abortion is the taking of a human life, no one has the right to perform or assist in any way in the performance of an abortion. And because abortion is a form of murder, it should be punished as severely as possible: with the death penalty.

The argument above can best be criticized as being

(A) an oversimplification

(B) an appeal to the emotions of the reader

(C) internally inconsistent

(D) needlessly abstract

(E) insufficiently detailed

The correct answer is (C). In the first sentence the author asserts that no one has the right to take a human life, but in the last sentence he calls for the death penalty.

12

EXERCISE

(Answers, page 319)

Directions: Below you will find 40 arguments, each of which illustrates one of the inferential errors discussed above. Beside each argument, indicate the type of error it contains.

(A) False Cause

(B) Hasty Generalization

(C) False Analogy

(D) Illegitimate Appeal to Authority

(E) Illegitimate *Ad Hominem* Attack

(F) False Dilemma

(G) Begging the Question

(H) Ambiguity

(I) Shifting the Burden of Proof

(J) Contradiction

1. The state has banned all smoking in railroad cars because of the threat posed by passive smoking to nonsmoking passengers. The city should learn from this lesson and pass an ordinance banning smoking in all restaurants and public meeting places.

2. Government programs often create or intensify existing problems rather than solve them. In the past five years, all levels of government have stepped up efforts to educate students about the dangers of drugs. And sure enough, the incidence of drug use among students has increased as well.

3. No one goes into that restaurant any more because it's too crowded.

4. This semester I am teaching Philosophy of Law at Bartlett College. On the first day I asked whether any of the students in the class owned a computer. No one raised a hand. It is clear, therefore, that no one at Bartlett College owns a computer.

5. The home team lost the game because its players were unable to score more points than the visiting team.

6. Every time that the mercury level in the thermometer drops, the temperature in the room becomes cooler. So the thermometer must be the machine that controls the temperature in the room.

7. A banana is yellow. Yellow is a color. Therefore, a banana is a color.

8. I don't think I'm going to take my parents to any more hockey games. Every time they go with me, our team loses; and I don't want to be the reason our team loses.

9. The sentence you are now reading is false.

10. I don't think it's true that Ivy League colleges give their students such good educations. It seems to me that they just pick the best students, and then when those students succeed later in life, the Ivy League colleges take credit for it.

11. The right half of the brain controls the left side of the body, and the left half of the brain controls the right side of the body. Therefore, left-handed people are the only people in their right minds.

12. Boxing is a sport in which one man fights with another. Cockfighting is a sport in which one rooster fights with another. Boxing is legal; cockfighting is not. But if it's all right for two human beings to fight, it should be all right for two animals to fight.

13. Last year our firm hired three graduates from Ipswich College, and they were very hard workers. Therefore, all graduates of Ipswich College must be very hard workers.

14. Defeated candidate: I have been asked why we lost the election. It was not for want of effort on the part of my staff, or because my position on the issues was not correct. Ultimately, I must attribute the loss to a shortage of ballots cast for me.

15. The State Commissioner of Insurance has asked the legislature to raise the minimum liability insurance required of all motorists. Twenty years ago, when the legislature passed the law requiring all motorists to carry insurance, it determined after careful study that $10,000 worth of liability insurance was sufficient. Given that such careful attention was given to the question then, I don't see any reason to change this policy.

16. The commission of a murder in Chicago is no news. Since no news is good news, the commission of a murder in Chicago is good news.

17. New Alphabeta 4 will help you sleep, because Alphabeta 4 contains a new secret ingredient which has the dormative property. What's the dormative property? That is the power a substance has to induce sleep. So get Alphabeta 4 and get a good night's sleep.

18. In the space of one hundred and seventy-six years, the Lower Mississippi has shortened itself two hundred and forty-two miles. That is an average of a trifle over one mile and a third per year. Therefore, any calm person, who is not blind or idiotic, can see that in the Old Oolitic Silurian Period, just a million years ago next November, the Lower Mississippi River was upward of one million three hundred thousand miles long. And by the same token, seven hundred and forty-two years from now the Lower Mississippi will be only a mile three-quarters long, and Cairo and New Orleans will have joined their streets together, and be plodding comfortably along under a single mayor and a mutual board of aldermen. —Mark Twain, from *Life on the Mississippi*.

19. A recent survey by the Department of Labor revealed that increases in the salaries of ministers are accompanied by increases in the average consumption of rum. It is evident, then, that when ministers have more money, they drink more rum.

20. Nothing is too good for my best friend. So for her birthday, I guess I'll have to get her something.

21. Statistics show that nearly 80 percent of all traffic accidents occur when the vehicle is being driven at speeds of less than 25 miles per hour. Therefore, driving slowly causes accidents.

22. In February, for the second straight month, the Consumer Price Index declined by 1 percent. By December, the CPI will have declined a total of 12 percent for the entire year.

23. My cat, Felix, has seemed lethargic recently, and he doesn't eat. I asked my neighbor George what it could be. George is a well-known dance critic for a national magazine, and he says that it's probably just a passing thing. So I'm not worried about Felix.

24. In June, a national television network aired a documentary about a case in which the victim of a rape testified against her assailant. Because of that testimony, the prosecutor won a conviction, and the assailant was sentenced to a lengthy jail term. In July, the number of rapes reported in our city increased by 20 percent. The network should never have aired the documentary because it resulted in an increase in the incidence of violence against women.

25. Perkins makes a very persuasive presentation for our company to retain his advertising agency, and I will grant that the firm has successfully handled similar accounts in the past. But I am leary of hiring an agency whose founding partner supported a communist candidate for Congress.

26. Mozart was the greatest composer of all time. He wrote the greatest music of any composer who ever lived, and the person who writes the greatest music must be considered the greatest composer.

27. Some judges have allowed hospitals to disconnect life-support equipment of patients who have no prospects for recovery. But I say this is murder. Either we put a stop to this practice now, or we will soon have programs of euthenasia for the old and infirm as well as others who might be considered a burden.

28. During a basketball game, I fell and got a bad wrist sprain. The medicine my doctor gave me is supposed to reduce the swelling of the soft tissue. I've been taking it for three days now, and my wrist isn't healed. I guess the medicine just doesn't work.

29. It's easy to prove that God exists. Most people do believe in God, even if they are not able to define exactly what they mean by that term. To some it means an all-powerful creator, to others it means a merciful forgiver, and to still others it means a supernatural force. But setting aside the differences in these interpretations, we can be confident that there is a divine being, because God would not cause so many people to believe in him if He did not exist.

30. The end of any process is its goal, and the end of life is death. Therefore, the goal of life is death.

31. A well-cooked steak is rare—having eaten many bad steaks, I know this is true. The statement, however, is logically equivalent to the statement "A rare steak is well-cooked." But how could a piece of meat that is rare be well-cooked?

32. Chief Justice Oliver Wendell Holmes once remarked, "Even a dog knows the difference between being kicked and tripped over." Yet, our society still allows thoroughbred horse racing. The jockeys whip these horses mercilessly just as though they were kicking a poor dog.

33. The Selective Service System uses a lottery to determine who will be drafted and who will not be drafted. One by one, dated balls are pulled at random from a drum. And persons with birthdays corresponding to the dates must report for induction in the order that the balls are drawn, until the need for draftees has been satisfied. Lotteries are a form of gambling, and gambling is immoral. Therefore, the Selective Service System is immoral.

34. Cross-country skiing is half physical training and 90 percent mental concentration.

35. One of the most well-entrenched concepts in our collective sense of justice is the right of self-defense. If a person is attacked and threatened with death or serious injury, he or she has a right to use deadly force against the attacker—even to kill. When a person commits a serious crime, he or she threatens each and every one of us. As a society, we have a right to defend ourselves. Therefore, using capital punishment against these individuals is justified.

36. The government is always looking for new sources of revenues. And one of the most equitable means of revenue-raising is users' fees, which require that people pay for what they use. A good example of a users' fee is a toll road or mass transit fares. Since we require people to pay for the water they use, we should also require that they pay for the air they breathe. Taxing air usage would help solve the problem of the deficit.

37. I oppose the idea of allowing doctors to take terminally ill people off life-support systems. Rather than disconnecting life-support equipment, we should let nature take its course. These people should die when their natural span of life is ended—not when some doctor thinks they should.

38. Grandpa is now 98 years old, so I figure he'll live to be at least 100. Since he didn't die in those first 98 years, I see no reason why he should in the next two years.

39. In 1950, Joe McCarthy claimed to have discovered 81 Communists in the State Department. Of one of these persons he said, "I do not have much information on this except the general statement of the agency that there is nothing in the files to disprove his Communist connections."

40. Advertisement: Do you want to present an image of a rising corporate executive destined for top-level management, or do you want to look like a totally ineffectual and incompetent nebbish? Don't be a nebbish. Dress for success. Come into Corporate Images today, and let us design your business wardrobe.

12

Summary

The inferential fallacies most commonly used on the LSAT are:
1. False Cause
2. Hasty Generalization
3. False Analogy
4. Illegitimate Appeal to Authority
5. Illegitimate *Ad Hominem* Attack
6. False Dilemma
7. Begging the Question
8. Ambiguity
9. Shifting the Burden of Proof
10. Contradiction

Answers

1. C	**11.** H	**21.** A	**31.** H
2. A	**12.** C	**22.** B	**32.** C
3. J	**13.** B	**23.** D	**33.** C
4. B	**14.** G	**24.** A	**34.** J
5. G	**15.** B	**25.** E	**35.** C
6. A	**16.** H	**26.** G	**36.** C
7. H	**17.** G	**27.** F	**37.** J
8. A	**18.** B	**28.** B	**38.** B
9. J	**19.** A	**29.** G	**39.** I
10. A	**20.** H	**30.** H	**40.** F

12

Logical Reasoning Drills

1. **Walk-Through Drill**
2. **Warm-Up Drills**

This chapter includes three logical reasoning drills. The first drill is a "walk-through," with answers and discussion in the column opposite the questions so that you can "walk through" the problems. The other two drills are "warm-up" drills that you should do within the specified time limit. The answers and explanations for the timed warm-up drills begin on page 350.

Walk-Through

Archaeologists have uncovered evidence that even as early as paleolithic times, human beings had a belief in an afterlife. Burial sites located close to ancient settlements have been found in which the dead were buried along with clothing, tools, and weapons. This is the earliest known evidence of a belief in life after death.

1. Which of the following is an assumption under-lying the argument above?

    (A) The placement of burial sites near settle-ments indicates a feeling of piety toward the dead.
    (B) Belief in life after death is a central tenet of most religious faiths.
    (C) The clothing, tools, and weapons found in the burial sites belonged to those buried nearby.
    (D) Religious belief is a characteristic of most civilized societies.
    (E) Only people who believe in life after death would bury artifacts with the dead.

1. (E) This is a question that asks you to identify a hidden assumption of the argument. (E) does this. The conclusion of the argument is that early humans believed in a life after death. The evidence for this conclusion is the discovery of certain articles buried with the dead. For this evidence to support the conclusion, the argument must implicitly presuppose that such articles would be buried with the dead only by people who had such beliefs.

    (A) is incorrect, for what is needed for this argument is a connection between the articles buried and a belief in an afterlife—not a feel-ing of piety toward the dead. After all, one might venerate one's ancestors even though one did not hold a belief in an afterlife. As for (B), this goes beyond the scope of the argu-ment. The author's conclusion, as delimited by the wording of the passage, is that certain early humans held a belief in the afterlife—not that such beliefs are widespread. (C) is incor-rect because the ownership of the articles is not important—only that the articles were placed there for use by the deceased. Finally, (D) makes essentially the same error that (B) does; it goes beyond the scope of the argument.

Some of the most popular television advertisements are those employing humor. But as an advertising technique, humor has its drawbacks. Studies have shown that, while many viewers of humorous advertisements vividly recall the commercials, far fewer recall the name of the product being promoted. This casts doubt on the ability of humorous commercials, no matter how funny or enjoyable, to increase product sales.

2. Which of the following is assumed by the passage above?
   (A) Humorous commercials tend to reduce the credibility of products in the eyes of viewers.
   (B) Though enjoyable, humorous commercials are often less memorable than serious commercials.
   (C) A commercial that fails to create product name recognition does not increase sales of the product.
   (D) Humorous commercials may alienate almost as many viewers as they entertain.
   (E) The ultimate goal of advertising is to increase the name recognition of the product being promoted.

Religious leaders in our country were once expected to express and articulate lasting moral values. This is no longer the case. Today, we see spokespersons for major religious denominations entering into debate over merely political matters formerly reserved for members of the secular community.

3. The logical structure of the passage above depends upon the author's assumption that the expression of lasting moral values is
   (A) a strictly religious function
   (B) no longer deeply valued
   (C) essentially nonpolitical
   (D) reserved for secular society
   (E) the most important role of religion

2. (C) This question, too, asks about a hidden assumption of the argument. The conclusion of the argument is that humorous ads are not effective. Supporting this conclusion is an explicit premise. Consumers remember the humor but not the product name. This conclusion also depends on a suppressed premise: name recognition is essential to sales. Answer (C) correctly identifies this hidden premise.

As for (A), this goes beyond the scope of the argument. The speaker merely says that such ads are not effective, not that they are damaging as well. As for (B), the author never states that viewers don't remember the ad, only that they don't remember the product. (D) makes the same error made by (A). The author does not say that the ads are damaging, only that they are ineffective in promoting the product.

(E) is perhaps the most attractive of the distractors here. But a careful reading of the argument will show that (E) is incorrect. The conclusion of the argument is that humorous ads do not *increase sales*. We should infer, therefore, that the ultimate objective of advertising is to increase sales and that name recognition is merely a means to that end.

3. (C) This item asks you to identify a hidden assumption of the argument. The speaker argues that religion is creeping into the political sphere. Critical to this argument is the assumption that there are two distinct and separate spheres, religion and politics. (C) correctly points out that this is an assumption of the argument.

Those in the business community who decry government regulation claim that it increases the costs of doing business and reduces beneficial competition, ultimately harming both business and the community as a whole. They point to industries such as trucking, airlines, and telecommunications, in which deregulation has apparently brought greater economic efficiency. These commentators ignore the industries, such as financial services, in which government regulation is essential; indeed, without government intervention in the 1930s, some whole segments of that industry might have permanently collapsed.

4.   The author's point is made primarily by

(A) offering a counterexample to rebut his opponents' argument

(B) calling into question the motives of his opponents

(C) pointing out an inconsistency in his opponents' use of terms

(D) drawing a distinction between valid and invalid methods of argument

(E) underscoring the subjectivity of his opponents' basic assumptions

Landmark preservation laws unfairly impinge on the freedom of owners to develop their own property as they see fit. In some cases, owners of hotels and office buildings designated as landmarks have been forbidden to make changes in the original facades or interiors, even though they reasonably believed that the changes would enhance the structures and make them more valuable.

5.   Which of the following statements, if true, seriously weakens the author's argument?

(A) Altering the appearance of a historic structure sometimes does not enhance its beauty or value.

(B) In traditional legal doctrine, ownership of a property implies the right to alter it at will.

(C) Only buildings over 75 years old are normally affected by landmark preservation laws.

(D) Landmark designations must be approved by a local regulatory body before taking effect.

(E) Historic buildings represent a cultural heritage which the community has a legitimate stake in preserving.

4. (A) This item asks you to describe the logical structure of the argument. The author cites the position of those who oppose government regulations and mentions some of the reasons they give for their position. Then the author introduces an example in which regulation was essential and successful. (A) best describes this tack.

As for (B), when you attack the motives of an opponent, as opposed to the argument of the opponent, you make what is called an *ad hominem* attack, but the speaker here doesn't make such an attack. As for (C), though the author does attack the position he cites, he does so by counterexample, not by pointing to any contradiction. As for (D), the author never raises the issue of what constitutes a proper mode of argumentation. Without any such theoretical justification, he simply launches his attack by counterexample. Finally, as for (E), the author never suggests that any of the terms or judgments involved are based on anything but objective, economic facts.

5. (E) This question asks that you weaken an argument. Often, the correct answer to such a question states that a key hidden assumption of the argument is false. In this case, the conclusion of the argument is that landmark preservation laws deprive landlords of their right to use their own property. This argument presupposes a clear distinction between public and private property and further that the building owned by a landlord is purely private property in which the community has no legitimate interest. (E) comes to grips with this assumption by noting that a landmark building may not be purely private property and that some part of the building (the heritage) may belong to the community at large.

(A) is perhaps the second-best response. It does seem to attack the landlord's judgment that his actions in altering a historical structure will be valuable. The difficulty with (A) is that it represents only a partial attack on the argument. It questions whether this or that alteration would be useful or valuable but seems to grant the main philosophical point that the community, in some cases, should be able to substitute its judgment for that of the landlord.

The cleaning and restoration of Michelangelo's frescoes on the ceiling of the Sistine Chapel were undertaken by some of the world's finest art restorers under the close supervision of an international team of art experts and historians. Nonetheless, the results have produced a storm of controversy. Most modern viewers, it seems, had become accustomed to seeing the frescoes with their colors dulled by layers of yellowing glue and varnish and with the contours of the figures obscured by centuries' accumulation of grime.

6. The passage implies that Michelangelo's frescoes

   (A) have been the subject of intense controversy over their artistic merit
   (B) suffered until recently from centuries of obscurity and neglect
   (C) should not have been cleaned and restored without more careful planning
   (D) have been obscured by dirt during the recent process of restoration
   (E) were originally much brighter and more vivid than most modern viewers realize

As for (B), this seems to strengthen the speaker's claim that landmark preservation laws represent an unwarranted interference with the rights of the landlord. (C) fails to come to grips with the issue here—even if the building is over 75 years old, doesn't it still belong to the owner and not to the community? Finally, (D) makes the same kind of error. Even if we grant that landmark status must be approved by a public body, that doesn't explain why a public body should be allowed to substitute its judgment for that of the building's owner in the first place.

6. (E) This item asks you to determine what is implied by the argument, that is, what is implicit in the argument. (E) is the correct choice. The speaker states that modern viewers, accustomed to the dull colors, were startled and even offended by the result of the restoration. We may infer from this that the cleaning restored the original, brighter colors.

As for (A), the passage deals with the restoration, not with the artistic merit of the work itself. (B) and (D) both represent misreadings of the paragraph. The author implies that the damage was the result of the natural process of the passing of centuries. Finally, as for (C), the author is not critical of the restoration. He even notes that it was conducted under the supervision of a team of experts. If anything, the author implies criticism of those who did not like the result of the restoration.

Questions 7–8

"In general," stated Professor Charney, "the athletes now attending the university are more interested in studies than athletes of ten years ago. The proof is that more and more of my students who are athletes attend class on a regular basis."

7. The conclusion of Professor Charney depends upon which of the following assumptions?

   (A) Professor Charney's student athletes show greater interest in studies because Professor Charney is a better teacher now than she was ten years ago.
   (B) Student athletes are more concerned about getting good grades because it is more difficult to become a professional athlete now than it was ten years ago.
   (C) Whether or not a student attends class on a regular basis is a good measure of whether a student is interested in his or her studies.
   (D) Professors should not expect the same commitment to studies from student athletes that they require of students in general.
   (E) An interest in studies is something that a student must learn very early in his or her academic career.

8. Which of the following is a possible weakness in Professor Charney's reasoning?

   (A) The athletes who enroll in her classes are not typical of students athletes in general.
   (B) Many other students who are not athletes are very interested in their studies.
   (C) Professor Charney does not take into account the special demands placed on students who are also athletes.
   (D) Professor Charney does not explain why student athletes are more motivated today than they were ten years ago.
   (E) Some student athletes may be provided with special tutoring to ensure that their grades will make them eligible for participation in athletics.

7. (C) This question asks about a hidden assumption. Start by isolating the conclusion of the line of reasoning:

   Athletes are now more interested in studies than before.

The explicit premise that supports that conclusion is:

   My student athletes are attending class more regularly.

Now you should look to each choice and ask yourself, "Is the speaker committed to this idea?"

   As for (A) and (B), the speaker is not necessarily committed to either of these ideas. The conclusion is a statement of fact: things have changed. The speaker is not necessarily committed to any particular explanation of that change. (D) makes the mistake of going beyond the scope of the statement. Although this is a judgment that someone might make, there is no warrant for attributing it to this particular speaker. For all we know, the speaker may think that student athletes should be held to the same standard as other students. Finally, (E) is a fairly weak response to the question, for nothing in the structure of the argument commits the author to analyze the development of study habits.

8. (A) The answer to this question is also a hidden assumption of the argument. The explicit premise of the argument is:

   My student athletes are attending class more regularly.

However, the conclusion is much broader, referring as it does to student athletes in general. Thus, the structure of the argument is a generalization; and, as you learned in the lesson on logical reasoning, often the best attack on such an argument is to point out that the sample is not representative of the population as a whole. This is the burden of choice (A).

   (D) and (E) will probably both attract some support as the correct choice, though neither is really a very good choice. (D), however, makes the error of trying to force the speaker to take on a greater burden than she has been willing to assume. The speaker says only,

"Student athletes are more interested in studies, and here is my proof." It is not a logical weakness in that claim that he has not also assumed the burden of explaining the "why" of this change. As for (E), this would be more relevant to an argument that claims "Athletes are now better students." (E) just isn't relevant to the claim actually made by the speaker.

(B) and (C) make the same kind of mistake made by (E)—they aren't really relevant to the statement made. As for (B), the speaker's comparison is of student athletes of today and those of another time—not of student athletes and other types of students. As for (C), the speaker does not analyze the reason for the change or for the original phenomenon.

In an effort to increase the number of taxicabs available during the hours from 8:00 p.m. to 6:00 a.m., the Taxi Commission, which sets fares, has proposed a $1.00-per-ride surcharge during those hours. This is unlikely to have any effect on the availability of taxis. The fleet owners who lease cabs to drivers on a shift basis will simply raise the per-shift charge for those hours, thus eliminating any incentive for the individual driver to work the nighttime hours.

9. Which of the following, if true, most weakens the argument above?

(A) Fleet owners usually have unleased cars during the nighttime hours covered by the Commission's proposal.

(B) Most people who need a taxi during the nighttime hours would not mind paying the $1.00 surcharge.

(C) The majority of licensed cabs are owned by individual drivers who do not lease them from fleet owners.

(D) The previous year the Commission approved a 10-percent increase in taxi fares.

(E) Passengers would not treat the surcharge as part of the driver's tip.

9. (C) The correct answer to this question aims at a hidden assumption of the argument. The argument offers a causal analysis: the fleet owners will raise the rent on cabs, so drivers will pay more, thus there will be no additional economic incentive to drive at night. (C) attacks this analysis by suggesting that a substantial number of cabs are owned by individual drivers and not fleets. This would mean the increase would go directly into the pocket of the driver, thus providing an economic incentive to drive at night.

As for (A), this seems to strengthen the proposal rather than weaken it (and thereby it weakens the speaker's analysis). If cabs are idle during the night hours, then raising the price that can be charged for those hours should increase the supply of cabs during those hours. As for (B), this too seems to strengthen the Commission's proposal by eliminating a possible objection to the surcharge. (D) is not clearly relevant to the argument, and to attempt to justify (D) as the correct choice, you would have to engage in considerable speculation, thus taking you far beyond the scope of the argument as given. Finally, (E) seems to strengthen rather than weaken the argument by precluding a possible unforeseen consequence of the proposal that would render it ineffective.

A landlord was recently found guilty of hiring thugs to harass legal tenants to force them from a decaying building so that the apartments could be renovated and sold as high-priced cooperatives. The judge sentenced the landlord to convey ownership of the property to a nonprofit organization that would convert the building into housing for the homeless. Yet, the sentence will not deter other landlords in the future from trying similar strongarm tactics.

10. The argument above is most strengthened if which of the following is true?

(A) The current tenants will be allowed to continue to live in their apartments even after the transfer of ownership.

(B) The value of the unrenovated building to the landlord was virtually nothing.

(C) The landlord could have continued to make a profit on the rental units in the building even without improving the property.

(D) Tenants have clearly defined rights under the landlord–tenant law including the right to quiet enjoyment of the premises.

(E) A building begins to decay only when the rental income from the property is insufficient to justify further investment in the property.

If Robert attends the party, then Sally, Tess, and Victor will also attend the party.

11. If the statement above is true, which of the following statements must also be true?

(A) If Robert does not attend the party, then Sally does not attend the party.

(B) If Sally, Tess, and Victor attend the party, then Robert will also attend the party.

(C) If Robert and Sally attend the party, then Tess and Victor will not attend the party.

(D) If Victor does not attend the party, then Robert does not attend the party.

(E) If Tess does not attend the party, then Sally does not attend the party.

10. (B) This question asks you to strengthen the argument. The conclusion of the argument is: Landlords will not be deterred by this sentence, but the speaker does not explain why not. There must be a hidden assumption, as (B) correctly points out. If the forfeiture of a building is not painful to a landlord, it must be the case that the building isn't worth anything in the first place.

   (A) and (D), although generally related to the subject matter of the statement, are irrelevant to the structure of the argument. They don't aim at the connection between the sentence and deterrence. (C) and (E) at least have the merit of bearing on that connection, but (C) seems to weaken the speaker's argument. If the building is valuable, then the landlord did lose something of value, and the sentence might have some deterrent value. As for (E), to the extent that it hints at what (B) states specifically, (E) is an interesting answer. But the very fact that (B) makes the point explicitly makes (B) a better choice.

11. (D) This is a logical deduction question, focusing on the structure of an "if, then" statement. The correct choice is (D). If Robert attends the party, then the other three also do. From this we can infer "If it is not the case that Sally, Tess, and Victor attend, then Robert does not attend." The conditional element of this statement is equivalent to "If Sally does not attend, or Tess does not attend, or Victor does not attend." Thus, if Victor does not attend, Robert does not attend.

Based on the results of a pilot program providing health care for elderly patients in their homes, the state concludes that such a system is considerably cheaper than providing the same care in a nursing home. The study does not mention, however, that the dramatic cost savings are achieved by severely undervaluing the work of home attendants. A system which perpetuates low wages is not the best way of providing health care services to the elderly.

12. The criticism above would be most strengthened if which of the following were true?

(A) Approximately 90 percent of the cost of providing health care to elderly patients in their homes is compensation for home attendants.

(B) Many elderly patients would prefer to live in communities with others of similar age and receive health care there.

(C) Most elderly patients lack the financial resources to purchase at-home health care without some government assistance.

(D) The state is planning to implement a testing and licensing procedure for home attendants who provide health care services to the elderly.

(E) In the past decade, unions representing hospital and nursing home workers have been able to secure substantial increases in wages and fringe benefits for their members.

Researchers have found that cushioned running shoes absorb energy, thus working against the runner. A highly elastic, rather than soft, sole would return energy to the runner's leg, allowing the runner to run faster. It is clear that the best running shoes in the future will be those that have highly elastic soles.

13. Which of the following, if true, would most weaken the argument above?

(A) Running shoes with highly elastic soles will be cheaper to manufacture than those with soft soles.

(B) With better training techniques, runners today are already breaking more and more track records.

(C) A highly elastic sole places great stress on joints and increases significantly the chance of serious injury.

(D) Many people who purchase running shoes use them as everyday shoes and not for training purposes.

(E) Present-day soft-soled running shoes represent a considerable advance over the leather-soled running shoes of thirty years ago.

12. (A) The conclusion of the argument is that the cost savings claimed are obtainable only by undervaluing the services of some workers. The conclusion depends on the hidden assumptions that the cost of those services is an important component of the total cost of care and therefore of the total savings that are obtained by alternative care programs. (A) strengthens this argument because it documents this hidden assumption.

(B), (C), and (D) fail to come to grips with the logical structure of the argument. (E) is perhaps the second-best answer, for it at least has the merit of focusing upon the economics of the argument. As for (E), that workers received wage increases in the past does not necessarily mean that current levels are not still too low.

13. (C) This question asks for you to identify an unforeseen causal consequence. As (C) correctly points out, a stiffer sole may have advantages in efficiency but disadvantages in other ways. Thus, (C) weakens the argument.

(A), if anything, seems to strengthen the argument by pointing to another advantage of stiffer soles. (B), (D), and (E) are all irrelevant to the question of the value of elastic versus inelastic soles.

A recent study conducted by a national market research firm reported that only 11 percent of college-bound women would consider an all-women's college. It is clear that women's colleges must become coeducational if they are to survive.

14. Which of the following, if true, most weakens the reasoning above?

   (A) Graduates of women's colleges have better records for getting into medical and other professional schools than do women graduates of coeducational colleges.

   (B) Fewer than 10 percent of all college-bound men would consider attending an all-men's college.

   (C) The total capacity of all-women's colleges can accommodate only 2 percent of the nation's college-bound female students.

   (D) Many women's colleges report a decline in the number of large alumnae contributions over the past few years.

   (E) The total pool of college-bound high school graduates is projected to shrink during the next ten years.

When a large manufacturing business decides to relocate, the community suffers an economic loss beyond that of the immediate unemployment of those who had been employed at the factory. For example, the automotive service industry in the area is depressed as well. Unemployed workers no longer use their cars for the daily commute to and from work, thus reducing the need for fuel and tires and for services to maintain the cars.

15. The author's point is made primarily by

   (A) posing a question and answering it
   (B) appealing to an authority
   (C) attacking the credibility of a speaker
   (D) presenting an analogy
   (E) analyzing a causal relationship

14. (C) This argument rests upon a hidden assumption: fewer women want to attend an all-women's college than there are seats available. The support for this conclusion, however, is a percentage figure—not an absolute number. The argument works only if the number of interested applicants (11 percent of the total pool) is less than the number of available seats. But the total pool may be so large than even a relatively small percentage, such as 11 percent, means more applicants than seats. (C) correctly points out this weakness.

As for (A), the quality of education is irrelevant to the speaker's claim that there aren't enough applicants. As for (B), conditions for all-men colleges are not relevant to the argument. As for (D), although this is not related to the logical structure of the argument, as an independent point it would, if anything, actually strengthen the argument: not only are there fewer applicants, there are budgetary pressures as well. The same reasoning applies to (E). This, if anything, strengthens the argument: and the number of interested women will decline.

15. (E) This question just asks that you describe the argument. The author traces out the causal implications of a certain phenomenon, so (E) is the best description.

College tuition has risen sharply over the past decade and will continue to rise in the future. Yet colleges and universities have the means to reverse this trend. Every such institution has a considerable endowment. They should use these funds to reduce tuition costs.

16. Which of the following, if true, would most weaken the argument above?

   (A) Most college students are able to meet tuition and other educational expenses even if they have to take out student loans.
   (B) The costs incurred by colleges in providing educational services have risen more rapidly than have tuition costs to students.
   (C) Donors who make gifts to the endowment funds usually restrict the uses to which their gifts can be put by the institution.
   (D) More college students are able to find part-time work during the academic year, which helps them to meet the rising costs of an education.
   (E) Non-tuition costs of a college education have increased more rapidly than the cost of tuition.

Some people argue that state lotteries are immoral because they are a form of regressive taxation. It is true that poor people purchase proportionately larger numbers of tickets than do the middle class or wealthy, but for that reason, they also win lotto jackpots relatively more often than do wealthier people. So the system is not regressive.

17. The argument above can be most weakened by pointing out that

   (A) a person who wins a large lottery prize can no longer be considered poor
   (B) only a few of the poor who buy lottery tickets win large lottery prizes
   (C) many of the middle class and rich do not buy lottery tickets
   (D) the United States does not have a national lottery
   (E) the revenues generated by lotteries serve to reduce taxes for everyone

16. (C) The conclusion of this argument is that colleges could slow the increase in tuition by dipping into their endowments. This conclusion rests upon the hidden assumption that colleges have the authority to use their endowments in this way. (C) weakens the argument by attacking this assumption. As for (A) and (D), the author doesn't claim that students cannot find ways of meeting increasing tuitions—only that colleges should not force them to do so. As for (B), the fact that institutional costs are increasing doesn't deny the author's point. In fact, the author might accept (B) and simply add "Yes, I know that, but still tuition doesn't have to increase at all." Finally, as for (E), again the author might accept this and add "Yes, and this makes it all the more urgent to hold the line on tuition."

17. (B) The objection to the lottery is that the poor pay proportionately more into it than do the middle class or the rich. The speaker attempts to defend the lottery by pointing out that because the poor pour more money into the lottery, they get more money back. But this defense of the lottery is successful only if the prize money returned offsets the disproportionate amount paid in by the poor. (B) points this out.

When the International Restaurant serves bacalao and mondongo on the same day, it also serves empanadas. Empanadas are never served on Tuesday. Manuel will eat at the International only if bacalao is being served.

18. If the statements above are true, which of the following must also be true?

   (A) Manuel does not eat at the International on Tuesday.
   (B) Manuel does not eat both bacalao and mondongo on the same day at the International.
   (C) The International does not serve mondongo on Tuesday.
   (D) Tuesday is the only day that the International does not serve bacalao.
   (E) Bacalao and mondongo are not both served at the International on Tuesday.

Questions 19– 20

   Eight authors are in competition for a literary prize, to be awarded according to the votes of a panel of judges. The panel is divided into various voting blocs.

   If Anderson receives more votes than Benchley, and Carson receives more votes than Dinsmore, Ellman will win the prize.

   If Benchley receives more votes than Anderson, or Farley receives more votes than Gonzalez, Hawthorne will win the prize.

   If Dinsmore receives more votes than Carson, Farley will win the prize.

19. If Hawthorne wins the prize, which of the following must be true?

   (A) Anderson received more votes than Benchley.
   (B) Benchley received more votes than Anderson.
   (C) Farley received more votes than Gonzalez.
   (D) Carson received more votes than Dinsmore.
   (E) Dinsmore did not receive more votes than Carson.

18. (E) Let us summarize the first statement as follows:

$$(B + M) \supset E$$

From this we can infer:

$$\sim E \supset \sim (B + M)$$

Since the restaurant does not serve empañadas on Tuesday, it is not the case that it serves both bacalao and mondongo on Tuesday.

19. (E) This item asks you to draw logical inferences from the information given. The first statement establishes conditions that are sufficient for Ellman to win, the second statement conditions sufficient for Hawthorne to win, and the third conditions sufficient for Farley to win. None of the statements, however, sets forth necessary conditions for those results. In other words, if the specified conditions are met, then the result follows; but the conditions do not establish that these are the only conditions that might result in the described outcomes. Thus, Farley will win the prize if Dinsmore receives more votes than Carson, but Farley might receive the prize anyway.

   The question stem stipulates that Hawthorne wins the prize, but we cannot infer from that whether or not the conditional part of the second statement was fulfilled. Thus, (A), (B), and (C) are not inferable. We can infer, however, from the statement that Hawthorne won the prize that Farley did not. And from that statement we can infer that it is not the case that Dinsmore received more votes than Carson. Notice that both (D) and (E) are very close to this idea. There is, however, a subtle but very important difference between them. While we can infer from the statement that Farley did not win the prize and that Dinsmore did not receive more votes than Carson, we cannot infer that Carson received more votes than Dinsmore —there could have been a tie.

20. If Carson received more votes than Dinsmore but Ellman did not win the prize, which of the following must be true?

   (A) Farley won the prize.
   (B) Hawthorne won the prize.
   (C) Farley received more votes than Gonzalez.
   (D) Anderson did not receive more votes than Benchley.
   (E) Benchley did not receive more votes than Farley.

The reason that the President nominated Judge Bork to the Supreme Court and the reason that conservatives are happy about the choice is that they believe this nominee, if confirmed by the Senate, will tip the balance on the Court solidly to the right for many years to come. The reason Judge Bork is so vehemently opposed by liberals is that they believe the conservatives are right.

21. The speaker in the paragraph above implies that

   (A) liberals believe that Judge Bork would make a good Supreme Court Justice
   (B) liberals believe that Judge Bork would make conservative decisions
   (C) liberals would not oppose Judge Bork's nomination if conservatives did not support it
   (D) conservatives would not support Judge Bork's nomination if liberals did not oppose it
   (E) Judge Bork should attempt to persuade liberals to support his nomination

---

20. (D) The first condition states that if Carson receives more votes than Dinsmore *and* Anderson receives more votes than Benchley, then Ellman will win. The question stem stipulates that Carson did receive more votes than Dinsmore, but Ellman lost. We can infer, therefore, that the other part of that condition was not fulfilled, namely, Anderson did not receive more votes than Benchley.

21. (B) This item asks you to draw a further conclusion from the initial paragraph. The correct choice is (B). According to the speaker, conservatives support the nomination because they think Judge Bork would make politically conservative decisions, and liberals oppose the nomination because they think the conservatives are right—not right in the sense of politically correct, but right in the sense that they have made a realistic assessment of the situation. Thus, the author implies that the liberals, too, believe that Judge Bork would make conservative decisions. Given this analysis of the paragraph, (A) must be incorrect. (C) seems to be the second-best choice, but (C) goes beyond the scope of the passage. Liberals oppose the nomination not because conservatives favor it but because they don't want a conservative Supreme Court Justice. It is not the belief of the conservatives that prompts liberal opposition but the fear that the belief is correct. Presumably, if the liberals believed that the conservatives were wrong and that Judge Bork would actually be a liberal influence on the Court, then the liberals would support the nomination. (D), too, is shown to be incorrect by this reasoning. Finally, (E) goes beyond the scope of the passage. The author makes an observation, but there is nothing in that observation to support a recommendation of the sort contained in this choice.

When the mayor appointed a Hispanic principal to the board of education, many whites and blacks decried the appointment as political; and when the mayor appointed a black businessman as director of franchises, many whites and Hispanics made the same charge. They are all correct, but what is wrong with that? The appointments were political acts well within the mayor's rights as defined by the City Charter.

22. Which of the following, if true, most strengthens the argument above?

(A) The principal appointed to the board of education and the businessman appointed director of franchises were as well qualified as any other candidate for the position.

(B) Shortly after making the appointments mentioned, the mayor appointed a white attorney from a powerful law firm to serve as the city's corporation counsel.

(C) Blacks who opposed the appointment of the Hispanic principal favored the appointment of a black who was a school district superintendent.

(D) The actions of an elected official should be judged by how well they serve the needs of the people and not just by whether the actions are legal.

(E) Three of the mayor's key aides were forced to resign and now face criminal indictments when it was discovered that they solicited a bribe from a cable television company seeking a city franchise.

22. (A) The point of the paragraph is that there is nothing wrong with taking into account political considerations when one is making what is essentially a political decision. This argument has some persuasive appeal: all other things being equal, why not take the politically expedient route? But the argument, as (A) points out, assumes (implicitly) that all other things are equal. (A) strengthens the argument by bolstering this hidden premise: since candidates all were equally well qualified, there was nothing wrong with making a political decision. (B) may be the second-best answer, but (B) fails to distinguish between the arguments of the groups mentioned in the initial paragraph and the argument itself. While (B) might be used to respond to the groups mentioned in the paragraph (no one should complain, because everyone eventually gets a political favor), (B) doesn't address the argument of the paragraph. The argument in the paragraph is not that some groups have legitimate complaints because they have not been represented in the appointment process, but that it is not an indictment of a political decision that it is political. As for (C), this would hardly be surprising; and, in any event, it doesn't address the argument of the speaker (as opposed to the thinking of those who accused the mayor of political decisions). Finally, (D) and (E) both seem to undermine the argument, not strengthen it.

Questions 23–24

There is a vague popular belief that lawyers are necessarily dishonest. I say vague, because when we consider to what extent clients inform their counselors of the most intimate details of their personal and financial lives, it appears improbable that the impression is very distinct and vivid. Yet the impression is common, almost universal. Let no young person choosing the law as a profession for a moment yield to the popular belief. Resolve to be honest at all events; and if in your own judgment you cannot be an honest lawyer, then resolve to be honest without being a lawyer.

23. Which of the following, if true, most weakens the speaker's claim that most people have no specific reason for distrusting lawyers?

    (A) Most people would not confide in a person they did not trust.
    (B) Most people believe that a dishonest lawyer is better than no lawyer at all.
    (C) Most people have had little direct contact with lawyers.
    (D) Most people do not seek the assistance of a lawyer unless they have been arrested.
    (E) Few people have ever been the victim of a dishonest lawyer.

24. The advice offered by the speaker to young people considering a career in law implies that

    (A) being honest is more important than being a lawyer
    (B) being a lawyer is more important than being honest
    (C) it is virtually impossible to be an honest lawyer
    (D) most people find it very difficult to be honest
    (E) practicing law makes it especially difficult to be honest

23. **(B)** The author of the initial paragraph concludes (in the middle of the paragraph) that the vague feeling that lawyers are dishonest is just that, a vague feeling. His evidence for this conclusion is the fact that people are willing to confide in their lawyers. This line of reasoning rests upon a hidden assumption: people would not confide in lawyers if they did not trust them. (B) weakens the argument by attacking this hidden assumption: people might distrust lawyers and confide in them anyway because they have no choice. (A), too, aims at the hidden assumption but strengthens rather than weakens the argument. (C) and (E) both mention ideas generally related to the topic of the initial paragraph, but it is difficult to see how either (C) or (E) weakens the argument. If anything, (C) and (E) are consistent with the speaker's claim: Most people's feelings are vague because they have never had direct contact with a bad lawyer. Finally, as for (D), to the extent that it tries to say something like (B), then (D) could weaken the argument, but by that same token, (B) would have to be considered a broader and therefore more general attack on the argument.

24. **(A)** This question asks you to reach a further conclusion. The speaker says it is better to be honest though not a lawyer than to be a lawyer and not honest. This idea is summarized by (A). (B) reverses this judgment and therefore must be incorrect. (C) and (E) go too far. In fact, the speaker implies that it is possible to be both honest and a lawyer. Finally, (D) is irrelevant because the speaker is discussing the practice of law in particular, not people in general.

I once heard an attorney in a criminal case offer the following defense on his client's behalf: "My client wasn't at the scene of the crime; and if he was, he didn't do it; and if he did it, he was insane at the time."

25. Which of the following is most similar to the argument mentioned above?

(A) Doctor: "This patient was admitted complaining of nausea, dizziness, and stomach cramps, the classic signs of food poisoning. For dinner he ate a shrimp cocktail, baked chicken, and ice cream. One of those three dishes caused the food poisoning."

(B) Forensic expert: "An examination of the body shows three bullet wounds to the head, which I have labeled A, B, and C. Any one of them could have caused death. If it wasn't A, then it was either B or C; and if it wasn't B, it was C."

(C) Stock market analyst: "The sudden drop in stock market prices was caused by three factors: the President's announcement of his intention to intervene in Central America; the release of government statistics showing virtually no economic growth for the past six months; and massive selling due to programmed trading. If any one of the three factors had not been working, the drop would have been much less severe."

(D) Neighbor: "I didn't borrow your snowblower; and if I did, I am sure that it was not broken when I returned it; and if it was broken when I returned it, it was broken when I borrowed it."

(E) Child: "I never tell a lie; and if I ever did tell a lie, I'm not lying now; and if I am lying now, you'll never find out."

25. (D) An accepted strategy in legal and other kinds of arguments is to argue in the alternative, but arguments in the alternative are persuasive when they are about interpretations or theories. The initial statement, however, begins with a statement of fact: He wasn't there. If the statement is true as a matter of fact, then the rest of the argument is superfluous; but if the speaker believes that the rest of the argument is not superfluous, then the first statement is false. Thus the speaker involves himself in an inconsistency. (D) is the choice that best parallels this inconsistency. As for (A) and (B), these are legitimate uses of the technique of arguing in the alternative, for they are arguments about possible theories. As for (C), this is not an argument in the alternative at all but just an analysis of an event with three necessary causes, none of which, according to the speaker, was sufficient to have caused the result. (E) is perhaps the second-best answer, but the parallelism breaks down in the final statement of (E).

Directions: In this section, the questions ask you to analyze and evaluate the reasoning presented in a statement or short paragraph. For some questions, all of the choices may arguably be answers to the question asked, but you are to select the best answer to the question. In evaluating the choices to a question, do not make assumptions that violate common standards by being implausible, redundant, irrevelant, or inconsistent.

The existence of flying saucers, unidentified flying objects supposedly piloted by extraterrestrial beings, has been shown to be illusory. Skeptical researchers have demonstrated that a number of photographs purportedly showing flying saucers are either crude forgeries or misinterpreted images of such earthly objects as clouds, birds, weather balloons, or small private planes.

1. If the photographs mentioned above are accurately explained in the passage, which of the following is the best argument AGAINST the conclusion drawn?

(A) Some purported unidentified flying objects have proved to be natural phenomena rather than manmade objects.
(B) The fact that a number of photographs of flying saucers are fake does not generally disprove the phenomenon.
(C) Some of those who claim to have witnessed flying saucers have no apparent motive for lying.
(D) Given the size and complexity of the universe, it seems unreasonable to assume that life exists only on Earth.
(E) Researchers who are skeptical about flying saucers inevitably bring their own biases and preconceptions to their work.

All the members of the Student Rights Coalition signed the petition calling for a meeting with the university trustees. Philip must be a member of the Student Rights Coalition, since his signature appears on the petition.

2. Which of the following best states the central flaw in the reasoning above?

(A) Some members of the Student Rights Coalition may not support all of the organization's positions.
(B) Philip's signature on the petition was not forged by a member of the Student Rights Coalition.
(C) No member of the university's faculty signed the petition.
(D) Philip may also be a member of the school's debating society.
(E) Some of those who signed the petition may not be members of the Student Rights Coalition.

For the purposes of the executive relocator study, ten qualities of a livable city were chosen, including a low crime rate, cleanliness, cultural attractions, and other amenities. For each city in the study, scores from 1 (lowest) to 10 (highest) were assigned for each of the ten qualities. The ten scores for each city were then averaged, yielding a total livability score for each city. We hope the resulting ratings will help readers in choosing their next place of residence.

3. The passage above makes which of the following assumptions?

I. It is possible to assign an accurate numerical score to each of a city's amenities.
II. Each of the ten qualities of a livable city is equally important.
III. Most people enjoy some degree of personal choice in where they reside.

(A) I only
(B) II only
(C) III only
(D) I and II only
(E) II and III only

Foreign-made electronics products gained popularity in the United States during the 1970s primarily because of their low cost. In recent years, changes to the exchange rates of United States and other currencies have increased the prices of imported electronics products relative to those produced in the United States. However, sales of imported electronics products have not declined in recent years.

4. Which of the following, if true, would help to explain why sales of imported electronics products remain high?

(A) Trade ministries in foreign nations have pursued policies that prevented prices of electronics products from rising even faster.
(B) The cost of manufacturing electronics products abroad is rising faster than it is in the United States.
(C) A coming shortage in consumer credit in the United States is expected to depress sales of imported products during the next two years.
(D) American consumers now perceive the quality of imports as being high enough to justify the increased prices.
(E) U.S. manufacturers have attempted to persuade Americans to buy electronics products made in the United States.

Young people who imagine that the life of a writer is one of glamor, riches, or fame soon discover not only the difficulties of the craft but the long odds against achieving any measure of recognition or financial security. Upon being asked, "Aren't most editors failed writers?" T.S. Eliot is said to have remarked, "Yes, but so are most writers."

5. The statement by T.S. Eliot conveys which of the following ideas?

   (A) Editing can be just as creative and challenging as writing.
   (B) Few writers are fortunate enough to attain real success in their profession.
   (C) For a writer, success is measured more by influence exerted than by material gain achieved.
   (D) Many writers find that a stint at editorial work is a beneficial apprenticeship for their craft.
   (E) There are no clear-cut standards of success and failure for writers, but there are such standards for editors.

In an extensive study of the reading habits of magazine subscribers, it was found that an average of between four and five people actually read each copy of the most popular weekly news magazine. On this basis, we estimate that the 12,000 copies of *Poets and Poetry* that are sold each month are actually read by 48,000 to 60,000 people.

6. The estimate above assumes that

   (A) individual magazine readers generally enjoy more than one type of magazine
   (B) most of the readers of *Poets and Poetry* subscribe to the magazine
   (C) the ratio of readers to copies is the same for *Poets and Poetry* as for the weekly news magazine
   (D) the number of readers of the weekly news magazine is similar to the number of readers of *Poets and Poetry*
   (E) most readers enjoy sharing copies of their favorite magazines with friends and family members

In reaction against the heavy, ornate designs favored by the neoclassical architects of the Victorian era, architectural critics and historians in the first half of this century went to the opposite extreme, declaring that only what was stripped-down, light, and free of decoration could be beautiful. Today, an overdue reevaluation of this esthetic is under way, as exemplified by the current exhibition of designs from the Beaux Arts school of the nineteenth century.

7. It can be inferred from the passage above that the present movement among architectural critics is toward

   (A) a renewed appreciation of the use of decorative motifs in building designs
   (B) a rejection of neoclassical standards of beauty in architectural design
   (C) a greater admiration of the light, simple designs characteristic of the early twentieth century
   (D) the adaptation of Victorian styles in the work of today's younger architects
   (E) a deeper understanding of the esthetic values of underlying post-neoclassical theory

In national surveys taken between 1970 and 1985, the percentage of respondents who reported that they regularly attended weekly religious services rose from 28 percent to 34 percent. However, statistics compiled during the same period by the nation's major religious denominations showed a gradual decline in attendance at weekly services.

8. Each of the following, if true, could help explain the apparent contradiction in the statements above EXCEPT

   (A) There was a sharp drop in the number of persons who attended religious services on an occasional basis.
   (B) Attendance statistics compiled by the religious denominations are often highly inaccurate.
   (C) As older churchgoers died, they were replaced by an equal number of younger churchgoers.
   (D) There was a significant increase in attendance among religious groups outside the major denominations.
   (E) Those responding to the surveys were not representative of the population as a whole.

If Whirlaway wins the Georgia Derby, then the Georgia Derby must be a fixed race.

9. The statement above depends upon which of the following assumptions?

   (A) Whirlaway can win a race only if the race is fixed.
   (B) Whirlaway can win the Georgia Derby only if the Georgia Derby is fixed.
   (C) No horse can win the Georgia Derby unless the race is fixed.
   (D) No horse can win any race unless the race is fixed.
   (E) Whirlaway will not win the Georgia Derby.

Philosophy should be taught to students at a very early age. It will instill in them a healthy skepticism toward values that they might otherwise accept without question.

10. The argument above makes which of the following assumptions?

   I. Unless students are exposed to philosophy at an early age, they will accept every idea.
   II. Even at an early age, students are able to understand some philosophical concepts.
   III. It is a good idea for students to question traditional values.

   (A) II only   (B) III only   (C) I and II only
   (D) II and III only   (E) I, II, and III

A: The plays and poems attributed to William Shakespeare, a poorly educated country bumpkin, were in fact written by Queen Elizabeth I, who had the intelligence and learning demanded by such works of genius.
B: Your claim is highly unlikely. If Elizabeth I had written plays such as *Hamlet* and *Macbeth*, she would quickly have become known as the greatest woman author in history. Yet, she has no such reputation.

11. B's argument assumes that it is improbable that

   (A) Elizabeth I's authorship of the plays would have been kept a secret
   (B) an uneducated person could have written plays like *Hamlet* and *Macbeth*
   (C) Elizabeth I had the artistic gifts necessary for great literary achievement
   (D) education and talent as a creative writer necessarily go hand in hand
   (E) a woman in Elizabethan times could not have attained greatness as an author

Between 1960 and 1970, ivory poachers in the African nation of Zinbaku killed over 6,500 elephants. During that period, the total elephant population in Zinbaku fell from about 35,000 to just under 30,000. In 1970, new antipoaching measures were implemented in Zinbaku, and between 1970 and 1980 over 800 poachers were arrested and expelled from the country. Nevertheless, by 1980, the elephant population in Zinbaku had fallen to about 21,000.

12. Which of the following, if true, would best help to explain the apparent paradox presented above?

   (A) The poachers arrested in Zinbaku between 1970 and 1980 were usually sentenced to long prison terms.
   (B) Because of highly publicized campaigns against the slaughter of elephants, demand for ivory fell between 1970 and 1980.
   (C) The elephant population in neighboring Mombasa rose slightly between 1970 and 1980.
   (D) Prior to 1970, the antipoaching laws passed by parliament in Zinbaku were rarely enforced.
   (E) In Zinbaku, between 1970 and 1980, thousands of acres of forest, the elephant's natural habitat, were cleared for farming.

Secondary school graduates in Japan score significantly higher on tests of science and mathematics than do students at the same level in the United States. Some educational reformers in the United States attribute this difference to the more rigid and rigorous Japanese secondary school program, which emphasizes required courses, long hours of study and homework, and memorization to a far greater degree than do schools in the United States.

13. Which of the following, if true, would most seriously weaken the conclusion drawn by the educational reformers cited?

   (A) The Japanese elementary school program is far less rigid and structured than the elementary school programs in most U.S. schools.
   (B) Many Japanese parents and educators decry the Japanese educational system, saying that it stifles independent thinking on the part of students.
   (C) Secondary schools in the U.S. that emphasize creativity and flexible student schedules usually produce students with science and math scores higher than those earned by their Japanese counterparts.
   (D) On average, Japanese students score lower than U.S. students on tests of logical thinking, language arts, and communications skills.
   (E) A higher percentage of U.S. students go on to higher education than in Japan.

If the wind is strong, kites are flown.
If the sky is not clear, kites are not flown.
If the temperature is high, kites are flown.

14. Assuming the statements above are true, if kites are flown, which of the following statements must be true?

   I. The wind is strong.
   II. The sky is clear.
   III. The temperature is high.

   (A) I only   (B) II only   (C) III only
   (D) I and III only   (E) II and III only

341

Last year, the number of cases of rape reported by women in this city increased by 20 percent. Ironically, these statistics have been cited with approval by advocates of women's rights.

15. Which of the following, if true, would logically explain the seemingly paradoxical approval of the women's rights advocates?

(A) A new city policy of encouraging women to report cases of rape has sharply diminished the number of unreported cases.

(B) The rate of convictions in rape cases in the city has increased steadily over the past three years.

(C) Rape prevention has long been a high priority for leaders of women's rights organizations.

(D) Most of the increase in reported cases of rape occurred in three particularly dangerous neighborhoods of the city.

(E) Local judges have begun to deal more harshly with those found guilty of committing rape.

Superficially, today's problems with the abuse of illegal drugs such as heroin and cocaine resemble the problems of alcohol abuse during the 1920s, when many people kept drinking in spite of Prohibition. There is, however, a significant difference. The use of drugs such as heroin and cocaine has never been a widespread, socially accepted practice among most middle-class, otherwise law-abiding Americans.

16. An underlying assumption of the passage is that

(A) during Prohibition, drinking of alcohol was commonly accepted among most Americans

(B) as long as drugs are available, they will be used despite laws to the contrary

(C) most Americans consider heroin and cocaine to be in the same category as alcohol

(D) in a democracy, laws must be based on the fundamental beliefs and values of the majority of citizens

(E) American popular opinion has always been molded primarily by the values of the middle class

Some scientists believe that, in certain species of birds, particles of metal within the brain react to the presence of the Earth's magnetic field in the same way as the needle in a compass. It is this mechanism that is thought to underlie the birds' amazing ability to navigate accurately over distances of thousands of miles by day and night during migration. To test this theory, researchers surgically removed the metal particles from the heads of some birds and then released them, along with a number of untreated birds, at the usual time and place of their annual winter migration.

17. Which of the following results would most seriously weaken the theory being tested?

(A) The unaltered birds were irritated by the erratic flight patterns of the altered birds and drove them away from the main flock.

(B) The altered birds were able to follow their usual migratory path by day but not at night.

(C) The altered birds formed their own flock and followed the usual migratory path two weeks after the main flock.

(D) The altered birds were able to migrate successfully only when closely following a group of unaltered birds.

(E) The altered birds were not able to maintain a straight course of flight when skies were overcast.

For our nation to compete successfully in the high-technology enterprises of the future, workers with skills in math and science will be needed. But it is doubtful that they will be available, since there is a shortage of high school math and science teachers that shows no signs of improving. Industry can help alleviate this problem by funding scholarship grants and aid to college students who major in math and science with the hope of pursuing teaching careers.

18. Which of the following, if true, would most probably prevent the proposed plan from achieving its intended effect?

(A) After graduation from college, most math and science majors opt for jobs in industry rather than in teaching.

(B) Many high schools have been forced to lower their standards in hiring math and science teachers.

(C) Less scholarship money is available for students of math and science than is available for those in the humanities.

(D) Population statistics show that the number of high school students is expected to increase over the next ten years.

(E) Many experts say that businesses of the future will require many semiskilled and purely technical employees.

Pollution control can no longer be viewed as a national problem to be dealt with by individual countries on the basis of national sovereignty. As the international effects of the Chernobyl nuclear accident made clear, pollutants do not respect political boundaries; thus, every nation has a legitimate stake in the environmental practices and policies of its neighbors.

19. Which of the following would be the most logical continuation of the argument above?

(A) So, growth of the nuclear power industry should be halted until more rigorous safety procedures have been developed.

(B) Hence, attempts made by one nation to impose its environmental policies on another should be resisted—if necessary, by force.

(C) Consequently, issues of pollution should be handled by an international commission with the authority to set policies for all nations.

(D) Thus, every nation should pledge itself to environmental policies that will minimize the danger to its neighbors.

(E) As a result, only the ultimate emergence of a sovereign world government will resolve to-day's most pressing environmental dilemmas.

20. Which of the following, if true, most strongly supports the view expressed in the passage?

(A) Acid rain from factories in the midwestern United States pollutes lakes in Canada.

(B) Soviet leaders refused western reporters access to safety records after the Chernobyl accident.

(C) Neighboring states within the United States are often unable to agree on joint pollution-control efforts.

(D) Some countries have unilaterally taken steps to curtail emission of pollutants that might travel.

(E) Fishers from Japanese fleets have increasingly depleted fish supplies in United States territorial waters.

The percentage of family income spent on entertainment has remained almost the same over the past 20 years—about 12 percent. When new forms of entertainment become popular, they do not expand this percentage. Therefore, film exhibitors have observed the video boom with concern, fearing that every dollar spent on rental of videos could mean a dollar less spent on movie theater admissions.

21. Which of the following, if true, most forcefully undermines the argument of the passage above?

(A) The cost of renting a video is generally substantially less than the price of movie theater admission.

(B) Most film producers receive a portion of the income from the sale of video rights to their movies.

(C) People with videocassette players watch fewer hours of broadcast television than do people without such machines.

(D) Since the start of the video boom, money spent on forms of entertainment other than videos and movies has dropped.

(E) Some movies that were unprofitable when shown in theaters have become successful when released in video form.

The use of petroleum products in the manufacture of plastics should be regulated and limited by law. Our country's need for petroleum for energy production is more vital than our need for plastics, and our growing dependence on foreign sources of petroleum could have serious consequences if, for example, a war cut off our access to those imports. By reducing our use of petroleum products in making plastics, we can take a major step toward national energy independence and so enhance our country's security.

22. Which of the following, if true, would most greatly weaken the argument above?

(A) Only a small fraction of the petroleum products consumed in this country is used in making plastics.

(B) New methods of plastics manufacturing can somewhat reduce the amount of petroleum needed.

(C) The development of atomic energy as an alternative to petroleum-based energy has been slowed by legitimate concerns over safety.

(D) In time of war, combatant nations would be seriously tempted to seize forcibly the territories of petroleum-producing nations.

(E) Some plastic products, such as aircraft and motor vehicles parts, play vital roles in our nation's defense.

It is a truism of military science that "Generals always prepare for the *last* war." In much the same way, public officials generally spend their efforts on problems that were resolved—one way or another—years before. By the time a public issue reaches the consciousness of enough of the citizenry to become a high priority of our elected leaders, the problem is usually past the point at which government efforts can significantly affect it.

23. All of the following are assumed in the argument above EXCEPT

    (A) Most public problems tend to evolve toward a point at which the government can do little to control them.

    (B) Political and military leaders are both prone to react tardily to changes in their fields.

    (C) Issues attain importance for public officials when large numbers of citizens are concerned about them.

    (D) Planning policies solely on the basis of past experiences is likely to be ineffective.

    (E) Government officials can generally do little to influence directly the course of public policy.

Government spending in support of pure research is often treated as somehow wasteful, as though only immediate technological application can justify any scientific endeavor. Yet, unless the well of basic knowledge is continually replenished through pure research, the flow of beneficial technology will soon dry up. Today's pure research may appear to be of little use; but no one can tell what good it may someday yield. One might just as well ask: "Of what use is a newborn baby?"

24. The argument above depends on which of the following assumptions?

    I. There is a time lag between the discovery of a new phenomenon and the discovery of a practical application for it.

    II. Pure research is more costly and time-consuming than the attempt to develop new technologies.

    III. Most pure research will eventually benefit future generations but will not be of use to people currently alive.

    (A) I only   (B) II only   (C) I and II only
    (D) I and III only   (E) I, II, and III

25. To which of the following would the author compare the "new-born baby" mentioned in the last sentence of the passage?

    (A) A technological breakthrough based on pure research

    (B) Government funding in support of scientific endeavors

    (C) Public support for spending on pure research

    (D) The flow of public benefits from new technological developments

    (E) A scientific discovery with no immediately apparent application

Directions: In this section, the questions ask you to analyze and evaluate the reasoning presented in a statement or short paragraph. For some questions, all of the choices may arguably be answers to the question asked, but you are to select the best answer to the question. In evaluating the choices to a question, do not make assumptions that violate common standards by being implausible, redundant, irrevelant, or inconsistent.

A Supreme Court Justice once observed, "We are not the last word because we are infallible; we are infallible because we are the last word."

1. Which of the following most closely parallels the logic of the statement above?

   (A) Congressperson: Although I may make some mistakes, I will always use my best judgment to protect the interests of my constituents.
   (B) Teacher: My ideas may not always be correct, but students obey me because I am the teacher.
   (C) Doctor: Doctors make life and death decisions every day, so we are the most powerful judges in this society.
   (D) Lawyer: I cannot assure my client of victory, because I cannot predict with certainty what a judge will do.
   (E) Pilot: In an emergency, the ground control crew is not in the plane with me, so I have to make the final decision and hope I have not made a mistake.

It is truly folly that when we are sick in fortune—often the surfeit of our own behavior—we make guilty of our disasters the sun, the moon, and the stars, as if we were villains of necessity, fools by heavenly compulsion, knaves and treachers by spherical predominance, drunkards, liars, and adulterers by enforced obedience of planetary influence, and all that we are evil in by a divine thrusting on.

2. It can be inferred that the speaker above believes which of the following?

   I. There is no substance to astrology.
   II. Many people are reluctant to accept the consequences of their actions.
   III. Most people are evil.

   (A) I only   (B) II only   (C) I and II only
   (D) I and III only   (E) I, II, and III

Philosophical ideals, as they find embodiment in political action, cannot be confined to a single geographical region. This is particularly true where two countries undergo a period of parallel development. The seed will necessarily be blown to other regions where, if the conditions are favorable, it will take root. Nowhere is this seen better than in the Irish Revolution of the late 18th century. The seed of revolution blown from France found fertile ground and favorable climatic conditions in Ireland, so it flowered.

3. Which of the following statements, if true, most weakens the argument above?

   (A) French political treatises were not widely read by most of Ireland's population.
   (B) Conditions similar to those in Ireland and France existed at the same time in Poland and Austria, but those countries did not experience revolutions.
   (C) Much of the revolutionary rhetoric in Ireland was drawn from the American Revolution.
   (D) A substantial number of people in Ireland opposed the revolution.
   (E) The revolt in Ireland ultimately failed because the English were too powerful.

If Peter graduated from college, he must have studied a foreign language.

4. Which of the following, if true, is sufficient to guarantee the truth of the statement above?

   (A) Only college students study foreign languages.
   (B) All foreign languages are studied by some college students.
   (C) All college students are allowed to study a foreign language.
   (D) All college students are required to study a foreign language before graduation.
   (E) Some foreign languages are studied by no college students.

At a recent art auction, a large canvas painted in many colors sold for $100,000. At the same auction, a simple pen-and-ink drawing by the same artist sold for $105,000, because it was more beautiful. Whatever it is that is beauty, that is, whatever it is that we prize so highly, it is not necessarily the product of a lifetime of work but rather the gift of a moment.

5. The speaker above is making what point?

   (A) Art collectors often do not know the true value of a work of art.
   (B) Prices for rare objects of art are governed by market forces.
   (C) What one person considers beautiful, another may consider not beautiful.
   (D) Artistic achievement requires creative insight and not just technique.
   (E) There is a direct correlation between the price of a work of art and the time the artist required to produce the object.

All bushes that bear red roses have thorns. This bush has no thorns. Therefore, this bush cannot bear roses.

6. The logic of the argument above is most nearly paralleled by which of the following?

   (A) All Sandarac automobiles have three wheels. This car has three wheels. Therefore, this car is a Sandarac automobile.
   (B) All brides wear white. This woman is not wearing white. Therefore, this woman must be the maid of honor.
   (C) All professional tennis players use metal rackets. This player does not use a metal racket. Therefore, this player is not a professional tennis player.
   (D) All Scottish ivy is heliotropic. This plant is not heliotropic. Therefore, this plant is not ivy.
   (E) All pencils have rubber erasers. This eraser is not attached to a pencil. Therefore, this eraser is not made of rubber.

The single greatest weakness of American parties is their inability to achieve cohesion in the legislature. Although there is some measure of party unity, it is not uncommon for the majority party to be unable to implement important legislation. The unity is strongest during the election campaigns. After the primary elections, the losing candidates all promise their support to the party nominee. By the time the Congress convenes, however, the unity has dissipated. This phenomenon is attributable to the fragmented nature of political parties. The national committees are no more than feudal lords who receive nominal fealty from their vassals. A Congressperson builds his or her power upon a local base. Consequently, he or she is likely to be responsive to locally based special-interest groups. Evidence of this is seen in the differences in voting patterns between the upper and lower houses. In the Senate, where terms are longer, there is more party unity.

7. Which of the following, if true, would most strengthen the author's argument?

   (A) On 30 key issues, 18 of the 67 majority party members in the Senate voted against the party leaders.
   (B) On 30 key issues, 70 of the 305 majority party members in the House voted against the party leaders.
   (C) On 30 key issues, over half of the members of the minority party in both houses voted with the majority party against the leaders of the minority party.
   (D) Of 30 key legislative proposals introduced by the President, only eight passed both houses.
   (E) Of 30 key legislative proposals introduced by a President whose party controlled a majority in both houses, only four passed both houses.

Hamlet: Watchman, tell me of the night.
Horatio: I see nothing, my Prince.
Hamlet: Your eyes are much better than mine. In this darkness, I can scarcely see anything.

8. It can be inferred that the first speaker in the exchange above believes that

   (A) Horatio is not really the watchman
   (B) nothing is something that can be seen
   (C) something is more easily seen in darkness than in light
   (D) the night conceals a serious danger
   (E) the watchman is concealing something from him

Senator: It is my understanding that you have memberships in several private clubs that do not allow anyone other than members of the white race to join. Can you reconcile this fact with your desire to be confirmed as Director of the Bureau of Racial Equality?

Nominee: Senator, that is no longer true. Last week I resigned my membership in those clubs.

9. Which of the following is the best explanation for why the Senator might find the response to his question unsatisfactory?

   (A) The Senator was concerned not so much with the nominee's present affiliations as with the nominee's attitudes on race relations.
   (B) The nominee is attempting to conceal his affiliations in clubs that refuse to accept non-whites for membership.
   (C) The nominee attempts to escape moral responsibility for his actions on the grounds that he was unaware that the clubs discriminated against non-whites.
   (D) The nominee believes incorrectly that the Senator himself endorses the existence of clubs that select membership on the basis of race.
   (E) The nominee believes that the Senator believes that there is no inconsistency between such memberships and being Director of the Bureau of Racial Equality.

Al: Why did you return my lawn mower with a broken blade?

David: First, I never borrowed your mower. Second, when I returned it, it wasn't broken. Third, when I borrowed it, it was already broken.

10. Which of the following best describes the weakness in David's response?

    (A) It is internally inconsistent.
    (B) It makes an unproved assumption.
    (C) It contains circular reasoning.
    (D) It leads to no definite conclusion.
    (E) It seeks to evade the issue.

It is not always the case that the whole is equal to the sum of the parts. For example, we speak of Impressionist painting. The elements of such a painting are a certain choice of colors, the use of particular brush strokes and other techniques of paint application, and the selection of a certain subject matter. But the painting cannot be reduced to just these elements.

11. Which of the following would the speaker regard as most similar to the notion of Impressionist painting?

    (A) The steps in a geometry proof
    (B) The volumes in an encyclopedia
    (C) The notion of a national character
    (D) The instructions for assembling a toy
    (E) The molecules that make up an atom

Questions 12–13

Some snakes are amphibians.
Some amphibians are intelligent.
Some intelligent creatures are not snakes.

12. If the statements above are true, which of the following could also be true?

    (A) No amphibians are intelligent.
    (B) No snakes are amphibians.
    (C) No intelligent creatures are amphibians.
    (D) No amphibians are snakes.
    (E) All snakes are intelligent.

13. If the statements above are true, which of the following must be false?

    (A) All snakes are not intelligent.
    (B) All intelligent creatures are snakes.
    (C) A rat is an amphibious snake.
    (D) All amphibians are snakes.
    (E) All intelligent creatures are amphibians.

I recall my first encounter with philosophy. Professor Elmendorff, who taught all of the introductory philosophy classes at the University, strode into the room and began, "The end of any philosophical inquiry is truth. Now, you may wonder why it is that a university, whose very reason for existence is the dissemination of learning, would offer a class in philosophy—not only allowing but even inviting the wolf into the fold. This has always been a great mystery to me."

14. It can be inferred that Professor Elmendorff believes that

    (A) philosophy should not be a required course at the university
    (B) philosophy has few if any practical applications
    (C) truth and learning are not the same thing
    (D) truth can be discovered only by the process of learning
    (E) learning is more important than philosophy

15. Although alcohol seems to make you sleepy, it is actually an antisoporific.

    The logic of the statement above is most closely paralleled by the logic of which of the following statements?

    (A) Although some people still believe in God, most people have accepted science as supreme.
    (B) Although sea water will not quench thirst, it will extinguish fires.
    (C) Although dry ice seems to burn the skin, it is actually quite cold.
    (D) Although all states have a capital, no state has the same capital as any other.
    (E) Although heroin induces a state of euphoria, the drug is highly addictive.

Can you answer *this* question?

16. Which of the following would be a logically permissible response to the question posed?

   I. Yes
  II. No
 III. Perhaps

(A) I only   (B) II only   (C) III only
(D) I and III only   (E) I, II, and III

17. According to the tenor of the following statements and the apparent authoritativeness of the source, which of the following statements is the most reliable?

(A) Professor Adams, Ph.D in biochemistry: "Manet's contributions to 19th-century French painting are negligible."
(B) Cobbler: "This rubber heel is not only less expensive but is also longer-wearing than leather heels."
(C) Student: "I am sorry, teacher, but I cannot turn in my assignment today. I finished it, but my baby brother tore it up."
(D) Oscar Nominee: "I don't believe that Edgar should have won the award for best actor. I think my own performance was more deserving."
(E) Radio Announcer: "The next record is destined to be a big hit. It was written and recorded by a very close friend of mine."

Advertisement: For fast, fast, fast relief of pain, take Miracle Drug. Per dose, Miracle Drug has twice as much of the pain reliever most recommended by doctors as any other brand.

18. All of the following weaken the advertising claim above EXCEPT

(A) The pain reliever most recommended by doctors is nothing but aspirin.
(B) Most doctors prescribe brand-name drugs instead of generic drugs.
(C) The body can absorb only 25 percent of the pain reliever in Miracle Drug and passes through the rest.
(D) Most other commercial pain relievers contain the same main ingredient as Miracle Drug.
(E) Miracle Drug costs twice as much as other medicines with the same ingredients.

When did you stop beating your wife?

19. The form of the question above most closely resembles which of the following?

(A) Do you believe that parents should pay for their children's educations?
(B) When is the best time for planting corn?
(C) Is it true that the assassination of the Archduke Ferdinand triggered World War I?
(D) Did your company profit by its attempts to illegally fix prices?
(E) When did you first discover that your basement was leaking?

Joe is the village idiot, which would not be remarkable except that Joe lives in New York City.

20. The author makes his point by

(A) illustration
(B) documentation
(C) overstatement
(D) syllogism
(E) deduction

The following instructions recently discovered in an attic are said to be those given by the famous composer Sergie Brandon born in 1750:
The opening passages should serve to establish the framework within which the listener can evaluate the thematic variations. Importantly, much emphasis should be given to the clavichord, an 18th-century piano, for it governs the timbric qualities of the opening. Later in the piece, subtle distinctions are made between the color and intensity of the instruments. To highlight these, I would suggest that the performers be seated not on a stage but on the same level as the audience.

21. Which of the following phrases was probably not a part of the original document?

(A) thematic
(B) 18th-century piano
(C) later
(D) color and intensity
(E) but on the same level as the audience

Television Announcer: Are you fond of the finer things in life? Classical music? Beautiful paintings? Fine wines? Good scotch? A good scotch whiskey need not be expensive! A&B Scotch sells for $12.50 a liter, about half of what you would expect to pay for 12-year-old scotch. Your friends will not be able to taste the difference. But if you would be embarrassed, serve it from a cut-glass decanter.

22. Which of the following assumptions were made by the author of this advertisement?

   I. Many people who purchase scotch are likely to judge a product on the basis of price.
  II. It is possible to sell a 12-year-old scotch for $12.50 a liter and still make a profit.
 III. People who imagine themselves to be consumers of "the finer things in life" are likely to purchase scotch whiskey.

(A) III only   (B) I and II only
(C) I and III only   (D) II and III only
(E) I, II, and III

Mr. Carpenter: Research has demonstrated that the United States, which has the most extensive health care industry in the world, has only the 17th-lowest infant mortality rate. This forces me to conclude that medical technology causes babies to die.

Mr. Adams: That is ludicrous. We know that medical care is not equally available to all. Infant mortality is more likely to be caused by low income than medical technology.

23. Mr. Adams attacks Mr. Carpenter's reasoning by

(A) questioning the validity of his data
(B) offering an alternative interpretation of the data
(C) suggesting that the argument is circular
(D) redefining an important term
(E) implying that the argument is internally inconsistent

The Constitution establishes three *coequal* branches of government: a legislature charged with making laws, an executive branch charged with enforcing the laws, and a judiciary charged with applying those laws. The officers of each branch are sworn to uphold the Constitution. The legislature passed and the executive branch attempted to enforce a law that the Supreme Court refused to apply because it thought that the law was contrary to the Constitution. The Court's reasoning arguably demonstrated that the law did violate the Constitution. Ultimately, however, the Court's reasoning was flawed because it failed to explain why . . . .

24. Which of the following best completes the paragraph above?

(A) the framers of the Constitution created three branches of government
(B) the President did not veto the legislation
(C) its judgment regarding the constitutionality of the law should supersede that of the Congress and the President
(D) the Constitution should not be changed to allow the governmental actions authorized by the law
(E) the Congress should not be allowed to pass a revised statute that would conform to the dictates of the Constitution

Explanatory Answers

DRILL 1

1. (B) The logical structure of this argument is an attempt to conclude from the failure to prove "A," that "not A" is true. It says, in essence, "No one has proved that flying saucers exist; therefore, they do not exist." (B) correctly notes this logical structure.

2. (E) This argument has the following logical structure:

   > All *S* are *P*.
   > *F* is a *P*.

   Therefore, *F* is an *S*.
   The argument is fatally flawed. It's like arguing:

   > All soft drinks are liquids.
   > Water is a liquid.
   > Therefore, water is a soft drink.

   (E) correctly notes this logical flaw.

3. (D) This item asks you to identify hidden assumptions in the argument. Test each statement. Statement I is an assumption of the argument, for the author states that he has assigned numerical values for the various aspects, which assumes that some sort of quantitative measure is possible. II, also, is an assumption, for the author treats each variable as a separate, independent measure, and the scores were averaged. Finally, however, III is not necessarily an assumption of the argument. The author does address those who do have flexibility in their living plans (otherwise he would not have prepared the study), but this does not commit him to the assumption that people in general enjoy such flexibility.

4. (D) This question asks you to examine a causal linkage. Ordinarily, we would expect higher prices to result in less demand for a product. Yet, according to the speaker, in the face of higher prices for imported electronics, demand has not weakened. (D) gives a good alternative causal explanation that could account for this.

5. (B) The main point of the passage is that most writers don't fare well. And this is why the author quotes T. S. Eliot, who, somewhat ironically, points out that even most people who claim to be writers really aren't *successful* writers.

6. (C) This argument is really kind of a generalization. It assumes that what is true of one magazine is true of other magazines as well. (C) points out that the argument is implicitly committed to this idea.

7. (A) This item asks that you draw a further inference from the material given. The speaker claims that for years architects were not interested in ornamentation, but instead wanted simple, light lines. Then the author states that we are seeing a reevaluation of this attitude—as exemplified by a current exhibit. We may infer from this that the reexamination is prompting a renewed appreciation of the function of ornamentation.

8. (C) This is one of those items that asks you to find alternative causal explanations. Here you are asked to find the one choice that does not provide an alternative explanation that would help eliminate the paradox. Every choice but (C) suggests a way of eliminating the paradox. (C), however, if anything, strengthens the paradox by eliminating a possible way of explaining away the paradox.

9. (B) This item asks you to identify a hidden assumption of the claim. The claim states that Whirlaway's winning entails that the race be fixed. So the claim depends on the hidden assumption that Whirlaway can win the Georgia Derby only if the race is fixed. (A) is incorrect, for the speaker claims only that Whirlaway's winning means that this particular race is fixed. (C) is incorrect because the speaker claims only that Whirlaway's winning (and not some other horse's winning) means that the race is fixed. (D) is wrong for the reasons that both (A) and (B) are wrong. Finally, as for (E), the author specifically allows that Whirlaway might win.

10. (D) This item asks you to identify hidden assumptions in the argument. Test each statement. Statement I is not an assumption of the argument, for the author need not commit himself to the view that children accept *every* idea—just that, given philosophical training, they would be more critical of ideas. The author is, however, committed to II. If children were not able to grasp philosophical concepts, then it would make no sense to try to teach them the concepts. The author is also committed to III. Implicit in the argument is the premise that it is a good idea to have students question ideas—otherwise, the author would be content to let them absorb the ideas without question.

11. (A) This item asks you to identify the assumptions made by B. B merely denies A's claim that Elizabeth I wrote the works ordinarily attributed to Shakespeare. In other words, B says "Elizabeth I did not write Shakespeare. Had she, she would have been famous." B doesn't have to take on any other burden. He doesn't have to prove who actually wrote the works—only that Elizabeth I did not write them.

12. (E) This question asks you to look for an alternative causal linkage. The passage implies that, given the legal actions to stop poaching, the elephant population should not have declined, but it did. What would explain that? (E) gives a very good explanation—another cause was working at the same time.

13. (C) Focus on the claim that you are asked to assess. The reformers claim that the critical difference between the math and science scores of Japanese and American children is the discipline of the Japanese educational system. (C) directly contradicts this claim. It says, in essence, that this cannot be the proper causal explanation because American students, in their highly flexible environments, actually outscore the Japanese students in their rigid environments.

14. (B) This is a problem involving deductive arguments. Assume that the initial statements are true; then test each choice. Statement I is not necessarily true. For example, even though it is true that when it is raining, there are clouds in the sky, you cannot conclude from the fact that there are clouds in the sky that it is raining. And III makes the same error. II, however, is inferable. It follows this reasoning: When there are no clouds in the sky, it is not raining. It is raining; therefore, there are clouds in the sky.

13

15. (A) Again, you are looking for an alternative causal explanation. The explanation for the paradoxical result is that there was no increase in the *incidence* of rape, but there was an increase in the *number of cases reported*.

16. (A) This item asks for an underlying assumption. The author claims that the situation with the abuse of heroin and cocaine is unlike that which existed with respect to alcohol during Prohibition. What is the difference? According to the author, heroin and cocaine are not middle-class drugs of preference. Thus, we can infer (though the author never specifically says so) that alcohol, even during Prohibition, was a middle-class drug of preference.

17. (C) The question stem here asks for the evidence that would most *weaken* the theory that metal particles are important to some birds' navigational mechanisms. The best refutation of the theory would be a finding that when the particles were removed, the birds continued to migrate as effectively as before. (C) is tantamount to saying that this was the case.

18. (A) The correct response to this question is a statement that focuses upon an unforeseen causal outcome. We might quote somewhat whimsically, "The best-laid plans of mice and men. . . ." What (A) asserts is that you can pour the money into the system, and you can train students in math and science, but they will not go into teaching. Thus, your plan will not achieve the desired result.

19. (C) This question asks that you draw a further conclusion from the premises given. The argument is leading up to a call for some sort of international agency to control pollution, which, as the author claims, is an international problem. Thus, (C) is the best response. As for (A), the author would consider the Chernobyl incident merely one example of the problem he is addressing; and, in fact, he may or may not oppose nuclear power per se. (B) and (D) are in tension with the paragraph, for the author is skeptical of the ability of a nation as an individual nation to solve the problems of pollution. Finally, however, (E) overstates the case. The author is concerned with a specific subject area—not world government in general.

20. (A) The author cites one example of international pollution, so another example would help strengthen his claim. (A) provides such an example. As for (B), the fact that journalists were not given access to the Chernobyl plant does not show that the incident had international repercussions. As for (C), this is a problem within a nation state, but the author is addressing the problem of international pollution. (D) actually weakens the argument by suggesting that the problem can be solved unilaterally. Finally, (E), too, is a problem that can be handled completely within the jurisdiction of a single nation: stop the fishers from fishing in the territorial waters.

21. (D) This is one of those questions, typical of the LSAT, that is answered by finding an alternative causal explanation. The author argues for the following connection: videos take money away from movies. What choice (D) asserts, in effect, is that the monies spent on videos came from some other source. So the projected cause-effect sequence was incorrect.

22. (A) This item asks you to find a hidden assumption of the argument. The speaker claims that in order to ensure we have sufficient energy, we should quit using petroleum as an energy source to manufacture plastics. If we do so, he claims, we will have made a significant step towards energy independence. This argument, however, assumes that we use a lot of petroleum in the manufacturing of plastic, which is what (A) points out.

23. (E) Here you are looking for the one idea that is not assumed by the speaker, and this is articulated by (E). The paragraph is really an argument for the position that government leaders *should* address problems more quickly. The author, then, is committed to the idea that public policy is under the control of the government. It just hasn't been effectively used in the past.

24. (A) Test each statement. Statement I is an assumption of the argument. If there were no such time lag, then the distinction between pure research and application would be nonexistent. It is the lag that creates the distinction. II, however, is not an assumption of the argument. The author assumes only that pure research seems "pure" because its applications are not immediately obvious, but he is not necessarily committed to the idea that it is more expensive than any other kind of research. Finally, III is not an assumption of the speaker. Although the time lag creates the distinction between the types of research, the author doesn't say how long the time period is that separates the types.

25. (E) Once you understand the main point of the passage, you also understand the answer to this question. The author is arguing that "pure" research, with no obvious, immediate applications, is still valuable—like a baby, it has potential.

DRILL 2

1. (B) The initial statement contains an interesting twist of reasoning. The Supreme Court Justice is making the point that the Supreme Court is the highest authority. This doesn't mean that the Court is infallible, but it does mean that it has the last word. In (B), the teacher makes a similar statement. The teacher will be obeyed because she is the highest authority for the students.

2. (C) This item is very much like something you would find in a Reading Comprehension section. You must read the paragraph and recognize that the speaker is criticizing the notion that the heavenly bodies influence human behavior. Therefore, the speaker probably would accept statement I. Also, the author implies that people attempt to escape responsibility for their actions by blaming the influence of the heavenly bodies. So II also would be endorsed by the speaker. III, however, overstates the case. The speaker does not imply that people are always evil, only that when they suffer misfortune or do something evil, they blame the stars.

3. (B) The author of the paragraph makes the general claim that revolution will spread from one country to another, and he documents that claim with a specific example. The best attack on this line of reasoning is provided by (B), which gives two counterexamples to the author's claim. (A) is, at best, a very weak attack. The author could turn aside this attack by simply saying, "But the leaders of the revolution were familiar with events in France." (C), too, is only a weak objection. The author could say, "It is true that the rhetoric was English, but the political ideas were derived from France." As for (D) and (E), the author doesn't contend that the revolution was successful, only that revolutionary activity occurred.

13

4. (D) The question stem really asks for you to find a hidden assumption of the argument. The claim assumes that the status of being a college graduate is sufficient to guarantee that Peter studied a foreign language. So you need a premise that is tantamount to saying all college graduates have studied a foreign language. (D) provides the missing link.

5. (D) This question asks you to identify the conclusion of the argument. Although the conclusion is not signalled by any word such as *therefore*, it is contained in the final sentence of the paragraph: beauty "is not necessarily the work of a lifetime but the gift of a moment." (D) best summarizes this idea. As for (A), the author does not imply any criticism of art collectors, and in fact seems to suggest that the prices paid were fair ones. As for (B), though the author might accept this statement, it is not the main point or conclusion of the argument as written. (C), too, might be a statement the author would accept, but (C) is not the conclusion of the argument as written. Finally, (E) seems to be directly contradicted by the passage.

6. (D) This item asks for you to find another argument that contains the same error found in the initial paragraph. You could describe the error of the initial paragraph as ambiguity, for the argument moves from a premise about "red rose bushes" to a conclusion about "rose bushes." (D) makes the same mistake. There the premise uses the term "Scottish ivy," but the conclusion uses the term "ivy."

7. (E) The conclusion of the argument is contained in the first sentence of the initial paragraph: American political parties are not unified. The best support for this conclusion will be a statement that is evidence of this disunity. All of the choices provide some support for the author's claim because each shows that party members do not always toe the party line. (E), however, provides the greatest support. (E) clearly shows that the party leader was unable to control the members of his own party. As for (A) and (B), the defections mentioned here are insignificant when compared with those cited by (E). As for (D), this result could be explained by the fact that the President's party did not control the legislature. (C) is perhaps the second-best response. But to assess the real strength of (C) you would need to know how many key issues were decided. If there were 300 key issues during the period studied, and on only 30 of them party members did not vote with the party leaders, then that would not provide much strength for the author's position.

8. (B) This is a problem similar to one you studied in the Logical Reasoning lesson. The exchange contains an ambiguity. The watchman says he sees nothing and means by that that he doesn't see anything. The other speaker interprets the watchman's remark to mean that the watchman is able to see something he calls "nothing."

9. (A) The nominee attempts a little fancy footwork to get around the issue. The Senator has asked the nominee to explain how he could be a member of all-white clubs and still want to head an agency that is supposed to promote racial equality. The nominee attempts to evade the question by noting that he is no longer a member of the clubs. The issue, however, as (A) correctly points out, is the nominee's attitudes. As for (B) and (C), the nominee has implicitly admitted that he previously held such memberships and that he was aware of what those memberships signified. (D) and (E) are incorrect because the nominee evidently understands only too well that the Senator does not endorse such clubs and, further, that the Senator does believe that there is an inconsistency between membership in such clubs and the ability to head the Bureau.

10. (A) The speaker makes three different statements—all as assertions of fact. But the three statements cannot all be true, so the speaker has contradicted himself.

11. (C) This is a kind of further application question. The point of the paragraph is that a concept that defines a school of painting cannot be completely reduced to other concepts. The speaker would say that the whole is more than the sum of the parts. The only situation given that is at all similar to the idea of a school of painting is the notion of a national character. So (C) is the best response. The ideas mentioned in each of the other choices can be reduced to individual parts, and once the individual components are isolated, there is nothing left to explain.

12. (E) Here you might want to make use of circle diagrams:

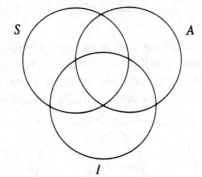

The three circles show the possible overlap of the categories "snakes," "amphibians," and "intelligent creatures." Now enter on the diagram the information provided by the first statement:

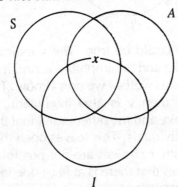

The x indicates that there is at least one individual in that region. I have placed the x on the circumference of the "intelligent creatures" circle, because we don't know whether the individual that is both a snake and an amphibian is also an intelligent creature. Now enter the information provided by the second statement:

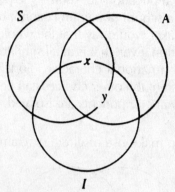

Again, the y indicates that there is at least one individual who has the characteristics "amphibian" and "intelligent creature." And again, I have placed the y on one of the borderlines to indicate we don't know whether the individual shares the third characteristic as well. Finally, complete the diagram:

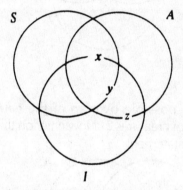

The diagram shows that (E) could be true. The x indicates that there is an individual that is both a snake and an amphibian. And it might belong in the circle for intelligent creatures as well — we don't know. The y might also be a snake, but if y is a snake, then y is also intelligent. Therefore, the one individual known to be a snake and the other individual that might be a snake could both be intelligent individuals. This leaves open the possibility that all snakes are intelligent. The other choices are not possible. As for the wrong choices, the diagram indicates that there is at least one individual that shares each of those pairs of characteristics.

13. (B) The z indicates that there is at least one individual that is intelligent and not a snake. Therefore, it must be false that all intelligent creatures are snakes. (A) is equivalent to "no snakes are intelligent," and according to the diagram, that statement could be true (if the x falls outside of the circle for intelligent creatures). As for (C), we have no information about rats, so this statement could be true. As for (D), the x indicates there is at least one amphibian that is a snake, and the y indicates there is at least one individual that is both amphibian and intelligent, and it could also be a snake. And the z indicates

that there is a creature that is not a snake and might or might not be an amphibian. Thus it is possible for (D) to be true. Finally, as for (E), this could be true depending on whether z belongs inside the amphibian circle.

Using circle diagrams is one way to attack these two problems. You can also attack them by using verbal logic. You should use the technique you feel more comfortable with.

14. (C) The professor states that the goal of philosophy is truth and draws a distinction between truth and learning. Thus, (C) is the best response. As for (A), the professor seems to favor philosophy over learning. He probably thinks that the head of the university would not allow philosophy to be a required course, but this doesn't mean he believes philosophy should not be required. As for (B), this goes considerably beyond the scope of the initial paragraph. To be sure, you can probably make an argument that the professor might accept this statement, but part of your justification will have to be that learning and truth are distinct. And that indicates that (B) is further removed from the explicit text, so (C) is a better choice. (D) and (E) must surely be false since the professor seems to accord priority to truth over learning.

15. (C) Although all of the answer choices have a grammatical structure similar to that of the initial statement, only one makes a claim that is substantively similar to the initial statement. The initial statement claims that X seems to have one characteristic but actually has the opposite—in other words, the sense is wrong. (C) makes a similar claim.

16. (A) This is a nice little problem in logic. If you answer "no" to the statement, then you have contradicted yourself because you have answered the question. Similarly, if you answer "perhaps" to the question, you have also contradicted yourself because you have definitely answered the question—not possibly answered it. You could, however, answer "yes" to the question without contradicting yourself.

17. (B) This item asks you to assess the credibility of five statements. You should keep in mind the considerations presented in the Logical Reasoning lesson in connection with *ad hominem* reasoning and arguments that rely on authority. (See Lesson 12.) The best choice is (B). Here you have an expert in a particular field (a cobbler would be an expert on shoes), and there can't be any question about self-interest, since the cobbler is touting the less expensive alternative. You should eliminate (A) because the speaker is not addressing a topic within his or her expertise. And you should eliminate (C), (D), and (E) because each implies that the speaker is probably not completely objective.

18. (B) In the Logical Reasoning lesson, I mentioned some of my favorite advertisements. Here is another. (B) fails to weaken the advertising claim because it doesn't come to grips with the claim at all. (A) is a good attack on the claim, because it makes it clear that the main ingredient of Miracle Drug is common aspirin. (C) weakens the claim by asking what good more medicine is if the body can't use it. (D) weakens the claim by showing that Miracle Drug is no better than any other similar remedy. And of course (E) weakens the claim by noting that Miracle Drug is more expensive than other remedies with the same ingredient.

13

19. (D) This is a "trick" question, the kind of question some people associate with "lawyering." The "trick" is that the question presumes that the person being interrogated admits that he beat his wife. (D) contains a similar hidden presupposition. In fact, a lawyer probably wouldn't get away with asking either question unless the truth of the hidden presupposition had already been established. If it had not already been proved that the man beat his wife, you can just bet his lawyer would object to the question.

20. (C) This is a fun little item. In fact, if you read this seriously you might have trouble answering it correctly. The statement, however, is intended ironically; and once you see that, you should be able to recognize that the speaker is exaggerating. So "overstatement" is the best description of the method by which the speaker makes his point.

21. (B) A person actually writing in the 18th century would not be likely to add the comment cited by (B). "Eighteenth-century piano" looks like a comment that would have been added by an editor for readers of a later period.

22. (C) Statement I must be a presupposition of the advertisement. Otherwise, the speaker would not mention price as a reason for buying A&B Scotch. III must also be a presupposition of the advertisement. Otherwise, the advertisement would not begin by appealing to people who have such notions. II, however, is not a presupposition of the advertisement. The author never states that A&B is a 12-year-old scotch.

23. (B) In Lesson 12, I described and presented examples of different types of reasoning. The response of Mr. Adams, here, is an attempt to question the causal linkage identified by Mr. Carpenter, and it does appear that Mr. Carpenter has committed the fallacy of the false cause. If you are unclear about the meanings of the remaining choices, I refer you to Lesson 12.

24. (C) The author states that all three of the branches of government are sworn to uphold the Constitution. Thus, when the Congress passed and the President signed the law in question, all of those officers were implicitly saying that they believed the law was Constitutional. Then, according to the author, the Supreme Court gave some powerful reasons why it believed the law to be unconstitutional and struck it down. The one thing the Court did not do was explain why its judgment about the constitutionality of the law was better than those of the other two branches.

Writing Sample: Part I

14

Part of your LSAT will be the Writing Sample. The time limit for the Writing Sample is 30 minutes, and during that time, you will write an essay on an assigned topic.

1. Anatomy of the Writing Sample

The Writing Sample is the last part of the LSAT. You will be given a Writing Sample booklet and a ball-point pen. The Writing Sample booklet contains the topic on which you are to write, two lined pages for your essay, and scratch paper. The lined paper on which you write is backed by paper that makes a carbonless copy so that you can keep a copy of your Writing Sample. The Writing Sample is not graded, but copies of your essay will be forwarded to the law schools that you designate to receive copies of your LSAT score.

Here are the general instructions for the Writing Sample:

> You are to complete the brief writing exercise on the topic inside. You will have 30 minutes in which to plan and write the exercise. Read the topic carefully. You will probably find it best to spend a few minutes considering the topic and organizing your thoughts before you begin writing. DO NOT WRITE ON A TOPIC OTHER THAN THE ONE SPECIFIED. WRITING ON A TOPIC OF YOUR OWN CHOICE IS NOT ACCEPTABLE.
>
> There is no "right" or "wrong" answer to this question. Law schools are interested in how carefully you support the position you take and how clearly you express that position. How well you write is much more important than how much you write. No special knowledge is required or expected. Law schools are interested in organization, vocabulary, and writing mechanics. They understand the short time available to you and the pressured circumstances under which you will write.
>
> Confine your writing to the lined area inside this booklet. Only the blocked lined area will be reproduced for the law schools. You will find that you have enough space in this booklet if you plan your writing carefully, write on every line, avoid wide margins, and keep your handwriting a reasonable size. Be sure that your writing is legible.

2. Three Important Facts about the Writing Sample

A. The Writing Sample is not usually an important factor in the admissions decision. The Writing Sample was added to the LSAT because law schools wanted an opportunity to see how different applicants write within the same time limit and under the same circumstances. But from the information provided by law schools in *The Official Guide to U.S. Law Schools,* it doesn't appear that the Writing Sample plays a very importnat role in the admissions process. Most law schools briefly describe the admission decision in terms such as these:

The Admissions Committee places primary emphasis on the undergraduate GPA and the score on the LSAT. The Committee also takes into account other factors, such as a substantial improvement in undergraduate grades, outstanding contributions to the student community, and motivation. Letters of recommendation can also be valuable.

Notice that there is no mention of the Writing Sample. Although the Writing Sample is not the most important factor in the admissions decision, in some cases it could prove decisive. Imagine that you are an admissions officer and that you have two applications that are very similar. The two applicants have GPAs and LSAT scores that are comparable, both have good letters of recommendation, and both have extensive extracurricular and community activities. Suppose also that you can accept only one of the two applications. Because of space limitations, the other must be rejected. What should you do? You could use their Writing Sample essays as the "tie-breaker." In such a situation, the Writing Sample would be the crucial factor.

In the "thought experiment" above, I asked you to assume that you had two, equally well-qualified applicants. I tried to show that the Writing Sample could very well be crucial. There it was crucial because our hypothetical admissions officer was faced with a difficult choice. I do not think that the reverse is true. If an admissions officer has an applicant who is well qualified in terms of the LSAT, GPA, and additional factors and another who is less well qualified, I doubt that the admissions officer is going to look at the Writing Samples of the two applicants hoping to reject the seemingly better-qualified applicant in favor of the seemingly less well-qualified applicant. In other words, I doubt seriously that writing a good essay is going to get you into a law school where you are not otherwise competitive. (Given the 30-minute time limit and the nature of the topic, I doubt that Oliver Wendell Holmes could get himself into law school with his Writing Sample essay if he were not already a serious candidate.) But a bad essay might keep you out.

14

B. The topic on which you will write will be a decision-problem topic.

EXAMPLE:

Read the following summaries of proposals submitted by Knight and Carpenter, each of whom wishes to lease the vacant store space in a co-op building located at 850 Seventh Avenue. Then, in the space provided, write an argument for the building's governing board in favor of leasing the space to either Knight or Carpenter. The following criteria are relevant to your decision:

1. The co-op board prefers to grant a long-term lease to a tenant who is financially secure and whose use would not unduly disturb residents of the building.

2. The co-op board wants the space used by a tenant who will provide a product or service that is not currently readily available to the 250 families who live in the building.

KNIGHT proposes to use the space for a delicatessen. The store will offer high-priced imported and specialty items. Knight has owned and operated a similar store on the other side of town for 18 years, and some of the building's residents are regular customers at that store. Knight is relocating his business because his lease has expired and the landlord is demanding an increase in monthly rent from $1,500 to $3,500. The monthly rental for the vacant store at 850 Seventh Avenue is $2,800. Knight is eager for a longer-term lease. He has also agreed to have included in the lease a provision that will govern the timing and frequency of truck deliveries and a provision allowing the co-op board to inspect the premises to make sure that the foodstuffs are not attracting rats.

CARPENTER proposes to use the store for a card and gift shop. For the past five years, Carpenter has managed a shoe store, handling all aspects of the business, including purchasing, sales, payroll, and other record keeping. Although there is already a card and gift shop in the neighborhood, Carpenter notes that its owner plans to retire in two years and close the store. Additionally, Carpenter will stock a greater variety of, and better-quality, merchandise. Since he is just starting his business, Carpenter would prefer a three- to five-year lease with an option to renew.

There is no right or wrong position. Instead, the topic is just the "excuse" you need to write something. And you can see from the nature of the topic that you don't need any special knowledge to write about it. In the next lesson, I will have more to say about what you should write.

C. You are not expected to be able to write a brilliant piece of prose. The directions specifically state that law schools "understand the short time available to you and the pressured circumstances under which you will write." Law schools are primarily interested in "organization, vocabulary, and writing mechanics." Your main goal, then, is to write something that is reasonably coherent and grammatically correct.

3. English Diagnostic Test

Half of the battle in this section is to make sure that what you write is written correctly. Below you will find a diagnostic test that will help you determine whether you need to do additional work on the basics of English grammar and punctuation. If you do reasonably well on the diagnostic test, missing only two or three items, you almost certainly do not need to do any review of the basic rules. If you miss more than a few items, you should probably find a grammar book and brush up on those areas in which you are weak.

ENGLISH DIAGNOSTIC TEST
35 Questions
No Time Limit

Directions: Each of the following sentences contains an error of grammar, sentence structure, usage, or punctuation. Circle the letter of the underlined part of the sentence containing the error. Although there is no time limit, you should work as quickly as possible. After you have finished, review your work using the explanations that follow.

1. Her and the other members of the team spoke to the press after their final victory.
   A   B   C   D

2. In early America, there has been very little to read except for the books sent from
                     A   B   C   D
   Europe.

3. Still remaining in the ancient castle are the Duke's collection of early Dutch
   A   B
   paintings, which will be donated to a museum.
              C   D

4. After having took the entrance examination, she was absolutely sure that she
              A   B   C
   would be admitted to the college.
   D

5. Most students preferred courses in the liberal arts to courses in science—unless
                  A   B   C
   they are science majors.
   D

6. The point of the coach's remarks were obviously to encourage the team and
                              A   B
   to restore its competitive spirit.
   C   D

7. When Mozart wrote The Marriage of Figaro, the Emperor was shocked at him using
               A   B   C
   mere servants as main characters.
                  D

8. Since he was called back for a third reading, the actor expected being chosen for the
   A   B   C   D
   part.

9. For a young woman who is ready to join the work force, there now exists many more
                    A   B   C
   opportunities than existed for her mother.
                D

10. Movie fans claim there is no greater director than him, although most critics
                A   B   C
    would mention the names of Bergman or Kurosawa.
    D

11. When the Senate meeting was televised, the first issue to be discussed were Federal
                   A   B   C   D
    grants and loans for higher education.

12. Although the average person watches a news program every day, they do not always
    A   B   C
    understand the issues discussed.
    D

13. It was said of the noted author Marcel Proust that he goes out only at night.
                                                   A B C   D

14. Most people do not realize that white wines, including champagne, are often made
                   A   B   C
    of red grapes.
    D

15. The earliest architecture in the New World <u>resembled</u> neither <u>that</u> of the European
    A   B
    Renaissance <u>or that</u> of the early Baroque period, <u>but rather</u> the medieval architecture
                  C   D
    of European towns.

16. <u>Like</u> many composers of the period, Debussy <u>was familiar</u> and <u>admired</u> contemporary
    A   B   C
    poetry and <u>used it as</u> the inspiration for his music.
                 D

17. Americans used to go to the movies <u>as often</u> as they watched television; but now that
                                          A
    <u>they</u> can watch movies in <u>their</u> homes, they <u>are doing more of it</u>.
      B   C   D

18. <u>After hearing</u> Joan Sutherland perform <u>live</u> at the Metropolitan Opera on
      A   B
    December 1, 1984, I am convinced that she is <u>greater than any prima donna</u>
                                                    C
    <u>of this century</u>.
      D

19. Like Andy Warhol, the "pop art" <u>of</u> Roy Lichtenstein <u>is filled with</u> familiar <u>images</u>
                                       A   B   C
    <u>such as</u> cartoon characters.
      D

20. <u>Because</u> the project had been a team effort, we <u>had divided</u> the bonus equally <u>among</u>
      A   B   C
    the <u>five of us</u>.
          D

21. <u>Postponing marriage</u> and having <u>little or no</u> children <u>are</u> not revolutionary choices for
      A   B   C
    women; <u>they were</u> choices made by the grandmothers of many postwar women.
             D

22. <u>Being that</u> black bears <u>are</u> large and powerful, most people fear <u>them</u> even though the
      A   B   C
    bears <u>are really</u> quite shy.
             D

23. <u>Because</u> consumers <u>believe</u> there <u>to be</u> a correlation between price and quality, the cost
      A   B   C
    of computer software <u>is steadily raising</u>.
                            D

24. <u>Travel to countries</u> with <u>less than</u> ideal sanitary conditions <u>increases</u> the <u>amount of</u>
      A   B   C   D
    victims of hepatitis.

25. The fuel truck <u>overturned</u> on the <u>highway, stopped</u> traffic for over four hours <u>during</u>
                     A   B   C
    the <u>busiest part</u> of the day.
          D

26. <u>Primarily found</u> in the remote mountainous regions of the southeastern states, very few
      A
    people <u>die</u> of the bite of the copperhead or highland moccasin because <u>very few</u>
             B   C
    people come into contact with <u>them</u>.
                                     D

27. <u>When Peter started the business in 1982</u>, it was <u>hardly nothing</u> more than a one-room operation
      A   B
    with a single telephone line, <u>but</u> today Peter <u>has</u> offices in six different states.
                                     C   D

28. <u>Unlike the 1960s, when drugs were used primarily</u> by "hippies," cocaine <u>is used</u> today
      A   B
    <u>by people</u> in all walks of life, <u>including</u> lawyers.
      C   D

29. While the Reagan–Gorbachev summit cannot be <u>described</u> as a complete waste of
                                                  A   B
    time, <u>nothing</u> <u>particular</u> significant was accomplished during the ten-day meeting.
            C   D

30. There are some people who are unusually sensitive to bee stings and who
                A   B
    may experience allergic reactions including swelling, chills, nausea, fever, and
                          C
    they may even become delirious.
                D

31. When Robert introduced the guest speaker he described his accomplishments in great
      A   B   C
    detail but then forgot to mention the speaker's name.
                 D

32. The fog was very dense, they were unable to make out the beacon light
         A   B   C
    on the opposite shore.
          D

33. Gordon told the clerk that he wanted to order three bottles of Beaujolais two bottles
         A   B   C
    of port, and one bottle of claret.
      D

34. "Guernica," one of Picasso's many masterpieces was exhibited in the New York
                       A   B
    Museum of Modern Art until, as specified in Picasso's will, it was returned to Spain
                 C   D
    once democracy was reinstated.

35. Mary Alice who is the dean's choice has indicated that she would be willing to serve
             A   B
    as chairperson *pro tem* only on the condition that a search committee be formed within
     C   D
    the next three weeks.

14

Explanatory Answers

1. (A) *Her* is an object pronoun and cannot be used as a subject.

2. (A) The verb tense is incorrect. The past tense, *was*, is needed here.

3. (B) The subject here is the collection of paintings, which is singular; therefore the verb should be singular.

4. (A) The past participle for *to take* is *taken*, not *took*.

5. (A) The sentence suffers from an illogical combination of verb tenses, a problem that can be corrected by changing *preferred* to *prefer*.

6. (A) The subject here is *point*, which is singular; therefore, the plural verb *were* is incorrect.

7. (C) The modifier is intended to modify the gerund; *him* should be *his*.

8. (D) The infinitive is required here; *he expected to be chosen*.

9. (B) The subject is *many opportunities*, which is plural. The verb should be *exist*.

10. (C) The subject pronoun is required for the predicate nominative; *him* should be *he*.

11. (D) The subject here is *issue*, which is singular, so the verb should also be singular—*was*.

12. (C) *They* represents a shift in subject from *the average person*. The correct pronoun would be *he or she*.

13. (C) Since the first verb is in the past tense, the second verb cannot be in the present tense.

14. (D) This is an error of idiomatic expression. The wines are made *from* red grapes, not *of* red grapes.

15. (C) The correct expression in English is *neither/nor*; here, *or* is incorrect.

16. (C) This is an incomplete construction. The sentence should say that Debussy was familiar *with* and admired.

17. (D) Here, the pronoun *it* has no specific referent.

18. (C) This is not a logical statement. The sentence says that Joan Sutherland is greater than herself. It should say that she is greater than any other prima donna.

19. (A) This is an illogical comparison; the sentence compares the art of Lichtenstein to Andy Warhol, not to his art.

20. (B) The use of the past perfect tense here is unnecessary. The simple past is required.

21. (B) This is a mistake of expression. The correct expression is *few*, not *little*.

22. (A) *Being that* is colloquial usage for *since* or *because* and should not be used.

23. (D) This is an error in diction. The correct word here is *rising*.

24. (D) The sentence contains an error in diction. The correct word is *number*, not *amount*.

25. (B) *Stopping* should be used instead of *stopped* to indicate simultaneous action and to avoid a run-on sentence.

26. (A) The sentence contains a dangling modifier. The writer does not mean to say that people are found in the remote mountainous regions but that the snakes are found in those regions.

27. (B) The sentence contains a double negative: *hardly nothing*.

28. (A) The sentence contains a dangling modifier. The phrase *the 1960s* cannot modify *cocaine*.

29. (D) *Particular* is an adjective and cannot be used to modify another adjective. The correct word would be *particularly*.

30. (D) The sentence suffers from faulty parallelism.

31. (B) A long introductory phrase or dependent clause must be separated from the main clause by a comma: "When Robert introduced the guest speaker, he . . . ."

32. (B) This sentence contains a comma splice. You cannot join two independent clauses (independent thoughts) with a comma. You must either use a semicolon instead of a comma or include a conjunction: "The fog was very dense; they were . . . ."

33. (C) You must set off a series of three or more similar elements with commas. Although a comma is not required between the final two elements, commas are required between the other elements. Thus, the comma following *port* is optional, but you do need a comma following *Beaujolais*.

34. (A) An appositive should be set off by commas: "'Guernica,' one of Picasso's many masterpieces, was . . . ." The other two commas are correct. They set off a parenthetical expression.

35. (A) A nonrestrictive clause must be set off by commas: "Mary, who is the dean's choice, ..."

14

4. Common Grammatical Errors to Avoid

A. Subject–Verb Agreement

As you know, a subject must agree with its verb.

> **EXAMPLE:**
>
> The professor were traveling in Europe when she received notice of her promotion.

The construction *were traveling* is an error. The subject is *professor*, a singular noun. The verb *were traveling* should be *was traveling*. The sentence should read: "The professor was traveling in Europe." This example is very simple; the error is easy to spot because the subject and verb are next to each other. Most errors occur when the subject and the verb are separated, when the sentence structure is inverted, or when you cannot recognize whether the subject is singular or plural.

First, the connection between the subject and the verb may be obscured because the subject and the verb are separated.

> **EXAMPLES:**
>
> The professor voted Teacher of the Year by the students were traveling in Europe when she received notice of her promotion.

Professor is singular, yet the verb *were traveling* is plural. This is more difficult to spot in this version of the sentence because of the proximity of the noun *students*, which might be mistaken for the subject of the verb. The sentence sounds correct to the ear: "...students were...." The sentence should read: "The professor voted Teacher of the Year by the students was traveling in Europe when she received notice of her promotion."

> Most teachers, unless they have an appointment to a prestigious university, earns relatively less as a teacher than they might in business.

The subject of *earns* is *teachers*. *Teachers earns* is incorrect. The correct construction is *teachers earn*. But it's easy to mistake *university* for the true subject of the sentence. The sentence should read: "Most teachers, unless they have an appointment to a prestigious university, earn relatively less as a teacher than they might in business."

> Many nutritionists now believe that a balanced diet and not large doses of vitamins are the best guarantee of health.

The true subject of the verb *are* is *diet*. The phrase *not large doses* is not part of the subject. The correct construction is: "diet...is." The corrected sentence should read: "Many nutritionists now believe that a balanced diet and not large doses of vitamins is the best guarantee of health."

> Television comedies in which there is at least one really detestable character captures the interest of viewers.

The true subject of the verb *captures* is *comedies*. The correct construction is "comedies...capture." The correct sentence is: "Television comedies in which there is at least one really detestable character capture the interest of the viewers."

Second, the connection between the subject and verb may be obscured by an inverted structure. An inverted sentence is one in which the verb comes before the subject.

EXAMPLES:

Although this is the wealthiest country in the world, within a few blocks of the White House there is scores of homeless people who live on the streets.

The subject of the verb *is* is not *there* but *scores*, which is plural. The correct construction is: "there are scores." The sentence should read: "Although this is the wealthiest country in the world, within a few blocks of the White House there are scores of homeless people who live on the streets."

Just a few miles from the factories and skyscrapers stand a medieval castle that looks exactly as it did in the 12th century.

The subject of the verb *stand* is *castle*. The correct construction is: "stands a medieval castle." The sentence should read: "Just a few miles from the factories and skyscrapers stands a medieval castle that looks exactly as it did in the 12th century."

Third, there are some subjects that are a bit tricky.

EXAMPLES:

Either the governor or one of his close aides prefer not to have the senator at the head table.

When a subject consists of two or more parts joined by *or*, the verb must agree with the element that follows the *or*. So for the purpose of agreement, the subject of the sentence is *one*. The correct construction is: "one . . . prefers." The sentence should read: "Either the governor or one of his close aides prefers not to have the senator at the head table."

Surrounded by layers of excelsior, none of the crystal goblets were broken when the workers dropped the crate.

The subject of the verb *were broken* is *none*, and *none* is singular. The correct construction is: "none . . . was broken." The corrected sentence is: "Surrounded by layers of excelsior, none of the crystal goblets was broken when the workers dropped the crate."

John, his wife, and the rest of his family plans to attend the awards dinner to be given by the company for the employees with the most seniority.

A subject consisting of two or more elements joined by *and* is plural. The correct construction is: "John, his wife, and the rest of his family plan to attend the awards dinner to be given by the company for the employees with the most seniority."

14

B. Pronoun Usage

There are three areas of pronoun usage that frequently cause problems and should be reviewed: whether a pronoun has a proper antecedent, agreement between pronoun and antecedent, and choice of pronoun case.

1. A pronoun is a word that takes the place of a noun, so a properly used pronoun will have an antecedent (also called a referent). This is the word the pronoun substitutes for. Setting aside certain idioms— such as *It's raining*, in which the *it* does not have an identifiable antecedent—a pronoun that lacks a clear antecedent is used incorrectly.

EXAMPLES:

During her rise to fame, she betrayed many of her friends; and because of it, very few people trust her.

A pronoun must have an antecedent, but *it* doesn't refer to anything. It "wants" to refer to the woman's *behavior*, but that word doesn't appear in the original sentence. Corrected, the sentence reads "During her rise to fame, she betrayed many of her friends; and because of her behavior, very few people trust her."

In New York City, they are brusque and even rude but quick to come to one another's assistance in a time of crisis.

This construction might be called the "ubiquitous they." "They" are everywhere: In New York, *they* are rude; in Chicago, *they* like the Cubs; in Atlanta, *they* speak with a southern accent; in California, *they* like parties. "They" do get around! The trouble with this use of "they" is that "they" has no antecedent.

In conversation, the "ubiquitous they" may be acceptable, but not in standard written English. The sentence above is corrected by using the word *people* in place of *they.* So the sentence should read: "In New York City, the people are brusque and even rude but quick to come to one another's assistance in a time of crisis."

Ten years ago, the United States imported ten times as much French wine as Italian wine, but today Americans are drinking more of it.

Here, the antecedent of *it* is unclear. Does the sentence mean to state that Americans are drinking more French wine or more Italian wine? It could be either. The sentence is corrected by specifying which. Corrected, the sentence reads: "Ten years ago, the United States imported ten times as much French wine as Italian wine, but today Americans are drinking more Italian wine."

2. A pronoun must agree with its antecedent, both in number and person.

EXAMPLES:

Although a police officer used to be a symbol of authority, today they receive little respect from most people.

In this sentence the pronoun *they* refers to *police officer*, which is singular. The best way to correct it is to say "he or she is." So, the sentence should read: "Although a police officer used to be a symbol of authority, today he or she receives little respect from most people."

The Abbot was an effective administrator who attempted to assign each monk a task particularly suited to their talents and training.

In this sentence, *their* refers to *each monk*. But *their* is plural and *each monk* is singular. The sentence is corrected by changing *their* to *his*: "The Abbot was an effective administrator who attempted to assign each monk a task particularly suited to his talents and training."

After three years of college education, a person should be allowed to apply to graduate school, because by that time you are ready to choose a profession.

In the third sentence, *you* refers to *person*. But *you* is a second person pronoun and *person* requires a third person pronoun. This is called the error of shifting subject. The sentence could be corrected by changing *you are* to *one is* or vice versa: "After three years of college education, a person should be allowed to apply to graduate school, because by that time one is ready to choose a profession."

If one wishes to apply for a scholarship, you must submit a completed application by March 1.

The error can be corrected by eliminating the incorrect pronoun altogether: "If one wishes to apply for a scholarship, a completed application must be submitted by March 1."

3. Pronouns have case, and a pronoun's function in a sentence determines which case should be used. Subjective case (also called nominative case) pronouns are used as subjects of sentences; objective case pronouns are used as objects (direct objects, indirect objects, and objects of prepositions); and possessive case pronouns are used to show possession.

EXAMPLES:

The judges were unable to make a final decision on a single winner, so they divided first prize between John and he.

In this sentence, *he* cannot serve as the object of a preposition since it is a subject pronoun. The correct pronoun here is the object pronoun *him*. Corrected, the sentence reads: "The judges were unable to make a final decision on a single winner, so they divided first prize between John and him."

Although Peter had been looking forward to the debate for weeks, a sore throat prevented him taking part.

In this sentence, *him* modifies *taking*, but the correct choice of pronoun is *his*. (When a pronoun modifies a gerund, the *-ing* form of a verb, you must use the possessive case.) The sentence should read: "Although Peter had been looking forward to the debate for weeks, a sore throat prevented his taking part."

C. *Adjective versus Adverb*

Adjectives are used to modify nouns. Adverbs are used to modify verbs and to modify adjectives.

EXAMPLES:

Some psychologists maintain that a child who has seen violence on television is more likely to react violent in situations of stress.

Violent is intended to modify *to react*, a verb form. So the adverb *violently* is required. The sentence should read: "Some psychologists maintain that a child who has seen violence on television is more likely to react violently in situations of stress."

The recent created commission has done nothing to address the problem except to approve the color of its stationery.

In this sentence, *recent* is intended to modify *created*, which is itself an adjective form modifying *commission*. So *recent* should be *recently*. The corrected sentence reads: "The recently created commission has done nothing to address the problem except to approve the color of its stationery."

14

D. Double Negatives

Double negatives are not acceptable usage in standard written English.

> **EXAMPLES:**
>
> Not hardly a sound could be heard in the auditorium when the speaker approached the dais to announce the result of the contest.

In this sentence, *not hardly* is a double negative. The sentence must read: "Hardly a sound could be heard in the auditorium when the speaker approached the dais to announce the result of the contest."

> Although she had been hired by the magazine to write book reviews, she knew scarcely nothing about current fiction.

Scarcely nothing is a double negative. The sentence must read: "Although she had been hired by the magazine to write book reviews, she knew scarcely anything about current fiction."

(Answers, page 389)

> *Directions:* The following exercise contains 25 sentences. Each sentence makes a grammatical error of the sort just reviewed. Circle the letter of the underlined part of the sentence containing the error.

1. The professor deals <u>harsh</u> with students <u>who are not prepared</u> and <u>he is</u> even
   A   B   C
   <u>more severe</u> with those who plagiarize.
   D

2. A recent study <u>indicates</u> that the average person <u>ignores</u> most commercial advertising
   A   B
   and <u>does not buy</u> products <u>because of them.</u>
   C   D

3. <u>Despite the fact that</u> New York City is <u>one of the most</u> densely populated areas in the
   A   B
   world, <u>there are</u> many parks where one can sit on a bench under the trees and <u>you can</u>
   C   D
   read a book.

4. Charles Dickens <u>wrote</u> about the <u>horrifying</u> conditions in the English boarding
   A   B
   <u>schools which</u> he learned about on one <u>of his</u> trips to Yorkshire.
   C   D

5. André Breton <u>initiated</u> the Surrealist movement <u>with the publication</u> of a manifesto,
   A   B
   and <u>it</u> incorporated the theories of Freud <u>as well as</u> his own.
   C   D

6. The review of the concert <u>published</u> in the morning's paper mentioned that the soloist <u>is</u>
   A   B
   a very promising talent and <u>that</u> the orchestra <u>played capable.</u>
   C   D

7. <u>During the war,</u> there were many people in the Polish countryside <u>that</u> sheltered <u>those</u>
   A   B   C
   who <u>had escaped</u> from concentration camps.
   D

8. The dean <u>lectured</u> to <u>we students</u> on the privilege and responsibility <u>of attending</u> the
   A   B   C   D
   university.

9. <u>You taking</u> the initiative in the <u>negotiations</u> will <u>profit</u> the company <u>to a great degree.</u>
   A   B   C   D

10. The members of the club <u>insisted that</u> <u>I be</u> the representative of the organization at the
    A   B
    <u>conference which</u> was something <u>I had hoped</u> to avoid.
    C   D

11. <u>No one</u> knows for sure <u>whether there was</u> a real <u>person about which</u> Michelangelo
    A   B   C
    <u>wrote</u> his sonnets.
    D

12. <u>Although</u> the director of the zoo <u>takes</u> great pains <u>to recreate</u> the natural habitats of the
    A   B   C
    animals, none of the exhibits <u>are completely</u> accurate in every detail.
    D

13. Climatic differences between the north and south of <u>some</u> countries <u>helps to account</u>
    A   B
    <u>for the differences</u> in temperament of the inhabitants <u>of the two</u> regions.
    C   D

14

14. The month of August <u>was particularly cold</u>; <u>hardly no</u> daily temperatures <u>were recorded</u>
                      A   B   C
    above 80 degrees, and <u>none was</u> recorded above 90 degrees.
                           D

15. The diaries of Stendhal, <u>which make entertaining reading</u>, <u>also provides</u> a great wealth of
                                      A   B
    information <u>about musical taste</u> and performance practice <u>in the last century</u>.
                    C   D

16. <u>Given the evidence</u> of the existence of a complicated system of communication
        A
    <u>used by whales</u>, <u>it is necessary</u> to acknowledge <u>its</u> intelligence.
         B   C   D

17. <u>Him being at the rally</u> does not necessarily mean <u>that</u> the Congressman <u>agrees</u> with the
               A   B   C   D
    President's entire platform.

18. Although there is no perfect form of government, representative democracy,
    <u>as it is practiced in America</u>, <u>is a system</u> that is <u>working well</u> and <u>more than satisfactorily</u>.
                     A   B   C   D

19. Alfred Stieglitz <u>launched</u> the career of Georgia O'Keeffe, <u>who</u> <u>he</u> <u>later married</u>, by
                      A   B C   D
    exhibiting her paintings in his gallery.

20. After driving past Trinity Church, the bus <u>stopped</u> at the <u>recent constructed</u> World Trade
                                     A   B
    Tower, the <u>tallest</u> building in the world, <u>to allow the passengers to take</u> the special
                C   D
    elevators to the observation tower.

21. The student senate <u>passed</u> the resolution <u>banning smoking in the cafeteria</u>
                       A   B
    <u>with scarcely any</u> dissenting <u>votes which angered</u> many members of the faculty.
                C   D

22. Most employers <u>assume</u> that one's professional personality and work habits <u>are formed</u>
                     A   B
    <u>as a result</u> of <u>your</u> early work experience.
              C   D

23. <u>Only a small number</u> of taxi drivers <u>fail to insure</u> their vehicles, but usually
                A   B
    <u>these are the ones</u> who need <u>it</u> most.
              C   D

24. <u>Angered</u> by the double standard society <u>imposed on</u> women, Edna St. Vincent Millay
       A   B
    <u>wrote candid about</u> her opinions and <u>her</u> personal life.
            C   D

25. Unless <u>they</u> hire players <u>who</u> <u>are</u> better hitters, the fans <u>will gradually lose</u> interest in the
           A   B C   D
    team despite the fine efforts of the pitching staff.

5. Avoiding Common Problems with
Sentence Structure

A. Faulty Parallelism

In a correctly written sentence, similar elements must have a similar form.

> **EXAMPLES:**
>
> To abandon their homes, leave behind their families, and traveling across the ocean required great courage on the part of the immigrants who moved to America.

In this, the three verb forms *abandon*, *leave*, and *traveling* should be parallel. The sentence is corrected by changing *traveling* to *travel* so that the sentence reads: "To abandon their homes, leave behind their families, and travel across the ocean required great courage on the part of the immigrants who moved to America."

> The review praised the wit, charm, and interpreting of the recitalist but never once mentioned her voice.

In this sentence, *wit* and *charm* are nouns, so *interpreting*, too, should be a noun. The sentence is corrected by changing *interpreting* to *interpretation*. So, the corrected sentence reads: "The review praised the wit, charm, and interpretation of the recitalist, but never once mentioned her voice."

> To acknowledge that one has something to learn is taking the first step on the road to true wisdom.

This sentence has a structure similar to a mathematical equation: *This* is the same as *that*. Both parts of the "equation" must have the same form. The sentence is corrected by changing *taking* to *to take*. Corrected, the sentence reads: "To acknowledge that one has something to learn is to take the first step on the road to true wisdom."

B. Incomplete Split Constructions

A split construction is a sentence structure in which two otherwise separate ideas are joined together by a later element. For example, "The Mayor knew or should have known about the corruption." This is a perfectly acceptable split construction in which the ideas *knew* and *should have known* are joined together by the single object *corruption*. In some split constructions, one half or the other never gets completed.

14

> **EXAMPLES:**
>
> The students are critical of the dean because he is either unfamiliar or doesn't care about the urgent need for new student housing on campus.

The split construction, *is either unfamiliar or doesn't care*, never gets completed. Leave out the idea following the *or* and the sentence reads: "is unfamiliar the urgent need." Nonsense! The sentence should read: "The students are critical of the dean because he is either unfamiliar with or doesn't care about the urgent need for new student housing on campus."

| Baseball has and probably always will be the sport that symbolizes for people in other countries the American way of life.

The first half of the split verb construction is never completed. Leave out the second idea and the sentence reads "Baseball has the sport." The sentence should read "Baseball has been and probably always will be the sport that symbolizes for people in other countries the American way of life."

C. Verb Tense

The choice of verb tenses in a correctly written sentence reflects the sequence of events described.

| **EXAMPLES:**

The teacher began to discuss the homework assignment when he will be interrupted by the sound of the fire alarm.

The sentence reads "The teacher began . . . and will be interrupted." One or the other verb tense is wrong. The sentence can be corrected by changing *will be interrupted* to *was interrupted*. Corrected, the sentence reads: "The teacher began to discuss the homework assignment when he was interrupted by the sound of the fire alarm."

| The conductor announced that the concert would resume as soon as the soloist replaces the broken string on her violin.

There is a mismatch between the verbs *would resume* and *replaces* in the second sentence. The sentence reads: *the concert would resume as soon as the soloist replaces*. Corrected, the sentence might read: "The conductor announced that the concert would resume as soon as the soloist replaced the broken string on her violin."

| Many patients begin to show symptoms again after they stopped taking the drug.

This sentence reads: *patients show symptoms after they stopped*. The sentence can be corrected by changing *stopped* to *stop*. The sentence would read: "Many patients begin to show symptoms again after they stop taking the drug."

D. Logical Errors

Sometimes a sentence will "want" to say one thing but end up saying something completely illogical.

| **EXAMPLES:**

The great pianist Vladimir Horowitz played the music of the romantic era better than any pianist in history.

As written, the first sentence asserts that Vladimir Horowitz was better than anyone —including himself. But that is a logical impossibility. The sentence should read: "The great pianist Vladimir Horowitz played the music of the romantic era better than any other pianist in history."

| Educators are now expressing their concern that American schoolchildren prefer watching television to books.

The sentence makes an illogical comparison between *watching television* and *books*. Watching television is an activity; the books are objects. The sentence should read: "Educators are now expressing their concern that American schoolchildren prefer watching television to reading books."

> The novels of Nathaniel Hawthorne contain characters that are every bit as sinister and frightening as the master of cinematic suspense, Alfred Hitchcock.

This sentence, too, commits the error just discussed. The sentence literally compares the characters in the novels of Nathaniel Hawthorne to Alfred Hitchcock, the person. The sentence should read: "The novels of Nathaniel Hawthorne contain characters that are every bit as sinister and frightening as those of the master of cinematic suspense, Alfred Hitchcock."

> A Japanese firm has developed a computer so small that users can carry it in their briefcase.

As written, the sentence asserts that all of the users have but a single, jointly owned briefcase. What the sentence means to say is that users can carry the new computer in their briefcases (plural). It should read: "A Japanese firm has developed a computer so small that users can carry it in their briefcases."

E. Sentence Fragment

A sentence must have a main verb.

> **EXAMPLE:**
>
> Post-modern art, with its vibrant colors and bold shapes, taking its inspiration from artists such as Cézanne but reacting against the pastel indistinctness of the Impressionist canvases.

The original sentence lacks a main verb. This is corrected by changing *taking* and *reacting* (which function as adjectives modifying *art*) to *took* and *reacted*. So, the corrected sentence reads: "Post-modern art, with its vibrant colors and bold shapes, took its inspiration from artists such as Cézanne but reacted against the pastel indistinctness of the Impressionist canvases."

6. Avoiding Problems of Awkward or
Unclear Expression

A. Directness and Conciseness

Your essays should demonstrate clarity of expression, which means that your writing should be clear and concise. Avoid awkward constructions and needlessly wordy sentences.

> **EXAMPLES:**
>
> After months of separation, Gauguin finally joined Van Gogh in Arles in October of 1888, although Gauguin left a few weeks later.

This sentence is awkward and needlessly wordy. It would be more concise to say: "After months of separation, Gauguin finally joined Van Gogh in Arles but left a few weeks later."

| The nineteenth-century composers Wagner and Mahler did more than just write music; as composers they did their own works.

This sentence is also awkward and needlessly wordy. The very same idea can be expressed more directly: "The nineteenth-century composers Wagner and Mahler did more than just write music; they conducted their own works."

B. Misplaced Modifiers

Another error that is frequently made by writers is the problem of the misplaced modifier.

| **EXAMPLES:**
| Wrapped in several thicknesses of newspaper, packed carefully in a strong cardboard carton, and bound securely with tape, the worker made sure that the fragile figurines would not be broken.

The sentence as originally written suggests that it was the worker who was wrapped, packed, and bound. In general, a modifier should be placed as closely as possible to the part of the sentence it is to modify. The corrected version of this sentence reads: "To make sure that the figurines would not be broken, the worker wrapped them in several thicknesses of newspaper, packed them carefully in a strong cardboard carton, and securely bound the carton with tape."

| Riding in a coach and wearing the crown jewels, the crowd cheered the royal couple.

The sentence as originally written suggests that the crowd is wearing the crown jewels and riding in the carriage. This sentence can be made clear by changing it to: "Riding in a coach and wearing the crown jewels, the royal couple was cheered by the crowd."

EXERCISE 2

(Answers, page 390)

━━

Directions: The following exercise contains 25 sentences. Each sentence makes a grammatical error of the sort just reviewed. Circle the letter of the underlined part of the sentence containing the error.

1. The owner of the collection <u>requested that</u> the museum <u>require</u> <u>all people with a camera</u> to leave them at the door.
   A — B — C — D

2. The young comic <u>found</u> that capturing the audience's attention was easy, <u>but to maintain</u> <u>their interest was</u> difficult.
   A — B — C — D

3. <u>Written in almost total isolation from the world</u>, Emily Dickinson <u>spoke of</u> love <u>and</u> death in <u>her</u> poems.
   A — B — C — D

4. <u>Early in his career</u>, the pianist entertained thoughts <u>of becoming</u> a composer; but after receiving bad reviews for his own work, <u>he</u> <u>had given it up</u>.
   A — B — C — D

5. The praying mantis is <u>welcomed by</u> homeowners for <u>its</u> ability <u>to control</u> destructive garden pests, <u>unlike the cockroach which serves no useful function</u>.
   A — B — C — D

6. The fact that she is bright, articulate, and <u>has charisma</u> <u>will serve</u> her well in her campaign for governor, <u>particularly</u> since her opponent <u>has none</u> of those qualities.
   A — B — C — D

7. Puritans such as William Bradford <u>displaying</u> the courage and piety <u>needed to survive</u> in the New World, a world <u>both</u> promising and threatening <u>which</u> offered unique challenges to their faith.
   A — B — C — D

8. The baseball game was halted due to rain and <u>rescheduled</u> for the following day, even though <u>the fans</u> <u>would not leave</u> the stadium.
   A — B — C — D

9. Unfortunately, <u>before</u> cures are found for diseases such as cancer, many lives <u>would have been</u> lost and millions of dollars in medical services <u>spent</u> to treat symptoms <u>rather than</u> provide a cure.
   A — B — C — D

10. <u>Being highly qualified for the position</u>, the bank president <u>will conduct</u> a final interview of the new candidate tomorrow, <u>after which</u> <u>he will make</u> her a job offer.
    A — B — C — D

11. For many people it is difficult <u>to accept</u> compliments graciously and <u>even more difficult</u> <u>taking</u> criticism <u>graciously</u>.
    A — B — C — D

12. The literature of Native Americans <u>has been overlooked</u> by <u>most</u> scholars, and the reason is <u>because</u> most university courses in literature <u>are taught</u> in departments that also teach a language, such as French.
    A — B — C — D

14

379

13. The French poet Artaud believed that, following the climax of a drama, the audience
    _____   ____   _____
         A   B   C
    experienced a violent catharsis and is thereby "reborn."
    _____
         D

14. In broken English, the police officer patiently listened to the tourist ask for directions to
    _____
         A
    Radio City Music Hall, after which she motioned the tourist and his family into the
                          _____   _____
                               B   C
    squad car and drove them to their destination.
                        ____
                         D

15. Bullfighting remains a controversial sport and many are repulsed by it, since Hemingway
                 _____   ____   _____
                    A   B   C
    was an aficionado of the sport and glorified it in his writing.
                                                 __
                                                  D

16. Wagering on the Kentucky Derby favorite is a bad betting proposition, for in the last
    _____   __   _____
       A   B   C
    fifteen years, the horse that was the crowd favorite at post time of the Kentucky Derby
    loses the race.
    _____
      D

17. Following the recent crash of the stock market, Peter bought a book on portfolio
    _____   _____
                           A   B
    management in order to learn methods to protect his investments
               _____
                     C
    from a well-known investment banker.
    _____
                     D

18. During the years she spent searching for a cure for the disease, Dr. Thompson
    _____   _____
           A   B
    interviewed hundreds of patients, ran thousands of tests, and cross-checking millions
                                                                  _____
                                                                        C
    of bits of data.
    _____
          D

19. Since we have a broader technological base, American scientists believe that our space
    _____   _____
      A   B
    program will ultimately prove superior to the Soviet Union.
            _____   _____
                      C   D

20. Although a person may always represent himself in a judicial proceeding, licensed
                                          _____
                                             A
    lawyers only may represent others in such proceedings for a fee.
           ____   _____   ____
            B   C   D

21. Unlike the pale and delicately built ballerinas of romantic ballet, Judith Jamison's
    _____
                                    A
    movement seems more African than European-American, and her physical appearance
             _____ _____
               B   C
    reinforces the contrast.
    _____
        D

22. Market experts predict that in ten years, when the harmful effects of caffeine become
                  _____
                     A
    more generally known, the number of tons of decaffeinated coffee consumed by
    _____   _____
             B   C
    Americans each year will exceed coffee containing caffeine.
                                    _____
                                             D

23. Illiteracy, a widespread problem in the United States, undermines productivity because
                _____   _____
                               A   B
    many mistakes are made by workers who do not know how to read on the job.
                  _____   _____
                     C   D

24. Because sailors are often assigned to ships that remain at sea for months at a time, men
                  _____   _____
                        A   B
    in the Navy spend more time away from home than any branch of the service.
                _____   _____
                  C   D

25. Like A.J. Ayer, much of Gilbert Ryle's philosophical argumentation relies on an analysis
    _____   _____
         A   B
    of the way people ordinarily use language.
                _____ _____
                  C   D

7. Avoiding Nonidiomatic Expressions

Often, sentences are not correct because they are not "idiomatic." An expression that is not idiomatic is one that is not acceptable English for any of several reasons.

A. Wrong Prepositions

In English, as in other languages, only certain prepositions can be used with certain verbs.

> **EXAMPLES:**
>
> In contrast of the prevailing opinion, the editorial places the blame for the strike on the workers and their representatives.

In this sentence, the expression *in contrast of* is not idiomatic. The expression should be *in contrast to*. So the sentence would read: "In contrast to the prevailing opinion, the editorial places the blame for the strike on the workers and their representatives."

> Although ballet and modern dance are both concerned in movement in space to musical accompaniment, the training for ballet is more rigorous than that for modern dance.

The expression *concerned in* is not idiomatic. The sentence should read: "Although ballet and modern dance are both concerned with movement in space to musical accompaniment, the training for ballet is more rigorous than that for modern dance."

B. Right Idea, Wrong Word

Make sure the you use words that mean what you intend to say. Be careful not to use an incorrect word that sounds like the word you really mean to use.

> **EXAMPLES:**
>
> By midnight the guests still had not been served anything to eat and they were ravishing.

The first sentence intends to state that the guests were very hungry, but that is not the meaning of the word *ravishing*. The sentence can be corrected by changing *ravishing* to *ravenous*. Corrected, the sentence reads: "By midnight the guests still had not been served anything to eat and they were ravenous."

> The raise in the number of accidents attributable to drunk drivers has prompted a call for stiffer penalties for driving while intoxicated.

This sentence can be corrected by changing *raise* to *rise*. The correct sentence reads: "The rise in the number of accidents attributable to drunk drivers has prompted a call for stiffer penalties for driving while intoxicated."

C. Gerund versus Infinitive

The infinitive is the "to" form of a verb, and the gerund is one of the "-ing" forms of a verb. Both are used as nouns. In some circumstances you can use either: "Adding an extra room to the house is the next project," or "To add an extra room to the house is the next project." In some circumstances, however, gerund and infinitive are not interchangeable.

14

EXAMPLES:

> The idea of trying completing the term paper by Friday caused Ken to cancel his plans for the weekend.

Although *completing* can be a noun, here you need the infinitive. The first sentence should read: "The idea of trying to complete the term paper by Friday caused Ken to cancel his plans for the weekend."

> Psychologists think that many people eat satisfying a need for affection that is not otherwise fulfilled.

Again you need the infinitive, not the gerund. The sentence should read: "Psychologists think that many people eat to satisfy a need for affection that is not otherwise fulfilled."

D. Unacceptable Expressions

There are a few expressions that are heard frequently in conversation that are regarded as low-level usage and unacceptable in standard written English, and they should be avoided in your essay.

EXAMPLES:

> Being that the hour was late, we agreed to adjourn the meeting and reconvene at nine o'clock the following morning.

Being that is not acceptable in standard written English. The sentence is corrected by changing the phrase to *Since*. The sentence should read: "Since the hour was late, we agreed to adjourn the meeting and reconvene at nine o'clock the following morning."

> Why some whales beach themselves in what seems to be a kind of suicide remains a mystery to marine biologists.

Why cannot be the subject of a sentence. The sentence is corrected by changing *Why* to *That*. So, the sentence now reads: "That some whales beach themselves in what seems to be a kind of suicide remains a mystery to marine biologists."

> The reason Harriet fired her secretary is because he was frequently late and spent too much time on personal phone calls.

Because cannot introduce a noun clause. The sentence is corrected by changing *because* to *that*. The corrected sentence reads: "The reason Harriet fired her secretary is that he was frequently late and spent too much time on personal phone calls."

> I read in a magazine where scientists believe that they have discovered a new subatomic particle.

Where cannot introduce a noun clause. The sentence is corrected by changing *where* to *that*. So the corrected sentence reads: "I read in a magazine that scientists believe that they have discovered a new subatomic particle."

(Answers, page 392)

Directions: The following exercise contains 15 sentences. Each sentence makes a grammatical error of the sort just reviewed. Circle the letter of the underlined part of the sentence containing the error.

1. Economists have established that there is a relation—albeit an indirect one—between
   <u>have established</u> [A] <u>relation</u> [B]
   the amount of oil imported into this country and the number of traffic accidents.
   <u>amount</u> [C] <u>number</u> [D]

2. Ironically, Elizabeth I and her rival for the English throne, Mary Stuart, whom she had
   <u>her</u> [A] <u>whom</u> [B] <u>she</u> [C]
   executed, lay side by side in Westminster Abbey.
   <u>lay</u> [D]

3. Although the script is interesting and well-written, it is not clear whether it can be
   <u>whether</u> [A]
   adopted for television since the original story contains scenes that could not be broadcast
   <u>adopted</u> [B] <u>could not be broadcast</u> [C]
   over the public airwaves.
   <u>over</u> [D]

4. If he had known how difficult law school would be, he would of chosen a different
   <u>had known</u> [A] <u>would of chosen</u> [B]
   profession or perhaps even have followed the tradition of going into the family business.
   <u>have followed</u> [C] <u>tradition</u> [D]

5. When shopping malls and business complexes get built, quite often the needs of the
   <u>get built</u> [A]
   handicapped are not considered; as a result, it later becomes necessary to make costly
   <u>are</u> [B] <u>costly</u> [C]
   modifications to structures to make them accessible to persons of impaired mobility.
   <u>accessible</u> [D]

6. Researchers have found that children experience twice as much deep sleep than
   <u>have found</u> [A] <u>experience</u> [B] <u>than</u> [C]
   adults, a fact which may teach us something about the connection between age and
   <u>a fact which may</u> [D]
   learning ability.

7. Despite the ample evidence that smoking is hazardous to one's health, many people
   <u>Despite</u> [A] <u>is hazardous to</u> [B] <u>many</u> [C]
   seem to find the warnings neither frightening or convincing.
   <u>or</u> [D]

8. No matter how many encores the audience demands, Helen Walker is always willing
   <u>many</u> [A] <u>is always willing</u> [B]
   to sing yet another song which pleases the audience.
   <u>yet</u> [C] <u>which pleases</u> [D]

9. In light of recent translations of stone carvings describing scenes of carnage, scholars
   <u>recent</u> [A] <u>describing</u> [B]
   are now questioning as to whether the Incas were really a peace-loving civilization.
   <u>as to whether</u> [C] <u>really</u> [D]

10. In galleries containing works of both Gauguin and Cézanne, you will find an equal
    number of admirers in front of the works of each, but most art critics agree that
    <u>number</u> [A] <u>in front of</u> [B] <u>each</u> [C]
    Gauguin is not of the same artistic stature with Cézanne.
    <u>with</u> [D]

11. The Board of Education will never be fully responsive to the needs of Hispanic children
    <u>will never be</u> [A] <u>fully</u> [B] <u>responsive</u> [C]
    in the school system so long that the Mayor refuses to appoint a Hispanic educator to
    <u>that</u> [D]
    the Board.

14

12. The judge <u>sentenced</u> the president of the corporation to ten years in prison for
    <u>A</u>
    <u>embezzling</u> corporate funds but <u>gave</u> his partner in crime <u>less of a sentence</u>.
    <u>B</u>   <u>C</u>   <u>D</u>

13. Scientists <u>have recently discovered</u> that mussels <u>secrete</u> a powerful adhesive that
    <u>A</u>   <u>B</u>
    allows them <u>attaching</u> themselves to rocks, concrete pilings, and <u>other</u> stone or masonry
    <u>C</u>   <u>D</u>
    structures.

14. Wall paintings found recently in the caves of Brazil are <u>convincing</u> evidence that cave art
    <u>A</u>
    <u>developed</u> in the Americas at an earlier time <u>as</u> <u>it</u> did on other continents.
    <u>B</u>   <u>C</u> <u>D</u>

15. The <u>drop</u> in oil prices and the slump in the computer industry <u>account for</u> the recent
    <u>A</u>   <u>B</u>
    <u>raise</u> in unemployment in Texas and the <u>associated</u> decline in the value of real
    <u>C</u>   <u>D</u>
    estate in the region.

8. Avoiding Punctuation Errors

In your Writing Sample essay, you will probably need to use only three different kinds of punctuation marks: period, comma, and semicolon. While there are other punctuation marks available to you (such as the dash and the exclamation point), you can avoid errors in punctuation by using only these three.

Use a comma before *and*, *but*, *so*, *yet*, *or*, and *nor* when those words are used to join two main clauses.

EXAMPLES:

I think that Doré's illustrations of Dante's *Divine Comedy* are excellent, but my favorite drawing is "Don Quixote in His Library."

Practically all nitrates are crystalline and readily soluble, and they are characterized by marked decrepitation when heated on charcoal by a blowpipe.

The general rule stated above should be qualified in two respects. First, when the two clauses joined by the conjunction are very short, the comma is optional.

EXAMPLE:

The door was ajar and the house had been ransacked.
The door was ajar, and the house had been ransacked.

Each of the sentences is correct.

For clarity, if either clause itself contains commas, you may need to use a semicolon before the conjunction.

EXAMPLE:

Because many diseases and insects cause serious damage to crops, special national legislation has been passed to provide for the quarantine of imported plants; and under provisions of various acts, inspectors are placed at ports of entry to prevent smugglers from bringing in plants that might be dangerous.

Given the length of the two clauses and the fact that each clause contains a comma, you should use a semicolon following *plants*, rather than a comma.

Use commas to separate the elements of a series.

EXAMPLES:

A full train crew consists of a motorman, a brakeman, a conductor, and two ticket takers.

The procedure requires that you open the outer cover plate, remove the thermostat, replace the broken switch, and then replace the thermostat.

Use a comma to separate a subordinate clause at the beginning of a sentence from the main clause.

EXAMPLES:

After Peter finished painting the bird feeder, he and Jack hung it from a limb of the oak tree.

When Pat explained to his mother that ten was the highest mark given on the entrance test, she breathed a sigh of relief.

If the subordinate clause follows the main clause, you do not need to set it off with a comma.

EXAMPLE:

Tim hopes to score well on the exam because he plans to go to an Ivy League school.

Use a comma after a long introductory phrase.

EXAMPLES:

In this impoverished region with its arid soil, a typical diet may contain only 800 calories per day.

At the height of the moral war against sensational journalism, Horace Greeley moved into the forefront of the journalistic picture.

Regardless of their length, use a comma after introductory gerunds, participles, and infinitives.

EXAMPLES:

Begun in 1981 and completed in 1985, the bridge provided the first link between the island and the mainland.

To slow the bleeding, Van tied a tourniquet around the lower portion of the leg.

Use commas to set off nonrestrictive clauses and phrases and other parenthetical elements.

EXAMPLES:

Niagara Falls, which forms part of the border between the United States and Canada, was the site of a saw mill built by the French in 1725.

The second Nicene Council, the seventh ecumenical council of the Church, was summoned by the Empress Irene and her son Constantine.

The last hope of the French expired when Metz, along with 180,000 soldiers, was surrendered by Bazaine.

Secretary of State Acheson, however, made a reasoned defense of the treaty.

14

(Nonrestrictive clauses and phrases are ones not essential to the meaning of the main clause. In general, if you can omit the material without changing the meaning of the main clause, then the material is nonrestrictive and should be set off by commas.)

These rules summarize the most important uses of commas. If you use them in just these situations, then you won't make a mistake in their use. In particular, do **NOT** use commas in the following situations.

Do not use a comma to separate a subject from its verb.

EXAMPLE:

Until the end of the 18th Century, the only musicians in Norway, were simple unsophisticated peasants who traveled about.

(The underlined comma is incorrect.)

Do not use commas to set off restrictive or necessary clauses or phrases.

EXAMPLES:

Prizes will be awarded in each event, and the participant, who compiles the greatest overall total, will receive a special prize.

Since learning of the dangers of caffeine, neither my wife nor I has consumed any beverage, containing caffeine.

(The underlined commas are incorrect.)

Do not use a comma in place of a conjunction.

EXAMPLE:

After months of separation, Gauguin finally joined Van Gogh in Arles in October of 1888, Gauguin left a few weeks later.

The sentence is incorrect because clauses cannot be spliced together using only a comma. If you want to join two main clauses, you can use a conjunction (such as *and*) plus a comma or semicolon or even just a semicolon. The sentence above could have been written: "After months of separation, Gauguin finally joined Van Gogh in Arles in October of 1888, but Gauguin left a few weeks later."

(Answers, page 393)

Directions: Punctuate the following sentences using commas, semicolons, and periods.

1. Neurology is the science that deals with the anatomy physiology and pathology of the nervous system

2. Nursery lore like everything human has been subject to many changes over long periods of time

3. In order to provide more living space we converted an attached garage into a den

4. Begun while Dickens was still at work on *Pickwick Papers Oliver Twist* was published in 1837 and is now one of the author's most widely read works

5. Given the great difficulties of making soundings in very deep water it is not surprising that few such soundings were made until the middle of this century

6. The root of modern Dutch was once supposed to be Old Frisian but the general view now is that the characteristic forms of Dutch are at least as old as those of Old Frisian

7. Moose once scarce because of indiscriminate hunting are protected by law and the number of moose is once again increasing

8. Perhaps the most interesting section of New Orleans is the French Quarter which extends from North Rampart Street to the Mississippi River

9. Writing for a skeptical and rationalizing age Shaftesbury was primarily concerned with showing that goodness and beauty are not determined by revelation authority opinion or fashion

10. A great deal of information regarding the nutritional requirements of farm animals has been accumulated over countless generations by trial and error but most recent advances have come as the result of systematic studies at schools of animal husbandry

11. *Omoo* Melville's sequel to *Typee* appeared in 1847 and went through five printings in that year alone.

12. Although the first school for Blacks was a public school established in Virginia in 1620 most educational opportunities for Blacks prior to the Civil War were provided by private agencies

13. As the climate of Europe changed the population became too dense for the supply of food obtained by hunting and other means of securing food such as the domestication of animals were necessary

14. In Faulkner's poetic realism the grotesque is somber violent and often inexplicable in Caldwell's writing it is lightened by a balladlike humorous sophisticated detachment

15. The valley of the Loir a northern tributary of the Loire at Angers abounds in rock villages and they occur in many other places in France Spain and northern Italy

14

Summary

The following is a checklist of items to look for as you write your essay.

1. Subject–verb agreement
2. Pronoun usage (antecedents, ambiguity, case)
3. Adjectives and adverbs (correct modification)
4. Double negatives (incorrect)
5. Parallelism (similar elements in similar form)
6. Split constructions properly completed
7. Logical choice of verb tenses
8. Logical expression
9. Sentence fragments
10. Conciseness and awkwardness
11. Misplaced modifiers
12. Prepositions (idiomatic usage)
13. Correct choice of words
14. Gerund versus infinitive
15. Low-level usage (*being that, why* as a subject, *because* in a noun phrase, *where* in a noun phrase)
16. Correct punctuation

Explanatory Answers

EXERCISE 1

1. (A) *Harsh* is intended to modify *deals*, a verb. The adverb *harshly* is needed here.

2. (D) *Them* is intended to be a pronoun substitute for *advertising*, but *advertising* is singular, not plural. *It* should replace *them*.

3. (D) *You* is intended to refer to *one*, but *one* is in the third person while *you* is in the second person. The sentence could be corrected simply by omitting the second pronoun altogether.

4. (C) *Which* has no clear referent. *Which* might refer either to *horrifying conditions* or to *English boarding schools*. The ambiguity could be avoided by rewording the sentence: "...about the horrifying conditions in the English boarding schools, conditions which he learned about...."

5. (C) *It* has no clear referent. *It* might refer either to the movement or to the manifesto. The sentence can be corrected by including an appropriate noun to clarify the speaker's meaning, e.g., "...of a manifesto, a work that incorporated...."

6. (D) *Capable* is intended to modify *played*, a verb. So the adverb form must be used: "...played capably."

7. (B) *Who* and *whom* are the correct pronouns to use for people: "...countryside who sheltered ...."

8. (B) *We* cannot be used as the object of *to*. The correct choice of pronoun is *us*.

9. (A) When a pronoun is used to modify a gerund, the pronoun must be in the possessive case: "Your taking the initiative...."

10. (C) *Which* has no clear antecedent. Had the speaker hoped to avoid the conference or just being selected to be the representative of the group at the conference? To avoid the ambiguity, the sentence will have to be substantially revised: "...at the conference, and I had hoped to avoid the conference altogether."

11. (C) *Whom* should be used here instead of *which*, since the pronoun refers to *person*.

12. (D) The subject of the main clause is *none*, a singular pronoun, so the verb should be *is* rather than *are*.

13. (B) The subject of the sentence is *differences*, a plural noun, so the verb should be *help* rather than *helps*.

14. (B) *Hardly no* is a double negative. The sentence should read *hardly any*.

15. (B) The subject of the sentence is *diaries*, a plural noun. So the verb should be *provide* rather than *provides*.

16. (D) *Its* intends to refer to *whales*, so the sentence should use the plural pronoun *their*.

17. (A) A pronoun used to modify a gerund must be in the possessive case: "His being at the rally...."

14

18. (D) *Satisfactory* is either intended to modify *working* or *system*. If it modifies *working*, then the adverb should be used: "...and more than satisfactorily." If the word modifies *system*, then another verb is required: "...and is more than satisfactory."

19. (B) *Who* is intended to be the object of the verb *married*, so the objective case pronoun *whom* is required.

20. (B) *Recent* is intended to modify *constructed*, an adjective. But an adjective cannot be used to modify another adjective. Here the adverb *recently* should be used.

21. (D) *Which* has no clear referent. Were the faculty angry because the resolution passed or because it passed with few dissenting votes? The sentence must be rewritten to clarify the speaker's intention.

22. (D) *Your* is intended to refer *one's*, so you need some kind of third person pronoun, for example, *his or her*.

23. (D) *It* lacks a referent. *It* seems to refer to something like *insurance*, but there is no such noun in the sentence. The sentence could be corrected by using the noun *insurance* in place of the pronoun *it*.

24. (C) *Candid* is intended to modify *wrote*, so the sentence must use the adverb *candidly*.

25. (A) The sentence commits the error of the "ubiquitous they." The sentence can be corrected by using a noun in place of the *they*.

EXERCISE 2

1. (C) The sentence commits an error of logical expression, because it implies that all the people coming into the museum have but a single camera. It could be corrected by changing *camera* to *cameras*.

2. (B) The sentence is flawed by faulty parallelism. It could be corrected by changing *to maintain* to *maintaining*.

3. (A) The sentence is afflicted with a dangling modifier. As written, the sentence implies that Emily Dickinson herself was written. To correct this error, it would have to be rewritten to bring the introductory modifier closer to the noun it modifies (*poems*): "The poems by Emily Dickinson, written in almost total isolation from the world, spoke of love and death."

4. (D) The use of the perfect tense *had given up* is not consistent with the use of the past tense *entertained*, for the use of the perfect tense implies that the pianist gave up his attempt to become a composer before he even entertained the idea of becoming one. The sentence can be corrected by substituting *gave up* for *had given up*.

5. (D) The final phrase is out of place. As written, the sentence implies that the cockroach is unlike destructive garden pests, but the speaker means to say that the cockroach is not like the praying mantis. The sentence can be corrected by relocating the offending phrase closer to the noun it modifies: "The praying mantis, unlike the cockroach, which serves no useful function, is welcomed by homeowners...."

6. (A) The sentence is flawed by a lack of parallelism, an error that can be corrected by substituting the adjective *charismatic* for the phrase *has charisma*.

7. (A) This item is a sentence fragment that lacks a conjugated verb. The fragment can be changed into a complete sentence by substituting *displayed* for *displaying*.

8. (B) The sentence commits an error of illogical expression, for, as written, it implies that the fans' leaving the stadium would ordinarily be sufficient to halt a game and reschedule it for later. The problem of illogical expression can be corrected by substituting the conjunction *but* for *even though*. (This particular error of logical expression is called illogical subordination.)

9. (B) The use of the subjunctive *would have been* is illogical. The use of the subjunctive incorrectly implies that the loss of lives and money is contingent upon some event, but no such event is mentioned in the sentence. The sentence can be corrected by substituting *will have been*.

10. (A) The sentence is afflicted with a dangling modifier. As written, it implies that the bank president is highly qualified for the position. The sentence needs substantial revision: "The bank president will conduct a final interview of the new candidate tomorrow. Since the candidate is highly qualified for the position, the president will make her a job offer after the interview."

11. (C) The sentence suffers from a lack of parallelism. This deficiency can be corrected by changing *taking* to *to take*. (In any event, the use of the gerund, *taking*, instead of the infinitive, *to take*, is not idiomatic, a point taken up in the next part of this lesson.)

12. (C) The sentence commits an error of logical expression by implying that the *reason* is an effect of some other cause, when the speaker really means to say that the *reason* and the *cause* are the same thing, the explanation for the phenomenon. The error can be corrected by substituting *that* for *because*. (**Note:** This use of *because* to introduce a noun clause can also be considered an example of an expression that is not acceptable in English usage, a point taken up in the next part of this lesson.)

13. (D) The tense of the first verb is not consistent with the tense of the second verb. The sentence can be corrected by substituting *experiences* for *experienced*.

14. (A) The sentence contains a dangling modifier. As written, it implies that the police officer is listening *in* broken English (not listening *to* broken English). The sentence can be corrected by relocating the modifier: "The police officer patiently listened to the tourist ask in broken English for directions to Radio City Music Hall, ..."

15. (C) The choice of *since* is illogical, because *since* implies that there is a causal or explanatory connection between Hemingway's view of bullfighting and the fact that bullfighting is a controversial sport that repulses some people. The problem of illogical subordination can be corrected by substituting *but* for *since*.

16. (D) The use of the present tense *loses* is illogical and inconsistent with the use of the past tense *was* earlier in the sentence. The error can be corrected by substituting *lost* for *loses*.

17. (D) The sentence contains a misplaced modifier. As written, it implies that Peter hopes to learn how to protect his investments from the threat posed by a well-known investment banker. The sentence must be rewritten: ". . . in order to learn from a well-known investment banker methods to protect his investments."

18. (C) The elements of the sentence are not parallel. The sentence would be correct if *cross-checked* were substituted for *cross-checking*.

14

19. (D) The sentence makes an error of logical expression, for it seems to compare our space program to the Soviet Union. The error can be eliminated by using the phrase *to that of* instead of *to* immediately after *superior*.

20. (B) The sentence contains a misplaced modifier. The placement of *only* seems to imply a restriction on the verb rather than on the subject. The sentence can be easily corrected by moving *only* and placing it just before *licensed lawyers*.

21. (A) The sentence contains a dangling modifier and seems to compare ballerinas of the romantic ballet with the movement of Judith Jamison. To correct this error, the sentence would have to be substantially rewritten: "Judith Jamison's movement seems more African than European-American, and her physical appearance, which is unlike the pale and delicately built ballerinas of romantic ballet, reinforces the contrast."

22. (D) The sentence contains an error of logical expression. It attempts to compare an amount of decaffeinated coffee with coffee containing caffeine. The sentence can be corrected by inserting clarifying phrases: ". . . the number of tons of coffee containing caffeine consumed by Americans."

23. (D) The sentence contains a misplaced modifier. As written, it implies that the workers are illiterate because they don't know how to read on the job. The sentence can be corrected by relocating the offending phrase so that it is closer to the noun it modifies: ". . . many mistakes are made on the job by workers . . . ."

24. (D) The sentence makes an illogical statement. It attempts to compare *time* and *branch of the service*. The sentence can be corrected by inserting a clarifying phrase: ". . . than do men in any other branch . . . ."

25. (A) The sentence contains a dangling modifier. As written, it implies a comparison between A.J. Ayer, the person, and the philosophical writings of Gilbert Ryle. The error can be corrected in the following way: "Like the writing of A.J. Ayer, much of . . . ."

EXERCISE 3

1. (B) Substitute *relationship*.
2. (D) Substitute *lie*.
3. (B) Substitute *adapted*.
4. (B) Substitute *would have chosen*.
5. (A) Substitute *are built*.
6. (C) Substitute *as*.
7. (D) Substitute *nor*.
8. (D) Substitute *to please*.
9. (C) Substitute *whether*.
10. (D) Substitute *as*.
11. (D) Substitute *as*.
12. (D) Substitute *a shorter sentence*.
13. (C) Substitute *to attach*.
14. (C) Substitute *than*.
15. (C) Substitute *rise*.

EXERCISE 4

1. Neurology is the science that deals with the anatomy, physiology, and pathology of the nervous system.

2. Nursery lore, like everything human, has been subject to many changes over long periods of time.

3. In order to provide more living space, we converted an attached garage into a den.

4. Begun while Dickens was still at work on *Pickwick Papers*, *Oliver Twist* was published in 1837 and is now one of the author's most widely read works.

5. Given the great difficulties of making soundings in very deep water, it is not surprising that few such soundings were made until the middle of this century.

6. The root of modern Dutch was once supposed to be Old Frisian, but the general view now is that the characteristic forms of Dutch are at least as old as those of Old Frisian.

7. Moose, once scarce because of indiscriminate hunting, are protected by law; and the number of moose is once again increasing. (You could use a comma in place of the semicolon.)

8. Perhaps the most interesting section of New Orleans is the French Quarter, which extends from North Rampart Street to the Mississippi River.

9. Writing for a skeptical and rationalizing age, Shaftesbury was primarily concerned with showing that goodness and beauty are not determined by revelation, authority, opinion, or fashion. (The final comma is optional.)

10. A great deal of information regarding the nutritional requirements of farm animals has been accumulated over countless generations by trial and error, but most recent advances have come as the result of systematic studies at schools of animal husbandry.

11. *Omoo*, Melville's sequel to *Typee*, appeared in 1847 and went through five printings in that year alone.

12. Although the first school for Blacks was a public school established in Virginia in 1620, most educational opportunities for Blacks prior to the Civil War were provided by private agencies.

13. As the climate of Europe changed, the population became too dense for the supply of food obtained by hunting; and other means of securing food, such as the domestication of animals, were necessary. (Here, given the complexity of the independent clauses, you should use a semicolon and not a comma.)

14. In Faulkner's poetic realism, the grotesque is somber, violent, and often inexplicable; in Caldwell's writing, it is lightened by a balladlike, humorous, sophisticated detachment. (The comma following *violent* is optional, but the comma following *humorous* is required—because there is no conjunction between *humorous* and *sophisticated*. The semicolon is required here. A comma would create a comma splice, because there is no conjunction to join the two clauses.)

15. The valley of the Loir, a northern tributary of the Loire at Angers, abounds in rock villages; and they occur in many other places in France, Spain, and northern Italy.

14

Writing Sample: Part II

1. **What to Say**
2. **How to Say It**
3. **An Attack Strategy for the Writing Sample**
4. **Writing Sample Drills**

Lesson 15

In the previous lesson, you reviewed the important elements of sentence construction. In this lesson, we discuss what to say in your Writing Sample essay and how to say it.

1. What to Say

You might think that finding something to say in your essay will be the most difficult aspect of the Writing Sample exercise. In fact, I think that finding something to say is the easiest aspect of the exercise—for three reasons.

In the first place, the topic asks you to evaluate a decisional situation; but the directions specifically state: "There is no 'right' or 'wrong' answer to this question." This is good news: you can't possibly "miss" this question. And the essay topic is drafted so that there are advantages and disadvantages to both of the options you are asked to evaluate. Neither option can be considered conclusively better than the other.

Second, you only have 30 minutes to read the topic, do your analysis, outline the essay, and write and proofread it. So you really don't have time to write more than a couple of hundred words. And that means that you don't want to have too many ideas. In fact, if you try to include too many ideas, you won't have time to finish the essay—and that would be a big mistake.

Third, the topic itself will suggest ideas to you. Consider again the sample topic introduced in the last lesson:

> Read the following summaries of proposals submitted by Knight and Carpenter, each of whom wishes to lease the vacant store space in a co-op building located at 850 Seventh Avenue. Then, in the space provided, write an argument for the building's governing board in favor of leasing the space to either Knight or Carpenter. The following criteria are relevant to your decision:
>
> 1. The co-op board prefers to grant a long-term lease to a tenant who is financially secure and whose use would not unduly disturb residents of the building.
>
> 2. The co-op board wants the space used by a tenant who will provide a product or service that is not currently readily available to the 250 families who live in the building.
>
> KNIGHT proposes to use the space for a delicatessen. The store will offer high-priced imported and specialty items. Knight has owned and operated a similar store on the other side of town for 18 years, and some of the building's residents are regular customers of that store. Knight is relocating his business because his lease has expired and the landlord is demanding an increase in monthly rent from $1,500 to $3,500. The monthly rental for the vacant store at 850 Seventh Avenue is $2,800. Knight is eager for a long-term lease. He has also agreed to have included in the lease a provision that will govern the timing and frequency of truck deliveries and to a provision allowing the co-op board to inspect the premises to make sure that the foodstuffs are not attracting pests.

CARPENTER proposes to use the store for a card and gift shop. For the past five years, Carpenter has managed a shoe store, handling all aspects of the business, including purchasing, sales, payroll, and other record-keeping. Although there is already a card and gift shop in the neighborhood, Carpenter notes that its owner plans to retire in two years and close the store. Additionally, Carpenter will stock a greater variety of, and better-quality, merchandise. Since he is just starting his business, Carpenter would prefer a three- to five-year lease with an option to renew.

The topic itself is about as long as any essay you could expect to write in 30 minutes, and it is sufficiently rich in detail to suggest many points that you might make in your essay.

You should take your cue from the two, numbered criteria. These general considerations will provide categories into which you can sort some of the details mentioned in the description of each option.

On Knight's behalf, you could point out the following:

Criterion 1. Knight has been in the delicatessen business for a considerable time, so he is likely to be a better financial risk than Carpenter, who is starting a new business. Additionally, Knight is willing to enter into a long-term agreement.

Criterion 2. Knight would provide a service not currently available to the residents of the building. Moreover, some residents are even willing to travel across town to get the products Knight carries.

On Carpenter's behalf, you could note:

Criterion 1: A card and gift shop would probably require fewer deliveries than a delicatessen and would therefore be less disturbing to the tenants. Additionally, a card and gift shop will not be likely to attract pests.

Criterion 2: Carpenter's store will eventually make up for the loss of the card and gift shop that presently does business in the neighborhood.

Given that there are advantages and disadvantages to each proposal, you may feel uncomfortable selecting and defending one side or the other. You may feel that you can't really determine which is the better option and would prefer to say so. I have two recommendations on this point. First, don't waffle; that is, don't try to avoid taking a position. The directions clearly state you are to pick a side and present an argument in favor of it, so that's what the admission committee wants to see. Do this even though you don't find either side of the issue particularly persuasive. (Oftentimes lawyers find themselves defending positions they don't like—because that's the position a client happens to be in.) Second, if in your practice in this book you find that you have difficulty choosing one position over the other, resolve to take the first option given in your exam topic and present arguments in favor of it. This way, you will know in advance what your strategy will be.

2. How to Say It

I suspect that the Writing Sample topics are carefully drafted so that neither of the positions is clearly superior to the other and such that there is not enough information for one side to be "right" and the other "wrong." In this section, the law schools are not so much interested in penetrating and sophisticated analysis (you don't really have enough information for that). According to the general instructions for the Writing Sample, "law schools are interested in organization, vocabulary, and writing mechanics."

Writing mechanics were discussed in the previous lesson, and I doubt there is much you can do in a short time to improve your vocabulary. You should just use the words you would ordinarily use. You should not attempt to work into your essay any legal terminology. Given the nature of the topic, legal terms would be out of place in your essay. And a law school admissions committee is not going to be impressed by an essay just because it contains a few "wheretoforeabovementioneds."

The key to writing a good essay for the Writing Sample is that first element mentioned in the excerpt from the instructions set out above: *organization*. In fact, I think it is possible to reduce the entire Writing Sample exercise to a simple formula: tell the reader what you're going to say, say it, and then remind the reader of what you've said. As simple as this little formula is, it can be applied successfully in many different areas—exams, speeches, letters, and, most importantly, the LSAT Writing Sample.

The very crudest formula for an essay is parasitic upon the two, numbered criteria given in the topic. In this formula, the essay offers two arguments for a position and is broken into four paragraphs. The first paragraph contains a statement of your position (which position you have chosen) and a summary of the two reasons you will offer in support of that position. (The two reasons correspond to the two criteria given in the topic.) The second paragraph presents points showing that your choice meets the first criterion. The third paragraph presents points showing that your choice meets the second criterion. The fourth paragraph contains a summary and a conclusion. Here is a sample outline for this approach:

I. Introduction
II. Carpenter would be a better tenant.
    A. A card and gift shop would not require frequent deliveries.
    B. A card and gift shop would not attract pests.
    C. Carpenter has experience in running a business, so he will probably succeed.
III. Carpenter would provide a needed service.
    A. The neighborhood will soon need another card and gift shop.
    B. Carpenter will carry better merchandise.
    C. Carpenter will carry a greater variety of merchandise.
IV. Conclusion

The beauty of this approach is that the essay almost writes itself:

    The co-op board should choose Carpenter over Knight for two reasons. One, Carpenter will be the better tenant; and two, Carpenter will offer a product needed by the residents of the building.

    Carpenter will be the better tenant because a card and gift shop will not require frequent deliveries and will therefore be less disturbing to residents of the building. In addition, a card and gift shop contains no foodstuffs to attract pests. Finally, although Carpenter has never owned a card and gift shop before, his experience suggests that his business will succeed.

    There are three ways in which Carpenter will provide residents of the building with a product they need. First, the neighborhood will need another card and gift shop within two years. Second, Carpenter will offer higher-quality merchandise than that currently available in the neighborhood. Third, Carpenter will offer a greater variety of merchandise.

    On balance, then, Carpenter will make a better tenant while offering the residents of the building a needed product. So the board should choose Carpenter.

Admittedly, the essay is not very imaginative; but given the topic, you're just not going to be able to sound brilliant.

15

If the two-point essay just described seems to you to be a little too simplistic, you might try the following three-point formula. The three-point essay also begins with an introduction and ends with a conclusion. Each of the three paragraphs between the introduction and the conclusion offers a different reason in support of your position.

As with the two-point approach, the first paragraph of the three-point approach consists of two sentences. The first sentence will state briefly the position you advocate. The second sentence will summarize the three points you are going to offer in support of that position. So in its simplest form, the first paragraph will look like this:

The xxxxxxxx should choose xxxxxx for three reasons. First, xxxx xxxx xxxxxxxx xxxxx xxxx xxxxxxx; second, xxxx xxxxx xxxxxxx xxx xxxxx xxxxxx xxx xxx xx xxxxx; and third, xxx xxx xxx xxxxxxxxxx xxx xxxx.

The second paragraph will consist of three sentences. The first sentence will be the topic sentence for the paragraph—a statement of the first reason offered in support of the position you have taken. The second sentence will be the first point you offer in support of your first reason. The third sentence will be the second point you offer in support of your first reason. Mark the transition from the first supporting point to the second supporting point with a word such as *additionally, further, furthermore,* or *moreover.*

The third and fourth paragraphs will be parallel in structure to the second paragraph: a topic sentence stating a point in support of your overall position and two supporting points.

The final paragraph will summarize and close. It will be one or perhaps two sentences.

Outlined, your essay will look like this:
 I. Introduction
 II. First Point
     A. Supporting Point
     B. Supporting Point
III. Second Point
     A. Supporting Point
     B. Supporting Point
IV. Third Point
     A. Supporting Point
     B. Supporting Point
 V. Conclusion

Here is a sample essay using the Writing Sample topic above that slavishly follows the formula:

The co-op board should lease the vacant space to Knight for three reasons. One, Knight is a better choice for a tenant in terms of financial considerations; two, Knight will provide residents of the building with a service they need; three, Knight's willingness to schedule deliveries and allow inspection of the premises means that his use will not disturb residents.

First, Knight is a better choice for a tenant in terms of financial considerations. Knight has 18 years of experience in operating a delicatessen, and during that time he has built up considerable good will. Additionally, Knight is willing to enter into a long-term lease, which means that it will not be necessary to face this problem again in the near future.

Second, Knight will provide a service needed by the residents of the building. At present, there does not appear to be any business in the neighborhood that sells exactly the same sort of products Knight would sell. Additionally, the fact that residents of the building are now willing to travel across town for his products indicates that residents want his products.

Third, although it might be thought that a delicatessen could disturb some residents in the building, Knight has shown he is willing to take steps to avoid this. He is willing to agree to inspections. Further, Knight will work out delivery schedules so that residents are not needlessly bothered.

On balance, Knight would be a better choice for tenant. He is financially a better choice; he would provide a useful service; and he would not disturb the residents of the building.

Again, this is admittedly not terribly imaginative. But you must remember that you don't have enough time to do anything very imaginative. And keep in mind also that a good essay is not by itself going to get you into a law school and that a bad essay could keep you out of school.

If you doubt that the two essays above would be sufficient, try copying them over in your own handwriting—in neat handwriting of the sort that you should use on the exam. You'll find that you require at least eight to ten minutes just to write out the sentences I have already written. Given, then, that on the exam you'll have to do an analysis of the topic, outline your approach, compose your sentences, write them out, and proofread your essay, you can begin to understand why the general directions for this part of the exam state: How well you write is much more important than how much you write.

You can, of course, mitigate the extreme severity of the formulaic approach. For example, make sure that your topic sentences are not simply exact restatements of the formulation you have given in the opening paragraph—vary the wording slightly. And try to avoid using the same wording in your conclusion. Again, vary the language slightly, and try in the conclusion to convey a sense of closure—that you have proved your point. For this, you may use phrases such as "on balance," "therefore," or "For these reasons, it follows that . . . ."

15

3. An Attack Strategy for the Writing Sample

A half-hour is not a lot of time in which to do the things you have to do for the Writing Sample, so you have to budget your time wisely. You should be particularly careful to make sure that you finish your essay. It does not look good to write eight and a half paragraphs and have the essay end abruptly in midsentence because you ran out of time.

I recommend the following time schedule:

Time in Minutes	Task
3	Read the topic through quickly to familiarize yourself with it. Then reread the topic more carefully. Underline the statement that tells you what you must write about.
4	Make a list of ideas on both sides of the issue on the scratch paper provided. Decide which side you prefer.
3	Make an outline of your argument. Arrange the ideas you plan to use in a logical sequence.
15	Write the essay. Try to compose each sentence in your head *before* you begin writing. Write legibly.
5	Proofread and edit the essay. Make neat corrections by drawing a single line through words and by inserting omitted material.

Summary

1. The Writing Sample topic itself will suggest to you ideas you should incorporate into your essay. Sort these ideas into the two categories suggested by the criteria.

2. Organize your ideas into outline form. Use either the two-point approach or the three-point approach. Begin with an introduction and end with a conclusion.

3. Budget your time so that you make sure you write a completed essay and have time to edit it.

---

4. Writing Sample Drills

This part includes three Writing Sample drills. The first drill is a "walk-through," with an outline and an essay on the page opposite the topic so that you can "walk through" the writing of an essay. The other two drills are "warm-up" drills that you should do within the specified time limit.

15

Walk-Through

No Time Limit
LSAT WRITING SAMPLE TOPIC

Read the following descriptions of Henri Bernard and Mary Stuart, applicants for a job as a French teacher in a private high school. Then, in the space provided, write an argument for hiring either Henri or Mary. The following criteria are relevant to your decision:

1. The school is concerned that students learn to speak fluent and idiomatic French. The chairperson of the languages department also hopes that the new teacher will be able to revise the audio tapes currently used in the school's language lab.
2. The school would like to hire a new teacher who is able to take on fund-raising duties including canvassing parents and graduates, preparing literature for fund-raising campaigns, and planning social functions to raise money.

HENRI was born in a small village in France and was educated in Paris, where he studied English literature. Following his graduation from college, Henri came to the United States to get a master's degree in business administration. After getting his MBA, he worked for the Société Française, a Washington, D.C.-based nonprofit association that provides informational services to American companies doing business with French firms. Among his other duties, Henri had responsibility for preparing a weekly newsletter that was distributed to several hundred readers. Although Henri has no classroom teaching experience, while in graduate school he was employed by the university on a part-time basis as a tutor to help students having difficulty with French.

MARY was born in Wisconsin and went to a state college, where she took four semesters of French. She also has a master's degree in education. She was teaching English literature on the high school level when the principal of her school imposed on Mary to teach beginning French for two months during the illness of the regular French teacher. Mary found she enjoyed teaching French and took a leave of absence for a year of intensive study at a French university in Lyons. She is considered fluent in the language. Two summers ago, Mary published a small book entitled *Essential French for the English-Speaking Traveler*. Presently, Mary is teaching French in a public high school and is the president of the regional association of French language teachers. One of the association's activities is finding scholarships and grants for high school students to study in France.

Explanation

After you have familiarized yourself with the topic, sort some ideas into the two categories suggested:
1. Who would be the better teacher?
   Henri is a native-speaker; Mary studied in France.
   Mary has formal teaching experience; Henri tutored.
   Henri would be good for the tapes; Mary is fluent.
2. Who would be better for the additional duties?
   Henri has an MBA; Mary has administrative experience.
   Henri published a newsletter; Mary published a book.
   Mary found scholarships and grants.

Then make a decision in favor of one or the other applicant and outline your argument. Since there is no really good reason to prefer one applicant over the other, I will choose the first one described, Henri. Here is a sample outline for an essay using the three-point approach:

I. Introduction
II. Henri will be a good teacher.
   A. Students will learn to speak well.
   B. He has tutoring experience.
III. Henri can redo the tapes.
   A. His accent must be perfect.
   B. He knows current usage.
IV. Henri can perform the additional duties.
   A. He has administrative experience.
   B. He can prepare written material.
V. Conclusion
   The next step is to write the essay.

> The school should hire Henri for three reasons. One, Henri would be an excellent teacher; two, Henri will be able to redo the tapes for the language lab; and three, Henri can perform the additional fundraising duties.
> First, Henri promises to be an excellent teacher. Obviously, he will be able to teach students current, idiomatic French and teach them to speak with a correct accent. Additionally, Henri has experience tutoring French and should be aware of special problems that students have.

Second, Henri is a good person to have redo the tapes in the language lab. A native-speaker will provide a good model for students to imitate. Furthermore, as a native-speaker, Henri will be able to make sure the tapes reflect current usage.

Third, Henri will be able to take over the additional duties described. As an MBA, he has the administrative skills needed to do things such as fundraising. Moreover, his experience in writing a newsletter demonstrates that he can prepare any written materials that might be needed.

Therefore, Henri should be the school's choice. He would be a good teacher; he can improve the quality of the tapes in the language lab; and he has the skills needed for fundraising and other similar activities.

DRILL 1

The Garden City Opera Guild, a small company that performs the standard Italian opera repertoire, is looking for a new tenor for its upcoming season. After auditioning many candidates, the music director has narrowed his choice to two singers, DWAYNE LUKAS and GASPARO MOCHERA. Write an essay arguing for the selection of one of the two singers. Two considerations should guide your decision:

1. The music director would like to hire a singer who could assist him in preparing other singers for their roles, either by accompanying them on the piano or by coaching Italian diction, or both.
2. The music director is trying to improve the quality of the company's performances in order to attract national attention. By gaining greater notoriety, the music director hopes to attract funding for the company from private sources.

DWAYNE is a young tenor who graduated from the Cincinnati Conservatory with a dual major in singing and piano. After leaving the Conservatory, Dwayne sang for two years in an apprentice program with a major opera company. He left the apprentice program when it became clear to him than another young tenor was being groomed for lead roles. Dwayne has been told by knowledgeable people that his voice will allow him to become a leading singer in some other company. The two years in the apprenticeship program is Dwayne's only stage experience. Dwayne is familiar with the standard Italian operatic repertoire but has not studied Italian formally.

GASPARO, a 40-year-old tenor from Naples, Italy, has been singing professionally for 15 years. Gasparo has worked extensively in the smaller opera houses of Italy, France, Spain, and Germany and has sung all the major roles of the Italian repertory. He received excellent reviews from European music critics for his acting ability as well as for his fine voice. He is now trying to establish a reputation in the United States. Gasparo has never studied at a conservatory and has only a limited ability to read music. Virtually all of his training has come through studying with former singers who turned to teaching. Gasparo has been in the United States for only a short time and still has difficulty with the language.

DRILL 2

The Board of Trustees for the new Native American Museum in Albuquerque wants to commission a mural for the lobby of the museum. After reviewing sketches submitted by many artists, the Board has narrowed the choice to two artists, SIMON ORTIZ and BURTON SCOTT. Write an essay arguing for the selection of one of the artists. The following criteria should guide your decision:

1. The Board would prefer a work by an established artist, because such a work would add prestige to the new museum.
2. The Board would like the subject matter of the mural to reflect the location and function of the museum.

SIMON is a Navajo artist from New Mexico who studied art at the University of Arizona. He currently teaches painting at a southwestern college. His ultra-modern, abstract canvases and sculptures are devoted primarily to representing the history of Native Americans. Two of Simon's paintings hang in the university's art museum, and one of his steel sculptures stands near the entrance to the university. Recently, knowledgeable collectors have come to regard Simon's works as good investments and have begun purchasing them with the expectation that they will increase in value as Simon's fame grows. Simon proposes an abstract mural painted in tones suggestive of the landscape of the southwest and incorporating images from Navajo traditions.

BURTON was born in Los Angeles and educated at Harvard. He currently lives in western Massachusetts. His paintings hang in museums in Boston, New York, and Washington; and he has done several murals for libraries and other public buildings. Burton's grandfather was a Hopi. Recently, Burton has become interested in his own family history and has made several trips to New Mexico and Arizona to meet with relatives who knew his grandfather. Burton's style is highly realistic, and he proposes a mural depicting several scenes of life in the Southwest over the last 500 years.

408

Warm-Up Drills

DRILL 1

DRILL 2

PART THREE

Practice Tests

Practice Test 1

Use a No. 2 pencil only. Be sure each mark is dark and completely fills the intended oval. Completely erase any errors or stray marks.

☐ A R C O ☐

DATE TAKEN:

ARCO TEST NO.

YOUR NAME:

Start with number 1 for each new section. If a section has fewer than 30 questions, leave the extra answer spaces blank.

SECTION 1

1 Ⓐ Ⓑ Ⓒ Ⓓ Ⓔ
2 Ⓐ Ⓑ Ⓒ Ⓓ Ⓔ
3 Ⓐ Ⓑ Ⓒ Ⓓ Ⓔ
4 Ⓐ Ⓑ Ⓒ Ⓓ Ⓔ
5 Ⓐ Ⓑ Ⓒ Ⓓ Ⓔ
6 Ⓐ Ⓑ Ⓒ Ⓓ Ⓔ
7 Ⓐ Ⓑ Ⓒ Ⓓ Ⓔ
8 Ⓐ Ⓑ Ⓒ Ⓓ Ⓔ
9 Ⓐ Ⓑ Ⓒ Ⓓ Ⓔ
10 Ⓐ Ⓑ Ⓒ Ⓓ Ⓔ
11 Ⓐ Ⓑ Ⓒ Ⓓ Ⓔ
12 Ⓐ Ⓑ Ⓒ Ⓓ Ⓔ
13 Ⓐ Ⓑ Ⓒ Ⓓ Ⓔ
14 Ⓐ Ⓑ Ⓒ Ⓓ Ⓔ
15 Ⓐ Ⓑ Ⓒ Ⓓ Ⓔ
16 Ⓐ Ⓑ Ⓒ Ⓓ Ⓔ
17 Ⓐ Ⓑ Ⓒ Ⓓ Ⓔ
18 Ⓐ Ⓑ Ⓒ Ⓓ Ⓔ
19 Ⓐ Ⓑ Ⓒ Ⓓ Ⓔ
20 Ⓐ Ⓑ Ⓒ Ⓓ Ⓔ
21 Ⓐ Ⓑ Ⓒ Ⓓ Ⓔ
22 Ⓐ Ⓑ Ⓒ Ⓓ Ⓔ
23 Ⓐ Ⓑ Ⓒ Ⓓ Ⓔ
24 Ⓐ Ⓑ Ⓒ Ⓓ Ⓔ
25 Ⓐ Ⓑ Ⓒ Ⓓ Ⓔ
26 Ⓐ Ⓑ Ⓒ Ⓓ Ⓔ
27 Ⓐ Ⓑ Ⓒ Ⓓ Ⓔ
28 Ⓐ Ⓑ Ⓒ Ⓓ Ⓔ
29 Ⓐ Ⓑ Ⓒ Ⓓ Ⓔ
30 Ⓐ Ⓑ Ⓒ Ⓓ Ⓔ

SECTION 2

1 Ⓐ Ⓑ Ⓒ Ⓓ Ⓔ
2 Ⓐ Ⓑ Ⓒ Ⓓ Ⓔ
3 Ⓐ Ⓑ Ⓒ Ⓓ Ⓔ
4 Ⓐ Ⓑ Ⓒ Ⓓ Ⓔ
5 Ⓐ Ⓑ Ⓒ Ⓓ Ⓔ
6 Ⓐ Ⓑ Ⓒ Ⓓ Ⓔ
7 Ⓐ Ⓑ Ⓒ Ⓓ Ⓔ
8 Ⓐ Ⓑ Ⓒ Ⓓ Ⓔ
9 Ⓐ Ⓑ Ⓒ Ⓓ Ⓔ
10 Ⓐ Ⓑ Ⓒ Ⓓ Ⓔ
11 Ⓐ Ⓑ Ⓒ Ⓓ Ⓔ
12 Ⓐ Ⓑ Ⓒ Ⓓ Ⓔ
13 Ⓐ Ⓑ Ⓒ Ⓓ Ⓔ
14 Ⓐ Ⓑ Ⓒ Ⓓ Ⓔ
15 Ⓐ Ⓑ Ⓒ Ⓓ Ⓔ
16 Ⓐ Ⓑ Ⓒ Ⓓ Ⓔ
17 Ⓐ Ⓑ Ⓒ Ⓓ Ⓔ
18 Ⓐ Ⓑ Ⓒ Ⓓ Ⓔ
19 Ⓐ Ⓑ Ⓒ Ⓓ Ⓔ
20 Ⓐ Ⓑ Ⓒ Ⓓ Ⓔ
21 Ⓐ Ⓑ Ⓒ Ⓓ Ⓔ
22 Ⓐ Ⓑ Ⓒ Ⓓ Ⓔ
23 Ⓐ Ⓑ Ⓒ Ⓓ Ⓔ
24 Ⓐ Ⓑ Ⓒ Ⓓ Ⓔ
25 Ⓐ Ⓑ Ⓒ Ⓓ Ⓔ
26 Ⓐ Ⓑ Ⓒ Ⓓ Ⓔ
27 Ⓐ Ⓑ Ⓒ Ⓓ Ⓔ
28 Ⓐ Ⓑ Ⓒ Ⓓ Ⓔ
29 Ⓐ Ⓑ Ⓒ Ⓓ Ⓔ
30 Ⓐ Ⓑ Ⓒ Ⓓ Ⓔ

SECTION 3

1 Ⓐ Ⓑ Ⓒ Ⓓ Ⓔ
2 Ⓐ Ⓑ Ⓒ Ⓓ Ⓔ
3 Ⓐ Ⓑ Ⓒ Ⓓ Ⓔ
4 Ⓐ Ⓑ Ⓒ Ⓓ Ⓔ
5 Ⓐ Ⓑ Ⓒ Ⓓ Ⓔ
6 Ⓐ Ⓑ Ⓒ Ⓓ Ⓔ
7 Ⓐ Ⓑ Ⓒ Ⓓ Ⓔ
8 Ⓐ Ⓑ Ⓒ Ⓓ Ⓔ
9 Ⓐ Ⓑ Ⓒ Ⓓ Ⓔ
10 Ⓐ Ⓑ Ⓒ Ⓓ Ⓔ
11 Ⓐ Ⓑ Ⓒ Ⓓ Ⓔ
12 Ⓐ Ⓑ Ⓒ Ⓓ Ⓔ
13 Ⓐ Ⓑ Ⓒ Ⓓ Ⓔ
14 Ⓐ Ⓑ Ⓒ Ⓓ Ⓔ
15 Ⓐ Ⓑ Ⓒ Ⓓ Ⓔ
16 Ⓐ Ⓑ Ⓒ Ⓓ Ⓔ
17 Ⓐ Ⓑ Ⓒ Ⓓ Ⓔ
18 Ⓐ Ⓑ Ⓒ Ⓓ Ⓔ
19 Ⓐ Ⓑ Ⓒ Ⓓ Ⓔ
20 Ⓐ Ⓑ Ⓒ Ⓓ Ⓔ
21 Ⓐ Ⓑ Ⓒ Ⓓ Ⓔ
22 Ⓐ Ⓑ Ⓒ Ⓓ Ⓔ
23 Ⓐ Ⓑ Ⓒ Ⓓ Ⓔ
24 Ⓐ Ⓑ Ⓒ Ⓓ Ⓔ
25 Ⓐ Ⓑ Ⓒ Ⓓ Ⓔ
26 Ⓐ Ⓑ Ⓒ Ⓓ Ⓔ
27 Ⓐ Ⓑ Ⓒ Ⓓ Ⓔ
28 Ⓐ Ⓑ Ⓒ Ⓓ Ⓔ
29 Ⓐ Ⓑ Ⓒ Ⓓ Ⓔ
30 Ⓐ Ⓑ Ⓒ Ⓓ Ⓔ

SECTION 4

1 Ⓐ Ⓑ Ⓒ Ⓓ Ⓔ
2 Ⓐ Ⓑ Ⓒ Ⓓ Ⓔ
3 Ⓐ Ⓑ Ⓒ Ⓓ Ⓔ
4 Ⓐ Ⓑ Ⓒ Ⓓ Ⓔ
5 Ⓐ Ⓑ Ⓒ Ⓓ Ⓔ
6 Ⓐ Ⓑ Ⓒ Ⓓ Ⓔ
7 Ⓐ Ⓑ Ⓒ Ⓓ Ⓔ
8 Ⓐ Ⓑ Ⓒ Ⓓ Ⓔ
9 Ⓐ Ⓑ Ⓒ Ⓓ Ⓔ
10 Ⓐ Ⓑ Ⓒ Ⓓ Ⓔ
11 Ⓐ Ⓑ Ⓒ Ⓓ Ⓔ
12 Ⓐ Ⓑ Ⓒ Ⓓ Ⓔ
13 Ⓐ Ⓑ Ⓒ Ⓓ Ⓔ
14 Ⓐ Ⓑ Ⓒ Ⓓ Ⓔ
15 Ⓐ Ⓑ Ⓒ Ⓓ Ⓔ
16 Ⓐ Ⓑ Ⓒ Ⓓ Ⓔ
17 Ⓐ Ⓑ Ⓒ Ⓓ Ⓔ
18 Ⓐ Ⓑ Ⓒ Ⓓ Ⓔ
19 Ⓐ Ⓑ Ⓒ Ⓓ Ⓔ
20 Ⓐ Ⓑ Ⓒ Ⓓ Ⓔ
21 Ⓐ Ⓑ Ⓒ Ⓓ Ⓔ
22 Ⓐ Ⓑ Ⓒ Ⓓ Ⓔ
23 Ⓐ Ⓑ Ⓒ Ⓓ Ⓔ
24 Ⓐ Ⓑ Ⓒ Ⓓ Ⓔ
25 Ⓐ Ⓑ Ⓒ Ⓓ Ⓔ
26 Ⓐ Ⓑ Ⓒ Ⓓ Ⓔ
27 Ⓐ Ⓑ Ⓒ Ⓓ Ⓔ
28 Ⓐ Ⓑ Ⓒ Ⓓ Ⓔ
29 Ⓐ Ⓑ Ⓒ Ⓓ Ⓔ
30 Ⓐ Ⓑ Ⓒ Ⓓ Ⓔ

SECTION 5

1 Ⓐ Ⓑ Ⓒ Ⓓ Ⓔ   16 Ⓐ Ⓑ Ⓒ Ⓓ Ⓔ
2 Ⓐ Ⓑ Ⓒ Ⓓ Ⓔ   17 Ⓐ Ⓑ Ⓒ Ⓓ Ⓔ
3 Ⓐ Ⓑ Ⓒ Ⓓ Ⓔ   18 Ⓐ Ⓑ Ⓒ Ⓓ Ⓔ
4 Ⓐ Ⓑ Ⓒ Ⓓ Ⓔ   19 Ⓐ Ⓑ Ⓒ Ⓓ Ⓔ
5 Ⓐ Ⓑ Ⓒ Ⓓ Ⓔ   20 Ⓐ Ⓑ Ⓒ Ⓓ Ⓔ
6 Ⓐ Ⓑ Ⓒ Ⓓ Ⓔ   21 Ⓐ Ⓑ Ⓒ Ⓓ Ⓔ
7 Ⓐ Ⓑ Ⓒ Ⓓ Ⓔ   22 Ⓐ Ⓑ Ⓒ Ⓓ Ⓔ
8 Ⓐ Ⓑ Ⓒ Ⓓ Ⓔ   23 Ⓐ Ⓑ Ⓒ Ⓓ Ⓔ
9 Ⓐ Ⓑ Ⓒ Ⓓ Ⓔ   24 Ⓐ Ⓑ Ⓒ Ⓓ Ⓔ
10 Ⓐ Ⓑ Ⓒ Ⓓ Ⓔ   25 Ⓐ Ⓑ Ⓒ Ⓓ Ⓔ
11 Ⓐ Ⓑ Ⓒ Ⓓ Ⓔ   26 Ⓐ Ⓑ Ⓒ Ⓓ Ⓔ
12 Ⓐ Ⓑ Ⓒ Ⓓ Ⓔ   27 Ⓐ Ⓑ Ⓒ Ⓓ Ⓔ
13 Ⓐ Ⓑ Ⓒ Ⓓ Ⓔ   28 Ⓐ Ⓑ Ⓒ Ⓓ Ⓔ
14 Ⓐ Ⓑ Ⓒ Ⓓ Ⓔ   29 Ⓐ Ⓑ Ⓒ Ⓓ Ⓔ
15 Ⓐ Ⓑ Ⓒ Ⓓ Ⓔ   30 Ⓐ Ⓑ Ⓒ Ⓓ Ⓔ

Directions: Each passage in this group is followed by questions based on its content. After reading a passage, choose the best answer to each question and blacken the corresponding space on the sheet. Answer all questions following a passage on the basis of what is <u>stated</u> or <u>implied</u> in that passage.

In North America, black slaves were isolated psychologically from their masters despite their physical proximity. Racism guaranteed this kind of distance because, even under the most generous slaveholder,
(5) slaves were made to "know their place." Every slave narrative attests to this reality. Slave children might sometimes enjoy a few early years during which they were not fully conscious of their status; but, even in the "best" of such cases, this situation did not last beyond
(10) early adolescence. Blacks in various conditions of subjugation gradually began to establish social systems. Many slaveholders fancied themselves as having exposed so-called heathen and primitive people to civilization. They were convinced of the childish, impulsive, and
(15) helpless natures of blacks and therefore assumed the appropriateness of social distance and control (in spite of ubiquitous sexual intimacy, which is a subject of considerable psychological interest in itself). They approved of only that behavior which was conforming and recognized
(20) only those relationships the existence of which was sanctioned by their own social codes. They were therefore ignorant of a great deal of what went on in the minds and in the lives of their slaves, whose behavior toward their masters was transposed into terms the slaveholders could
(25) understand. Ironically, then, the slaveholders' social attitudes unwittingly contributed to the development of a black social structure, which was a great source of practical and psychological strength.

In other parts of the Americas, however, an emerging
(30) mulatto class gained legal and social recognition between that of pure blacks and pure whites. The racial behavior stimulated by this development aided social communication between blacks and whites in those areas, while in North America the racial isolation created a profound social
(35) and psychological distance. Fantasies about the other race became, on both sides, gross exaggerations of the reality which rigid segregation had helped to create. The stereotyped white view of blacks characterized them as primitive, while the stereotyped black view of whites
(40) emphasized individual white power.

For blacks, however, the dominant effect of the racial isolation during slavery was the stimulation of a unique black culture. The more black cultural forms differed from those of the masters, the more immune
(45) they were from the control of whites and the more they gained in personal autonomy and self-esteem. As Robert Jones pointed out, "In British North America the peculiar isolation of blacks caused them to take a unique emotional and intellectual perspective on their Africanity."

(50) This helps account for the extraordinary vitality and creativity of the slave communities and subsequent black communities. Afro-American folktales, music, drama, religion, and language all reveal the creative merger of what is traditionally African with the North American
(55) slave experience.

1. The author's primary purpose is to

   (A) contrast two different views of a social issue
   (B) describe a social phenomenon
   (C) present new research to support a theory
   (D) argue in favor of social change
   (E) illustrate a moral dilemma

2. The author apparently regards Robert Jones (lines 46–47) as

   (A) an important historical personage
   (B) an opponent of segregation
   (C) an authority on the social effects of slavery
   (D) a spokesperson for black communities
   (E) a defender of the attitudes of white slaveholders

3. Which of the following statements can be inferred from the passage?

   (A) Since blacks outside of North America were not as racially isolated as North American blacks, they did not develop the same vital black communities.
   (B) Some areas outside of North America had a mulatto class, so there was no racial tension between blacks and whites in those areas.
   (C) Because of the racial separation of blacks and whites in North America, blacks thought that most whites were also oppressed by powerful whites.
   (D) Black communities in North America incorporated more African elements into their cultural forms than they drew from the slavery experience.
   (E) Blacks intentionally invented new cultural forms that were unlike those of whites, so that whites could not understand their culture.

GO ON TO THE NEXT PAGE

4. The author most probably puts the word *best* (line 9) in quotation marks to
   (A) acknowledge that he is quoting from another source
   (B) emphasize that no aspect of slavery could ever be good
   (C) remind the reader that the word is ambiguous
   (D) alert the reader that a definition will follow
   (E) show his support for the black communities

5. The author's attitude toward North American black communities can best be described as
   (A) enthusiastic
   (B) neutral
   (C) disinterested
   (D) deprecatory
   (E) admiring

6. The author implies that the eagerness of white slaveholders to be sexually intimate with black slaves was
   (A) inconsistent with the attitude of white slaveholders that they were superior to blacks
   (B) a contributing factor in the eventual breakdown of the psychological barriers separating whites and blacks
   (C) more prevalent in British North America than in other parts of the Americas
   (D) a reinforcement of the negative attitudes of white slaveholders toward blacks
   (E) a reason for white slaveholders to reassess their attitudes about blacks

Man, so the truism goes, lives increasingly in a man-made environment. This places a special burden on human immaturity, for it is plain that adapting to such variable conditions must depend very heavily on opportunities for learning, or whatever the processes are that are operative during immaturity. It must also mean that during immaturity man must master knowledge and skills that are neither stored in the gene pool nor learned by direct encounter, but that are contained in the culture pool—knowledge about values and history, skills as varied as an obligatory natural language or an optional mathematical one, as mute as levers or as articulate as myth telling.

Yet, it would be a mistake to leap to the conclusion that because human immaturity makes possible high flexibility, therefore anything is possible for the species. Human traits were selected for their survival value over a four- to five-million-year period with a great acceleration of the selection process during the last half of that period. There were crucial, irreversible changes during that final man-making period: recession of formidable dentition, 50-percent increase in brain volume, the obstetrical paradox—bipedalism and strong pelvic girdle, larger brain through a smaller birth canal—immature brain at birth, and creation of what Washburn has called a "technical-social way of life," involving tool and symbol use.

Note, however, that hominidization consisted principally of adaptations to conditions in the Pleistocene.

These preadaptations, shaped in response to earlier habitat demands, are part of man's evolutionary inheritance. This is not to say that close beneath the skin of man is a naked ape, that civilization is only a veneer. The technical-social way of life is a deep feature of the species adaptation. But we would err if we assumed *a priori* that man's inheritance placed no constraint on his power to adapt. Some of the preadaptations can be shown to be presently maladaptive. Man's inordinate fondness for fats and sweets no longer serves his individual survival well. And the human obsession with sexuality is plainly not fitted for survival of the species now, however well it might have served to populate the upper Pliocene and the Pleistocene. Nevertheless, note that the species responds typically to these challenges by technical innovation rather than by morphological or behavioral change. Contraception dissociates sexuality from reproduction. We do not, of course, know what kinds and what range of stresses are produced by successive rounds of such technical innovation. Dissociating sexuality and reproduction, for example, surely produces changes in the structure of the family, which in turn redefine the role of women, which in turn alters the authority pattern affecting the child, etc. Continuing and possibly accelerating change seems inherent in such adaptation. And this, of course, places an enormous pressure on man's uses of immaturity, preparing the young for unforeseeable change—the more so if there are severe restraints imposed by human preadaptations to earlier conditions of life.

7. The primary purpose of the passage is to
   (A) refute some misconceptions about the importance of human immaturity
   (B) introduce a new theory of the origins of the human species
   (C) describe the evolutionary forces that formed the physical appearance of modern humans
   (D) discuss the importance of human immaturity as an adaptive mechanism
   (E) outline the process by which humans mature into social beings

8. It can be inferred that the obstetrical paradox is puzzling because
   (A) it occurred very late during the evolution of the species
   (B) evolutionary forces seemed to work at cross purposes to each other
   (C) technological innovations have made the process of birth easier
   (D) an increase in brain size is not an ordinary evolutionary event
   (E) a strong pelvic girdle is no longer necessary to the survival of the species

GO ON TO THE NEXT PAGE

9. Which of the following statements can be inferred from the passage?

    (A) Human beings are today less sexually active than were our ancestors during the Pleistocene era.

    (B) During the Pleistocene era, a fondness for fats and sweets was a trait that contributed to survival of humans.

    (C) Mathematics was invented by human beings during the latter half of the Pleistocene era.

    (D) The use of language and tools is a trait that is genetically transmitted from one generation to the next.

    (E) During immaturity, human beings gain knowledge and learn skills primarily through the process of direct encounter.

10. The author uses the term *preadaptation* to describe traits that

    (A) were useful to earlier human beings but have since lost their utility

    (B) appeared in response to the need to learn a natural language and the use of tools

    (C) humans currently exhibit but that developed in response to conditions of an earlier age

    (D) are disadvantageous to creatures whose way of life is primarily technical and social

    (E) continue to exist despite evolutionary pressures that threaten to erase them

11. The author mentions contraception to demonstrate that

    (A) human beings may adapt to new conditions by technological invention rather than by changing their behavior

    (B) sexual promiscuity is no longer an aid to the survival of the human species

    (C) technological innovation is a more important adaptive mechanism than either heredity or direct encounter

    (D) conditions during the upper Pliocene and Pleistocene eras no longer affect the course of human evolution

    (E) morphological change is a common response to new demands placed on a creature by its environment

12. With which of the following statements would the author LEAST likely agree?

    (A) The technical-social way of life of humans is an adaptive mechanism that arose in response to environmental pressures.

    (B) The possibility of technical innovation makes it unlikely that the physical appearance of humans will change radically in a short time.

    (C) Technological innovations can result in changes in the social structures in which humans live.

    (D) New demands created by changes in the social structure are sometimes met by technological innovation.

    (E) The fact that humans have a technical-social way of life makes the species immune from evolutionary pressures.

13. The author is most probably addressing which of the following audiences?

    (A) Medical students in a course on human anatomy

    (B) College students in an introductory course on archaeology

    (C) Psychologists investigating the uses of human immaturity

    (D) Biologists trying to trace the course of human evolution

    (E) Linguists doing research on the origins of natural languages

The uniqueness of the Japanese character is the result of two, seemingly contradictory forces: the strength of traditions, and selective receptivity to foreign achievements and inventions. As early as the 1860s, there were counter movements to the traditional orientation. Yukichi Fukuzawa, the most eloquent spokesman of Japan's "Enlightenment," claimed "The Confucian civilization of the East seems to me to lack two things possessed by Western civilization: science in the material sphere and a sense of independence in the spiritual sphere." Fukuzawa's great influence is found in the free and individualistic philosophy of the Education Code of 1872, but he was not able to prevent the government from turning back to the canons of Confucian thought in the Imperial Rescript of 1890. Another interlude of relative liberalism followed World War I, when the democratic idealism of President Woodrow Wilson had an important impact on Japanese intellectuals and, especially, students; but more important was the Leninist ideology of the 1917 Bolshevik Revolution. Again, in the early 1930s, nationalism and militarism became dominant, largely as a result of failing economic conditions.

Following the end of World War II, substantial changes were undertaken in Japan to liberate the individual from authoritarian restraints. The new democratic value system was accepted by many teachers, students, intellectuals, and old liberals, but it was not immediately embraced by the society as a whole. Japanese traditions

GO ON TO THE NEXT PAGE

were dominated by group values, and notions of personal freedom and individual rights were unfamiliar.

Today, democratic processes are clearly evident in the widespread participation of the Japanese people in social and political life; yet, there is no universally accepted and stable value system. Values are constantly modified by strong infusions of Western ideas, both democratic and Marxist. School textbooks expound democratic principles, emphasizing equality over hierarchy and rationalism over tradition; but in practice these values are often misinterpreted and distorted, particularly by the youth who translate the individualistic and humanistic goals of democracy into egoistic and materialistic ones.

Most Japanese people have consciously rejected Confucianism, but vestiges of the old order remain. An important feature of relationships in many institutions such as political parties, large corporations, and university faculties is the *oyabun-kobun* or parent–child relation. A party leader, supervisor, or professor, in return for loyalty, protects those subordinate to him and takes general responsibility for their interests throughout their entire lives, an obligation that sometimes even extends to arranging marriages. The corresponding loyalty of the individual to his patron reinforces his allegiance to the group to which they both belong. A willingness to cooperate with other members of the group and to support without qualification the interests of the group in all its external relations is still a widely respected virtue. The *oyabun-kobun* creates ladders of mobility which an individual can ascend, rising as far as abilities permit, so long as he maintains successful personal ties with a superior in the vertical channel, the latter requirement usually taking precedence over a need for exceptional competence. As a consequence, there is little horizontal relationship between people even within the same profession.

14. Which of the following is most like the relationship of the *oyabun-kobun* described in the passage?

   (A) A political candidate and the voting public
   (B) A gifted scientist and his protégé
   (C) Two brothers who are partners in a business
   (D) A judge presiding at the trial of a criminal defendant
   (E) A leader of a musical ensemble who is also a musician in the group

15. According to the passage, Japanese attitudes are influenced by which of the following?

   I. Democratic ideals
   II. Elements of modern Western culture
   III. Remnants of an earlier social structure

   (A) I only   (B) II only   (C) I and II only
   (D) II and III only   (E) I, II, and III

16. The author implies that

   (A) decisions about promotions are often based on personal feelings
   (B) students and intellectuals do not understand the basic tenets of Western democracy
   (C) Western values have completely overwhelmed traditional Japanese attitudes
   (D) respect for authority was introduced into Japan following World War II
   (E) most Japanese workers are members of a single political party

17. In developing the passage, the author does which of the following?

   (A) Introduce an analogy
   (B) Define a term
   (C) Present statistics
   (D) Cite an authority
   (E) Issue a challenge

18. It can be inferred that the Imperial Rescript of 1890

   (A) was a protest by liberals against the lack of individual liberty in Japan
   (B) marked a return in government policies to conservative values
   (C) implemented the ideals set forth in the Education Code of 1872
   (D) was influenced by the Leninist ideology of the Bolshevik Revolution
   (E) prohibited the teaching of Western ideas in Japanese schools

19. Which of the following is the most accurate description of the organization of the passage?

   (A) A sequence of inferences in which the conclusion of each successive step becomes a premise in the next argument
   (B) A list of generalizations, most of which are supported by only a single example
   (C) A chronological analysis of historical events leading up to a description of the current situation
   (D) A statement of a commonly accepted theory that is then subjected to a critical analysis
   (E) An introduction of a key term that is then defined by giving examples

GO ON TO THE NEXT PAGE

20. Which of the following best states the central thesis of the passage?

    (A) The value system of Japan is based upon traditional and conservative values that have, in modern times, been modified by Western and other liberal values.
    (B) Students and radicals in Japan have used Leninist ideology to distort the meaning of democratic, Western values.
    (C) The notions of personal freedom and individual liberty did not find immediate acceptance in Japan because of the predominance of traditional group values.
    (D) Modern Japanese society is characterized by hierarchical relationships in which a personal tie to a superior is often more important than merit.
    (E) The influence on Japanese values of the American ideals of personal freedom and individual rights is less important than the influence of Leninist ideology.

21. The tone of the passage can best be described as

    (A) neutral and objective
    (B) disparaging and flippant
    (C) critical and demanding
    (D) enthusiastic and supportive
    (E) skeptical and questioning

In the 1950s, the development of antipsychotic drugs called neuroleptics radically changed the clinical outlook for patients in mental institutions who had previously been considered hopelessly psychotic. Daily medication controlled delusions and made psychotherapy possible. Many who otherwise might never have left institutions returned to society. Now physicians have learned that there is a price to be paid for these benefits. Approximately 10 to 15 percent of patients who undergo long-term treatment with antipsychotic drugs develop a cluster of symptoms called tardive dyskinesia, the most common symptoms of which are involuntary repetitive movement of the tongue, mouth, and face, and sometimes the limbs and trunk.

Neuroleptic drugs interfere with the action of dopamine, an important neurotransmitter in the brain, by binding to the dopamine receptors of nerve cells, and dopamine is a prime suspect in the pathophysiology of schizophrenia. Large doses of drugs such as amphetamines, which stimulate secretion of dopamine, produce a psychosis resembling schizophrenia. Reducing the activity of this neurotransmitter alleviates the delusions that cause psychotic behavior. Although the inhibition of dopamine activity can control psychotic behavior, researchers now believe that the central nervous system of some patients adapts to long-term therapy by increasing the number of specific dopamine binding sites. The net result is dopamine hypersensitivity, which is correlated with the subsequent appearance of tardive dyskinesia.

The risk of developing tardive dyskinesia is not so great that doctors have considered abandoning the use of antipsychotic drugs. Patients generally are bothered only slightly by the physical side effects, though the abnormal movements are troubling and may hinder social adjustment. Additionally, early diagnosis and prompt discontinuation of the neuroleptics might decrease the incidence of the movement disorders. Unfortunately, without neuroleptic drugs, psychotic behavior returns. So researchers have tried to achieve a satisfactory balance between the two effects, lowering dosages to a level that minimizes movement disorders yet controls psychosis. In a five-year study of twenty-seven psychiatric patients treated with neuroleptics representing all classes of antipsychotic drugs, researchers attempted to decrease drug doses to their lowest effective levels. Patient responses suggested that low to moderate doses of antipsychotic drugs could control psychoses just as well as high doses, and tardive dyskinesia symptoms stabilized and gradually diminished or completely disappeared.

The fact that psychoses can be controlled at the same time that tardive dyskinesia symptoms are reduced suggests that a drug more specifically affecting the mechanism of psychoses might not cause movement disorders. Sulpiride, a drug not available in the United States but widely used in Europe, where it was developed, may be one such alternative. The drug selectively blocks $D-2$ dopamine receptors, perhaps especially those in the limbic area of the brain, which is involved in emotion and behavior. It does not adversely affect the adenylate cyclase-linked $D-1$ dopamine receptors. Sulpiride has proven effective in the short term, but whether it suppresses tardive dyskinesia over a long period of treatment is not yet known.

22. Which of the following titles best describes the content of the passage?

    (A) The Therapeutic Value of Antipsychotic Drugs
    (B) The Tradeoff in the Use of Neuroleptic Drugs
    (C) The Connection between Psychotherapy and Neuroleptic Drugs
    (D) Recent Developments in the Treatment of Mental Illness
    (E) Techniques for Treating Tardive Dyskinesia

23. It can be inferred that neuroleptic drugs control psychosis by

    (A) suppressing the production of dopamine in the brain
    (B) blocking the nerve impulses transmitted to the muscles
    (C) preventing the absorption of dopamine by brain cells
    (D) creating a hypersensitivity to dopamine
    (E) counteracting the effect of other prescription drugs

GO ON TO THE NEXT PAGE

24. According to the passage, neuroleptic drugs are

    (A) generally effective but have unwanted side
        effects
    (B) gradually replacing psychotherapy
    (C) experimental and still not widely accepted
    (D) reserved for the most serious cases of psychosis
    (E) clinically effective but too expensive

25. It can be inferred that the primary danger of tardive
    dyskinesia is the

    (A) psychological effect on the patient
    (B) long-term therapeutic use of drugs
    (C) addiction of a patient to dopamine
    (D) physical injuries caused by violent muscle
        spasms
    (E) inability of the patient to remain in therapy

26. If a patient showed symptoms of tardive dyskinesia,
    a doctor would probably

    (A) discontinue the use of all antipsychotic drugs
    (B) increase the dosage of dopamine
    (C) confine the patient to an institution
    (D) reduce the dosage of any neuroleptic drug
    (E) recommend psychotherapy and counseling

27. The author cites the effects of large doses of drugs
    such as amphetamines in order to

    (A) demonstrate that dopamine may be the cause
        of some psychotic behavior
    (B) prove that neuroleptic drugs produce symp-
        toms of tardive dyskinesia
    (C) give an example of a neuroleptic drug that
        does not necessarily cause tardive dyskinesia
    (D) show that smaller dosages of neuroleptic
        drugs can effectively control psychotic behavior
    (E) persuade the reader that the drug sulpiride
        should be available in the United States

28. According to the passage, which of the following
    statements about D−2 dopamine receptors are true?

    I.   They are located only in the limbic area of the
         brain.
    II. Their functioning is affected by the drug sulpiride.
    III. They are responsible for initiating motor
         movements.

    (A) I only
    (B) II only
    (C) I and II only
    (D) II and III only
    (E) I, II, and III

IF YOU FINISH BEFORE TIME IS CALLED, YOU MAY CHECK YOUR WORK ON THIS SECTION ONLY. DO NOT WORK ON ANY OTHER SECTION IN THE TEST. **S T O P**

SECTION 2   Time—35 Minutes   In this section solve each problem, using any available space on the
             24 Questions   page for scratchwork. Then decide which is the best of the choices
                                given and fill in the corresponding oval on the answer sheet.

Directions: Each question or group of questions is based on a passage or set of conditions. In answering some of the questions, it may be useful to draw a rough diagram. For each question, select the best answer choice given.

Questions 1–6
A business executive must visit four clients in four different cities—Atlanta, Boston, Detroit, and Charleston—in a single week, Monday through Friday. She will visit only one client on any given day, and on one day she will return to her office in New York. Her schedule is subject to the following restrictions:

She cannot visit Atlanta until she has already visited both Boston and Detroit.

She cannot visit Charleston until she has visited Detroit and returned to her office in New York.

She will visit each city only once during the week.

1. Which of the following is an acceptable schedule for the visits, listed from left to right for Monday through Friday?

   (A) Atlanta, Charleston, New York, Detroit, Boston
   (B) Boston, Detroit, New York, Charleston, Atlanta
   (C) Charleston, Boston, Detroit, New York, Atlanta
   (D) New York, Charleston, Detroit, Boston, Atlanta
   (E) New York, Charleston, Atlanta, Detroit, Boston

   Which of the following cities could be visited on Thursday and Friday, respectively?

   (A) Atlanta and Charleston
   (B) Boston and Charleston
   (C) Charleston and Detroit
   (D) Detroit and Atlanta
   (E) Detroit and New York

3. If the executive visits Boston and New York on Monday and Tuesday, respectively, which of the following must be true?

   (A) On Wednesday she visits Atlanta.
   (B) On Wednesday she visits Detroit.
   (C) On Thursday she visits Atlanta.
   (D) On Thursday she visits Detroit.
   (E) On Friday she visits Charleston.

4. If the executive visits Charleston before Boston, then it must also be true that she visits

   (A) Atlanta before Detroit
   (B) Boston before Detroit
   (C) Charleston before Atlanta
   (D) Charleston before New York
   (E) Detroit before New York

5. Which of the following could be part of an acceptable schedule for the executive?

   (A) Atlanta on Monday
   (B) Boston on Thursday
   (C) Charleston on Tuesday
   (D) Detroit on Friday
   (E) New York on Friday

6. The one day of the week on which any of the five cities could be visited is

   (A) Monday   (B) Tuesday   (C) Wednesday
   (D) Thursday   (E) Friday

Questions 7–12
Six people—J, K, L, M, N, and O—are to be assigned to two three-person committees, according to the following conditions:

Each person will serve on one committee or the other.

N and O cannot serve on the same committee.

Whichever committee includes L must also include either J or K.

7. Which of the following groups of people could serve together on a committee?

   (A) J, K, N
   (B) J, K, O
   (C) J, L, K
   (D) K, N, O
   (E) L, K, O

GO ON TO THE NEXT PAGE

8. If L and O serve on the same committee, which of the following pairs must serve on the other committee?

(A) J and K
(B) J and M
(C) J and N
(D) K and N
(E) M and N

9. If M and O serve on one committee, which of the following pairs must serve on the other committee?

(A) J and L
(B) J and N
(C) K and L
(D) K and N
(E) L and N

10. Which of the following pairs CANNOT serve on the same committee?

(A) J and K
(B) J and M
(C) L and O
(D) M and N
(E) M and O

11. If J and M serve on different committees, which of the following must be true?
  I. M and K serve on the same committee.
  II. N and L serve on the same committee.
  III. J and N serve on the same committee.

(A) I only   (B) III only   (C) I and II only
(D) II and III only   (E) I, II, and III

12. If L and J serve on the same committee, which of the following must be true?
  I. M and K serve on the same committee.
  II. M and N serve on the same committee.
  III. J and O serve on the same committee.

(A) I only   (B) II only   (C) III only
(D) I and III only   (E) II and III only

Questions 13–19
A university committee consists of three students, J, K, and L, three faculty members, P, Q, and R, and two members of the administration, X and Y. The eight committee members are to be seated about a perfectly round table with eight equally spaced chairs. X chairs the meeting, and her chair is arbitrarily designated 1. The other chairs are numbered consecutively, from 2 to 8, in a clockwise direction. Seating must observe the following requirements:

No faculty member can be seated next to another faculty member.
K cannot be seated next to P.
L cannot be seated next to J or next to Q.

13. Which of the following is an acceptable seating arrangement for seats 2 through 8, respectively?

(A) J, K, P, Y, Q, R, L
(B) K, P, J, Q, L, R, Y
(C) L, J, Y, R, K, Q, P
(D) P, L, R, K, Q, Y, J
(E) P, L, Q, J, Y, R, K

14. All of the following are acceptable seating arrangements for seats 2 through 8, respectively, EXCEPT

(A) J, Y, P, R, K, L, Q
(B) K, Q, J, P, Y, R, L
(C) L, K, R, Y, P, J, Q
(D) K, L, P, J, R, Y, Q
(E) Y, P, L, R, J, Q, K

15. If P is seated in seat 4 and J is seated in seat 6, then who must be seated in seat 5?

(A) K (B) L (C) Q (D) R (E) Y

16. If J is seated in seat 5 and Q is seated in seat 6 and no faculty member is seated directly across from another faculty member, then which of the following must be true?

(A) Seat 2 is occupied by L.
(B) Seat 3 is occupied by P.
(C) Seat 4 is occupied by K.
(D) Seat 7 is occupied by Y.
(E) Seat 8 is occupied by R.

17. If both P and R are seated in even-numbered seats and no faculty member is seated directly across from another faculty member, which of the following must be true?

(A) J is seated in an odd-numbered seat.
(B) K is seated in an odd-numbered seat.
(C) Q is seated in an odd-numbered seat.
(D) L is seated in an even-numbered seat.
(E) Q is seated in an even-numbered seat.

18. If K is seated in seat 3 and L is seated in seat 5 and no faculty member is seated directly across from another faculty member, then the correct seating pattern for seats 2, 4, 6, 7, and 8, respectively, is

(A) J, R, Y, P, Q
(B) P, R, Y, Q, J
(C) Q, R, Y, P, J
(D) R, Q, Y, P, J
(E) Y, Q, R, P, J

GO ON TO THE NEXT PAGE

19. If *J* and *L* are seated directly opposite each other, then *J* cannot be seated in seat

(A) 2 (B) 3 (C) 4 (D) 5 (E) 6

Questions 20-24

Six different sales representatives—Bradey, Daniels, Fowler, Gibson, Martin, and Wright—are all employed by the same company, and each representative receives both a salary and commissions. These are their only sources of compensation. During a certain week:

The amount earned by Bradey in commissions was equal to the amount Wright earned in salary, and the amount earned by Wright in commissions was equal to the amount Bradey earned in salary.

Daniels earned $200 in salary, and Bradey earned $100 more in commissions than Daniels earned in salary.

Martin earned $50 more in salary than Fowler earned in commissions, and Gibson earned $100 more in commissions than Martin earned in salary.

Wright earned $100 more in commissions than Bradey.

20. How much did Wright earn in commissions?

(A) $50 (B) $200 (C) $300
(D) $400 (E) $700

21. Which of the following statements can be inferred from the information given above?

I. Gibson earned $150 more in commissions than Fowler did.
II. Martin earned more in salary than Wright earned in commissions.
III. Bradey earned more in salary than in commissions.

(A) I only (B) I and II only
(C) I and III only (D) II and III only
(E) I, II, and III

22. If Martin earned $300 in commissions, an amount twice what he earned in salary, then which of the following must be true?

(A) Martin earned more in salary than Fowler did.
(B) Martin earned more in salary than Wright did.
(C) Martin earned more in commissions that Daniels did.
(D) Daniels earned less in salary than Gibson earned in commissions.
(E) Bradey earned less in salary than Martin earned in commissions.

23. If Gibson and Wright each earned the same amount in commissions, then which of the following must be true?

I. Fowler earned $250 in commissions.
II. Martin earned $300 in salary.
III. Daniels earned $150 in salary.

(A) I only (B) II only (C) I and II only
(D) II and III only (E) I, II, and III

24. If the amount earned by Fowler in commissions was $150 more than the amount earned by Daniels in salary, then which of the following must be true?

I. The amount earned by Martin in salary was equal to the amount earned by Bradey in salary.
II. The amount earned by Wright in salary was equal to the amount earned by Fowler in commissions.
III. The amount earned by Martin in commissions was equal to the amount earned by Wright in commissions.
IV. The amount earned by Wright in commissions was equal to the amount earned by Gibson in commissions.

(A) I only (B) I and IV only (C) III and IV only
(D) II, III, and IV only (E) I, II, III, and IV

Directions: The questions in this section require you to follow or evaluate the reasoning contained in brief statements or passages. In some questions, each of the choices is a conceivable solution to the particular problem posed. However, you are to select the one that answers the question best, that is, the one that does not require you to make what are by common-sense standards implausible, superfluous, or incompatible assumptions. After you have chosen the best answer, blacken the corresponding space on the answer sheet.

The editor of a newspaper received the following letter:

Dear Editor:

This holiday season I think we should make a serious effort to recapture the true spirit of giving. Each of us should resolve to give gifts and expect none. And if someone offers us a gift, we should refuse it and suggest that it be given to someone else. In this way, we would all experience a feeling of pure giving.

1. Which of the following statements points out the most serious logical flaw in the letter?

(A) If no one accepted any gifts, it would be impossible for anyone to give a gift.
(B) The holiday season is not the only time of year when people give and receive gifts.
(C) Often people receive gifts that are really not very useful, so it would not be a great sacrifice to part with them.
(D) Sometimes a person may make a gift to someone in the hope of later receiving something in exchange for it.
(E) Gift-giving is a tradition that is thousands of years old and a characteristic of virtually every human community.

Recently credit card companies have come under attack by consumer groups who argue that the interest rates charged by these companies are unconscionably high. In fact, the rates are generally several percentage points above those charged by banks for ordinary personal loans. But consumer groups overlook the fact that credit cards afford the user great flexibility. A user can purchase an item while it is on sale. So the lower cost of the item offsets the extra cost of the credit.

2. The argument above makes which of the following assumptions?

(A) The cost savings of buying an item at a reduced price are at least equal to the excess interest that a consumer pays on purchases made with a credit card.
(B) A credit card application is not rejected unless the applicant has a long history of late payments and other credit problems.
(C) The prices of items on sale purchased by consumers are still sufficiently high to enable sellers to recoup their costs and make a modest profit.
(D) The consumers who make purchases of sale items with credit cards are persons who might not qualify for bank loans with a lower interest rate.
(E) The average outstanding balance of the ordinary credit card user is no greater than the total non-credit-card debt of the credit card user.

Bob and Cindy are each older than both Diane and Ellen.

3. If the statement above is true, then which of the following additional statements ensures the truth of the conclusion "Allen is older than Ellen"?

(A) Allen is younger than Bob.
(B) Cindy is older than Bob.
(C) Cindy is younger than Bob.
(D) Allen is older than Diane.
(E) Allen is older than Cindy.

GO ON TO THE NEXT PAGE

Despite seductive advertisements, so-called low tar and nicotine cigarettes are really no safer than other cigarettes. The seemingly lower levels of tar and nicotine reported by the Federal Trade Commission are attributable to the FTS use of smoking machines, not human beings, to determine tar and nicotine levels. But people do not smoke like machines. A study of blood samples of smokers found no significant differences among smokers of the various brands and a direct relationship between nicotine intake and the number of cigarettes smoked, regardless of brand.

4. Someone wishing to defend a low tar and nicotine cigarette as a safer smoking alternative could point out that

   (A) most people who smoke give little consideration to the health risks involved in smoking
   (B) in confined spaces the health of even non-smokers is endangered by tobacco smoke
   (C) a smoker could choose to make his smoking habits similar to the methods of the testing machines
   (D) most cigarette companies offer smokers several different brands, including low tar and nicotine cigarettes
   (E) cigarette companies are required by law to include tar and nicotine content on the labels of cigarette packages

Many countries that rely on the United States for military assistance request the same sophisticated weapons systems used by United States forces. But experience shows the folly of this policy. Because their armed forces lack the training and parts needed to maintain them, the weapons systems are often totally ineffective when installed or become ineffective shortly thereafter.

5. The problem described above is most like which of the following situations?

   (A) An antique car collector who purchases two old sports cars of the same model and cannibalizes one for spare parts for the other.
   (B) A business corporation that decides to lease a fleet of cars rather than purchase them with the understanding that the leasing company will service and repair them.
   (C) A university physics professor who hires graduate students to do research work but finds that she must first train them in their new duties.
   (D) A parent who purchases a personal computer for a child's education only to find that the available software is too complex for the child to use.
   (E) A captain of a large ship who is forced to return to port for repairs after an accident caused by a failure of the ship's radar.

Dr. Esterhaus is an extremely competent administrator. In the twelve months following her appointment as Chief Executive Officer of the History Department, the number of applications for admission to the program was nearly 150 above that of the previous year.

6. The reasoning above makes which of the following assumptions?

   I. The increase in the number of applications for admissions is attributable to Dr. Esterhaus' efforts.
   II. Dr. Esterhaus is well-respected in the academic community as a history scholar.
   III. The number of applications for admission to a program is a good measure of the effectiveness of the Chief Executive Officer.

   (A) I only   (B) II only   (C) III only
   (D) I and III   (E) I, II, and III

The recent 40-percent reduction in airfares represents an attempt by the airlines to encourage impulse traveling. Because the lower-fare tickets need to be purchased only two days in advance of the flight, the companies hope to increase volume, thereby boosting overall revenues. The policy is ill-conceived, however, because business travelers, who would normally pay full fare, will now purchase discount fares, thus depressing revenues.

7. Which of the following, if true, would most weaken the argument above?

   (A) Some people would prefer to pay a higher fare if the additional cost ensured better schedules and service.
   (B) The number of business travelers who will purchase discount tickets is greater than the number of additional passengers who will be attracted by the lower fares.
   (C) An airplane must be operated at or near capacity for the airline to show a profit on a particular flight.
   (D) Impulse travelers are persons whose schedules are highly flexible and who are anxious to find lower fares.
   (E) Most business travelers must arrange their travel schedules more than two days in advance.

GO ON TO THE NEXT PAGE

The United States Postal Service is drowning in junk mail. The average postal carrier delivers more junk mail, or third-class letters, than first-class mail. The result is a rapid decline in the quality of all postal services because first-class mail in effect subsidizes third-class mail.

8. Which of the following, if true, would most strengthen the argument above?

(A) It costs twice as much to mail a first-class letter as a third-class letter, yet per piece handling cost for each is the same.

(B) Members of the postal workers union have opposed deregulation of third-class delivery services because such a move threatens the jobs of postal workers.

(C) Since private companies were allowed to compete with the Postal Service for overnight letter business, the Postal Service's share of that market fell off by 60 percent.

(D) The cost of first-class postage has risen at a rate twice that of inflation while the delivery time for first-class mail has increased by 10 percent.

(E) An audit conducted by the General Accounting Office revealed that 80 percent of all first-class letters are delivered within five days of postmark while only 20 percent of all third-class mail is delivered within five days of postmark.

Questions 9–10

Negative consumer reaction to a product is not generated solely by critical negative appraisal of a product's performance. Rather, negative reaction is generated by a perceived gap between consumer expectation and product performance. Businesses should use advertising to adjust consumer expectations to coincide with their products' performances.

9. Which of the following is (are) implied by the passage above?

   I. If consumer expectations are sufficiently reduced, then negative consumer reaction to products will disappear even though product performance remains unchanged.

   II. If product performances are sufficiently improved, negative consumer reaction to products will disappear no matter how high expectations remain.

   III. When consumer expectations about product performance increase, negative consumer reaction may persist despite improvements in product performance.

(A) I only   (B) III only   (C) I and III only
(D) II and III only   (E) I, II, and III

10. Which of the following, if true, would most weaken the argument above?

(A) Most consumers are able to make informed judgments about the actual performance of the products they purchase.

(B) The expectations of most consumers are influenced to a large extent by the claims made for those products by the manufacturers.

(C) Unless consumer expectations about a product are sufficiently high, consumers will not purchase that product.

(D) Government agencies prosecute businesses that make fraudulent advertising claims about product performances.

(E) Most consumers purchase products based upon their recognition of a particular brand name, not on a critical evaluation of the product's past performance.

The bills produced by a truly great counterfeiter are never discovered. So a counterfeiter whose product has been learned to be fraudulent is not a very good counterfeiter. The truly great ones never get caught.

11. Which of the following arguments supports its conclusion in the same way as the argument above?

(A) This government agency has been infiltrated by spies from a foreign power. The three who were caught have given the names of several other spies.

(B) A reliable security guard always patrols his or her assigned territory. Ellen, who is a security guard, did not patrol her assigned territory. Therefore, Ellen is not a good security guard.

(C) Drug usage is on the increase. Over the past few years, drug enforcement agents have arrested more and more people attempting to smuggle drugs into the country.

(D) The CIA is accused of bungling its attempted covert operations in several foreign countries. But this is not fair to the CIA. The agency conducts many successful covert operations; but by definition, a successful covert operation never comes to light, so the agency cannot take credit for them.

(E) The state legislature should pass a law requiring all restaurants with a seating capacity of a certain minimum to set aside a section for nonsmokers. There is ample scientific evidence that passive smoking is harmful to nonsmokers.

GO ON TO THE NEXT PAGE

Production of chlorofluorocarbons (CFCs) is believed to cause the breakdown of fragile ozone molecules in the Earth's atmosphere. During the 1970s, when production of CFCs was high, especially in the United States, scientists found that the quantity of ozone in the atmosphere dropped by an average of about 2 percent. In 1981, a ban on the use of CFCs in aerosol spray cans went into effect in the United States. In 1986, new measurements showed that ozone levels in the atmosphere had fallen by another 1 percent as compared to 1981.

12. Which of the following, if true, could help provide an explanation for this finding?

    I. Production of CFCs in Japan and Western Europe rose sharply between 1981 and 1986.
    II. Climatic changes occurring during the early 1980s have contributed to the breakdown of atmospheric ozone.
    III. During the early 1980s, several new and important uses were found for CFCs.

    (A) I only　(B) III only　(C) I and III only
    (D) II and III only　(E) I, II, and III

In a study of crime, it was estimated that over 60 percent of all major property crimes—auto thefts, burglaries, and robberies—in the city during 1986 were committed by a group of 350 persistent offenders. It was also found that over half of the major property crimes were committed by individuals who were addicted to drugs.

13. If the statements above are true, which of the following must also be true?

    (A) Some of the 350 persistent offenders in the city are also drug addicts.
    (B) All of the 350 persistent offenders in the city are also drug addicts.
    (C) Most drug addicts eventually become persistent offenders.
    (D) Most persistent offenders became criminals because they were drug addicts.
    (E) Persistent offenders and drug addicts do not commit crimes other than major property crimes.

During the past ten years, the number of semiconductors manufactured by the United States semiconductor industry has grown by 200 percent, but the number of semiconductors manufactured by the Japanese semiconductor industry has grown by 500 percent. Therefore, Japan now produces more semiconductors than the United States.

14. Which of the following, if true, most weakens the argument above?

    (A) In the past five years, the number of semiconductors manufactured by the United States semiconductor industry has grown by only 100 percent.
    (B) The dollar value of the semiconductors produced in the United States over the past ten years was greater than the dollar value of semiconductors produced in Japan during the same time.
    (C) Exports of semiconductors today represent a higher proportion of total United States exports than they did ten years ago.
    (D) Ten years ago, the United States produced 90 percent of the world's semiconductors while Japan produced only 2 percent.
    (E) Ten years ago, Japan ranked fourth in the world in the production of semiconductors while the United States ranked first.

Government spending on education does not really benefit students. During the 1960s and 1970s, spending by the federal government on education programs rose by over 150 percent. During the same period, students' scores on standardized tests dropped nearly every year.

15. The argument above depends upon which of the following assumptions?

    (A) The scores students achieve on standardized examinations are a good measure of the effectiveness of educational programs.
    (B) During the 1960s and 1970s, progressively more students were able to take advantage of federally funded educational programs.
    (C) The proportion of the United States population classified as students did not increase appreciably during the 1960s and 1970s.
    (D) The money spent by the federal government on educational programs during the 1960s and 1970s could have been better spent on health and welfare programs.
    (E) The number of college graduates who chose teaching as a profession declined during the 1960s and 1970s.

GO ON TO THE NEXT PAGE

16. Which of the following arguments is directed against the proponent of an idea rather than against the idea itself?

   (A) Allowing the Soviet Union to join our nation in peacekeeping efforts in the Middle East will serve only to increase the Soviet profile there and strengthen the hand of the communists in a vital region of the world.

   (B) Advocates of capital punishment argue that the fear of the death penalty will frighten potential criminals sufficiently to deter them from committing crimes, but the proponents of the death penalty fail to recognize that statistics demonstrate that the death penalty actually does nothing to deter crime.

   (C) Free trade must not be a one-way street. Before the United States drops its barriers against imports, our trading partners must offer firm guarantees that they will do the same. Otherwise, our balance of trade will suffer greatly.

   (D) The voters should reject the bond issue proposed to finance the new, multi-million-dollar sports complex. The mayor would never have proposed this project were it not that real estate developers are among the chief contributors to his campaigns.

   (E) Much of the money spent on defense projects is wasteful. First, a lot of money is spent by the different services working on essentially the same projects. Second, defense contractors understand that government audits rarely uncover overbilling, so the contractors routinely submit inflated demands for payment.

It is essential that school children learn important facts about their country's history, and it may be salutary for them to learn, in time, of its follies and misdeeds, so as not to repeat them. But it is important, above all, for the very young to learn something of their nation's heroes; for only in this way are the virtues that make us fully human transmitted from one generation to the next.

17. The speaker above would most likely agree with which of the following statements?

   (A) Children should first be taught about the positive aspects of their country's history and only later about the negative aspects of its history.

   (B) The school system should not provide information to students about historical incidents which might be considered to have been mistakes.

   (C) The development of moral virtue and civic character is a task for the classroom rather than for the parents in the home.

   (D) Writers of histories for children should strive for a well-balanced and objective presentation of historical facts.

   (E) The primary function of the educational system is the inculcation of moral and social values.

Local governments frequently offer tax incentives, changes in zoning restrictions, and the loosening of environmental regulations to large local corporations in an effort to keep these firms from relocating, thereby hoping to maintain employment possibilities for its citizens. Yet most new jobs today are created not by large corporations but by smaller, new ones, and these are the firms most likely to be hurt by burdensome taxes and government regulations. Therefore, the inducements offered to large corporations ultimately hurt local economies.

18. Which of the following, if true, would most weaken the argument above?

   (A) Large corporations provide considerably more job opportunities than those created by smaller enterprises.

   (B) Most small businesses fail during the first year because their owners lack needed managerial experience.

   (C) The federal government's Small Business Administration offers low-cost loans and other services for newly created small businesses.

   (D) The economic growth of the country as a whole depends more upon the success or failure of the largest corporations than it does upon the success or failure of small businesses.

   (E) Tax breaks and other economic incentives help small businesses survive for a longer period than they would otherwise remain economically viable.

This last season, the Youth League baseball team sponsored by Cantrell Bootery included four players who pitched, seven who played the outfield, five who played the infield, and three who played catcher. The league rules state that a player may not play more than one position during a game and that a player must play the entire game unless injured. From these figures, we can conclude that the Cantrell Bootery team included nineteen different players.

19. Which of the following, if true, most seriously weakens the conclusion above?

   (A) When a player is injured during a game, a substitute may be provided.

   (B) Some players on the Cantrell Bootery did not play in every game during the season.

   (C) The number of players on a Youth League team may fluctuate during the course of the season.

   (D) A particular player in the league may play different positions in different games.

   (E) According to league rules, only nine players may be on the playing field at any one time.

GO ON TO THE NEXT PAGE

Whenever possible, our nation's founders reserved political powers to state and local governments. Their assumption was that the officers in these governments, being chosen by smaller and more geographically compact bodies of citizens, would be "closer" to the people and more responsive to their interests. However, in today's era of mass media and national broadcast coverage of politics, most citizens are better informed about government on the national level than they are about local governments. Consequently, corrupt or incompetent public officials are more likely to thrive at the state and local levels.

20. The argument above assumes that
   (A) voters are generally incapable of understanding local issues
   (B) the mass media are usually eager to publicize charges of governmental corruption and incompetence
   (C) state and local officials are likely to be more honest and competent than those at the national level
   (D) the founders were unaware of the extent of the corruption and incompetence that characterized their own local governments
   (E) citizen awareness is likely to help deter or reduce corruption and incompetence in government

Proponents of the use of air bags in automobiles claim that these units, designed to inflate automatically in case of a crash, can cushion passengers against the impact of the collision, thereby saving lives. They say that, like seat belts, air bags should be required in every new car. Opponents argue that air bags would add hundreds of dollars to the cost of a new car, putting domestic producers at a competitive disadvantage, since foreign producers are not required by their governments to include the air-bag safety feature.

21. Which of the following, if true, most weakens the argument given above by the opponents of the air-bag requirement?

   (A) A majority of drivers polled responded that they believe that air bags offer no additional safety advantage over that already provided by seat belts.
   (B) In nine out of ten automobile accidents, the use of a seat belt significantly reduces the risk of serious injury or death.
   (C) In manufacturers' tests of air bags, the air bags spontaneously inflated on the average about once every 350,000 miles.
   (D) A law requiring domestic manufacturers to include air bags could also require that all cars imported into the country also be equipped with air bags.
   (E) The lobbyists for the automobile industry have thus far been successful in convincing certain powerful figures in the legislature to veto any proposed air-bag legislation.

The average salary of major league baseball players is so high because they represent the cream of their profession, the very best among the many thousands of aspiring baseball players produced in this country each year. The salaries of major leaguers should be compared, not with those of typical businesspeople, doctors, or lawyers, but with only the top business executives, the finest surgeons, or the partners of leading law firms.

22. The author is most likely trying to make which of the following points?

   (A) Playing baseball at the major league level requires the same kinds of skills required of highly paid business executives, doctors, and lawyers.
   (B) In a market economy, the price paid for any good or service is subject to the laws of supply and demand.
   (C) The salaries of major league baseball players are not overly inflated when compared to those of other highly skilled professionals.
   (D) The services provided by professional baseball players are as important to the team as those provided by executives, doctors, and lawyers are to their businesses, patients, and clients.
   (E) Baseball players who seek to maximize their compensation are responding to the same economic pressures that motivate business executives, doctors, and lawyers.

GO ON TO THE NEXT PAGE

Questions 23–24

According to a recent study, the gap between the average starting salaries of teachers and those of other professionals has shrunk in recent years. Among ten other professions requiring comparable levels of education, teaching ranked ninth in starting salaries in 1975; today, it ranks sixth. Moreover, the average starting salary for a teacher is now 82 percent of the average for the other professionals included in the study. Therefore, it can no longer be argued that starting teachers are underpaid.

23. The argument above depends upon which of the following assumptions?

    (A) The extent of a person's formal education is an appropriate measure by which to determine the level of his salary.

    (B) The purchasing power of the dollars paid to teachers has not changed significantly since 1975.

    (C) The average age of first-year teachers is the same today as it was in 1975.

    (D) The profession with the highest average starting salary today is the same profession with the highest average starting salary in 1975.

    (E) The average starting salary for a teacher should be equal to the average starting salary in the highest-paid profession.

24. Which of the following conclusions can be most reliably inferred from the passage above?

    (A) Eighty-two percent of teachers earn more than the average salary of other professionals.

    (B) Starting salaries for teachers have grown more quickly since 1975 than those of any other professionals.

    (C) The salaries of teachers may soon be expected to equal those of most other professionals.

    (D) Teachers today earn starting salaries less than those earned by some other professionals with comparable levels of education.

    (E) The dollar increase in teachers' salaries since 1975 has been greater than those of most other professionals.

The Bill of Rights establishes freedom of speech as an absolute value which may not be abridged by any actions of the government. In interpreting and applying this provision of the Constitution, the courts have wisely held that exceptions to this rule must be rare, chiefly occurring under clearly defined circumstances in which unlimited freedom of speech would pose a clear and immediate danger to the safety of society at large.

25. The author of the statement above would most likely agree with which of the following?

    (A) Freedom of speech may reasonably be restricted to those forms of speech generally judged by the courts to be beneficial to society as a whole.

    (B) The absolute protection of freedom of speech set forth in the Constitution must be modified in certain situations.

    (C) The courts have usurped the power to determine what will and will not be considered "protected speech" under the Constitution.

    (D) Freedom of speech is the single most important guarantee included in the Bill of Rights.

    (E) Government will always tend to abridge freedom of speech unless legal impediments exist to prevent it from doing so.

IF YOU FINISH BEFORE TIME IS CALLED, YOU MAY CHECK YOUR WORK ON THIS SECTION ONLY. DO NOT WORK ON ANY OTHER SECTION IN THE TEST. **S T O P**

Sid is traveling in the land of Sasnak. His destination is Nocam, but he has encountered a fork in the road and doesn't know which route leads to his destination. In the land of Sasnak there are two clans; members of one clan always speak the truth, while members of the other clan always speak the opposite of the truth. It is impossible to tell who is a member of which clan simply by looking at them. At the fork is a man, and Sid wants to ask him for directions.

1. The answer to which of the following questions, if asked by Sid, will ensure that Sid will find the right road?

   I. Is the left fork the road to Nocam?
   II. If I asked you whether the left fork is the road to Nocam, would you tell the truth?
   III. If I asked you whether the left fork is the road to Nocam, would you say yes?

(A) II only   (B) III only   (C) I and III only
(D) II and III only   (E) I, II, and III

Questions 2 and 3

(A) City Council member Ruth Jerome has introduced a proposal for commercial rent control that would limit the increases landlords can charge to small businesses. Of course, Ms. Jerome would favor such a plan because she and her husband own two small grocery stores.

(B) On each of the three occasions I met John, he was wearing a hat. The first time it was a derby, the second time it was a beret, and the third time it was a baseball cap. I conclude, therefore, that John always wears a hat of some sort.

(C) Mary has suggested that the Clippers finished in fifth place last season because they scored too few runs during the season. In fact, the Clippers' total run production for the season was the second highest in the league. So the Clippers failed to do better than fifth because their defense was inadequate.

(D) Eighty-seven percent of the voters surveyed thought that Mr. Herman's views on foreign policy were better than those of Mr. Smith, and 91 percent thought Mr. Herman's views

on domestic policy superior to those of Mr. Smith. On this basis, we can conclude that Mr. Herman is likely to make a better senator than Mr. Smith.

(E) It is sometimes argued that the best way to stop drug-related crime is to legalize all drugs. But that's like giving away money to bank robbers and pickpockets.

2. Which of the arguments above relies upon a questionable analogy?

3. Which of the arguments above attacks the credibility of a person rather than the merits of a proposal?

Jorge: To be a good carpenter, one must have patience.
   Gloria: That's not so; a good carpenter must also have the right tools.

4. Gloria has understood Jorge's statement to mean that

(A) if a person is a good carpenter, she will have the right tools
(B) if a person is a good carpenter, she will have patience
(C) if a person has patience, she will be a good carpenter
(D) if a person has the right tools, she will be a good carpenter
(E) if a person does not have the right tools, she cannot be a good carpenter

GO ON TO THE NEXT PAGE

The country of West Umberland imports no copper. Private industry's use of copper in West Umberland equals 85 percent of the amount of copper produced by the country's mines each year, while government use of copper equals 23 percent of the amount of copper produced by the country's mines each year.

5. If the information above is true, then which of the following conclusions can most reliably be drawn?

(A) West Umberland imports copper ore from other countries.
(B) Some copper in West Umberland is recycled.
(C) West Umberland's industry wastes substantial amounts of copper.
(D) Copper is in short supply in West Umberland.
(E) Each year, West Umberland produces more copper than the previous year.

At a time when New York City is going through a budgetary crisis, it is cutting its funding of the one agency that helps put more than half a billion dollars into its coffers: the Convention and Visitors Bureau. The proposed $1 million cut comes on the heels of last year's $250,000 funding cut. The debilitating effect of that cut is now obvious. Hotel occupancy rates shrank by 7 percent over last year, resulting in $10 million in taxes not realized by the city.

6. Which of the following, if true, would most weaken the argument above?

(A) New York City spends less than other less populated cities such as Louisville and Dayton to attract visitors and conventions.
(B) The proposed $1 million cut in the budget of the Convention and Visitors Bureau's budget would do little to help balance the city's budget.
(C) The entire country is experiencing an economic downturn, and during an economic downturn people travel less than during times of prosperity.
(D) Adverse publicity about the crime rate in New York discourages some people and organizations from visiting the city.
(E) Many people and organizations would visit New York City even if it were not for the public relations efforts of the Convention and Visitors Bureau.

Within a scheme of criminal penalties, some penalties are more severe than others. A logical consequence of this hierarchy is that one penalty must be the most severe or ultimate penalty. Since the death penalty is the ultimate penalty, we can see that the death penalty is justified as a matter of logic.

7. Which of the following observations most weakens the argument above?

(A) Not everyone believes that the death penalty is effective in deterring crime.
(B) Some people incorrectly convicted of a crime might receive the death penalty.
(C) The most severe penalty in a system of punishments could be something other than the death penalty.
(D) For a person serving a life sentence with no chance of parole, only the death penalty is greater punishment.
(E) No two punishments can be ranked equally severe in their effects on a person.

Gloria's office is in Atlanta, but she must spend most of her time traveling. Every time I get a card from her, it has been mailed from some other city where she is staying on business.

8. It can be inferred from the passage above that Gloria

(A) does not work in Atlanta
(B) sends cards frequently
(C) does not write letters
(D) travels only on business
(E) has offices in other cities

Advocates for the homeless attempt to portray homeless persons as victims of social and economic circumstances beyond their control. A recent survey of the homeless in major cities found that a high percentage are addicted to alcohol or other drugs. Rather than innocent victims, these are people who are solely responsible for their own plights.

9. Which of the following, if true, would most weaken the argument above?

(A) A large number of homeless persons turn to drugs and alcohol out of despair after becoming homeless.
(B) Several government programs are designed to help the homeless find jobs and new housing.
(C) Most cities offer shelter to the homeless on a night-by-night basis.
(D) Alcoholism and other drug addictions can cause erratic and even violent behavior.
(E) As much as 60 percent of any community's homeless population are local people.

GO ON TO THE NEXT PAGE

434

New York and several other states have wisely refused to raise the highway speed limit above 55 miles per hour despite calls by motorists for an increase. Although the 55-mile-per-hour speed limit was initially enacted by the Federal government as a conservation measure, it soon became clear that a felicitous consequence of the measure was considerably fewer traffic fatalities.

10. The speaker above is arguing that states that have a 55-mile-per-hour highway speed limit should

    (A) raise the highway speed limit
    (B) further reduce the highway speed limit
    (C) retain the 55-mile-per-hour highway speed limit
    (D) enact other measures to improve fuel conservation
    (E) find other ways of reducing highway fatalities

The quality of life provided by a government depends not so much upon its formal structure as upon the ability and temperament of those who serve as its officers.

11. The author of the paragraph above would most likely agree with which of the following statements?

    (A) A written constitution is essential to ensure the liberty of citizens against a strong government.
    (B) Universal suffrage is the best guarantee that the general will of the people will become legislation.
    (C) A government with good leaders is likely to survive for a longer time than a government with incompetent leaders.
    (D) Poor leadership in a hierarchical organization threatens the ability of the organization to achieve results.
    (E) The quality of the leadership of a government is the main determinant of whether the citizens will be happy.

Your chart listing winners of the Most Valuable Player award states that one designated hitter won the award: Don Baylor in 1979. This is erroneous. No designated hitter has ever won the M.V.P., and it is extremely doubtful that a player who does not serve the team in the field will ever win it.

12. Which of the following, if true, would most strengthen the argument above?

    (A) In 1979, Don Baylor played one game as first baseman.
    (B) In 1979, Don Baylor played 97 games as an outfielder versus 65 as a designated hitter.
    (C) Don Baylor won the Most Valuable Player award only once in his career.
    (D) Of the two major baseball leagues, only the American League allows the use of a designated hitter.
    (E) The Most Valuable Player award can be given to any player on the team.

"Most people like pennies," says Hamilton Dix, spokesperson for the United States Mint. "In March 1986 we did a survey at the Epcot Center at Walt Disney World, and half of all the adults said they use pennies daily."

13. Which of the following observations most undermines the position of the speaker above?

    (A) Most of the people who visit Walt Disney World are on vacation.
    (B) The survey covered people only at a single location in one state.
    (C) The survey included adults visiting Epcot Center but not children.
    (D) The speaker is a representative of the agency that manufactures pennies.
    (E) Many purchases require the use of pennies either as payment or as change.

As a citizen who values individual rights, I am appalled at the growing use of random or mandatory drug testing. What is needed is a screening test for impaired function, not for drug use per se. For example, it would be easy to design a computerized test for reaction time. Such a test should be simple to administer and would be nonintrusive. Anyone failing the test could then be required to submit to the more invasive drug test.

14. Which of the following, if true, would most weaken the argument above?

    (A) Administrations of a reaction test could be arranged randomly, so that a drug-user could not alter his or her habits.
    (B) A reaction test measures capacity only at that time, but a drug test may show that a person is likely to be a future risk.
    (C) The Supreme Court has refused to rule that mandatory drug tests for employees in sensitive positions are unconstitutional.
    (D) A person might fail a reaction test for a reason other than impairment due to the use of illegal drugs.
    (E) A person who has ingested an illegal substance might have sufficient self-control to pass a reaction test.

GO ON TO THE NEXT PAGE

Computer colorization of black-and-white film is an important tool for making historical events seem real to students who live in an age of color movies and color television. A colorized version of the footage of Jack Ruby's assassination of Lee Harvey Oswald or of the first manned space shot will help students today understand what it was like for the millions of Americans who actually saw those events on television.

15. Which of the following, if true, most weakens the conclusion of the argument above?

(A) The people who saw those events live saw them in black and white, not in color.
(B) The events mentioned occurred before most of today's students were born.
(C) Many important historical events were never recorded on film.
(D) Modern techniques can improve the quality of the sound of old film footage.
(E) Colorization can be accomplished by a computer process that is relatively inexpensive.

Five United States representatives are jointly sponsoring a bill that would provide federal funds to municipalities that will replace steps to public buildings with ramps in order to provide greater access to disabled persons. This is another example of a proposal to use public funds to provide advantages to some special-interest group while burdening the general public.

16. Which of the following observations would most weaken the conclusion of the argument above?

(A) Although a disabled person may not be able to use steps, both disabled and nondisabled people can use a ramp.
(B) The funds would be made available to all states and districts and not just to those represented by the bill's sponsors.
(C) An audit of government programs by an independent citizens' watchdog group uncovered billions of dollars spent for special-interest groups.
(D) Congressional lobbyists for associations representing disabled persons have alleged that the bill is underfunded.
(E) The federal funds will be available only on a matching basis to states and cities which provide funds of their own.

For over a week, we have been listening to news reports of the "heroic" efforts to save the two whales trapped in the arctic ice. Thousands of working hours were invested by Eskimos cutting a path through the ice, and icebreaking ships were called in at a cost of hundreds of thousands of dollars. Why spend a million dollars to save two whales when people are starving to death every day in Sudan?

17. The argument above makes the unsupported assumption that

(A) the people who worked to save the whales do not care about human suffering
(B) though the whales were rescued, they will not survive very much longer
(C) icebreaking efforts can somehow stop starvation in the Sudan
(D) Eskimos no longer rely heavily on whales as a source of nourishment
(E) the rescue operation to save the whales was mounted with government funds

Until the 1986 federal tax reform law, the maximum tax on gains from investment like securities, real estate, works of art, and herds of cattle was only 20 percent, while ordinary income was taxed at rates as high as 50 percent. The reform law eliminated the capital gains tax advantage. Now the President proposes a 15-percent cap on taxes on personal investment in securities and homes. This new capital gains tax will create an incentive for investment, and investment spurs growth and creates jobs.

18. Which of the following, if true, most undermines the proposal for the new tax?

(A) The major investors in today's markets are tax-free institutional investors such as pension funds and endowments.
(B) Since the repeal of favorable treatment of capital gains, real economic growth has not declined considerably.
(C) The rate of inflation since the repeal of the capital gains tax has been the same as before the repeal.
(D) The President promised during the election campaign that there would be no new taxes during his administration.
(E) Interest rates have recently begun to drift upward in response to a tightening of the money supply by the Federal Reserve Board.

GO ON TO THE NEXT PAGE ⇨

Questions 19–20

Biological functions can ultimately be explained in chemical terms. And chemical reactions can ultimately be explained by the laws of physics. Since biological function is dictated by physical laws, we should eventually discover life in other galaxies that functions very much like that here on earth.

19. The argument above assumes that

(A) life on other planets will be equally advanced
(B) chemistry and biology are not separate disciplines
(C) physics is a more important science than biology
(D) physical laws are the same throughout the universe
(E) physical laws can be explained in biological terms

20. Which of the following, if true, would most weaken the argument above?

(A) Physical laws permit many different organizations for life processes.
(B) In our solar system, only earth can support life as we know it.
(C) Scientists have not yet successfully created life in a laboratory.
(D) Space travel is not advanced enough to transport people to other galaxies.
(E) Physicists have advanced many different theories of subatomic particles.

A Federal judge has ordered the county to house prisoners for whom there are no beds at the County Detention Facility at motels and inns until such time as beds become available. This will cost the county anywhere between $30 and $60 per night. I say it's time to punish criminals. Why shouldn't robbers, thieves, rapists, and murderers have to sleep on the floor for a couple of nights?

21. Which of the following, if true, would most weaken the argument above?

(A) The suit against the county was brought by a group of prisoners' rights activists concerned about jail overcrowding.
(B) The Federal judge who issued the order is known for her strong position against crime and her severe sentences.
(C) Very few hotel rooms in the county are available at rates of less than $30 per night.
(D) The cost of housing prisoners in double-occupancy rooms would be only $20 per night per prisoner.
(E) The Federal judge's order applies only to persons who have been charged with but not yet convicted of a crime.

Questions 22–23

Speaker X: Given the rising crime rate and the increased tendency for criminals to be heavily armed, our city's police officers need more powerful weapons. The standard six-shot .38 Special revolver should be replaced by the powerful 9-millimeter semiautomatic handgun. With the 9-millimeter, a criminal who is hit will stay down.

Speaker Y: To incapacitate, a handgun bullet must expend its full energy within the body cavity, creating hydrostatic pressures that result in trauma. The velocity of the bullet fired from a 9-millimeter handgun is so great that the bullet exits the body cavity too swiftly. A better use of public funds would be to retrain police officers to shoot well with the six-shot .38 Special revolvers. Each shot in a vital zone will change the attitude of any criminal.

22. Speaker Y challenges Speaker X's assumption that

(A) police ought to be effectively armed against criminals
(B) criminals are armed with powerful weapons
(C) a 9-millimeter handgun has more effective stopping power than a .38 Special revolver
(D) a 9-millimeter handgun fires a bullet with a higher velocity than a .38 Special revolver
(E) a 9-millimeter handgun is more accurate than a .38 Special revolver

23. An answer to which of the following questions would be LEAST relevant to the debate above?

(A) What is the cost of the 9-millimeter semiautomatic handgun compared to that of the .38 Special revolver?
(B) What is the risk of injuring a bystander with a 9-millimeter semiautomatic handgun compared to that of the .38 Special revolver?
(C) Over the past ten years, for how many of the occasions in which a police officer has used armed force would the 9-millimeter semiautomatic handgun have been more effective than the .38 Special revolver?
(D) By how much would a police officer's ability to incapacitate an attacker be improved by a retraining program on how to use the .38 Special revolver?
(E) How many civilians are intentionally killed each year by criminals who carry 9-millimeter semiautomatic handguns compared with all other handguns?

GO ON TO THE NEXT PAGE

A chemist knows the following about the colorless liquid in a certain beaker:

1. If chemical X is added to the liquid, it will turn red.
2. If chemical Y is added to the liquid, it will turn blue.
3. If both chemical X and chemical Y are added to the liquid, it will turn green.

24. Given the statements above, which of the following must be true?

(A) If the liquid remains colorless, then no chemicals were added.
(B) If the liquid turned green, then both chemical X and chemical Y were added.
(C) If the liquid turned blue, then chemical X was not added.
(D) If the liquid turned blue, then it is possible that chemical Y was added.
(E) If the liquid remained colorless, then it is possible that chemical X and only chemical X was added.

IF YOU FINISH BEFORE TIME IS CALLED, YOU MAY CHECK YOUR WORK ON THIS SECTION ONLY. DO NOT WORK ON ANY OTHER SECTION IN THE TEST. **S T O P**

438

SECTION **5** Time—35 Minutes
24 Questions

In this section solve each problem, using any available space on the page for scratchwork. Then decide which is the best of the choices given and fill in the corresponding oval on the answer sheet.

Directions: Each question or group of questions is based on a passage or set of conditions. In answering some of the questions, it may be useful to draw a rough diagram. For each question, select the best answer choice given.

Questions 1–6

The interoffice telephone system of a certain business is malfunctioning:

Beth can receive calls from every other person in the system but cannot call anyone in the system.

Fred can call every other person in the system but cannot receive any calls.

Gary can call Helen and Mike.

Helen can call Gary and Mike.

Mike can call Paul and Susan.

Susan can call Paul.

These are the only direct calls that can be made.

A worker can relay a message to another worker.

1. How many people in the system can call Mike directly?

   (A) 1   (B) 2   (C) 3   (D) 4   (E) 5

2. How many workers in the system are unable to make any direct calls?

   (A) 0   (B) 1   (C) 2   (D) 3   (E) 4

3. How many people in the system can call someone directly who can also call them directly?

   (A) 0   (B) 1   (C) 2   (D) 3   (E) 4

4. Using the system, which of the following communications can be sent, either directly or indirectly?

   (A) Beth to Gary
   (B) Gary to Paul
   (C) Helen to Fred
   (D) Paul to Gary
   (E) Susan to Mike

5. How many people using the system can telephone directly a person other than Beth who cannot telephone them directly?

   (A) 2   (B) 3   (C) 4   (D) 5   (E) 6

6. Which of the following repairs would ensure that Susan can call directly or have a message relayed to everyone else in the system?

   (A) Beth can call Fred.
   (B) Beth can call Gary.
   (C) Helen can call Paul.
   (D) Paul can call Mike.
   (E) Susan can call Gary.

Questions 7–12

In a certain wooded area, six forest rangers—Ed, Grant, Helen, Jill, Maria, and Pedro—are assigned to six different watchtowers. Each morning they report to a central headquarters building and then hike to their assignments.

Ed's tower is southwest of headquarters, and Grant's tower is southeast of headquarters.

Helen's tower is southwest of headquarters, but Ed's tower is farther south than Helen's.

Jill's tower is somewhere to the north of headquarters, and Maria's tower is northeast of headquarters.

Jill's tower is farther east than Ed's tower and farther south than Maria's tower.

Pedro's tower is somewhere east of headquarters and farther south than Jill's tower.

7. Pedro's tower cannot be located

   (A) due east of headquarters
   (B) due north of Grant's tower
   (C) due east of Maria's tower
   (D) northeast of Ed's tower
   (E) northeast of Helen's tower

8. If Maria walks a straight course from her tower to headquarters and continues on that same course, then it is possible that she would come to all of the following towers EXCEPT:

   (A) Ed's   (B) Grant's   (C) Helen's
   (D) Jill's   (E) Pedro's

GO ON TO THE NEXT PAGE

9. If a tower is located exactly halfway between Maria's tower and Grant's tower, then that tower could be staffed by

    I. Jill
    II. Ed
    III. Pedro

(A) I only   (B) III only   (C) I and III only
(D) II and III only   (E) I, II, and III

10. Which of the following cannot be true?

(A) Helen's tower is exactly halfway between Jill's tower and Ed's tower.
(B) Ed's tower is exactly halfway between Helen's tower and Grant's tower.
(C) Jill's tower is exactly halfway between Ed's tower and Maria's tower.
(D) Jill's tower is exactly halfway between Maria's tower and Pedro's tower.
(E) Jill's tower is exactly halfway between Ed's tower and Grant's tower.

11. Which of the following statements could be true of the six towers?

    I. There are more towers east of headquarters than west of headquarters.
    II. There are more towers west of headquarters than east of headquarters.
    III. There are more towers south of headquarters than north of headquarters.

(A) I only   (B) II only   (C) I and II only
(D) I and III only   (E) I, II, and III

12. If a seventh tower is constructed somewhere west of headquarters, then which of the following could be true of the new tower?

    I. It is located due east of Jill's tower.
    II. It is located due south of Ed's tower.
    III. It is located due west of Maria's tower.

(A) I only
(B) I and II only
(C) I and III only
(D) II and III only
(E) I, II, and III

Questions 13–18

Six people—J, K, L, M, N, and O—are to be seated in a row of theater seats. Facing the stage, the three seats to the left of the aisle are numbered 1 through 3, from left to right. And the three seats to the right of the aisle are numbered 4 through 6, also from left to right.

L and N will not sit on the same side of the aisle.

Either J or M must sit on the same side of the aisle as O.

13. Which of the following pairs CANNOT sit on the same side of the aisle?

(A) J and M
(B) J and N
(C) K and N
(D) L and M
(E) L and O

14. Which of the following must be true?

    I. If L and O sit on the right side of the aisle, then K must sit on the left side of the aisle.
    II. If L and K sit on the right side of the aisle, then O must sit on the left side of the aisle.
    III. If J and O sit on the right side of the aisle, then L must sit on the left side of the aisle.

(A) I only   (B) II only   (C) I and II only
(D) II and III only   (E) I, II, and III

15. If N and O sit on the left side of the aisle, then which of the following pairs must sit on the right side of the aisle?

(A) J and K
(B) J and L
(C) J and M
(D) K and L
(E) K and M

16. If K and N are seated in seats 1 and 2, then which of the following pairs must be seated on the right side of the aisle?

(A) J and L
(B) J and M
(C) L and M
(D) L and O
(E) M and O

17. If M and K are seated in center seats on either side of the aisle, then which of the following must be true?

    I. J is seated next to M.
    II. O is seated next to K.
    III. N is seated next to M.

(A) I only   (B) II only   (C) I and II only
(D) I and III only   (E) II and III only

18. If M and N are seated in seats 3 and 6, respectively, and O is not seated next to N, then all of the following must be true EXCEPT:

(A) If K is seated next to M, then O is seated in seat 4.
(B) If L is seated next to M, then J is seated next to N.
(C) If J is seated next to L, then K is seated next to N.
(D) If J is seated in seat 4, then K is seated in seat 5.
(E) If O is seated in seat 4, then K is seated next to L.

GO ON TO THE NEXT PAGE

Questions 19–24

A certain school system has twelve grades. At the end of certain grades, students are required to take the following comprehensive exams:

A math exam every other year starting in the second grade

A vocabulary exam every other year starting in the third grade

An English exam every three years starting in the third grade

A science exam every four years starting in the fourth grade

19. A student who finishes every grade in the school system would take how many exams?

(A) 15   (B) 18   (C) 20   (D) 22   (E) 24

20. A student who takes only a math and an English exam at the end of the year must be in grade

(A) 2   (B) 6   (C) 8   (D) 9   (E) 12

21. A student who takes a science exam and an English exam at the end of the year must be in grade

(A) 4   (B) 6   (C) 8   (D) 10   (E) 12

22. A student who takes a vocabulary exam but not an English exam could be in which of the following grades?

  I. 5
 II. 7
III. 11

(A) I only   (B) II only   (C) III only
(D) I and III only   (E) I, II, and III

23. In how many years does a student take no exams?

(A) 0   (B) 1   (C) 2   (D) 3   (E) 4

24. In all of the following grades, a battery of subject tests is given that matches exactly a battery given in another grade EXCEPT:

(A) 2   (B) 3   (C) 4   (D) 5   (E) 6

IF YOU FINISH BEFORE TIME IS CALLED, YOU MAY CHECK YOUR WORK ON THIS SECTION ONLY. DO NOT WORK ON ANY OTHER SECTION IN THE TEST. **S T O P**

441

LSAT® WRITING SAMPLE BOOKLET

**WAIT FOR THE SUPERVISOR's INSTRUCTIONS BEFORE YOU TURN THE PAGE TO THE TOPIC.
PLEASE SIGN YOUR NAME AND NOTE THE DATE AT THE TOP OF PAGE ONE BEFORE YOU START TO WORK.**

TIME: 30 MINUTES

GENERAL DIRECTIONS

You are to complete the brief writing exercise on the topic inside. You will have 30 minutes in which to plan and write the exercise. Read the topic carefully. You will probably find it best to spend a few minutes considering the topic and organizing your thoughts before you begin writing. DO NOT WRITE ON A TOPIC OTHER THAN THE ONE SPECIFIED. WRITING ON A TOPIC OF YOUR OWN CHOICE IS NOT ACCEPTABLE.

There is no "right" or "wrong" answer to this question. Law schools are interested in how carefully you support the position you take and how clearly you express that position. How well you write is much more important than how much you write. No special knowledge is required or expected. Law schools are interested in organization, vocabulary, and writing mechanics. They understand the short time available to you and the pressured circumstances under which you will write.

Confine your writing to the lined area inside this booklet. Only the blocked lined area will be reproduced for the law schools. You will find that you have enough space in this booklet if you plan your writing carefully, write on every line, avoid wide margins, and keep your handwriting a reasonable size. Be sure that your writing is legible.

LSAT WRITING SAMPLE TOPIC

Read the following descriptions of Midtown High School and John Jay High School, two schools in which Olivia, who moved during the summer and is entering her junior year, is considering enrolling. **Then, in the space provided, write an argument for the choice you think Olivia should make.** The following considerations should guide your thinking:

1. Olivia wants a curriculum that will prepare her for college.
2. Olivia wants to participate in extracurricular activities, particularly gymnastics.
3. Olivia is worried that she will not make friends quickly.

   MIDTOWN HIGH SCHOOL has a student body of 10,000, and average class size is 35 to 37. Because it is a large school, Midtown offers a wide variety of courses, including vocational training and advanced courses in chemistry, physics, and math. Each year students from Midtown capture several of the state's top academic awards. Midtown offers a wide range of extracurricular activities, and its gymnastics team placed third in state competition last year.

   JOHN JAY HIGH SCHOOL has a student body of 2,000, and average class size is 15 to 17. The school was established to offer academically challenging courses for talented students. In the senior year, a student is allowed to register for courses at the community college across the street from John Jay. Because the primary focus of the school is on academics, its few clubs are oriented toward areas of academic interest; for example, the school has a Science Club, a Math Club, and a Latin Club. Last year, one of the teachers, a former college gymnast, started a gymnastic team. John Jay does not have a gymnasium of its own, but its students are allowed to practice with the members of the community college's gymnastics team.

Answer Key

SECTION 1	SECTION 2	SECTION 3	SECTION 4	SECTION 5
1. B	1. B	1. A	1. B	1. C
2. C	2. A	2. A	2. E	2. B
3. A	3. B	3. E	3. A	3. C
4. B	4. C	4. C	4. C	4. B
5. E	5. B	5. D	5. B	5. D
6. A	6. C	6. D	6. C	6. A
7. D	7. E	7. E	7. C	7. C
8. B	8. E	8. A	8. B	8. B
9. B	9. E	9. B	9. A	9. C
10. C	10. A	10. C	10. C	10. E
11. A	11. A	11. D	11. E	11. D
12. E	12. A	12. E	12. B	12. E
13. C	13. D	13. A	13. E	13. A
14. B	14. A	14. D	14. B	14. C
15. E	15. E	15. A	15. A	15. D
16. A	16. A	16. D	16. A	16. D
17. B	17. C	17. A	17. C	17. C
18. B	18. C	18. A	18. A	18. B
19. C	19. D	19. D	19. D	19. B
20. A	20. D	20. E	20. A	20. B
21. A	21. C	21. D	21. E	21. E
22. B	22. D	22. C	22. C	22. E
23. C	23. C	23. A	23. E	23. B
24. A	24. A	24. D	24. D	24. E
25. A		25. B		
26. D				
27. A				
28. B				

Explanatory Answers

SAMPLE ESSAY

Olivia should enroll at John Jay High School for three reasons: first, John Jay offers a curriculum that will prepare her for college; second, at John Jay, Olivia will make friends easily; and third, she will have the opportunity to participate in gymnastics.

John Jay will prepare Olivia for the challenges of college in two respects. The courses at John Jay are designed for talented students, so they must be difficult. Additionally, in her senior year, Olivia can learn firsthand what college is like.

Olivia will have the opportunity to make friends at John Jay because the size of the student body is not overwhelmingly large. Moreover, the fact that the average class size is only fifteen to seventeen students suggests that classes will not be very formal.

Finally, John Jay has a relatively new gymnastics team, so Olivia should be able to participate in many events. Further, she will be able to learn by watching college gymnasts practice.

Although Midtown does offer some advantages, Olivia would be better able to achieve her goals at John Jay.

1. The author's primary purpose is to

(A) contrast two different views of a social issue
(B) describe a social phenomenon
(C) present new research to support a theory
(D) argue in favor of social change
(E) illustrate a moral dilemma

(B) This is a main idea question. The author focuses on an important feature of black slavery in America, racial separation, and he describes some of the implications of that social structure. (B) correctly points out that the author's burden is to describe something and that what the author describes is a social phenomenon.

2. The author apparently regards Robert Jones (lines 46–47) as

(A) an important historical personage
(B) an opponent of segregation
(C) an authority on the social effects of slavery
(D) a spokesperson for black communities
(E) a defender of the attitudes of white slaveholders

(C) This is a logical detail question. The author has made an assertion about the development of black cultural forms, and then he cites an authority to back him up. Thus the author regards Jones as an authority on the topic.

3. Which of the following statements can be inferred from the passage?

(A) Since blacks outside of North America were not as racially isolated as North American blacks, they did not develop the same vital black communities.
(B) Some areas outside of North America had a mulatto class, so there was no racial tension between blacks and whites in those areas.
(C) Because of the racial separation of blacks and whites in North America, blacks thought that most whites were also oppressed by powerful whites.
(D) Black communities in North America incorporated more African elements into their cultural forms than they drew from the slavery experience.
(E) Blacks intentionally invented new cultural forms that were unlike those of whites, so that whites could not understand their culture.

(A) This is an implied idea question. The author never specfically states the conclusion given in (A), but it can be inferred from the passage. The author states that racial separation was one of the important factors in the development of the uniquely North American black cultural forms. He also states that

this separation, which was so important in North America, did not exist to the same extent elsewhere. We may infer, therefore, that since the important factor is missing in other regions, black cultural forms did not develop in the same way.

4. The author most probably puts the word *best* (line 9) in quotation marks to

(A) acknowledge that he is quoting from another source
(B) emphasize that no aspect of slavery could ever be good
(C) remind the reader that the word is ambiguous
(D) alert the reader that a definition will follow
(E) show his support for the black communities

(B) This is a logical detail question. There are many reasons why an author might place a word in quotations. In this case, the author has put "scare" quotes around the word. "Scare" quotes are used to alert the reader that the word in quotes is being used in an unusual way. The author has used the word *best* to describe slavery, but he doesn't want readers to misunderstand him and infer that he thinks slavery was in any way good.

5. The author's attitude toward North American black communities can best be described as

(A) enthusiastic
(B) neutral
(C) disinterested
(D) deprecatory
(E) admiring

(E) This is an attitude question. In the final paragraph the author mentions that black communities in North America have a particularly rich cultural heritage. We may conclude on this basis that he regards them with a positive attitude. (A) overstates the case. (E) is a more appropriate description.

6. The author implies that the eagerness of white slaveholders to be sexually intimate with black slaves was

(A) inconsistent with the attitude of white slave-holders that they were superior to blacks
(B) a contributing factor in the eventual breakdown of the psychological barriers separating whites and blacks
(C) more prevalent in British North America than in other parts of the Americas
(D) a reinforcement of the negative attitudes of white slaveholders toward blacks
(E) a reason for white slaveholders to reassess their attitudes about blacks

(A) This is an implied idea question. In the first paragraph, the author states that many white slave-holders were sexually intimate with black slaves in spite of their attitude of superiority. We can infer, therefore, that the author detects an inconsistency in white attitudes. The whites regarded blacks as less than fully adult human beings but were nonetheless willing to be sexually intimate with them. (B) is incorrect because the author doesn't talk about any such breakdown in barriers; and, in any event, the sexual intimacy mentioned belongs to a specific historical period. As for (C), although we can infer from the existence of a mulatto class in other parts of the Americas that there was sexual intimacy between blacks and whites, there is nothing in the passage to suggest that such intimacy was more frequent in British North America than elsewhere in the Americas. As for (D) and (E), the author does mention that white slaveholders did hold negative attitudes about blacks, but the author does not imply that these attitudes were in any way changed by sexual intimacy between the races.

The primary purpose of the passage is to

(A) refute some misconceptions about the importance of human immaturity
(B) introduce a new theory of the origins of the human species
(C) describe the evolutionary forces that formed the physical appearance of modern humans
(D) discuss the importance of human immaturity as an adaptive mechanism
(E) outline the process by which humans mature into social beings

(D) This is a main idea question. The author begins by noting that the fact that man lives in an increasingly man-made world places special burdens on human immaturity, because it is during this period that people must learn things that are not already innate in the organism. Then the author goes on to discuss the importance of the technical-social way of life as an adaptive mechanism. Finally, he returns to his starting point, the importance of the period of immaturity. (D) best describes this development.

As for (A), the author does discuss some ideas about human immaturity, so it is possible to argue that he (at least implicitly) corrects misconceptions. There is the further point that the author does seem to open paragraph two with an attempt to pre-empt a possible misconception, but correcting misconceptions is at best incidental to the main theme of the passage, which is positive, not remedial. As for (B), though the author does theorize, he does not offer a new theory of the *origins of the human species*. As for (C), the general topic is evolution, and the author does mention some of the physical changes that oc-

curred in the species. Nevertheless, the wording of (C) does not accurately describe the main development of the selection. Finally, as for (E), though the topic of the selection is the importance of immaturity in humans, the author doesn't describe any specific mechanisms by which humans mature.

8. It can be inferred that the obstetrical paradox is puzzling because

(A) it occurred very late during the evolution of the species
(B) evolutionary forces seemed to work at cross purposes to each other
(C) technological innovations have made the process of birth easier
(D) an increase in brain size is not an ordinary evolutionary event
(E) a strong pelvic girdle is no longer necessary to the survival of the species

(B) This is an inference question, and the key word here is *paradox*. A paradox is a seeming contradiction, so the correct choice must explain why this phenomenon is puzzling. (B) does this. The essence of the paradox is that the species changed in two different directions. On the one hand, the brain got larger, and on the other, the birth canal got smaller —the net result being that birth became more difficult. That is puzzling because one would expect evolutionary forces to work to avoid such difficulties.

As for (A) and (D), these choices at least have the merit of attempting to respond to the question asked. They try to explain why the paradox is puzzling, but the difficulty with these choices is that there is no support in the text for either of them. As for (A), though this change did occur late in the evolutionary process, there is nothing in the selection to suggest that this is surprising. Similarly, as for (D), though the passage does state that the brain got larger, there is nothing in the passage to suggest that an evolutionary move toward a larger brain is *per se* puzzling.

9. Which of the following statements can be inferred from the passage?

(A) Human beings are today less sexually active than were our ancestors during the Pleistocene era.

(B) During the Pleistocene era, a fondness for fats and sweets was a trait that contributed to survival of humans.

(C) Mathematics was invented by human beings during the latter half of the Pleistocene era.

(D) The use of language and tools is a trait that is genetically transmitted from one generation to the next.

(E) During immaturity, human beings gain knowledge and learn skills primarily through the process of direct encounter.

(B) This is an inference question. In the third paragraph, where the author is discussing traits that developed during the Pleistocene era, he states that man's fondness for fats and sweets *no longer* serves him well. From this, we can infer that this fondness was at one time a valuable adaptive trait—as (B) states.

(A) represents a confused reading of the rest of the passage. The author does state that an obsession with sexuality was a valuable trait during an earlier era, for it helped to ensure the growth of the human population. According to the author, this obsession is no longer a valuable trait. But this shift has not resulted in a decrease in sexual activity but the dissociation of sexuality from reproduction by contraception. As for (C), nothing in the passage indicates when mathematics was first studied. (D) is specifically contradicted by the passage, for the ability to use language is (according to the first paragraph) something that is not in the gene pool but something that must be learned during immaturity. Finally, (E) represents a confused reading of that first paragraph. Learning by direct encounter is one way of gaining knowledge, but the author does not state that this is the most important way of gaining knowledge. In fact, given that the emphasis of the selection is on the use of immaturity to educate humans to things that cannot be learned by direct encounter, we are probably justified in concluding that (E) is contradicted by the passage.

10. The author uses the term *preadaptation* to describe traits that

(A) were useful to earlier human beings but have since lost their utility

(B) appeared in response to the need to learn a natural language and the use of tools

(C) humans currently exhibit but that developed in response to conditions of an earlier age

(D) are disadvantageous to creatures whose way of life is primarily technical and social

(E) continue to exist despite evolutionary pressures that threaten to erase them

(C) This is a specific detail question. What is the meaning of the term *preadaptation*? The author states that preadaptations occurred during an earlier period in response to the conditions that prevailed then (and may not exist now). This idea is summarized by choice (C). It is true that the author then goes on to point out that preadaptations may no longer be useful and may in fact be harmful, but the fact that an adaptation to an earlier condition is no longer currently useful is not the defining characteristic of *preadaptation*. In fact, for the specific situation in which a preadaptation is now harmful, the author uses the term *maladaptation*. Thus, (A) is a good second choice but is still wrong, and this reasoning allows us to eliminate (D) as well. The other two choices do use language from the selection, but neither is at all responsive to the question.

11. The author mentions contraception to demonstrate that

(A) human beings may adapt to new conditions by technological invention rather than by changing their behavior

(B) sexual promiscuity is no longer an aid to the survival of the human species

(C) technological innovation is a more important adaptive mechanism than either heredity or direct encounter

(D) conditions during the upper Pliocene and Pleistocene eras no longer affect the course of human evolution

(E) morphological change is a common response to new demands placed on a creature by its environment

(A) This is a logical detail question, asking *why* the author mentions contraception. In the sentence before, when the author uses the term *contraception*, he states "the species responds typically to these challenges by technical innovation rather than morphological or behavioral change." Contraception is intended to be an example of this contention, as (A) correctly notes. (Uncontrolled sexual activity is no longer necessary to further the goal of increased population; but instead of modifying their behavior in response to this pressure—as other animals would —humans use a technical innovation, birth control, to get around the pressure.)

(B) is perhaps the second-best answer. It is true that the author states that unbridled sexual activity is no longer a valuable adaptive mechanism, but this is not why he mentions contraception. He mentions contraception to show that the response of humans to such a situation is often technological innovation. Thus, (B) is true but not responsive to the question. As for (C), though contraception is an example of technical innovation, the author does not use the example to prove that technical innovation is *more important* than other mechanisms by which knowledge is transmitted or acquired. As for (D), while it is true that this is part of the author's point (the need for uncontrolled sexual activity has disappeared), this statement is not responsive to the question asked. Finally, as for (E), the author's point is that with humans, morphological change is not the typical response to a new environmental demand.

12. With which of the following statements would the author LEAST likely agree?

(A) The technical-social way of life of humans is an adaptive mechanism that arose in response to environmental pressures.

(B) The possibility of technical innovation makes it unlikely that the physical appearance of humans will change radically in a short time.

(C) Technological innovations can result in changes in the social structures in which humans live.

(D) New demands created by changes in the social structure are sometimes met by technological innovation.

(E) The fact that humans have a technical-social way of life makes the species immune from evolutionary pressures.

(E) This is a further application question. Based on your understanding of the text, you have to find the one the author would be least likely to endorse. This is (E). In fact, in his closing remarks, the author states that humans are subject to the special pressure of accelerating change. As for (A), this is a statement the author would surely accept. The author cites Washburn as authority for the contention that the technical-social way of life is a form of adaptation. Similarly, the author would probably accept (B), since he states that humans typically respond to environmental challenges with technical innovation rather than physical adaptation. As for (C) and (D), the discussion of the effects of contraception suggests that the author would accept both of these statements.

13. The author is most probably addressing which of the following audiences?

(A) Medical students in a course on human anatomy

(B) College students in an introductory course on archaeology

(C) Psychologists investigating the uses of human immaturity

(D) Biologists trying to trace the course of human evolution

(E) Linguists doing research on the origins of natural languages

(C) This is another further application question. The most likely audience is that described by (C), because it specifically focuses on the idea of human immaturity. As for (A), although this is a paper that might be presented to medical students, its subject matter is not anatomy. Similarly, as for (B), though this would be an appropriate lecture to give college students, the topic doesn't seem to belong in a course on archaeology. As for (D), although this is a paper that would be suitable to read to biologists, the discussion focuses on current problems—not the origins of the species. Finally, as for (E), though the selection does mention language, that is not the main focus of the selection.

14. Which of the following is most like the relationship of the *oyabun-kobun* described in the passage?

(A) A political candidate and the voting public

(B) A gifted scientist and his protege

(C) Two brothers who are partners in a business

(D) A judge presiding at the trial of a criminal defendant

(E) A leader of a musical ensemble who is also a musician in the group

(B) This is a further application question. You must take what you have learned about the *oyabun-kobun* and apply it to a new situation. What are the defining characteristics of this relationship? First, the *oyabun-kobun* is like a parent–child relationship; one person is superior to the other. On this ground, you can eliminate both (C) and (E). They describe situations in which people behave more or less as equals. Another aspect of the parent–child relation is intimacy. So you can eliminate (A), which is a relationship between one and many. Although (D) describes a one-on-one situation in which one party is in charge, the situation lacks the element of intimacy. This leaves (B). And (B) describes a relationship that is personal, in which the interests of the parties are similar, and in which one party is superior to the other.

451

15. According to the passage, Japanese attitudes are influenced by which of the following?

 I. Democratic ideals
 II. Elements of modern Western culture
 III. Remnants of an earlier social structure

 (A) I only (B) II only (C) I and II only
 (D) II and III only (E) I, II, and III

(E) This is a specific detail question. To be part of the correct answer, an idea must have been specifically mentioned in the selection. I is specifically mentioned in the first and second paragraphs. II also is specifically mentioned in the first and second paragraphs. III is the topic of the remaining paragraphs.

16. The author implies that

 (A) decisions about promotions are often based on personal feelings
 (B) students and intellectuals do not understand the basic tenets of Western democracy
 (C) Western values have completely overwhelmed traditional Japanese attitudes
 (D) respect for authority was introduced into Japan following World War II
 (E) most Japanese workers are members of a single political party

(A) This is an implied idea question. You will find the basis for the conclusion expressed in (A) in the final paragraph. There the author states that maintaining a successful personal relationship with a superior may be more important than having exceptional abilities. We can infer, therefore, that superiors may make decisions based on their personal preferences for subordinates.

(B) represents a misunderstanding of the second and third paragraphs. The author states that students and intellectuals did embrace the basic ideas of democracy, but young people have distorted certain Western ideas.

(C) is actually in contradiction to the passage. The second half of the selection is devoted to a discussion of the influence of traditional values. So Western influences cannot have completely obliterated those values.

(D) represents a misreading of the passage. Respect for authority is a traditional value that predates the introduction of democratic ideas following the war.

As for (E), there is nothing in the passage to support such a conclusion. If you selected (E), perhaps you misread something in the discussion of the *oyabun-kobun*. Although someone in a political party may establish a parent–child relationship with a senior member of the party, this does not imply that everyone belongs to the same political party.

17. In developing the passage, the author does which of the following?

 (A) Introduce an analogy
 (B) Define a term
 (C) Present statistics
 (D) Cite an authority
 (E) Issue a challenge

(B) This is a logical structure question. In the passage the author does define a term, the *oyabun-kobun*. But the author uses none of the other devices.

18. It can be inferred that the Imperial Rescript of 1890

 (A) was a protest by liberals against the lack of individual liberty in Japan
 (B) marked a return in government policies to conservative values
 (C) implemented the ideals set forth in the Education Code of 1872
 (D) was influenced by the Leninist ideology of the Bolshevik Revolution
 (E) prohibited the teaching of Western ideas in Japanese schools

(B) This is an inference question based on the first paragraph. The key sentence is the one that reads "[Fukuzawa] was not able to prevent the government from turning back to the canons of Confucian thought in the Imperial Rescript of 1890." Since Fukuzawa represented liberal thought and Confucianism was the source of traditional values, we can infer that the Imperial Rescript represented a return to traditional values. Thus, (A) and (C) both reach clearly wrong conclusions. (D) represents a confused reading of the selection. The Bolshevik Revolution did not occur until 1917. Finally, (E) represents the second most attractive answer. It at least has the merit of noting that the Imperial Rescript represented a reaction to liberal ideas. The difficulty with (E) is that it goes too far beyond the explicit text. While we can infer the general conclusion that the Imperial Rescript represented a reaction to liberal thinking, there is nothing in the selection to support the very specific conclusion given in (E).

19. Which of the following is the most accurate description of the organization of the passage?

 (A) A sequence of inferences in which the conclusion of each successive step becomes a premise in the next argument
 (B) A list of generalizations, most of which are supported by only a single example
 (C) A chronological analysis of historical events leading up to a description of the current situation
 (D) A statement of a commonly accepted theory that is then subjected to a critical analysis
 (E) An introduction of a key term that is then defined by giving examples

(C) This is a logical structure question that asks about the overall development of the selection. One of the most important structural features of the selection is its chronological approach. It begins sometime in the late nineteenth century and then traces important developments to the present, at which point it provides a more detailed description of the current situation. This development is correctly described by (C).

(A) is incorrect because there is no sequence of interrelated deductive links. (B) is perhaps the second-best choice. It is true that the passage contains several very general claims, some of which are supported by examples. The difficulty with (B) is first that a general claim is not the same thing as a generalization. (A generalization is a type of reasoning that moves from one or more examples to a conclusion about an entire population.) Additionally, (B) fails to make mention of that very striking stylistic feature of the selection, the chronological development. As for (D), the author does not introduce a competing theory. And finally, as for (E), though the author does define an important term (*oyabun-kobun*), providing this definition is not the main structural feature of the selection.

20. Which of the following best states the central thesis of the passage?

    (A) The value system of Japan is based upon traditional and conservative values that have, in modern times, been modified by Western and other liberal values.
    (B) Students and radicals in Japan have used Leninist ideology to distort the meaning of democratic, Western values.
    (C) The notions of personal freedom and individual liberty did not find immediate acceptance in Japan because of the predominance of traditional group values.
    (D) Modern Japanese society is characterized by hierarchical relationships in which a personal tie to a superior is often more important than merit.
    (E) The influence on Japanese values of the American ideals of personal freedom and individual rights is less important that the influence of Leninist ideology.

(A) This is a main idea question. Remember, the task is to find a description of the selection that is neither too broad nor too narrow. (A) fits the bill. The very first sentence summarizes the author's thesis. Japanese values are the product of two seemingly contradictory forces, traditional values and modern values. (B) and (E) are incorrect because they refer to but minor points in the development of

the selection. (C) and (D) make the same mistake, though less egregiously. (D) refers only to the final paragraph of the selection. (C) does seem to be the second most attractive answer, for it is one of the important points the author makes. But the description of the *initial* reception of the new values is not the main point of the selection.

21. The tone of the passage can best be described as

    (A) neutral and objective
    (B) disparaging and flippant
    (C) critical and demanding
    (D) enthusiastic and supportive
    (E) skeptical and questioning

(A) The tone of the passage is scholarly, so the best available description is that provided by (A). (B) and (C) can be eliminated because there are no such negative attitudes suggested by the selection. (D) can be eliminated for the opposite reason. Finally, as for (E), there is nothing in the passage that suggests the author refuses to believe any of the ideas he discusses.

22. Which of the following titles best describes the content of the passage?

    (A) The Therapeutic Value of Antipsychotic Drugs
    (B) The Tradeoff in the Use of Neuroleptic Drugs
    (C) The Connection between Psychotherapy and Neuroleptic Drugs
    (D) Recent Developments in the Treatment of Mental Illness
    (E) Techniques for Treating Tardive Dyskinesia

(B) This is a main idea question that asks for an appropriate title. The strategy is to find a title that describes the main point of the passage. The author discusses the use of neuroleptic drugs, their benefits, and some disadvantages of their use. Finally, he suggests possible solutions to the dilemma created by the unwanted effects. (B) correctly describes this development; the word "tradeoff" is particularly well-chosen.

(A) is too narrow. The description of the benefits of the drugs is only one-half of the selection. (C) is wrong because it takes one relatively minor point from the passage and elevates that point to the status of main idea. The author does mention that these drugs make psychotherapy possible, but that is not the main point of the selection. (D) is overly broad. The author focuses on the tradeoff in the use of neuroleptic drugs, one particular kind of drug. So the passage is not a general discussion of recent developments in treatments for mental illness. Finally, (E) is too narrow. It is true that the author mentions a technique for minimizing the effects of tardive dyskinesia, but that is not the main point of the passage.

23. It can be inferred that neuroleptic drugs control psychosis by

(A) suppressing the production of dopamine in the brain
(B) blocking the nerve impulses transmitted to the muscles
(C) preventing the absorption of dopamine by brain cells
(D) creating a hypersensitivity to dopamine
(E) counteracting the effect of other prescription drugs

(C) The word *inferred* signals that this is an implied idea question. The author does not specifically describe the mechanism by which neuroleptic drugs have their effect, but we will be able to deduce some conclusion about that mechanism. The second paragraph describes the functioning of neuroleptic drugs. Such drugs interfere with the action of dopamine by binding to the dopamine receptors. We can infer that this means the drugs *coat* the receptors so the dopamine cannot be absorbed, the process described by (C).

(A) is incorrect. The passage does not state that less dopamine is produced, only that the existing dopamine is rendered relatively ineffective. (B) shows some promise of being correct by using the word *blocking,* but neuroleptic drugs *block* the absorption of dopamine by the nerve cells, not the impulses going to the muscles. (D) is incorrect since this is an unwanted side effect of the drugs, not the method by which psychosis is controlled. Finally, as for (E), the passage describes the operation of the drugs in terms of dopamine, a chemical produced by the brain itself. Dopamine is not another drug introduced from outside the body.

24. According to the passage, neuroleptic drugs are

(A) generally effective but have unwanted side effects
(B) gradually replacing psychotherapy
(C) experimental and still not widely accepted
(D) reserved for the most serious cases of psychosis
(E) clinically effective but too expensive

(A) This is a specific idea question, and the author specifically states that neuroleptic drugs are effective but have the unwanted side effect called tardive dyskinesia. (B) is wrong since the drugs are used in conjunction with psychotherapy. (C) is specifically contradicted by the passage, since the drugs have been in use since the 1950s.

As for (D), you might point to the problem of

tardive dyskinesia and argue that the drugs are probably used only in extreme cases. This line of reasoning is interesting but wrong for two reasons. First, as a matter of reading, the general success of the drugs suggests that they are probably widely used. Second, as a matter of test-taking strategy, the correct answer to a specific detail question does not require an argument to support it. So even though the line of reasoning suggested is interesting, it is wrong as a matter of test-taking tactics.

Finally, (E) is incorrect since expense is not said to be a problem. If (E) were the correct answer to this specific detail question, somewhere in the passage the author would have raised the topic of cost.

25. It can be inferred that the primary danger of tardive dyskinesia is the

(A) psychological effect on the patient
(B) long-term therapeutic use of drugs
(C) addiction of a patient to dopamine
(D) physical injuries caused by violent muscle spasms
(E) inability of the patient to remain in therapy

(A) The word *inferred* signals that this is an implied idea question. The correct conclusion will not have been specifically stated in the passage, but it will be deducible from the information provided by the author. The correct answer is (A). In the third paragraph, the author states that the physical effects of tardive dyskinesia are slight, but patients are bothered by the effects and the abnormal movements may hinder social adjustment. We may infer, therefore, that the most serious problem is psychological. Given this, we can easily eliminate (D), the only other likely choice. As for (B), long-term use is the cause of tardive dyskinesia, not one of its effects. As for (C), dopamine is a substance produced by the brain itself, not a drug. (E) is incorrect since an inability to remain in therapy is not mentioned as an effect of tardive dyskinesia.

26. If a patient showed symptoms of tardive dyskinesia, a doctor would probably

(A) discontinue the use of all antipsychotic drugs
(B) increase the dosage of dopamine
(C) confine the patient to an institution
(D) reduce the dosage of any neuroleptic drug
(E) recommend psychotherapy and counseling

(D) This is a further application question. In the third paragraph, the author suggests that a possible solution to the dilemma is finding an optimal dosage, one that controls psychosis while minimizing the symptoms of tardive dyskinesia. This idea of *balancing* is the key to this question. Given that a balance must be struck, the most reasonable course of action in the situation described is to reduce the dosage of the drug, hoping that the lower dosage will be effective and will result in a reduction of the unwanted side effects.

(A) must be incorrect because the course of action it suggests completely ignores the idea of finding an appropriate balance. (B) is wrong because increasing the dosage would likely result in more severe symptoms of tardive dyskinesia. (C) and (E) are related to the general idea of psychosis, but neither suggests a course of action that addresses the dilemma created by the use of neuroleptic drugs.

27. The author cites the effects of large doses of drugs such as amphetamines in order to

(A) demonstrate that dopamine may be the cause of some psychotic behavior
(B) prove that neuroleptic drugs produce symptoms of tardive dyskinesia
(C) give an example of a neuroleptic drug that does not necessarily cause tardive dyskinesia
(D) show that smaller dosages of neuroleptic drugs can effectively control psychotic behavior
(E) persuade the reader that the drug sulpiride should be available in the United States

(A) This is a logical structure question. The question stem cites an idea mentioned in the passage and then asks *why* that idea was introduced. In the second paragraph, where the author is discussing the effect of neuroleptic drugs, the author states that dopamine is considered a likely cause of schizophrenia. The author says that amphetamines cause the secretion of dopamine and are associated with psychosis. We conclude that the author mentions the effect of amphetamines in order to show that dopamine is related to schizophrenia.

(B) is an idea mentioned in the passage, but (B) is not responsive to the question. As for (C), the author does mention a drug that does not necessarily cause tardive dyskinesia (sulpiride), but sulpiride is not said to be an amphetamine. As for (D), this, too, is a point mentioned in the selection, but this idea is not responsive to the question asked. Finally, as for (E), though the author might agree with this conclusion, this is not the reason that the author mentions the effects of amphetamines.

28. According to the passage, which of the following statements about D−2 dopamine receptors are true?

I. They are located only in the limbic area of the brain.
II. Their functioning is affected by the drug sulpiride.
III. They are responsible for initiating motor movements.

(A) I only   (B) II only   (C) I and II only
(D) II and III only   (E) I, II, and III

(B) This is a specific detail question. The reference you need is in the final paragraph of the selection, where the author discusses the effect of sulpiride. The author states that sulpiride primarily affects D−2 receptors *perhaps especially those in the limbic area of the brain*. That statement says that some D−2 receptors are located in the limbic area, but it does not say that *all* D−2 receptors are located in the region. So statement I is not part of the correct choice, and you can eliminate (A), (C), and (E). As for II, that part of the selection does specifically state that sulpiride acts on the D−2 receptors, so II must be part of the correct choice. Finally, as for III, the selection states that the limbic area of the brain is involved in emotion and behavior. Since some D−2 receptors are located in that region, you would be entitled to infer that they are involved in emotion and behavior. But nothing in the passage identifies the part of the brain that is responsible for motor actions.

SECTION 2

ANALYTICAL REASONING

Questions 1–6

This is a simple linear ordering set. Begin by summarizing the initial conditions:

$(B + D) < A$
$(D + NY) < C$

The initial conditions don't seem to fix the date of any appointment, so we will go directly to the questions.

1. Which of the following is an acceptable schedule for the visits, listed from left to right for Monday through Friday?

    (A) Atlanta, Charleston, New York, Detroit, Boston
    (B) Boston, Detroit, New York, Charleston, Atlanta
    (C) Charleston, Boston, Detroit, Boston, Atlanta
    (D) New York, Charleston, Detroit, New York, Atlanta
    (E) New York, Charleston, Atlanta, Detroit, Boston

    (B) This question provides no additional information, so just check each answer choice by the initial conditions. First, B and D must be scheduled before A, so we eliminate choices (A) and (E). Next, D and NY must be scheduled before C, and we eliminate choices (C) and (D). Thus, (B) is the answer.

2. Which of the following cities could be visited on Thursday and Friday, respectively?

    (A) Atlanta and Charleston
    (B) Boston and Charleston
    (C) Charleston and Detroit
    (D) Detroit and Atlanta
    (E) Detroit and New York

    (A) Scheduling A and C on Thursday and Friday, respectively, makes it possible to schedule both B and D before A and D and NY before C. For example:

M	Tu	W	Th	Fri
B	D	NY	A	C

    The remaining choices are not possible. As for (B), if B is scheduled on Thursday with C on Friday, then B is not scheduled before A. As for (C), C cannot be scheduled before D. As for (D) and (E), if D is scheduled on Thursday with a city other than C on Friday, then D is not scheduled before C.

3. If the executive visits Boston and New York on Monday and Tuesday, respectively, which of the following must be true?

    (A) On Wednesday she visits Atlanta.
    (B) On Wednesday she visits Detroit.
    (C) On Thursday she visits Atlanta.
    (D) On Thursday she visits Detroit.
    (E) On Friday she visits Charleston.

    (B) This question provides additional information. We'll use a diagram to keep track of our further deductions:

M	Tu	W	Th	F
B	NY			

    Given the initial conditions, since D must be scheduled before both A and C, D will be scheduled for Wednesday:

M	Tu	W	Th	F
B	NY	D		

    A and C will be scheduled for Thursday and Friday, though not necessarily in that order:

M	Tu	W	Th	F
B	NY	D	A/C	A/C

    Thus, (B) is necessarily true, while (A) and (D) are necessarily false and (C) and (E) are only possibly true.

4. If the executive visits Charleston before Boston, then it must also be true that she visits

    (A) Atlanta before Detroit
    (B) Boston before Detroit
    (C) Charleston before Atlanta
    (D) Charleston before New York
    (E) Detroit before New York

    (C) If C is scheduled before B, then NY is also scheduled before B. For example:

D	NY	C	B

    Notice that D and NY are not necessarily in that order. Since A must follow B, there are only two possible orders:

M	Tu	W	Th	F
D	NY	C	B	A
NY	D	C	B	A

    The diagrams show that (C) is necessarily true, while (A), (B), and (D) are false and (E) is only possibly true.

5. Which of the following could be part of an acceptable schedule for the executive?

(A) Atlanta on Monday
(B) Boston on Thursday
(C) Charleston on Tuesday
(D) Detroit on Friday
(E) New York on Friday

(B) This question provides no additional information, so we check the choices against the initial conditions. (A) is not a possible choice since A cannot be scheduled until after two other cities (so A cannot be scheduled for Monday). (C) is not possible since C must be scheduled after two other cities (so C cannot be scheduled before Wednesday). Neither (D) nor (E) is possible because D and NY must both be scheduled before some other city (so neither can be last). (B) is possible as shown by the following diagram:

M	Tu	W	Th	F
D	NY	C	B	A

6. The one day of the week on which any of the five cities could be visited is

(A) Monday   (B) Tuesday   (C) Wednesday
(D) Thursday   (E) Friday

(C) Neither A nor C (both of which must be scheduled later than two of the other cities) can be scheduled for either Monday or Tuesday, so we eliminate (A) and (B). Then, Thursday is not acceptable for D, which must be scheduled before both A and C. Finally, Friday is not acceptable for B, D, or NY. Wednesday is an acceptable day for any of the five cities as shown by the following diagrams:

M	Tu	W	Th	F
B	D	A	NY	C
NY	D	B	A	C
NY	D	C	B	A
NY	B	D	A	C
B	D	NY	A	C

Questions 7–12

This is a selection set. You should begin by summarizing the initial conditions:

$$N \neq O$$
$$L \supset J \text{ or } K$$

This last condition seems to be ambiguous: can both J and K serve on a committee with L? The answer is no. For placing J, K, and L on the same committee would place N and O on a committee together in violation of the first condition. Aside from this, there don't appear to be any further obvious conclusions, so we go to the questions.

7. Which of the following groups of people could serve together on a committee?

(A) J, K, N
(B) J, K, O
(C) J, L, K
(D) K, N, O
(E) L, K, O

(E) Since no additional information is provided by the stem, check each group against the initial conditions. (C) and (D) violate the first condition. The remaining choices do not directly contradict any condition, but (A) and (B) indirectly contradict the second condition, for the other committee must include L without either J or K.

8. If L and O serve on the same committee, which of the following pairs must serve on the other committee?

(A) J and K
(B) J and M
(C) J and N
(D) K and N
(E) M and N

(E) If L and O are on one committee, then obviously N must be on the other committee:

$$L, O \qquad N$$

There is only one other initial condition, so the solution to this item must involve the placement of J and K relative to L. Either J or K must be on the committee with L and the other on the committee with N. This means that M is on the committee with N.

457

9. If *M* and *O* serve on one committee, which of the following pairs must serve on the other committee?

    (A) *J* and *L*
    (B) *J* and *N*
    (C) *K* and *L*
    (D) *K* and *N*
    (E) *L* and *N*

(E) If *M* and *O* serve on one committee, then *N* must serve on the other committee:

  M,O *N*

Again, the key to the problem must be the second condition. Since *L* must be with either *J* or *K*, *L* cannot be on a committee with *M* and *O*. So *L* must be on the committee with *N*:

  M,O *N,L*

Then, *J* will be on one committee with *K* on the other (though which cannot be determined from the information given). This is sufficient, however, to answer the question.

10. Which of the following pairs CANNOT serve on the same committee?

    (A) *J* and *K*
    (B) *J* and *M*
    (C) *L* and *O*
    (D) *M* and *N*
    (E) *M* and *O*

(A) Test each choice by trying to construct possible committees using the pairs. The correct choice will be the one for which a permissible arrangement is NOT possible. (A) is not a possibility. *L* would also have to be on the same committee, but if one committee consists of *J*, *K*, and *L*, then the other committee would include both *N* and *O* in violation of the first condition. As for (B), *J,M,N* and *L,K,O* are possible committees; and this arrangement also shows that (C) and (D) are also possible. Then to prove that (E) is possible, simply switch the positions of *N* and *O*: *J,M,O* and *L,K,N*.

11. If *J* and *M* serve on different committees, which of the following must be true?

    I. *M* and *K* serve on the same committee.
    II. *N* and *L* serve on the same committee.
    III. *J* and *N* serve on the same committee.

    (A) I only (B) III only (C) I and II only
    (D) II and III only (E) I, II, and III

(A) If *J* and *M* serve on different committees, then since *N* and *O* also serve on different committees, it is also true that the remaining two persons, *K* and *L*, must serve on different committees:

  J/M, N/O, K/L *J/M, N/O, K/L*

But *K* must serve with either *L*, who must serve with either *J* or *K*. Since *L* is not going to be on the same committee as *K*, *L* must be on the same committee as *J*, and the following must be true:

  J,L, N/O *M, K, N/O*

Thus, only statement I is necessarily true.

12. If *L* and *J* serve on the same committee, which of the following must be true?

    I. *M* and *K* serve on the same committee.
    II. *M* and *N* serve on the same committee.
    III. *J* and *O* serve on the same committee.

    (A) I only (B) II only (C) III only
    (D) I and III only (E) II and III only

(A) If *L* and *J* are on the same committee, then either *N* or *O* must also be on that committee (to respect the first condition), and this means that both *M* and *K* are on the other committee:

  L, J, N/O *M, K, N/O*

Thus, only statement I is necessarily true.

Questions 13–19

This set is a variation on the linear ordering theme. But here the individuals are arranged in a circle rather than in a single line. Of course, you may want to use a diagram such as:

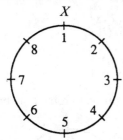

We begin by summarizing the information:

students = J,K,L

faculty = P,Q,R

admin. = X,Y

fac. ≠ fac.

K ≠ P

L ≠ J

L ≠ Q

13. Which of the following is an acceptable seating arrangement for seats 2 through 8, respectively?

    (A) J, K, P, Y, Q, R, L
    (B) K, P, J, Q, L, R, Y
    (C) L, J, Y, R, K, Q, P
    (D) P, L, R, K, Q, Y, J
    (E) P, L, Q, J, Y, R, K

    (D) This set provides no additional information, so just use the initial conditions to eliminate choices. Using the first condition (that no faculty member can be seated next to another faculty member), we eliminate (A) and (C). Then, using the second condition, that K not sit next to P, we eliminate (B). And finally, using the fourth condition, that L not sit next to Q, we eliminate (E). Only (D) meets all of the initial conditions.

14. All of the following are acceptable seating arrangements for seats 2 through 8, respectively, EXCEPT

    (A) J, Y, P, R, K, L, Q
    (B) K, Q, J, P, Y, R, L
    (C) L, K, R, Y, P, J, Q
    (D) K, L, P, J, R, Y, Q
    (E) Y, P, L, R, J, Q, K

    (A) We attack this question in the same way, but here the correct choice is the one that violates one of the restrictions. We start with the first condition and immediately see that (A) is not a possible order. (P cannot be seated next to R.) (A) also violates the last condition. The other choices respect all of the initial conditions.

15. If P is seated in seat 4 and J is seated in seat 6, then who must be seated in seat 5?

    (A) K (B) L (C) Q (D) R (E) Y

    (E) One way of approaching this item is to try to use the additional information coupled with the initial conditions to deduce which individual must be seated in chair 5. You would reason that neither Q nor R can be in 5 (for they are faculty, as is P). Further, K cannot be in 5 (next to P), and L cannot be in 5 (next to J). Since X is in seat 1, the only person left to occupy seat 5 is Y.

    Or, you can reach the same conclusion by working backwards from the choices. You can eliminate (A) through (D), so the one remaining choice, (E), must be correct.

16. If J is seated in seat 5 and Q is seated in seat 6, and if no faculty member is seated directly across the table from another faculty member, then which of the following must be true?

    (A) Seat 2 is occupied by L.
    (B) Seat 3 is occupied by P.
    (C) Seat 4 is occupied by K.
    (D) Seat 7 is occupied by Y.
    (E) Seat 8 is occupied by R.

    (A) Here you will probably want to use a rough diagram:

    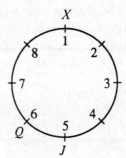

    Given the additional stipulation that faculty members cannot sit opposite one another, we know that P and R cannot occupy seat 2. Now where should

459

you look for further conclusions? The most powerful condition is the first, since it governs the placement of three individuals. So that should be your starting point. Neither P nor R can occupy seat 7. Given, then, that only seats 3, 4, and 8 remain available, to respect that first condition either P or R will have to occupy seat 8 and the other seat 3, though which will occupy which seat is not determined.

Now work with the other conditions. As for the second, since neither K nor P is already placed on the diagram, this condition doesn't help us. So try the next two conditions. Since L cannot sit next to either J or P, L must be seated in seat 2. At last we have another definite conclusion. Is it enough to answer the question? Check the choices. Only (A) apears to be necessarily true, while the other choices are only possibly true. So (A) must be the correct one.

17. If no faculty member sits directly across the table from another faculty member and both P and R are seated in even-numbered seats, which of the following must be true?

(A) J is seated in an odd-numbered seat.
(B) K is seated in an odd-numbered seat.
(C) Q is seated in an odd-numbered seat.
(D) L is seated in an even-numbered seat.
(E) Q is seated in an even-numbered seat.

(C) If P and R are both seated in even-numbered seats, then (given that they cannot be seated opposite one another) they must be separated by exactly one seat; for example:

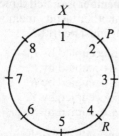

Now use the additional information to try to place Q. Q cannot be in an even-numbered seat, for that would put Q directly opposite either P or R. So Q is in an odd-numbered seat, and this conclusion is sufficient to answer the question.

18. If K is seated in seat 3 and L is seated in seat 5 and no faculty member is seated directly across the table from another faculty member, then the correct seating pattern for seats 2, 4, 6, 7, and 8, respectively, is

(A) J, R, Y, P, Q
(B) P, R, Y, Q, J
(C) Q, R, Y, P, J
(D) R, Q, Y, P, J
(E) Y, Q, R, P, J

(C) Again, you will probably need a diagram:

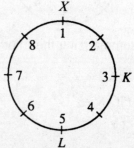

Again, you should start with the conditions that govern the placement of the faculty members. Given the first initial condition and the additional stipulation of this question regarding the seating of faculty members, the faculty members must be in seats 2, 4, and 7. Try some other arrangements, and you will see they are not possible because they either put a faculty member next to or directly across from another faculty member:

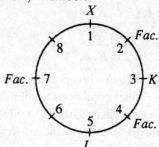

Now use the other conditions. According to the second condition, K cannot sit next to P, which means that P must be in seat 7:

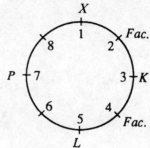

Since Q cannot sit next to L, Q must be in seat 2 with R in seat 4:

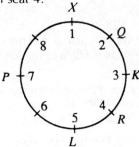

Given the third condition, J must be in seat 8 with Y in seat 6. So (C) gives the correct order.

19. If J and L are seated directly opposite each other, then J cannot be seated in seat

(A) 2
(B) 3
(C) 4
(D) 5
(E) 6

(D) Since X is in seat 1, J cannot be seated in seat 5.

First, it is possible for J and L to be in seats 4 and 8, respectively:

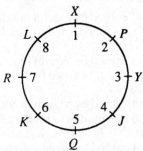

It is not possible, however, for L and J to occupy seats 5 and 1, for X is assigned to seat 1.

Finally, it is possible for J and L to occupy seats 6 and 2, respectively:

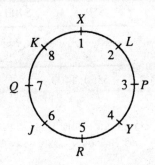

Questions 20–24

This is a set that uses relationships such as "greater than" and "less than." Notice that there are two elements to keep track of, salary and commission:

Salary ——————————————→
Commission ——————————————→

It's not possible to enter the first condition on the diagram, since you don't know the relationship between the amounts described in that statement. It is possible, however, to enter the information provided by the second condition. Daniels' salary = $200, and Bradey's commissions = $200 + $100 = $300.

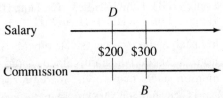

Now try the third condition. It isn't possible to place this information on the diagram you already have, so sketch a second diagram:

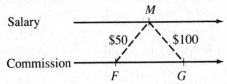

Now you can enter the last condition on the first diagram:

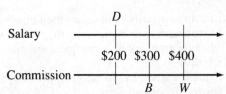

And then pick up the rest of the information from the first condition:

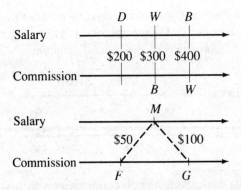

It is typical of a problem set like this that you may have to work back and forth between different conditions to extract all of the information from them. Whatever other conclusions there are to be drawn are already implicitly contained in the diagram, so we should go to the questions.

20. How much did Wright earn in commissions?

(A) $50　(B) $200　(C) $300
(D) $400　(E) $700

(D) This is made clear by the first diagram.

21. Which of the following statements can be inferred from the information given above?

I. Gibson earned $150 more in commissions than Fowler did.
II. Martin earned more in salary than Wright earned in commissions.
III. Bradey earned more in salary than in commissions.

(A) I only　(B) I and II only　(C) I and III only
(D) II and III only　(E) I, II, and III

(C) Test each of the statements. Statement I is inferable from the second diagram. Since Martin made $50 more in salary than Fowler made in commissions and Gibson made $100 more in commissions than Martin made in salary, Gibson must have made $150 more in commissions than Fowler did. Statement III is clearly inferable from the first diagram. Statement II, however, is not inferable, because there is no information that allows us to compare data given in the first diagram with data given in the second diagram.

22. If Martin earned $300 in commissions, an amount twice what he earned in salary, then which of the following must be true?

(A) Martin earned more in salary than Fowler did.
(B) Martin earned more in salary than Wright did.
(C) Martin earned more in commissions that Daniels did.
(D) Daniels earned less in salary than Gibson earned in commissions.
(E) Bradey earned less in salary than Martin earned in commissions.

(D) The additional information provided by this stem establishes that Martin's salary was $150. Enter the new information on the second diagram:

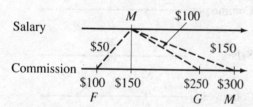

The first diagram taken in conjunction with this diagram shows that (D) is necessarily true. (A) might or might not be true (we have no information about Fowler's salary). (B) is necessarily false (Wright earned $300 in salary, Martin only $150). (C) might or might not be true (we have no information about Daniels'

commissions). And (E) is necessarily false (Bradey earned $400 in salary and Martin only $300 in commissions).

23. If Gibson and Wright each earned the same amount in commissions, then which of the following must be true?

I. Fowler earned $250 in commissions.
II. Martin earned $300 in salary.
III. Daniels earned $150 in salary.

(A) I only　(B) II only　(C) I and II only
(D) II and III only　(E) I, II, and III

(C) Erase the information from item 22 from the diagram and enter the new information:

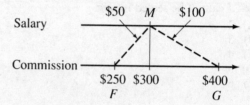

Thus, statements I and II are necessarily true. Statement III might or might not be true (no information is given about Daniels' salary).

24. If the amount earned by Fowler in commissions was $150 more than the amount earned by Daniels in salary, then which of the following must be true?

I. The amount earned by Martin in salary was equal to the amount earned by Bradey in salary.
II. The amount earned by Wright in salary was equal to the amount earned by Fowler in commissions.
III. The amount earned by Martin in commissions was equal to the amount earned by Wright in commissions.
IV. The amount earned by Wright in commissions was equal to the amount earned by Gibson in commissions.

(A) I only　(B) I and IV only
(C) III and IV only　(D) II, III, and IV only
(E) I, II, III, and IV

(A) Again, erase the information from the previous problem and enter the new information on the second diagram:

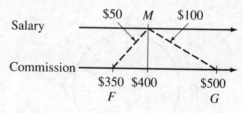

Therefore, statement I must be true (Martin's salary was $400, and Bradey's salary was $400). State-

462

ment II is false (Wright's salary was $300, but Fowler earned $350 in commissions). Statement III might or might not be true; we have no information about Martin's commissions. Finally, statement IV must be false (Wright earned $400 in commissions, but Gibson earned $500 in commissions).

SECTION 3

LOGICAL REASONING

The editor of a newspaper received the following letter:

Dear Editor:

This holiday season I think we should make a serious effort to recapture the true spirit of giving. Each of us should resolve to give gifts and expect none. And if someone offers us a gift, we should refuse it and suggest that it be given to someone else. In this way, we would all experience a feeling of pure giving.

1. Which of the following statements points out the most serious logical flaw in the letter?

    (A) If no one accepted any gifts, it would be impossible for anyone to give a gift.
    (B) The holiday season is not the only time of year when people give and receive gifts.
    (C) Often people receive gifts that are really not very useful, so it would not be a great sacrifice to part with them.
    (D) Sometimes a person may make a gift to someone in the hope of later receiving something in exchange for it.
    (E) Gift-giving is a tradition that is thousands of years old and a characteristic of virtually every human community.

    (A) There is a logical flaw in the argument. If everyone refused to accept gifts, there would be no one to whom to give gifts. Thus, the whole idea of gift-giving breaks down. The reasoning put forth in the letter is internally inconsistent.

Recently credit card companies have come under attack by consumer groups who argue that the interest rates charged by these companies are unconscionably high. In fact, the rates are generally several percentage points above those charged by banks for ordinary personal loans. But consumer groups overlook the fact that credit cards afford the user great flexibility. A user can purchase an item while it is on sale. So the lower cost of the item offsets the extra cost of the credit.

2. The argument above makes which of the following assumptions?

    (A) The cost savings of buying an item at a reduced price are at least equal to the excess interest that a consumer pays on purchases made with a credit card.

    (B) A credit card application is not rejected unless the applicant has a long history of late payments and other credit problems.
    (C) The prices of items purchased by consumers on sale are still sufficiently high to enable sellers to recoup their costs and make a modest profit.
    (D) The consumers who make purchases of sale items with credit cards are persons who might not qualify for bank loans with a lower interest rate.
    (E) The average outstanding balance of the ordinary credit card user is no greater than the total non-credit-card debt of the credit card user.

(A) The conclusion of the argument is that despite the comparatively high interest rates charged by credit card companies, on balance consumers are not harmed because they save money by buying items on sale. For this conclusion to be true, it must be the case that the amount of money saved by purchasing items on sale is sufficient to offset the additional cost of the credit. (A) makes this hidden assumption explicit. (B) and (C) are both fairly weak responses. As for (B), the speaker claims only that those who have and use credit cards are not disadvantaged by the high interest rates. He doesn't make any claim about the availability of cards. As for (C), the speaker claims only that items are offered on sale. He doesn't have to commit himself to any position on the wisdom of the seller's marketing strategy.

(D) and (E) are somewhat attractive because they both mention the idea of ordinary loans and the idea of credit cards. The difficulty with (D) is that this is a position to which the speaker need not commit, and you can prove this by making the opposite assumption. Even if all credit card users could qualify for ordinary bank loans, this doesn't affect the speaker's conclusion that the flexibility afforded by credit cards offsets the additional cost of using them. (E) is wrong for a similar reason; even if (E) is false, the conclusion of the argument is not affected one way or the other.

Bob and Cindy are each older than both Diane and Ellen.

3. If the statement above is true, then which of the following *additional* statements ensures the truth of the conclusion "Allen is older than Ellen"?

   (A) Allen is younger than Bob.
   (B) Cindy is older than Bob.
   (C) Cindy is younger than Bob.
   (D) Allen is older than Diane.
   (E) Allen is older than Cindy.

   (E) This item is like an analytical reasoning problem, so you may find that a simple diagram is useful:

   $(D + E) < (B + C)$

   Now test each answer choice:

   (A) $A < (D + E) < (B + C)$

   This shows that (A) does not *guarantee* that A is older than E. (B) and (C) must be incorrect since neither places A on the diagram. As for (D):

   $D < A < E < (B + C)$

   This shows that (D) does not guarantee that A is older than E. (E), however, does guarantee that A is older than E:

   $(D + E) < (B + C) < A$

   Even if A is not older than B, he must be older than E.

Despite seductive advertisements, so-called low tar and nicotine cigarettes are really no safer than other cigarettes. The seemingly lower levels of tar and nicotine reported by the Federal Trade Commission are attributable to the FTS use of smoking machines, not human beings, to determine tar and nicotine levels. But people do not smoke like machines. A study of blood samples of smokers found no significant differences among smokers of the various brands and a direct relationship between nicotine intake and the number of cigarettes smoked, regardless of brand.

4. Someone wishing to defend a low tar and nicotine cigarette as a safer smoking alternative could point out that

   (A) most people who smoke give little consideration to the health risks involved in smoking
   (B) in confined spaces the health of even non-smokers is endangered by tobacco smoke
   (C) a smoker could choose to make his smoking habits similar to the methods of the testing machines
   (D) most cigarette companies offer smokers several different brands, including low tar and nicotine cigarettes
   (E) cigarette companies are required by law to include tar and nicotine content on the labels of cigarette packages

(C) The logical structure of the original statement is an attempt to discredit an argument from analogy by pointing out that machines don't smoke like human beings. You could strengthen the argument under attack (that is, you can strengthen the claim that low tar and nicotine cigarettes are an improvement over regular cigarettes) by repairing the analogy. This is what (C) attempts to do. As for (A), asserting that smokers just don't care about their health is not going to do very much to repair the argument for the claim that low tar and nicotine cigarettes have health advantages. As for (D) and (E), these two fail to advance the issue, for neither is connected with the question of whether light cigarettes really have any significant advantage in terms of health. (B) is perhaps the second-best choice. You might attempt to defend light cigarettes by arguing that, even though they don't offer any real advantage over regular cigarettes in terms of the health of the smoker, non-smokers might benefit from them if they are exposed to less tar and nicotine than they otherwise would be. There are two things wrong with this line of thinking. First, you would still have the burden of showing that so-called light cigarettes emit lower levels of tar and nicotine, but (B) doesn't make any such claim. Second, as a matter of test-taking strategy, you should prefer choice (C) because (C) comes to grips with the internal logical structure of the statement.

Many countries that rely on the United States for military assistance request the same sophisticated weapons systems used by United States forces. But experience shows the folly of this policy. Because their armed forces lack the training and parts needed to maintain them, the weapons systems are often totally ineffective when installed or become ineffective shortly thereafter.

5. The problem described above is most like which of the following situations?

   (A) An antique car collector who purchases two old sports cars of the same model and cannibalizes one for spare parts for the other.
   (B) A business corporation that decides to lease a fleet of cars rather than purchase them with the understanding that the leasing company will service and repair them.
   (C) A university physics professor who hires graduate students to do research work but finds that she must first train them in their new duties.
   (D) A parent who purchases a personal computer for a child's education only to find that the available software is too complex for the child to use.
   (E) A captain of a large ship who is forced to return to port for repairs after an accident caused by a failure of the ship's radar.

(D) This is a logical similarity question. The problem described by the initial statement is that the armed forces of the beneficiary nation lack the know-how needed to operate the sophisticated equipment. A similar situation is described by (D)—the child lacks the know-how to operate the computer.

Dr. Esterhaus is an extremely competent administrator. In the twelve months following her appointment as Chief Executive Officer of the History Department, the number of applications for admission to the program was nearly 150 above that of the previous year.

6. The reasoning above makes which of the following assumptions?

    I. The increase in the number of applications for admissions is attributable to Dr. Esterhaus's efforts.

    II. Dr. Esterhaus is well-respected in the academic community as a history scholar.

    III. The number of applications for admission to a program is a good measure of the effectiveness of the Chief Executive Officer.

    (A) I only   (B) II only   (C) III only
    (D) I and III   (E) I, II, and III

(D) This question asks that you identify hidden assumptions of the argument. The conclusion of the argument is that Dr. Esterhaus is an effective administrator, and the support for that conclusion is the explicit premise that, following her appointment, the number of applications increased. This assumes (as statement I points out) that Dr. Esterhaus was responsible for the increase. If the increase had some other cause, then the conclusion regarding Dr. Esterhaus' effectiveness would not follow. The argument also assumes (as III notes) that the number of applications received is a good measure of an administrator's effectiveness. If the number of applications received is not necessarily a good measure of effectiveness, then the conclusion does not follow from the premises. II, however, is not a hidden premise of the argument. Whether or not Dr. Esterhaus is a good scholar is irrelevant to her effectiveness as an administrator, at least as that term is used in the initial statement.

The recent 40-percent reduction in airfares represents an attempt by the airlines to encourage impulse traveling. Because the lower-fare tickets need to be purchased only two days in advance of the flight, the companies hope to increase volume, thereby boosting overall revenues. The policy is ill-conceived, however, because business travelers, who would normally pay full fare, will now purchase discount fares, thus depressing revenues.

7. Which of the following, if true, would most weaken the argument above?

    (A) Some people would prefer to pay a higher fare if the additional cost ensured better schedules and service.

    (B) The number of business travelers who will purchase discount tickets is greater than the number of additional passengers who will be attracted by the lower fares.

    (C) An airplane must be operated at or near capacity for the airline to show a profit on a particular flight.

    (D) Impulse travelers are persons whose schedules are highly flexible and who are anxious to find a lower fare.

    (E) Most business travelers must arrange their travel schedules more than two days in advance.

(E) This item asks you to find a good attack on the initial argument, and, as you have been instructed, the correct answer to such an item is often the denial of a hidden assumption of the argument. This is why (E) is an effective attack. The conclusion of the argument is that the airlines will lose money. Why? Because business travelers will take advantage of the reduced fares. This argument assumes, however, that business travelers are able to take advantage of the reduced fares. (E) attacks this hidden assumption by noting that business travelers must arrange their schedules in advance, which effectively precludes them from taking advantage of the lower fares.

(A) may have some merit as a choice. You might argue that some people would avoid using discount fares, preferring better service. The difficulty with this line of thinking is that it attempts to provide a counterexample to a claim that is not universal in the first place. The speaker never claims that everyone will take advantage of the lower fares, only that enough people will to depress revenues. (B) seems to be the second-best choice because it at least has the merit of trying to come to grips with the logical structure of the initial statement. (It tries to analyze the probable effect of the new policy.) The difficulty with (B), and this is a fatal difficulty, is that it actually strengthens the initial argument. In essence, (B) is arguing that revenues will be depressed by the discount fares. (C) does not come to grips with the logic of the argument. The airlines' cost structure does not necessarily dictate consumer behavior. Finally, (D) just seems to provide a definition of *impulse traveler* that is consistent with the usage the speaker makes of that term, so (D) does not weaken the argument.

The United States Postal Service is drowning in junk mail. The average postal carrier delivers more junk mail, or third-class letters, than first-class mail. The result is a rapid decline in the quality of all postal services because first-class mail in effect subsidizes third-class mail.

8. Which of the following, if true, would most strengthen the argument above?

(A) It costs twice as much to mail a first-class letter as a third-class letter, yet per piece handling cost for each is the same.

(B) Members of the postal workers union have opposed deregulation of third-class delivery services because such a move threatens the jobs of postal workers.

(C) Since private companies were allowed to compete with the Postal Service for overnight letter business, the Postal Services share of that market fell off by 60 percent.

(D) The cost of first-class postage has risen at a rate twice that of inflation while the delivery time for first-class mail has increased by 10 percent.

(E) An audit conducted by the General Accounting Office revealed that 80 percent of all first-class letters are delivered within five days of postmark while only 20 percent of all third-class mail is delivered within five days of postmark.

(A) This item asks for you to stengthen the argument, so the correct choice may articulate a hidden assumption of the argument. The conclusion of the argument is that the quality of postal service has declined. What has caused this? According to the argument, the decline in service stems from the fact that first-class mail subsidizes third-class mail. This assertion rests on the hidden assumption that funds that would otherwise be spent on first-class service are being used to pay for the servicing of third-class mail. (A) correctly identifies this assumption: third-class mail doesn't pay for itself.

As for (B), the fact that the postal workers union opposes a change in policy doesn't reveal anything about the cost structure of the post office one way or the other. As for (C), the argument concerns the relationship between first- and third-class mail, so a point about overnight mail service is irrelevant. (D) at least has the merit of addressing the issue of the cost of first-class mail, but it is not clear how this bears on the question of whether first-class mail is subsidizing third-class mail. Finally, (E) is perhaps

the second-best response. (E) at least makes an attempt to compare some aspect of first-class mail with third-class mail, but (E) (which refers to delivery time) doesn't analyze the relative cost of mailing and handling the two classes of mail.

Questions 9–10

Negative consumer reaction to a product is not generated solely by critical negative appraisal of a product's performance. Rather, negative reaction is generated by a perceived gap between consumer expectation and product performance. Businesses should use advertising to adjust consumer expectations to coincide with their products' performances.

9. Which of the following is (are) implied by the passage above?

I. If consumer expectations are sufficiently reduced, then negative consumer reaction to products will disappear even though product performance remains unchanged.

II. If product performances are sufficiently improved, negative consumer reaction to products will disappear no matter how high expectations remain.

III. When consumer expectations about product performance increase, negative consumer reaction may persist despite improvements in product performance.

(A) I only   (B) III only   (C) I and III only
(D) II and III only   (E) I, II, and III

(B) This item asks you to draw a further conclusion from the premises given. With an item like this, you must make sure that your further conclusions are adequately supported by the premises contained in the initial statement. In particular, you want to make sure your further conclusions do not go beyond the scope of the initial statement. It is for this reason that we can eliminate both I and II. The initial statement says that negative consumer reaction is a function of expectation as well as product performance. Statement I makes the mistake of concluding that expectation is the sole factor in consumer reaction and that product performance is completely irrelevant—a conclusion not supported by the initial statement. II errs in the other direction. It concludes that performance is the only relevant factor and that expectations can be ignored—again, a conclusion that goes beyond the scope of the initial statement. III, however, is implied by the initial statement. Since two factors are operating to determine consumer reaction, adjusting the one but not the other may leave a residuum of dissatisfaction.

10. Which of the following, if true, would most weaken the argument above?

(A) Most consumers are able to make informed judgments about the actual performance of the products they purchase.

(B) The expectations of most consumers are influenced to a large extent by the claims made for those products by the manufacturers.

(C) Unless consumer expectations about a product are sufficiently high, consumers will not purchase that product.

(D) Government agencies prosecute businesses that make fraudulent advertising claims about product performances.

(E) Most consumers purchase products based upon their recognition of a particular brand name, not on a critical evaluation of the product's past performance.

(C) A common way of attacking an argument that makes a proposal for some sort of policy is to determine whether the proposal would entail any unwanted side effects. This is the strategy employed by (C). The initial statement says, in effect, that by reducing consumer expectations, the consumer won't be disappointed in the product. An unwanted consequence of reducing expectations, however, may be that consumers simply will not buy the product in the first place.

Here, both (A) and (B) seem to support rather than weaken the argument. As for (A), it is a hidden assumption of the argument that consumers are able to make judgments about product quality. But this choice provides support for that assumption, so it strengthens rather than weakens the argument. (B) makes a similar error. The argument presupposes that it is possible to manipulate consumer expectations, but this choice strengthens that assumption. (D) is fairly clearly irrelevant to the issue raised in the initial statement. Finally, (E) is perhaps the second-best choice. It seems to say that consumers don't make judgments about quality; compare choice (A). The difficulty with (E) is that brand name comes to stand for performance expectation and that is presumably something that can be manipulated.

The bills produced by a truly great counterfeiter are never discovered. So a counterfeiter whose product has been learned to be fraudulent is not a very good counterfeiter. The truly great ones never get caught.

11. Which of the following arguments supports its conclusion in the same way as the argument above?

(A) This government agency has been infiltrated by spies from a foreign power. The three who were caught have given the names of several other spies.

(B) A reliable security guard always patrols his or her assigned territory. Ellen, who is a security guard, did not patrol her assigned territory. Therefore, Ellen is not a good security guard.

(C) Drug usage is on the increase. Over the past few years, drug enforcement agents have arrested more and more people attempting to smuggle drugs into the country.

(D) The CIA is accused of bungling its attempted covert operations in several foreign countries. But this is not fair to the CIA. The agency conducts many successful covert operations, but by definition, a successful covert operation never comes to light, so the agency cannot take credit for them.

(E) The state legislature should pass a law requiring all restaurants with a seating capacity of a certain minimum to set aside a section for nonsmokers. There is ample scientific evidence that passive smoking is harmful to nonsmokers.

(D) The logical structure of the initial statement reminds me of what parents tell their children as the Christmas holiday approaches: Santa Claus is watching you; but no matter how quick you are, you'll never get a glimpse of him, because he's too fast. In other words, the claim that Santa Claus is watching is, in principle, unverifiable. So, too, is the claim in (D): there are CIA successes, but you can never learn about them because they are successful. None of the other choices exhibit this logical flaw.

Production of chlorofluorocarbons (CFCs) is believed to cause the breakdown of fragile ozone molecules in the Earth's atmosphere. During the 1970s, especially in the United States, scientists found that the quantity of ozone in the atmosphere dropped by an average of about 2 percent. In 1981, a ban on the use of CFCs in aerosol spray cans went into effect in the United States. In 1986, new measurements showed that ozone levels in the atmosphere had fallen by another 1 percent as compared to 1981.

12. Which of the following, if true, could help provide an explanation for this finding?

I. Production of CFCs in Japan and Western Europe rose sharply between 1981 and 1986.

II. Climatic changes occurring during the early 1980s have contributed to the breakdown of atmospheric ozone.

III. During the early 1980s, several new and important uses were found for CFCs.

(A) I only   (B) III only   (C) I and III only
(D) II and III only   (E) I, II, and III

(E) This question asks that you find possible causal explanations for a phenomenon. Statement I is a possible explanation. For even though the United States may have reduced its production of CFCs, it is possible that production increased elsewhere and that this accounted for damage to the ozone layer. II is another possible explanation: natural phenomena were at work as well. Finally, III also is a possible explanation: although one use was prohibited, CFCs were manufactured in increasing amounts to satisfy other uses.

In a study of crime, it was estimated that over 60 percent of all major property crimes—auto thefts, burglaries, and robberies—in the city during 1986 were committed by a group of 350 persistent offenders. It was also found that over half of the major property crimes were committed by individuals who were addicted to drugs.

13. If the statements above are true, which of the following must also be true?

(A) Some of the 350 persistent offenders in the city are also drug addicts.
(B) All of the 350 persistent offenders in the city are also drug addicts.
(C) Most drug addicts eventually become persistent offenders.
(D) Most persistent offenders became criminals because they were drug addicts.
(E) Persistent offenders and drug addicts do not commit crimes other than major property crimes.

(A) We can eliminate (C), (D), and (E) because they go beyond the scope of the initial statement. There is just not enough evidence provided to support them. (A), however, is supported by the evidence cited. Since 60 percent of the crimes in question were committed by persistent offenders, and since over half were committed by drug addicts, there must be some overlap between the two populations. Thus, we can conclude that at least some of the persistent offenders are drug addicts. We cannot, however, conclude that all of the persistent offenders are drug addicts.

If this is not clear to you, try thinking of an analogous case. For example, in a certain group of ten people, six are wearing hats and five are wearing gloves. Thus, you know at least one person is wearing both.

During the past ten years, the number of semiconductors manufactured by the United States semiconductor industry has grown by 200 percent, but the number of semiconductors manufactured by the Japanese semiconductor industry has grown by 500 percent. Therefore, Japan now produces more semiconductors than the United States.

14. Which of the following, if true, most weakens the argument above?

(A) In the past five years, the number of semiconductors manufactured by the United States semiconductor industry has grown by only 100 percent.
(B) The dollar value of the semiconductors produced in the United States over the past ten years was greater than the dollar value of semiconductors produced in Japan during the same time.
(C) Exports of semiconductors today represent a higher proportion of total United States exports than they did ten years ago.
(D) Ten years ago, the United States produced 90 percent of the world's semiconductors while Japan produced only 2 percent.
(E) Ten years ago, Japan ranked fourth in the world in the production of semiconductors while the United States ranked first.

(D) The fallacy in the argument is the common one of confusing percents with absolute numbers. The conclusion of the argument is that Japan produces more semiconductors than the United States, but the support for that argument would be a comparison of the percentage increase. It is easy to illustrate the fallacy using numbers. Assume, for example, that ten years ago the United States produced 90 semiconductors and Japan produced only two semiconductors. Ten years later, given a 200-percent growth rate, the United States would produce 90 + 180 = 270 units. Given a 500-percent growth rate, Japan would produce 2 + 10 = 12 units.

This explains why people on opposite sides of an issue reach seemingly different conclusions based on the same facts. For example:

X: During the past five years, we have held the line on costs. The cost of a subway token has increased by only 15 cents during this period.
Y: The cost of riding the subway has soared over the past five years by a whopping 25 percent.

Both of the claims could very well be true, if the original cost of the token was 60 cents and the new cost is 75 cents. (D) correctly focuses on this fallacy.

(A) does not contradict the statements contained in the argument. It is possible that the growth rate over the past five years was only half of what it was for the entire ten-year period. (B) doesn't come to grips with the argument, for the speaker has chosen to make a point about the number of semiconductors—not their dollar value. As for (C), this point may very well be true; but it doesn't address the comparison made in the initial paragraph. Finally, as for (E), this, if anything, seems completely consistent with the information provided in the initial paragraph.

Government spending on education does not really benefit students. During the 1960s and 1970s, spending by the federal government on education programs rose by over 150 percent. During the same period, students' scores on standardized tests dropped nearly every year.

15. The argument above depends upon which of the following assumptions?

(A) The scores students achieve on standardized examinations are a good measure of the effectiveness of educational programs.

(B) During the 1960s and 1970s, progressively more students were able to take advantage of federally funded educational programs.

(C) The proportion of the United States population classified as students did not increase appreciably during the 1960s and 1970s.

(D) The money spent by the federal government on educational programs during the 1960s and 1970s could have been better spent on health and welfare programs.

(E) The number of college graduates who chose teaching as a profession declined during the 1960s and 1970s.

(A) This item asks for you to identify a hidden premise of the argument. Examine the structure of the argument. The conclusion is "Government spending on education does not really benefit students." The explicit premises are (a) spending has increased and (b) standardized test scores have not. The conclusion rests upon the suppressed premise that standardized test scores are an appropriate measure of how well students are doing. (A) correctly points this out.

(B) is not completely irrelevant to the argument, but its significance is not clear. It could be used to support the argument: the money reached more and more students but still did no good. It could also be used to undermine the argument: the funds were not ineffective, but they were spread too thinly, so that overall results were disappointing. Since the point seems to cut both ways, we cannot say that it definitely weakens the argument.

(C) and (E) can be analyzed in the same way. Both are generally related to the problem discussed by the speaker, but it is not clear how each is directly relevant to the point made. Finally, as for (D), the author is not necessarily committed to the view that the money could have been better spent elsewhere. The author might very well think that virtually all such spending is a waste.

16. Which of the following arguments is directed against the proponent of an idea rather than against the idea itself?

(A) Allowing the Soviet Union to join our nation in peace-keeping efforts in the Middle East will serve only to increase the Soviet profile there and strengthen the hand of the communists in a vital region of the world.

(B) Advocates of capital punishment argue that the fear of the death penalty will frighten potential criminals sufficiently to deter them from committing crimes, but the proponents of the death penalty fail to recognize that statistics demonstrate that the death penalty actually does nothing to deter crime.

(C) Free trade must not be a one-way street. Before the United States drops its barriers against imports, our trading partners must offer firm guarantees that they will do the same. Otherwise, our balance of trade will suffer greatly.

(D) The voters should reject the bond issue proposed to finance the new, multi-million-dollar sports complex. The mayor would never have proposed this project were it not that real estate developers are among the chief contributors to his campaigns.

(E) Much of the money spent on defense projects is wasteful. First, a lot of money is spent by the different services working on essentially the same projects. Second, defense contractors understand that government audits rarely uncover overbilling, so the contractors routinely submit inflated demands for payment.

(D) The question stem asks you to identify the argument that is directed against the proponent of the idea rather than against the merit of the idea itself. This is (D). The argument in (D) never addresses the consequences of building the proposed sports complex. Instead, the argument states that the proposal should be rejected because its defender, the mayor, is biased. Notice that each of the other arguments addresses the merits of an issue by describing some of the results of taking a certain course of action.

It is essential that school children learn important facts about their country's history, and it may be salutary for them to learn, in time, of its follies and misdeeds, so as not to repeat them. But it is important, above all, for the very young to learn something of their nation's heroes; for only in this way are the virtues that make us fully human transmitted from one generation to the next.

17. The speaker above would most likely agree with which of the following statements?

   (A) Children should first be taught about the positive aspects of their country's history and only later about the negative aspects of its history.
   (B) The school system should not provide information to students about historical incidents that might be considered to have been mistakes.
   (C) The development of moral virtue and civic character is a task for the classroom rather than for the parents in the home.
   (D) Writers of histories for children should strive for a well-balanced and objective presentation of historical facts.
   (E) The primary function of the educational system is the inculcation of moral and social values.

(A) This question asks what further conclusion can be inferred from the paragraph. The key to such a problem is to find a further conclusion that is strongly supported by the explicit text, that is, a conclusion that does not go very far beyond the text. Here, the best choice is (A). The speaker claims that it is important for school children to learn about their country's history, especially about its heroes, but only later about its failings. From this we can infer that school children should be taught about the favorable aspects of their country's history and only later, when they are older, about unfavorable aspects.

(B) is contradicted by the explicit wording of the claim, for the speaker allows that students should be taught about their country's failings—but only when they are older. (C) goes far beyond the explicit wording of the claim. The author might very well insist that parents as well as teachers have the responsibility to teach children of their country's history. As for (D), the speaker apparently believes that a balanced view of history is not necessarily the best view to give school children. And finally, (E) goes too far beyond the specific claim. While the author obviously believes that it is a function of the educational system to provide moral and social instruction, nothing in the text suggests that the author thinks this is the primary function of the educational system.

Local governments frequently offer tax incentives, changes in zoning restrictions, and the loosening of environmental regulations to large local corporations in an effort to keep these firms from relocating, thereby hoping to maintain employment possibilities for its citizens. Yet most new jobs today are created not by large corporations but by smaller, new ones, and these are the firms most likely to be hurt by burdensome taxes and government regulations. Therefore, the inducements offered to large corporations ultimately hurt local economies.

18. Which of the following, if true, would most weaken the argument above?

   (A) Large corporations provide considerably more job opportunities than those created by smaller enterprises.
   (B) Most small businesses fail during the first year because their owners lack needed managerial experience.
   (C) The federal government's Small Business Administration offers low-cost loans and other services for newly created small businesses.
   (D) The economic growth of the country as a whole depends more upon the success or failure of the largest corporations than it does upon the success or failure of small businesses.
   (E) Tax breaks and other economic incentives help small businesses survive for a longer period than they would otherwise remain economically viable.

(A) The weakness in this argument is that it oversimplifies matters. The speaker argues that smaller firms are responsible for creating new jobs, so legislation that is protective of large firms (and presumably injures small ones) is economically harmful. Here is the oversimplification. The speaker fails to recognize that large firms, even though they don't create new jobs, do employ large numbers of people. (A) focuses on this weakness.

(B) mentions an idea that is related to the idea of small firms, but (B) is not immediately relevant to the question discussed in the paragraph. (C) is incorrect for a similar reason. (D) fails because the speaker has made a claim that is carefully limited to the effects of such policies on local economies. (D) just shifts the focus of the discussion but doesn't attack the original argument. Finally, as for (E), the fact that small businesses may be the beneficiaries of some government policies has no bearing on the analysis made by the speaker (of policies aimed at large businesses).

This last season, the Youth League baseball team sponsored by Cantrell Bootery included four players who pitched, seven who played the outfield, five who played the infield, and three who played catcher. The league rules state that a player may not play more than one position during a game and that a player must play the entire game unless injured. From these figures, we can conclude that the Cantrell Bootery team included nineteen different players.

19. Which of the following, if true, most seriously weakens the conclusion above?

   (A) When a player is injured during a game, a substitute may be provided.
   (B) Some players on the Cantrell Bootery did not play in every game during the season.
   (C) The number of players on a Youth League team may fluctuate during the course of the season.
   (D) A particular player in the league may play different positions in different games.
   (E) According to league rules, only nine players may be on the playing field at any one time.

(D) The argument above is characterized by a logical flaw. It fails to recognize that an individual may have more than one of the enumerated characteristics. For example, a player might pitch, catch, and play the infield and outfield. The rules of the league provide only that a player may not do this within a particular game, but they do not preclude a player's playing different positions in different games. (D) correctly focuses on this logical weakness.

Whenever possible, our nation's founders reserved political powers to state and local governments. Their assumption was that the officers in these governments, being chosen by smaller and more geographically compact bodies of citizens, would be "closer" to the people and more responsive to their interests. However, in today's era of mass media and national broadcast coverage of politics, most citizens are better informed about government on the national level than they are about local governments. Consequently, corrupt or incompetent public officials are more likely to thrive at the state and local levels.

20. The argument above assumes that

   (A) voters are generally incapable of understanding local issues
   (B) the mass media are usually eager to publicize charges of governmental corruption and incompetence
   (C) state and local officials are likely to be more honest and competent than those at the national level
   (D) the founders were unaware of the extent of the corruption and incompetence that characterized their own local governments
   (E) citizen awareness is likely to help deter or reduce corruption and incompetence in government

(E) This question asks you to identify a hidden assumption of the argument, so begin by analyzing the structure of the argument. The conclusion of the argument is contained in the final sentence of the initial paragraph and is signaled by the word *consequently*: "corrupt or incompetent officials are more likely to be found at the local level." The speaker argues to this conclusion in the following way. First, in theory, the closer the government is to its citizens, the better it will govern. Second, citizens today are generally ignorant of what goes on in local government. For this to be an explanation of corruption in local government, the author must believe also that it is the ignorance of citizens about local affairs that permits local governments to be corrupt. (E) articulates this hidden assumption.

(A) seems to be contradicted by the initial paragraph. As we have just seen, the author believes that voters can make a difference. As for (B), the speaker might or might not accept this, but his position on this issue is irrelevant to the claim made in the initial paragraph. To prove this to yourself, assume first that the author would agree with the statement in (B) and then that he would not. You will find the author's position on this related issue is not essential to the argument in the initial paragraph. As for (C), this statement is directly contradicted by the conclusion of the initial paragraph. Finally, as for (D), the author states that the phenomenon of local corruption is a modern one.

Proponents of the use of air bags in automobiles claim that these units, designed to inflate automatically in case of a crash, can cushion passengers against the impact of the collision, thereby saving lives. They say that, like seat belts, air bags should be required in every new car. Opponents argue that air bags would add hundreds of dollars to the cost of a new car, putting domestic producers at a competitive disadvantage, since foreign producers are not required by their governments to include the air bag safety feature.

21. Which of the following, if true, most weakens the argument given above by the opponents of the air bag requirement?

(A) A majority of drivers polled responded that they believe that air bags offer no additional safety advantage over that already provided by seat belts.

(B) In nine out of ten automobile accidents, the use of a seat belt significantly reduces the risk of serious injury or death.

(C) In manufacturers' tests of air bags, the air bags spontaneously inflated on the average about once every 350,000 miles.

(D) A law requiring domestic manufacturers to include air bags could also require that all cars imported into the country also be equipped with air bags.

(E) The lobbyists for the automobile industry have thus far been successful in convincing certain powerful figures in the legislature to veto any proposed air bag legislation.

(D) This question asks for you to weaken the argument above. As was stressed in the chapter "Logical Reasoning I," the answer to a question like this often focuses on a hidden assumption of an argument. (D) does this. The conclusion of the argument is that requiring domestic manufacturers to incorporate air bags into the design of their cars would put these manufacturers at a competitive disadvantage vis-a-vis foreign manufacturers. But this is true only if it is also true that foreign manufacturers do not also include air bags. (D) attacks this assumption by pointing out that the law could also require that imported cars be equipped with air bags.

As for (A), what drivers believe about the effectiveness of air bags is not relevant to the issue of whether the cost of air bags would be a disadvantage to domestic producers. Similarly, as for (B), whether or not seat belts are effective is not relevant to the issue of whether the additional cost of air bags would harm domestic manufacturers. As for (C), though this is a point that might be relevant to a discussion of the effectiveness of air bags, it is not relevant to the question of their cost. Finally, as for (E), the fact that lobbyists have in the past been successful in preventing the passage of a law does not mean that the law should not be passed.

The average salary of major league baseball players is so high because they represent the cream of their profession, the very best among the many thousands of aspiring baseball players produced in this country each year. The salaries of major leaguers should be compared not with those of typical businesspeople, doctors, or lawyers, but with only top business executives, the finest surgeons, or the partners of leading law firms.

22. The author is most likely trying to make which of the following points?

(A) Playing baseball at the major league level requires the same kinds of skills required of highly paid business executives, doctors, and lawyers.

(B) In a market economy, the price paid for any good or service is subject to the laws of supply and demand.

(C) The salaries of major league baseball players are not overly inflated when compared with those of other highly skilled professionals.

(D) The services provided by professional baseball players are as important to the team as those services provided by executives, doctors, and lawyers are to their businesses, patients, and clients.

(E) Baseball players who seek to maximize their compensation are responding to the same economic pressures that motivate business executives, doctors, and lawyers.

(C) This question asks you to draw a further conclusion from the initial paragraph. Remember that the key to this type of question is finding a choice that is strongly supported by the text. Avoid choices that are overly broad, and pay careful attention to the way that the choices and the initial paragraph are worded.

(C) is strongly supported by the text. The speaker argues that it is wrong to compare highly paid baseball players with businesspeople, doctors, and lawyers in general. Since major league players are not ordinary players, the appropriate comparison would be between major league players and extraordinary business people, doctors, and lawyers. Once this comparison is made, the high salaries of baseball players will not seem so high by comparison.

A careful reading of (A) will show that it is incorrect. The speaker argues that major league baseball players, like high-powered business executives, doctors, and lawyers, are extremely skilled. Although he would acknowledge that these groups are highly skilled, nothing in the text suggests he would insist that they have the same skills. (B) is much too general a conclusion. This might be a statement the speaker would endorse but would not be a conclusion of the highly specific information contained in this initial statement. (D) is perhaps the second-best

answer. The author might very well agree with this statement, but (D), if it is truly relevant to the argument, is actually a hidden assumption of the argument. When the speaker argues that the proper comparison is between big-league players and other high-powered professionals, he implicitly assumes that their value in their respective professions is similar. Since this is really a hidden assumption of the argument, it cannot be the conclusion to which the speaker is leading. Finally, as for (E), though the author might also accept this statement, it is not the point to which he is leading.

Questions 23–24

According to a recent study, the gap between the average starting salaries of teachers and those of other professionals has shrunk in recent years. Among ten other professions requiring comparable levels of education, teaching ranked ninth in starting salaries in 1975; today, it ranks sixth. Moreover, the average starting salary for a teacher is now 82 percent of the average for the other professionals included in the study. Therefore, it can no longer be argued that starting teachers are underpaid.

23. The argument above depends upon which of the following assumptions?

(A) The extent of a person's formal education is an appropriate measure by which to determine the level of his salary.

(B) The purchasing power of the dollars paid to teachers has not changed significantly since 1975.

(C) The average age of first-year teachers is the same today as it was in 1975.

(D) The profession with the highest average starting salary today is the same profession with the highest average starting salary in 1975.

(E) The average starting salary for a teacher should be equal to the average starting salary in the highest-paid profession.

(A) This question asks you to identify a suppressed premise of the argument. Analyze the structure of the argument. The conclusion is that starting teachers are no longer underpaid. The premise supporting this conclusion asserts, in essence, that the starting salaries for teachers are roughly equivalent to those for professions requiring the same education. For this comparison to support the conclusion, the author must assume that years of education is an appropriate way of determining how much someone should earn (as opposed to factors like hours worked, working conditions, risk, etc.). (A) articulates this hidden assumption.

(B) is incorrect because the author's only concern is to make a comparison of salary levels, not real purchasing power. As for (C), it is difficult to

473

see what relevance age has to starting salary. As for (D), the author compares starting salaries in teaching with the *average* of those in other professions. He does not need to analyze starting salaries within any other specific industry in order to make his point. Finally, (E) attributes to the author a value judgment that the text strongly suggests the author would reject. (The text states that starting teachers are no longer underpaid.)

24. Which of the following conclusions can be most reliably inferred from the passage above?

   (A) Eighty-two percent of teachers earn more than the average salary of other professionals.
   (B) Starting salaries for teachers have grown more quickly since 1975 than those of any other professionals.
   (C) The salaries of teachers may soon be expected to equal those of most other professionals.
   (D) Teachers today earn starting salaries lower than those earned by some other professionals with comparable levels of education.
   (E) The dollar increase in teachers' salaries since 1975 has been greater than those of most other professionals.

(D) This question asks you to analyze the data given in the initial paragraph and find a conclusion that it will support. (D) is the best response. The paragraph specifically states that the average starting salary for a teacher is now 82 percent of the average for the other professionals included in the study. From this you can conclude that there are some professions in which the average starting salary is higher than that for teaching.

(A) is incorrect for two reasons. First, this statement refers to "teachers" in general, but the initial paragraph discusses "starting salaries." Second, the 82-percent figure given in the passage means that the average starting salary for a teacher is 82 percent of the average starting salary of the other professions —not that 82 percent of all teachers earn a certain salary. (B) makes a claim that is not supported by the specific text. The text states only that relative to salary levels in certain other professions, those in teaching have increased—not that they have increased more than those in any other profession. (C) is a weak answer for two reasons. First, it refers to teachers' salaries in general, rather than starting salaries. Second, it makes a prediction for which there is no support in the text. The speaker gives us no reason to believe that the trend will continue. Finally, (E) is a weak response for two reasons. First, it refers generally to teachers' salaries, rather than to starting salaries. Second, (E) refers to "most other professionals,"

but the claim in the initial paragraph cites a study that focused upon ten other professions requiring comparable levels of education.

The Bill of Rights establishes freedom of speech as an absolute value that may not be abridged by any actions of the government. In interpreting and applying this provision of the Constitution, the courts have wisely held that exceptions to this rule must be rare, chiefly occurring under clearly defined circumstances in which unlimited freedom of speech would pose a clear and immediate danger to the safety of society at large.

25. The author of the statement above would most likely agree with which of the following?

   (A) Freedom of speech may reasonably be restricted to those forms of speech generally judged by the courts to be beneficial to society as a whole.
   (B) The absolute protection of freedom of speech set forth in the Constitution must be modified in certain situations.
   (C) The courts have usurped the power to determine what will and will not be considered "protected speech" under the Constitution.
   (D) Freedom of speech is the single most important guarantee included in the Bill of Rights.
   (E) Government will always tend to abridge freedom of speech unless legal impediments exist to prevent it from doing so.

(B) This question asks you to draw a further conclusion from the paragraph. The key to a question like this is to find an answer choice that is solidly supported by the explicit text of the paragraph. Carefully avoid choices that attribute too much to the speaker.

The correct answer is (B). The author notes that the language of the Bill of Rights establishes an unqualified right of free speech. He then states that courts have *wisely* limited this right, but only in very special circumstances. This language implies that though the author greatly values free speech, he recognizes that there must be some limitations on this right.

(A) attributes too much to the author. The author is very cautious in allowing restrictions on the right of free speech. (C) errs in the opposite direction. Though the author is cautious in allowing exceptions to the right of free speech, he does recognize that some exceptions are necessary and that courts have generally done a good job of defining them. (D) goes beyond the text of the paragraph. We would be entitled to conclude that the author values very highly the right to free speech, but there is nothing in the text to support this very grand conclusion. For all we know, the speaker may regard the right to due process as more important than the right to free speech. Finally, (E), too, goes beyond the scope of the speaker's claim. The author seems to think that a proper balance has been struck by the courts.

SECTION 4

LOGICAL REASONING

Sid is traveling in the land of Sasnak. His destination is Nocam, but he has encountered a fork in the road and doesn't know which route leads to his destination. In the land of Sasnak there are two clans. Members of one clan always speak the truth; members of the other clan always speak the opposite of the truth. It is impossible to tell who is a member of which clan simply by looking at them. At the fork is a man, and Sid wants to ask him for directions.

1. The answer to which of the following questions, if asked by Sid, will ensure that Sid will find the right road?

    I. Is the left fork the road to Nocam?
    II. If I asked you whether the left fork is the road to Nocam, would you tell the truth?
    III. If I asked you whether the left fork is the road to Nocam, would you say yes?
    (A) II only   (B) III only   (C) I and III only
    (D) II and III only   (E) I, II, and III

(B) This question is a logical teaser. Try each question. Statement I won't do the trick. If the man is a member of the truth-telling clan, Sid will obviously get the right answer; but if the man is a member of the other clan, he will get the wrong answer. But he has no way of determining whether he is getting a right or wrong answer. Nor will statement II do the trick, because it doesn't even tell the man about the particular roads in question. Statement III, however, will solve Sid's problem. If the man is a member of the truth-telling clan, Sid will get the right response. If the man is a member of the other clan, and if the left fork is the correct route, what will the man say? To answer the question "Is the left fork the correct route?" the liar would ordinarily respond "no," because it is the correct route. But if you ask at the same time "Would you say yes?" then the liar must respond "yes," because he would ordinarily say "no." Conversely, if the left fork is not the correct route, the liar will be tricked into saying "no." So regardless of the man's clan Sid gets a "yes" response if the road is the right one and a "no" response if it is not.

Questions 2 and 3

    (A) City Council member Ruth Jerome has introduced a proposal for commercial rent control that would limit the increases landlords can charge to small businesses. Of course, Ms. Jerome would favor such a plan because she and her husband own two small grocery stores.

    (B) On each of the three occasions I met John, he was wearing a hat. The first time it was a derby, the second time it was a beret, and the third time it was a baseball cap. I conclude, therefore, that John always wears a hat of some sort.

    (C) Mary has suggested that the Clippers finished in fifth place last season because they scored too few runs during the season. In fact, the Clippers' total run production for the season was the second highest in the league. So the Clippers failed to do better than fifth because their defense was inadequate.

    (D) Eighty-seven percent of the voters surveyed thought that Mr. Herman's views on foreign policy were better than those of Mr. Smith, and 91 percent thought Mr. Herman's views on domestic policy superior to those of Mr. Smith. On this basis, we can conclude that Mr. Herman is likely to make a better senator than Mr. Smith.

    (E) It is sometimes argued that the best way to stop drug-related crime is to legalize all drugs. But that's like giving away money to bank robbers and pickpockets.

2. Which of the arguments above relies upon a questionable analogy?

(E) The argument presented in (E) likens the proposal to legalize drugs to a proposal to legalize bank robbery and pickpocketing. The best description of this kind of argument is analogy, and the analogy is very weak. The criminal aspect of the ordinary drug transaction is the transfer of a substance that is illegal. In a robbery, a legal item (money) is illegally transferred.

3. Which of the arguments above attacks the credibility of a person rather than the merits of a proposal?

(A) In (A), the speaker never addresses the merits of the Council member's proposal. The speaker just attacks her motivation for making it, hoping to discredit her. As for the other choices, (B) is an argument based on generalization. There, the speaker reaches a very general conclusion (John always wears a hat of some type) based upon only three observations. As for (C), this speaker offers an alternative explanation for a phenomenon: the Clippers were good hitters, but other teams frequently outscored them because the defense was weak. As for

(D), this argument uses popular opinion to support its conclusion: Herman will be the better senator because people think more highly of him. (D), as written, therefore is a weak argument. Had (D) read "Herman will probably be elected," then the conclusion would seem justified.

Jorge: To be a good carpenter, one must have patience.
Gloria: That's not so; a good carpenter must also have the right tools.

4. Gloria has understood Jorge's statement to mean that

(A) if a person is a good carpenter, she will have the right tools
(B) if a person is a good carpenter, she will have patience
(C) if a person has patience, she will be a good carpenter
(D) if a person has the right tools, she will be a good carpenter
(E) if a person does not have the right tools, she cannot be a good carpenter

(C) In this verbal exchange, Gloria has evidently misunderstood what Jorge has said. The best way to attack the problem is to put each choice into Jorge's mouth. When you find one that makes sense of Gloria's response, you've found the right response (Jorge: If a person has patience, she will be a good carpenter. Gloria: That's not so; a good carpenter must also have the right tools.). This exchange makes sense. Gloria believes that she is correcting Jorge: No, patience alone is not enough; you also need the right tools.

The country of West Umberland imports no copper. Private industry's use of copper in West Umberland equals 85 percent of the amount of copper produced by the country's mines each year, while government use of copper equals 23 percent of the amount of copper produced by the country's mines each year.

5. If the information above is true, then which of the following conclusions can most reliably be drawn?

(A) West Umberland imports copper ore from other countries.
(B) Some copper in West Umberland is recycled.
(C) West Umberland's industry wastes substantial amounts of copper.
(D) Copper is in short supply in West Umberland.
(E) Each year, West Umberland produces more copper than the previous year.

(B) The paragraph asserts that West Umberland's use is equal to more than 100 percent of what its mines produce, so West Umberland must get some copper from a source other than its mines. The paragraph specifically denies that West Umberland im-

ports any copper, so (A) must be wrong. Only (B) mentions a possible source for the extra copper. (C) uses the word *waste*, but there is nothing in the initial paragraph to support the conclusion that industry wastes copper. (D) is perhaps the second-best answer. When read carefully, however, it turns out to be wrong. (D) asserts that there is a shortage of copper. But the fact that a commodity is recycled does not necessarily mean it is in short supply. (Recycling may simply be cheaper than mining ore.) Finally, (E) is wrong because the paragraph implies no year-to-year comparison. It is conceivable, for all we are told, that both use and production of copper are falling steadily in West Umberland.

At a time when New York City is going through a budgetary crisis, it is cutting its funding of the one agency that helps put more than half a billion dollars into its coffers: the Convention and Visitors Bureau. The proposed $1 million cut comes on the heels of last year's $250,000 funding cut. The debilitating effect of that cut is now obvious. Hotel occupancy rates shrank by 7 percent over last year, resulting in $10 million in taxes not realized by the city.

6. Which of the following, if true, would most weaken the argument above?

(A) New York City spends less than other less populated cities such as Louisville and Dayton to attract visitors and convention.
(B) The proposed $1 million cut in the budget of the Convention and Visitors Bureau's budget would do little to help balance the city's budget.
(C) The entire country is experiencing an economic downturn, and during an economic downturn people travel less than during times of prosperity.
(D) Adverse publicity about the crime rate in New York discourages some people and organizations from visiting the city.
(E) Many people and organizations would visit New York City even if it were not for the public relations efforts of the Convention and Visitors Bureau.

(C) The speaker asserts a causal connection between last year's cut of the Bureau's budget and the drop in tourism. The question stem then asks you to weaken this argument. Often, the correct answer to a question like this will be an alternative explanation for the phenomenon. (C) provides one: the drop is due to a general economic downturn, not to the cut in the Bureau's budget. (A) is irrelevant to the speaker's claim. The speaker has made a statement about what happened in New York—not in other cities. (B) and (E) both seem to strengthen the speaker's argument—(B) by stating that the city is being penny wise and pound foolish and (E) by stating that the Bureau is effective. (D) is perhaps the second-best response, for it might be read to suggest that adverse publicity is the reason for the drop. But notice that (D) talks about a chronic condition, so it does not explain the sudden one-year drop in tourism.

Within a scheme of criminal penalties, some penalties are more severe than others. A logical consequence of this hierarchy is that one penalty must be the most severe or ultimate penalty. Since the death penalty is the ultimate penalty, we can see that the death penalty is justified as a matter of logic.

7. Which of the following observations most weakens the argument above?

   (A) Not everyone believes that the death penalty is effective in deterring crime.
   (B) Some people incorrectly convicted of a crime might receive the death penalty.
   (C) The most severe penalty in a system of punishments could be something other than the death penalty.
   (D) For a person serving a life sentence with no chance of parole, only the death penalty is greater punishment.
   (E) No two punishments can be ranked equally severe in their effects on a person.

(C) The argument commits the fallacy of ambiguity. The speaker uses the term *ultimate* the first time to mean "most severe within the system." And it is true that in a system of punishments, there will be a most severe punishment. The second time, the speaker uses *ultimate* to mean "the most severe penalty possible." It is this equivocation that gives the argument its seemingly persuasive force. (A) is irrelevant to the speaker's claim. (If you picked [A], reread the choice carefully. [A] does not say that the death penalty is ineffective—only that some people don't believe that it is effective.) (B) is an argument that is often used by opponents of the death penalty, but it doesn't attack the logical structure of this particular argument. The observation made by (D) seems plausible, but it is irrelevant to the speaker's claim. Finally, (E) actually seems to strengthen that part of the speaker's claim that talks about a hierarchy of punishments.

Gloria's office is in Atlanta, but she must spend most of her time traveling. Every time I get a card from her, it has been mailed from some other city where she is staying on business.

8. It can be inferred from the passage above that Gloria

   (A) does not work in Atlanta

   (B) sends cards frequently
   (C) does not write letters
   (D) travels only on business
   (E) has offices in other cities

(B) This argument rests upon a suppressed or hidden premise: Gloria sends cards when she travels. (Gloria sends a lot of cards.) Therefore, Gloria must travel a lot.

(B) highlights this hidden assumption. (A) is specifically contradicted by the speaker's remarks. (C) is outside the scope of the argument. The argument says that Gloria sends cards—not that she sends only cards. (D) makes the same kind of error. The speaker states that Gloria travels on business—not that she travels only on business. And (E) is wrong because the speaker says only that Gloria travels on business and nothing about where she does her work while traveling.

Advocates for the homeless attempt to portray homeless persons as victims of social and economic circumstances beyond their control. A recent survey of the homeless in major cities found that a high percentage are addicted to alcohol or other drugs. Rather than innocent victims, these are people who are solely responsible for their own plights.

9. Which of the following, if true, would most weaken the argument above?

   (A) A large number of homeless persons turn to drugs and alcohol out of despair after becoming homeless.
   (B) Several government programs are designed to help the homeless find jobs and new housing.
   (C) Most cities offer shelter to the homeless on a night-by-night basis.
   (D) Alcoholism and other drug addictions can cause erratic and even violent behavior.
   (E) As much as 60 percent of any community's homeless population are local people.

(A) This argument also rests upon a hidden assumption. The speaker must believe (though does not say so specifically) that the homeless people in question were addicted to drugs or alcohol before they became homeless. (A) attacks this premise by indicating that the addiction may have taken place after the homelessness occurred. (B), (C), and (E) are irrelevant to the speaker's claim. The speaker is talking about the causes of homelessness, not about what is done for the homeless after the fact nor about where the people lived when they had homes. (D) at least has the merit of focusing on addiction, but it, too, is irrelevant because it does not address the issue of addiction as a cause of homelessness.

New York and several other states have wisely refused to raise the highway speed limit above 55 miles per hour despite calls by motorists for an increase. Although the 55-mile-per-hour speed limit was initially enacted by the Federal government as a conservation measure, it soon became clear that a felicitous consequence of the measure was considerably fewer traffic fatalities.

10. The speaker above is arguing that states that have a 55-mile-per-hour highway speed limit should

(A) raise the highway speed limit
(B) further reduce the highway speed limit
(C) retain the 55-mile-per-hour highway speed limit
(D) enact other measures to improve fuel conservation
(E) find other ways of reducing highway fatalities

(C) The question asks that you state the speaker's conclusion. The speaker states that some states have "wisely" refused to raise the speed limit because a higher speed limit would result in more fatalities. (C) is most likely the conclusion of this thinking. (A) must surely be wrong because the speaker is clearly opposed to raising the speed limit. (B) overstates the speaker's case. The speaker may believe that 55 miles per hour is the optimum speed limit: it saves lives while not being overly inconvenient. (D) and (E) may be ideas that the speaker would endorse, but the evidence presented about the 55-mile-per-hour speed limit does not lead in either of these directions.

The quality of life provided by a government depends not so much upon its formal structure as upon the ability and temperament of those who serve as its officers.

11. The author of the paragraph above would most likely agree with which of the following statements?

(A) A written constitution is essential to ensure the liberty of citizens against a strong government.
(B) Universal suffrage is the best guarantee that the general will of the people will become legislation.
(C) A government with good leaders is likely to survive for a longer time than a government with incompetent leaders.
(D) Poor leadership in a hierarchical organization threatens the ability of the organization to achieve results.
(E) The quality of the leadership of a government is the main determinant of whether the citizens will be happy.

(E) The initial statement asserts that the primary determinant of a government's ability to provide for its citizens is the skill of its administrators and not the formal structure of the government. Thus, (A) and (B) are incorrect. Those choices refer to formal elements of a government. (C) and (D) are more interesting but can be eliminated after careful reading. As for (C), the author states that the ability of the leaders determines the quality of life of the citizens—not whether the government will survive for a long period. It seems to me that (D) is the second-best choice. The author might very well apply his analysis of governmental structures to other hierarchical structures. But that requires that you go beyond the scope of the passage. By contrast, (E) is more clearly supported by the text because it is a statement about government. Another way of expressing this idea is to say that if (D) is arguably a correct choice, then (E) must be even better.

Your chart listing winners of the Most Valuable Player award states that one designated hitter won the award: Don Baylor in 1979. This is erroneous. No designated hitter has ever won the M.V.P., and it is extremely doubtful that a player who does not serve the team in the field will ever win it.

12. Which of the following, if true, would most strengthen the argument above?

(A) In 1979, Don Baylor played one game as first baseman.
(B) In 1979, Don Baylor played 97 games as an outfielder versus 65 as a designated hitter.
(C) Don Baylor won the Most Valuable Player award only once in his career.
(D) Of the two major baseball leagues, only the American League allows the use of a designated hitter.
(E) The Most Valuable Player award can be given to any player on the team.

(B) The argument as written is ambiguous. Is the speaker denying that Don Baylor was given the M.V.P. award in 1979, or is the speaker denying that Don Baylor was a designated hitter when he won it in 1979? If we adopt the first interpretation, there is no correct answer, so we must adopt the second interpretation. Now (B) appears to strengthen the argument: Don Baylor was an outfielder when he won the 1979 M.V.P., not a designated hitter. As for (A), this idea is consistent with the speaker's point but doesn't really strengthen the argument. The fact that Don Baylor played one game at first base doesn't prove that Don Baylor was not a designated hitter. (C) and (D) are irrelevant to the speaker's claim. Finally, as for (E), this point seems to suggest that it is theoretically possible for a designated hitter to be given the M.V.P. award, but that doesn't strengthen the argument that practically speaking, a designated hitter would never win the award.

"Most people like pennies," says Hamilton Dix, spokesperson for the United States Mint. "In March 1986 we did a survey at the Epcot Center at Walt Disney World, and half of all the adults said they use pennies daily."

13. Which of the following observations most undermines the position of the speaker above?

   (A) Most of the people who visit Walt Disney World are on vacation.
   (B) The survey covered people only at a single location in one state.
   (C) The survey included adults visiting Epcot Center but not children.
   (D) The speaker is a representative of the agency that manufactures pennies.
   (E) Many purchases require the use of pennies either as payment or as change.

(E) The argument above is a non sequitur; that is, the conclusion does not follow from the premises. The speaker claims that people *like* pennies, but the proof for that claim is that people *use* pennies. A person might be compelled to do something that he or she doesn't like at all, as choice (E) suggests. It is difficult to imagine how (A) can be read to contradict the argument. To the extent that you read (A) as indicting the survey (vacationers are not representative of people in general?), (B) is surely a better choice. At least (B) suggests that there is something specifically wrong with the survey. The weakness with (B), however, is that it doesn't carry the issue far enough. To be an effective attack on the argument, (B) would have to explain why the people surveyed do not reflect the population as a whole. (C) is weak for the same reason: how does this prove that the survey is inaccurate? As for (D), this does constitute an attack on the argument by suggesting that the speaker may have some reason to misrepresent the results of the survey. The trouble with (D), however, is that it is nowhere nearly so powerful an attack as (E). Whereas (D) only hints that the speaker *may* be misrepresenting the results, (E) points out the logical fallacy in the argument.

As a citizen who values individual rights, I am appalled at the growing use of random or mandatory drug testing. What is needed is a screening test for impaired function, not for drug use per se. For example, it would be easy to design a computerized test for reaction time. Such a test would be simple to administer and would be nonintrusive. Anyone failing the test could then be required to submit to the more invasive drug test.

14. Which of the following, if true, would most weaken the argument above?

   (A) Administrations of a reaction test could be arranged randomly, so that a drug-user could not alter his or her habits.
   (B) A reaction test measures capacity only at that time, but a drug test may show that a person is likely to be a future risk.
   (C) The Supreme Court has refused to rule that mandatory drug tests for employees in sensitive positions are unconstitutional.
   (D) A person might fail a reaction test for a reason other than impairment due to the use of illegal drugs.
   (E) A person who has ingested an illegal substance might have sufficient self-control to pass a reaction test.

(B) The speaker's argument assumes that the purpose of drug testing is to detect impairment at a particular moment, but drug testing may also serve to identify persons who, though not impaired at the time of testing, might be impaired at some future time. This is in essence what (B) argues. (A) seems to strengthen the speaker's position by stating that the reaction test could be used effectively. (C) doesn't constitute an attack on the argument at all. The fact that the Supreme Court has not held mandatory testing unconstitutional does not mean that a reaction test is not a better alternative than mandatory drug testing. On the surface, (D) does seem to attack the speaker's position, but closer study shows that (D) is actually consistent with the spirit of the speaker's proposal. While it may be true that a person might incorrectly be required to take a drug test (because she or he failed the reaction test for a reason unrelated to drug use), even a flawed reaction test is less intrusive than mandatory drug testing: with a flawed reaction test, a few people are needlessly tested for drugs, but with mandatory drug testing everyone is subject to the drug test. Finally, (E) also seems to attack the speaker's argument by saying that the reaction test would not necessarily detect all drug use. But the speaker can easily absorb this attack: true, but if the person tested can pass the reaction test, then the person is not impaired and shouldn't be required to take the drug test.

Computer colorization of black-and-white film is an important tool for making historical events seem real to students who live in an age of color movies and color television. A colorized version of the footage of Jack Ruby's assassination of Lee Harvey Oswald or of the first manned space shot will help students today understand what it was like for the millions of Americans who actually saw those events on television.

15. Which of the following, if true, most weakens the conclusion of the argument above?

(A) The people who saw those events live saw them in black and white, not in color.

(B) The events mentioned occurred before most of today's students were born.

(C) Many important historical events were never recorded on film.

(D) Modern techniques can improve the quality of the sound of old film footage.

(E) Colorization can be accomplished by a computer process that is relatively inexpensive.

(A) The speaker argues that colorization of film footage of historical events will help students today understand what people who originally viewed those events on television felt. The fallacy in this argument is that the people who saw the original events saw them in black and white, not in color. So if you really want to understand what is was like to watch the first manned space shot on television, you should watch it in black and white. This is the point made by (A). (B) is simply irrelevant to the argument. That today's students were not yet born at the time of the events in question doesn't address the speaker's point that colorization would be a good way of educating those students. Similarly, (C) is irrelevant. The fact that some events were not recorded doesn't address the speaker's point that the film that does exist should be colorized. (D) seems to make the same kind of mistake as the initial paragraph. Improving the quality of the soundtrack of old film will not give the same impression as the original soundtrack. And finally, as for (E), the fact that colorization is technologically feasible is certainly not a argument against colorization.

Five United States representatives are jointly sponsoring a bill that would provide federal funds to municipalities that will replace steps to public buildings with ramps in order to provide greater access to disabled persons. This is another example of a proposal to use public funds to provide advantages to some special-interest group while burdening the general public.

16. Which of the following observations would most weaken the conclusion of the argument above?

(A) Although a disabled person may not be able to use steps, both disabled and nondisabled people can use a ramp.

(B) The funds would be made available to all states and districts and not just to those represented by the bill's sponsors.

(C) An audit of government programs by an independent citizens' watchdog group uncovered billions of dollars spent for special-interest groups.

(D) Congressional lobbyists for associations representing disabled persons have alleged that the bill is underfunded.

(E) The federal funds will be available only on a matching basis to states and cities which provide funds of their own.

(A) The burden of the speaker's position is that installing ramps unfairly favors one group over another. What (A) points out is that stairs have the effect of favoring nondisabled persons over disabled persons (because disabled persons cannot negotiate the steps), but ramps do not disadvantage anyone for either group can utilize them. (B), (D), and (E) don't constitute an attack at all. The funding structure of the program is irrelevant to the speaker's point that the program favors a special-interest group. As for (C), this seems like an idea that the speaker would probably endorse, so it hardly constitutes an attack on the initial argument.

For over a week, we have been listening to news reports of the "heroic" efforts to save the two whales trapped in the arctic ice. Thousands of working hours were invested by Eskimos cutting a path through the ice, and icebreaking ships were called in at a cost of hundreds of thousands of dollars. Why spend a million dollars to save two whales when people are starving to death every day in Sudan?

17. The argument above makes the unsupported assumption that

(A) the people who worked to save the whales do not care about human suffering
(B) though the whales were rescued, they will not survive very much longer
(C) icebreaking efforts can somehow stop starvation in the Sudan
(D) Eskimos no longer rely heavily on whales as a source of nourishment
(E) the rescue operation to save the whales was mounted with government funds

(C) The speaker argues that the human effort and cost of equipment could better have been spent combatting starvation in the Sudan rather than in saving the lives of two whales. The fallacy of this argument is that it assumes that those efforts and costs could somehow have been utilized elsewhere. But it is difficult to imagine how an icebreaker could be used to combat starvation in the Sudan. (C) correctly highlights this unsupported assumption. (A) goes beyond the scope of the argument. Although the speaker does argue that the resources might have been better allocated, he is not committed to the idea that those who used the resources to save the whales did so perversely. (B) is wrong because the speaker is not arguing that the rescue of the whales was ineffective. (D) is completely irrelevant to the speaker's claim. (E) is perhaps the second-most-attractive answer, for it might prompt you to start thinking along the lines suggested by (C). But the speaker is not logically committed to the idea that government funds were used. The proof of this is that he would probably insist that even if private funds were used, those funds could better have been used elsewhere.

Until the 1986 federal tax reform law, the maximum tax on gains from investment like securities, real estate, works of art, and herds of cattle was only 20 percent, while ordinary income was taxed at rates as high as 50 percent. The reform law eliminated the capital gains tax advantage. Now the President proposes a 15-percent cap on taxes on personal investment in securities and homes. This new capital gains tax will create an incentive for investment, and investment spurs growth and creates jobs.

18. Which of the following, if true, most undermines the proposal for the new tax?

(A) The major investors in today's markets are tax-free institutional investors such as pension funds and endowments.
(B) Since the repeal of favorable treatment of capital gains, real economic growth has not declined considerably.
(C) The rate of inflation since the repeal of the capital gains tax has been the same as before the repeal.
(D) The President promised during the election campaign that there would be no new taxes during his administration.
(E) Interest rates have recently begun to drift upward in response to a tightening of the money supply by the Federal Reserve Board.

(A) The argument depends upon the assumption that significant investment decisions are affected by the tax treatment given to certain investments. (A) attacks this assumption by noting that most major investment decisions today are not influenced by tax considerations. (B) is perhaps the second-most-attractive answer. One way of attacking the proposal would be to show that the economy fares just as well without a capital gains tax as with it. Notice, however, that (B) doesn't say that. As for (C) and (E), these choices do mention economic trends but don't make any attempt to connect them to the repeal of the capital gains tax. Finally, (D) is fairly clearly irrelevant to the argument of lowering taxes by capping the tax on capital gains.

Questions 19 and 20

Biological functions can ultimately be explained in chemical terms. And chemical reactions can ultimately be explained by the laws of physics. Since biological function is dictated by physical laws, we should eventually discover life in other galaxies that functions very much like that here on earth.

19. The argument above assumes that

(A) life on other planets will be equally advanced
(B) chemistry and biology are not separate disciplines
(C) physics is a more important science than biology
(D) physical laws are the same throughout the universe

(E) physical laws can be explained in biological terms

(D) The speaker argues that physical laws dictate biological function, so we will find similar life in other parts of the universe. This assumes, as (D) notes, that other parts of the universe are governed by the same physical laws. (A) overstates the speaker's point. The speaker expects to find similar life in other parts of the universe, but he is not necessarily committed to the idea that this life will be at the same level on the evolutionary scale. (B) is a misreading of the initial paragraph. Though the speaker insists that the concepts of biology and chemistry can ultimately be explained in terms of physics, this is not to say that biology and chemistry do not exist as separate disciplines. (C) also overstates the speaker's point. There is no basis for the conclusion that one of the disciplines is more important than the other two. Finally, (E) reverses the connection made by the speaker.

20. Which of the following, if true, would most weaken the argument above?

(A) Physical laws permit many different organizations for life processes.
(B) In our solar system, only earth can support life as we know it.
(C) Scientists have not yet successfully created life in a laboratory.
(D) Space travel is not advanced enough to transport people to other galaxies.
(E) Physicists have advanced many different theories of subatomic particles.

(A) The problem with the initial argument is that it goes too far. The speaker is surely correct to note that biological processes depend upon the laws of physics, but this is not equivalent to saying that physical laws dictate a single "correct" organization for life processes. (A) focuses on this weakness in the argument. (B) is not an effective attack on the argument, for the speaker refers to other *galaxies,* not to other planets. (C), too, is irrelevant. The fact that scientists have not yet created life in a test tube does not counteract any point made by the speaker. Nor does (D) attack the speaker's argument. The speaker argues only that we will eventually find other life forms, not that we are presently equipped to find them. (E) is perhaps the second best answer, for it could be read to suggest that there is no one set of physical laws. But (E) does not really say that. It says not that the universe might have different sets of physical laws but that scientists have not yet agreed on how to describe these laws.

A Federal judge has ordered the county to house prisoners for whom there are no beds at the County Detention Facility at motels and inns until such time as beds become available. This will cost the county anywhere between $30 and $60 per night. I say it's time to punish criminals. Why shouldn't robbers, thieves, rapists, and murderers have to sleep on the floor for a couple of nights?

21. Which of the following, if true, would most weaken the argument above?

(A) The suit against the county was brought by a group of prisoners' rights activists concerned about jail overcrowding.
(B) The Federal judge who issued the order is known for her strong position against crime and her severe sentences.
(C) Very few hotel rooms in the county are available at rates of less than $30 per night.
(D) The cost of housing prisoners in double-occupancy rooms would be only $20 per night per prisoner.
(E) The Federal judge's order applies only to persons who have been charged with but not yet convicted of a crime.

(E) The correct answer to this item attacks a hidden assumption of the argument, namely, the assumption that the prisoners who are the subject of the judge's order are criminals. Any persuasive appeal the argument might have evaporates once it is made clear that the prisoners are merely accuseds and not criminals at all. As for (A) and (B), it is difficult to see what the genesis of the suit or the characteristics of the judge who issued the ruling have to do with the speaker's point. (C) and (D) at least have the merit of addressing some element of the argument; though ultimately, they are not serious attacks on the argument. As for (C), the fact that hotel rooms in general are expensive doesn't undermine the speaker's contention that hotel rooms ought not to be used because they do cost money. (D) is surely the second best answer here. It does tend to undermine somewhat the speaker's position: you have overstated your case; the cost will be $20 per night–not $30. Even so, it is easy to see that the speaker can respond "Even $20 per night is too much for criminals." (E) is by far the strongest argument. Rather than quibble over details, (E) attacks a premise—the foundation—of the argument.

Speaker X: Given the rising crime rate and the increased tendency for criminals to be heavily armed, our city's police officers need more powerful weapons. The standard six-shot .38 Special revolver should be replaced by the powerful 9-millimeter semiautomatic handgun. With the 9-millimeter, a criminal who is hit will stay down.

Speaker Y: To incapacitate, a handgun bullet must expend its full energy within the body cavity, creating hydrostatic pressures that result in trauma. The velocity of the bullet fired from a 9-millimeter handgun is so great that the bullet exits the body cavity too swiftly. A better use of public funds would be to retrain police officers to shoot well with the six-shot .38 Special revolvers. Each shot in a vital zone will change the attitude of any criminal.

22. Speaker Y challenges Speaker X's assumption that

(A) police ought to be effectively armed against criminals
(B) criminals are armed with powerful weapons
(C) a 9-millimeter handgun has more effective stopping power than a .38 Special revolver
(D) a 9-millimeter handgun fires a bullet with a higher velocity than a .38 Special revolver
(E) a 9-millimeter handgun is more accurate than a .38 Special revolver

(C) Speaker X's case for the 9-millimeter rests on the assumption that a criminal who is shot with such a gun will be incapacitated. Speaker Y attacks this assumption by explaining that the velocity of the bullet fired by the 9-millimeter is so great that the power of the bullet is wasted. (C) summarizes this strategy. As for (A), the second speaker agrees with the first that police ought to be "effectively" armed; the two disagree about how to achieve that goal. As for (B), the second speaker implicitly agrees with the first on this point by not attacking the point and by agreeing that police should be effectively armed. As for (D), to the extent that "more powerful" means "greater muzzle velocity," both speakers are agreed on this point. The first speaker considers the greater velocity an advantage, while the second considers it a disadvantage. Finally, as for (E), this choice misreads the second speaker's call for more training. The two speaker's disagree about the importance of "power" in a handgun, not about the relative accuracy of the two guns mentioned.

23. An answer to which of the following questions would be LEAST relevant to the debate above

(A) What is the cost of the 9-millimeter semiautomatic handgun compared to that of the .38 Special revolver?
(B) What is the risk of injuring a bystander with a 9-millimeter semiautomatic handgun compared to that of the .38 Special revolver?
(C) Over the past ten years, for how many of the occasions in which a police officer has used armed force would the 9-millimeter semiautomatic handgun have been more effective than the .38 Special revolver?
(D) By how much would a police officer's ability to incapacitate an attacker be improved by a retraining program on how to use the .38 Special revolver?
(E) How many civilians are intentionally killed each year by criminals who carry 9-millimeter semiautomatic handguns compared with all other handguns?

(E) The two speakers agree that criminals are heavily armed. They disagree on how best to neutralize their fire power. An answer to this question would neither strengthen nor weaken either speaker's position. As for (C) and (D), these two questions bear directly on the point at issue: is the 9-millimeter better than the .38. As for (A), the issue of cost is made relevant by the second speaker. Finally, as for (B), though neither speaker specifically mentions this issue, it is implicitly raised by the idea of the "power" of a handgun: if increased power means more civilian casualties, then that is a disadvantage of increased power.

A chemist knows the following about the colorless liquid in a certain beaker:

1. If chemical X is added to the liquid, it will turn red.
2. If chemical Y is added to the liquid, it will turn blue.
3. If both chemical X and chemical Y are added to the liquid, it will turn green.

24. Given the statements above, which of the following must be true?

(A) If the liquid remains colorless, then no chemicals were added.
(B) If the liquid turned green, then both chemical X and chemical Y were added.
(C) If the liquid turned blue, then chemical X was not added
(D) If the liquid turned blue, then it is possible that chemical Y was added.
(E) If the liquid remained colorless, then it is possible that chemical X and only chemical X was added.

(D) When dealing with statements of the sort used in this problem, you must be careful to distinguish between what are called "sufficient" and what are called "necessary" causes or conditions. Statement 1, for example, asserts that the addition of X will cause the liquid to turn red. That statement sets up a sufficient condition: adding X is sufficient to cause the liquid to turn red. Statement 1, however, does not assert that X is necessary to turn the liquid red. There could be many other chemicals that would also turn the liquid red. Compare the following: If X, then red. (sufficient but not necessary cause) Red only if X. (necessary but not sufficient cause) Red if and only if X. (necessary and sufficient cause) All three statements set up sufficient causes, as (D) correctly takes into account: Y is one, though perhaps not the only, possible cause for the liquid's turning red. As for (A), (B), and (C), these all treat the statements as setting up necessary conditions. Take (B) for example. Statement 3 asserts that the addition of both X and Y will turn the liquid green, but statement 3 does not assert that the only thing that will turn the liquid green is adding X and Y. As for (E), this is specifically contradicted by statement 1.

SECTION 5

ANALYTICAL REASONING

Questions 1–6

Use arrows to show the network of relations:

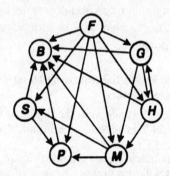

1. How many people in the system can call Mike directly?

   (A) 1   (B) 2   (C) 3   (D) 4   (E) 5

   (C) As the diagram shows, Mike can be reached directly by three people: Gary, Helen, and Fred.

2. How many workers in the system are unable to make any direct calls?

   (A) 0   (B) 1   (C) 2   (D) 3   (E) 4

   (B) The diagram shows one person with no outgoing arrows: Beth.

3. How many people in the system can call someone directly who can also call them directly?

   (A) 0   (B) 1   (C) 2   (D) 3   (E) 4

   (C) The diagram shows only one pair of reciprocal arrows: between Gary and Helen. So Gary can call Helen and vice versa.

4. Using the system, which of the following communications can be sent, either directly or indirectly?

   (A) Beth to Gary
   (B) Gary to Paul
   (C) Helen to Fred
   (D) Paul to Gary
   (E) Susan to Mike

   (B) Gary can call Mike directly, and Mike can in turn relay the message to Paul.

5. How many people using the system can telephone directly persons other than Beth who cannot telephone them directly?

   (A) 2   (B) 3   (C) 4   (D) 5   (E) 6

   (D) Five people can make direct calls to persons other than Beth who cannot return a direct call: Fred (to everyone else), Gary (to Mike), Helen (to Mike), Mike (to Paul and to Susan), and Susan (to Paul).

6. Which of the following repairs would ensure that Susan can call directly or have a message relayed to everyone else in the system?

   (A) Beth can call Fred.
   (B) Beth can call Gary.
   (C) Helen can call Paul.
   (D) Paul can call Mike.
   (E) Susan can call Gary.

   (A) Since Susan can call Beth directly, and since Fred can call everyone else, if Beth can call Fred, then Susan's message can be relayed to everyone else.

Questions 7–12

In a certain wooded area, six forest rangers—Ed, Grant, Helen, Jill, Maria, and Pedro—are assigned to six different watchtowers. Each morning they report to a central headquarters building and then hike to their assignments.

Ed's tower is southwest of headquarters, and Grant's tower is southeast of headquarters.

Helen's tower is southwest of headquarters, but Ed's tower is farther south than Helen's.

Jill's tower is somewhere to the north of headquarters, and Maria's tower is northeast of headquarters.

Jill's tower is farther east than Ed's tower and farther south than Maria's tower.

Pedro's tower is somewhere east of headquarters

484

and farther south than Jill's tower.

This problem requires a map:

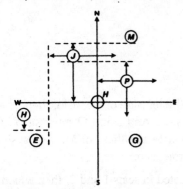

7. Pedro's tower cannot be located

(A) due east of headquarters
(B) due north of Grant's tower
(C) due east of Maria's tower
(D) northeast of Ed's tower
(E) northeast of Helen's tower

(C) Pedro's tower is south of Jill's tower and Jill's tower is south of Maria's tower. So Pedro's tower must be somewhere to the south of Maria's tower.

8. If Maria walks a straight course from her tower to headquarters and continues on that same course, then it is possible that she would come to all of the following towers EXCEPT:

(A) Ed's   (B) Grant's   (C) Helen's
(D) Jill's   (E) Pedro's

(B) Sketch the course on the map with a pencil. Maria would be walking in a southwesterly direction. While still in the northeast sector she could encounter either Jill or Pedro. On the other side of headquarters she would be in the southwest sector and could encounter either Helen or Ed. She could not, however, encounter Grant. Grant is in the southeast sector, and Maria would pass from the northeast to the southwest without entering the southeast sector.

9. If a tower is located exactly halfway between Maria's tower and Grant's tower, then that tower could be staffed by

I. Jill
II. Ed
III. Pedro

(A) I only   (B) III only   (C) I and III only
(D) II and III only   (E) I, II, and III

(C) Our map shows that Pedro might be midway between Maria and Grant. Also note that Jill could be east of headquarters, so she could be midway between Maria and Pedro. Ed, however, is in the southwest sector, so he cannot be midway between Maria and Grant.

10. Which of the following cannot be true?

(A) Helen's tower is exactly halfway between Jill's tower and Ed's tower.
(B) Ed's tower is exactly halfway between Helen's tower and Grant's tower.
(C) Jill's tower is exactly halfway between Ed's tower and Maria's tower.
(D) Jill's tower is exactly halfway between Maria's tower and Pedro's tower.
(E) Jill's tower is exactly halfway between Ed's tower and Grant's tower.

(E) Ed and Grant are both south of headquarters, while Jill is north of headquarters. So Jill could not be located halfway between Ed and Grant. The other choices make statements that could be true. As for (A), Helen must be north of Ed and south of Jill, so she could be halfway between the two of them. As for (B), Grant's position is not fixed, so Ed could be halfway between Helen and Grant. As for (C), Ed is in the southwest sector and Maria in the northeast sector, so it is possible to position Jill midway between them. Finally, as for (D), Jill could be east of headquarters and halfway between Maria and Pedro.

11. Which of the following statements could be true of the six towers?

I. There are more towers east of headquarters than west of headquarters.
II. There are more towers west of headquarters than east of headquarters.
III. There are more towers south of headquarters than north of headquarters.

(A) I only   (B) II only   (C) I and II only
(D) I and III only   (E) I, II, and III

(D) Maria, Pedro, and Grant are east of headquarters, so statement I will be true if Jill is also east of headquarters. Helen, Ed, and Grant are south of headquarters, so statement III will be true if Pedro is also south of headquarters. Statement II, however, cannot be true. At least three towers must be east of headquarters.

12. If a seventh tower is constructed somewhere west of headquarters, then which of the following could be true of the new tower?

I. It is located due east of Jill's tower.
II. It is located due south of Ed's tower.
III. It is located due west of Maria's tower.

(A) I only
(B) I and II only
(C) I and III only
(D) II and III only
(E) I, II, and III

(E) A seventh tower could be located due east of Jill's tower but to the west of headquarters, since

485

Jill's tower could also be west of headquarters. So statement I could be true. As for II, a new tower could be located due south of Ed's. And as for III, a new tower could also be located due west of Maria's tower (so long as it is also west of headquarters).

Questions 13–18

This is a selection set. The theater seats look like this:

STAGE

1   2   3   Aisle   4   5   6

And the other two conditions are:
$L \neq N$ $O = (J$ or $M)$

13. Which of the following pairs CANNOT sit on the same side of the aisle?

(A) J and M
(B) J and N
(C) K and N
(D) L and M
(E) L and O

(A) If J and M are on the same side of the aisle, then given the second condition, O must also be on that side of the aisle. But if J, M, and O sit on the same side of the aisle, then L and N will be together on the other side of the aisle—in violation of the first condition. The other pairings are possible:

(B) J, N, and O; K, L, and M
(C) K, N, and M; J, O, and L
(D) L, M, and K; J, O, and N
(E) L, O, and J; K, N, and M

14. Which of the following must be true?

I. If L and O sit on the right side of the aisle, then K must sit on the left side of the aisle.
II. If L and K sit on the right side of the aisle, then O must sit on the left side of the aisle.
III. If J and O sit on the right side of the aisle, then L must sit on the left side of the aisle.

(A) I only   (B) II only   (C) I and II only
(D) II and III only   (E) I, II, and III

(C) Statement I is true. If L and O sit on one side of the aisle, then either J or M must also sit on that side of the aisle. That makes three people on that side of the aisle, so N, K, and either J or M must sit on the other side of the aisle. II is also true. If L and K sit on the right side of the aisle, then (given the second condition) O must sit on the left so as to be with either J or M. III, however, is not necessarily true. If J and O sit on the right side of the aisle, either L or N sits with them.

15. If N and O sit on the left side of the aisle, then which of the following pairs must sit on the right side of the aisle?

(A) J and K
(B) J and L
(C) J and M
(D) K and L
(E) K and M

(D) If N sits on the left side of the aisle, then L must sit on the right side. And since O must sit on the same side of the aisle as either J or M, K must sit on the right side of the aisle.

16. If K and N are seated in seats 1 and 2, then which of the following pairs must be seated on the right side of the aisle?

(A) J and L
(B) J and M
(C) L and M
(D) L and O
(E) M and O

(D) If N sits on the left side of the aisle, then L must sit on the right side. And if K and N are on the left side, O cannot be on the left side. (O must be with either J or M.)

17. If M and K are seated in center seats on either side of the aisle, then which of the following must be true?

I. J is seated next to M.
II. O is seated next to K.
III. N is seated next to M.

(A) I only   (B) II only   (C) I and II only
(D) I and III only   (E) II and III only

(C) The additional information stipulates that M and K are on opposite sides of the aisle, and the initial conditions stipulate that L and N are on opposite sides of the aisle. This gives us two people on each side, and this means that J and O must be on opposite sides. But since O must be seated with either J or M, O must be seated on the same side of the aisle as M. And since M has the middle seat on the side of the aisle, J must be seated next to N. Therefore, statement I is true. Then, since O is on the same side of the aisle as K, and since K is in the middle seat, O must be seated next to K. So statement II is true. Statement III, however, is not true because we don't know which side of the aisle N will be seated on.

18. If M and N are seated in seats 3 and 6, respectively, and O is not seated next to N, then all of the following must be true EXCEPT:

(A) If K is seated next to M, then O is seated in seat 4.

(B) If L is seated next to M, then J is seated next to N.

(C) If J is seated next to L, then K is seated next to N.

(D) If J is seated in seat 4, then K is seated in seat 5.

(E) If O is seated in seat 4, then K is seated next to L.

(B) The initial conditions stipulate the following:

$$1 \quad 2 \quad 3 \quad \quad 4 \quad 5 \quad 6$$
$$\quad \quad \quad M \quad \quad \quad \quad \quad \quad N$$

And O is not seated in seat 5. Since N is in seat 6, we know that L must be on the left side of the aisle. (A) is necessarily true. If K is seated in seat 2, then L is seated in seat 1. This means that both O and J are on the right side of the aisle, and O must be in seat 4. (C) is also necessarily true. If J is seated next to L, then that fills up the seats to the left of the aisle. This means that J and O sit on the right side and that J must be next to N. (D) is necessarily true as well. If J is in seat 4, then, since O must be with either J or M, O must be on the left side of the aisle with M and L. This means that K is in the middle seat on the right side of the aisle. Finally, (E) is also necessarily true. With O in seat 4, J must be in seat 5. This means that K and L will occupy seats 1 and 2 (though not necessarily in that order) and be next to each other. (B), however, is not necessarily true. If L is seated next to M, then O could be seated in seat 1.

Questions 19–24

This is not a difficult problem set, but it becomes very easy if you find the right diagram:

1	2	3	4	5	6	7	8	9	10	11	12
	M		M		M		M		M		M
		V		V		V		V		V	
		E			E			E			E
			S				S				S

19. A student who finishes every grade in the school system would take how many exams?

(A) 15 (B) 18 (C) 20 (D) 22 (E) 24

(B) The table makes it easy to count them.

20. A student who takes only a math and an English exam at the end of the year must be in grade

(A) 2 (B) 6 (C) 8 (D) 9 (E) 12

(B) The table shows that only in grade six does a student take only math and English exams.

21. A student who takes a science exam and an English exam at the end of the year must be in grade

(A) 4 (B) 6 (C) 8 (D) 10 (E) 12

(E) Only in the twelfth grade does a student take both science and English exams. (The student would also take a math exam, but notice the difference in wording between this question and the preceding one.)

22. A student who takes a vocabulary exam but not an English exam could be in which of the following grades?

I. 5
II. 7
III. 11

(A) I only (B) II only (C) III only
(D) I and III only (E) I, II, and III

(E) Students take vocabulary exams in grades 5, 7, and 11, and in those grades they do not take English exams.

23. In how many years does a student take no exams?

(A) 0 (B) 1 (C) 2 (D) 3 (E) 4

(B) Only first-graders take no exams.

24. In all of the following grades, a battery of subject tests is given that matches exactly a battery given in another grade EXCEPT:

(A) 2 (B) 3 (C) 4 (D) 5 (E) 6

(E) In the sixth grade, a student takes exams in math and English only. In no other grade do students take exactly this battery. As for choice (A), the battery given to second-graders matches the battery given to tenth-graders. As for (B), the battery given to third-graders matches the battery given to ninth-graders. As for (C), the battery given to fourth-graders matches the battery given to eighth-graders. And as for (D), the battery given to fifth-graders matches the battery given to eleventh-graders.

Practice Test 2

Use a No. 2 pencil only. Be sure each mark is dark and completely fills the intended oval. Completely erase any errors or stray marks.

☐ A R C O ☐

Start with number 1 for each new section. If a section has fewer than 30 questions, leave the extra answer spaces blank.

SECTION 1

1. Ⓐ Ⓑ Ⓒ Ⓓ Ⓔ
2. Ⓐ Ⓑ Ⓒ Ⓓ Ⓔ
3. Ⓐ Ⓑ Ⓒ Ⓓ Ⓔ
4. Ⓐ Ⓑ Ⓒ Ⓓ Ⓔ
5. Ⓐ Ⓑ Ⓒ Ⓓ Ⓔ
6. Ⓐ Ⓑ Ⓒ Ⓓ Ⓔ
7. Ⓐ Ⓑ Ⓒ Ⓓ Ⓔ
8. Ⓐ Ⓑ Ⓒ Ⓓ Ⓔ
9. Ⓐ Ⓑ Ⓒ Ⓓ Ⓔ
10. Ⓐ Ⓑ Ⓒ Ⓓ Ⓔ
11. Ⓐ Ⓑ Ⓒ Ⓓ Ⓔ
12. Ⓐ Ⓑ Ⓒ Ⓓ Ⓔ
13. Ⓐ Ⓑ Ⓒ Ⓓ Ⓔ
14. Ⓐ Ⓑ Ⓒ Ⓓ Ⓔ
15. Ⓐ Ⓑ Ⓒ Ⓓ Ⓔ
16. Ⓐ Ⓑ Ⓒ Ⓓ Ⓔ
17. Ⓐ Ⓑ Ⓒ Ⓓ Ⓔ
18. Ⓐ Ⓑ Ⓒ Ⓓ Ⓔ
19. Ⓐ Ⓑ Ⓒ Ⓓ Ⓔ
20. Ⓐ Ⓑ Ⓒ Ⓓ Ⓔ
21. Ⓐ Ⓑ Ⓒ Ⓓ Ⓔ
22. Ⓐ Ⓑ Ⓒ Ⓓ Ⓔ
23. Ⓐ Ⓑ Ⓒ Ⓓ Ⓔ
24. Ⓐ Ⓑ Ⓒ Ⓓ Ⓔ
25. Ⓐ Ⓑ Ⓒ Ⓓ Ⓔ
26. Ⓐ Ⓑ Ⓒ Ⓓ Ⓔ
27. Ⓐ Ⓑ Ⓒ Ⓓ Ⓔ
28. Ⓐ Ⓑ Ⓒ Ⓓ Ⓔ
29. Ⓐ Ⓑ Ⓒ Ⓓ Ⓔ
30. Ⓐ Ⓑ Ⓒ Ⓓ Ⓔ

SECTION 2

1. Ⓐ Ⓑ Ⓒ Ⓓ Ⓔ
2. Ⓐ Ⓑ Ⓒ Ⓓ Ⓔ
3. Ⓐ Ⓑ Ⓒ Ⓓ Ⓔ
4. Ⓐ Ⓑ Ⓒ Ⓓ Ⓔ
5. Ⓐ Ⓑ Ⓒ Ⓓ Ⓔ
6. Ⓐ Ⓑ Ⓒ Ⓓ Ⓔ
7. Ⓐ Ⓑ Ⓒ Ⓓ Ⓔ
8. Ⓐ Ⓑ Ⓒ Ⓓ Ⓔ
9. Ⓐ Ⓑ Ⓒ Ⓓ Ⓔ
10. Ⓐ Ⓑ Ⓒ Ⓓ Ⓔ
11. Ⓐ Ⓑ Ⓒ Ⓓ Ⓔ
12. Ⓐ Ⓑ Ⓒ Ⓓ Ⓔ
13. Ⓐ Ⓑ Ⓒ Ⓓ Ⓔ
14. Ⓐ Ⓑ Ⓒ Ⓓ Ⓔ
15. Ⓐ Ⓑ Ⓒ Ⓓ Ⓔ
16. Ⓐ Ⓑ Ⓒ Ⓓ Ⓔ
17. Ⓐ Ⓑ Ⓒ Ⓓ Ⓔ
18. Ⓐ Ⓑ Ⓒ Ⓓ Ⓔ
19. Ⓐ Ⓑ Ⓒ Ⓓ Ⓔ
20. Ⓐ Ⓑ Ⓒ Ⓓ Ⓔ
21. Ⓐ Ⓑ Ⓒ Ⓓ Ⓔ
22. Ⓐ Ⓑ Ⓒ Ⓓ Ⓔ
23. Ⓐ Ⓑ Ⓒ Ⓓ Ⓔ
24. Ⓐ Ⓑ Ⓒ Ⓓ Ⓔ
25. Ⓐ Ⓑ Ⓒ Ⓓ Ⓔ
26. Ⓐ Ⓑ Ⓒ Ⓓ Ⓔ
27. Ⓐ Ⓑ Ⓒ Ⓓ Ⓔ
28. Ⓐ Ⓑ Ⓒ Ⓓ Ⓔ
29. Ⓐ Ⓑ Ⓒ Ⓓ Ⓔ
30. Ⓐ Ⓑ Ⓒ Ⓓ Ⓔ

SECTION 3

1. Ⓐ Ⓑ Ⓒ Ⓓ Ⓔ
2. Ⓐ Ⓑ Ⓒ Ⓓ Ⓔ
3. Ⓐ Ⓑ Ⓒ Ⓓ Ⓔ
4. Ⓐ Ⓑ Ⓒ Ⓓ Ⓔ
5. Ⓐ Ⓑ Ⓒ Ⓓ Ⓔ
6. Ⓐ Ⓑ Ⓒ Ⓓ Ⓔ
7. Ⓐ Ⓑ Ⓒ Ⓓ Ⓔ
8. Ⓐ Ⓑ Ⓒ Ⓓ Ⓔ
9. Ⓐ Ⓑ Ⓒ Ⓓ Ⓔ
10. Ⓐ Ⓑ Ⓒ Ⓓ Ⓔ
11. Ⓐ Ⓑ Ⓒ Ⓓ Ⓔ
12. Ⓐ Ⓑ Ⓒ Ⓓ Ⓔ
13. Ⓐ Ⓑ Ⓒ Ⓓ Ⓔ
14. Ⓐ Ⓑ Ⓒ Ⓓ Ⓔ
15. Ⓐ Ⓑ Ⓒ Ⓓ Ⓔ
16. Ⓐ Ⓑ Ⓒ Ⓓ Ⓔ
17. Ⓐ Ⓑ Ⓒ Ⓓ Ⓔ
18. Ⓐ Ⓑ Ⓒ Ⓓ Ⓔ
19. Ⓐ Ⓑ Ⓒ Ⓓ Ⓔ
20. Ⓐ Ⓑ Ⓒ Ⓓ Ⓔ
21. Ⓐ Ⓑ Ⓒ Ⓓ Ⓔ
22. Ⓐ Ⓑ Ⓒ Ⓓ Ⓔ
23. Ⓐ Ⓑ Ⓒ Ⓓ Ⓔ
24. Ⓐ Ⓑ Ⓒ Ⓓ Ⓔ
25. Ⓐ Ⓑ Ⓒ Ⓓ Ⓔ
26. Ⓐ Ⓑ Ⓒ Ⓓ Ⓔ
27. Ⓐ Ⓑ Ⓒ Ⓓ Ⓔ
28. Ⓐ Ⓑ Ⓒ Ⓓ Ⓔ
29. Ⓐ Ⓑ Ⓒ Ⓓ Ⓔ
30. Ⓐ Ⓑ Ⓒ Ⓓ Ⓔ

SECTION 4

1. Ⓐ Ⓑ Ⓒ Ⓓ Ⓔ
2. Ⓐ Ⓑ Ⓒ Ⓓ Ⓔ
3. Ⓐ Ⓑ Ⓒ Ⓓ Ⓔ
4. Ⓐ Ⓑ Ⓒ Ⓓ Ⓔ
5. Ⓐ Ⓑ Ⓒ Ⓓ Ⓔ
6. Ⓐ Ⓑ Ⓒ Ⓓ Ⓔ
7. Ⓐ Ⓑ Ⓒ Ⓓ Ⓔ
8. Ⓐ Ⓑ Ⓒ Ⓓ Ⓔ
9. Ⓐ Ⓑ Ⓒ Ⓓ Ⓔ
10. Ⓐ Ⓑ Ⓒ Ⓓ Ⓔ
11. Ⓐ Ⓑ Ⓒ Ⓓ Ⓔ
12. Ⓐ Ⓑ Ⓒ Ⓓ Ⓔ
13. Ⓐ Ⓑ Ⓒ Ⓓ Ⓔ
14. Ⓐ Ⓑ Ⓒ Ⓓ Ⓔ
15. Ⓐ Ⓑ Ⓒ Ⓓ Ⓔ
16. Ⓐ Ⓑ Ⓒ Ⓓ Ⓔ
17. Ⓐ Ⓑ Ⓒ Ⓓ Ⓔ
18. Ⓐ Ⓑ Ⓒ Ⓓ Ⓔ
19. Ⓐ Ⓑ Ⓒ Ⓓ Ⓔ
20. Ⓐ Ⓑ Ⓒ Ⓓ Ⓔ
21. Ⓐ Ⓑ Ⓒ Ⓓ Ⓔ
22. Ⓐ Ⓑ Ⓒ Ⓓ Ⓔ
23. Ⓐ Ⓑ Ⓒ Ⓓ Ⓔ
24. Ⓐ Ⓑ Ⓒ Ⓓ Ⓔ
25. Ⓐ Ⓑ Ⓒ Ⓓ Ⓔ
26. Ⓐ Ⓑ Ⓒ Ⓓ Ⓔ
27. Ⓐ Ⓑ Ⓒ Ⓓ Ⓔ
28. Ⓐ Ⓑ Ⓒ Ⓓ Ⓔ
29. Ⓐ Ⓑ Ⓒ Ⓓ Ⓔ
30. Ⓐ Ⓑ Ⓒ Ⓓ Ⓔ

SECTION 5

1. Ⓐ Ⓑ Ⓒ Ⓓ Ⓔ
2. Ⓐ Ⓑ Ⓒ Ⓓ Ⓔ
3. Ⓐ Ⓑ Ⓒ Ⓓ Ⓔ
4. Ⓐ Ⓑ Ⓒ Ⓓ Ⓔ
5. Ⓐ Ⓑ Ⓒ Ⓓ Ⓔ
6. Ⓐ Ⓑ Ⓒ Ⓓ Ⓔ
7. Ⓐ Ⓑ Ⓒ Ⓓ Ⓔ
8. Ⓐ Ⓑ Ⓒ Ⓓ Ⓔ
9. Ⓐ Ⓑ Ⓒ Ⓓ Ⓔ
10. Ⓐ Ⓑ Ⓒ Ⓓ Ⓔ
11. Ⓐ Ⓑ Ⓒ Ⓓ Ⓔ
12. Ⓐ Ⓑ Ⓒ Ⓓ Ⓔ
13. Ⓐ Ⓑ Ⓒ Ⓓ Ⓔ
14. Ⓐ Ⓑ Ⓒ Ⓓ Ⓔ
15. Ⓐ Ⓑ Ⓒ Ⓓ Ⓔ
16. Ⓐ Ⓑ Ⓒ Ⓓ Ⓔ
17. Ⓐ Ⓑ Ⓒ Ⓓ Ⓔ
18. Ⓐ Ⓑ Ⓒ Ⓓ Ⓔ
19. Ⓐ Ⓑ Ⓒ Ⓓ Ⓔ
20. Ⓐ Ⓑ Ⓒ Ⓓ Ⓔ
21. Ⓐ Ⓑ Ⓒ Ⓓ Ⓔ
22. Ⓐ Ⓑ Ⓒ Ⓓ Ⓔ
23. Ⓐ Ⓑ Ⓒ Ⓓ Ⓔ
24. Ⓐ Ⓑ Ⓒ Ⓓ Ⓔ
25. Ⓐ Ⓑ Ⓒ Ⓓ Ⓔ
26. Ⓐ Ⓑ Ⓒ Ⓓ Ⓔ
27. Ⓐ Ⓑ Ⓒ Ⓓ Ⓔ
28. Ⓐ Ⓑ Ⓒ Ⓓ Ⓔ
29. Ⓐ Ⓑ Ⓒ Ⓓ Ⓔ
30. Ⓐ Ⓑ Ⓒ Ⓓ Ⓔ

SECTION **1** Time—35 Minutes
24 Questions

In this section solve each problem, using any available space on the page for scratchwork. Then decide which is the best of the choices given and fill in the corresponding oval on the answer sheet.

Directions: Each group of questions is based on a set of conditions. In answering some of the questions it may be useful to draw a rough diagram. Choose the best answer for each question and blacken the corresponding space on your answer sheet.

Questions 1–6

Players in a certain card game are given cards, each card a solid color—blue, green, orange, red, or yellow. In each turn, a player plays five of his cards, one at a time, in succession according to the following rules:

A player may not play a red card immediately before or after a yellow card.

A player may not play a blue card first unless he also holds and later plays an orange card.

A player may not play a green unless he holds and later plays another green card.

An orange card may not be played as the last card of a turn unless a green card has been played during that turn.

1. Which of the following is an acceptable sequence of cards for a player's turn?

   (A) green, red, yellow, blue, green
   (B) green, red, orange, blue, yellow
   (C) orange, green, green, blue, yellow
   (D) bluc, red, green, green, yellow
   (E) blue, blue, yellow, blue, orange

2. All of the following are acceptable sequences of cards for a player's turn EXCEPT

   (A) red, orange, green, green, yellow
   (B) orange, green, yellow, green, red
   (C) blue, red, blue, yellow, orange
   (D) red, green, yellow, green, red
   (E) blue, green, green, yellow, orange

3. If a player has already played, in order, a yellow card, a green card, a blue card, and a green card, then which of the following is a complete and accurate listing of the cards he could play as the fifth and last card of his turn?

   (A) green
   (B) green, blue
   (C) green, blue, orange
   (D) green, blue, orange, yellow
   (E) green, blue, orange, yellow, red

4. If a player holds seven cards—one green card, one red card, one blue card, and four yellow cards—then which of the following could be the first card the player plays?

   I. A bluc card
   II. A green card
   III. A red card

   (A) I only   (B) III only   (C) I and III only
   (D) II and III only   (E) I, II, and III

5. Which of the following sequences of cards could be turned into an acceptable play by rearranging the cards indicated?

   (A) green, blue, blue, red, yellow
   (B) yellow, red, yellow, red, yellow
   (C) red, green, green, red, yellow
   (D) orange, blue, orange, blue, green
   (E) blue, red, orange, green, yellow

6. If a player plans to play three red cards, an orange card, and one other card, then which of the following must be true?

   (A) He cannot play a yellow card.
   (B) He cannot play a blue card third .
   (C) He cannot play an orange card last.
   (D) He cannot play a blue card first.
   (E) He cannot play a red card third.

Questions 7–12

Six students, $J, K, L, M, N,$ and O, took a test with the following results:

J scored higher than N but lower than O.
K scored higher than L but lower than O.
M scored higher than L but lower than J.

7. Which of the following could be the rank ordering of the students' scores, from lowest to highest?

   (A) K, L, N, M, J, O
   (B) L, K, N, J, M, O
   (C) N, K, O, J, L, M
   (D) N, L, M, K, J, O
   (E) N, M, L, K, J, O

GO ON TO THE NEXT PAGE

8. Which of the following must be true of the scores received by the students?

   (A) *O* received the highest score.
   (B) *J* received the second-highest score.
   (C) *K* received the third-highest score.
   (D) *N* received the lowest score.
   (E) *L* received the lowest score.

9. Which of the following could be true?

   I. *J* and *K* received the same score.
   II. *N* and *L* received the same score.
   III. *M* and *L* received the same score.

   (A) I only   (B) II only   (C) I and II only
   (D) II and III only   (E) I, II, and III

10. If two students received scores higher than *L* but lower than *M*, they must be

    (A) *J* and *K*   (B) *J* and *L*   (C) *K* and *J*
    (D) *K* and *N*   (E) *K* and *O*

11. What is the maximum number of students who could have scored higher than *K*?

    (A) 5   (B) 4   (C) 3   (D) 2   (E) 1

12. Which of the following provides a complete and accurate description of those students who could have scored higher than *M*?

    (A) *J*   (B) *J,O*   (C) *J,O,K*
    (D) *J,O,K,N*   (E) *J,O,K,N,L*

Questions 13–18

Six diplomats—*P, Q, R, S, T,* and *U*—are to be seated around a circular table. Six chairs are evenly spaced around the table so that each chair is directly opposite one other chair.

   P cannot be seated next to *Q*.
   R cannot be seated next to *S*.
   T must be seated next to *S*.

13. Which of the following seating arrangements is acceptable?

14. If *P* is seated next to *T*, then which of the following CANNOT be true?

    (A) *U* sits next to *S*.
    (B) *U* sits next to *R*.
    (C) *R* sits next to *P*.
    (D) *Q* sits between *U* and *T*.
    (E) *U* sits between *R* and *Q*.

15. If *Q* is seated next to *T* and *S* is seated next to *U*, who is seated directly across from *R*?

    (A) *P*   (B) *Q*   (C) *R*   (D) *S*   (E) *U*

16. If *U* and *T* are seated in adjacent seats, who could be seated next to *U*?

    I. *P*
    II. *Q*
    III. *R*

    (A) I only   (B) II only   (C) III only
    (D) I and II only   (E) II and III only

17. If *R* is seated directly across from *Q*, in how many different orders can the rest of the diplomats be seated?

    (A) 1   (B) 2   (C) 3   (D) 4   (E) 5

18. If *P* is seated directly across from *T*, then which of the following is seated directly across from *S*?

    (A) *P*   (B) *Q*   (C) *R*   (D) *T*   (E) *U*

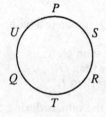

(A)

(B)

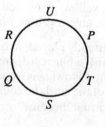

(C)

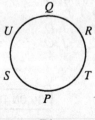

(D)

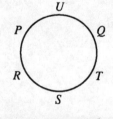

(E)

GO ON TO THE NEXT PAGE

Questions 19–24

In a certain society, everyone belongs to one of three marital groups—*J, K,* or *L*—and the only marriages permitted are the following:

Marriages between males of group *K* and females of group *L*.

Marriages between males of group *L* and females of group *J*.

Marriages between males of group *J* and females of group *K*.

Divorce and remarriage are permitted. Upon birth, a child becomes a member of the group to which neither of his parents belongs.

19. Which of the following are prohibited by the rules above?

   I. All marriages between brother and sister
  II. All marriages between a woman and her ex-husband's brother
 III. All marriages between a woman and her sister's ex-husband

  (A) I only (B) III only (C) I and II only
  (D) II and III only (E) I, II, and III

20. Which of the following must be true of the grandparents of someone who is a member of group J?

  (A) Both grandfathers belong to group J.
  (B) Both grandmothers belong to group K.
  (C) One grandfather belongs to group J and the other to group L.
  (D) One grandmother belongs to group J and the other to group L.
  (E) One grandmother belongs to group L and the other to group L.

21. Which of the following is a complete and accurate list of the groups to which the grandchild of a person belonging to group L could possibly belong?

  (A) J (B) J,L (C) K,L
  (D) J,K (E) J,K,L

22. A man would be permitted to marry which of the following?

   I. His brother's wife's sister
  II. His sister's husband's sister
 III. His son's wife's mother

  (A) I only (B) III only (C) I and III only
  (D) II and III only (E) I, II, and III

23. In a group consisting of a woman, her sister, her husband, her husband's parents, and all of her husband's grandparents, what is the largest number of people that will belong to any one of the three groups?

  (A) 3 (B) 4 (C) 5 (D) 6 (E) 7

24. Which of the following marriages between cousins are prohibited by the rules?

    I. A marriage between a man and a daughter of his mother's sister.
   II. A marriage between a man and a daughter of his father's brother.
  III. A marriage between a woman and a son of her mother's brother.
  IV. A marriage between a woman and a son of her father's sister.

  (A) I only (B) IV only (C) I and IV only
  (D) I, II, and III only (E) I, II, III, and IV

IF YOU FINISH BEFORE TIME IS CALLED, YOU MAY CHECK YOUR WORK ON THIS SECTION ONLY. DO NOT WORK ON ANY OTHER SECTION IN THE TEST. **STOP**

495

SECTION 2   Time—35 Minutes
25 Questions

For each question in this section, choose the best answer and blacken the corresponding space on the answer sheet.

The questions in this section require you to follow or evaluate the reasoning contained in brief statements or passages. In some questions, each of the choices is a conceivable solution to the particular problem posed. However, you are to select the one that answers the question best, that is, the one that does not require you to make what are by common-sense standards implausible, superfluous, or incompatible assumptions. After you have chosen the best answer, blacken the corresponding space on the answer sheet.

If Karen was selected for the committee, she must be a sophomore.

1. The statement above makes which of the following assumptions?

   (A) Only Karen can be selected for the committee.
   (B) Only sophomores can be selected for the committee.
   (C) Some sophomores must be selected for the committee.
   (D) Some sophomores might not be selected for the committee.
   (E) Karen did not refuse to serve on the committee.

The use of statistical data gathered from historical sources such as census reports and commercial registers and analyzed with the help of sophisticated computer programs has permeated the study of history in recent years. Now it would appear that the new statistical methods have begun to generate major breakthroughs in historical research, which brings us to Dr. Kramer's fascinating new book on the nineteenth-century settlement of the American frontier.

2. Which of the following conclusions is best supported by the passage above?

   (A) Statistical data from historical sources are the single most important form of information underpinning current historical research.
   (B) Dr. Kramer is the first major historian to apply the new statistical techniques to the study of the settlement of the American frontier.
   (C) Historians have begun to make major contributions to the science of statistical analysis.
   (D) Today, writers of histories must be skilled as computer programmers as well as knowledgeable about a particular era of history.
   (E) Dr. Kramer's book offers important new insights into its subject, based on analysis of historical statistics.

Some people oppose special college admissions programs for minority students on the ground that merit alone—as measured by high school grades, scores on entrance exams, and other objective standards—should be used in admissions decisions. This argument ignores the facts that non-merit factors—the applicant's place of origin, whether a parent is a graduate of the college, and so on—have always been considered by colleges. These subjective factors are usually such as to exclude minority-group students.

3. Which of the following would best complete the paragraph above?

   (A) Therefore, merit plays no substantive role in the majority of college admissions decisions.
   (B) Therefore, subjective factors should be completely removed from the college admissions process.
   (C) Therefore, the concept of merit is merely a subterfuge by which minority students may be excluded.
   (D) Therefore, it is not inappropriate to use special admissions programs for minority students to help redress an imbalance.
   (E) Therefore, high school grades alone are an inadequate measure of a student's past academic performance.

Government involvement in industry is more detrimental than helpful to that industry. As proof of this, consider two comparable industries: urban mass transit and the airline business. The former has generally been subsidized and operated by local governments, and in most cities service is poor and deteriorating. By contrast, the privately owned and operated airlines earn profits and provide, for the most part, fast and efficient service.

GO ON TO THE NEXT PAGE

4. Which of the following, if true, would LEAST weaken the argument above?

(A) Passenger complaints about airline scheduling and service have increased rapidly and are now greater than ever before.

(B) Privately owned mass transit systems do not have problems similar to those of government-operated systems.

(C) The government subsidizes airport construction and operation and offers tax breaks to airlines.

(D) Technological advances in air travel have allowed airlines to operate more efficiently, but no similar advances have occurred in rail travel.

(E) On average, airline ticket prices have increased faster than mass transit fares over the past ten years.

Neither artifacts, personal messages, nor historical documents from any human civilization would be likely to have any meaning for intelligent extraterrestrial beings. Therefore, the probe to be sent into interstellar space in the hope that alien beings may find it will contain a plaque inscribed with certain scientific and mathematical formulas, for example, a statement of the value of π or the molecular weight of water.

5. The argument above depends upon which of the following assumptions?

(A) Somewhere in the universe there is at least one intelligent race other than the human race living on Earth.

(B) Extraterrestrial beings probably have civilizations that are not as technically advanced as those on Earth.

(C) Life on other worlds is likely to be dependent upon the presence of water just as it is on Earth.

(D) Intelligent beings on other worlds have probably developed means of interstellar space travel.

(E) Some symbols used by human beings will be meaningful to intelligent extraterrestrial beings.

Studies of twins separated at or shortly after birth have played a major role in attempts to measure the relative influence of genetic and environmental factors on personal development. Those who consider environment all-important would predict that separately reared twins would exhibit no more similarity than another two unrelated individuals brought up under the same conditions. The data do not support this extreme position, but neither do they support the opposite fallacy, the belief that "genetics is destiny."

6. Which of the following statements would be the most reasonable conclusion to draw from the argument above?

(A) More study of the relationship between genetics and environment is needed before it can be determined whether one or the other of the two extreme positions is correct.

(B) Studies of twins separated at birth show that environmental factors are the most important factor in later personal development.

(C) Twin studies suggest that both genetic and environmental factors play an important part in the development of personality.

(D) Attempts to modify personal development by making changes in the environment of an individual are misguided and doomed to failure.

(E) Twin studies are inherently unsatisfactory as a research tool because of the ambiguity that infects the results obtained.

We hear it said that, for all the social progress America has made over the past thirty years—for all the toppling of racial and ethnic barriers that we have witnessed—this remains an inherently racist society, in which the white majority has never fully accepted the equal humanity of the minority. Those who repeat this slander against America ignore the fact that, as I write, the most popular television program in the country focuses on the lives of a proud middle-class black family, whose members have become some of the best-recognized —and most widely admired—people in America.

7. The argument above assumes that

(A) television acting is a challenging and financially rewarding profession

(B) thirty years ago a television show with black characters would not have been popular

(C) those who label America a racist society seek to foment unrest and disrupt the fabric of American society

(D) a person's attitude toward a character on a television show is like his attitude toward real people with similar characteristics

(E) the television program is more popular among white viewers than among black viewers

GO ON TO THE NEXT PAGE

Foods that are high in fat, salt, or sugar content have been shown to be deleterious to health. If the government can forbid the sale to minors of other harmful products, such as cigarettes and alcoholic beverages, why not treat dangerous foods in the same way? Children under 18 should be allowed to purchase only foods that are nutritious and healthful.

8. The author of the statement above makes his point primarily by

(A) analyzing a cause-and-effect relationship
(B) drawing an analogy
(C) appealing to the emotions of the audience
(D) offering a counterexample
(E) making a generalization

By studying census data, demographers are able to develop lists of counties and communities throughout the country whose populations have specific economic characteristics—for example, high or low median age, large numbers of families with children, a high percentage of two-career couples, or particularly affluent households. Lists such as these can be especially useful to political organizations that are promoting candidates who have particular appeal to voters with specific characteristics.

9. Which of the following, if true, best supports the claim that the demographic information mentioned in the passage may be valuable to political organizations?

(A) Affluent citizens are known to be more likely to vote in local elections than are those who are less affluent.
(B) Because census data are compiled by the federal government, they must legally be made available to all who request them.
(C) Voters tend to be heavily influenced in their thinking by the opinions and preferences of their friends and neighbors.
(D) Research shows that the economic and social characteristics of differing groups can be closely correlated with specific political views.
(E) Several of today's most significant political issues have particular impact on the interests of families with children.

Some people oppose testing of employees for use of illegal drugs on the ground that the tests sometimes produce false results. These fears are without basis. The newest tests can detect over 99 percent of the cases in which a person has used one of the most common illegal drugs at any time during the previous 48 hours.

10. Which of the following, if true, would most weaken the argument above?

(A) The best drug tests available today return a significant number of positive results even when the person has not used drugs.
(B) The best drug tests available today cannot reliably identify every form of illegal drug that a person might have used.
(C) The best drug tests available today cannot identify an illegal drug if the subject took that drug more than 48 hours prior to the test.
(D) An employee who occasionally uses an illegal drug may still be a valuable worker.
(E) Some employers still continue to use older and less reliable drug tests.

One of the most influential studies of the ancient construction known as Stonehenge was conducted by Professor Gerald Hawkins. Hawkins used computer calculations to compare the locations of stones in Stonehenge with the positions of stars, planets, and the sun at the time the structure was built. He concluded that the stones could have been used to mark viewing angles along which the rising and setting of heavenly bodies could be observed, making Stonehenge a kind of primitive "computer" for predicting astronomical events.

11. Which of the following, if true, most seriously weakens Hawkins' argument?

(A) There is no reliable scientific evidence that the ancient people who built Stonehenge worshipped heavenly bodies.
(B) Hawkins' computer calculations, though on their face accurate, have not been independently verified.
(C) The positions of heavenly bodies have shifted slightly in the thousands of years since Stonehenge was built.
(D) The fragility of the already-damaged stones of Stonehenge has caused authorities to limit the access of scholars to the site.
(E) Any structure as complex as that at Stonehenge must inevitably contain some astronomical viewing angles, even if they were not intended by the builders.

The tendency toward political tyranny increases in periods of economic collapse. When most people have homes and jobs and when families anticipate a better life for their children, citizens support moderate policies that promise peaceful growth and gradual development. When work is scarce, prices are rising, and prospects for the future seem bleak, desperate measures begin to seem attractive, and the would-be totalitarian's promise of drastic upheaval holds appeal.

GO ON TO THE NEXT PAGE

12. The claim made in the argument above would be most seriously weakened by evidence of which of the following?

(A) Countries undergoing economic collapse in which democratic institutions were strengthened
(B) Countries in which periods of drastic economic change had little apparent political effect
(C) Countries in which totalitarian governments were established with little basis in popular support
(D) Examples of tyrannical governments that arose during periods of prosperity
(E) Examples of totalitarian leaders who actually kept the promises they made before attaining power

A basic social function of the university is to provide a setting within which all points of view may be freely debated, including those whose radical nature may offend some or even most members of the community. Unfortunately, this mandate includes totalitarian views that might themselves threaten the freedom and diversity of expression to which the university is dedicated.

13. The speaker in the paragraph above is most concerned with discussing a(n)

(A) dilemma   (B) contradiction   (C) paradox
(D) analogy   (E) generalization

Questions 14–15
Colleges are doing a poor job of imparting basic skills. According to a recent survey of personnel directors of major corporations, large numbers of entry-level workers lack ability in writing, mathematics, and reasoning skills.

14. Which of the following must be true if the argument above is valid?

(A) College students today are no longer required to take courses in basic skills.
(B) Few entry-level workers today have college degrees.
(C) Basic skills in writing, mathematics, and reasoning are important for success in most jobs.
(D) Entry-level workers at major corporations are generally representative of today's college graduates.
(E) College students in the past received better training in basic skills than students of today.

15. Which of the following questions would be most relevant in determining the validity of the argument above?

(A) What kinds of training programs are provided by major corporations for their entry-level workers?
(B) Do colleges have the responsibility for teaching students basic skills in writing, mathematics, and reasoning?
(C) How closely correlated are workers' levels of skill in writing, mathematics, and reasoning?
(D) Do major corporations today demand a higher level of basic skills from entry-level workers than in the past?
(E) How do the skill levels of workers at major corporations compare with those at smaller companies?

Lawyers are sometimes asked, "How can you, in good conscience, defend a person whom you know to be guilty?" One answer lies in the nature of our adversary system of justice. Believing that justice is best served through the open clash of opposing arguments, we hold it to be important that all persons should be given a voice in court—not just those who are popular or "known" to be in the right. Only when every side has a reasonable chance to be heard, we believe, can truth most fully emerge.

16. The passage above justifies the lawyers' practice of defending guilty persons on the ground that it is

(A) deeply rooted in our society's customs and traditions
(B) the most effective means of determining what is the truth
(C) a means by which unpopular social and political views may gain a fair hearing
(D) necessary to satisfy society's inherent sense of fair play
(E) unlikely to lead to any serious miscarriage of justice

GO ON TO THE NEXT PAGE

During the past three years, an increasing number of youths between thirteen and sixteen years of age have been injured or killed in accidents while driving or riding on lightweight motorcycles called dirt bikes. These motorcycles are simply too powerful for children under the age of sixteen, for even the most skillful riders of their age group lack the maturity of judgment to use them wisely.

17. The speaker in the paragraph above would most likely favor a law that prohibited

    (A) children under the age of sixteen from owning a dirt bike
    (B) children under the age of thirteen from operating a dirt bike
    (C) children between the ages of thirteen and sixteen from operating a dirt bike
    (D) children under the age of sixteen from riding on a dirt bike
    (E) children under the age of sixteen from operating a dirt bike

Questions 18–19
When the military forces of the Soviet Union are compared directly with those of the United States, the two superpowers appear to be about equal, with each side leading and trailing in several categories of weapons, equipment, and manpower. When the forces of the other Warsaw Pact nations are added to those of the Soviet Union, and the forces of the NATO allies of the United States are added to those of the United States, a substantial advantage for the NATO side in nearly every category is found to exist. We can conclude, therefore, that the United States actually enjoys military superiority over the Soviet Union.

18. From the information provided above, which of the following can be most reliably inferred?

    (A) In a war between the Warsaw Pact nations and the NATO countries, the NATO countries would prevail.
    (B) The military forces of the NATO allies of the United States are greater than those of the Soviet Union's Warsaw Pact allies.
    (C) The NATO allies of the United States have combined military forces that are greater than those of the United States itself.
    (D) A portion of the military forces of the Soviet Union are deployed for the purpose of deterring an attack by the NATO countries.
    (E) There are more member countries in the NATO alliance than there are in the Warsaw Pact.

19. Which of the following, if true, would most seriously weaken the argument above?

    (A) The military forces of the NATO allies are not under the direct control of the United States, but those of the Warsaw Pact are under the direct control of the Soviet Union.
    (B) Although the United States has fewer missiles than the Soviet Union, it has a comparable number of nuclear warheads.
    (C) The NATO allies of the United States have grown reluctant to allow the United States to deploy nuclear weapons on their soils.
    (D) Much of the military equipment of the Warsaw Pact nations is older than that of the NATO allies and therefore technologically less advanced.
    (E) The Warsaw Pact nations spend a proportionately larger share of their budgets each year on the military than do the NATO countries.

Mycroft's role in the government is unique. Whereas all other state officials are specialists in one area or another, Mycroft is the supreme generalist, the single person who can determine how various interrelated areas of government are likely to be affected by a particular course of action. As a consequence, Mycroft is the only truly indispensable person in the government.

20. If the statements above are true, which of the following statements must also be true?

    I. It would be easier to replace or do without a person with general knowledge than a person with specialized knowledge.
    II. A decision that affected only one area of government would not require Mycroft's expertise.
    III. Mycroft's knowledge of each separate area of government is as profound as that of a specialist.

    (A) I only   (B) II only   (C) III only
    (D) II and III only   (E) I, II, and III

Questions 21–22
Some politicians are boating enthusiasts.
All Republocrats favor industrial development along the shoreline.
All boating enthusiasts oppose industrial development along the shoreline.

21. If the statements above are true, which of the following must be true?

    (A) All politicians are Republocrats.
    (B) Some Republocrats are boating enthusiasts.
    (C) Some politicians are not Republocrats.
    (D) Not all Republocrats are politicians.
    (E) Some boating enthusiasts are Republocrats.

GO ON TO THE NEXT PAGE

22. If, in addition to the statements above, it is true that all politicians are boating enthusiasts, which of the following must be FALSE?

(A) Some politicians are not Republocrats.
(B) Not all boating enthusiasts are politicians.
(C) Some Republocrats are politicians.
(D) All politicians oppose industrial development along the shoreline.
(E) Some boating enthusiasts are not Republocrats.

Questions 23–24

Historically, our nation's prosperity has been based on a continuous flow of new inventions that have spurred the creation of new industries, from the automotive and aircraft industries to the fields of chemicals, pharmaceuticals, and electronics. Therefore, the best guarantee of continued economic strength is increased spending by businesses on scientific research and development.

23. The author of the passage above makes which of the following assumptions?

   I. Scientific research and development can ensure a flow of new inventions.
   II. The chemical, pharmaceutical, and electronics industries will provide most of the new technology over the next few years.
   III. The amount of money now spent by businesses on scientific research and development is not adequate to ensure a flow of new inventions.

(A) I only   (B) III only   (C) I and II only
(D) I and III only   (E) I, II, and III

24. Which of the following, if true, would most seriously weaken the argument above?

(A) The research and development divisions of most businesses concentrate on making minor improvements to existing products rather than developing new technologies.
(B) At current levels of spending, corporate research and development divisions are applying for fewer patents each year than they were a decade ago.
(C) Historically, only a few new major industries have been based directly on the work of technical breakthroughs achieved by corporate research and development divisions.
(D) Levels of corporate spending on scientific research and development are directly related to the number of new inventions patented each year.
(E) Government spending on scientific research and development will be sharply curtailed over the next five years.

It is true that the striking textile workers have agreed to return to work with a contract that is little better than the contract they could have obtained three weeks ago at the onset of the strike. But the workers have shown an ability to maintain their own unity under extremely difficult circumstances, a fact that will help them in the next set of negotiations when this contract expires a year from now.

25. The argument above depends on which of the following assumptions?

   I. The labor unity achieved during this strike will not disappear within the year.
   II. When the current contract expires, management will take into account the fact that labor maintained its unity in the previous strike.
   III. Labor will call another strike upon the expiration of the current contract to force management to make concessions.

(A) I only   (B) II only   (C) I and II only
(D) II and III only   (E) I, II, and III

IF YOU FINISH BEFORE TIME IS CALLED, YOU MAY CHECK YOUR WORK ON THIS SECTION ONLY. DO NOT WORK ON ANY OTHER SECTION IN THE TEST. **S T O P**

Directions: Each passage in this group is followed by questions based on its content. After reading a passage, choose the best answer to each question and blacken the corresponding space on the answer sheet. Answer all questions following a passage on the basis of what is <u>stated</u> or <u>implied</u> in that passage.

The service of philosophy towards the human spirit is to startle it into sharp and eager observation. Every moment, and for that moment only, some form grows perfect in hand or face; some tone on the hills or the sea
(5) is choicer than the rest. Not the fruit of experience, but experience itself is the end. Only a counted number of pulses is given to us of a variegated, dramatic life. How shall we pass most quickly from point to point, and be present always at the focus where the greatest number of
(10) vital forces unite in their purest energy?

To burn always with this hard, gemlike flame, to maintain this ecstasy, is success in life. It is only the roughness of the eye that makes any two persons, things, or situations seem alike. While all melts under our feet,
(15) we may well catch at any exquisite passion, or any knowledge that seems by a lifted horizon to set the spirit free for a moment, or any stirring of the senses, strange dyes, strange colors, curious odors, or work of the artist's hands or the faces of one's friends. Not to discriminate
(20) every moment some passionate attitude in those about us, and in the brilliancy of their gifts some tragic dividing of forces of their ways is, on this short day of the frost and sun, to sleep before evening. With this sense of the splendor of our experience and of its awful brevity,
(25) gathering all we are into one desperate effort to see and touch, we shall hardly have time to make theories about the things we see and touch.

We are all under sentence of death but with a sort of indefinite reprieve; we have an interval and then our
(30) place knows us no more. Some spend this interval in listlessness, others in high passions, the wisest—at least among the "children of this world"—in art and song. For our one chance lies in expanding this interval, in getting as many pulsations as possible into the given
(35) time. Great passions may give us this quickened sense of life, ecstasy, sorrow, and love, the various forms of enthusiastic activity. Of this wisdom, the poetic passion, the desire of beauty, the love of art for art's sake has most; for art comes to you professing frankly to give
(40) nothing but the highest quality to your moments as they pass, and simply for the sake of those moments.

1. Which of the following best describes the overall structure of the passage?

(A) The author raises a question and then provides an answer.
(B) The author presents a theory, which he then proves.
(C) The author studies a widely held belief and then rejects it.
(D) The author defines a term and then provides examples.
(E) The author tells an anecdote and then explains its significance.

2. In the passage, the author uses the word *pulsations* (line 34) to mean

(A) heartbeats   (B) children   (C) lives
(D) death   (E) experiences

3. According to the author, the function of art is to

(A) depict reality accurately
(B) stimulate strong emotions
(C) encourage social reform
(D) express the artist's feelings
(E) provide a means of escape

4. With which of the following statements would the author most likely agree?

(A) A person's lifetime is merely preparation for what comes after death.
(B) Only an artist can truly enjoy life.
(C) The original experience is more important than the memory of it.
(D) A perceptive person understands that all experience is repetitious.
(E) The best life is a life of meditation and contemplation.

5. The tone of the passage can best be described as

(A) impassioned   (B) scholarly   (C) informative
(D) speculative   (E) detached

GO ON TO THE NEXT PAGE →

6. In the context of this passage, the phrase "short day of the frost and sun" refers to

    (A) the transient effect of poetry
    (B) a brief moment of passion
    (C) the life of a person
    (D) stimulation of the senses
    (E) a midwinter day

The founders of the Republic viewed their revolution primarily in political rather than economic or social terms. And they talked about education as essential to the public good—a goal that took precedence over knowledge as occupational training or as a means to self-fulfillment or self-improvement. Over and over again, the Revolutionary generation, both liberal and conservative in outlook, asserted its conviction that the welfare of the Republic rested upon an educated citizenry and that schools, especially free public schools, would be the best means of educating the citizenry in civic values and the obligations required of everyone in a democratic republican society. All agreed that the principal ingredients of a civic education were literacy and the inculcation of patriotic and moral virtues, some others adding the study of history and the study of principles of the republican government itself.

The founders, as was the case with almost all their successors, were long on exhortation and rhetoric regarding the value of civic education, but they left it to the textbook writers to distill the essence of those values for school children. Texts in American history and government appeared as early as the 1790s. The textbook writers turned out to be very largely of conservative persuasion, more likely Federalist in outlook than Jeffersonian, and almost universally agreed that political virtue must rest upon moral and religious precepts. Since most textbook writers were New Englanders, this meant that the texts were infused with Protestant, and above all Puritan, outlooks.

In the first half of the Republic, civic education in the schools emphasized the inculcation of civic values and made little attempt to develop participatory political skills. That was a task left to incipient political parties, town meetings, churches, and the coffee or ale houses where men gathered for conversation. Additionally, as a reading of certain Federalist papers of the period would demonstrate, the press probably did more to disseminate realistic as well as partisan knowledge of government than the schools. The goal of education, however, was to achieve a higher form of *unum* for the new Republic. In the middle half of the nineteenth century, the political values taught in the public and private schools did not change substantially from those celebrated in the first fifty years of the Republic. In the textbooks of the day, their rosy hues if anything became golden. To the resplendent values of liberty, equality, and a benevolent Christian morality were now added the middle-class virtues—especially of New England—of hard work, honesty and integrity, the rewards of individual effort, and obedience to parents and legitimate authority. But of all the political values taught in school, patriotism was preeminent; and whenever teachers explained to school children why they should love their country above all else, the idea of liberty assumed pride of place.

7. The passage deals primarily with the

    (A) content of textbooks used in early American schools
    (B) role of education in late eighteenth- and early to mid-nineteenth-century America
    (C) influence of New England Puritanism on early American values
    (D) origin and development of the Protestant work ethic in modern America
    (E) establishment of universal, free public education in America

8. According to the passage, the founders of the Republic regarded education primarily as

    (A) a religious obligation
    (B) a private matter
    (C) an unnecessary luxury
    (D) a matter of individual choice
    (E) a political necessity

9. The author states that textbooks written in the middle part of the nineteenth century

    (A) departed radically in tone and style from earlier textbooks
    (B) mentioned for the first time the value of liberty
    (C) treated traditional civic virtues with even greater reverence
    (D) were commissioned by government agencies
    (E) contained no reference to conservative ideas

10. Which of the following would LEAST likely have been the subject of an early American textbook?

    (A) Basic rules of English grammar
    (B) The American Revolution
    (C) Patriotism and other civic virtues
    (D) Vocational education
    (E) Principles of American government

11. The author's attitude toward the educational system she discusses can best be described as

    (A) cynical and unpatriotic
    (B) realistic and analytical
    (C) pragmatic and frustrated
    (D) disenchanted and bitter
    (E) idealistic and naive

GO ON TO THE NEXT PAGE

12. The passage provides information that would be helpful in answering which of the following questions?

(A) Why was a disproportionate share of early American textbooks written by New England authors?

(B) Was the Federalist party primarily a liberal or conservative force in early American politics?

(C) How many years of education did the founders believe were sufficient to instruct young citizens in civic virtue?

(D) What were the names of some of the Puritan authors who wrote early American textbooks?

(E) Did most citizens of the early Republic agree with the founders that public education was essential to the welfare of the Republic?

13. The author implies that an early American Puritan would likely insist that

(A) moral and religious values are the foundation of civic virtue

(B) textbooks should instruct students in political issues of vital concern to the community

(C) textbooks should give greater emphasis to the value of individual liberty than to the duties of patriotism

(D) private schools with a particular religious focus are preferable to public schools with no religious instruction

(E) government and religion are separate institutions and the church should not interfere in political affairs

The health-care economy is replete with unusual and even unique economic relationships. One of the least understood involves the peculiar roles of producer or "provider" and purchaser or "consumer" in the typical doctor–patient relationship. In most sectors of the economy, it is the seller who attempts to attract a potential buyer with various inducements of price, quality, and utility, and it is the buyer who makes the decision. Where circumstances permit the buyer no choice because there is effectively only one seller and the product is relatively essential, government usually asserts monopoly and places the industry under price and other regulations. Neither of these conditions prevails in most of the health-care industry.

In the health-care industry, the doctor–patient relationship is the mirror image of the ordinary relationship between producer and consumer. Once an individual has chosen to see a physician—and even then there may be no real choice—it is the physician who usually makes all significant purchasing decisions: whether the patient should return "next Wednesday," whether X-rays are needed, whether drugs should be prescribed, etc. It is a rare and sophisticated patient who will challenge such professional decisions or raise in advance questions about price, especially when the ailment is regarded as serious.

This is particularly significant in relation to hospital care. The physician must certify the need for hospitalization, determine what procedures will be performed, and announce when the patient may be discharged. The patient may be consulted about some of these decisions, but in the main it is the doctor's judgments that are final. Little wonder, then, that in the eyes of the hospital it is the physician who is the real "consumer." As a consequence, the medical staff represents the "power center" in hospital policy and decision-making, not the administration.

Although usually there are in this situation four identifiable participants—the physician, the hospital, the patient, and the payer (generally an insurance carrier or government)—the physician makes the essential decisions for all of them. The hospital becomes an extension of the physician; the payer generally meets most of the bona fide bills generated by the physician/hospital; and for the most part the patient plays a passive role. In routine or minor illnesses, or just plain worries, the patient's options are, of course, much greater with respect to use and price. In illnesses that are of some significance, however, such choices tend to evaporate, and it is for these illnesses that the bulk of the health-care dollar is spent. We estimate that about 75–80 percent of health-care expenditures are determined by physicians, not patients. For this reason, economy measures directed at patients or the general public are relatively ineffective.

14. The author's primary purpose is to

(A) speculate about the relationship between a patient's ability to pay and the treatment received

(B) criticize doctors for exercising too much control over patients

(C) analyze some important economic factors in health care

(D) urge hospitals to reclaim their decision-making authority

(E) inform potential patients of their health-care rights

15. It can be inferred that doctors are able to determine hospital policies because

(A) it is doctors who generate income for the hospital

(B) most of a patient's bills are paid by his health insurance

(C) hospital administrators lack the expertise to question medical decisions

(D) a doctor is ultimately responsible for a patient's health

(E) some patients might refuse to accept their physician's advice

GO ON TO THE NEXT PAGE

16. According to the author, when a doctor tells a patient to "return next Wednesday," the doctor is in effect

(A) taking advantage of the patient's concern for his health
(B) instructing the patient to buy more medical services
(C) warning the patient that a hospital stay might be necessary
(D) advising the patient to seek a second opinion
(E) admitting that the initial visit was ineffective

17. The author is most probably leading up to

(A) a proposal to control medical costs
(B) a discussion of a new medical treatment
(C) an analysis of the causes of inflation in the United States
(D) a study of lawsuits against doctors for malpractice
(E) a comparison of hospitals and factories

18. The tone of the passage can best be described as

(A) whimsical
(B) cautious
(C) analytical
(D) inquisitive
(E) defiant

19. With which of the following statements would the author be likely to agree?

I. Most patients are reluctant to object to the course of treatment prescribed by a doctor or to question the cost of the services.
II. The more serious the illness of a patient, the less likely it is that the patient will object to the course of treatment prescribed or to question the cost of services.
III. The payer, whether insurance carrier or the government, is less likely to acquiesce to demands for payment when the illness of the patient is regarded as serious.

(A) I only   (B) II only   (C) I and II only
(D) II and III only   (E) I, II, and III

20. The author's primary concern is to

(A) define a term
(B) clarify a misunderstanding
(C) refute a theory
(D) discuss a problem
(E) announce a new discovery

About twice every century, one of the massive stars in our galaxy blows itself apart in a supernova explosion that sends massive quantities of radiation and matter into space and generates shock waves that sweep through the (5) arms of the galaxy. The shock waves heat the interstellar gas, evaporate small clouds, and compress larger ones to the point at which they collapse under their own gravity to form new stars. The general picture that has been developed for the supernova explosion and its aftermath (10) goes something like this. Throughout its evolution, a star is much like a leaky balloon. It keeps its equilibrium figure through a balance of internal pressure against the tendency to collapse under its own weight. The pressure is generated by nuclear reactions in the core of the star (15) which must continually supply energy to balance the energy that leaks out in the form of radiation. Eventually the nuclear fuel is exhausted, and the pressure drops in the core. With nothing to hold it up, the matter in the center of the star collapses inward, creating higher and (20) higher densities and temperatures, until the nuclei and electrons are fused into a superdense lump of matter known as a neutron star.

As the overlying layers rain down on the surface of the neutron star, the temperature rises until, with a (25) blinding flash of radiation, the collapse is reversed. A thermonuclear shock wave runs through the now expanding stellar envelope, fusing lighter elements into heavier ones and producing a brilliant visual outburst that can be as intense as the light of 10 billion suns. The (30) shell of matter thrown off by the explosion plows through the surrounding gas, producing an expanding bubble of hot gas, with gas temperatures in the millions of degrees. This gas will emit most of its energy at X-ray wavelengths, so it is not surprising that X-ray observato- (35) ries have provided some of the most useful insights into the nature of the supernova phenomenon. More than twenty supernova remnants have now been detected in X-ray studies.

Recent discoveries of meteorites with anomalous (40) concentrations of certain isotopes indicate that a supernova might have precipitated the birth of our solar system more than four and a half billion years ago. Although the cloud that collapsed to form the Sun and the planets was composed primarily of hydrogen and helium, it also (45) contained carbon, nitrogen, and oxygen, elements essential for life as we know it. Elements heavier than helium are manufactured deep in the interior of stars and would, for the most part, remain there if it were not for the cataclysmic supernova explosions that blow giant stars (50) apart. Additionally, supernovas produce clouds of high-energy particles called cosmic rays. These high-energy particles continually bombard the Earth and are responsible for many of the genetic mutations that are the driving force of the evolution of species.

GO ON TO THE NEXT PAGE

21. According to the passage, we can expect a supernova to occur in our galaxy about

(A) twice each year
(B) 100 times each century
(C) once every 50 years
(D) once every other century
(E) once every four to five billion years

22. According to the passage, all of the following are true of supernovas EXCEPT that they

(A) are extremely bright
(B) are an explosion of some sort
(C) emit large quantities of X-rays
(D) result in the destruction of a neutron star
(E) are caused by the collision of large galaxies

23. The author employs which of the following to develop the first paragraph?

(A) Analogy
(B) Deduction
(C) Generalization
(D) Example
(E) Refutation

24. It can be inferred from the passage that the meteorites mentioned by the author at line 39

(A) contain dangerous concentrations of radioactive materials
(B) give off large quantities of X-rays
(C) include material not created in the normal development of our solar system
(D) are larger than the meteors normally found in a solar system like ours
(E) contain pieces of a supernova that occurred several billion years ago

25. The author implies that

(A) it is sometimes easier to detect supernovas by observation of the X-ray spectrum than by observation of visible wavelengths of light
(B) life on Earth is endangered by its constant exposure to radiation forces that are released by a supernova
(C) recently discovered meteorites indicate that the Earth and other planets of our solar system survived the explosion of a supernova several billion years ago
(D) lighter elements are formed from heavier elements during a supernova as the heavier elements are torn apart
(E) the core of a neutron star is composed largely of heavier elements such as carbon, nitrogen, and oxygen

26. According to the passage, what is the first event in the sequence that leads to the occurrence of a supernova?

(A) An ordinary star begins to emit tremendous quantities of X-rays.
(B) A neutron star is enveloped by a superheated cloud of gas.
(C) An imbalance between light and heavy elements causes an ordinary star to collapse.
(D) A cloud of interstellar gas, rich in carbon, nitrogen, and oxygen, collapses to form a neutron star.
(E) An ordinary star exhausts its supply of nuclear fuel and begins to collapse.

27. According to the passage, a neutron star is

(A) a gaseous cloud containing heavy elements
(B) an intermediate stage between an ordinary star and a supernova
(C) the residue that is left by a supernova
(D) the core of an ordinary star that houses the thermonuclear reactions
(E) one of billions of meteors that are scattered across the galaxy by a supernova

28. The author is primarily concerned with

(A) speculating about the origins of our solar system
(B) presenting evidence proving the existence of supernovas
(C) discussing the nuclear reaction that occurs in the core of a star
(D) describing the sequence of scientific events
(E) disproving a theory about the causes of supernovas

IF YOU FINISH BEFORE TIME IS CALLED, YOU MAY CHECK YOUR WORK ON THIS SECTION ONLY. DO NOT WORK ON ANY OTHER SECTION IN THE TEST. **S T O P**

Bernie was stopped on the street by a man in dark glasses. The man offered to sell Bernie an Epsilon watch, which normally retails for $750, for $50. Bernie gave the man $50 for the watch. Later that day, Bernie learned the watch was actually an Upsilon watch, which normally retails for $19.95.

1. Which of the following adages is an appropriate criticism of Bernie's action?

   I. You must look before you leap.
   II. A fool and his money are soon parted.
   III. There is a sucker born every minute.
   IV. Nothing ventured, nothing gained.

   (A) I and II, only   (B) I and IV only
   (C) I, II, and III only   (D) II, III, and IV only
   (E) I, II, III, and IV

The Governor claims that the state faces a drought and has implemented new water-use restrictions; but that's just a move to get some free publicity for his re-election campaign. So far this year we have had 3.5 inches of rain, slightly more than the average amount of rain for the same period over the last three years.

2. Which of the following, if true, would most weaken the conclusion of the argument above?

   (A) The governor did not declare drought emergencies in the previous three years.
   (B) City officials who have the authority to mandate water-use restrictions have not done so.
   (C) The snowmelt that usually contributes significantly to the state's reservoirs is several inches below normal.
   (D) The amount of water the state can draw from rivers that cross state boundaries is limited by federal law.
   (E) Water-use restrictions are short-term measures and do little to reduce long-term water consumption.

Clean-Well is a company that offers cleaning services. The agency's fee is $25 per hour per employee used to do a job plus $5 car fare for each employee. Customers must provide cleaning supplies. I use the service to clean the windows of my store. Over the years, I have found that one worker can do the job in eight hours, while two workers can do the job in only three hours, making it cheaper to hire two workers than one. I conclude that two workers function as a team, making them more efficient than a single worker.

3. Which of the following, if true, would most weaken the conclusion of the argument above?

   (A) The cost of cleaning supplies to do the job is the same for one worker as for a team of two workers.
   (B) At the end of an eight-hour day a worker is only ⅓ as efficient as at the beginning of the day.
   (C) The workers provided by the service are paid only $7 of the $25-per-hour charge assessed by the company.
   (D) A team of four workers requires two hours and thirty minutes to complete the job.
   (E) A team of two workers from a competitor of Clean-Well will take four hours to do the job.

In general, the per-hour cost of operating a device by solar energy is more expensive than using the power supplied by the public utility. But for some purposes, such as adding a new outdoor light to a house, a solar-powered unit is actually cheaper.

4. Which of the following, if true, probably underlies the conclusion above?

   (A) Solar energy is more efficient in the southern latitudes than in the northern latitudes.
   (B) A solar-powered light is a self-contained unit and does not require the installation of a power line.
   (C) New technology will eventually reduce the cost of solar power below that of other energy sources.
   (D) The most costly components of any solar-powered system are the solar cells that convert sunlight to electricity.
   (E) A solar-powered system can be installed only in areas that receive considerable direct sunlight.

The Commission on Public Service recently recommended that federal judges be given a substantial pay increase. For many years, however, there have been many applicants for each new vacancy on the federal bench, proving that a pay increase is not needed.

5. Which of the following, if true, most weakens the argument above?

   (A) Salaries for federal judges are higher than those for state and municipal judges.
   (B) Salaries for the federal judiciary are established by the legislative branch.
   (C) A federal judgeship is a very prestigious position in the legal community.
   (D) Salaries for federal judges are too low to attract qualified lawyers.
   (E) Most federal judges are former practitioners, teachers, or state judges.

When it rains, my car gets wet. Since it hasn't rained recently, my car can't be wet.

6. Which of the following is logically most similar to the argument above?

   (A) Whenever critics give a play a favorable review, people go to see it; Pinter's new play did not receive favorable reviews, so I doubt that anyone will go to see it.
   (B) Whenever people go to see a play, critics give it a favorable review; people did go to see Pinter's new play, so it did get a favorable review.
   (C) Whenever critics give a play a favorable review, people go to see it; Pinter's new play got favorable reviews, so people will probably go see it.
   (D) Whenever a play is given favorable reviews by the critics, people go to see it; since people are going to see Pinter's new play, it will probably get favorable reviews.
   (E) Whenever critics give a play a favorable review, people go to see it; people are not going to see Pinter's new play, so it did not get favorable reviews.

"Channel One" is a 12-minute school news show that includes two minutes of commercials. The show's producers offer high schools $50,000 worth of television equipment to air the program. Many parents and teachers oppose the use of commercial television in schools, arguing that advertisements are tantamount to indoctrination. But students are already familiar with television commercials and know how to distinguish programming from advertising.

7. The argument assumes that

   (A) the effects of an advertisement viewed in a classroom would be similar to those of the same advertisement viewed at home
   (B) many educators would be willing to allow the indoctrination of students in exchange for new equipment for their schools
   (C) television advertising is a more effective way of promoting a product to high school students than print advertising
   (D) high school students are sufficiently interested in world affairs to learn from a television news program
   (E) a television news program produced especially for high school students is an effective teaching tool

Questions 8–9

The spate of terrorist acts against airlines and their passengers raises a new question: should government officials be forced to disclose the fact that they have received warning of an impending terrorist attack? The answer is "yes." The government currently releases information about the health hazards of smoking, the ecological dangers of pesticides, and the health consequences of food.

8. The argument above relies primarily on

   (A) circular reasoning
   (B) generalization
   (C) authority
   (D) analogy
   (E) causal analysis

9. All of the following, if true, would weaken the argument above EXCEPT

   (A) Public disclosure of threats would encourage more threats by giving terrorists greater publicity.
   (B) Information about terrorist acts is gained from intelligence gathering, not research studies.
   (C) Information about possible terrorist acts is routinely distributed to the staff of U.S. embassies.
   (D) Making public terrorist threats would allow terrorists to identify sources who had leaked the information.
   (E) Public disclosure of threats would encourage false threats designed to disrupt air travel.

GO ON TO THE NEXT PAGE

Some residents of San Juan Capistrano, California have suggested that government take some action to prevent the swallows from returning there each year because the birds constitute a nuisance. This suggestion ignores the important role the birds play in the environment. Swallows feed almost exclusively on flying insects, including many species that are annoying or harmful to human beings. The abundance of the birds in that region indicates an abundance of insects that are controlled through predation.

10. The speaker above implies that

   (A) without swallows, the region would be infested with insects
   (B) the majority of residents favor limiting the swallow population
   (C) the economic damage caused by the swallows is negligible
   (D) swallows are less destructive than other species of birds
   (E) pesticides would be ineffective against the species of insects eaten by the swallows

Susan: International Cosmetics is marketing a new treatment for cellulite called Fango Italiano. It's a cream that is spread on the affected area, allowed to dry, and then washed off. The treatment is very expensive—$250 per month—but it comes with a money-back guarantee. If Fango Italiano doesn't reduce your cellulite, the company will give you all of your money back. Since the company gives such a guarantee, the treatment must work.

Tom: I doubt that the treatment works. "Fango" is just the Italian word for *mud*. But it does seem to me that the company has found a brilliant marketing scheme. People who are so worried about their physical appearance that they are willing to spend $250 a month to get rid of cellulite are people who, while using the treatment, will also start eating less and exercising more. Thus, the treatment will appear to be successful and International Cosmetics will be that much richer.

11. Which of the following best characterizes the position Tom takes with regard to Susan's statement?

   (A) He denies that Fango Italiano will be effective and questions whether or not International Cosmetics really intends to refund the money of dissatisfied customers.
   (B) He denies that International Cosmetics really intends to market Fango Italiano, but suspects that the treatment is not effective.
   (C) He questions whether or not the treatment is effective and denies that it is possible to do anything about cellulite.
   (D) He agrees that people who purchase Fango Italiano may very well lose cellulite, but is skeptical that the treatment will be the reason.
   (E) He argues that $250 per month is too expensive for a treatment for cellulite and encourages people with cellulite to eat less and exercise more.

The National Research Council has recommended against requiring seat belts in school buses because only one life would be saved per year at a cost of $40 million annually. This analysis is shortsighted. Children who are required to use seat belts in school buses will remember to use them when they are old enough to drive.

12. The speaker above assumes that

   (A) installing seat belts in school buses will not cost $40 million per year
   (B) requiring seat belts in school buses would save many lives each year
   (C) most schoolchildren are transported to and from school in buses
   (D) states should require the use of seat belts in private vehicles
   (E) behavior learned as a child may affect adulthood behavior

A decade ago, "earn your age" was the immediate goal of every recent business school graduate. For example, a 26-year-old M.B.A. expected to earn $26,000 per year. This standard no longer holds true in America—a newly graduated M.B.A. in America would want to earn much more—but it is still the norm in England. It seems, therefore, that a starting M.B.A. in America is economically better off than one in England.

13. Which of the following, if true, most weakens the argument above?

   (A) Many students from England earn their M.B.A.s in the United States.
   (B) Most students in American business schools have had prior work experience.
   (C) The British pound is worth almost twice as much as the American dollar.
   (D) Graduates from American law schools earn more than graduates from American business schools.
   (E) England produces fewer M.B.A.s each year than the United States.

GO ON TO THE NEXT PAGE

The United States is currently faced with a shortage of qualified math and science teachers. A Rand Corporation study indicates that graduates of traditional undergraduate schools of education are expected to fill only half the 20,000 vacancies for math and science teachers. One way of addressing this problem is to provide scholarships for math and science majors to finish their educations and graduate without accumulating massive debts. If they are freed of the burdens of college loans, they will be more likely to consider careers in teaching.

14. Which of the following, if true, would most weaken the argument above?

   (A) Public school teachers earn starting salaries that are well above the average wage in the United States.
   (B) Large numbers of graduates in math and science in prior years created a surplus pool from which teaching jobs are filled.
   (C) The cost of an undergraduate education in math or science is comparable to that for other majors.
   (D) Faculty at colleges and universities generally earn higher salaries than teachers in public schools.
   (E) There is no shortage of teachers in areas such as history, literature, and vocational training.

Questions 15 and 16

   Helium-filled balloons rise because helium is a light gas, much lighter than air. Glass tubes filled with neon gas can be charged with electricity to make light, so neon is also a light gas. Therefore, there is one respect in which both helium gas and neon gas are alike: they are both light gases.

15. Which of the following arguments most closely parallels the argument above?

   (A) The Empire State Building is a tall building, and Peter is a tall man. Therefore, there is one respect in which both the Empire State Building and Peter are alike: they are both tall.
   (B) Mary is a law school professor, and her daughter is a medical school professor. So there is one respect in which Mary and her daughter are alike: they are both professors.
   (C) A good steak must be rare, and total lunar eclipses are rare. So there is one respect in which a good steak and total lunar eclipses are alike: they are both rare.
   (D) All whales are mammals, and all bats are mammals. Since all mammals are warm-blooded, there is one respect in which whales and bats are alike: they are both warm-blooded.
   (E) Susan ate half of the melon, and Nancy ate the other half of the melon. So there is one respect in which Susan and Nancy are alike: each ate half a melon.

16. The conclusion of the argument above does not follow from the premises because the speaker

   (A) mistakes a cause for an effect
   (B) may not be a scientific authority
   (C) fails to use statistics
   (D) contradicts herself
   (E) uses a term in an ambiguous way

   Marvin is a senior, so he must have gone to the senior prom.

17. The statement above assumes that

   (A) Marvin is the only senior who went to the prom
   (B) all seniors went to the prom
   (C) only seniors went to the prom
   (D) some seniors did not go to the prom
   (E) no seniors went to the prom

   When a vicious animal attacks a human being, we justifiably kill that animal to protect others. So, too, is the death penalty morally justified.

18. The speaker above relies primarily upon

   (A) a questionable analogy
   (B) circular reasoning
   (C) second-hand data
   (D) logical deduction
   (E) generalization

   The nobility of the effort to protect minors from capitalistic exploitation by means of child labor laws has arguably become an easy camouflage for attempts by organized labor and government to preserve the semblance of nearly full employment. The introduction of a majority of women into the workplace has further reinforced a social need to prevent teenagers from working.

19. The argument above assumes that

   (A) minors and women would compete for jobs
   (B) child labor laws should be repealed
   (C) women should not enter the work force
   (D) women do not want teenagers to work
   (E) unions and government disagree on child labor

GO ON TO THE NEXT PAGE

The air around us is getting cleaner. In 1980, only 53 percent of American industry was able to comply with Federal standards on air pollutants, but now over 75 percent are in complete compliance.

20. Which of the following, if true, would most weaken the argument above?

(A) Since 1980, manufacturers have spent large sums of money to comply with Federal air pollution standards.
(B) Other nations have passed stringent air pollution control laws and have begun to enforce them.
(C) In the 1980s, the Federal government eased tight restrictions on particulate emissions into the air.
(D) Since 1980, the Federal government has entered into treaties with other countries to control ocean dumping.
(E) Energy demands by United States industry have increased drastically since 1980.

Beginning in two years, in the areas of the United States that have not yet met the standards of the Environmental Protection Agency for carbon monoxide emissions, gasoline sold during the winter months must be oxygenated. There is no doubt that the oxygenated gasoline will reduce the amount of carbon monoxide discharged from vehicle tailpipes, but the benefit will be short lived. Older vehicles emit more carbon monoxide than newer ones. As older vehicles are replaced by newer ones, the same level of reduction in carbon monoxide will be achieved without any change in the content of gasoline.

21. Which of the following, if true, would undermine the argument above?

I. According to current estimates, petroleum refiners do not now have the capacity to meet the demand for oxygenated gasoline projected by the EPA under its new regulations.
II. Carbon monoxide build-up is cumulative, and once created years must pass before the deleterious effects have disappeared.
III. Requiring the use of oxygenated gasoline in newer cars will reduce carbon monoxide emissions more than allowing regular gasoline to be used in new cars.

(A) II only   (B) III only   (C) I and II only
(D) II and III only   (E) I, II, and III

Helen told me that she retired after 30 years as a city police officer with a pension of $80,000 per year. I checked with the city's Civil Service Commission and learned that the annual salary for someone in Helen's position would have been only $60,000 per year and that her pension should be equal to 80 percent of what she earned in her last year on the job. So Helen's pension has been wrongly computed.

22. Which of the following, if true, would most weaken the conclusion of the argument above?

(A) Some city police officers with higher ranks than that held by Helen in her last year earn $100,000 per year and more.
(B) Had Helen retired after only 25 years on the city police force her pension would have been only $50,000 per year.
(C) Helen will not begin to collect her pension until she reaches the age of 58, 7 years from now.
(D) During her last year on the force, Helen earned $40,000 in overtime.
(E) The estimated total cost to the city of Helen's pension benefits, based on actuarial tables, is $275,000.

Hume proved that it is impossible to deduce any "ought" statement from statements about what "is." That is to say, whatever is has no implication about what should or should not be. It is no part of an argument about what "should" be that something "is." Any line of reasoning that moves from statements of fact to a normative conclusion is not, strictly speaking, a logical argument.

23. Which of the following lines of reasoning runs afoul of Hume's restriction, as described above?

(A) The dean is opposed to letting the students have any say on the curriculum changes. Therefore, the students will probably stage a protest rally.
(B) The minister said in her sermon that anyone who is able to help collect food for the needy should do so. Since I have a lot of free time, the minister would probably say that I should help collect food for the needy.
(C) If an employee does a good job, then that employee will receive a promotion. Robert has just received a promotion. Therefore, Robert does a good job.
(D) The teeth of human beings are intended to grind vegetable matter—not to tear meat. Additionally, we find the notion of tearing a piece of meat off a freshly killed animal and eating it raw a repulsive thought. Therefore, humans should eat only plants.
(E) If a person should not deceive someone else, then that person should not tell a lie. A person should not deceive someone else. Therefore, no one should tell a lie.

GO ON TO THE NEXT PAGE

As a real estate agent in this city, I can personally attest to the recession that now afflicts the nation's housing market. Last year, the number of houses I was able to sell was 7 percent less than the number I was able to sell the year before.

24. Which of the following is NOT an assumption made by the speaker above?

(A) The speaker's experience in her city is typical of that of real estate agents around the country.

(B) The efforts made by the speaker last year to sell houses were equivalent to those she made the year before.

(C) No significant changes in the structure of the city's real estate market deprived the speaker of her share of the market.

(D) Sales recorded by the speaker two years ago were not the result of a boom that artificially inflated the number of sales.

(E) The average price of the homes sold by the speaker declined last year compared with the year before.

SECTION 5   Time—35 Minutes
28 Questions

For each question in this section, choose the best answer and blacken the corresponding space on the answer sheet.

The basic objective of the antitrust laws is to achieve desirable economic performance as measured by such criteria as efficient manufacturing and distributive processes, rapid technological progress, economic growth, and equity in the distribution of the fruits of progress. A society may achieve these objectives in a variety of ways. The government may specify performance by telling business what and how much to produce, or it may itself undertake the performance of certain functions. The basic philosophy of the antitrust laws, however, is to attempt to maintain sufficiently competitive market structure and market conduct to insure that private enterprise performs in a socially acceptable manner. The assumption is that we can avoid government intervention in the economically and politically hazardous thicket of specifying industrial performance by controlling certain aspects of industrial structure and competitive conduct. Hence, the antitrust approach is not regulation, per se.

Much of the job of antitrust enforcement involves formulating rules that govern the ways in which the competitive game is played. Economic theory suggests, and business experience verifies, that market structure plays a powerful role in determining or conditioning business conduct and that business conduct, in turn, determines the ultimate quality of industrial performance. This is not to say that an industry's structure and conduct are the only factors determining ultimate performance, but the available empirical evidence indicates that such structural characteristics as the height of entry barriers facing potential competitors, the degree of product differentiation, and the level of market concentration always are of some importance, and often are of decisive importance, in determining industry performance. There is also general agreement that certain forms of business conduct result in undesirable performance. For example, restrictive agreement among competitors may result in monopoly pricing even in industries that would otherwise generate competitive prices. Other forms of conduct may adversely affect market structure and thereby ultimate industry performance. Predatory pricing is an example. Although in the short run such conduct may give consumers low prices, it may also destroy competitors and result in higher prices in the long run.

Antitrust policy does not involve exhaustive investigation or analysis of all the factors that conceivably might have a bearing on industrial performance, nor does it involve direct specification of desired performance. This is both the great strength and the great weakness of the antitrust approach. Its strength derives from the fact that a maximum effect may flow from a minimum of government intervention. It is not necessary to assemble and maintain a vast bureaucracy that exercises continued intervention in and surveillance of the affairs of business. The Interstate Commerce Commission, whose major responsibilities involve setting of rates and other performance characteristics, has twice as many employees as the combined employees in antitrust enforcement at the Federal Trade Commission and the Department of Justice—and the ICC has responsibility for just a part of the field of transportation.

While the great virtue of the antitrust approach is that it requires a minimum of regulatory resources and intervention into business affairs, this is also its Achilles' heel. Because there are no precise causal links between market structure, conduct, and performance, rules of law controlling or modifying market structure and conduct are necessarily vulnerable to criticism.

1. The author of the passage is primarily concerned with

   (A) arguing against direct government intervention in the marketplace
   (B) explaining the underlying philosophy of the antitrust laws
   (C) outlining different theories of government regulation of markets
   (D) criticizing government agencies such as the Interstate Commerce Commission
   (E) justifying the enforcement of antitrust legislation

2. It can be inferred from the passage that predatory pricing

   (A) occurs only when a single firm has control of a large share of a market
   (B) is a type of business conduct best eliminated by direct government regulation
   (C) allows a large number of firms to distribute products over a broad region
   (D) improves an industry's ability to deliver a variety of goods and services
   (E) aims at eliminating competition so that the surviving firm can raise prices

3. The author cites the Interstate Commerce Commission to prove that

(A) direct government intervention requires a large bureaucracy
(B) antitrust enforcement is not an exact science
(C) controlling market structures is more effective than regulation
(D) antitrust laws can eliminate entry barriers for business
(E) some government agencies intervene directly in the marketplace

4. The author's attitude toward the theory of antitrust laws is best described as

(A) wary acceptance
(B) categorical rejection
(C) cautious skepticism
(D) qualified endorsement
(E) reluctant dismissal

5. The author mentions all of the following as measures of economic performance EXCEPT:

(A) high industry profits
(B) manufacturing efficiency
(C) technological progress
(D) distributional efficiency
(E) distributional equity

6. The author would most likely agree with which of the following statements?

(A) An effective antitrust policy depends on having as much information about market structure and conduct as possible.
(B) An antitrust approach to controlling market structure and conduct is only marginally more effective than regulation.
(C) Direct government intervention in the marketplace is cumbersome and never warranted.
(D) Antitrust policies are inherently arbitrary because no one can be certain what factors influence market structure and conduct.
(E) Market structure and market conduct are two independent variables and must be regulated separately.

7. The author mentions which of the following as factors that may affect industry performance?

I. The ease with which new firms can enter the market
II. The number of firms already in the market
III. The uniqueness of the product

(A) I only   (B) I and II only   (C) I and III only
(D) II and III only   (E) I, II, and III

A National Industrial Conference Board study prepared by Bock and Forkas examined the relationship between average productivity measured in terms of labor inputs of the top companies in an industry and other companies in the same industry and the relationship between industry concentration and industry productivity. The study shows that, on the average, the top companies

in an industry had higher rates of productivity than the remaining companies in the same industry and that the industries with the highest productivity tended, on the average, to have high concentration ratios. This prompted the nation's most sophisticated weekly business magazine to title its story on the NICB study ''Bigness Means Efficiency.''

The NICB study does find that there is a tendency for concentration to be higher in industries with high shipments per employee (or value added per employee) and lowest in industries with low shipments per employee. But this does not establish a causal link. The observed weak association between ''productivity'' and concentration is due mainly to two factors. First, the reason many industries are relatively unconcentrated is that the capital requirements for entry are very low. Frequently such industries are relatively labor-intensive and therefore have relatively low shipments or value added per employee—the measures of ''productivity'' used in the NICB study. It is not surprising, therefore, that the study found that of the 35 industries with the lowest productivity, 90 percent were located in areas such as textiles and apparel, lumber and wood products, and miscellaneous products such as lampshades and umbrellas. Once these industries are excluded from the analysis, the statistical association between concentration and shipments per employee disappears entirely, and that between concentration and value added per employee very nearly disappears. Additionally, the study's measure of ''productivity'' includes not only output per employee but also profits and advertising outlay per employee. (In some manufactured goods, advertising and profits may run as high as 50 percent of value added.) Hence, the higher productivity observed in the study is partly due to the presence of noncompetitive profits and greater advertising outlays in the more concentrated industries.

The NICB study also found that in 87 percent of the industries studied, the top four companies had greater ''productivity'' than other firms in their industries, but the observed association between size and productivity is misleading. Comparing the labor productivity of the top companies in a Census industry with ''all others'' generates questionable results. Often the smaller companies in a Census industry are actually in a different industry than the leading companies. For example, according to the Census of Manufacturers there are 158 companies competing with the four largest operators of blast furnaces and steel mills. Many of the smaller companies are actually in different, more labor-intensive industries than the top four. It is more relevant to compare large companies with medium-sized ones. When the top four are compared with the second four companies, their apparent superiority disappears. The one exception to this finding is consumer goods industries. This may seem surprising, since the requirements of large-scale production generally are less important in consumer goods than in producer goods industries. But the answer to this paradox lies in the fact that leading manufacturers of differentiated goods often have greater profits and advertising outlays than do smaller companies.

Finally, if the study's measure of productivity is a meaningful one, then the leading companies have such a decided advantage over their smaller rivals that they should be increasing their market share of the industry. Yet, since 1947 the leading companies have lost ground in most producer goods industries, the very industries where technology is most important. Only in consumer goods have they made net gains, but the reasons for this are not to be found in technology.

8. The primary purpose of the selection is to

(A) demonstrate that the NICB study does not prove that efficiency results from concentration
(B) argue that less concentrated industries are as efficient as highly concentrated ones
(C) prove that smaller companies are as efficient as the largest firms in any given industry
(D) explain why labor-intensive industries are likely to have low shipments per employee
(E) criticize the nation's leading business magazine for printing its story about the NICB study

9. The author places the word *productivity* in quotation marks when referring to the NICB study in order to

(A) remind the reader that the word is taken from another source
(B) express disagreement with the definition used by the study
(C) imply that the word is not susceptible to clear definition
(D) indicate that the magazine did not understand the word
(E) suggest that economic concepts have no content

10. The passage implies all of the following conclusions about the textile and apparel industry EXCEPT:

(A) It is relatively labor intensive.
(B) It is relatively unconcentrated.
(C) It has low shipments per employee.
(D) It is relatively easy for a firm to enter the industry.
(E) It has high profits and advertising expenditures per employee.

11. According to the passage, the study's findings that large firms have greater productivity than other firms is misleading for which of the following reasons?

I. It failed to include the consumer goods industries.
II. It included small firms not properly belonging to the studied industries.
III. It compared medium-sized firms to the four largest firms in certain industries.

(A) I only
(B) II only
(C) I and II only
(D) II and III only
(E) I, II, and III

12. According to the selection, the study tends to overstate shipments per employee in some industries because

(A) productivity included profits and advertising outlays
(B) captital requirements for entry are low
(C) the category ''all other'' industries is overly inclusive
(D) top companies, on the average, have higher rates of productivity
(E) low-productivity industries are relatively unconcentrated

13. In the final paragraph, the author

(A) indicts the motives of the people who prepared the NICB study
(B) criticizes the methodology of the NICB study
(C) offers affirmative evidence to disprove the conclusions of the NICB study
(D) cites other studies that contradict the conclusions of the NICB study
(E) describes the difference between consumer and producer goods industries

14. The author regards the conclusions of the NICB study as

(A) open to debate
(B) conclusively disproved
(C) probably true
(D) possibly true
(E) not subject to verification

GO ON TO THE NEXT PAGE

Is the Constitution of the United States a mechanism or an organism? Does it furnish for the American community a structure or a process? The Constitution is Newtonian in that it establishes a set of forces and counter-forces. These confer power and impose limitations on power, and one of the great virtues of the Newtonian model is that correctives can be self-generated. They do not have to be imposed from without. The homely illustration is the cutting of a pie into two pieces so that brother and sister will have equal shares. Rather than setting up a system of judicial review under an equal-protection clause—a device that might not work until the pie has become stale—you simply let one sibling cut the pie and the other choose a piece.

The Newtonian system assumes that each branch has a capacity to act that is commensurate with its authority to act and to improve its ability to discharge its constitutional responsibilities. For example, on the Congressional side, this means a rationalizing of the legislative process to improve its capability to formulate and carry through a legislative program that is coherent in policies and technically proficient. The goal involves better access to disinterested information through better research staffs and facilities, as well probably as the selection of committee chairs on a basis other than simple seniority. Other devices might alleviate the overburdened executive branch: a strengthened Cabinet, with a smaller, executive Cabinet of respected statesmen to serve as a link between the White House and the departments, and between the President and the Congress. No constitutional impediment stands in the way of any of the structural changes on either the legislative or the executive side.

In a Newtonian constitution, extraordinary force in one direction is likely to produce extraordinary, and sometimes excessive, force in another direction. In the early years of the New Deal, the Supreme Court, generally over the dissent of its most respected members, engaged in a series of judicial vetoes that reflected an unjudicial approach to the function of judging. The President, on his part, countered with the Court reorganization plan, which seriously threatened the independence of the judiciary. A Newtonian system demands constitutional morality. It would be possible, by excessive use of legal power, to bring the system to a standstill. Congress might refuse to appropriate for executive departments. The President might ignore Supreme Court decisions. The Court might declare unconstitutional all laws that a majority of its members would not have voted for. Without constitutional morality, the system breaks down.

The constitution is also Darwinian and stresses process and adaptation. Justice Holmes remarked that "the provisions of the Constitution are not mathematical formulas having their essence in their form; they are organic living institutions." Growth and adaptation, to be sure, have sometimes been seen as mutations, threatening the constitutional order. Chief Justice Marshall, near the close of his life, viewing with despair the developments of the Jacksonian era, confided to Justice Story, "The Union has been preserved thus far by miracles. I fear they cannot continue."

It must be admitted that we have all too readily assigned responsibility for the Darwinian constitutional evolution to the Supreme Court. Congress has too often either neglected its opportunities and responsibilities or has acted tentatively. When Congress does legislate, it is apt to regard its own constitutional judgment as only provisional, to await as a matter of course a submission to the Supreme Court. A striking example is the recent campaign finance law. But in the final analysis, is the Constitution a mechanism or an organism? If light can be viewed as both wave and particles, depending on which analysis is the more serviceable for a given problem, why cannot the Constitution be seen as both a mechanism and an organism, a structure and a process?

15. The main purpose of the selection is to

   (A) discuss two models of constitutional law
   (B) criticize Congress and the executive branch for inaction
   (C) suggest a new role for the Supreme Court
   (D) challenge the validity of Supreme Court rulings
   (E) call for a revised Constitution

16. In the first paragraph, the author makes use of

   (A) circular reasoning
   (B) authority
   (C) analogy
   (D) generalization
   (E) ambiguity

17. With which of the following statements would the author most likely agree?

   (A) The Darwinian model and the Newtonian model produce almost identical interpretations of the Constitution.
   (B) A constitutionally permissible action might still be constitutionally immoral.
   (C) One branch of government is morally obligated not to criticize the actions of another.
   (D) The Newtonian model of the Constitution is superior to the Darwinian model.
   (E) The Supreme Court should have primary responsibility for evolving a Darwinian model of government.

18. The author regards the President's attempt to reorganize the Supreme Court as

   (A) understandable but wrong
   (B) ineffective but correct
   (C) impractical but well-intentioned
   (D) necessary but misguided
   (E) half-hearted but moral

19. In the final sentence, the author

   (A) poses a question for future research
   (B) introduces a new problem of constitutional theory
   (C) rejects the Darwinian model
   (D) suggests ways for improving governmental efficiency
   (E) asks a rhetorical question

20. The passage implies that

    (A) Congress is more important than either the executive or the judiciary
    (B) branches of government may have more constitutional authority than they use
    (C) the earliest Supreme Court justices were more sincere than today's justices
    (D) the Constitution sets up a very simple system for governmental decisions
    (E) constitutionally created hurdles block needed improvements in governmental efficiency

21. The author is primarily concerned with

    (A) creating a dilemma
    (B) evading a question
    (C) answering a question
    (D) pointing out a contradiction
    (E) reporting on a development

What we expect of translation is a reasonable facsimile of something that might have been said in our language, but there is involved in this notion of reasonable facsimile a debate between critics as to what constitutes a reasonable facsimile. Most of us at heart belong to the "soft-line" party: a given translation may not be exactly "living language," but the facsimile is generally reasonable. The "hard-line" party aims only for the good translation. The majority of readers never notice the difference, as they read passively, often missing stylistic integrity so long as the story holds them. Additionally, a literature like Japanese may even be treated to an "exoticism handicap."

Whether or not one agrees with Roy A. Miller's postulation of an attitude of mysticism by the Japanese toward their own language, it is true that the Japanese have special feelings toward the possibilities of their language and its relation to life and art, and these feelings have an effect on what Japanese writers write about and how they write. Many of the special language relationships are not immediately available to the non-Japanese (which is only to say that the Japanese language, like every other, has some unique features). For example, in my own work on Dazai Osamu, I have found how close to the sense of the rhythms of spoken Japanese his writing is, and how hard that is to duplicate in English. Juda's cackling hysterically, "Heh, heh, heh" (in *Kakekomi uttae*), or the coy poutings of a schoolgirl (in *Joseito*) have what Masao Miyoshi has called, in *Accomplices of Silence,* an "embarrassing" quality. It is, however, the embarrassment of recognition that the reader of Japanese feels. The moments simply do not work in English.

Even the orthography of written Japanese is a resource not open to us. Tanizaki Jun'ichirō, who elsewhere laments the poverty of "indigenous" Japanese vocabulary, writes in *Bunshō tokuhon* of the contribution to literary effect—to "meaning," if you will—made simply by the way a Japanese author chooses to "spell" a word. In Shiga Naoya's *Kinosaki nite,* for example, the onomatopoeic "bu—n" with which a honeybee takes flight has a different feeling for having been written in *hiragana* instead of *katakana*. I read, and I am convinced. Arishima Takeo uses onomatopoeic words in his children's story *Hitofusa no budō,* and the effect is not one of baby talk, but of gentleness and intimacy that automatically pulls the reader into the world of childhood fears, tragedies, and consolations, memories of which lie close under the surface of every adult psyche.

This, of course, is hard to reproduce in translation, although translators labor hard to do so. George Steiner speaks of an "intentional strangeness," a "creative dislocation," that sometimes is invoked in the attempt. He cites Chateaubriand's 1836 translation of Milton's *Paradise Lost,* for which Chateaubriand "created" a Latinate French to approximate Milton's special English as an example of just such a successful act of creation. He also laments what he calls the " 'moon in pond like blossom weary' school of instant exotica," with which we are perhaps all too familiar.

22. The author is primarily concerned with

    (A) criticizing translators who do not faithfully reproduce the style of works written in another language
    (B) suggesting that Japanese literature is more complex than English literature
    (C) arguing that no translation can do justice to a work written in another language
    (D) demonstrating that Japanese literature is particularly difficult to translate into English
    (E) discussing some of the problems of translating Japanese literature into English

23. It can be inferred that *Accomplices of Silence* is

    (A) an English translation of Japanese poetry
    (B) a critical commentary on the work of Dazai Osamu
    (C) a prior publication by the author on Japanese literature
    (D) a text on Japanese orthography
    (E) a general work on the problem of translation

24. The author cites Shiga Naoya's *Kinosaki nite* in order to

    (A) illustrate the effect that Japanese orthography has on meaning
    (B) demonstrate the poverty of indigenous Japanese vocabulary
    (C) prove that it is difficult to translate Japanese into English
    (D) acquaint the reader with an important work of Japanese literature
    (E) impress upon the reader the importance of faithfully translating a work from one language into another

GO ON TO THE NEXT PAGE

25. With which of the following statements would the author most likely agree?

(A) The Japanese language is the language best suited to poetry.
(B) English is one of the most difficult languages into which to translate any work written in Japanese.
(C) It is impossible for a person not fluent in Japanese to understand the inner meaning of Japanese literature.
(D) Most Japanese people think that their language is uniquely suited to conveying mystical ideas.
(E) Every language has its own peculiar potentialities which present challenges to a translator.

26. It can be inferred that the Japanese word "bu—n" is most like which of the following English words?

(A) bee
(B) honey
(C) buzz
(D) flower
(E) moon

27. The author uses all of the following EXCEPT

(A) examples to prove a point
(B) citation of authority
(C) analogy
(D) personal knowledge
(E) contrasting two viewpoints

28. It can be inferred that the "exoticism handicap" mentioned by the author is

(A) the tendency of some translators of Japanese to render Japanese literature in a needlessly awkward style
(B) the attempt of Japanese writers to create for their readers a world characterized by mysticism
(C) the lack of literal, word-for-word translational equivalents for Japanese and English vocabulary
(D) the expectation of many English readers that Japanese literature can only be understood by someone who speaks Japanese
(E) the difficulty a Japanese reader encounters in trying to penetrate the meaning of difficult Japanese poets

TEST CENTER NUMBER

TEST DATE

MO. DAY YR.

LSAT/LSDAS NUMBER

SOCIAL SECURITY / SOCIAL INS. NO.

LAST NAME (PRINT)

FIRST NAME (PRINT)

MIDDLE INITIAL

IMPORTANT: Please complete the above area in clear legible PRINT!
(THIS INFORMATION SHOULD BE THE SAME AS THAT ON YOUR LSAT ADMISSION TICKET/IDENTIFICATION CARD)

LSAT® WRITING SAMPLE BOOKLET

WAIT FOR THE SUPERVISOR's INSTRUCTIONS BEFORE YOU TURN THE PAGE TO THE TOPIC. PLEASE SIGN YOUR NAME AND NOTE THE DATE AT THE TOP OF PAGE ONE BEFORE YOU START TO WORK.

TIME: 30 MINUTES

GENERAL DIRECTIONS

You are to complete the brief writing exercise on the topic inside. You will have 30 minutes in which to plan and write the exercise. Read the topic carefully. You will probably find it best to spend a few minutes considering the topic and organizing your thoughts before you begin writing. DO NOT WRITE ON A TOPIC OTHER THAN THE ONE SPECIFIED. WRITING ON A TOPIC OF YOUR OWN CHOICE IS NOT ACCEPTABLE.

There is no "right" or "wrong" answer to this question. Law schools are interested in how carefully you support the position you take and how clearly you express that position. How well you write is much more important than how much you write. No special knowledge is required or expected. Law schools are interested in organization, vocabulary, and writing mechanics. They understand the short time available to you and the pressured circumstances under which you will write.

Confine your writing to the lined area inside this booklet. Only the blocked lined area will be reproduced for the law schools. You will find that you have enough space in this booklet if you plan your writing carefully, write on every line, avoid wide margins, and keep your handwriting a reasonable size. Be sure that your writing is legible.

LSAT WRITING SAMPLE TOPIC

Read the following proposals of ABC Food and Beverages and Tri-County Caterers to operate a concession in the student union building of Lamar College. **Then, in the space provided, write an argument in favor of the company you think the president of the student senate should choose.** The following considerations should be taken into account:

1. The concession should offer students food at a reasonable price and should provide jobs for students.
2. The concession should provide a place for students to socialize.

ABC Food and Beverages proposes to operate an Italian restaurant. The menu would include pizza, pasta, heros, and one or two dinner plates such as eggplant parmigiana. The average price for a meal would be $4 to $5, including a beverage. ABC would hire four students to work in the kitchen and another three students to wait on tables. The dining room of the restaurant would close at 10:00 p.m. on weekdays and 11:00 p.m. on weekends, but the kitchen would be open until midnight every day for take-out service.

Tri-County Caterers proposes to place food vending machines in the student union. The vending machines would dispense cold sandwiches, fresh fruit, yogurt, and snacks, with one machine dispensing hot soup. Tri-County would also provide a microwave oven, so that students can heat up prepared platters of food. A typical platter would include turkey with stuffing and gravy and a vegetable. The prices for food would range from fifty cents for a piece of fruit to $2.00 for a sandwich and $3.50 for a platter. All of the food preparation would be done in Tri-County's kitchen, but Tri-County would employ two students to help clean up. Additionally, the vending machine area would be open to students all night.

Answer Key

SECTION 1	SECTION 2	SECTION 3	SECTION 4	SECTION 5
1. C	1. B	1. A	1. C	1. B
2. C	2. E	2. E	2. C	2. E
3. E	3. D	3. B	3. B	3. A
4. B	4. B	4. C	4. B	4. D
5. C	5. E	5. A	5. D	5. A
6. C	6. C	6. C	6. A	6. A
7. D	7. D	7. A	7. A	7. E
8. A	8. B	8. E	8. D	8. A
9. C	9. D	9. C	9. C	9. B
10. D	10. A	10. D	10. A	10. E
11. B	11. E	11. B	11. D	11. B
12. D	12. A	12. B	12. E	12. A
13. C	13. A	13. A	13. C	13. C
14. D	14. D	14. C	14. B	14. B
15. D	15. B	15. A	15. C	15. A
16. D	16. B	16. B	16. E	16. C
17. B	17. E	17. A	17. B	17. B
18. C	18. B	18. C	18. A	18. A
19. A	19. A	19. C	19. A	19. E
20. C	20. B	20. D	20. C	20. B
21. E	21. C	21. C	21. D	21. C
22. A	22. C	22. E	22. D	22. E
23. B	23. D	23. A	23. D	23. B
24. D	24. A	24. C	24. E	24. A
	25. C	25. A		25. E
		26. E		26. C
		27. B		27. C
		28. D		28. A

Explanatory Answers

SAMPLE ESSAY

The president of the student senate should accept the proposal submitted by ABC for three reasons: first, the proposed Italian restaurant would provide meals well-suited to the needs of students; second, a restaurant would employ more students; and third, the restaurant would add to the social life on campus.

The prices at the Italian restaurant are within the means of most students, and take-out service would be even less expensive. Also, the food is typical student fare, and the food would be freshly prepared. Because of this, the Italian restaurant would be well received by students.

The restaurant also would provide employment for several students. Some students would be hired as cooks and others as dishwashers. In addition, some students would be hired to wait on tables, and these students would earn tips.

Finally, the restaurant would provide a good meeting place for students. Students would enjoy sharing a pizza and soft drinks around a table, and the restaurant would be open late enough for most of them. Further, even after the dining area has closed, students could still use take-out service and share a pizza in a dormitory lounge.

Although the proposed vending-machine canteen has certain advantages, a restaurant, for the reasons just given, would best serve the needs of the students.

SECTION 1

ANALYTICAL REASONING

Questions 1–6

This set is a variation on the idea of a linear ordering. In fact, it is very much like the "word games" type discussed in the lesson on Analytical Reasoning. Begin by summarizing the information:

$$Y \neq R$$
$$(B = 1) \supset O$$
$$G \supset G$$
$$(O = 5) \supset G$$

There do not appear to be any further obvious conclusions to be drawn, so go to the questions.

1. Which of the following is an acceptable sequence of cards for a player's turn?

   (A) green, red, yellow, blue, green
   (B) green, red, orange, blue, yellow
   (C) orange, green, green, blue, yellow
   (D) blue, red, green, green, yellow
   (E) blue, blue, yellow, blue, orange

   (C) Just test the choices against the initial conditions. Using the first condition, eliminate choice (A). The other choices are consistent with the first requirement. Now use the second condition. Both (D) and (E) include blue cards as the first card played. (E) meets the second condition, but (D) fails to meet it. So we eliminate (D). Next, we use the third condition, and we eliminate (B) because that series includes but one green card. Finally, use the last condition to eliminate (E). By the process of elimination, the correct choice is (C).

2. All of the following are acceptable sequences of cards for a player's turn EXCEPT

   (A) red, orange, green, green, yellow
   (B) orange, green, yellow, green, red
   (C) blue, red, blue, yellow, orange
   (D) red, green, yellow, green, red
   (E) blue, green, green, yellow, orange

   (C) Again you will use the initial conditions to screen choices. This question, however, contains a thought-reverser, so the correct choice will be the one sequence that violates one or more of the initial conditions. All choices meet the first three conditions. Choice (C), however, fails to meet the final condition, so it must be the correct answer.

3. If a player has already played, in order, a yellow card, a green card, a blue card, and a green card, then which of the following is a complete and accurate listing of the cards he could play as the fifth and last card of his turn?

   (A) green
   (B) green, blue
   (C) green, blue, orange
   (D) green, blue, orange, yellow
   (E) green, blue, orange, yellow, red

   (E) One way of attacking this item is to take each color in turn and determine whether a card of that color played last is consistent with all of the initial conditions. You will find that every color creates an acceptable sequence. Or you might reason that the first four cards of the sequence have already satisfied the second and third conditions. (Blue is not the first card, and two green cards have already been played.) Then, the first condition requires only that red and yellow cards not be played in succession; but since the fourth card is a green one, this condition is no longer important. Finally, the last condition requires that an orange card played as the final card be preceded by a green card—and that requirement has already been satisfied. Thus, any color will create an acceptable sequence.

4. If a player holds seven cards—one green card, one red card, one blue card, and four yellow cards—then which of the following could be the first card the player plays?

    I. A blue card
   II. A green card
  III. A red card

(A) I only   (B) III only   (C) I and III only
(D) II and III only   (E) I, II, and III

(B) Test each Roman-numeraled statement. As for statement I, the player cannot play a blue card first. The second initial condition states that a blue card played first must be followed at some time in the turn by an orange card; but the player doesn't have an orange card in his holding. (Since statement I is not part of the correct choice, you can eliminate choices [A], [C], and [E].) As for II, a green card must be accompanied by another green card. Since the player has but one green card in his holding, he cannot play that card. (Since II is not part of the correct choice, you can eliminate [D].) We have thus established that the correct answer is (B). For the purpose of explanation, however, let us examine III. The player could play the following sequence of cards: red, blue, yellow, yellow, yellow.

5. Which of the following sequence of cards could be turned into an acceptable play by rearranging the cards indicated?

(A) green, blue, blue, red, yellow
(B) yellow, red, yellow, red, yellow
(C) red, green, green, red, yellow
(D) orange, blue, orange, blue, green
(E) blue, red, orange, green, yellow

(C) Examine each of the sequences. As for (A), (D), and (E), these sequences contain only one green card, so just rearranging the cards will not bring them into conformity with the third initial condition. As for (B), in this sequence we have yellow and red cards played in sequence, in violation of the first initial condition. Since there are only red and yellow cards in the sequence, no arrangement will rectify this defect. As for (C), we have a yellow card following a red card, but that problem can be corrected by rearranging the order of play: red, green, red, green, yellow. This sequence is also consistent with the other conditions.

6. If a player plans to play three red cards, an orange card, and one other card, then which of the following must be true?

(A) He cannot play a yellow card.
(B) He cannot play a blue card third .
(C) He cannot play an orange card last.
(D) He cannot play a blue card first.
(E) He cannot play a red card third.

(C) If an orange card is played last, then a green card must also be played. If a green card is played, then two green cards must be played. But the player already plans to play three red cards and one orange card, so he cannot play three other cards. To prove that the other choices are not necessarily true, construct acceptable sequences using the cards in the positions they specify:

(A)   yellow, orange, red, red, red

(B)   orange, blue, red, red, red

(D)   blue, red, red, orange, red

(E)   orange, red, red, red, blue

Questions 7–12

This is a variation on the idea of linear ordering. Here it appears that students could have the same scores. Begin by summarizing the information:

$$N < J < O$$

$$L < K < O$$

$$L < M < J$$

There is one further conclusion that you should see. Since O scored higher than J, O must have also scored higher than M and L:

$$L < M < J < O$$

This means that O received the highest score. There do not appear to be any further conclusions to be drawn, so we go to the questions.

7. Which of the following could be the rank ordering of the students' scores, from lowest to highest?

    (A) *K, L, N, M, J, O*
    (B) *L, K, N, J, M, O*
    (C) *N, K, O, J, L, M*
    (D) *N, L, M, K, J, O*
    (E) *N, M, L, K, J, O*

    (D) Just test each choice by the initial conditions. (A) violates the second condition (*K* scores higher than *L*). (B) violates the third condition (*J* scores higher than *M*). (C) violates each of the three conditions (*O* received the highest score). (E) violates the third condition (*M* scored higher than *L*). (D), however, is consistent with all three conditions.

8. Which of the following must be true of the scores received by the students?

    (A) *O* received the highest score.
    (B) *J* received the second-highest score.
    (C) *K* received the third-highest score.
    (D) *N* received the lowest score.
    (E) *L* received the lowest score.

    (A) In the overview of this set, we deduced that *O* must have received the highest score. You can prove that the other choices are not necessarily true by constructing counterexamples to those claims. The possible order *L, M, N, J, K, O* proves that (B), (C) and (D) are not necessarily true. The sequence *N, L, M, K, J, O* proves that (E) is not necessarily true.

9. Which of the following could be true?
    I. *J* and *K* received the same score.
    II. *N* and *L* received the same score.
    III. *M* and *L* received the same score.

    (A) I only   (B) II only   (C) I and II only
    (D) II and III only   (E) I, II, and III

    (C) III is not possible, since the third condition states that *M* received a higher score than *L*. That the other two statements are possible can be shown by an example:

    $$(L \text{ and } N) < M < (J \text{ and } K) < O$$

    Notice that this order is consistent with the initial conditions.

10. If two students received scores higher than *L* but lower than *M*, they must be

    (A) *J* and *K*   (B) *J* and *L*   (C) *K* and *J*
    (D) *K* and *N*   (E) *K* and *O*

    (D) Where should you start? With either *L* or *M*; as it turns out, one line of attack is better than the other, but you have no way of knowing which until you try them. Let us start with *L*. Consulting the summarized information, we see that every other student could have scored higher than *L*. This first line of attack is not that helpful, so we change our focus to *M*. Since *J* scored higher than *M*, and since *O* received the highest score of all the students, we know that neither *J* nor *O* scored lower than *M*. This leaves only two other students, *K* and *N*, so they must be the two who scored lower than *M* and yet higher than *L*.

11. What is the maximum number of students who could have scored higher than *K*?

    (A) 5   (B) 4   (C) 3   (D) 2   (E) 1

    (B) Attack this problem by trying to determine which students could have scored higher than *K*. First, we know that *L* cannot have scored higher than *K*. (See the second condition.) Next, try to find a possible order in which every other student scored higher than *K*:

    L, K, M, N, J, O

    This shows that four students could have scored higher than *K*.

12. Which of the following provides a complete and accurate description of those students who could have scored higher than *M*?

(A) *J*   (B) *J,O*   (C) *J,O,K*
(D) *J,O,K,N*   (E) *J,O,K,N,L*

(D) Here we can use the same reasoning that we used for question 11, above. Given the third condition, *M* scored higher than *L*. Next, we construct a scenario in which other students scored higher than *M*: *L, M, N, K, J, O*.

Questions 13–19

This is a variation on the idea of a linear ordering set. Here, however, in addition to the relationship "beside," there is the relationship "across from." Begin by summarizing the information:

$P \neq Q$

$R \neq S$

$T = S$

There do not appear to be any further conclusions to be drawn, so go to the questions.

13. Which of the following seating arrangements is acceptable?

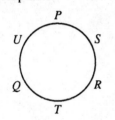

(A)

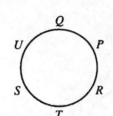

(B)

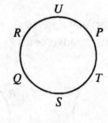

(C)

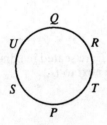

(D)

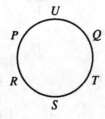

(E)

(C) Just use the initial conditions to test each choice. Using the first condition, we eliminate choice (B). Next, using the second condition, we eliminate (A) and (E). Finally, using the third condition, we eliminate (D). Only (C) meets all three of the initial conditions.

14. If *P* is seated next to *T*, then which of the following cannot be true?

(A) *U* sits next to *S*.
(B) *U* sits next to *R*.
(C) *R* sits next to *P*.
(D) *Q* sits between *U* and *T*.
(E) *U* sits between *R* and *Q*.

(D) Begin by entering the new information on a diagram:

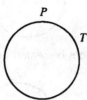

(**Note:** Since the positions around the table are not distinguished from each other, you can put P and T anywhere.) Now look at the initial conditions for further conclusions. The third condition states that S is seated next to T:

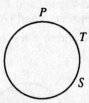

Next, Q cannot be seated next to P:

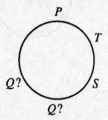

R cannot be seated next to S:

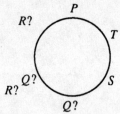

Thus, given the additional stipulation that P sits next to T, there are three possible seating arrangements:

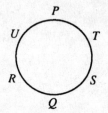 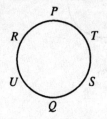 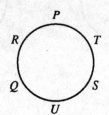

Now you can see that (A), (B), (C), and (E) are possible arrangements, but (D) is not.

15. If Q is seated next to T and S is seated next to U, who is seated directly across from R?

(A) P (B) Q (C) R (D) S (E) U

(**D**) Here you have two pieces of information to be entered on a diagram. You can enter them both on a diagram simultaneously because T must be seated next to S:

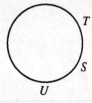

To complete the diagram, return to the initial conditions. Since Q cannot be seated next to P, there is but one possible order:

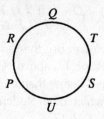

As the diagram shows, S is seated directly opposite R.

16. If U and T are seated in adjacent seats, who could be seated next to U?

I. P
II. Q
III. R

(A) I only (B) II only (C) III only
(D) I and II only (E) II and III only

(**D**) Enter the new information on a diagram:

Of course, T is seated next to S.

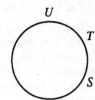

Now return to the initial conditions. The first states that P and Q cannot be seated together. Since there are only three seats left, P and Q must be seated next to U and S, respectively, or vice versa. This means that R must sit between P and Q. Therefore, either P or Q, though not R, could sit next to U.

17. If R is seated directly across from Q, in how many different orders can the rest of the diplomats be seated?

(A) 1 (B) 2 (C) 3 (D) 4 (E) 5

(B) Start by entering the new information on a diagram:

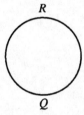

Since T and S must be seated together, they must sit on one side of R or the other and in such a way that S is not next to R:

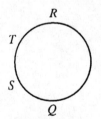 or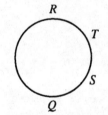

This means that P must be seated on the other side of R from T and S and in such a way that P is not next to Q (and U occupies the remaining seat):

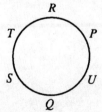 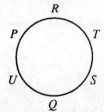

Given the additional stipulation that R is seated directly across from Q, exactly two different seating arrangements are possible.

18. If P is seated directly across from T, then which of the following is seated directly across from S?

(A) P (B) Q (C) R (D) T (E) U

(C) Begin by entering the new information on a diagram:

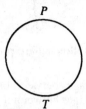

S is seated next to T:

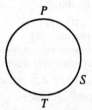

Since Q cannot be seated next to P, Q must be seated as follows:

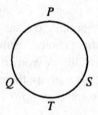

Since R cannot sit next to S, R must be seated next to Q, with U in the remaining seat:

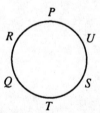

As the diagram shows, given that P is seated directly across from T, it is R who sits directly opposite S.

529

Questions 19–24

Start by summarizing the initial conditions:

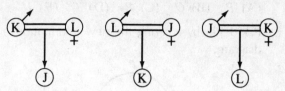

19. Which of the following are prohibited by the rules above?

   I. All marriages between brother and sister
   II. All marriages between a woman and her ex-husband's brother
   III. All marriages between a woman and her sister's ex-husband

   (A) I only (B) III only (C) I and II only
   (D) II and III only (E) I, II, and III

   (A) Since a brother and sister are always of the same group, they cannot marry, so statement I must be part of the correct choice. As for statement II, this kind of marriage is not prohibited. The brother of a woman's ex-husband will belong to the same group as her ex-husband (since they are both offspring of the same set of parents); therefore, he is a member of the eligible group. So statement II should not be part of the correct choice. Similar reasoning eliminates statement III. A woman and her sister both belong to the same group; therefore, they must both marry into the same group.

20. Which of the following must be true of the grandparents of someone who is a member of group J?

   (A) Both grandfathers belong to group J.
   (B) Both grandmothers belong to group K.
   (C) One grandfather belongs to group J and the other to group L.
   (D) One grandmother belongs to group J and the other to group L.
   (E) One grandmother belongs to group L and the other to group K.

   (C) Extend the relationships shown in our overview back one generation:

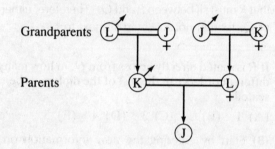

21. Which of the following is a complete and accurate list of the groups to which the grandchild of a person belonging to group L could possibly belong?

(A) J   (B) J,L   (C) K,L
(D) J,K   (E) J,K,L

(E) Extend the relationships shown in the initial overview forward by two generations:

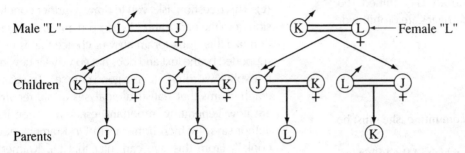

22. A man would be permitted to marry which of the following?

   I. His brother's wife's sister
  II. His sister's husband's sister
 III. His son's wife's mother

(A) I only   (B) III only   (C) I and III only
(D) II and III only   (E) I, II, and III

(A) As for statement I, a man and his brother belong to the same group, and a man's wife and her sister belong to the same group. Therefore, a man is allowed to marry the sister of his brother's wife. As for statement II, a man and his sister belong to the same group, and his sister's husband and his sister belong to the same group. The rules, however, apply differently to different sexes. For example, if a man and his sister belong to group J, then she marries into group L, but a man belonging to group J marries into group K—not group L. The best way to assess the truth of statement III is to apply a specific example. Take a man who is a member of group K. His son is a member of group J and marries a woman who is a member of group K. A woman who is a member of group K has a mother who is a member of group J. Can a man who is a member of group K marry a woman who is a member of group J? No. So the correct answer consists of statement I only.

23. In a group consisting of a woman, her sister, her husband, her husband's parents, and all of her husband's grandparents, what is the largest number of people that will belong to any one of the three groups?

(A) 3   (B) 4   (C) 5   (D) 6   (E) 7

(B) Again, perhaps the best way to handle the problem is to use an example:

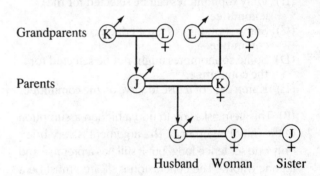

24. Which of the following marriages between cousins are prohibited by the rules?

    I. A marriage between a man and a daughter of his mother's sister.
   II. A marriage between a man and a daughter of his father's brother.
 III. A marriage between a woman and a son of her mother's brother.
 IV. A marriage between a woman and a son of her father's sister.

(A) I only   (B) IV only   (C) I and IV only
(D) I, II, and III only   (E) I, II, III, and IV

(D) As for statement I, this type of marriage is not permitted. For example, if a man belongs to group J, his mother belongs to group L, and her sister is also a member of group L. Her sister's children will belong to group J, so this is not a permitted marriage. As for statement II, this marriage is not permitted. For example, if a man belongs to group J, his father and father's brother both belong to group K, and the daughter of a man belonging to group K is also J. So this type of marriage is prohibited. As for statement III, this is not a permitted marriage. For example, if a woman belongs to group J, her mother and her mother's brother both belong to group L, and her mother's brother's son belongs to group K. And a male (K)–female (J) marriage is not allowed. Finally, as for statement IV, this is a permitted marriage. If a daughter belongs to group J, her father and his sisters belong to group K. And the son of a woman belonging to group K belongs to group L. And a male (L)–female (J) marriage is permitted. So only the first three types of marriages are prohibited.

SECTION 2

LOGICAL REASONING

If Karen was selected for the committee, she must be a sophomore.

1. The statement above makes which of the following assumptions?

    (A) Only Karen can be selected for the committee.
    (B) Only sophomores can be selected for the committee.
    (C) Some sophomores must be selected for the committee.
    (D) Some sophomores might not be selected for the committee.
    (E) Karen did not refuse to serve on the committee.

(B) This item asks you to find a hidden assumption of the initial argument. The argument is very brief, only one sentence long, but it still has a premise and a conclusion. The conclusion is "Karen must be a sophomore," and the premise is "Karen was selected for the committee." Thus, the argument has the structure:

Premise: Karen was selected for the committee.
Conclusion: Karen must be a sophomore.

The hidden assumption of this argument is articulated by (B).

The use of statistical data gathered from historical sources such as census reports and commercial registers and analyzed with the help of sophisticated computer programs has permeated the study of history in recent years. Now it would appear that the new statistical methods have begun to generate major breakthroughs in historical research, which brings us to Dr. Kramer's fascinating new book on the nineteenth-century settlement of the American frontier.

2. Which of the following conclusions is best supported by the passage above?

    (A) Statistical data from historical sources are the single most important form of information underpinning current historical research.
    (B) Dr. Kramer is the first major historian to apply the new statistical techniques to the study of the settlement of the American frontier.

    (C) Historians have begun to make major contributions to the science of statistical analysis.
    (D) Today, writers of histories must be skilled as computer programmers as well as knowledgeable about a particular era of history.
    (E) Dr. Kramer's book offers important new insights into its subject, based on analysis of historical statistics.

(E) This question asks you to draw a further conclusion from the paragraph. When you analyze a question like this, look for an answer choice that is well supported by the text and does not go very far beyond its explicit wording. (E) is a good choice. The paragraph claims that statistical analyses of old records are now generating important research. Then the author says, "which brings us to Dr. Kramer's new book." From this, we can infer that Dr. Kramer's new book is an example of the general trend cited by the author.

(A) overstates the author's point. The author does not claim that this new research technique is now the single most important source of historical research. (B) avoids the error of (A) but makes a different mistake. To be sure, Dr. Kramer's book is evidently an example of the general trend described by the author, but there is nothing in the paragraph to suggest that Dr. Kramer is the very first to use it. Choice (C) gets the causal sequence reversed. Existing statistical methods are now being applied to historical research, but the paragraph does not say that historians discovered new statistical techniques. Finally, (D) overstates the case. Though the new research technique requires researchers who understand statistics, this does not necessarily mean that they have to be able to program a computer.

Some people oppose special college admissions programs for minority students on the ground that merit alone—as measured by high school grades, scores on entrance exams, and other objective standards—should be used in admissions decisions. This argument ignores the facts that non-merit factors—the applicant's place of origin, whether a parent is a graduate of the college, and so on—have always been considered by colleges. And these subjective factors are usually such as to exclude minority-group students.

3. Which of the following would best complete the paragraph above?

    (A) Therefore, merit plays no substantive role in the majority of college admissions decisions.
    (B) Therefore, subjective factors should be completely removed from the college admissions process.
    (C) Therefore, the concept of merit is merely a subterfuge by which minority students may be excluded.

(D) Therefore, it is not inappropriate to use special admissions programs for minority students to help redress an imbalance.

(E) Therefore, high school grades alone are an inadequate measure of a student's past academic performance.

(D) This question also asks that you draw a conclusion, and the criteria for evaluating answer choices were given in our analysis of the preceding question. Eliminate (A) because it goes too far beyond the text. The paragraph suggests that factors other than merit play a role in admissions decisions, but not that merit plays absolutely no role at all. (B) makes a recommendation, but one that is not strongly supported by the text (especially given the recommendation made by [D]). The author says that colleges use subjective factors, but there is nothing to suggest he favors eliminating them from the admissions decision entirely—as opposed to using them in a new way. (C) really overstates the author's case. Nothing in the paragraph suggests a conclusion that uses emotional terms such as *subterfuge*. Though the author would surely endorse (E), it is not the point toward which this paragraph is leading.

The point toward which the paragraph is leading is nicely stated by (D). The author cites a position: some people oppose the use of special admissions criteria. He then notes that colleges have always used subjective considerations. Given the opening sentence of the paragraph, (D) is a conclusion toward which the author is probably working.

Government involvement in industry is more detrimental than helpful to that industry. As proof of this, consider two comparable industries: urban mass transit and the airline business. The former has generally been subsidized and operated by local governments, and in most cities service is poor and deteriorating. By contrast, the privately owned and operated airlines earn profits and provide, for the most part, fast and efficient service.

4. Which of the following, if true, would LEAST weaken the argument above?

(A) Passenger complaints about airline scheduling and service have increased rapidly and are now greater than ever before.

(B) Privately owned mass transit systems do not have problems similar to those of government-operated systems.

(C) The government subsidizes airport construction and operation and offers tax breaks to airlines.

(D) Technological advances in air travel have allowed airlines to operate more efficiently, but no similar advances have occurred in rail travel.

(E) On average, airline ticket prices have increased faster than mass transit fares over the past ten years.

(B) This question asks you to attack this argument. The conclusion of the argument is contained in the first sentence: government involvement is harmful. The proof of this conclusion is a comparison of urban mass transit and airlines. The author claims that the quality of service provided by urban mass transit, which receives government aid, is deteriorating while costs have increased. On the other hand, according to the argument, the airlines, which receive no government aid, provide good service and make a profit.

(A) provides a good attack on this final point: airline service is not that good. (C) attacks the argument by claiming that the successful operations of the airlines are actually dependent upon government support and involvement. (D) attacks the argument by pointing to an alternative causal explanation: it is not management but technological breakthroughs that account for the difference. Finally, (E) argues that the economic performance of airlines is, in at least one respect, no better than that of urban mass transit.

(B) actually strengthens the argument by suggesting that government interference is the cause of the differences in performances between government-owned rapid transit and privately owned airlines: publicly owned mass transit has these problems, but privately owned mass transit does not.

Neither artifacts, personal messages, nor historical documents from any human civilization would be likely to have any meaning for intelligent extraterrestrial beings. Therefore, the probe to be sent into interstellar space in the hope that alien beings may find it will contain a plaque inscribed with certain scientific and mathematical formulas, for example, a statement of the value of π or the molecular weight of water.

5. The argument above depends upon which of the following assumptions?

(A) Somewhere in the universe there is at least one intelligent race other than the human race living on Earth.

(B) Extraterrestrial beings probably have civilizations that are not as technically advanced as those on Earth.

(C) Life on other worlds is likely to be dependent upon the presence of water just as it is on Earth.

(D) Intelligent beings in other worlds have probably developed means of interstellar space travel.

(E) Some symbols used by human beings will be meaningful to intelligent extraterrestrial beings.

(E) This question asks you to find a hidden assumption of the argument. The conclusion of the argument (although not stated very precisely) is that alien beings will be able to read mathematical and scientific formulas. But these formulas are written in human symbols. Thus, the argument implicitly presupposes that the aliens will be able to read (at least some) symbols used by humans.

(A) is incorrect, for the probe is launched with the hope that such races exist. But that they exist is just that—a hope, not a presupposition. As for (B) and (D), the argument depends upon the assumption that an alien race is different—not that it is less or more technically advanced than we are. Finally, as for (C), though one of the formulas is the molecular weight of water, the argument assumes only that alien races would recognize it as the molecular weight of water—not that they depend on water in the same way that we do.

Studies of twins separated at or shortly after birth have played a major role in attempts to measure the relative influence of genetic and environmental factors on personal development. Those who consider environment all-important would predict that separately reared twins would exhibit no more similarity than another two unrelated individuals brought up under the same conditions. The data do not support this extreme position, but neither do they support the opposite fallacy, the belief that "genetics is destiny."

6. Which of the following statements would be the most reasonable conclusion to draw from the argument above?

(A) More study of the relationship between genetics and environment is needed before it can be determined whether one or the other of the two extreme positions is correct.
(B) Studies of twins separated at birth show that environmental factors are the most important factor in later personal development.
(C) Twin studies suggest that both genetic and environmental factors play an important part in the development of personality.
(D) Attempts to modify personal development by making changes in the environment of an individual are misguided and doomed to failure.
(E) Twin studies are inherently unsatisfactory as a research tool because of the ambiguity that infects the results obtained.

(C) This item asks you to draw a further conclusion from the initial paragraph. The speaker mentions two competing theories: heredity is all-important and environment is all-important. The evidence provided by studies of twins, according to the author, does not support either view. The most reasonable conclusion to draw is that the truth is somewhere in between—as (C) suggests. You can eliminate (A) be-

cause the author does not believe either of the extreme positions is correct. For the same reason, you can eliminate both (B) and (D). Finally, as for (E), nothing in the paragraph suggests that the studies are unreliable.

We hear it said that, for all the social progress America has made over the past thirty years—for all the toppling of racial and ethnic barriers that we have witnessed—this remains an inherently racist society, in which the white majority has never fully accepted the equal humanity of the minority. Those who repeat this slander against America ignore the fact that, as I write, the most popular television program in the country focuses on the lives of a proud middle-class black family, whose members have become some of the best-recognized—and most widely admired—people in America.

7. The argument above assumes that

(A) television acting is a challenging and financially rewarding profession
(B) thirty years ago a television show with black characters would not have been popular
(C) those who label America a racist society seek to foment unrest and disrupt the fabric of American society
(D) a person's attitude toward a character on a television show is like his attitude toward real people with similar characteristics
(E) the television program is more popular among white viewers than among black viewers

(D) This question asks that you find a hidden assumption of the argument. The conclusion of the argument is that America is not a racist society (or at least not so racist as some would contend). The proof for this conclusion is that a popular television show depicts successful black people. Thus, the argument implicitly assumes that what people find attractive in a television character, they also find attractive in a real person—a point made by (D).

As for (A), the important fact, according to the speaker, is that the fictional characters are successful—not that the actors are successful. On first reading, (B) might seem to be an implicit assumption of the argument, but a closer reading shows that it is not. You might think that the author is logically committed to the proposition that black characters would not have been popular thirty years ago. (Otherwise, why would the fact that this particular series is popular indicate that racism is on the decline?) The difficulty with (B) is that it fails to distinguish between possible portrayals of black characters, and one of the most important features of the argument is that the characters mentioned are successful. Thus, the author might allow that thirty years ago there were popular black characters but these were racist stereotypes. (C) overstates the case. Although there is some indication in the paragraph that the author regards this as an emotional issue (he uses the term *slander*), (C) goes too far beyond the text. Finally, as for (E), this is not an idea to which the author is logically committed. The author could allow that the white and black viewers alike enjoy the program and still argue that the fact that since whites like it at all, it shows that racism is on the wane.

Foods that are high in fat, salt, or sugar content have been shown to be deleterious to health. If the government can forbid the sale to minors of other harmful products, such as cigarettes and alcoholic beverages, why not treat dangerous foods in the same way? Children under 18 should be allowed to purchase only foods that are nutritious and healthful.

8. The author of the statement above makes his point primarily by

    (A) analyzing a cause-and-effect relationship
    (B) drawing an analogy
    (C) appealing to the emotions of the audience
    (D) offering a counterexample
    (E) making a generalization

    (B) This is a fairly easy critical thinking question. The speaker draws an analogy between harmful substances such as tobacco and alcohol and foods that might be harmful. Admittedly, the argument from analogy is not very persuasive, but (B) does correctly describe the form of the argument.

By studying census data, demographers are able to develop lists of counties and communities throughout the country whose populations have specific economic characteristics—for example, high or low median age, large numbers of families with children, a high percentage of two-career couples, or particularly affluent households. Lists such as these can be especially useful to political organizations that are promoting candidates who have particular appeal to voters with specific characteristics.

9. Which of the following, if true, best supports the claim that the demographic information mentioned in the passage may be valuable to political organizations?

    (A) Affluent citizens are known to be more likely to vote in local elections than are those who are less affluent.
    (B) Because census data are compiled by the federal government, they must legally be made available to all who request them.
    (C) Voters tend to be heavily influenced in their thinking by the opinions and preferences of their friends and neighbors.
    (D) Research shows that the economic and social characteristics of differing groups can be closely correlated with specific political views.
    (E) Several of today's most significant political issues have particular impact on the interests of families with children.

(D) This item asks us to strengthen the argument, so we are anticipating an answer choice that proves a hidden assumption of the argument. The conclusion of the argument is that the lists mentioned can be helpful to political organizations in targeting certain voters. Since the lists contain demographic information, the speaker must believe that demographic characteristics can be used to predict voting patterns. (D) provides support for this critical assumption.

(A) uses language that is generally relevant to the argument, but (A) doesn't weaken or strengthen the argument. One way of proving this to yourself is to try to explain how (A) is relevant to the argument. Then try to explain how the negation of (A) is also relevant to the argument. Both (A) and its negation are equally uninteresting. As for (B), this may be true of census data, but it does not explain why lists of demographic characteristics would be valuable to political organizations. As for (C), this at least has the merit of suggesting that demographic information (who the neighbors are and what they think) may have something to do with voting patterns. And, in the absence of (D), you might make a good argument for the correctness of (C). The difficulty with (C) is that it merely suggests that demographic data is important, whereas (D) states this specifically. So on balance (D) is a better choice than (C). Finally, as for (E), to the extent that you can argue that it would be useful to know which families have children because they might be predisposed to vote a certain way on some issues, you are really making an argument for (D).

Some people oppose testing of employees for use of illegal drugs on the ground that the tests sometimes produce false results. These fears are without basis. The newest tests can detect over 99 percent of the cases in which a person has used one of the most common illegal drugs at any time during the previous 48 hours.

10. Which of the following, if true, would most weaken the argument above?

    (A) The best drug tests available today return a significant number of positive results even when the person has not used drugs.
    (B) The best drug tests available today cannot reliably identify every form of illegal drug that a person might have used.
    (C) The best drug tests available today cannot identify an illegal drug if the subject took that drug more than 48 hours prior to the test.
    (D) An employee who occasionally uses an illegal drug may still be a valuable worker.
    (E) Some employers still continue to use older and less reliable drugs tests.

(A) The argument claims that drug testing is fairly reliable, and the proof given for this is that the tests are able to detect accurately when someone has used drugs within a certain time period before the test. The difficulty with this analysis is that it addresses only half of the issue of reliability. The real concern over drug testing is not whether the tests return a positive most or all of the time that the person tested has used drugs, but whether the tests return a positive on only those occasions. This is the issue of false positives, and (A) points out that this is a weakness in the argument about reliability.

(B) and (C) are incorrect for the same reason. Each does cite a weakness in drug testing, but the wording of the speaker's claim really pre-empts these objections. The speaker says that drug testing is fairly reliable for the most common illegal drugs taken within a certain time before the test. (D) makes a claim that is irrelevant to the issue of reliability. As for (E), the fact that some employers use unreliable tests does not weaken the author's claim that reliable tests are available.

One of the most influential studies of the ancient construction known as Stonehenge was conducted by Professor Gerald Hawkins. Hawkins used computer calculations to compare the locations of stones in Stonehenge with the positions of stars, planets, and the sun at the time the structure was built. He concluded that the stones could have been used to mark viewing angles along which the rising and setting of heavenly bodies could be observed, making Stonehenge a kind of primitive "computer" for predicting astronomical events.

11. Which of the following, if true, most seriously weakens Hawkins' argument?

   (A) There is no reliable scientific evidence that the ancient people who built Stonehenge worshipped heavenly bodies.
   (B) Hawkins' computer calculations, though on their face accurate, have not been independently verified.
   (C) The positions of heavenly bodies have shifted slightly in the thousands of years since Stonehenge was built.
   (D) The fragility of the already-damaged stones of Stonehenge has caused authorities to limit the access of scholars to the site.
   (E) Any structure as complex as that at Stonehenge must inevitably contain some astronomical viewing angles, even if they were not intended by the builders.

(E) One of the techniques discussed in the chapter on logical reasoning is to attack an argument by looking for an alternative causal explanation. This is what choice (E) does. Hawkins explains the structure at Stonehenge by reference to the intentions of the builders. (E) suggests that a different explanation is possible: the viewing lines are merely a coincidence.

(A) is a fairly weak attack on the argument. A people might construct something with astronomical significance even if they did not worship heavenly bodies. (B), too, is not much of an attack on the argument, for even if true, it does not mean that Hawkins is wrong. (C) would be more interesting if Hawkins had contended that Stonehenge has no astronomical significance. A good attack on that argument would then explain that the lines of viewing had significance thousands of years ago, even if they do not have significance now. But (C) does nothing to the argument actually made by Hawkins. (D) is very much like (B).

The tendency toward political tyranny increases in periods of economic collapse. When most people have homes and jobs and when families anticipate a better life for their children, citizens support moderate policies that promise peaceful growth and gradual development. When work is scarce, prices are rising, and prospects for the future seem bleak, desperate measures begin to seem attractive, and the would-be totalitarian's promise of drastic upheaval holds appeal.

12. The claim made in the argument above would be most seriously weakened by evidence of which of the following?

   (A) Countries undergoing economic collapse in which democratic institutions were strengthened
   (B) Countries in which periods of drastic economic change had little apparent political effect
   (C) Countries in which totalitarian governments were established with little basis in popular support
   (D) Examples of tyrannical governments that arose during periods of prosperity
   (E) Examples of totalitarian leaders who actually kept the promises they made before attaining power

(A) To answer this item correctly, you have to read the initial paragraph with some care. The conclusion of the argument is contained in the first sentence: poor economic conditions are conducive to the rise of tyranny. Counterexamples in which poor economic conditions actually lead to a strengthening of democratic institutions would be the best refutation of this theory. (A) provides them.

(D) is surely the second-best answer but would have been more nearly correct if the conclusion of the initial paragraph had been "During times of economic prosperity, tyranny rarely flourishes." That is not the conclusion of the initial paragraph, although it is an idea related to the topic discussed in the paragraph and an idea the author would probably accept. (A) is a stronger attack than (D) because (A)

536

aims at the precise conclusion of the argument and not at a collateral issue.

(B), (C), and (E) are weaker responses. (B) is generally related to the topic of the paragraph, but (B) doesn't specify (as [A] and [D] do) the kinds of economic changes that occurred. As for (C), the author would probably respond to this statement by agreeing that it is possible for tyrannies to exist without popular support, but he claims only that when economic conditions are poor, they receive popular support. Finally, as for (E), the author never analyzes the features of tyrannical governments.

A basic social function of the university is to provide a setting within which all points of view may be freely debated, including those whose radical nature may offend some or even most members of the community. Unfortunately, this mandate includes totalitarian views which might themselves threaten the freedom and diversity of expression to which the university is dedicated.

13. The speaker in the paragraph above is most concerned with discussing a(n)

(A) dilemma (B) contradiction (C) paradox
(D) analogy (E) generalization

(A) Let's begin by eliminating (D) and (E), since they are fairly obviously not descriptions of the paragraph. The remaining choices, (A), (B), and (C), are fairly close.

What makes this item difficult is the fact that dilemma, contradiction, and paradox share a common logical feature. Each involves a pair of ideas. Dilemma is the best description of the problem discussed in the initial paragraph, because the paragraph describes two possible courses of action, neither of which is a happy choice. On the one hand, the university cannot suppress ideas without failing in its function. On the other hand, the university cannot allow the expression of totalitarian ideas without also jeopardizing its function. This "damned if you do, and damned if you don't" situation is the defining characteristic of a dilemma.

A contradiction, on the other hand, is simply the conjunction of two statements, the one of which is the negative to the other: I will go, but I won't go. A paradox is a special logical form, the most famous example of which is the Liar's Paradox:

The sentence you are now reading is false.

Questions 14–15

Colleges are doing a poor job of imparting basic skills. According to a recent survey of personnel directors of major corporations, large numbers of entry-level workers lack ability in writing, mathematics, and reasoning skills.

14. Which of the following must be true if the argument above is valid?

(A) College students today are no longer required to take courses in basic skills.
(B) Few entry-level workers today have college degrees.
(C) Basic skills in writing, mathematics, and reasoning are important for success in most jobs.
(D) Entry-level workers at major corporations are generally representative of today's college graduates.
(E) College students in the past received better training in basic skills than those of today.

(D) This question asks you to identify a hidden assumption of the argument. Test each of the choices to see whether or not the author is committed to that idea. As for (A), the author says only that colleges today are not teaching important basic skills, and that's as far as he needs to go. For his purposes, he doesn't need to explain the cause of that failure, so (A) is not an idea the author is necessarily committed to. As for (B), the author is committed to the idea that some entry-level workers have college degrees. Otherwise, it would be irrational to blame the colleges for the workers' lack of training. As for (C), although the author might agree that these skills are important, he is not logically committed to this idea by the structure of the argument. The author says only that entry-level workers in large corporations lack these important skills—not that the skills are important for *most* jobs. Finally, (E) has some merit, for, given the general tone of the paragraph, this is something we might anticipate the author would endorse. But again, he is not committed to this idea by the structure of the argument. (The author could conceivably believe that colleges have always done a poor job of teaching basic skills.)

(D) is an idea the author is committed to. The conclusion of the argument is "Colleges are doing a poor job." The evidence for this conclusion is "This group of people is poorly trained." For this conclusion to follow, the group cited must be representative of college graduates in general.

15. Which of the following questions would be most relevant in determining the validity of the argument above?

    (A) What kinds of training programs are provided by major corporations for their entry-level workers?

    (B) Do colleges have the responsibility for teaching students basic skills in writing, mathematics, and reasoning?

    (C) How closely correlated are workers' levels of skill in writing, mathematics, and reasoning?

    (D) Do major corporations today demand a higher level of basic skills from entry-level workers than in the past?

    (E) How do the skill levels of workers at major corporations compare with those at smaller companies?

(B) This question, too, focuses upon a hidden assumption of the argument. The conclusion of the argument is that colleges are doing a poor job of teaching basic skills, and the evidence for this is that certain college graduates today lack these skills. Obviously, the argument rests upon the implicit premise that it is the job of the colleges to provide these skills. (Otherwise, the author would not blame the colleges.)

The question posed by (A) is not immediately relevant to the argument. Whether or not corporations are forced to provide training programs is not relevant to the issue of whether or not new workers come to them with basic skills. As for (C), the author says that college graduates are weak in all three areas, but he does not need to insist that there is a correlation of skills in these three areas. He might very well think that the three areas are completely independent of each other and that colleges are failing on three different counts—not just on one. As for (D), we noted in the discussion of the preceding item that the author does not imply a comparison of the quality of college education today with that of an earlier time. Be careful that you don't read something into the paragraph that is not there. To be sure, many people might use the information provided to support an argument having the form "Things today are much worse than they used to be...," but this is not the argument advanced in this particular case. Finally, as for (E), the author focuses on entry-level workers, not on workers in general.

Lawyers are sometimes asked, "How can you, in good conscience, defend a person whom you know to be guilty?" One answer lies in the nature of our adversary system of justice. Believing that justice is best served through the open clash of opposing arguments, we hold it to be important that all persons should be given a voice in court—not just those who are popular or "known" to be in the right. Only when every side has a reasonable chance to be heard, we believe, can truth most fully emerge.

16. The passage above justifies the lawyers' practice of defending guilty persons on the ground that it is

    (A) deeply rooted in our society's customs and traditions

    (B) the most effective means of determining what is the truth

    (C) a means by which unpopular social and political views may gain a fair hearing

    (D) necessary to satisfy society's inherent sense of fair play

    (E) unlikely to lead to any serious miscarriage of justice

(B) The argument justifies the practice of defending guilty persons by claiming that this is the best way of ensuring that the truth is found. (B) correctly points out that this is the support for the conclusion.

As for (A), the author never defends lawyers by simply saying "This is what we have always done." (C) has some merit. But (C) is incorrect because the defense of the practice is not that this is one means among others of accomplishing a certain end, but that this is the best way of doing it. Further, the goal of the practice is not simply to provide a forum for unpopular viewpoints. According to the author, the practice is calculated to arrive at the truth. (D), too, has some merit, but it is incorrect because the justification for the practice is that it serves the truth—not just a sense of fair play. And finally, (E) also understates the author's point. The author doesn't merely say "This isn't such a terrible idea; it won't cause any grave injustice." The author asserts affirmatively that this is the best way to arrive at the truth.

During the past three years, an increasing number of youths between thirteen and sixteen years of age have been injured or killed in accidents while driving or riding on lightweight motorcycles called dirt bikes. These motorcycles are simply too powerful for children under the age of sixteen, for even the most skillful riders of their age group lack the maturity of judgment to use them wisely.

17. The speaker in the paragraph above would most likely favor a law that prohibited

    (A) children under the age of sixteen from owning a dirt bike
    (B) children under the age of thirteen from operating a dirt bike
    (C) children between the ages of thirteen and sixteen from operating a dirt bike
    (D) children under the age of sixteen from riding on a dirt bike
    (E) children under the age of sixteen from operating a dirt bike

(E) This question asks you to draw a further conclusion from the initial statements. The author says that dirt bikes are the cause of a large number of deaths among children aged thirteen to sixteen, and he adds that the vehicles are "simply too powerful for even the most skillful riders" of this age group. This strongly suggests that the author would favor a ban on such vehicles—in particular, a law to prohibit children under the age of sixteen from operating such vehicles.

To eliminate the remaining choices, you must read carefully. As for (A), the issue addressed in the initial paragraph is not that of *ownership* but *operation*. (Owning a bike doesn't kill anyone, but riding it does.) As for (B), this proposal doesn't go far enough. The author would certainly agree that children younger than thirteen should not operate dirt bikes, but the problem discussed requires a broader solution. As for (C), this is the mirror image of (B). Yes, the author would agree that children between the ages of thirteen and sixteen should not operate the bikes, but he would also agree that children younger than that should not operate them either. As for (D), the author might applaud this proposal as well, but it goes a bit beyond the scope of the passage. The author's primary concern is that children in the age group discussed are operating the bikes. The author might allow that it would be all right for a child to ride on a bike when an adult is operating it.

Questions 18–19

When the military forces of the Soviet Union are compared directly with those of the United States, the two superpowers appear to be about equal, with each side leading and trailing in several categories of weapons, equipment, and manpower. When the forces of the other Warsaw Pact nations are added to those of the Soviet Union, and the forces of the NATO allies of the United States are added to those of the United States, a substantial advantage for the NATO side in nearly every category is found to exist. We can conclude, therefore, that the United States actually enjoys military superiority over the Soviet Union.

18. From the information provided above, which of the following can be most reliably inferred?

    (A) In a war between the Warsaw Pact nations and the NATO countries, the NATO countries would prevail.
    (B) The military forces of the NATO allies of the United States are greater than those of the Soviet Union's Warsaw Pact allies.
    (C) The NATO allies of the United States have combined military forces that are greater than those of the United States itself.
    (D) A portion of the military forces of the Soviet Union are deployed for the purpose of deterring an attack by the NATO countries.
    (E) There are more member countries in the NATO alliance than there are in the Warsaw Pact.

(B) This question asks you to draw a further conclusion from the initial paragraph. The speaker points out that United States forces are approximately equal to those of the Soviet Union but goes on to note that total United States and NATO forces are superior to total Soviet Union and Warsaw Pact forces. For this to be true, it must be the case that non-U.S. NATO forces are greater than non-Soviet Warsaw Pact Forces.

(A) is incorrect, for simple military superiority may not be sufficient to win a war. As for (C), this choice misconstrues the comparison. (D), of course, goes far beyond the scope of the paragraph. And as for (E), you can only infer from the premise that one group of countries is militarily superior to another group, not that the first group is numerically superior to the second.

19. Which of the following, if true, would most seriously weaken the argument above?

(A) The military forces of the NATO allies are not under the direct control of the United States, but those of the Warsaw Pact are under the direct control of the Soviet Union.

(B) Although the United States has fewer missiles than the Soviet Union, it has a comparable number of nuclear warheads.

(C) The NATO allies of the United States have grown reluctant to allow the United States to deploy nuclear weapons on their soils.

(D) Much of the military equipment of the Warsaw Pact nations is older than that of the NATO allies and therefore technologically less advanced.

(E) The Warsaw Pact nations spend a proportionately larger share of their budgets each year on the military than do the NATO countries.

(A) The correct answer to this question focuses upon a hidden assumption of the argument. The conclusion of the argument is that the United States is militarily superior to the Soviet Union. The basis for this conclusion is the assumption that total NATO forces are superior to total Warsaw Pact forces. But the inference depends on equating United States forces with NATO forces. If the United States could count the allies' military forces as its own, then the inference would be strong. (A) attacks the argument by weakening this critical assumption: those military forces do not belong to the United States and are not under its control.

(B) is generally relevant to the issue but doesn't do much to weaken the argument. If anything, (B) is consistent with the argument, since the author allows that the United States is ahead in some respects. As for (C), to the extent that this statement weakens the argument, (A) is a much better answer than (C). For (C) is really just a specific example of the general idea expressed by (A). As for (D), this, if anything, strengthens the author's conclusion that the United States enjoys military superiority. As for (E), this idea is generally relevant to the issue discussed, and you might argue that the amount of money spent on the military has something to do with the quantity and quality of military forces. (This is a debatable assertion.) Even so, this answer choice makes a statement about the *proportion* of the budget allocated to the military and not the actual *amount* spent. So compared with (A), this is not a very strong attack on the argument.

Mycroft's role in the government is unique. Whereas all other state officials are specialists in one area or another, Mycroft is the supreme generalist, the single person who can determine how various interrelated areas of government are likely to be affected by a particular course of action. As a consequence, Mycroft is the only truly indispensable person in the government.

20. If the statements above are true, which of the following statements must also be true?

I. It would be easier to replace or do without a person with general knowledge than a person with specialized knowledge.

II. A decision that affected only one area of government would not require Mycroft's expertise.

III. Mycroft's knowledge of each separate area of government is as profound as that of a specialist.

(A) I only   (B) II only   (C) III only
(D) II and III only   (E) I, II, and III

(B) This question asks you to draw inferences from the initial statement. Test each of the statements. Statement I is actually contradicted by the passage, for the passage emphasizes the importance of the generalist. Since I is not part of the correct choice, you can eliminate choices (A) and (E). Statement II is inferable from the initial statement. The special function of a generalist is to determine how an action will affect different areas of the government. If the effect of the action is confined to a single area, then there is no need for the generalist. Since II is a part of the correct choice, you should eliminate (C). Finally, statement III is not inferable from the initial statement. Mycroft's special function is coordinating information. To see the large picture, it is not necessary that he know every single detail. Thus, the correct choice consists of II only.

Questions 21–22

Some politicians are boating enthusiasts.
All Republocrats favor industrial development along the shoreline.
All boating enthusiasts oppose industrial development along the shoreline.

21. If the statements above are true, which of the following must be true?

(A) All politicians are Republocrats.
(B) Some Republocrats are boating enthusiasts.
(C) Some politicians are not Republocrats.
(D) Not all Republocrats are politicians.
(E) Some boating enthusiasts are Republocrats.

(C) This is a logical deduction problem. A good way of attacking problems like this is to use a diagram to exhibit the logical relationships described. The diagram we will use is a variation on Venn diagrams. Venn diagrams are often taught in college logic courses but were not included in the instructional material of this book for two reasons. First, Venn diagrams were developed to handle highly specific logical deductions and are not perfectly suited to the problems that ordinarily are used on the exam. Second, the device can be adapted for use on the exam in a fairly intuitive way, which we will call circle diagrams. (**Note**: If you don't find circle diagrams a useful technique, you can solve problems such as this by reasoning about the logical relations verbally.)

In the technique of circle diagrams, you use a circle to describe a logical space. For example, the circle:

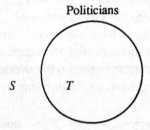

Politicians

represents the entire universe of the category "politicians." Since letter T is inside the circle, the individual designated by T (say, Tim) is a politician, while the individual designated by S (say, Sam) is not a politician. (S is outside the circle.)

To represent the three categories, politicians, boating enthusiasts, and Republocrats, we need three circles. (Actually, "people who favor industrial development" and "people who oppose industrial development" are also categories, but the circle diagram technique cannot be used with more than three categories at any given time.) We will draw the three circles so that they overlap:

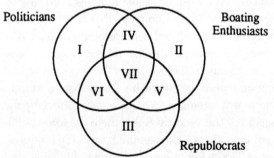

The three overlapping circles allow us to keep track of the various possible overlaps between categories, e.g., whether a person who is a politician is also a boating enthusiast or whether a person who is a boating enthusiast is not a politician. Region I is reserved

for those individuals who are politicians but are not boating enthusiasts or Republocrats:

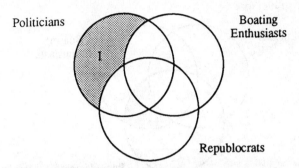

Region II is reserved for those individuals who are boating enthusiasts but not politicians or Republocrats:

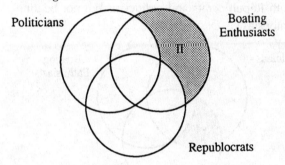

Region III is reserved for those individuals who are Republocrats but not politicians or boating enthusiasts:

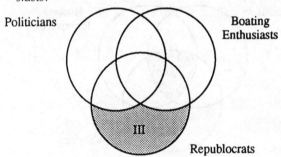

Region IV is reserved for those individuals who are both politicians and boating enthusiasts but not Republocrats:

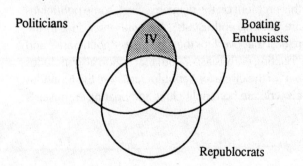

Region V is reserved for those individuals who are both boating enthusiasts and Republocrats but not politicians:

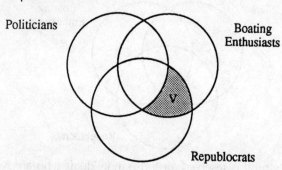

Region VI is reserved for those individuals who are both Republocrats and politicians but not boating enthusiasts:

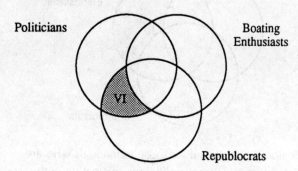

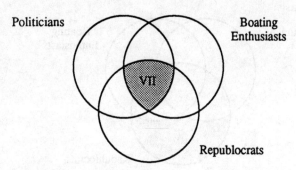

Region VII is reserved for those individuals who fall into all three categories.

Now that you understand the principle of circle diagrams, we can enter the logical relationships of this problem on the diagram. First, some politicians are boating enthusiasts. We will enter an x in the region that overlaps the categories "politicians" and "boating enthusiasts." But that region also includes part of the circle for Republocrats. Are the individuals who are both politicians and boating enthusiasts

also Republocrats? We don't know, so we will enter the x on the circumference of the Republocrat circle:

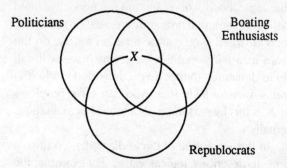

The next two statements establish that there is no overlap between the Republocrat and boating enthusiast categories. (One group favors industrial development of the shoreline, the other opposes it.) So that part of the diagram which is the overlap of the Republocrats circle and the boating enthusiasts circle is void:

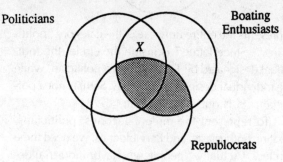

Notice that the x has been relocated, for we now know that those persons who are politicians and boating enthusiasts are not also Republocrats.

We can use the diagram to analyze the answer choices. As for (A), this statement is proven false by the diagram. The x indicates that there are some people (at least one and perhaps more) who are politicians but not Republocrats. (B), too, is proven false by the diagram. The overlap of the Republocrat and boating enthusiast circles has been shaded to indicate that it is empty. (C) is proven correct by the diagram. The x indicates that there are some politicians who are not also Republocrats. (D) is equivalent to "Some Republocrats are not politicians," but this is not proven correct nor incorrect by the diagram. Even though the area of the diagram that is within the Republocrat circle but not within the politician circle is empty, this does not prove that no such people exist. There may be some, there may not be any—we just don't have information about this possibility. Finally, (E) is proved wrong by the diagram, since that part of the diagram has been shaded to indicate that no individual possesses both characteristics.

22. If, in addition to the statements above, it is true that all politicians are boating enthusiasts, which of the following must be FALSE?

    (A) Some politicians are not Republocrats.
    (B) Not all boating enthusiasts are politicians.
    (C) Some Republocrats are politicians.
    (D) All politicians oppose industrial development along the shoreline.
    (E) Some boating enthusiasts are not Republocrats.

(C) Add the new information to the diagram:

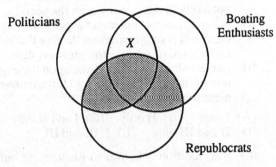

(A), (D), and (E) are all proved true by the diagram. As for (A), the x indicates that there are some politicians (who happen to be boating enthusiasts as well) who are not Republocrats. As for (D), the only area of the politician circle left unshaded is that which overlaps the boating enthusiast circle. This means that all politicians are boating enthusiasts. Since boating enthusiasts universally oppose industrial development of the shoreline, we can conclude that all politicians oppose such development. As for (E), the x also shows that some boating enthusiasts (those who are also politicians) are not Republocrats. (B) is not proved either true or false by the diagram. (B) is equivalent to "Some boating enthusiasts are not politicians." That region is empty, but it could be occupied by individuals (the existence of whom we are ignorant). (C), however, is proved false by the diagram. No overlap between the Republocrat and the politician circle remains.

Questions 23–24

Historically, our nation's prosperity has been based on a continuous flow of new inventions that have spurred the creation of new industries, from the automotive and aircraft industries to the fields of chemicals, pharmaceuticals, and electronics. Therefore, the best guarantee of continued economic strength is increased spending by businesses on scientific research and development.

23. The author of the passage above makes which of the following assumptions?

    I. Scientific research and development can ensure a flow of new inventions.
    II. The chemical, pharmaceutical, and electronics industries will provide most of the new technology over the next few years.
    III. The amount of money now spent by businesses on scientific research and development is not adequate to ensure a flow of new inventions.

    (A) I only   (B) III only   (C) I and II only
    (D) I and III only   (E) I, II, and III

(D) This question asks you to identify hidden assumptions of the argument. The conclusion of the argument is "For economic growth, we need increased spending on R and D." The explicit premise on which this conclusion is based is "New inventions spur new industries." For the conclusion to follow from the explicit premise, the author must also believe that R and D creates new inventions, as noted by statement I. Notice also that the conclusion calls for *increased* spending on R and D, so the author apparently also believes that current spending is not sufficient, as noted by III. Statement II, however, is not an assumption of the argument. These three industries are simply used by the author as examples to illustrate a point.

24. Which of the following, if true, would most seriously weaken the argument above?

(A) The research and development divisions of most businesses concentrate on making minor improvements to existing products rather than developing new technologies.

(B) At current levels of spending, corporate research and development divisions are applying for fewer patents each year than they were a decade ago.

(C) Historically, only a few new major industries have been based directly on the work of technical breakthroughs achieved by corporate research and development divisions.

(D) Levels of corporate spending on scientific research and development are directly related to the number of new inventions patented each year.

(E) Government spending on scientific research and development will be sharply curtailed over the next five years.

(A) The correct answer to a question such as this (which asks that you attack an argument) often focuses on a hidden assumption. Above, we saw that the author implicitly assumes that R and D results in new inventions. Answer choice (A) specifically attacks that assumption by suggesting that R-and-D money is spent on perfecting existing technology rather than on creating new technology. (B) is incorrect and actually seems to strengthen the argument by suggesting that the flow of new technology has slowed down. (C) is perhaps the second-best response, for it might be read to suggest that new technology does not create new industry. A closer reading of (C) shows that it will not support this conclusion. The fact that only a few new major industries have resulted from breakthroughs by corporate R and D does not mean that these were not significant in economic terms. Consider, for example, a breakthrough in electronics such as the telephone, which creates a huge industry. Finally, (D) and (E) both fairly clearly help prove the author's point.

It is true that the striking textile workers have agreed to return to work with a contract that is little better than the contract they could have obtained three weeks ago at the onset of the strike. But the workers have shown an ability to maintain their own unity under extremely difficult circumstances, a fact that will help them in the next set of negotiations when this contract expires a year from now.

25. The argument above depends on which of the following assumptions?

I. The labor unity achieved during this strike is not likely to disappear within the year.

II. When the current contract expires, management will take into account the fact that labor maintained its unity in the previous strike.

III. Labor will call another strike upon the expiration of the current contract to force management to make concessions.

(A) I only   (B) II only   (C) I and II only
(D) II and III only   (E) I, II, and III

(C) This question asks you to identify the hidden assumptions of this argument. Statement I is a hidden assumption. The author argues that the labor unity achieved during this strike will aid the union in its next negotiations, but that conclusion rests on the assumption that the unity will continue. II also is an assumption of the argument. In order for the unity achieved in this strike to benefit labor, management must be aware of it and take it into account in future negotiations. III, however, is not an assumption of the argument. The new unity may actually prove useful to labor in exacting concessions from management in the next round of negotiations without having to resort to a strike.

SECTION 3
READING COMPREHENSION

1. Which of the following best describes the overall structure of the passage?

(A) The author raises a question and then provides an answer.

(B) The author presents a theory, which he then proves.

(C) The author studies a widely held belief and then rejects it.

(D) The author defines a term and then provides examples.

(E) The author tells an anecdote and then explains its significance.

(A) This is a logical structure question that asks about the general organization of the selection. At the end of the first paragraph, the author raises a question, which he then proceeds to answer. (A) correctly describes this development.

(B) is incorrect because the author does not present a theory as such. Though you might argue that we, the readers, can learn from the passage about the author's theory of life, the method of presentation used by the author is not the presentation of a theory as such. As for (C), the author does not contrast his own views with other views. As for (D), the author does not define a term. Finally, as for (E), the author doesn't tell an anecdote.

2. In the passage, the author uses the word *pulsations* (line 34) to mean

(A) heartbeats   (B) children   (C) lives
(D) death   (E) experiences

(E) This is an inference question. What does the author mean by the word *pulsations*? In that final paragraph, the author explains that life is much too short. And he introduces his discussion by stating that experience is the end or goal of life. To get the most out of life, one must pack it with as many pulsations as possible. We may infer that by this term he means experiences.

3. According to the author, the function of art is to

(A) depict reality accurately
(B) stimulate strong emotions
(C) encourage social reform
(D) express the artist's feelings
(E) provide a means of escape

(B) The discussion of art is found in the closing sentences of the passage. Having said that the best life is one packed with experiences (pulsations), the author goes on to say how one can have these intense experiences. This is one function of art, he says—to do nothing but provoke feelings—not to depict reality (A); not to encourage reform (C); not as a means of expression (D); and not as an escape from life (E).

4. With which of the following statements would the author most likely agree?

(A) A person's lifetime is merely preparation for what comes after death.
(B) Only an artist can truly enjoy life.
(C) The original experience is more important than the memory of it.
(D) A perceptive person understands that all experience is repetitious.
(E) The best life is a life of meditation and contemplation.

(C) This is a further application question, and our discussion thus far has set the stage for this explanation. Experience is everything according to the au-

thor, so he would probably agree with (C). It is the feeling of the moment, not the memory of the feeling, that is important. Once the feeling is past, you should be looking for new feelings, not thinking about past ones.

The author certainly would not agree with (A). Everything he says contradicts (A). Nor would he agree with (B). In fact, he implies that anyone with a passion for life can use art to increase that passion. As for (D), the author specifically states that experience should not be repetitious. Anyone who thinks experience is repetitious just isn't looking closely enough. Finally, as for (E), the author emphasizes experience and feeling, not contemplation and meditation.

5. The tone of the passage can best be described as

(A) impassioned   (B) scholarly   (C) informative
(D) speculative   (E) detached

(A) This is a tone question. The writing is highly impassioned. The intensity of the writing is evident in every sentence. The issues are those of life and death. The author uses phrases such as "awful brevity" and "splendor of experience." Thus, we can eliminate (E). As for (B), though the author discusses important issues, he does not do so in a scholarly tone. As for (C), though the passage conveys information, its tone is not informative. Finally, we can also eliminate (D). Although one may speculate in writing about a topic, the writing style of the selection is not speculative.

6. In the context of this passage, the phrase "short day of the frost and sun" refers to

(A) the transient effect of poetry
(B) a brief moment of passion
(C) the life of a person
(D) stimulation of the senses
(E) a midwinter day

(C) This is an explicit idea question. In the second paragraph, the author argues that the best life is one filled with experiences of every sort. Not to seek after a variety of experiences is, in the author's words, "on this short day of the frost and sun, to sleep before evening." The phrase "to sleep before evening" must mean to stop living even before death. So the "short day of the frost and sun" must refer to a person's life.

7. The passage deals primarily with the
   (A) content of textbooks used in early American schools
   (B) role of education in late eighteenth- and early to mid-nineteenth-century America
   (C) influence of New England Puritanism on early American values
   (D) origin and development of the Protestant work ethic in modern America
   (E) establishment of universal, free public education in America

(A) This is a main idea question. The passage is primarily a discussion of what was contained in school textbooks in the late eighteenth and early nineteenth centuries. (A) correctly summarizes this. You can eliminate (B) because the passage is more focused than (B) suggests. It does not discuss the role of education generally, except to mention in passing that its main objective was to teach civic virtue. (C) makes the mistake of elevating one part of the passage to the status of main idea. You can eliminate (D) because this is not the main point of the discussion. Though you do learn something about the origin of the work ethic by reading the passage, that is not the author's goal. Finally, (E) is incorrect because the focus of the passage is not the establishment of schools but what material was included in textbooks.

8. According to the passage, the founders of the Republic regarded education primarily as
   (A) a religious obligation
   (B) a private matter
   (C) an unnecessary luxury
   (D) a matter of individual choice
   (E) a political necessity

(E) This is a specific detail question. In the first paragraph, the author specifically states that the founders regarded education as a political necessity, not as a means to gain knowledge or a skill. So you can eliminate all choices but (E). The obligation was political, not religious (A), and was therefore a public obligation (B). As an obligation, it was a matter of necessity, not a luxury (C) and not a matter of choice (D).

9. The author states that textbooks written in the middle part of the nineteenth century
   (A) departed radically in tone and style from earlier textbooks
   (B) mentioned for the first time the value of liberty
   (C) treated traditional civic virtues with even greater reverence
   (D) were commissioned by government agencies
   (E) contained no reference to conservative ideas

(C) This, too, is a specific detail question. In the middle of the last paragraph, the author states that textbooks did not change during the first half of the nineteenth century. So you can eliminate (A). As for (D) and (E), these ideas are not specifically mentioned, so neither can be the correct answer to a specific detail question. Finally, (B) represents a confused reading of the third paragraph. The author says that liberty was even more revered in later books, not that it was first mentioned in later books.

10. Which of the following would LEAST likely have been the subject of an early American textbook?
    (A) Basic rules of English grammar
    (B) The American Revolution
    (C) Patriotism and other civic virtues
    (D) Vocational education
    (E) Principles of American government

(D) This is a further application question. There is ample support for (A) (literacy), (B) (American history), (C) (patriotic and moral virtues), and (E) (principles of republican government) in the first and second paragraphs. As for (D), the first paragraph specifically states that at that time education would not have included occupational training.

11. The author's attitude toward the educational system she discusses can best be described as
    (A) cynical and unpatriotic
    (B) realistic and analytical
    (C) pragmatic and frustrated
    (D) disenchanted and bitter
    (E) idealistic and naive

(B) This is an attitude question. You can eliminate (A), (C), and (D) because there are no negative elements in the selection. Although (A) is wrong for the reason given, you might argue that the idea that education is a political tool smacks of cynicism. The problem with this reasoning is that you are asked about the author's attitude—not the beliefs of the founders. The author describes the pragmatism of the founders in objective terms. So (A) and also (E) are incorrect, and by the same reasoning (B) is correct.

12. The passage provides information that would be helpful in answering which of the following questions?

(A) Why was a disproportionate share of early American textbooks written by New England authors?

(B) Was the Federalist party primarily a liberal or conservative force in early American politics?

(C) How many years of education did the founders believe were sufficient to instruct young citizens in civic virtues?

(D) What were the names of some of the Puritan authors who wrote early American textbooks?

(E) Did most citizens of the early Republic agree with the founders that public education was essential to the welfare of the Republic?

(B) This is a specific detail question. In the second paragraph the author equates the Federalists with conservatives, so the passage contains information that would answer the question posed by (B). As for (A), though the passage does state that most early textbooks were written by New Englanders, the author doesn't explain why this happened. As for (C), the passage does state that the founders believed education to be important to the welfare of the Republic, but the passage doesn't say how much education the founders wanted children to have. As for (D), the passage doesn't mention any authors by name. Finally, as for (E), the passage doesn't talk about the attitudes of the majority of citizens—as opposed to the attitudes of the founders themselves.

13. The author implies that an early American Puritan would likely insist that

(A) moral and religious values are the foundation of civic virtue

(B) textbooks should instruct students in political issues of vital concern to the community

(C) textbooks should give greater emphasis to the value of individual liberty than to the duties of patriotism

(D) private schools with a particular religious focus are preferable to public schools with no religious instruction

(E) government and religion are separate institutions and the church should not interfere in political affairs

(A) This is an implied idea question. In the second paragraph, the author states that the textbook writers, most of whom were Puritans, believed that political virtue rests upon moral and religious precepts. We can infer, therefore, that other Puritans would agree with this position as well.

14. The author's primary purpose is to

(A) speculate about the relationship between a patient's ability to pay and the treatment received

(B) criticize doctors for exercising too much control over patients

(C) analyze some important economic factors in health care

(D) urge hospitals to reclaim their decision-making authority

(E) inform potential patients of their health care rights

(C) This is a main idea question presented in sentence completion form. Surveying the opening words of each choice, we can eliminate (D), and probably (A) and (B) as well. As for (D), although a reader might use the information supplied in the passage to support some action, the primary purpose of the passage itself is not to "urge" anything. Similarly, although someone might use the information supplied to criticize doctors, criticism is not the author's primary goal. You can eliminate (A) because the author may be said to investigate or analyze a phenomenon, but he does not speculate about it.

Of the other two choices, which begin with *analyze* and *inform*, (E) can be eliminated because the author is not addressing his remarks to patients. He assumes his reader is someone within the health-care industry or someone who has an interest in the economics of the industry (e.g., a government official).

15. It can be inferred that doctors are able to determine hospital policies because

(A) it is doctors who generate income for the hospital

(B) most of a patient's bills are paid by his health insurance

(C) hospital administrators lack the expertise to question medical decisions

(D) a doctor is ultimately responsible for a patient's health

(E) some patients might refuse to accept their physician's advice

(A) This is an implied idea question. In the second paragraph the author states that it is the physician who is the real "consumer." So it is not surprising that physicians would make key decisions. Although the author does not specifically say so, we may infer that physicians control power because they control the money. This is choice (A).

(B) mentions a related issue. But the author states that carriers are generally rubber stamps, paying whatever is approved by the physician. Thus, it is the physician, not the carrier, who has the real power. As for (C), this may very well be true in the real world, but this choice illustrates the limit of what is a correct answer to an implied idea question. The passage nowhere mentions anything about the expertise of hospital administrators nor anything related to that topic. (D) is arguably an explanation for the phenomenon mentioned, but it is not the one given by the author. The author cites economic factors, not professional ones; though this may be a true statement, it is not a response to the question asked.

Finally, as for (E), though it might be true that some patients do not follow their doctor's advice, this fact does not explain why doctors control *hospital* policies.

16. According to the author, when a doctor tells a patient to "return next Wednesday," the doctor is in effect

   (A) taking advantage of the patient's concern for his health
   (B) instructing the patient to buy more medical services
   (C) warning the patient that a hospital stay might be necessary
   (D) advising the patient to seek a second opinion
   (E) admitting that the initial visit was ineffective

   (B) This is an explicit idea question. The reference you need is in the second paragraph. The author states that it is the physician who makes the purchasing decisions on behalf of the patient. One of his examples is whether to schedule a return visit. So when the doctor tells a patient to make another appointment, he is telling the patient to buy more of his services.

   As for (A), the author does not indict the motives of the doctor. A doctor may believe a patient badly needs another visit. Still, it is the doctor making the decision, not the patient. As for (C), there is no hidden meaning in the doctor's statement. As for (E), to suggest another visit is needed does not necessarily mean that the earlier treatment was ineffective, just incomplete. Finally, (D) is certainly not the meaning of the statement. The doctor is making the decision for the patient without giving the patient any option.

17. The author is most probably leading up to

   (A) a proposal to control medical costs
   (B) a discussion of a new medical treatment
   (C) an analysis of the causes of inflation in the United States
   (D) a study of lawsuits against doctors for malpractice
   (E) a comparison of hospitals and factories

   (A) This is a further application question. The author concludes the passage with the statement that,

because of the factors cited, cost control measures aimed at patients are ineffective. Patients do not decide what medical services to buy. Logically, the author could be leading up to a discussion of a plan to solve this problem. (B) would not be a logical extension of the argument. Though the passage discusses medicine, it analyzes the economics of health care, not medical knowledge. (C) goes beyond the scope of the passage. The selection focuses specifically on the problem of cost control in the health-care industry. As for (D), although in the real world medical malpractice suits may be tied to problems of cost control, there is nothing in the passage to suggest that this is the direction in which the author is moving. Finally, (E) is incorrect. The author analyzes the economics of the health-care industry. His initial comparison of this industry and the rest of the economy was made to introduce the reader to the special problems of the health-care industry.

18. The tone of the passage can best be described as

   (A) whimsical   (B) cautious   (C) analytical
   (D) inquisitive   (E) defiant

   (C) The statements in the passage—though critical in their content—are made in an analytical tone. So (C) is the best description of the tone of the passage. (A) and (E) can easily be eliminated. There is neither whimsy nor defiance in the passage. As for (D), though the author does answer some questions, the tone of the passage is not inquisitive but assertive. For this reason, (B), too, must be wrong. The author confidently makes some bold claims.

19. With which of the following statements would the author be likely to agree?

   I. Most patients are reluctant to object to the course of treatment prescribed by a doctor or to question the cost of the services.
   II. The more serious the illness of a patient, the less likely it is that the patient will object to the course of treatment prescribed or to question the cost of services.
   III. The payer, whether insurance carrier or the government, is less likely to acquiesce to demands for payment when the illness of the patient is regarded as serious.

   (A) I only   (B) II only   (C) I and II only
   (D) II and III only   (E) I, II, and III

   (C) This is a further application question. Statement I is something the author would agree with. In the second paragraph, the author states that it is a "rare and sophisticated" patient who challenges a doctor's decision regarding treatment. Thus, we can infer that the author believes that few people make such challenges; you can eliminate choices (B) and (D). Statement II is also something the author would accept. In that same sentence, he notes that this problem is particularly pronounced when the ailment is a serious one. Statement III, however, is not something the author would likely accept. In the fourth paragraph, the author states that the payer generally meets most of the bona fide bills of a patient. Here the author does not draw a distinction between serious and not-so-serious illnesses.

20. The author's primary concern is to

   (A) define a term
   (B) clarify a misunderstanding
   (C) refute a theory
   (D) discuss a problem
   (E) announce a new discovery

   (D) This is a main idea question. Some of the choices here are fairly similar, and we will have to distinguish them carefully to find the correct one. It's fairly easy to eliminate (A). Even if we allow that the author does define a term (for example, *payer*), providing a definition is not the main point of the selection. (B) is a little more difficult to eliminate. It is true that the author argues that the ordinary economic relationships are, in the health-care sector, reversed. But the fact that the relationships are unusual does not mean that they are misunderstood. (B) would have been more nearly correct had the author cited a theory which holds authority maintains that the health-care sector is similar to other sectors of the economy. Then you could say that the author is attempting to correct a misunderstanding. (C) is incorrect for pretty much the same reason. The author does not attack the economic theory that applies to most sectors of the economy. Indeed, he is implicitly committed to the assumption that the general theory of economic relations is correct. (Otherwise, he would not contrast the health-care sector with the other sectors in terms of the general theory.) (E), too, has some merit. The author is presenting information, but there is nothing in the selection to support the conclusion that this information about the health-care industry is newly discovered. And even if you think that the author is about to draw some new conclusions based on his observations, a new conclusion is not the same thing as a new discovery. (D) is the best description of the passage. The author does discuss the problem of the cost structure of the health-care industry.

21. According to the passage, we can expect a supernova to occur in our galaxy about

   (A) twice each year
   (B) 100 times each century
   (C) once every 50 years
   (D) once every other century
   (E) once every four to five billion years

   (C) This is a specific detail question. In the first sentence of the passage the author says a supernova occurs about twice every century, which is about once every fifty years.

22. According to the passage, all of the following are true of supernovas EXCEPT that they

   (A) are extremely bright
   (B) are an explosion of some sort
   (C) emit large quantities of X-rays
   (D) result in the destruction of a neutron star
   (E) are caused by the collision of large galaxies

   (E) This, too, is a specific idea question. (A) is stated in the second paragraph. (B) is specifically stated in the first paragraph. (C) and (D) are both stated in the second paragraph. Although the word *galaxy* is used in the selection, the author does not say that supernovas are caused by colliding galaxies. So (E) is the one detail not mentioned in the selection.

23. The author employs which of the following to develop the first paragraph?

   (A) Analogy
   (B) Deduction
   (C) Generalization
   (D) Example
   (E) Refutation

   (A) This is a logical structure question. In the first paragraph the author compares a star to a leaky balloon. That is an analogy. There is neither deduction nor refutation in that paragraph, so (B) and (E) are wrong. As for (D), the author speaks in general about stars, not about specific stars. But (C), too, is wrong. To speak in categorical terms is not to generalize. Generalization is a method of reasoning that bases broad conclusions on one or two examples.

24. It can be inferred from the passage that the meteorites mentioned by the author at line 39

   (A) contain dangerous concentrations of radioactive materials
   (B) give off large quantities of X-rays
   (C) include material not created in the normal development of our solar system
   (D) are larger than the meteors normally found in a solar system like ours
   (E) contain pieces of a supernova that occurred several billion years ago

(C) This is an implied idea question. The key word for this question is *anomalous*. The author states that the unexpected makeup of the meteorites is evidence that a supernova helped form our solar system. However, this evidence supports the conclusion only if the strange content is foreign to our solar system. So (C) is a correct inference. None of the other choices explains the connection between the theory of the origin of our solar system and the strange makeup of the meteors.

25. The author implies that
    (A) it is sometimes easier to detect supernovas by observation of the X-ray spectrum than by observation of visible wavelengths of light
    (B) life on Earth is endangered by its constant exposure to radiation forces that are released by a supernova.
    (C) recently discovered meteorites indicate that the Earth and other planets of our solar system survived the explosion of a supernova several billion years ago
    (D) lighter elements are formed from heavier elements during a supernova as the heavier elements are torn apart
    (E) the core of a neutron star is composed largely of heavier elements such as carbon, nitrogen, and oxygen

(A) In the last two sentences of the second paragraph, the author states that supernovas emit most of their energy as X-rays and notes that X-ray observations provide the most useful insights into the nature of supernovas. He adds that remnants of supernovas have been found using X-ray studies. We can infer from these remarks that it is easier to find a supernova using equipment that detects X-rays than it is using equipment for viewing visible light.

(B) is not implied by the author. In fact, in the last paragraph, the author states that cosmic radiation is essential to the evolution of life. As for (C), we have already discussed the significance of the meteorites, above. It is also noteworthy that the author does not imply that the Earth survived a supernova explosion but that the Earth was formed from the residue of such an explosion. As for (D), in the second paragraph, the author states that one effect of the supernova is to form heavier elements by fusion, not to split heavier elements into lighter ones. Finally, as for (E), the author does state that these elements are manufactured in the cores of stars, but he does not imply that these are the only elements found in the cores.

26. According to the passage, what is the first event in the sequence that leads to the occurrence of a supernova?
    (A) An ordinary star begins to emit tremendous quantities of X-rays.
    (B) A neutron star is enveloped by a superheated cloud of gas.
    (C) An imbalance between light and heavy elements causes an ordinary star to collapse.
    (D) A cloud of interstellar gas, rich in carbon, nitrogen, and oxygen, collapses to form a neutron star.
    (E) An ordinary star exhausts its supply of nuclear fuel and begins to collapse.

(E) This is a specific detail question. In the first paragraph, the author describes the start of the sequence of events that leads to a supernova. It begins when a star runs out of fuel and collapses.

27. According to the passage, a neutron star is
    (A) a gaseous cloud containing heavy elements
    (B) an intermediate stage between an ordinary star and a supernova
    (C) the residue that is left by a supernova
    (D) the core of an ordinary star that houses the thermonuclear reactions
    (E) one of billions of meteors that are scattered across the galaxy by a supernova

(B) This is a specific detail question. In the first paragraph, the author describes the collapse of an ordinary star. The result is a neutron star. Then, in the second paragraph, the author describes what follows: a supernova. Thus, the neutron star is an intermediate stage between the ordinary star and its final phase, a supernova.

28. The author is primarily concerned with
    (A) speculating about the origins of our solar system
    (B) presenting evidence proving the existence of supernovas
    (C) discussing the nuclear reaction that occurs in the core of a star
    (D) describing the sequence of scientific events
    (E) disproving a theory about the causes of supernovas

(D) This is a main idea question. (A), (B), and (C) are all incorrect, and each makes the mistake of elevating a part of the passage to the status of main idea. As for (E), the author discusses only one theory, his own. (D) is the best description of the passage. The author describes the sequence of events that leads to a supernova and then describes what events follow the supernova.

SECTION 4

LOGICAL REASONING

Bernie was stopped on the street by a man in dark glasses. The man offered to sell Bernie an Epsilon watch, which normally retails for $750, for $50. Bernie gave the man $50 for the watch. Later that day, Bernie learned the watch was actually an Upsilon watch, which normally retails for $19.95.

1. Which of the following adages is an appropriate criticism of Bernie's action?

    I. You must look before you leap.
    II. A fool and his money are soon parted.
    III. There is a sucker born every minute.
    IV. Nothing ventured, nothing gained.

    (A) I and II only   (B) I and IV only
    (C) I, II, and III only   (D) II, III, and IV only
    (E) I, II, III, and IV

    (C) Bernie was obviously conned. You could use I, II, and III to criticize Bernie's behavior because each of those adages cautions against being overly trusting. IV, however, could only be used to *defend* Bernie's behavior—not to criticize it.

The Governor claims that the state faces a drought and has implemented new water-use restrictions; but that's just a move to get some free publicity for his re-election campaign. So far this year we have had 3.5 inches of rain, slightly more than the average amount of rain for the same period over the last three years.

2. Which of the following, if true, would most weaken the conclusion of the argument above?

    (A) The governor did not declare drought emergencies in the previous three years.
    (B) City officials who have the authority to mandate water-use restrictions have not done so.
    (C) The snowmelt that usually contributes significantly to the state's reservoirs is several inches below normal.
    (D) The amount of water the state can draw from rivers that cross state boundaries is limited by federal law.
    (E) Water-use restrictions are short-term measures and do little to reduce long-term water consumption.

    (C) The argument above depends upon a hidden and unsupported assumption: rainfall is the only source of water for the reservoirs. (C) effectively attacks the argument by attacking this hidden assumption. (A) is an interesting observation, but it is difficult to see in which direction it cuts. Does (A) tend to show that the governor is declaring a drought emergency in this year as a political maneuver, or does it tend to show that this year there really is a drought? As for (B), if this has any relevance at all, it

actually strengthens the argument: if city officials have not declared a drought emergency, then maybe there really is no emergency. (D) and (E) mention ideas that are generally related to the problem discussed by the speaker, but they have no specific relevance to the points made by him.

Clean-Well is a company that offers cleaning services. The agency's fee is $25 per hour per employee used to do a job plus $5 car fare for each employee. Customers must provide cleaning supplies. I use the service to clean the windows of my store. Over the years, I have found that one worker can do the job in eight hours, while two workers can do the job in only three hours, making it cheaper to hire two workers than one. I conclude that two workers function as a team, making them more efficient than a single worker.

3. Which of the following, if true, would most weaken the conclusion of the argument above?

    (A) The cost of cleaning supplies to do the job is the same for one worker as for a team of two workers.
    (B) At the end of an eight-hour day a worker is only ⅓ as efficient as at the beginning of the day.
    (C) The workers provided by the service are paid only $7 of the $25-per-hour charge assessed by the company.
    (D) A team of four workers requires two hours and thirty minutes to complete the job.
    (E) A team of two workers from a competitor of Clean-Well will take four hours to do the job.

    (B) Begin your attack on this item by finding the conclusion of the argument. It's not difficult to find, for the speaker signals it with the phrase "I conclude that." The conclusion is that a team of workers requires fewer working hours to complete the project than a single worker because they work as a team. One way of attacking this argument is to look for an alternative causal linkage. (B) does this. The real reason that two workers take less time is that they are fresher. Each works only three hours, while a single worker works eight hours, becoming less efficient later in the day. (A), (C), and (E) have nothing to do with why two workers from Clean-Well appear to be more efficient than a single worker. (D) is probably the second-best answer choice here. The group of four workers requires a total of ten hours to do the job, and this suggests that four workers may not be an efficient team. But the speaker has made a point about a group of two people working as a team. He might readily acknowledge that four is too large a group to work as a team, but that point does not score against his explanation about the efficiency of a two-person work group.

In general, the per-hour cost of operating a device by solar energy is more expensive than using the power supplied by the public utility. But for some purposes, such as adding a new outdoor light to a house, a solar-powered unit is actually cheaper.

4. Which of the following, if true, probably underlies the conclusion above?

(A) Solar energy is more efficient in the southern latitudes than in the northern latitudes.
(B) A solar-powered light is a self-contained unit and does not require the installation of a power line.
(C) New technology will eventually reduce the cost of solar power below that of other energy sources.
(D) The most costly components of any solar-powered system are the solar cells that convert sunlight to electricity.
(E) A solar-powered system can be installed only in areas that receive considerable direct sunlight.

(B) The speaker notes that the cost of electricity supplied by a public utility is generally lower than that for solar power but concludes that there are some exceptions to this rule, such as an outdoor light. Why would an outdoor light be such an exception? (B) gives us a possible explanation: it doesn't incur the cost of running a wire. (A) is irrelevant, since the speaker does not contrast solar power in northern and southern latitudes. (C) is also irrelevant, since the speaker is talking about technology that is presently in use. (D) helps explain why solar power is generally more expensive but doesn't explain why the exception mentioned is an exception to the general rule. Finally, (E) certainly discusses a limitation of solar power, but it does nothing to explain the exception mentioned by the speaker.

The Commission on Public Service recently recommended that federal judges be given a substantial pay increase. For many years, however, there have been many applicants for each new vacancy on the federal bench, proving that a pay increase is not needed.

5. Which of the following, if true, most weakens the argument above?

(A) Salaries for federal judges are higher than those for state and municipal judges.
(B) Salaries for the federal judiciary are established by the legislative branch.
(C) A federal judgeship is a very prestigious position in the legal community.
(D) Salaries for federal judges are too low to attract qualified lawyers.
(E) Most federal judges are former practitioners, teachers, or state judges.

(D) The speaker argues that there is no need to raise salaries for federal judges because there are many applicants who want these positions at existing salaries. The problem with this reasoning is that it equates quantity with quality. (D) focuses on this weakness. As for (A), this idea seems to strengthen the speaker's claim: you don't need to raise salaries for federal judges because their salaries are already higher than those for other judges. (B) has nothing to do with the question of whether or not judges *should* be given raises. (C) seems to strengthen the speaker's claim: you don't need to raise salaries because the prestige of the position is sufficient to ensure that qualified applicants will seek federal judgeships. Finally, (E) is irrelevant to the speaker's claim.

When it rains, my car gets wet. Since it hasn't rained recently, my car can't be wet.

6. Which of the following is logically most similar to the argument above?

(A) Whenever critics give a play a favorable review, people go to see it; Pinter's new play did not receive favorable reviews, so I doubt that anyone will go to see it.
(B) Whenever people go to see a play, critics give it a favorable review; people did go to see Pinter's new play, so it did get a favorable review.
(C) Whenever critics give a play a favorable review, people go to see it; Pinter's new play got favorable reviews, so people will probably go see it.
(D) Whenever a play is given favorable reviews by the critics, people go to see it; since people are going to see Pinter's new play, it will probably get favorable reviews.
(E) Whenever critics give a play a favorable review, people go to see it; people are not going to see Pinter's new play, so it did not get favorable reviews.

(A) The fallacy of the initial argument is confusing a sufficient with a necessary cause. A sufficient cause is an event that is sufficient to guarantee some effect; for example, rain is a sufficient cause for getting a car wet. A necessary cause is one that is required for some event; for example, oxygen is a necessary condition for combustion. The initial argument mentions a sufficient cause (rain will wet a car) but erroneously concludes that that cause is a necessary cause (a car might be hosed down). (A) parallels this error. According to (A), favorable reviews are sufficient to prompt people to see a play. (A) goes on to say that since the play did not receive favorable reviews, people will not go to see it. But favorable reviews are a sufficient cause for people's going to see the play, not a necessary cause.

"Channel One" is a 12-minute school news show that includes two minutes of commercials. The show's producers offer high schools $50,000 worth of television equipment to air the program. Many parents and teachers oppose the use of commercial television in schools, arguing that advertisements are tantamount to indoctrination. But students are already familiar with television commercials and know how to distinguish programming from advertising.

7. The argument assumes that

(A) the effects of an advertisement viewed in a classroom would be similar to those of the same advertisement viewed at home
(B) many educators would be willing to allow the indoctrination of students in exchange for new equipment for their schools
(C) television advertising is a more effective way of promoting a product to high school students than print advertising
(D) high school students are sufficiently interested in world affairs to learn from a television news program
(E) a television news program produced especially for high school students is an effective teaching tool

(A) The speaker addresses a concern voiced by some parents and teachers about commercial television in school. She argues that students already understand the difference between commercials and programming. But this argument depends upon the unsupported assumption that the student will be able to apply that distinction in the classroom situation. You might argue on the other side that students have been taught to accept information provided in a classroom setting and that they will not be able to draw the distinction as easily. So the speaker is logically committed to the idea expressed by (A), not to the ideas expressed by the other choices. As for (B), the speaker assumes that indoctrination will not be a necessary consequence of the new program (not that educators are willing to accept the indoctrination). As for (C), the speaker is not committed to any comparison between print and television advertising. As for (D) and (E), the speaker does not commit herself one way or the other on the effectiveness of the program.

Questions 8–9

The spate of terrorist acts against airlines and their passengers raises a new question: should government officials be forced to disclose the fact that they have received warning of an impending terrorist attack? The answer is "yes." The government currently releases information about the health hazards of smoking, the ecological dangers of pesticides, and the health consequences of food.

8. The argument above relies primarily on

(A) circular reasoning
(B) generalization
(C) authority
(D) analogy
(E) causal analysis

(D) The author draws an analogy between releasing information about terrorist threats and the publication of warnings of other types. For an explanation of the meanings of the other terms, consult the chapters on logical reasoning in the instructional portion of this book.

9. All of the following, if true, would weaken the argument above EXCEPT

(A) Public disclosure of threats would encourage more threats by giving terrorists greater publicity.
(B) Information about terrorist acts is gained from intelligence gathering, not research studies.
(C) Information about possible terrorist acts is routinely distributed to the staff of U.S. embassies.
(D) Making public terrorist threats would allow terrorists to identify sources who had leaked the information.
(E) Public disclosure of threats would encourage false threats designed to disrupt air travel.

(C) Choices (A) and (E) clearly undermine the speaker's proposal, for they point out disadvantages associated with releasing the information. (D) also undermines the argument, for (D) suggests that sources of information would dry up. And since this argument is based on an analogy, (B) also weakens the argument by pointing out a dissimilarity between the two situations compared. (C), however, actually seems to strengthen the argument: the information is already available to some and should be available to others.

Some residents of San Juan Capistrano, California have suggested that government take some action to prevent the swallows from returning there each year because the birds constitute a nuisance. This suggestion ignores the important role the birds play in the environment. Swallows feed almost exclusively on flying insects, including many species that are annoying or harmful to human beings. The abundance of the birds in that region indicates an abundance of insects that are controlled through predation.

10. The speaker above implies that

   (A) without swallows, the region would be infested with insects
   (B) the majority of residents favor limiting the swallow population
   (C) the economic damage caused by the swallows is negligible
   (D) swallows are less destructive than other species of birds
   (E) pesticides would be ineffective against the species of insects eaten by the swallows

(A) The speaker argues that swallows help to control a large insect population. Thus, we can infer that without the swallows the insect population would be considerably larger than it is. So (A) is a conclusion that can be drawn from the material given. (B) cannot be logically inferred. The speaker refers to "some residents" only. As for (C), the speaker implies that the harm of attacking the swallows would not be negligible. As for (D), no such comparison is implied by the initial paragraph. (E) is perhaps the second-best answer, but carefully compare (A) and (E). Had (E) read "the city would have to use pesticides to combat the insects," then (E) would be more nearly correct. Notice, however, that this is not what (E) says.

Susan: International Cosmetics is marketing a new treatment for cellulite called Fango Italiano. It's a cream that is spread on the affected area, allowed to dry, and then washed off. The treatment is very expensive—$250 per month—but it comes with a money-back guarantee. If Fango Italiano doesn't reduce your cellulite, the company will give you all of your money back. Since the company gives such a guarantee, the treatment must work.
Tom: I doubt that the treatment works. "Fango" is just the Italian word for *mud*. But it does seem to me that the company has found a brilliant marketing scheme. People who are so worried about their physical appearance that they are willing to spend $250 a month to get rid of cellulite are people who, while using the treatment, will also start eating less and exercising more. Thus, the treatment will appear to be successful and International Cosmetics will be that much richer.

11. Which of the following best characterizes the position Tom takes with regard to Susan's statement?

   (A) He denies that Fango Italiano will be effective and questions whether or not International Cosmetics really intends to refund the money of dissatisfied customers.
   (B) He denies that International Cosmetics really intends to market Fango Italiano, but suspects that the treatment is not effective.
   (C) He questions whether or not the treatment is effective and denies that it is possible to do anything about cellulite.
   (D) He agrees that people who purchase Fango Italiano may very well lose cellulite, but is skeptical that the treatment will be the reason.
   (E) He argues that $250 per month is too expensive for a treatment for cellulite and encourages people with cellulite to eat less and exercise more.

(D) In the very first sentence of Tom's statement, he says that he doubts the treatment will be effective. He goes on to explain that he imagines that the people who use the treatment will lose cellulite because they are the people who have probably also made a decision to begin losing weight and toning muscle. (D) best describes this position (Tom finds a different causal linkage). (B) captures Tom's skepticism regarding the effectiveness of the treatment, but Tom does not suggest that the company will not actually market the product. In fact, his statement that the company will be richer because of its sales indicates that he thinks the company will market the product. As for (A), although Tom seems to think that the company will market the product, it is not the case that he believes the company will not honor the guarantee. Rather, Tom evidently thinks the company will not often have to honor the guarantee because the treatment will seem to be effective. As for (C), while Tom evidently thinks the treatment will not be effective, it is not the case that he thinks there is no effective treatment for cellulite. He thinks that dieting and exercise will be effective. Finally, as for (E), while it is true that Tom thinks that dieting and exercise are effective treatments for cellulite, he does not encourage anyone to undertake such a regimen.

The National Research Council has recommended against requiring seat belts in school buses because only one life would be saved per year at a cost of $40 million annually. This analysis is shortsighted. Children who are required to use seat belts in school buses will remember to use them when they are old enough to drive.

12. The speaker above assumes that

 (A) installing seat belts in school buses will not cost $40 million per year
 (B) requiring seat belts in school buses would save many lives each year
 (C) most schoolchildren are transported to and from school in buses
 (D) states should require the use of seat belts in private vehicles
 (E) behavior learned as a child may affect adulthood behavior

(E) The question asks you to find a hidden assumption of the argument. The speaker assumes, without saying so specifically, that what a person learns as a child will carry over to adulthood. (A) and (B) are incorrect because the speaker does not choose to quarrel with the specifics of the report. As for (C), the speaker does claim that the policy would benefit a certain group of the population, but she is not logically committed to any position on the number of persons in that group. As for (D), the speaker might very well accept this notion, but it has nothing to do with putting seat belts in school buses.

A decade ago, "earn your age" was the immediate goal of every recent business school graduate. For example, a 26-year-old M.B.A. expected to earn $26,000 per year. This standard no longer holds true in America—a newly graduated M.B.A. in America would want to earn much more—but it is still the norm in England. It seems, therefore, that a starting M.B.A. in America is **economically** better off than one in England.

13. Which of the following, if true, most weakens the argument above?

 (A) Many students from England earn their M.B.A.s in the United States.
 (B) Most students in American business schools have had prior work experience.
 (C) The British pound is worth almost twice as much as the American dollar.
 (D) Graduates from American law schools earn more than graduates from American business schools.
 (E) England produces fewer M.B.A.s each year than the United States.

(C) This problem involves a cute little twist of reasoning; and once you see that, the problem becomes easy. The speaker is saying that "earn your age" is the standard in England and concludes on that basis that M.B.A.s are paid less in England. The

fallacy is that there is a big difference between earning 26,000 dollars and 26,000 pounds—as (C) points out.

The United States is currently faced with a shortage of qualified math and science teachers. A Rand Corporation study indicates that graduates of traditional undergraduate schools of education are expected to fill only half the 20,000 vacancies for math and science teachers. One way of addressing this problem is to provide scholarships for math and science majors to finish their educations and graduate without accumulating massive debts. If they are freed of the burdens of college loans, they will be more likely to consider careers in teaching.

14. Which of the following, if true, would most weaken the argument above?

 (A) Public school teachers earn starting salaries that are well above the average wage in the United States.
 (B) Large numbers of graduates in math and science in prior years created a surplus pool from which teaching jobs are filled.
 (C) The cost of an undergraduate education in math or science is comparable to that for other majors.
 (D) Faculty at colleges and univerities generally earn higher salaries than teachers in public schools.
 (E) There is no shortage of teachers in areas such as history, literature, and vocational training.

(B) The correct answer to a "weakening" question often attacks a hidden premise of the argument. Here the speaker claims that there is a shortage of math and science teachers because there are not enough math and science majors now. This assumes that the only source of math and science teachers is the math and science majors now graduating. (B) attacks this assumption: there is another source of math and science teachers. The other choices make statements that are generally related to the ideas of teaching and recruitment but do not address the specific claims of this speaker.

Questions 15 and 16

Helium-filled balloons rise because helium is a light gas, much ligher than air. Glass tubes filled with neon gas can be charged with electricity to make light, so neon is also a light gas. Therefore, there is one respect in which both helium gas and neon gas are alike: they are both light gases.

15. Which of the following arguments most closely parallels the argument above?

    (A) The Empire State Building is a tall building, and Peter is a tall man. Therefore, there is one respect in which both the Empire State Building and Peter are alike: they are both tall.
    (B) Mary is a law school professor, and her daughter is a medical school professor. So there is one respect in which Mary and her daughter are alike: they are both professors.
    (C) A good steak must be rare, and total lunar eclipses are rare. So there is one respect in which a good steak and total lunar eclipses are alike: they are both rare.
    (D) All whales are mammals, and all bats are mammals. Since all mammals are warm-blooded, there is one respect in which whales and bats are alike: they are both warm-blooded.
    (E) Susan ate half of the melon, and Nancy ate the other half of the melon. So there is one respect in which Susan and Nancy are alike: each ate half a melon.

    (C) This is a logical similarity question. The most striking thing about the stimulus argument is that it uses a term in an ambiguous fashion. It uses *light* the first time to mean "lacking weight," but it uses the word the second time to mean "illumination." Only (C) contains a similar error. The first use of *rare* means "undercooked," while its second use means "not common."

16. The conclusion of the argument above does not follow from the premises because the speaker

    (A) mistakes a cause for an effect
    (B) may not be a scientific authority
    (C) fails to use statistics
    (D) contradicts herself
    (E) uses a term in an ambiguous way

    (E) The analysis of the preceding item explains why (E) is the correct answer here.

Marvin is a senior, so he must have gone to the senior prom.

17. The statement above assumes that

    (A) Marvin is the only senior who went to the prom
    (B) all seniors went to the prom
    (C) only seniors went to the prom
    (D) some seniors did not go to the prom
    (E) no seniors went to the prom

    (B) This argument rests upon a hidden assumption: Marvin is a senior.
    (All seniors went to the prom.)
    Therefore, Marvin went to the prom.
    Only this premise is sufficient to guarantee that the conclusion will follow.

When a vicious animal attacks a human being, we justifiably kill that animal to protect others. So, too, is the death penalty morally justified.

18. The speaker above relies primarily upon

    (A) a questionable analogy
    (B) circular reasoning
    (C) second-hand data
    (D) logical deduction
    (E) generalization

    (A) In this argument, the author points to the similarity between two situations. This type of argument is called analogy. And this analogy, while it has some emotional appeal, is really very weak. To compare a criminal with an animal is overly simplistic.

The nobility of the effort to protect minors from capitalistic exploitation by means of child labor laws has arguably become an easy camouflage for attempts by organized labor and government to preserve the semblance of nearly full employment. The introduction of a majority of women into the workplace has further reinforced a social need to prevent teenagers from working.

19. The argument above assumes that

    (A) minors and women would compete for jobs
    (B) child labor laws should be repealed
    (C) women should not enter the work force
    (D) women do not want teenagers to work
    (E) unions and government disagree on child labor

    (A) The speaker here is arguing that unions and government try to keep minors from working. Why? So that it looks like everyone who wants to work, including the women who have recently joined the labor force, is working. This argument assumes implicitly that both all minors and all women could not have jobs. (A) articulates this suppressed premise. As for (B), the speaker might or might not endorse this idea. To the extent that you believe the speaker would agree with (B), you are highlighting a further conclusion of the argument—not an assumption. The same analysis can be applied to (C). If you think the speaker would accept this idea, then you are attributing a further conclusion to the speaker, not an assumption. As for (D), the argument specifically states that it is government and unions that insist upon the child labor laws, not women. And finally, (E) must be wrong because the author implies that government and unions are in agreement on this policy.

The air around us is getting cleaner. In 1980, only 53 percent of American industry was able to comply with Federal standards on air pollutants, but now over 75 percent are in complete compliance.

20. Which of the following, if true, would most weaken the argument above?

   (A) Since 1980, manufacturers have spent large sums of money to comply with Federal air pollution standards.
   (B) Other nations have passed stringent air pollution control laws and have begun to enforce them.
   (C) In the 1980s, the Federal government eased tight restrictions on particulate emissions into the air.
   (D) Since 1980, the Federal government has entered into treaties with other countries to control ocean dumping.
   (E) Energy demands by United States industry have increased drastically since 1980.

(C) This argument draws a causal connection between compliance and air quality. (C) offers an alternative explanation: the air is not cleaner—the standards are just lower. (A) and (B) would seem to strengthen rather than weaken the conclusion that the air is getting cleaner. (D) is clearly irrelevant, since it talks about ocean pollution rather than air pollution. And (E) is also irrelevant. The increased demand might have been met with cleaner sources of energy.

Beginning in two years, in the areas of the United States that have not yet met the standards of the Environmental Protection Agency for carbon monoxide emissions, gasoline sold during the winter months must by oxygenated. There is no doubt that the oxygenated gasoline will reduce the amount of carbon monoxide discharged from vehicle tailpipes, but the benefit will be short lived. Older vehicles emit more carbon monoxide than newer ones. As older vehicles are replaced by newer ones, the same level of reduction in carbon monoxide will be achieved without any change in the content of gasoline.

21. Which of the following, if true, would undermine the argument above?

   I. According to current estimates, petroleum refiners do not now have the capacity to meet the demand for oxygenated gasoline projected by the EPA under its new regulations.
   II. Carbon monoxide build-up is cumulative, and once created years must pass before the deleterious effects have disappeared.
   III. Requiring the use of oxygenated gasoline in newer cars will reduce carbon monoxide emissions more than allowing regular gasoline to be used in new cars.

   (A) II only   (B) III only   (C) I and II only
   (D) II and III only   (E) I, II, and III

(D) Examine each of the statements. Statement I does not undermine the argument. The fact that the capacity does not exist now doesn't effect the speaker's position one way or the other. (Had Statement I read "The capacity won't exist for 10 years," then it would seem to support the speaker's position, not weaken it.) Statement II does attack the speaker's position by suggesting that every little bit helps: oxygenated gasoline will avoid several year's worth of CO emissions during the transition from older to newer cars. And statement III attacks the speaker's position by noting that the two methods of reducing pollution are not mutually exclusive: with oxygenated gasoline you get the time savings plus a double reduction in the future.

Helen told me that she retired after 30 years as a city police officer with a pension of $80,000 per year. I checked with the city's Civil Service Commission and learned that the annual salary for someone in Helen's position would have been only $60,000 per year and that her pension should be equal to 80 percent of what she earned in her last year on the job. So Helen's pension has been wrongly computed.

22. Which of the following, if true, would most weaken the conclusion of the argument above?

(A) Some city police officers with higher ranks than that held by Helen in her last year earn $100,000 per year and more.
(B) Had Helen retired after only 25 years on the city police force her pension would have been only $50,000 per year.
(C) Helen will not begin to collect her pension until she reaches the age of 58, 7 years from now.
(D) During her last year on the force, Helen earned $40,000 in overtime.
(E) The estimated total cost to the city of Helen's pensions benefits, based on actuarial tables, is $275,000.

(D) The speaker misinterprets the rules for calculating pension benefits. According to the information obtained by the speaker, Helen's pension should be a percentage of what she "earned" in her last year, not 80 percent of her base salary. If (D) is true, then Helen's pension has not been incorrectly calculated.

As for (A), the speaker addresses the issue of Helen's pension. The fact that other retirees might have a different pension doesn't affect the speaker's analysis of the pension Helen says she is entitled to. Similarly, as for (B), the speaker is concerned with the pension Helen says she is entitled to after 30 years—not what she might have been entitled to after only 25 years. As for (C), this may very well be true of Helen's pension, but it relates to the timing of the benefits, not to annual value of the benefits. And finally, as for (E), the estimated cost of Helen's pension doesn't address the issue of whether or not it was correctly calculated.

Hume proved that it is impossible to deduce any "ought" statement from statements about what "is." That is to say, whatever is has no implication about what should or should not be. It is no part of an argument about what "should" be that something "is." Any line of reasoning that moves from statements of fact to a normative conclusion is not, strictly speaking, a logical argument.

23. Which of the following lines of reasoning runs afoul of Hume's restriction, as described above?

(A) The dean is opposed to letting the students have any say on the curriculum changes. Therefore, the students will probably stage a protest rally.
(B) The minister said in her sermon that anyone who is able to help collect food for the needy should do so. Since I have a lot of free time, the minister would probably say that I should help collect food for the needy.
(C) If an employee does a good job, then that employee will receive a promotion. Robert has just received a promotion. Therefore, Robert does a good job.
(D) The teeth of human beings are intended to grind vegetable matter—not to tear meat. Additionally, we find the notion of tearing a piece of meat off a freshly killed animal and eating it raw a repulsive thought. Therefore, humans should eat only plants.
(E) If a person should not deceive someone else, then that person should not tell a lie. A person should not deceive someone else. Therefore, no one should tell a lie.

(D) The arguments proscribed by Hume's analysis are those that move from "is" statements to "ought" statements. (D) is just such an argument: human beings are like this, therefore we should do something.

As for (A), the conclusion here is a statement about the future. It may prove right or wrong, but it is still a statement about what will be—not about what should be. As for (B), although the argument includes an element about what the minister *thinks* should be done, a statement about the minister's thoughts is one that is either true or false—a matter of fact. As for (C), these statements are matters of fact and can be proved or disproved. Finally, as for (E), every statement in that argument uses a "should." Therefore, it cannot possibly proceed from a descriptive statement to a normative one.

As a real estate agent in this city, I can personally attest to the recession that now afflicts the nation's housing market. Last year, the number of houses I was able to sell was 7 percent less than the number I was able to sell the year before.

24. Which of the following is NOT an assumption made by the speaker above?

(A) The speaker's experience in her city is typical of that of real estate agents around the country.

(B) The efforts made by the speaker last year to sell houses were equivalent to those she made the year before.

(C) No significant changes in the structure of the city's real estate market deprived the speaker of her share of the market.

(D) Sales recorded by the speaker two years ago were not the result of a boom that artificially inflated the number of sales.

(E) The average price of the homes sold by the speaker declined last year compared with the year before.

(E) The speaker's claim is specifically restricted to the "number of houses" she was able to sell. She makes no mention of the value of those houses. So (E) is not an assumption of the argument.

As for the other choices, each focuses upon an assumption that is essential to the speaker's conclusion. As for (A), the speaker must assume that her experience is typical—otherwise, she would not have reached a conclusion about the *national* market. As for (B), the speaker must assume that the decline in sales was attributable to a decline in the market—not to a decline in her efforts. As for (C), the speaker must also assume that no external event—say the entry of new and powerful competition—took business from her. (Otherwise, her experience is not typical of the market in general.) And finally, as for (D), since the speaker believes last year's sales were below normal, she must believe that the previous year's sales (which are her benchmark) were normal.

SECTION 5

READING COMPREHENSION

1. The author of the passage is primarily concerned with

(A) arguing against direct government intervention in the marketplace

(B) explaining the underlying philosophy of the antitrust laws

(C) outlining different theories of government regulation of markets

(D) criticizing government agencies such as the Interstate Commerce Commission

(E) justifying the enforcement of antitrust legislation

(B) This is a main idea question. In the first paragraph the author distinguishes antitrust actions from regulation per se. In the second paragraph he talks about the basic functioning of antitrust laws. In the third and fourth paragraphs, the author mentions some pros and cons of the antitrust philosophy. (B) provides the best description of this development. As for (A), you might argue that the author's favorable review of antitrust law implies that he would look with disfavor on direct intervention. And you might even cite his mention of the ICC. The difficulty with this reasoning is twofold. First, the author may not be opposed to all government intervention. He may, for example, regard the ICC as a necessary evil because antitrust laws would be ineffective in the transportation sector. Second, even if the first point is conceded, you still haven't found the main idea of the selection. The focus of the argument is antitrust, not regulation per se. (C) is wrong for this second reason as well. It is true that in the first paragraph the author does distinguish between antitrust and regulation, but the main focus of the passage then becomes antitrust. (D) is wrong for both of the reasons discussed in connection with choice (A): One, we can't be sure that the author is critical of the ICC; and two, this wouldn't be considered the main point of the selection anyway. Finally, (E) is wrong because the word *justification* is inappropriate. Further, while you might conclude from the passage that having a system of antitrust laws is justifiable, persuading you of that is not the author's main burden.

2. It can be inferred from the passage that predatory pricing

   (A) occurs only when a single firm has control of a large share of a market
   (B) is a type of business conduct best eliminated by direct government regulation
   (C) allows a large number of firms to distribute products over a broad region
   (D) improves an industry's ability to deliver a variety of goods and services
   (E) aims at eliminating competition so that the surviving firm can raise prices

   (E) This is an implied idea question. The information we need is found at the end of the second paragraph. The author states that the effect of predatory pricing is to lower prices in the short run. This eliminates competition. Then the survivors raise prices. (E) describes this process. (A) is the second-best choice, but the word *only* makes it wrong. We can certainly infer that predatory pricing could occur when a single firm is very powerful, but we should not conclude that this is the only circumstance under which it occurs. It might also occur with two or three very powerful firms. (B) must be wrong because the author seems to think that this type of conduct is best controlled by the antitrust laws. (C) and (D) have nothing to do with the concept of predatory pricing. And from what we have just learned, nothing good comes from predatory pricing—at least not in the long run.

3. The author cites the Interstate Commerce Commission to prove that

   (A) direct government intervention requires a large bureaucracy
   (B) antitrust enforcement is not an exact science
   (C) controlling market structures is more effective than regulation
   (D) antitrust laws can eliminate entry barriers for business
   (E) some government agencies intervene directly in the marketplace

   (A) This is a logical structure question. The author cites the ICC in the third paragraph. Why? There, he is making the point that antitrust policy, because it is not direct government intervention, does not require a large bureaucracy. He then mentions that the ICC does have a large bureaucracy. This example helps prove the point that antitrust policy does not require as large a bureaucracy. (B), (C), and (D) are ideas found at various points in the selection, but those choices are not responsive to the question: Why does the author mention the ICC? Finally, (E) is surely the second-best choice. The ICC is an example of a government agency that intervenes directly. But he is not saying: Sometimes the government intervenes directly, e.g., through the ICC. (A) better explains why the author mentions the ICC.

4. The author's attitude toward the theory of antitrust laws is best described as

   (A) wary acceptance
   (B) categorical rejection
   (C) cautious skepticism
   (D) qualified endorsement
   (E) reluctant dismissal

   (D) This is an author's attitude question. In the first paragraph, the author outlines the basic philosophy of antitrust policy and notes that it avoids the "politically hazardous thicket" of direct intervention. This is a positive attitude. In the third and fourth paragraphs, the author dicusses advantages of antitrust policy (it is not a large bureaucracy) and also some disadvantages (antitrust policy is not an exact science). We can conclude, therefore, that the author's attitude is a positive one tempered by the realization that antitrust policy is not perfect. (D) best describes this attitude.

5. The author mentions all of the following as measures of economic performance EXCEPT:

   (A) high industry profits
   (B) manufacturing efficiency
   (C) technological progress
   (D) distributional efficiency
   (E) distributional equity

   (A) This is a specific detail question with a thought reversal. In the very first sentence of the selection, the author mentions (B) through (E) as desirable qualities of economic performance. He never mentions high profits as desirable from a public policy standpoint. (Indeed, the author might think high profits to be bad because they might be the result of monopolistic practices.)

6. The author would most likely agree with which of the following statements?

(A) An effective antitrust policy depends on having as much information about market structure and conduct as possible.
(B) An antitrust approach to controlling market structure and conduct is only marginally more effective than regulation.
(C) Direct government intervention in the marketplace is cumbersome and never warranted.
(D) Antitrust policies are inherently arbitrary because no one can be certain what factors influence market structure and conduct.
(E) Market structure and market conduct are two independent variables and must be regulated separately.

(A) This is a further application question. In the third and fourth paragraphs, the author makes the point that antitrust is not an exact science because there are no easily definable causal connections between market structure and conduct. Thus, the author would probably agree that your policy is only as good as the information you have. (B) overstates the case. Our analysis of the preceding question revealed that the author believes that antitrust policy is effective. (C) also overstates the author's case. The author would prefer to avoid direct intervention, but we should not conclude that the author believes intervention is NEVER justified. And (D) overstates the case. Although the author recognizes that antitrust policy cannot be perfect, he certainly doesn't regard it as arbitrary. As for (E), the author would surely reject this statement, for he specifically states that structure can affect conduct and vice versa.

7. The author mentions which of the following as factors that may affect industry performance?

I. The ease with which new firms can enter the market
II. The number of firms already in the market
III. The uniqueness of the product

(A) I only   (B) I and II only   (C) I and III only
(D) II and III only   (E) I, II, and III

(E) This is a specific detail question set up in numbered-statement-format. In the middle of the second paragraph, the author mentions entry barriers (I), product differentiation (III), and market concentration (II).

8. The primary purpose of the selection is to

(A) demonstrate that the NICB study does not prove that efficiency results from concentration
(B) argue that less concentrated industries are as efficient as highly concentrated ones
(C) prove that smaller companies are as efficient as the largest firms in any given industry
(D) explain why labor-intensive industries are likely to have low shipments per employee
(E) criticize the nation's leading business magazine for printing its story about the NICB study

(A) This is a main idea question. The author begins by citing the NICB study. The study found correlations between concentration and productivity and between size and productivity. This prompted the NICB and the magazine to conclude that size equals efficiency. In the second paragraph the author attacks the study's claim that concentration is correlated with productivity; and in the third paragraph, he attacks the study's claim that size is correlated with productivity. In the final paragraph, the author directly contradicts the claim that size means efficiency. (A) best describes this development. (B) and (C) both overstate points made by the author. Even if they were toned down somewhat, neither could be considered the overall theme of the selection. (D) and (E) are only small points made in the passage.

9. The author places the word *productivity* in quotation marks when referring to the NICB study in order to

(A) remind the reader that the word is taken from another source
(B) express disagreement with the definition used by the study
(C) imply that the word is not susceptible to clear definition
(D) indicate that the magazine did not understand the word
(E) suggest that economic concepts have no content

(B) The study uses as a measure of productivity "shipments per employee" and "value added per employee." The author argues that this is not an appropriate measure of productivity for several reasons. The best explanation for his decision to put the term into quotation marks is to show the reader that he does not accept the study's definition of it. Once we understand this, we can see that (A) is incorrect. (C), (D), and (E), however, overstate the author's point. The author would not deny that the term *productivity* can be defined. Rather, he is objecting to the particular content given the term by this study.

561

10. The passage implies all of the following conclusions about the textile and appparel industry EXCEPT:

(A) It is relatively labor intensive.
(B) It is relatively unconcentrated.
(C) It has low shipments per employee.
(D) It is relatively easy for a firm to enter the industry.
(E) It has high profits and advertising expenditures per employee.

(E) This is an implied idea question. In the second paragraph, the author mentions textiles and apparel as examples of industries with low productivity as defined by the study (low shipments per employee). The list of low-productivity industries consists of examples of industries that are relatively unconcentrated because entry barriers are fairly low. And entry barriers are fairly low because the industries are labor intensive. Thus, we can see that (A), (B), (C), and (D) are all mentioned in that paragraph. As for (E), this idea is mentioned in conjunction with some manufactured goods later in the second paragraph, but it is not said to be a general characteristic of low-concentration industry.

11. According to the passage, the study's finding that large firms have greater productivity than other firms is misleading for which of the following reasons?

I. It failed to include the consumer goods industries.
II. It included small firms not properly belonging to the studied industries.
III. It compared medium-sized firms to the four largest firms in certain industries.

(A) I only
(B) II only
(C) I and II only
(D) II and III only
(E) I, II, and III

(B) This is a specific detail question. In the third paragraph, the author objects that the study included smaller firms that should not have been taken into account. (Those firms really should be classified as belonging to a different industry.) Thus, II is specifically mentioned in the selection. As for statement I, the author does single out the consumer goods industries, but he does not say the study failed to include those industries. As for III, it is the author of this selection (not the study) that compares large firms with medium-sized firms.

12. According to the selection, the study tends to overstate shipments per employee in some industries because

(A) productivity included profits and advertising outlays
(B) capital requirements for entry are low
(C) the category "all other" industries is overly inclusive
(D) top companies, on the average, have higher rates of productivity
(E) low-productivity industries are relatively unconcentrated

(A) This is a specific idea question. The last three sentences of the second paragraph specifically make the point suggested by (A). The other choices make statements that are to be found in the selection (made by the author or by the study), but those choices are not responsive to this question.

13. In the final paragraph, the author

(A) indicts the motives of the people who prepared the NICB study
(B) criticizes the methodology of the NICB study
(C) offers affirmative evidence to disprove the conclusions of the NICB study
(D) cites other studies that contradict the conclusions of the NICB study
(E) describes the difference between consumer and producer goods industries

(C) This is a logical structure question. Having demolished the study in the second and third paragraphs, the author then goes one step further: not only does the study not prove that bigger is better, but it can be proven that bigger is not necessarily better. (C) describes this strategy. (A) is incorrect because the author carries out the attack in a very scholarly way—attacking the study itself, not the motives of those who wrote it. (B) correctly describes the second and third paragraphs, but not the final paragraph. (D) and (E) are incorrect because these ideas do not appear in the final paragraph.

14. The author regards the conclusions of the NICB study as

(A) open to debate
(B) conclusively disproved
(C) probably true
(D) possibly true
(E) not subject to verification

(B) Our analysis thus far shows that the author disagrees with both the methodology and the conclusion of the study, so we can eliminate (C) and (D). As for (A) and (E), in the last paragraph the author offers evidence that he believes deals the death blow to the idea that size equals efficiency. So the best description of the author's attitude is given by (B).

15. The main purpose of the selection is to

(A) discuss the two models of constitutional law
(B) criticize Congress and the executive for inaction
(C) suggest a new role for the Supreme Court
(D) challenge the validity of Supreme Court rulings
(E) call for a revised Constitution

(A) This is a main idea question. The author begins by asking which of two models better describes the Constitution. The selection then examines both models. And the author ends by creating an analogy between constitutional theory and physics that suggests that both models have uses. The best description of this development is provided by (A). (B) is too narrow to be a correct description of the main idea of the selection. The author also criticizes the judiciary, and the main emphasis of the passage is theoretical. (C) is also too narrow. The author suggests obliquely that the Supreme Court has perhaps taken too much responsibility for evolving constitutional doctrine, but that is not the main point of the passage. Finally, (E) is surely wrong, for the author is concerned about how to interpret the existing Constitution.

16. In the first paragraph, the author makes use of

(A) circular reasoning
(B) authority
(C) analogy
(D) generalization
(E) ambiguity

(C) This is a logical structure question. In the first paragraph the author likens a certain view of the Constitution to dividing a pie between two siblings. The best description of this strategy is analogy.

17. With which of following statements would the author most likely agree?

(A) The Darwinian model and the Newtonian model produce almost identical interpretations of the Constitution.
(B) A constitutionally permissible action might still be constitutionally immoral.
(C) One branch of government is morally obligated not to criticize the actions of another.
(D) The Newtonian model of the Constitution is superior to the Darwinian model.
(E) The Supreme Court should have primary responsibility for evolving a Darwinian model of government.

(B) This is a further application question. In the third paragraph, the author states that a Newtonian system requires "constitutional morality" or restraint. He explains that a branch of government might well have the legal authority to do acts that would interfere with the proper functioning of government. Thus the author would likely agree with the statement in (B). Conversely, the author would almost surely reject (A). In the final paragraph, the analogy between constitutional theory and physics implies that both models are useful—one has advantages that the other lacks and vice versa. (C) represents a misreading of the phrase "constitutional morality." The "morality" called for in the third paragraph is restraint, but not restraint from criticism. "Constitutional morality" is restraint from legal but counterproductive actions. (D) makes the same type of mistake made by (B). The author states that both models have their advantages and that both should be used. Finally, (E) is directly contradicted by the first sentence of the final paragraph. There the author states that it is unfortunate that the Court has had so much responsibility for the Darwinian model.

18. The author regards the President's attempt to reorganize the Supreme Court as

(A) understandable but wrong
(B) ineffective but correct
(C) impractical but well-intentioned
(D) necessary but misguided
(E) half-hearted but moral

(A) This is an attitude question. In the third paragraph, the author notes that in a Newtonian model extraordinary action may trigger excessive reaction. And the author uses the Court reorganization plan as an example. Since the plan was an excessive reaction, we know the author would condemn it. Further, the author uses terms such as "unjudicial" and "seriously threatened." The best description of this attitude is provided by (A): the author understands why the President acted as he did but disagrees with the policy. The remaining choices are incorrect because the author thinks the policy was wrong.

19. In the final sentence, the author

    (A) poses a question for future research
    (B) introduces a new problem of constitutional theory
    (C) rejects the Darwinian model
    (D) suggests ways for improving governmental efficiency
    (E) asks a rhetorical question

(E) In the final paragraph, having discussed the merits of the two models, the author draws an analogy between physics and constitutional theory. A physicist might, suggests the author, use either of two models depending on the need. With the analogy, the author implies that the same is true of constitutional theory. So the author asks a question in the final sentence that he believes has already been answered. (A) is wrong because the author apparently believes the analogy disposes of the problem introduced in the first paragraph. (B) is wrong because the problem addressed by the selection was introduced in the first paragraph. (C) is wrong because the author regards both models as useful. And (D) is a description of some of the other paragraphs in the selection—but not of the final sentence.

20. The passage implies that

    (A) Congress is more important than either the executive or the judiciary
    (B) branches of government may have more constitutional authority than they use
    (C) the earliest Supreme Court justices were more sincere than today's justices
    (D) the Constitution sets up a very simple system for governmental decisions
    (E) constitutionally created hurdles block needed improvements in governmental efficiency

(B) This is an inference question. In the second paragraph the author suggests some things that the executive and legislative branches might do to make government better, things that are constitutionally permissible. Thus, we can infer that the branches of government may have more authority than they are using. (A) is incorrect because the author seems to regard all three branches as equally important. (That is part of the Newtonian model.) (C) is wrong because the only part of the passage that even hints that judges might be "insincere" is the discussion about the New Deal decisions—and that compares

members of the same Court. (D) must be incorrect because the author implies that the constitutional process is sufficiently complex that it cannot be explained by a single model. And our analysis of the correct choice shows that (E) is wrong. The author believes that governmental efficiency can be improved by taking constitutionally permissible action.

21. The author is primarily concerned with

    (A) creating a dilemma
    (B) evading a question
    (C) answering a question
    (D) pointing out a contradiction
    (E) reporting on a development

(C) This is a main idea question. Our analysis thus far shows that the author's main purpose is to answer the questions posed at the beginning of the selection. As for (A), a dilemma occurs when a person finds herself in an "either/or" situation and neither alternative is particularly attractive. Here, rather than creating a dilemma, the author avoids one by arguing it is not necessary to embrace one model to the exclusion of the other: you can use them both. As for (B), the author does not explicitly answer the question posed in the last sentence because it is rhetorical. This is not because he wishes to evade the question; the author doesn't answer because he thinks the answer is obvious. As for (D), though the author discusses two different models, he doesn't examine points of inconsistency between them. And finally, as for (E), though the author does state that the Darwinian model talks of "process," it would be incorrect to say that he is reporting on a development.

22. The author is primarily concerned with

    (A) criticizing translators who do not faithfully reproduce the style of works written in another language
    (B) suggesting that Japanese literature is more complex than English literature
    (C) arguing that no translation can do justice to a work written in another language
    (D) demonstrating that Japanese literature is particularly difficult to translate into English
    (E) discussing some of the problems of translating Japanese literature into English

(E) This is a main idea queston. (A) is not correct because although the author discusses the difficulty of making a translation, he does not criticize translators. In fact, he seems sympathetic to their problems since he is a translator himself. (B) is not correct since he mentions the fact that all languages have their particular difficulties and uses the poetry of Milton—an English poet—as an example of a difficult text to translate. (C) is wrong because although the author says it is difficult to do justice to a work in another language, he refers to some translations that are successful—those that please the "hard-liners," for instance. He also mentions Chateaubriand's translation of *Paradise Lost* as a successful translation. (D) is incorrect because although the author mentions some of the difficulties of translating Japanese into English, the point of the passage is not that Japanese is particularly difficult—just that it is difficult in some particular ways. (E) is the correct answer.

23. It can be inferred that *Accomplices of Silence* is

   (A) an English translation of Japanese poetry
   (B) a critical commentary on the work of Dazai Osamu
   (C) a prior publication by the author on Japanese literature
   (D) a text on Japanese orthography
   (E) a general work on the problem of translation

(B) This is an implied idea question. The author mentions the fact that he has done some translating of work by Dazai Osamu. He then mentions another book, *Accomplices of Silence*, which talks about certain aspects of Osamu's work. We may infer, then, that the book mentioned is a critical commentary on the work of Osamu. It is certainly not an English translation of Japanese poetry since it is clear that this book talks *about* the literature. It is not a prior publication by the author because the author names another author—Masao Miyoshi; thus, (C) is incorrect. (D) is wrong because the author gives examples of the things mentioned in Miyoshi's book and they have nothing to do with orthography. Finally, (E) is wrong because it is clear that Miyoshi's comments as quoted by the author are about Osamu's effects *in Japanese*, not in English; therefore, he is not talking about the problems of translation.

24. The author cites Shiga Naoya's *Kinosaki nite* in order to

   (A) illustrate the effect that Japanese orthography has on meaning
   (B) demonstrate the poverty of indigenous Japanese vocabulary
   (C) prove that it is difficult to translate Japanese into English
   (D) acquaint the reader with an important work of Japanese literature
   (E) impress upon the reader the importance of faithfully translating a work from one language into another

(A) This is a logical detail question. The author uses an example taken from *Kinosaki nite* to illustrate the onomatopoeic effect of writing a word in one system of orthography rather than another. (B) is incorrect because although the author mentions the fact that a Japanese writer laments the poverty of indigenous Japanese vocabulary, this is not the point of his example. In fact, the example actually demonstrates a certain richness of the Japanese language. (C) is incorrect because the example has nothing to do with translation. It is an example of an effect rendered in Japanese. (D) is not correct since the reader actually learns nothing at all about this work of literature except that this literary device appears in it. Finally, (E) is wrong because, again, the example has nothing to do with translation.

25. With which of the following statements would the author most likely agree?

   (A) The Japanese language is the language best suited to poetry.
   (B) English is one of the most difficult languages into which to translate any work written in Japanese.
   (C) It is impossible for a person not fluent in Japanese to understand the inner meaning of Japanese literature.
   (D) Most Japanese people think that their language is uniquely suited to conveying mystical ideas.
   (E) Every language has its own peculiar potentialities which present challenges to a translator.

(E) This is a further application question. (A) is incorrect because although the author says that the Japanese people have special feelings about the possibilities of their language, he does not say that he shares these feelings. (B) is wrong because although the author discusses the difficulties of translating Japanese, he says that the difficulty stems from the peculiarities of the Japanese language, not from the limitations of the English. There is no reason to assume that the author thinks it would be easier to translate Japanese into any other language. (C) is wrong because it overstates the case. The author might say that it is difficult, but not necessarily impossible, for someone not fluent in Japanese to understand Japanese literature. (D) is wrong because the author specifically brackets the question of the truth of this hypothesis. (E) is correct because the author states that although Japanese has "special language relationships," he just means that like any other language, it has unique features. Thus, the author seems to feel that all languages have special qualities and they all present special challenges to a translator.

26. It can be inferred that the Japanese word ''bu—n''
is most like which of the following English words?

   (A) bee
   (B) honey
   (C) buzz
   (D) flower
   (E) moon

(C) This is an implied idea question. Since the author cites this word as an example of onomatopoeia (a poetic device in which the word used to describe an action *sounds* like the action itself), the answer can only be (C): buzz. In English, the word ''buzz'' sounds like the flight of a bee.

27. The author uses all of the following EXCEPT

   (A) examples to prove a point
   (B) citation of authority
   (C) analogy
   (D) personal knowledge
   (E) contrasting two viewpoints

(C) This is a logical structure question. The author uses many examples to illustrate his points. He cites the example of onomatopoeia in *Kinosaki nite*, for instance. He also cites the particular effects which are difficult to translate in the work of Osamu. He cites several authorities. He cites Miyoshi on the subject of Osamu, and George Steiner on the subject of translation. As for (D), the author discusses his personal experience in translating the work of Osamu. Finally, as for (E), the author contrasts two viewpoints in the first paragraph (the hard line and the soft line).

28. It can be inferred that the ''exoticism handicap'' mentioned by the author is

   (A) the tendency of some translators of Japanese to render Japanese literature in a needlessly awkward style
   (B) the attempt of Japanese writers to create for their readers a world characterized by mysticism
   (C) the lack of literal, word-for-word translational equivalents for Japanese and English vocabulary
   (D) the expectation of many English readers that Japanese literature can only be understood by someone who speaks Japanese
   (E) the difficulty a Japanese reader encounters in trying to penetrate the meaning of difficult Japanese poets

(A) This is an implied idea question. (B) cannot be correct since the handicap referred to is the result of translating the poetry, not the result of the Japanese writer's intention. (C) is incorrect because although there may be no word-for-word equivalents, that is a general problem of translation, not just a problem of translating Japanese into English. (D) is incorrect because the handicap is not related to the expectations of the reader. (E) is obviously incorrect since the problem is related to translation and has nothing to do with the problems of a Japanese reader reading in Japanese. The example quoted by the author is obviously a translator's attempt to make the English sound ''oriental,'' or what a Western audience thinks ''oriental'' sounds like. So (A) is the correct response.

Practice Test 3

☐ A R C O ☐

YOUR NAME:

ARCO TEST NO.

DATE TAKEN:

Start with number 1 for each new section. If a section has fewer than 30 questions, leave the extra answer spaces blank.

SECTION 1

1 Ⓐ Ⓑ Ⓒ Ⓓ Ⓔ
2 Ⓐ Ⓑ Ⓒ Ⓓ Ⓔ
3 Ⓐ Ⓑ Ⓒ Ⓓ Ⓔ
4 Ⓐ Ⓑ Ⓒ Ⓓ Ⓔ
5 Ⓐ Ⓑ Ⓒ Ⓓ Ⓔ
6 Ⓐ Ⓑ Ⓒ Ⓓ Ⓔ
7 Ⓐ Ⓑ Ⓒ Ⓓ Ⓔ
8 Ⓐ Ⓑ Ⓒ Ⓓ Ⓔ
9 Ⓐ Ⓑ Ⓒ Ⓓ Ⓔ
10 Ⓐ Ⓑ Ⓒ Ⓓ Ⓔ
11 Ⓐ Ⓑ Ⓒ Ⓓ Ⓔ
12 Ⓐ Ⓑ Ⓒ Ⓓ Ⓔ
13 Ⓐ Ⓑ Ⓒ Ⓓ Ⓔ
14 Ⓐ Ⓑ Ⓒ Ⓓ Ⓔ
15 Ⓐ Ⓑ Ⓒ Ⓓ Ⓔ
16 Ⓐ Ⓑ Ⓒ Ⓓ Ⓔ
17 Ⓐ Ⓑ Ⓒ Ⓓ Ⓔ
18 Ⓐ Ⓑ Ⓒ Ⓓ Ⓔ
19 Ⓐ Ⓑ Ⓒ Ⓓ Ⓔ
20 Ⓐ Ⓑ Ⓒ Ⓓ Ⓔ
21 Ⓐ Ⓑ Ⓒ Ⓓ Ⓔ
22 Ⓐ Ⓑ Ⓒ Ⓓ Ⓔ
23 Ⓐ Ⓑ Ⓒ Ⓓ Ⓔ
24 Ⓐ Ⓑ Ⓒ Ⓓ Ⓔ
25 Ⓐ Ⓑ Ⓒ Ⓓ Ⓔ
26 Ⓐ Ⓑ Ⓒ Ⓓ Ⓔ
27 Ⓐ Ⓑ Ⓒ Ⓓ Ⓔ
28 Ⓐ Ⓑ Ⓒ Ⓓ Ⓔ
29 Ⓐ Ⓑ Ⓒ Ⓓ Ⓔ
30 Ⓐ Ⓑ Ⓒ Ⓓ Ⓔ

SECTION 2

1 Ⓐ Ⓑ Ⓒ Ⓓ Ⓔ
2 Ⓐ Ⓑ Ⓒ Ⓓ Ⓔ
3 Ⓐ Ⓑ Ⓒ Ⓓ Ⓔ
4 Ⓐ Ⓑ Ⓒ Ⓓ Ⓔ
5 Ⓐ Ⓑ Ⓒ Ⓓ Ⓔ
6 Ⓐ Ⓑ Ⓒ Ⓓ Ⓔ
7 Ⓐ Ⓑ Ⓒ Ⓓ Ⓔ
8 Ⓐ Ⓑ Ⓒ Ⓓ Ⓔ
9 Ⓐ Ⓑ Ⓒ Ⓓ Ⓔ
10 Ⓐ Ⓑ Ⓒ Ⓓ Ⓔ
11 Ⓐ Ⓑ Ⓒ Ⓓ Ⓔ
12 Ⓐ Ⓑ Ⓒ Ⓓ Ⓔ
13 Ⓐ Ⓑ Ⓒ Ⓓ Ⓔ
14 Ⓐ Ⓑ Ⓒ Ⓓ Ⓔ
15 Ⓐ Ⓑ Ⓒ Ⓓ Ⓔ
16 Ⓐ Ⓑ Ⓒ Ⓓ Ⓔ
17 Ⓐ Ⓑ Ⓒ Ⓓ Ⓔ
18 Ⓐ Ⓑ Ⓒ Ⓓ Ⓔ
19 Ⓐ Ⓑ Ⓒ Ⓓ Ⓔ
20 Ⓐ Ⓑ Ⓒ Ⓓ Ⓔ
21 Ⓐ Ⓑ Ⓒ Ⓓ Ⓔ
22 Ⓐ Ⓑ Ⓒ Ⓓ Ⓔ
23 Ⓐ Ⓑ Ⓒ Ⓓ Ⓔ
24 Ⓐ Ⓑ Ⓒ Ⓓ Ⓔ
25 Ⓐ Ⓑ Ⓒ Ⓓ Ⓔ
26 Ⓐ Ⓑ Ⓒ Ⓓ Ⓔ
27 Ⓐ Ⓑ Ⓒ Ⓓ Ⓔ
28 Ⓐ Ⓑ Ⓒ Ⓓ Ⓔ
29 Ⓐ Ⓑ Ⓒ Ⓓ Ⓔ
30 Ⓐ Ⓑ Ⓒ Ⓓ Ⓔ

SECTION 3

1 Ⓐ Ⓑ Ⓒ Ⓓ Ⓔ
2 Ⓐ Ⓑ Ⓒ Ⓓ Ⓔ
3 Ⓐ Ⓑ Ⓒ Ⓓ Ⓔ
4 Ⓐ Ⓑ Ⓒ Ⓓ Ⓔ
5 Ⓐ Ⓑ Ⓒ Ⓓ Ⓔ
6 Ⓐ Ⓑ Ⓒ Ⓓ Ⓔ
7 Ⓐ Ⓑ Ⓒ Ⓓ Ⓔ
8 Ⓐ Ⓑ Ⓒ Ⓓ Ⓔ
9 Ⓐ Ⓑ Ⓒ Ⓓ Ⓔ
10 Ⓐ Ⓑ Ⓒ Ⓓ Ⓔ
11 Ⓐ Ⓑ Ⓒ Ⓓ Ⓔ
12 Ⓐ Ⓑ Ⓒ Ⓓ Ⓔ
13 Ⓐ Ⓑ Ⓒ Ⓓ Ⓔ
14 Ⓐ Ⓑ Ⓒ Ⓓ Ⓔ
15 Ⓐ Ⓑ Ⓒ Ⓓ Ⓔ
16 Ⓐ Ⓑ Ⓒ Ⓓ Ⓔ
17 Ⓐ Ⓑ Ⓒ Ⓓ Ⓔ
18 Ⓐ Ⓑ Ⓒ Ⓓ Ⓔ
19 Ⓐ Ⓑ Ⓒ Ⓓ Ⓔ
20 Ⓐ Ⓑ Ⓒ Ⓓ Ⓔ
21 Ⓐ Ⓑ Ⓒ Ⓓ Ⓔ
22 Ⓐ Ⓑ Ⓒ Ⓓ Ⓔ
23 Ⓐ Ⓑ Ⓒ Ⓓ Ⓔ
24 Ⓐ Ⓑ Ⓒ Ⓓ Ⓔ
25 Ⓐ Ⓑ Ⓒ Ⓓ Ⓔ
26 Ⓐ Ⓑ Ⓒ Ⓓ Ⓔ
27 Ⓐ Ⓑ Ⓒ Ⓓ Ⓔ
28 Ⓐ Ⓑ Ⓒ Ⓓ Ⓔ
29 Ⓐ Ⓑ Ⓒ Ⓓ Ⓔ
30 Ⓐ Ⓑ Ⓒ Ⓓ Ⓔ

SECTION 4

1 Ⓐ Ⓑ Ⓒ Ⓓ Ⓔ
2 Ⓐ Ⓑ Ⓒ Ⓓ Ⓔ
3 Ⓐ Ⓑ Ⓒ Ⓓ Ⓔ
4 Ⓐ Ⓑ Ⓒ Ⓓ Ⓔ
5 Ⓐ Ⓑ Ⓒ Ⓓ Ⓔ
6 Ⓐ Ⓑ Ⓒ Ⓓ Ⓔ
7 Ⓐ Ⓑ Ⓒ Ⓓ Ⓔ
8 Ⓐ Ⓑ Ⓒ Ⓓ Ⓔ
9 Ⓐ Ⓑ Ⓒ Ⓓ Ⓔ
10 Ⓐ Ⓑ Ⓒ Ⓓ Ⓔ
11 Ⓐ Ⓑ Ⓒ Ⓓ Ⓔ
12 Ⓐ Ⓑ Ⓒ Ⓓ Ⓔ
13 Ⓐ Ⓑ Ⓒ Ⓓ Ⓔ
14 Ⓐ Ⓑ Ⓒ Ⓓ Ⓔ
15 Ⓐ Ⓑ Ⓒ Ⓓ Ⓔ
16 Ⓐ Ⓑ Ⓒ Ⓓ Ⓔ
17 Ⓐ Ⓑ Ⓒ Ⓓ Ⓔ
18 Ⓐ Ⓑ Ⓒ Ⓓ Ⓔ
19 Ⓐ Ⓑ Ⓒ Ⓓ Ⓔ
20 Ⓐ Ⓑ Ⓒ Ⓓ Ⓔ
21 Ⓐ Ⓑ Ⓒ Ⓓ Ⓔ
22 Ⓐ Ⓑ Ⓒ Ⓓ Ⓔ
23 Ⓐ Ⓑ Ⓒ Ⓓ Ⓔ
24 Ⓐ Ⓑ Ⓒ Ⓓ Ⓔ
25 Ⓐ Ⓑ Ⓒ Ⓓ Ⓔ
26 Ⓐ Ⓑ Ⓒ Ⓓ Ⓔ
27 Ⓐ Ⓑ Ⓒ Ⓓ Ⓔ
28 Ⓐ Ⓑ Ⓒ Ⓓ Ⓔ
29 Ⓐ Ⓑ Ⓒ Ⓓ Ⓔ
30 Ⓐ Ⓑ Ⓒ Ⓓ Ⓔ

SECTION 5

1 Ⓐ Ⓑ Ⓒ Ⓓ Ⓔ   16 Ⓐ Ⓑ Ⓒ Ⓓ Ⓔ
2 Ⓐ Ⓑ Ⓒ Ⓓ Ⓔ   17 Ⓐ Ⓑ Ⓒ Ⓓ Ⓔ
3 Ⓐ Ⓑ Ⓒ Ⓓ Ⓔ   18 Ⓐ Ⓑ Ⓒ Ⓓ Ⓔ
4 Ⓐ Ⓑ Ⓒ Ⓓ Ⓔ   19 Ⓐ Ⓑ Ⓒ Ⓓ Ⓔ
5 Ⓐ Ⓑ Ⓒ Ⓓ Ⓔ   20 Ⓐ Ⓑ Ⓒ Ⓓ Ⓔ
6 Ⓐ Ⓑ Ⓒ Ⓓ Ⓔ   21 Ⓐ Ⓑ Ⓒ Ⓓ Ⓔ
7 Ⓐ Ⓑ Ⓒ Ⓓ Ⓔ   22 Ⓐ Ⓑ Ⓒ Ⓓ Ⓔ
8 Ⓐ Ⓑ Ⓒ Ⓓ Ⓔ   23 Ⓐ Ⓑ Ⓒ Ⓓ Ⓔ
9 Ⓐ Ⓑ Ⓒ Ⓓ Ⓔ   24 Ⓐ Ⓑ Ⓒ Ⓓ Ⓔ
10 Ⓐ Ⓑ Ⓒ Ⓓ Ⓔ   25 Ⓐ Ⓑ Ⓒ Ⓓ Ⓔ
11 Ⓐ Ⓑ Ⓒ Ⓓ Ⓔ   26 Ⓐ Ⓑ Ⓒ Ⓓ Ⓔ
12 Ⓐ Ⓑ Ⓒ Ⓓ Ⓔ   27 Ⓐ Ⓑ Ⓒ Ⓓ Ⓔ
13 Ⓐ Ⓑ Ⓒ Ⓓ Ⓔ   28 Ⓐ Ⓑ Ⓒ Ⓓ Ⓔ
14 Ⓐ Ⓑ Ⓒ Ⓓ Ⓔ   29 Ⓐ Ⓑ Ⓒ Ⓓ Ⓔ
15 Ⓐ Ⓑ Ⓒ Ⓓ Ⓔ   30 Ⓐ Ⓑ Ⓒ Ⓓ Ⓔ

SECTION 1   Time—35 Minutes   In this section solve each problem, using any available space on the
24 Questions   page for scratchwork. Then decide which is the best of the choices
given and fill in the corresponding oval on the answer sheet.

Directions: Each group of questions is based on a set of conditions. In answering some of the questions it may be useful to draw a rough diagram. Choose the best answer for each question and blacken the corresponding space on your answer sheet.

Questions 1–7

Eight people—J, K, L, M, N, O, P, and Q—are making a long driving trip in two cars. Each car seats four people, two in the front seat and two in the back seat. Every two hours, the cars stop and the people change their seating arrangements.

J must always sit in the same car as N, directly behind N.

Q and P cannot sit in the same car.

The driver of a car sits on the left side of the front seat.

1. Which of the following groups of four people could ride in one of the cars?

   (A) J, L, O, P
   (B) J, M, O, Q
   (C) K, L, P, Q
   (D) K, P, J, N
   (E) L, M, N, P

2. If P is sitting in a seat behind O and Q is sitting in a seat next to M, then which of the following must be true?

   (A) J is sitting next to K.
   (B) K is sitting next to L.
   (C) K is sitting behind Q.
   (D) L is sitting behind Q.
   (E) L is sitting behind M.

3. If P is sitting in a seat next to N and K is sitting in a seat next to L, then which of the following must be true?

   (A) M and Q are sitting in different cars.
   (B) O and M are sitting in different cars.
   (C) O and P are sitting in different cars.
   (D) M is sitting behind L.
   (E) Q is sitting behind K.

4. If K is sitting in the front seat of a car that Q is driving and O is driving the other car, then all of the following must be true EXCEPT

   (A) M is sitting next to L.
   (B) O is sitting next to N.
   (C) O is sitting in front of P.
   (D) P is sitting next to J.
   (E) Q is sitting in front of L.

5. If K is sitting behind P in a car that M is driving, then all of the following could be true EXCEPT

   (A) L is sitting behind M.
   (B) L is sitting behind Q.
   (C) L is sitting next to O.
   (D) O is sitting next to J.
   (E) O is sitting next to N.

6. If J is riding in a car driven by K and O is driving the other car, then all of the following could be true EXCEPT

   (A) L is sitting behind P.
   (B) L is sitting behind Q.
   (C) M is sitting behind K.
   (D) M is sitting next to P.
   (E) Q is sitting next to J.

7. If M is driving one car and K is driving the other, which of the following must be true?

   (A) J is sitting next to either P or Q.
   (B) K is sitting next to either L or O.
   (C) L is sitting next to either K or O.
   (D) O is sitting behind either P or Q.
   (E) Q is sitting behind either L or O.

GO ON TO THE NEXT PAGE

Questions 8–13

Four people—*J*, *K*, *L*, and *M*—are competing in a speech contest. Each person will read two speeches. The order in which the speeches are read must conform to the following conditions:

Either *L* will read first and *M* will read last, or *M* will read first and *L* will read last.

K's second reading must follow *K*'s first reading with no intervening readings.

L's second reading must follow *L*'s first reading with no intervening readings.

J's second reading cannot follow directly *J*'s first reading.

8. Which of the following is an acceptable order for the speeches?

   (A) *J, K, K, J, L, L, M, M*
   (B) *L, L, J, K, K, M, M, J*
   (C) *L, K, J, L, J, M, K, M*
   (D) *M, K, K, J, J, M, L, L*
   (E) *M, J, K, K, M, J, L, L*

9. All of the following are acceptable orders for the speeches EXCEPT

   (A) *L, L, M, J, K, K, J, M*
   (B) *L, L, J, M, K, K, J, M*
   (C) *L, L, K, K, J, M, J, M*
   (D) *M, M, J, K, K, L, J, L*
   (E) *M, K, K, J, M, J, L, L*

10. If *M* reads the fourth and eighth speeches, which of the following must be true?

    (A) *J* reads the fifth speech.
    (B) *J* reads the seventh speech.
    (C) *K* reads the third speech.
    (D) *K* reads the fifth speech.
    (E) *K* reads the sixth speech.

11. If *J* reads the second speech, which of the following COULD NOT be true?

    (A) *J*'s second speech comes sometime after *M*'s second speech.
    (B) *J*'s second speech comes sometime after *K*'s second speech.
    (C) *K*'s second speech comes sometime after *J*'s second speech.
    (D) *M*'s second speech comes after *J*'s second speech and *K*'s second speech.
    (E) *J*'s second speech comes before *M*'s second speech and before *K*'s first speech.

12. If *M* reads both of his speeches before *J* reads his first speech, the fourth and fifth speeches are read by

    (A) *J*
    (B) *K*
    (C) *J* and *K*, respectively
    (D) *K* and *J*, respectively
    (E) *M* and *J*, respectively

13. Which of the following conditions is sufficient to determine the complete order for the reading of the speeches?

    I. *M* reads the second speech.
    II. *K* reads the seventh speech.
    III. *J* reads the sixth speech.

    (A) I only   (B) II only   (C) I and II only
    (D) II and III only   (E) I, II, and III

Questions 14–19

In a certain society, each person belongs to a clan, and each clan has one of the following five totems: bear, wolf, elk, bird, fish. Marriage in the society is governed by the following rules:

A member of one clan can marry a person who is also a member of his or her clan.

Men who are members of the wolf clan can marry women who are members of the elk and bird clans.

Women who are members of the wolf clan can marry men who are members of the bird and fish clans.

Men who are members of the bird clan can marry women who are members of the fish clan.

These are the only marriages permitted. A son belongs to the same clan as his father, and a daughter belongs to the same clan as her mother.

14. Which of the following provides a complete and accurate list of the totems of men to whom a woman of the fish clan could be married?

    (A) Wolf
    (B) Bird
    (C) Fish
    (D) Bird, fish
    (E) Wolf, bird, fish

15. If a man whose totem is the wolf wishes to marry a woman outside of his own clan, then he could marry a woman with which of the following totems?

    I. Bear
    II. Elk
    III. Bird

    (A) I only   (B) II only   (C) III only
    (D) II and III only   (E) I, II, and III

16. The son of a woman whose totem is the fish could be a member of which of the following clans?

    I. Elk
    II. Bird
    III. Fish

    (A) I, but not II or III
    (B) II, but not I or III
    (C) I and II, but not III
    (D) II and III, but not I
    (E) I, II, or III

GO ON TO THE NEXT PAGE

17. If a man's totem is the wolf, then which of the following could be his sister's totem?

    I. Wolf
   II. Elk
  III. Bird

(A) I only   (B) II only   (C) I and II only
(D) II and III only   (E) I, II, and III

18. The daughter of a man whose totem is the elk could only marry a man with which of following totems?

    I. Wolf
   II. Elk
  III. Bird

(A) I only   (B) III only   (C) I and II only
(D) II and III only   (E) I, II, and III

19. If a man's totem is the fish, then which of the following is a complete and accurate list of the clans to which his wife's father could belong?

(A) Wolf, bird
(B) Wolf, bird, fish
(C) Bear, wolf, bird
(D) Bear, wolf, fish
(E) Bear, wolf, elk, bird, fish

Questions 20–24

A newspaper, which is published seven days a week, employs six full-time writers who contribute columns on a regular basis. In a certain week:

Munick's column appeared every day except for Tuesday, Thursday, and Friday.

Harris's column appeared only on Tuesday, Thursday, and Saturday.

Roe's column appeared on every day that Munick's did not appear and appeared on Sunday as well.

Cavanaugh's column appeared every day except for Tuesday and Thursday.

Clock's column appeared on Monday, Wednesday, Friday, and Saturday.

Areff's column appeared on Tuesday, Thursday, and Sunday.

20. What is the total number of columns by the six columnists published by the paper during the week?

(A) 15   (B) 17   (C) 19   (D) 23   (E) 26

21. Which of the following statements can be deduced from the information given above?

    I. Any day that Munick's column appeared, Cavanaugh's column also appeared.
   II. Any day that Harris's column did not appear, Clock's column appeared.
  III. Areff had the fewest number of columns published during the week.

(A) I only   (B) II only   (C) I and II only
(D) II and III only   (E) I, II, and III

22. If on a certain day neither Roe's column nor Areff's column appeared, then that day could have been which of the following?

    I. Monday
   II. Wednesday
  III. Saturday

(A) I only   (B) II only   (C) III only
(D) II and III only   (E) I, II, and III

23. If the paper contained columns by Clock and Cavanaugh, then knowing that columns by which of the following had also appeared would be sufficient to determine what day the paper had been published?

    I. Munick
   II. Harris
  III. Roe

(A) I only   (B) II only   (C) III only
(D) II and III only   (E) I, II, and III

24. If a paper contained neither a column by Munick nor one by Areff, then that paper was published on

(A) Monday   (B) Tuesday   (C) Thursday
(D) Friday   (E) Saturday

IF YOU FINISH BEFORE TIME IS CALLED, YOU MAY CHECK YOUR WORK ON THIS SECTION ONLY. DO NOT WORK ON ANY OTHER SECTION IN THE TEST.   **S T O P**

The questions in this section require you to follow or evaluate the reasoning contained in brief statements or passages. In some questions, each of the choices is a conceivable solution to the particular problem posed. However, you are to select the one that answers the question _best_, that is, the one that does not require you to make what are by common-sense standards implausible, superfluous, or incompatible assumptions. After you have chosen the best answer, blacken the corresponding space on the answer sheet.

In an attempt to predict the future course of consumer spending, _Investment Monthly_ magazine surveyed its readers. Of those surveyed, over 60 percent reported that they planned to buy a new automobile or at least one major appliance within the next three months. From these results, the magazine concluded that consumer spending for the next quarter was likely to be high.

1. Which of the following, if true, would most weaken the conclusion above?

   (A) The cost of a new automobile is much greater than that of a major appliance.

   (B) A person who plans to make a major purchase at some time in the future may not yet have settled on a brand.

   (C) The readers of _Investment Monthly_ are more affluent than the average consumer.

   (D) Some of the items to be purchased will be imports and will not stimulate markets in the United States.

   (E) Not all readers of _Investment Monthly_ magazine responded to the survey.

Questions 2–3

Every member of the New York Burros, a team in the Big Apple Softball League, who wears wristbands when batting wears either red wristbands or white wristbands.

2. If the statement above is true, which of the following must be true?

   I. A member of the New York Burros who does not wear red wristbands while batting wears white wristbands while batting.

   II. No member of the New York Burros wears blue wristbands while batting.

   III. Some members of the New York Burros do not wear wristbands when batting.

   (A) I only
   (B) II only
   (C) III only
   (D) I and III only
   (E) I, II, and III

3. If any player in the Big Apple Softball League who wears red wristbands while batting also wears blue batting gloves, and if no member of the New York Burros wears blue batting gloves, which of the following must be true?

   (A) Every member of the New York Burros wears white wristbands when batting.

   (B) No member of the New York Burros wears white wristbands.

   (C) Some members of the New York Burros wear red wristbands when batting.

   (D) Some members of the New York Burros do not wear batting gloves.

   (E) Every member of the New York Burros who wears wristbands wears white wristbands when batting.

A bill now pending before the Congress would give physicians the option of prescribing heroin as a painkiller for terminally ill patients. The Congress should refuse to pass the bill, because there is a serious danger that the heroin would be stolen and wind up being sold on the streets.

4. Which of the following, if true, would most weaken the argument above?

   (A) Other prescription painkillers are available for terminally ill patients that in most cases provide relief of pain as effective as that provided by heroin.

   (B) The addictive effects of heroin are inconsequential considering that the patients who would be scheduled for treatment are terminally ill.

   (C) The amount of heroin that would be required for terminally ill patients is insignificant when compared with the amount of heroin sold illegally.

   (D) Heroin sold illegally varies widely in quality and purity and can easily cause death by overdose, because it is taken without proper measurement.

   (E) Over the past five years, the number of deaths attributable to heroin overdose has declined slightly, but the total number of deaths by drug overdose has increased significantly because of increased use of cocaine.

It used to be said that artistic creativity is the province solely of human beings and that it is, in fact, one of the marks that distinguishes humans from all other creatures. Today, cleverly programmed computers can create images that are indistinguishable from paintings by contemporary abstract artists. Thus, the traditional argument that artistic creativity is the province of humans is proved incorrect.

5. Which of the following, if true, most weakens the argument above?

(A) Most human beings have never produced a creative work that others would regard as a work of art.

(B) The image produced by a computer is an image that it was directed to create by the human programmer.

(C) Many people are unfamiliar with abstract art and so are unable to distinguish good modern art from bad modern art.

(D) Human beings engage in many activities other than the creation of art, activities such as production, warfare, and building.

(E) A program designed to produce a computerized image will produce the same image on any computer that can accept the program.

The right to work under humane conditions is a fundamental right of all people.

Therefore, all men and women have the right to a job and to decent conditions of employment.

6. Which of the following arguments most closely parallels the reasoning of the argument above?

(A) The expression of anger is a natural instinct of human beings who feel threatened. Therefore, Smith is not to be blamed for expressing anger when she felt threatened.

(B) Johnson is one of the most honest legislative leaders ever to serve this state. Therefore, Johnson could not have committed the dishonest acts of which he has been accused.

(C) The Bill of Rights protects the free practice of religion in this country. Therefore, all people have the right to worship God in a manner of their own choosing.

(D) Children are human beings who have the potential for adult behavior. Therefore, any right or privilege that is granted to adults ought, in fairness, to be granted to children as well.

(E) The President has the duty of defending the country from any external enemy. Therefore, the President acted properly in ordering our army to repel the invading forces.

Amid great fanfare, the Taxi and Limousine Commission announced last June that a new dress code for taxi drivers would be incorporated into the Commission's rules. After six months, no driver has lost his license or even been fined under the new dress code. Evidently, drivers have chosen to comply with the new dress code.

7. Which of the following, if true, would most weaken the argument above?

(A) Prior to the announcement of the new dress code, an average of 16 cab drivers each month lost their licenses for various violations of the Commission's rules.

(B) Inspectors routinely stop cab drivers to inspect licenses, safety, and cleanliness of the vehicle and the driver's record of fares.

(C) The Commission's lawyers have refused to prosecute drivers cited under the new dress code, because they believe that the law is unconstitutional.

(D) A survey of passengers who say they regularly use taxi cabs shows that 45 percent of the riders don't believe that drivers are better dressed.

(E) During July and August, the number of cab drivers available for work is less than that during the other months of the year.

Questions 8–9

The existence of our state's inefficient and wasteful automobile accident liability system can be easily explained. As long as most of our legislators are lawyers, the system will never be reformed, because litigation creates more work for lawyers.

8. Which of the following, if true, would most weaken the argument above?

(A) Most judges in the state are members of the legal profession as well.

(B) Few of the state's legislators are among the relatively small percentage of lawyers who handle automobile accident cases.

(C) Under the customary fee arrangement, a lawyer receives one-third of any monetary award made to a client.

(D) The state legislature allocates funds to pay for defense attorneys who represent indigent clients.

(E) Any reform legislation could be vetoed by the governor of the state, who is also an attorney.

9. The argument above rests on the assumption that

(A) given the opportunity, most lawyers would want to be members of the state legislature

(B) legislation to reform the state's automobile accident liability system could be introduced by a legislator who is not a lawyer

(C) state laws set minimum fees that attorneys are permitted to charge in cases arising from automobile accidents

(D) the state's automobile accident liability system encourages litigation

(E) state laws governing the ownership and operation of motor vehicles encourage unsafe driving practices

Premises: All weavers are members of the union.
Some carders are women.
Some weavers are women.
All union members are covered by health insurance.
No carders are covered by health insurance.

10. All of the following conclusions can be drawn from the statements above EXCEPT

(A) All weavers are covered by health insurance.
(B) Some women are covered by health insurance.
(C) Some women are not covered by health insurance.
(D) Some members of the union are not covered by health insurance.
(E) No carders are members of the union.

11. Which of the following workers would provide a counterexample to the statements above?

(A) A man who is a carder
(B) A weaver who is not covered by health insurance
(C) A carder who is not covered by health insurance
(D) A worker covered by health insurance who is not a weaver
(E) A worker covered by health insurance who is not a carder

The Olympic Games represent a first step in the historic movement away from war and toward the substitution for war of peaceful competition among nations. Just as professional sports in the United States provide a field in which local, regional, and even racial and ethnic hostilities may be sublimated and expressed in a controlled, harmless form, so international athletic competition may help to abolish war between nations by providing a sphere in which chauvinistic hostilities may be harmlessly discharged.

12. Which of the following, if true, would weaken the argument in the passage?

(A) The existence of professional sports in the United States has not completely eliminated regional and ethnic conflicts.
(B) The Olympic Games themselves generate intense international rivalries and emotional responses by spectators.
(C) On several occasions, the Olympic Games have been cancelled or reduced in scope because of international conflicts or wars.
(D) Unlike professional sports, the Olympic Games are conducted on a purely amateur, not-for-profit basis.
(E) War is caused primarily by objective conflicts between nations over political and economic advantages.

Psychology originated in the attempts of researchers to describe, record, classify, and explain their own mental impressions, thoughts, and feelings and those of others as they described them verbally. It matured into a science only when the reliance on subjective impressions was gradually abandoned and researchers concentrated on human behavior. Then, psychology truly became a science of mental activity.

13. The passage makes which of the following assumptions?

I. It is not possible to observe episodes of mental activity directly.
II. Early research was unreliable because researchers gave less-than-candid accounts of their mental experiences.
III. Human behavior is an expression of mental activity.

(A) I only
(B) III only
(C) I and II only
(D) I and III only
(E) II and III only

Many people who describe themselves as authors do not belong in that category at all, since writing is not their main source of income.

14. The paragraph above makes the assumption that

(A) many of those who consider themselves authors lack the skills and training needed to write professionally
(B) the average income of professional writers is higher than that for most other professions
(C) professional authors are motivated to become writers primarily by the prospect of financial gain
(D) to be considered an author, a person must publish writings on a regular basis
(E) a person cannot be considered an author unless he or she derives most of his or her income from writing

A poll taken ten days before the election showed that 36 percent of the people surveyed planned to vote for Green and 42 percent planned to vote for his opponent. When the votes were finally tallied, Green received 52 percent of the vote, while his opponent received only 46 percent. Thus, the survey method used for the preelection poll was flawed.

15. Which of the following, if true, would most weaken the conclusion of the argument above?

(A) A poll taken 21 days before the election showed that 32 percent of the people surveyed planned to vote for Green.
(B) At the time the preelection poll was taken, many voters had not yet made up their minds about which candidate to vote for.
(C) During the week just before the election, Green's opponent received an important endorsement from a major newspaper.
(D) The voter turnout for the election in question was extremely light due to inclement weather.
(E) The preelection survey also questioned voters about their attitudes toward a referendum authorizing the legislature to legalize pari-mutuel gambling.

Some attorneys wear beards. Therefore, some bearded people favor brown tweed jackets.

16. Which of the following, if true, is sufficient to guarantee the truth of the conclusion?

   (A) Some attorneys favor brown tweed jackets.
   (B) Some of those attorneys who favor brown tweed jackets do not wear beards.
   (C) All attorneys favor brown tweed jackets.
   (D) Some attorneys do not wear beards.
   (E) All of those who favor brown tweed jackets are attorneys.

Socrates: Is it raining?
Plato: Yes.
Socrates: Is your response correct?
Plato: No.

17. Which of the following best describes Plato's responses?

   I. If his first response is true, then his second response is false.
   II. If his second response is false, then his first response is true.
   III. If his first response is false, then his second response is true.

   (A) I only   (B) III only   (C) I and II only
   (D) II and III only   (E) I, II, and III

Questions 18–19

Knowledge and study of ethical principles does not resolve in any permanent way the ethical dilemmas a person may face in his or her life. On the contrary, the more one knows about ethics, the more acutely one is aware of one's own ethical problems. A person who does not know how to count is "free" of mathematical problems; it is the person who has devoted a lifetime of study to mathematics who is most apt to wrestle with the knottiest problems of the subject. In the same way, the only type of person who is free of ethical dilemmas is one who _____18_____ .

18. Which of the following best completes the paragraph above?

   (A) is ignorant of the ethical principles that give rise to such dilemmas
   (B) has studied ethics extensively and fully mastered its intricacies
   (C) has withdrawn so completely from life as to avoid all troublesome situations
   (D) acts in every situation only in accordance with the strictest ethical principles
   (E) follows instinct and emotion rather than reason when making ethical decisions

19. In the paragraph above, the speaker makes use of which of the following?

   (A) Counterexample
   (B) Generalization
   (C) Deduction
   (D) Paradox
   (E) Analogy

One of the problems faced by government planners is the so-called NIMBY, or "Not in My Back Yard," Syndrome. For example, although poll after poll shows that the majority of citizens in this state favor the construction of new prisons, whenever plans are announced to construct a new prison somewhere in the state, residents of nearby communities protest and often succeed in blocking the project.

20. Which of the following also illustrates the NIMBY Syndrome described above?

   (A) A parent who insists that students with AIDS should not be allowed to attend public schools and withdraws his own child from school when an infected child is admitted to the public school
   (B) A politician who argues that all candidates for public office should be required to file financial disclosure forms and submits a fraudulent disclosure form
   (C) A minister who preaches that religious groups have an obligation to do charitable work but refuses to donate money to the Salvation Army
   (D) An auto dealer who favors free trade with other countries as a means to a healthy United States economy but urges the government to restrict imports of foreign-made cars
   (E) A military strategist who thinks that a nuclear war would leave no survivors but argues the United States should maintain a strong nuclear arsenal to deter other countries from war

During the past 20 years, the number of black members of state legislatures has increased by over 100 percent while the number of white members has declined slightly. This strongly suggests that the political power of blacks will soon be roughly equal to that of whites.

21. Which of the following, if true, would most weaken the argument above?

   (A) The total number of seats available in state legislatures has remained virtually constant for the last 20 years.
   (B) Twenty years ago, 168 blacks and 7,614 whites were members of state legislatures.
   (C) Fewer than five states have elected blacks as governors over the past 20 years.
   (D) During the past 20 years, median family income for both whites and blacks has risen by approximately 80 percent.
   (E) During the past 20 years, the percentage of blacks who say they are registered to vote has increased, while the percentage of whites who say they are registered to vote has decreased.

A 15-year study of more than 45,000 Swedish soldiers suggests that heavy marijuana users are six times more likely than nonusers to develop schizophrenia. The authors of the study said the statistical association between schizophrenia and marijuana, or *cannabis*, does not necessarily mean that the drug causes schizophrenia. On the contrary, the study may suggest that consumption of marijuana is caused by emerging schizophrenia.

22. Which of the following is most similar in its structure to the argument above?

    (A) The trainer explained to me that it may not be the excessive wear on the side of my sneaker that causes my ankle to ache. Instead, in response to the ache in my ankle, I may subconsciously shift the weight to the outside of my foot, which in turn would cause the sneaker to wear down.

    (B) The judge found the defendant guilty of possession of stolen property and of conspiracy to buy and sell stolen property and sentenced her to five years' imprisonment on each count, the prison terms to run concurrently.

    (C) The gardener always plants marigolds around the tomatoes. For years, we believed that this was simply to make the garden beautiful; but the gardener explained to us that the marigolds help to protect the tomatoes from nematodes, a pest which attacks the tomato plants.

    (D) The recent increase in the incidence of street crimes such as robberies is attributable to two factors: the increased use of drugs such as cocaine and heroin, and the higher unemployment rate.

    (E) To the primitive consciousness, all actions and movements were generated by spirits; for example, the tree swayed not because it was blown by the wind but because the spirit of the tree responded in harmony to the movement of the spirit of the wind.

An inventor protects his rights by obtaining a patent; and to do this, he must exhibit a working model of the invention and demonstrate that the invention is original by showing that it represents a significant departure from other similar devices. The law also protects industrial trade secrets such as the chemical formula for a soft drink, but businesses are not required to register these secrets. As a result, one business could find that it has inadvertently used the trade secret of another business and wind up on the losing end of a law suit. It would be better for all if trade secrets were registered with a Trade Secrets Office, so that a business could regularly check to determine that it was not infringing upon another business's trade secrets.

23. The main weakness of the argument above is that it

    (A) relies upon a questionable analogy
    (B) reverses a cause-and-effect connection
    (C) generalizes on the basis of a single example
    (D) contains a logical contradiction
    (E) relies upon circular reasoning

Telephone sales representative: You can take advantage of a special introductory offer. You can get 26 weekly issues of the magazine for only $52. The regular subscription price is $104 per year.

Prospective subscriber: That's not a special offer. Under either plan the cost is $2 per issue.

24. Which of the following, if true, most weakens the response of the prospective subscriber?

    (A) Normally, the minimum length of a subscription is a full year.
    (B) The magazine is available only on a subscription basis.
    (C) Recently, the price of the magazine increased from $1.75 to $2 per issue.
    (D) The year in which the exchange takes place is a leap year.
    (E) Other, similar magazines are available for $48 for a six-month subscription.

IF YOU FINISH BEFORE TIME IS CALLED, YOU MAY CHECK YOUR WORK ON THIS SECTION ONLY. DO NOT WORK ON ANY OTHER SECTION IN THE TEST. **S T O P**

578

Directions: Each passage in this group is followed by questions based on its content. After reading a passage, choose the best answer to each question and blacken the corresponding space on the answer sheet. Answer all questions following a passage on the basis of what is stated or implied in that passage.

Nothing can please many and please long but the just representation of general nature. Shakespeare is, above all writers, the poet of nature; the poet that holds up to his readers a faithful mirror of manners and life. His characters are not modified by the customs of particular places unknown to the rest of the world; by peculiarities of studies or professions known to just a few; or by the latest fashions of popular opinions: they are all genuine representations of common humanity, such as the world will always supply and observation will always find. His characters act and speak by the influence of those general passions and the principles by which all minds are agitated and the whole system of life is continued in motion. In the writings of other poets a character is too often an individual; in those of Shakespeare's it is commonly a species. It is from this wide extension of design that so much instruction is derived. It is this which fills the plays of Shakespeare with practical axioms and domestic wisdom. It was said of Euripides that every verse was a precept; and it may be said of Shakespeare that from his works may be collected a system of civil and economical prudence. Yet his real power is not shown in the splendor of particular passages, but by the progress of his fable and the tenor of his dialogue; and he that tries to recommend him by select quotations will succeed like the pedant in Hierocles who, when he offered his house for sale, carried a brick in his pocket as a specimen.

Other dramatists can gain attention only by hyperbolical or aggravated characters, by their fabulous and unexampled excellence or depravity, as the writers of barbarous romances invigorated the reader by the giant or the dwarf; and who should form his expectations of human affairs from the play or from the tale would be equally deceived. Shakespeare has no such heroes; his scenes are occupied only by men who act and speak as the reader thinks that he should himself have spoken or acted on the same occasion. His adherence to general nature may have exposed him to the censure of critics who form their judgments on narrower principles; Voltaire thinks that his kings are not royal enough. But Shakespeare always makes nature predominate over accident. This, therefore, is the praise of Shakespeare, that his drama is the mirror of life. The reader who has amazed his imagination in following the phantoms which other writers raise up before him may, by reading Shakespeare, be cured of these delirious ecstasies by reading human sentiments in human language; by scenes from which a hermit may estimate the transactions of the world, and a confessor predict the progress of passions.

1. The author is primarily concerned with

   (A) explaining dramatic conventions
   (B) contrasting the works of two great writers
   (C) defending the work of one writer
   (D) disparaging the writing of one author
   (E) extolling nature as the perfect model for art

2. According to the author, which of the following is true of Shakespeare's characters?

   (A) They are all members of the nobility.
   (B) They are larger than life.
   (C) They are exotic and unfamiliar to the audience.
   (D) They do not exhibit emotion.
   (E) They are typical human beings.

3. The author develops his theme primarily by

   (A) presenting comparison and contrast
   (B) mentioning specific characters and analyzing them
   (C) quoting from other critics
   (D) attacking popular opinion
   (E) raising a point and then refuting it

4. The author cites Voltaire because he is

   (A) a friend of Shakespeare
   (B) a teacher of Shakespeare
   (C) an admirer of Shakespeare
   (D) a critic of Shakespeare
   (E) a Shakespearean actor

5. The author uses the examples of hermit and confessor in the final sentence in order to

   (A) emphasize that Shakespeare's plays are so true to life that one could learn about real people by reading them
   (B) prove that Shakespeare's work was condemned by some critics for failing to include heroic characters
   (C) call attention to the religious and mystical elements in Shakespeare's plays
   (D) show that interesting characters such as hermits and confessors appear infrequently in Shakespeare's plays
   (E) give examples of the hyperbolical and exaggerated characters he mentions as being typical of the work of other authors

GO ON TO THE NEXT PAGE

6. Which of the following best describes the analogy the author wishes to draw by introducing the pedant of Hierocles?

(A) Shakespeare is to Hierocles as one of Shakespeare's plays is to the pedant
(B) Shakespeare is to Hierocles as one of Shakespeare's characters is to the pedant
(C) Shakespeare is to the pedant as Hierocles is to the brick
(D) Shakespeare's plays are to Hierocles's writings as Shakespeare's characters are to the pedant
(E) Lines from Shakespeare's plays are to the plays as the pedant's brick is to his house

Public general hospitals originated in the almshouse infirmaries established as early as colonial times by local governments to care for the poor. Later, in the late eighteenth and early nineteenth centuries, the infirmary separated from the almshouse and became an independent institution supported by local tax money. At the same time, private charity hospitals began to develop. Both private and public hospitals provided mainly food and shelter for the impoverished sick, since there was little that medicine could actually do to cure illness, and the middle class was treated at home by private physicians.

Late in the nineteenth century, the private charity hospital began trying to attract middle-class patients. Although the depression of 1890 stimulated the growth of charitable institutions and an expanding urban population became dependent on assistance, there was a decline in private contributions to these organizations which forced them to look to local government for financial support. Since private institutions had also lost benefactors, they began to charge patients. In order to attract middle-class patients, private institutions provided services and amenities that distinguished between paying and nonpaying patients and made the hospital a desirable place for private physicians to treat their own patients. As paying patients became more necessary to the survival of the private hospital, the public hospitals slowly became the only place for the poor to get treatment. By the end of the nineteenth century, cities were reimbursing private hospitals for their care of indigent patients and the public hospitals remained dependent on the tax dollars.

The advent of private hospital health insurance, which provided middle-class patients with the purchasing power to pay for private hospital services, guaranteed the private hospital a regular source of income. Private hospitals restricted themselves to revenue-generating patients, leaving the public hospitals to care for the poor. Although public hospitals continued to provide services for patients with communicable diseases and outpatient and emergency services, the Blue Cross plans developed around the needs of the private hospitals and the inpatients they served. Thus, reimbursement for ambulatory care has been minimal under most Blue Cross plans, and provision of outpatient care has not been a major function of the private hospital, in part because private patients can afford to pay for the services of private physicians. Additionally, since World War II, there has been a tremendous influx of federal money into private medical schools and the hospitals associated with them. Further, large private medical centers with expensive research equipment and programs have attracted the best administrators, physicians, and researchers. As a result of the greater resources available to the private medical centers, public hospitals have increasing problems attracting highly qualified research and medical personnel. With the mainstream of health care firmly established in the private medical sector, the public hospital has become a "dumping ground."

7. According to the passage, the very first private hospitals

(A) developed from almshouse infirmaries
(B) provided better care than public infirmaries
(C) were established mainly to service the poor
(D) were supported by government revenues
(E) catered primarily to the middle-class patients

8. It can be inferred that the author believes the differences that currently exist between public and private hospitals are primarily the result of

(A) political considerations
(B) economic factors
(C) ethical concerns
(D) legislative requirements
(E) technological developments

9. It can be inferred that the growth of private health insurance

(A) relieved local governments of the need to fund public hospitals
(B) guaranteed that the poor would have access to medical care
(C) forced middle-class patients to use public hospitals
(D) prompted the closing of many charitable institutions
(E) reinforced the distinction between public and private hospitals

10. Which of the following would be the most logical topic for the author to introduce in the next paragraph?

(A) A plan to improve the quality of public hospitals
(B) An analysis of the profit structure of health insurance companies
(C) A proposal to raise taxes on the middle class
(D) A discussion of recent developments in medical technology
(E) A list of the subjects studied by students in medical school

GO ON TO THE NEXT PAGE

11. The author's primary concern is to

(A) describe the financial structure of the health-care industry
(B) demonstrate the importance of government support for health-care institutions
(C) criticize wealthy institutions for refusing to provide services to the poor
(D) identify the historical causes of the division between private and public hospitals
(E) praise public hospitals for their willingness to provide health care for the poor

12. The author cites all of the following as factors contributing to the decline of public hospitals EXCEPT

(A) Government money was used to subsidize private medical schools and hospitals to the detriment of public hospitals.
(B) Public hospitals are not able to compete with private institutions for top-flight managers and doctors.
(C) Large private medical centers have better research facilities and more extensive research programs than public hospitals.
(D) Public hospitals accepted the responsibility for treating patients with certain diseases.
(E) Blue Cross insurance coverage does not re-imburse subscribers for medical expenses incurred in a public hospital.

13. The author's attitude toward public hospitals can best be described as

(A) contemptuous and prejudiced
(B) apprehensive and distrustful
(C) concerned and understanding
(D) enthusiastic and supportive
(E) unsympathetic and annoyed

14. The author implies that any outpatient care provided by a hospital is

(A) paid for by private insurance
(B) provided in lieu of treatment by a private physician
(C) supplied primarily by private hospitals
(D) a source of revenue for public hospitals
(E) no longer provided by hospitals, public or private

The National Security Act of 1947 created a national military establishment headed by a single Secretary of Defense. The legislation had been a year-and-a-half in the making—beginning when President Truman first recommended that the armed services be reorganized into a single department. During that period the President's concept of a unified armed service was torn apart and put back together several times, the final measure to emerge from Congress being a compromise. Most of the opposition to the bill came from the Navy and its numerous civilian spokesmen, including Secretary of the Navy James Forrestal. In support of unification (and a separate air force that was part of the unification package)

were the Army air forces, the Army, and, most importantly, the President of the United States.

Passage of the bill did not bring an end to the bitter interservice disputes. Rather than unify, the act served only to federate the military services. It neither halted the rapid demobilization of the armed forces that followed World War II nor brought to the new national military establishment the loyalties of officers steeped in the traditions of the separate services. At a time when the balance of power in Europe and Asia was rapidly shifting, the services lacked any precise statement of United States foreign policy from the National Security Council on which to base future programs. The services bickered unceasingly over their respective roles and missions, already complicated by the Soviet nuclear capability that for the first time made the United States subject to devastating attack. Not even the appointment of Forrestal as First Secretary of Defense allayed the suspicions of naval officers and their supporters that the role of the U.S. Navy was threatened with permanent eclipse. Before the war of words died down, Forrestal himself was driven to resignation and then suicide.

By 1948, the United States military establishment was forced to make do with a budget approximately 10 percent of what it had been at its wartime peak. Meanwhile, the cost of weapons procurement was rising geometrically as the nation came to put more and more reliance on the atomic bomb and its delivery systems. These two factors inevitably made adversaries of the Navy and the Air Force as the battle between advocates of the B−36 and the supercarrier so amply demonstrates. Given severe fiscal restraints on the one hand, and on the other the nation's increasing reliance on strategic nuclear deterrence, the conflict between these two services over roles and missions was essentially a contest over slices of an ever-diminishing pie.

Yet if in the end neither service was the obvious victor, the principle of civilian dominance over the military clearly was. If there had ever been any danger that the United States military establishment might exploit, to the detriment of civilian control, the good-will it enjoyed as a result of its victories in World War II, that danger disappeared in the interservice animosities engendered by the battle over unification.

15. According to the passage, the interservice strife that followed unification occurred primarily between the

(A) Army and Army Air Forces
(B) Army and Navy
(C) Army Air Forces and Navy
(D) Navy and Army
(E) Air Force and Navy

GO ON TO THE NEXT PAGE

16. It can be inferred from the passage that For-restal's appointment as Secretary of Defense was expected to

(A) placate members of the Navy
(B) result in decreased levels of defense spending
(C) outrage advocates of the Army Air Forces
(D) win Congressional approval of the unification plan
(E) make Forrestal a Presidential candidate against Truman

17. According to the passage, President Truman sup-ported which of the following?
   I. Elimination of the Navy
   II. A unified military service
   III. Establishment of a separate air force

(A) I only   (B) II only   (C) I and II only
(D) II and III only   (E) I, II, and III

18. With which of the following statements about defense unification would the author most likely agree?

(A) Unification ultimately undermined United States military capability by inciting interser-vice rivalry.
(B) The unification legislation was necessitated by the drastic decline in appropriations for the military services.
(C) Although the unification was not entirely successful, it had the unexpected result of ensuring civilian control of the military.
(D) In spite of the attempted unification, each service was still able to pursue its own objec-tives without interference from the other branches.
(E) Unification was in the first place unwarranted and in the second place ineffective

19. According to the selection, the political situation following the passage of the National Security Act of 1947 was characterized by all of the following EXCEPT

(A) a shifting balance of power in Europe and in Asia
(B) fierce interservice rivalries
(C) lack of strong leadership by the National Security Council
(D) shrinking postwar military budgets
(E) a lame-duck President who was unable to unify the legislature

20. The author cites the resignation and suicide of Forrestal in order to

(A) underscore the bitterness of the interservice rivalry surrounding the passage of the Na-tional Security Act of 1947
(B) demonstrate that the Navy eventually emerged as the dominant branch of service after the passage of the National Security Act of 1947
(C) suggest that the nation would be better served by a unified armed service under a single command
(D) provide an example of a military leader who preferred to serve his country in war rather than in peace
(E) persuade the reader that Forrestal was a victim of political opportunists and an un-scrupulous press

21. The author is primarily concerned with

(A) discussing the influence of personalities on political events
(B) describing the administration of a powerful leader
(C) criticizing a piece of legislation
(D) analyzing a political development
(E) suggesting methods for controlling the military

The theory of stellar evolution predicts that when the core of a star has used up its nuclear fuel, the core will collapse. If the star is about the size of the Sun, it will turn into a degenerate dwarf star. If it is somewhat larger, it may undergo a supernova explosion that leaves behind a neutron star. But if the stellar core has a mass greater than about three solar masses, gravitational forces overwhelm nuclear forces and the core collapses. Since nuclear forces are the strongest repulsive forces known, nothing can stop the continued collapse of the star. A black hole in space is formed.

Because of the intense gravitational forces near the black hole, nothing can escape from it, not even light. If we were to send a probe toward an isolated black hole, the probe would detect no radiation from the black hole. It would, however, sense a gravitational field like the one that would be produced by a normal star of the same mass. As the probe approached the black hole, the gravitational forces would increase inexorably. At a distance of a few thousand kilometers, the gravitational forces would be so great that the side of the probe closest to the black hole would literally be torn away from the side furthest away from the black hole. Eventually, at a distance of a few kilometers from the black hole, the particles that made up the probe would pass the point of no return, and the particles would be lost forever down the black hole. This point of no return is called the gravitational radius of the black hole.

But how can we hope to observe such an object? Nature, herself, could conceivably provide us with a "probe" of a black hole: a binary star system in which one of the stars has become a black hole and is absorbing the mass of its companion star. As the matter of the companion star fell into the black hole, it would accelerate. This increased energy of motion would be changed into heat energy. Near the gravitational radius the matter would move at speeds close to the speed of light, and temperatures would range from tens of millions of degrees to perhaps as much as a billion degrees. At these temperatures, X and gamma radiation are produced. Further, since the matter near the gravitational radius would be orbiting the black hole about once every millisecond, the X-radiation should show erratic, short-term variability unlike the regular or periodic variability associated with neutron stars and degenerate dwarfs.

The X-ray source Cygnus X−1 fulfills these "experimental" conditions. It is part of a binary star system in which a blue supergiant star is orbiting an invisible companion star. This invisible companion has a mass greater than about nine times the mass of the Sun, and it is a strong X-ray source that shows rapid variations in the intensity of its X-ray flux. Most astronomers believe that Cygnus X−1 is a black hole; but this belief is tempered with a dose of caution. The idea of a black hole is still difficult to swallow, but theorists can think of no other object that could explain the phenomenon of Cygnus X−1. For this reason, in most scientific papers, Cygnus X−1 is referred to simply as a black hole "candidate."

22. Which of the following best describes the logical structure of the passage?

(A) The author presents a theory and then describes the kind of evidence that would support the theory.
(B) The author outlines a widely accepted theory and then introduces evidence to refute it.
(C) The author describes a phenomenon and then formulates a theory to explain it.
(D) The author introduces statistical studies to support a theory that is highly speculative.
(E) The author describes the result of an experiment that he conducted to prove a theory.

23. According to the passage, a black hole would

(A) be most likely to develop in a binary star system
(B) emit large quantities of X and gamma rays
(C) be observable through a powerful telescope
(D) be formed from a degenerate dwarf star
(E) be invisible even at close range

24. It can be inferred from the passage that a neutron star originated as a

(A) degenerate dwarf star of any size
(B) normal star with a mass less than one-third that of our sun
(C) normal star with a mass greater than that of our sun but less than three times that of our sun
(D) normal star with a mass at least three times greater than that of our sun
(E) supernova with a mass at least three times greater than that of our sun

25. It can be inferred that a black hole has

(A) no mass at all
(B) a mass only one-third of the mass of the normal star from which it was formed
(C) approximately the same mass as the normal star from which it was formed
(D) a mass approximately equal to the mass of two binary stars
(E) a mass equal to the mass of our sun

26. The author regards the existence of black holes as

(A) in principle unprovable
(B) theoretically possible
(C) extremely unlikely
(D) experimentally confirmed
(E) a logical contradiction

27. All of the following are mentioned by the author as evidence to suggest that the Cygnus X−1 source might be a black hole EXCEPT

(A) Cygnus X−1 is a source of powerful X-ray radiation.
(B) The companion star of Cygnus X−1 has a mass sufficiently large to create a black hole.
(C) The intensity of the X-rays emanating from Cygnus X−1 exhibits short-term variability.
(D) The star around which the visible star of Cygnus X−1 is orbiting is not itself visible.
(E) The visible star of the Cygnus X−1 system is a blue supergiant.

28. According to the passage, the gravitational radius of a black hole is the

(A) orbital distance separating a visible star from a black hole in a binary star system
(B) distance at which matter is irreversibly drawn into the black hole by gravitational forces
(C) distance from the black hole at which an approaching rocket would first start to disintegrate
(D) radius of the massive star that created the black hole when it collapsed in upon itself
(E) scale for measuring the short-term variability of X-radiation emitted by a black hole

Directions: The questions in this section require you to follow or evaluate the reasoning contained in brief statements or passages. In some questions, each of the choices is a conceivable solution to the particular problem posed. However, you are to select the one that answers the question best, that is, the one that does not require you to make what are by common-sense standards implausible, superfluous, or incompatible assumptions. After you have chosen the best answer, blacken the corresponding space on the answer sheet.

There is a tendency in intelligence-gathering communities for the members of each lower level of bureaucracy to filter information before it is passed to the next higher level. Thus, the information is colored so that it meets the expectation of a superior. A good example of this tendency is the Gulf of Tonkin incident. Although the Destroyer Maddox transmitted a second message recanting the first and requesting time for reevaluation of data, the second message was blocked by the bureaucracy. Intermediate bureau chiefs failed to relay the information to the President because they knew he _____.

1. Which of the following best completes the paragraph above?

   (A) was already aware of the content of the second message
   (B) had already made his decision on the basis of the first messagge
   (C) would have been displeased by the carelessness of the crew in sending the first message
   (D) was not interested in the content of the first message
   (E) was pleased with the content of the first message

PETER: Seventy percent of the people we surveyed stated that they would use Myrdal for relief of occasional headache pain, while only 30 percent of those surveyed indicated that they would take Burphin for such pain.

RON: Then over twice as many people preferred Myrdal to Burphin.

PETER: No, 25 percent of those surveyed stated that they never took any such medication.

2. Which of the following, if true, best explains the reason for the seeming inconsistency in Peter's claim?

   (A) The survey included more than 1,000 people.
   (B) Fifty percent of the people surveyed mentioned neither Myrdal nor Burphin.
   (C) Some of the people surveyed indicated that they would take both medications.
   (D) None of the people who said they would take Myrdal indicated that they would also take Burphin.
   (E) All of the people who said that they would take Myrdal also responded that they would take Burphin.

Some legislators have proposed raising the gasoline tax to help reduce the Federal budget deficit. The Federal gasoline tax is already nine cents per gallon. In addition, states tax gasoline at an average of more than 15 cents per gallon. In fact, the gasoline tax rates are as high as the so-called "sin" taxes on alcohol and tobacco. Gasoline, however, is not a "sinful" commodity. It is practically a necessity, and any increase in the gasoline tax would be unfair.

3. The speaker above is arguing primarily

   (A) for the repeal of the gasoline tax
   (B) for a reduction in the gasoline tax rate
   (C) against an increase in the gasoline tax rate
   (D) against taxes on alcohol and tobacco
   (E) against the sale of alcohol and tobacco

GO ON TO THE NEXT PAGE

As part of a Federal package to aid beleaguered savings and loan institutions, Congress has proposed prohibiting these institutions from investing in high-yield junk bonds. Thrifts would be barred from investing in companies that fail to earn a "higher bond-rating," that is, a triple-B rating or higher. This will put savings and loans on a more conservative and more secure footing. Additionally, Congress has seized the opportunity to help redress some of the inequalities of the American economy by requiring savings and loans to direct more investment toward minority groups, women, and inner-city areas.

4. Which of the following, if true, would be the best criticism of the proposal discussed above?

   (A) Many savings and loan institutions failed when Latin American countries defaulted on their obligations.
   (B) Savings and loan institutions are a major source of investment in the American economy.
   (C) Savings and loans institutions are geographically diversified and serve localized areas.
   (D) No business owned largely by blacks, Hispanics, or women qualifies for the higher bond ratings.
   (E) Adjustable rate mortgages commonly offered by savings and loans are considered risky loans.

The death penalty is not really effective in protecting society. In 1972, the death sentences of 558 murderers were automatically commuted to prison terms by a Supreme Court decision. Since then, four of those inmates have committed murders in prison, and another committed a murder after his release. It is foolish to kill over 550 people just to save the lives of 5 people.

5. The argument above assumes that

   (A) some of the death row inmates were improperly convicted
   (B) the Supreme Court should not have commuted the death sentences
   (C) the life of a convicted murderer is as valuable as that of a victim
   (D) more murders take place inside of prison walls than outside of them
   (E) few people would object to the death penalty if it protected them

Four students are competing in the final round of a debating match:
If Alan scores more points than Beth or if Cathy scores more points than David, then Cathy will be the winner.
If David scores more points than Alan, then Beth will be the winner.
If Cathy scores more points then Beth, then Alan will be the winner.

6. If David is the winner, then which of the following statements must be true?

   I. David scored more points than Cathy.
   II. Neither Cathy nor Alan scored more points than Beth.
   III. David did not score more points than Alan.

   (A) III only
   (B) I and II only
   (C) I and III only
   (D) II and III only
   (E) I, II, and III

I had planned to vote for Smith in the upcoming election for the Senate, but I have changed my mind. The *Morning News* endorsed Smith, and I disagree with the *Morning News* on just about every issue.

7. Which of the following, if true, would weaken the argument above?

   (A) Smith did not solicit the endorsement.
   (B) Many political leaders have endorsed Smith.
   (C) Smith is the incumbent in the race.
   (D) Smith's main opponent has no previous political experience.
   (E) No other newspaper has yet endorsed Smith.

The rusty crayfish outcompetes blue and fantail crayfish. Consequently, it has become the top feeder on plants. It also eats fish eggs and the plants that form the habitat of fish that prey on crayfish. This limits the habitat of fish. In lakes with rusty crayfish, muddy bottoms with layers of muck and many plants have now given way to clean, sandy bottoms with few plants.

8. The speaker above is primarily concerned with

   (A) outlining a causal chain
   (B) advancing a new proposal
   (C) speculating about the future
   (D) attacking a government policy
   (E) defending a generalization

Mary Cassatt, like Edgar Degas, was impressed by the exhibition of Japanese *ukiyo-e* prints at the Ecole des Beaux-Arts in Paris during the spring of 1890. By April of 1891, she had finished a set of prints of her own depicting scenes of domestic life. These describe moments such as a woman washing her little boy or a woman mailing a letter. The women depicted all seem emotionally removed from the scene and introspective. Cassatt eschewed the more traditional poses in favor of a casual representation—a technique used also by Degas. Consequently, even the most sweetly colored of the works do not appear in the least saccharine or sentimental.

9. The paragraph above implies that

   (A) Degas and Cassatt collaborated on the prints
   (B) the prints were produced in a great hurry
   (C) Cassatt rarely depicted everyday life
   (D) more formal poses might have made the works sentimental
   (E) the *ukiyo-e* prints treated official or formal moments

One of the most effective ways to reduce street sales of crack is interdiction of supplies at the border. Interdiction raises the price of crack by increasing the cost of smuggling, and higher cost decreases demand.

10. Which of the following, if true, most weakens the argument above?

    (A) Arrests of street-level dealers and users have created a problem of state and Federal prison overcrowding.
    (B) Smuggling costs account for only 1 percent of the street price of crack.
    (C) Drugs are grown, processed, and transported in countries where bribery of government officials is common.
    (D) A successful interdiction effort requires a nationally coordinated Federal effort.
    (E) Increased use of crack has lead to an increase in supply, which in turn lowers the cost of crack.

Every business executive carries a briefcase, and these briefcases are invariably brown or black.

11. Which of the following conclusions most reliably follows from the statement above?

    (A) All briefcases are either brown or black.
    (B) Some business executives carry briefcases that are neither brown nor black.
    (C) Some people carry brown briefcases, and some people carry black briefcases.
    (D) All brown and black briefcases are carried by business executives.
    (E) All briefcases are carried by business executives.

All statements about truth are inherently subjective and therefore purely a matter of individual opinion. Such statements carry no moral authority for any but the individual who makes them.

12. A logical weakness in the claim above is that it

    (A) is internally inconsistent
    (B) is a hasty generalization
    (C) mistakes a cause for an effect
    (D) relies upon an unproved assumption
    (E) assumes what it hopes to prove

One man can dig a posthole in four minutes; therefore, four men can dig a posthole in one minute.

13. The argument above is weak because it

    (A) makes a questionable assumption
    (B) is internally inconsistent
    (C) relies on questionable authority
    (D) uses its conclusion as one of its premises
    (E) confuses an effect with its cause

The President has done a remarkable job of holding the line on military expenditures. Last year, defense expenditures in constant dollars were just about what they were in 1970.

14. Which of the following statements, if true, represents the most serious criticism of the claim above?

    (A) The President promised during the election campaign that the defense budget would be carefully scrutinized for waste.
    (B) In 1970, the United States was devoting extraordinary military resources to fighting a war in Southeast Asia.
    (C) Since 1970, the average salary increase for personnel in the military has paralleled the rise in the cost-of-living index.
    (D) Several proposals for complex weapons systems have been delayed for one year or more in order to hold the line on defense expenditures.
    (E) When measured as a proportion of Gross National Product, military expenditures by other Western nations have declined since 1970.

Guns don't kill people—people do! If a gun is not available, a person intent on doing someone else bodily harm will turn to the next-best available weapon, a knife. So banning guns will not help prevent homicides.

15. The argument above assumes that

    (A) people who are violent are likely to commit several crimes
    (B) knives are used more frequently in crimes than guns
    (C) guns are more widely available than other weapons
    (D) knives are equally as deadly as guns
    (E) dangerous knives should be banned

If Alice told Bob about the surprise party, then Bob told Carl about the surprise party. And if Carl knew about the party, then Danielle knew about it. But Danielle did not know about the surprise party.

16. Which of the following statements can be deduced from the information given above?

    I. Alice did not tell Carl about the party.
    II. Alice did not tell Bob about the party.
    III. Carl did not know about the party.

    (A) I only   (B) II only   (C) I and II only
    (D) I and III only   (E) I, II, and III

GO ON TO THE NEXT PAGE

Patty: Administration officials know the identity of the students who painted grafitti on campus buildings during the recent demonstrations. Those students should be expelled from school. This will discourage other students from doing the same thing in the future.

Randy: But if those students are expelled, students in the future might be tempted to do worse damage because they know they will be expelled anyway.

17. The speakers above both agree that

(A) expulsion from school is a severe penalty
(B) no future demonstrations will cause vandalism
(C) the administration should deal more harshly with vandals
(D) students are justified in using vandalism as a protest tool
(E) some students will commit criminal acts despite sanctions

When I need to get a letter to a business associate as fast as possible, I use an overnight express service no matter what the cost. Otherwise, I use the postal service, because it is cheaper.

18. The speaker's remark assumes that

(A) the postal service is generally less efficient than overnight express services
(B) an overnight express service is less expensive than the postal service
(C) cost and delivery time are the two most important factors to consider
(D) cost is a more important consideration for important packages than delivery time
(E) the postal service is sometimes able to deliver sooner than an overnight express service

In 1983, 75 percent of the employees in the garment center were resident aliens. In 1989, only 60 percent were resident aliens.

19. If the statements above are true, all of the following could be true about the 1983-to-1989 period EXCEPT:

(A) The number of people employed in the garment center increased.
(B) The total resident alien population of the country increased.
(C) The number of resident aliens employed in the garment center increased while the total number of persons employed declined.
(D) The number of firms in the garment center declined while the total number of persons employed there increased.
(E) The value of imported garments increased while the total value of production by the garment center also increased.

You can fool all of the people some of the time, and some of the people all of the time.

20. Which of the following conclusions can be logically deduced from the statement above?

(A) No one can be fooled all of the time.
(B) Everyone can be fooled most of the time.
(C) Someone can be fooled all of the time.
(D) All of the time no one can be fooled.
(E) At no time can anyone be fooled.

I know that when my children grow up they will become lawyers, because my parents, my wife, and I are all lawyers.

21. The argument above can be best criticized because it

(A) fails to define the term *lawyer*
(B) oversimplifies a causal connection
(C) does not rely upon statistics
(D) uses an ambiguous term
(E) uses circular reasoning

My favorite color is red, and I don't like the color green. My wife's favorite color is green, and she doesn't like the color red. Is what she sees as red what I experience when I see green, thus accounting for the difference in our preferences? Or do we both see red and green alike, but have different reactions to the two stimuli? It is impossible to justify one explanation over the other, for there is no possibility of verifying one answer or the other.

22. The speaker above assumes that

  I. some experiences are entirely subjective
 II. everyone has a favorite color
III. no one can like both red and green

(A) I only (B) II only (C) III only
(D) I and III only (E) I, II, and III

Kevin: I think that Martha is an excellent parent. She is a full-time professional and offers a wonderful role-model for her children. Additionally, she earns a very nice living and is able to provide her children with a nice home and virtually every educational advantage possible.

Mark: I don't think Martha is a good parent. Counting commuting time, she spends over ten hours a day away from home and sometimes must travel out of town overnight. If she worked fewer hours and closer to home, she could be more of a mother.

23. The two speakers above disagree primarily about

(A) how much time Martha spends with her children
(B) what Martha's children think of her
(C) whether Martha is happy in her career
(D) how to define a good parent
(E) whether a working mother can be a good parent

A survey of 1,000 college students were asked about a non-existent campus agency. Six percent of those surveyed said they thought the agency was doing an excellent job.

24. Which of the following can be most reliably inferred from the information above?

    (A) Six percent of those surveyed deliberately lied to the questioners.
    (B) Sixty college students are unaware that the agency asked about did not exist.
    (C) Almost all of those surveyed knew that the agency asked about did not exist.
    (D) A survey of the sort mentioned is likely to contain an error in measurement.
    (E) Ninety-four percent of those surveyed responded that they had never heard of the agency.

Steve: Since the beginning of the massive emergency relief effort, planes have flown 300 blankets and 200 pounds of food to the beleaguered country.

Lorraine: You call a few blankets and some food a massive relief effort? That's not even a full plane load of cargo.

25. Which of the following, if true, would most weaken Lorraine's objection to Steve's statement?

    (A) Three planes were used to ferry the cargo to the country in question.
    (B) The country receiving the aid was hit by a devastating earthquake.
    (C) International relief agencies have tons of relief cargo ready for shipment as soon as planes are available.
    (D) The country receiving the aid also needs medical supplies.
    (E) The aid already delivered has already been distributed to those who need it.

IF YOU FINISH BEFORE TIME IS CALLED, YOU MAY CHECK YOUR WORK ON THIS SECTION ONLY. DO NOT WORK ON ANY OTHER SECTION IN THE TEST. **S T O P**

SECTION **5**   Time—35 Minutes
24 Questions

In this section solve each problem, using any available space on the page for scratchwork. Then decide which is the best of the choices given and fill in the corresponding oval on the answer sheet.

Directions: Each question or group of questions is based on a passage or set of conditions. In answering some of the questions, it may be useful to draw a rough diagram. For each question, select the best answer choice given.

Questions 1–6

Twelve people waiting for sales assistance in a store have each taken a slip with a number on it. The slips are numbered 1 through 12, and each person has a different number.

The people with numbers 2, 4, 6, 9, and 11 are the only ones wearing hats.

The people with numbers 1, 3, 6, 8, 10, and 12 are the only ones wearing gloves.

The people with numbers 3, 6, 9, and 12 are the only ones wearing raincoats.

The people with numbers 4, 8, and 12 are the only ones wearing scarves.

1. The person wearing a hat and a raincoat but no gloves or scarf is holding what number?

   (A) 2   (B) 4   (C) 6   (D) 9   (E) 11

2. Which of the following is true?

   (A) Exactly one person is wearing gloves but no hat, scarf, or raincoat.
   (B) Exactly two people are wearing gloves but no hat.
   (C) Exactly one person is wearing both a hat and a scarf.
   (D) Exactly two persons are wearing both gloves and a hat.
   (E) Exactly three people are wearing both hats and raincoats.

3. The person with number 9 is wearing

   (A) a hat and gloves but no raincoat or scarf
   (B) a hat and raincoat but no gloves or scarf
   (C) a hat and scarf but no gloves or raincoat
   (D) a raincoat and gloves but no hat or scarf
   (E) a raincoat and scarf but no hat or gloves

4. How many people are wearing both gloves and a raincoat?

   (A) 0   (B) 1   (C) 2   (D) 3   (E) 4

5. A person wearing neither a hat nor gloves could be holding number

   I. 5
   II. 7
   III. 10

   (A) I only   (B) II only   (C) I and II only
   (D) I and III only   (E) I, II, and III

6. If a person is wearing neither gloves nor a raincoat, then which of the following would be sufficient to establish what number that person is holding?

   (A) The person is wearing a hat.
   (B) The person is wearing a scarf.
   (C) The person is not wearing a hat.
   (D) The person is not wearing a scarf.
   (E) The person is wearing a hat but not a scarf.

Questions 7–12

Seven colleges, *J, K, L, M, N, O,* and *P,* are all located in the same city. Under a cooperative program, students are allowed to cross-register for courses offered at other colleges. All students are permitted to take courses at *K.* In addition, the following opportunities for cross-registration are offered:

Students at *J* can take courses at *L.*
Students at *L* can take courses at *M* and *O.*
Students at *M* can take courses at *L, N, O,* and *P.*
Students at *O* can take courses at *P.*

7. A class given at *P* could contain, at most, students from how many different colleges other than *P*?

   (A) 0   (B) 1   (C) 2   (D) 3   (E) 4

8. A class given at *O* could include students from which of the following colleges?

   I. L
   II. M
   III. N

   (A) I only   (B) II only   (C) I and II only
   (D) I and III only   (E) I, II, and III

GO ON TO THE NEXT PAGE

9. How many of the colleges accept visiting students from a school at which its own students are not allowed to cross-register?

(A) 1   (B) 2   (C) 3   (D) 4   (E) 5

10. Which of the following pairs of students could register for the same class at one of their colleges?

(A) *L* and *P*   (B) *L* and *N*   (C) *M* and *J*
(D) *N* and *O*   (E) *O* and *L*

11. How many colleges both accept visiting students from another college and allow their students to cross-register for courses at that college?

(A) 0   (B) 1   (C) 2   (D) 3   (E) 4

12. Which of the following could be true?

(A) Students from *J* and *L* are registered for a class offered at *J*.
(B) Students from *K* and *L* are registered for a class offered at *L*.
(C) Students from *L* and *M* are registered for a class offered at *P*.
(D) Students from *M* and *O* are registered for a class offered at *P*.
(E) Students from *N* and *P* are registered for a class offered at *J*.

Questions 13–18

A wine importer is arranging two wine tastings, one for Monday and one for Wednesday. Each tasting will include exactly three wines, and no wine will be sampled on both days. The importer is considering two wines from France, *G* and *M*, three wines from Spain, *F*, *H*, and *J*, and three wines from Italy, *I*, *K*, and *L*.

The red wines, *G*, *I*, *H*, and *J*, were bottled in 1984, 1985, 1986, and 1987, respectively.

The white wines, *K*, *L*, *F*, and *M*, were bottled in 1984, 1985, 1986, and 1987, respectively.

Monday's tasting must include at least two red wines; Wednesday's tasting must included at least two white wines.

Both tastings must include at least one wine from each of the three countries.

13. Which of the following groups of wines could be tested on Monday?

(A) *F, G, H*   (B) *G, H, I*   (C) *H, K, J*
(D) *J, K, M*   (E) *G, M, J*

14. If *M* is included in Monday's tasting, then which of the following must be true?

(A) The oldest red wine tasted on Monday is *I*.
(B) The oldest red wine tasted on Monday is *H*.
(C) The oldest white wine tasted on Wednesday is *K*.
(D) The oldest white wine tasted on Wednesday is *L*.
(E) The youngest red wine tasted on Monday is *J*.

15. If *F* is the oldest white wine tasted on Wednesday, then which of the following must be true?

(A) *H* is tasted on Monday.
(B) *I* is tasted on Wednesday.
(C) *J* is tasted on Monday.
(D) *K* is tasted on Wednesday.
(E) *L* is tasted on Wednesday.

16. Which of the following CANNOT be true?

(A) *F* is the youngest wine tasted on Monday.
(B) *H* is the youngest wine tasted on Monday.
(C) *L* is the youngest wine tasted on Wednesday.
(D) *L* is the oldest wine tasted on Wednesday.
(E) *I* is the oldest wine tasted on Wednesday.

17. If *F* is not included in either tasting, then which of the following must be included in one tasting or the other?

I. *H*
II. *J*
III. *M*
(A) I only   (B) III only   (C) I and III only
(D) II and III only   (E) I, II, and III

18. If *I* is the oldest red wine tasted on Monday, then all of the following must be true EXCEPT

(A) *F* is tasted on Wednesday.
(B) *G* is tasted on Wednesday.
(C) *M* is tasted on Monday.
(D) *F* is the youngest wine in its tasting.
(E) *K* is included in a tasting with either *J* or *H*.

Questions 19–24

Nine people—P, Q, R, S, T, U, V, W, and X—are to be seated at three tables with three different colored table cloths—red, blue, and green. Exactly three of the people will be seated at each table.

W and V must sit at the same table.
X and T must sit at the same table.
R and U cannot sit at the same table.
Either R or S must sit at the same table as Q.
S must sit at the green table.

19. Which of the following people could sit at the same table?

(A) P, R, S
(B) P, U, V
(C) S, W, X
(D) T, X, R
(E) U, X, R

20. Which of the following CANNOT be true?

(A) Q sits at the red table.
(B) U sits at the red table.
(C) X sits at the green table.
(D) P sits at the red table, and W sits at the blue table.
(E) R sits at the red table, and Q sits at the blue table.

590

21. All of the following groups of persons could sit at the blue table EXCEPT

   (A) P, Q, R
   (B) P, R, X
   (C) R, T, X
   (D) R, V, W
   (E) U, V, W

22. All of the following could sit at the same table as W EXCEPT

   (A) P
   (B) R
   (C) S
   (D) U
   (E) X

23. If R and W sit at the blue table, then which of the following must sit at the green table?

   (A) P
   (B) Q
   (C) U
   (D) V
   (E) X

24. If S and T sit at the same table, and if Q sits at the red table, which of the following must sit at the blue table?

   (A) R, V
   (B) R, X
   (C) U, X
   (D) P, V, W
   (E) U, V, W

TEST CENTER NUMBER

TEST DATE

MO.　DAY　YR.

LSAT/LSDAS NUMBER

SOCIAL SECURITY / SOCIAL INS. NO.

LAST NAME (PRINT)

FIRST NAME (PRINT)

MIDDLE INITIAL

IMPORTANT: Please complete the above area in clear legible PRINT!
(THIS INFORMATION SHOULD BE THE SAME AS THAT ON YOUR LSAT ADMISSION TICKET/IDENTIFICATION CARD)

LSAT® WRITING SAMPLE BOOKLET

WAIT FOR THE SUPERVISOR's INSTRUCTIONS BEFORE YOU TURN THE PAGE TO THE TOPIC. PLEASE SIGN YOUR NAME AND NOTE THE DATE AT THE TOP OF PAGE ONE BEFORE YOU START TO WORK.

TIME: 30 MINUTES

GENERAL DIRECTIONS

You are to complete the brief writing exercise on the topic inside. You will have 30 minutes in which to plan and write the exercise. Read the topic carefully. You will probably find it best to spend a few minutes considering the topic and organizing your thoughts before you begin writing. DO NOT WRITE ON A TOPIC OTHER THAN THE ONE SPECIFIED. WRITING ON A TOPIC OF YOUR OWN CHOICE IS NOT ACCEPTABLE.

There is no "right" or "wrong" answer to this question. Law schools are interested in how carefully you support the position you take and how clearly you express that position. How well you write is much more important than how much you write. No special knowledge is required or expected. Law schools are interested in organization, vocabulary, and writing mechanics. They understand the short time available to you and the pressured circumstances under which you will write.

Confine your writing to the lined area inside this booklet. Only the blocked lined area will be reproduced for the law schools. You will find that you have enough space in this booklet if you plan your writing carefully, write on every line, avoid wide margins, and keep your handwriting a reasonable size. Be sure that your writing is legible.

593

LSAT WRITING SAMPLE TOPIC

Read the following proposals of Johnson and Edwards, two members of the village of Coventry Town Council, who have to decide how to spend the $100,000 that Mrs. Whitmore left the village in her will. **Then, in the space provided, write an argument in favor of the proposal you think the Town Council should choose.** The following considerations must be taken into account:

1. The will stipulates that the money must be used for the benefit of the children of Coventry.
2. The Town Council wants to spend the money on a project that will benefit business in Coventry.

JOHNSON has proposed that the money be used for a park. Part of the park would be set aside as a play area for children and their parents. At present, there is a schoolyard in the village and an athletic field but no playground. The park would also include picnic shelters that could be used by families. The land for the park is now owned by a large real estate firm located in the state capital and would be purchased at a cost of $38,000. The playground equipment would have to be purchased from a playground equipment supply company in another state at a cost of $12,000. The grading and other site preparation could be done by a construction firm based in Coventry at a cost of $23,000. The remaining money would be used to hire local carpenters to build the picnic shelters and to hire a local nursery to plant flowers and shrubs in the park.

EDWARDS has proposed that the money be used to build a special children's wing on the public library. At present, there is a children's room in the library, but it is small. The number of books that can be housed in the room is limited, and the room is not suitable for special reading programs. A new wing, which could be built at a cost of $83,000, would be used to house additional books and for special children's programs. Edwards anticipates that volunteers could use the wing on weekends to assist children having trouble with their schoolwork. Additionally, the remaining $17,000 could be used to purchase more books and to buy several computers with educational software.

Answer Key

SECTION 1	SECTION 2	SECTION 3	SECTION 4	SECTION 5
1. D	1. C	1. C	1. E	1. D
2. B	2. B	2. E	2. C	2. C
3. B	3. E	3. A	3. C	3. B
4. E	4. C	4. D	4. D	4. D
5. C	5. B	5. A	5. C	5. C
6. C	6. C	6. E	6. D	6. B
7. A	7. C	7. C	7. A	7. C
8. E	8. B	8. B	8. A	8. C
9. D	9. D	9. E	9. D	9. E
10. E	10. D	10. A	10. B	10. E
11. E	11. B	11. D	11. C	11. C
12. B	12. E	12. E	12. A	12. D
13. C	13. D	13. C	13. A	13. B
14. D	14. E	14. B	14. B	14. A
15. D	15. B	15. E	15. D	15. B
16. D	16. C	16. A	16. E	16. C
17. E	17. E	17. B	17. A	17. E
18. C	18. A	18. C	18. C	18. E
19. B	19. E	19. E	19. C	19. D
20. D	20. D	20. A	20. C	20. E
21. A	21. B	21. D	21. B	21. B
22. E	22. A	22. A	22. A	22. E
23. D	23. A	23. E	23. D	23. B
24. D	24. A	24. C	24. D	24. E
		25. C	25. C	
		26. B		
		27. E		
		28. B		

Explanatory Answers

SAMPLE ESSAY

The City Council should adopt the proposal submitted by Edwards for three reasons: first, a new children's wing to the library will more directly benefit the village's children than a park would; second, the educational value of expanded library facilities outweighs the benefits of a play area; and third, the cost of building a library wing would directly benefit the village economy.

A new library wing will directly benefit children since it will contain books for children and will allow room for educational programs specifically designed for them. By contrast, only part of the proposed park is specifically for children. Although picnic shelters and flowers indirectly benefit children, they do not meet their needs in the same way that books and educational programs do.

The educational value of a new wing is greater than the recreational value of a park. The village already has some recreational areas for children, but the existing library facilities are inadequate. Also, the value of learning about computers and getting extra help with schoolwork is greater than that of fancier playground equipment.

Finally, the construction of a new wing will directly benefit the economy of Coventry. Most of the construction cost of a new library wing would go into the local economy.

Although a park would in some ways benefit the children and economy of Coventry, the construction of a new wing on the library would provide even greater benefits for the children and businesses of the village.

SECTION 1

ANALYTICAL REASONING

Questions 1–7

This is a selection set. Begin by summarizing the initial conditions:

J behind *N*
Q ≠ *P*

1. Which of the following groups of four people could ride in one of the cars?

   (A) *J, L, O, P*
   (B) *J, M, O, Q*
   (C) *K, L, P, Q*
   (D) *K, P, J, N*
   (E) *L, M, N, P*

   (D) Since this stem provides no additional information, just use the initial conditions to eliminate choices. Using the first condition that *J* and *N* must ride in the same car with *J* behind *N*, we eliminate (A), (B), and (E). Using that other condition, we eliminate (C).

2. If *P* is sitting in a seat behind *O* and *Q* is sitting in a seat next to *M*, then which of the following must be true?

   (A) *J* is sitting next to *K*.
   (B) *K* is sitting next to *L*.
   (C) *K* is sitting behind *Q*.
   (D) *L* is sitting behind *Q*.
   (E) *L* is sitting behind *M*.

   (B) Given that *Q* and *M* occupy the same seat in one of the cars, *J* and *N* must be in the other car. (Otherwise, *J* could not sit directly behind *N*.) So in one car, *O* and *N* sit in the front seat, and *P* and *J* sit in the back seat. In the other car, *Q* and *M* sit in one seat, which means that *K* and *L* are sitting in the other seat. Thus, (B) is necessarily true. As for the other choices, (A) is necessarily false, while (C), (D), and (E) are possibly, though not necessarily, true.

3. If *P* is sitting in a seat next to *N* and *K* is sitting in a seat next to *L*, then which of the following must be true?

   (A) *M* and *Q* are sitting in different cars.
   (B) *O* and *M* are sitting in different cars.
   (C) *O* and *P* are sitting in different cars.
   (D) *M* is sitting behind *L*.
   (E) *Q* is sitting behind *K*.

   (B) Since *J* must sit behind *N*, given the additional information, *J*, *N*, and *P* sit in one car, while *K* and *L* sit in the other. Since *Q* must not be in the same car as *P*, the second car includes *Q* as well as *K* and *L*. This leaves *M* and *O*, and one must sit in one car

and the other in the other car—as (B) correctly points out. The remaining choices are possibly, though not necessarily, true.

4. If *K* is sitting in the front seat of a car that *Q* is driving and *O* is driving the other car, then all of the following must be true EXCEPT

   (A) *M* is sitting next to *L*.
   (B) *O* is sitting next to *N*.
   (C) *O* is sitting in front of *P*.
   (D) *P* is sitting next to *J*.
   (E) *Q* is sitting in front of *L*.

   (E) Since *Q* and *K* are sitting beside each other in one car, *N* and *J* must be in the other car (because *J* must sit behind *N*), and *N* is sitting beside the driver. Since *P* and *Q* must be in different cars, *P* is in the same car as *O*, *N*, and *J*, sitting directly behind *O*, the driver. Finally, the other two individuals, *M* and *L*, are sitting together in the back seat of the other car:

Q	*K*	*O*	*N*
L/M	*L/M*	*P*	*J*

   The diagram shows that (A), (B), (C), and (D) are necessarily true. (E) is possibly, though not necessarily, true.

5. If *K* is sitting behind *P* in a car that *M* is driving, then all of the following could be true EXCEPT

   (A) *L* is sitting behind *M*.
   (B) *L* is sitting behind *Q*.
   (C) *L* is sitting next to *O*.
   (D) *O* is sitting next to *J*.
   (E) *O* is sitting next to *N*.

   (C) Given that *K*, *P*, and *M* are in one car, then *J*, *N*, and *Q* must be in the other; and this means that *L* and *O* are in different cars, though which is in which is not determined by the information given. These conclusions, however, are sufficient to find the correct choice. Since *L* and *O* are sitting in different cars, they cannot be sitting next to each other. You can demonstrate that the other choices are possible by constructing examples.

6. If *J* is riding in a car driven by *K* and *O* is driving the other car, then all of the following could be true EXCEPT

(A) *L* is sitting behind *P*.
(B) *L* is sitting behind *Q*.
(C) *M* is sitting behind *K*.
(D) *M* is sitting next to *P*.
(E) *Q* is sitting next to *J*.

(C) If *J* is riding in a car with *K*, then that car includes *N* as well, and therefore *J*, *K*, and *N* plus either *P* or *Q*. The other car must include *O*, *L*, *M*, and either *P* or *Q*. Thus, *M* and *K* are in different cars, so (C) is not a possible arrangement of passengers. Again, you can prove that the other choices describe possible arrangements by constructing examples.

7. If *M* is driving one car and *K* is driving the other, which of the following must be true?

(A) *J* is sitting next to either *P* or *Q*.
(B) *K* is sitting next to either *L* or *O*.
(C) *L* is sitting next to either *K* or *O*.
(D) *O* is sitting behind either *P* or *Q*.
(E) *Q* is sitting behind either *L* or *O*.

(A) Since *J* sits behind *N*, and given that *M* and *K* are the two drivers, one of the cars must include *M*, *N*, and *J* or *K*, *N*, and *J*, with *N* in the front seat with the driver and *J* in the back seat with the fourth passenger. Since *P* and *Q* cannot be in the same car, one or the other must occupy the fourth seat in one of the cars and sit next to *J*. The other choices describe arrangements that are possible but not necessary.

Questions 8–13

This is a linear ordering set. Begin by summarizing the information:

$L = 1$ and $M = 8$; or $M = 1$ and $L = 8$
$K = K$
$L = L$
$J \neq J$

Since the initial conditions do not dictate any part of the order for the speeches, go to the questions.

8. Which of the following is an acceptable order for the speeches?

(A) *J, K, K, J, L, L, M, M*
(B) *L,L, J, K, K, M, M, J*
(C) *L, K, J, L, J, M, K, M*
(D) *M, K, K, J, J, M, L, L*
(E) *M, J, K, K, M, J, L, L*

(E) This question stem does not provide any additional information, so use the initial conditions to

eliminate choices. Using the first condition, eliminate (A) and (B). Using the second condition, eliminate (C). And using the fourth condition, eliminate (D).

9. All of the following are acceptable orders for the speeches EXCEPT

(A) *L, L, M, J, K, K, J, M*
(B) *L,L, J, M, K, K, J, M*
(C) *L, L, K, K, J, M, J, M*
(D) *M, M, J, K, K, L, J, L*
(E) *M, K, K, J, M, J, L, L*

(D) Use the initial conditions to find the one choice that contains an arrangement that is not possible. (D) violates the requirement that $L = L$.

10. If *M* reads the fourth and eighth speeches, which of the following must be true?

(A) *J* reads the fifth speech.
(B) *J* reads the seventh speech.
(C) *K* reads the third speech.
(D) *K* reads the fifth speech.
(E) *K* reads the sixth speech.

(E) This stem provides additional information, so enter it on a diagram:

1	2	3	4	5	6	7	8
			M				M

And this means that *L* must give the first and second speeches:

1	2	3	4	5	6	7	8
L	L		M				M

Since *K*'s speeches must come one after another, *K* either gives the fifth and sixth speeches or the sixth and seventh speeches:

1	2	3	4	5	6	7	8
L	L	J	M	K	K	J	M
L	L	J	M	J	K	K	M

As the diagram shows, (A), (B), and (D) are possibly, though not necessarily, true, while (C) is false. (E), however, is necessarily true.

11. If *J* reads the second speech, which of the following must be true?

    (A) *J*'s second speech comes sometime after *M*'s second speech.

    (B) *J*'s second speech comes sometime after *K*'s second speech.

    (C) *K*'s second speech comes sometime after *J*'s second speech.

    (D) *M*'s second speech comes after *J*'s second speech and *K*'s second speech.

    (E) *J*'s second speech comes before *M*'s second speech and before *K*'s first speech.

(E) Enter the new information on a diagram:

1	2	3	4	5	6	7	8
	J						

This means that *M* must speak first and that *L* must speak seventh and eighth:

1	2	3	4	5	6	7	8
M	*J*					*L*	*L*

Given that *K* = *K*, there are the following possible orders:

1	2	3	4	5	6	7	8
M	*J*	*K*	*K*	*M/J*	*M/J*	*L*	*L*
M	*J*	*M*	*K*	*K*	*J*	*L*	*L*
M	*J*	*M*	*J*	*K*	*K*	*L*	*L*

As the diagram shows, (A), (B), (C), and (D) are possibly true but (E) cannot be true.

12. If *M* reads both of his speeches before *J* reads his first speech, then the fourth and fifth speeches are read by

    (A) *J*

    (B) *K*

    (C) *J* and *K*, respectively

    (D) *K* and *J*, respectively

    (E) *M* and *J*, respectively

(B) If *M* reads both of his speeches before *J* reads his first speech, then *M* must read first and *L* seventh and eighth:

1	2	3	4	5	6	7	8
M						*L*	*L*

The most powerful condition remaining is that *K* = *K*, so try to find all the possible placements of *K*. At first, there seem to be four:

1	2	3	4	5	6	7	8
M	*K*	*K*				*L*	*L*
M		*K*	*K*			*L*	*L*
M			*K*	*K*		*L*	*L*
M				*K*	*K*	*L*	*L*

The first of these, however, is not possible. Given the additional stipulation that *M* read both of his speeches before *J* reads his first speech, the resulting order would be:

1	2	3	4	5	6	7	8
M	*K*	*K*	*M*	*J*	*J*	*L*	*L*

This is a violation of the last condition. The second is not possible for the same reason:

1	2	3	4	5	6	7	8
M	*M*	*K*	*K*	*J*	*J*	*L*	*L*

The fourth is not possible:

1	2	3	4	5	6	7	8
M	*M*	*J*	*J*	*K*	*K*	*L*	*L*

So only the third is possible:

1	2	3	4	5	6	7	8
M	*M*	*J*	*K*	*K*	*J*	*L*	*L*

13. Which of the following conditions is sufficient to determine the complete order for the reading of the speeches?

    I. *M* reads the second speech.
   II. *K* reads the seventh speech.
  III. *J* reads the sixth speech.

(A) I only   (B) II only   (C) I and II only
(D) II and III only   (E) I, II, and III

(C) Test each of the statements. Statement I guarantees a complete order:

```
1   2   3   4   5   6   7   8
    M
```

This means that *M* must read first and *L*, seventh and eighth:

```
1   2   3   4   5   6   7   8
M   M                   L   L
```

Since *J* cannot follow *J*:

```
1   2   3   4   5   6   7   8
M   M   J   K   K   J   L   L
```

Statement II also provides information that fixes the entire schedule:

```
1   2   3   4   5   6   7   8
                    K
```

This means that *K* reads sixth, *L* reads first and second, and *M* reads eighth:

```
1   2   3   4   5   6   7   8
L   L               K   K   M
```

Since *J* cannot follow *J*:

```
1   2   3   4   5   6   7   8
L   L   J   M   J   K   K   M
```

III, however, does not fix an order:

```
1   2   3   4   5   6   7   8
L   L   J   K   K   J   M   M
M   M   J   K   K   J   L   L
```

Questions 14–19

Begin by summarizing the initial conditions in a table:

Women

		Bear	Wolf	Elk	Bird	Fish
Men	Bear	✔				
	Wolf		✔	✔	✔	
	Elk			✔		
	Bird		✔		✔	✔
	Fish		✔			✔

Whatever further conclusions might be drawn are already implicit in the table, so go directly to the questions.

14. Which of the following provides a complete and accurate list of the totems of men to whom a woman of the fish clan could be married?

(A) Wolf
(B) Bird
(C) Fish
(D) Bird, Fish
(E) Wolf, Bird, Fish

(D) As the table shows, a woman of the fish clan can marry a man of the bird clan or the fish clan.

15. If a man whose totem is the wolf wishes to marry a woman outside of his own clan, then he could marry a woman with which of the following totems?

    I. Bear
  II. Elk
 III. Bird

(A) I only   (B) II only   (C) III only
(D) II and III only   (E) I, II, and III

(D) The table shows that a man of the wolf totem can marry a woman with the wolf totem, or the elk totem, or the bird totem.

16. The son of a woman whose totem is the fish could be a member of which of the following clans?

    I. Elk
  II. Bird
 III. Fish

(A) I but not II or III
(B) II but not I or III
(C) I and II but not III
(D) II and III but not I
(E) I, II, or III

(D) A son's totem is the same as that of his father, and the husband of a woman whose totem is the fish has either the bird or the fish as his totem.

17. If a man's totem is the wolf, then which of the following could be his sister's totem?

   I. Wolf
  II. Elk
 III. Bird

(A) I only (B) II only (C) I and II only
(D) II and III only (E) I, II, and III

(E) A man's totem is the same as that of his father, and a man whose totem is the wolf can marry a woman whose totem is the wolf, the elk, or the bird. Since the woman assumes the same totem as her mother, the sister of a man whose totem is the wolf could have as her totem any one of the following: wolf, elk, or bird.

18. The daughter of a man whose totem is the elk could marry a man with which of the following totems?

   I. Wolf
  II. Elk
 III. Bird

(A) I only (B) II only (C) I and II only
(D) II and III only (E) I, II, and III

(C) A man whose totem is the elk can marry only a woman whose totem is the elk; but her daughter, who is also an elk, can marry a man from either the wolf clan or the elk clan.

19. If a man's totem is the fish, then which of the following is a complete and accurate list of the clans to which his wife's father can belong?

(A) Wolf, bird
(B) Wolf, bird, fish
(C) Bear, wolf, bird
(D) Bear, wolf, fish
(E) Bear, wolf, elk, bird, fish

(B) A man whose totem is the fish can marry a woman from the wolf clan or the fish clan, and her mother would have been a member of one of those two clans. If her totem were the wolf, she would have married either a member of the wolf clan, the bird clan, or the fish clan, and if her totem were a fish, she would have married a member of either the bird or the fish clan.

Questions 20–24

The best way to help you answer this set is to put the information in usable form. I would suggest using a table:

✓		✓			✓	✓
	✓		✓		✓	
	✓		✓	✓		✓
✓		✓		✓	✓	✓
✓		✓		✓	✓	
	✓		✓			✓

There are no further inferences to be drawn. Everything you need to know is in the table.

20. What is the total number of columns by the six columnists published by the paper during the week?

(A) 15 (B) 17 (C) 19 (D) 23 (E) 26

(D) Just count or add them up. The total is 23.

21. Which of the following statements can be deduced from the information given above?

   I. Any day that Munick's column appeared, Cavanaugh's column also appeared.
  II. Any day that Harris's column did not appear, Clock's column appeared.
 III. Areff had published the fewest number of columns during the week.

(A) I only (B) II only (C) I and II only
(D) II and III only (E) I, II, and III

(A) Check each statement by the table. Statement I can be inferred from the table. Munick's column appeared on Monday, Wednesday, Saturday, and Sunday; Cavanaugh's column appeared on Monday, Wednesday, Friday, Saturday, and Sunday. So each time Munick's column appeared, so did one by Cavanaugh. Statement II is not inferable. Harris's column did not appear on Sunday, and Clock's column did appear on Sunday. Statement III is not inferable. Areff and Harris both published only three columns.

22. If on a certain day neither Roe's column nor Areff's column appeared, then that day could have been which of the following?

    I. Monday
   II. Wednesday
  III. Saturday

(A) I only (B) II only (C) III only
(D) II and III only (E) I, II, and III

(E) On Monday neither a column by Roe nor a column by Areff appeared, so statement I must be part of the correct choice. On Wednesday, neither published a column, so statement II is part of the correct choice. Finally, on Saturday, neither published a column. So statement III also belongs in the correct choice.

23. If the paper contained columns by Clock and Cavanaugh, then knowing that columns by which of the following had also appeared would be sufficient to determine what day the paper had been published?

    I. Munick
   II. Harris
  III. Roe

(A) I only (B) II only (C) III only
(D) II and III only (E) I, II, and III

(D) Both Clock's and Cavanaugh's columns appeared on Monday, Wednesday, Friday, and Saturday. As for statement I, knowing that Munick had a column also would not settle the issue, for Munick published on Monday, Wednesday, Saturday, and Sunday. So, on three days all three of the writers had columns. Therefore, statement I is not part of the correct choice. As for statement II, Harris's column appeared on Tuesday, Thursday, and Saturday. So there was only one day on which a paper included a column by Harris as well as a column by both Clock and Cavanaugh: Saturday. So statement II is part of the correct choice. Finally, as for statement III, Roe's column appeared on Tuesday, Thursday, Friday, and Sunday. Only one of those days coincides with a day on which appeared a column by both Clock and Cavanaugh: Friday. So statement III is part of the correct choice as well.

24. If a paper contained neither a column by Munick nor one by Areff, then that paper was published on

(A) Monday (B) Tuesday (C) Thursday
(D) Friday (E) Saturday

(D) The only day on which neither a column by Munick nor a column by Areff appeared was Friday.

SECTION 2

LOGICAL REASONING

In an attempt to predict the future course of consumer spending, *Investment Monthly* magazine surveyed its readers. Of those surveyed, over 60 percent reported that they planned to buy a new automobile or at least one major appliance within the next three months. From these results, the magazine concluded that consumer spending for the next quarter was likely to be high.

1. Which of the following, if true, would most weaken the conclusion above?

(A) The cost of a new automobile is much greater than that of a major appliance.

(B) A person who plans to make a major purchase at some time in the future may not yet have settled on a brand.

(C) The readers of *Investment Monthly* are more affluent than the average consumer.

(D) Some of the items to be purchased will be imports and will not stimulate markets in the United States.

(E) Not all readers of *Investment Monthly* magazine responded to the survey.

(C) In the lesson, I talked about the nature of generalization and stressed that the strength of a generalization depends on the representativeness of the examples on which it is based. Here the conclusion is that consumer spending in general will be high for the upcoming quarter, and the basis for that general conclusion is a sampling of readers of a magazine called *Investment Monthly*. (C) attacks the generalization by suggesting that the sample is not representative of consumers in general. (A), (B), and (D) are all irrelevant to the argument, since the speaker does not distinguish types of consumer purchases, e.g., automobile versus refrigerator, Brand X versus Brand Y, or imported versus domestically produced goods. (E) is perhaps the second-best answer, for at least it has the merit of addressing the sampling procedure. (E), however, represents a questioning of the argument rather than an outright attack. Even if the survey covered only a part of the readership, if that survey was unbiased, the fact that not everyone responded is not important. (E) would have been a much stronger answer had it been phrased "Only the wealthiest readers responded." But then, that would be very much like (C), and the test-writers would never include two answers so similar to each other.

Every member of the New York Burros, a team in the Big Apple Softball League, who wears wristbands when batting wears either red wristbands or white wristbands.

2. If the statement above is true, which of the following must be true?

    I. A member of the New York Burros who does not wear red wristbands while batting wears white wristbands while batting.

    II. No member of the New York Burros wears blue wristbands while batting.

    III. Some members of the New York Burros do not wear wristbands when batting.

    (A) I only
    (B) II only
    (C) III only
    (D) I and III only
    (E) I, II, and III

(B) The result of your attack on a question like this usually depends on a careful reading of the initial statements. I and III are not inferable for essentially the same reason. The initial statement has the general form "All individuals with characteristic X also have characteristic Y or Z." (All individuals who wear wristbands while batting wear either red ones or blue ones.) But you cannot infer from such a statement that everyone in the population has characteristic X, so you cannot infer that everyone in the population has either Y or Z. On the other hand, you cannot conclude that some individuals do not have characteristic X. Therefore, neither I nor III is inferable. II, however, is inferable. Any Burro who wears wristbands while batting wears either red ones or white ones. So no Burro wears blue wristbands while batting.

3. If any player in the Big Apple Softball League who wears red wristbands while batting also wears blue batting gloves, and if no member of the New York Burros wears blue batting gloves, which of the following must be true?

    (A) Every member of the New York Burros wears white wristbands when batting.

    (B) No member of the New York Burros wears white wristbands.

    (C) Some members of the New York Burros wear red wristbands when batting.

    (D) Some members of the New York Burros do not wear batting gloves.

    (E) Every member of the New York Burros who wears wristbands wears white wristbands when batting.

(E) What can be inferred using the additional information? Since no Burro wears blue batting gloves, no Burro wears red wristbands when batting. Coupling this conclusion with the initial statements, we can infer that those Burros who wear wristbands while batting wear white wristbands. This is the conclusion set forth in (E). (A) is incorrect for the same reason that statement I of the preceding item is not inferable, and (B) makes the opposite error. (C) is necessarily false (given the additional information of this question stem). Finally, (D) is not inferable. Although (D) is possibly true, it is not necessarily true.

A bill now pending before the Congress would give physicians the option of prescribing heroin as a painkiller for terminally ill patients. The Congress should refuse to pass the bill, because there is a serious danger that the heroin would be stolen and wind up being sold on the streets.

4. Which of the following, if true, would most weaken the argument above?

    (A) Other prescription painkillers are available for terminally ill patients that in most cases provide relief of pain as effective as that provided by heroin.

    (B) The addictive effects of heroin are inconsequential considering that the patients who would be scheduled for treatment are terminally ill.

    (C) The amount of heroin that would be required for terminally ill patients is insignificant when compared with the amount of heroin sold illegally.

    (D) Heroin sold illegally varies widely in quality and purity and can easily cause death by overdose, because it is taken without proper measurement.

    (E) Over the past five years, the number of deaths attributable to heroin overdose has declined slightly, but the total number of deaths by drug overdose has increased significantly because of increased use of cocaine.

(C) The speaker opposes the proposal of a limited legalization of heroin because he or she fears that any quantities earmarked for legal use might be diverted to illegal street sales. And this is a legitimate objection to the plan. (C), however, points out that although the objection is not illogical, it is not a serious objection because of the limited quantities that would be required. (A) does not weaken the speaker's objection. If anything, the point made by (A) strengthens the speaker's objection by claiming that there is no particular need for legalized heroin. (B) is generally related to the topic of the initial paragraph, but (B) seems to be a response to a possible objection to the plan to legalize heroin. As such, it is a point that a defender of the plan might make, but it is not a response to the particular point made in this initial paragraph. (D) and (E) may both be true, but they aren't arguments directed against the use of legalized heroin.

It used to be said that artistic creativity is the province solely of human beings and that it is, in fact, one of the marks that distinguishes humans from all other creatures. Today, cleverly programmed computers can create images that are indistinguishable from paintings by contemporary abstract artists. Thus, the traditional argument that artistic creativity is the province of humans is proved incorrect.

5. Which of the following, if true, most weakens the argument above?

   (A) Most human beings have never produced a creative work that others would regard as a work of art.
   (B) The image produced by a computer is an image that it was directed to create by the human programmer.
   (C) Many people are unfamiliar with abstract art and so are unable to distinguish good modern art from bad modern art.
   (D) Human beings engage in many activities other than the creation of art, activities such as production, warfare, and building.
   (E) A program designed to produce a computerized image will produce the same image on any computer that can accept the program.

(B) The point of the initial argument is that computers can generate what seems to be art and that artistic creativity is therefore not just the province of humans. (B) weakens the argument by attacking the evidence for the claim, namely, that computers can generate art. It does this not by denying that art emerges from a computer, but by arguing that it is not the machine but a human being who is ultimately responsible for the image. (A) sounds like an attack on the argument only if you misread the argument. The speaker attacks the claim "Only humans can produce art," not the claim "All humans produce art." (C) and (D) are incorrect for substantially the same reason. The claim under attack is not "Everyone has good artistic judgment" nor "Humans create only art." Finally, as for (E), this idea, if anything, seems to strengthen rather than weaken the speaker's point by suggesting that computer-generated images are produced by a purely mechanical process completely devoid of any creative urge.

The right to work under humane conditions is a fundamental right of all people.

Therefore, all men and women have the right to a job and to decent conditions of employment.

6. Which of the following arguments most closely parallels the reasoning of the argument above?

   (A) The expression of anger is a natural instinct of human beings who feel threatened. Therefore, Smith is not to be blamed for expressing anger when she felt threatened.
   (B) Johnson is one of the most honest legislative leaders ever to serve this state. Therefore, Johnson could not have committed the dishonest acts of which he has been accused.
   (C) The Bill of Rights protects the free practice of religion in this country. Therefore, all people have the right to worship God in a manner of their own choosing.
   (D) Children are human beings who have the potential for adult behavior. Therefore, any right or privilege that is granted to adults ought, in fairness, to be granted to children as well.
   (E) The President has the duty of defending the country from any external enemy. Therefore, the President acted properly in ordering our army to repel the invading forces.

(C) The initial argument is not very complex. The conclusion really amounts to little more than a restatement of the premise. (C) parallels this structure, because the conclusion of (C) is little more than a restatement of the premise. The other four choices do not parallel the initial argument as closely because in each of those choices, the conclusion is something more than a restatement of the premise.

Amid great fanfare, the Taxi and Limousine Commission announced last June that a new dress code for taxi drivers would be incorporated into the Commission's rules. After six months, no driver has lost his license or even been fined under the new dress code. Evidently, drivers have chosen to comply with the new dress code.

7. Which of the following, if true, would most weaken the argument above?

    (A) Prior to the announcement of the new dress code, an average of 16 cab drivers each month lost their licenses for various violations of the Commission's rules.
    (B) Inspectors routinely stop cab drivers to inspect licenses, safety, and cleanliness of the vehicle and the driver's record of fares.
    (C) The Commission's lawyers have refused to prosecute drivers cited under the new dress code, because they believe that the law is unconstitutional.
    (D) A survey of passengers who say they regularly use taxi cabs shows that 45 percent of the riders don't believe that drivers are better dressed.
    (E) During July and August, the number of cab drivers available for work is less than that during the other months of the year.

(C) This item asks you to find an alternative causal explanation for the phenomenon described. (C) provides an alternative explanation: There have been no convictions not because drivers have complied with the law but because the law has not been enforced. As for (A), the fact that drivers were in the past disciplined for other reasons has no bearing on the patterns of enforcement of the dress code. As for (B), this idea seems to strengthen rather than weaken the argument by suggesting that inspectors are in a position to detect violations of the dress code. (D) is perhaps the second-best answer, for (D) at least has the merit of suggesting that drivers are not better dressed. But (D) relies on a survey of attitudes, and the attitudes might or might not be well founded. A driver might be in compliance with a dress code and still not meet a passenger's expectation of "better dressed." Finally, it is difficult to imagine how (E) could be construed to be an attack on the argument.

Questions 8–9

The existence of our state's inefficient and wasteful automobile accident liability system can be easily explained. As long as most of our legislators are lawyers, the system will never be reformed, because litigation creates more work for lawyers.

8. Which of the following, if true, would most weaken the argument above?

    (A) Most judges in the state are members of the legal profession as well.
    (B) Few of the state's legislators are among the relatively small percentage of lawyers who handle automobile accident cases.
    (C) Under the customary fee arrangement, a lawyer receives one-third of any monetary award made to a client.
    (D) The state legislature allocates funds to pay for defense attorneys who represent indigent clients.
    (E) Any reform legislation could be vetoed by the governor of the state, who is also an attorney.

(B) The initial argument tries to provide an explanation for a certain situation: The lawyers in the legislatures refuse to reform the law because reform would reduce the income of lawyers. In other words, the initial argument suggests that the lawyers in the legislature act out of self-interest. The argument implicitly assumes that the lawyers in the legislature derive financial benefit from the existing laws. (B) attacks this hidden assumption of the argument. The remaining answer choices are generally relevant to the topic of the initial paragraph but do not constitute an attack on the speaker's reasoning.

9. The argument above rests on the assumption that

    (A) given the opportunity, most lawyers would want to be members of the state legislature
    (B) legislation to reform the state's automobile accident liability system could be introduced by a legislator who is not a lawyer
    (C) state laws set minimum fees that attorneys are permitted to charge in cases arising from automobile accidents
    (D) the state's automobile accident liability system encourages litigation
    (E) state laws governing the ownership and operation of motor vehicles encourage unsafe driving practices

(D) The argument above has the structure: Litigation creates work for lawyers; therefore, these laws will not be reformed. The speaker apparently believes, though he does not say so explicitly, that the existing system of laws encourages litigation. Thus, (D) highlights a suppressed premise of the argument. The speaker is not, however, logically committed to the idea mentioned in (A). Instead, the speaker is committed only to the proposition that those lawyers who are legislators refuse to reform the laws. As for (B), this might be a way of attacking the speaker's position (though probably not a very effective way of attacking it), so (B) is not a hidden assumption made by the speaker. As for (C), if this were true, the speaker's position would probably be strengthened somewhat; but the speaker is not logically committed to each and every point that might help his position. Finally, (E) seems to represent a misreading of the initial paragraph. The author is not claiming that existing laws cause accidents, only that those accidents that do occur often become the basis for litigation.

Questions 10–11

Premises: All weavers are members of the union.
Some carders are women.
Some weavers are women.
All union members are covered by health insurance.
No carders are covered by health insurance.

10. All of the following conclusions can be drawn from the statements above EXCEPT

    (A) All weavers are covered by health insurance.
    (B) Some women are covered by health insurance.
    (C) Some women are not covered by health insurance.
    (D) Some members of the union are not covered by health insurance.
    (E) No carders are members of the union.

    (D) (D) cannot be inferred from the statements. In fact, the fourth statement implies that (D) is false. As for (A), since all weavers are union members and all union members are covered by health insurance, it follows that all weavers are covered by health insurance. As for (B), since some women are weavers and all weavers are covered by health insurance, it follows that some women are covered by health insurance. As for (C), since some women are carders and no carder is covered by health insurance, it follows that some women are not covered by health insurance. Finally, as for (E), since no carder is covered by health insurance but all union members are covered by health insurance, it follows that no carder is a member of the union.

11. Which of the following workers would provide a counterexample to the statements above?

    (A) A man who is a carder
    (B) A weaver who is not covered by health insurance
    (C) A carder who is not covered by health insurance
    (D) A worker covered by health insurance who is not a weaver
    (E) A worker covered by health insurance who is not a carder

    (B) (B) provides a counterexample to the first and fourth statements. Those two statements together imply that all weavers are covered by health insurance.

The Olympic Games represent a first step in the historic movement away from war and toward the substitution for war of peaceful competition among nations. Just as professional sports in the United States provide a field in which local, regional, and even racial and ethnic hostilities may be sublimated and expressed in a controlled, harmless form, so international athletic competition may help to abolish war between nations by providing a sphere in which chauvinistic hostilities may be harmlessly discharged.

12. Which of the following, if true, would weaken the argument in the passage?

    (A) The existence of professional sports in the United States has not completely eliminated regional and ethnic conflicts.
    (B) The Olympic Games themselves generate intense international rivalries and emotional responses by spectators.
    (C) On several occasions, the Olympic Games have been cancelled or reduced in scope because of international conflicts or wars.
    (D) Unlike professional sports, the Olympic Games are conducted on a purely amateur, not-for-profit basis.
    (E) War is caused primarily by objective conflicts between nations over political and economic advantages.

    (E) The argument implicitly assumes that nations are moved to go to war by the same emotions that generate regional and ethnic rivalries, and (E) attacks this hidden premise. (A) may be read as weakening the argument, but the attack is not very serious. The speaker could easily reply, "That's true. I didn't claim that sports can eliminate all conflict. I claimed only that they may help accomplish that." As for (B), the speaker could also claim that this idea is consistent with his argument: "True, but these emotional responses are controlled and channeled into an acceptable outlet." As for (C), the speaker argues that the games could have a certain effect, but the speaker does not claim that the games will necessarily take place. Finally, while (D) is generally relevant to the topic of the initial paragraph, it is difficult to see the immediate relevance of this idea to the initial argument.

Psychology originated in the attempts of researchers to describe, record, classify, and explain their own mental impressions, thoughts, and feelings and those of others as they described them verbally. It matured into a science only when the reliance on subjective impressions was gradually abandoned and researchers concentrated on human behavior. Then, psychology truly became a science of mental activity.

13. The passage makes which of the following assumptions?

    I. It is not possible to observe episodes of mental activity directly.
    II. Early research was unreliable because researchers gave less-than-candid accounts of their mental experiences.
    III. Human behavior is an expression of mental activity.

(A) I only   (B) III only   (C) I and II only
(D) I and III only   (E) II and III only

(D) This question asks that you identify suppressed premises of the argument. Statement I is a suppressed premise. The speaker claims that psychology could become a science only when researchers abandoned the attempt to study mental impressions. Thus, the speaker evidently believes that mental impressions are not observable as scientific phenomena. Similarly, III, too, is a suppressed premise. The speaker claims that psychology became a true science of mental activity only when it concentrated on observable events such as human behavior. Thus, the speaker must believe that behavior is tied to mental activity. Finally, II is not a suppressed premise of the argument. The weakness of early psychology, according to the speaker, was that it tried to study subjective impressions rather than observable phenomena. A subjective impression is just that, regardless of whether the person describing the feeling is being candid or not.

Many people who describe themselves as authors do not belong in that category at all, since writing is not their main source of income.

14. The paragraph above makes the assumption that

(A) many of those who consider themselves authors lack the skills and training needed to write professionally
(B) the average income of professional writers is higher than that for most other professions
(C) professional authors are motivated to become writers primarily by the prospect of financial gain
(D) to be considered an author, a person must publish writings on a regular basis
(E) a person cannot be considered an author unless he or she derives most of his or her income from writing

(E) The initial argument has the structure: Writing is not the main source of income for a certain group of people; therefore, these people are not really authors.

The argument implicitly assumes that a person is not an author unless he derives most of his income from his writing. (A) is not an assumption of the argument. The speaker assumes only that such people do not derive most of their income from writing, not that they cannot do so. As for the remaining choices, the speaker's definition of *author* requires that a person derive most of his income from writing, not that he have a large income, nor that the prospect of financial gain be his motivation for writing, nor that the income derive from a series of regularly published writings.

A poll taken ten days before the election showed that 36 percent of the people surveyed planned to vote for Green and 42 percent planned to vote for his opponent. When the votes were finally tallied, Green received 52 percent of the vote, while his opponent received only 46 percent. Thus, the survey method used for the preelection poll was flawed.

15. Which of the following, if true, would most weaken the conclusion of the argument above?

(A) A poll taken 21 days before the election showed that 32 percent of the people surveyed planned to vote for Green.

(B) At the time the preelection poll was taken, many voters had not yet made up their minds about which candidate to vote for.

(C) During the week just before the election, Green's opponent received an important endorsement from a major newspaper.

(D) The voter turnout for the election in question was extremely light due to inclement weather.

(E) The preelection survey also questioned voters about their attitudes toward a referendum authorizing the legislature to legalize pari-mutuel gambling.

(B) This question asks you to find an alternative explanation (an explanation for the result other than a flawed study). (B) provides this alternative. The findings were correct as reported: at the time of the survey, 36 percent of the people were committed to Green and 42 percent were committed to Green's opponent (36% + 42% = 78%), but over the next ten days, many of those who were previously undecided determined to vote for Green. As for (A), while this is consistent with the results and suggests that Green was picking up votes as the election date grew nearer, this does not explain what happened in the ten days between the date of the survey and the election. As for (C), this seems to strengthen the conclusion that the survey was inaccurate, for this suggests that Green's opponent should have had even more votes than predicted by the survey. As for (D), weather certainly could affect the outcome of the election, but it's impossible to say given the available facts which of the candidates (if either) would have been aided by a light turnout. Therefore, this idea neither weakens nor strengthens the argument. Finally, (E) is generally related to the topic of the passage but has no bearing on the specific issue being discussed.

Some attorneys wear beards. Therefore, some bearded people favor brown tweed jackets.

16. Which of the following, if true, is sufficient to guarantee the truth of the conclusion?

(A) Some attorneys favor brown tweed jackets.

(B) Some of those attorneys who favor brown tweed jackets do not wear beards.

(C) All attorneys favor brown tweed jackets.

(D) Some attorneys do not wear beards.

(E) All of those who favor brown tweed jackets are attorneys.

(C) The argument depends upon a suppressed premise: Some attorneys wear beards; all attorneys favor brown tweed jackets; therefore, some bearded people favor brown tweed jackets. (C) correctly points out that the argument depends on this hidden assumption. (A), however, is not sufficient to guarantee the truth of the conclusion, for it is possible that those attorneys who favor brown tweed jackets are not those who also wear beards.

Socrates: Is it raining?
Plato: Yes.
Socrates: Is your response correct?
Plato: No.

17. Which of the following best describes Plato's responses?

I. If his first response is true, then his second response is false.

II. If his second response is false, then his first response is true.

III. If his first response is false, then his second response is true.

(A) I only (B) III only (C) I and II only
(D) II and III only (E) I, II, and III

(E) I is a correct description of the responses. If the first response is true, then it is in fact raining; so the denial that is the second response is necessarily false. As for II, if the denial that is the second response is false, then the first response must be true. Finally, as for III, if the first response is false, then it is in fact not raining; so the denial that is the second response is true.

Knowledge and study of ethical principles do not resolve in any permanent way the ethical dilemmas a person may face in his or her life. On the contrary, the more one knows about ethics, the more acutely one is aware of one's own ethical problems. A person who does not know how to count is "free" of mathematical problems; it is the person who has devoted a lifetime of study to mathematics who is most apt to wrestle with the knottiest problems of the subject. In the same way, the only type of person who is free of ethical dilemmas is one who _____(18)_____.

18. Which of the following best completes the paragraph above?

(A) is ignorant of the ethical principles that give rise to such dilemmas

(B) has studied ethics extensively and fully mastered its intricacies

(C) has withdrawn so completely from life as to avoid all troublesome situations

(D) acts in every situation only in accordance with the strictest ethical principles

(E) follows instinct and emotion rather than reason when making ethical decisions

(A) This question asks you to draw a further conclusion from the initial statement. The speaker claims that the study of ethical principles does not eliminate ethical problems. Then the speaker introduces an analogy. He compares the study of ethics to the study of math, noting that a person who has never really studied math is not aware that there are difficult mathematical problems. Thus, the conclusion the speaker is probably leading to is that someone who doesn't realize how many ethical problems there are is someone who hasn't studied ethics seriously. Thus, (A) provides a logical completion of the paragraph. (B) and (D) are directly contradicted by this analysis and so must be wrong. As for (C) and (E), though these may be ways of avoiding ethical dilemmas, they are not methods suggested by the speaker.

19. In the paragraph above, the speaker makes use of which of the following?

(A) Counterexample
(B) Generalization
(C) Deduction
(D) Paradox
(E) Analogy

(E) As indicated above, the speaker draws an analogy between the study of ethical principles and the study of math. As for (A) and (B), the speaker doesn't mention any particular examples or counterexamples of ethical problems and doesn't reach any general conclusions based on examples. As for (C), though the speaker reasons logically, he does not use

deductive inferences. Finally, as for (D), though the speaker refers to ethical dilemmas, he never refers to any paradox.

One of the problems faced by government planners is the so-called NIMBY, or "Not in My Back Yard," Syndrome. For example, although poll after poll shows that the majority of citizens in this state favor the construction of new prisons, whenever plans are announced to construct a new prison somewhere in the state, residents of nearby communities protest and often succeed in blocking the project.

20. Which of the following also illustrates the NIMBY Syndrome described above?

(A) A parent who insists that students with AIDS should not be allowed to attend public schools and withdraws his own child from school when an infected child is admitted to the public school

(B) A politician who argues that all candidates for public office should be required to file financial disclosure forms and submits a fraudulent disclosure form

(C) A minister who preaches that religious groups have an obligation to do charitable work but refuses to donate money to the Salvation Army

(D) An auto dealer who favors free trade with other countries as a means to a healthy United States economy but urges the government to restrict imports of foreign-made cars

(E) A military strategist who thinks that a nuclear war would leave no survivors but argues the United States should maintain a strong nuclear arsenal to deter other countries from launching a nuclear attack

(D) The essence of the NIMBY Syndrome is that the person who is afflicted with the syndrome falls into inconsistency. He insists on a certain course of action, say, building more prisons, but also adopts a posture that, if assumed by everyone, would make that course of action impossible. (D) parallels this thinking. The car dealer is in favor of a policy of free trade so long as there is free trade in other sectors of the economy but not in his own. (A) does not illustrate the NIMBY attitude. Rather, the parent is acting in an entirely consistent (if perhaps irrational) manner. (B) is perhaps the second-best answer, for the hypocrisy of the politician is at least suggestive of the inconsistency of those with the NIMBY attitude. But the politician of (B) is not quite like the homeowner of the initial paragraph. The politician implicitly acknowledges that he is subject to the law and then violates that law. The situation would be much closer to the NIMBY attitude if an incumbent politician said, "I think all politicians except incumbents should file disclosure forms." As for (C), the minister is not necessarily inconsistent in his actions, for he might advocate charity and still believe that a particular charitable institution was not the best vehicle for that charity. As for (E), the strategist is consistent in his actions, for he hopes to deter war by presenting a creditable threat.

During the past 20 years, the number of black members of state legislatures has increased by over 100 percent while the number of white members has declined slightly. This strongly suggests that the political power of blacks will soon be roughly equal to that of whites.

21. Which of the following, if true, would most weaken the argument above?

(A) The total number of seats available in state legislatures has remained virtually constant for the last 20 years.

(B) Twenty years ago, 168 blacks and 7,614 whites were members of state legislatures.

(C) Fewer than five states have elected blacks as governors over the past 20 years.

(D) During the past 20 years, median family income for both whites and blacks has risen by approximately 80 percent.

(E) During the past 20 years, the percentage of blacks who say they are registered to vote has increased, while the percentage of whites who say they are registered to vote has decreased.

(B) The conclusion of the argument is that the political power of blacks will soon be equal to that of whites. The support for this argument is the percent increase in the number of black legislators. The problem with statistics that describe percent changes is that the statistics provide no information about the actual quantities involved. Here, for example, as (B) points out, a 100-percent increase from a very low level is not very significant in terms of the actual numbers involved. Thus, if there are now around 350 black legislators and over 7,000 white ones, it's difficult to believe that blacks will soon have political power equal to that of whites.

A 15-year study of more than 45,000 Swedish soldiers suggests that heavy marijuana users are six times more likely than nonusers to develop schizophrenia. The authors of the study said the statistical association between schizophrenia and marijuana, or *cannabis*, does not necessarily mean that the drug causes schizophrenia. On the contrary, the study may suggest that consumption of marijuana is caused by emerging schizophrenia.

22. Which of the following is most similar in its structure to the argument above?

(A) The trainer explained to me that it may not be the excessive wear on the side of my sneaker that causes my ankle to ache. Instead, in response to the ache in my ankle, I may subconsciously shift the weight to the outside of my foot, which in turn would cause the sneaker to wear down.

(B) The judge found the defendant guilty of possession of stolen property and of conspiracy to buy and sell stolen property and sentenced her to five years' imprisonment on each count, the prison terms to run concurrently.

(C) The gardener always plants marigolds around the tomatoes. For years, we believed that this was simply to make the garden beautiful; but the gardener explained to us that the marigolds help to protect the tomatoes from nematodes, a pest which attacks the tomato plants.

(D) The recent increase in the incidence of street crimes such as robberies is attributable to two factors: the increased use of drugs such as cocaine and heroin, and the higher unemployment rate.

(E) To the primitive consciousness, all actions and movements were generated by spirits; for example, the tree swayed not because it was blown by the wind but because the spirit of the tree responded in harmony to the movement of the spirit of the wind.

(A) The initial argument is concerned with interpreting evidence and describing a cause-and-effect sequence. The researchers caution that the statistical association between schizophrenia and marijuana use does not demonstrate that marijuana use causes schizophrenia. It is also possible that people who have a tendency to be schizophrenic begin to use more and more marijuana as their condition worsens. In other words, it's not clear which is the cause and which is the effect. (A) is the only choice that offers a similar analysis: the ankle doesn't hurt because the sneaker is worn down; the sneaker gets worn down because the ankle hurts. (B) doesn't even discuss a cause-and-effect sequence. (C) does discuss a causal sequence, but (C) discusses which of two causes is the true explanation of an effect, not whether the seeming effect is really the explanation of the seeming cause. As for (D), this choice simply identifies some causes of a phenomenon, but it does not discuss a situation in which cause and effect might be incorrectly interpreted. Finally, (E) mentions a world view in which there are no causal relations as we know them, but that description is not parallel to the initial statement.

An inventor protects his rights by obtaining a patent; and to do this, he must exhibit a working model of the invention and demonstrate that the invention is original by showing that it represents a significant departure from other similar devices. The law also protects industrial trade secrets such as the chemical formula for a soft drink, but businesses are not required to register these secrets. As a result, one business could find that it has inadvertently used the trade secret of another business and wind up on the losing end of a law suit. It would be better for all if trade secrets were registered with a Trade Secrets Office, so that a business could regularly check to determine that it was not infringing upon another business's trade secrets.

23. The main weakness of the argument above is that it

    (A) relies upon a questionable analogy
    (B) reverses a cause-and-effect connection
    (C) generalizes on the basis of a single example
    (D) contains a logical contradiction
    (E) relies upon circular reasoning

    (A) The speaker draws an analogy between patents and trade secrets, but the analogy is flawed. A trade secret is just that, a secret, and if it were registered and readily available to everyone, then it would no longer be a secret. As for (B), problem 22, above, would be a good example of such reasoning. As for the remaining choices, the speaker does not make any generalizations, he does not contradict himself, and he doesn't beg any question.

Telephone Sales Representative: You can take advantage of a special introductory offer. You can get 26 weekly issues of the magazine for only $52. The regular subscription price is $104 per year.
Prospective Subscriber: That's not a special offer. Under either plan the cost is $2 per issue.

24. Which of the following, if true, most weakens the response of the prospective subscriber?

    (A) Normally, the minimum length of a subscription is a full year.
    (B) The magazine is available only on a subscription basis.
    (C) Recently, the price of the magazine increased from $1.75 to $2 per issue.
    (D) The year in which the exchange takes place is a leap year.
    (E) Other, similar magazines are available for $48 for a six-month subscription.

    (A) The prospective subscriber apparently believes that the essence of the "special" offer is a lower price. (A) is aimed at this hidden assumption. An offer could be special for reasons other than cost savings. (B)

and (C) are generally related to the idea discussed, but they neither strengthen nor weaken the prospective subscriber's response. (D) might at first attract your attention, for you might jump to the conclusion that the would-be subscriber is being offered more issues. But the magazine is issued on a weekly basis, so the subscriber would get one issue for each of the 26 weeks regardless of how many days there are in the year. Finally, (E) if anything strengthens the prospective subscriber's response: That's not so special, I can get the same thing even cheaper.

SECTION 3

READING COMPREHENSION

1. The author is primarily concerned with

    (A) explaining dramatic conventions
    (B) contrasting the works of two great writers
    (C) defending the work of one writer
    (D) disparaging the writing of one author
    (E) extolling nature as the perfect model for art

    (C) This is a main idea question. The main purpose of this passage is to argue that Shakespeare was a great writer. (A) is incorrect because it goes beyond the scope of the passage. The author does not discuss dramatic "conventions." (B) is incorrect because the single mention of Voltaire does not turn the entire passage into a contrast of two authors. As for (D), the main purpose is the defense of a writer, not the disparagement of a writer. Finally, the author praises Shakespeare for his fidelity to nature, but nature as a suitable topic of art is not the main point.

2. According to the author, which of the following is true of Shakespeare's characters?

    (A) They are all members of the nobility.
    (B) They are larger than life.
    (C) They are exotic and unfamiliar to the audience.
    (D) They do not exhibit emotion.
    (E) They are typical human beings.

    (E) This is an explicit idea question. In the second paragraph, the author specifically says that other writers use hyperbolic, aggravated, fabulous, or depraved characters, but not Shakespeare. So Shakespeare's characters would not be larger than life and would not be exotic, such as a dwarf or a giant. Thus, we eliminate (B), (C), and (D). As for (A), the passage never states that all Shakespearean characters are nobles. (And you shouldn't leap to such a conclusion just because Voltaire did not like Shakespeare's kings.) Thus, (E) is the best answer; the author does argue that Shakespeare's characters are ordinary people.

3. The author develops his theme primarily by

(A) presenting comparison and contrast
(B) mentioning specific characters and analyzing them
(C) quoting from other critics
(D) attacking popular opinion
(E) raising a point and then refuting it

(A) This is a logical structure question that asks about the overall development of the selection. The defense of Shakespeare's writing is carried out by contrasting it and comparing it with that of others whom the author considers to be inferior. So (A) correctly describes this development. (B) must be incorrect since the discussion is general. The author never mentions a single Shakespearean character by name. (C) must also be incorrect since the author never quotes anyone. And in any event, the passing reference to Voltaire hardly qualifies as the main theme of the passage. As for (D), the author does not mention any *popular* opinions. Finally, the author offers no refutation of a point, so (E) must be wrong.

4. The author cites Voltaire because he is

(A) a friend of Shakespeare
(B) a teacher of Shakespeare
(C) an admirer of Shakespeare
(D) a critic of Shakespeare
(E) a Shakespearean actor

(D) This is a logical structure question that asks *why* the author makes a specific point. Voltaire is mentioned in conjunction with critics of Shakespeare, and he says that Shakespeare's characters are defective (kings are not royal enough). So the author must have mentioned Voltaire as an example of a critic. By this reasoning, (B) and (C) must surely be wrong. And we can eliminate (A) and (E) since there is nothing in the selection to support such a conclusion.

5. The author uses the examples of hermit and confessor in the final sentence in order to

(A) emphasize that Shakespeare's plays are so true to life that one could learn about real people by reading them
(B) prove that Shakespeare's work was condemned by some critics for failing to include heroic characters
(C) call attention to the religious and mystical elements in Shakespeare's plays
(D) show that interesting characters such as hermits and confessors appear infrequently in Shakespeare's plays
(E) give examples of the hyperbolical and exaggerated characters he mentions as being typical of the work of other authors

(A) This is also a logical structure question. To answer, you must first determine what the final clause of the paragraph means. The hermit may estimate the transactions of the world, or we might say a hermit could learn about the world. A confessor may predict the progress of passion, or we might say, a confessor could learn about a person's feelings and thoughts—and all this from a play. The author is saying that a hermit (who supposedly knows nothing about the world) could learn about the world from Shakespeare since his plays accurately reflect nature (the world). And a confessor could learn about the hidden thoughts of another in the same way.

Of course, the author probably does not mean this literally. Rather, this is an attempt to underscore the main point of the passage, that Shakespeare's characters and action are reflective of the world as it is.

(A) nicely summarizes this point. (B) can be eliminated since this does not answer the "why" of the question. Though the author does say that Shakespeare was criticized, this is not why the author introduces the hermit and the confessor. As for (C), the author does not discuss any such features. As for (D) and (E), the author insists that exotic characters are not a part of Shakespeare's plays, so this is not why he introduces the confessor and the hermit.

6. Which of the following best describes the analogy the author wishes to draw by introducing the pedant of Hierocles?

(A) Shakespeare is to Hierocles as one of Shakespeare's plays is to the pedant
(B) Shakespeare is to Hierocles as one of Shakespeare's characters is to the pedant
(C) Shakespeare is to the pedant as Hierocles is to the brick
(D) Shakespeare's plays are to Hierocles's writings as Shakespeare's characters are to the pedant
(E) Lines from Shakespeare's plays are to the plays as the pedant's brick is to his house

(E) At the end of the first paragraph, the author makes the point that the most important feature of Shakespeare's plays is not isolated passages but the whole story and the entire dialogue. He notes that anyone who tries to prove that Shakespeare is a great writer by producing pithy quotations will fail to demonstrate what is really great in Shakespeare's writings. It is at this point that he mentions the pedant of Hierocles. The pedant attempted to give people an idea of his house by showing them an isolated brick. So the author intends to draw an analogy between the whole of a play and the house and a pithy quotation and a single brick.

7. According to the passage, the very first private hospitals

    (A) developed from almshouse infirmaries
    (B) provided better care than public infirmaries
    (C) were established mainly to service the poor
    (D) were supported by government revenues
    (E) catered primarily to the middle-class patients

    (C) This is a specific idea question. According to the first paragraph, private charity hospitals were established about the same time that public hospitals split off from the almshouses. Both had the same objective, to provide for the poor.

8. It can be inferred that the author believes the differences that currently exist between public and private hospitals are primarily the result of

    (A) political considerations
    (B) economic factors
    (C) ethical concerns
    (D) legislative requirements
    (E) technological developments

    (B) This is an inference question that covers the entire passage. The entire analysis is done in economic terms, such as the need for income and the attempt to attract paying patients. So though the author never specifically states that he considers economic factors to be the primary determinants of the present situation, we may infer such a conclusion from the passage.

9. It can be inferred that the growth of private health insurance

    (A) relieved local governments of the need to fund public hospitals
    (B) guaranteed that the poor would have access to medical care
    (C) forced middle-class patients to use public hospitals
    (D) prompted the closing of many charitable institutions
    (E) reinforced the distinction between public and private hospitals

    (E) This is an implied idea question. In the final paragraph the author states that health insurance provided the middle class with the ability to purchase services from private hospitals. This guaranteed private hospitals a source of income. So private hospitals chose to treat only income-producing patients, which left the poor to seek care at public hospitals. Then the author jumps to the conclusion that public hospitals have become a dumping ground. Though the author does not specifically say so, we may infer that he believes that private health insurance is in large measure responsible for the distinction between public and private hospitals and for the plight of public hospitals.

10. Which of the following would be the most logical topic for the author to introduce in the next paragraph?

    (A) A plan to improve the quality of public hospitals
    (B) An analysis of the profit structure of health insurance companies
    (C) A proposal to raise taxes on the middle class
    (D) A discussion of recent developments in medical technology
    (E) A list of the subjects studied by students in medical school

    (A) This is a further application question. The author begins and ends with public hospitals. Every time that he mentions private hospitals, it is only to compare them with public hospitals. Given this, and that he concludes by saying that public hospitals have suffered as a result of the events described, it is not unlikely that he is leading up to a discussion of how to rectify the situation.

11. The author's primary concern is to

    (A) describe the financial structure of the health-care industry
    (B) demonstrate the importance of government support for health-care institutions
    (C) criticize wealthy institutions for refusing to provide services to the poor
    (D) identify the historical causes of the division between private and public hospitals
    (E) praise public hospitals for their willingness to provide health care for the poor

    (D) This is a main idea question. The passage provides a brief history of public hospitals, a history which, according to the author, ends unsatisfactorily. A fair description of that development is provided by (D).

12. The author cites all of the following as factors contributing to the decline of public hospitals EXCEPT

    (A) Government money was used to subsidize private medical schools and hospitals to the detriment of public hospitals.
    (B) Public hospitals are not able to compete with private institutions for top flight managers and doctors.
    (C) Large private medical centers have better research facilities and more extensive research programs than public hospitals.
    (D) Public hospitals accepted the responsibility for treating patients with certain diseases.
    (E) Blue Cross insurance coverage does not reimburse subscribers for medical expenses incurred in a public hospital.

    (E) This is a specific detail question—with a thought-reverser. (A), (B), (C), and (D) are all mentioned in the third paragraph. (E), however, is an idea never mentioned in the selection. Though the author does state that Blue Cross plans covered patients likely to use private hospitals, he does not say that these plans did not cover expenses incurred in public hospitals.

13. The author's attitude toward public hospitals can best be described as

   (A) contemptuous and prejudiced
   (B) apprehensive and distrustful
   (C) concerned and understanding
   (D) enthusiastic and supportive
   (E) unsympathetic and annoyed

   (C) This is a tone question. Although the author discusses the plight of the public hospital, he does so as an interested third party. He recognizes that public hospitals are not the equal of private hospitals, but he understands the economic factors that created this problem. Thus, we can eliminate those choices with highly negative overtones, specifically, (A), (B), and (E). (D) overstates the case in the opposite directions. The tone of the selection is not enthusiastic.

14. The author implies that any outpatient care provided by a hospital is

   (A) paid for by private insurance
   (B) provided in lieu of treatment by a private physician
   (C) supplied primarily by private hospitals
   (D) a source of revenue for public hospitals
   (E) no longer provided by hospitals, public or private

   (B) This is an implied idea question. In the fourth sentence of the third paragraph, the author states: "... provision of outpatient care has not been a major function of the private hospital, in part, because private patients can afford to pay for the services of private physicians." From this, we can infer that the outpatient care provided by public hospitals is the same sort of care that would otherwise be provided by a private doctor. Since this type of care is provided by public hospitals, the remaining answer choices must be wrong.

15. According to the passage, the interservice strife that followed unification occurred primarily between the

   (A) Army and Army Air Forces
   (B) Army and Navy
   (C) Army Air Forces and Navy
   (D) Navy and Army
   (E) Air Force and Navy

   (E) This is a specific detail question. In the third paragraph, it is specifically stated that the Navy and the Air Force became adversaries.

16. It can be inferred from the passage that Forrestal's appointment as Secretary of Defense was expected to

   (A) placate members of the Navy
   (B) result in decreased levels of defense spending
   (C) outrage advocates of the Army Air Forces
   (D) win Congressional approval of the unification plan
   (E) make Forrestal a Presidential candidate against Truman

   (A) This is an implied idea. The reference you need is in the second paragraph. There the author states that not even the appointment of Forrestal allayed the suspicions of Navy officers and their allies. The words *not even* allow us to infer that the appointment of Forrestal was intended to have a placating effect on those people.

17. According to the passage, President Truman supported which of the following?

   I. Elimination of the Navy
   II. A unified military service
   III. Establishment of a separate air force

   (A) I only
   (B) II only
   (C) I and II only
   (D) II and III only
   (E) I, II, and III

   (B) This is a specific detail question. In the first paragraph it is stated that Truman recommended the unification of the military services and a separate air force.

18. With which of the following statements about defense unification would the author most likely agree?

   (A) Unification ultimately undermined United States military capability by inciting interservice rivalry.
   (B) The unification legislation was necessitated by the drastic decline in appropriations for the military services.
   (C) Although the unification was not entirely successful, it had the unexpected result of ensuring civilian control of the military.
   (D) In spite of the attempted unification, each service was still able to pursue its own objectives without interference from the other branches.
   (E) Unification was in the first place unwarranted, and in the second place ineffective.

   (C) This is a further application question. In the closing paragraph the author states that an unexpected result of the unification battle was that the military would never be able to establish itself as a power independent of and outside civilian control.

19. According to the selection, the political situation following the passage of the National Security Act of 1947 was characterized by all of the following EXCEPT

(A) a shifting balance of power in Europe and in Asia
(B) fierce interservice rivalries
(C) lack of strong leadership by the National Security Council
(D) shrinking postwar military budgets
(E) a lame-duck President who was unable to unify the legislature

(E) This is a specific detail question—with a thought-reverser. Four of the five ideas are mentioned in the selection. The one that is not is the correct choice. (A) and (C) are mentioned in the second paragraph. (D) is mentioned in the third paragraph. (B) is mentioned at several points in the selection. (E), however, is not mentioned.

20. The author cites the resignation and suicide of Forrestal in order to

(A) underscore the bitterness of the interservice rivalry surrounding the passage of the National Security Act of 1947
(B) demonstrate that the Navy eventually emerged as the dominant branch of service after the passage of the National Security Act of 1947
(C) suggest that the nation would be better served by a unified armed service under a single command
(D) provide an example of a military leader who preferred to serve his country in war rather than in peace
(E) persuade the reader that Forrestal was a victim of political opportunists and an unscrupulous press

(A) This is a logical structure question. Why does the author mention this fact? In the first paragraph, the author is describing the bitter rivalries that surround the passage of the NSA, and it is at the end of that paragraph that he mentions the resignation and suicide of Forrestal. The reason, therefore, he mentioned Forrestal must have been to underscore the bitterness of the interservice fighting.

21. The author is primarily concerned with

(A) discussing the influence of personalities on political events
(B) describing the administration of a powerful leader
(C) criticizing a piece of legislation
(D) analyzing a political development
(E) suggesting methods for controlling the military

(D) This is a main idea question. Although the ideas contained in the wrong choices are mentioned in the discussion (personalities, the President, a law, and the military), the author views the events primarily in political terms.

22. Which of the following best describes the logical structure of the passage?

(A) The author presents a theory and then describes the kind of evidence that would support the theory.
(B) The author outlines a widely accepted theory and then introduces evidence to refute it.
(C) The author describes a phenomenon and then formulates a theory to explain it.
(D) The author introduces statistical studies to support a theory that is highly speculative.
(E) The author describes the result of an experiment that he conducted to prove a theory.

(A) This is a logical structure question. The author begins by theorizing that black holes may represent a possible course in a star's evolution. Then he describes the properties of a black hole. Nothing that goes in can get out, so it is impossible to see them. Next, he asks how one could possibly prove the existence of a black hole (and live to tell about it). In the final paragraph, he suggests that certain natural events might set up a kind of "experiment" that would permit us to determine that black holes do, in fact, exist. (A) correctly describes this development.

23. According to the passage, a black hole would

(A) be most likely to develop in a binary star system
(B) emit large quantities of X and gamma rays
(C) be observable through a powerful telescope
(D) be formed from a degenerate dwarf star
(E) be invisible even at close range

(E) This is a specific detail question. The author specifically states that nothing (not even light) can escape from a black hole. A probe nearing a black hole, he explains, would detect a gravitational field, but it would not "see" anything.

24. It can be inferred from the passage that a neutron star originated as a

(A) degenerate dwarf star of any size
(B) normal star with a mass less than one-third that of our sun
(C) normal star with a mass greater than that of our sun but less than three times that of our sun
(D) normal star with a mass at least three times greater than that of our sun
(E) supernova with a mass at least three times greater than that of our sun

(C) This is a specific detail question. The answer is given in the first paragraph. The author states that stars the size of our sun or smaller become dwarf stars. Stars with a mass greater than three times that of our sun become black holes. And stars with a mass in between those two limits become neutron stars.

25. It can be inferred that a black hole has

(A) no mass at all
(B) a mass only one-third of the mass of the normal star from which it was formed
(C) approximately the same mass as the normal star from which it was formed
(D) a mass approximately equal to the mass of two binary stars
(E) a mass equal to the mass of our sun

(C) This is an implied idea question. In describing what a probe might find as it neared a black hole, the author states that it would detect a gravitational field that would be associated with a normal star of the same mass. We may infer, therefore, that the black hole keeps the same mass (approximately) that it had when it was a normal star before it became a black hole.

26. The author regards the existence of black holes as

(A) in principle unprovable
(B) theoretically possible
(C) extremely unlikely
(D) experimentally confirmed
(E) a logical contradiction

(B) This is an attitude question. The author discusses the existence of black holes only in theoretical terms. He gives reason to believe that they might exist and describes the conditions that might prove their existence. (B) is the best description of this attitude.

27. All of the following are mentioned by the author as evidence to suggest that the Cygnus X−1 source might be a black hole EXCEPT

(A) Cygnus X−1 is a source of powerful X-ray radiation.
(B) The companion star of Cygnus X−1 has a mass sufficiently large to create a black hole.
(C) The intensity of the X-rays emanating from Cygnus X−1 exhibits short-term variability.
(D) The star around which the visible star of Cygnus X−1 is orbiting is not itself visible.
(E) The visible star of the Cygnus X−1 system is a blue supergiant.

(E) This is a specific detail question with a thought-reverser. In the second paragraph the author describes the "experimental" conditions that might confirm the existence of a black hole, and in the final paragraph he describes a star system that seems to fit these conditions. He mentions that such a system would be a source of X-radiation (A) and that this radiation would exhibit variation (C), as Cygnus X−1 does. He mentions that one of the stars is invisible (D)—an important characteristic of a black hole—and that this invisible star has a mass of the requisite weight (B). The author also states that the other star in the system is a blue supergiant, but that is not one of the features of the system that suggests that the system includes a black hole. So (E) is true but not responsive to the question.

28. According to the passage, the gravitational radius of a black hole is the

(A) orbital distance separating a visible star from a black hole in a binary star system
(B) distance at which matter is irreversibly drawn into the black hole by gravitational forces
(C) distance from the black hole at which an approaching rocket would first start to disintegrate
(D) radius of the massive star that created the black hole when it collapsed in upon itself
(E) scale for measuring the short-term variability of X-radiation emitted by a black hole

(B) This is a specific detail question. In the last sentence of the second paragraph, the author states that the gravitational radius is the "point of no return," meaning the distance at which objects are irresistibly drawn in by the forces of the black hole. Notice that the other choices use language that appears in the selection, but they either represent misreadings of the passage or are not responsive to the question asked.

SECTION 4

LOGICAL REASONING

There is a tendency in intelligence-gathering communities for the members of each lower level of bureaucracy to filter information before it is passed to the next higher level. Thus, the information is colored so that it meets the expectation of a superior. A good example of this tendency is the Gulf of Tonkin incident. Although the Destroyer Maddox transmitted a second message recanting the first and requesting time for reevaluation of data, the second message was blocked by the bureaucracy. Intermediate bureau chiefs failed to relay the information to the President because they knew he ____(25)____.

1. Which of the following best completes the paragraph above?

   (A) was already aware of the content of the second message
   (B) had already made his decision on the basis of the first message
   (C) would have been displeased by the carelessness of the crew in sending the first message
   (D) was not interested in the content of the first message
   (E) was pleased with the content of the first message

(E) This item asks you to draw a conclusion from the statements given. The essence of the tendency described is that bureaucracies create self-fulfilling prophecies. Someone in the bureaucracy knows what his superior wants to hear, so he makes sure that's what he hears. Applying this analysis to the specific example of the Gulf of Tonkin incident, the intermediate bureau chiefs failed to pass information along to their superior, the President, because they had already told him what he wanted to hear. The initial paragraph implies that the President did not know of the second message until later, so (A) is incorrect. As for (B), while this may be a reason not to forward information, this completion does not create an example that illustrates the general problem described in the initial paragraph. As for (C), while it is true that the bureau chiefs did not want to disappoint the President, the disappointment would have been generated by the contradiction of his pet views, not by dissatisfaction with the crew's efficiency. Finally, (D) is specifically contradicted by our analysis above. The President was very interested in the first message.

PETER: Seventy percent of the people we surveyed stated that they would use Myrdal for relief of occasional headache pain, while only 30 percent of those surveyed indicated that they would take Burphin for such pain.

RON: Then over twice as many people preferred Myrdal to Burphin.

PETER: No, 25 percent of those surveyed stated that they never took any such medication.

2. Which of the following, if true, best explains the reason for the seeming inconsistency in Peter's claim?

   (A) The survey included more than 1,000 people.
   (B) Fifty percent of the people surveyed mentioned neither Myrdal nor Burphin.
   (C) Some of the people surveyed indicated that they would take both medications.
   (D) None of the people who said that they would take Myrdal indicated that they would also take Burphin.
   (E) All of the people who said that they would take Myrdal also responded that they would take Burphin.

(C) Peter's claim may at first seem to be inconsistent because he denies that over twice as many respondents preferred Myrdal to Burphin even though 70 percent of the people responded they would take Myrdal and only 30 percent responded they would take Burphin. The key to eliminating the seeming contradiction is Peter's remark that 25 percent of the people responded that they took neither Myrdal nor Burphin. This indicates that the two groups (those who take Myrdal and those who take Burphin) are not mutually exclusive. So some of the people surveyed must have mentioned both medicines—as noted by (C).

Some legislators have proposed raising the gasoline tax to help reduce the Federal budget deficit. The Federal gasoline tax is already nine cents per gallon. In addition, states tax gasoline at an average of more than 15 cents per gallon. In fact, the gasoline tax rates are as high as the so-called "sin" taxes on alcohol and tobacco. Gasoline, however, is not a "sinful" commodity. It is practically a necessity, and any increase in the gasoline tax would be unfair.

3. The speaker above is arguing primarily

   (A) for the repeal of the gasoline tax
   (B) for a reduction in the gasoline tax rate
   (C) against an increase in the gasoline tax rate
   (D) against taxes on alcohol and tobacco
   (E) against the sale of alcohol and tobacco

(C) The speaker begins by identifying the issue she will address: the proposed increase in the gasoline tax. She then proceeds to attack that proposal. Thus,

(C) provides the best description of the paragraph. (A) and (B) both overstate the case. To be opposed to a plan to do something is not equivalent to proposing a different plan. As for (D) and (E), the speaker uses the tax rates on alcohol and tobacco as a standard by which to measure the fairness of the tax on gasoline, but she doesn't argue against such taxes or against the sale of those commodities.

As part of a Federal package to aid beleaguered savings and loan institutions, Congress has proposed prohibiting these institutions from investing in high-yield junk bonds. Thrifts would be barred from investing in companies that fail to earn a "higher bond-rating," that is, a triple-B rating or higher. This will put savings and loans on a more conservative and more secure footing. Additionally, Congress has seized the opportunity to help redress some of the inequalities of the American economy by requiring savings and loans to direct more investment toward minority groups, women, and inner-city areas.

4. Which of the following, if true, would be the best criticism of the proposal discussed above?

(A) Many savings and loan institutions failed when Latin American countries defaulted on their obligations.
(B) Savings and loan institutions are a major source of investment in the American economy.
(C) Savings and loans institutions are geographically diversified and serve localized areas.
(D) No business owned largely by blacks, Hispanics, or women qualifies for the higher bond ratings.
(E) Adjustable rate mortgages commonly offered by savings and loans are considered risky loans.

(D) The speaker states that the plan to aid savings and loans contains two valuable provisions. What (D) points out is that the two provisions work against each other. If savings and loans cannot invest in risky ventures, then they cannot fulfill the goal of aiding businesses owned by minority groups and women. (A) and (E) are wrong for the same reason. Although both cite factors contributing to the problems experienced by savings and loans, the speaker is not addressing the genesis of the problem but rather a possible solution. And (B) and (C) are wrong for the same reason. Both mention characteristics of savings and loans, but those characteristics are not immediately relevant to the argument made by the speaker.

The death penalty is not really effective in protecting society. In 1972, the death sentences of 558 murderers were automatically commuted to prison terms by a Supreme Court decision. Since then, four of those inmates have committed murders in prison, and another committed a murder after his release. It is foolish to kill over 550 people just to save the lives of 5 people.

5. The argument above assumes that

(A) some of the death row inmates were improperly convicted
(B) the Supreme Court should not have commuted the death sentences
(C) the life of a convicted murderer is as valuable as that of a victim
(D) more murders take place inside of prison walls than outside of them
(E) few people would object to the death penalty if it protected them

(C) This argument asks you to identify a hidden assumption of the argument. The speaker does a calculation: 550 is greater than 5. For this calculation to work, the two quantities compared must be of similar types. (You can't compare apples and oranges.) Therefore, the speaker is logically committed to the notion that the lives of the convicted murderers have as much value as those of the victims. (For example, someone might argue that it is worth the lives of 550 murderers to save the lives of 5 future victims.) As for (A), although the speaker is opposed to the death penalty, the objection does not depend on this argument. As for (B), this idea actually seems to contradict the speaker's position, for he is opposed to the death penalty. As for (D), though the author cites four murders in prison and one outside of prison, remember that this is a special subgroup of the population—convicted murderers. Since most of those are probably in prison, it would not be surprising to learn that any crimes committed by them would be committed in prison. So the speaker is not logically committed to the notion that more murders—in general—are committed within prison than without. Finally, as for (E), although the speaker's argument against the death penalty is couched in terms of deterrence, he is not logically committed to any position about what other people think.

Four students are competing in the final round of a debating match:

If Alan scores more points than Beth or if Cathy scores more points than David, then Cathy will be the winner.

If David scores more points than Alan, then Beth will be the winner.

If Cathy scores more points than Beth, then Alan will be the winner.

6. If David is the winner, then which of the following statements must be true?

    I. David scored more points than Cathy.
    II. Neither Cathy nor Alan scored more points than Beth.
    III. David did not score more points than Alan.

    (A) III only
    (B) I and II only
    (C) I and III only
    (D) II and III only
    (E) I, II, and III

(D) The information establishes conditions under which David would not be the winner. (Cathy, Beth, or Alan would be the winner under conditions one, two, and three, respectively.) If David is the winner, then none of those conditions obtains. The first and third conditions establish that if either Alan or Cathy beats Beth, then someone other than David is the winner. Since David is the winner, we can infer statement II. Similarly, given the second condition, had David scored more points than Alan, David would not have been the winner. So statement III is inferable. Statement I, however, is not inferable. We do know that Cathy did not score more points than David, but we cannot infer from that that David scored more points than Cathy. Perhaps David and Cathy scored the same number of points.

I had planned to vote for Smith in the upcoming election for the Senate, but I have changed my mind. The *Morning News* endorsed Smith and I disagree with the *Morning News* on just about every issue.

7. Which of the following, if true, would weaken the argument above?

    (A) Smith did not solicit the endorsement.
    (B) Many political leaders have endorsed Smith.
    (C) Smith is the incumbent in the race.
    (D) Smith's main opponent has no previous political experience.
    (E) No other newspaper has yet endorsed Smith.

(A) The speaker's argument makes sense only if the speaker assumes that the endorsement was given because the paper agrees with Smith's views. Choice (A) attacks that assumption by stating that

Smith did not want to be endorsed by a newspaper with those views, suggesting that Smith's views are different from those held by the newspaper. None of the other answer choices is relevant to the logical structure of the argument.

The rusty crayfish outcompetes blue and fantail crayfish. Consequently, it has become the top feeder on plants. It also eats fish eggs and the plants that form the habitat of fish that prey on crayfish. This limits the number of fish. In lakes with rusty crayfish, muddy bottoms with layers of muck and many plants have now given way to clean, sandy bottoms with few plants.

8. The speaker above is primarily concerned with

    (A) outlining a causal chain
    (B) advancing a new proposal
    (C) speculating about the future
    (D) attacking a government policy
    (E) defending a generalization

(A) This question asks only that you describe the type of analysis used by the speaker. The speaker explains the causal consequences of having the rusty crayfish in a lake, so (A) is the best response. As for (B), the speaker doesn't present any plan. (You don't even know whether she thinks the presence of the rusty crayfish is a good idea or a bad one.) (C) is wrong because the speaker is not speculating. Rather, she describes a known causal sequence. (D) is wrong because no government policy is mentioned. And (E) is incorrect because the speaker does not reach a general conclusion based on a few examples.

Mary Cassatt, like Edgar Degas, was impressed by the exhibition of Japanese *ukiyo-e* prints at the Ecole des Beaux-Arts in Paris during the spring of 1890. By April of 1891, she had finished a set of prints of her own depicting scenes of domestic life. These describe moments such as a woman washing her little boy or a woman mailing a letter. The women depicted all seem emotionally removed from the scene and introspective. Cassatt eschewed the more traditional poses in favor of a casual representation—a technique used also by Degas. Consequently, even the most sweetly colored of the works do not appear in the least saccharine or sentimental.

9. The paragraph above implies that

    (A) Degas and Cassatt collaborated on the prints
    (B) the prints were produced in a great hurry
    (C) Cassatt rarely depicted everyday life
    (D) more formal poses might have made the works sentimental
    (E) the *ukiyo-e* prints treated official or formal moments

(D) In the final sentence, the speaker states that a

consequence of Cassatt's decision not to use formal poses is that the works are not sentimental. We can infer from this that formal poses might have made the works sentimental. As for (A), although the speaker mentions that both Cassatt and Degas were impressed by the exhibition, there is nothing in the paragraph to suggest that they worked together to create Cassatt's prints. As for (B), the speaker does say that the prints were finished by April of 1891 — but is that a short time or a long time to produce prints? As for (C), the speaker does state that these particular works depicted scenes from everyday life, but that is not sufficient information from which to conclude that Cassatt rarely did this. And as for (E), the passage does not say what the Japanese prints depicted.

One of the most effective ways to reduce street sales of crack is interdiction of supplies at the border. Interdiction raises the price of crack by increasing the cost of smuggling, and higher cost decreases demand.

10. Which of the following, if true, most weakens the argument above?

   (A) Arrests of street-level dealers and users have created a problem of state and federal prison overcrowding
   (B) Smuggling costs account for only 1 percent of the street price of crack.
   (C) Drugs are grown, processed, and transported in countries where bribery of government officials is common.
   (D) A successful interdiction effort requires a nationally coordinated Federal effort.
   (E) Increased use of crack has led to an increase in supply, which in turn lowers the cost of crack.

(B) The argument above depends upon the assumption that the cost of smuggling is sufficiently important to have some effect on the final cost of street transactions. (B) attacks this assumption. If the cost of smuggling is only 1 percent of the cost of the drug at street level, then even doubling the cost of smuggling would have only a very small impact on the final cost of the drug. (A), (C), and (E) are problems associated with drug sales, but they are not connected to the speaker's analysis of the problem. (D) is perhaps the second-best answer, but it doesn't really attack the speaker's position. It states that a nationally coordinated Federal effort is required but does not say that such an effort is impossible or even difficult.

Every business executive carries a briefcase, and these briefcases are invariably brown or black.

11. Which of the following conclusions most reliably follows from the statement above?

   (A) All briefcases are either brown or black.
   (B) Some business executives carry briefcases that are neither brown nor black.
   (C) Some people carry brown briefcases, and some people carry black briefcases.
   (D) All brown and black briefcases are carried by business executives.
   (E) All briefcases are carried by business executives.

(C) The initial statement asserts that all business executives carry either a brown or a black briefcase. Therefore, at least some people are known to carry brown briefcases, and some people are known to carry black briefcases. (A) is wrong because the initial statement refers only to those briefcases carried by business executives. (B) is directly contradicted by the initial statement. (All briefcases carried by business executives are either brown or black.) (D) and (E) both make this kind of error: All whales are mammals; therefore, all mammals are whales.

All statements about truth are inherently subjective and therefore purely a matter of individual opinion. Such statements carry no moral authority for any but the individual who makes them.

12. A logical weakness in the claim above is that it

   (A) is internally inconsistent
   (B) is a hasty generalization
   (C) mistakes a cause for an effect
   (D) relies upon an unproved assumption
   (E) assumes what it hopes to prove

(A) The statement is equivalent to saying there is no such thing as a true statement. If the statement is true, then what it says must be the case, namely, that no statement is true. But if what it says is the case, namely, that no statement is true, then it must be false. So the statement winds up contradicting itself. The technical term used to describe the initial statement is paradox, but the best response is "internally inconsistent."

One man can dig a posthole in four minutes; therefore, four men can dig a posthole in one minute.

13. The argument above is weak because it

(A) makes a questionable assumption
(B) is internally inconsistent
(C) relies on questionable authority
(D) uses its conclusion as one of its premises
(E) confuses an effect with its cause

(A) The weakness of the argument is that it assumes that four people can work together as efficiently as one person working alone. If you are not clear about the meanings of the other choices, see Lesson 12.

The President has done a remarkable job of holding the line on military expenditures. Last year, defense expenditures in constant dollars were just about what they were in 1970.

14. Which of the following statements, if true, represents the most serious criticism of the claim above?

(A) The President promised during the election campaign that the defense budget would be carefully scrutinized for waste.
(B) In 1970, the United States was devoting extraordinary military resources to fighting a war in Southeast Asia.
(C) Since 1970, the average salary increase for personnel in the military has paralleled the rise in the cost-of-living index.
(D) Several proposals for complex weapons systems have been delayed for one year or more in order to hold the line on defense expenditures.
(E) When measured as a proportion of Gross National Product, military expenditures by other Western nations have declined since 1970.

(B) This question asks that you weaken the argument. Often the correct answer to such a question attacks a hidden assumption of the argument. Here, the speaker's claim rests upon an implicit or hidden assumption that 1970 is a legitimate year for comparison. (B) attacks this by pointing out that 1970 was an unusual year: military expenditures were especially high. This considerably undermines that speaker's claim that military expenditures now are not excessive. As for (A), (C), and (D), these choices fail to come to grips with the specific claim made by the speaker. And to the extent that you think one of these three statements might be relevant, the statement is more likely to support the speaker's claim than to undermine it. And (E) is simply irrelevant, since the speaker is not talking about "other Western nations."

Guns don't kill people—people do! If a gun is not available, a person intent on doing someone else bodily harm will turn to the next-best available weapon, a knife. So banning guns will not help prevent homicides.

15. The argument above assumes that

(A) people who are violent are likely to commit several crimes
(B) knives are used more frequently in crimes than guns
(C) guns are more widely available than other weapons
(D) knives are equally as deadly as guns
(E) dangerous knives should be banned

(D) Again we are asked to identify a hidden assumption of an argument. Here, the speaker claims that someone intent on doing someone else bodily harm will use whatever means are available and that gun control would therefore be ineffective. This reasoning depends upon the unarticulated premise that the result will be the same whether the person reaches for a gun or for a knife. This is specifically made clear by (D). (Whether or not this is a correct assumption is not relevant to this question. All we have to see is that the speaker does make such an assumption.) (A) is an answer that you might find attractive if you are not reading carefully. Had (A) read "people who are violent are likely to commit a crime," it would have been more nearly correct. But that is not what (A) says. As for (B) and (C), the speaker claims that a person intent on committing a crime will find the means (knife or gun) but is not committed to any comparison of the frequency with which weapons are now used. Finally, as for (E), this is a sentiment with which the speaker would likely disagree since he seems to have the attitude that nothing will deter someone who is intent on injuring someone else.

If Alice told Bob about the surprise party, then Bob told Carl about the surprise party. And if Carl knew about the party, then Danielle knew about it. But Danielle did not know about the surprise party.

16. Which of the following statements can be deduced from the information given above?

   I. Alice did not tell Carl about the party.
  II. Alice did not tell Bob about the party.
 III. Carl did not know about the party.

(A) I only (B) II only (C) I and II only
(D) I and III only (E) I, II, and III

(E) This argument is a variation on what is known as the hypothetical syllogism:

If A, then B.
If B, then C.
A.
Therefore C.

(I say it is a variation because the argument in this problem does not have this precise structure.) It is important to remember that an argument like this is *hypothetical*. It reads *"if* a certain condition obtains, *then* another also obtains." Here we are told that Danielle did not know about the party. Given that information, we can conclude that Carl also did not know. (Otherwise, Danielle would have known.) And we can conclude that Bob did not know. (Otherwise, he would have told Carl.) And we can conclude that Alice did not tell Carl. (Otherwise Carl would have known and so, too, would Danielle). So all three statements can be deduced.

Patty: Administration officials know the identity of the students who painted grafitti on campus buildings during the recent demonstrations. Those students should be expelled from school. This will discourage other students from doing the same thing in the future.

Randy: But if those students are expelled, students in the future might be tempted to do worse damage because they know they will be expelled anyway.

17. The speakers above both agree that

(A) expulsion from school is a severe penalty
(B) no future demonstrations will cause vandalism
(C) the administration should deal more harshly with vandals
(D) students are justified in using vandalism as a protest tool
(E) some students will commit criminal acts despite sanctions

(A) The two speakers here have different opinions about what the administration should do, but they both share the opinion that expulsion is a serious punishment. Their different opinions are about whether or not that serious sanction should be used.

(B) is incorrect because it is not clear that either speaker knows what will happen in the future. (C) is wrong because the second speaker seems to think that harsh sanctions should not be used. As for (D) and (E), if anything, both speakers agree implicitly that vandalism is something that should be deterred (but they disagree about how to accomplish that).

When I need to get a letter to a business associate as fast as possible, I use an overnight express service no matter what the cost. Otherwise, I use the postal service, because it is cheaper.

18. The speaker's remark assumes that

(A) the postal service is generally less efficient than overnight express services
(B) an overnight express service is less expensive than the postal service
(C) cost and delivery time are the two most important factors to consider
(D) cost is a more important consideration for important packages than delivery time
(E) the postal service is sometimes able to deliver sooner than an overnight express service

(C) The speaker here sets up an "either/or" proposition: either speed at any cost or minimum cost regardless of speed. So speed and cost are the only two factors this speaker would consider—as noted by (C). (A) is incorrect because it uses the word *efficient*. The speaker does assume that ordinary postal service is not as *fast* as express service, but speed and efficiency are not the same thing. (B) and (E) are both specifically contradicted by the speaker's remarks. Finally, as for (D), the speaker is not committed to a position such as this. She considers two factors, but the weight accorded to each will depend upon the situation. Sometimes cost will be more important than speed.

In 1983, 75 percent of the employees in the garment center were resident aliens. In 1989, only 60 percent were resident aliens.

19. If the statements above are true, all of the following could be true about the 1983-to-1989 period EXCEPT:

(A) The number of people employed in the garment center increased.
(B) The total resident alien population of the country increased.
(C) The number of resident aliens employed in the garment center increased while the total number of persons employed declined.
(D) The number of firms in the garment center declined while the total number of persons employed there increased.

(E) The value of imported garments increased while the total value of production by the garment center also increased.

(C) According to this claim, the *percentage* of the work force in the garment center classified as resident alien declined during a certain period. This claim is therefore consistent with every statement except that given by (C). It is possible that the number of people employed in the industry increased (and that many of the new employees were not resident aliens). Thus, (A) is possible. As for (B), it is possible that the total resident alien population increased, but those people simply didn't find jobs in the garment center. As for (D), it is possible that the number of businesses in the garment center declined and that the others provided more jobs (most of which were filled by persons other than resident aliens). Finally, as for (E), the value of goods produced is not relevant to a claim about the status of the workers. (C), however, is not possible. If the total number of persons employed in the industry declined while the number of resident aliens increased, the resident aliens would have counted for an increasing proportion of the work force.

You can fool all of the people some of the time, and some of the people all of the time.

20. Which of the following conclusions can be logically deduced from the statement above?

(A) No one can be fooled all of the time.
(B) Everyone can be fooled most of the time.
(C) Someone can be fooled all of the time.
(D) All of the time no one can be fooled.
(E) At no time can anyone be fooled.

(C) According to the speaker, you can fool some of the people all of the time—as (C) correctly notes. As for (A), the speaker specifically says that some people can be fooled all of the time. (B) overstates the claim. The speaker says only that some (not all) of the people can be fooled all of the time. As for (D) and (E), since some people can be fooled all of the time, at all times someone is fooled.

I know that when my children grow up they will become lawyers, because my parents, my wife, and I are all lawyers.

21. The argument above can be best criticized because it

(A) fails to define the term *lawyer*
(B) oversimplifies a causal connection
(C) does not rely upon statistics
(D) uses an ambiguous term
(E) uses circular reasoning

(B) This argument is fairly simplistic and the weakness should be obvious to you: the speaker oversimplifies a causal connection. As for (A) and (C), it is true that the speaker doesn't define *lawyer* and doesn't use statistics, but why should he? As for (D), there is no term in the argument that doesn't have a fairly clear meaning. And as for (E), although the argument is weak, it doesn't have the structure of a circular argument. (If you are not clear about what constitutes a circular argument, look up that topic in the chapters devoted to Logical Reasoning in this book.)

My favorite color is red, and I don't like the color green. My wife's favorite color is green, and she doesn't like the color red. Is what she sees as red what I experience when I see green, thus accounting for the difference in our preferences? Or do we both see red and green alike, but have different reactions to the two stimuli? It is impossible to justify one explanation over the other, for there is no possibility of verifying one answer or the other.

22. The speaker above assumes that

　I. some experiences are entirely subjective
　II. everyone has a favorite color
　III. no one can like both red and green

(A) I only　(B) II only　(C) III only
(D) I and III only　(E) I, II, and III

(A) This argument is a simple version of a standard "Introduction to Philosophy" problem: Is what you see as red the same thing I see as red? (We both identify the same things as red, but maybe my experience of those things is different from yours.) A key assumption of this problem is that a personal experience is just that. I can't know exactly what you experience and vice versa, as statement I points out. As for II and III, the argument does not assume that every person has a favorite color, only that what you experience as red or green may be different from what I experience. (I could like all colors, and you could hate all colors.)

Kevin: I think that Martha is an excellent parent. She is a full-time professional and offers a wonderful role-model for her children. Additionally, she earns a very nice living and is able to provide her children with a nice home and virtually every educational advantage possible.

Mark: I don't think Martha is a good parent. Counting commuting time, she spends over ten hours a day away from home and sometimes must travel out of town overnight. If she worked fewer hours and closer to home, she could be more of a mother.

23. The two speakers above disagree primarily about

    (A) how much time Martha spends with her children
    (B) what Martha's children think of her
    (C) whether Martha is happy in her career
    (D) how to define a good parent
    (E) whether a working mother can be a good parent

(D) The difficulty with the exchange above is that the two speakers seem to have different ideas about what it means to be a good parent—as (D) notes. As for (A), although Mark objects that Martha spends too much time on her career, there is nothing in the exchange to suggest that the two speakers disagree over exactly how much time Martha spends with her children. As for (B), both speakers seem to agree that there is some objective standard which determines what constitutes a good parent, and neither includes the children's opinions in that standard. And the same reasoning can be applied to (C). As for (E), both speakers seem to assume that a working mother can be a good parent. They disagree, however, about how much time a good working parent should commit to the home.

A survey of 1,000 college students was asked about a non-existent campus agency. Six percent of those surveyed said they thought the agency was doing an excellent job.

24. Which of the following can be most reliably inferred from the information above?

    (A) Six percent of those surveyed deliberately lied to the questioners.
    (B) Sixty college students are unaware that the agency asked about did not exist.
    (C) Almost all of those surveyed knew that the agency asked about did not exist.
    (D) A survey of the sort mentioned is likely to contain an error in measurement.
    (E) Ninety-four percent of those surveyed responded that they had never heard of the agency.

(D) This is a good point at which to stop and remind ourselves that the object of the exam is to pick the BEST answer available. I am not a statistician, and I don't really know anything about public opinion polls (and their statistics). I do know, however, that of the choices presented, (D) is the most reasonable: somewhere there is an error. Examine the wrong choices and you will see that (D) must be the best response. As for (A), we certainly cannot conclude that the six percent in question deliberately lied. As for (B), although 60 students responded that they thought the agency was doing an excellent job, we cannot infer that each of those 60 students thought the agency exists. It could very well be that some or all knew full well that the agency did not exist and were teasing the questioner. Or perhpas some or all just didn't understand the question. As for (C), we don't know what the other responses were. (Suppose that the other 94 percent responded that they thought the agency was doing a very poor job?) Finally, (E) can be eliminated for the same reason.

Steve: Since the beginning of the massive emergency relief effort, planes have flow 300 blankets and 200 pounds of food to the beleaguered country.

Lorraine: You call a few blankets and some food a massive relief effort? That's not even a full plane load of cargo.

25. Which of the following, if true, would most weaken Lorraine's objection to Steve's statement?

    (A) Three planes were used to ferry the cargo to the country in question.
    (B) The country receiving the aid was hit by a devastating earthquake.
    (C) International relief agencies have tons of relief cargo ready for shipment as soon as planes are available.
    (D) The country receiving the aid also needs medical supplies.
    (E) The aid already delivered has already been distributed to those who need it.

(C) The second speaker makes an assumption about the first speaker's remarks: the aid mentioned is the whole relief effort. (C) corrects this misapprehension: the blankets and food mentioned are just the beginning. As for (A), this certainly doesn't weaken Lorraine's point that the 300 blankets and 200 pounds of food don't constitute a full plane load. As for (B), the reason the country needs the aid is irrelevant to the dispute between Steve and Lorraine: is the relief effort a "massive" one? As for (D), this idea, if anything, seems to support Lorraine's objection that not enough is being done. And finally, as for (E), the fact that the aid already sent was distributed doesn't bear on the disagreement between the two speakers as to what constitutes a "massive" relief effort.

SECTION 5

ANALYTICAL REASONING

Questions 1–6

Twelve people waiting for sales assistance in a store have each taken a slip with a number on it. The slips are numbered 1 through 12, and each person has a different number.

The people with numbers 2, 4, 6, 9, and 11 are the only ones wearing hats.

The people with numbers 1, 3, 6, 8, 10, and 12 are the only ones wearing gloves.

The people with numbers 3, 6, 9, and 12 are the only ones wearing raincoats.

The people with numbers 4, 8, and 12 are the only ones wearing scarves.

1. The person wearing a hat and a raincoat but no gloves or scarf is holding what number?

    (A) 2 (B) 4 (C) 6 (D) 9 (E) 11

    (D) Two people are wearing both a hat and a raincoat: those holding numbers 6 and 9. The person with 6, however, is wearing gloves. So the only person wearing a hat and raincoat but no gloves or scarf is the person holding number 9.

2. Which of the following is true?

    (A) Exactly one person is wearing gloves but no hat, scarf, or raincoat.
    (B) Exactly two people are wearing gloves but no hat.
    (C) Exactly one person is wearing both a hat and a scarf.
    (D) Exactly two persons are wearing both gloves and a hat.
    (E) Exactly three people are wearing both hats and raincoats.

    (C) Only one person, 4, is wearing both a hat and a scarf. As for (A), two people are wearing gloves but no hat, scarf, or raincoat: 1 and 10. As for (B), five people are wearing gloves but no hat: 1, 3, 8, 10, and 12. As for (D), only one person is wearing a hat and gloves: 6. And as for (E), only two people are wearing both hats and raincoats: 6 and 9.

3. The person with number 9 is wearing

    (A) a hat and gloves but no raincoat or scarf
    (B) a hat and raincoat but no gloves or scarf
    (C) a hat and scarf but no gloves or raincoat
    (D) a raincoat and gloves but no hat or scarf
    (E) a raincoat and scarf but no hat or gloves

    (B) The diagram shows that number 9 is wearing a hat and a raincoat and is not wearing gloves or a scarf.

4. How many people are wearing both gloves and a raincoat?

    (A) 0 (B) 1 (C) 2 (D) 3 (E) 4

    (D) Three people are wearing both gloves and a raincoat: 3, 6, and 12.

5. A person wearing neither a hat nor gloves could be holding number

    I. 5
    II. 7
    III. 10
    (A) I only (B) II only (C) I and II only
    (D) I and III only (E) I, II, and III

    (C) The only two people wearing neither a hat nor gloves are holding numbers 5 and 7. The person holding number 10 is wearing gloves.

6. If a person is wearing neither gloves nor a raincoat, then which of the following would be sufficient to establish what number that person is holding?

    (A) The person is wearing a hat.
    (B) The person is wearing a scarf.
    (C) The person is not wearing a hat.
    (D) The person is not wearing a scarf.
    (E) The person is wearing a hat but not a scarf.

    (B) Five people, numbers 2, 4, 5, 7, and 11, are wearing neither gloves nor a raincoat. Of that group, only 4 is wearing a scarf. So (B) is sufficient to establish the identity of the person in question. (A) is not, for of the group just defined, numbers 2, 4, and 11 are wearing hats. As for (C), the other two members of the group are not wearing hats. As for (D), four of the five are not wearing scarves. And as for (E), of the three members of the group just defined who are wearing hats, two of them are not wearing scarves.

Questions 7–12

This is a "network" set. You could use the following diagram:

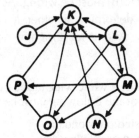

Each arrow indicates that a student from one college may go to the other college. "Network" sets are usually fairly stable, that is, the relationships don't change from question to question. Consequently, the information you need to answer questions is contained in the picture itself.

7. A class given a *P* could contain, at most, students from how many different colleges other than *P*?

   (A) 0
   (B) 1
   (C) 2
   (D) 3
   (E) 4

   (C) The diagram shows two arrows aimed at *P*, one from *M* and one from *O*. So a class at *P* could contain cross-registered students from *M* and *O* only.

8. A class given at *O* could include students from which of the following colleges?

   I. L
   II. M
   III. N

   (A) I only   (B) II only   (C) I and II only
   (D) I and III only   (E) I, II, and III

   (C) The diagram shows that it is possible for students from *L* and *M* to attend classes at *O*, but students from *N* cannot do so.

9. How many of the colleges accept visiting students from a school at which its own students are not allowed to cross-register?

   (A) 1
   (B) 2
   (C) 3
   (D) 4
   (E) 5

   (E) To answer this question, count the number of colleges that have arrows coming in but not going out. They are *K, L, N, O,* and *P*. For example, *L* accepts visiting students from *J*, but students from *L* are not allowed to attend classes at *J*.

10. Which of the following pairs of students could register for the same class at one of their colleges?

    (A) *L* and *P*
    (B) *L* and *N*
    (C) *M* and *J*
    (D) *N* and *O*
    (E) *O* and *L*

    (E) Only one of the pairs listed above is connected by an arrow on the diagram: a student from *L* could attend a class at *O*.

11. How many colleges both accept visiting students from another college and allow their students to cross-register for courses at that college?

    (A) 0
    (B) 1
    (C) 2
    (D) 3
    (E) 4

    (C) For this question, look for colleges that are connected by arrows running in both directions. There is only one set: the arrows connecting *L* and *M*. Therefore, there are two colleges that accept visiting students from another college and allow their students to cross-register for courses at that college.

12. Which of the following could be true?

    (A) Students from *J* and *L* are registered for a class offered at *J*.
    (B) Students from *K* and *L* are registered for a class offered at *L*.
    (C) Students from *L* and *M* are registered for a class offered at *P*.
    (D) Students from *M* and *O* are registered for a class offered at *P*.
    (E) Students from *N* and *P* are registered for a class offered at *J*.

    (D) The diagram shows that students from both *M* and *O* are allowed to attend classes at *P*, so (D) makes a statement that could be true. (A) must be false. Although students from *J* and *L* might be in the same classroom, that would occur on *L*'s campus. The same is true of (B). Students from *K* and *L* might be in the same classroom, but that classroom would be at *K*. Similarly, as for (C), students from both *L* and *M* might be in the same class at either *L* or *M* but not at *P*, since students from *L* cannot attend classes at *P*. And finally, as for (E), students from *N* and *P* could only be in the same class as *K*.

This is a selection set. Begin by summarizing the information:

France	Spain	Italy
G (R, '84)	F (W, '86)	I (R, '85)
M (W, '87)	H (R, '86)	K (W, '84)
	J (R, '87)	L (W, '85)

Mon: 2 or 3 reds
Wed: 2 or 3 whites
1 from each country

13. Which of the following groups of wines could be tested on Monday?

    (A) *F, G, H*
    (B) *G, H, I*
    (C) *H, K, J*
    (D) *J, K, M*
    (E) *G, M, J*

    (B) This problem provides no additional information, so you can test answer choices using the conditions summarized above. Monday must include at least two reds, so we eliminate choice (D). (Only *J* is red.) And we must have one wine from each country, so we eliminate (A) (no wine from Italy), (C) (no wine from France), and (E) (no wine from Italy). By the process of elimination, we learn that (B) is the only acceptable combination.

14. If *M* is included in Monday's tasting, then which of the following must be true?

    (A) The oldest red wine tasted on Monday is *I*.
    (B) the oldest red wine tasted on Monday is *H*.
    (C) The oldest white wine tasted on Wednesday is *K*.
    (D) The oldest white wine tasted on Wednesday is *L*.
    (E) The youngest red wine tasted on Monday is *J*.

    (A) If *M* is used on Monday, then to ensure that each country is represented on Wednesday, *G* must be included on Wednesday. Since *M* is white, the other two wines used on Monday must be red, one from Spain (either *H* or *J*) and the other from Italy (*I*). And Wednesday must include two white wines, one from Spain (*F*) and one from Italy (either *K* or *L*):

	France	Spain	Italy
Mon:	M	H or J	I
Wed:	G	F	K or L

    From this, we learn that *I* is the oldest red wine tast-

ed on Monday. (*I* was bottled in 1985, while *H* and *J* were bottled in 1986 and 1987, respectively.) Since (A) is correct, (B) must be wrong. As for (C) and (D), we cannot determine whether *K* or *L* is used on Wednesday. And as for (E), *J* may not be used even on Monday.

15. If *F* is the oldest white wine tasted on Wednesday, then which of the following must be true?

    (A) *H* is tasted on Monday.
    (B) *I* is tasted on Wednesday.
    (C) *J* is tasted on Monday.
    (D) *K* is tasted on Wednesday.
    (E) *L* is tasted on Wednesday.

    (B) If *F* is the oldest white wine used on Wednesday, then since *F* was bottled in 1986, the other white wine used on Wednesday has to be *M* (bottled in 1987). This means that the third wine for Wednesday is the red wine from Italy. And the other wine from France is used on Monday:

	France	Spain	Italy
Mon:	G	H or J	K or L
Wed:	M	F	I

    Our diagram shows that only (B) must be true. (A) and (C) are possibly, though not necessarily, true, while both (D) and (E) are necessarily false.

16. Which of the following CANNOT be true?

    (A) *F* is the youngest wine tasted on Monday.
    (B) *H* is the youngest wine tasted on Monday.
    (C) *L* is the youngest wine tasted on Wednesday.
    (D) *L* is the oldest wine tasted on Wednesday.
    (E) *I* is the oldest wine tasted on Wednesday.

    (C) If *L* is used on Wednesday, then either *M* or *F* or both must also be used on Wednesday. But both *M* and *F* were bottled after *L* was bottled. As for (A), *F* could be tasted on Monday with *G* and *I*. As for (B), *H* could be tasted on Monday with *G* and any Italian wine. As for (D), *L* could be tasted on Wednesday with *M* and either *H* or *J*. As for (E), *I* could be included with *M* and *F* for a Wednesday tasting, and *I* would be the oldest wine on that day.

17. If *F* is not included in either tasting, then which of the following must be included in one tasting or the other?

    I. H
   II. J
  III. M

(A) I only (B) III only (C) I and III only
(D) II and III only (E) I, II, and III

(E) Each country must be represented at each tasting. If *F* is not used at all, both *H* and *J* must be used. Likewise, since there are only two French wines, *M* must be used on one day or the other.

18. If *I* is the oldest red wine tasted on Monday, then all of the following must be true EXCEPT

(A) *F* is tasted on Wednesday.
(B) *G* is tasted on Wednesday.
(C) *M* is tasted on Monday.
(D) *F* is the youngest wine in its tasting.
(E) *K* is included in a tasting with either *J* or *H*.

(E) If *I* is the oldest red wine tasted on Monday, then *G* cannot be tasted Monday. Either *H* or *J* will be the other red wine tasted Monday. And if *G* is tasted on Wednesday, then *M* is tasted on Monday:

	France	Spain	Italy
Mon:	*M*	*H* or *J*	*I*
Wed:	*G*	*F*	*K* or *L*

Our diagram shows that (A), (B), (C), and (D) (*F* is younger than *K* or *L*) must be true. (E), however, is necessarily false. *H* and *J* could be used only on Monday and *K* and *L* only on Wednesday.

Questions 19–24
Start by summarizing the information:

W = V
X = T
R ≠ U
(R or S) = Q
S = Green

19. Which of the following people could sit at the same table?

(A) P, R, S
(B) P, U, V
(C) S, W, X
(D) T, X, R
(E) U, X, R

(D) Use the initial conditions to eliminate choices. Using the first condition, eliminate (B) and (C).

Using the second condition, eliminate (E). And using the fourth condition, eliminate (A). (D) is a possible seating arrangement:

Red	Green	Blue
TXR	QSU	WVP

20. Which of the following CANNOT be true?

(A) Q sits at the red table.
(B) U sits at the red table.
(C) X sits at the green table.
(D) P sits at the red table, and W sits at the blue table.
(E) R sits at the red table, and Q sits at the blue table.

(E) Since S sits at the green table, if R sits at the red table and Q at the blue table, then neither R nor S sits with Q—a violation of the fourth condition.

21. All of the following groups of persons could sit at the blue table EXCEPT

(A) P, Q, R
(B) P, R, X
(C) R, T, X
(D) R, V, W
(E) U, V, W

(B) X must sit with T. Since only three people can be accommodated at each table, (B) is not a possible arrangement.

22. All of the following could sit at the same table as W EXCEPT

(A) P
(B) R
(C) S
(D) U
(E) X

(E) Since W must sit with V and X sit with T, those pairs cannot be seated at the same table.

23. If R and W sit at the blue table, then which of the following must sit at the green table?

(A) P
(B) Q
(C) U
(D) V
(E) X

(B) If R and W sit at the blue table, then V is also seated at the blue table. Thus, since Q must sit with either S or R, Q is left to sit at the green table with S.

24. If S and T sit at the same table, and if Q sits at the red table, which of the following must sit at the blue table?

(A) R, V
(B) R, X
(C) U, X
(D) P, V, W
(E) U, V, W

(E) S and T must be joined at the green by X, and this means that R and Q must sit at the same table, the red table. Therefore, V and W sit at the blue table:

Red	Green	Blue
RQ—	STX	VW—

And since U will not sit with R, the blue table consists of U, V, and W.

Practice Test 4

Use a No. 2 pencil only. Be sure each mark is dark and completely fills the intended oval. Completely erase any errors or stray marks.

ARCO TEST NO.

YOUR NAME:

Start with number 1 for each new section. If a section has fewer than 30 questions, leave the extra answer spaces blank.

SECTION 1

1 Ⓐ Ⓑ Ⓒ Ⓓ Ⓔ
2 Ⓐ Ⓑ Ⓒ Ⓓ Ⓔ
3 Ⓐ Ⓑ Ⓒ Ⓓ Ⓔ
4 Ⓐ Ⓑ Ⓒ Ⓓ Ⓔ
5 Ⓐ Ⓑ Ⓒ Ⓓ Ⓔ
6 Ⓐ Ⓑ Ⓒ Ⓓ Ⓔ
7 Ⓐ Ⓑ Ⓒ Ⓓ Ⓔ
8 Ⓐ Ⓑ Ⓒ Ⓓ Ⓔ
9 Ⓐ Ⓑ Ⓒ Ⓓ Ⓔ
10 Ⓐ Ⓑ Ⓒ Ⓓ Ⓔ
11 Ⓐ Ⓑ Ⓒ Ⓓ Ⓔ
12 Ⓐ Ⓑ Ⓒ Ⓓ Ⓔ
13 Ⓐ Ⓑ Ⓒ Ⓓ Ⓔ
14 Ⓐ Ⓑ Ⓒ Ⓓ Ⓔ
15 Ⓐ Ⓑ Ⓒ Ⓓ Ⓔ
16 Ⓐ Ⓑ Ⓒ Ⓓ Ⓔ
17 Ⓐ Ⓑ Ⓒ Ⓓ Ⓔ
18 Ⓐ Ⓑ Ⓒ Ⓓ Ⓔ
19 Ⓐ Ⓑ Ⓒ Ⓓ Ⓔ
20 Ⓐ Ⓑ Ⓒ Ⓓ Ⓔ
21 Ⓐ Ⓑ Ⓒ Ⓓ Ⓔ
22 Ⓐ Ⓑ Ⓒ Ⓓ Ⓔ
23 Ⓐ Ⓑ Ⓒ Ⓓ Ⓔ
24 Ⓐ Ⓑ Ⓒ Ⓓ Ⓔ
25 Ⓐ Ⓑ Ⓒ Ⓓ Ⓔ
26 Ⓐ Ⓑ Ⓒ Ⓓ Ⓔ
27 Ⓐ Ⓑ Ⓒ Ⓓ Ⓔ
28 Ⓐ Ⓑ Ⓒ Ⓓ Ⓔ
29 Ⓐ Ⓑ Ⓒ Ⓓ Ⓔ
30 Ⓐ Ⓑ Ⓒ Ⓓ Ⓔ

SECTION 2

1 Ⓐ Ⓑ Ⓒ Ⓓ Ⓔ
2 Ⓐ Ⓑ Ⓒ Ⓓ Ⓔ
3 Ⓐ Ⓑ Ⓒ Ⓓ Ⓔ
4 Ⓐ Ⓑ Ⓒ Ⓓ Ⓔ
5 Ⓐ Ⓑ Ⓒ Ⓓ Ⓔ
6 Ⓐ Ⓑ Ⓒ Ⓓ Ⓔ
7 Ⓐ Ⓑ Ⓒ Ⓓ Ⓔ
8 Ⓐ Ⓑ Ⓒ Ⓓ Ⓔ
9 Ⓐ Ⓑ Ⓒ Ⓓ Ⓔ
10 Ⓐ Ⓑ Ⓒ Ⓓ Ⓔ
11 Ⓐ Ⓑ Ⓒ Ⓓ Ⓔ
12 Ⓐ Ⓑ Ⓒ Ⓓ Ⓔ
13 Ⓐ Ⓑ Ⓒ Ⓓ Ⓔ
14 Ⓐ Ⓑ Ⓒ Ⓓ Ⓔ
15 Ⓐ Ⓑ Ⓒ Ⓓ Ⓔ
16 Ⓐ Ⓑ Ⓒ Ⓓ Ⓔ
17 Ⓐ Ⓑ Ⓒ Ⓓ Ⓔ
18 Ⓐ Ⓑ Ⓒ Ⓓ Ⓔ
19 Ⓐ Ⓑ Ⓒ Ⓓ Ⓔ
20 Ⓐ Ⓑ Ⓒ Ⓓ Ⓔ
21 Ⓐ Ⓑ Ⓒ Ⓓ Ⓔ
22 Ⓐ Ⓑ Ⓒ Ⓓ Ⓔ
23 Ⓐ Ⓑ Ⓒ Ⓓ Ⓔ
24 Ⓐ Ⓑ Ⓒ Ⓓ Ⓔ
25 Ⓐ Ⓑ Ⓒ Ⓓ Ⓔ
26 Ⓐ Ⓑ Ⓒ Ⓓ Ⓔ
27 Ⓐ Ⓑ Ⓒ Ⓓ Ⓔ
28 Ⓐ Ⓑ Ⓒ Ⓓ Ⓔ
29 Ⓐ Ⓑ Ⓒ Ⓓ Ⓔ
30 Ⓐ Ⓑ Ⓒ Ⓓ Ⓔ

SECTION 3

1 Ⓐ Ⓑ Ⓒ Ⓓ Ⓔ
2 Ⓐ Ⓑ Ⓒ Ⓓ Ⓔ
3 Ⓐ Ⓑ Ⓒ Ⓓ Ⓔ
4 Ⓐ Ⓑ Ⓒ Ⓓ Ⓔ
5 Ⓐ Ⓑ Ⓒ Ⓓ Ⓔ
6 Ⓐ Ⓑ Ⓒ Ⓓ Ⓔ
7 Ⓐ Ⓑ Ⓒ Ⓓ Ⓔ
8 Ⓐ Ⓑ Ⓒ Ⓓ Ⓔ
9 Ⓐ Ⓑ Ⓒ Ⓓ Ⓔ
10 Ⓐ Ⓑ Ⓒ Ⓓ Ⓔ
11 Ⓐ Ⓑ Ⓒ Ⓓ Ⓔ
12 Ⓐ Ⓑ Ⓒ Ⓓ Ⓔ
13 Ⓐ Ⓑ Ⓒ Ⓓ Ⓔ
14 Ⓐ Ⓑ Ⓒ Ⓓ Ⓔ
15 Ⓐ Ⓑ Ⓒ Ⓓ Ⓔ
16 Ⓐ Ⓑ Ⓒ Ⓓ Ⓔ
17 Ⓐ Ⓑ Ⓒ Ⓓ Ⓔ
18 Ⓐ Ⓑ Ⓒ Ⓓ Ⓔ
19 Ⓐ Ⓑ Ⓒ Ⓓ Ⓔ
20 Ⓐ Ⓑ Ⓒ Ⓓ Ⓔ
21 Ⓐ Ⓑ Ⓒ Ⓓ Ⓔ
22 Ⓐ Ⓑ Ⓒ Ⓓ Ⓔ
23 Ⓐ Ⓑ Ⓒ Ⓓ Ⓔ
24 Ⓐ Ⓑ Ⓒ Ⓓ Ⓔ
25 Ⓐ Ⓑ Ⓒ Ⓓ Ⓔ
26 Ⓐ Ⓑ Ⓒ Ⓓ Ⓔ
27 Ⓐ Ⓑ Ⓒ Ⓓ Ⓔ
28 Ⓐ Ⓑ Ⓒ Ⓓ Ⓔ
29 Ⓐ Ⓑ Ⓒ Ⓓ Ⓔ
30 Ⓐ Ⓑ Ⓒ Ⓓ Ⓔ

SECTION 4

1 Ⓐ Ⓑ Ⓒ Ⓓ Ⓔ
2 Ⓐ Ⓑ Ⓒ Ⓓ Ⓔ
3 Ⓐ Ⓑ Ⓒ Ⓓ Ⓔ
4 Ⓐ Ⓑ Ⓒ Ⓓ Ⓔ
5 Ⓐ Ⓑ Ⓒ Ⓓ Ⓔ
6 Ⓐ Ⓑ Ⓒ Ⓓ Ⓔ
7 Ⓐ Ⓑ Ⓒ Ⓓ Ⓔ
8 Ⓐ Ⓑ Ⓒ Ⓓ Ⓔ
9 Ⓐ Ⓑ Ⓒ Ⓓ Ⓔ
10 Ⓐ Ⓑ Ⓒ Ⓓ Ⓔ
11 Ⓐ Ⓑ Ⓒ Ⓓ Ⓔ
12 Ⓐ Ⓑ Ⓒ Ⓓ Ⓔ
13 Ⓐ Ⓑ Ⓒ Ⓓ Ⓔ
14 Ⓐ Ⓑ Ⓒ Ⓓ Ⓔ
15 Ⓐ Ⓑ Ⓒ Ⓓ Ⓔ
16 Ⓐ Ⓑ Ⓒ Ⓓ Ⓔ
17 Ⓐ Ⓑ Ⓒ Ⓓ Ⓔ
18 Ⓐ Ⓑ Ⓒ Ⓓ Ⓔ
19 Ⓐ Ⓑ Ⓒ Ⓓ Ⓔ
20 Ⓐ Ⓑ Ⓒ Ⓓ Ⓔ
21 Ⓐ Ⓑ Ⓒ Ⓓ Ⓔ
22 Ⓐ Ⓑ Ⓒ Ⓓ Ⓔ
23 Ⓐ Ⓑ Ⓒ Ⓓ Ⓔ
24 Ⓐ Ⓑ Ⓒ Ⓓ Ⓔ
25 Ⓐ Ⓑ Ⓒ Ⓓ Ⓔ
26 Ⓐ Ⓑ Ⓒ Ⓓ Ⓔ
27 Ⓐ Ⓑ Ⓒ Ⓓ Ⓔ
28 Ⓐ Ⓑ Ⓒ Ⓓ Ⓔ
29 Ⓐ Ⓑ Ⓒ Ⓓ Ⓔ
30 Ⓐ Ⓑ Ⓒ Ⓓ Ⓔ

SECTION 5

1 Ⓐ Ⓑ Ⓒ Ⓓ Ⓔ   16 Ⓐ Ⓑ Ⓒ Ⓓ Ⓔ
2 Ⓐ Ⓑ Ⓒ Ⓓ Ⓔ   17 Ⓐ Ⓑ Ⓒ Ⓓ Ⓔ
3 Ⓐ Ⓑ Ⓒ Ⓓ Ⓔ   18 Ⓐ Ⓑ Ⓒ Ⓓ Ⓔ
4 Ⓐ Ⓑ Ⓒ Ⓓ Ⓔ   19 Ⓐ Ⓑ Ⓒ Ⓓ Ⓔ
5 Ⓐ Ⓑ Ⓒ Ⓓ Ⓔ   20 Ⓐ Ⓑ Ⓒ Ⓓ Ⓔ
6 Ⓐ Ⓑ Ⓒ Ⓓ Ⓔ   21 Ⓐ Ⓑ Ⓒ Ⓓ Ⓔ
7 Ⓐ Ⓑ Ⓒ Ⓓ Ⓔ   22 Ⓐ Ⓑ Ⓒ Ⓓ Ⓔ
8 Ⓐ Ⓑ Ⓒ Ⓓ Ⓔ   23 Ⓐ Ⓑ Ⓒ Ⓓ Ⓔ
9 Ⓐ Ⓑ Ⓒ Ⓓ Ⓔ   24 Ⓐ Ⓑ Ⓒ Ⓓ Ⓔ
10 Ⓐ Ⓑ Ⓒ Ⓓ Ⓔ   25 Ⓐ Ⓑ Ⓒ Ⓓ Ⓔ
11 Ⓐ Ⓑ Ⓒ Ⓓ Ⓔ   26 Ⓐ Ⓑ Ⓒ Ⓓ Ⓔ
12 Ⓐ Ⓑ Ⓒ Ⓓ Ⓔ   27 Ⓐ Ⓑ Ⓒ Ⓓ Ⓔ
13 Ⓐ Ⓑ Ⓒ Ⓓ Ⓔ   28 Ⓐ Ⓑ Ⓒ Ⓓ Ⓔ
14 Ⓐ Ⓑ Ⓒ Ⓓ Ⓔ   29 Ⓐ Ⓑ Ⓒ Ⓓ Ⓔ
15 Ⓐ Ⓑ Ⓒ Ⓓ Ⓔ   30 Ⓐ Ⓑ Ⓒ Ⓓ Ⓔ

The questions in this section require you to follow or evaluate the reasoning contained in brief statements or passages. In some questions, each of the choices is a conceivable solution to the particular problem posed. However, you are to select the one that answers the question best, that is, the one that does not require you to make what are by common-sense standards implausible, superfluous, or incompatible assumptions. After you have chosen the best answer, blacken the corresponding space on the answer sheet.

Questions 1–2

The Robin sedan is a better car than the Eagle hatchback. Robin owners report fewer mechanical repairs for their cars than do Eagle owners, so the Robin is cheaper to maintain.

1. The argument above assumes one car is better than another if it

   (A) is cheaper to manufacture than another car
   (B) suffers less damage in an accident than another car
   (C) gets better gas mileage than another car
   (D) is cheaper to maintain than another car
   (E) is covered by a more extensive warranty than another car

2. Which of the following, if true, points out a possible logical flaw in the argument above?

   I. The Robin can carry fewer passengers and less cargo than the Eagle can.
   II. Robin owners report fewer repairs, but the average cost per repair is higher than that reported by Eagle owners.
   III. Comparably equipped Robin and Eagle models cost about the same.

   (A) I only   (B) II only   (C) III only
   (D) I and II only   (E) II and III only

The question of the extent to which differing groups in our society share the same background knowledge of history, culture, and the sciences is not a question that is internal to the field of education. Without a body of shared assumptions and values, a nation may easily dissolve into a chaos of warring interest groups, unable to reach joint decisions for the long-run benefit of the entire community.

3. With which of the following statements is the author of the passage above most likely to disagree?

   (A) Decisions as to what curriculum is taught in the schools are best left in the hands of professional educators.
   (B) A body of shared values is essential for the existence of a unified society.
   (C) Knowledge of both humanities and science is a prerequisite for effective participation in a society.
   (D) The ethical and moral assumptions of an individual are likely to be affected by his or her educational background.
   (E) Groups representing the interests of different segments of society are likely to differ over what should be taught in schools.

The day following her absence from school, a student gave this note to her teacher:

To Whom It May Concern:

Please excuse Susan for her absence yesterday from her classes. She was at home ill with a viral infection. If you have any questions, you should not hesitate to call my office.

Sincerely,
Susan's Mother

4. Which of the following phrases suggests that the note is not authentic?

   (A) To Whom It May Concern
   (B) yesterday
   (C) viral infection
   (D) call my office
   (E) Susan's Mother

GO ON TO THE NEXT PAGE

John: No women received scholarships from the Cart Fund this year.

Elaine: Then I assume that no Cart Fund awards were made.

John: No; in fact, several men received scholarships this year from the Cart Fund.

5. Elaine's response might be premised on all of the following beliefs EXCEPT

(A) The Cart Fund awards were restricted to women.

(B) Only women were under consideration for the Cart Fund awards.

(C) All female applicants for Cart Fund awards were better qualified for the awards than the male applicants.

(D) Some female applicants for Cart Fund awards were better qualified for the awards than some male applicants.

(E) An equal number of awards would be made to men and women.

A Roman poet wrote, "It is sweet and noble to die for one's country." It is hard to see how any sensation of sweetness could be involved in the experience of dying in battle, in excruciating pain, in a muddy ditch miles from home, hearth, and family. Therefore, we may well doubt that nobility may be said to inhere in the act of dying itself.

6. The main point of the argument is that

(A) it is the consequence of the act of dying in defense of one's country that is important, not the act of dying itself

(B) the political and military objectives of war may not be evident to each individual soldier

(C) the word *sweetness* is ambiguous when it is used to describe actions rather than taste sensations

(D) the consequences of war have changed little since ancient times

(E) dying in defense of one's country is an action that may or may not be noble depending on whether the cause of the war is just

An international conference on the development of the world's undersea resources has proposed that all future use of these resources through undersea mining, harvesting of food in international waters, or other forms of development be subject to an international tax, to be set at a fixed percentage of the profits. The revenues from this tax would be used to support industrial development in the poorest nations of the world. This scheme, if adopted, will probably halt all future development of undersea resources. By removing the profit incentive, the proposed tax will discourage industrial nations from making the investments needed to exploit these valuable but remote undersea resources.

7. Which of the following questions would be most relevant in evaluating the validity of the conclusion reached above?

(A) What kinds of development projects would be supported by the proposed tax?

(B) What percentage of the profits derived from exploitation of undersea resources would be taken by the proposed tax?

(C) What position has been taken on the issue of the tax by the representatives of the nations that would benefit from the tax?

(D) What definition of *international waters* will be used for purposes of levying the proposed tax?

(E) What international agency would have the responsibility for assessing the tax and redistributing the revenues?

If zebras have feathers, they are birds; and if zebras are birds, they have long, pointed beaks. Zebras do not have feathers. Therefore, zebras do not have long, pointed beaks.

8. Which of the following arguments most closely parallels the argument above?

(A) If Carter enjoys cold weather, he will enjoy skiing; and if he enjoys skiing, he will enjoy a trip to Vermont. Carter enjoys cold weather, so he will enjoy a trip to Vermont.

(B) If the earth is flat, Columbus was wrong; and if Columbus was wrong, Ptolemy was right. Columbus was right, so the earth must actually be round.

(C) If Susan is a physician, her sister Kate is an accountant; if Kate is an accountant, Kate's husband, Martin, is an electrician. Martin is not an electrician, so Susan must not be a physician.

(D) If Brown is a Republocrat, he believes in free trade; and if he believes in free trade, he is no friend of labor. Brown is not a Republocrat, so he must be a friend of labor.

(E) If Matthew likes a sport, he plays it every weekend; if he plays a sport every weekend, he buys his own equipment. Matthew likes golf, so he must own a set of golf clubs.

GO ON TO THE NEXT PAGE

Television Advertisement: Here is news for all coffee drinkers. In 17 cities across the nation, we tested our instant coffee against perked coffee and we won! In a survey of thousands of coffee drinkers, two out of every five expressed a preference for Flash Instant Coffee over perked coffee. Shouldn't you try Flash, the coffee with the same rich taste as perked coffee?

9. Which of the following, if true, would most weaken the claim above?

 (A) The 17 cities were concentrated primarily in the midwest and west.
 (B) The survey included 150 people in each of the 17 cities.
 (C) The taste tests used a medium-priced brand of perked coffee.
 (D) For purposes of the survey, "coffee drinker" was defined as anyone who drinks at least one cup of coffee per day.
 (E) Those coffee drinkers who preferred Flash over perked coffee were already instant-coffee drinkers.

Those who say that underhand pitching in baseball is not dangerous must be unaware of the case of Ray Chapman. In 1920, Chapman was struck by a pitch thrown by underhand pitcher Carl Mays and subsequently died of head injuries. Underhand pitching should be banned.

10. The argument above may best be described as one that

 (A) applies a general principle to a specific instance
 (B) confuses cause and effect
 (C) attacks the proponent of an idea on personal rather than logical grounds
 (D) relies on a confusion between two similar but distinct terms
 (E) draws a general conclusion from a specific example

The preeminence of television in modern political campaigns has produced several deleterious effects on our democratic system. Because the attention span of television-trained audiences has been artificially shortened, candidates are forced to encapsulate their programs and ideas in 30- or 60-second summaries—mere slogans embellished with emotionally evocative imagery. And because television commercials are so costly, candidates must spend much of their campaign time raising money rather than delving deeply into the issues confronting our nation and its leaders.

11. According to the passage above, the negative effects of television on political campaigns are attributable to which of the following?

 I. The high cost of television commercials
 II. The influence of television on the ability of viewers to absorb complex ideas
 III. The complexity of today's political issues

 (A) I only   (B) II only   (C) I and II only
 (D) II and III only   (E) I, II, and III

The doctrine of civil disobedience requires, paradoxically, the utmost respect for the system of law, even when a higher moral obligation demands that a particular law be broken. A true proponent of civil disobedience never claims to go beyond the reach of the law or to be exempt from any of its penalties.

12. Which of the following best explains why the speaker above regards the doctrine of civil disobedience as paradoxical?

 (A) A law that is unjust is no law at all, so no one has a moral obligation to obey an unjust law.
 (B) Respect for the law is the highest civic virtue, but certain moral virtues are more important than any civic virtue.
 (C) One who engages in civil disobedience must insist that the law be enforced even as he breaks it.
 (D) A proponent of civil disobedience is hypocritical because he claims to be acting morally when he breaks a law.
 (E) The doctrine of civil disobedience entails that every individual has the right to judge whether or not a law is just.

Questions 13–14

Beauty depends on a pleasing blend of regularity or symmetry with irregularity or asymmetry. In poetry, for example, the most beautiful rhythms are those that, while fitting into an overall metrical pattern, vary line by line in the specific stresses, accents, and lengths that mark particular syllables. Without these subtle variations, pure metric regularity would quickly pall; without the overarching regularity, the verses would appear chaotic and ugly.

13. Which of the following, if true, would most weaken the argument above?

 (A) The beauty of poetry arises from imagery and syntax as well as from rhythm.
 (B) No arrangement of words, however carefully planned, can ever be absolutely regular in its rhythmic patterns.
 (C) Critics often disagree as to which poems appear beautiful and which do not.
 (D) Poetry in different languages generally follows different metrical arrangements.
 (E) Some poems that follow no regular metrical pattern have rhythms that are very beautiful.

GO ON TO THE NEXT PAGE

14. The argument above assumes which of the following to be true?

(A) A blend of symmetry with asymmetry will always be esthetically pleasing.

(B) A rhythmical arrangement that is uninteresting may nevertheless be beautiful.

(C) The qualities that make poetry beautiful cannot necessarily be generalized to other types of beauty.

(D) Variations in poetic rhythm are most effective when they underscore the meaning of the lines.

(E) Regularity may be varied without losing its fundamentally regular quality.

Anyone who is planning on a career as an investment banker wants to receive an M.B.A. degree from an Ivy League university. Phyllis wants an M.B.A. from Dartmouth, which is an Ivy League university. Therefore, Phyllis must be planning on a career as an investment banker.

15. Which of the following, if true, most strengthens the conclusion of the argument above?

(A) All of those who want M.B.A. degrees from Ivy League universities are planning careers as investment bankers.

(B) Some investment bankers have M.B.A. degrees from Ivy League universities.

(C) All investment bankers with M.B.A. degrees attended Ivy League universities.

(D) Only those planning on careers as investment bankers want M.B.A. degrees from Ivy League universities.

(E) Only those with M.B.A. degrees from Ivy League universities are fully qualified for careers as investment bankers.

Questions 16–17

The Sandersons must be planning to sell their house on Lincoln Place, since they visited the office of the local real estate agent yesterday.

16. Which of the following states the conclusion of the argument above?

(A) The Sandersons visited the office of the local real estate agent yesterday.

(B) The Sandersons want to sell their house on Lincoln Place.

(C) The local real estate agent will be handling the sale of the Sandersons' house.

(D) The Sandersons own a house on Lincoln Place.

(E) The local real estate agent could assist the Sandersons in selling their house on Lincoln Place.

17. The argument above assumes which of the following to be true?

I. The Sandersons own a house on Lincoln Place.

II. The Sandersons live on Lincoln Place.

III. The Sandersons would not visit the office of the local real estate agent unless they were planning to sell their house.

(A) I only (B) I and II only (C) I and III only (D) II and III only (E) I, II, and III

Questions 18–19

Professor Gilmartin gives good grades only to students of Irish descent. After all, last term he gave grades of A to Kathleen and Mary, both of whom are of Irish descent.

18. A critique of the logic of the argument above would most likely emphasize the fact that the speaker

(A) fails to define the term "good grades"

(B) reverses the most likely causal relationship

(C) criticizes Professor Gilmartin on personal rather than logical grounds

(D) fails to explain Professor Gilmartin's motivation in favoring students of Irish descent

(E) generalizes on the basis of limited evidence

19. Which of the following questions would be most relevant in examining the validity of the conclusion drawn above?

(A) Has Professor Gilmartin given grades of A to any students who are not of Irish descent?

(B) Is Professor Gilmartin generally considered a stricter grader than any other teacher at the school?

(C) Did Kathleen and Mary produce any extra projects while students of Professor Gilmartin?

(D) How many students of Irish descent have received grades of D or less from Professor Gilmartin?

(E) From what ethnic background is Professor Gilmartin descended?

GO ON TO THE NEXT PAGE

Some doctors drive fancy cars, and all extremely wealthy people drive fancy cars. Therefore, some doctors are extremely wealthy.

20. Which of the following arguments most closely parallels the reasoning in the argument above?

(A) Some Italians are socialists, and all members of the Red Students League are socialists. Therefore, some Italians are members of the Red Students League.

(B) Some politicians are dishonest, and all members of Congress are politicians. Therefore, some members of Congress are dishonest.

(C) Some dentists like to cook, and Dr. Gomez is a dentist. Therefore, Dr. Gomez likes to cook.

(D) Some farmers wear green overalls, and all farmers wear visored caps. Therefore, some people who wear visored caps wear green overalls.

(E) Some baseball players chew tobacco, and all those who chew tobacco have stained teeth. Therefore, some baseball players have stained teeth.

Since the structure and functioning of living tissue is governed by the laws of physics, the same combination of conditions that gave rise to life here on Earth could also occur other places in the universe and also give rise to life. Given an infinite amount of time, this possibility becomes a certainty. Thus, it is almost certain that life exists elsewhere in the universe.

21. Which of the following statements, if true, would weaken the above argument?

I. The universe is a finite number of years old.

II. The conditions that gave rise to life on Earth were unique to a particular epoch in the history of the universe and are not likely to be repeated.

III. Scientists have no real evidence that life exists anywhere except on Earth.

(A) I only   (B) II only   (C) I and II only
(D) I and III only   (E) II and III only

Those who deny the existence of miracles say that miraculous events are impossible because they violate the laws of nature. However, we know from personal experience that laws are violated every day; otherwise, there would be no need for police, judges, and prisons. Therefore, there is no reason to believe that the laws of nature may not be violated as well.

22. Which of the following best states the central weakness in the argument above?

(A) It places a divine being, who might bring about a miraculous event, on the same moral level as a human criminal.

(B) The term *law*, when applied to the laws of nature, has a different meaning than when applied to human laws.

(C) It assumes that miraculous events have taken place without offering substantive proof for their occurrence.

(D) It ignores the fact that under unusual circumstances natural events may occur that appear to violate natural laws without actually doing so.

(E) It attacks the motivations of those who deny the miraculous rather than analyzing the evidence for and against their arguments.

Questions 23–24

Without fully considering the question, we tend to assume that consciousness is necessary for purposeful behavior. We regard the actions of a well-regulated marching band or those of a flock of geese flying in formation as purposeful, while those of the molecules that form an intricate mineral crystal we consider non-purposeful. Yet, on reflection, this assumption seems unwarranted. Consciousness may be merely epiphenomenal, occurring alongside of but not directing behavior. When we look at consciousness in this light, we must consider the possibility that a chicken is, in reality, merely an egg's way of making another egg.

23. The speaker above implies that consciousness

(A) cannot occur without purposeful behavior
(B) is not essential to purposeful behavior
(C) directs all purposeful behavior
(D) is merely an illusion
(E) is capable of reproduction

24. The speaker implies that an egg is

(A) capable of purposeful behavior
(B) characterized by consciousness
(C) less intelligent than a chicken
(D) less complex than a mineral crystal
(E) more intelligent than a chicken

IF YOU FINISH BEFORE TIME IS CALLED, YOU MAY CHECK YOUR WORK ON THIS SECTION ONLY. DO NOT WORK ON ANY OTHER SECTION IN THE TEST. **S T O P**

SECTION **2**   Time—35 Minutes   For each question in this section, choose the best answer and
28 Questions   blacken the corresponding space on the answer sheet.

Directions: Each passage in this group is followed by questions based on its content. After reading a passage, choose the best answer to each question and blacken the corresponding space on the answer sheet. Answer all questions following a passage on the basis of what is stated or implied in that passage.

Galaxies come in a variety of sizes and shapes: majestic spirals, ruddy disks, elliptically shaped dwarfs and giants, and a menagerie of other, more bizarre forms. Most currently popular theories suggest that conditions prior to birth—mass of the protogalactic cloud, its size, its rotation—determine whether a galaxy will be large or small, spiral or elliptical; but about ten percent of all galaxies are members of rich clusters of thousands of galaxies. Galaxies in the crowded central region of rich clusters are constantly distorted by the gravitational forces of fields of nearby galaxies. In addition, rich clusters of galaxies are pervaded by a tenuous gas with a temperature of up to 100 million degrees. Galaxies are blasted and scoured by a hot wind created by their motion through the gas. In crowded conditions such as these, environment becomes a more important determinant of the size and shape of a galaxy than heredity. In fact, if our galaxy had happened to form well within the core of a cluster such as Virgo, the Sun would probably never have formed, because the Sun, a second- or third-generation star located in the disk of the galaxy, was formed from leftover gas five billion years or so after the initial period of star formation. By that time, in a rich cluster, the galaxy may well have already been stripped of its gas.

As a galaxy moves through the core of a rich cluster, it is not only scoured by hot gas; it encounters other galaxies as well. If the collision is a one-on-one affair at moderate to high speeds of galaxies of approximately the same size, both galaxies will emerge relatively intact, if a little distorted and ragged about the edges. If, however, a galaxy coasts by a much larger one in a slow, grazing collision, the smaller one can be completely disrupted and assimilated by the larger.

Under the right conditions, these cosmic cannibals can consume 50 to 100 galaxies. The accumulative effect of these collisions is to produce a dynamic friction on the large galaxy, slowing it down. As a result, it gradually spirals in toward the center of the cluster. Eventually the gravitational forces that bind the stars to the infalling galaxy are overwhelmed by the combined gravity of the galaxies in the core of the cluster—just as the ocean is pulled away from the shore at ebb tide by the Moon, the stars are pulled away from their infalling parent galaxy. If there is a large galaxy at the center of the cluster, it may ultimately capture these stars. With the passage of time, many galaxies will be torn asunder in the depths of this gravitational maelstrom and be swallowed up in the ever-expanding envelope of the central cannibal galaxy.

Galactic cannibalism also explains why there are few if any bright galaxies in these clusters other than the central supergiant galaxy. That is because the bright galaxies, which are the most massive, experience the greatest dynamical friction. They are the first to go down to the gravitational well and be swallowed up by the central galaxies.

Over the course of several billion years, 50 or so galaxies may be swallowed up, leaving only the central supergiant and, say, the 51st, the 52nd, etc., brightest galaxies. And given time, all the massive galaxies in the cluster will be absorbed, leaving a rather sparse cluster of a supergiant galaxy surrounded by clouds of small, dim galaxies.

1. It can be inferred from the passage that the physical features of a galaxy that does not belong to a rich cluster are determined primarily by the

    (A) size and rotation of the protogalactic cloud
    (B) intensity of light emanating from the galaxy
    (C) temperature of the interstellar gas
    (D) age of the protogalactic cloud
    (E) speed at which the protogalactic cloud is moving through space

2. The author implies that the currently accepted theories on galaxy formation are

    (A) completely incorrect and misguided
    (B) naive and out-of-date
    (C) speculative and unsupported by observation
    (D) substantially correct but in need of modification
    (E) accurate and adequate to explain all known observations

3. According to the passage, a cluster with a central, supergiant galaxy will

    (A) contain no intermediately bright galaxies
    (B) have 50 to 100 galaxies of all sizes and intensities
    (C) consist solely of third- and fourth- generation stars
    (D) produce only spiral and disk-shaped galaxies
    (E) be surrounded by galaxies of all sizes and shapes

GO ON TO THE NEXT PAGE

4. According to the passage, the outcome of a collision between galaxies depends on which of the following?

   I. The relative velocities of the galaxies
   II. The relative ages of the galaxies
   III. The relative sizes of the galaxies

   (A) I only   (B) II only   (C) III only
   (D) I and III only   (E) I, II, and III

5. According to the passage, as a galaxy falls inward toward the center of a cluster, it

   (A) collides with the central core and emerges relatively intact
   (B) absorbs superheated gases from the interstellar medium
   (C) is broken apart by the gravitational forces of the core
   (D) is transformed by collisions into a large, spiral galaxy
   (E) captures unattached stars that have been ejected from the galaxy's core

6. The passage provides information that will answer which of the following questions?

   I. What is the age of our sun?
   II. What proportion of all galaxies are found in clusters?
   III. Approximately how many galaxies would be found in a rich cluster?

   (A) I only   (B) II only   (C) I and III only
   (D) II and III only   (E) I, II, and III

Behavior is one of two general responses available to endothermic (warm-blooded) species for the regulation of body temperature, the other being innate (reflexive) mechanisms of heat production and heat loss. Human
(5) beings rely primarily on the first to provide a hospitable thermal microclimate for themselves, in which the transfer of heat between the body and the environment is accomplished with minimal involvement of innate mechanisms of heat production and loss. Thermoregulatory
(10) behavior *anticipates* hyperthermia, and the organism adjusts its behavior to avoid becoming hyperthermic: it removes layers of clothing, it goes for a cool swim, etc. The organism can also respond to changes in the temperature of the body core, as is the case during exercise; but
(15) such responses result from the direct stimulation of thermoreceptors distributed widely within the central nervous system, and the ability of these mechanisms to help the organism adjust to gross changes in its environment is limited.
(20) Until recently it was assumed that organisms respond to microwave radiation in the same way that they respond to temperature changes caused by other forms of radiation. After all, the argument runs, microwaves are radiation and heat body tissues. This theory ignores the
(25) fact that the stimulus to a behavioral response is normally a temperature change that occurs at the surface of the organism. The thermoreceptors that prompt behavioral changes are located within the first millimeter of the skin's surface, but the energy of a microwave field
(30) may be selectively deposited in deep tissues, effectively bypassing these thermoreceptors, particularly if the field is at near-resonant frequencies. The resulting temperature profile may well be a kind of reverse thermal gradient in which the deep tissues are warmed more than
(35) those of the surface. Since the heat is not conducted outward to the surface to stimulate the appropriate receptors, the organism does not "appreciate" this stimulation in the same way that it "appreciates" heating and cooling of the skin. In theory, the internal organs of a
(40) human being or an animal could be quite literally cooked well-done before the animal even realizes that the balance of its thermomicroclimate has been disturbed.

   Until a few years ago, microwave irradiations at equivalent plane-wave power densities of about 100
(45) mW/cm^2 were considered unequivocally to produce "thermal" effects; irradiations within the range of 10 to 100 mW/cm^2 might or might not produce "thermal" effects; while effects observed at power densities below 10 mW/cm^2 were assumed to be "nonthermal" in na-
(50) ture. Experiments have shown this to be an oversimplification, and a recent report suggests that fields as weak as 1 mW/cm^2 can be thermogenic. When the heat generated in the tissues by an imposed radio frequency (plus the heat generated by metabolism) exceeds the heat-loss
(55) capabilities of the organism, the thermoregulatory system has been compromised. Yet surprisingly, not long ago, an increase in the internal body temperature was regarded merely as "evidence" of a thermal effect.

7. The author is primarily concerned with

   (A) showing that behavior is a more effective way of controlling bodily temperature than innate mechanisms
   (B) criticizing researchers who will not discard their theories about the effects of microwave radiation on organisms
   (C) demonstrating that effects of microwave radiation are different from those of other forms of radiation
   (D) analyzing the mechanism by which an organism maintains its bodily temperature in a changing thermal environment
   (E) discussing the importance of thermoreceptors in the control of the internal temperature of an organism

8. The author makes which of the following points about innate mechanisms for heat production?

   I. They are governed by thermoreceptors inside the body of the organism rather than at the surface.
   II. They are a less effective means of compensating for gross changes in temperature than behavioral strategies.
   III. They are not affected by microwave radiation.

   (A) I only   (B) I and II only   (C) I and III only
   (D) II and III only   (E) I, II, and III

GO ON TO THE NEXT PAGE

9. Which of the following would be the most logical topic for the author to take up in the paragraph following the final paragraph of the selection?

(A) A suggestion for new research to be done on the effects of microwaves on animals and human beings
(B) An analysis of the differences between microwave radiation and other forms of radiation
(C) A proposal that the use of microwave radiation be prohibited because it is dangerous
(D) A survey of the literature on the effects of microwave radiation on human beings
(E) A discussion of the strategies used by various species to control hyperthermia

10. The author's strategy in lines 39–42 is to

(A) introduce a hypothetical example to dramatize a point
(B) propose an experiment to test a scientific hypothesis
(C) cite a case study to illustrate a general contention
(D) produce a counterexample to disprove an opponent's theory
(E) speculate about the probable consequences of a scientific phenomenon

11. The author implies that the proponents of the theory that microwave radiation acts on organisms in the same way as other forms of radiation based their conclusions primarily on

(A) laboratory research
(B) unfounded assumption
(C) control group surveys
(D) deductive reasoning
(E) causal investigation

12. The tone of the passage can best be described as

(A) genial and conversational
(B) alarmed and disparaging
(C) facetious and cynical
(D) scholarly and noncommittal
(E) analytical and concerned

13. The author is primarily concerned with

(A) pointing out weaknesses in a popular scientific theory
(B) developing a hypothesis to explain a scientific phenomenon
(C) reporting on new research on the effects of microwave radiation
(D) criticizing the research methods of earlier investigators
(E) clarifying ambiguities in the terminology used to describe a phenomenon

Since World War II, considerable advances have been made in the area of health-care services. These include better access to health care (particularly for the poor and minorities), improvements in physical plants,
(5) and increased numbers of physicians and other health personnel. All have played a part in the recent improve-
ment in life expectancy. But there is mounting criticism of the large remaining gaps in access, unbridled cost inflation, the further fragmentation of service, excessive
(10) indulgence in wasteful high-technology "gadgeteering," and a breakdown in doctor-patient relationships. In recent years proposed panaceas and new programs, small and large, have proliferated at a feverish pace and disappointments multiply at almost the same rate. This has
(15) led to an increased pessimism—"everything has been tried and nothing works"—which sometimes borders on cynicism or even nihilism.

It is true that the automatic "pass through" of rapidly spiraling costs to government and insurance carri-
(20) ers, which was set in a publicized environment of "the richest nation in the world," produced for a time a sense of unlimited resources and allowed to develop a mood whereby every practitioner and institution could "do his own thing" without undue concern for the "Medical
(25) Commons." The practice of full-cost reimbursement encouraged capital investment and now the industry is overcapitalized. Many cities have hundreds of excess hospital beds; hospitals have proliferated a superabundance of high-technology equipment; and structural os-
(30) tentation and luxury were the order of the day. In any given day, one-fourth of all community beds are vacant; expensive equipment is underused or, worse, used unnecessarily. Capital investment brings rapidly rising operating costs.
(35) Yet, in part, this pessimism derives from expecting too much of health care. It must be realized that care is, for most people, a painful experience, often accompanied by fear and unwelcome results. Although there is vast room for improvement, health care will always retain
(40) some unpleasantness and frustration. Moreover, the capacities of medical science are limited. Humpty Dumpty cannot always be put back together again. Too many physicians are reluctant to admit their limitations to patients; too many patients and families are unwilling to
(45) accept such realities. Nor is it true that everything has been tried and nothing works, as shown by the prepaid group practice plans of the Kaiser Foundation and at Puget Sound. In the main, however, such undertakings have been drowned by a veritable flood of public and
(50) private moneys which have supported and encouraged the continuation of conventional practices and subsidized their shortcomings on a massive, almost unrestricted scale. Except for the most idealistic and dedicated, there were no incentives to seek change or to practice self-
(55) restraint or frugality. In this atmosphere, it is not fair to condemn as failures all attempted experiments; it may be more accurate to say many never had a fair trial.

14. The tone of the passage can best be described as

(A) light-hearted and amused
(B) objective but concerned
(C) detached and unconcerned
(D) cautious but sincere
(E) enthusiastic and enlightened

GO ON TO THE NEXT PAGE →

15. According to the author, the "pessimism" mentioned at line 35 is partly attributable to the fact that

(A) there has been little real improvement in health-care services
(B) expectations about health-care services are sometimes unrealistic
(C) large segments of the population find it impossible to get access to health-care services
(D) advances in technology have made health-care service unaffordable
(E) doctors are now less concerned with patient care

16. The author cites the prepaid plans in lines 46–48 as

(A) counterexamples to the claim that nothing has worked
(B) examples of health-care plans that were overfunded
(C) evidence that health-care services are fragmented
(D) proof of the theory that no plan has been successful
(E) experiments that yielded disappointing results

17. It can be inferred that the sentence "Humpty Dumpty cannot always be put back together again" means that

(A) the cost of health-care services will not decline
(B) some people should not become doctors
(C) medical care is not really essential to good health
(D) illness is often unpleasant and even painful
(E) medical science cannot cure every ill

18. With which of the following descriptions of the system for the delivery of health-care services would the author most likely agree?

(A) It is biased in favor of doctors and against patients.
(B) It is highly fragmented and completely ineffective.
(C) It has not embraced new technology rapidly enough.
(D) It is generally effective but can be improved.
(E) It discourages people from seeking medical care.

19. Which of the following best describes the logical structure of the selection?

(A) The third paragraph is intended as a refutation of the first and second paragraphs.
(B) The second and third paragraphs are intended as a refutation of the first paragraph.
(C) The second and third paragraphs explain and put into perspective the points made in the first paragraph.
(D) The first paragraph describes a problem, and the second and third paragraphs present two horns of a dilemma.
(E) The first paragraph describes a problem, the second its causes, and the third a possible solution.

20. The author's primary concern is to

(A) criticize physicians and health-care administrators for investing in technologically advanced equipment
(B) examine some problems affecting delivery of health-care services and assess their severity
(C) defend the medical community from charges that health-care has not improved since World War II
(D) analyze the reasons for the health-care industry's inability to provide quality care to all segments of the population
(E) describe the peculiar economic features of the health-care industry that are the causes of spiraling medical costs

When we are speaking casually, we call *Nineteen Eighty-Four* a novel, but in a more exacting context we call it a political fable. This requirement is not refuted by the fact that the book is preoccupied with an individ-
(5) ual, Winston Smith, who suffers from a varicose ulcer, nor by the fact that it takes account of other individuals, including Julia, Mr. Charrington, Mrs. Parsons, Syme, and O'Brien. The figures claim our attention, but they exist mainly in their relation to the political system that
(10) determines them. It would indeed be possible to think of them as figures in a novel, though in that case they would have to be imagined in a far more diverse set of relations. They would no longer inhabit or sustain a fable, because a fable is a narrative relieved of much
(15) contingent detail so that it may stand forth in an unusual degree of clarity and simplicity. A fable is a structure of types, each of them deliberately simplified lest a sense of difference and heterogeneity reduce the force of the typical. Let us say, then, that *Nineteen Eighty-Four* is a
(20) political fable, projected into a near future and incorporating historical references mainly to document a canceled past.

Since a fable is predicated upon a typology, it must be written from a certain distance. The author cannot
(25) afford the sense of familiarity which is induced by detail and differentiation. A fable, in this respect, asks to be compared to a caricature, not to a photograph. It follows that in a political fable there is bound to be some tension between a political sense, which deals in the multiplicity

(30) of social and personal life, and a sense of fable, which is committed to simplicity of form and feature. If the political sense were to prevail, the narrative would be drawn away from fable into the novel, at some cost to its simplicity. If the sense of fable were to prevail, the

(35) fabulist would station himself at such a distance from any imaginary conditions in the case that his narrative would appear unmediated, free or bereft of conditions. The risk in that procedure would be considerable: a reader might feel that the fabulist has lost interest in the variety

(40) of human life and fallen back upon an unconditioned sense of its types, that he has become less interested in lives than in a particular idea of life. The risk is greater still if the fabulist projects his narrative into the future: the reader can't question by appealing to the conditions

(45) of life he already knows. He is asked to believe that the future is another country and that "they just do things differently there."

In a powerful fable the reader's feeling is likely to be mostly fear: he is afraid that the fabulist's vision of any

(50) life that is likely to arise may be accurate and will be verified in the event. The fabulist's feeling may be more various. Such a fable as *Nineteen Eighty-Four* might arise from disgust, despair, or world-weariness induced by evidence that nothing, despite one's best efforts, has

(55) changed and that it is too late now to hope for the change one wants.

21. In drawing an analogy between a fable and a caricature (lines 26–27), the author would most likely regard which of the following pairs of ideas as also analogous?

   (A) The subject of a caricature and the topic of a fable
   (B) The subject of a caricature and the main character in *Nineteen Eighty-Four*
   (C) The subject of a fable and the artist who draws the caricature
   (D) The artist who draws the caricature and a novelist
   (E) The minor characters in a fable and a photographer

22. Which of the following would be the most appropriate title for the passage?

   (A) A Critical Study of the Use of Characters in *Nineteen Eighty-Four*
   (B) *Nineteen Eighty-Four*: Political Fable Rather Than Novel
   (C) *Nineteen Eighty-Four*: Reflections on the Relationship of the Individual to Society
   (D) The Use of Typology in the Literature of Political Fables
   (E) Distinguishing a Political Fable from a Novel

23. According to the passage, which of the following are characteristics of a political fable?

   I. Its characters are defined primarily by their relationship to the social order.
   II. The reader is likely to experience fear as his reaction to the political situation described.
   III. Its time frame must treat events that occur at some point in the future.

   (A) I only   (B) II only   (C) I and II only
   (D) I and III only   (E) I, II, and III

24. Which of the following best explains why the author mentions that Winston Smith suffers from a varicose ulcer?

   (A) To demonstrate that a political fable must emphasize type over detail
   (B) To show that Winston Smith has some characteristics that distinguish him as an individual
   (C) To argue that Winston Smith is no more important than any other character in *Nineteen Eighty-Four*
   (D) To illustrate one of the features of the political situation described in *Nineteen Eighty-Four*
   (E) To suggest that *Nineteen Eighty-Four* is too realistic to be considered a work of fiction

25. The "tension" that the author mentions in line 28 refers to the

   (A) necessity of striking a balance between the need to describe a political situation in simple terms and the need to make the description realistic
   (B) reaction the reader feels because he is drawn to the characters of the fable as individuals but repulsed by the political situation
   (C) delicate task faced by a literary critic who must interpret the text of a work while attempting to describe accurately the intentions of the author
   (D) danger that too realistic a description of a key character will make the reader feel that the fable is actually a description of his own situation
   (E) conflict of aspirations and interests between characters that an author creates to motivate the action of the narrative

26. The author's attitude toward *Nineteen Eighty-Four* can best be described as

   (A) condescending   (B) laudatory
   (C) disparaging   (D) scholarly   (E) ironic

GO ON TO THE NEXT PAGE

27. The author uses the phrase "another country" to describe a political fable in which

(A) political events described in a fable occur in a place other than the country of national origin of the author

(B) a lack of detail makes it difficult for a reader to see the connection between his own situation and the one described in the book

(C) too many minor characters create the impression of complete disorganization, leading the reader to believe he is in a foreign country

(D) the author has allowed his personal political convictions to infect his description of the political situation

(E) an overabundance of detail prevents the reader from appreciating the real possibility that such a political situation could develop

28. The author's primary concern is to

(A) define and clarify a concept

(B) point out a logical inconsistency

(C) trace the connection between a cause and an effect

(D) illustrate a general statement with examples

(E) outline a proposal for future action

SECTION 3 — Time—35 Minutes, 24 Questions

In this section solve each problem, using any available space on the page for scratchwork. Then decide which is the best of the choices given and fill in the corresponding oval on the answer sheet.

Directions: Each group of questions is based on a set of conditions. In answering some of the questions it may be useful to draw a rough diagram. Choose the best answer for each question and blacken the corresponding space on your answer sheet.

Questions 1–6

The owner of a vending machine company is placing a new snack machine in a college dormitory. He plans to stock the machine with three of six different snacks—J, K, L, M, N, and O—according to the following rules.

The array of snacks will be changed every week after the first week.

If L is stocked in the machine during a week, then N must also be stocked in the machine during that week.

M can only be stocked in the machine in a week following a week in which K is stocked in the machine.

When J is stocked in the machine in one week, it cannot be stocked in the machine the following week.

Only one of the three snacks from a previous week can be stocked in the machine in the following week.

1. Which of the following groups of snacks could be stocked in the machine during weeks two and three?

    (A) $L, N, J; N, L, O$
    (B) $L, N, O; L, J, K$
    (C) $M, L, N; J, K, M$
    (D) $N, O, J; K, L, N$
    (E) $O, M, J; J, L, N$

2. If J, L, and N are stocked in the machine one week, which three snacks must be stocked in the machine the following week?

    (A) K, M, O
    (B) K, N, O
    (C) L, M, N
    (D) L, N, O
    (E) M, N, O

3. If J, N, and O are stocked in the machine in the first week, then which three snacks must be stocked in the machine in week two?

    (A) J, L, N
    (B) K, L, N
    (C) L, N, O
    (D) M, L, N
    (E) M, N, O

4. If L and O are stocked in the machine in the first week, which of the following snacks must be stocked in the machine in the second week?

    I. J
    II. K
    III. O

    (A) I only   (B) II only   (C) I and II only
    (D) II and III only   (E) I, II, and III

5. If K is stocked in the machine in the first week, and neither N nor K is stocked in the machine in the second week, how many different combinations of snacks are possible for the second week?

    (A) 1   (B) 2   (C) 3   (D) 4   (E) 5

6. If L is stocked in the machine in the first week, and J, M, and O are stocked in the second week, which of the following pairs of snacks must also have been stocked in the first week?

    (A) K and N
    (B) K and O
    (C) M and N
    (D) M and O
    (E) N and O

GO ON TO THE NEXT PAGE

Questions 7–11

Six acrobats—J, K, L, M, N, and O—form a human pyramid. Three acrobats form the bottom tier, two acrobats standing on their shoulders form the second tier, and one acrobat standing on the shoulders of the second tier is the third tier.

    O is not in the same tier as M.
    N is in the same tier as M.

7. Which of the following are acceptable pyramids?

   (A)
$$J$$
$$L \quad K$$
$$M \quad N \quad O$$

   (B)
$$J$$
$$K \quad N$$
$$O \quad M \quad L$$

   (C)
$$L$$
$$M \quad N$$
$$J \quad O \quad K$$

   (D)
$$K$$
$$O \quad M$$
$$N \quad J \quad L$$

   (E)
$$M$$
$$N \quad L$$
$$J \quad O \quad K$$

8. Which of the following could be true of the human pyramid?

   (A) J, K, and M form the bottom tier.
   (B) K, M, and O form the bottom tier.
   (C) M and K form the second tier.
   (D) K forms the top tier.
   (E) N forms the top tier.

9. If J is standing on N's shoulders, then which of the following is a complete and accurate list of the acrobats who could be the top tier of the pyramid?

   (A) J (B) K (C) J, K
   (D) J, K, L (E) J, K, L, O

10. If K is standing on L's shoulder, then all of the following could be true EXCEPT

   (A) J is standing on M's shoulder.
   (B) L is standing on M's shoulder.
   (C) K is standing on N's shoulder.
   (D) M is standing on K's shoulder.
   (E) O is standing on K's shoulder.

11. If K is in the middle tier of the pyramid, all of the following could be true EXCEPT

   (A) J is standing on L's shoulder.
   (B) K is standing on O's shoulder.
   (C) L is standing on M's shoulder.
   (D) L is standing on the ground.
   (E) J is standing on the ground.

Questions 12–15

A gardener is planting a flower bed. He has six types of flowers—T, U, V, X, Y, and Z. The planting is subject to the following restrictions:

    X cannot be planted in the bed with either Y or Z.
    T cannot be planted in the bed with U.
    If U is planted in the bed, then Z must also be planted in the bed.

12. Which of the following must be true?

    I. T cannot be planted with Z.
    II. T cannot be planted with Y.
    III. X cannot be planted with U.

   (A) I only   (B) III only   (C) I and III only
   (D) II and III only   (E) I, II, and III

13. Which of the following is an acceptable combination of flowers for the bed?

   (A) T, U, X
   (B) T, X, Z
   (C) T, V, Z
   (D) U, X, Y
   (E) Z, U, X

14. What is the largest number of different varieties of flowers that could be planted together in the bed?

   (A) 2   (B) 3   (C) 4   (D) 5   (E) 6

15. If the gardener wishes to plant X and one other variety, how many different combinations of flowers are possible?

   (A) 1   (B) 2   (C) 3   (D) 4   (E) 5

Questions 16–19

Six people, John, Ken, Leroy, Mark, Ned, and Oscar, are sitting at a table.

    John speaks only English, Italian, and French.
    Ken speaks only German.
    Leroy speaks only English, Italian, and German.
    Mark speaks only French and Spanish.
    Ned speaks only English, German, and Spanish.
    Oscar speaks only English and Italian.

16. Which language is spoken by the largest number of people at the table?

   (A) English   (B) French   (C) German
   (D) Italian   (E) Spanish

17. Leroy could converse directly with Ned in how many different languages?

   (A) 0   (B) 1   (C) 2   (D) 3   (E) 4

GO ON TO THE NEXT PAGE

18. Which of the following is a complete and accurate list of the persons sitting at the table who can converse directly with Mark?

(A) John, Ken
(B) John, Ned
(C) Leroy, Ned
(D) John, Ken, Ned
(E) Leroy, Ken, Ned

19. Which of the following people could function as a translator in a conversation between Ken and Oscar?

I. John
II. Leroy
III. Ned

(A) I only   (B) II only   (C) III only
(D) I and III only   (E) II and III only

Questions 20–24

A certain law firm consists of seven senior partners—J, M, P, R, S, T, and U—and five junior partners—K, L, N, O, and Q. The firm is divided into three departments:
J, O, P, and U work in litigation.
L, K, M, and T work in taxation.
N, Q, R, and S work in corporations.
The firm is forming a hiring committee to interview prospective employees. The committee must conform to the following restrictions:
There must be at least as many senior partners on the committee as junior partners.
At least one partner from each department must be on the committee.
If either J or P serves on the committee, then the other must also serve on the committee.
If either L or N serves on the committee, then the other must also serve on the committee.
If either R or S serves on the committee, then the other must also serve on the committee.
M cannot serve on the committee with T, and P cannot serve on the committee with S.

20. Which of the following committees is acceptable?

(A) J, K, L, M, N, U
(B) K, L, M, N, R, S
(C) K, L, M, N, Q, U
(D) L, M, N, O, R, T
(E) M, O, Q, R, S, U

21. Which of the following statements about the committee must be true?

(A) O cannot serve on the committee with K.
(B) L cannot serve on the committee with U.
(C) M cannot serve on the committee with Q.
(D) R cannot serve on the committee with J.
(E) T cannot serve on the committee with U.

22. The largest committee consistent with the requirements above would consist of how many people?

(A) 6   (B) 7   (C) 8   (D) 9   (E) 10

23. If J serves on the committee but L does not, which of the following must be true?

(A) M serves on the committee.
(B) T serves on the committee.
(C) Q serves on the committee.
(D) U does not serve on the committee.
(E) O does not serve on the committee.

24. If the committee is to include L, K, and R, then which partners must also be on the committee?

I. O
II. U
III. M

(A) I only   (B) II only   (C) I and II only
(D) II and III only   (E) I, II, and III

IF YOU FINISH BEFORE TIME IS CALLED, YOU MAY CHECK YOUR WORK ON THIS SECTION ONLY. DO NOT WORK ON ANY OTHER SECTION IN THE TEST. **S T O P**

Directions: The questions in this section require you to follow or evaluate the reasoning contained in brief statements or passages. In some questions, each of the choices is a conceivable solution to the particular problem posed. However, you are to select the one that answers the question best, that is, the one that does not require you to make what are by common-sense standards implausible, superfluous, or incompatible assumptions. After you have chosen the best answer, blacken the corresponding space on the answer sheet.

Speaker X: The dinosaurs died out because of some major climatic change that diminished the formerly abundant food supplies.

Speaker Y: That's incorrect. Dinosaurs died out because of competition for food from a new family of animals—the mammals.

Speaker Z: I believe that a massive asteroid struck the Earth, raising a worldwide cloud of smoke and dust that darkened the skies for months or even years. The dense cloud blocked sunlight, killing off much of the plant life that the dinosaurs used as food.

1. Which of the following best describes the disagreement among the three speakers?

(A) The speakers agree that starvation caused the dinosaurs to become extinct but don't agree about the cause of the drop in their food supply.

(B) The speakers agree that climatic changes caused a drop in the food supply of dinosaurs but don't agree that this drop caused the dinosaurs to become extinct.

(C) Speakers X and Z agree that major climatic changes caused the extinction of the dinosaurs but offer different explanations for those changes.

(D) Speakers Y and Z agree that starvation caused the extinction of the dinosaurs and agree that this was caused by a decline in the total amount of plant life on Earth.

(E) Speakers X and Y agree that starvation was responsible for the extinction of the dinosaurs but disagree with Z that a meteor was responsible for climatic changes that reduced the food supply of the dinosaurs.

A cryptographer has intercepted a message that is in code. She knows that the code is a simple substitution of numbers for letters in the words of a foreign language.

2. Which of the following would be the LEAST helpful to the cryptographer in breaking the code?

(A) Knowing the frequency with which each vowel in the language is used

(B) Knowing the frequency with which two vowels appear together in the language

(C) Knowing the frequency with which odd numbers appear relative to even numbers in the message

(D) Knowing the conjugation of the equivalent for the verb *to be* in the language on which the code is based

(E) Knowing every word in the language that begins with the letter ''R''

All the books shelved in the library's west wing are works of fiction. *David Copperfield* is shelved in the library's east wing. Therefore, *David Copperfield* is not a work of fiction.

3. Which of the following is most similar to the argument above?

(A) All automobiles manufactured in the United States come equipped with radial tires. The Mandate is manufactured in Italy. Therefore, the Mandate is not equipped with radial tires.

(B) Only new written works are covered by copyrights. A machine is not a written work. Therefore, a machine is not covered by a copyright.

(C) All bananas are yellow. Yellow is a color. Therefore, all bananas are colors.

(D) All of the seniors are seated in the cafeteria. Mary is seated in the gymnasium. Therefore, Mary is not a senior.

(E) All legal government actions must be consistent with the Constitution. The Constitution requires the separation of church and state. Therefore, establishment of a state church would be an illegal government action.

GO ON TO THE NEXT PAGE

It is sometimes argued that a national lottery would cut into revenues generated by state lotteries. As a consequence, according to the argument, there would be no net increase in the amount of money going to government, just a redistribution of funds from the state to the federal level. This argument ignores the fact that federal and state governments share personal and corporate income taxes and certain excise taxes. Similarly, lottery states could piggyback on a federal lottery, increasing the total participation in both.

4. The speaker above argues primarily by

(A) citing an authority
(B) relying on statistics
(C) creating a distinction
(D) drawing an analogy
(E) proposing a change

Some people have argued that mental events can be explained in terms of brain events. Brain events can all be located in space, but no one has been able to pinpoint the physical location of a mental event.

5. The speaker above is most likely arguing that

(A) it will eventually be possible to locate brain events
(B) mental events are more important than brain events
(C) brain events are the only events that are locatable
(D) brain events cannot be explained as mental events
(E) mental events are not identical to brain events

All homework is tedious.
Some biology assignments are homework.
No lab assignments are homework.

6. Which of the following conclusions can be deduced from the statements above?

(A) Some biology assignments are not homework.
(B) Some biology assignments are tedious.
(C) Some biology assignments are not tedious.
(D) Some biology assignments are lab assignments.
(E) No lab assignments are tedious.

Martin: Mayor Clark was the most popular mayor this city ever had. He was elected by 93 percent of the vote.

Victor: But the total population of this city then was only 42,000. The current mayor, Nancy Short, won by only a couple of percentage points, but she received the votes of over 150,000 people. That makes her the most popular mayor ever.

7. In the exchange above, the two speakers

(A) agree that Clark and Short are the two most popular mayors in the city's history
(B) concur that only a popular mayor should be mayor of the city
(C) disagree about the identity of the current mayor
(D) attack each other's sincerity
(E) give different meanings to a key term

Smokers often claim that they have a right to smoke and use the word *right* as though it implies an unqualified permission to smoke whenever and wherever they choose. Thus, they argue, they have a "right" to smoke in public places such as restaurants. This idea is mistaken. After all, no one has a "right" to smoke when smoking represents a clear danger to the safety of others, for example, during the takeoff and landing of a plane or while a motor vehicle is being refueled.

8. The speaker attempts to show that

(A) a person may have a right that cannot be legally protected
(B) a certain concept of "right" leads to an absurd conclusion
(C) one person's right may endanger the safety of someone else
(D) no person has a right to endanger the safety of another
(E) some people may have rights that others do not have

GO ON TO THE NEXT PAGE

Questions 9-10

(A) In his concession speech, the candidate explained that he lost the election not because the people did not think him best qualified for the position and not because they did not endorse his view. The candidate lost the election because he had insufficient vote-getting power. As we all know, the candidate who gets the most votes wins.

(B) Human life is sacred; that is why we must punish murderers severely. Taking the life of another human being is something no one has the right to do. The crime of murder is so heinous that it deserves the strongest punishment imaginable, and that is why I favor the death penalty for murderers.

(C) Senator Jensen issued a statement denouncing the Committee's decision to recommend the closing of three naval bases, arguing that the bases are essential to the security of the nation. Of course the senator would likely oppose the recommendation, because two of the three bases are located in the state he represents.

(D) Our school system should spend whatever money is needed to purchase computer systems for student use. Our standardized test scores in reading and math for the past three years have been several points below those of our neighboring system, which has computers for student use.

(E) The mayor announced yesterday that a major corporation has changed its plans to move its offices from the city because of certain tax incentives granted by him. The mayor should realize that the corporation's actions are tantamount to blackmail: announcing plans to leave the city in order to extort favorable tax treatment for remaining.

9. Which of the arguments above is self-contradictory?

10. Which of the arguments above attacks the motives of the proponent of the argument?

The Census Bureau described the period of 10.7-percent growth of median real family income between 1982 and 1986 as the "longest period of sustained income growth" since the 1960s. They failed to note, however, that in 1982 the economy experienced the most serious recession since World War II and that median real family income in 1982 had dropped to its lowest level in 14 years.

11. The speaker is arguing that

(A) real median income did not increase from 1982 to 1986
(B) the Census Bureau was unaware of the 1982 recession
(C) it is difficult to measure real median family income
(D) economic growth can be achieved only following a severe recession
(E) the growth only recaptured what had been lost in the recession

Speaker X: I'm afraid I won't be able to get into State University.

Speaker Y: Relax. State University's brochure states that no one will be accepted after May 1. So just make sure that your application is received before then, and you'll definitely be accepted.

12. Which of the following lines of reasoning is LEAST similar to that contained in Speaker Y's reply.

(A) The professor stated that any one who failed to submit a term paper would fail the course. I submitted a term paper. Therefore, I will pass the course.
(B) Overwatering a house plant is sure to kill it. Since I never overwater my house plants, they should never die.
(C) Any employee who is detected falsifying time records will be fired. Since Mary is scrupulously honest about her time card, she will never be fired.
(D) Every time it snows the sky is cloudy and the weather is cold. Today the weather is warm and the sky is clear, so we won't have snow.
(E) Anyone who attends every class will pass the course. Evan did not attend every class. Therefore, Evan will not pass the course.

GO ON TO THE NEXT PAGE

You have stated that our charity wrongly passes off routine mailing costs as public education. But you are wrong, and your example proves that you are wrong. The letter you cite was four pages long. Three pages detail the problems of animal abuse. One page asks for a $5 contribution and encourages the recipient to send a detachable postcard of protest to Congress. Since over 20,000 people who received the mailing did both, it is obvious that the letter had a very valuable educational impact.

13. The response set forth above assumes that

   (A) the members of Congress who receive the post-cards will change their minds on the issue in question

   (B) problems of animal abuse can only be solved by Federal legislation

   (C) the charity only needs $100,000 in contributions

   (D) those who responded with contributions and postcards of protests were not already advocates of the charity's position

   (E) everyone who received the mailing made a charitable contribution to the organization

Questions 14-15
The library is requesting an increase in its budget for next year. With the additional funds, the library hopes to add a video tape section that will allow library patrons to borrow, free of charge, video tapes that they would otherwise have to rent from one of the several retail stores here in town. The library's request should be rejected. If the library offers free video tapes, local merchants who rent such tapes will lose sales. And if local merchants lose sales, the town will lose tax revenues, and everyone will suffer.

14. The author above is ultimately trying to prove that

   (A) local merchants will lose sales if the library's budget request is approved

   (B) the town will lose tax revenues if the library's budget request is approved

   (C) some people who would otherwise rent video tapes from merchants will borrow them from the library

   (D) the library's request for a budget increase to fund free video tapes should be rejected

   (E) the library should not be allowed to rent video tapes in competition with local merchants

15. The argument above makes which of the following assumptions?

   I. The tapes that would be available for loan from the library are similar to those rented by local merchants.

   II. The lost tax revenues are more significant than the savings to the town's people.

   III. The library will offer tapes that are culturally superior to those offered by the local merchants.

   (A) I only   (B) II only   (C) I and II only
   (D) II and III only   (E) I, II, and III

The philosopher Immanuel Kant distinguished between what he called analytic statements and what he called synthetic statements. According to Kant, a statement of the form:

   Subject . . . is . . . predicate

is analytic if negating the statement results in a contradiction. For example, the following statement, in Kant's analysis, is analytic:

   All bachelors are unmarried.

The statement is analytic because its negation--it is not the case that all bachelors are unmarried--is a contradiction.

16. According to the analysis of Kant given above, which of the following statements is also an analytic statement?

   I. All widows have been married at least once.
   II. Every daughter has at least one brother.
   III. Every father has at least one child.

   (A) I only   (B) III only   (C) I and II only
   (D) I and III only   (E) I, II, and III

Delbert: A professor of journalism checked the tapes of interviews of several prominent people against the published interviews and found that only 3 percent of the statements that appeared inside of quotation marks were actually quoted verbatim.

Linda: Yet in every one of the cases studied, the person interviewed reviewed the manuscript and had the power to edit the remarks before they finally appeared in print.

17. If both speakers above are correct, which of the following conclusions is best supported by the exchange?

   (A) Most prominent people do not care what is said about them in print.

   (B) Most prominent people are reluctant to say what they really believe in an interview.

   (C) Most journalists intentionally distort the responses of interviewees.

   (D) The interviewees in question were satisfied that the interviewer accurately rendered their thoughts.

   (E) The interviewer unconsciously distorted the responses obtained during the interview.

Any oil painting signed by Alain was painted after 1962.

18. Which of the following can be logically deduced from the statement above?

   (A) Alain signed only the paintings he painted after 1962.

   (B) Alain signed only the paintings he did in oils.

   (C) After 1962, Alain painted only oil paintings.

   (D) Alain never signed an oil painting before 1962.

   (E) Alain never signed any painting before 1962.

A woman who was seriously injured in a fall on a staircase remarked, "I'm glad this is behind me because I am terribly afraid of elevators. Yet, statistics show that a person is ten times as likely to be seriously injured while using stairs as while riding in an elevator. Now that I've had my fall, I can use stairs without fear."

19. The conclusion above is erroneous because the woman

    (A) ignores the possibility of serious injury while using a ramp
    (B) assumes that all accidents are equally serious
    (C) misuses the concept of probability
    (D) fails to connect the possibility of accident with personal fear
    (E) makes no reference to the fact that stairs are not mechanical devices

Parent: I am very worried that your school is not providing my daughter with the best possible college preparatory education.

Headmaster: Rest assured that we are. Last year, the average score of our students on the college entrance exam was in the top five percent.

20. The Headmaster's response assumes that

    (A) the daughter is performing below the school average
    (B) scores on the college entrance exam measure academic achievement
    (C) the parent is unaware of the importance of entrance exam scores
    (D) an exam score below the top five percent is evidence of academic failure
    (E) the parent believes that the daughter's performance is average

To the editor—

I must respond to the letter you published from a group of writers in my country. They allege that Francesco Humberto's most recent novel was censored. It is true that Basitia Press refused to publish the novel, but at worst that raises the possibility of breach of contract—not censorship. Basitia and Humberto entered into a contract: Humberto was given an advance to write the novel, and Basitia agreed to publish it. After reading the manuscript, however, corporate officials at Basitia feared that the content of the novel would offend many people and decided not to publish it. But since this was a matter of contract between private parties, it can hardly be called censorship.

Constantus Adolphus
New Balkan

21. Which of the following, if true, would most weaken the analysis set forth in the letter above?

    (A) Basitia has published novels by authors other than Humberto that offended some readers.
    (B) Basitia has published other novels by Humberto that offended very few people.
    (C) The officials of Basitia, the only publisher in New Balkan, are appointed by the government.

    (D) Critics who reviewed the manuscript of the novel agreed that certain parts were offensive.
    (E) Humberto was eventually able to publish the novel in another country.

All those who support nuclear energy will vote either for Perkins or for Hughes for president. Some isolationists will vote for Hughes and others will vote for Sutherland.

22. Given the statements above, which of the following must be true?

    I. Some isolationists do not support nuclear energy.
    II. Some supporters of nuclear energy are isolationists.
    III. If Perkins withdraws from the election, all supporters of nuclear energy will vote for Hughes.

    (A) I only   (B) II only   (C) III only
    (D) I and III only   (E) I, II, and III

Gun control is one of those ideas that is nice in theory but won't work in practice. The number of guns, both legal and illegal, already in private hands is enough to arm every person in the United States several times over. Even if no new guns were manufactured in or imported into the United States, there is a gun available for anyone who wants one.

23. Which of the following is NOT an assumption of the argument above?

    (A) Those who currently have guns would be willing to transfer them illegally.
    (B) Everyone wanting an illegal gun could afford to pay the black market price.
    (C) Owners of guns made illegal under gun control would not voluntarily surrender them.
    (D) Guns do not deteriorate and eventually become unoperational.
    (E) After gun control, everyone in the United States would want a gun.

GO ON TO THE NEXT PAGE

Whenever Bart is bluffing, he folds his cards into his left hand. Since Bart just folded his cards into his left hand, he must be bluffing.

24. The logic of which of the following is most like that of the thinking above?

    (A) All deciduous trees lose their leaves in the winter. It's mid-winter, and the tree by the pond has no leaves. Therefore, the tree by the pond must be a deciduous tree.

    (B) All candies produced by the Candy Kitchen use only fresh fruits. Since this chocolate was made by the Candy Kitchen, the cherry in the middle must be fresh.

    (C) Every great detective encounters some cases that cannot be solved. Since Sherlock Holmes was a great detective, he must have had some cases he could not solve.

    (D) It's always easy to tell when the home team is winning because the crowd is very loud. Since the crowd is now silent, the home team must not be ahead.

    (E) Tourists only come to the island when the weather is good. Since the weather is bad, we don't expect to see very many tourists.

IF YOU FINISH BEFORE TIME IS CALLED, YOU MAY CHECK YOUR WORK ON THIS SECTION ONLY. DO NOT WORK ON ANY OTHER SECTION IN THE TEST. **S T O P**

SECTION **5**   Time—35 Minutes
28 Questions

For each question in this section, choose the best answer and blacken the corresponding space on the answer sheet.

Directions: Each passage in this group is followed by questions based on its content. After reading a passage, choose the best answer to each question and blacken the corresponding space on the sheet. Answer all questions following a passage on the basis of what is <u>stated</u> or <u>implied</u> in that passage.

A fundamental principle of pharmacology is that all drugs have multiple actions. Actions that are desirable in the treatment of disease are considered therapeutic, while those that are undesirable or pose
(5) risks to the patient are called "effects." Adverse drug effects range from the trivial, for example, nausea or dry mouth, to the serious, such as massive gastrointestinal bleeding or thromboembolism; and some drugs can be lethal. Therefore, an effective system for
(10) the detection of adverse drug effects is an important component of the health-care system of any advanced nation. Much of the research conducted on new drugs aims at identifying the conditions of use that maximize beneficial effects and minimize the risk of
(15) adverse effects. The intent of drug labeling is to reflect this body of knowledge accurately so that physicians can properly prescribe the drug or, if it is to be sold without perscription, so that consumers can properly use the drug.
(20)   The current system of drug investigation in the United States has proved very useful and accurate in identifying the common side effects associated with new prescription drugs. By the time a new drug is approved by the Food and Drug Administration, its
(25) side effects are usually well described in the package insert for physicians. The investigational process, however, cannot be counted on to detect all adverse effects because of the relatively small number of patients involved in premarketing studies and the
(30) relatively short duration of the studies. Animal toxicology studies are, of course, done prior to marketing in an attempt to identify any potential for toxicity, but negative results do not guarantee the safety of a drug in humans, as evidenced by such well-known exam-
(35) ples as the birth deformities due to thalidomide.
    This recognition prompted the establishment in many countries of programs to which physicians report adverse drug effects. The United States and other countries also send reports to an international
(40) program operated by the World Health Organization. These programs, however, are voluntary reporting programs and are intended to serve a limited goal: alterting a government or private agency to adverse drug effects detected by physicians in the course of
(45) practice. Other approaches must be used to confirm suspected drug reactions and to estimate incidence rates. These other approaches include conducting

retrospective control studies, for example, the studies associating endometrial cancer with estrogen use, and
(50) systematically monitoring hospitalized patients to determine the incidence of acute common side effects, as typified by the Boston Collaborative Drug Surveillance Program.
    Thus, the overall drug surveillance system of the
(55) United States is composed of a set of information bases, special studies, and monitoring programs, each contributing in its own way to our knowledge about marketed drugs. The system is decentralized among a number of governmental units and is not administered
(60) as a coordinated function. Still, it would be inappropriate at this time to attempt to unite all of the disparate elements into a comprehensive surveillance program. Instead, the challenge is to improve each segment of the system and to take advantage of new
(65) computer strategies to improve coordination and communication.

1. The author's primary concern is to discuss

   (A) methods for testing the effects of new drugs on humans
   (B) the importance of having accurate information about the effects of drugs
   (C) procedures for determining the long-term effects of new drugs
   (D) attempts to curb the abuse of prescription drugs
   (E) the difference between the therapeutic and nontherapeutic actions of drugs

2. The author implies that a drug with adverse side effects

   (A) will not be approved for use by consumers without a doctor's prescription
   (B) must wait for approval until lengthy studies prove the effects are not permanent
   (C) should be used only if its therapeutic value outweighs its adverse effects
   (D) should be withdrawn from the marketplace pending a government investigation
   (E) could be used in foreign countries even though it is not approved for use in the United States

GO ON TO THE NEXT PAGE ⟹

3. Which of the following can be inferred from the passage?

   I. Some adverse drug effects cannot be detected prior to approval because they take a long time to develop.

   II. Drugs with serious adverse side effects are never approved for distribution.

   III. Some adverse drug effects are not discovered during testing because they are very rare.

   (A) I only
   (B) II only
   (C) III only
   (D) I and III only
   (E) II and III only

4. The author introduces the examples of thalidomide (line 35) to show that some

   (A) drugs do not have the same actions in humans as they do in animals
   (B) drug testing procedures are ignored by careless laboratory workers
   (C) drugs have no therapeutic value for humans
   (D) drugs have adverse side effects as well as beneficial actions
   (E) physicians prescribe drugs without first reading the manufacturer's recommendations

5. It can be inferred that the estrogen study mentioned in line 49

   (A) uncovered long-term side effects of a drug that had already been approved for sale by the Food and Drug Administration
   (B) discovered potential side effects of a drug that was still awaiting approval for sale by the Food and Drug Administration
   (C) revealed possible new applications of a drug that had previously been approved for a different treatment
   (D) is an example of a study that could be more efficiently conducted by a centralized authority than by volunteer reporting
   (E) proved that the use of the drug estrogen was not associated with side effects such as thromboembolism

6. The author is most probably leading up to a discussion of some suggestions about how to

   (A) centralize authority for drug surveillance in the United States
   (B) centralize authority for drug surveillance among international agencies
   (C) coordinate better the sharing of information among the drug surveillance agencies
   (D) eliminate the availability and sale of certain drugs now on the market
   (E) improve drug-testing procedures to detect dangerous effects before drugs are approved

7. The author makes use of which of the following devices in the passage?

   I. Definition of terms
   II. Examples
   III. Analogy

   (A) I only (B) II only (C) I and II only
   (D) II and III only (E) I, II, and III

At Nuremberg, 210 individuals were tried before thirteen military tribunals. The International Military Tribunal (IMT) tried the major German war criminals, including Hermann Goering, Rudolph Hess, and Joachim von Ribbentrop, from November 1945 to October 1946. Subsequently, another 185 defendants, grouped by organization or by type of crime, were tried before twelve United States military tribunals. Robert H. Jackson, the United States chief of counsel and an associate justice of the United States Supreme Court, decided for the IMT that in order to obtain convictions of the officials who gave the orders but did not themselves execute them, the prosecution would rely heavily upon documentary evidence. Such evidence was presumably more persuasive than affidavits and direct testimony of witnesses who might easily be brought by defense lawyers to waver in their statements.

In the course of the various trials, the prosecution chose from the millions of records available to them about 18,000 to be presented as evidence. Only 2,500 of these were affidavits or interrogation transcripts. Of the total number of defense exhibits, about one-half were affidavits. The rest of the documentary evidence came from a variety of sources, often from the defendant's personal files, the materials in the tribunal library file, and prosecution records and resources. Heavy reliance on the latter often placed the defense in a position of dependence on the good will of the prosecution.

The prosecution staff of the IMT established an elaborate system requiring the cooperation of many government agencies for processing documents, and the prosecution at the 12 United States trials at Nuremberg inherited this system. The resources of the defense were, of course, considerably more limited. Though defendants were given the right to present evidence to the tribunal, they were often compelled to engage in a long and often futile struggle to obtain records. Rulings were often affected by factors not directly related to courtroom and document-handling procedures. Some former members of the IMT defense counsel had acquired more expertise than others by defending several of the accused before the various United States tribunals at different times. As the crimes of the Nazis became more remote in time and the differences among the Allies in the cold-war period increased, a strong, rearmed Germany that could serve as an integral part of Western European defense became desirable. Correspondingly, it became difficult to try German military leaders before United States military tribunals while reestablishing a German military force. Sentences were progressively lightened and procedures softened. Sometimes, however, the nature of the crimes committed precluded the chance of the defendants to receive lighter sentences. Many harsh sentences resulted from the trial of 24 SS Einsatzgruppen for exterminating approximately one million Soviet citizens. In general, SS defendants received severe sentences, often the death penalty, and had greater difficulty in obtaining documents than other defendants.

The judges themselves were also of considerable importance. Judge Toms, from Michigan's third judicial district, Judge Phillips, from North Carolina's thirteenth district, Judge Musamanno, from the court of common pleas in Pennsylvania, and John J. Speight, admitted to the bar of Alabama, adjudicated the Milch and Pohl cases. In addition, judges Musamanno and Speight were on the bench in the Ohlendorf case. Their rulings on document-handling procedures were often more rigid and disadvantageous to defendants than were those of other judges. Among the latter were judges Wennerstrum, Shake, and Christianson of the Supreme Court of Minnesota, who presided over the Weizaecker case.

Although one might say that greater lenience in document procedures might have resulted in better defense, considering the crimes charged, there is no assurance that even the most liberal procedure would have produced exonerating records. The prosecution's greater control of documents in the earlier cases, acting under rules similar to adversary proceedings, tainted the trials. Yet, despite these flaws, the procedures devised at Nuremberg pioneered the massive use of records as court evidence with large groups of defendants. In the face of the terrible hatred engendered by the inhumanities of the Second World War, the tribunals succeeded in dispensing, essentially, justice.

8. The author is primarily concerned with

   (A) describing a historical event
   (B) developing a theory of jurisprudence
   (C) analyzing courtroom procedures
   (D) criticizing a government policy
   (E) interpreting a legal principle

9. According to the author, which of the following factors affected the severity of the sentences received by those convicted at Nuremberg?

   I. The number of documents submitted by the defense
   II. The time elapsed between the trial and the end of the war
   III. The nature of the crimes committed

   (A) III only   (B) I and II   (C) I and III
   (D) II and III   (E) I, II, and III

10. Which of the following conclusions can be inferred about the Milch, Pohl, Ohlendorf, and Weizaecker cases?

   (A) Milch, Pohl, and Ohlendorf were convicted, but Weizaecker was acquitted.
   (B) Although all four defendants were convicted, Weizaeker received a lighter sentence.
   (C) The Milch, Pohl, and Ohlendorf trials took place before the Weizaecker trial.
   (D) The defense attorneys in the Weizaecker case were given more liberal access to documents than in the other cases.
   (E) Milch, Pohl, and Ohlendorf were tried by the IMT, but Weizaecker was not.

11. According to the passage, defendants at the Nuremberg trials

   (A) were not given the opportunity to present evidence
   (B) frequently had difficulty obtaining documents
   (C) were not represented by counsel
   (D) were tried in absentia
   (E) were prosecuted by officers of the United States military

12. It can be inferred from the selection that defendants

   (A) called more witnesses than the prosecution
   (B) submitted more affidavits than the prosecution
   (C) did not have access to the tribunal libraries
   (D) were not permitted to testify on their own behalfs
   (E) relied more heavily on affidavits than the prosecution

13. The author's attitude toward the military tribunals can best be described as

   (A) restrained contempt
   (B) evident awe
   (C) uncontrolled rage
   (D) profound amusement
   (E) qualified endorsement

14. The author would be most likely to agree with which of the following statements?

   (A) Members of the SS were unfairly punished more severely than other war criminals
   (B) The IMT was more effective than the 12 United States military tribunals.
   (C) Many war criminals would have received harsher sentences had they been tried earlier.
   (D) Counsel who represented the defendants at Nuremberg were often incompetent.
   (E) Trial by documentary evidence is inherently prejudicial to the rights of a defendant.

A single tax is a tax levied upon a single item or a single type of transaction that is intended to meet all or at least the principal revenue needs of a nation or other political jurisdiction. The concept of a single tax on the rent of land was introduced into general economic discussion about the middle of the 18th century by the Physiocrats and was popularized in the late 19th century by Henry George, particularly in his *Progress and Poverty* and in his New York mayoralty campaign of 1886. George advocated the abolition of all taxes on industry and its products and the appropriation by taxation of the annual rental value of all the various forms of natural opportunities embraced under the general term "land."

The single tax proposed by Henry George was defended by its supporters as consonant with the theory of natural rights. A human being, they asserted, has an absolute inalienable right to life, equality of opportunity, and the pursuit of property. By virtue of these general rights, a person may claim access to land, which is necessary for the maintenance of life. But land, most of which is privately held, differs in fertility and value. Thus, those who hold poorer land or no land at all are denied their natural rights of life, equality of opportunity, and pursuit of property. These natural rights, argued the supporters of the single tax, give everyone a joint claim to the difference between the value of the worst and the best lands. This differential value, called economic rent, belongs to the community as a whole.

Against this position, it was argued that the theory of natural rights also holds that a person is entitled to the fruits of his or her labor and that the taking of property created by individual effort is confiscatory. Supporters of the single tax argued, however, that any scheme of private ownership was inherently unjust. Because of the scarcity of land and because of the differences in productivity among various parcels of land, some people are necessarily denied their right of equality of opportunity. Consequently, a single tax on land would not confiscate that which belongs rightly to the land owner but would merely reclaim from the landowner that which by natural right belonged to the entire community.

A second general argument for the single tax on land rested upon the economic theory of distribution. With increases in population, people are forced to bring into cultivation poorer and poorer lands. But as this is done, economic rent—the difference between the productivity of the best and the worst lands under cultivation—increases. As a result, wages decrease because wages in general are fixed by the income that can be earned by occupiers and tillers of freely held land. The share of capital in the product of industry, George maintained, follows the same course as wages (capital being in all essential respects simply labor impressed or congealed into matter). Thus wages and interest rates rise and fall together, varying inversely with rent.

Not only does rent increase with the increase in population, according to supporters of the single tax on land, every invention involves a further demand upon the soil for raw produce, thus increasing rent. Everything that lowers interest rates depresses wages and elevates rent; every increment of capital, being a demand for land, and every additional laborer has the same effect. Under private ownership of land, increases in population, science that stimulates invention, frugality that multiplies capital—in short, material progress itself—is synonymous with poverty.

Finally, advocates of the single tax on land argued that it would be more expeditious than other methods of taxation. First, it would eliminate a large army of tax collectors. Second, it would enormously increase the production of wealth by removing the taxes upon capital, production, and consumption which, they theorized, repressed or discouraged industry and by forcing into use lands held idle for speculative purposes.

15. The author of the selection is primarily concerned to

   (A) persuade the reader that a single tax on land is economically efficient
   (B) encourage legislators to adopt a single tax on land in lieu of other taxes
   (C) describe some 19th century arguments in favor of a single tax on land
   (D) discuss the relationship between tax rates and other economic factors such as interest rates
   (E) employ the concept of a natural right to justify government confiscation of private property

16. According to the passage, Henry George regarded which of the following as the primary determinant of the wage level?

   (A) amount of income produced by owners of freely held land
   (B) number of employers in a geographical region
   (C) rate of taxation by the government of wages and salaries
   (D) level of rents paid by renters for the use of land owned by others
   (E) availability of government jobs as an alternative to private employment

17. It can be inferred from the passage that Henry George entitled his work *Progress and Poverty* because he thought that under the existing tax structure

   (A) progress would inevitably lead to greater proverty
   (B) poverty would inevitably lead to more progress
   (C) progress would inevitably lead to a reduction in poverty
   (D) higher interest rates would inevitably lead to lower wages
   (E) higher taxes would inevitably lead to greater progress and to greater poverty

18. It can be inferred that an opponent of the single tax on land would regard the economic value created by the efforts of a landowner to improve that land as a

(A) property right
(B) loss of capital
(C) legitimately taxable transaction
(D) cause of unemployment
(E) diminution of rental value

19. If a government makes available to the general population fertile lands previously unoccupied, then economic rent, as that term was used by the supporters of a single tax on land, should

(A) increase
(B) decrease
(C) remain unchanged
(D) become zero
(E) cause wages to decrease

20. According to the supporters of a single tax on land, an increase in wages should be accompanied by

(A) a decrease in interest rates
(B) an increase in rent
(C) an increase in interest rates
(D) an increase in population
(E) a decrease in capital

21. According to the selection, supporters of a single tax on land claimed that the single tax would do all of the following EXCEPT:

(A) reduce government bureaucracy
(B) discourage land speculation
(C) increase production of wealth
(D) burden poor laborers
(E) stimulate production

Antitrust suits are easy to bring and costly to defend. The defendant's exposure includes treble damages, injunction, and plaintiff's attorney's fees. The defendant bears the principal burden of discovery and must pay his or her own attorneys. The plaintiff can litigate on a comparative shoestring and may pass even these costs on to the defendant. Thus, one firm may find suing its business rival a worthwhile strategic move. If the plaintiff wins, the rival is burdened; if the litigation drags on, the rival is burdened; and if the rival backs off from the challenged conduct to relieve these burdens, the plaintiff may benefit from a reduction in competition. Even the sharing of information in discovery may help rivals to collude. It seems possible, then, that the filing of an antitrust suit might tend to lessen competition in violation of the antitrust laws themselves. Is such conduct actionable?

We protect untruth, if at all, only because of concern that attempts to separate truth from untruth will lead to condemnation of truth by mistake and will prompt people to be too cautious and thus desist from making even true—because debatable—statements. A rule that requires someone to spend hours in research or contemplation before speaking, the better to avoid untruthful statements, raises the costs of all speech and ensures that we will have less of it. The compromise struck in the constitutional libel cases is a rule that discriminates honest statements—those that are not made recklessly or with knowledge of falsehood—from deliberately untruthful ones. All but the deliberately untruthful are protected.

Similarly, we protect petitioning the government by interest groups for private favors, it at all, only to give shelter to other speech. There is no abstract First Amendment right to seek transfer payments or economic rents. The framers of the Constitution saw political and economic factions as a danger to be overcome, not as a desirable end. They divided the powers of government in the belief that this would reduce the power of self-interested factions. They wrote constitutional prohibitions such as the contract clause in the hope that the limits on the power of government to transfer wealth and undercut property would aid the welfare of all. Yet a court cannot confidently separate appeals for transfers and other rents from the kind of appeals to the joint welfare that the First Amendment was designed to protect. There may be no line between the two, let alone a line that could be maintained in litigation. Thus, the Constitution protects both kinds of petitions. This protection requires "victims" to bear some or all of the costs of the political process, whether wisely or selfishly used. Similarly, they must bear part of the cost of the judicial process under the American rule. The next question is whether there is a good parallel in antitrust to the "honest statement" rule used in libel to allocate these costs.

We may quickly discard a rule that turns on whether the plaintiff (or administrative protestant) wins on the merits. That would be the equivalent of a "truth" rule for other First Amendment purposes; it would impose excessive risks or resort to the political and judicial process. We may also discard a rule that turns on whether the plaintiff or protestant had a colorable claim, something that could survive dismissal on the pleading. Noncolorable claims impose no loss on business rivals, because they may be disposed of by court or agency quickly. The only claims we need to worry about are the ones with just enough merit to linger and impose loss on one's rivals.

The tort of abuse of process offers a useful way to strike the balance. It is tortious—and the injured party can recover damages for any loss—to employ litigation in pursuit of an objective other than the one ostensibly sought. This tort offers the victim of an illegitimate suit the protection of the law yet does not endanger First Amendment rights.

22. Which of the following best describes the primary purpose of the passage?

(A) Antitrust claims may be used as a weapon by one business entity against its competitors.
(B) The tort of abuse of process is the best way to discourage spurious antitrust suits.
(C) The First Amendment does not necessarily protect statements that are untrue.
(D) Antitrust suits can impose considerable economic burdens on those sued.
(E) Some businesses may file antitrust claims against competitors to reduce competition.

23. According to the passage, the American rule requires

(A) plaintiffs to prove the truth of their claims
(B) defendants to pay their own costs in litigation
(C) each party to a lawsuit to pay the other's costs
(D) a judge to determine which party is at fault
(E) the government to grant favors to petitioners

24. The author mentions all of the following as burdens placed on a defendant in an antitrust suit EXCEPT:

(A) The possibility of being assessed treble damages
(B) The possibility of having to pay plaintiff's attorney's fees
(C) The possibility of having to file a petition for economic rents
(D) The cost of discovery
(E) The cost of its attorney's fees

25. Which of the following best describes the structure of the passage?

(A) The author focuses on an ambiguous term and provides a definition.
(B) The author identifies a problem and suggests a solution.
(C) The author introduces an analogy and attacks it.
(D) The author mentions an example and extrapolates a conclusion.
(E) The author defends a theory against someone else's attacks.

26. The author of the passage would most likely agree with which of the following statements?

(A) Because of the defendant's exposure, the American rule should be suspended in antitrust litigation.
(B) The Constitution should be amended to create a right to seek transfer payments and economic rents.
(C) In antitrust suits, the "honest statement" rule should be replaced by a "truth" rule.
(D) The tort of abuse of process can eventually eliminate the need for antitrust litigation.
(E) Some false statements must be protected in order to ensure that freedom of speech is not restricted.

27. It can be inferred from the passage that a "truth" rule would

(A) impose liability for litigation costs on a plaintiff if the plaintiff lost
(B) create a buffer zone between statements that are true and those that are honest but untrue
(C) increase the economic and financial risks incurred by defendants in antitrust suits
(D) encourage businesses to file frivolous antitrust claims against rival businesses
(E) reduce the power of the government to control markets through antitrust policy

28. The author regards using the tort of abuse of process in antitrust cases as a

(A) dangerous precedent
(B) recent innovation
(C) practical compromise
(D) costly error
(E) risky proposition

IF YOU FINISH BEFORE TIME IS CALLED, YOU MAY CHECK YOUR WORK ON THIS SECTION ONLY. DO NOT WORK ON ANY OTHER SECTION IN THE TEST. **S T O P**

TEST CENTER NUMBER

TEST DATE

MO. DAY YR.

LSAT/LSDAS NUMBER

SOCIAL SECURITY/ SOCIAL INS. NO.

LAST NAME (PRINT)

FIRST NAME (PRINT)

MIDDLE INITIAL

IMPORTANT: Please complete the above area in clear legible PRINT!
(THIS INFORMATION SHOULD BE THE SAME AS THAT ON YOUR LSAT ADMISSION TICKET/IDENTIFICATION CARD)

LSAT® WRITING SAMPLE BOOKLET

WAIT FOR THE SUPERVISOR's INSTRUCTIONS BEFORE YOU TURN THE PAGE TO THE TOPIC. PLEASE SIGN YOUR NAME AND NOTE THE DATE AT THE TOP OF PAGE ONE BEFORE YOU START TO WORK.

TIME: 30 MINUTES

GENERAL DIRECTIONS

You are to complete the brief writing exercise on the topic inside. You will have 30 minutes in which to plan and write the exercise. Read the topic carefully. You will probably find it best to spend a few minutes considering the topic and organizing your thoughts before you begin writing. DO NOT WRITE ON A TOPIC OTHER THAN THE ONE SPECIFIED. WRITING ON A TOPIC OF YOUR OWN CHOICE IS NOT ACCEPTABLE.

There is no "right" or "wrong" answer to this question. Law schools are interested in how carefully you support the position you take and how clearly you express that position. How well you write is much more important than how much you write. No special knowledge is required or expected. Law schools are interested in organization, vocabulary, and writing mechanics. They understand the short time available to you and the pressured circumstances under which you will write.

Confine your writing to the lined area inside this booklet. Only the blocked lined area will be reproduced for the law schools. You will find that you have enough space in this booklet if you plan your writing carefully, write on every line, avoid wide margins, and keep your handwriting a reasonable size. Be sure that your writing is legible.

LSAT WRITING SAMPLE TOPIC

Read the following proposals of Jackson and Simon, which were submitted to the city of Sparta's Department of Housing, to renovate an abandoned structure in one of the city's poorer neighborhoods and then operate a business in it. **Then, in the space provided, write an argument in favor of the proposal you think the Department of Housing should choose.** The following considerations should guide your decision:

1. The Department of Finance eventually wants to transfer ownership of the structure to the business as soon as the business is able to pay the back taxes on the property.
2. The Department of Housing wants a business that will benefit the community.

JACKSON plans to operate a hardware store in the building. He will use the ground floor for retail displays and the second floor and basement for storing stock. Jackson has $100,000 of his own money for purchasing stock and for other start-up costs, plus a letter of credit from a local bank that will allow him to borrow up to $150,000 for renovation. Jackson is willing to open a new business in the neighborhood because he believes the neighborhood is about to experience a renaissance. Jackson worked for ten years as the manager of a hardware store that is part of a large chain.

SIMON plans to operate a personal financial consulting firm in the building. The firm will offer budget counseling, tax preparation, advice on completing loan applications, and help with legal documents for a fee. The size of the fee will depend on the service rendered and the ability of a client to pay. Simon has $50,000 to cover the cost of renovating the building and has received a grant of $75,000 from the state's Human Resources Center to purchase computers and cover other start-up costs. Simon's plan is initially just to renovate the ground floor and then open for business. The second floor would be renovated once the business generated sufficient income. Simon worked for three years as a legal aid attorney and is familiar with the problems of the people in the neighborhood.

Answer Key

SECTION 1	SECTION 2	SECTION 3	SECTION 4	SECTION 5
1. D	1. A	1. D		1. B
2. B	2. D	2. B	1. A	2. C
3. A	3. A	3. B	2. C	3. D
4. E	4. D	4. C	3. A	4. A
5. D	5. C	5. A	4. D	5. A
6. A	6. B	6. A	5. E	6. C
7. B	7. C	7. C	6. B	7. C
8. D	8. B	8. D	7. E	8. A
9. E	9. A	9. E	8. B	9. D
10. E	10. A	10. D	9. B	10. D
11. C	11. B	11. B	10. C	11. B
12. C	12. E	12. B	11. E	12. E
13. E	13. A	13. C	12. D	13. E
14. E	14. B	14. C	13. D	14. C
15. A	15. B	15. B	14. D	15. C
16. B	16. A	16. A	15. C	16. A
17. C	17. E	17. C	16. D	17. A
18. E	18. D	18. B	17. D	18. A
19. A	19. C	19. E	18. D	19. B
20. A	20. B	20. E	19. C	20. C
21. C	21. A	21. D	20. B	21. D
22. B	22. B	22. C	21. C	22. B
23. B	23. C	23. C	22. D	23. B
24. A	24. B	24. B	23. E	24. C
	25. A		24. A	25. B
	26. D			26. E
	27. B			27. A
	28. A			28. C

Explanatory Answers

SAMPLE ESSAY

The Department of Housing should accept the proposal submitted by Jackson for two reasons: first, Jackson's proposal will prove beneficial to the neighborhood; and second, Jackson is likely to be in a position to pay the city the back taxes it is owed.

Jackson's proposal will benefit the community both in the short run and the long run. In the short run, Jackson has the money to do a complete renovation of the building, which will improve the appearance of the neighborhood. In the long run, he will stock supplies that other residents will need in order to improve their properties, and one successful business will attract other businesses.

In addition, Jackson is more likely than Simon to be able to pay off the back taxes. Jackson has the experience to run a successful business, and he has more money to invest in the business. Also, as the neighborhood begins to change, Jackson's goods will be in demand, so the hardware store will become more profitable.

Although Simon's plan would provide a service that some members of the community might need, Jackson's hardware store will also provide something needed in the area, and Jackson is more likely to pay the city the money it is owed.

SECTION 1

LOGICAL REASONING

Questions 1–2

The Robin sedan is a better car than the Eagle hatchback. Robin owners report fewer mechanical repairs for their cars than do Eagle owners, so the Robin is cheaper to maintain.

1. The argument above assumes one car is better than another if it

    (A) is cheaper to manufacture than another car
    (B) suffers less damage in an accident than another car
    (C) gets better gas mileage than another car
    (D) is cheaper to maintain than another car
    (E) is covered by a more extensive warranty than another car

(D) The argument has the structure: Robin owners report fewer mechanical repairs than do Eagle owners; the Robin is cheaper to maintain than the Eagle; therefore, Robin is a better car. The first statement is a premise that has as its conclusion the second statement, and the second statement in turn functions as a premise for the ultimate conclusion of the argument (the third statement). The ultimate conclusion of the argument depends upon a hidden, definitional assumption: cheaper to maintain is equivalent to better; the Robin is cheaper to maintain than the Eagle; a car that is cheaper to maintain is a better car; therefore, the Robin is a better car.

2. Which of the following, if true, points out a possible logical flaw in the argument above?

    I.   The Robin can carry fewer passengers and less cargo than the Eagle can.
    II. Robin owners report fewer repairs, but the average cost per repair is higher than that reported by Eagle owners.
    III. Comparably equipped Robin and Eagle models cost about the same.

    (A) I only
    (B) II only
    (C) III only
    (D) I and II only
    (E) II and III only

(B) Keep in mind the structure of the argument as outlined above. Statement I does not point out a logical flaw in the argument. Although some people might prefer a larger car and therefore prefer the

Eagle to the Robin, that does not constitute a logical weakness in the argument. (After all, other people would be just as happy with the smaller car.) Similarly, III is wide of the mark, for the speaker never makes any claim about purchase price. II, however, would weaken the argument. The claim depends on a second hidden assumption: the number of repairs determines how costly a car is to maintain. II points out that one car could require fewer repairs than another car and yet be more costly to maintain.

The question of the extent to which differing groups in our society share the same background knowledge of history, culture, and the sciences is not a question that is internal to the field of education. Without a body of shared assumptions and values, a nation may easily dissolve into a chaos of warring interest groups, unable to reach joint decisions for the long-run benefit of the entire community.

3. With which of the following statements is the author of the passage above most likely to disagree?

    (A) Decisions as to what curriculum is taught in the schools are best left in the hands of professional educators.
    (B) A body of shared values is essential for the existence of a unified society.
    (C) Knowledge of both humanities and science is a prerequisite for effective participation in a society.
    (D) The ethical and moral assumptions of an individual are likely to be affected by his or her educational background.
    (E) Groups representing the interests of different segments of society are likely to differ over what should be taught in schools.

(A) The speaker begins by stating that the extent to which groups in a society share values is more than just a question about education. The degree to which members of a society share common values determines, according to the speaker, the coherence of the society. Given this emphasis on shared values, we may infer that the author believes that decisions about the values to be inculcated should not be left to professional educators but should be made by the people who direct the course of the society. Every other choice mentions an idea the speaker is likely to endorse. As for (B), the paragraph specifically states that shared values are essential for the survival of a society. As for (C), the speaker specifically states that knowledge of history, culture, and science is not just a matter internal to education but a matter that is essential to the survival of our society. As for (D), though the speaker does not explicitly make such a statement, we can infer that he or she would be likely to agree with this idea, since the speaker argues that without shared values a society becomes splintered. Finally, the speaker would probably also agree with (E). The paragraph implies that shared values are needed to overcome the tendency of groups to isolate themselves from the rest of society.

The day following her absence from school, a student gave this note to her teacher:

To Whom It May Concern:

Please excuse Susan for her absence yesterday from her classes. She was at home ill with a viral infection. If you have any questions, you should not hesitate to call my office.

Sincerely,
Susan's Mother

4. Which of the following phrases suggests that the note is not authentic?

(A) To Whom It May Concern
(B) yesterday
(C) viral infection
(D) call my office
(E) Susan's Mother

(E) The note purports to be from the student's mother, but a parent would probably not sign such a note "Susan's Mother." A parent would use his or her own name. The presence of the phrase "Susan's Mother" suggests that Susan wrote the note herself.

John: No women received scholarships from the Cart Fund this year.
Elaine: Then I assume that no Cart Fund awards were made.
John: No; in fact, several men received scholarships this year from the Cart Fund.

5. Elaine's response might be premised on all of the following beliefs EXCEPT

(A) The Cart Fund awards were restricted to women.
(B) Only women were under consideration for the Cart Fund awards.
(C) All female applicants for Cart Fund awards were better qualified for the awards than the male applicants.
(D) Some female applicants for Cart Fund awards were better qualified for the awards than some male applicants.
(E) An equal number of awards would be made to men and women.

(D) Elaine's response demonstrates that she believes that some women would necessarily receive awards if any awards were given. Thus, when she hears that no women received awards, she concludes that no awards were given at all. (A) and (B) could each explain this reaction: if only women were eligible or under consideration and no women received awards, then no awards were given at all. (C) also accounts for the reaction: if any awards were given, they would have been given to women; so since no women received awards, none were given. And (E) also can explain the reaction: awards would be given only in equal numbers, and since no women received awards, no men received them either. (D), however, cannot explain the reaction, for (D) leaves open the possibility that awards were made to some men who were better qualified than the best-qualified female applicants.

A Roman poet wrote, "It is sweet and noble to die for one's country." It is hard to see how any sensation of sweetness could be involved in the experience of dying in battle, in excruciating pain, in a muddy ditch miles from home, hearth and family. Therefore, we may well doubt that nobility may be said to inhere in the act of dying itself.

6. The main point of the argument is that

(A) it is the consequence of the act of dying in defense of one's country that is important, not the act of dying itself
(B) the political and military objectives of war may not be evident to each individual soldier
(C) the word *sweetness* is ambiguous when it is used to describe actions rather than taste sensations
(D) the consequences of war have changed little since ancient times
(E) dying in defense of one's country is an action that may or may not be noble depending on whether the cause of the war is just

(A) The speaker seeks to draw a distinction between the simple fact of death, which he argues can in no way be pleasant, and the result accomplished by that act. (A) summarizes this distinction. As for (B), this statement is probably correct, but it does not describe the distinction drawn in the paragraph. As for (C), the author would probably deny that *sweetness* is ambiguous, even though it is used metaphorically. Instead, it seems that the author understands well what is intended by that term and denies that it accurately describes the act of dying in war. (D) is not a distinction made by the speaker. And finally, as for (E), though this might be a distinction someone would want to make, it is not the distinction made by the speaker here.

An international conference on the development of the world's undersea resources has proposed that all future use of these resources through undersea mining, harvesting of food in international waters, or other forms of development be subject to an international tax, to be set at a fixed percentage of the profits. The revenues from this tax would be used to support industrial development in the poorest nations of the world. This scheme, if adopted, will probably halt all future development of undersea resources. By removing the profit incentive, the proposed tax will discourage industrial nations from making the investments needed to exploit these valuable but remote undersea resources.

7. Which of the following questions would be most relevant in evaluating the validity of the conclusion reached above?

(A) What kinds of development projects would be supported by the proposed tax?

(B) What percentage of the profits derived from exploitation of undersea resources would be taken by the proposed tax?

(C) What position has been taken on the issue of the tax by the representatives of the nations that would benefit from the tax?

(D) What definition of *international waters* will be used for purposes of levying the proposed tax?

(E) What international agency would have the responsibility for assessing the tax and redistributing the revenues?

(B) The conclusion of the argument above is that nations will not invest money in the development projects because the tax to be imposed would make the projects unprofitable. The argument, however, rests on a very important assumption: the tax would be so great as to eliminate all potential for profit. Thus, having an answer to the question raised by (B) is very important in assessing the strength of the argument. As for (A), this question is relevant to the issue of whether the proposed tax can produce benefits, but it is not relevant to the speaker's claim that the tax would be self-defeating. As for (C), what the would-be beneficiaries of the proposed tax think of the tax will not determine whether the development projects can attract investors. Finally, (D) and (E) are both questions that you might want to ask about the proposed tax, but the answers you would get to those questions are not nearly as critical to the feasibility of the project as the answer to the question raised by (B).

If zebras have feathers, they are birds; and if zebras are birds, they have long, pointed beaks. Zebras do not have feathers. Therefore, zebras do not have long, pointed beaks.

8. Which of the following arguments most closely parallels the argument above?

(A) If Carter enjoys cold weather, he will enjoy skiing; and if he enjoys skiing, he will enjoy a trip to Vermont. Carter enjoys cold weather, so he will enjoy a trip to Vermont.

(B) If the earth is flat, then Columbus was wrong; and if Columbus was wrong, Ptolemy was right. Columbus was right, so the earth must actually be round.

(C) If Susan is a physician, her sister Kate is an accountant; if Kate is an accountant, Kate's husband, Martin, is an electrician. Martin is not an electrician, so Susan must not be a physician.

(D) If Brown is a Republocrat, he believes in free trade; and if he believes in free trade, he is no friend of labor. Brown is not a Republocrat, so he must be a friend of labor.

(E) If Matthew likes a sport, he plays it every weekend; if he plays a sport every weekend, he buys his own equipment. Matthew likes golf, so he must own a set of golf clubs.

(D) One way to attack a question like this is to use capital letters to represent the parts of the argument:

Z = zebras have feathers
B = zebras are birds
P = zebras have long, pointed beaks

The initial argument has the structure:

$Z \supset B$
$B \supset P$
$\sim Z$
Therefore, $\sim P$.

Now we will use the same technique to describe the arguments of the answer choices:

(A) C = Carter enjoys cold weather
 S = Carter enjoys skiing
 V = Carter will enjoy a trip to Vermont.
$C \supset S$
$S \supset V$
C
Therefore, V.

(B) E = Earth is flat
 C = Columbus was wrong
 P = Ptolemy was right
$E \supset C$
$C \supset P$
$\sim C$
Therefore, $\sim E$.

(C) S = Susan is a physician
   K = Kate is an accountant
   M = Martin is an electrician
   $S \supset K$
   $K \supset M$
   $\sim M$
Therefore, $\sim S$.

(D) R = Brown is a Republocrat
   F = Brown believes in free trade
   L = Brown is no friend of labor
   $R \supset F$
   $F \supset L$
   $\sim R$
Therefore, $\sim L$.

(E) S = Matthew likes a sport
   P = Matthew plays it every weekend
   E = Matthew buys his own equipment
   G = Matthew likes golf
   O = Matthew owns a set of golf clubs
   $M \supset P$
   $P \supset E$
   G
Therefore, O.

(Notice that this argument has five different terms.)

Television Advertisement: Here is news for all coffee drinkers. In 17 cities across the nation, we tested our instant coffee against perked coffee and we won! In a survey of thousands of coffee drinkers, two out of every five expressed a preference for Flash Instant Coffee over perked coffee. Shouldn't you try Flash, the coffee with the same rich taste as perked coffee?

9. Which of the following, if true, would most weaken the claim above?

(A) The 17 cities were concentrated primarily in the midwest and west.
(B) The survey included 150 people in each of the 17 cities.
(C) The taste tests used a medium-priced brand of perked coffee.
(D) For purposes of the survey, "coffee drinker" was defined as anyone who drinks at least one cup of coffee per day.
(E) Those coffee drinkers who preferred Flash over perked coffee were already instant-coffee drinkers.

(E) The advertisement is apparently aimed at people who drink brewed coffee, and it attempts to persuade them that an instant coffee has the same sort of flavor as brewed coffee. (E) considerably undermines this attempt by pointing out that those people who preferred Flash to the brewed coffee did so because they already liked the taste of instant coffee. The other choices are generally relevant to the advertising claim, but none of them makes a very powerful attack on the claim.

Those who say that underhand pitching in baseball is not dangerous must be unaware of the case of Ray Chapman. In 1920, Chapman was struck by a pitch thrown by underhand pitcher Carl Mays and subsequently died of head injuries. Underhand pitching should be banned.

10. The argument above may best be described as one that

(A) applies a general principle to a specific instance
(B) confuses cause and effect
(C) attacks the proponent of an idea on personal rather than logical grounds
(D) relies on a confusion between two similar but distinct terms
(E) draws a general conclusion from a specific example

(E) This item merely asks that you describe the initial argument. In the initial paragraph, the speaker cites a specific example and draws a general conclusion from it. Thus, (E) is the best description of the initial paragraph.

The preeminence of television in modern political campaigns has produced several deleterious effects on our democratic system. Because the attention span of television-trained audiences has been artificially shortened, candidates are forced to encapsulate their programs and ideas in 30- or 60-second summaries—mere slogans embellished with emotionally evocative imagery. And because television commercials are so costly, candidates must spend much of their campaign time raising money rather than delving deeply into the issues confronting our nation and its leaders.

11. According to the passage above, the negative effects of television on political campaigns are attributable to which of the following?

  I. The high cost of television commercials
  II. The influence of television on the ability of viewers to absorb complex ideas
  III. The complexity of today's political issues

(A) I only (B) II only (C) I and II only
(D) II and III only (E) I, II, and III

(C) The initial paragraph states that television has artificially shortened the attention spans of viewers; therefore, II is one of the problems mentioned by the speaker. Additionally, the initial paragraph states that the high cost of television advertising forces candidates to spend time raising money instead of learning about issues. So item I is also a problem mentioned by the author. III, however, is not a problem created by television.

The doctrine of civil disobedience requires, paradoxically, the utmost respect for the system of law, even when a higher moral obligation demands that a particular law be broken. A true proponent of civil disobedience never claims to go beyond the reach of the law or to be exempt from any of its penalties.

12. Which of the following best explains why the speaker above regards the doctrine of civil disobedience as paradoxical?

(A) A law that is unjust is no law at all, so no one has a moral obligation to obey an unjust law.

(B) Respect for the law is the highest civic virtue, but certain moral virtues are more important than any civic virtue.

(C) One who engages in civil disobedience must insist that the law be enforced even as he breaks it.

(D) A proponent of civil disobedience is hypocritical because he claims to be acting morally when he breaks a law.

(E) The doctrine of civil disobedience entails that every individual has the right to judge whether or not a law is just.

(C) The essence of civil disobedience is that the person who breaks the law expects to incur the penalty for breaking it. He does not consider himself above the law or beyond its reach. This is why civil disobedience is not simply lawlessness. (C) nicely describes this seemingly paradoxical position: I will break the law to show it is unjust, but I also insist that the law be enforced. As for (A) and (B), while these are positions that some philosophers have maintained, neither explains why civil disobedience is a paradoxical act. As for (D), it is the fact that the person who commits an act of civil disobedience expects to be punished for breaking the law that prevents civil disobedience from being hypocritical. And finally, as for (E), though this might also be a tenet of the proponent of civil disobedience, this does not explain the speaker's description of civil disobedience as paradoxical.

Questions 13–14

Beauty depends on a pleasing blend of regularity or symmetry with irregularity or asymmetry. In poetry, for example, the most beautiful rhythms are those that, while fitting into an overall metrical pattern, vary line by line in the specific stresses, accents, and lengths that mark particular syllables. Without these subtle variations, pure metric regularity would quickly pall; without the overarching regularity, the verses would appear chaotic and ugly.

13. Which of the following, if true, would most weaken the argument above?

(A) The beauty of poetry arises from imagery and syntax as well as from rhythm.

(B) No arrangement of words, however carefully planned, can ever be absolutely regular in its rhythmic patterns.

(C) Critics often disagree as to which poems appear beautiful and which do not.

(D) Poetry in different languages generally follows different metrical arrangements.

(E) Some poems that follow no regular metrical pattern have rhythms that are very beautiful.

(E) The main point of the paragraph is that beauty in general and in poetry in particular depends upon variation presented in the context of regularity. According to the speaker, regularity without variation is boring, but variation without regularity is chaotic and ugly. (E) challenges this point by arguing that some beautiful poetry lacks the regularity insisted upon by the speaker. As for (A), the speaker never claims that beauty derives solely from variation in the context of regularity, only that this is necessary. As for (B), at best this objection only means that it is impossible to achieve perfection, not that beauty does not depend on variation in the context of regularity. As for (C), that critics may disagree does not mean that there are no standards by which a poem may be judged; and, more specifically, their disagreement does not mean that the standard proposed by the speaker is invalid. As for (D), this seems consistent with the speaker's point, for it suggests that poetry in other languages also depends on the general principle of variation in a context of regularity.

14. The argument above assumes which of the following to be true?

   (A) A blend of symmetry with asymmetry will always be esthetically pleasing.
   (B) A rhythmical arrangement that is uninteresting may nevertheless be beautiful.
   (C) The qualities that make poetry beautiful cannot necessarily be generalized to other types of beauty.
   (D) Variations in poetic rhythm are most effective when they underscore the meaning of the lines.
   (E) Regularity may be varied without losing its fundamentally regular quality.

(E) As noted above, the central point of the paragraph is that beauty depends upon variation in a context of regularity. Thus, (E) is an assumption made by the speaker. As for (A), the author claims only that beauty depends on variation in a context of regularity, not that every mix of variety and regularity is beautiful. As for (B), the speaker implies that a boring rhythmical pattern is not beautiful. As for (C), the speaker makes a general claim about the nature of beauty and then illustrates that claim with some remarks about poetry. Thus, the speaker evidently believes that the rules that govern poetry can be generalized to other areas. Finally, as for (D), though this is a nice idea, the speaker never commits himself to it.

Anyone who is planning on a career as an investment banker wants to receive an M.B.A. degree from an Ivy League university. Phyllis wants an M.B.A. from Dartmouth, which is an Ivy League university. Therefore, Phyllis must be planning on a career as an investment banker.

15. Which of the following, if true, most strengthens the conclusion of the argument above?

   (A) All of those who want M.B.A. degrees from Ivy League universities are planning careers as investment bankers.
   (B) Some investment bankers have M.B.A. degrees from Ivy League universities.
   (C) All investment bankers with M.B.A. degrees attended Ivy League universities.
   (D) Only those planning on careers as investment bankers want M.B.A. degrees from Ivy League universities.
   (E) Only those with M.B.A. degrees from Ivy League universities are fully qualified for careers as investment bankers.

(A) The initial argument has (more or less) the following structure:

All *IB* are *MBA*s.

P is an *MBA*.

Therefore, *P* is an *IB*.

where *IB* stands for people who are planning careers as investment bankers, *MBA* stands for people who want M.B.A. degrees from Ivy League schools, and *P* stands for Phyllis. As you can see, the argument is not valid. (It's similar to the argument: All whales are mammals; Tony is a mammal; therefore, Tony is a whale. Tony may be a chimpanzee!) Choice (A) strengthens the argument:

All *MBA*s are *IB*.

P is an *MBA*.

Therefore, *P* is an *IB*.

This is now a valid argument.

The Sandersons must be planning to sell their house on Lincoln Place, since they visited the office of the local real estate agent yesterday.

16. Which of the following states the conclusion of the argument above?

(A) The Sandersons visited the office of the local real estate agent yesterday.
(B) The Sandersons want to sell their house on Lincoln Place.
(C) The local real estate agent will be handling the sale of the Sandersons' house.
(D) The Sandersons own a house on Lincoln Place.
(E) The local real estate agent could assist the Sandersons in selling their house on Lincoln Place.

(B) In this argument there is an explicit premise signalled by *since* (they visited the office of the local real estate agent yesterday). The other statement in the argument is the conclusion (as [B] correctly points out). (A) is the explicit premise of the argument, so it cannot be the conclusion. (D) and (E) are implicit premises of the argument. (C) goes beyond the scope of the argument. (Compare [C] with [E].)

17. The argument above assumes which of the following to be true?

I. The Sandersons own a house on Lincoln Place.
II. The Sandersons live on Lincoln Place.
III. The Sandersons would not visit the office of the local real estate agent unless they were planning to sell their house.

(A) I only
(B) I and II only
(C) I and III only
(D) II and III only
(E) I, II, and III

(C) This item asks you to identify the assumptions of the initial argument. Statement I must be an assumption of the argument, since the speaker says that the Sandersons are planning to sell their house. III is also an assumption of the argument. The argument has the form: The Sandersons visited the real estate agent; therefore, they are planning to sell their house. And that conclusion also rests on the hidden assumption articulated by III. II, however, is not an assumption of the argument. The Sandersons could own the house on Lincoln Place even if they do not live in it.

Professor Gilmartin gives good grades only to students of Irish descent. After all, last term he gave grades of A to Kathleen and Mary, both of whom are of Irish descent.

18. A critique of the logic of the argument above would most likely emphasize the fact that the speaker

(A) fails to define the term *good grades*
(B) reverses the most likely causal relationship
(C) criticizes Professor Gilmartin on personal rather than logical grounds
(D) fails to explain Professor Gilmartin's motivation in favoring students of Irish descent
(E) generalizes on the basis of limited evidence

(E) This argument is a good example of the fallacy of hasty generalization. The speaker cites two examples and then reaches a very general conclusion. As for (A), while it is true that you could ask for a more precise definition of the term *good grades*, the speaker's failure to define that term initially doesn't seem to be the most glaring weakness of the argument. After all, the term is not completely ambiguous, and the speaker does imply that he considers a grade of A to be a good grade. As for (B), the speaker doesn't identify any causal relation. He does not, for example, say, "And Gilmartin does this because he is Irish." As for (C), you might correctly describe the argument as an attack on Gilmartin, but that does not prove the argument is weak. In fact, it seems to be the speaker's intention to attack Gilmartin for his grading policies. As for (D), before you would accept the conclusion of the argument, you might very well want to know why Gilmartin grades the way he does. But the fact that the author has not offered all of the reasons for the conclusion that could possibly be offered is not a logical weakness in the argument.

19. Which of the following questions would be most relevant in examining the validity of the conclusion drawn above?

    (A) Has Professor Gilmartin given grades of A to any students who are not of Irish descent?

    (B) Is Professor Gilmartin generally considered a stricter grader than any other teacher at the school?

    (C) Did Kathleen and Mary produce any extra projects while students of Professor Gilmartin?

    (D) How many students of Irish descent have received grades of D or less from Professor Gilmartin?

    (E) From what ethnic background is Professor Gilmartin descended?

(A) Several of the questions presented in the answer choices are relevant to the speaker's claim, but an answer to the question raised by (A) would be most likely to prove or disprove the conclusion of the initial argument. The speaker claims, "Gilmartin gives good grades only to students of Irish descent." A "yes" answer to the question raised by (A) would disprove that conclusion, while a "no" answer would prove the conclusion. As for (B), whether Gilmartin is stricter or more lenient than other teachers is irrelevant. The speaker questions the fairness of Gilmartin's grading as applied to his own students. As for (C), an answer to this question would help you evaluate the significance of the examples adduced in support of the claim. By comparison, however, (A), which aims directly at the conclusion, is more directly relevant than (C), which aims only at the proof for the conclusion. (D) is at best only remotely related to the speaker's claim. The speaker claims that only students of Irish descent receive high grades, not that all students of Irish descent receive high grades. Finally, (E) is somewhat like (C). While it is true that an answer to this question might cast some light on the issue raised by the speaker, an answer to (A) would provide much more information.

Some doctors drive fancy cars, and all extremely wealthy people drive fancy cars. Therefore, some doctors are extremely wealthy.

20. Which of the following arguments most closely parallels the reasoning in the argument above?

    (A) Some Italians are socialists, and all members of the Red Students League are socialists. Therefore, some Italians are members of the Red Students League.

    (B) Some politicians are dishonest, and all members of Congress are politicians. Therefore, some members of Congress are dishonest.

    (C) Some dentists like to cook, and Dr. Gomez is a dentist. Therefore, Dr. Gomez likes to cook.

    (D) Some farmers wear green overalls, and all farmers wear visored caps. Therefore, some people who wear visored caps wear green overalls.

    (E) Some baseball players chew tobacco, and all those who chew tobacco have stained teeth. Therefore, some baseball players have stained teeth.

(A) One way to attack this item is to use capital letters to represent the logical structure of the arguments. The initial argument has the structure: Some *D* are *FC* (some doctors are drivers of fancy cars); all *WP* are *FC* (all extremely wealthy people are drivers of fancy cars); therefore, some *D* are *WP*.

Some *D* are *FC*.
All *WP* are *FC*.
Therefore, some *D* are *WP*.

    (A) Some *I* are *S*.
          All *R* are *S*.
          Therefore, some *I* are *R*.

    (B) Some *P* are *D*.
          All *C* are *P*.
          Therefore, some *C* are *D*.

    (C) Some *D* are *C*.
          G is a *D*.
          Therefore, *G* is a *C*.

    (D) Some *F* are *GO*.
          All *F* are *VC*.
          Therefore, some *PVC* are *GO*.

(**Note:** The conclusion requires the use of another letter because it includes a new term. *People* is not logically equivalent to *farmers*.)

    (E) Some *P* are *TC*.
          All *TC* are *ST*.
          Therefore, some *P* are *ST*.

You can see that (A) makes the same kind of mistake as the original argument.

Since the structure and functioning of living tissue is governed by the laws of physics, the same combination of conditions that gave rise to life here on Earth could also occur other places in the universe and also give rise to life. Given an infinite amount of time, this possibility becomes a certainty. Thus, it is almost certain that life exists elsewhere in the universe.

21. Which of the following statements, if true, would weaken the above argument?

    I. The universe is a finite number of years old.
    II. The conditions that gave rise to life on Earth were unique to a particular epoch in the history of the universe and are not likely to be repeated.
    III. Scientists have no real evidence that life exists anywhere except on Earth.

    (A) I only
    (B) II only
    (C) I and II only
    (D) I and III only
    (E) II and III only

(C) The argument rests on two hidden assumptions: first, that the conditions that gave rise to life on Earth can be repeated elsewhere; and second, that an infinite time has elapsed during which these conditions could have occurred. Statements I and II attack these assumptions. III, however, does not weaken the argument. The fact that no one yet has proved the existence of other life does not undermine the logical structure of the argument. (Notice that the conclusion of the argument is that life now exists elsewhere. Had the conclusion read that life would exist elsewhere at some point in the future, then II would not be a very powerful attack on the argument.)

Those who deny the existence of miracles say that miraculous events are impossible because they violate the laws of nature. However, we know from personal experience that laws are violated every day; otherwise, there would be no need for police, judges, and prisons. Therefore, there is no reason to believe that the laws of nature may not be violated as well.

22. Which of the following best states the central weakness in the argument above?

    (A) It places a divine being, who might bring about a miraculous event, on the same moral level as a human criminal.
    (B) The term *law*, when applied to the laws of nature, has a different meaning than when applied to human laws.
    (C) It assumes that miraculous events have taken place without offering substantive proof for their occurrence.
    (D) It ignores the fact that under unusual circumstances natural events may occur that appear to violate natural laws without actually doing so.
    (E) It attacks the motivations of those who deny the miraculous rather than analyzing the evidence for and against their arguments.

(B) The initial argument commits the fallacy of ambiguity. It uses the term *law* in two different senses. The first occurrence of the term in the phrase "laws of nature" implies orderly regularities that are without exceptions. In other words, a law of nature is not something that can be broken. The second occurrence refers to statutes and implies that this sort of law can be broken.

Questions 23–24

Without fully considering the question, we tend to assume that consciousness is necessary for purposeful behavior. We regard the actions of a well-regulated marching band or those of a flock of geese flying in formation as purposeful, while those of the molecules that form an intricate mineral crystal we consider nonpurposeful. Yet, on reflection, this assumption seems unwarranted. Consciousness may be merely epiphenomenal, occurring alongside of but not directing behavior. When we look at consciousness in this light, we must consider the possibility that a chicken is, in reality, merely an egg's way of making another egg.

23. The speaker above implies that consciousness

    (A) cannot occur without purposeful behavior
    (B) is not essential to purposeful behavior
    (C) directs all purposeful behavior
    (D) is merely an illusion
    (E) is capable of reproduction

(B) The speaker suggests that consciousness might be merely epiphenomenal, that is, that episodes of consciousness take place parallel to purposeful behavior but do not cause it. The point of mentioning the egg is to suggest that an activity (such as reproduction) can be regarded as purposeful even without introducing the idea of consciousness. (B) summarizes this idea. (A) and (C) misinterpret the main point of the paragraph. The speaker suggests that purposeful behavior does not depend on consciousness. (D) overstates the speaker's point. The speaker does not deny that consciousness occurs, only that it does not direct purposeful behavior. Finally, (E) represents a misinterpretation of the point made in the last sentence of the selection.

24. The speaker implies that an egg is

(A) capable of purposeful behavior
(B) characterized by consciousness
(C) less intelligent than a chicken
(D) less complex than a mineral crystal
(E) more intelligent than a chicken

(A) As noted above, the point of the example of the egg is to suggest that purposeful behavior can take place without consciousness. Therefore, (A) is the best response. (B) is incorrect, for the speaker intends to suggest that the egg, which lacks consciousness, is still capable of purposeful behavior, namely reproduction.

SECTION 2

READING COMPREHENSION

1. It can be inferred from the passage that the physical features of a galaxy that does not belong to a rich cluster are determined primarily by the

(A) size and rotation of the protogalactic cloud
(B) intensity of light emanating from the galaxy
(C) temperature of the interstellar gas
(D) age of the protogalactic cloud
(E) speed at which the protogalactic cloud is moving through space

(A) This is an implied idea question. In the first paragraph, the author states that the generally accepted theory of galaxy formation maintains that the size and shape of a galaxy is determined by the size and rotation of the protogalactic cloud. The author then states that this theory must be qualified for those galaxies that are members of clusters, because other forces such as the hot, scouring gas and collisions with other galaxies become more important than the preconditions. Thus, we can infer that the author believes that the size and shape of a galaxy that is not a member of a rich cluster is determined by those features cited by the generally accepted theory. As for (B), the author never states that the intensity of light emanating from a galaxy contributes to its shape

or size. Instead, the author implies that the intensity of light emanating from a galaxy is a function of the size of the galaxy. As for (C), though the author mentions that the temperature of the tenuous interstellar gas found in clusters is very high (maybe 100 million degrees), the author does not suggest that size or shape of a galaxy varies according to the temperature of that gas. As for (D), though the author mentions that the Sun was formed at a certain period in the history of the galaxy, he does not state that the size or shape of a galaxy depends on the age of the protogalactic cloud. Finally, as for (E), though the author states that hot wind scours galaxies moving through clusters of galaxies, he does not state that the speed of a protogalactic cloud has any effect on the resulting galaxy.

2. The author implies that the currently accepted theories on galaxy formation are

(A) completely incorrect and misguided
(B) naive and out-of-date
(C) speculative and unsupported by observation
(D) substantially correct but in need of modification
(E) accurate and adequate to explain all known observations

(D) This is an implied idea question. As noted above, the author states that the currently accepted theories do not account for all that is known about galaxy formation. In particular, those theories do not take account of what goes on in a rich cluster of galaxies. Thus, we can eliminate choice (A). But the author also notes that only about 10 percent of all galaxies are members of rich clusters, so we can infer that he believes that the theories are largely correct and just fail to take account of the special conditions in clusters. Therefore, (D), rather than (A), (B), or (C), is the best choice.

3. According to the passage, a cluster with a central, supergiant galaxy will

(A) contain no intermediately bright galaxies
(B) have 50 to 100 galaxies of all sizes and intensities
(C) consist solely of third- and fourth-generation stars
(D) produce only spiral and disk-shaped galaxies
(E) be surrounded by galaxies of all sizes and shapes

(A) This is an explicit idea question. In the final paragraph, the author states that the result of this galactic cannibalism will be a central supergiant (which has reached that size by devouring other galaxies), surrounded by a sparse cluster of dim galaxies (the other large galaxies having been dragged into the central supergiant).

4. According to the passage, the outcome of a collision between galaxies depends on which of the following?

   I. The relative velocities of the galaxies
   II. The relative ages of the galaxies
   III. The relative sizes of the galaxies

   (A) I only   (B) II only   (C) III only
   (D) I and III only   (E) I, II, and III

   (D) This is an explicit idea question. In the second paragraph the author mentions the factors that will determine the outcome of a collision between two galaxies, and he mentions the speeds at which they are moving and their sizes. He does not, however, mention age as a factor.

5. According to the passage, as a galaxy falls inward toward the center of a cluster, it

   (A) collides with the central core and emerges relatively intact
   (B) absorbs superheated gases from the interstellar medium
   (C) is broken apart by the gravitational forces of the core
   (D) is transformed by collisions into a large, spiral galaxy
   (E) captures unattached stars that have been ejected from the galaxy's core

   (C) This is an explicit idea question. In the third paragraph the author specifically states that as a galaxy slows and spirals in toward the center of a cluster, the gravitational forces that hold the stars to the galaxy are overcome by the gravitational attraction of the core of the cluster. The stars are then pulled away from the infalling galaxy. Also, in the next sentence the author mentions that many galaxies may be "torn asunder" in this fashion.

6. The passage provides information that will answer which of the following questions?

   I. What is the age of our sun?
   II. What proportion of all galaxies are found in clusters?
   III. Approximately how many galaxies would be found in a rich cluster?

   (A) I only   (B) II only   (C) I and III only
   (D) II and III only   (E) I, II, and III

   (B) In the first paragraph the author states that about 10 percent of all galaxies are members of rich clusters, so II must be part of the correct answer. No information, however, is provided to answer the question posed in I. Although the author states that the sun was formed some five billion years after the initial period of star formation, this information will not answer the question asked. As for III, the passage never states how many galaxies would be found in a rich cluster.

7. The author is primarily concerned with

   (A) showing that behavior is a more effective way of controlling bodily temperature than innate mechanisms
   (B) criticizing researchers who will not discard their theories about the effects of microwave radiation on organisms
   (C) demonstrating that effects of microwave radiation are different from those of other forms of radiation
   (D) analyzing the mechanism by which an organism maintains its bodily temperature in a changing thermal environment
   (E) discussing the importance of thermoreceptors in the control of the internal temperature of an organism

   (C) This is a main idea question. Choice (A) describes a point made in the selection (in the last sentence in the first paragraph), but that idea is not the overall or main point of the selection. The idea suggested by choice (B) is certainly one that is consistent with the overall tone of the passage, but again, the idea is not the main point of the selection. The author is not just concerned with criticizing those who won't abandon their theories; he is more concerned with demonstrating that those theories are in fact wrong. And this is the idea mentioned by (C): the main point of the passage is that the popular theories are incorrect. Choices (D) and (E) are like choice (A). They mention ideas covered in the passage, but neither describes the main point of the passage.

8. The author makes which of the following points about innate mechanisms for heat production?

   I. They are governed by thermoreceptors inside the body of the organism rather than at the surface.
   II. They are a less effective means of compensating for gross changes in temperature than behavioral strategies.
   III. They are not affected by microwave radiation.

   (A) I only   (B) I and II only   (C) I and III only
   (D) II and III only   (E) I, II, and III

   (B) This is a specific detail question. In the opening sentence, the author establishes that there are two general responses available to warm-blooded animals for regulating body temperature: behavior and innate mechanisms. The author goes on to state that humans rely primarily on the first type of response but adds that the organism also responds to changes in temperature in the core of the body (the second type of response) and that these changes are triggered by thermoreceptors distributed throughout the central nervous system. Thus, statement I must be part of the correct answer choice. In the final sentence of the first paragraph, the author states that the second type of mechanism for regulating temperature is less effective for adjusting to gross changes in temperature than the first type. Thus, II must be part of the correct response. Finally, the author does not state that the internal thermoreceptors are not affected by microwave radiation. The problem cited by the author is not that internal thermoreceptors do not respond to changes in the temperature of the core of the body but that they do not trigger the type of response needed to counteract gross changes in environmental temperatures.

9. Which of the following would be the most logical topic for the author to take up in the paragraph following the final paragraph of the selection?

   (A) A suggestion for new research to be done on the effects of microwaves on animals and human beings
   (B) An analysis of the differences between microwave radiation and other forms of radiation
   (C) A proposal that the use of microwave radiation be prohibited because it is dangerous
   (D) A survey of the literature on the effects of microwave radiation on human beings
   (E) A discussion of the strategies used by various species to control hyperthermia

   (A) This is a further application question. Since the last paragraph deals with a recent report suggesting that previous assumptions about microwaves were incorrect, the author would probably go on to talk about the need for more research. (B) is incorrect because the author is dealing with microwave radiation and there would be no reason at this point to compare it to other forms of radiation. Besides, the author made the comparison earlier in the passage. (C) is incorrect because it overstates the case. There is no evidence to suggest that microwave radiation is so dangerous that it should be prohibited—just understood and regulated. (D) is incorrect because clearly the author is concerned with new information about microwave radiation. He has already suggested that what we now believe is erroneous. Finally, (E) is incorrect because a discussion of the strategies used by various species to control hyperthermia would not follow logically from his remarks that microwave radiation has not been correctly understood. In any event, the discussion of such strategies early in the passage is intended to set the stage for the main point of the selection. (See the discussion of question 7, above.)

10. The author's strategy in lines 39–42 is to

    (A) introduce a hypothetical example to dramatize a point
    (B) propose an experiment to test a scientific hypothesis
    (C) cite a case study to illustrate a general contention
    (D) produce a counterexample to disprove an opponent's theory
    (E) speculate about the probable consequences of a scientific phenomenon

    (A) In the lines indicated, the author states that it is possible that an organism could be cooked by microwave radiation (because the radiation penetrates into the core) before it even realizes its temperature is rising. The verb tense here (could) clearly indicates that the author is introducing a hypothetical possibility. Given the shocking nature of the example, we should conclude that he has introduced it to dramatize a point.

11. The author implies that the proponents of the theory that microwave radiation acts on organisms in the same way as other forms of radiation based their conclusions primarily on

    (A) laboratory research
    (B) unfounded assumption
    (C) control group surveys
    (D) deductive reasoning
    (E) causal investigation

    (B) In the first sentence of the second paragraph the author remarks that proponents of the generally accepted theory (which treats microwave radiation like other radiation) simply assumed that one type of radiation would have the same thermal effect as other types of radiation. Then the author goes on to demonstrate that this assumption is wrong. Thus, (B) is the best description of the error identified by the author. Certainly, there is no suggestion that the proponents of the accepted theory did special laboratory research, control group surveys, or causal investigation. As for choice (D), while the proponents of the accepted theory may have used deductive reasoning to reach their conclusion, this would not have been the main basis for their conclusions. (Note the wording of the question stem.)

12. The tone of the passage can best be described as

   (A) genial and conversational
   (B) alarmed and disparaging
   (C) facetious and cynical
   (D) scholarly and noncommittal
   (E) analytical and concerned

   (E) This is a tone question. The author gives facts and analyzes or discusses a problem, so the tone could be called scholarly or analytical. The author is clearly concerned that other scientists made an error in their assessment of the effects of microwave radiation. (A) is incorrect because the tone is not conversational at all, but expository. (B) is incorrect because although the author seems disturbed by the ignorance of the scientists, he is never disparaging. He is also never facetious or cynical (C). (D) is close because the tone is scholarly, but (E) is the best choice because the author is more "concerned" than he is "noncommittal."

13. The author is primarily concerned with

   (A) pointing out weaknesses in a popular scientific theory
   (B) developing a hypothesis to explain a scientific phenomenon
   (C) reporting on new research on the effects of microwave radiation
   (D) criticizing the research methods of earlier investigators
   (E) clarifying ambiguities in the terminology used to describe a phenomenon

   (A) This is a main idea question. The passage explains why microwave radiation is not like other radiation and why it is therefore dangerous to warm-blooded species. Since it was until recently assumed that microwave radiation was like other radiation, the author is concerned with pointing out the weaknesses of this theory.

14. The tone of the passage can best be described as

   (A) light-hearted and amused
   (B) objective but concerned
   (C) detached and unconcerned
   (D) cautious but sincere
   (E) enthusiastic and enlightened

   (B) This is a tone question. We can immediately eliminate (A) as inconsistent with the topic of the selection and (E) as inconsistent with the neutral tone of the passage. As for (C), this choice overstates the case. Though the author adopts the stance of a commentator, he is not detached or unconcerned. You can eliminate (D) because the author does seem sincere, but there is nothing to warrant the description *cautious*. (B) is the best choice. The statements are made in an objective and analytical way, and the author is concerned with the topic he has chosen.

15. According to the author, the "pessimism" mentioned at line 35 is partly attributable to the fact that

   (A) there has been little real improvement in health-care services
   (B) expectations about health-care services are sometimes unrealistic
   (C) large segments of the population find it impossible to get access to health-care services
   (D) advances in technology have made health-care service unaffordable
   (E) doctors are now less concerned with patient care

   (B) This is a specific detail question. In the first paragraph, the author states that some problems do remain, and he gives some examples. In the second paragraph, he discusses some of the causes of the problems. In the third paragraph, he says that the problems are not as bad as they sometimes seem. Some of the disappointment in health-care services must be attributable to the fact that people expect too much from health care. (A) is specifically contradicted by the first paragraph where the author states there have been improvements. As for (C), (D), and (E), even if these statements were true (but ultimately they seem inconsistent with the first paragraph), they are not responsive to this question.

16. The author cites the prepaid plans (lines 46–48) as

   (A) counterexamples to the claim that nothing has worked
   (B) examples of health-care plans that were overfunded
   (C) evidence that health-care services are fragmented
   (D) proof of the theory that no plan has been successful
   (E) experiments that yielded disappointing results

   (A) This is a logical detail question. In the first paragraph, the author states that there have been disappointments which have led to pessimism. In the second paragraph, he explains why this pessimism is at least in part unfounded. He begins the third paragraph by saying it is not true that nothing works. At this point he mentions the prepaid plans. So they must be examples of the ideas that worked. As for (B), this is a problem with other experiments, not the prepaid plans the author mentions by name. As for (C), though the author mentions this as a complaint sometimes heard, the sentence appears in the first paragraph so it is not an answer to this logical detail question. (D) and (E) are contradicted by our analysis of the correct answer.

678

17. It can be inferred that the sentence "Humpty Dumpty cannot always be put back together again" means that

(A) the cost of health-care services will not decline
(B) some people should not become doctors
(C) medical care is not really essential to good health
(D) illness is often unpleasant and even painful
(E) medical science cannot cure every ill

(E) This is an inference question. In the third paragraph the author is explaining why the pessimism is not totally justified. He gives as one reason the fact that a person who is sick is not in the best frame of mind anyway. He goes on to say, Humpty Dumpty cannot always be put back together again—too many doctors won't admit they have limitations. The reference to Humpty Dumpty and the observation that doctors do in fact have limitations implies that some illnesses just cannot be cured and this is stated by choice (E). As for (A), though the author may believe this conclusion, it is not responsive to this inference question. As for (B), though the author implies criticism of a doctor who will not admit the limitations of medicine, that falls short of the conclusion actually stated in (B). As for (C), this, too, overstates the case. The fact that there are limits to what medicine can do does not imply that it does nothing at all. As for (D), though this is a true statement, it is not responsive to the question asked.

18. With which of the following descriptions of the system for the delivery of health-care services would the author most likely agree?

(A) It is biased in favor of doctors and against patients.
(B) It is highly fragmented and completely ineffective.
(C) It has not embraced new technology rapidly enough.
(D) It is generally effective but can be improved.
(E) It discourages people from seeking medical care.

(D) This is a further application question. We are looking for the statement the author would be most likely to accept. In the first paragraph the author specifically states that improvements have been made, that these improvements have led to greater life expectancies, and that there are still gaps. Thus, there is reason to believe the author would say the system is generally effective but can still be improved. As for (A), nothing in the passage suggests that the system favors one party over the other. As for (B), this overstates the case. Though the author acknowledges that problems remain, he would not go so far as to say the system is completely ineffective. As for (C),

this seems contradicted by the first paragraph. One of the problems cited is the tendency to spend too much money on new technology. Finally, as for (E), though there are problems of access for some people, the author does not say that the system itself discourages people from trying to get access to health care.

19. Which of the following best describes the logical structure of the selection?

(A) The third paragraph is intended as a refutation of the first and second paragraphs.
(B) The second and third paragraphs are intended as a refutation of the first paragraph.
(C) The second and third paragraphs explain and put into perspective the points made in the first paragraph.
(D) The first paragraph describes a problem, and the second and third paragraphs present two horns of a dilemma.
(E) The first paragraph describes a problem, the second its causes, and the third a possible solution.

(C) In the first paragraph the author describes several negative aspects of the health-care system. In the second paragraph, he acknowledges that there are problems and discusses their causes. But in the third paragraph he argues that things are not as bad as they seem. The best description of this development is provided by (C). (A) and (B) are incorrect, for, though the author does, in the third paragraph, say that things are not as bad as they seem, this is not a refutation of the claim that there are some problems. As for (D), though the author strives to present an objective and balanced picture, the fact that there are two perspectives on a problem does not constitute a dilemma. As for (E), though the first paragraph does discuss a problem and the second the causes of the problem, the third paragraph is not a proposal to solve the problem.

20. The author's primary concern is to
    (A) criticize physicians and health care administrators for investing in technologically advanced equipment
    (B) examine some problems affecting delivery of health-care services and assess their severity
    (C) defend the medical community from charges that health-care has not improved since World War II
    (D) analyze the reasons for the health-care industry's inability to provide quality care to all segments of the population
    (E) describe the peculiar economic features of the health-care industry that are the causes of spiraling medical costs

(B) This is a main idea question. You should eliminate (A) because it is too narrow. It is true that the author criticizes doctors and administrators for spending too much on expensive equipment, but that criticism is not the main point of the selection. You should eliminate (C) and (E) for the same reason. There are elements in the passage to suggest both (C) and (E), but neither is the main point of the passage. As for (D), this is outside the scope of the passage. Though the author may agree that more could be done in this area, he doesn't offer a detailed analysis of this problem. Given our analysis of question 15, above, you should be able see that (B) is the best description of the selection.

21. In drawing an analogy between a fable and a caricature (lines 26–27), the author would most likely regard which of the following pairs of ideas as also analogous?
    (A) The subject of a caricature and the topic of a fable
    (B) The subject of a caricature and the main character in *Nineteen Eighty-Four*
    (C) The subject of a fable and the artist who draws the caricature
    (D) The artist who draws the caricature and a novelist
    (E) The minor characters in a fable and a photographer

(A) This is an implied idea question. The author draws an analogy between a political fable and a caricature because the political fable emphasizes certain points over others; it paints with a very broad brush, dealing in types rather than characters. Similarly, a caricature emphasizes certain personal characteristics over others. Thus, this is the analogy: society:political fable::person:caricature.

22. Which of the following would be the most appropriate title for the passage?
    (A) A Critical Study of the Use of Characters in *Nineteen Eighty-Four*
    (B) *Nineteen Eighty-Four*: Political Fable Rather Than Novel
    (C) *Nineteen Eighty-Four*: Reflections on the Relationship of the Individual to Society
    (D) The Use of Typology in the Literature of Political Fables
    (E) Distinguishing a Political Fable from a Novel

(B) This is a main idea question of the variation "pick the best title." The author begins by announcing that *Nineteen Eighty-Four* is not a novel in the strict sense of that term but really a political fable. (B) echoes the author's statement of his own purpose.

(A) is incorrect because it is too narrow. The author barely mentions in passing some of the characters in the book. (C) also is too narrow. Although it is true that the author does state that one of the characteristics of a political fable is that characters are defined in relation to their society, that is but one of many points made in the selection. (D) suffers from the same defect. There are several other points made by the author in the passage. In addition, (D) is in a sense too broad, for the author takes as the focus for his discussion the particular work *Nineteen Eighty-Four*—not political fables in general. Finally, (E) suffers from both of the ills that afflict (D). (E) is both too narrow because the distinction between novel and political fable is but one part of the discussion and too broad because it fails to acknowledge that the author has chosen to focus on a particular work.

23. According to the passage, which of the following are characteristics of a political fable?

    I. Its characters are defined primarily by their relationship to the social order.

    II. The reader is likely to experience fear as his reaction to the political situation described.

    III. Its time frame must treat events that occur at some point in the future.

(A) I only   (B) II only   (C) I and II only
(D) I and III only   (E) I, II, and III

(C) This is a specific detail question. In the second sentence (among other places), the author states that characters in a political fable are defined by their position in their society, so statement I must be a part of the correct answer; you can eliminate (B). In the third paragraph, the author mentions that a reader is likely to feel fear when reading a political fable, so II also belongs in the correct choice; you eliminate (A) and (D). III, however, represents a misreading of two references in the selection. In the last sentence of the first paragraph, the author states that *Nineteen Eighty-Four* is a political fable projected in the near future. Notice, however, that the selection does not say there that it is a requirement of political fables that the action take place in the future. The other reference to the future is in the middle of the second paragraph. There, the author states that the risk of not striking the proper balance between the demands of fable and the need to describe a political society (and its individuals and their interactions) is compounded *if* the situation is projected into the future. From this, we may conclude that a political fable need not take place in the future.

24. Which of the following best explains why the author mentions that Winston Smith suffers from a varicose ulcer?

(A) To demonstrate that a political fable must emphasize type over detail
(B) To show that Winston Smith has some characteristics that distinguish him as an individual
(C) To argue that Winston Smith is no more important than any other character in *Nineteen Eighty-Four*
(D) To illustrate one of the features of the political situation described in *Nineteen Eighty-Four*
(E) To suggest that *Nineteen Eighty-Four* is too realistic to be considered a work of fiction

(B) This is a logical detail question. Why does the author mention this characteristic of Winston Smith? The answer to this question doesn't become clear until you have read the entire selection. One important feature of a political fable is that characters are reduced to mere types. They don't have the idiosyncrasies that they would have in a novel. The function of that part of the first sentence which begins, "a requirement not refuted . . . ." is to preempt an objection to this claim: Winston Smith is described in some detail. So the author mentions this to let the audience know that he is aware that Winston Smith is described in some detail and to insist that this makes no difference to his argument.

Given this analysis, (A) must be incorrect. Small details like an ulcer would not be characteristic of a type but of an individual. (C) simply represents a confused reading of that section of the passage. The author implies there that Winston Smith is the main character of the work. As for (D) and (E), though these echo some of the ideas developed in the selection, they are not responsive to the question.

25. The "tension" that the author mentions in line 28 refers to the

(A) necessity of striking a balance between the need to describe a political situation in simple terms and the need to make the description realistic
(B) reaction the reader feels because he is drawn to the characters of the fable as individuals but repulsed by the political situation
(C) delicate task faced by a literary critic who must interpret the text of a work while attempting to describe accurately the intentions of the author
(D) danger that too realistic a description of a key character will make the reader feel that the fable is actually a description of his own situation
(E) conflict of aspirations and interests between characters that an author creates to motivate the action of the narrative

(A) The tension the author describes is between the

political sense of a political fable (the political element which must be conveyed by talking about individual people in their social situation) and the sense of fable (which must rely on type). The passage then states that the author faces a difficult task. If he errs on the side of the political sense, the value of the work as a fable is lost; if he errs on the side of the fable, the reader can't identify with the situation described. This dilemma is described by (A).

(B) does refer to ideas mentioned in the text, but (B) is not responsive to the question. (C) describes a "tension" that might exist in other situations, but this is not the situation the author describes. (D) is contradicted by our analysis above, for the danger is that the reader won't find the situation realistic enough. Finally, though (E) does echo the idea of "tension," this is not the kind of tension the author is discussing.

26. The author's attitude toward *Nineteen Eighty-Four* can best be described as

(A) condescending (B) laudatory
(C) disparaging (D) scholarly (E) ironic

(D) This is an author's attitude question. The tone of the passage is neutral. The author makes neither positive nor negative comments about the particular work, *Nineteen Eighty-Four.* So the best description is *scholarly.*

27. The author uses the phrase "another country" to describe a political fable in which

(A) political events described in a fable occur in a place other than the country of national origin of the author
(B) a lack of detail makes it difficult for a reader to see the connection between his own situation and the one described in the book
(C) too many minor characters create the impression of complete disorganization, leading the reader to believe he is in a foreign country
(D) the author has allowed his personal political convictions to infect his description of the political situation
(E) an overabundance of detail prevents the reader from appreciating the real possibility that such a political situation could develop

(B) This specific detail question asks that you show an understanding of the meaning of a particular part of the selection. Our analysis of question 25, above, will help us here. The dilemma faced by the political fabulist is the danger of too much versus too little detail. In discussing this dilemma, the author says that too little detail will leave the reader without a sense of connection to life. The author continues to say that this is particularly true if the writer projects

his narrative into the future. Then the reader may conclude that the situation described by the fable is completely alien to him—just a foreign country with strange customs, meaning that he can't understand why anyone does anything so their actions are really not connected with his. (B) summarizes this idea.

(A) is incorrect because the author does not mean that the action literally takes place in another country but that the reader feels no connection with the situation. As for (C), it is the lack of detail (e.g., interacting characters) that creates the problem mentioned in this reference. (D) finds no support in the passage; and, indeed, the political fabulist is actually presenting his own political vision. Finally, as for (E), it is the lack of detail, not the overabundance of detail, that creates the "foreign country" problem.

28. The author's primary concern is to

(A) define and clarify a concept
(B) point out a logical inconsistency
(C) trace the connection between a cause and an effect
(D) illustrate a general statement with examples
(E) outline a proposal for future action

(A) This is a logical structure question that asks about the overall development of the selection. As we have seen, the author is concerned with discussing the elements of a political fable, and this development is described by (A). (B) and (C) are incorrect because the author doesn't mention a logical inconsistency or a cause-and-effect connection. As for (D), to the extent that the author does introduce examples (the characters of the book), this is not the main concern of the selection. Finally, though the selection discusses a political fable that projects its situation into the future, the author doesn't introduce any proposals for future action himself.

SECTION 3

ANALYTICAL REASONING

Questions 1–6

This is a selection set. Begin by summarizing the initial conditions.

L⊃N
K←M
J↦~J
At most, one carry over

1. Which of the following groups of snacks could be stocked in the machine during weeks two and three?

   (A) *L, N, J; N, L, O*
   (B) *L, N, O; L, J, K*
   (C) *M, L, N; J, K, M*
   (D) *N, O, J; K, L, N*
   (E) *O, M, J; J, L, N*

   (D) Since no additional information is provided here, just use the initial conditions to eliminate choices. Using the first condition, eliminate (B). Using the second condition, eliminate (C). Using the third, eliminate (E). Using the last, eliminate (A).

2. If *J, L,* and *N* are stocked in the machine one week, which three snacks must be stocked in the machine the following week?

   (A) *K, M, O*
   (B) *K, N, O*
   (C) *L, M, N*
   (D) *L, N, O*
   (E) *M, N, O*

   (B) If *J, L,* and *N* are used in one week, then neither *J* (by the third condition) nor *L* (because *L* requires *N* and that would be two carry over products) can be used in the following week. Additionally, since *K* is not used in the first week, *M* cannot be used in the following week. By the process of elimination, then, the products offered in the second week must be *K, N,* and *O.*

3. If *J, N,* and *O* are stocked in the machine in the first week, then which three snacks must be stocked in the machine in week two?

   (A) *J, L, N*
   (B) *K, L, N*
   (C) *L, N, O*
   (D) *M, L, N*
   (E) *M, N, O*

   (B) Start by eliminating those snacks that cannot be offered in the second week. Since *J* is offered in the first week, *J* cannot be offered in the second week; and since *K* is not offered in the first week, *M* cannot

be offered in the second. This leaves us with *L, M, N,* and *O* for the second week, and of *N* and *O* only one can be carried over from the first week. We cannot use *O,* for that would leave us with *L* and *K*—without *N.* Therefore, *N* must be used (and not *O*) along with *L* and *K.*

4. If *L* and *O* are stocked in the machine in the first week, which of the following snacks must be stocked in the machine in the second week?

   I. *J*
   II. *K*
   III. *O*

   (A) I only   (B) II only   (C) I and II only
   (D) II and III only   (E) I, II, and III

   (C) Since *L* is offered in the first week, *N* must also be offered. Then for the second week, *L* cannot be offered again, for that would require *N* as well (in violation of the condition that at most one snack can be carried over). Further, *M* cannot be offered in the second week, for *K* is not offered in the first week. This leaves us with *J, K, N,* and *O* for the second, and we need three of those four. Since we can only carry over one from the first week, we must use *J* and *K,* and we have a choice of whether to use *N* or *O.* So both *J* and *K* must be used in the second week.

5. If *K* is stocked in the machine in the first week, and neither *N* nor *K* is stocked in the machine in the second week, how many different combinations of snacks are possible for the second week?

   (A) 1   (B) 2   (C) 3   (D) 4   (E) 5

   (A) If *N* is not stocked in the second week, then *L* cannot be used in the second week either. This, coupled with the rest of the information provided by this stem, eliminates *K, L,* and *N.* So there is only one possible group of snacks for use in the second week: *J, M,* and *O.*

6. If *L* is stocked in the machine in the first week, and *J, M,* and *O* are stocked in the second week, which of the following pairs of snacks must also have been stocked in the first week?

   (A) *K* and *N*
   (B) *K* and *O*
   (C) *M* and *N*
   (D) *M* and *O*
   (E) *N* and *O*

   (A) Since *L* is stocked in the first week, *N* too must be stocked in the first week. Then, since *M* is stocked in the second week, *K* must have been stocked in the first week.

Questions 7–11

This set combines elements of spatial ordering with rules of selection. Begin by summarizing the initial conditions:

$O \neq M$

$N = M$

There is one further conclusion you might see: N and M must be in the bottom or middle tier. If you missed this, it would probably occur to you as you answer particular questions.

7. Which of the following are acceptable pyramids?

  (A)   J
           L   K
       M   N   O

  (B)   J
         K   N
       O   M   L

  (C)   L
         M   N
       J   O   K

  (D)   K
        O   M
      N   J   L

  (E)   M
        N   L
      J   O   K

(C) This stem provides no additional information, so use the initial conditions to eliminate choices. Using the first condition, eliminate (A), (B), and (D). Using the second, eliminate (E).

8. Which of the following could be true of the human pyramid?

(A) J, K, and M form the bottom tier.
(B) K, M, and O form the bottom tier.
(C) M and K form the second tier.
(D) K forms the top tier.
(E) N forms the top tier.

(D) Again, the question provides no additional information, so use the initial conditions to eliminate choices. (A), (B), (C), and (E) violate the condition that M and N are in the same tier.

9. If J is standing on N's shoulders, then which of the following is a complete and accurate list of the acrobats who could be the top tier of the pyramid?

(A) J   (B) K   (C) J, K
(D) J, K, L   (E) J, K, L, O

(E) If J is standing on N's shoulders, then either J is the top of the pyramid and M and N the second tier, or J is in the second tier. If J is in the second tier, since there are no restrictions on the placement of the other individuals (except that O cannot be in the same tier with M), K, L, or O could be the top of the pyramid.

10. If K is standing on L's shoulder, then all of the following could be true EXCEPT

(A) J is standing on M's shoulder.
(B) L is standing on M's shoulder.
(C) K is standing on N's shoulder.
(D) M is standing on K's shoulder.
(E) O is standing on K's shoulder.

(D) If K is standing on L's shoulder, then either K is the top of the pyramid with L in the second tier or K is in the second tier with L on the bottom. On either assumption, M and N must be in the bottom tier, which means that M cannot stand on anyone's shoulders.

You can prove to yourself that the remaining choices are possible by constructing examples:

  (A)   O
        K   J
      L   M   N

  (B)   K
        L   O
     M   N   J

  (C)   O
        K   J
      L   N   M

  (E)   O
        J   K
     M   N   L

11. If K is in the middle tier of the pyramid, all of the following could be true EXCEPT

(A) J is standing on L's shoulder.
(B) K is standing on O's shoulder.
(C) L is standing on M's shoulder.
(D) L is standing on the ground.
(E) J is standing on the ground.

(B) If K is in the middle tier of the pyramid, then M and N must be in the bottom tier, and O must be either in the second tier or the top of the pyramid. Thus, (B) is not possible. You can construct examples to prove to yourself that the other choices are possible.

Questions 12–15

This is a fairly standard selection set. Begin by summarizing the initial conditions:

(1) $X \neq Y$
(2) $X \neq Z$
(3) $T \neq U$
(4) $U \supset Z$

There is one further conclusion to be drawn from this information. Since U requires Z, and since Z cannot be planted with X, U cannot be planted with X.

12. Which of the following must be true?

   I. T cannot be planted with Z.
   II. T cannot be planted with Y.
   III. X cannot be planted with U.

   (A) I only   (B) III only   (C) I and III only
   (D) II and III only   (E) I, II, and III

   (B) This question focuses upon the further conclusion drawn in the overview of this set. III is necessarily true. I, however, is not necessarily true. T and Z could be planted together, for example, with no other varieties. II is not true for the same reason.

13. Which of the following is an acceptable combination of flowers for the bed?

   (A) T, U, X
   (B) T, X, Z
   (C) T, V, Z
   (D) U, X, Y
   (E) Z, U, X

   (C) This stem provides no additional information, so use the initial conditions to eliminate choices. Using the first two conditions (that X cannot be planted with Y or Z), eliminate (B), (D), and (E). Using the third condition, eliminate (A).

14. What is the largest number of different varieties of flowers that could be planted together in the bed?

   (A) 2   (B) 3   (C) 4   (D) 5   (E) 6

   (C) There is no single, uniquely correct way to approach a question like this, but a good start would be to see that using X precludes the use of both Y and Z. So the group with the maximum number of different flowers will likely not include X. This leaves T, U, V, Y, and Z. The flowers that exclude each other are T and U. You can take either of those but not both. So the maximum number of varieties is four.

15. If the gardener wishes to plant X and one other variety, how many different combinations of flowers are possible?

   (A) 1   (B) 2   (C) 3   (D) 4   (E) 5

   (B) If the gardener plants X, he cannot plant either Y or Z; and since he cannot plant Z, neither can he plant U. Thus, in addition to X, he can plant only T and V. Thus, he can plant either X and T or X and V.

Questions 16–19

Use a table to summarize the information:

	Eng.	Ita.	Fr.	Ger.	Sp.
J	✔	✔	✔		
K				✔	
L	✔	✔		✔	
M			✔		✔
N	✔			✔	✔
O	✔	✔			

16. Which language is spoken by the largest number of people at the table?

   (A) English   (B) French   (C) German
   (D) Italian   (E) Spanish

   (A) As the table shows, a total of four people speak English, the largest number who speak any of the languages.

17. Leroy could converse directly with Ned in how many different languages?

   (A) 0   (B) 1   (C) 2   (D) 3   (E) 4

   (C) Leroy speaks English, Italian, and German, and Ned speaks English, German, and Spanish. So the two could converse in English and German.

18. Which of the following is a complete and accurate list of the persons sitting at the table who can converse directly with Mark?

   (A) John, Ken   (B) John, Ned   (C) Leroy, Ned
   (D) John, Ken, Ned   (E) Leroy, Ken, Ned

   (B) Mark speaks French and Spanish:
   John can converse with Mark in French.
   Ken cannot speak either French or Spanish.
   Leroy cannot speak either French or Spanish.
   Ned can converse with Mark in Spanish.
   Oscar cannot speak either French or Spanish.

19. Which of the following people could function as a translator in a conversation between Ken and Oscar?

    I. John
   II. Leroy
  III. Ned

(A) I only   (B) II only   (C) III only
(D) I and III only   (E) II and III only

(E) Ken speaks only German, and Oscar speaks only English and Italian. So a translator must speak German and either English or Italian. So either Leroy or Ned could serve as translator between Ken and Oscar.

Questions 20–24

This set involves selecting members for a committee. Here is one way of summarizing the information:

Litigation	O			J P	U
Taxation	L	K	×	M ≠	T
Corporations	N	Q		R S	

The boxes around pairs of individuals indicate that those individuals, if they serve, must serve together. The "≠" between M and T is our standard symbol for showing that two individuals cannot be used together. And finally, the additional notes should be self-explanatory.

There is one further obvious conclusion to be drawn from the diagram: R and J cannot serve together. If you missed this inference at this point, it is probably because it is already implicitly contained in the diagram, so you didn't feel the need to draw it explicitly. But this conclusion is the key to item 21 below.

20. Which of the following committees is acceptable?

(A) J, K, L, M, N, U
(B) K, L, M, N, R, S
(C) K, L, M, N, Q, U
(D) L, M, N, O, R, T
(E) M, O, Q, R, S, U

(E) Here you should simply take each initial condition and apply it to each choice, eliminating choices as you go. When you have finally eliminated four choices, the remaining one will be the correct answer.

First, we must have at least as many senior partners as junior partners. (A), (B), (D), and (E) meet this requirement, but (C) does not, so eliminate (C). Next, there must be at least one partner from each department. (A), (D), and (E) meet this requirement, but (B) does not—(B) does not include a partner from

litigation—so eliminate (B). Now check to determine whether the remaining committees respect the requirement that J and P serve together if they do serve. (D) and (E) respect this requirement (because neither J nor P appears), but (A) does not—J appears in that choice without P. So eliminate (A). Next, determine whether the remaining choices respect the requirement that R and S serve together if they serve. (D) does not. So the correct choice must be (E).

21. Which of the following statements about the committee must be true?

(A) O cannot serve on the committee with K.
(B) L cannot serve on the committee with U.
(C) M cannot serve on the committee with Q.
(D) R cannot serve on the committee with J.
(E) T cannot serve on the committee with U.

(D) This is one of those problems for which you should seek an obvious solution before you start working out a lot of possible committee arrangements. The correct answer, (D), contains the fairly obvious conclusion that we reached in our overview of this set. Look for a conclusion like this before you start working out a lot of detailed possibilities.

For purposes of explanations, the following committees demonstrate that the other choices are wrong:

(A) O, K, Q, J, P, M (So O can serve with K.)
(B) L, N, U, M, R, S (So L can serve with U.)
(C) O, M, Q, R, S (So M can serve with Q.)
(E) T, U, R, S, O (So T can serve with U.)

22. The largest committee consistent with the requirements above would consist of how many people?

(A) 6   (B) 7   (C) 8   (D) 9   (E) 10

(C) Because of the restrictions on the pairs J and P and R and S, the maximum number of senior partners who could be assembled for a committee is four (e.g., J, P, U, and M or R, S, U, and M). Therefore, the maximum number of junior partners who could serve on a committee is also four. So the largest committee would consist of eight people.

23. If *J* serves on the committee but *L* does not, which of the following must be true?

    (A) *M* serves on the committee.
    (B) *T* serves on the committee.
    (C) *Q* serves on the committee.
    (D) *U* does not serve on the committee.
    (E) *O* does not serve on the committee.

(C) Using the new information that this question stem provides, see what other conclusions you can deduce. If *J* serves on the committee, then *P* also serves on the committee, but neither *R* nor *S* serves on the committee. If *L* does not serve on the committee, then neither does *N*. So far we have learned:

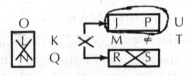

Litigation   O   J P U
Taxation   L K   M ≠ T
Corporations   N Q   R S

This leaves only one member of the Corporations department. So, given the requirement that at least one partner from each department be included on the committee, we can deduce that the committee must include *Q*. As for (A) and (B), either *M* or *T* can serve on the committee (e.g., *J, P, M, O, K, Q*), but neither must serve on the committee (e.g., *J, P, U, O, K, Q*). As for (D) and (E), the examples just given show that *O* and *U* can serve on the committee.

24. If the committee is to include *L*, *K*, and *R*, then which partners must also be on the committee?

    I. *O*
    II. *U*
    III. *M*

    (A) I only   (B) II only   (C) I and II only
    (D) II and III only   (E) I, II, and III

(B) Begin by using the additional information to draw further conclusions:

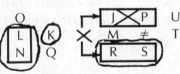

Litigation   O   J P U
Taxation   L K   M ≠ T
Corporations   N Q   R S

We now have selected three junior partners and two senior partners, and we have two requirements left to fulfill. We must choose at least one more senior partner, and we must select someone from Litigation. If we select *O* from Litigation, then we need two more senior partners, *U* and either *M* or *T*. Or we can select *U* from Litigation to complete the committee. Therefore, *U* must be selected for the committee. As for *O* and *M*, they may be selected (*L, N, K, R, S, U, O, M*), but they do not have to be selected (*L, N, K, R, S, U*).

LOGICAL REASONING

Speaker X: The dinosaurs died out because of some major climatic change that diminished their formerly abundant food supplies.

Speaker Y: That's incorrect. Dinosaurs died out because of competition for food from a new family of animals—the mammals.

Speaker Z: I believe that a massive asteroid struck the Earth, raising a worldwide cloud of smoke and dust that darkened the skies for months or even years. The dense cloud blocked sunlight, killing off much of the plant life that the dinosaurs used for food.

1. Which of the following best describes the disagreement among the three speakers?

    (A) The speakers agree that starvation caused the dinosaurs to become extinct but don't agree about the cause of the drop in their food supply.
    (B) The speakers agree that climatic changes caused a drop in the food supply of dinosaurs but don't agree that this drop caused the dinosaurs to become extinct.
    (C) Speakers X and Z agree that major climatic changes caused the extinction of the dinosaurs but offer different explanations for those changes.
    (D) Speakers Y and Z agree that starvation caused the extinction of the dinosaurs and agree that this was caused by a decline in the total amount of plant life on Earth.
    (E) Speakers X and Y agree that starvation was responsible for the extinction of the dinosaurs but disagree with Z that a meteor was responsible for climatic changes that reduced the food supply of the dinosaurs.

(A) All three speakers mention that the immediate cause for the extinction of the dinosaurs was a lack of food. Speaker X, however, cites as the cause for that condition some unknown climatic change. Speaker Y cites as the cause for that condition competition for food from a new group. Speaker Z cites as the cause for that condition climatic changes caused by a giant asteroid collision. Thus, all three speakers agree on the immediate cause of extinction (starvation), but not on what caused the starvation.

A cryptographer has intercepted a message that is in code. She knows that the code is a simple substitution of numbers for letters in the words of a foreign language.

2. Which of the following would be the LEAST helpful to the cryptographer in breaking the code?

(A) Knowing the frequency with which each vowel in the language is used
(B) Knowing the frequency with which two vowels appear together in the language
(C) Knowing the frequency with which odd numbers appear relative to even numbers in the message
(D) Knowing the conjugation of the equivalent for the verb *to be* in the language on which the code is based
(E) Knowing every word in the language that begins with the letter ''R''

(C) To break the code, the cryptographer must find which numbers represent which letters in the foreign language. She will have to look for patterns in the numbers; for example, a single number standing alone in a sentence in the message would have to represent a single letter that could stand alone in the language, and two consecutive numbers in the same word in the message would have to represent double letters in the language. So anything that she could learn about the language itself would be useful. Knowing the frequency of odd versus even numbers in the coded message would not, however, be particularly useful, for that information tells her nothing about the content of the message.

All the books shelved in the library's west wing are works of fiction. *David Copperfield* is shelved in the library's east wing. Therefore, *David Copperfield* is not a work of fiction.

3. Which of the following is most similar to the argument above?

(A) All automobiles manufactured in the United States come equipped with radial tires. The Mandate is manufactured in Italy. Therefore, the Mandate is not equipped with radial tires.
(B) Only new written works are covered by copyrights. A machine is not a written work. Therefore, a machine is not covered by a copyright.
(C) All bananas are yellow. Yellow is a color. Therefore, all bananas are colors.
(D) All of the seniors are seated in the cafeteria. Mary is seated in the gymnasium. Therefore, Mary is not a senior.
(E) All legal government actions must be consistent with the Constitution. The Constitution requires the separation of church and state. Therefore, establishment of a state church would be an illegal government action.

(A) This is a logical similarity question. The stimulus material has the form:

All *BW* are *F*.
DC is not *BW*.
Therefore, *DC* is not *F*.

(*BW* stands for books shelved in the west wing.) This argument is fallacious. Although all books in the west wing are fiction, this does not mean all fiction is shelved in the west wing. (A) gives us an argument with a similar structure:

All *US* are *RT*.
M is not *US*.
Therefore, *M* is not *RT*.

(All U.S.-made cars are ones with radial tires. Since the Mandate is made in Italy, the Mandate is not a U.S.-made car. Therefore, the Mandate is not a car with radial tires.) The argument makes the same error as the stimulus material. You cannot get from ''All U.S.-made cars have radial tires'' to ''All cars with radial tires are made in the U.S.''
(B) has the structure:

Only *WW* are *C*.
M is not a *WW*.
Therefore, *M* is not *C*.

And that is a valid argument.
The structure of (C) is difficult to describe, because (C) commits the fallacy of ambiguity. (D) has the following structure:

All *S* are *C*.
M is not *C*.
Therefore, *M* is not *S*.

(That Mary is seated in the gymnasium means she is not sitting in the cafeteria.) And this argument is valid. Finally, (E) has this structure:

All *LGA* are *C*.
SC is not *C*.
Therefore, *SC* is not *LGA*.

(The second premise is equivalent to ''A state church is not constitutional.'')

It is sometimes argued that a national lottery would cut into revenues generated by state lotteries. As a consequence, according to the argument, there would be no net increase in the amount of money going to government, just a redistribution of funds from the state to the federal level. This argument ignores the fact that federal and state governments share personal and corporate income taxes and certain excise taxes. Similarly, lottery states could piggyback on a federal lottery, increasing the total participation in both.

4. The speaker above argues primarily by

   (A) citing an authority
   (B) relying on statistics
   (C) creating a distinction
   (D) drawing an analogy
   (E) proposing a change

(D) This argument proceeds by comparing our experience with taxes to lotteries. Such arguments (as you probably know by now) are arguments based on analogy. (And remember that their strength or weakness is a function of the similarity or dissimilarity between the two situations compared.) (A) and (B) must surely be wrong since the speaker mentions neither authority nor statistics. As for (C), the speaker does talk about two different programs, but he regards them as similar and does not distinguish between them. (E) is probably the second-best answer, but the word *propose* makes it wrong. The speaker is defending a proposal for a change but is not himself proposing the change.

Some people have argued that mental events can be explained in terms of brain events. Brain events can all be located in space, but no one has been able to pinpoint the physical location of a mental event.

5. The speaker above is most likely arguing that

   (A) it will eventually be possible to locate brain events
   (B) mental events are more important than brain events
   (C) brain events are the only events that are locatable
   (D) brain events cannot be explained as mental events
   (E) mental events are not identical to brain events

(E) This question asks that you identify the conclusion the speaker is probably leading up to. Notice the first sentence. The speaker states that some people have argued that mental events are really just brain events. Then she gives us a reason to believe that that conclusion might be false: you can locate a brain event in space but not a mental event. (A) is incorrect because this is the position against which the speaker is arguing. (B) goes beyond the scope of

the paragraph. The speaker is arguing that brain events and mental events are distinct but does not suggest that one is more important than the other. (C) also goes beyond the scope of the argument. The speaker does say that brain events are locatable in space, but this does not mean that they are the only events locatable in space. Finally, (D) reverses the connection studied by the speaker. The speaker is arguing against the conclusion that mental events can be explained as brain events. No one has suggested that brain events can be explained as mental events.

All homework is tedious.
Some biology assignments are homework.
No lab assignments are homework.

6. Which of the following conclusions can be deduced from the statements above?

   (A) Some biology assignments are not homework.
   (B) Some biology assignments are tedious.
   (C) Some biology assignments are not tedious.
   (D) Some biology assignments are lab assignments.
   (E) No lab assignments are tedious.

(B) For this problem we can use a circle diagram:

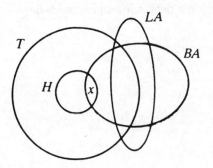

The x indicates that some biology assignments are homework. It also allows us to infer (B) that some biology assignments are tedious. (The x is in the overlap of the homework and biology circles.) As for the remaining choices, there are overlaps on the diagram that show that these are possibly though not necessarily true.

Martin: Mayor Clark was the most popular mayor this city ever had. He was elected by 93 percent of the vote.

Victor: But the total population of the city then was only 42,000. The current mayor, Nancy Short, won by only a couple of percentage points, but she received the votes of over 150,000 people. That makes her the most popular mayor ever.

7. In the exchange above, the two speakers

(A) agree that Clark and Short are the two most popular mayors in the city's history
(B) concur that only a popular mayor should be mayor of the city
(C) disagree about the identity of the current mayor
(D) attack each other's sincerity
(E) give different meanings to a key term

(E) For the first speaker, "popularity" is measured by the percentage of votes won. For the second speaker, it is measured by the number of votes won. Thus, the two speakers give different meanings to a key term. As for (A), the speakers agree on nothing. Each claims a different person as the most popular mayor in the city's history. (B) goes beyond the scope of the discussion, for neither makes any such judgment. And (C) is wrong since Martin never mentions the identity of the current mayor. Finally, (D) is incorrect because neither questions the motives of the other person in making the claim.

Smokers often claim that they have a right to smoke and use the word *right* as though it implies an unqualified permission to smoke whenever and wherever they choose. Thus, they argue, they have a "right" to smoke in public places such as restaurants. This idea is mistaken. After all, no one has a "right" to smoke when smoking represents a clear danger to the safety of others, for example, during the takeoff and landing of a plane or while a motor vehicle is being refueled.

8. The speaker attempts to show that

(A) a person may have a right that cannot be legally protected
(B) a certain concept of "right" leads to an absurd conclusion
(C) one person's right may endanger the safety of someone else
(D) no person has a right to endanger the safety of another
(E) some people may have rights that others do not have

(B) The speaker introduces a certain concept of "right," an idea she says is mistaken. Then she illustrates the logical limits of such a concept: smokers would have a right to smoke even while creating a serious and immediate danger to others. The best description of this strategy is provided by (B). (A) is incorrect because the speaker is attempting to show that smokers do not have any unqualified right to smoke, so there is no right to be protected. (C) is a pretty good wrong answer. Had it read: one person's CONDUCT may endanger the safety of someone else, (C) would have been more attractive. But it is wrong because the speaker implies that one does not have a right to endanger someone else. (D) is also somewhat attractive, for it is a statement the speaker would probably endorse. The problem with (D) is that it is really a hidden assumption of the argument. The speaker thinks that once a listener realizes that the unqualified interpretation of a "right to smoke" might endanger lives, the listener will see that no one has a "right" to smoke, as such. This depends on an implicit understanding that no person should be allowed to harm another. The idea expressed by (D), therefore, is not what the speaker attempts to show but a hidden supposition used to support that conclusion. Finally, (E) is incorrect because the speaker denies that anyone has an unqualified right to smoke.

(A) In his concession speech, the candidate explained that he lost the election not because the people did not think him best qualified for the position and not because they did not endorse his view. The candidate lost the election because he had insufficient vote-getting power. As we all know, the candidate who gets the most votes wins.

(B) Human life is sacred; that is why we must punish murderers severely. Taking the life of another human being is something no one has the right to do. The crime of murder is so heinous that it deserves the strongest punishment imaginable, and that is why I favor the death penalty for murderers.

(C) Senator Jensen issued a statement denouncing the Committee's decision to recommend the closing of three naval bases, arguing that the bases are essential to the security of the nation. Of course the senator would likely oppose the recommendation, because two of the three bases are located in the state he represents.

(D) Our school system should spend whatever money is needed to purchase computer systems for student use. Our standardized test scores in reading and math for the past three years have been several points below those of our neighboring system, which has computers for student use.

(E) The mayor announced yesterday that a major corporation has changed its plans to move its offices from the city because of certain tax incentives granted by him. The mayor should realize that the corporation's actions are tantamount to blackmail: announcing plans to leave the city in order to extort favorable tax treatment for remaining.

9. Which of the arguments above is self-contradictory?

(B) The speaker begins by saying that no one has the right to take the life of another human being but ends by saying that murderers should be killed by other human beings. And that is a logical contradiction.

10. Which of the arguments above attacks the motives of the proponent of the argument?

(C) The speaker here never addresses the merits of Senator Jensen's opposition to the plan to close bases. Instead, the speaker merely implies that Senator Jensen's opposition to the closures is self-serving.

As for the other choices, the speaker in (A) says something like this: the candidate lost because he got an insufficient number of votes. You might call that statement a tautology. (It is very much like a circular argument.) The tautology has no explanatory power. As for (D), this speaker makes an ordinary argument. (The argument does depend on the hidden premise that the important difference in the school systems is the computers.) Finally, (E) is also an ordinary argument. (It might be strong or weak, depending on many other factors.)

The Census Bureau described the period of 10.7-percent growth of median real family income between 1982 and 1986 as the "longest period of sustained income growth" since the 1960s. They failed to note, however, that in 1982 the economy experienced the most serious recession since World War II and that median real family income in 1982 had dropped to its lowest level in 14 years.

11. The speaker is arguing that

(A) real median income did not increase from 1982 to 1986
(B) the Census Bureau was unaware of the 1982 recession
(C) it is difficult to measure real median family income
(D) economic growth can be achieved only following a severe recession
(E) the growth only recaptured what had been lost in the recession

(E) The speaker cites the Census Bureau's claim of extraordinary economic growth. Then he says that the Bureau failed to mention the fact that the growth began at a fairly low level. What is the speaker trying to do? The best explanation is given by (E). As for (A), the speaker does not deny the facts adduced by the Bureau. Rather, he accepts the facts presented but offers a different interpretation. (B) goes beyond the scope of the argument. The speaker states that the Bureau failed to mention the recession in its report—not that the Bureau was unaware of it. (C) introduces a concept totally irrelevant to the discussion. Finally, as for (D), although the speaker does state that this period of growth followed a recession, he does not say that growth comes only after a recession.

Speaker X: I'm afraid I won't be able to get into State University.

Speaker Y: Relax. State University's brochure states that no one will be accepted after May 1. So just make sure that your application is received before then, and you'll definitely be accepted.

12. Which of the following lines of reasoning is LEAST similar to that contained in Speaker Y's reply.

(A) The professor stated that any one who failed to submit a term paper would fail the course. I submitted a term paper. Therefore, I will pass the course.

(B) Overwatering a house plant is sure to kill it. Since I never overwater my house plants, they should never die.

(C) Any employee who is detected falsifying time records will be fired. Since Mary is scrupulously honest about her time card, she will never be fired.

(D) Every time it snows the sky is cloudy and the weather is cold. Today the weather is warm and the sky is clear, so we won't have snow.

(E) Anyone who attends every class will pass the course. Evan did not attend every class. Therefore, Evan will not pass the course.

(D) Speaker Y makes an error. Failure to submit the application on time means it will be rejected but meeting the deadline doesn't mean an automatic acceptance. There are many other reasons an applications may be rejected. Every choice but (D) makes a similar error. The reasoning in (D), however, is valid.

You have stated that our charity wrongly passes off routine mailing costs as public education. But you are wrong, and your example proves that you are wrong. The letter you cite was four pages long. Three pages detail the problems of animal abuse. One page asks for a $5 contribution and encourages the recipient to send a detachable postcard of protest to Congress. Since over 20,000 people who received the mailing did both, it is obvious that the letter had a very valuable educational impact.

13. The response set forth above assumes that

(A) the members of Congress who receive the postcards will change their minds on the issue in question

(B) problems of animal abuse can only be solved by Federal legislation

(C) the charity only needs $100,000 in contributions

(D) those who responded with contributions and postcards of protests were not already advocates of the charity's position

(E) everyone who received the mailing made a charitable contribution to the organization

(D) The burden of the defense above is that the solicitation and political element was merely incidental to the educational intent of the letter. And the proof is that people acted as the letter suggested. But that demonstrates that the letter educated readers only if we assume that they were not already inclined to make a donation and send a postcard. As for (A), it is the addressee of the original mailing that the organization purports to educate. (B) overstates the speaker's case. The speaker apparently believes that Federal legislation is important, but nothing in the paragraph suggests that the speaker believes it is the only way of solving the problem. As for (C), though we know that the organization did receive this amount in donations prompted by the mailing, we know nothing more about its finances. Finally, as for (E), we don't know how many of the original mailings were sent.

Questions 14-15

The library is requesting an increase in its budget for next year. With the additional funds, the library hopes to add a video tape section that will allow library patrons to borrow, free of charge, video tapes that they would otherwise have to rent from one of the several retail stores here in town. The library's request should be rejected. If the library offers free video tapes, local merchants who rent such tapes will lose sales. And if local merchants lose sales, the town will lose tax revenues, and everyone will suffer.

14. The author above is ultimately trying to prove that

    (A) local merchants will lose sales if the library's budget request is approved
    (B) the town will lose tax revenues if the library's budget request is approved
    (C) some people who would otherwise rent video tapes from merchants will borrow them from the library
    (D) the library's request for a budget increase to fund free video tapes should be rejected
    (E) the library should not be allowed to rent video tapes in competition with local merchants

(D) This item asks you to distinguish the ultimate conclusion of the argument from its assumptions and from intermediate conclusion that functions as assumptions for the main conclusion. What is the point at which the speaker is ultimately aiming? The library's request should be rejected. (A) and (C) are both assumptions made by the speaker without any proof. (B) is a further step in the argument but is not the final conclusion. Rather, the author uses the idea expressed by (B) to prove (D). As for (E), this idea is outside the scope of the speaker's remarks. To be sure, the speaker might endorse a rule forbidding the library from "renting" tapes, but that is not a burden the speaker chose to assume in this paragraph.

15. The argument above makes which of the following assumptions?

    I. The tapes that would be available for loan from the library are similar to those rented by local merchants.
    II. The lost tax revenues are more significant than the savings to the town's people.
    III. The library will offer tapes that are culturally superior to those offered by the local merchants.

    (A) I only (B) II only (C) I and II only
    (D) II and III only (E) I, II, and III

(C) This item asks you to identify assumptions of the argument. Statement I is an assumption made by the speaker. The speaker asserts, without proof, that the

library would take business from local merchants. Thus, the speaker must assume that the tapes offered by the library would be similar to those rented by merchants. Statement II is also an assumption of the argument. The speaker offers as an intermediate step the conclusion that "everyone will suffer." But if lost tax revenue is less than what the town's people pay to rent videos, not everyone is worse off. The merchants may be worse off, but the rest of the people are better off. Statement III is not an assumption of the argument. In fact, the argument assumes that the library's tapes would not be significantly different.

The philosopher Immanuel Kant distinguished between what he called analytic statements and what he called synthetic statements. According to Kant, a statement of the form:
Subject . . . is . . . predicate
is analytic if negating the statement results in a contradiction. For example, the following statement, in Kant's analysis, is analytic:
All bachelors are unmarried.
The statement is analytic because its negation—it is not the case that all bachelors are unmarried—is a contradiction.

16. According to the analysis of Kant given above, which of the following statements is also an analytic statement?

    I. All widows have been married at least once.
    II. Every daughter has at least one brother.
    III. Every father has at least one child.

    (A) I only (B) III only (C) I and II only
    (D) I and III only (E) I, II, and III

(D) Statement I is analytic because denying it results in a contraction. A person cannot be a widow unless she has been married. Similarly, statement III is analytic. A person cannot be a father unless he has at least one child. Statement II, however, is not analytic. It is not a contradiction for parents to have one or more daughters and no sons.

Delbert: A professor of journalism checked the tapes of interviews of several prominent people against the published interviews and found that only 3 percent of the statements that appeared inside of quotation marks were actually quoted verbatim.

Linda: Yet in every one of the cases studied, the person interviewed reviewed the manuscript and had the power to edit the remarks before they finally appeared in print.

17. If both speakers above are correct, which of the following conclusions is best supported by the exchange?

(A) Most prominent people do not care what is said about them in print.
(B) Most prominent people are reluctant to say what they really believe in an interview.
(C) Most journalists intentionally distort the responses of interviewees.
(D) The interviewees in question were satisfied that the interviewer accurately rendered their thoughts.
(E) The interviewer unconsciously distorted the responses obtained during the interview.

(D) If both speakers are correct, then the most reasonable conclusion to draw is that the interviewees did not object to the way the interviewer had reported their comments—even though the printed words did not echo exactly what they had said.

Any oil painting signed by Alain was painted after 1962.

18. Which of the following can be logically deduced from the statement above?

(A) Alain signed only the paintings he painted after 1962.
(B) Alain signed only the paintings he did in oils.
(C) After 1962, Alain painted only oil paintings.
(D) Alain never signed an oil painting before 1962.
(E) Alain never signed any painting before 1962.

(D) If the stimulus statement is true, then it must also be true that Alain signed no oil painting before 1962. As for the other choices, there are three important elements in the stimulus statement: signed, oil, and 1962. Each of the other choices fails to take account of one or more of these elements.

A woman who was seriously injured in a fall on a staircase remarked, "I'm glad this is behind me because I am terribly afraid of elevators. Yet, statistics show that a person is ten times as likely to be seriously injured while using stairs as while riding in an elevator. Now that I've had my fall, I can use stairs without fear."

19. The conclusion above is erroneous because the woman

(A) ignores the possibility of serious injury while using a ramp
(B) assumes that all accidents are equally serious
(C) misuses the concept of probability
(D) fails to connect the possibility of accident with personal fear
(E) makes no reference to the fact that stairs are not mechanical devices

(C) The weakness in the reasoning above is that it ignores the fact that the probability of falling on stairs is not erased just because one has had an accident. Each time you mount the stairs, you still face the risk of an accident.

Parent: I am very worried that your school is not providing my daughter with the best possible college preparatory education.

Headmaster: Rest assured that we are. Last year, the average score of our students on the college entrance exam was in the top five percent.

20. The Headmaster's response assumes that

(A) the daughter is performing below the school average
(B) scores on the college entrance exam measure academic achievement
(C) the parent is unaware of the importance of entrance exam scores
(D) an exam score below the top five percent is evidence of academic failure
(E) the parent believes that the daughter's performance is average.

(B) This item asks you to identify a hidden assumption of the Headmaster's response, and (B) does this. The Headmaster offers as evidence of academic excellence student scores on an admission test. Thus, the Headmaster apparently assumes that there is some connection between the two. As for (A) and (E), the response implies nothing about the daughter's standing in her class nor about what her parent knows about that standing. As for (C), the Headmaster's remark assumes that the parent does appreciate the importance of exam scores. Finally, (D) overstates the case. The Headmaster implicitly recognizes that some students at the school score below the top 5 percent because he mentions an average.

To the editor—

I must respond to the letter you published from a group of writers in my country. They allege that Francesco Humberto's most recent novel was censored. It is true that Basitia Press refused to publish the novel, but at worst that raises the possibility of breach of contract—not censorship. Basitia and Humberto entered into a contract: Humberto was given an advance to write the novel, and Basitia agreed to publish it. After reading the manuscript, however, corporate officials at Basitia feared that the content of the novel would offend many people and decided not to publish it. But since this was a matter of contract between private parties, it can hardly be called censorship.

Constantus Adolphus
New Balkan

21. Which of the following, if true, would most weaken the analysis set forth in the letter above?

(A) Basitia has published novels by authors other than Humberto that offended some readers.
(B) Basitia has published other novels by Humberto that offended very few people.
(C) The officials of Basitia, the only publisher in New Balkan, are appointed by the government.
(D) Critics who reviewed the manuscript of the novel agreed that certain parts were offensive.
(E) Humberto was eventually able to publish the novel in another country.

(C) The defense offered in the letter above depends on distinguishing a private concern from the New Balkan government. If that distinction can be defended, then the difference between breach of contract and censorship also can be defended. (C) attacks this important point: since the government controls the publishing house, refusing to publish Humberto's novel is a form of censorship.

All those who support nuclear energy will vote either for Perkins or for Hughes for president. Some isolationists will vote for Hughes and others will vote for Sutherland.

22. Given the statements above, which of the following must be true?

   I. Some isolationists do not support nuclear energy.
  II. Some supporters of nuclear energy are isolationists.
 III. If Perkins withdraws from the election, all supporters of nuclear energy will vote for Hughes.

(A) I only   (B) II only   (C) III only
(D) I and III only   (E) I, II, and III

(D) Examine each of the statements. Statement I is deducible from the stimulus material: since some isolationists vote for someone other than Perkins or Hughes, they cannot support nuclear energy. Statement III is also deducible: supporters of nuclear energy vote either for Perkins or Hughes; if they can't vote for Perkins, they vote for Hughes. Statement II, however, is not deducible. While statement II is possibly true, it is not necessarily true.

Gun control is one of those ideas that is nice in theory but won't work in practice. The number of guns, both legal and illegal, already in private hands is enough to arm every person in the United States several times over. Even if no new guns were manufactured in or imported into the United States, there is a gun available for anyone who wants one.

23. Which of the following is NOT an assumption of the argument above?

(A) Those who currently have guns would be willing to transfer them illegally.
(B) Everyone wanting an illegal gun could afford to pay the black market price.
(C) Owners of guns made illegal under gun control would not voluntarily surrender them.
(D) Guns do not deteriorate and eventually become unoperational.
(E) After gun control, everyone in the United States would want a gun.

(E) The one statement that is not an assumption of the argument is (E). (E) overstates the speaker's case. The speaker does assume those who would want a gun could obtain one illegally. But the speaker does not assume that everyone would want one. The other choices are assumptions of the speaker's argument. As for (A) and (B), the speaker assumes that a black market would develop. As for (C) and (D), the speaker assumes that the supply of existing guns would not diminish.

Whenever Bart is bluffing, he folds his cards into his left hand. Since Bart just folded his cards into his left hand, he must be bluffing.

24. The logic of which of the following is most like that of the thinking above?

(A) All deciduous trees lose their leaves in the winter. It's mid-winter, and the tree by the pond has no leaves. Therefore, the tree by the pond must be a deciduous tree.

(B) All candies produced by the Candy Kitchen use only fresh fruits. Since this chocolate was made by the Candy Kitchen, the cherry in the middle must be fresh.

(C) Every great detective encounters some cases that cannot be solved. Since Sherlock Holmes was a great detective, he must have had some case he could not solve.

(D) It's always easy to tell when the home team is winning because the crowd is very loud. Since the crowd is now silent, the home team must not be ahead.

(E) Tourists only come to the island when the weather is good. Since the weather is bad, we don't expect to see very many tourists.

(A) The reasoning in the stimulus material contains an error:

All S are P.

X is a P.

Therefore, X is also an S.

In the case of the stimulus material, although Bart folds his cards in a certain way when he is bluffing, he may fold them that way at other times. As for (A), there may be other explanations for the tree's lack of leaves: it died, an animal ate them, a vandal stripped them, etc.

SECTION 5

READING COMPREHENSION

1. The author's primary concern is to discuss

(A) methods for testing the effects of new drugs on humans

(B) the importance of having accurate information about the effects of drugs

(C) procedures for determining the long-term effects of new drugs

(D) attempts to curb the abuse of prescription drugs

(E) the difference between the therapeutic and nontherapeutic actions of drugs

(B) This is a main idea question. (B) correctly describes the overall point of the passage. The author starts by stating that all drugs have both good and bad effects and that correct use of a drug requires balancing the effects. For such a balancing to take place, it is essential to have good information about how the drugs work. Some of this can be obtained prior to approval of the drug, but some information will not become available until after years of use.

(A) is incorrect, for the different methods for testing drugs are mentioned only as a part of the development just described. The author is not concerned with talking about how drugs are tested but about why it is important that they be tested. (C) is incorrect for the same reason.

As for (E), this is the starting point for the discussion—not its main point. Finally, as for (D), drug abuse is not discussed in the passage at all.

2. The author implies that a drug with adverse side effects

(A) will not be approved for use by consumers without a doctor's prescription

(B) must wait for approval until lengthy studies prove the effects are not permanent

(C) should be used only if its therapeutic value outweighs its adverse effects

(D) should be withdrawn from the marketplace pending a government investigation

(E) could be used in foreign countries even though it is not approved for use in the United States

(C) This is an implied idea question. In the first paragraph, the author states that all drugs have side effects and that these effects range from the unimportant to the very important. One purpose of drug labeling is to ensure that physicians (and ultimately consumers) are aware of these effects. We can infer, therefore, that drugs with side effects are used—provided the gain is worth the risk. And this is what (C) says.

(A) seems to be contradicted by the passage. One purpose of labeling, according to the author, is to let consumers of nonprescription drugs know of possible side effects of those drugs. As for (B) and (D), the analysis in the preceding paragraph clearly shows that drugs are approved for use and used even though they have unwanted side effects. Finally, there is nothing in the passage to support the conclusion expressed in (E).

3. Which of the following can be inferred from the passage?

   I. Some adverse drug effects cannot be detected prior to approval because they take a long time to develop.
   II. Drugs with serious adverse side effects are never approved for distribution.
   III. Some adverse drug effects are not discovered during testing because they are very rare.

   (A) I only
   (B) II only
   (C) III only
   (D) I and III only
   (E) II and III only

   (D) This is an implied idea question. Statement I can be inferred from the passage. The author does not state this conclusion in so many words, but he says that some effects are not uncovered because of the short duration of the studies. We may therefore infer that some effects do not manifest themselves for a long period. III is inferable in the same fashion. The author states that the size of the groups studied makes it difficult to uncover some effects, so we may infer that some effects are rare. II, however, is not inferable, as our analysis of the preceding question shows.

4. The author introduces the example of thalidomide (line 35) to show that some

   (A) drugs do not have the same actions in humans that they do in animals
   (B) drug testing procedures are ignored by careless laboratory workers
   (C) drugs have no therapeutic value for humans
   (D) drugs have adverse side effects as well as beneficial actions
   (E) physicians prescribe drugs without first reading the manufacturer's recommendations

   (A) This is a logical detail question. The author introduces the example at line 30, where he is discussing animal studies. He says the fact that a drug shows no dangerous effects in animals does not necessarily mean that it will not adversely affect humans. Then he gives the example. Thus, the example proves that a drug does not necessarily work in humans the same way it does in animals.

5. It can be inferred that the estrogen study mentioned in line 49

   (A) uncovered long-term side effects of a drug that had already been approved for sale by the Food and Drug Administration
   (B) discovered potential side effects of a drug that was still awaiting approval for sale by the Food and Drug Administration
   (C) revealed possible new applications of a drug that had previously been approved for a different treatment
   (D) is an example of a study that could be more efficiently conducted by a centralized authority than by volunteer reporting
   (E) proved that the use of the drug estrogen was not associated with side effects such as thromboembolism

   (A) This is an implied question. The key to this question is the word *retrospective*. This tells you that the control study mentioned was done after the drug was already in use. (B) is incorrect because although the study uncovered harmful side effects, according to the passage, the drug was already in use. (C) is incorrect because the paragraph in which this study is mentioned deals with methods of reporting adverse drug effects, not new applications for drugs. (D) is incorrect first because the author does not mention the efficiency of the study and second because the author is not in favor of a centralized authority. In fact, in the last paragraph the author says that it would be inappropriate at this time to attempt to unite all of the disparate elements into a comprehensive surveillance program. Finally, (E) is incorrect because although thromboembolism is mentioned in the passage as one of the possible harmful side effects of drugs, it is not mentioned in connection with estrogen. The use of estrogen is mentioned in connection with endometrial cancer.

6. The author is most probably leading up to a discussion of some suggestions about how to

   (A) centralize authority for drug surveillance in the United States
   (B) centralize authority for drug surveillance among international agencies
   (C) coordinate better the sharing of information among the drug surveillance agencies
   (D) eliminate the availability and sale of certain drugs now on the market
   (E) improve drug-testing procedures to detect dangerous effects before drugs are approved

   (C) This is a further application question. In the last paragraph the author suggests that uniting disparate elements into a comprehensive surveillance program is inappropriate at this time. This eliminates choices (A) and (B). He suggests, however, that improvements are possible in each segment of the system and urges reliance on computers to improve coordination and communication, so (C) is the correct answer. (D) is wrong because although the author might advocate the elimination of the availability of certain drugs, that is not what the passage is leading up to. As for (E), although the author acknowledges that preapproval studies are not infallible, this notion is too narrow in scope to be the next logical topic for discussion.

7. The author makes use of which of the following devices in the passage?

    I. Definition of terms
    II. Examples
    III. Analogy

    (A) I only   (B) II only   (C) I and II only
    (D) II and III only   (E) I, II, and III

(C) The author defines terms in the passage. For example, in the first paragraph he defines *effects* as undesirable actions of a drug. The author also makes use of examples. He cites thalidomide as an example of a drug that was released for sale because the animal toxicology studies were negative, and yet the drug proved very harmful to humans. The author does not use analogy as a device, so the answer is (C).

8. The author is primarily concerned with

    (A) describing a historical event
    (B) developing a theory of jurisdprudence
    (C) analyzing courtroom procedures
    (D) criticizing a government policy
    (E) interpreting a legal principle

(A) This is a main idea question. Using the first words of the choices, you should be able to eliminate (D). Although the author does make one or two remarks that are critical of the tribunals, it is not the main purpose of the passage to criticize anything. The first words of the remaining choices are consistent with the development of the passage, so we must look at those choices in their entirety. The best choice is (A). The author treats the Nuremberg trials as a historical occurrence. We can eliminate (B) as too broad. Though the topic of the selection is law, the author is not concerned with the broad topic of jurisprudence. (C), too, is overly broad. The selection does talk about problems of proof at the Nuremberg trials, but those problems were unique to those tribunals. So the phrase "courtroom procedures" is not particularly apt. And we eliminate (E) because

the author doesn't mention any legal principle as such.

9. According to the author, which of the following factors affected the severity of the sentences received by those convicted at Nuremberg?

    I. The number of documents submitted by the defense
    II. The time elapsed between the trial and the end of the war
    III. The nature of the crimes committed

    (A) III only   (B) I and II   (C) I and III
    (D) II and III   (E) I, II, and III

(D) This is a specific detail question, and the answer to such a question will always be found in the text. The ideas mentioned by statements II and III are specifically discussed in the third paragraph. The idea mentioned by statement I is discussed in the first paragraph but not in connection with the sentences handed down by the tribunals.

10. Which of the following conclusions can be inferred about the Milch, Pohl, Ohlendorf, and Weizaecker cases?

    (A) Milch, Pohl, and Ohlendorf were convicted, but Weizaecker was acquitted.
    (B) Although all four defendants were convicted, Weizaecker received a lighter sentence.
    (C) The Milch, Pohl, and Ohlendorf trial took place before the Weizaecker trial.
    (D) The defense attorneys in the Weizaecker case were given more liberal access to documents than in the other cases.
    (E) Milch, Pohl, and Ohlendorf were tried by the IMT, but Weizaecker was not.

(D) This is an implied idea question. In the last paragraph of the selection, the author states that some judges (and mentions those who tried Weizaecker) granted to defendants more liberal access to documents than other judges did (and mentions those who tried Milch, Pohl, and Ohlendorf). (A) goes beyond the scope of the passage. Although you are entitled to infer that Weizaecker was able to mount a better defense than the other three, you cannot conclude that he was acquitted. As for (B), the information just cited talks about liberality with respect to access to documents, not about sentencing. (C) is an interesting choice, for the passage does state that judges became more liberal with the passing of time. But the last paragraph refers to two groups of judges, one liberal, the other more restrictive, implying that their views were a matter of judicial temperament. Finally, as for (E), the passage actually implies the opposite of this statement since the IMT was used for the major war criminals. The names in this question were introduced in the last paragraph, not in the first, where the author discusses the IMT.

11. According to the passage, defendants at the Nuremberg trials

   (A) were not given the opportunity to present evidence
   (B) frequently had difficulty obtaining documents
   (C) were not represented by counsel
   (D) were tried in absentia
   (E) were prosecuted by officers of the United States military

(B) This is a specific detail question. In the third paragraph, the author specifically states that procedures established to handle documents made it difficult for the defense to get access to the documents. (A) is specifically contradicted by the selection. The defendants did present evidence. As for (C), the passage specifically refers to defense counsel in the third paragraph. As for (D), though the passage doesn't specifically state that the defendants were present at the trials, it doesn't state that they were absent either. Finally, (E) is perhaps the most attractive of the wrong answers because the passage talks about "military tribunals." But the passage doesn't specifically state that the lawyers who prosecuted the cases were themselves members of the military. In fact, it indicates that the head of the prosecution for the IMT was a justice of the Supreme Court of the United States.

12. It can be inferred from the selection that defendants

   (A) called more witnesses than the prosecution
   (B) submitted more affidavits than the prosecution
   (C) did not have access to the tribunal libraries
   (D) were not permitted to testify on their own behalves
   (E) relied more heavily on affidavits than the prosecution

(E) This is an inference question. In the second paragraph, the author states that the prosecution presented about 18,000 documents, of which 2,500 were affidavits. So a relatively small share of the prosecution's documents were affidavits. But according to the selection, about half of the defendants' documents were affidavits. Thus, we can conclude that the defendants relied more heavily on affidavits than did the prosecutors. As for (A) and (D), the passage clearly indicates that documentary evidence was the primary form of proof used at the trials, but it does not go so far as to say that no one

called any witnesses or that one side called more witnesses than the other or that the defendants did not themselves testify. (B) goes too far. Although we know that affidavits constituted a larger portion of the documents submitted by the defendants than those submitted by the prosecutors, we don't know how many documents defendants submitted. (C) overstates a point made by the author. The author acknowledges that it was often difficult for defendants to obtain documents in the custody of the prosecutors but does not say that they did not have access to tribunal libraries.

13. The author's attitude toward the military tribunals can best be described as

   (A) restrained contempt
   (B) evident awe
   (C) uncontrolled rage
   (D) profound amusement
   (E) qualified endorsement

(E) This is an author's attitude question. You have everything you need to answer this question in the last paragraph, even in the last sentence, where the author says that in spite of the difficulties, the tribunals were successful. This is clearly a positive attitude, so you can eliminate choices (A), (C), and (D). Answer choice (B) overstates the case. (E) is the best choice because it notes that the author generally agrees with the results of the tribunal even though he has some misgivings.

14. The author would be most likely to agree with which of the following statements?

   (A) Members of the SS were unfairly punished more severely than other war criminals.
   (B) The IMT was more effective than the 12 United States military tribunals.
   (C) Many war criminals would have received harsher sentences had they been tried earlier.
   (D) Counsel who represented the defendants at Nuremberg were often incompetent.
   (E) Trial by documentary evidence is inherently prejudicial to the rights of a defendant.

(C) This is a further application question. In the third paragraph, the author notes that the passing of time and changing political conditions resulted in lighter sentences. We can conclude that had defendants been tried before these factors began to mitigate the severity of the sentencing process, they would have received stiffer sentences. Thus, the author would endorse the statement suggested by (C). You can eliminate (A) because it uses the word *unfairly*. While the author acknowledges that members of the SS were generally treated more harshly, the author does not suggest that the difference was in any way unfair. As for (B), the author does mention that the IMT tried the major war criminals, but that does not mean it was any more effective than the other tribunals. As for (D), the author acknowledges that defense counsel often had difficulty obtaining documents, but the difficulty is attributed to the procedures, not to any lack of ability on the part of the lawyers. And it is true that the author later states that some defense counsel were more experienced with the procedures than others (and more effective), but that does not mean that those who were new to the procedures were not competent. Finally, (E) seems to be contradicted by the selection.

15. The author of the selection is primarily concerned to

(A) persuade the reader that a single tax on land is economically efficient
(B) encourage legislators to adopt a single tax on land in lieu of other taxes
(C) describe some 19th century arguments in favor of a single tax on land
(D) discuss the relationship between tax rates and other economic factors such as interest rates
(E) employ the concept of a natural right to justify government confiscation of private property

(C) This is a main idea question. We can eliminate (A), (B), and (E) because those choices go beyond the scope of the passage. The passage is purely descriptive. The author never makes an argument in favor of or against any economic policy. On the other hand, (D) is too narrow. While the author does mention this idea, it is but a small part of the overall development of the selection. The best choice is (C). It correctly notes that the author is interested only in describing some arguments in favor of a particular policy.

16. According to the passage, Henry George regarded which of the following as the primary determinant of the wage level?

(A) amount of income produced by owners of freely held land
(B) number of employers in a geographical region
(C) rate of taxation by the government of wages and salaries
(D) level of rents paid by renters for the use of land owned by others
(E) availability of government jobs as an alternative to private employment

(A) This is a specific detail question, so the correct answer is explicitly stated somewhere in the selection. In the fourth paragraph, the author specifically states that supporters of the single tax on land theorized that "wages in general are fixed by

the income that can be earned by occupiers and tillers of freely held land."

17. It can be inferred from the passage that Henry George entitled his work *Progress and Poverty* because he thought that under the existing tax structure

(A) progress would inevitably lead to greater poverty
(B) poverty would inevitably lead to more progress
(C) progress would inevitably lead to a reduction in poverty
(D) higher interest rates would inevitably lead to lower wages
(E) higher taxes would inevitably lead to greater progress and to greater poverty

(A) This is an inferred idea question. Although the author never explicitly tells us why George selected the title *Progress and Poverty*, the final sentence of the penultimate paragraph strongly suggests the reason. There the author states that a central tenet of George's theory is that all material progress results in further poverty. We can infer, therefore, that the title of the work is intended to highlight this connection.

18. It can be inferred that an opponent of the single tax on land would regard the economic value created by the efforts of a landowner to improve that land as a

(A) property right
(B) loss of capital
(C) legitimately taxable transaction
(D) cause of unemployment
(E) diminution of rental value

(A) The argument from natural rights against the single tax on land is mentioned in the third paragraph. There it is stated that opponents of the single tax on land argued that the landowner who labors to improve the land is by natural law entitled to the fruits of that labor. In other words, by working the landowner creates a property right in the land.

19. If a government makes available to the general population fertile lands previously unoccupied, then economic rent, as that term was used by the supporters of a single tax on land, should

(A) increase
(B) decrease
(C) remain unchanged
(D) become zero
(E) cause wages to decrease

(B) This is a further application question. You must take what you have learned about the economic theory underlying the proposal for a single tax on land and apply it to a new situation. In

700

terms of the theory discussed in the selection, economic rent is the advantage enjoyed by those who hold more productive lands over those who hold less productive lands or no land at all. If productive land were so abundant that anyone who wanted it could have it, then no one would be disadvantaged by another's private ownership of any particular parcel. In other words, a situation of pure equality of opportunity would prevail, and economic rent would equal zero. An increase, therefore, in the availability of productive land should tend to decrease the differential between the haves and the have nots and decrease economic rent.

20. According to the supporters of a single tax on land, an increase in wages should be accompanied by

    (A) a decrease in interest rates
    (B) an increase in rent
    (C) an increase in interest rates
    (D) an increase in population
    (E) a decrease in capital

    (C) The answer to this specific detail question is found in the final sentence of the third paragraph. There it is explicitly stated that according to the single tax theory wages and interest rates rise and fall together.

21. According to the selection, supporters of a single tax on land claimed that the single tax would do all of the following EXCEPT:

    (A) reduce government bureaucracy
    (B) discourage land speculation
    (C) increase production of wealth
    (D) burden poor laborers
    (E) stimulate production

    (D) This is a specific detail question with a thought-reverser. The ideas described by choices (A), (B), (C), and (E) are specifically mentioned in the final paragraph. The idea described by (D) is not.

22. Which of the following best describes the primary purpose of the passage?

    (A) Antitrust claims may be used as a weapon by one business entity against its competitors.
    (B) The tort of abuse of process is the best way to discourage spurious antitrust suits.
    (C) The First Amendment does not necessarily protect statements that are untrue.

    (D) Antitrust suits can impose considerable economic burdens on those sued.
    (E) Some businesses may file antitrust claims against competitors to reduce competition.

    (B) This is a main idea question. The author begins by noting that antitrust laws may be unfairly used by one business against another. In the final sentence of that paragraph, the author asks what we can do about this problem. The second, third, and fourth paragraphs discuss some philosophical problems associated with discouraging parties from seeking government relief (either legislative or judicial). Finally, the author concludes that the best solution is the tort of abuse of process: it won't deter people from filing claims, but it will protect innocent defendants. The other choices do refer to ideas mentioned in the selection, but none of them describes the overall development of the selection. In short, the other choices are too narrow.

23. According to the passage, the American rule requires

    (A) plaintiffs to prove the truth of their claims
    (B) defendants to pay their own costs in litigation
    (C) each party to a lawsuit to pay the other's costs
    (D) a judge to determine which party is at fault
    (E) the government to grant favors to petitioners

    (B) This is a specific detail question. Use the wording of the question to find the material you need. You will find it at the end of the third paragraph. The author states that under the American rule, the "victim" may have to bear some of the cost of the dispute. The "victim" is the defendant. So the American rule requires defendants to bear their own costs.

24. The author mentions all of the following as burdens placed on a defendant in an antitrust suit EXCEPT:

    (A) The possibility of being assessed treble damages
    (B) The possibility of having to pay plaintiff's attorney's fees
    (C) The possibility of having to file a petition for economic rents
    (D) The cost of discovery
    (E) The cost of attorney's fees

    (C) This is also a special detail question—but one with a thought-reverser. In the first few sentences you will find mentioned (A), (B), (D), and (E). The idea of filing a petition for economic rents doesn't come up until the third paragraph, well beyond the discussion of defendants' burdens.

701

25. Which of the following best describes the structure of the passage?

   (A) The author focuses on an ambiguous term and provides a definition.
   (B) The author identifies a problem and suggests a solution.
   (C) The author introduces an analogy and attacks it.
   (D) The author mentions an example and extrapolates a conclusion.
   (E) The author defends a theory against someone else's attacks.

(B) This is a logical structure question that asks about the overall development of the selection. Refer to our analysis of the main idea question above. (B) best describes that development. (A) is incorrect because the author does not examine an ambiguous term. (A problem is not equivalent to an ambiguity.) As for (C), the author does rely on analogy (e.g., between antitrust law and libel law), but he does not attack this analogy. As for (D), you might argue that the author introduces examples (of the defendant's exposure in an antitrust suit). And even if we grant for argument's sake that he draws further conclusions based on those examples, that is not the principle that governs the overall structure of the selection. Finally, as for (E), though the author does have a position he defends, the selection never mentions someone else's attacks on the author's position.

26. The author of the passage would most likely agree with which of the following statements?

   (A) Because of the defendant's exposure, the American rule should be suspended in antitrust litigation.
   (B) The Constitution should be amended to create a right to seek transfer payments and economic rents.
   (C) In antitrust suits, the "honest statement" rule should be replaced by a "truth" rule.
   (D) The tort of abuse of process can eventually eliminate the need for antitrust litigation.
   (E) Some false statements must be protected in order to ensure that freedom of speech is not restricted.

(E) This is a further application question. In the second and third paragraphs, the author makes the point that we tolerate some false accusations or petitions. If we punished—economically or otherwise—all false statements, then people might be unwilling to make a statement they knew or believed to be true for fear of such sanctions if they were unable to prove the truth of the state-

ment conclusively. Thus, the author would likely agree with (E). As for (A), the author does mention the American rule, but the statements about the rule are factual only. There is no hint of a judgment in the selection, so there is no reason to believe the author would accept this statement. (B) makes the same error as (A). Yes, the author does say that there is no constitutional right to petition the government for these things, but there is nothing in the paragraph to suggest that he thinks there should be such a right—much less that there should be a constitutional amendment. (C) is a statement the author would surely reject. In the fourth paragraph, the author specifically says "we may quickly discard a rule that . . . ." And then the next sentence refers to the "truth" rule. Finally, as for (D), the author does say that the tort of abuse of process can protect defendants from spurious antitrust claims, but he does not say that it will ELIMINATE the need for antitrust litigation.

27. It can be inferred from the passage that a "truth" rule would

   (A) impose liability for litigation costs on a plaintiff if the plaintiff lost
   (B) create a buffer zone between statements that are true and those that are honest but untrue
   (C) increase the economic and financial risks incurred by defendants in antitrust suits
   (D) encourage businesses to file frivolous antitrust claims against rival businesses
   (E) reduce the power of the government to control markets through antitrust policy

(A) This is an implied idea question. At the end of the third paragraph, the author is wrestling with the problem of how to allocate costs in an antitrust suit. At the beginning of the fourth paragraph, he says we must reject a rule that would impose costs on a plaintiff simply because the plaintiff does not win. The next sentence refers to this as the "truth" rule. Thus, we can infer that the "truth" rule would require the plaintiff to pay all costs if it doesn't win. (B) is surely wrong because a "truth" rule would impose risks on speech. (C) is incorrect because the rule would increase the risk for plaintiffs and reduce the risk for defendants and potential defendants. (D) is incorrect because the rule, by placing the risk on the plaintiff, would discourage suits. Finally, (E) is wrong because the rule as applied to antitrust law would affect the parties, not the government.

28. The author regards using the tort of abuse of process in antitrust cases as a

   (A) dangerous precedent
   (B) recent innovation
   (C) practical compromise
   (D) costly error
   (E) risky proposition

(C) This is a tone question. The author wrestles with the problem of how to protect innocent victims against spurious antitrust litigation without discouraging legitimate claims. In the final paragraph, the author proposes a solution to this dilemma: the tort of abuse of process. The author clearly favors this approach, so we can eliminate choices (A), (D), and (E). As for (B), the author never says that this is a new idea. It may be an old idea that she thinks should be more widely used.

Use a No. 2 pencil only. Be sure each mark is dark and completely fills the intended oval. Completely erase any errors or stray marks.

□ A R C O □

Start with number 1 for each new section. If a section has fewer than 30 questions, leave the extra answer spaces blank.

SECTION 1

1. Ⓐ Ⓑ Ⓒ Ⓓ Ⓔ
2. Ⓐ Ⓑ Ⓒ Ⓓ Ⓔ
3. Ⓐ Ⓑ Ⓒ Ⓓ Ⓔ
4. Ⓐ Ⓑ Ⓒ Ⓓ Ⓔ
5. Ⓐ Ⓑ Ⓒ Ⓓ Ⓔ
6. Ⓐ Ⓑ Ⓒ Ⓓ Ⓔ
7. Ⓐ Ⓑ Ⓒ Ⓓ Ⓔ
8. Ⓐ Ⓑ Ⓒ Ⓓ Ⓔ
9. Ⓐ Ⓑ Ⓒ Ⓓ Ⓔ
10. Ⓐ Ⓑ Ⓒ Ⓓ Ⓔ
11. Ⓐ Ⓑ Ⓒ Ⓓ Ⓔ
12. Ⓐ Ⓑ Ⓒ Ⓓ Ⓔ
13. Ⓐ Ⓑ Ⓒ Ⓓ Ⓔ
14. Ⓐ Ⓑ Ⓒ Ⓓ Ⓔ
15. Ⓐ Ⓑ Ⓒ Ⓓ Ⓔ
16. Ⓐ Ⓑ Ⓒ Ⓓ Ⓔ
17. Ⓐ Ⓑ Ⓒ Ⓓ Ⓔ
18. Ⓐ Ⓑ Ⓒ Ⓓ Ⓔ
19. Ⓐ Ⓑ Ⓒ Ⓓ Ⓔ
20. Ⓐ Ⓑ Ⓒ Ⓓ Ⓔ
21. Ⓐ Ⓑ Ⓒ Ⓓ Ⓔ
22. Ⓐ Ⓑ Ⓒ Ⓓ Ⓔ
23. Ⓐ Ⓑ Ⓒ Ⓓ Ⓔ
24. Ⓐ Ⓑ Ⓒ Ⓓ Ⓔ
25. Ⓐ Ⓑ Ⓒ Ⓓ Ⓔ
26. Ⓐ Ⓑ Ⓒ Ⓓ Ⓔ
27. Ⓐ Ⓑ Ⓒ Ⓓ Ⓔ
28. Ⓐ Ⓑ Ⓒ Ⓓ Ⓔ
29. Ⓐ Ⓑ Ⓒ Ⓓ Ⓔ
30. Ⓐ Ⓑ Ⓒ Ⓓ Ⓔ

SECTION 2

1. Ⓐ Ⓑ Ⓒ Ⓓ Ⓔ
2. Ⓐ Ⓑ Ⓒ Ⓓ Ⓔ
3. Ⓐ Ⓑ Ⓒ Ⓓ Ⓔ
4. Ⓐ Ⓑ Ⓒ Ⓓ Ⓔ
5. Ⓐ Ⓑ Ⓒ Ⓓ Ⓔ
6. Ⓐ Ⓑ Ⓒ Ⓓ Ⓔ
7. Ⓐ Ⓑ Ⓒ Ⓓ Ⓔ
8. Ⓐ Ⓑ Ⓒ Ⓓ Ⓔ
9. Ⓐ Ⓑ Ⓒ Ⓓ Ⓔ
10. Ⓐ Ⓑ Ⓒ Ⓓ Ⓔ
11. Ⓐ Ⓑ Ⓒ Ⓓ Ⓔ
12. Ⓐ Ⓑ Ⓒ Ⓓ Ⓔ
13. Ⓐ Ⓑ Ⓒ Ⓓ Ⓔ
14. Ⓐ Ⓑ Ⓒ Ⓓ Ⓔ
15. Ⓐ Ⓑ Ⓒ Ⓓ Ⓔ
16. Ⓐ Ⓑ Ⓒ Ⓓ Ⓔ
17. Ⓐ Ⓑ Ⓒ Ⓓ Ⓔ
18. Ⓐ Ⓑ Ⓒ Ⓓ Ⓔ
19. Ⓐ Ⓑ Ⓒ Ⓓ Ⓔ
20. Ⓐ Ⓑ Ⓒ Ⓓ Ⓔ
21. Ⓐ Ⓑ Ⓒ Ⓓ Ⓔ
22. Ⓐ Ⓑ Ⓒ Ⓓ Ⓔ
23. Ⓐ Ⓑ Ⓒ Ⓓ Ⓔ
24. Ⓐ Ⓑ Ⓒ Ⓓ Ⓔ
25. Ⓐ Ⓑ Ⓒ Ⓓ Ⓔ
26. Ⓐ Ⓑ Ⓒ Ⓓ Ⓔ
27. Ⓐ Ⓑ Ⓒ Ⓓ Ⓔ
28. Ⓐ Ⓑ Ⓒ Ⓓ Ⓔ
29. Ⓐ Ⓑ Ⓒ Ⓓ Ⓔ
30. Ⓐ Ⓑ Ⓒ Ⓓ Ⓔ

SECTION 3

1. Ⓐ Ⓑ Ⓒ Ⓓ Ⓔ
2. Ⓐ Ⓑ Ⓒ Ⓓ Ⓔ
3. Ⓐ Ⓑ Ⓒ Ⓓ Ⓔ
4. Ⓐ Ⓑ Ⓒ Ⓓ Ⓔ
5. Ⓐ Ⓑ Ⓒ Ⓓ Ⓔ
6. Ⓐ Ⓑ Ⓒ Ⓓ Ⓔ
7. Ⓐ Ⓑ Ⓒ Ⓓ Ⓔ
8. Ⓐ Ⓑ Ⓒ Ⓓ Ⓔ
9. Ⓐ Ⓑ Ⓒ Ⓓ Ⓔ
10. Ⓐ Ⓑ Ⓒ Ⓓ Ⓔ
11. Ⓐ Ⓑ Ⓒ Ⓓ Ⓔ
12. Ⓐ Ⓑ Ⓒ Ⓓ Ⓔ
13. Ⓐ Ⓑ Ⓒ Ⓓ Ⓔ
14. Ⓐ Ⓑ Ⓒ Ⓓ Ⓔ
15. Ⓐ Ⓑ Ⓒ Ⓓ Ⓔ
16. Ⓐ Ⓑ Ⓒ Ⓓ Ⓔ
17. Ⓐ Ⓑ Ⓒ Ⓓ Ⓔ
18. Ⓐ Ⓑ Ⓒ Ⓓ Ⓔ
19. Ⓐ Ⓑ Ⓒ Ⓓ Ⓔ
20. Ⓐ Ⓑ Ⓒ Ⓓ Ⓔ
21. Ⓐ Ⓑ Ⓒ Ⓓ Ⓔ
22. Ⓐ Ⓑ Ⓒ Ⓓ Ⓔ
23. Ⓐ Ⓑ Ⓒ Ⓓ Ⓔ
24. Ⓐ Ⓑ Ⓒ Ⓓ Ⓔ
25. Ⓐ Ⓑ Ⓒ Ⓓ Ⓔ
26. Ⓐ Ⓑ Ⓒ Ⓓ Ⓔ
27. Ⓐ Ⓑ Ⓒ Ⓓ Ⓔ
28. Ⓐ Ⓑ Ⓒ Ⓓ Ⓔ
29. Ⓐ Ⓑ Ⓒ Ⓓ Ⓔ
30. Ⓐ Ⓑ Ⓒ Ⓓ Ⓔ

SECTION 4

1. Ⓐ Ⓑ Ⓒ Ⓓ Ⓔ
2. Ⓐ Ⓑ Ⓒ Ⓓ Ⓔ
3. Ⓐ Ⓑ Ⓒ Ⓓ Ⓔ
4. Ⓐ Ⓑ Ⓒ Ⓓ Ⓔ
5. Ⓐ Ⓑ Ⓒ Ⓓ Ⓔ
6. Ⓐ Ⓑ Ⓒ Ⓓ Ⓔ
7. Ⓐ Ⓑ Ⓒ Ⓓ Ⓔ
8. Ⓐ Ⓑ Ⓒ Ⓓ Ⓔ
9. Ⓐ Ⓑ Ⓒ Ⓓ Ⓔ
10. Ⓐ Ⓑ Ⓒ Ⓓ Ⓔ
11. Ⓐ Ⓑ Ⓒ Ⓓ Ⓔ
12. Ⓐ Ⓑ Ⓒ Ⓓ Ⓔ
13. Ⓐ Ⓑ Ⓒ Ⓓ Ⓔ
14. Ⓐ Ⓑ Ⓒ Ⓓ Ⓔ
15. Ⓐ Ⓑ Ⓒ Ⓓ Ⓔ
16. Ⓐ Ⓑ Ⓒ Ⓓ Ⓔ
17. Ⓐ Ⓑ Ⓒ Ⓓ Ⓔ
18. Ⓐ Ⓑ Ⓒ Ⓓ Ⓔ
19. Ⓐ Ⓑ Ⓒ Ⓓ Ⓔ
20. Ⓐ Ⓑ Ⓒ Ⓓ Ⓔ
21. Ⓐ Ⓑ Ⓒ Ⓓ Ⓔ
22. Ⓐ Ⓑ Ⓒ Ⓓ Ⓔ
23. Ⓐ Ⓑ Ⓒ Ⓓ Ⓔ
24. Ⓐ Ⓑ Ⓒ Ⓓ Ⓔ
25. Ⓐ Ⓑ Ⓒ Ⓓ Ⓔ
26. Ⓐ Ⓑ Ⓒ Ⓓ Ⓔ
27. Ⓐ Ⓑ Ⓒ Ⓓ Ⓔ
28. Ⓐ Ⓑ Ⓒ Ⓓ Ⓔ
29. Ⓐ Ⓑ Ⓒ Ⓓ Ⓔ
30. Ⓐ Ⓑ Ⓒ Ⓓ Ⓔ

SECTION 5

1. Ⓐ Ⓑ Ⓒ Ⓓ Ⓔ
2. Ⓐ Ⓑ Ⓒ Ⓓ Ⓔ
3. Ⓐ Ⓑ Ⓒ Ⓓ Ⓔ
4. Ⓐ Ⓑ Ⓒ Ⓓ Ⓔ
5. Ⓐ Ⓑ Ⓒ Ⓓ Ⓔ
6. Ⓐ Ⓑ Ⓒ Ⓓ Ⓔ
7. Ⓐ Ⓑ Ⓒ Ⓓ Ⓔ
8. Ⓐ Ⓑ Ⓒ Ⓓ Ⓔ
9. Ⓐ Ⓑ Ⓒ Ⓓ Ⓔ
10. Ⓐ Ⓑ Ⓒ Ⓓ Ⓔ
11. Ⓐ Ⓑ Ⓒ Ⓓ Ⓔ
12. Ⓐ Ⓑ Ⓒ Ⓓ Ⓔ
13. Ⓐ Ⓑ Ⓒ Ⓓ Ⓔ
14. Ⓐ Ⓑ Ⓒ Ⓓ Ⓔ
15. Ⓐ Ⓑ Ⓒ Ⓓ Ⓔ
16. Ⓐ Ⓑ Ⓒ Ⓓ Ⓔ
17. Ⓐ Ⓑ Ⓒ Ⓓ Ⓔ
18. Ⓐ Ⓑ Ⓒ Ⓓ Ⓔ
19. Ⓐ Ⓑ Ⓒ Ⓓ Ⓔ
20. Ⓐ Ⓑ Ⓒ Ⓓ Ⓔ
21. Ⓐ Ⓑ Ⓒ Ⓓ Ⓔ
22. Ⓐ Ⓑ Ⓒ Ⓓ Ⓔ
23. Ⓐ Ⓑ Ⓒ Ⓓ Ⓔ
24. Ⓐ Ⓑ Ⓒ Ⓓ Ⓔ
25. Ⓐ Ⓑ Ⓒ Ⓓ Ⓔ
26. Ⓐ Ⓑ Ⓒ Ⓓ Ⓔ
27. Ⓐ Ⓑ Ⓒ Ⓓ Ⓔ
28. Ⓐ Ⓑ Ⓒ Ⓓ Ⓔ
29. Ⓐ Ⓑ Ⓒ Ⓓ Ⓔ
30. Ⓐ Ⓑ Ⓒ Ⓓ Ⓔ

☐ A R C O ☐

... number 1 for each new section. If a section has fewer than 30 questions, leave the extra answer spaces blank.

SECTION 1

	A	B	C	D	E
1	Ⓐ	Ⓑ	Ⓒ	Ⓓ	Ⓔ
2	Ⓐ	Ⓑ	Ⓒ	Ⓓ	Ⓔ
3	Ⓐ	Ⓑ	Ⓒ	Ⓓ	Ⓔ
4	Ⓐ	Ⓑ	Ⓒ	Ⓓ	Ⓔ
5	Ⓐ	Ⓑ	Ⓒ	Ⓓ	Ⓔ
6	Ⓐ	Ⓑ	Ⓒ	Ⓓ	Ⓔ
7	Ⓐ	Ⓑ	Ⓒ	Ⓓ	Ⓔ
8	Ⓐ	Ⓑ	Ⓒ	Ⓓ	Ⓔ
9	Ⓐ	Ⓑ	Ⓒ	Ⓓ	Ⓔ
10	Ⓐ	Ⓑ	Ⓒ	Ⓓ	Ⓔ
11	Ⓐ	Ⓑ	Ⓒ	Ⓓ	Ⓔ
12	Ⓐ	Ⓑ	Ⓒ	Ⓓ	Ⓔ
13	Ⓐ	Ⓑ	Ⓒ	Ⓓ	Ⓔ
14	Ⓐ	Ⓑ	Ⓒ	Ⓓ	Ⓔ
15	Ⓐ	Ⓑ	Ⓒ	Ⓓ	Ⓔ
16	Ⓐ	Ⓑ	Ⓒ	Ⓓ	Ⓔ
17	Ⓐ	Ⓑ	Ⓒ	Ⓓ	Ⓔ
18	Ⓐ	Ⓑ	Ⓒ	Ⓓ	Ⓔ
19	Ⓐ	Ⓑ	Ⓒ	Ⓓ	Ⓔ
20	Ⓐ	Ⓑ	Ⓒ	Ⓓ	Ⓔ
21	Ⓐ	Ⓑ	Ⓒ	Ⓓ	Ⓔ
22	Ⓐ	Ⓑ	Ⓒ	Ⓓ	Ⓔ
23	Ⓐ	Ⓑ	Ⓒ	Ⓓ	Ⓔ
24	Ⓐ	Ⓑ	Ⓒ	Ⓓ	Ⓔ
25	Ⓐ	Ⓑ	Ⓒ	Ⓓ	Ⓔ
26	Ⓐ	Ⓑ	Ⓒ	Ⓓ	Ⓔ
27	Ⓐ	Ⓑ	Ⓒ	Ⓓ	Ⓔ
28	Ⓐ	Ⓑ	Ⓒ	Ⓓ	Ⓔ
29	Ⓐ	Ⓑ	Ⓒ	Ⓓ	Ⓔ
30	Ⓐ	Ⓑ	Ⓒ	Ⓓ	Ⓔ

SECTION 2

	A	B	C	D	E
1	Ⓐ	Ⓑ	Ⓒ	Ⓓ	Ⓔ
2	Ⓐ	Ⓑ	Ⓒ	Ⓓ	Ⓔ
3	Ⓐ	Ⓑ	Ⓒ	Ⓓ	Ⓔ
4	Ⓐ	Ⓑ	Ⓒ	Ⓓ	Ⓔ
5	Ⓐ	Ⓑ	Ⓒ	Ⓓ	Ⓔ
6	Ⓐ	Ⓑ	Ⓒ	Ⓓ	Ⓔ
7	Ⓐ	Ⓑ	Ⓒ	Ⓓ	Ⓔ
8	Ⓐ	Ⓑ	Ⓒ	Ⓓ	Ⓔ
9	Ⓐ	Ⓑ	Ⓒ	Ⓓ	Ⓔ
10	Ⓐ	Ⓑ	Ⓒ	Ⓓ	Ⓔ
11	Ⓐ	Ⓑ	Ⓒ	Ⓓ	Ⓔ
12	Ⓐ	Ⓑ	Ⓒ	Ⓓ	Ⓔ
13	Ⓐ	Ⓑ	Ⓒ	Ⓓ	Ⓔ
14	Ⓐ	Ⓑ	Ⓒ	Ⓓ	Ⓔ
15	Ⓐ	Ⓑ	Ⓒ	Ⓓ	Ⓔ
16	Ⓐ	Ⓑ	Ⓒ	Ⓓ	Ⓔ
17	Ⓐ	Ⓑ	Ⓒ	Ⓓ	Ⓔ
18	Ⓐ	Ⓑ	Ⓒ	Ⓓ	Ⓔ
19	Ⓐ	Ⓑ	Ⓒ	Ⓓ	Ⓔ
20	Ⓐ	Ⓑ	Ⓒ	Ⓓ	Ⓔ
21	Ⓐ	Ⓑ	Ⓒ	Ⓓ	Ⓔ
22	Ⓐ	Ⓑ	Ⓒ	Ⓓ	Ⓔ
23	Ⓐ	Ⓑ	Ⓒ	Ⓓ	Ⓔ
24	Ⓐ	Ⓑ	Ⓒ	Ⓓ	Ⓔ
25	Ⓐ	Ⓑ	Ⓒ	Ⓓ	Ⓔ
26	Ⓐ	Ⓑ	Ⓒ	Ⓓ	Ⓔ
27	Ⓐ	Ⓑ	Ⓒ	Ⓓ	Ⓔ
28	Ⓐ	Ⓑ	Ⓒ	Ⓓ	Ⓔ
29	Ⓐ	Ⓑ	Ⓒ	Ⓓ	Ⓔ
30	Ⓐ	Ⓑ	Ⓒ	Ⓓ	Ⓔ

SECTION 3

	A	B	C	D	E
1	Ⓐ	Ⓑ	Ⓒ	Ⓓ	Ⓔ
2	Ⓐ	Ⓑ	Ⓒ	Ⓓ	Ⓔ
3	Ⓐ	Ⓑ	Ⓒ	Ⓓ	Ⓔ
4	Ⓐ	Ⓑ	Ⓒ	Ⓓ	Ⓔ
5	Ⓐ	Ⓑ	Ⓒ	Ⓓ	Ⓔ
6	Ⓐ	Ⓑ	Ⓒ	Ⓓ	Ⓔ
7	Ⓐ	Ⓑ	Ⓒ	Ⓓ	Ⓔ
8	Ⓐ	Ⓑ	Ⓒ	Ⓓ	Ⓔ
9	Ⓐ	Ⓑ	Ⓒ	Ⓓ	Ⓔ
10	Ⓐ	Ⓑ	Ⓒ	Ⓓ	Ⓔ
11	Ⓐ	Ⓑ	Ⓒ	Ⓓ	Ⓔ
12	Ⓐ	Ⓑ	Ⓒ	Ⓓ	Ⓔ
13	Ⓐ	Ⓑ	Ⓒ	Ⓓ	Ⓔ
14	Ⓐ	Ⓑ	Ⓒ	Ⓓ	Ⓔ
15	Ⓐ	Ⓑ	Ⓒ	Ⓓ	Ⓔ
16	Ⓐ	Ⓑ	Ⓒ	Ⓓ	Ⓔ
17	Ⓐ	Ⓑ	Ⓒ	Ⓓ	Ⓔ
18	Ⓐ	Ⓑ	Ⓒ	Ⓓ	Ⓔ
19	Ⓐ	Ⓑ	Ⓒ	Ⓓ	Ⓔ
20	Ⓐ	Ⓑ	Ⓒ	Ⓓ	Ⓔ
21	Ⓐ	Ⓑ	Ⓒ	Ⓓ	Ⓔ
22	Ⓐ	Ⓑ	Ⓒ	Ⓓ	Ⓔ
23	Ⓐ	Ⓑ	Ⓒ	Ⓓ	Ⓔ
24	Ⓐ	Ⓑ	Ⓒ	Ⓓ	Ⓔ
25	Ⓐ	Ⓑ	Ⓒ	Ⓓ	Ⓔ
26	Ⓐ	Ⓑ	Ⓒ	Ⓓ	Ⓔ
27	Ⓐ	Ⓑ	Ⓒ	Ⓓ	Ⓔ
28	Ⓐ	Ⓑ	Ⓒ	Ⓓ	Ⓔ
29	Ⓐ	Ⓑ	Ⓒ	Ⓓ	Ⓔ
30	Ⓐ	Ⓑ	Ⓒ	Ⓓ	Ⓔ

SECTION 4

	A	B	C	D	E
1	Ⓐ	Ⓑ	Ⓒ	Ⓓ	Ⓔ
2	Ⓐ	Ⓑ	Ⓒ	Ⓓ	Ⓔ
3	Ⓐ	Ⓑ	Ⓒ	Ⓓ	Ⓔ
4	Ⓐ	Ⓑ	Ⓒ	Ⓓ	Ⓔ
5	Ⓐ	Ⓑ	Ⓒ	Ⓓ	Ⓔ
6	Ⓐ	Ⓑ	Ⓒ	Ⓓ	Ⓔ
7	Ⓐ	Ⓑ	Ⓒ	Ⓓ	Ⓔ
8	Ⓐ	Ⓑ	Ⓒ	Ⓓ	Ⓔ
9	Ⓐ	Ⓑ	Ⓒ	Ⓓ	Ⓔ
10	Ⓐ	Ⓑ	Ⓒ	Ⓓ	Ⓔ
11	Ⓐ	Ⓑ	Ⓒ	Ⓓ	Ⓔ
12	Ⓐ	Ⓑ	Ⓒ	Ⓓ	Ⓔ
13	Ⓐ	Ⓑ	Ⓒ	Ⓓ	Ⓔ
14	Ⓐ	Ⓑ	Ⓒ	Ⓓ	Ⓔ
15	Ⓐ	Ⓑ	Ⓒ	Ⓓ	Ⓔ
16	Ⓐ	Ⓑ	Ⓒ	Ⓓ	Ⓔ
17	Ⓐ	Ⓑ	Ⓒ	Ⓓ	Ⓔ
18	Ⓐ	Ⓑ	Ⓒ	Ⓓ	Ⓔ
19	Ⓐ	Ⓑ	Ⓒ	Ⓓ	Ⓔ
20	Ⓐ	Ⓑ	Ⓒ	Ⓓ	Ⓔ
21	Ⓐ	Ⓑ	Ⓒ	Ⓓ	Ⓔ
22	Ⓐ	Ⓑ	Ⓒ	Ⓓ	Ⓔ
23	Ⓐ	Ⓑ	Ⓒ	Ⓓ	Ⓔ
24	Ⓐ	Ⓑ	Ⓒ	Ⓓ	Ⓔ
25	Ⓐ	Ⓑ	Ⓒ	Ⓓ	Ⓔ
26	Ⓐ	Ⓑ	Ⓒ	Ⓓ	Ⓔ
27	Ⓐ	Ⓑ	Ⓒ	Ⓓ	Ⓔ
28	Ⓐ	Ⓑ	Ⓒ	Ⓓ	Ⓔ
29	Ⓐ	Ⓑ	Ⓒ	Ⓓ	Ⓔ
30	Ⓐ	Ⓑ	Ⓒ	Ⓓ	Ⓔ

SECTION 5

	A	B	C	D	E		A	B	C	D	E
1	Ⓐ	Ⓑ	Ⓒ	Ⓓ	Ⓔ	16	Ⓐ	Ⓑ	Ⓒ	Ⓓ	Ⓔ
2	Ⓐ	Ⓑ	Ⓒ	Ⓓ	Ⓔ	17	Ⓐ	Ⓑ	Ⓒ	Ⓓ	Ⓔ
3	Ⓐ	Ⓑ	Ⓒ	Ⓓ	Ⓔ	18	Ⓐ	Ⓑ	Ⓒ	Ⓓ	Ⓔ
4	Ⓐ	Ⓑ	Ⓒ	Ⓓ	Ⓔ	19	Ⓐ	Ⓑ	Ⓒ	Ⓓ	Ⓔ
5	Ⓐ	Ⓑ	Ⓒ	Ⓓ	Ⓔ	20	Ⓐ	Ⓑ	Ⓒ	Ⓓ	Ⓔ
6	Ⓐ	Ⓑ	Ⓒ	Ⓓ	Ⓔ	21	Ⓐ	Ⓑ	Ⓒ	Ⓓ	Ⓔ
7	Ⓐ	Ⓑ	Ⓒ	Ⓓ	Ⓔ	22	Ⓐ	Ⓑ	Ⓒ	Ⓓ	Ⓔ
8	Ⓐ	Ⓑ	Ⓒ	Ⓓ	Ⓔ	23	Ⓐ	Ⓑ	Ⓒ	Ⓓ	Ⓔ
9	Ⓐ	Ⓑ	Ⓒ	Ⓓ	Ⓔ	24	Ⓐ	Ⓑ	Ⓒ	Ⓓ	Ⓔ
10	Ⓐ	Ⓑ	Ⓒ	Ⓓ	Ⓔ	25	Ⓐ	Ⓑ	Ⓒ	Ⓓ	Ⓔ
11	Ⓐ	Ⓑ	Ⓒ	Ⓓ	Ⓔ	26	Ⓐ	Ⓑ	Ⓒ	Ⓓ	Ⓔ
12	Ⓐ	Ⓑ	Ⓒ	Ⓓ	Ⓔ	27	Ⓐ	Ⓑ	Ⓒ	Ⓓ	Ⓔ
13	Ⓐ	Ⓑ	Ⓒ	Ⓓ	Ⓔ	28	Ⓐ	Ⓑ	Ⓒ	Ⓓ	Ⓔ
14	Ⓐ	Ⓑ	Ⓒ	Ⓓ	Ⓔ	29	Ⓐ	Ⓑ	Ⓒ	Ⓓ	Ⓔ
15	Ⓐ	Ⓑ	Ⓒ	Ⓓ	Ⓔ	30	Ⓐ	Ⓑ	Ⓒ	Ⓓ	Ⓔ

☐ A R C O ☐

YOUR NAME: _____

ARCO
TEST NO. _____

DATE
TAKEN: _____

Start with number 1 for each new section. If a section has fewer than 30 questions, leave the extra answer spaces blank.

	SECTION 1		SECTION 2		SECTION 3		SECTION 4
1	Ⓐ Ⓑ Ⓒ Ⓓ Ⓔ	1	Ⓐ Ⓑ Ⓒ Ⓓ Ⓔ	1	Ⓐ Ⓑ Ⓒ Ⓓ Ⓔ	1	Ⓐ Ⓑ Ⓒ Ⓓ Ⓔ
2	Ⓐ Ⓑ Ⓒ Ⓓ Ⓔ	2	Ⓐ Ⓑ Ⓒ Ⓓ Ⓔ	2	Ⓐ Ⓑ Ⓒ Ⓓ Ⓔ	2	Ⓐ Ⓑ Ⓒ Ⓓ Ⓔ
3	Ⓐ Ⓑ Ⓒ Ⓓ Ⓔ	3	Ⓐ Ⓑ Ⓒ Ⓓ Ⓔ	3	Ⓐ Ⓑ Ⓒ Ⓓ Ⓔ	3	Ⓐ Ⓑ Ⓒ Ⓓ Ⓔ
4	Ⓐ Ⓑ Ⓒ Ⓓ Ⓔ	4	Ⓐ Ⓑ Ⓒ Ⓓ Ⓔ	4	Ⓐ Ⓑ Ⓒ Ⓓ Ⓔ	4	Ⓐ Ⓑ Ⓒ Ⓓ Ⓔ
5	Ⓐ Ⓑ Ⓒ Ⓓ Ⓔ	5	Ⓐ Ⓑ Ⓒ Ⓓ Ⓔ	5	Ⓐ Ⓑ Ⓒ Ⓓ Ⓔ	5	Ⓐ Ⓑ Ⓒ Ⓓ Ⓔ
6	Ⓐ Ⓑ Ⓒ Ⓓ Ⓔ	6	Ⓐ Ⓑ Ⓒ Ⓓ Ⓔ	6	Ⓐ Ⓑ Ⓒ Ⓓ Ⓔ	6	Ⓐ Ⓑ Ⓒ Ⓓ Ⓔ
7	Ⓐ Ⓑ Ⓒ Ⓓ Ⓔ	7	Ⓐ Ⓑ Ⓒ Ⓓ Ⓔ	7	Ⓐ Ⓑ Ⓒ Ⓓ Ⓔ	7	Ⓐ Ⓑ Ⓒ Ⓓ Ⓔ
8	Ⓐ Ⓑ Ⓒ Ⓓ Ⓔ	8	Ⓐ Ⓑ Ⓒ Ⓓ Ⓔ	8	Ⓐ Ⓑ Ⓒ Ⓓ Ⓔ	8	Ⓐ Ⓑ Ⓒ Ⓓ Ⓔ
9	Ⓐ Ⓑ Ⓒ Ⓓ Ⓔ	9	Ⓐ Ⓑ Ⓒ Ⓓ Ⓔ	9	Ⓐ Ⓑ Ⓒ Ⓓ Ⓔ	9	Ⓐ Ⓑ Ⓒ Ⓓ Ⓔ
10	Ⓐ Ⓑ Ⓒ Ⓓ Ⓔ	10	Ⓐ Ⓑ Ⓒ Ⓓ Ⓔ	10	Ⓐ Ⓑ Ⓒ Ⓓ Ⓔ	10	Ⓐ Ⓑ Ⓒ Ⓓ Ⓔ
11	Ⓐ Ⓑ Ⓒ Ⓓ Ⓔ	11	Ⓐ Ⓑ Ⓒ Ⓓ Ⓔ	11	Ⓐ Ⓑ Ⓒ Ⓓ Ⓔ	11	Ⓐ Ⓑ Ⓒ Ⓓ Ⓔ
12	Ⓐ Ⓑ Ⓒ Ⓓ Ⓔ	12	Ⓐ Ⓑ Ⓒ Ⓓ Ⓔ	12	Ⓐ Ⓑ Ⓒ Ⓓ Ⓔ	12	Ⓐ Ⓑ Ⓒ Ⓓ Ⓔ
13	Ⓐ Ⓑ Ⓒ Ⓓ Ⓔ	13	Ⓐ Ⓑ Ⓒ Ⓓ Ⓔ	13	Ⓐ Ⓑ Ⓒ Ⓓ Ⓔ	13	Ⓐ Ⓑ Ⓒ Ⓓ Ⓔ
14	Ⓐ Ⓑ Ⓒ Ⓓ Ⓔ	14	Ⓐ Ⓑ Ⓒ Ⓓ Ⓔ	14	Ⓐ Ⓑ Ⓒ Ⓓ Ⓔ	14	Ⓐ Ⓑ Ⓒ Ⓓ Ⓔ
15	Ⓐ Ⓑ Ⓒ Ⓓ Ⓔ	15	Ⓐ Ⓑ Ⓒ Ⓓ Ⓔ	15	Ⓐ Ⓑ Ⓒ Ⓓ Ⓔ	15	Ⓐ Ⓑ Ⓒ Ⓓ Ⓔ
16	Ⓐ Ⓑ Ⓒ Ⓓ Ⓔ	16	Ⓐ Ⓑ Ⓒ Ⓓ Ⓔ	16	Ⓐ Ⓑ Ⓒ Ⓓ Ⓔ	16	Ⓐ Ⓑ Ⓒ Ⓓ Ⓔ
17	Ⓐ Ⓑ Ⓒ Ⓓ Ⓔ	17	Ⓐ Ⓑ Ⓒ Ⓓ Ⓔ	17	Ⓐ Ⓑ Ⓒ Ⓓ Ⓔ	17	Ⓐ Ⓑ Ⓒ Ⓓ Ⓔ
18	Ⓐ Ⓑ Ⓒ Ⓓ Ⓔ	18	Ⓐ Ⓑ Ⓒ Ⓓ Ⓔ	18	Ⓐ Ⓑ Ⓒ Ⓓ Ⓔ	18	Ⓐ Ⓑ Ⓒ Ⓓ Ⓔ
19	Ⓐ Ⓑ Ⓒ Ⓓ Ⓔ	19	Ⓐ Ⓑ Ⓒ Ⓓ Ⓔ	19	Ⓐ Ⓑ Ⓒ Ⓓ Ⓔ	19	Ⓐ Ⓑ Ⓒ Ⓓ Ⓔ
20	Ⓐ Ⓑ Ⓒ Ⓓ Ⓔ	20	Ⓐ Ⓑ Ⓒ Ⓓ Ⓔ	20	Ⓐ Ⓑ Ⓒ Ⓓ Ⓔ	20	Ⓐ Ⓑ Ⓒ Ⓓ Ⓔ
21	Ⓐ Ⓑ Ⓒ Ⓓ Ⓔ	21	Ⓐ Ⓑ Ⓒ Ⓓ Ⓔ	21	Ⓐ Ⓑ Ⓒ Ⓓ Ⓔ	21	Ⓐ Ⓑ Ⓒ Ⓓ Ⓔ
22	Ⓐ Ⓑ Ⓒ Ⓓ Ⓔ	22	Ⓐ Ⓑ Ⓒ Ⓓ Ⓔ	22	Ⓐ Ⓑ Ⓒ Ⓓ Ⓔ	22	Ⓐ Ⓑ Ⓒ Ⓓ Ⓔ
23	Ⓐ Ⓑ Ⓒ Ⓓ Ⓔ	23	Ⓐ Ⓑ Ⓒ Ⓓ Ⓔ	23	Ⓐ Ⓑ Ⓒ Ⓓ Ⓔ	23	Ⓐ Ⓑ Ⓒ Ⓓ Ⓔ
24	Ⓐ Ⓑ Ⓒ Ⓓ Ⓔ	24	Ⓐ Ⓑ Ⓒ Ⓓ Ⓔ	24	Ⓐ Ⓑ Ⓒ Ⓓ Ⓔ	24	Ⓐ Ⓑ Ⓒ Ⓓ Ⓔ
25	Ⓐ Ⓑ Ⓒ Ⓓ Ⓔ	25	Ⓐ Ⓑ Ⓒ Ⓓ Ⓔ	25	Ⓐ Ⓑ Ⓒ Ⓓ Ⓔ	25	Ⓐ Ⓑ Ⓒ Ⓓ Ⓔ
26	Ⓐ Ⓑ Ⓒ Ⓓ Ⓔ	26	Ⓐ Ⓑ Ⓒ Ⓓ Ⓔ	26	Ⓐ Ⓑ Ⓒ Ⓓ Ⓔ	26	Ⓐ Ⓑ Ⓒ Ⓓ Ⓔ
27	Ⓐ Ⓑ Ⓒ Ⓓ Ⓔ	27	Ⓐ Ⓑ Ⓒ Ⓓ Ⓔ	27	Ⓐ Ⓑ Ⓒ Ⓓ Ⓔ	27	Ⓐ Ⓑ Ⓒ Ⓓ Ⓔ
28	Ⓐ Ⓑ Ⓒ Ⓓ Ⓔ	28	Ⓐ Ⓑ Ⓒ Ⓓ Ⓔ	28	Ⓐ Ⓑ Ⓒ Ⓓ Ⓔ	28	Ⓐ Ⓑ Ⓒ Ⓓ Ⓔ
29	Ⓐ Ⓑ Ⓒ Ⓓ Ⓔ	29	Ⓐ Ⓑ Ⓒ Ⓓ Ⓔ	29	Ⓐ Ⓑ Ⓒ Ⓓ Ⓔ	29	Ⓐ Ⓑ Ⓒ Ⓓ Ⓔ
30	Ⓐ Ⓑ Ⓒ Ⓓ Ⓔ	30	Ⓐ Ⓑ Ⓒ Ⓓ Ⓔ	30	Ⓐ Ⓑ Ⓒ Ⓓ Ⓔ	30	Ⓐ Ⓑ Ⓒ Ⓓ Ⓔ

	SECTION 5		
1	Ⓐ Ⓑ Ⓒ Ⓓ Ⓔ	16	Ⓐ Ⓑ Ⓒ Ⓓ Ⓔ
2	Ⓐ Ⓑ Ⓒ Ⓓ Ⓔ	17	Ⓐ Ⓑ Ⓒ Ⓓ Ⓔ
3	Ⓐ Ⓑ Ⓒ Ⓓ Ⓔ	18	Ⓐ Ⓑ Ⓒ Ⓓ Ⓔ
4	Ⓐ Ⓑ Ⓒ Ⓓ Ⓔ	19	Ⓐ Ⓑ Ⓒ Ⓓ Ⓔ
5	Ⓐ Ⓑ Ⓒ Ⓓ Ⓔ	20	Ⓐ Ⓑ Ⓒ Ⓓ Ⓔ
6	Ⓐ Ⓑ Ⓒ Ⓓ Ⓔ	21	Ⓐ Ⓑ Ⓒ Ⓓ Ⓔ
7	Ⓐ Ⓑ Ⓒ Ⓓ Ⓔ	22	Ⓐ Ⓑ Ⓒ Ⓓ Ⓔ
8	Ⓐ Ⓑ Ⓒ Ⓓ Ⓔ	23	Ⓐ Ⓑ Ⓒ Ⓓ Ⓔ
9	Ⓐ Ⓑ Ⓒ Ⓓ Ⓔ	24	Ⓐ Ⓑ Ⓒ Ⓓ Ⓔ
10	Ⓐ Ⓑ Ⓒ Ⓓ Ⓔ	25	Ⓐ Ⓑ Ⓒ Ⓓ Ⓔ
11	Ⓐ Ⓑ Ⓒ Ⓓ Ⓔ	26	Ⓐ Ⓑ Ⓒ Ⓓ Ⓔ
12	Ⓐ Ⓑ Ⓒ Ⓓ Ⓔ	27	Ⓐ Ⓑ Ⓒ Ⓓ Ⓔ
13	Ⓐ Ⓑ Ⓒ Ⓓ Ⓔ	28	Ⓐ Ⓑ Ⓒ Ⓓ Ⓔ
14	Ⓐ Ⓑ Ⓒ Ⓓ Ⓔ	29	Ⓐ Ⓑ Ⓒ Ⓓ Ⓔ
15	Ⓐ Ⓑ Ⓒ Ⓓ Ⓔ	30	Ⓐ Ⓑ Ⓒ Ⓓ Ⓔ

☐ A R C O ☐

...with number 1 for each new section. If a section has fewer than 30 questions, leave the extra answer spaces blank.

SECTION 1

1. Ⓐ Ⓑ Ⓒ Ⓓ Ⓔ
2. Ⓐ Ⓑ Ⓒ Ⓓ Ⓔ
3. Ⓐ Ⓑ Ⓒ Ⓓ Ⓔ
4. Ⓐ Ⓑ Ⓒ Ⓓ Ⓔ
5. Ⓐ Ⓑ Ⓒ Ⓓ Ⓔ
6. Ⓐ Ⓑ Ⓒ Ⓓ Ⓔ
7. Ⓐ Ⓑ Ⓒ Ⓓ Ⓔ
8. Ⓐ Ⓑ Ⓒ Ⓓ Ⓔ
9. Ⓐ Ⓑ Ⓒ Ⓓ Ⓔ
10. Ⓐ Ⓑ Ⓒ Ⓓ Ⓔ
11. Ⓐ Ⓑ Ⓒ Ⓓ Ⓔ
12. Ⓐ Ⓑ Ⓒ Ⓓ Ⓔ
13. Ⓐ Ⓑ Ⓒ Ⓓ Ⓔ
14. Ⓐ Ⓑ Ⓒ Ⓓ Ⓔ
15. Ⓐ Ⓑ Ⓒ Ⓓ Ⓔ
16. Ⓐ Ⓑ Ⓒ Ⓓ Ⓔ
17. Ⓐ Ⓑ Ⓒ Ⓓ Ⓔ
18. Ⓐ Ⓑ Ⓒ Ⓓ Ⓔ
19. Ⓐ Ⓑ Ⓒ Ⓓ Ⓔ
20. Ⓐ Ⓑ Ⓒ Ⓓ Ⓔ
21. Ⓐ Ⓑ Ⓒ Ⓓ Ⓔ
22. Ⓐ Ⓑ Ⓒ Ⓓ Ⓔ
23. Ⓐ Ⓑ Ⓒ Ⓓ Ⓔ
24. Ⓐ Ⓑ Ⓒ Ⓓ Ⓔ
25. Ⓐ Ⓑ Ⓒ Ⓓ Ⓔ
26. Ⓐ Ⓑ Ⓒ Ⓓ Ⓔ
27. Ⓐ Ⓑ Ⓒ Ⓓ Ⓔ
28. Ⓐ Ⓑ Ⓒ Ⓓ Ⓔ
29. Ⓐ Ⓑ Ⓒ Ⓓ Ⓔ
30. Ⓐ Ⓑ Ⓒ Ⓓ Ⓔ

SECTION 2

1. Ⓐ Ⓑ Ⓒ Ⓓ Ⓔ
2. Ⓐ Ⓑ Ⓒ Ⓓ Ⓔ
3. Ⓐ Ⓑ Ⓒ Ⓓ Ⓔ
4. Ⓐ Ⓑ Ⓒ Ⓓ Ⓔ
5. Ⓐ Ⓑ Ⓒ Ⓓ Ⓔ
6. Ⓐ Ⓑ Ⓒ Ⓓ Ⓔ
7. Ⓐ Ⓑ Ⓒ Ⓓ Ⓔ
8. Ⓐ Ⓑ Ⓒ Ⓓ Ⓔ
9. Ⓐ Ⓑ Ⓒ Ⓓ Ⓔ
10. Ⓐ Ⓑ Ⓒ Ⓓ Ⓔ
11. Ⓐ Ⓑ Ⓒ Ⓓ Ⓔ
12. Ⓐ Ⓑ Ⓒ Ⓓ Ⓔ
13. Ⓐ Ⓑ Ⓒ Ⓓ Ⓔ
14. Ⓐ Ⓑ Ⓒ Ⓓ Ⓔ
15. Ⓐ Ⓑ Ⓒ Ⓓ Ⓔ
16. Ⓐ Ⓑ Ⓒ Ⓓ Ⓔ
17. Ⓐ Ⓑ Ⓒ Ⓓ Ⓔ
18. Ⓐ Ⓑ Ⓒ Ⓓ Ⓔ
19. Ⓐ Ⓑ Ⓒ Ⓓ Ⓔ
20. Ⓐ Ⓑ Ⓒ Ⓓ Ⓔ
21. Ⓐ Ⓑ Ⓒ Ⓓ Ⓔ
22. Ⓐ Ⓑ Ⓒ Ⓓ Ⓔ
23. Ⓐ Ⓑ Ⓒ Ⓓ Ⓔ
24. Ⓐ Ⓑ Ⓒ Ⓓ Ⓔ
25. Ⓐ Ⓑ Ⓒ Ⓓ Ⓔ
26. Ⓐ Ⓑ Ⓒ Ⓓ Ⓔ
27. Ⓐ Ⓑ Ⓒ Ⓓ Ⓔ
28. Ⓐ Ⓑ Ⓒ Ⓓ Ⓔ
29. Ⓐ Ⓑ Ⓒ Ⓓ Ⓔ
30. Ⓐ Ⓑ Ⓒ Ⓓ Ⓔ

SECTION 3

1. Ⓐ Ⓑ Ⓒ Ⓓ Ⓔ
2. Ⓐ Ⓑ Ⓒ Ⓓ Ⓔ
3. Ⓐ Ⓑ Ⓒ Ⓓ Ⓔ
4. Ⓐ Ⓑ Ⓒ Ⓓ Ⓔ
5. Ⓐ Ⓑ Ⓒ Ⓓ Ⓔ
6. Ⓐ Ⓑ Ⓒ Ⓓ Ⓔ
7. Ⓐ Ⓑ Ⓒ Ⓓ Ⓔ
8. Ⓐ Ⓑ Ⓒ Ⓓ Ⓔ
9. Ⓐ Ⓑ Ⓒ Ⓓ Ⓔ
10. Ⓐ Ⓑ Ⓒ Ⓓ Ⓔ
11. Ⓐ Ⓑ Ⓒ Ⓓ Ⓔ
12. Ⓐ Ⓑ Ⓒ Ⓓ Ⓔ
13. Ⓐ Ⓑ Ⓒ Ⓓ Ⓔ
14. Ⓐ Ⓑ Ⓒ Ⓓ Ⓔ
15. Ⓐ Ⓑ Ⓒ Ⓓ Ⓔ
16. Ⓐ Ⓑ Ⓒ Ⓓ Ⓔ
17. Ⓐ Ⓑ Ⓒ Ⓓ Ⓔ
18. Ⓐ Ⓑ Ⓒ Ⓓ Ⓔ
19. Ⓐ Ⓑ Ⓒ Ⓓ Ⓔ
20. Ⓐ Ⓑ Ⓒ Ⓓ Ⓔ
21. Ⓐ Ⓑ Ⓒ Ⓓ Ⓔ
22. Ⓐ Ⓑ Ⓒ Ⓓ Ⓔ
23. Ⓐ Ⓑ Ⓒ Ⓓ Ⓔ
24. Ⓐ Ⓑ Ⓒ Ⓓ Ⓔ
25. Ⓐ Ⓑ Ⓒ Ⓓ Ⓔ
26. Ⓐ Ⓑ Ⓒ Ⓓ Ⓔ
27. Ⓐ Ⓑ Ⓒ Ⓓ Ⓔ
28. Ⓐ Ⓑ Ⓒ Ⓓ Ⓔ
29. Ⓐ Ⓑ Ⓒ Ⓓ Ⓔ
30. Ⓐ Ⓑ Ⓒ Ⓓ Ⓔ

SECTION 4

1. Ⓐ Ⓑ Ⓒ Ⓓ Ⓔ
2. Ⓐ Ⓑ Ⓒ Ⓓ Ⓔ
3. Ⓐ Ⓑ Ⓒ Ⓓ Ⓔ
4. Ⓐ Ⓑ Ⓒ Ⓓ Ⓔ
5. Ⓐ Ⓑ Ⓒ Ⓓ Ⓔ
6. Ⓐ Ⓑ Ⓒ Ⓓ Ⓔ
7. Ⓐ Ⓑ Ⓒ Ⓓ Ⓔ
8. Ⓐ Ⓑ Ⓒ Ⓓ Ⓔ
9. Ⓐ Ⓑ Ⓒ Ⓓ Ⓔ
10. Ⓐ Ⓑ Ⓒ Ⓓ Ⓔ
11. Ⓐ Ⓑ Ⓒ Ⓓ Ⓔ
12. Ⓐ Ⓑ Ⓒ Ⓓ Ⓔ
13. Ⓐ Ⓑ Ⓒ Ⓓ Ⓔ
14. Ⓐ Ⓑ Ⓒ Ⓓ Ⓔ
15. Ⓐ Ⓑ Ⓒ Ⓓ Ⓔ
16. Ⓐ Ⓑ Ⓒ Ⓓ Ⓔ
17. Ⓐ Ⓑ Ⓒ Ⓓ Ⓔ
18. Ⓐ Ⓑ Ⓒ Ⓓ Ⓔ
19. Ⓐ Ⓑ Ⓒ Ⓓ Ⓔ
20. Ⓐ Ⓑ Ⓒ Ⓓ Ⓔ
21. Ⓐ Ⓑ Ⓒ Ⓓ Ⓔ
22. Ⓐ Ⓑ Ⓒ Ⓓ Ⓔ
23. Ⓐ Ⓑ Ⓒ Ⓓ Ⓔ
24. Ⓐ Ⓑ Ⓒ Ⓓ Ⓔ
25. Ⓐ Ⓑ Ⓒ Ⓓ Ⓔ
26. Ⓐ Ⓑ Ⓒ Ⓓ Ⓔ
27. Ⓐ Ⓑ Ⓒ Ⓓ Ⓔ
28. Ⓐ Ⓑ Ⓒ Ⓓ Ⓔ
29. Ⓐ Ⓑ Ⓒ Ⓓ Ⓔ
30. Ⓐ Ⓑ Ⓒ Ⓓ Ⓔ

SECTION 5

1. Ⓐ Ⓑ Ⓒ Ⓓ Ⓔ
2. Ⓐ Ⓑ Ⓒ Ⓓ Ⓔ
3. Ⓐ Ⓑ Ⓒ Ⓓ Ⓔ
4. Ⓐ Ⓑ Ⓒ Ⓓ Ⓔ
5. Ⓐ Ⓑ Ⓒ Ⓓ Ⓔ
6. Ⓐ Ⓑ Ⓒ Ⓓ Ⓔ
7. Ⓐ Ⓑ Ⓒ Ⓓ Ⓔ
8. Ⓐ Ⓑ Ⓒ Ⓓ Ⓔ
9. Ⓐ Ⓑ Ⓒ Ⓓ Ⓔ
10. Ⓐ Ⓑ Ⓒ Ⓓ Ⓔ
11. Ⓐ Ⓑ Ⓒ Ⓓ Ⓔ
12. Ⓐ Ⓑ Ⓒ Ⓓ Ⓔ
13. Ⓐ Ⓑ Ⓒ Ⓓ Ⓔ
14. Ⓐ Ⓑ Ⓒ Ⓓ Ⓔ
15. Ⓐ Ⓑ Ⓒ Ⓓ Ⓔ
16. Ⓐ Ⓑ Ⓒ Ⓓ Ⓔ
17. Ⓐ Ⓑ Ⓒ Ⓓ Ⓔ
18. Ⓐ Ⓑ Ⓒ Ⓓ Ⓔ
19. Ⓐ Ⓑ Ⓒ Ⓓ Ⓔ
20. Ⓐ Ⓑ Ⓒ Ⓓ Ⓔ
21. Ⓐ Ⓑ Ⓒ Ⓓ Ⓔ
22. Ⓐ Ⓑ Ⓒ Ⓓ Ⓔ
23. Ⓐ Ⓑ Ⓒ Ⓓ Ⓔ
24. Ⓐ Ⓑ Ⓒ Ⓓ Ⓔ
25. Ⓐ Ⓑ Ⓒ Ⓓ Ⓔ
26. Ⓐ Ⓑ Ⓒ Ⓓ Ⓔ
27. Ⓐ Ⓑ Ⓒ Ⓓ Ⓔ
28. Ⓐ Ⓑ Ⓒ Ⓓ Ⓔ
29. Ⓐ Ⓑ Ⓒ Ⓓ Ⓔ
30. Ⓐ Ⓑ Ⓒ Ⓓ Ⓔ

Use a No. 2 pencil only. Be sure each mark is dark and completely fills the intended oval. Completely erase any errors or stray marks.

□ A R C O □

Start with number 1 for each new section. If a section has fewer than 30 questions, leave the extra answer spaces blank.

SECTION 1

1 Ⓐ Ⓑ Ⓒ Ⓓ Ⓔ
2 Ⓐ Ⓑ Ⓒ Ⓓ Ⓔ
3 Ⓐ Ⓑ Ⓒ Ⓓ Ⓔ
4 Ⓐ Ⓑ Ⓒ Ⓓ Ⓔ
5 Ⓐ Ⓑ Ⓒ Ⓓ Ⓔ
6 Ⓐ Ⓑ Ⓒ Ⓓ Ⓔ
7 Ⓐ Ⓑ Ⓒ Ⓓ Ⓔ
8 Ⓐ Ⓑ Ⓒ Ⓓ Ⓔ
9 Ⓐ Ⓑ Ⓒ Ⓓ Ⓔ
10 Ⓐ Ⓑ Ⓒ Ⓓ Ⓔ
11 Ⓐ Ⓑ Ⓒ Ⓓ Ⓔ
12 Ⓐ Ⓑ Ⓒ Ⓓ Ⓔ
13 Ⓐ Ⓑ Ⓒ Ⓓ Ⓔ
14 Ⓐ Ⓑ Ⓒ Ⓓ Ⓔ
15 Ⓐ Ⓑ Ⓒ Ⓓ Ⓔ
16 Ⓐ Ⓑ Ⓒ Ⓓ Ⓔ
17 Ⓐ Ⓑ Ⓒ Ⓓ Ⓔ
18 Ⓐ Ⓑ Ⓒ Ⓓ Ⓔ
19 Ⓐ Ⓑ Ⓒ Ⓓ Ⓔ
20 Ⓐ Ⓑ Ⓒ Ⓓ Ⓔ
21 Ⓐ Ⓑ Ⓒ Ⓓ Ⓔ
22 Ⓐ Ⓑ Ⓒ Ⓓ Ⓔ
23 Ⓐ Ⓑ Ⓒ Ⓓ Ⓔ
24 Ⓐ Ⓑ Ⓒ Ⓓ Ⓔ
25 Ⓐ Ⓑ Ⓒ Ⓓ Ⓔ
26 Ⓐ Ⓑ Ⓒ Ⓓ Ⓔ
27 Ⓐ Ⓑ Ⓒ Ⓓ Ⓔ
28 Ⓐ Ⓑ Ⓒ Ⓓ Ⓔ
29 Ⓐ Ⓑ Ⓒ Ⓓ Ⓔ
30 Ⓐ Ⓑ Ⓒ Ⓓ Ⓔ

SECTION 2

1 Ⓐ Ⓑ Ⓒ Ⓓ Ⓔ
2 Ⓐ Ⓑ Ⓒ Ⓓ Ⓔ
3 Ⓐ Ⓑ Ⓒ Ⓓ Ⓔ
4 Ⓐ Ⓑ Ⓒ Ⓓ Ⓔ
5 Ⓐ Ⓑ Ⓒ Ⓓ Ⓔ
6 Ⓐ Ⓑ Ⓒ Ⓓ Ⓔ
7 Ⓐ Ⓑ Ⓒ Ⓓ Ⓔ
8 Ⓐ Ⓑ Ⓒ Ⓓ Ⓔ
9 Ⓐ Ⓑ Ⓒ Ⓓ Ⓔ
10 Ⓐ Ⓑ Ⓒ Ⓓ Ⓔ
11 Ⓐ Ⓑ Ⓒ Ⓓ Ⓔ
12 Ⓐ Ⓑ Ⓒ Ⓓ Ⓔ
13 Ⓐ Ⓑ Ⓒ Ⓓ Ⓔ
14 Ⓐ Ⓑ Ⓒ Ⓓ Ⓔ
15 Ⓐ Ⓑ Ⓒ Ⓓ Ⓔ
16 Ⓐ Ⓑ Ⓒ Ⓓ Ⓔ
17 Ⓐ Ⓑ Ⓒ Ⓓ Ⓔ
18 Ⓐ Ⓑ Ⓒ Ⓓ Ⓔ
19 Ⓐ Ⓑ Ⓒ Ⓓ Ⓔ
20 Ⓐ Ⓑ Ⓒ Ⓓ Ⓔ
21 Ⓐ Ⓑ Ⓒ Ⓓ Ⓔ
22 Ⓐ Ⓑ Ⓒ Ⓓ Ⓔ
23 Ⓐ Ⓑ Ⓒ Ⓓ Ⓔ
24 Ⓐ Ⓑ Ⓒ Ⓓ Ⓔ
25 Ⓐ Ⓑ Ⓒ Ⓓ Ⓔ
26 Ⓐ Ⓑ Ⓒ Ⓓ Ⓔ
27 Ⓐ Ⓑ Ⓒ Ⓓ Ⓔ
28 Ⓐ Ⓑ Ⓒ Ⓓ Ⓔ
29 Ⓐ Ⓑ Ⓒ Ⓓ Ⓔ
30 Ⓐ Ⓑ Ⓒ Ⓓ Ⓔ

SECTION 3

1 Ⓐ Ⓑ Ⓒ Ⓓ Ⓔ
2 Ⓐ Ⓑ Ⓒ Ⓓ Ⓔ
3 Ⓐ Ⓑ Ⓒ Ⓓ Ⓔ
4 Ⓐ Ⓑ Ⓒ Ⓓ Ⓔ
5 Ⓐ Ⓑ Ⓒ Ⓓ Ⓔ
6 Ⓐ Ⓑ Ⓒ Ⓓ Ⓔ
7 Ⓐ Ⓑ Ⓒ Ⓓ Ⓔ
8 Ⓐ Ⓑ Ⓒ Ⓓ Ⓔ
9 Ⓐ Ⓑ Ⓒ Ⓓ Ⓔ
10 Ⓐ Ⓑ Ⓒ Ⓓ Ⓔ
11 Ⓐ Ⓑ Ⓒ Ⓓ Ⓔ
12 Ⓐ Ⓑ Ⓒ Ⓓ Ⓔ
13 Ⓐ Ⓑ Ⓒ Ⓓ Ⓔ
14 Ⓐ Ⓑ Ⓒ Ⓓ Ⓔ
15 Ⓐ Ⓑ Ⓒ Ⓓ Ⓔ
16 Ⓐ Ⓑ Ⓒ Ⓓ Ⓔ
17 Ⓐ Ⓑ Ⓒ Ⓓ Ⓔ
18 Ⓐ Ⓑ Ⓒ Ⓓ Ⓔ
19 Ⓐ Ⓑ Ⓒ Ⓓ Ⓔ
20 Ⓐ Ⓑ Ⓒ Ⓓ Ⓔ
21 Ⓐ Ⓑ Ⓒ Ⓓ Ⓔ
22 Ⓐ Ⓑ Ⓒ Ⓓ Ⓔ
23 Ⓐ Ⓑ Ⓒ Ⓓ Ⓔ
24 Ⓐ Ⓑ Ⓒ Ⓓ Ⓔ
25 Ⓐ Ⓑ Ⓒ Ⓓ Ⓔ
26 Ⓐ Ⓑ Ⓒ Ⓓ Ⓔ
27 Ⓐ Ⓑ Ⓒ Ⓓ Ⓔ
28 Ⓐ Ⓑ Ⓒ Ⓓ Ⓔ
29 Ⓐ Ⓑ Ⓒ Ⓓ Ⓔ
30 Ⓐ Ⓑ Ⓒ Ⓓ Ⓔ

SECTION 4

1 Ⓐ Ⓑ Ⓒ Ⓓ Ⓔ
2 Ⓐ Ⓑ Ⓒ Ⓓ Ⓔ
3 Ⓐ Ⓑ Ⓒ Ⓓ Ⓔ
4 Ⓐ Ⓑ Ⓒ Ⓓ Ⓔ
5 Ⓐ Ⓑ Ⓒ Ⓓ Ⓔ
6 Ⓐ Ⓑ Ⓒ Ⓓ Ⓔ
7 Ⓐ Ⓑ Ⓒ Ⓓ Ⓔ
8 Ⓐ Ⓑ Ⓒ Ⓓ Ⓔ
9 Ⓐ Ⓑ Ⓒ Ⓓ Ⓔ
10 Ⓐ Ⓑ Ⓒ Ⓓ Ⓔ
11 Ⓐ Ⓑ Ⓒ Ⓓ Ⓔ
12 Ⓐ Ⓑ Ⓒ Ⓓ Ⓔ
13 Ⓐ Ⓑ Ⓒ Ⓓ Ⓔ
14 Ⓐ Ⓑ Ⓒ Ⓓ Ⓔ
15 Ⓐ Ⓑ Ⓒ Ⓓ Ⓔ
16 Ⓐ Ⓑ Ⓒ Ⓓ Ⓔ
17 Ⓐ Ⓑ Ⓒ Ⓓ Ⓔ
18 Ⓐ Ⓑ Ⓒ Ⓓ Ⓔ
19 Ⓐ Ⓑ Ⓒ Ⓓ Ⓔ
20 Ⓐ Ⓑ Ⓒ Ⓓ Ⓔ
21 Ⓐ Ⓑ Ⓒ Ⓓ Ⓔ
22 Ⓐ Ⓑ Ⓒ Ⓓ Ⓔ
23 Ⓐ Ⓑ Ⓒ Ⓓ Ⓔ
24 Ⓐ Ⓑ Ⓒ Ⓓ Ⓔ
25 Ⓐ Ⓑ Ⓒ Ⓓ Ⓔ
26 Ⓐ Ⓑ Ⓒ Ⓓ Ⓔ
27 Ⓐ Ⓑ Ⓒ Ⓓ Ⓔ
28 Ⓐ Ⓑ Ⓒ Ⓓ Ⓔ
29 Ⓐ Ⓑ Ⓒ Ⓓ Ⓔ
30 Ⓐ Ⓑ Ⓒ Ⓓ Ⓔ

SECTION 5

1 Ⓐ Ⓑ Ⓒ Ⓓ Ⓔ   16 Ⓐ Ⓑ Ⓒ Ⓓ Ⓔ
2 Ⓐ Ⓑ Ⓒ Ⓓ Ⓔ   17 Ⓐ Ⓑ Ⓒ Ⓓ Ⓔ
3 Ⓐ Ⓑ Ⓒ Ⓓ Ⓔ   18 Ⓐ Ⓑ Ⓒ Ⓓ Ⓔ
4 Ⓐ Ⓑ Ⓒ Ⓓ Ⓔ   19 Ⓐ Ⓑ Ⓒ Ⓓ Ⓔ
5 Ⓐ Ⓑ Ⓒ Ⓓ Ⓔ   20 Ⓐ Ⓑ Ⓒ Ⓓ Ⓔ
6 Ⓐ Ⓑ Ⓒ Ⓓ Ⓔ   21 Ⓐ Ⓑ Ⓒ Ⓓ Ⓔ
7 Ⓐ Ⓑ Ⓒ Ⓓ Ⓔ   22 Ⓐ Ⓑ Ⓒ Ⓓ Ⓔ
8 Ⓐ Ⓑ Ⓒ Ⓓ Ⓔ   23 Ⓐ Ⓑ Ⓒ Ⓓ Ⓔ
9 Ⓐ Ⓑ Ⓒ Ⓓ Ⓔ   24 Ⓐ Ⓑ Ⓒ Ⓓ Ⓔ
10 Ⓐ Ⓑ Ⓒ Ⓓ Ⓔ   25 Ⓐ Ⓑ Ⓒ Ⓓ Ⓔ
11 Ⓐ Ⓑ Ⓒ Ⓓ Ⓔ   26 Ⓐ Ⓑ Ⓒ Ⓓ Ⓔ
12 Ⓐ Ⓑ Ⓒ Ⓓ Ⓔ   27 Ⓐ Ⓑ Ⓒ Ⓓ Ⓔ
13 Ⓐ Ⓑ Ⓒ Ⓓ Ⓔ   28 Ⓐ Ⓑ Ⓒ Ⓓ Ⓔ
14 Ⓐ Ⓑ Ⓒ Ⓓ Ⓔ   29 Ⓐ Ⓑ Ⓒ Ⓓ Ⓔ
15 Ⓐ Ⓑ Ⓒ Ⓓ Ⓔ   30 Ⓐ Ⓑ Ⓒ Ⓓ Ⓔ